The Princeton Review®

ACT®

PREP

2021 Edition

The Staff of The Princeton Review

PrincetonReview.com

Penguin
Random
House

Editorial
Rob Franek, Editor-in-Chief
Deborah Weber, Director of Production
Gabriel Berlin, Production Design Manager
David Soto, Director of Content Development
Stephen Koch, Student Survey Manager
Selena Coppock, Managing Editor
Aaron Riccio, Senior Editor
Meave Shelton, Senior Editor
Chris Chimera, Editor
Orion McBean, Editor
Anna Goodlett, Editor
Eleanor Green, Editor
Patricia Murphy, Editorial Assistant

Penguin Random House Publishing Team
Tom Russell, VP, Publisher
Alison Stoltzfus, Publishing Director
Amanda Yee, Associate Managing Editor
Ellen Reed, Production Manager
Suzanne Lee, Designer

Published in the United States by Penguin Random House LLC, New York and in Canada by Random House of Canada, a division of Penguin Random House Ltd., Toronto.

ISBN: 978-0-525-57011-0
eBook ISBN: 978-0-525-57021-9
ISSN: 2644-3643

ACT is a registered trademark of ACT, Inc.

The Princeton Review is not affiliated with Princeton University.

Editor: Orion McBean
Production Editors: Kathy Carter and Sarah Litt
Production Artist: Kris Ogilvie

Printed in the United States of America.

10 9 8 7 6 5 4 3 2 1

2021 Edition

Acknowledgments

The completion of this book would not have been possible without the help and dedication of several individuals. In particular, we would like to thank Aaron Lindh, High School Content Director for The Princeton Review.

Special thanks to Amy Minster, Cat Healey, Sara Kuperstein, and Cynthia Ward for their expert review and contributions to the content of the book. Thanks also to Aleksei Alferiev, Kevin Baldwin, Emily Baumbach, Gabby Budzon, Nicole Cosme, Stacey Cowap, Lori DesRochers, Elizabeth Evangelista, Anne Goldberg-Baldwin, Brad Kelly, Jomil London, Scott O'Neal, Danielle Perrini, Sara Soriano, Jess Thomas, and Jimmy Williams for their contributions to this book. Also thanks to Kris Oglivie, Kathy Carter, and Sarah Litt for their work on the production of this book.

Special thanks to Adam Robinson, who conceived of and perfected the Joe Bloggs approach to standardized tests and many other successful techniques used by The Princeton Review.

Contents

(Free) Content
at **PrincetonReview.com/prep**

As easy as **1·2·3**

1 Go to PrincetonReview.com/prep and enter the following ISBN for your book:
9780525570110

2 Answer a few simple questions to set up an exclusive Princeton Review account. *(If you already have one, you can just log in.)*

3 Enjoy access to your **FREE** content!

Once you've registered, you can...

- Access two more full-length practice tests

- Find any late-breaking information released about the ACT

- Read our special "College Admissions Insider" and get valuable advice about the college application process, including tips for writing a great essay and where to apply for financial aid

- Check to see if there have been any corrections or updates to this edition

- Sort colleges by whatever you're looking for (such as Best Theater or Dorm), learn more about your top choices, and see how they all rank according to *The Best 386 Colleges*

- Check out bonus features in your Student Tools, including comprehensive study guides, additional bubble sheets, and more

Need to report a potential **content** issue?

Contact **EditorialSupport@review.com** and include:

- full title of the book
- ISBN
- page number

Need to report a **technical** issue?

Contact **TPRStudentTech@review.com** and provide:

- your full name
- email address used to register the book
- full book title and ISBN
- Operating system (Mac/PC) and browser (Firefox, Safari, etc.)

Look For These Icons Throughout The Book

 PROVEN TECHNIQUES

 APPLIED STRATEGIES

 WATCH OUT

 STUDY BREAK

 OTHER REFERENCES

 ONLINE ARTICLES

Part I
Orientation

Chapter 1
Introduction to
the ACT

So you're taking the ACT. What will you need to do first? This chapter presents an overview of the ACT as a whole and discusses registration requirements, when to take the test, how to have your scores reported to colleges (or how not to), and the ways in which colleges use your scores.

THE ACT

Welcome to *ACT Prep, 2021 Edition.* The ACT is a standardized test used for college admissions. But you probably already knew that. In this book, we'll tell you all the things you didn't know about the ACT, all to show you how to crack the test and get your best score.

The ACT has traditionally been a pencil-and-paper exam but is now also available on the computer (what ACT calls the "ACT Online Test," which still needs to be taken at a test center and not at home). While the pencil-and-paper test is usually taken on Saturday mornings, some states offer a special state-administration during the school day. Non-Saturday testing is available but only for students who live in remote areas or who can't test on Saturdays for religious reasons.

Where Does the ACT Come From?

The ACT is written by a nonprofit organization that used to call itself American College Testing but now just calls itself ACT. The company has been producing the ACT since it introduced the test in 1959 as an alternative to the College Board's SAT. ACT also writes ACT Aspire and PreACT, which are tests you may have taken earlier in your academic career. The organization also provides a broad range of services to educational agencies and business institutions.

What Does the ACT Test?

The nice people who write the ACT—we'll refer to them as "ACT" from now on—describe it as an assessment of college readiness, "a curriculum- and standards-based educational and career planning tool that assesses students' academic readiness for college."

We at The Princeton Review have always been skeptical when any standardized test makes broad claims of what it can measure. In our opinion, a standardized test is just a measure of how well you take that test. Granted, ACT has spent an extraordinary amount of time analyzing data and providing the results of their research to various educational institutions and agencies. In fact, ACT has contributed to the development of the Common Core Standards Initiative, an educational reform that aligns diverse state curricula into national uniform standards.

With all due respect to ACT and the various state and federal agencies working on the Common Core, we still think the ACT is just a measure of how well you take the ACT. Many factors other than mastery of the "curriculum-based" content determine your performance on a standardized test. That's why we'll teach you both the content you need as well as crucial test-taking strategies.

Focus!
If you were getting ready to take a history test, you'd study history. If you were preparing for a basketball game, you'd practice basketball. So if you're preparing for the ACT, study the ACT!

What's on the ACT?

The ACT consists of four multiple-choice, timed tests: English, Math, Reading, and Science, always given in that order. The ACT Plus Writing also includes an essay, with the Writing Test given after the Science Test. (ACT calls them tests, but we may also use the term "sections" in this book to avoid confusion.) In Parts II–VI, we'll thoroughly review the content and strategies you need for each test.

1. English Test (45 minutes—75 questions)

You will be given 5 essays total with some words or phrases underlined. The essays will be situated on the left side of the page, while on the right side of the page you will be asked whether each underlined portion is correct as written or whether one of the three alternatives listed would be better. The English Test is a test of grammar, punctuation, sentence structure, and rhetorical skills. Throughout each essay, commonly known as a passage, there will also be questions about overall organization and style or perhaps about how the writing could be revised or strengthened.

2. Math Test (60 minutes—60 questions)

These are the regular, multiple-choice math questions you've been doing all your life. The easier questions, which test basic math proficiency, *tend* to come first, but the folks at ACT can mix in easy, medium, and difficult problems throughout the Math test. A good third of the test covers pre-algebra and elementary algebra. Slightly less than a third covers intermediate algebra and coordinate geometry (graphing). Regular geometry accounts for less than a quarter of the questions, and there are typically four questions that cover trigonometry.

3. Reading Test (35 minutes—40 questions)

In this test, there will be four reading passages of about 800 words each—the average length of a magazine article but maybe not as entertaining to read. There is always one prose fiction (or literary narrative) passage, one social science passage, one humanities passage, and one natural science passage, and they are always in that order. One of these passages will consist of a dual passage in which the *total* length of the two passages will still be about 800 words. Each passage will be followed by 10 questions.

4. Science Test (35 minutes—40 questions)

No specific scientific knowledge is necessary to do well on the Science test. You won't need to know the chemical makeup of hydrochloric acid or any formulas. Instead, you will be asked to understand scientific information presented in graphs, charts, tables, and research summaries, and you will have to make sense of one disagreement between two to four scientists.

5. Optional Writing Test (40 minutes)

The ACT Plus Writing contains an "optional" writing test featuring a single essay. We recommend you take the "ACT Plus Writing" version of the test because many schools require or recommend it. On test day you may think that you don't need it, but you might later decide to apply to a school that requires a writing score. The last thing you want is to be forced into taking the whole ACT all over again...this time *with* the Writing test. The essay requires that you consider a socially relevant prompt and three perspectives on that prompt. The essay is scored by two graders who will each assign four scores of 1–6 that are then averaged and combined for a total score of 2–12. This score will NOT factor into your composite score.

How Is the ACT Scored?

Scores for each of the four multiple-choice tests are reported on a scale of 1 to 36 (36 being the highest score possible). The four scores are averaged to yield your composite score, which is the score colleges and universities use to help determine admission. An average ending in .5 or .75 is rounded up, whereas an average ending in .25 is rounded down. Next to each score is a percentile ranking. Percentile ranking refers to how you performed on the test relative to other people who took it at the same time. For instance, a percentile ranking of 87 indicates that you scored higher than 87 percent of the people who took the test, and the other 13 percent scored equal to or higher than you.

Some of the scores have subcategories. For instance, English is broken down into Usage/Mechanics and Rhetorical Skills. In these subcategories, scores are reported on a scale of 1 to 18 (18 being the highest score possible). They are also reported as percentiles.

ACT will also give two cross-test scores called "STEM" (Science, Technology, Engineering, Mathematics) and "ELA" (English, Language Arts). Your STEM score is simply an average of your Math and Science scores. Your ELA score is taken from your English, Reading, and Writing scores. (If you don't take the Writing test, you won't receive an ELA score.) Neither score has any influence on your composite, nor, frankly, as far as we can tell, on your college admission.

On your score report, ACT also indicates if you met their "College Readiness Benchmark Scores": 18 in English, 22 in Math, 22 in Reading, and 23 in Science. ACT maintains that these benchmarks can predict college "success," defined as a "50 percent or higher probability of earning a B or higher in the corresponding college course or courses." These scores and their meaning have been determined by ACT's own research and data, not by any studies done by colleges and universities themselves.

When Should You Take the ACT?

If you haven't already, go to ACTStudent.org and create your free ACT Web Account. You can register for tests, view your scores, and request score reports for colleges through this account. You can also view the specific test dates and centers for the upcoming academic year.

The ACT is given seven times a year: September, October, December, February, April, June, and July. The February and July administrations are not available in New York.

Many states also offer an additional ACT as part of their state testing. Check with your high school to see if and when your state offers a special ACT. Your school will register you automatically for a state ACT. You must register yourself for all other administrations.

Traditionally, most students wait until the spring of their junior year to take the ACT. Many high schools still recommend the spring of the junior year because the content of the Math test includes topics some curricula do not cover before then. However, these topics appear in only a handful of questions, and many juniors take their first ACT in the fall or winter.

We recommend that you consider your own schedule when picking your test dates. Do you play a fall sport and carry a heavier load of extracurricular activities in the fall? Is winter a quiet time in between semesters? Do you act in the spring musical and plan to take several AP exams? Have you been dreaming of attending Big State University since you were a toddler and already plan to apply for early decision? Let the answers to these questions determine your test dates. But we recommend taking your first test after you've done some prep and feel comfortable that you've learned enough in school to achieve your goal score. For most students, this is sometime in junior year (grade 11).

How Many Times Should You Take the ACT?

For security reasons, ACT will not let you take the exam more than 12 times in your lifetime. But we certainly hope no one is dismayed by this restriction. There are certainly better things to do with your time on a Saturday morning, and we don't believe any college will accept "taking the ACT" as an extracurricular activity!

Looking for more help on the ACT? Check out princetonreview.com for information on self-paced courses, live courses, and tutoring!

The Princeton Review recommends that you plan to take the ACT two to three times. If you achieve your goal score in your first administration, great. Take the money and run. On the other hand, if after three tests you have reason and motivation to take the ACT again, do it. On your first day of college, you will neither remember nor care how many times you had to take the ACT.

In fact, at many colleges, the median number of times admitted students took the ACT (or SAT) is 3. In other words, it's perfectly fine (and normal!) to retake the ACT.

Does ACT "Super Score"?

Starting in September 2020, ACT will "superscore" students' results upon request. What's a superscore? A superscore is a new score report (including a new composite score) that takes the best results in every section (English, Math, Reading, Science, and Writing (if you took it)) over any number of test dates. In other words, if you did better on Reading and Science in February, but better on English and Math in April, ACT will take your February Reading and Science scores and combine them with your April English and Math scores to create a new, higher superscore. This is also how single-section tests (see the following page) will be incorporated into your scores.

In addition, many schools (and the Common Application) will ask you to list the score and test date of your English, Math, Reading, and Science and then calculate a superscore based on these scores, separate from ACT. Therefore, if you worry that some scores will rise as others fall when you take the ACT again, the superscore will reflect your best results.

However, not every college will accept ACT superscores. Therefore, The Princeton Review strongly recommends that you research each school you're applying to. While ACT will send the results only from the test dates you request or ACT's generated superscore, you should decide which and how many dates to send based on your scores and the school's guidelines about superscoring. Moreover, some schools require that you submit all test scores from every administration, and you should abide by any such requirements.

WHAT IS THE ACT ONLINE TEST?

The ACT Online Test is the ACT that you take on a computer, rather than with pencil and paper. Despite the name, you can't take the ACT from the comfort of your own home; rather, you'll have to go to a testing center (possibly your high school) and take the test on the center's computer.

The ACT Online Test has the same overall structure, timing, and number of questions as the pencil-and-paper ACT. The scoring, score range, and scoring method are also the same. If the ACT Online Test is basically the same as the pencil-and-paper ACT, who would take the ACT Online Test?

WHO TAKES THE ACT ONLINE TEST?

ACT has been offering versions of the ACT on the computer since about 2016. The first group of students to take the ACT on the computer were students taking the test at school. Schools and school districts decided whether to give the test on the computer.

As of September 2018, all students taking the ACT outside of the United States take the test on a computer (except for those students with accommodations requiring the use of a traditional pencil-and-paper test).

Starting sometime in 2021, students in the United States will have the option to take the ACT Online Test instead of the traditional pencil-and-paper version. Students choosing this option will get their scores in about two to three business days (e.g., take the test on Saturday, have your score the next Wednesday). In addition, any students taking advantage of the Single-Section Retesting must do so on the computer.

> Single-Section Retesting will be an incredible option for students in 2021. However, colleges still have the the option as to whether to accept these new scores. Research your target schools early so you know your options!

Single-Section Retesting

Students who have already taken the full ACT may choose to take one, two, or three sections again using Single-Section Retesting. ACT will then produce a superscore consisting of your best results in all tests (English, Math, Reading, Science, and Writing took it)). Note that not all colleges accept a superscored ACT, so do your research before taking advantage of this option. ACT had originally planned to roll out this option along with the ACT Online Test and Superscoring; however, Single-Section Retesting has been delayed until 2021 to allow more students to take the full-length ACT in the fall of 2020.

ACT ONLINE TEST FEATURES

So, then, besides the obvious "it's on the computer," what are the differences between taking the ACT on the computer and taking it on paper? Let's start with what you can't do on the ACT Online Test. You can't "write" on the screen in a freehand way. You're limited in how you're able to mark the answer choices, and each question appears on its own screen (so you can't see multiple questions at one glance). You will also be given a small "whiteboard" and dry erase pen with which to make notes and do work.

The ACT Online Test will have some useful features and some you may never use. You can flag questions to come back to them later, eliminate answers on the screen, or even hide the answers until you are ready for them. You will also be able to highlight the text, magnify it, or cover part of the screen to focus on one relevant window. To see all these features in action, go to ACT's website at http://www.act.org/content/act/en/products-and-services/the-act-non-us/test-preparation.html. If you are registered for a Princeton Review course or tutorial, you will also have access to more ACT Online Tests on our website, http://www.princetonreview.com.

HOW TO PREPARE FOR THE ACT ONLINE TEST

If you are going to take the ACT Online Test, you will want to incorporate some computer-based practice into your prep plan. ACT's website has practice sections for each of the four multiple-choice parts of the test and for the essay. We recommend that you do those sections toward the end of your preparation (and close to your test date) to give you an opportunity to practice what you've learned on a platform similar to the one you'll be using on the day of the test.

If you are planning to take the ACT online, you should practice as if you're doing all your work on the computer, even when you're working in a physical book. Use a highlighter, but don't use the highlighter on any figures (as the ACT Online Test won't let you do so). Use your pencil to eliminate answer choices and have a separate sheet of paper or a whiteboard to do any work you need to do, instead of writing on the problem itself.

> **Remember!**
> Your goal is to get the best possible score on the ACT. ACT's goal is to assign a number to you that (supposedly) means something to colleges. Focus on your goal!

Also, remember that our approaches work. Don't get misled by ACT's instructions on the day of the test–their way of approaching the test won't give you the best results!

How Do You Register for the ACT?

The fastest way to register is online, through your ACT Web Account. You can also obtain a registration packet at your high school guidance office, online at **ACTStudent.org/forms/stud_req**, or by writing or calling ACT at the address and phone number below.

ACT Student Services
2727 Scott Blvd
PO Box 414
Iowa City, IA 52243-0414

319.337.1270

> **Registration Tip #1**
> The registration includes ACT's survey on your grades and interests, but you are not required to answer these questions. To save time, you can provide only the required information, marked by an asterisk.

Registration Tip #2

If you take the December, April, or June test, sign up for the Test Information Release. Six to eight weeks after the test, you'll receive a copy of the test, the answer key, and your answers. This service costs an additional fee and is available only on these test dates. You can order the Test Information Release up to 3 months after the test date, but it's easier to order it at the time you register. It's a great tool to help you prepare for your next ACT.

Bookmark **ACTStudent.org**. You will start at this portal to view test dates, fees, and registration deadlines. You can also research the requirements and processes to apply for extended time or other accommodations. You will also start at ACTStudent.org to access your account to register, view your scores, and order score reports.

Check the site for the latest information about fees. The ACT Plus Writing costs more than the ACT (No Writing), but ACT also offers a fee waiver service. While you can choose four schools to send a score report to at no charge, there are fees for score reports sent to additional schools. As of July 2019, students with ACT waivers are able to send scores to up to 20 schools.

Test Security Changes

As part of the registration process, you have to upload or mail a photograph that will be printed on your admissions ticket. On test day, you have to take the ticket and acceptable photo identification with you.

Standby testing is available, but you have to register in advance, usually before the prior Monday. Check ACTStudent.org for more information.

HOW TO PREPARE FOR THE ACT

The Princeton Review materials and test-taking techniques contained in this book should give you all the information you need to improve your score on the ACT. For more practice materials, The Princeton Review also publishes *1,523 Practice ACT Questions*, which includes more than six tests' worth of material.

Other popular coaching books contain several complete practice ACT exams. We strongly advise you *not* to waste your time taking these tests. In some cases, the questions in these books are not modeled on real ACT questions. Some of them cover material that is not even on the real ACT. Others give the impression that the ACT is much easier or more difficult than it really is. Taking the practice tests offered in these books could actually hurt your score.

More great titles by The Princeton Review

1,523 ACT Practice Questions offers the equivalent of 6 whole ACT practice tests.

Cynics might suggest that no one else can license ACT exams because ACT sells its own review book called *The Official ACT Prep Guide*. We think *The Official ACT Prep Guide* is well worth the price for the three real tests it contains (make sure you buy the most recent edition). We recommend that you either buy the book or ask your high school to send away to ACT for actual ACT tests. You should get a copy of *Preparing for the ACT Test* from your counselor. It's free, and it contains a complete, real ACT. The same test can be downloaded for free from ACT's website.

While we advise you to obtain these practice tests to further your preparation for the ACT, it is important that you use them properly. Many students like to think that they can prepare by simply taking test after test until they get the scores they want. Unfortunately, this doesn't work all that well. Why? Well, in many instances, repetitive test-taking only reinforces some of the bad test-taking habits that we address in this book. You should use practice tests for the following three key purposes:

- to build up familiarity with the exam
- to learn how to avoid the types of mistakes you are currently making
- to master our techniques and strategies so you can save time and earn more points

Do I Need to Prepare If I Have Good Grades?

Let's take the hypothetical case of Sid. Sid is valedictorian of his class, editor of the school paper, and the only teenager ever to win the Nobel Prize. To support his widowed mother, he sold more magazine subscriptions and gift wrap than any other person in recorded history. He speaks eight languages in addition to being able to communicate with dolphins and wolves. He has recommendations from Elon Musk *and* Bill Gates. So if Sid had a bad day when he took the ACT (the plane bringing him back from his Medal of Freedom award presentation was late), we are pretty sure that he is going to be just fine anyway. But Sid wants to ensure that when his colleges look at his ACT score, they see the same high-caliber student they see when they look at the rest of his application, so he carefully reviews the types of questions asked and learns some useful test-taking strategies.

I Have Lousy Grades in School. Is There Any Hope?

Let's take the case of Tom. Tom didn't do particularly well in high school. In fact, he has been on academic probation since kindergarten. He has caused four of his teachers to give up teaching as a profession, and he prides himself on his perfect homework record: he's never done any, not ever. But if Tom aces his ACT, a college might decide that he is actually a misunderstood genius and give him a full scholarship. Tom decides to learn as much as he can about the ACT.

Most of us, of course, fall between these two extremes. So is it important to prepare for the ACT?

If you were to look in the information bulletin of any of the colleges in which you are interested, we can pretty much guarantee that somewhere you would find the following paragraph:

> Many factors go into a college's acceptance of a student. Test scores are *only one* of these factors. Grades in high school, extracurricular activities, essays, and recommendations are also important and may in some cases outweigh test scores.
>
> (2021 University of Anywhere Bulletin)

Truer words were never written. In our opinion, just about *every* other element in your application "package" is more important than your test scores. The Princeton Review (among other organizations) has been telling colleges for years that scores on the ACT or the SAT are pretty incomplete measures of a student's overall academic abilities. Some colleges have stopped looking at test scores entirely, and others are downplaying their importance.

Want to know which colleges are best for you? Check out our College Search engine at princetonreview.com for information on over 1,000 schools.

So Why Should You Spend Any Time Preparing for the ACT?

Out of all the elements in your application "package," your ACT score is the easiest to change. The grades you've received up to now are written in stone. You aren't going to become captain of the soccer team or editor of the school paper overnight. Your essays will be only as good as you can write them, and recommendations are only as good as your teachers' memories of you.

On the contrary, in a few weeks you can substantially change your score on the ACT (and the way colleges look at your applications). The test does not pretend to measure analytic ability or intelligence. It measures your knowledge of specific skills such as grammar, algebra, and reading comprehension. Mostly, it measures how good you are at taking this test.

Need a Study Plan?
Go to your Student Tools to download our study plans tailored specifically for 4, 8, or 12 weeks of available prep time!

THE ACT VS. THE SAT

You may have to take the ACT anyway, but most of the schools in which you're interested also accept the SAT. In order to determine which test may be better for you to take, invest the time to take a full-length, timed practice test for each to (1) see how you score on each test and (2) assess how you *feel* during each test. The time spent on this exercise will be incredibly beneficial for your test preparation planning. You can take these tests as part of your free Student Tools at princetonreview.com. Once you've decided which test is the better fit for you, you can then use that initial score as a baseline for planning your preparation to hit the target score for your dream college.

What Exactly Are the Differences?

Both the SAT and ACT can be pressure-packed tests, so knowing the structures of each can help you decide which test may be better for you. Let's take the Reading Tests for the SAT and the ACT as an example. The SAT's Reading Test is 65 minutes long and has 52 questions covering 5 passages; the ACT's Reading Test is 35 minutes long and has 40 questions covering 4 passages. In short, you have an average of 75 seconds to answer each SAT Reading question, whereas you have an average of about 53 seconds to answer each ACT Reading question. However, ACT Reading questions tend to be more directly answered by the passage, whereas SAT Reading questions can require a bit more close reading to determine the right answer. In general, students who prefer more straightforward but faster-paced questions lean towards the ACT, whereas those who appreciate a bit more time with each question, even if those questions themselves require a bit more effort, gravitate towards the SAT. Our advice – take a practice test of each and see which one you prefer.

In terms of subject matter though, both tests will generally test the same types of content. The biggest differences are in the areas of math and science. The SAT will have two math sections, one of which is a no calculator section. The ACT Math section tests a few more advanced concepts than the SAT does, such as matrices and logs. The ACT also has a Science section that is basically a reading comprehension

More great titles by The Princeton Review
The Best 386 Colleges

test. However, if the thought of a science section truly makes you uncomfortable, you should seriously consider doing the SAT instead.

Both tests include an optional Essay at the end of the test. For each test, the Essay score has no bearing on the composite (ACT) or total (SAT) score. Check with your prospective colleges and universities to determine whether they need you to take the essay for either the ACT or SAT. This is especially important to know *before* you take the ACT or SAT because you can't register for a future test date to take just the essay—you'd have to take the whole test again!

To find out whether the schools in which you are interested require the ACT essay, consult their admissions webpages.

While the tests may sound similar to you, you should know that some students end up scoring substantially higher on the SAT than they do on the ACT and vice versa. It may be to your advantage to take a practice test for each one to see which is more likely to get you a better score.

ADDITIONAL RESOURCES

In addition to the material in this book, we offer a number of other resources to aid you during your ACT preparation.

Register your book at **PrincetonReview.com** to gain access to your Student Tools, the companion website to this book. There you will find more ACT practice tests, additional bubble sheets, and useful articles on the college application process.

WHAT IS THE PRINCETON REVIEW?

The Princeton Review is the world's leading test-preparation and educational services company. We run courses at hundreds of locations worldwide and offer Web-based instruction at PrincetonReview.com. Our test-taking techniques and review strategies are unique and powerful. We developed them after studying all the real ACTs we could get our hands on. For more information about our programs and services, feel free to call us at **800-2Review**.

A FINAL THOUGHT BEFORE YOU BEGIN

The ACT does not measure intelligence, nor does it predict your ultimate success or failure as a human being. No matter how high or how low you score on this test initially, and no matter how much you may increase your score through preparation, you should *never* consider the score you receive on this or any other test a final judgment of your abilities.

Chapter 2
ACT Strategy

You will raise your ACT score by working smarter, not harder, and a smart test-taker is a strategic test-taker. You will target specific content to review, you will apply an effective and efficient approach, and you will employ common sense.

Each test on the ACT demands a specific approach, and even the most universal strategies vary in their applications. In Parts II–VI, we'll discuss these strategies in greater detail customized to English, Math, Reading, Science, and Writing.

THE BASIC APPROACH

The ACT test is different from the tests you take in school, so you need to approach it differently. The Princeton Review's strategies are not arbitrary. To be effective, ACT strategies have to be based on the ACT and not on any other test.

You need to know how the ACT is scored and how it's constructed.

Scoring

When students and schools talk about ACT scores, they typically mean the composite score, a range of 1–36. The composite is an average of the four multiple-choice tests, each scored on the same 1–36 scale. Neither the Writing test score nor the combined English plus Writing score affects the composite.

The Composite

When you look at your score online, the biggest number on the page is always the composite. While admissions offices will certainly see the individual scores of all five tests (and their subscores), schools will use the composite to evaluate your application, and that's why in the end it's the only one that matters.

The composite is an average. Add the scores for the English, Math, Reading, and Science tests, and divide the total by four. Do you add one test twice? Um, no. Do you omit one of the tests in the total? Er, no again. The four tests are weighted equally to calculate the composite. But do you need to bring up all four equally to raise your composite? Do you need to be a superstar in all four tests? Should you focus more on your weakest tests than your strongest tests? No, no, and absolutely not. The best way to improve your composite is to shore up your weaknesses but exploit your strengths as much as possible.

> To lift the composite score as high as possible,
> maximize the scores of your strongest tests.

You don't need to be a rock star on all four tests. Identify two, maybe three tests, and focus on raising those scores as much as you can to raise your composite score. Work on your weakest scores to keep them from pulling you down. Are you strongest in English and Math, or maybe in English, Reading, and Science? Then work to raise those scores as high as you can. You shouldn't ignore your weaknesses, but recognize that the work you put in on your strengths will yield greater dividends. Think of it this way. If you had only one hour to devote to practice the week before the ACT, you would put that hour toward your best subjects.

Structure

Let's review quickly the structure of the ACT. The five tests are always given in the same order.

English	Math	Reading	Science	Writing
45 minutes	60 minutes	35 minutes	35 minutes	40 minutes
75 questions	60 questions	40 questions	40 questions	1 essay

Enemy #1: Time

How much time do you have per question on the Math test? You have just one minute, and that's generous compared with the time given per question on the English, Reading, and Science tests. But how often do you take a test in school with a minute or less per question? If you do at all, it's maybe on a multiple-choice quiz but probably not on a major exam or final. Time is your enemy on the ACT, and you have to use it wisely and be aware of how that time pressure can bring out your worst instincts as a test taker.

Enemy #2: Yourself

Many people struggle with test anxiety in school and on standardized tests. But there is something particularly evil about tests like the ACT and SAT. The skills you've been rewarded for throughout your academic career can easily work against you on the ACT. You've been taught since birth to follow directions, go in order, and finish everything. But that approach won't necessarily earn you your highest ACT score.

On the other hand, treating the ACT as a scary, alien beast can leave your brain blank and useless and can incite irrational, self-defeating behavior. When you pick up a No. 2 pencil or sit in front of the computer, you may tend to leave your common sense at the door. Test nerves and anxieties can make you misread a question, commit a careless error, see something that isn't there, blind you to what is there, talk you into a bad answer, and worst of all, convince you to spend good time after bad.

There is good news. You can—and will—crack the ACT. You will learn how to approach it differently than you would a test in school, and you won't let the test crack you.

ACT STRATEGIES

Personal Order of Difficulty (POOD)

If time is going to run out, would you rather it run out on the hardest questions or the easiest? Of course you want it to run out on the questions you are less likely to get right.

You can easily fall into the trap of spending too much time on the hardest problems and either never getting to or rushing through the easiest. You shouldn't work in the order ACT provides just because the test is in that order. Instead, find your own Personal Order of Difficulty (POOD).

Make smart decisions quickly for good reasons as you move through each test.

The Best Way to Bubble In

If you're taking the pencil-and-paper ACT, work a page at a time, circling your answers right on the booklet. Transfer a page's worth of answers to the answer document at one time. It's better to stay focused on working questions rather than disrupt your concentration to find where you left off on the answer document. You'll be more accurate at both tasks. Do not wait to the end, however, to transfer all the answers of that test on your answer document. Go one page at a time on English and Math, a passage at a time on Reading and Science. In the last few minutes, though, bubble the answer after working each question.

Letter of the Day (LOTD)

Just because you don't *work* a question doesn't mean you don't *answer* it. There is no penalty for wrong answers on the ACT, so you should never leave any blanks on your answer document. When you guess on Never questions, pick your favorite letter or, on the pencil-and-paper ACT, two-letter combo of answers and stick with it. For example, always choose A/F or C/H. If you're consistent, you're more likely to pick up more points.

Now

Does a question look okay? Do you know how to do it? Do it *Now*.

Later

Will this question take a long time to work? Leave it and come back to it *Later*. Circle the question number or flag the question on the computer for easy reference to return.

Never

Test taker, know thyself. Know the topics that are your worst, and learn the signs that flash danger. Don't waste time on questions you should *Never* do. Instead, use more time to answer the Now and Later questions accurately.

Pacing

The ACT may be designed for you to run out of time, but you can't rush through it as fast as possible. All you'll do is make careless errors on easy questions you should get right and spend way too much time on difficult ones you're unlikely to get right. Let your POOD help determine your pacing. Go slowly enough to answer correctly all the Now questions but quickly enough to get to the number of Later questions you need to reach your goal score.

In Chapter 3, we'll teach you how to identify the number of questions you need to reach your goal score. You'll practice your pacing in practice tests, going slowly enough to avoid careless errors and quickly enough to reach your goal scores.

Process of Elimination (POE)

Multiple-choice tests offer one great advantage: they provide the correct answer right there on the page. Of course, they hide the correct answer amid 3–4 incorrect answers. It's often easier to spot the wrong answers than it is to identify the right ones, particularly when you apply a smart Process of Elimination (POE).

POE works differently on each test on the ACT, but it's a powerful strategy on all of them. For some question types, you'll always use POE rather than wasting time trying to figure out the answer on your own. For other questions, you'll use POE when you're stuck. ACT hides the correct answer behind wrong ones, but when you eliminate just one or two wrong answers, the correct answer can become more obvious, sometimes jumping right off the page or screen.

POOD, Pacing, and POE all work together to help you spend your time where it does the most good: on the questions you can and should get right.

> **Use Your Pencil**
> If you take the pencil-and-paper test, you own the test booklet, and you should write where and when it helps you. Use your pencil to literally cross off wrong answers on the page.

Be Ruthless

The worst mistake a test taker can make is to throw good time at bad questions. You read a question but don't understand it, so you read it again. And again. If you stare at it really hard, you know you're going to just *see* the answer. And you can't move on, because really, after spending all that time it would be a waste not to keep at it, right?

Wrong. You can't let one tough question drag you down, and you can't let your worst instincts tempt you into self-defeating behavior. Instead, the best way to improve your ACT score is to follow our advice.

- Use the techniques and strategies in the lessons to work efficiently and accurately through all your Now and Later questions.
- Know your Never questions, and use your LOTD.
- Know when to move on. Use POE, and guess from what's left.

In Parts II–VI, you'll learn how POOD, Pacing, and POE work on each test. In Chapter 3, we'll discuss in greater detail how to use your Pacing to hit your target scores.

> **... or Your Tools**
> When you take the test on a computer, you can't write on the computer screen, but you can eliminate answers using the Answer Eliminator tool. Additionally, use the highlighter tool in the passage, question, and answer choices, and use the whiteboard for any work you need to do.

Chapter 3
Score Goals

To hit your target score, you have to know how many raw points you need. Your goals and pacing for English, Math, Reading, and Science will vary depending on the test and your own individual strengths.

SCORE GRIDS

On each test of the ACT, the number of correct answers converts to a scaled score 1–36. ACT works hard to adjust the scale of each test at each administration as necessary to make all scaled scores comparable, smoothing out any differences in level of difficulty across test dates. There is thus no truth to any one test date being "easier" than the others, but you can expect to see slight variations in the scale from test to test. Because these variations are slight, we'll use the same scoring conversion table for each of our Practice Tests in this book; keep in mind that your results will therefore be approximately what you would have scored on the real ACT.

Where Will Your Scores Take You?
Check out our College Search Engine on princetonreview.com for information on more than 1,000 schools. There, you'll find info on average test scores and admission rate.

This is the score grid from the free test ACT makes available on its website, ACT.org. We're going to use it to explain how to pick a target score and pace yourself.

Scale Score	Test 1 English	Test 2 Math	Test 3 Reading	Test 4 Science	Scale Score
36	75	60	40	40	36
35	73–74	59	39	39	35
34	72	58	38	38	34
33	71	57	37	37	33
32	70	56	36	—	32
31	69	54–55	34–35	36	31
30	68	53	33	35	30
29	67	51–52	32	34	29
28	65–66	49–50	30–31	33	28
27	64	46–48	29	32	27
26	62–63	44–45	28	30–31	26
25	60–61	41–43	27	28–29	25
24	58–59	39–40	26	27	24
23	55–57	37–38	24–25	25–26	23
22	53–54	35–36	23	23–24	22
21	50–52	33–34	22	21–22	21
20	47–49	31–32	21	19–20	20
19	44–46	28–30	19–20	17–18	19
18	42–43	25–27	18	15–16	18
17	40–41	22–24	17	14	17
16	37–39	18–21	16	13	16
15	34–36	15–17	15	12	15
14	31–33	11–14	13–14	11	14
13	29–30	9–10	12	10	13
12	27–28	7–8	10–11	9	12
11	25–26	6	8–9	8	11
10	23–24	5	7	7	10
9	21–22	4	6	6	9

PACING STRATEGIES

Focus on the number of questions you need to hit your goal scores.

English

For English, there is no order of difficulty of the passages or their questions. The most important thing is to finish, finding all the Now questions you can throughout the whole test.

Math

Spend more time to do fewer questions, and you'll raise your accuracy. Let's say your goal on Math is a 24. Find 24 under the scaled score column, and you'll see that you need 39–40 raw points. Take all 60 minutes and work 45 questions, using your Letter of the Day (LOTD) on 15 Never questions. You'll get most of the questions you work right, some wrong, and pick up a couple points on the LOTDs.

Look at it this way: how many *more* questions do you need to answer correctly to move from a 24 to a 27? As few as six. Do you think you could find six careless errors on a practice test that you *should* have gotten right?

Reading

When it comes to picking a pacing strategy for Reading, you have to practice extensively and figure out what works best for you.

Some students are slow but good readers. If you take 35 minutes to do fewer passages, you could get all of the questions right for each passage you do. Use your LOTD for the passages you don't work, and you should pick up a few additional points.

Other students could take hours to work each passage and never get all the questions right. But if you find all the questions you can do on many passages, using your LOTD on all those Never questions, you could hit your target score.

Which is better? There is no set answer to that. True ACT score improvement will come with a willingness to experiment and analyze what works.

More Great Titles By The Princeton Review
English and Reading Workout for the ACT and *Math and Science Workout for the ACT*

Science

In the Science lessons, you'll learn how to identify your Now, Later, and Never passages.

Our advice is to be aggressive. Spend the time needed on the easiest passages first, but keep moving to get to your targeted raw score. Identify Never questions on Now Passages, and use your LOTD. Use your remaining time to find the Now questions on as many Later passages as you can get to.

PACING CHARTS

Revisit these pages as you practice. Record your scores from practice. Set a goal of 1–3 point improvement in your scale score for the next practice test. Identify the number of questions you need to answer correctly to reach that goal. The score grids provided in Part VIII come with their specific scales. You can use those, or use the score grids in this chapter.

English Pacing

Scale Score	Raw Score	Scale Score	Raw Score	Scale Score	Raw Score
36	75	24	58–59	12	27–28
35	73–74	23	55–57	11	25–26
34	72	22	53–54	10	23–24
33	71	21	50–52	9	21–22
32	70	20	47–49	8	18–20
31	69	19	44–46	7	15–17
30	68	18	42–43	6	12–14
29	67	17	40–41	5	9–11
28	65–66	16	37–39	4	7–8
27	64	15	34–36	3	5–6
26	62–63	14	31–33	2	3–4
25	60–61	13	29–30	1	0–2

Remember that in English, your pacing goal is to finish.

Prior Score (if applicable): _____

Practice Test 1 Goal: _____   Practice Test 2 Goal: _____

# of Questions Needed: _____   # of Questions Needed: _____

Practice Test 1 Score: _____   Practice Test 2 Score: _____

Math Pacing

Scale Score	Raw Score	Scale Score	Raw Score	Scale Score	Raw Score
36	60	24	39–40	12	7–8
35	59	23	37–38	11	6
34	58	22	35–36	10	5
33	57	21	33–34	9	4
32	56	20	31–32	8	3
31	54–55	19	28–30	7	—
30	53	18	25–27	6	2
29	51–52	17	22–24	5	—
28	49–50	16	18–21	4	1
27	46–48	15	15–17	3	—
26	44–45	14	11–14	2	—
25	41–43	13	9–10	1	0

Our advice is to add 5 questions to your targeted raw score. You have a cushion to get a few wrong—nobody's perfect—and you're likely to pick up at least a few points from your LOTDs. Track your progress on practice tests to pinpoint your target score.

Prior Score (if applicable): _____

Practice Test 1 Goal: _____   Practice Test 2 Goal: _____

# of Questions Needed: _____   # of Questions Needed: _____

+5   +5

= # of Questions to Work:_____   = # of Questions to Work: _____

Practice Test 1 Score: _____   Practice Test 2 Score: _____

Reading Pacing

Scale Score	Raw Score	Scale Score	Raw Score	Scale Score	Raw Score
36	40	24	26	12	10–11
35	39	23	24–25	11	8–9
34	38	22	23	10	7
33	37	21	22	9	6
32	36	20	21	8	5
31	34–35	19	19–20	7	—
30	33	18	18	6	4
29	32	17	17	5	3
28	30–31	16	16	4	2
27	29	15	15	3	—
26	28	14	13–14	2	1
25	27	13	12	1	0

Experiment with Reading by trying fewer passages, taking more time per passage, and then adding more passages and more questions. Identify first how many questions you need.

Prior Score (if applicable): _____

Practice Test 1 Goal: _____   Practice Test 2 Goal: _____

# of Questions Needed: _____   # of Questions Needed: _____

How many passages to work: _____   How many passages to work: _____

Practice Test 1 Score: _____   Practice Test 2 Score: _____

Science Pacing

Scale Score	Raw Score	Scale Score	Raw Score	Scale Score	Raw Score
36	40	24	27	12	9
35	39	23	25–26	11	8
34	38	22	23–24	10	7
33	37	21	21–22	9	6
32	—	20	19–20	8	5
31	36	19	17–18	7	4
30	35	18	15–16	6	3
29	34	17	14	5	2
28	33	16	13	4	—
27	32	15	12	3	1
26	30–31	14	11	2	—
25	28–29	13	10	1	0

More great titles from The Princeton Review
Feeling confident? *ACT Elite 36* is designed specifically for advanced students who want to push themselves toward that perfect ACT score.

ACT Science tests generally have 6 passages but may have 7.

Use the chart below to figure out how many passages to work if there are 6 passages.

Target Score	# of passages to attempt
< 20	4 passages
20–27	4–5 passages
> 27	5–6 passages

Prior Score (if applicable): _____

Practice Test 1 Goal: _____   Practice Test 2 Goal: _____

# of Questions Needed: _____   # of Questions Needed: _____

How many passages to work: _____   How many passages to work: _____

Practice Test 1 Score: _____   Practice Test 2 Score: _____

Chapter 4
Taking the ACT

Preparing yourself both mentally and physically to take the ACT is important. This chapter helps you learn exactly what you're in for, so you can plan ahead and be as comfortable as possible on test day. We talk about not only what to do but also what *not* to do.

PREPARING FOR THE ACT

The best way to prepare for any test is to find out exactly what is going to be on it. This book provides you with just that information. In the following chapters, you will find a comprehensive review of all the question types on the ACT, complete information on all the subjects covered by the ACT, and some powerful test-taking strategies developed specifically for the ACT.

To take full advantage of the review and techniques, you should practice on the tests in this book as well as on real ACT questions. We've already told you how to obtain copies of real ACT exams. Taking full practice exams allows you to chart your progress (with accurate scores for each test), gives you confidence in our techniques, and develops your stamina.

The Night Before the Test

Unless you are the kind of person who remains calm only by staying up all night to do last-minute studying, we recommend that you take the evening off. Go see a movie or read a good book (besides this one), and make sure you get to bed at a normal hour. No final, frantically memorized math formula or grammatical rule is going to make or break your score. A positive mental attitude comes from treating yourself decently. If you've prepared over the last several weeks or months, then you're ready.

If you haven't really prepared, there will be other opportunities to take the test, so get some rest and do the best you can. Remember, colleges will see only the score you choose to let them see. No *single* ACT is going to be crucial. We don't think night-before-the-test cramming is very effective. For example, we would not recommend that you try going through this book in one night.

Don't Leave Home Without 'Em

Here are some items you'll want to have on test day.

- Admissions ticket
- Photo ID or letter of identification
- Plenty of sharpened No. 2 pencils (if you're taking the pencil-and-paper ACT)
- A watch
- An acceptable calculator with new batteries

On the Day of the Test

It's important that you eat a real breakfast, even if you normally don't. We find that about two-thirds of the way through the test, people who didn't eat something beforehand suddenly lose their will to go on. Equally importantly, take a snack to the test center. You will get a break during which food is allowed. Some people spend the break out in the hallways comparing answers and getting upset when their answers don't match. Ignore the people around you, and eat your snack. Why assume they know any more than you do?

Warming Up

While you're having breakfast, get your mind going by doing a couple of questions from an ACT on which you've already worked. You don't want to use the first test on the real exam to warm up. And please don't try a hard question you've never done before. If you miss it, your confidence will be diminished, and that's not something you want on the day of the test.

At the test center, you'll be asked to show some form of picture ID or provide a note from your school—on school stationery—describing what you look like. You'll also need to take a calculator. Check ACTStudent.org/faq to see if your calculator model is permitted. If you haven't changed the batteries recently (or ever), you should do that before the test or take a back-up calculator. Finally, if you're taking the pencil-and-paper ACT, you'll need to take No. 2 pencils and an eraser. You'll also want to take a reliable watch—not the beeping kind—because the time remaining is not always announced during the test sections.

When you get into the actual room in which you'll be taking the exam, make sure you're comfortable. Is there enough light? Is your desk sturdy? Do the mouse and keyboard work? Don't be afraid to speak up; after all, you're going to be spending three and a half hours at that desk. And it's not a bad idea to go to the bathroom *before* you get to the room. It's a long haul to that first break.

While your college search may be the furthest thing from your mind on test day, don't forget that your Student Tools is a great resource for informative articles and advice on financial aid, the application process, letters of recommendation, and much more!

ZEN AND THE ART OF TEST TAKING

Once the exam begins, tune out the rest of the world. That girl with the annoying cough in the next row? You don't hear her. That guy who is fidgeting in the seat ahead of you? You don't see him. It's just you and the exam. Everything else should be a blur.

As soon as one section ends, erase it completely from your mind. It no longer exists. The only thing that matters is the one you are taking right now. Even if you are upset about a particular section, try to forget about it. If you are busy thinking about the last section, you cannot focus on the one on which you are currently working, and that's a sure-fire way to make costly mistakes. Most people aren't very good at assessing how they performed on a given section of the exam, especially while they're still taking it, so don't waste your time and energy trying.

Some Things to Remember
- Make sure you know where the test center is located and where you need to go once you are there.
- Show up early; you can't show up right when the test is scheduled to begin and expect to get in.
- Lay out everything you need, including your calculator, admission ticket, and photo identification, the night before the test. The last thing you want to do on the morning of the test is run around looking for a calculator. Also, it's important to take your own watch if you're taking the pencil-and-paper ACT because there's no requirement for the room you're in to have a working clock.
- Take a snack and a bottle of water just in case you get hungry. There's nothing worse than testing on an empty stomach.

Keep Your Answers to Yourself

Please don't let anyone cheat off you. Test companies have developed sophisticated anti-cheating measures that go way beyond having a proctor walk around the room. We know of one test company that gets seating charts of each testing room. Its computers analyze the results of people sitting in the immediate vicinity for correlations of wrong answer choices. Innocent and guilty are invited to take the exam over again, and their scores from the first exam are invalidated.

Using the Nav Tool On the ACT Online Test, use the Nav Tool to make sure you've answered every question before time runs out. We recommend doing so at the 5 minute warning.

Beware of Misbubbling Your Answer Sheet

Probably the most painful kind of mistake you can make on the ACT is to bubble in choice (A) with your pencil when you really mean choice (B), or to have your answers one question number off (perhaps because you skipped one question on the test but forgot to skip it on the answer sheet). Aargh! The proctor isn't allowed to let you change your answers after a section is over, so it is critical that you either catch yourself before a test section ends or—even better—that you don't make a mistake in the first place.

We suggest to our students that they write down their answers in their test booklets. This way, whenever you finish a page of questions in the test booklet, you can transfer all your answers from that page in a group. We find that this method minimizes the possibility of misbubbling, and it also saves time. Of course, as you get near the end of a test, you should go back to bubbling question by question.

Write Now Feel free to write all over your test booklet. Don't do computations in your head. Put them in the booklet; you paid for it. Go nuts!

If you get back your ACT scores and they seem completely out of line, you can ask the ACT examiners to look over your answer sheet for what are called "gridding errors." If you want to, you can even be there while they look. If it is clear that there has been an error, ACT will change your score. An example of a gridding error would be a test in which, if you moved all the responses over by one, they would suddenly all be correct.

Should I Ever Cancel My Scores?

We recommend against canceling your scores, even if you feel you've done poorly. If you have registered as we recommended and not sent the scores to any colleges and possibly not to your high school, then the score you receive won't go anywhere unless you send it on later. There is no need to panic and cancel your score without knowing what it is if no one will ever see it. You never know—perhaps you did better than you think. Furthermore, if you've taken the ACT two or more times (something we heartily recommend), you can choose which score you want colleges to see or send a superscore when you request reports from ACT.

If you do decide to cancel your scores, ACT allows you to do it only at the test center itself. However, you can stop scores from reaching colleges if you call ACT by 12:00 P.M. (CST) on the *Thursday* following the test. The number to call is 319-337-1270.

Part II
How to Crack the ACT English Test

Chapter 5
Introduction to the ACT English Test

The English test is not a grammar test. It's also not a test of how well you write. In fact, it tests your editing skills: your ability to fix errors in grammar and punctuation and to improve the organization and style of five different passages. In this chapter, you'll learn the basic strategy of how to crack the passages and review the grammar you need to know.

WHAT'S ON THE ENGLISH TEST

Before we dive into the details of the content and strategy, let's review what the English test looks like. Remember, the five tests on the ACT are always given in the same order, and English is always first.

The English test includes five prose passages on topics ranging from historical essays to personal narratives. Each passage is typically accompanied by 15 questions for a total of 75 questions that you must answer in 45 minutes. Portions of each passage are underlined, and you must decide if these are correct as written or if one of the other answers would fix or improve the selection. Other questions will ask you to add, cut, or reorder text, while still others will ask you to evaluate the passage as a whole.

WRITING

While the idea of English grammar makes most of us think of persnickety, picky rules long since outdated, English is actually a dynamic, adaptive language. We add new vocabulary all the time, and we let common usage influence and change many rules. Pick up a handful of style books, and you'll find very few rules that everyone agrees upon. This is actually good news for studying for the ACT: you're unlikely to see questions testing the most obscure or most disputed rules. However, few of us follow ALL of even the most basic, universally accepted rules when we speak, much less when we email, text, or Snapchat.

The 4 C's: Complete, Consistent, Clear, and Concise

ACT test writers will never make you name a particular error. But with 75 questions, they can certainly test a lot of different rules—and yes, that's leaving out the obscure and debated rules. You would drive yourself crazy if you tried to learn, just for the ACT, all of the grammar you never knew in the first place. You're much better off with a common-sense approach. We'll teach you the rules that show up the most often, and we'll show you how to crack the questions that test them. What about all the rest of the questions? That's where the 4 C's come in.

Good writing should be in **complete** sentences; everything should be **consistent**; the meaning should be **clear**. The correct answer, free of any errors, will be the most **concise**. All of the rules we'll review fall under one or more of the 4 C's. But even when you can't identify what a question is testing, apply the 4 C's, and you'll be able to answer even the most difficult questions.

We'll explain in greater detail what the 4 C's mean in the grammar review and in the following lessons. But first, let's discuss your general strategies and overall approach to the English test.

HOW TO CRACK THE ENGLISH TEST

The Passages

As always on the ACT, time is your enemy. With only 45 minutes to review five passages and answer 75 questions, you can't read a passage in its entirety and then go back to do the questions. For each passage, work the questions as you make your way through the passage. Read from the beginning until you get to the end of a sentence with an underlined selection, work that question, and then resume reading until the next underlined portion and the next question.

The Questions

Not all questions are created equal. In fact, ACT divides the questions on the English test into two categories: (1) usage and mechanics and (2) rhetorical skills. These designations will mean very little to you when you're taking the test. All questions are worth the same number of points, after all, and you'll crack most of the questions the same way, regardless of what ACT calls them. Many of the rhetorical skills questions, however, are on organization and style, and some take longer to answer than other questions. Since there is no order of difficulty of the passages or of the questions, all that matters is that you identify your *Now, Later, Never* questions and make sure you finish.

The best way to make sure you finish with as many correct answers as possible is to use our 5-step Basic Approach.

Step 1: Identify the Topic

For each underlined portion, finish the sentence, and then look at the answers. The answers are your clues to identifying what the question is testing. Let's start off with this first question.

Nigerian author Chimamanda Ngozi Adichie,
<u>   </u>
                    1
is highly acclaimed for her novels, short stories,

and essays.

1. **A.** NO CHANGE
   B. author, Chimamanda Ngozi Adichie
   C. author Chimamanda Ngozi Adichie
   D. author, Chimamanda Ngozi Adichie,

Do any of the words change? No. What is the only thing that does change? Commas. So what must be the topic of the question? Commas.

Always identify the topic of the question first. Pay attention to what changes versus what stays the same in the answers.

> **Same Approach**
> You'll use the same approach for both the pencil-and-paper ACT and the ACT Online Test. The questions are the same on both tests!

Step 2: Use POE

You may have chosen an answer for question 1 already. If you haven't, don't worry: we'll review all the rules of commas in the next lesson. But let's use question 1 to learn the next step, POE. To go from good to great on the English test, you can't just fix a question in your head and then find an answer that matches. Instead, after you've identified what's wrong, eliminate all the choices that do not fix the error.

For question 1, the comma after *Adichie* is unnecessary and should be deleted. Use your pencil or the Answer Eliminator to cross off the answers that leave it in, (A) and (D).

1. **A.** ~~NO CHANGE~~
   B. author, Chimamanda Ngozi Adichie
   C. author Chimamanda Ngozi Adichie
   D. ~~author, Chimamanda Ngozi Adichie,~~

Now compare the two that remain, (B) and (C). Do you need the comma after *author*? No, you don't need any commas, so (C) is the correct answer. Here's where you could have messed up if you didn't use POE: if you knew all along you didn't need any commas, you could have easily missed that new comma in (B) and chosen incorrectly. POE on English isn't optional or a backup when you're stuck. You have to first eliminate wrong answers and then compare what's left.

Let's go on to the next step.

Step 3: Use the Context

Even though you may struggle with time on the English test, you can't skip the non-underlined text in between questions in order to save yourself a few minutes. Take a look at this next question.

After Adichie won a MacArthur

Genius Grant in 2008, she <u>will publish</u> a book of

short stories called *The Thing Around Your Neck*.

2. F. NO CHANGE
    G. published
    H. was published
    J. publishes

Use your pencil or the Highlighter tool to help you focus on the context needed to answer the question.

Don't forget to apply the first two steps. The verb in the answer choices is changing, specifically verb tense. How do you know which tense to use? Look at the beginning of the sentence: the phrase *After Adichie won* tells us we want past tense, so eliminate the choices that don't use past tense.

2. F. ~~NO CHANGE~~
    G. published
    H. was published
    J. ~~publishes~~

The is one of the 4 C's in action: *consistent*. The correct tense has to be consistent with the clues in the non-underlined portion. Next, compare (G) and (H). Choice (H) says that Adichie *was published a book*, which isn't a correct phrasing--it should be "published" a book. Therefore, (G) is correct.

Don't skip from question to question. The non-underlined text provides context you need.

Let's move on to the next step.

Step 4: Trust Your Ear, But Verify

For question 2, you may have never even considered (H) as serious competition for (G). It just sounds wrong, doesn't it? Well, it turned out you were right. In fact, your ear is pretty reliable at raising the alarm for outright errors and clunky, awkward phrasing.

You should, however, always verify what your ear signals by confirming the actual error. Steps 1 and 2 will help with that: use the answers to identify the topic, and use POE heavily.

But remember to be careful for errors your ear *won't* catch. Using the answers to identify the topic will save you there as well.

Let's try another question.

In March 2017, a panel chose Adichie's book

Americanah <u>as their</u> selection for a citywide

book club.

3. A. NO CHANGE
    B. it's
    C. they're
    D. its

That sounded pretty good to us, how about you? But before we circle NO CHANGE and go on our merry way, look at the answers to identify the topic and confirm there is no error. Only the pronoun changes, so the question is testing pronouns. We'll go over all the rules about pronouns a little later in this chapter and in Chapter 7, so we'll just give a short explanation here. *Their* is a plural pronoun, but *a panel* is singular. Cross off (A) and (C)—(C) isn't even the right type of pronoun, plural or not. Since we need a possessive pronoun, cross off (B) as well. Choice (D) is the correct answer.

Let's move on to our last step.

Step 5: Don't Fix What Isn't Broken

Read the next question.

Among a generation of new writers, Adichie

has <u>emerged as one of the freshest, most original</u>
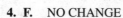
voices.

4. F. NO CHANGE
G. been distinguished and deemed
H. come on the scene as
J. made a strong case to be called

Sounds okay, so go to Step 1, identify the topic. Remember that saved us with question 3. *Everything* seems to be changing in the answers for question 4: what the question is testing isn't obvious at all. You can't confirm what you can't identify, so leave "NO CHANGE," and apply the 4 C's.

Does one of the answers fix something you missed?

Does one of the answers make the sentence better by making it more concise?

If the answer to both questions is No for all three other answers, the correct answer is (A), NO CHANGE.

NO CHANGE *is* a legitimate answer choice. Don't make the mistake of assuming that all questions have an error that you just can't spot. If you use the five steps of our Basic Approach, you'll catch errors your ear would miss, and you'll confidently choose NO CHANGE when it's the correct answer.

Pace Yourself

Repeat Steps 1–5 as you make your way through all the questions on all five passages. Since there is no order of difficulty in the passages or questions, your pacing goal is to finish.

Goal Score

Use the pacing strategies and score grid on page 22 to find your goal score for each practice test and, eventually, the ACT.

GRAMMAR REVIEW

This is not an exhaustive review of English grammar. It is an overview of the most common rules tested on the English test. We focus on the rules that show up the most AND that we know you can easily identify. In the next two chapters, we'll teach you how to crack those questions on the ACT. For now, we'll introduce you to the terms and rules you need to know.

Verbs

What's wrong with the following sentences?

1. Ryan play soccer.
2. Mary and Allison practices every day.
3. Next week, the team traveled to play its bitter rival.
4. Shivani has became the star of the team.

If you read thoughtfully, your ear probably caught all of the verb errors in these sentences. Remember, your ear will pretty reliably raise the alarm with many errors you'll encounter on the English test. You don't always need to know why a sentence is wrong to get the right answer, but the more you know why, the more you can count on getting that question right the next time it appears, and every time after that. Know the likely errors for verbs.

Subject-Verb Agreement

First, know your terms. A *subject* is the performer of an action. A *verb* is an action, feeling, or state of being. Verbs have to be consistent with their subjects. Singular subjects take the singular forms of verbs, and plural subjects take plural forms of verbs.

> ### The Rule
> Your ear can alert you to many, if not most, subject-verb agreement errors.
> **As a general rule, singular verbs end with *s* and plural verbs do not.**

*Ryan **plays** soccer.*

*Mary and Allison **practice** every day.*

Verb Tense

The tense of the verb changes with the time of the event.

Simple Tense

ACT tests your ability to choose from among the three simple tenses.

Past: *Last year, the team **finished** in last place.*

Present: *This year, the team **plays** a demanding schedule.*

Future: *Next week, the team **will travel** to play its bitter rival.*

Perfect Tenses

The perfect tenses provide additional ways to place an event in time. On the ACT, the perfect tenses appear less often than do the simple tenses.

Past perfect: *Before I went to the performance with Kelly, I **had** never **appreciated** ballet.*

Use the past perfect to make clear the chronology of two events completed at a definite time in the past, one before the other.

Present perfect: *I **have lived** in Chicago for ten years. I **have read** all the Harry Potter books.*

Use the present perfect to describe an event that began in the past and continues into the present, or to describe an event that was completed at some indefinite time before the present.

Future perfect: *Jim **will have left** by the time I arrive.*

Use the future perfect to describe an event that will be completed at a definite later time.

Irregular Verbs

ACT tests heavily the correct past *participles* of irregular verbs. Participle refers to the form the verb takes when it's paired with the helping verb *to have* to form a perfect tense. For regular verbs, the simple past tense and the past participle are the same.

*I **called** you last night. I **have called** you several times today.*

For irregular verbs, the two are different.

*Shivani **became** the star of the team*, or *Shivani **has become** the star of the team.*

Here is a list of some common irregular verbs.

Infinitive	Simple Past	Past Participle
become	became	become
begin	began	begun
blow	blew	blown
break	broke	broken
bring	brought	brought
choose	chose	chosen
come	came	come
drink	drank	drunk
drive	drove	driven
eat	ate	eaten
fall	fell	fallen
fly	flew	flown
forbid	forbade	forbidden
forget	forgot	forgotten
forgive	forgave	forgiven
freeze	froze	frozen
get	got	gotten
give	gave	given
go	went	gone
grow	grew	grown

Infinitive	Simple Past	Past Participle
hide	hid	hidden
know	knew	known
lay	laid	laid
lead	led	led
lie	lay	lain
ride	rode	ridden
ring	rang	rung
rise	rose	risen
run	ran	run
see	saw	seen
shake	shook	shaken
sing	sang	sung
speak	spoke	spoken
spring	sprang	sprung
steal	stole	stolen
swim	swam	swum
take	took	taken
teach	taught	taught
tear	tore	torn
throw	threw	thrown
wear	wore	worn
write	wrote	written

Pronouns

What's wrong with the following sentences?

1. The team nominated their goalie the most valuable player.
2. My friends and me took the train downtown.
3. Her and I worked on the group project together.
4. The crowd pushed Cesar and I onto the stage.

Pronoun Agreement

First, know your terms. *Pronouns* take the place of nouns. Pronouns have to be consistent with the nouns they replace in number and in gender.

	Female	Male	Things
Singular	she, her, hers	he, him, his	it, its
Plural	they, them, their	they, them, their	they, them, their

*The team nominated **its** goalie the most valuable player.*

Pronoun Case

Pronouns also need to be consistent with the function they perform in a sentence. There are three different cases of pronouns: *subject*, *object*, and *possessive*.

	1st person	2nd person	3rd person
Subject	I, we	you	she, he, it, they
Object	me, us	you	her, him, it, them
Possessive	my, mine, our, ours	your, yours	her, hers, his, its, their, theirs

*My friends and **I** took the train downtown.*

***She** and I worked on the group project together.*

*The crowd pushed Cesar and **me** onto the stage.*

Modifying Words

What's wrong with these sentences?

1. No one took her warnings serious.
2. Blizzard is a charmingly energetically puppy.
3. Farid is more busy than Wesley is.
4. Lara was the beautifulest girl at the prom.

Adjectives and Adverbs

Adjectives modify nouns. *Adverbs* modify everything else, including verbs, adjectives, and other adverbs. Most adverbs are formed by adding *-ly* to the end of an adjective.

*No one took her warnings **seriously**.*

*Blizzard is a charmingly **energetic** puppy.*

Comparisons and Superlatives

For most adjectives, an *-er* at the end makes a comparison, and an *-est* makes a superlative. But some adjectives need instead the word *more* for a comparison and the word *most* for a superlative.

*Farid is **busier** than Wesley is.*

*Lara was the **most beautiful** girl at the prom.*

In the following chapters, we'll show you how these rules appear on the ACT and how to crack those questions. We'll also discuss some of the more difficult and challenging concepts that you may face.

Summary

- Identify what the question is testing by examining the changes in the answer choices.

- Use POE heavily.

- Don't skip the non-underlined text: use it for context.

- Trust your ear, but verify by the rules.

- NO CHANGE is a legitimate answer choice.

- Good writing should be complete, consistent, clear, and concise.

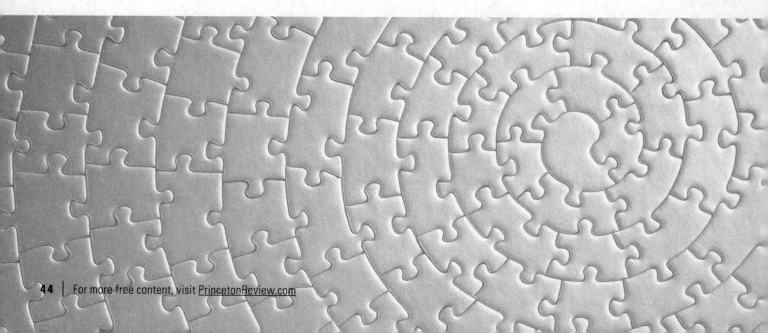

Chapter 6
Complete

The ACT English test contains a number of questions that test sentence structure and punctuation. This chapter discusses how to identify ideas as complete or incomplete and then explains how to punctuate different ideas. In addition to covering punctuation, the chapter also covers how to change ideas with the addition or removal of conjunctions.

COMPLETE AND INCOMPLETE IDEAS

Many questions on the English test involve sentence structure and punctuation. The correct structure and punctuation all depend on whether the ideas are complete or incomplete.

A complete idea can stand on its own, whether it's the entire sentence or just one part. Let's look at some examples.

1.   *Amanda throws strikes.*
2.   *Go Bears!*
3.   *Who won the game?*
4.   *The players celebrated after they won the game.*

Think of a complete idea as one part of a conversation. You don't have to say a lot to hold up one side of a conversation, but you can't leave your listener hanging. You have to finish your sentence. You can give commands, and you can ask questions too. Your listeners don't have to know what you're talking about: they just have to wait for you to finish to ask questions of their own. *What game are you asking me about? How did the team celebrate?*

In grammar terms, a complete idea must have a subject and a verb. Let's break down the examples above.

	Subject	Verb
1	*Amanda*	*throws*
2	*You* (understood)	*Go*
3	*Who*	*won*
4	*players* and *they*	*celebrated* and *won*

An incomplete idea can't stand on its own. Look at the following examples.

1.   *The batter who hit second*
2.   *Since you bought the hotdogs*
3.   *To get a batter out*
4.   *The team grabbed*

If anyone began a conversation with any of these, you would be waiting for the speaker to finish before you could speak. That's a sure sign all of the examples are incomplete: all of them are unfinished, and all would leave you hanging as a listener.

Now, in real-life terms, we may think some of those examples could be fine as answers to these questions: *Who got the run? Why did you buy the sodas? Why did he pitch a fastball?* Remember, however, that in real life we don't always follow the conventional rules when we speak. So let's define an incomplete idea in grammatical terms.

An incomplete idea is always missing something, whether a subject and verb (example #3), the main idea (example #2), or the rest of an idea (examples #1 and #4). None of these could stand on its own, and each would need to link up with another idea to make a sentence. ACT tests heavily how to link ideas with punctuation and conjunctions, so let's see how that works.

STOP PUNCTUATION

Imagine two trucks heading toward a busy intersection, one from the south and one from the west. If there were no traffic signals at the intersection, the two trucks would crash. Writing is just like traffic, depending on punctuation to prevent ideas from crashing into each other.

Two complete ideas are like two trucks and need the strongest punctuation to separate them. All of the punctuation in the box below can come in between only two complete ideas.

> ### STOP Punctuation
> Period (.) Semicolon (;) Question mark (?) Exclamation mark (!) comma + FANBOYS

Let's see how this works in a question.

> **FANBOYS** stands for For, And, Nor, But, Or, Yet, So.

After the thumping music <u>started. The bird</u>
<u>began to dance.</u>
1

1. **A.** NO CHANGE
   B. started, the bird began,
   C. started; the bird began
   D. started, the bird began

Here's How to Crack It

Begin with Step 1 of the Basic Approach you learned in Chapter 5. Use the differences and similarities in the answer choices to identify the topic. Whenever a question is testing STOP punctuation, use the Vertical Line Test. On the pencil-and-paper ACT, draw a vertical line where the Stop punctuation is to help you determine whether the ideas before and after the line are complete or incomplete.

After the thumping music <u>started.</u>│<u>The</u>
<u>bird began</u> to dance.
1

On the ACT Online Test, draw a "t" on your whiteboard. In the lower-left corner, write "started." In the lower-right corner, write "The."

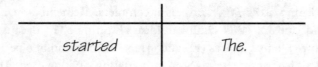

After the thumping music started is incomplete. *The bird began to dance* is complete. Mark the left side of the vertical line with an "I" and the right side with a "C." Stop punctuation can come in between *only* two complete ideas, go to Step 2 and use POE. Eliminate all the answers that don't fix the error (that is, the answers that include Stop punctuation), and compare those that are left.

1. ~~**A.** NO CHANGE~~
   B. started, the bird began,
   ~~**C.** started; the bird began~~
   D. started, the bird began

Using Steps 3 and 4, we can use the context of the rest of the sentence to confirm that we don't need the second comma that (B) offers. Choice (D) is the correct answer.

―――――――――――○―――――――――――

GO PUNCTUATION

Let's go back to the traffic analogy. Imagine a road with a stop sign at every block. Those stop signs prevent accidents, but when rush hour hits, traffic backs up. Stop signs need to be used strategically, so that they don't cause more problems than they solve. Punctuation functions the same way: use it to prevent accidents, but don't slow down ideas and make the sentence longer than necessary, or just plain incomprehensible.

> Go punctuation could be either a comma or no punctuation at all, depending on the sentence. Go punctuation can link anything EXCEPT two complete ideas.

A sentence is a complete idea, regardless of how many complete and incomplete ideas it's made of, so it will always end with Stop punctuation. Within a sentence, use punctuation only to avoid an error or to make your meaning clear. Use Stop punctuation in between two complete ideas. Use a comma to slow down, but not stop, ideas. If you don't need to stop or slow down, don't use any punctuation. Keep traffic moving, and keep ideas flowing.

Here's another example.

―――――――――――○―――――――――――

I wondered how Snowball had learned to
dance, and asked his trainer.
‾‾‾‾‾‾‾‾‾‾
    2

2. **F.** NO CHANGE
   G. dance and
   H. dance; and
   J. dance. And

Here's How to Crack It

Use the Vertical Line Test whenever you see Stop punctuation, either in the test booklet or on your whiteboard. Because *and* is a FANBOYS word, draw two lines around the word *and*. The word *and* connects the ideas, so we won't consider it when we do the Vertical Line Test. The part before the first line, *I wondered how Snowball had learned to dance, is complete.* The part after the second line, *asked his trainer,* is incomplete. Remember, a comma plus *and* is Stop punctuation and can only link complete ideas. Eliminate (F) because the comma plus FANBOYS is not allowed here. Choices (H) and (J) use a semicolon or a period, but the second part of the sentence still isn't complete, so Stop punctuation can't be used. Therefore, (G) is the correct answer. In this case, Go punctuation (which here is no punctuation at all) is needed.

―――――――――――○―――――――――――

Commas

Commas work like blinking yellow lights: they slow down but do not stop ideas. In the real world, there is variation in when writers use commas, but when it comes to the ACT, all commas must be in the sentence for a reason. On the ACT, there are only four reasons to use a comma.

Stop

A comma by itself can't come in between two complete ideas, but it can when it's paired with what we call FANBOYS: *for, and, nor, but, or, yet, so.* A comma plus any of these is the equivalent of Stop punctuation. These words also impact direction, which might influence the correct answer.

> *The music changed suddenly, but Snowball picked up the new beat.*

Draw a vertical line on either side of *but* (either on the page or on your whiteboard) to help break the sentence into separate ideas. *The music changed suddenly* is complete. *Snowball picked up the new beat* is complete.

For the record, all conjunctions link things, but coordinating conjunctions—that is, FANBOYS—specifically come in between two ideas and are never a part of either idea.

Go

A comma can link an incomplete idea to a complete idea, in either order.

> *After Snowball stopped dancing, the trainer gave the bird another treat.*

> *Snowball rocked out to Lady Gaga, oblivious to the growing crowd of fans.*

Lists

Use a comma to separate items in a list.

> *Snowball prefers songs with a regular, funky beat.*

Regular and *funky* are both describing *beat*. If you would say *regular and funky* then you can say *regular, funky.*

> *Snowball seems to like best the music of Backstreet Boys, Lady Gaga, and Queen.*

Whenever you have three or more items in a list, always use a comma before the *and* preceding the final item. This is a rule that not everyone agrees on, but if you apply the 4 C's, the extra comma makes your meaning *Clear.* On the ACT, always use the comma before the word *and* or the word *or* in a list of three or more things.

Check for Commas

Look out for:

- words and phrases in a series
- introductory phrases and words
- mid-sentence phrases that are not essential to the sentence

---

For the Record

Semicolons can be used to separate items in a very complicated list, but ACT almost never tests this. Exclamation points and question marks show up only occasionally.

Unnecessary Info

Use a pair of commas around unnecessary information.

> *Further research has shown that parrots, including cockatoos, can dance in perfect sync to music.*

If information is necessary to the sentence in either meaning or structure, don't use the commas. If the meaning would be exactly the same but the additional information makes the sentence more interesting, use a pair of commas—or a pair of dashes—around the information.

Try the next questions.

_____

Many people point to dog dancing competitions to <u>argue that birds are not the</u> <u>only animals</u> that can dance.
                                        3

3. A. NO CHANGE
B. argue, that birds are not the only animals,
C. argue, that birds are not the only animals
D. argue that birds are not the only animals,

Here's How to Crack It

The changes in the answers identify the topic of the question: commas. Remember, there are only four reasons to use a comma on the ACT, and if you can't name the reason to use one, don't use one. If you thought the sentence was fine, leave NO CHANGE, and confirm none of the answers fixed something you missed. Think of ACT's comma rules, and determine whether any apply here. With neither STOP punctuation nor FANBOYS in play, it can't be two complete ideas or a list. If the Unnecessary Info rule is in play, (B) would mean *that birds are not the only animals* isn't necessary, but the sentence would make no sense without this phrase, so eliminate (B). The only other possible rule is GO, linking a complete idea to an incomplete idea. Neither (C) nor (D) offers a complete idea on one side of a comma, so eliminate both. The correct answer is (A), NO CHANGE.

_____

_____

Scientists now believe that the ability to <u>mimic, which only some creatures are capable,</u> of acquiring, is necessary for an animal to keep a synchronized beat.
                                        4

4. F. NO CHANGE
G. mimic, which only some creatures are capable
H. mimic, which, only some creatures are capable
J. mimic which only some creatures are capable

Here's How to Crack It

The changes in the answers identify the topic of the question: commas. By reading to the end of the sentence, you catch the comma that isn't underlined. Since the Unnecessary Info rule requires two commas, not three, check that rule first. The extra information is *which only some creatures are capable of acquiring,* and thus the correct answer is (G).

HALF-STOP

Colons and single dashes are very specific pieces of punctuation, and they are very flexible. They can link a complete idea to either an incomplete idea or another complete idea. The complete idea must come first, and the second idea will be a definition, explanation, or list. Since they are always used with at least one complete idea, use the Vertical Line Test whenever they appear in and out of answer choices.

Let's see two examples.

Parrots don't respond well to genres with the

least noticeable 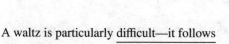upbeat; waltzes and salsa.
⁵

5. **A.** NO CHANGE
   B. upbeat, waltzes,
   C. upbeat: waltzes,
   D. upbeat: waltzes

Here's How to Crack It

Draw the vertical line in between *upbeat* and *waltzes*. The first idea is complete, but the second is incomplete. Eliminate (A). The list isn't *upbeat, waltzes, and salsa,* so eliminate (B). The list is only two things, so the comma in (C) is unnecessary. The correct answer is (D).

A waltz is particularly difficult—it follows
⁶

a three-beat pattern.

6. **F.** NO CHANGE
   G. difficult it follows
   H. difficult, it follows
   J. difficult, it follows,

Here's How to Crack It

Draw the vertical line between *difficult* and *it*. Both are complete ideas, so eliminate (G), (H), and (J). Choice (F) is correct.

―――――――――○―――――――――

Identical Punctuation

In question 6, a period, a semicolon, or a colon could have been used. Notice, however, that none of those appeared among the answer choices. ACT won't make you evaluate those subtle differences that might make one punctuation mark better than the others when they all perform essentially identical functions. Knowing which forms of punctuation are identical is a powerful POE tool. After all, you can't have two right answers, so if two or more choices are identical, they all must be wrong.

CONJUNCTIONS

Punctuation isn't the only way to link ideas. On some of the more difficult questions on sentence structure, you have to change the ideas by adding or deleting the conjunction.

Here are some of the more common conjunctions you may see.

> although, as, because, if, since, that, until, what,
> when, where, which, while, who, whom

Proper grammarians might object to calling *what, which, when, where, who,* and *whom* conjunctions, but the technical terms aren't important on the English test. It's not as if ACT makes you name any part of speech, and all that matters is that those words, when they are used in a sentence instead of a question, act just like conjunctions. They make an idea incomplete. (Look at how we used *when* in the next-to-last sentence in this paragraph!)

Add a conjunction to make an idea incomplete, or take one out to make the idea complete.

Let's see how this works in a few questions.

―――――――――○―――――――――

The African grey parrot, which also mimics human speech and therefore can dance.
[7]

7. **A.** NO CHANGE
   B. parrot which
   C. parrot that
   D. parrot

Here's How to Crack It

If conjunctions change in the answer choices, the question is likely testing Complete. When you read to the end of the sentence, you're left hanging, waiting for the main point about African grey parrots. The sentence is incomplete, and the only way to fix it is to take out the conjunction. Choice (D) is correct.

Try another.

The videos of Snowball dancing have sparked a serious area of study, researchers admit they appreciate the sheer entertainment value.

8. **F.** NO CHANGE
   G. Although the videos
   H. The videos appearing all over the Internet
   J. Since the videos

Here's How to Crack It

If it sounded fine to your ear, using the answers to identify the topic will help you either spot something you missed or verify that NO CHANGE is correct. If conjunctions change in the answer choices, it is likely testing Complete. Check whether the entire sentence makes a complete idea and that all ideas within are joined correctly. There are two complete ideas in the sentence, separated only by a comma. A comma alone is GO punctuation, so eliminate (F) and (H). You need a choice with a conjunction added to the first idea, making it incomplete. Conjunctions vary by direction, which we'll discuss in the next lesson. The two ideas show a contrast—*serious* and *entertainment*—so (G) is correct.

English Drill 1

Try an English passage on your own. Use the Basic Approach explained in Chapter 5. Answers are in Chapter 25.

Portraiture for the Common Man

Kehinde Wiley's paintings are powerfully disorienting for the way they blur the lines between new and old styles. Wiley paints large canvases that watch the many
$\underline{}$
1

achievement's of African-American men. His portrait of
2

Ice-T, the rapper and reality-TV star, draws from a nineteenth-
3
century portrait of Napoleon. His striking portrayal of singer

Michael Jackson drawing on the influence of Peter Paul
4

Rubens. Although each of Wiley's subjects is famous, his
5
portraits cannot help but make his audience see them in new ways.

In these paintings, Wiley uses very traditional techniques. Inspired by the Dutch masters, Wiley oversees a painting workshop: the ideas are his own, but the artisan assistants in his workshop aid in the completion of the paintings. This
6
collaborative process allows for Wiley's vast output and allows him to impartially oversee the quality of the work. In addition,

1. **A.** NO CHANGE
   B. color
   C. celebrate
   D. speak

2. **F.** NO CHANGE
   G. achievements's
   H. achievements'
   J. achievements

3. **A.** NO CHANGE
   B. Ice-T
   C. Ice-T:
   D. Ice-T;

4. **F.** NO CHANGE
   G. drawn
   H. draws
   J. while drawing

5. **A.** NO CHANGE
   B. Often painted in large dimensions,
   C. Born in 1977 in Los Angeles,
   D. Loved and adored by art critics,

6. **F.** NO CHANGE
   G. complete
   H. end with completing
   J. complete the end of

Wiley's assistants <u>gather</u> the raw materials and mix the paints,
₇

thereby making <u>them</u> a classical work from start to finish. This
₈
attention to detail and process made Wiley an art-world

celebrity <u>in the time of life known as the early 20s.</u> Wiley has
₉
forced art lovers to reconsider the relationship between the old
and the new. After all, paintings created by such profoundly
traditional means do not usually have the faces of contemporary
celebrities staring out of them.

    <u>Wiley's father was Nigerian, and Wiley did not meet him</u>
₁₀
<u>until a trip to Africa in his early 20s.</u> Some of his most famous
₁₀

works <u>of Harlem</u> portray various, anonymous men Wiley has
₁₁

seen on the streets. In <u>his</u> more recent work, Wiley brings his
₁₂
classic style to the common people of Israel and the West

Indies. [13] To glorify people from oppressed cultures all over

7. **A.** NO CHANGE
    B. have gathered
    C. were gathering
    D. gathered

8. **F.** NO CHANGE
    G. it
    H. each
    J. each painting

9. **A.** NO CHANGE
    B. at the young age of being in his 20s.
    C. in his 20s.
    D. between the ages of 20 and 30.

10. Given that all the choices are true, which one most effectively introduces the paragraph?

    F. NO CHANGE
    G. Wiley grew up in South Central Los Angeles, but he made his name in Harlem.
    H. Although it was difficult financially for his mother, Wiley received the best art education money could buy.
    J. However, Wiley's focus is not exclusively on celebrities, and he is just as interested in "average" people.

11. The best placement for the underlined portion would be:

    A. where it is now.
    B. after the word *portray*.
    C. after the word *Wiley*.
    D. after the word *streets* (and before the period).

12. **F.** NO CHANGE
    G. its
    H. them
    J. their

13. At this point, the writer is considering adding the following true statement:

    His paintings were shown in the National Portrait Gallery in Washington, D.C., in 2008.

Should the writer make this addition here?

    A. Yes, because it gives another instance of Wiley's popularity.
    B. Yes, because it demonstrates why Kehinde Wiley traveled abroad.
    C. No, because it strays from the paragraph's focus on Wiley's body of work.
    D. No, because it shifts the focus of the paragraph from the streets of Harlem to a museum in D.C.

the world, by depicting his subjects in the types of poses and
<u>14</u>
backgrounds usually reserved for royalty. He shows that even

those to whom history pays no attention can have their own

regal dignity.

　　Wiley's works can be seen in galleries all over the world

because the everyday appearance of those he portrays has an

almost universal appeal. Wiley may draw on the work of many

earlier artists, but his unique contribution is to show that art

need not be restricted to those who can afford to commission it,

or even those who are interested in viewing it.

14. **F.** NO CHANGE
　　G. depicting
　　H. by which Wiley depicted
　　J. Wiley depicts

15. The writer is considering deleting the underlined portion
(adjusting the punctuation as needed). Should the underlined portion be kept or deleted?

　　A. Kept, because it gives additional information about how
Wiley chooses his subjects.
　　B. Kept, because it offers one idea for why Wiley's popular-
ity is so far-reaching.
　　C. Deleted, because it repeats other information given in the
previous paragraph.
　　D. Deleted, because it undermines claims made in the previ-
ous paragraph about Wiley's importance.

Summary

o ACT writers like to test your knowledge of whether sentences are put together and punctuated correctly.

o A complete idea can stand on its own as a complete sentence even though it may be part of a longer sentence. An incomplete idea can't stand on its own as a complete sentence and must be appropriately linked to another idea.

o Stop punctuation includes a period, a semicolon, an exclamation mark, a question mark, and a comma plus FANBOYS. Stop punctuation can only come between complete ideas.

o Go punctuation includes a comma and nothing at all. Go punctuation can link anything except two complete ideas.

o Always put a comma before *and* at the end of a list with three or more items.

o Always put a pair of commas (or a pair of dashes or parentheses) around unnecessary info.

o Colons and single dashes must follow a complete idea but can precede a complete or incomplete idea.

o Conjunctions make an idea incomplete.

Chapter 7
Consistent, Clear, and Concise

The key to an outstanding ACT English score is to focus on the topics that show up the most often *and* which are both easy to identify and simple to fix. In this chapter, we'll teach you how to crack questions on verbs, pronouns, apostrophes, and transitions. For each topic, following the rules makes good writing consistent, clear, and concise.

VERBS

A verb expresses an action, feeling, or state of being. The form of a verb depends on the number of the subject—singular or plural—the time of the event, and the presence of helping verbs. Whenever you spot the verb changing among the answer choices, use these three steps along with your Basic Approach.

1. Identify the subject. The verb must be consistent with its subject: singular subject with a singular verb, and plural subject with a plural verb.
2. Check the tense. The tense must be consistent with the setting and the participle. Use the context of the non-underlined portion to determine whether the verb should be past, present, or future.
3. Be concise. Pick the shortest answer free of any errors.

Here's an example.

Each of the first three taxis I saw <u>were</u> too far away to hail.
₁

1. **A.** NO CHANGE
   B. are
   C. is
   D. was

Here's How to Crack It

Use the changes in the answers to identify verbs as the topic ACT is testing. Both tense and number seem to be changing, so find the subject first. What was too far away? *Each* of the taxis. *Each* is singular, so eliminate the plural forms of the verb, (A) and (B). Now check the tense. *Saw* is past tense, so choose the past tense, (D).

Tricky Pronouns

Question 1 wasn't testing pronouns directly—the changes among the answer choices were verbs. To answer correctly, however, you had to know that the pronoun *each* is singular. The following pronouns are all singular.

anybody	either	nobody
anyone	everybody	somebody
each	everyone	someone

Your ear should reliably raise the alarm over a subject-verb agreement error, both for tricky pronouns and regular nouns. Consider the following examples.

*Somebody **love** me.*
*Everyone **like** ice cream.*
*Each **are** beautiful.*
*Nobody **do** it better.*

Your ear probably automatically fixed these.

*Somebody **loves** me.*
*Everyone **likes** ice cream.*
*Each **is** beautiful.*
*Nobody **does** it better.*

This is why your ear can frequently help you eliminate the wrong answers on verb questions. But remember Step 4 of the Basic Approach: trust, but verify, your ear. Confirm the error by making sure you have correctly identified the subject.

Prepositional Phrases

Another way ACT made question 1 confusing was by burying the subject to the left of the prepositional phrase. *Each **of the first three taxis** I saw were too far away to hail.* Prepositions are little words that show a relationship between nouns. Some examples are *at, between, by, in, of, on, to,* and *with*. A prepositional phrase modifies—that is, describes—a noun. ACT will add prepositional phrases to distract you from the subject, so be on the lookout for them. Always look to the left of the preposition to find your subject. Try the following examples. Does the subject agree with its verb?

Only one of the dresses fit me.
A selection of fruit, cheese, and nuts were served at the party.
The argument between Pat and Ron sadden all of us.
The books on the table is due back to the library.

Cross out the prepositional phrases to find the subject and confirm the verb.

*Only **one** ~~of the dresses~~ **fits** me.*
*A **selection** ~~of fruit, cheese, and nuts~~ **was** served at the party.*
*The **argument** ~~between Pat and Ron~~ **saddens** all of us.*
*The **books** ~~on the table~~ **are** due back to the library.*

Irregular Verb Participles

ACT can make verb tense difficult as well. Most tense questions are straightforward choices of past, present, or future. However, ACT sometimes likes to test the correct past participle for irregular verbs.

Let's try another ACT question.

I <u>woken up</u> at 10:30 to find that my alarm
₂
clock had failed to go off.

2. **F.** NO CHANGE
   G. had woke
   H. woke
   J. waked

Here's How to Crack It

The changes in the answers identify verbs as the topic. The subject, *I*, doesn't change the form, and all of the choices are in past tense. Use POE to get rid of all the wrong answers that do not use the correct form of the irregular verb, *to wake*. The simple past tense of *wake* is *woke*, so cross off (J) because *waked* isn't a word. The past participle of *wake* is *woken*: this word must go along with a helping verb such as *has*, *have*, or *had*. Therefore, (F) is wrong because it doesn't contain the helping verb. Choice (G) contains the helping verb *had* but uses the simple past *woke* instead of the past participle *woken*. Only the past participle can go with the helping verb *had*, so eliminate (G). Choice (H) is the only correct form.

Regular verbs follow a predictable pattern.

You Don't Have to Be Perfect

The perfect tenses change the time of an event in subtle ways. You will never need to identify by name a particular tense on the ACT, nor choose between the present and present perfect. Choose the past perfect to establish an order of one event happening in the past before another.

*Present: I **study** for the ACT every day.*
*Present perfect: I **have studied** for months.*
*Simple past: I **studied** all day yesterday.*
*Past perfect: I **had studied** for the SAT before I decided to switch to the ACT.*

Irregular verbs are the problem. While you can usually use your ear to find the correct participle, you can look over the list on page 41 for some of the most common irregular verbs. The *infinitive* is the form of the verb used with *to*; the simple past works on its own, without a helping verb; and the *past participle* works with a form of the helping verb *to have*.

Need a refresher on irregular verbs? Check out the table in Chapter 5.

*Infinitive: Jacob would like **to become** a biotech engineer.*
*Present perfect: Hannah **has become** a star swimmer.*
*Simple past: Samara **became** a voracious reader.*
*Past perfect: Jonah **had become** tired of practicing.*

Let's try another ACT question.

My boss was mad that I had forgot to
bring the report I had been preparing at home.
(underlined segment marked 3)

3. **A.** NO CHANGE
   B. forgotten to bring the report that I had prepared at home.
   C. forgotten to bring the report that had been prepared at home by me.
   D. forgotten to bring the report I had been preparing at home.

Here's How to Crack It

The changes in the answer choices identify verbs as the topic, specifically past participles. Choice (A) incorrectly uses the simple past *forgot* with the helping verb *had*, so you can eliminate it right away. Choices (B), (C), and (D) all fix that error, so compare the differences among them. Choice (B) works, so keep it. Choice (C) uses passive voice, making the sentence unnecessarily longer, so eliminate it. Choice (D) replaces *had prepared* with *had been preparing*, which is a more awkward phrasing as the point is that the report was prepared at home, not "being prepared" at home. The correct answer is (B).

Passive Voice

In question 3, (B) was the most concise in part because it uses the active voice. Choice (C) is passive, which makes the sentence much longer. Both active and passive voice are grammatically correct—they just describe one event in two different ways. Compare the following sentences:

Beatrice prepared the fine meal.

The fine meal was prepared by Beatrice.

Beatrice makes the meal in both sentences. Active voice preserves the performer of the action, *Beatrice,* as the subject. Passive voice promotes the receiver of the action, in this case *the meal,* to subject and changes the verb by adding the helping verb *was.*

How to Spot Passive Voice

Look for forms of the verb *to be* and the preposition *by.*

How to Crack It

Choose passive voice *only* when you're confident that the other three choices contain a grammatical error. Otherwise, go with active voice. While there can be good reasons to use passive voice, ACT generally prefers active voice.

PRONOUNS

Pronouns take the place of nouns and make your writing more concise. On the ACT, several questions will test the correct usage of pronouns. Whenever you spot pronouns changing among the answers, use these two steps with your Basic Approach.

> Revisit Chapter 5 for lists of different types of pronouns.

1. Find the original. The pronoun has to be consistent in number and gender with the noun it replaces and other related pronouns.
2. Check the case. Choose the correct pronoun based on its specific function in the sentence.

Let's try a few examples.

----○----

Have you ever had a day when you wished

<u>you could have</u> just stayed in bed?
   4

4. **F.** NO CHANGE
     G. you could of
     H. one could of
     J. one could have

Here's How to Crack It

Nothing seems obviously wrong, so leave (F) and use the answers to see if you missed something. Pronouns and verbs are changing—sort of; *of* is not a verb, even if it sounds like *have*. Eliminate (G) and (H). The pronoun should be consistent with the *you* in the non-underlined portion, so eliminate (J). Choice (F) is correct.

----○----

Try another.

----○----

The taxi driver <u>who finally picked up my</u>
                   5

<u>boss and I</u> wouldn't take credit cards.
  5

5. **A.** NO CHANGE
     B. whom finally picked up my boss and I
     C. who finally picked up my boss and me
     D. which finally picked up my boss and myself

Here's How to Crack It

The changes in the answers identify pronouns as the topic of the sentence. There are two pronouns in the underlined portion, so consider both and follow your two steps. *Taxi driver* is a person, and *which* is used only for things. *Myself* is correct only for emphasis (I myself don't know the answer) or when the subject and object are the same (I corrected myself). Cross off (D). Check the case for *who* and *I,* and don't worry—it's perfectly okay to check *I* first since everyone is scared of "who" versus "whom" (see "Who Versus Whom" below). For case, cross off everything except the pronoun and the verb. *Picked up I* is incorrect because *I* is a subject pronoun, so eliminate (A) and (B). The correct choice is (C), and you didn't even have to worry about "who" and "whom." Now go learn about them so you don't have to depend on luck the next time.

----○----

Who Versus Whom

Who is the subject pronoun. *Whom* is the object pronoun. Why do they seem so hard to all of us? Very few movies and television shows use *whom* when it's needed, and most of us do the same in our regular conversations.

How to Crack It

Whenever you see *who* and *whom* tested on the ACT, try *he* and *him* in their place. If you would say *he called me*, you would say *who called me*. If you would say *I called him*, you would say *whom I called*. Don't worry about how the words flip: just match your "m" pronouns and you'll be fine.

APOSTROPHES

Similar to pronouns, apostrophes make your writing more concise. They have two uses: possession and contraction.

Possession

To show possession with singular nouns, add *'s*, and with plural nouns ending with *s*, add just the apostrophe after the *s*. For tricky plurals that do not end in *s*, add *'s*.

Consider the following examples.

The new car of Peter = *Peter's new car*
The room of the girls = *the girls' room*
The room of the men = *the men's room*

To show possession with pronouns, never use apostrophes. Use the appropriate possessive pronoun.

His car
Their room
Its door

> **Pronouns Most Frequently Misused**
> The ACT test writers will sometimes try to confuse you by presenting both a possessive pronoun and the same pronoun in a contraction as answer choices. Do you know the difference between these words: *whose, who's; its, it's*?

Contractions

Whenever you see a pronoun with an apostrophe, it's (it is) a contraction, which means the apostrophe takes the place of at least one letter.

Consider the following examples.

It is important. = ***It's** important.*
They are happy to help. = ***They're** happy to help.*
Who is the leader of the group? = ***Who's** the leader of the group?*

Because these particular contractions sound the same as some possessive pronouns, these questions can be very tricky on the ACT. You can't use your ear—you have to know the rules above. Let's look at some sample ACT questions.

I watched in dismay as my laptop was

crushed beneath the <u>taxis wheels'.</u>
₆

6. **F.** NO CHANGE
   G. taxis' wheels.
   H. taxi's wheels'.
   J. taxi's wheels.

Here's How to Crack It

The changes in the answer choices identify apostrophes as the topic. Use POE heavily with apostrophes: eliminate all the answers that are wrong. If you just try to fix it in your head and find a match, you'll likely miss something. *Wheels* don't "possess" anything in this sentence, so eliminate (F) and (H). The wheels belong to the taxi, so an apostrophe is needed on that word. Eliminate (F), and (J) is the correct answer.

Its' screen was smashed to pieces.
7

7. **A.** NO CHANGE
   B. Their
   C. It's
   D. Its

Here's How to Crack It

The changes in the answer choices identify apostrophes/pronouns as the topic. There is no such word as *its'*, so eliminate (A). The *laptop* (context from the non-underlined portion in the previous question) is singular, so eliminate (B). To determine whether you need the possessive or a contraction, expand out to *it is*. *It is screen* makes no sense, so choose the possessive pronoun, (D).

TRANSITIONS

In Chapter 6, we used traffic as an analogy to explain punctuation. If good writing is like a pleasant drive, then transitions are road signs, preventing you from getting lost and helping you make important turns. Good transitions are consistent with the flow of ideas.

Many words can act as transitions. Some are specific to the context, where only one word will fit the precise meaning. But others are just slight variations, giving you directions: *turn around* or *keep going*. Here's a partial list.

> ### Turn Around
> although, but, despite, even though, however, nonetheless, nevertheless, or, yet
>
> ### Keep Going
> and, because, finally, furthermore, moreover, since, so, thus, therefore

Try an example.

I apologized for not having the report ready,

since she had told me the report wasn't due for
8
another week.

8. **F.** NO CHANGE
    G. even though
    H. because
    J. and

Here's How to Crack It

The changes in the answer choices are transition words, but they are also a mix of FANBOYS and conjunctions. Before you consider direction, make sure the sentence is complete and that all ideas within the sentence are joined correctly. All are correct and complete, but the sentence doesn't make sense because the direction is wrong. It is a transitions question. The two ideas on either side of the transition word disagree, so choose a *turn around* word. Only (G) makes sense.

CONCISION

All the 4 C's are important on the ACT. They are your framework for understanding the topics that you can identify and your strategy to conquer the questions whose topics you can't identify. But concise isn't just a strategy or a tool used to understand certain grammar rules. Sometimes, ACT tests it directly.

Try the following examples.

Next, my boss was furious that I was late.
9

9. **A.** NO CHANGE
    B. My
    C. Then, my
    D. Next my

Here's How to Crack It

The changes in the answer choices identify transitions as the topic, possibly with commas as well. Use POE. The words *then* and *next* mean the same thing when used in this context. If both could be right, both must be wrong. Eliminate (A) and (C). *Next* should have a comma after it because it's an introductory idea, so eliminate (D) also. The correct answer is (B) because you do not need a transition word here.

ACT will frequently test concise in a question concerning transitions. If you don't need a transition word for your sentence to be either complete or clear, don't use it. In the answer choices for question 9, note how *my boss* appeared in each, and one choice featured only *my boss* (and was correct). That is a reliable sign ACT is testing concise.

Try these additional questions.

———————————○———————————

I was already an hour and a half late for <u>work</u>

<u>and not on time.</u>
₁₀

10. **F.** NO CHANGE
    G. work, and behind schedule.
    H. work and delayed in getting the morning started.
    J. work.

Here's How to Crack It

The appearance of *work* in every choice and by itself in one identifies the topic as concise. Use POE and pay attention to the non-underlined portion of the sentence for context. The narrator has already established she's late, so all of the other choices are unnecessarily wordy. The correct answer is (J).

———————————○———————————

English Drill 2

Try another English passage on your own. Answers are in Chapter 25.

A Tunnel to History

After school let out, my best <u>friend and I,</u> used to go to one
of the oldest parts of the city. From the little trail beside the
school, we'd climb down to the old railway tunnel that had

gone dark many years <u>before that</u> pitch darkness was terrifying
and mysterious. We would go down, staring into that darkened

tunnel, <u>having</u> our flashlights. We would leave our backpacks
at the edge of the tunnel, knowing that they would be good
landmarks when we re-emerged. As the throng of New Jersey

Turnpike traffic roared overhead, we would enter. 〔4〕 But we
were always looking for the traces of the history of our city.

[1] When we first started going down into the tunnel, we

didn't do so with any specific <u>purpose really</u> we just liked
going to this place that everyone else was too scared to visit.
[2] Our history teacher directed us to some books at the public
library. [3] We learned that this railroad used to be a very busy
one, shipping goods from the western states to New York City.
[4] The long highway ramp that passed over the tunnel and
the whole area was actually pretty new: as recently as thirty
years ago, <u>there</u> had been no ramp at all. [5] What was now all
abandoned marshland had once been its own neighborhood,

1. A. NO CHANGE
   B. friend, and I
   C. friend and I
   D. friend, and I—

2. F. NO CHANGE
   G. before, the
   H. before. The
   J. before, yet the

3. Which choice best conveys the idea that the narrator and
   his friend held their flashlights nervously?

   A. NO CHANGE
   B. clutching
   C. carrying
   D. donning

4. Which of the following true statements, if added here,
   would most effectively continue the narration of what happened during the summer walks the friends took?

   F. We were friends throughout most of middle school and
      high school.
   G. The tunnel was wide enough for two tracks, but it con-
      tained only one.
   H. Sometimes, we'd cast eerie shadows on the walls or listen
      to the echo of our voices in the long tunnels.
   J. Many rail lines have been shut down since the advent of
      trucking in the United States.

5. A. NO CHANGE
   B. purpose real
   C. purpose: really,
   D. purposely: really,

6. F. NO CHANGE
   G. they're
   H. their
   J. it is

lined with streets and houses. [6] After a few aimless visits, though, we started to look more into the history of the area. 7

7. For the sake of the logic and coherence of the paragraph, Sentence 6 should be placed:

A. where it is now.
B. before Sentence 1.
C. before Sentence 2
D. before Sentence 4.

Being a teenager in New Jersey, history is everywhere.
8

8. F. NO CHANGE
G. Being raised in
H. Raising a family
J. Where I grew up

Four centuries earlier our history teacher told us that our town
9
had been settled by Dutch traders. But the Lenape tribes had already been living there for many thousands of years. In fact, in the early seventeenth century, when the Dutch arrived, the

9. The writer wants to stress the amount of time that had passed since his city had first been settled by Europeans. Assuming that the capitalization would be adjusted as needed, where should the underlined portion be placed?

A. Where it is now
B. After the word *teacher*
C. After the word *us*
D. After the word *settled*

Lenape were one of the most powerful tribes in the region: an
10
area that spread from Delaware to Massachusetts to upstate New York. The tribe's influence is still with us. The Dutch

10. F. NO CHANGE
G. region
H. region;
J. region is

settlers were ruthless in the conquest of the region, which they
11
held on to many Lenape names, such as Manhattan, Raritan,

11. A. NO CHANGE
B. and
C. but
D. then

and Tappan. Lah-di-dah, the area looks so different now, but the
12
Lenape influence is still undeniably there,

12. F. NO CHANGE
G. Moving right along, the
H. Meanwhile, the
J. The

commemorated by the names.
13

13. A. NO CHANGE
B. commemorate
C. commemorating
D. in memoriam

This history lesson enriched our trips around the secret
<u>corridors</u> of the city because we began to feel all of our town's
14
historical layers at once. We became so enmeshed in the history

of our city that we were invited <u>to give presentations, to our</u>
15
fellow classmates and teachers. A little curiosity goes a long
way: you never know what you'll find in a place that people
have ignored for many years.

14. Which of the following alternatives to the underlined portion would NOT be acceptable?

    F. hidden
    G. lesser-known
    H. classified
    J. secluded

15. **A.** NO CHANGE
    B. to: give presentations
    C. to give: presentations
    D. to give presentations

Summary

- Verbs, pronouns, apostrophes, and transitions are heavily tested on the ACT.

- All four are readily identifiable from changes in the answer choices, and all have relatively few rules to use to evaluate the question.

- The 4 C's can be applied to evaluate any question whose topic you can't identify. ACT also tests concise as its own topic.

- When working on a concise problem, be biased toward the answer choice that says DELETE, but do not assume it will be the correct answer all or even half the time.

Chapter 8
Rhetorical Skills

ACT categorizes the questions on the English test as either Rhetorical Skills or Usage and Mechanics. For most questions, the Basic Approach used to crack them is the same, regardless of how ACT labels them. Some questions, however, require a different approach. In this chapter, we'll teach you how to crack questions that ask for wrong answers, as well as questions on strategy and order.

EXCEPT/LEAST/NOT

You know a question is tricky when the right answer is wrong. That is, if the question asks you to identify the choice that is "NOT acceptable," you have to cross off three answers that work and choose the one that doesn't.

For the Record

Not all EXCEPT/LEAST/NOT questions are Rhetorical Skills questions by ACT standards. Our argument is that when most of the "questions" are just four answer choices, the presence of a true question demands a different category and different approach.

The EXCEPT/LEAST/NOT questions, or E/L/N for short, hide in plain sight, posing a challenge to spot. Most of the "questions" on the ACT English section do not actually include a question: instead, they feature only answer choices and the task is to choose the best one. However, some questions will actually include a bona fide question, and if you're not careful, it's easy to jump straight to the answers and overlook the fact that your task is different on these questions. Moreover, many of the topics on E/L/N will look familiar: Stop/Go punctuation and transition questions are two topics heavily tested in this format, so the four answers look pretty much the same way they always do.

Since it can be tricky to think of answers that *do* work as the wrong answers, treat these as Yes/No questions. Cross off the EXCEPT/NOT/LEAST word; then go through the answers and write "Yes" by the ones that work and "No" by the ones that don't. The one "No" you have at the end is the one that isn't acceptable and is therefore the correct answer.

I gave my information to the director of the animal shelter. She promised to contact me if any French Bulldogs came in. ¹

1. Which of the following alternatives to the underlined portion would NOT be acceptable?

   A. shelter; she
   B. shelter, and she
   C. shelter, she
   D. shelter, who

Here's How to Crack It

Cross out NOT. Since the sentence used Stop punctuation, write "Yes" next to the answers that also use Stop punctuation, (A) and (B). Before you worry about (D), which changes the wording, focus on the remaining choice with the exact same wording as the original sentence. Remember that a comma alone can never be Stop Punctuation, so (C) is grammatically wrong. Write a "No" next to that one. That will be the odd one out, so it is the correct answer.

Word Choice and Idioms

Two of the most popular and challenging topics ACT tests are word choice and idioms, either in regular or E/L/N format. Word choice refers to selecting the precise word that fits with the context. An idiom is an expression that requires a specific preposition. Idioms follow no grammatical rules—they are what they are.

Both word choice and idioms will be easy to spot by the changes in the answers, but neither fits our standards for being easy to fix. Use POE heavily with these, and don't let them drag you down in your pacing.

Try some more examples.

> **Idioms**
> Idioms are expressions that require the use of a specific preposition. Fortunately, you'll be familiar with many of the idioms on the test. The best way to spot them is to look for prepositions in the answer choices.

I remember well the day I first saw Wheezie at the animal shelter. In truth, I think Wheezie is the one who <u>adopted me</u>.
₂

2. Which of the following alternatives to the underlined word would be LEAST acceptable?

   F. selected
   G. assumed
   H. picked
   J. chose

Here's How to Crack It

Cross out LEAST. Use POE, trying each answer choice in place of *adopted*. Choices (F), (H), and (J) could all mean the same thing, but *assumed* just doesn't work and is therefore the correct choice.

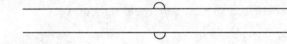

After an hour of play, chew toys, tennis balls, and stuffed animals were strewn <u>around</u> the
₃
living room.

3. Which of the following alternatives to the underlined word would be LEAST acceptable?

   A. on
   B. throughout
   C. all over
   D. about

Here's How to Crack It

Cross out LEAST. This is testing an idiom, specifically which prepositions work with *strewn*. Use POE, trying each answer choice in place of *around*. Choices (B), (C), and (D) could all work with *strewn*, but *on* doesn't work. Therefore (A) is the correct choice.

While idioms aren't repeated frequently on the ACT, there are several sets of frequently confused words that tend to show up. These are the most commonly tested ones.

Affect vs. Effect

Affect—(verb) to cause to happen or change
> *The rain did not **affect** my weekend plans.*

Effect—(noun) the result of something
> *The rain did not have any **effect** on my weekend plans.*

Allusion vs. Illusion vs. Elusion

Allusion—a reference to something
> *The mention of Mount Olympus was an **allusion** to Greek mythology.*

Illusion—a visual trick
> *The painting's use of perspective gives it the **illusion** of depth.*

Elusion—escaping or avoiding
> *After fifteen minutes of trying to catch my cat, I grew tired of his **elusion**.*

Cite vs. Site vs. Sight

Cite—to point to or show as a source
> *Opponents of the bill **cite** an increase in pollution as a potential downside.*

Site—the location of something
> *This lot is the future **site** of a new school.*

Sight—related to seeing
> *At the **sight** of the bus approaching, I began to run.*

Could/would/might/should of vs. Could/would/might/should have

The correct phrases are *could have*, *would have*, *might have*, and *should have*. *Could of* and any of the others with *of* are never correct, so eliminate them right away.

Lay vs. Lie vs. Laid

Lay—to place or put down
> *Please **lay** the papers on the table.*

Laid—past tense of *lay*
> *I **laid** the papers on the table as you asked me to.*

Lie—to recline
> *I like to **lie** on the couch while I watch TV.*

Lay—past tense of *lie*
> *Yesterday I **lay** on the couch while watching TV.*

Hint: In present tense, if you can replace the verb with *put*, you want *lay*. If not, it's *lie*. A few idioms to know are *lay the foundation for*, *lay the groundwork for*, and *lay claim to*.

Lead vs. Led

Lead—(rhymes with deed) to guide or be in charge of something

*Our choir teacher will **lead** us in the next song.*

Led—past tense of *lead*

*Our choir teacher **led** us in the last song.*

Hint: People get this one confused because of the word *lead*, which sounds like *led* but refers to a type of metal. When referring to leadership, *lead* is pronounced with a long -e sound. The past tense is *led*.

Passed vs. Past

Passed—went by

*The deadline for submissions to the contest has already **passed**.*

Past—previous, already happened

*Your **past** actions will be considered in your evaluation.*

Hint: *Passed* is a past-tense verb, while *past* is an adjective or noun. The meanings are somewhat similar, but you must choose the correct part of speech for the sentence. For *passed*, ask yourself: did something go by? If so, *passed* is correct.

Than vs. Then

Than—used to make a comparison

*I have seen more episodes **than** you have.*

Then—used to refer to time

*It was **then** that I decided to major in English.*

Bonus: "Rather then" is never correct. It's *rather than*.

STRATEGY QUESTIONS

Strategy questions come in many different forms, but they all revolve around the *purpose* of the text. Among the different types of Strategy questions, expect to see questions asking you to add and replace text, determine whether text should be added or deleted, evaluate the impact on the passage if text is deleted, or judge the overall effect of the passage on the reader.

Let's see some examples.

———○———

Many dog owners turn to animal trainers when they find they can no longer control their pets. Most experts find that a poorly trained dog has received plenty of affection but not enough discipline or exercise. ⁤4

4. Which of the following sentences provides new, specific guidelines about the proper training of a dog?

F. Behavior that was cute in a twenty-pound puppy is alarming in a one hundred-pound adult dog.

G. Would-be dog owners should consider their own lifestyles and the temperament of a specific breed before adopting the animal.

H. Dogs should be walked at least three times a day and should never be given a treat without first obeying a command.

J. Small children should never be left unsupervised with a dog.

Here's How to Crack It

Identify the purpose of the proposed text. According to the question, one of these choices *provides new, specific guidelines about the proper training of a dog*. We don't even need to go back into the passage: find an answer choice that fulfills the purpose. Choices (F), (G), and (J) all may be true, but they do not offer any *specific* information about training a dog. Only (H) does that, and it is the correct answer.

———○———

Try another.

Wheezie's puppy playfulness masked the steely determination of a true French bulldog, and she stubbornly resisted all the lessons from our obedience class. [5]

5. At this point, the writer is considering adding the following true statement:

> My nephews trained Blizzard, a black lab with a sweet disposition, very easily.

Should the writer add this sentence here?

A. Yes, because it explains why the author felt so insecure about her difficulties training her dog.

B. Yes, because it provides an important detail about another breed of dog.

C. No, because it doesn't explain how Blizzard was trained.

D. No, because it distracts the reader from the main point of this paragraph.

Here's How to Crack It

Whenever a strategy question asks if you should add or delete new text, evaluate the reasons in the answer choices carefully. The reason should correctly explain the purpose of the selected text. Here, choice (D) is correct because there is no reason to add text that is irrelevant to the topic.

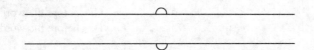 Most puppy books no longer recommend using newspapers to housebreak dogs. I bought three safety gates to block off the kitchen from the rest of the house. I also brought home a crate, baby blankets to make it cozy, a stylish collar and matching leash, several bags of food, and of course, plenty of toys.

6. Given that all choices are true, which one provides the best opening to this paragraph?

F. NO CHANGE

G. When I was growing up, my family had an Irish Setter and four cats.

H. I made sure I had all the supplies we'd need before bringing Wheezie home.

J. Many people prefer cats as pets.

Here's How to Crack It

In many strategy questions, the purpose is to add a sentence to open or close a paragraph or tie two paragraphs together. Use the context of the paragraph, and read through to the end before deciding. Since the author mentions several things she's bought in preparation, (H) provides the best introduction to the paragraph.

───────────○───────────

ORDER

There are also several types of Order questions, but they all involve the correct placement of ideas. Some order questions will ask you to correctly place a modifier or additional text. Other questions will ask you to evaluate and possibly correct the order of sentences within a paragraph or the paragraphs themselves.

All order questions work best with POE. Ideas should be consistent and the meaning should be clear, but that meaning can be difficult to understand until ideas are in their proper place.

Let's look at a few examples.

───────────○───────────

French bulldogs can face a serious number of health issues affecting the respiratory system, knees, and eyesight.

7. The best placement for the underlined word would be:
   A. where it is now.
   B. before the word *French* (revising the capitalization accordingly).
   C. before the word *health*.
   D. before the word *respiratory*.

Here's How to Crack It

Use POE, trying the word in the places suggested by each answer choice. The correct answer is (C) because it modifies health issues and therefore includes all three listed. "Serious" to mean "a lot of" is slang and thus appeals to your ear. But "large" is not a definition of serious, literally or figuratively, and none of the other definitions really apply to the figurative meaning of "large."

───────────○───────────

Order of Sentences

If there is a question on order of the sentences or placement of new text within a paragraph, all of the sentences in the passage will be numbered. NO CHANGE could be the answer to the order of the sentences, but if you're reading along and get confused by a sudden shift in the action, that's a good sign the sentences are in fact out of order. Do not go back and reread, but instead wait until you get to the question.

Don't waste time trying to reorder all of the sentences yourself. Look for transition words that indicate an introduction, a conclusion, or a pair of sentences that should go back to back, and use POE.

Try an example.

---

[4]

[1] He recommended an excellent specialist to perform the surgery. [2] When the day came, I drove to the hospital, dreading the moment I'd need to leave her behind. [3] While we waited for her to be admitted, Wheezie sensed something was wrong and curled up on my lap, trembling. [4] My vet broke the bad news that Wheezie would have to have surgery to correct the problems in her nasal passage and vocal chords.

8. Which of the following sequence of sentences will make the paragraph most logical?

   F. NO CHANGE
   G. 2, 3, 1, 4
   H. 4, 3, 2, 1
   J. 4, 1, 2, 3

Here's How to Crack It

Use POE. The surgery isn't properly introduced until the end, which means Sentence 4 should be the introduction. Eliminate (F) and (G), and determine whether Sentence 3 or 1 should be next. Sentence 1 should come before Sentence 3 because Sentence 1 happens before the surgery and Sentence 3 is on the day of the surgery, so the answer is (J).

Order of the Paragraphs

If there is a question on the order of the paragraphs, there will be a warning at the beginning of the passage, alerting you that the paragraphs may or may not be in the correct order and identifying which question will ask about which paragraph.

Almost no one ever spots this warning. Treat these the same way you treat the order of the sentences. If you suddenly find yourself confused by an inexplicable shift in the action, check above the title to see if the warning is there. Alternatively, continue reading and working the questions and bet safely you'll encounter a question on the order of the paragraphs at the end of the passage.

AND IN THE END...

> Questions 14 and 15 ask about the passage as a whole.

Other than order of the paragraphs, two other questions routinely appear at the end and are always preceded by the announcement above.

Placement of New Info

The paragraphs will also be numbered for a question testing the placement of additional info.

---

14. The writer is considering adding the following sentence to the essay:

    > After a night spent winning the hearts of all of the attendants, Wheezie bounded out of the recovery room and into my waiting arms.

    If the author were to add this sentence, it would most logically be placed at:

    F. Point A in Paragraph 1.
    G. Point B in Paragraph 3.
    H. Point C in Paragraph 3.
    J. Point D in Paragraph 5.

Here's How to Crack It

Okay, so this is a little unfair: we didn't give you the entire passage, so you can't answer this one. However, we'll give you some tips for answering these questions when you do have a whole passage. First off, if the topic of the sentence fits more with the ideas toward the beginning or end of the passage, or in a certain paragraph, you could start with those options. If you're not sure, go straight to POE. Then look for clues in the sentence. Pronouns and phrases beginning with *this* and *such* are good clues about what must have been mentioned in the previous sentence. Look at the sentences surrounding the bracketed letter in the passage to see how the new sentence fits in.

Grading the Passage

Questions at the end that ask you to evaluate the passage are another version of a strategy question. The question identifies the purpose of the passage and asks you to determine whether the author succeeded. These are always at the end, so we waited to show you here.

---

15. Suppose that one of the writer's goals had been to address the role obedience classes can play in the healthy development of dogs. Would this essay fulfill that goal?

   A. Yes, because the essay implies the writer and her dog benefited from obedience classes.
   B. Yes, because the essay indicates French bulldogs are not easily trained.
   C. No, because the essay is focused on one anecdote about one dog.
   D. No, because the essay indicates the dog displayed aggressive and territorial behavior.

Here's How to Crack It

With all strategy questions, identify the purpose in the question. With questions that use a Yes/No format, connect the purpose in the question to the reasons given in the answer choices. Choice (C) is the correct answer.

Rhetorical Skills Drill

In the drill below, you will find questions focusing only on Rhetorical Skills, so it is only 9 questions long. Before you start, take a few moments to go back over the review material and techniques. Answers are in Chapter 25.

> The following paragraphs may or may not be in the most logical order. Each paragraph is numbered, and question 9 will ask you to choose where Paragraph 2 should most logically be placed.

[1]

The golden age of television means many things to many people, but to the small band of actors, writers, and directors who would rise to prominence in the late '50s and early '60s, without a doubt it meant the television shows such as
$$\underline{1}$$

Playhouse 90, on which many of them worked for the first live time.
$$\underline{2}$$

[2]

Despite the undeniable risks of live performances—or perhaps because of them—the results rank among the greatest achievements in American entertainment. Many of the show's productions were later remade, for both television and film, including *Requiem for a Heavyweight, Judgment at Nuremberg,* and *Days of Wine and Roses.* [3] Many critics maintain none of the remakes could match the brilliance and electricity of the live performances displayed in *Playhouse 90.*

[3]

[1] Each week, a new "teleplay" was created from scratch—written, cast, rehearsed, and performed. [2] *Playhouse 90* was truly a remarkable training ground for young talents. [3] Such future luminaries as Rod Serling, Sidney Lumet, Paddy Chayefsky, Marlon Brando, and Patricia Neal worked long

1. Which of the following alternatives to the underlined word would be LEAST acceptable?
   A. fame
   B. projection
   C. stardom
   D. greatness

2. The best placement for the underlined word would be:
   F. where it is now.
   G. before the word *actors*.
   H. before the word *doubt*.
   J. before the word *television*.

3. The writer is considering deleting the preceding sentence. Should the sentence be kept or deleted?
   A. Kept, because it provides context for the reference to remakes in the next sentence.
   B. Kept, because it is crucial to understanding why *Playhouse 90* was a success.
   C. Deleted, because it does not match the objective tone of the essay.
   D. Deleted, because it contains information that has already been provided in the essay.

hours reading scripts. [4] In some cases, when there

were problems with the censors, it would have to be created

twice. |5|

[4]

Due to the frantic pace, accidents happened frequently.
David Niven once revealed that, during an early show, he
inadvertently locked his costume in his dressing room two
minutes before air time. As the announcer read the opening
credits, the sound of axes splintering the door to Niven's
dressing room could be heard in the background. |7|

4. Which choice would most clearly indicate that the actors,
   writers, and directors became extremely skilled?

   F. memorizing their lines.
   G. honing their craft.
   H. constructing the set.
   J. skimming the want-ads.

5. Which sequence of sentences makes the paragraph most
   logical?

   A. NO CHANGE
   B. 1, 2, 4, 3
   C. 2, 1, 4, 3
   D. 2, 3, 1, 4

6. Given that all choices are true, which one most effectively
   introduces this paragraph?

   F. NO CHANGE
   G. The ratings for *Playhouse 90* were unimpressive.
   H. Broadway has produced many famous actors as well.
   J. *Playhouse 90* ran on CBS from 1956 to 1961.

7. The writer is considering deleting the preceding sentence.
   If the writer were to make this deletion, the essay would
   primarily lose a statement that:

   A. explains the organization of the last paragraph.
   B. adds a much needed touch of humor to the essay.
   C. explains how one accident was resolved.
   D. adds nothing, since the information is provided elsewhere
      in the essay.

Questions 8 and 9 ask about the preceding
passage as a whole.

---

8. Suppose that one of the writer's goals had been to write a
   brief essay describing an influential program in television's
   history. Would this essay fulfill that goal?
   F. Yes, because it explains that many future stars underwent
      valuable training working on *Playhouse 90*.
   G. Yes, because it mentions that *Playhouse 90* had the greatest
      number of viewers in its time slot.
   H. No, because it fails to mention any future stars by name.
   J. No, because even though many future stars received their
      start on *Playhouse 90*, few ever returned to television.

9. For the sake of the logic and coherence of this essay, Paragraph 2 should be placed:

   A. where it is now.
   B. before Paragraph 1.
   C. after Paragraph 3.
   D. after Paragraph 4.

Summary

- o   The official categories of Usage and Mechanics and Rhetorical Skills do not matter if you use the same approach to cracking them.

- o   Questions that come with actual question marks—as opposed to just replacement options for an underlined portion—do need a different approach.

- o   For EXCEPT/LEAST/NOT questions, cross off the E/L/N word and use POE.

- o   All strategy questions involve a purpose.

- o   Order questions involve the correct placement of words, sentences, and paragraphs.

Part III
How to Crack the ACT Mathematics Test

Chapter 9
Introduction to the ACT Mathematics Test

The second section of the ACT will always be the Math test. To perform your best, you'll need to become familiar with the structure and strategy of the ACT Math test. In this chapter, we discuss the types of questions you can expect to see and how you can use organizational strategy, estimation, and elimination skills to improve your Math score.

WHAT TO EXPECT ON THE MATH TEST

You will have 60 minutes to answer 60 multiple-choice questions based on "topics covered in typical high school classes." For those of you who aren't sure if you went to a typical high school, these questions break down into rather precise areas of knowledge.

The Math section usually breaks down into the following:

Preparing for Higher Math (34–36 questions)
- Number & Quantity (4–6 questions)
- Algebra (7–9 questions)
- Functions (7–9 questions)
- Geometry (7–9 questions)
- Statistics and Probability (5–7 questions)

Integrating Essential Skills (24–26 questions)

Modeling (15+ questions)

What Not to Expect on the Math Test

The ACT does not provide any formulas at the beginning of the Math test. Before you panic, take a second look at the chart above. Because the ACT is so specific about the types of questions it expects you to answer, preparing to tackle ACT Math takes a few simple steps.

A NOTE ON CALCULATORS

Not all standardized tests allow calculators. Fortunately, ACT does. We're not about to give you the stodgy advice that you shouldn't use your calculator—quite the opposite, in fact. Your calculator can help to save a ton of time on operations that you may have forgotten how to do or that are easy to mess up. Adding fractions, multiplying decimals, doing operations with big numbers: why not use a calculator on these? The place where you have to be really careful with your calculator, though, is on the easy ones. Let's see an example.

1. What is the value of $3x^2 + 5x - 7$ when $x = -1$?
   A. -15
   B. -9
   C. -1
   D. 5
   E. 15

Here's How to Crack It

If you have your calculator handy, use it. This problem is pretty straightforward, but a calculator can help to put everything together. BUT, make sure you're treating the -1 with the respect it deserves. What you punch into your calculator should look something like this:

$$3(-1)^2 + 5(-1) - 7$$

When working with negative numbers or fractions, make doubly sure that you use parentheses. If not, a lot of weird stuff can happen, and unfortunately all of the weird, wrong stuff that can happen is reflected in the wrong answer choices. If you computed this expression and found -9, (B), you got the right answer. Well done. If not, try to go back and figure out where you made your calculator mistake.

Types of Calculators

Throughout the rest of the Math chapters, we discuss ways to solve calculator-friendly questions in an accurate and manageable way. Because TI-89 and TI-92 calculators are not allowed on the ACT, we will show you how to solve problems on the a TI-80 series calculator. If you don't plan to use a TI-80 series calculator on the test, we recommend you make sure your calculator is acceptable for use on the test and that it can do the following:

- handle positive, negative, and fractional exponents
- use parentheses
- graph simple functions
- convert fractions to decimals and vice versa

> Use your calculator, but use it wisely. Be careful with negative numbers and fractions.

THE PRINCETON REVIEW APPROACH

Because the test is so predictable, the best way to prepare for ACT Math is with:

- a thorough review of the very specific information and question types that come up repeatedly
- an understanding of The Princeton Review's test-taking strategies and techniques

In each Math chapter in this book, you'll find a mixture of review and technique, with a sprinkling of ACT-like problems. At the end of each chapter, there is a summary of the chapter and a drill designed to pinpoint your math test-taking strengths and weaknesses. In addition to working through the problems in this book, we strongly suggest you practice our techniques on some real ACT practice tests. Let's begin with some general strategies.

Order of Difficulty: Still Personal

The Math test is the only part of the ACT that is in Order of Difficulty (OOD). What this means is that the easier questions tend to be a bit earlier in the exam, and the harder questions are later. Usually, this means that question 1 is a freebie and question 60 is a doozy. None of the other tests have an OOD, unfortunately, so they are all about Personal Order of Difficulty (POOD). This OOD in and of itself is great to know when planning how you will attack this part of the ACT.

Now, we all love easy questions, but hold on for a second. If you and I both get a B on a math test at school, is it necessarily because we got exactly the same questions right or wrong? Unfortunately, no. What makes for a hard question? Is it hard because it's a long word problem, or is it hard because it tests some arcane concept that your teacher went over for like five seconds? Only the very hardest questions will be both. So even on the Math test of the ACT, you still need to use your POOD. The things you might find easy or hard won't necessarily jibe with ACT's OOD.

Now

Do the problems you're sure you can do quickly and accurately.

Later

If a problem looks time-consuming, save it for later. Do the Nows first.

Never

Sometimes it's better to just walk away. If a problem has you totally stumped, answer with your Letter of the Day and move on.

Now, Later, Never

Hard questions take a long time. Easy ones take a short time. That's obvious, but as we've seen, the definition of an "Easy" question is a tough one to pin down. That's why you should be careful trusting ACT's Order of Difficulty on the Math test. The no-brainer approach is to open the test booklet and work questions 1 through 60 in order, but you can get a lot of extra points by out-thinking this test. You'll have a much easier time drawing your own road map for this test than letting ACT guide you.

Clearly, many, but not all, of the easy questions will be right in the beginning. This is why when you arrive at each question, you should first determine whether it is a Now, Later, or Never question. Do the Now questions immediately: they're the freebies—the ones you know how to do and can do quickly and accurately. Skip any questions you think might take you a bit longer or which test unfamiliar concepts—save them for Later. Make sure you get all the points you can on the problems you know you can do, no matter what the question number.

Once you've done all the Now questions, go back to all the ones you left for Later. But here you should be careful as well. For both Now and Later questions, don't rush and make careless errors. On the other hand, don't get stuck on a particular problem. In a 60-minute exam, think of how much spending 5 minutes on a single problem can cost you!

Finally, there's no problem with leaving a few questions behind in the Never category. The good news here is that these problems are not necessarily totally lost. Fill them in with a Letter of the Day: choose one pair of letters and bubble in all the blanks this way. For example, always bubble in A or F, B or G, etc. ACT doesn't have a guessing penalty, so there's nothing to lose, and you can even get lucky and score a few free points.

> **Flag Later, Not Never**
> On the ACT Online Test, use the Flag tool on Later questions so you can easily go back. *Don't* flag the Never questions—you don't want to waste your time looking at those questions again! In either case, put in your LOTD as you skip the question.

USE PROCESS OF ELIMINATION (POE)

Remember the major technique we introduced in Chapter 2: POE, or Process of Elimination. ACT doesn't take away points for wrong answers, so you should always guess, and POE can help you improve those chances of guessing. Don't make the mistake of thinking that POE is a strategy reserved only for English, Reading, and Science. Math has its own kind of POE, one facet of which we like to call Ballparking.

BALLPARK

You can frequently get rid of several answer choices in an ACT math problem without doing any complicated math. Narrow down the choices by estimating your answer. We call this Ballparking. Let's look at an example.

3. There are 600 school children in the Lakeville district. If 54 of them are high school seniors, what is the percentage of high school seniors in the Lakeville district?

   A. 0.9%
   B. 2.32%
   C. 9%
   D. 11%
   E. 90%

> **Cross Out the Crazy Answers**
> What's the average of 100 and 200?
> A. 500
> B. 150
> C. a billion

Here's How to Crack It
Before we do any serious math on this problem, let's see if we can get rid of some answer choices by Ballparking.

First, we need to figure out what percent 54 is of 600. It's pretty small, definitely way less than 50%, so we can eliminate (E) right off the bat. Now, think about easy percentages that you know—10% and 25%—and start from there. What's 10% of 600? Just move the decimal one place to the left to get it, and you'll find that 10% of 600 is 60. Therefore, if the number from the problem is 54, the answer must be less than 10%. Let's get rid of (D). Now, we know that 54 is pretty close to 60, so we want something close to 10% but slightly less, and the only possible answer is (C).

It may feel like we somehow cheated the system by doing the problem that way, but here's what ACT doesn't want you to know: the quick, easy way and the "real" way get you the same number of points. Not all problems will be so easily ballparkable, but if you think before you start frantically figuring, you can usually eliminate at least an answer choice or two.

WORD PROBLEMS

You've seen the breakdown of the topics that are tested on the ACT Math test. At a glance, it actually looks like the ACT should be kind of an easy test: you've definitely learned a lot of this stuff in school, a lot of it by the end of middle school. So what's the deal? Well, part of the deal is that ACT makes familiar stuff really unfamiliar by putting it into word problems. Word problems add some confusing steps that mask the often simple concepts trapped in the problems. Trap answers, partial answers, and weird phrasing abound in word problems. Is anyone else getting the feeling that this whole exam is about reading comprehension?

Word problems look a lot of different ways and test a lot of different math concepts, but if you keep these three steps in mind, you should be able to get started on most word problems.

We'll demonstrate these steps in action on the next page.

When dealing with word problems on the ACT Math test
1. **Know the question.** Read the whole problem before calculating anything, and underline or highlight the actual question.
2. **Let the answers help.** Look for clues on how to solve and ways to use POE (Process of Elimination).
3. **Break the problem into bite-sized pieces.** When you read the problem a second time, calculate at each step necessary and watch out for tricky phrasing.

Let's try a problem.

---

8. Each member in a club had to choose an activity for a day of volunteer work. $\frac{1}{3}$ of the members chose to pick up trash. $\frac{1}{4}$ of the remaining members chose to paint fences. $\frac{5}{6}$ of the remaining members still without tasks chose to clean school buses. The rest of the members chose to plant trees. If the club has 36 members, how many of the members chose to plant trees?

F. 3
G. 6
H. 9
J. 12
K. 15

Here's How to Crack It

Step 1: Know the Question

There is actually a slightly tricky step on this one. First of all, the problem doesn't tell you until the very end that there are 36 students in this class. Without this piece of information, the fractions don't mean much of anything. Second, the question is asking for the number of members who chose to plant trees, and we're going to have to figure out a bunch of other things before we can figure that out.

Step 2: Let the Answers Help

There aren't any crazy answers in this one, though if you noticed how much we're subtracting from 36, you're probably thinking that the answer will be one of the smaller numbers.

Step 3: Break the Problem into Bite-Sized Pieces

The starting point of this word problem actually comes at the end: this club has 36 members. Once you've got that, work the problem sentence by sentence, and pay particular attention to the language of the problem.

$$\frac{1}{3} \text{ of the members chose to pick up trash.}$$

A nice easy way to start. There are 36 members, and $\frac{1}{3}$ of 36 is 12, so 12 members pick up trash.

$$\frac{1}{4} \text{ of the remaining members chose to paint fences.}$$

This is just like the last piece, except for one HUGE exception, which comes from the word *remaining*. First, we'll need to figure out how many remaining members there are from the first step. There are 36 total members and 12 of them are picking up trash, so there are 24 members remaining. $\frac{1}{4}$ of 24 is 6, so 6 members paint fences.

$\frac{5}{6}$ of the remaining members still without tasks chose to clean school buses.

Write it down!
Don't do the steps of a Math question in your head, especially on word problems. Write each step on your whiteboard or test booklet. You'll actually save time by not having to redo steps, to say nothing of increasing your accuracy.

There's that word *remaining* again. There were 24 members in the last step, but 6 of them chose to paint fences, so now there are 18 *remaining* members. $\frac{5}{6}$ of 18 is 15, so 15 members clean school buses.

The rest of the members chose to plant trees.

There were 18 members left over in the last step, and 15 of them chose to clean school buses, which means there must be 3 students left to plant trees. Choice (F) is the correct answer. Look at those other answers; then look at the numbers you were dealing with in the problem: what a mess of partial answers!

If it seems like this took kind of a long time to do, don't worry; they won't all take this long. Most of these steps will come naturally after a while, and you'll have a solid base with which to begin any ACT Math problem in such a way that enables you to get to the answer as efficiently as possible.

PACING

As you work through the following lessons, revisit your POOD. The more content you review and the more you practice, the more you may find more Now questions and fewer Never questions.

GOAL SCORE

Use the pacing strategies and score grid on page 22 to find your goal score for each practice test and, eventually, the ACT.

Summary

o   On the ACT Math test, you have 60 minutes to attempt 60 questions. The vast majority of these questions will cover math concepts you learned in middle and high school.

o   Use your Personal Order of Difficulty to determine if a question is for Now, Later, or Never.
  •   Just because the Math test is technically in order of difficulty doesn't mean you need to do it in order.
  •   Never leave any blanks! Fill in the Never questions with your Letter of the Day.

o   Remember the Basic Approach for Word Problems.
  •   **Know the question.** Read the problem all the way through and underline the question.
  •   **Let the answers help.** Look for clues on how to solve. Use POE and Ballparking.
  •   **Break the problem into bite-sized pieces.** Every problem has lots of information: process each piece one at a time and be careful of tricky phrasing.

o   Finally, use your calculator liberally but wisely!

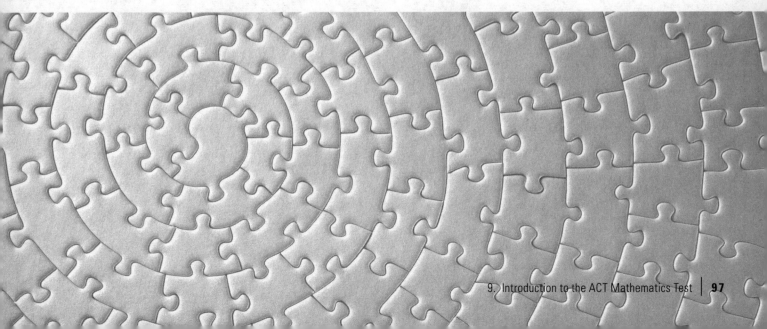

Chapter 10
Fundamentals

A solid base in the fundamentals of the math tested on the ACT is essential to getting a good score. We'll see a number of strategies that will help to work around some of the more advanced concepts, but there's often no way to work around questions that test the fundamentals.

VOCABULARY

Calculators can solve a lot of problems, but Vocabulary is one aspect of math with which a calculator can't help. Let's review some of the main terms.

A Note on Calculators

This chapter will deal mainly with concepts rather than operations. As mentioned in the previous chapter, we encourage you to use your calculator liberally but wisely. The operations discussed in this chapter will be those for which a calculator might be unhelpful or extra confusing.

Basics

Use the numbers below to answer questions 1 through 6 that follow. Check your answers against the Answer Key at the end of this chapter on page 122.

$$-81, -19, -9, -6, -\frac{1}{4}, -0.15, 0, 1.75, 2, 3, 12, 16, 81$$

1. List all the *positive numbers*. _____

2. List all the *negative integers*. _____

3. List all the *odd* integers. _____

4. List all the *even* integers. _____

5. List all the *positive, even* integers in *consecutive* order. _____
    _____

6. List all the numbers that are neither *positive* nor *negative*. _____
    _____

Now try these questions.

7. What is the *reciprocal* of $-\frac{1}{4}$? _____

8. What is the *opposite reciprocal* of 2? _____

9. When a number and its reciprocal are multiplied, what is the product?
    _____

10. How many times does 2 go into 15 evenly? _____

11. How much is left over? _____

12. What is 15 divided by 2? _____

Let's try it the other way. Use the following list of terms to answer questions 13 through 18.

> Number, Integer, Positive, Negative, Even, Odd,
> Consecutive, Reciprocal, Remainder

13. Which terms describe the number 6? _____

_____

14. Which terms describe the number $-\dfrac{1}{5}$? _____

_____

15. Which terms describe the number 0? _____

_____

16. When 14 is divided by 3, it has a _____ of 2.

17. The _____ of $-\dfrac{1}{4}$ is -4.

18. The numbers 2, 4, 6 are listed in _____ order, but the numbers 3, 1, 14 are not.

Factors and Multiples

Factors and multiples are all numbers that are divisible by other numbers. Start with examples, and the definitions will become easier.

> Example
> - The factors of 10 are 1, 2, 5, 10.
> - The first four positive multiples of 10 are 10, 20, 30, 40.

> **A Good Rule of Thumb**
> - The factors of a number are always equivalent to that number or *smaller*.
> - The multiples of a number are always equivalent to that number or *larger*.

1. List the factors of 12. _____
2. List the first four multiples of 12. _____
3. List the factors of 30. _____
4. List the first four multiples of 30. _____
5. Is 12 a multiple or factor of 24? _____
6. Is 8 one of the factors of 64? _____
7. What is the greatest common factor of 27 and 45? _____
8. What is the greatest common factor of 9 and 36? _____
9. What is the least common multiple of 9 and 12? _____
10. What is the least common multiple of 24 and 48? _____

Prime

> A prime number is any number with only two distinct factors: 1 and itself.

1. What are the single-digit prime numbers? _____
2. What is the only even prime number? _____
3. Is 1 a prime number? _____

The prime factorization of a number is the reduction of a number to its prime factors. Find the prime factorization of a number by using a factor tree. Consider this example:

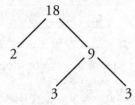

The prime factorization of 18 is $2 \times 3 \times 3$ or 2×3^2.

4.   What is the prime factorization of 36?

5.   What is the sum of all the prime factors of 36? _____

6.   What is the product of all the distinct prime factors of 36? _____

ADVANCED TERMS

Real Numbers and Their Imaginary Friends

ACT uses the term "real" a lot, but it's usually only there to scare you. Sometimes, though, ACT will test it directly, so it's good to have at least a sense of what the term means.

1.   How much would you like to earn in your eventual job?_____

2.   How much scholarship money do you want from your eventual college? _____

3.   What's the temperature in the Bahamas right now? (Ballpark it!) _____

4.   How many slices of pizza could you eat in a single sitting? _____

Unless you have some interesting ideas about money and/or pizza, ALL of the numbers above are real. The only numbers that aren't real are imaginary—a negative number under an even root.

5. What is $\sqrt{1}$? _____

6. What is -1×-1? _____

7. What is $-1 \times -1 \times -1$? _____

8. What is $\sqrt{-1}$? _____

9. What real number could you square to get a product of –1? _____

That last question was a trick: there is no real number that you can square and get a negative product. The only way to get the square root (or any even root) of a negative number is to *imagine* it.

$\sqrt{-1}$ is defined as the imaginary number *i*. All other imaginary numbers are something multiplied by *i*.

Rational Numbers and Their Irrational Friends

1. Write 0.5 as a fraction. _____

2. Write 3 as a fraction. _____

3. In the number $0.166\overline{6}$, what digit is coming next? _____

4. In the number, $0.1919\overline{19}$, what digit is coming next? _____

A *rational* number is any number that can be written as a fraction—that includes integers and repeating decimals. An *irrational* number is any number that cannot be written as a fraction because it goes on unpredictably. *Both* types of numbers are *real*.

Love Your Calculator for Real, but Be Rational

Your calculator can be a really handy tool for problems dealing with imaginary and irrational numbers. If you have a Texas Instruments TI-80 series calculator (such as the TI-84), the second function of the decimal is *i*. Use this function to solve the following problems.

5. $(2 + i)(2 - i)$? _____

6. $(3 + i)^2$? _____

Different calculator? No problem!
We're discussing the TI-80 series calculators in this book, but you should use the calculator that you're familiar with. Check out your calculator's manual or look up the calculator online to learn how to do these key operations.

To determine if a number is rational or irrational, it can help to try to convert it into a fraction. In the MATH menu, the first item is >*Frac*. This will convert a decimal to a fraction if the number is rational. For each question below, after you have typed in the number provided hit ENTER, then MATH>ENTER>ENTER. Give the result in the blank and identify whether it is rational or irrational.

7. 0.375 _____

8. 0.16666666666 (until the end of the screen) _____

9. π _____

10. 0.479109801431 _____

Exponents

Exponents are a shorthand way of indicating that a number is multiplied by itself. The exponent tells you how many times (for example, $5^4 = 5 \times 5 \times 5 \times 5$). Exponents are tricky when you have to combine them in some way. Here's a great way to remember all the rules.

> Remember MADSPM!
>
> * When you *multiply* two numbers with common bases, *add* the exponents.
> * When you *divide* two numbers with common bases, *subtract* the exponents.
> * When you raise an exponential number to a *power*, *multiply* the exponents.

Basic Rules

1. $(x^2)(x^3)$

2. $\dfrac{x^4}{x^3}$

3. $(x^4)^3$

4. $2x^2 \times 6x^3$

5. $(2x^2)^3$

6. $\dfrac{9x^6}{3x^2}$

7. $\dfrac{(x^2)(x^5)}{x^4}$

Special Rules

Follow the basic rules to see how some of these special rules are derived.

1. $\dfrac{x^4}{x^4}$

2. x^0

3. $\dfrac{x^2}{x^5}$

4. x^{-3}

5. x^1

6. 1^{513}

7. 0^{619}

8. $(-2)^2$

9. $(-2)^3$

10. -2^2

11. $\left(\dfrac{1}{2}\right)^2$

12. $\left(\dfrac{2}{3}\right)^2$

Scientific Notation

Scientific Notation is a way to concisely write very large or very small numbers.

Examples:

$$437{,}000{,}000{,}000{,}000 = 4.37 \times 10^{14}$$

$$0.000000000057 = 5.7 \times 10^{-11}$$

When representing a number with scientific notation, first move the decimal to the left or right until it creates a number from 1 up to, but not including, 10. In first the example, 437 trillion, the decimal was moved to the left 14 places so that the value was 4.37. Scientific notation always uses some multiple of 10 to represent the movement of the decimal. To determine the exponent of 10, simply count the number of places the decimal moved: in the first example, 14 places to the left. If the decimal moves to the left when creating scientific notation, the exponent will be positive. If it moves to the right when creating scientific notation, the exponent will be negative, as in the second example above.

The ACT may also contain problems that ask you to convert numbers from scientific notation back to the original number. To do that, work in reverse! If the number has a positive exponent of 10, move the decimal that many places to the right to make the number greater than 1.

$$3.9 \times 10^{6} = 3\underset{\cdots\cdots\cdots}{900000}$$

If the number has a negative exponent of 10, move the decimal that many places to the left to make the number less than 1.

$$2.5 \times 10^{-4} = 0.\underset{\cdots\cdots}{00025}$$

The ACT will also ask you to do calculations with numbers in scientific notation. The good news is that your calculator can do a lot of the work for you. Most calculators represent scientific notation by replacing × 10 with E. What your calculator returns will probably look like this:

$$7{,}320{,}000{,}000 = 7.32\text{E}9$$

Type the numbers below into your calculator and hit enter or = ; write what your calculator returns.

1. 37,600,000,000 _____

2. 0.00000000043 _____

3. 7.1×10^{-12} _____

4. 520,000 _____

In most calculators, the last number will come back as the same thing you typed in, 520,000. In situations like that it's important to know how to represent scientific notation without the help of your calculator.

Now that you know how to enter numbers in scientific notation, let's see how to use the calculator to do calculations on those numbers. First determine what the problem is asking and then plug the problem in exactly as you wrote it. Make sure you put parentheses around the numerator and denominator and close any parentheses your calculator opens.

But what if your calculator has trouble with scientific notation? Another option is to work the problem by hand. Let's simplify:

$$\frac{6.2\times10^5}{3.1\times10^3}$$

Here's how:

6.2×10^5 is the same as $6.2 \times 10 \times 10 \times 10 \times 10 \times 10$, and $3.1 \times 10^3 = 3.1 \times 10 \times 10 \times 10$.

If a question asks you to divide numbers in scientific notation, there are some shortcuts you can take to make the problem easier.

For example:

$$\frac{6.2\times10^5}{3.1\times10^3} = \frac{6.2\times10\times10\times10\times10\times10}{3.1\times10\times10\times10} = \frac{6.2\times10\times10}{3.1}\times\frac{10}{10}\times\frac{10}{10}\times\frac{10}{10}$$

And any number divided by itself is 1, so this expression simplifies to:

$$\frac{6.2\times10\times10}{3.1}\times 1 \times 1 \times 1 \text{ OR } \frac{6.2\times10\times10}{3.1}$$

One way to simplify this expression further is as follows:

$$\frac{6.2}{3.1}\times\frac{10}{1}\times\frac{10}{1} = 2 \times 10 \times 10 = 200$$

This process is time consuming, and time is a luxury on the ACT. Here's quicker version of the same solution:

$$\frac{6.2\times10^5}{3.1\times10^3} = \frac{6.2}{3.1}\times\frac{10^5}{10^3} = 2 \times 10^2 = 200$$

Let's try a problem:

———————————————◯———————————————

31. A warehouse ships out 5.3×10^4 packages per day during the holiday season. How many days will it take this company to ship out all of the 1.59×10^9 packages this holiday season?

   A. 3.3×10^5

   B. 3.0×10^4

   C. 3.3×10^8

   D. 3.0×10^{13}

   E. 3.3×10^{19}

Here's How to Crack It

The problem asks how many days it will take to ship 1.59×10^9 packages and states that the number of packages it can ship per day is 5.3×10^4. In order to determine the number of days it will take the factory to ship 1.59×10^9 packages, we need to divide 1.59×10^9 by the number of packages that the warehouse can ship each day, 5.3×10^4. The expression looks like this: $\frac{1.59 \times 10^9}{5.3 \times 10^4}$, and it can be rewritten as $\frac{1.59}{5.3} \times \frac{10^9}{10^4}$. The first fraction won't divide into an integer, so try writing the numbers out and cancelling the zeroes in the numerator and denominator: $\frac{1,590,000,000}{53,000} = \frac{1,590,000,\cancel{000}}{53,\cancel{000}} = \frac{1,590,000}{53} = 30,000$. This answer isn't in scientific notation, but the answer choices are, so it needs to be converted. Count the number of places the decimal needs to be moved to make a number between 1 and 10: $30{,}000$. It's 4 spaces to the left, so the exponent must be 4 and the value of the coefficient will be 3.0. The answer is 3.0×10^4, which is (B).

———————————————◯———————————————

Roots

You can add or subtract square roots only when the numbers under the square root sign are the same.

Example:

$$4\sqrt{x} + 2\sqrt{x} = 6\sqrt{x}$$

But $4\sqrt{x} + 2\sqrt{2x}$ can't be combined!

Multiplication and division are more flexible. Different values can be combined under the root, as long as the root has the same degree.

Example:

$$\left(\sqrt{x}\right)\left(\sqrt{y}\right) = \sqrt{xy}$$

$$\frac{\sqrt{x}}{\sqrt{y}} = \sqrt{\frac{x}{y}}$$

1. $\sqrt{x} + \sqrt{x} =$

2. $3\sqrt{x} + 5\sqrt{x} =$

3. $x\sqrt{3} + x\sqrt{5} =$

4. $\left(\sqrt{2x}\right)\left(\sqrt{y}\right) =$

5. $\left(\sqrt{x}\right)\left(\sqrt{xy}\right) =$

If ACT asks you to simplify exponents or roots with numbers instead of variables, use your calculator if necessary, but be extra careful with parentheses!

6. $4\sqrt{12} \times 2\sqrt{3} =$

7. $\dfrac{\sqrt{72}}{\sqrt{2}}$

8. $\left(\sqrt{529} - \sqrt{361}\right)^{\frac{1}{2}}$

Quadratic Formula

A quadratic equation is an equation of the second degree, which means that the highest exponent in the equation is 2. The standard form of a quadratic equation is $ax^2 + bx + c = 0$. On the ACT, you will need to know some important vocabulary associated with quadratic equations.

To give you an idea of how quadratics are sometimes calculated, let's first start by multiplying two binomials. A binominal is an expression of the sum or difference of two terms, and one example is $(x + 2)$.

Given the binomials $(x + 2)$ and $(x + 1)$, let's multiply to get a quadratic expression in standard form. We do this by using FOIL, an acronym standing for First, Outer, Inner, Last.

$$(x + 2)(x + 1)$$

FIRST: multiply the first terms of each binomial: $(x + 2)(x + 1)$

$$(x)(x) = x^2$$

OUTER: multiply the outer terms of each binominal: $(x + 2)(x + 1)$

$$(x)(1) = x$$

INNER: multiply the inner terms of each binominal: $(x + 2)(x + 1)$

$$(2)(x) = 2x$$

LAST: multiply the last terms of each binominal: $(x + 2)(x + 1)$

$$(2)(1) = 2$$

Now add those terms together and combine like terms:

$$x^2 + x + 2x + 2 = x^2 + 3x + 2$$

Factoring a quadratic is the opposite of FOILing it. When you are working with a quadratic equation in standard form, $ax^2 + bx + c = 0$, determine what the FIRST terms will be by looking at the coefficient of the x^2 term. Try the equation $x^2 + 5x - 6 = 0$. For this equation, the coefficient is 1, so the FIRST term of each binomial will be x. Write:

$$(x \quad)(x \quad) = 0$$

The second terms in each binomial will add up to b and multiply to c. One way to keep the work organized is to put it into a table with the first column representing the factor pairs that equal c and the second column representing the sums of those factors. Start by determining the factors of c, and then sum those factors in the second column.

In the equation $x^2 + 5x - 6 = 0$, $c = -6$, so the chart will look like this:

	Factors of –6	Sum of factors
I.	1, –6	$1 + (-6) = -5$
II.	2, –3	$2 + (-3) = -1$
III.	–1, 6	$-1 + 6 = 5$
IV.	–2, 3	$-2 + 3 = 1$

Row III gives factors of –6 that add up to 5, the b value in $x^2 + 5x - 6 = 0$. This means that the second terms in the binomials will be –1 and 6. Write:

$$(x - 1)(x + 6) = 0$$

Try a few yourself!

1. $x^2 + 7x + 12 = 0$ _____

2. $x^2 - 4x + 4 = 0$ _____

3. $x^2 - 6x - 16 = 0$ _____

Roots, Solutions, and *x*-intercepts

You may be wondering why the standard form of the quadratic equation is always set equal to 0, and that's a great question. A quadratic equation is another way to represent a parabola; you may also have seen it written $y = ax^2 + bx + c$. When you graph a parabola, in some cases it will intersect the *x*-axis. By setting $y = 0$, we can find the coordinates of *x* where the parabola crosses the *x*-axis, also known as the *x*-intercepts, roots, or solutions to the quadratic equation. One of the cool things about factoring a quadratic equation into binomials comes from the rule that anything multiplied by 0 is equal to zero.

Let's explore with the equation above.

$$x^2 + 5x - 6 = (x - 1)(x + 6) = 0$$

Since we are multiplying the binomials $(x - 1)(x + 6)$ and they are equal to 0, we know that one or both the binomials must be equal to 0.

$$x - 1 = 0 \qquad x + 6 = 0$$

Solving those binomials results in the following:

$$x = 1 \qquad x = -6$$

Therefore, the roots/solutions/*x*-intercepts of quadratic equation $x^2 + 5x - 6 = 0$ are 1 and −6.

Let's try a problem.

───────────────── ○ ─────────────────

6. What is one of the roots of the equation $3x^2 + 12x + 9 = 0$?
   F. −4
   G. −3
   H. 1
   J. 3
   K. 9

Here's How to Crack It

Notice that the coefficient in front of the x^2 is not equal to 1. Check to see if you can factor out a constant before factoring the quadratic. In this equation, 3 can be factored out: $3(x^2 + 4x + 3) = 0$. Now factor the quadratic.

	Factors of 3	Sum of factors
I.	1, 3	$1 + 3 = 4$

There is only one option for factors of 3, and the sum is correct! Rewrite the equation using the factors: $3(x + 1)(x + 3) = 0$. Set the factors equal to 0 and solve for x, ignoring 3 for now since $3 \neq 0$.

$$(x + 1) = 0 \qquad (x + 3) = 0$$

$$x = -1 \qquad x = -3$$

While both -1 and -3 are valid roots, ACT gives only one of the roots as an option: -3, (G).

But what happens if you have a quadratic equation that isn't so easy to factor? Well that's when the quadratic formula becomes your friend!

The quadratic formula is another way to solve for the roots, solutions, and x-intercepts of a quadratic equation in the standard form, $ax^2 + bx + c = 0$, and looks like this:

$$x = \frac{-b \pm \sqrt{b^2 - 4ac}}{2a}$$

Let's see how it works in a problem.

31. What are the solutions for $7x^2 - 3x + 15 = 0$?

First, notice that there isn't an easy way to factor out 7 in this equation, so it's faster and more accurate to use the quadratic formula to solve for the solutions. The equation is already in standard form, so we know $a = 7$, $b = -3$, and $c = 15$. Filling those numbers into the quadratic formula gives the following:

$$x = \frac{-(-3) \pm \sqrt{(-3)^2 - 4(7)(15)}}{2(7)}$$

Simplifying the equation gives:

$$x = \frac{3 \pm \sqrt{-411}}{14}$$

You may see the answer choices written in this form, or they may be separated into two solutions like this:

$$x = \frac{3 + \sqrt{-411}}{14} \qquad x = \frac{3 - \sqrt{-411}}{14}$$

Try a few yourself!

4. $4x^2 - 2x + 7 = 0$ _____

5. $x^2 - 3x - 23 = 0$ _____

Discriminant

You may be looking at the solutions to a couple of the last few equations wondering how there can be an x-intercept value that contains a negative under the square root. After all, negatives under a square root are imaginary numbers. You're absolutely correct! If you have a graphing calculator, go to the Y= screen and enter $y = 7x^2 - 3x + 15$ and hit GRAPH (you might have to zoom out to see the parabola). It should look like this:

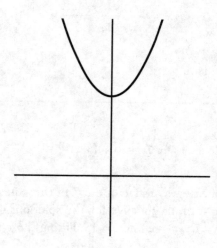

Well look at that! The parabola doesn't intersect the x-axis at all!

The portion of the quadratic formula that is under the radical, $b^2 - 4ac$, is called the discriminant, and we can use it to tell us about the number of x-intercepts a quadratic equation in standard form has without solving for the roots.

If the discriminant is:

- Positive, the quadratic has 2 distinct real roots
- Zero, the quadratic has 1 real root
- Negative, the quadratic has no real roots

Find the discriminants of the following quadratic equations and the number and type of roots:

6. $5x^2 + 4x + 9 = 0$ _____   roots: _____

7. $x^2 - 13x + 12 = 0$ _____   roots: _____

Remember: the Answer Keys for the preceding drills can be found at the end of this chapter after the Summary page.

Let's use our knowledge of discriminants on this problem.

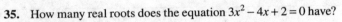

35. How many real roots does the equation $3x^2 - 4x + 2 = 0$ have?
- **A.** None
- **B.** One
- **C.** Two
- **D.** Three
- **E.** Four

Here's How to Crack It

Since the question asks for real roots, use the discriminant. For this quadratic, $a = 3$, $b = -4$, and $c = 2$. Plugging those numbers into the discriminant gives $(-4)^2 - 4(3)(2) = 16 - 24 = -8$. The value of the discriminant is negative, so there are no real roots for this quadratic equation, and the answer is (A).

FUNDAMENTALS VOCABULARY DRILL

Write out the definitions for each of the following math terms. If possible, write them in your own words.

Absolute Value: _____

_____

Consecutive: _____

_____

Decimal: _____

_____

Difference: _____

_____

Digits: _____

_____

Discriminant: _____

_____

Distinct: _____

_____

Divisible: _____

_____

Even: _____

_____

Exponent/Power: _____

_____

Factor: _____

_____

FOIL: _____

_____

Fraction: _____

_____

Greatest Common Factor: _____

_____

Imaginary: _____

_____

Integers: _____

_____

Irrational: _____

_____

Least Common Multiple: _____

_____

Multiple: _____

_____

Negative: _____

_____

Number: _____

_____

Odd: _____

_____

Opposite: _____

_____

Order of Operations: _____

_____

Positive: _____

_____

Prime: _____

_____

Product: _____

_____

Quadratic Formula: _____

_____

Quotient: _____

_____

Real: _____

_____

Radical: _____

_____

Rational: _____

_____

Reciprocal: _____

_____

Remainder: _____

_____

Roots (solutions, *x*-intercepts): _____

_____

Scientific Notation: _____

_____

Sum: _____

_____

GLOSSARY

Absolute Value	The distance from zero on the number line
Consecutive	An order in which numbers are arranged in increasing order with no gaps (e.g., 6, 7, 8)
Decimal	A way of expressing a fraction in which numbers are divided by ten, one hundred, one thousand, and other powers of ten
Difference	The result of subtraction
Digits	The integers 0 through 9
Discriminant	The portion of the quadratic formula under the radical sign $b^2 - 4ac$
Distinct	Different
Divisible	An integer can be divided by another integer evenly, with no fraction or decimal left over
Even	Divisible by 2
Exponent/Power	A number that indicates the number of times to multiply a base by itself
Factor	Integers that multiply together to make a given product
FOIL	First, Outer, Inner, Last—a method used to multiply binomials
Fraction	A way of expressing the division of numbers by stacking one over the other
Greatest Common Factor	The largest factor common to two numbers
Imaginary	The square (or any other even) root of a negative number
Integers	All real numbers other than decimals or fractions
Irrational	A number that can be expressed as a decimal but not a fraction
Least Common Multiple	The smallest multiple common to two numbers
Multiple	The product of an integer and another integer
Negative	Less than 0
Number	A count or measure, including zero, all positive and negative values, and all integers, fractions, and decimals
Odd	NOT divisible by 2
Opposite	Two numbers that have the same magnitude but are opposite in signs. That is, two numbers with the same distance from zero on the number line, but one is positive and the other negative.
Order of Operations	Parentheses, Exponents, Multiplication, Division, Addition, Subtraction
Positive	Greater than 0
Prime	A number that has itself and 1 as its only factors
Product	The result of multiplication

Quadratic Formula A formula used to solve for the roots of a quadratic equation in standard form:

$$x = \frac{-b \pm \sqrt{b^2 - 4ac}}{2a}$$

Quotient The result of division

Real Zero, all positive and negative integers, fractions, decimals, and roots

Radical Another word for the $\sqrt{}$ sign

Rational A number that can be expressed as the ratio of two other numbers, making a fraction

Reciprocal The inverse of a number—flip the numerator and denominator

Remainder The number left over when a number is not evenly divisible by another number

Roots (solutions, x-intercepts) The x-values of a quadratic equation in standard form: the x-value at which the quadratic equation crosses the x-axis

Scientific Notation A representation of a large number using fewer digits: a decimal number between 1 and 10 multiplied by 10 to a power

Sum The result of addition

Fundamentals Drill

In the drill below, you will find questions focusing only on fundamental skills. Before you start, take a few moments to go back over the review material and techniques. Answers are in Chapter 25.

1. What is the product of the distinct prime factors of 54 ?
   A. 2
   B. 3
   C. 6
   D. 11
   E. 54

2. If x is the least odd prime number and y is the least positive integer multiple of 10, what is the positive difference between x and y ?
   F. 3
   G. 7
   H. 11
   J. 15
   K. 17

3. For all x and y, $(x^{-1}y^{-3})^{-2}(x^4y^7)^3 = ?$
   A. $x^{10}y^{15}$
   B. x^5y^{10}
   C. x^3y^4
   D. $x^{14}y^{27}$
   E. $x^{-6}y^{18}$

4. In the complex numbers, where $i^2 = -1$, which of the following is equal to the result of squaring the expression $(i + 4)$?
   F. $4i$
   G. $16i$
   H. $15 + 8i$
   J. $16 + i$
   K. $17 - 18i$

5. What is the least possible sum of three distinct prime numbers between 10 and 20 ?
   A. 30
   B. 39
   C. 41
   D. 45
   E. 60

6. $\dfrac{9.1 \times 10^{-7}}{1.3 \times 10^3} =$
   F. 7.0×10^{-10}
   G. 7.0×10^{-4}
   H. 7.0×10^4
   J. 7.8×10^{-10}
   K. 7.8×10^{-4}

7. The graph of which of the following does not intersect the x-axis?
   A. $-x^2 + 5x - 1 = 0$
   B. $x^2 + 6x - 9 = 0$
   C. $x^2 - 3x + 10 = 0$
   D. $2x^2 + 3x - 11 = 0$
   E. $3x^2 + 12x + 12 = 0$

Summary

o Learn the basics for the ACT Math test before you move on to more difficult concepts. The Fundamentals are the one thing on the ACT that you can't fake!

o Know your vocabulary. The Math test requires its own Reading Comprehension.

o Know your rules for 0.
  - 0 is an even number.
  - 0 is neither positive nor negative.
  - Anything multiplied by 0 is 0.
  - 0 raised to any power is 0.
  - Anything raised to the 0 power is 1.

o A number's factors are always *smaller than* or the *same as* that number.

o A number's multiples are always *larger than* or the *same as* that number.

o A prime number has only two distinct factors: 1 and itself.
  - 1 is NOT a prime number.
  - 2 is the only even prime number.

o Use your calculator well and wisely. A calculator is particularly helpful with:
  - imaginary numbers (represented as i in problems)
  - square roots that don't contain variables (and often those that do)
  - converting decimals or other expressions into fractions
  - multiplying and dividing large numbers

o When combining numbers with exponents, remember MADSPM.

FUNDAMENTALS LESSON ANSWER KEY

Basics (page 100)

1. 1.75, 2, 3, 12, 16, 81
2. −81, −19, −9, −6
3. −81, −19, −9, 3, 81
4. −6, 0, 2, 12, 16
5. 2, 12, 16
6. 0
7. −4
8. $-\dfrac{1}{2}$
9. 1
10. 7
11. 1
12. 7 R 1 (7 *remainder* 1)
13. Number, Integer, Positive, Even
14. Number, Negative
15. Number, Integer, Even
16. Remainder
17. Reciprocal
18. Consecutive

Factors and Multiples (page 102)

1. 1, 2, 3, 4 , 6, 12
2. 12, 24, 36, 48
3. 1, 2, 3, 5, 6, 10, 15, 30
4. 30, 60, 90, 120
5. Factor
6. Yes
7. 9
8. 9
9. 36
10. 48

Prime (page 102-103)

1. 2, 3, 5, 7
2. 2
3. No, it does not have two *distinct* factors.
4. $2 \times 2 \times 3 \times 3$ or $2^2 \times 3^2$
5. $2 + 2 + 3 + 3 = 10$
6. $2 \times 3 = 6$

Real Numbers and Their Imaginary Friends (page 103-104)

5. 1
6. 1
7. −1
8. No answer, or imaginary, or i
9. None

Rational Numbers and Their Irrational Friends (page 104-105)

1. $\dfrac{1}{2}$
2. $\dfrac{3}{1}$
3. 6
4. 1

Love Your Calculator for Real, but Be Rational (page 105)

5. 5
6. $8 + 6i$
7. $\dfrac{3}{8}$ Rational.
8. $\dfrac{1}{6}$ Rational.
9. No result. Irrational.
10. $\dfrac{479,109,801,431}{10,000,000,000,000}$ Rational.

Basic Rules (page 106)

1. x^5
2. x^1, or x
3. x^{12}
4. $12x^5$. Don't forget the coefficients!
5. $8x^6$
6. $3x^4$
7. x^3

Special Rules (page 106)

1. x^0, or 1
2. 1
3. x^{-3}, or $\dfrac{1}{x^3}$
4. $\dfrac{1}{x^3}$

5. x
6. 1
7. 0
8. 4
9. -8
10. -4
11. $\dfrac{1}{4}$
12. $\dfrac{4}{9}$

Scientific Notation (page 107)

1. 3.76E10
2. 4.3E−10
3. 7.1E−12
4. 520,000

Roots (page 110)

1. $2\sqrt{x}$
2. $8\sqrt{x}$
3. Can't be combined!
4. $\sqrt{2xy}$
5. $\sqrt{x^2 y} = x\sqrt{y}$
6. $8\sqrt{36} = 8(6) = 48$
7. $\sqrt{36} = 6$
8. $\left(\sqrt{529} - \sqrt{361}\right)^{\frac{1}{2}} = (23 - 19)^{\frac{1}{2}} = (4)^{\frac{1}{2}} = 2$

Quadratic Formula (pages 112, 114, and 115)

1. $(x + 3)(x + 4)$
2. $(x - 2)(x - 2)$ or $(x - 2)^2$
3. $(x + 2)(x - 8)$
4. $\dfrac{2 \pm \sqrt{-108}}{8}$ or $\dfrac{1 \pm 3\sqrt{-3}}{4}$
5. $\dfrac{3 \pm \sqrt{101}}{2}$
6. -164; no real roots
7. 121; distinct real roots

Chapter 11
No More Algebra

Once you have a solid foundation in basic operations and vocabulary, you are well-equipped to solve a wide variety of problems. This chapter will look at some of the problems that test concepts you may have seen in Algebra classes, and it will show how to work around some of the toughest algebra problems.

ALGEBRA AND THE ACT

Plug-and-Chug questions are ones that look like questions that you might see in Math class. Rather than burying the math in a word problem, ACT puts the question in a more straightforward form. We've already seen some of the easier plug-and-chug algebra problems in Chapter 10. Most questions that ACT considers "algebra" questions won't be so straightforward. ACT expects you to use algebra to solve word problems as well as plug-and-chug questions. Let's see how you can make this work in your favor.

HOW I LEARNED TO STOP WORRYING AND LOVE VARIABLES

Let's look at the following problem:

21. John has x red pencils, and three times as many red pencils as blue pencils. If he has four more yellow pencils than blue pencils, then in terms of x, how many yellow pencils does John have?

A. $x + 4$

B. $x + 7$

C. $\dfrac{x}{6}$

D. $\dfrac{x + 12}{6}$

E. $\dfrac{x + 12}{3}$

Let's think about the bigger picture for a second here. We're all familiar with these x values from algebra class, but what we often forget is that x is substituting for some real value. Equations use x because that value is an unknown. The variable x could be 5 or 105 or 0.36491. In fact, the ACT writers are asking you to create an expression that will answer this question to find what that "certain number" is. And they want you to make it even harder on yourself by forgetting that x is a number at all.

PLUGGING IN

If you had 1 dollar and you bought 2 pieces of candy at 25 cents apiece, how much change would you have? 50 cents, of course. If you had d dollars and bought p pieces of candy at c cents apiece, how much change would you have? Um, Letter of the Day.

Numbers are a lot easier to work with than variables. Therefore, when you see variables on the ACT, you can usually make things a lot easier on yourself by using numbers instead. Whenever there are variables in the answer choices or the problem, you can use Plugging In.

Use Plugging In

- when there are variables in the answer choices
- when solving word problems or plug-and-chug questions
- for questions of any difficulty level

Let's go back to question 21.

21. John has x red pencils and three times as many red pencils as blue pencils. If he has four more yellow pencils than blue pencils, then in terms of x, how many yellow pencils does John have?

A. $x + 4$

B. $x + 7$

C. $\dfrac{x}{6}$

D. $\dfrac{x + 12}{6}$

E. $\dfrac{x + 12}{3}$

Here's How to Crack It

1. Know the Question. Underline "how many yellow pencils does John have?" We're not solving for x here; we need the number of yellow pencils. ACT just wants us to name the value "in terms of x."

2. Let the answers help. The answers help a lot here: each contains the variable x, which means we can plug in.

3. Break the problem into bite-sized pieces. We know we can plug in. Let's take it step by step from there.

Make sure to keep your work organized when Plugging In. Always circle your target answer.

We want to make the math easy on ourselves. Let's say $x = 3$, so John has 3 red pencils. Now that we've dispensed with the variable, let's work the rest of the problem.

John has 3 red pencils and *three times as many red pencils as blue pencils.* He therefore must have 1 blue pencil. He has *four more yellow pencils than blue pencils,* so he must have 5 yellow pencils.

Now we can answer the question with what is called our *target answer*. The question asks *How many yellow pencils does John have?*, to which our answer is 5. Circle this answer on your paper. Let's go to the answer choices to see which one gives us our target. Remember, $x = 3$.

A. $(3) + 4 = 7$ Not our target answer. Cross it off.

B. $(3) + 7 = 10$ Not our target answer. Cross it off.

C. $\dfrac{(3)}{6} = \dfrac{1}{2}$ Not our target answer. Cross it off.

D. $\dfrac{(3) + 12}{6} = \dfrac{15}{6}$ Not our target answer. Cross it off.

E. $\dfrac{(3) + 12}{3} = 5$ ✔

Only (E) works, so this is our correct answer. Look how easy that was, and not a bit of algebra necessary! Let's try another.

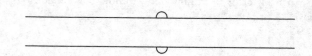

17. For all $x \neq 3$, which of the following is equivalent to the expression $\dfrac{3x^2 - 7x - 6}{x - 3}$?

A. $3x + 2$

B. $3x - 2$

C. $3(x - 2)$

D. $3(x + 2)$

E. $x^2 - 2$

Here's How to Crack It

This looks a lot more like a standard plug-and-chug than the last problem did, but remember, we can always plug in when there are variables in the answer choices. This will be a tough problem to factor, so Plugging In will probably be your best bet, even if you're an ace with quadratic equations. The only thing the problem tells us is that $x \neq 3$, so let's say $x = 2$.

$$\frac{3(2)^2 - 7(2) - 6}{(2) - 3}$$

$$\frac{3(4) - 14 - 6}{-1}$$

$$\frac{-8}{-1} = 8$$

We now know that for the value we've chosen, the value of this expression is 8. That means **8** is our target answer. Circle that number. Let's plug our *x* value into the answer choices to find the one that matches the target.

A.	$3(2) + 2 = 8$ ✔	This matches our target answer, but when you plug in, always check all 5 answers.
B.	$3(2) - 2 = 6 - 2 = 4$	Not our target answer. Cross it off.
C.	$3((2) - 2) = 3(0) = 0$	Not our target answer. Cross it off.
D.	$3((2) + 2) = 3(4) = 12$	Not our target answer. Cross it off.
E.	$(2)^2 - 2 = 2$	Not our target answer. Cross it off.

Only (A) worked, and it is the correct answer. So as we can see, Plugging In works for all kinds of algebra problems. Let's review what we've done so far.

What To Do When You Plug In

1. Identify the opportunity. Can you plug in on this question?

2. Choose a good number. Make the math easy on yourself.

3. Find a target answer. Answer the question posed in the problem with your number, and circle your target answer.

4. Test all the answer choices. If two of them work, try a new number.

Let's try a tougher one.

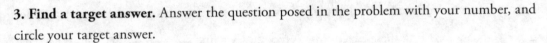

36. In my dear Aunt Sally's math class, there are four exams. The first three exam scores are averaged, and the resulting score is averaged with the final exam score. If *a*, *b*, and *c* are the first three exam scores, and *f* is the final exam score, which of the following gives a student's final score in the class?

F. $\dfrac{a + b + c}{3} + f$

G. $\dfrac{a + b + c + 3f}{6}$

H. $\dfrac{a + b + c + f}{4}$

J. $\dfrac{a + b + c + 3f}{4}$

K. $a + b + c + f$

Here's How to Crack It

This is a word problem, so remember the Basic Approach.

1. Know the question. Underline the question in this problem: *which of the following gives a student's final score in this class?*

2. Let the answers help. There are variables in each of these answer choices, which means we can plug in, so these answers will help a lot. If you want to do a bit of POE, you might notice that the problem is asking for an average, so (K) can't work. Also, something funny will need to happen with the *f* variable, so you can eliminate (H).

3. Break the problem into bite-sized pieces. If you rush through this problem, it's very easy to mess up. Let's go piece by piece as we did in the earlier problem.

The first three exam scores are averaged.

There's no reason to give realistic exam scores here: we can pick whatever numbers we want, so let's use numbers that make the math easy. We know from this problem that the first three exam scores are represented by *a*, *b*, and *c*, so let's say $a = 2$, $b = 3$, and $c = 4$. The average of these three numbers can be found as follows: $\frac{2 + 3 + 4}{3} = \frac{9}{3} = 3$.

The resulting score is then averaged with the final score.

The resulting score is 3, and we need to plug in some final score, *f*. Let's use another easy number and say $f = 5$. In averaging these two numbers together, we find $\frac{3 + 5}{2} = \frac{8}{2} = 4$. Thus, we have our target answer: a student's final score with these exam scores will be **4.** Circle that number.

Let's go to the answer choices and look for the one that matches the target. Remember, $a = 2$, $b = 3$, $c = 4$, and $f = 5$.

F. $\quad \dfrac{2 + 3 + 4}{3} + 5 = \dfrac{9}{3} + 5 = 8 \qquad ✗$

G. $\quad \dfrac{2 + 3 + 4 + 3(5)}{6} = \dfrac{24}{6} = 4 \qquad ✔$

H. $\quad \dfrac{2 + 3 + 4 + 5}{4} = \dfrac{14}{4} = 3.5 \qquad ✗$

J. $\quad \dfrac{2 + 3 + 4 + 3(5)}{4} = \dfrac{24}{4} = 6 \qquad ✗$

K. $\quad 2 + 3 + 4 + 5 = 14 \qquad ✗$

Choice (G) is the correct answer, and no tough algebra necessary!

Hidden Plug-Ins

Both of the above questions have had variables in the answer choices, which is a dead giveaway that we can plug in. The good news is that that's not the only time. In any problem in which there are hypothetical values or values relative to each other, Plugging In will work. Let's have a look at a problem.

---

25. If $x - z = 6$ and $y = 3x - 2 - 3z$, then $y = ?$

    A.   2
    B.   4
    C.   14
    D.   16
    E.   18

Here's How to Crack It

There aren't any variables in the answer choices, but notice all values in the problem are defined relative to one another. Let's plug in.

Using the first equation in the problem, let's make the numbers easy on ourselves and say $x = 8$ and $z = 2$. Using these values, let's find the value for the expression given in the problem: $y = 3(8) - 2 - 3(2) = 24 - 2 - 6 = 16$, (D).

It may feel like we just pulled these numbers out of thin air, but try any two numbers that work in the equation $x - z = 6$, and you'll find that it always works.

PLUGGING IN THE ANSWERS

So we've seen that Plugging In is a great strategy when there are variables in the question or the answers. How about when there aren't? Does that mean we have to go back to algebra? Of course not! On most problems on the ACT, there are a variety of ways to solve. Let's look at another one that helps to simplify the math in algebra-related problems.

2. If $600 were deposited in a bank account for one year and earned interest of $42, what was the interest rate?

    F.   6.26%
    G.   7.00%
    H.   8.00%
    J.   9.00%
    K.   9.50%

Before we get started cracking this problem, we should note a few things about it. First of all, there aren't any variables, but you get the feeling that you're going to have to put the $600 and the $42 in relationship to some other number by means of an algebraic expression. Then, notice that the problem is asking for a very specific number, the interest rate, and that the answer choices give possibilities for that specific number in ascending order. All of this taken together means that we can plug in the answers.

Use Plugging In The Answers (PITA) when

- answer choices are numbers in ascending or descending order
- the question asks for a specific amount. Questions will usually be "what?" or "how many?"
- you get the urge to do algebra even when there are no variables in the problem

---

Let's see what this looks like.

---

2. If $600 were deposited in a bank account for one year and earned interest of $42, what was the interest rate?

    F. 6.26%
    G. 7.00%
    H. 8.00%
    J. 9.00%
    K. 9.50%

Here's How to Crack It

1. Know the question. As we've already identified, we need to find the *interest rate*.

2. Let the answers help. The way the answer choices are listed has already indicated that we'll be able to use PITA on this problem, so we'll be using the answers a lot in this question.

3. Break the problem into bite-sized pieces. We're going to use the answer choices to walk through each step of the problem, working it in bite-sized pieces.

Because these answer choices are listed in ascending order, it will be best to start with the middle choice. That way, if it's too high or too low, we'll be able to use POE more efficiently.

Therefore, if we start with 8.00% as our interest rate, we can find what the annual interest on a $600 deposit would be by multiplying $600 × 0.08 = $48. Because the problem tells us that the deposit earned $42 of interest, we know (H) is too high, which also eliminates (J) and (K).

Let's try (G): you may find it helpful to keep your work organized in columns as shown below.

Interest Rate	Rate per $600	= $42?
F. 6.26%		
G. 7.00%	$42	Yes! ✔
H. 8.00%	$48	✗
J. 9.00%		
K. 9.50%		

We haven't introduced any of our own numbers into this problem, so once we find the correct answer, we can stop. The correct answer is (G).

Let's try a harder one.

49. In a piggy bank, there are pennies, nickels, dimes, and quarters that total $2.17 in value. If there are 3 times as many pennies as there are dimes, 1 more dime than nickels, and 2 more quarters than dimes, then how many pennies are in the piggy bank?

A. 12
B. 15
C. 18
D. 21
E. 24

Here's How to Crack It
1. Know the question. *How many pennies are in the bank?*

2. Let the answers help. There are no variables, but the very specific question coupled with the numerical answers in ascending order gives a pretty good indication that we can use PITA.

3. Break the problem into bite-sized pieces. Make sure you take your time with this problem; you'll need to multiply the number of each coin by its monetary value. In other words, don't forget that 1 nickel will count for 5 cents, 1 dime will count for 10 cents, and 1 quarter will count for 25 cents. As in the previous problem, let's set up some columns to keep our work organized and begin with (C).

Since ACT has already given us the answers, we will plug in the answers and work backward. Each of the answers listed gives a possible value for the number of pennies. Using the information in the problem, we can work backward from that number of pennies to find the number of nickels, dimes, and quarters. When the values for the number of coins add up to $2.17, we know we're done.

If we begin with the assumption that there are 18 pennies, then there must be 6 dimes (*3 times as many pennies as there are dimes*). 6 dimes means 5 nickels (*1 more dime than nickels*) and 8 quarters (*2 more quarters than dimes*).

Now multiply the number of coins by the monetary value of each to see if they total $2.17.

	Pennies ($P)	Dimes ($D)	Nickels ($N)	Quarters ($Q)	Total = $2.17?
C.	18 ($0.18)	6 ($0.60)	5 ($0.25)	8 ($2.00)	Total = $3.03

That's too high, so we can eliminate not only (C), but also (D) and (E). Cross them off, and try (B).

	Pennies ($P)	Dimes ($D)	Nickels ($N)	Quarters ($Q)	Total = $2.17?
A.	12 ($0.12)	4 ($0.40)	3 ($0.15)	6 ($1.50)	Total = $2.17 ✔
B.	15 ($0.15)	5 ($0.50)	4 ($0.20)	7 ($1.75)	Total = $2.60 ✗
C.	18 ($0.18)	6 ($0.60)	5 ($0.25)	8 ($2.00)	Total = $3.03 ✗
D.	21	Eliminated through POE			
E.	24	Eliminated through POE			

Only (A) works. No algebra necessary!

———————————◯———————————

A NOTE ON PLUGGING IN AND PITA

Need More Practice?
Math and Science Workout for the ACT has four full-length Math tests.

Plugging In and PITA are not the only ways to solve these problems, and it may feel weird using these methods instead of trying to do these problems "the real way." You may have even found that you knew how to work with the variables in Plugging In problems or how to write the appropriate equations for the PITA problems. If you can do either of those things, you're already on your way to a great Math score.

But think about it this way. We've already said that ACT doesn't give any partial credit. So do you think doing it "the real way" gets you any extra points? It doesn't: on the ACT, a right answer is a right answer, no matter how you get it. "The real way" is great, but unfortunately, it's often a lot more complex and offers many more opportunities to make careless errors.

The biggest problem with doing things the real way, though, is that it essentially requires that you invent a new approach for every problem. Instead, notice what we've given you here: two strategies that will work toward getting you the right answer on any number of questions. You may have heard the saying, "Give a man a fish and you've fed him for a day, but teach a man to fish and you've fed him for a lifetime." Now, don't worry; our delusions of grandeur are not quite so extreme, but Plugging In and PITA are useful in a similar way. Rather than giving you a detailed description of how to create formulas and work through them for these problems that won't themselves ever appear on an ACT again, we're giving you a strategy that will help you to work through any number of similar problems on future ACTs.

Try these strategies on your own in the drill that concludes this chapter.

Algebra Drill

For the answers to this drill, please go to Chapter 25.

1. What is the largest value of x that solves the equation $x^2 - 4x + 3 = 0$?

   A. 1
   B. 2
   C. 3
   D. 4
   E. 5

2. For all $\dfrac{x^2 + 6x - 27}{(x+9)} = ?$

   F. $x + 9$
   G. $x - 3$
   H. $x + 3$
   J. $2x - 4$
   K. $2x + 3$

3. If 2 less than 3 times a certain number is the same as 4 more than the product of 5 and 3, what is the number?

   A. 7
   B. 10
   C. 11
   D. 14
   E. 15

4. A certain number of books are to be given away at a promotion. If $\dfrac{2}{5}$ of the books are distributed in the morning and $\dfrac{1}{3}$ of the remaining books are distributed in the afternoon, what fraction of the books remains to be distributed the next day?

   F. $\dfrac{1}{5}$
   G. $\dfrac{2}{5}$
   H. $\dfrac{1}{3}$
   J. $\dfrac{5}{7}$
   K. $\dfrac{8}{9}$

5. In the equation $a = \dfrac{3}{b}$, b is a positive, real number. As the value of b is increased so it becomes closer and closer to infinity, what happens to the value of a ?

   A. It remains constant.
   B. It gets closer and closer to zero.
   C. It gets closer and closer to one.
   D. It gets closer and closer to three.
   E. It gets closer and closer to infinity.

Summary

o Remember the Basic Approach for Word Problems:
   - Know the question.
   - Let the answers help.
   - Break the problem into bite-sized pieces.

o Use Plugging In when there are variables in the answer choices or the problem. Keep the following pointers in mind:
   - Choose numbers that make the math easy.
   - Try all the answer choices.
   - On more complex problems, keep your variables straight!

o Use Plugging In the Answers (PITA) when answer choices are listed in ascending or descending order and when the question is asking for a specific number. Keep the following pointers in mind:
   - Start with choice (C) or (H) to help with POE.
   - When you find the correct answer, STOP!

Chapter 12
Plane Geometry

The ACT test writers tell us the breakdown of numbers of questions into broad categories like Preparing for Higher Math, Integrating Essential Skills, and Modeling. It's difficult to know where any one question may fall within these categories, though. For one thing, many problems incorporate several concepts: you even need algebra to solve many geometry questions, so would the ACT test writers count a question like that in the algebra or plane geometry column?

What matters most is that you can identify the topics that can make a question Now, Later, or Never for you.

While ACT test writers occasionally may throw in a more advanced formula or complex shape, the majority of the questions test the basic rules on the basic shapes. This chapter will review a cross section of those formulas and concepts and give you a strategic approach to apply those rules on the ACT.

CRACKING THE GEOMETRY ON THE ACT

Plug-and-chug geometry questions can have so much information in them that they feel like word problems. So treat them like word problems. Let's review the Basic Approach to word problems. We'll then add some points specific to geometry.

Step 1: Know the Question

Know the question. Read the whole problem before calculating anything, and underline the actual question.

Step 2: Let the Answers Help

Let the answers help. Look for clues on how to solve and ways to use POE (Process of Elimination).

Step 3: Break the Problem into Bite-Sized Pieces

Break the problem into bite-sized pieces. When you read the problem a second time, calculate at each step necessary and watch out for tricky phrasing.

For geometry questions, Step 3 has two specific additions:

> **Step 3a:** If you're taking the ACT Online Test, copy the figure onto your whiteboard. If there is no figure (regardless of which ACT you are taking), draw your own. Then, write all the information given in the problem on the figure.
>
> **Step 3b:** Write down any formulas you need, and fill in any information you have.

Geometry BFFs: POE and Ballparking

Step 2 of the Basic Approach is particularly important to geometry questions. In the last few chapters, we've seen how POE and Ballparking can help to narrow down the answer choices when you're confused. Before you rush to calculate, Ballparking in particular will help you a ton on geometry problems because most figures are drawn to scale.

To Scale or Not to Scale?

That is the question. The ACT makes a big deal in the instructions about the fact that their figures are "NOT necessarily drawn to scale." Here's the thing, though: they usually are drawn to scale or at least enough to use them in broad strokes. Use Ballparking to eliminate answers that are too big or too small rather than to determine a precise value. Questions on angles and area especially lend themselves to Ballparking. The main place to be skeptical is on those problems that ask questions like, "Which of the following must be true?" Those are the ones whose figures can be purposely misleading.

In most other cases, if you know how to use the figures that are given (or how to draw your own), you can eliminate several wrong answers before doing any math at all. Let's see how this works.

How Big Is Angle *NLM* ?

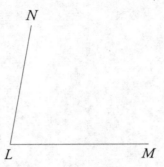

Obviously, you don't know exactly how big this angle is, but it would be easy to compare it with an angle whose measure you *do* know exactly. Let's compare it with a 90° angle.

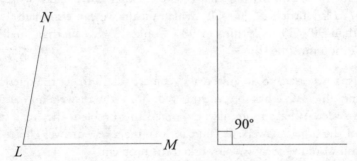

Angle *NLM* is clearly a bit less than 90°. Now look at the following problem, which asks about the same angle *NLM* .

1. In the figure below, *O*, *N*, and *M* are collinear. If the lengths of $\overline{ON}$ and $\overline{NL}$ are the same, the measure of angle *LON* is 30°, and angle *LMN* is 40°, what is the measure of angle *NLM* ?

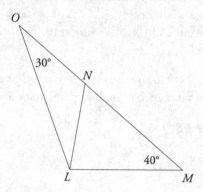

A. 30°
B. 80°
C. 90°
D. 110°
E. 120°

Here's How to Crack It

Start with Step 1: Know the question. Underline *what is the measure of angle NLM ?* and even mark the angle on your figure. You don't want to answer for the wrong angle. Now move to Step 2, and let's focus on eliminating answer choices that don't make sense. We've already decided that ∠*NLM* is a little less than 90°, which means we can eliminate (C), (D), and (E). How much less than 90°? 30° is a third of 90°. Could ∠*NLM* be that small? No way! The answer to this question must be (B).

In this case, it wasn't necessary to do any "real" geometry at all to get the question right, but it took about half the time. ACT has to give you credit for right answers no matter how you get them. Revenge is sweet. What's more, if you worked this problem the "real" way, you might have picked one of the other answers: as you can imagine, every answer choice gives some partial answer that you would've seen as you worked the problem.

Let's Do It Again

2. In the figure below, if $AB = 27$, $CD = 20$, and the area of triangle $ADC = 240$, what is the area of polygon $ABCD$?

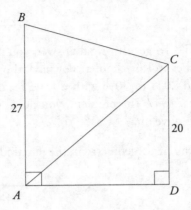

   F.   420
   G.   480
   H.   540
   J.   564
   K. 1,128

Here's How to Crack It

Start with Step 1: Know the question. Underline *what is the area of polygon ABCD ?* This polygon is not a conventional figure, but if we had to choose one figure that the polygon resembled, we might pick a rectangle. Try drawing a line at a right angle from the line segment $\overline{AB}$ so that it touches point C, thus creating a rectangle. It should look like the following:

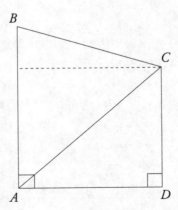

The area of polygon $ABCD$ is equal to the area of the rectangle you've just formed, plus a little bit at the top. The problem tells you that the area of triangle ADC is 240. What is the area of the rectangle you just created? If you said 480, you are exactly right, whether you knew the geometric rules that applied or whether you just measured it with your eyes.

What Should I Do If There Is No Diagram?
Draw one! It's always easier to understand a problem when you can see it in front of you. If possible, draw your figure to scale so that you can estimate the answer as well.

So the area of the rectangle is 480. Roughly speaking, then, what should the area of the polygon be? A little more. Let's look at the answer choices. Choices (F) and (G) are either less than or equal to 480; get rid of them. Choices (H) and (J) both seem possible; they are both a little more than 480; let's hold on to them. Choice (K) seems pretty unrealistic. We want more than 480, but 1,128 is ridiculous.

The answer to this question is (J). To get this final answer, you'll need to use a variety of area formulas, which we'll explore later in this chapter. For now, though, notice that your chances of guessing have increased from 20% to 50% with a little bit of quick thinking. Now what should you do? If you know how to do the problem, you do it. If you don't or if you are running out of time, you guess and move on.

However, even as we move into the "real" geometry in the remainder of this chapter, don't forget:

Always look for opportunities to Ballpark on geometry problems even if you know how to do them the "real" way.

GEOMETRY REVIEW

By using the diagrams ACT has so thoughtfully provided, and by making your own diagrams when they are not provided, you can often eliminate several of the answer choices. In some cases, you'll be able to eliminate every choice but one. Of course, you will also need to know the actual geometry concepts that ACT is testing. We've divided our review into the following four topics:

- Angles and lines
- Triangles
- Four-sided figures
- Circles

ANGLES AND LINES

Here is a line.

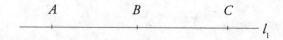

A line extends forever in either direction. This line, called l_1, has three points on it: A, B, and C. These three points are said to be **collinear** because they are all on the same line. The piece of the line in between points A and B is called a line **segment**. ACT will refer to it as segment AB or simply $\overline{AB}$. A and B are the **endpoints** of segment AB.

A line forms an angle of 180°. If that line is cut by another line, it divides that 180° into two angles that together add up to 180°.

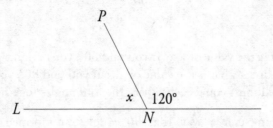

In the above diagram, what is the value of *x*? If you said 60°, you are correct. To find *x*, just subtract 120° from 180°.

An angle can also be described by points on the lines that intersect to form the angle and the point of intersection itself, with the middle letter corresponding to the point of intersection. For example, in the previous diagram, ∠*x* could also be described as ∠*LNP*. On the ACT, instead of writing out "angle *LNP*," they'll use math shorthand and put ∠*LNP* instead. So "angle *x*" becomes ∠*x*.

If there are 180° above a line, there are also 180° below the line, for a total of 360°.

When two lines intersect, they form four angles, represented below by letters *A*, *B*, *C*, and *D*. ∠*A* and ∠*B* together form a straight line, so they add up to 180°. Angles that add up to 180° are called **supplementary** angles.

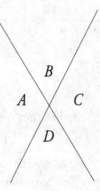

∠*A* and ∠*C* are opposite from each other and always equal each other, as are ∠*B* and ∠*D*. Angles like these are called **vertical** angles.

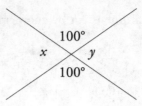

In the figure above, what is the value of $\angle x$? If you said 80°, you're right. Together with the 100° angle, x forms a straight line. What is the value of $\angle y$? If you said 80°, you're right again. These two angles are vertical and must equal each other. The four angles together add up to 360°.

When two lines meet in such a way that 90° angles are formed, the lines are called **perpendicular**. The little box at the point of intersection of two lines below indicates that they are perpendicular. It stands to reason that all four of these angles have measures of 90°.

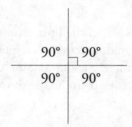

When two lines in the same plane are drawn so that they could extend into infinity without ever meeting, they are called **parallel**. In the figure below, l_1 is parallel to l_2. The symbol for parallel is | |.

When two parallel lines are cut by a third line, eight angles are formed, but in fact, there are really only two angle measures—a big one and a little one. Look at the diagram below.

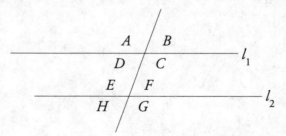

If $m\angle A = 110°$, then $m\angle B$ must equal 70° (together they form a straight line). $\angle D$ is vertical to $\angle B$, which means that it must also measure 70°. $\angle C$ is vertical to $\angle A$, so it must measure 110°.

The four angles $\angle E$, $\angle F$, $\angle G$, and $\angle H$ are in exactly the same proportion as the angles above. The little angles both measure 70°. The big angles both measure 110°.

Try the following problem.

1. In the figure below, line *L* is parallel to line *M*. Line *N* intersects both *L* and *M*, with angles *a*, *b*, *c*, *d*, *e*, *f*, *g*, and *h* as shown below. Which of the following lists includes all the angles that are supplementary to ∠*a* ?

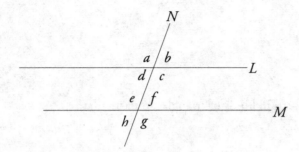

   A. Angles *b*, *d*, *f*, and *h*
   B. Angles *c*, *e*, and *g*
   C. Angles *b*, *d*, and *c*
   D. Angles *e*, *f*, *g*, and *h*
   E. Angles *d*, *c*, *h*, and *g*

Here's How to Crack It

An angle is supplementary to another angle if the two angle measures together add up to 180°. Because ∠*a* is one of the eight angles formed by the intersection of a line with two parallel lines, we know that there are really only two angle measures: a big one and a little one. ∠*a* is a big one. Thus, only the small angles would be supplementary to it. Which angles are those? The correct answer is (A). By the way, if you think back to the last chapter and apply what you learned there, could you have Plugged In on this problem? Of course you could have. After all, there are variables in the answer choices. Sometimes it is easier to see the correct answer if you substitute real values for the angles instead of just looking at them as a series of variables. Just because a problem involves geometry doesn't mean that you can't plug in.

N

a = 100° / *b* = 80° —— *L*
d = 80° / *c* = 100°

e = 100° / *f* = 80° —— *M*
h = 80° / *g* = 100°

TRIANGLES

A triangle is a three-sided figure whose inside angles always add up to 180°. The largest angle of a triangle is always opposite its longest side. Thus, in triangle *XYZ* below, *XY* would be the largest side, followed by *YZ*, followed by *XZ*. On the ACT, "triangle *XYZ*" will often be written as $\triangle XYZ$.

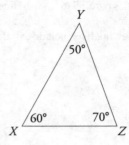

The ACT likes to ask about certain kinds of triangles in particular.

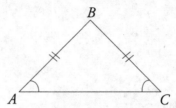

An **isosceles** triangle has two equal sides. The angles opposite those sides are also equal. In the isosceles triangle above, if $m\angle A = 50°$, then so does $m\angle C$. If $AB = 6$, then so does BC.

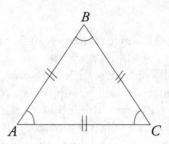

An **equilateral** triangle has three equal sides and three equal angles. Because measures of the three equal angles must add up to 180°, all three angles of an equilateral triangle always measure 60°.

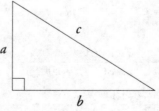

A **right triangle** has one inside angle that has measure equal to 90°. The longest side of a right triangle (the one opposite the 90° angle) is called the **hypotenuse**.

Pythagoras, a Greek mathematician, discovered that the sides of a right triangle are always in a particular proportion, which can be expressed by the formula $a^2 + b^2 = c^2$, where *a* and *b* are the shorter sides of the triangle, and c is the hypotenuse. This formula is called the **Pythagorean Theorem**.

There are certain right triangles that the test writers at ACT find endlessly fascinating. Let's test out the Pythagorean Theorem on the first of these.

$$3^2 + 4^2 = c^2$$

$$9 + 16 = 25$$

$$c^2 = 25, \text{ so } c = 5$$

The ACT writers adore the 3-4-5 triangle and use it frequently, along with its multiples, such as the 6-8-10 triangle and the 9-12-15 triangle. Of course, you can always use the Pythagorean Theorem to figure out the third side of a right triangle, as long as you have the other two sides, but because ACT problems almost invariably use "triples" like the ones we've just mentioned, it makes sense just to memorize them.

The ACT has three commonly used right-triangle triples.

3-4-5 (and its multiples)

5-12-13 (and its multiples)

7-24-25 (not as common as the other two)

Don't Get Snared

*   Is this a 3-4-5 triangle?

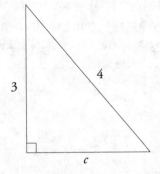

> **Pythagoras's *Other* Theorem**
> Pythagoras also developed a theory about the transmigration of souls. So far, this has not been proven, nor will it help you on this exam.

No, because the hypotenuse of a right triangle must be its *longest* side—the one opposite the 90° angle. In this case, we must use the Pythagorean Theorem to discover side c: $3^2 + c^2 = 16$, so $c = \sqrt{7}$.

- Is this a 5-12-13 triangle?

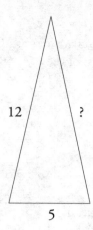

No, because the Pythagorean Theorem—and triples—apply only to *right* triangles. We can't determine definitively the third side of this triangle without knowing the specific angle measures.

The Isosceles Right Triangle (The 45-45-90 Triangle)

As fond as the ACT test writers are of triples, they are even fonder of two other right triangles. The first is called the **isosceles right triangle**. The sides and angles of the isosceles right triangle are always in a particular proportion.

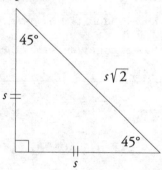

Be on the Lookout . . .

for problems in which the application of the Pythagorean Theorem is not obvious. For example, every rectangle contains two right triangles. That means that if you know the length and width of the rectangle, you also know the length of the diagonal, which is the hypotenuse of both triangles created by the diagonal.

You could use the Pythagorean Theorem to prove this (or you could just take our word for it). Whatever the length of the two equal sides of the isosceles right triangle, the length of the hypotenuse is always equal to one of those side lengths times $\sqrt{2}$. Here are two examples.

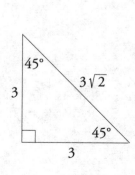

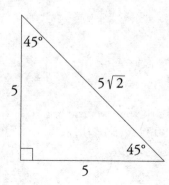

The 30-60-90 Triangle

The other right triangle tested frequently on the ACT is the **30-60-90 triangle**, which also has sides that are always in a particular proportion.

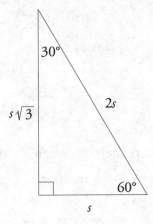

You can use the Pythagorean Theorem to prove this. Whatever the length of the short side of the 30-60-90 triangle, the hypotenuse is always twice as long. The length of the medium side is always equal to the length of the short side times $\sqrt{3}$. Here are two examples.

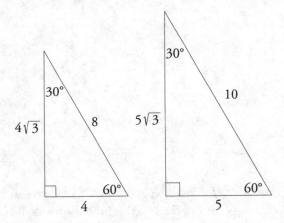

Because these triangles are tested so frequently, it makes sense to memorize the proportions, rather than waste time deriving them each time they appear.

Don't Get Snared

- In the isosceles right triangle below, are the sides equal to $3\sqrt{2}$?

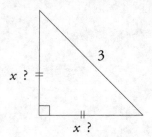

No. Remember, in an isosceles right triangle, hypotenuse = the side $\sqrt{2}$. In this case, 3 = the side $\sqrt{2}$. If we solve for the side, we get $\dfrac{3}{\sqrt{2}}$ = the side.

For arcane mathematical reasons, we are not supposed to leave a radical in the denominator, but we can multiply top and bottom by $\sqrt{2}$ to get $\dfrac{3\sqrt{2}}{2}$.

- In the right triangle below, is x equal to $4\sqrt{3}$?

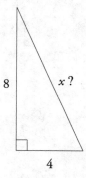

No. Even though it is one of ACT's favorites, you have to be careful not to see a 30-60-90 where none exists. In the triangle above, the length of the short side is half of the length of the *medium* side, not half of the length of the hypotenuse. This is some sort of right triangle all right, but it is not a 30-60-90. The hypotenuse, in case you're curious, is really $4\sqrt{5}$.

Area

The **area** of a triangle can be found with the following formula:

$$\text{area} = \frac{\text{base} \times \text{height}}{2}$$

Height is measured as the perpendicular distance from the base of the triangle to its highest point.

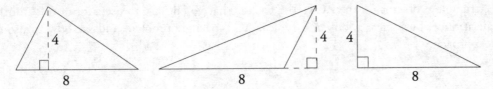

In all three of the above triangles, the area is

$$\frac{8 \times 4}{2} = 16$$

Don't Get Snared

- Sometimes the height of a triangle can be *outside* the triangle itself, as we just saw in the example above.
- In a right triangle, the height of the triangle can also be one of the sides of the triangle, as we just saw in the third example. However, be careful when finding the area of a *non-right* triangle. Simply because you know two sides of the triangle does not mean that you have the height of the triangle.

Similar Triangles

Two triangles are called similar if their angles have the same degree measures. This means their side lengths will be in proportion. For example, the two triangles below are similar.

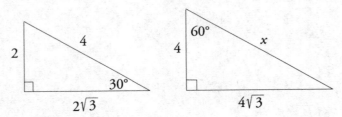

Because the side lengths of the two triangles are in the same proportion, you can find the missing side length, x, by setting up a proportion equation.

$$\frac{\text{short leg}}{\text{hypotenuse}} \quad \overset{\text{small triangle}}{\frac{2}{4}} = \overset{\text{big triangle}}{\frac{4}{x}}$$

$$x = 8$$

ACT TRIANGLE PROBLEMS

In this chapter, we've pretty much given you all the basic triangle information you'll need to do the triangle problems on the ACT. The trick is that you'll have to use a lot of this information all at once. Let's have a look at a typical ACT triangle problem and see how to use the Basic Approach.

3. In the figure below, square *ABCD* is attached to Δ*ADE* as shown. If ∠*EAD* measures 30° and *AE* is equal to $4\sqrt{3}$, then what is the area of square *ABCD* ?

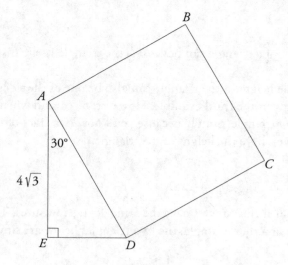

A. $8\sqrt{3}$

B. 16

C. 64

D. 72

E. $64\sqrt{2}$

Here's How to Crack It

Start with Step 1: Know the question. Underline *what is the area of square ABCD ?* Move to Step 2: Look at the answers. We don't have any values for areas of other shapes within the figure, so there is nothing to Ballpark. But note the presence of $\sqrt{2}$ and $\sqrt{3}$ in the answers: They're an additional clue, if you haven't absorbed the info given, that 30-60-90 and/or 45-45-90 triangles are in play.

The triangle in the figure is in fact a 30-60-90. Now move to Step 3: Break the problem into bite-sized pieces. Because angle *A* is the short angle, the side opposite that angle has length 4 and the hypotenuse has length 8. Now move on to Step 3a: Mark your figure with these values. Now move to Step 3b: Write down any formulas you need. The area for a square is s^2. Because that hypotenuse is also the side of the square, the area of the square must be 8 times 8, or 64. This is (C). If you forgot the ratio of the sides of a 30-60-90 triangle, go back and review it. You'll need it.

POE Pointers

If you didn't remember the ratio of the sides of a 30-60-90 triangle, could you have eliminated some answers using POE? Of course. Let's see if we can use the diagram to eliminate some answer choices.

The diagram tells us that $\overline{AE}$ has length $4\sqrt{3}$. A good approximation for $\sqrt{3}$ is 1.7. So $4\sqrt{3} \approx$ 6.8. We can now use this to estimate the lengths of the sides of square $ABCD$. Just using your eyes, would you say that $\overline{AD}$ is longer or shorter than $\overline{AE}$? Of course it's a bit longer; it's the hypotenuse of $\triangle ADE$. You decide to write down what you think its length might be. To find the area of the square, simply square whatever value you decided the side measured. This is your answer.

Now all you have to do is see which of the answer choices still makes sense. Could the answer be (A)? $8\sqrt{3}$ equals roughly 13.6. Is this close to your answer? No way. Could the answer be (B), which is 16? Still much too small. Could the answer be (C), which is 64? Quite possibly. Could the answer be 72? It might be. Could the correct answer be $64\sqrt{2}$? An approximation of $\sqrt{2}$ is 1.4, so $64\sqrt{2} \approx 89.6$. This seems rather large. Thus, on this problem, by using POE we could eliminate (A), (B), and (E).

FOUR-SIDED FIGURES

The interior angles of any four-sided figure (also known as a quadrilateral) add up to 360°. The most common four-sided figures on the ACT are the rectangle and the square, with the parallelogram and the trapezoid coming in a far distant third and fourth.

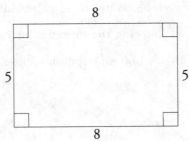

A **rectangle** is a four-sided figure whose four interior angles each measure 90°. The area of a rectangle is *base × height*. Therefore, the area of the rectangle above is 8 (*base*) × 5 (*height*) = 40. The perimeter of a rectangle is the sum of all four of its side lengths. The perimeter of the rectangle above is 8 + 8 + 5 + 5 = 26.

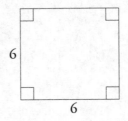

> **Your Friend the Triangle**
> Because a quadrilateral is really just two triangles, its interior angles must measure twice those of a triangle: 2(180) = 360.

> **D'oh, I'm in a Square!**
> To help you remember the area of a four-sided figure (a square, a rectangle, or a parallelogram), imagine that Bart and Homer Simpson are stuck inside of it. To get its area, just multiply **B**art times **H**omer, or (*b*)(*h*), or the base times the height.

A **square** is a rectangle whose four sides are all equal in length. You can think of the area of a square, therefore, as **side squared**. The area of the above square is 6 (*base*) × 6 (*height*) = 36. The perimeter is 24, or 4*s*.

A **parallelogram** is a four-sided figure made up of two sets of parallel lines. We said earlier that when parallel lines are crossed by a third line, eight angles are formed but that in reality there are only two angle measures—the big one and the little one. In a parallelogram, 16 angles are formed, but there are still, in reality, only two angle measures.

The area of a parallelogram is also *base × height*, but because of the shape of the figure, the height of a parallelogram is not necessarily equal to one of its side lengths. Height is measured by a perpendicular line drawn from the base to the top of the figure. The area of the parallelogram above is 9 × 5 = 45.

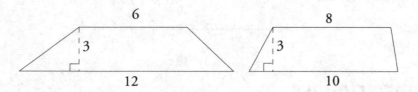

A **trapezoid** is a four-sided figure in which two sides are parallel. Both of the figures above are trapezoids. The area of a trapezoid is the *average of the two parallel sides × the height*, or $\frac{1}{2}$ (*base* 1 + *base* 2)(*height*), but on ACT problems involving trapezoids, there is almost always some easy way to find the area without knowing the formula (for example, by dividing the trapezoid into two triangles and a rectangle). In both trapezoids above, the area is 27.

CIRCLES

The distance from the center of a circle to any point on the circle is called the **radius**. The distance from one point on a circle through the center of the circle to another point on the circle is called the **diameter**. The diameter is always equal to twice the radius. In the circle on the left below, *AB* is called a **chord**. *CD* is called a **tangent** to the circle.

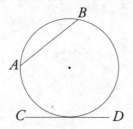

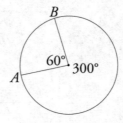

The curved portion of the right-hand circle between points A and B is called an **arc**. The angle formed by drawing lines from the center of the circle to points A and B is said to be **subtended** by the arc. There are 360° in a circle, so that if the angle we just mentioned measures 60°, it takes up $\frac{60}{360}$ or $\frac{1}{6}$ of the degrees in the entire circle. The area it sweeps out takes up $\frac{1}{6}$ of the area of the circle and the arc it forms takes up $\frac{1}{6}$ of the outer perimeter of the circle, called the **circumference**.

> The formula for the **area** of a circle is πr^2.
>
> The formula for the **circumference** is $2\pi r$.

In the circle below, if the radius is 4, then the area is 16π, and the circumference is 8π.

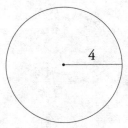

The key to circle problems on the ACT is to look for the word or phrase that tells you what to do. If you see the word *circumference*, immediately write down the formula for circumference, and plug in any numbers the problem has given you. By solving for whatever quantity is still unknown, you have probably already answered the problem. Another tip is to find the radius. The radius is the key to many circle problems.

1. If the area of a circle is 16 square meters, what is its radius in meters?

   A. $\dfrac{8}{\pi}$

   B. 12π

   C. $\dfrac{4\sqrt{\pi}}{\pi}$

   D. $\dfrac{16}{\pi}$

   E. $144\pi^2$

Here's How to Crack It

Step 1: Know the question. We need to solve for the radius.

Step 2: Let the answers help. We don't have a figure, so there's nothing to Ballpark. But no figure?

Step 3a: Draw your own.

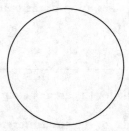

Step 3b: Write down any formulas you need and fill in the information you have. Plug the value you know into the formula for the area of a circle: $\pi r^2 = 16$. The problem is asking for the radius, so you have to solve for r. If you divide both sides by π, you get

$$r^2 = \frac{16}{\pi}$$

$$r = \sqrt{\frac{16}{\pi}}$$

$$= \frac{4}{\sqrt{\pi}}$$

$$= \frac{4\sqrt{\pi}}{\pi}$$

The correct answer is (C).

2. In the figure below, the circle with center O is inscribed inside square $ABCD$ as shown. If a side of the square measures 8 units, what is the area of the shaded region?

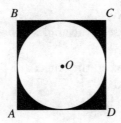

F. $8 - 16\pi$
G. 8π
H. $64 - 16\pi$
J. $64 - 8\pi$
K. 64π

Here's How to Crack It

Begin with Step 1, and underline *what is the area of the shaded region?* Step 2 brings us to the answers, and we see all of the answers have π in them. Since π is approximately 3, (F) would be a negative area. Eliminate this answer. If no other answer choice can be obviously eliminated via Ballparking, move to Step 3. Break the problem into bite-sized pieces, but don't get hung up on "inscribed." Yes, that's an important term to know, but since we have the figure, it's irrelevant. Move to Step 3a and 3b: mark the side of the square "8," and write down the formulas for the area of a circle and square: πr^2 and s^2.

Is there a formula for the shape made by the shaded region? Nope. We just need the basic formulas for the basic shapes. $8^2 = 64$, so we at least know the shaded region is less than 64, the area of the square. At this point we know that the answer must be 64 minus the area of the circle, so we can eliminate (G) and (K) because they do not match this format. What's the link between the square and the circle? The side length of the square equals the diameter. So if the diameter is 8, then the radius must be 4. Use that in the area formula: $4^2\pi = 16\pi$. Subtract the area of the circle from the area of the square, and we get (H).

FUN FACTS ABOUT FIGURES

Read and review the following facts you need to know about plane geometry.

Angle Facts

- There are 90° in a right angle.
- When two straight lines intersect, the angles opposite each other are equal.
- There are 180° in a straight line.
- Two lines are perpendicular when they meet at a 90° angle.
- The sign for perpendicular is ⊥.
- Bisect means to cut exactly in half.
- There are 180° in a triangle.
- There are 360° in any four-sided figure.

Triangle Facts

In any triangle:

- The longest side is opposite the largest angle.
- The shortest side is opposite the smallest angle.
- All angle measures add up to 180°.
- Area = $\frac{1}{2}$ (base × height) = $\frac{1}{2} bh$
- The height is the perpendicular distance from the base to the opposite vertex.
- Perimeter is the sum of the side lengths.
- The length of the third side of any triangle is always less than the sum and greater than the difference of the other two side lengths.

In an isosceles triangle:

- Two side lengths are equal.
- The two angles opposite the equal sides also have equal measures.

In an equilateral triangle:

- All three side lengths are equal.
- All angles measure 60°.

Four-Sided Figure Facts

In a quadrilateral:

- All four angle measures add up to 360°.

In a parallelogram:

- Opposite sides are parallel and have equal length.
- Opposite angles have equal measures.
- Adjacent angles are supplementary (their measures add up to 180°).
- Area = base × height = bh
- The height is the perpendicular distance from the base to the opposite side.

In a rhombus:
- Opposite sides are parallel.
- Opposite angles have equal measures.
- Adjacent angles are supplementary (their measures add up to 180°).
- All 4 sides have equal length.
- Area = base × height = bh
- The height is the perpendicular distance from the base to the opposite side.
- The diagonals are perpendicular.

In a rectangle:
- Rectangles are special parallelograms; thus, any fact about parallelograms also applies to rectangles.
- All 4 angles measure 90°.
- Area = length × width = lw
- Perimeter = 2(length) + 2(width) = $2l + 2w$
- The diagonals have equal length.

In a square:
- Squares are special rectangles; thus, any fact about rectangles also applies to squares.
- All 4 sides have equal length.
- Area = $(side)^2 = s^2$
- Perimeter = 4(side) = $4s$
- The diagonals are perpendicular.

Circle Facts

Circle:
- There are 360° in a circle.

Radius (r):
- The distance from the center to any point on the edge of the circle is the radius.
- All radii in a circle are equal.

Diameter (d):
- The length of a line that connects two points on the edge of the circle, passing through the center, is the diameter.
- The diameter is the longest line in a circle.
- The diameter is twice the radius.

Chord:
- Any line segment connecting two points on the edge of a circle is a chord.
- The longest chord is the diameter.

Circumference (C):
- The distance around the outside of the circle is the circumference.
- $C = 2\pi r = \pi d$

Arc:
- An arc is a part of the circumference.
- The length of an arc is proportional to the measure of the interior angle.

Area:
- The amount of space within the boundaries of the circle is its area.
- $A = \pi r^2$

Sector:
- A sector is a part of the area formed by two radii and the outside of the circle.
- The area of a sector is proportional to the measure of the interior angle.

Line Facts

Line:
- A line has no width and extends infinitely in both directions.
- The angle formed by a line measures 180°.
- A line that contains points A and B is called $\overleftrightarrow{AB}$ (line AB).
- If a figure on the ACT looks like a straight line, and that line looks like it contains a point, it does.

Ray:
- A ray extends infinitely in one direction but has an endpoint.
- The degree measure of a ray is 180°.
- A ray with endpoint A that goes through point B is called $\overrightarrow{AB}$. Pay attention to the arrow above the points and the order in which they are given; those will determine the direction the ray is pointing!

Line Segment:
- A line segment is a part of a line and has two endpoints.
- The degree measure of a line segment is 180°.
- A line segment, which has endpoints of A and B, is written as $\overline{AB}$.

Tangents:
- Tangent means intersecting at one point. For example, a line tangent to a circle intersects exactly one point on the circumference of the circle. Two circles that touch at just one point are also tangent.
- A line tangent to a circle is always perpendicular to the radius drawn to that point of intersection.
- If $\overline{AB}$ intersects a circle at point T, then you would say, "$\overline{AB}$ is tangent to the circle at point T."

PLANE GEOMETRY FORMULAS

Here's a list of all the plane geometry formulas that could show up on the ACT. Memorize the formulas for perimeter/circumference, area, and volume for basic shapes. ACT usually provides the more advanced formulas if they are needed.

You won't be able to take any notes into the test with you, so it's a good idea to make sure you know these formulas by heart!

Circles

- Area: $A = \pi r^2$
- Circumference: $C = 2\pi r = \pi d$

Triangles

- Area: $A = \dfrac{1}{2}bh$
- Perimeter: P = sum of the side lengths
- Pythagorean Theorem: $a^2 + b^2 = c^2$

SOHCAHTOA

- $\sin(\theta) = \dfrac{\text{opposite}}{\text{hypotenuse}}$
- $\cos(\theta) = \dfrac{\text{adjacent}}{\text{hypotenuse}}$
- $\tan(\theta) = \dfrac{\text{opposite}}{\text{adjacent}}$
- $\csc(\theta) = \dfrac{1}{\sin}$
- $\sec(\theta) = \dfrac{1}{\cos}$
- $\cot(\theta) = \dfrac{1}{\tan}$

Quadrilaterals

Parallelograms

- Area: $A = bh$
- Perimeter: P = sum of the side lengths

Rhombuses

- Area: $A = bh$
- Perimeter: P = sum of the side lengths

Trapezoids

- Area: $A = \dfrac{1}{2}h(b_1 + b_2)$
- Perimeter: P = sum of the side lengths

Rectangles

- Area: $A = lw$
- Perimeter: $P = 2(l + w)$

Squares

- Area: $A = s^2$
- Perimeter: $P = 4s$

Polygons

- Sum of angle measures in an n-sided polygon: $(n-2)180°$

- Angle measure of each angle in a regular n-sided polygon: $\dfrac{(n-2)180°}{n}$

3-D Figures

- Surface area of a rectangular solid: $S = 2(lw + lh + wh)$
- Surface area of a cube: $S = 6s^2$
- Surface area of a right circular cylinder: $S = 2\pi r^2 + 2\pi rh$
- Surface area of a sphere: $S = 4\pi r^2$
- Volume of a cube: $V = s^3$
- Volume of a rectangular solid: $V = lwh$
- Volume of a right circular cylinder: $V = \pi r^2 h$
- Volume of a sphere: $V = \dfrac{4\pi r^3}{3}$

GLOSSARY

Arc Any part of the circumference

Bisect To cut in half

Chord Any line segment connecting two points on the edge of a circle

Circumscribed Surrounded by a circle as small as possible

Collinear Lying on the same line

Congruent Equal in size and shape

Diagonal (of a polygon) A line segment connecting opposite vertices

Equilateral triangle A triangle in which all sides have equal length and each angle measures 60°

Inscribed (angle in a circle) An angle in a circle with its vertex on the circumference

Isosceles triangle A triangle with two equal side lengths

Parallel Two distinct lines that do not intersect

Perpendicular At a 90° angle

Plane A flat surface extending in all directions

Polygon A closed figure with three or more sides

Quadrilateral A four-sided figure

Regular polygon A figure with all sides equal in length and all angle measures equal

Sector Any part of the area formed by two radii and the outside of the circle

Similar Having equal angle measures and proportional sides

Surface area The sum of the areas of each face of a figure

Tangent Intersecting at one point

Vertex/Vertices A corner point. For angles, it's where two rays meet. For figures, it's where two adjacent sides meet.

Geometry Drill

For the answers to this drill, please go to Chapter 25.

1. In △*ABC* below, the measure of ∠*A* is equal to the measure of ∠*B*, and the measure of ∠*C* is twice the measure of ∠*B*. What is the measure, in degrees, of ∠*A* ?

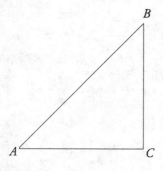

- **A.** 30
- **B.** 45
- **C.** 50
- **D.** 75
- **E.** 90

2. In the figure below, $l_1 \parallel l_2$. Which of the labeled angles must have equal measure?

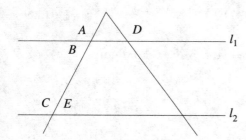

- **F.** *A* and *C*
- **G.** *D* and *E*
- **H.** *A* and *B*
- **J.** *D* and *B*
- **K.** *C* and *B*

3. In the figure below, right triangles *ABC* and *ACD* are drawn as shown below. If *AB* = 20, *BC* = 15, and *AD* = 7, then *CD* = ?

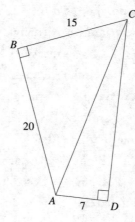

- **A.** 21
- **B.** 22
- **C.** 23
- **D.** 24
- **E.** 25

4. If the area of circle *A* is 16π, then what is the circumference of circle *B* if its radius is $\frac{1}{2}$ that of circle *A* ?

- **F.** 2π
- **G.** 4π
- **H.** 6π
- **J.** 8π
- **K.** 16π

5. In the figure below, $\overline{MO}$ is perpendicular to $\overline{LN}$, *LO* is equal to 4, *MO* is equal to *ON*, and *LM* is equal to 6. What is *MN* ?

- **A.** $2\sqrt{10}$
- **B.** $3\sqrt{5}$
- **C.** $4\sqrt{5}$
- **D.** $3\sqrt{10}$
- **E.** $6\sqrt{4}$

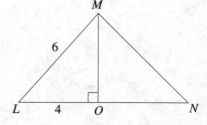

Summary

o   Use the Basic Approach.
-   **Step 1:** Know the question. Read the whole problem before calculating anything, and underline the actual question.
-   **Step 2:** Let the answers help. Look for clues on how to solve and ways to use Process of Elimination (POE). Ballparking works well on geometry questions on area and angles.
-   **Step 3:** Break the problem into bite-sized pieces. When you read the problem a second time, calculate at each step necessary and watch out for tricky phrasing. On geometry, this means
    o   **Step 3a:** Write all the information given in the problem on the figure. If there is no figure, draw your own.
    o   **Step 3b:** Write down any formulas you need and fill in any information you have.

o   There are several things to know about angles and lines.
-   A line is a 180° angle.
-   When two lines intersect, four angles are formed, but in reality there are only two distinct measures.
-   When two parallel lines are cut by a third line, eight angles are formed, but in reality there are still only two measures (a large one and a small one).

o   There are several things to know about triangles.
-   A triangle has three sides and three angles; the sum of the angle measures equals 180°.
-   An isosceles triangle has two equal side lengths and two equal angle lengths opposite those sides.
-   An equilateral triangle has three equal side lengths and three equal angle measures; each angle measures 60°.
-   A right triangle has one 90° angle. In a right triangle problem, you can use the Pythagorean Theorem to find the lengths of sides.
-   Some common right triangles are 3-4-5, 6-8-10, 5-12-13, and 7-24-25.
-   ACT test writers also like the isosceles right triangle, in which the sides are always in the ratio $s : s : s\sqrt{2}$, and the 30-60-90 triangle, in which the sides are always in the ratio $s : s\sqrt{3} : 2s$.

- Similar triangles have the same angle measurements and sides that are in the same proportion.
- The area of a triangle is equal to $\dfrac{(base \times height)}{2}$, with height measured perpendicular to the base.

o Four-sided objects are called quadrilaterals and have four angles, whose measures add up to 360°. There are several important things to remember.
- The area of a rectangle, a square, or a parallelogram can be found using the formula $base \times height = area$, with height measured perpendicular to the base.
- The perimeter of any object is the sum of the lengths of its sides.
- The area of a trapezoid is equal to the average of the lengths of the two bases times the height.

o For any circle problem, you need to know four basic things.
- Radius
- Diameter
- Area (πr^2)
- Circumference (πd or $2\pi r$)

o Don't forget that you can plug in on geometry questions that have variables in the answer choices.

Chapter 13
Word Problems

Now that you've refreshed some of the essential geometry concepts, we will see how to integrate those concepts with your test-taking strategy. In addition, we'll see some other Word Problem strategies that will help you to complete problems quickly and accurately.

PLUGGING IN: NOT JUST ALGEBRA

Remember what the main requirements are for a Plugging In problem. You need variables in the answer choices or question: that's it. It doesn't say anywhere that the problem needs to be a pure algebra problem. What is a pure algebra problem anyway? Don't forget: part of what makes this test so hard is that ACT piles concept on top of concept in its problems. In other words, word problems often *are* algebra problems.

WORD PROBLEMS VS. PLUG-AND-CHUG QUESTIONS

We prefer a simple definition of a word problem: it has to tell a story. We worked through some Geometry word problems in Chapter 12, but let's review the word problem Basic Approach again.

Step 1: Know the Question

Know the question. Read the whole problem before calculating anything, and underline the actual question.

Step 2: Let the Answers Help

Let the answers help. Look for clues on how to solve and ways to use POE.

Step 3: Break the Problem into Bite-Sized Pieces

Break the problem into bite-sized pieces. When you read the problem a second time, calculate at each step necessary and watch out for tricky phrasing.

For geometry questions, Step 3 has two specific additions:

Step 3a: If you're taking the ACT Online Test, copy the figure onto your whiteboard. If there is no figure (regardless of which ACT you are taking), draw your own. Write all the information given in the problem on the figure.

Step 3b: Write down any formulas you need and fill in any information you have.

Let's look at a short, straightforward example.

1. A circle with center O has a radius r. What is the area of a circle with a radius three times larger?

   A. $3\pi r$
   B. $9\pi r$
   C. $3\pi r^2$
   D. $6\pi r^2$
   E. $9\pi r^2$

Here's How to Crack It

Step 1: Know the question. You need to find the area of this new larger circle, not the larger radius.

Step 2: Let the answers help. First of all, you're looking for the area, which means something will have to be squared, so you can eliminate (A) and (B), which can't be right. Now, notice that each of these answer choices has a variable in it. If you're thinking Plugging In, you're thinking right.

Step 3: Break the problem into bite-sized pieces. Pick an easy value for r, like $r = 2$.

Step 3a: Write all the information given in the problem on the figure. There's no figure here, so draw 2 circles. Label the radius of the smaller one: $r = 2$.

Step 3b: Write down any formulas you need and fill in any information you have. The formula for the area of a circle that you'll need is $A = \pi r^2$.

If the original radius is 2, then the larger radius, which is three times larger, must be 6. Therefore, the area of the larger circle must be $A = \pi(6)^2 = 36\pi$. We've got a target answer, so let's try it in the answer choices. Remember, we've already eliminated (A) and (B).

   A. ~~$3\pi r$~~
   B. ~~$9\pi r$~~
   C. $3\pi(2)^2 = 12\pi$ ✗
   D. $6\pi(2)^2 = 24\pi$ ✗
   E. $9\pi(2)^2 = 36\pi$ ✔

Choice (E) is the correct answer. Have another look at those answer choices and think of all the ways you could make mistakes on this problem. Plugging In saves the day again by minimizing the possibility for algebra errors.

ARITHMETIC

When it comes to writing word problems, ACT test writers can draw on both algebra and geometry, as we've seen. But lots of word problems, and even some plug-and-chugs, will test a variety of arithmetic concepts. The rest of this chapter will review those topics.

PERCENTAGES, PROBABILITIES, AND RATIOS: DIDN'T WE JUST DO THIS?

Percentages, probabilities, and ratios can get mighty complex in your math classes at school. Do you want the good news or the bad news? Well, the bad news is that ratios, percentages, and probabilities will all appear on the ACT Math test, but the good news is that they're all testing the same basic concept: parts to wholes.

Let's say you're taking batting practice. You are thrown 100 pitches and hit 20 of them. Ignoring the fact that you're probably not ready for major league baseball, let's put this into some math language. Once we get the basics down, we'll try some more advanced problems.

First, what percentage of the pitches did you hit? Well, that's an easy one because we're dealing with 100. But you can always find percentages with this simple part-to-whole formula:

$$\frac{part}{whole} \times 100\%$$

Once we put the numbers in, we'll get this: $\frac{20}{100} \times 100\% = 0.2 \times 100\% = 20\%$. If you hit 20 of the 100 pitches, you hit 20% of them.

Next, what is the probability that you were to hit any given pitch? Remember, this is just a matter of parts to wholes, so we can find this probability as follows: $\frac{part}{whole} = \frac{hits}{pitches} = \frac{20}{100} = 0.2$. In other words, there's a 0.2, or $\frac{1}{5}$, probability you hit any given pitch during batting practice.

Ratios are a little different. Usually these will ask for the relationship of some part to some other part. If we're still using our batting practice statistics, we might want to know something like, what's the ratio of the pitches you hit to the pitches you missed?

Even though we're not dealing with the whole this time, we'll find the ratio the same way, but instead of $\frac{part}{whole}$, we'll use $\frac{part}{part} = \frac{hits}{misses} = \frac{20}{80} = \frac{1}{4}$. The ratio of hits to misses is $\frac{1}{4}$, or 1 to 4, or 1:4.

If it feels like we just did the same thing three times, it was supposed to. As we've seen a few times already, just because things have different names doesn't mean that they are unrelated. Let's try some problems.

Percentages

1. At a restaurant, diners enjoy an "early bird" discount of 10% off their bills. If a diner orders a meal regularly priced at $18 and leaves a tip of 15% of the discounted meal (no tax), how much does he pay in total?

   A. $13.50
   B. $16.20
   C. $18.63
   D. $18.90
   E. $20.70

Here's How to Crack It

Step 1: Know the question. We want the price of the discounted meal plus tip.

Step 2: Let the answers help. We are reducing a number by 10% and then increasing it by 15%, so it's not likely that the final number will be much less or much greater than $18. Let's eliminate (A) and (E).

Step 3: Break the problem into bite-sized pieces.

First, we'll need to figure out what the discounted price of the meal is. There are a number of ways to do this, but if you find this $\dfrac{part}{whole}$ method useful, you could find the discount this way:

$$10\% = discount$$

$$\frac{10}{100} = \frac{discount}{\$18}$$

$$discount = \$1.80$$

The price of the discounted meal, then, is $18 − $1.80 = $16.20. Let's find the tip the same way.

$$15\% = tip$$

$$\frac{15}{100} = \frac{tip}{\$16.20}$$

$$tip = \$2.43$$

The price of the discounted meal plus tip, therefore, is $16.20 + $2.43 = $18.63. The correct answer is (C).

Another Way to Deal with Percents

A percentage is a fraction in which the denominator equals 100. In literal terms, the word *percent* means "divided by 100," so any time you see a percentage in an ACT question, you can punch it into your calculator quite easily. If a question asks for 40 percent of something, for instance, you can express the percentage as a fraction: $\dfrac{40}{100}$. Any time you are looking for a percent, you can use your calculator to find the decimal equivalent and multiply the result by 100. If four out of five dentists recommend a particular brand of toothpaste, you can quickly determine the percent of doctors who recommend it by typing $\dfrac{4}{5} \times 100$ and hitting the $\boxed{\text{ENTER}}$ key. The resulting "80" just needs a percent sign tacked onto it. To properly translate all percent questions, it is helpful to have a decoding table for the various terms you'll come across.

English	Math Equivalent
percent	/100
of	multiplication ($\times$)
what	variable (y, z)
is, are, were	=
what percent	$\dfrac{y}{100}$

Percentage Shortcuts

In the last problem, we could have saved a little time if we had realized that $\dfrac{1}{5} = 20$ percent. Therefore, $\dfrac{4}{5}$ would be 4×20 percent, or 80 percent. On the next page you'll find some fractions and decimals whose percent equivalents you should know.

Another fast way to do percents is to move the decimal place. To find 10 percent of any number, move the decimal point of that number over one place to the left.

10% of 500 = 50

10% of 50 = 5

10% of 5 = 0.5

To find 1 percent of a number, move the decimal point of that number over two places to the left.

$$1\% \text{ of } 500 = 5$$
$$1\% \text{ of } 50 = 0.5$$
$$1\% \text{ of } 5 = 0.05$$

You can use a combination of these last two techniques to find even very complicated percentages by breaking them down into easy-to-find chunks.

- 20% of 500: 10% of 500 = 50, so 20% is twice 50, or 100.
- 30% of 70: 10% of 70 = 7, so 30% is three times 7, or 21.
- 32% of 400: 10% of 400 = 40, so 30% is three times 40, or 120. 1% of 400 = 4, so 2% is two times 4, or 8. Therefore, 32 percent of 400 = 120 + 8 = 128.

Let's have a look at another ACT percentage problem.

> **The Big Four: Fraction/Percent Equivalents You Should Know**
>
> $$\frac{1}{5} = 0.2 = 20\%$$
> $$\frac{1}{4} = 0.25 = 25\%$$
> $$\frac{1}{3} = 0.\overline{33} = 33\frac{1}{3}\%$$
> $$\frac{1}{2} = 0.5 = 50\%$$

---

2. When 15% of 40 is added to 5% of 260, the resulting number is:

    F.   19
    G.   40
    H.   95
    J.   180
    K.   260

Here's How to Crack It

Let's try this one using the decoding table. Although this isn't really a word problem, that doesn't mean we shouldn't be careful and break it into bite-sized pieces.

First, 15% of 40. Remember, % translates to divide by 100, and "of" translates to multiplication. Therefore, we can rewrite 15% of 40 as $\frac{15}{100} \times 40$. Put this expression in your calculator to find that $\frac{15}{100} \times 40 = 6$.

Now, find 5% of 260. Use the same translations to find $\frac{5}{100} \times 260 = 13$. We've done the tough part, so let's substitute what we've found back into the problem: *When 6 is added to 13, the resulting number is*: Now that's a problem we can handle! 6 + 13 = 19, so the answer is (F).

Now let's look at a harder one that takes several percentages in a row.

---

58. An elementary school class just finished its annual fundraiser that it has been running for several years. The changes in the money earned from one year to the next for the fundraiser were a 10% decrease, a 45% increase, and a 20% decrease. What was the percent increase in the class's fundraising money over the last 3 years?

   F. 4.4%
   G. 5.6%
   H. 15%
   J.   85%
   K. 95.6%

Here's How to Crack It

When faced with multiple percent changes, do each percent change calculation individually. Use the answer from the previous percent change calculation as the starting value for the next calculation. The difficulty here is that you aren't given the starting number! When dealing with a percent of an unknown total, what strategy do you use? Plugging In! The easiest number to plug in for a percent question is 100. If the class made $100 the first year, then it made 10% less, or 0.10(100) = $10 less the second year. Therefore, it made $100 − $10 = $90 the second year, and 45% more, or 0.45(90) = $40.50 more the third year. It made $90 + $40.50 = $130.50 the third year, and 20% less, or 0.20(130.50) = $26.10 less the final year. The final amount was $130.50 − $26.10 = $104.40. The difference between the starting amount and the final amount was $104.40 − $100 = $4.40, so the percent difference is $4.40 ÷ $100 = 0.044 or 4.4%. The correct answer is (F).

Probability

---

3. Herbie's practice bag contains 4 blue racquetballs, 1 red racquetball, and 6 green racquetballs. If he chooses a ball at random, which of the following is closest to the probability that the ball will NOT be green?

   A. 0.09
   B. 0.27
   C. 0.36
   D. 0.45
   E. 0.54

Here's How to Crack It

Step 1: Know the question. Make sure you read carefully! We want the probability that the chosen ball will NOT be green.

Step 2: Let the answers help. Green balls account for slightly more than half the number of balls in the bag, so the likelihood that the ball will NOT be green should be slightly less than half. That eliminates (A), (B), and (E). Not bad!

Step 3: Break the problem into bite-sized pieces. This is a pretty straightforward $\frac{part}{whole}$ problem: $\frac{part}{whole} = \frac{NOT\,green}{all} = \frac{5}{11}$. The only slight difficulty is that the answers are not listed as fractions, but it's nothing a calculator can't help. Find $5 \div 11 \approx 0.45$, (D).

Expected Value

Sometime the ACT will ask about the "expected value" of the results of a situation. The expected value is based on both the values and the probability that those values will occur.

To find the expected value, multiply each possibility by the probability that it will occur; then add those products together.

Here's what it looks like in practice:

Given the table below, what is the expected value of a number drawn at random?

Number	Probability
1	0.25
2	0.20
3	0.40
4	0.05
5	0.10

First, multiply each number by the probability of it being drawn.

$$1 \times 0.25 = 0.25$$
$$2 \times 0.20 = 0.40$$
$$3 \times 0.40 = 1.20$$
$$4 \times 0.05 = 0.20$$
$$5 \times 0.10 = 0.50$$

Now sum the results: $0.25 + 0.40 + 1.20 + 0.20 + 0.50 = 2.55$

The expected value for a number drawn is 2.55. You are probably thinking, but 2.55 isn't a value that I can draw. There's a good mathematical reason for how it can be the expected value, but luckily the ACT won't test that. For now, just know that your expected value can be something other than the values that are available!

Let's try another problem.

---

54. Lovell the Magician prepares a standard deck of cards by removing all of the face cards, aces, and tens, leaving 32 cards in the deck. An audience participant draws a card at random from the 32 remaining cards numbered 2 through 9. If the random variable c represents the value of the card drawn from the deck by the audience participant, what is the expected value of c?

F. 0.125
G. 4
H. 5
J. 5.5
K. 6

Here's How to Crack It

This question does not provide the probability of drawing each numbered card from the deck, so that must be found before the expected value can be calculated. Lovell the Magician has left only the numbered cards 2 through 9 in his deck of standard playing cards. That means there are 4 of each numbered card. The probability that an audience participant draws a card with a value of 2 is $\frac{4}{32} = 0.125$. Since there are 4 cards available for all the values 3 through 9, the probability of drawing a card of any of those values is also 0.125. The expected value of any one draw can be calculated by first multiplying the value of each card by its probability and then summing the results.

$(2)(0.125) + (3)(0.125) + (4)(0.125) + (5)(0.125) + (6)(0.125) + (7)(0.125) + (8)(0.125) + (9)(0.125) = 0.25 + 0.375 + 0.5 + 0.625 ++ 0.75 + 0.875 + 1 + 1.125 = 5.5$, which is (J).

Ratios

4. If the ratio of $2x$ to $5y$ is $\dfrac{1}{20}$, what is the ratio of x to y?

F. $\dfrac{1}{40}$

G. $\dfrac{1}{20}$

H. $\dfrac{1}{10}$

J. $\dfrac{1}{8}$

K. $\dfrac{1}{4}$

Here's How to Crack It

The difficulty of this problem is all in the setup. Just remember that you're comparing parts to parts, and you'll be fine.

$$\frac{2x}{5y} = \frac{1}{20}$$

To isolate $\dfrac{x}{y}$ on the left side of this equation, let's multiply both sides of the equation by $\dfrac{5}{2}$.

$$\frac{5}{2} \times \frac{2x}{5y} = \frac{1}{20} \times \frac{5}{2}$$

$$\frac{x}{y} = \frac{5}{40}$$

$\dfrac{5}{40}$ reduces to $\dfrac{1}{8}$. The answer is (J).

If you got stuck on this one, look at those answer choices: you could've used PITA!

Let's see how ACT might test ratios in a word problem.

5. If 3.7 inches of rain fell on Vancouver during the first 4 days of December, and the rain continues to fall at this pace for the rest of the month, approximately how many feet of rain will fall during December?

(Note: The month of December has 31 days.)

A. 2.4
B. 3.7
C. 9.5
D. 28.7
E. 114.7

Here's How to Crack It

Step 1: Know the question. It's in the last line: *how many feet of rain will fall in December?* But be careful: the value given in the problem is in inches. We're going to have to do some converting!

Step 2: Let the answers help. Since we know the problem is asking how many *feet* of rain will fall, and the problem tells us that 3.7 *inches* of rain will fall in 4 days, we can do some Ballparking. The number of inches will increase, but it will be reduced again when we convert it into feet. Choice (E) is definitely too big, and (D) probably is too.

Step 3: Break the problem into bite-sized pieces. There are going to be two main parts to this problem: first, we want to figure out how much rain will fall in 31 days; then we want to convert it to feet. We can do this by using ratios.

The ratio given in the problem is 3.7 inches every four days, or in math terms, $\dfrac{3.7 \text{ in.}}{4 \text{ days}}$. The ratio will remain the same no matter how many days there are, so let's use this ratio to find how many inches of rain will fall in December.

$$\frac{3.7 \text{ in.}}{4 \text{ days}} = \frac{? \text{ in.}}{31 \text{ days}}$$

We can rearrange the terms to find

$$? \text{ in.} = \frac{(3.7 \text{ in.})(31 \text{ days})}{4 \text{ days}} = 28.675 \text{ in.}$$

But we can't stop here! Remember, the problem is asking for a value in feet. (It's a good thing we did some early POE, isn't it?)

We'll use the same process, and this time we already know the ratio of inches to feet: $\dfrac{12 \text{ in.}}{1 \text{ ft}}$. As we did above, let's use this ratio to find our answer.

$$\frac{12 \text{ in.}}{1 \text{ ft}} = \frac{28.675 \text{ in.}}{? \text{ ft}}$$

Rearrange the equation to find

$$? \text{ ft} = \frac{28.675 \text{ in.}(1 \text{ ft})}{12 \text{ in.}} \approx 2.4 \text{ ft, (A)}$$

AVERAGES

There are only three parts to any average question. Fortunately for you, the ACT must give you two of these parts, which are all you need to find the third. For any question about averages, use the formula $T = AN$, in which T is the total, A is the average, and N in the number of things.

For example, if you want to find the average of 9, 12, and 6, you know you have 3 items with a total of 27. The formula becomes $27 = A(3)$. You can divide both sides by 3 to find that $A = 9$.

> **Playing the Averages**
>
> **Arithmetic mean**—just a fancy way of saying "average."
>
> **Median**—the one in the middle, like the median strip on the highway.
>
> **Mode**—you're looking for the element that appears most. Get it? MOde, MOst.

Although you probably could have done that without the formula, more difficult average questions involve multiple calculations and lend themselves particularly well to using the formula. Let's take a look at one:

3. Over 9 games, a baseball team had an average of 8 runs per game. If the average number of runs for the first 7 games was 6 runs per game and the same number of runs was scored in each of the last 2 games, how many runs did the team score during the last game?

   A.   5
   B.   15
   C.   26
   D.   30
   E.   46

> **The Missing Number**
> The ACT loves to leave out totals on average problems. You aren't done until you've found it.

Here's How to Crack It
Step 1: Know the question. *How many runs did the team score during the last game?*

Step 2: Let the answers help. Eliminate (A). Since the average for the first 7 is lower than all 9, the runs scored in the last two games can't be that few. Similarly, (E) is probably too big. If you don't trust your sense of numbers and you're not comfortable Ballparking here, however, leave both. It's a complicated question on a more advanced topic.

Step 3: Break the problem into bite-sized pieces. Let's use bite-sized pieces to plug the information from the first line of this question into our trusty average formula. We get $T = (8)(9) = 72$.

Now let's put the information from the second line into the formula. We get $T = (6)(7) = 42$.

If the number of runs scored in all 9 games added up to 72 and those of 7 of these games added up to 42, then the number of runs scored in the remaining 2 games had a total of $72 - 42$, or 30. In case you are feeling smug about getting this far, the ACT writers made 30 (D).

But of course you know that they only want the runs scored in the last game. Because the same number of runs was scored in each of the last two games, the answer is $\frac{30}{2}$ or 15, (B).

The Weighted Average

ACT writers have a particular fondness for "weighted average" problems. First, let's look at a regular unweighted average question.

> If Sally received a grade of 90 on a test last week and a grade of 100 on a test this week, what is her average for the two tests?

Piece of cake, right? The answer is 95. You added the scores and divided by 2. Now let's turn the same question into a weighted average question.

> If Sally's average for the entire year last year was 90 and her average for the entire year this year was 100, is her average for the two years combined equal to 95 ?

The answer is "not necessarily." If Sally took the same number of courses in both years, then yes, her average is 95. But what if last year she took 6 courses, while this year she took only 2 courses? Can you compare the two years equally? ACT likes to test your answer to this question. Here's an example.

1. The starting team of a baseball club has 9 members who have an average of 12 home runs apiece for the season. The second-string team for the baseball club has 7 members who have an average of 8 home runs apiece for the season. What is the average number of home runs for the starting team and the second-string team combined?

   A. 7.5
   B. 8
   C. 10
   D. 10.25
   E. 14.2

Here's How to Crack It

The ACT test writers want to see whether you spot this as a weighted average problem. If you thought the first-string team was exactly equivalent to the second-string team, then you merely had to take the average of the two averages, 12 and 8, to get 10. In weighted average problems, the ACT test writers always include the average of the two averages among the answer choices, and it is always wrong. 10 is choice (C). Cross off (C).

The two teams are not equivalent because there are different numbers of players on each team. To get the true average, we'll have to find the total number of home runs and divide by the total number of players. How do we do this? By using the trusty average formula as usual. The first line of the problem says that the 9 members on the first team have an average of 12 home runs apiece. The formula becomes $T = (12)(9) = 108$ home runs scored by the starting team.

The second sentence says that the 7 members of the second-string team have an average of 8 home runs each. The formula becomes $T = (8)(7) = 56$ home runs scored by the second-string team.

Now we can find the true average. Add all the home runs scored by the starting team to all the home runs scored by the second-string team: $108 + 56 = 164$. This is the true total. The total number of players is $9 + 7 = 16$, so the average formula becomes $164 = A(16)$. Divide both sides by 16 to find that $A = 10.25$, so the answer is (D).

CHARTS AND GRAPHS

Since calculators were added to the arsenal you're allowed to have with you when you take the ACT, more and more of the test has been composed of questions on which calculators are of little or no use, such as questions based on charts and graphs. On this type of question, your math skills aren't really being tested at all; what ACT is interested in is your ability to read a simple graph (not unlike on the Science Reasoning test, which we'll get to later in Part V). All of the questions we have seen in this format have been very direct. If you can read a simple graph, you can always get them right. What's most important on questions like these is paying attention to the labels on the information. Let's take a look at a graph question.

23. Between which two months was the change in total rainfall the greatest?

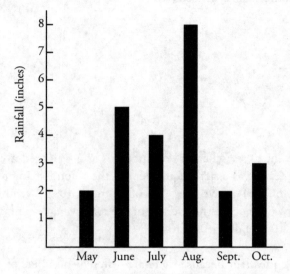

Average monthly rainfall in Belleville, IL.

A. May and June
B. June and July
C. July and August
D. August and September
E. September and October

Here's How to Crack It
The ACT test writers want to see if you can decipher the information presented in the graph. Before you read the question then, you need to take a look at the graph. What is measured here? It says on the bottom: *Average monthly rainfall in Belleville, IL.* You should look at the values along the left side and bottom of the graph as well. When you do, you'll see that the rain is measured in inches (left-hand side), and the measurements were made each month (bottom).

Now for the question. To determine which two months had the greatest change, we need to compare the change between each pair of months, discarding the smaller ones until we have only one left. The difference from May to June is about 3, and that's larger than June to July and September to October, so (B) and (E) are out. July to August is larger still, though, so (A) is out, leaving only (C) and (D). It should be pretty apparent that the August to September change is larger than the July to August change, though, so the correct answer must be (D).

Although most questions involving graphs on the Math test are this simple, you may see slightly more complicated variations. Here's another question based on the same bar graph.

---

24. Based on the information presented in the graph below, what is the approximate average monthly rainfall, in inches, in Belleville, IL, for the period given?

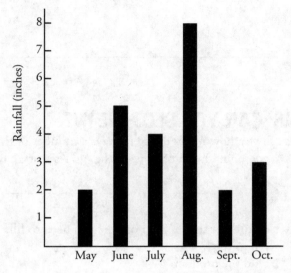

Average monthly rainfall in Belleville, IL.

F. 2
G. 3
H. 4
J. 5
K. 8

Here's How to Crack It

As with the last question, the first thing you want to do is examine the graph and figure out what information is being given to you and how it is being presented. Because you already did that for this graph, we'll skip that step on this one.

This question combines graph reading with average calculation, so the next thing you'll have to do is estimate the rainfall for each month. Because the question uses the word *approximate*, you don't have to worry too much about making super-exact measurements of the heights of the bar graphs. Eyeballing it and rounding to the closest value given on the left-hand side will be good enough to get you the right answer. Do that now before you read the next sentence.

To us, it looks like about 2 inches fell in May and September, and around 3 fell in October. July saw about 4, June roughly 5, and August about 8. Your estimates should be the same as ours. If they're not, go back now and figure out why not. You probably need to be a little more careful in your estimating. Use another piece of paper as a guide if necessary (you can use your answer sheet in this manner when taking the real ACT).

Now it's just a matter of calculating the average. Find the total first.

$$2 + 2 + 3 + 4 + 5 + 8 = 24$$

There are 6 months, so the formula becomes $T = AN$ becomes $24 = A(6)$, and you just need to divide both sides by 6.

So the answer is 4, or (H).

———————○———————

COMBINATIONS: CAN YOU SLOT ME IN?

Combination problems ask you how many different ways a number of things could be chosen or combined. The rules for combination problems on the ACT are straightforward.

---

1. Figure out the number of slots you need to fill.
2. Fill in those slots.
3. Find the product.

Seem confusing? It's not. Let's look at an example. This is what most combination problems on the ACT will look like:

———————○———————

6. At the school cafeteria, students can choose from 3 different salads, 5 different main dishes, and 2 different desserts. If Isabel chooses one salad, one main dish, and one dessert for lunch, how many different lunches could she choose?

   F. 10
   G. 15
   H. 25
   J. 30
   K. 50

Here's How to Crack It

We've got three slots to fill here, one for each item: salad, main dish, dessert. And the number of possibilities for each is pretty clear. Set up the slots and take the product as your answer.

$$\underset{\text{Salad}}{\underline{3}} \times \underset{\text{Main}}{\underline{5}} \times \underset{\text{Dessert}}{\underline{2}} = 30$$

The correct answer here is (J).

On a more difficult problem, you may run into a combination with more restricted elements. Just be sure to read the problem carefully before attempting it. If the question makes your head spin, leave it and return to it later, or pick your Letter of the Day and move on. For good measure, though, here's what one of those tougher ones might look like.

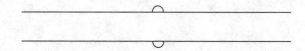

7. At the school cafeteria, 2 boys and 4 girls are forming a lunch line. If the boys must stand in the first and last places in line, how many different lines can be formed?

    A. 2
    B. 6
    C. 48
    D. 360
    E. 720

Here's How to Crack It

These restrictions might make this problem seem daunting, but this is where the slot method is really helpful. We have six spots in line to fill, so draw six slots:

——   ——   ——   ——   ——   ——

It even looks like the line the boys and girls are standing in! Do the restricted spots first. The problem tells us that the two boys *must stand in the first and last places in line*. This means that either of the boys could stand in first place, and then the other boy will stand in last. This means that we have two options for the first place, but only one for the last.

<u> 2 </u>   ——   ——   ——   ——   <u> 1 </u>

Now do the same with the unrestricted parts. Any of the four girls could stand in the second spot.

<u> 2 </u>   <u> 4 </u>   ——   ——   ——   <u> 1 </u>

Now, since one of the girls is standing in the second spot, there are only three left to stand in the third spot, and so on, and so on.

$$\underline{2}\quad\underline{4}\quad\underline{3}\quad\underline{2}\quad\underline{1}\quad\underline{1}$$

Now, as ever, just take the product, to find that the correct answer is (C), 48.

$$\underline{2}\times\underline{4}\times\underline{3}\times\underline{2}\times\underline{1}\times\underline{1}=48$$

Let's try one more that tests a few things.

8. Elias has to select one shirt, one pair of pants, and one pair of shoes. If he selects at random from his 8 shirts, 4 pairs of pants, and 3 pairs of shoes, and all his shirts, pants, and shoes are different colors, what is the likelihood that he will select his red shirt, black pants, and brown shoes?

    F. $\dfrac{1}{3}$

    G. $\dfrac{1}{4}$

    H. $\dfrac{1}{15}$

    J. $\dfrac{1}{32}$

    K. $\dfrac{1}{96}$

Here's How to Crack It

Step 1: Know the question. The problem is asking what the probability is that he will select this one group of clothes from all possible combinations of clothes.

Step 2: Let the answers help. The answers offer the important reminder that we're looking for a probability. We know that it will be only one arrangement out of a reasonably large number of them, so we should at least get rid of (F) and (G).

Step 3: Break the problem into bite-sized pieces. First, we should find the total number of possible combinations. Then, we can deal with the probability.

We have three slots to fill here, and we want to find the product of the three.

$$\underline{\quad 8 \quad}_{\text{Shirts}} \times \underline{\quad 4 \quad}_{\text{Pants}} \times \underline{\quad 3 \quad}_{\text{Shoes}} = 96 \text{ arrangements}$$

Of the 96 possible arrangements, an ensemble of red shirt, black pants, and brown shoes is only one. Therefore, we can go to our $\dfrac{part}{whole}$ ratio to find $\dfrac{part}{whole} = \dfrac{\text{red, black, brown}}{\text{ALL arrangements}} = \dfrac{1}{96}$, (K).

Combinations and Permutations

Another type of combination question given on the ACT involves the use of the notation for combinations, $_nC_r$, and permutations, $_nP_r$. In both notations, n is the number of items available to choose from, and r is the number of slots to fill.

A combination is a grouping of elements in which order doesn't matter. For example, a group of 3 people, Erin, Sarah, and Alex, is the same group of 3 people if you put their names in alphabetical order: Alex, Erin, and Sarah.

Permutations, on the other hand, are groups in which the order does matter. For example, if you unlock your phone with the pattern upper right, lower left, middle, you can't also unlock your phone with middle, upper right, lower left, because the order matters!

Let's see what that looks like in practice.

---

58. An animal trainer is selecting a group of animals for a feature film. The film's director requested three cats and four dogs. If the animal trainer has 15 cats and 7 dogs available, which of the following represents the number of different groupings of animals that can be created for the film?

F. $_{22}P_7$
G. $_{22}C_7$
H. $(_{15}P_3)(_7P_4)$
J. $(_{15}C_3)(_7C_4)$
K. $(_{22}C_7)^2$

Here's How to Crack it

This question is asking you to group together animals, so just as with the group of Sarah, Alex, and Erin, it doesn't matter what order the cats or dogs are in. You know this will be a combination problem and the notation will be in the form $_nC_r$. Eliminate answers (F) and (H). This question also tells you that you will be selecting cats and dogs separately, because the director is looking for a specific number of each animal. This is similar to problem 7 above, in which you had to deal with girls and boys separately. That means there will be one combination for the cats and a separate one for the dogs. Eliminate answer (G) because it has only one combination. Remember that in the combination notation, n represents the number of options available. For the cats that is 15, and for the dogs that is 7. The r represents the number of slots available to be filled by the cats, 3, and the dogs, 4. Therefore your combination notation for the cats will be $_{15}C_3$ and for the dogs, it will be $_7C_4$. You need to multiply those combinations to get $(_{15}C_3)(_7C_4)$, which is (J).

PATTERNS

A pattern as it is used on the ACT is a sequence or grouping of numbers that increases or decreases in a predictable way. There are two types of sequences that the ACT tests. The first is an arithmetic sequence, a sequence with a constant difference between subsequent terms. The second is a geometric sequence, a sequence with a constant ratio between subsequent terms.

Arithmetic and Geometric Sequences

Arithmetic sequence examples:

$$2, 7, 12, 17, 22...$$

Each term in this sequence is found by adding 5 to the previous term.

$$19, 17, 15, 13, 11...$$

Each term in this sequence is found by subtracting 2 from the previous term.

Geometric sequence examples:

$$2, 8, 32, 128, 512...$$

Each term in this sequence is found by multiplying the previous term by 4.

$$1{,}380, 230, 38\frac{1}{3}, 6\frac{7}{18}...$$

Each term in this sequence is found by dividing the previous term by 6.

Let's explore a problem dealing with an arithmetic sequence.

13. In January, a diner donated 300 meals to the local food bank. In February, the same diner donated 323 meals, and in March, the diner donated 346 meals. If the number of meals the diner donates each month increases by a constant amount, how many meals will the diner donate in July?

    A. 369
    B. 392
    C. 415
    D. 438
    E. 461

Here's How to Crack It

The problem states that the number of meals donated each month increases by a constant amount. That means there is a sequence being represented in the problem, and since the amount is constant, the sequence is an arithmetic sequence. Look at the number of donations in January. Comparing that to the number of meals donated in February gives you the difference, so calculate $323 - 300 = 23$ meals. Now that you know the difference between months, you can use that information to determine the number of meals donated in July. The last month the problem told you about is March, which was 346 meals, so add 23 to determine how many meals were donated in April: $346 + 23 = 369$. Add another 23 for May: $369 + 23 = 392$; June: $392 + 23 = 415$; and July: $415 + 23 = 438$. The correct answer is (D).

If there was more space between the terms, such as asking for the number in July 3 years from now, it wouldn't make sense to do each addition individually; it is way too time consuming for the ACT. There's a short cut you can use to make this type of calculation faster. Let's look at how to do that when asked, "What is the 89th term of an arithmetic sequence whose 5th and 6th terms are 12 and 15, respectively?"

This question is nice because the terms that were provided are right next to each other. It's very easy to find the constant difference in this arithmetic sequence: $15 - 12 = 3$.

But the next part of the process can be tricky. Finding the 89th term will be very time-consuming if you have to add $15 + 3 = 18$, $18 + 3 = 21$,…all the way up to the 89th term.

Let's make it easier by finding the number of "jumps" you take from the 6th term to the 89th term. To do so, subtract $89 - 6 = 83$. In this sequence, we would need to add 3 a total of 83 times, which is an additional $3 \times 83 = 249$ added to the 6th term of the sequence: $15 + 249 = 264$. The 89th term of the sequence is 264!

Let's try a problem dealing with a geometric sequence.

---

54. In a geometric sequence whose second term is $\dfrac{6}{5}$ and fifth term is $\dfrac{1,296}{5}$, what is the first term?

    F. $-\dfrac{12}{5}$

    G. $-\dfrac{6}{5}$

    H. $\dfrac{1}{6}$

    J. $\dfrac{1}{5}$

    K. $\dfrac{7,776}{5}$

Here's How to Crack It

This problem gave us the 2nd and 5th term of a geometric sequence. In a geometric sequence, the ratio between each term is constant, so you need to determine what that ratio is. First let's find the ratio between the 2nd and 5th terms: $\dfrac{\frac{1,296}{5}}{\frac{6}{5}} = \dfrac{1,296}{6} = 216$. Now take a look at how many "jumps" there are between the 2nd and 5th terms.

In order to move from the 2nd term to the 5th term, you would have multiplied each term by the ratio 3 times. Mathematically, if c is the ratio, the formula would be $\dfrac{6}{5} \times c \times c \times c = \dfrac{1,296}{5}$, which can also be written as $\dfrac{6}{5}c^3 = \dfrac{1,296}{5}$. You already determined that to get from the second term, $\dfrac{6}{5}$, to the 5th term, $\dfrac{1,296}{5}$, you need to multiply by 216, which is the same as c^3.

Set 216 = c^3 and solve to get $c = 6$. Now you know that to get from one term to the next you multiply by 6! The question asks for the first term. You are given the second term and asked for the first, moving backwards in the sequence. Therefore, you need to do the opposite of multiplication: divide the second term, $\frac{6}{5}$, by 6 to get $\frac{\frac{6}{5}}{6} = \frac{1}{5}$. The first term of the sequence is $\frac{1}{5}$, which is (J).

The above solution might seem a little complicated. What you hopefully discovered from the solution above is that when you find the ratio between non-subsequent terms in a geometric sequence and the difference between the term numbers, that is enough information to find the ratio for your geometric sequence. And don't forget to use your POOD and skip questions like this one if you are running short on time!

—————————————○—————————————

Word Problems Drill

For the answers to this drill, please go to Chapter 25.

1. The ratio of boys to girls at the Milwood School is 4 to 5. If there are a total of 27 children at the school, how many boys attend the Milwood School?

   A. 4
   B. 9
   C. 12
   D. 14
   E. 17

2. Aubrie computed the average of her six biology test scores by mistakenly adding the totals of five scores and dividing by five, giving her an average score of 88. When Aubrie realized her error, she recalculated and included the sixth test score of 82. What is the average of Aubrie's six biology tests?

   F. 82
   G. 85
   H. 86
   J. 87
   K. 88

3. In the process of milling grain, 3% of the original is lost because of spillage, and another 5% of the original is lost because of mildew. If the mill starts out with 490 tons of grain, how much (in tons) remains to be sold after milling?

   A. 425
   B. 426
   C. 420.5
   D. 440
   E. 450.8

4. A rectangular box has a base measuring a by a meters and height of b meters. Which of the following represents the surface area of the box?

   F. $6ab$
   G. a^2b
   H. $a^2 + 2ab$
   J. $2a(a + 2b)$
   K. $2(a^2 + b^2)$

5. In the word HAWKS, how many ways is it possible to rearrange the letters if none repeat and the letter W must go last?

   A. 5
   B. 15
   C. 24
   D. 120
   E. 650

6. An arcade game requires the participant to drop quarters into the machine; each quarter dropped into the machine will in turn push several quarters off the edge of a ledge, and the participant will win that many quarters. For each quarter dropped into the machine, the chance of a certain number of quarters falling off the ledge is represented in the table below. What is the expected number of quarters a participant will win for each quarter dropped into the machine?

# of Quarters	Probability
0	0.5
1	0.3
2	0.15
3	0.03
4	0.02

   F. 0
   G. 0.15
   H. 0.77
   J. 1
   K. 3

7. There are 7 terms in a finite arithmetic sequence, and the first term is 11. Which of the following is true about the median and the mean of the 7 terms?

   A. The median is 7 more than the mean.
   B. The median is 11 more than the mean.
   C. The median and the mean are equal.
   D. The median is 11 less than the mean.
   E. The median is 7 less than the mean.

Summary

o   Plugging In works on all kinds of problems, not just Algebra. Always look for opportunities to simplify the math by plugging in!

o   Percentages and probabilities are all based on a relationship of PART to WHOLE. Ratios are based on a relationship of PART to PART. Probabilities can be found by taking the part (the number of things that meet some given criteria) divided by the whole (all possibilities, including those that don't meet the criteria).

o   Percentages can typically be found by multiplying $\frac{part}{whole} \times 100\%$.

   •   When dealing with percentages, remember to convert English into Math with the handy chart.

English	Math Equivalent
percent	/100
of	multiplication (×)
what	variable (y, z)
is, are, were	=
what percent	$\frac{y}{100}$

o   On Combination problems
   1.   Figure out the number of slots you need to fill.
   2.   Fill in those slots.
   3.   Find the product.

o   On Average problems, use the average formula $T = AN$.

   T is the total.
   A is the average.
   N is the number of things.

Chapter 14
Graphing and Coordinate Geometry

We've covered most of what you'll need to get a great score on the ACT Math test. This chapter will give a brief overview of Coordinate Geometry. While it's not tested as heavily as Plane Geometry, Coordinate Geometry offers many fast plug-and-chug opportunities. Though we will be discussing the basic rules and formulas you need, we will always have an eye on how we can crack some of these problems more strategically as well.

COORDINATE GEOMETRY

As we saw in the first Math chapter, coordinate geometry will account for about 9 questions in any given exam. While ACT makes a big deal about how separate this is from plane geometry, the only major difference between the two is that you need more graph paper to do coordinate geometry. We'll cover the basics of graphing and its related functions, but don't forget, you know a lot of this stuff from the earlier geometry chapter already!

Graphing Inequalities

Here's a simple inequality:

$$3x + 5 > 11$$

Solve an inequality the same way that you solve an equality. By subtracting 5 from both sides and then dividing both sides by 3, you get the expression

$$x > 2$$

This can be represented on a number line as shown below.

An Open Circle
On the number line, a hollow circle means that point is *not* included in the graph.

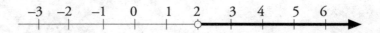

The open circle at 2 indicates that x can include every number greater than 2, but not 2 itself or anything less than 2.

If we had wanted to graph $x \geq 2$, the circle would have to be filled in, indicating that our graph includes 2 as well.

A Solid Dot
On the number line, a solid dot means that point is included in the graph.

An ACT graphing problem might look like this.

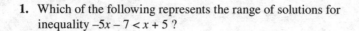

1. Which of the following represents the range of solutions for inequality $-5x - 7 < x + 5$?

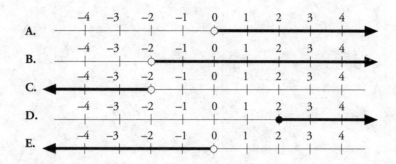

Here's How to Crack It

The ACT test writers want you first to simplify the inequality, and then figure out which of the answer choices represents a graph of the solution set of the inequality. To simplify, isolate x on one side of the inequality.

$$
\begin{array}{r}
-5x - 7 < x + 5 \\
-x \qquad -x \\
\hline
-6x - 7 < \qquad 5 \\
+7 \qquad +7 \\
\hline
-6x \qquad < \qquad 12
\end{array}
$$

Now divide both sides by −6. Note that when you multiply or divide an inequality by a negative, the sign flips over.

$$
\frac{-6x}{-6} < \frac{12}{-6}
$$
$$
x > -2
$$

Which of the choices answers the question? If you selected (B), you're right.

Flip Flop
When you multiply or divide an inequality by a negative, the sign flips.

Graphing in Two Dimensions

More complicated graphing questions concern equations with two variables, usually designated *x* and *y*. These equations can be graphed on a Cartesian grid, which looks like this.

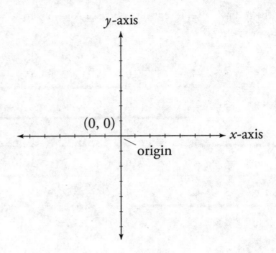

Every point (*x*, *y*) has a place on this grid. For example, the point *A* (3, 4) can be found by counting over on the *x*-axis 3 places to the right of (0, 0)—known as the **origin**—and then counting on the *y*-axis 4 places up from the origin, as shown below. Point *B* (5, –2) can be found by counting 5 places to the right on the *x*-axis and then down 2 places on the *y*-axis. Point *C* (–4, –1) can be found by counting 4 places to the left of the origin on the *x*-axis and then 1 place down on the *y*-axis.

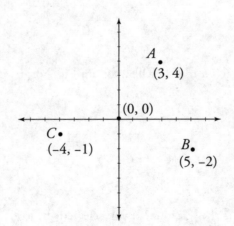

The grid is divided into four quadrants, which go counterclockwise.

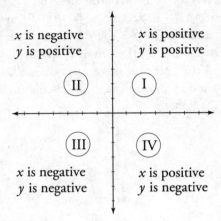

- In the first quadrant, both x and y are positive.
- In the second quadrant, x is negative but y is positive.
- In the third quadrant, both x and y are negative.
- In the fourth quadrant, x is positive but y is negative.

Note: This is when your graphing calculator (if you have one) will really get a chance to shine. Practice doing all the ACT coordinate geometry questions on your calculator now and you'll blow them away when you actually take the test.

Graphic Guesstimation

A few questions on the ACT might involve actual graphing, but it is more likely that you will be able to make use of graphing to *estimate* the answers to questions that the ACT test writers think are more complicated.

1. Point B (4,3) is the midpoint of line segment AC. If point A has coordinates (0,1), then what are the coordinates of point C ?

   A. $(-4, -1)$
   B. $(4, 1)$
   C. $(4, 4)$
   D. $(8, 5)$
   E. $(8, 9)$

Here's How to Crack It

You may or may not remember the midpoint formula: the ACT test writers expect you to use it to solve this problem. We'll go over it in a moment, along with the other formulas you'll need to solve coordinate geometry questions. However, it is worth noting that by drawing a rough graph of this problem, you can get the correct answer without the formula.

On your TI-80 series calculator, you can plot independent points to see what the graph should look like. To do this, hit [STAT] and select option [1:Edit]. Enter the *x*- and *y*-coordinate points in the first two columns; use [L1] for your *x*-coordinates and [L2] for the *y*-coordinates. After you enter the two points, hit [2nd] [Y=] to access the [STAT PLOT] menu. Select option [1:Plot1]. Change the [OFF] status to [ON] and hit [GRAPH]. You should now see the two points you entered. Now you can ballpark the answers based on where they are in the coordinate plane. Keep in mind that you can also plot all the points in the answers as well. Just be sure you keep track of all the *x*- and *y*-values. If you don't have a graphing calculator, use the grid we've provided below.

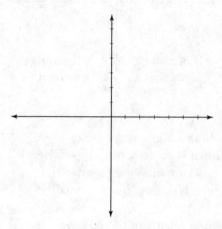

B is supposed to be the midpoint of a line segment *AC*. Draw a line through the two points you've just plotted and extend it upward until *B* is the midpoint of the line segment. It should look like this:

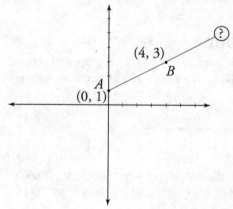

The place where you stopped drawing is the approximate location of point *C*. Now let's look at the answer choices to see if any of them are in the ballpark.

A. (−4, −1): These coordinates are in the wrong quadrant.
B. (4, 1): This point is way below where it should be.
C. (4, 4): This point does not extend enough to the right.
D. (8, 5): Definitely in the ballpark. Hold on to this answer choice.
E. (8, 9): Possible, although the *y*-coordinate seems a little high.

Which answer choice do you want to pick? If you said (D), you are right.

THE IMPORTANT COORDINATE GEOMETRY FORMULAS

By memorizing a few formulas, you will be able to answer virtually all of the coordinate geometry questions on this test. Remember, too, that in coordinate geometry you almost *always* have a fallback: just graph it out.

And always keep your graphing calculator handy on these types of problems. Graphing calculators are great for solving line equations and giving you graphs you can use to ballpark. Be sure you know how to solve and graph an equation for a line on your calculator before you take the ACT.

The following formulas are listed in order of importance.

The Slope-Intercept Form of a Line

$$y = mx + b$$

Using the form above, you can find two pieces of information that ACT likes to test: the **slope** and the **y-intercept**.

The **slope** is a number that tells you how sharply a line is inclining, and it is equivalent to the variable **m** in the equation above. For example, in the equation $y = 3x + 4$, the number 3 (think of it as $\frac{3}{1}$) tells us that from any point on the line, we can find another point on the line by going up 3 and over to the right 1.

In the equation $y = -\frac{4}{5}x - 7$, the slope $-\frac{4}{5}$ tells us that from any point on the line, we can find another point on the line by going up 4 and over 5 to the left.

The **y-intercept**, equivalent to the variable **b** in the equation above, is the point at which the line intercepts the y-axis. For example, in the equation $y = 3x + 4$, the line will strike the y-axis at a point 4 above the origin. In the equation $y = 2x - 7$, the line will strike the y-axis at a point 7 below the origin. A typical ACT $y = mx + b$ question might give you an equation in another form and ask you to find either the slope or the y-intercept. Simply put the equation into the form we've just shown you.

To find the x-intercept
Set *y* equal to zero, and solve for *x*.

2. What is the slope of the line with the equation
$5x - y = 7x + 6$?

    F.   −2
    G.   0
    H.   2
    J.   6
    K.   −6

Here's How to Crack It

Isolate y on the left side of the equation. Do it by hand by subtracting $5x$ from both sides.

> Sometimes, a line will be given in the standard form $Ax + By = C$. For the equation in question 2, the standard form is $-2x - y = 6$. In this form, the slope is $-\frac{A}{B}$, and the y-intercept is $\frac{C}{B}$.

$$
\begin{array}{rrrr}
5x & -\ y = & 7x & +\ 6 \\
-\ 5x & & -\ 5x & \\
\hline
& -y = & 2x & +\ 6
\end{array}
$$

We aren't quite done. The format we want is $y = mx + b$, not $-y = mx + b$. Let's multiply both sides by −1.

$$(-1)(-y) = (2x + 6)(-1)$$
$$y = -2x - 6$$

The slope of this line is −2, so the answer is (F).

The Slope Formula

You can find the slope of a line, even if all you have are two points on that line, by using the slope formula.

> **The Slippery Slope**
> A line going from bottom left to upper right has a positive slope. A line going from top left to bottom right has a negative slope.

$$\text{slope} = \frac{\text{change in } y}{\text{change in } x} \quad \text{or} \quad \frac{y_2 - y_1}{x_2 - x_1}$$

3. What is the slope of the straight line passing through the points (–2,5) and (6,4) ?

A. $-\dfrac{1}{16}$

B. $-\dfrac{1}{8}$

C. $\dfrac{1}{5}$

D. $\dfrac{2}{9}$

E. $\dfrac{4}{9}$

Parallel Tracks

If two lines have the same slope, those lines are *parallel* to one another.

If two lines have opposite reciprocal slopes, those lines are *perpendicular* to one another.

So how about if the question on this page asked for the slope of a line parallel to the one given in the problem? How about perpendicular?

A *parallel* line would have a slope of $-\dfrac{1}{8}$.

A *perpendicular* line would have a slope of 8.

Here's How to Crack It

Find the change in *y* and put it over the change in *x*. The change in *y* is the first *y*-coordinate minus the second *y*-coordinate. (It doesn't matter which point is first and which is second.) The change in *x* is the first *x* minus the second *x*.

$$\frac{y_2 - y_1}{x_2 - x_1} = \frac{5 - 4}{-2 - 6} = \frac{1}{-8}$$

The correct answer is (B).

If you take a look at the formula for finding slope, you'll see that the part on top ("change in *y*") is how much the line is rising (or falling, if the line points down and has a negative slope). That change in position on the *y*-axis is called the *rise*. The part on the bottom ("change in *x*") is how far along the *x*-axis you move and is called the *run*. So the slope of a line is sometimes referred to as "rise over run."

In the question we just did, then, the rise was 1 and the run was –8, giving us the slope $-\dfrac{1}{8}$. Same answer, different terminology.

Midpoint Formula

If you have the two endpoints of a line segment, you can find the midpoint of the segment by using the midpoint formula.

$$\left(x[m], y[m]\right) = \left(\frac{x_1 + x_2}{2}, \frac{y_1 + y_2}{2}\right)$$

It looks much more intimidating than it really is.

The Shortest Distance Between Two Points Is…a Calculator?

If you want to draw a line between two points on your TI-80 series calculator, you can use the Line function. To access this, press 2nd PRGM to access the [DRAW] menu. From there, select option [2:Line]. The format of the line function is Line (X1, Y1, X2, Y2); for example, if you wanted to view the line that passes through the points (–2, 5) and (6, 4), enter Line (–2,5,6,4). Hit ENTER to see your line.

To find the midpoint of a line, just take the *average* of the two x-coordinates and the *average* of the two y-coordinates. For example, the midpoint of the line segment formed by the coordinates (3, 4) and (9, 2) is just

$$\frac{(3+9)}{2} = 6 \text{ and } \frac{(4+2)}{2} = 3$$
$$\text{or } (6, 3)$$

Remember the first midpoint problem we did? Here it is again.

1. Point *B* (4,3) is the midpoint of line segment *AC*. If point *A* has coordinates (0,1), then what are the coordinates of point *C* ?

   A. (–4, –1)
   B. (4, 1)
   C. (4, 4)
   D. (8, 5)
   E. (8, 9)

Here's How to Crack It

You'll remember that it was perfectly possible to solve this problem just by drawing a quick graph of what it ought to look like. However, to find the correct answer using the midpoint formula, we first have to realize that, in this case, we already *have* the midpoint. We are asked to find one of the endpoints.

The midpoint is (4, 3). This represents the average of the two endpoints. The endpoint we know about is (0, 1). Let's do the x-coordinate first. The average of the x-coordinates of the two endpoints equals the x-coordinate of the midpoint. So $\frac{(0+?)}{2} = 4$. What is the missing x-coordinate? 8. Now let's do the y-coordinate. $\frac{(1+?)}{2} = 3$. What is the missing y-coordinate? 5. The answer is (D).

If you had trouble following that last explanation, just remember that you already understood this problem (and got the answer) using graphing. Never be intimidated by formulas on the ACT. There is usually another way to do the problem.

The Distance Formula

We hate the distance formula. We keep forgetting it, and even when we remember it, we feel like fools for using it because there are much easier ways to find the distance between two points. We aren't even going to tell you what the distance formula is. If you need to know the distance between two points, you can always think of that distance as being the hypotenuse of a right triangle. Here's an example.

○

4. What is the distance between points *A* (2,2) and *B* (5,6) ?

    F. 3
    G. 4
    H. 5
    J. 6
    K. 7

Here's How to Crack It

Let's make a quick graph of what this ought to look like.

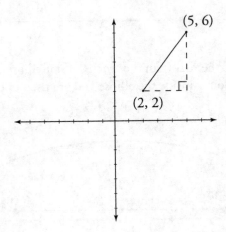

If we extend lines from the two points to form a right triangle under the line segment *AB*, we can use the Pythagorean Theorem to get the distance between the two points. What is the length of the base of the triangle? It's 3. What is the length of the height of the triangle? It's 4. So what is the length of the hypotenuse? It's 5. Of course, as usual, it is one of the triples of which ACT is so fond. The answer is (H). You could also have popped the points into your calculator and had it calculate the distance for you.

Here's the distance formula if you must know (or know how to program into your calculator):
$$d = \sqrt{(x_2 - x_1)^2 + (y_2 - y_1)^2}$$
Isn't the triangle method so much easier?

○

Circles, Ellipses, and Parabolas, Oh My!

You should probably have a *vague* idea of what the equations for these figures look like; just remember that there are very few questions concerning these figures, and when they do come up, in many cases you can figure them out by graphing or make good guesses using POE.

The standard equation for a circle is shown below.

$$(x - h)^2 + (y - k)^2 = r^2$$

(h, k) = center of the circle

r = radius

The standard equation for an ellipse (just a squat-looking circle-like shape) is shown below.

We include the ellipse formula because it has shown up on previous exams, but if you can't remember it, don't worry. It shows up only once in a blue moon, and you never need to reproduce it from memory.

$$\frac{(x - h)^2}{a^2} + \frac{(y - k)^2}{b^2} = 1$$

(h, k) = center of the ellipse

$2a$ = horizontal axis (width)

$2b$ = vertical axis (height)

The ACT can ask you about the foci (plural of focus) of an ellipse. Every ellipse has two foci. They are defined as 2 fixed points inside the ellipse and are used to create the curve. They look like this:

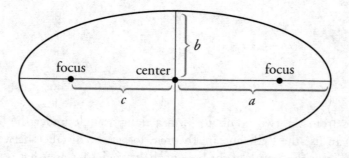

ACT could ask you to find the coordinates of the foci or ask you to determine something about the ellipse based on the location of the foci. If you know the foci are inside the ellipse and on the longest axis, you can probably use POE on at least a few answers. If you want to solve the problem, keep this formula in mind, and you'll have all you need.

$$c^2 = a^2 - b^2$$

a = half the length of the horizontal axis (width)

b = half the length of the vertical axis (height)

The basic equation for a parabola (just a U-shaped curve) is shown below.

$$y = x^2$$

5. If the equation $x^2 = 1 - y^2$ were graphed in the standard (x,y) coordinate plane, the graph would represent which of the following geometric figures?

   A. Square
   B. Straight line
   C. Circle
   D. Triangle
   E. Parabola

Here's How to Crack It

If you're familiar with what the equations of the various elements in the answer choices are supposed to look like, you may be able to figure out the problem without graphing at all. (However, that's why you bought a graphing calculator in the first place....) Let's consider what we know about the equations of geometric figures. If an equation has only x and y, we know that the graph of the equation is a straight line. (Think back to the $y = mx + b$ problems we did earlier.) However, in this equation, both x and y are squared, so we can rule out (B). There is no equation for a square, so we can rule out (A). Similarly, there's no equation for a triangle, so (D) is out. If only one of the variables were squared, this might be a parabola, but in this problem both are squared, which means we can eliminate (E). We are left with (C).

Graphing Circles on Your Calculator

To draw a circle on your TI-80 series calculator, you first need to alter the Zoom settings. Press [ZOOM] and select option [5:ZSquare]. Next, hit [2nd] [PRGM] to access the [DRAW] menu. Select option [9:Circle]. All you need to do is enter the coordinates of the circle's center and the value of its radius. If, for instance, you were trying to graph a circle with a center of (2, 3) and a radius of 5, your screen would say the following: Circle (2,3,5). Hit [ENTER] to see the resulting graph. You can draw as many circles as you like. To clear the graph, press [2nd] [DRAW] and select option [1:ClrDraw].

Estimating Note

Of course, we could also just plug some numbers into the equation and plot them out on a home-made (x, y) axis in the scratchwork column of the test booklet. Let's try this on the grid below.

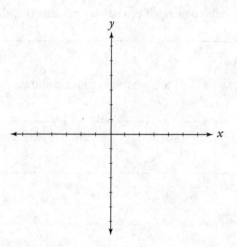

The easiest way to start is to let one of the variables equal 0. If $x = 0$, then y must equal 1. So one point of this equation is $(0, 1)$. If we let $y = 0$, then x must equal 1. So another point of this equation is $(1, 0)$. Plot out some other points of the equation. How about $(-1, 0)$ and $(0, -1)$? What kind of geometric figure do we appear to have? If you said a circle, you are correct.

Here's another question that combines circles and ellipses in the same problem:

6. Shown below in the standard (x,y) coordinate plane are a circle and an el-
    lipse, both centered at the origin. The circle has the equation $x^2 + y^2 = 100$
    and intersects the ellipse at only 2 points, both on the y-axis. Which of the
    following represents the equation of the ellipse?

    F. $\dfrac{x^2}{3} + \dfrac{y^2}{10} = 1$

    G. $\dfrac{x^2}{9} + \dfrac{y^2}{100} = 1$

    H. $\dfrac{x^2}{9} + \dfrac{y^2}{10} = 1$

    J. $\dfrac{x^2}{10} + \dfrac{y^2}{9} = 1$

    K. $\dfrac{x^2}{3} + \dfrac{y^2}{100} = 1$

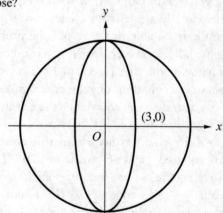

Here's How to Crack It

Your first inclination might be to reach for your graphing calculator, but unfortunately to graph the equations given you would have to first solve all the equations for y, which is time consuming and leaves a lot of room for error. If you remember the equations of a circle, $(x - h)^2 + (y - k)^2 = r^2$, and an ellipse, $\frac{(x-h)^2}{a^2} + \frac{(y-k)^2}{b^2} = 1$, there is a quicker solution. The question states that both the circle and the ellipse are centered at the origin, (0, 0). That's great news because (h, k) is equal to (0, 0) for both figures, and the circle and ellipse formulas simplify to $x^2 + y^2 = r^2$ and $\frac{x^2}{a^2} + \frac{y^2}{b^2} = 1$, respectively. The question also states that the figures intersect at only 2 points. Those points are collinear and on a diameter of the circle. You can tell from the picture that those points are also the end points of the vertical axis of the ellipse. Since the diameter and the axis are the same, the value of b in the ellipse equation is equal to the radius of the circle. The question has given you the radius disguised in the formula for the circle: $x^2 + y^2 = 100$. Therefore, $100 = r^2$, and the radius of the circle is 10. This means that $b = 10$ as well. Plugging b into the equation of the ellipse gives $\frac{x^2}{a^2} + \frac{y^2}{10^2} = 1$ or $\frac{x^2}{a^2} + \frac{y^2}{100} = 1$. The only answer choices that contain an equation in that format are (G) and (K). Comparing these shows that the only difference is the value of a, or half of the distance of the horizontal axis of the ellipse. Luckily, ACT has given you a point on the ellipse to help. Point (0, 3) is on the x-axis, 3 units from the center of the circle, (0, 0). The length from the center of the ellipse to a point on the edge along the horizontal axis is the same as a. Therefore $a = 3$. Plugging a into the equation of the ellipse gives you $\frac{x^2}{3^2} + \frac{y^2}{100} = 1$ or $\frac{x^2}{9} + \frac{y^2}{100} = 1$, which is (G).

Graphing and Coordinate Geometry Drill

For the answers to this drill, please go to Chapter 25.

1. Which of the following represents the solution of the inequality $-3x - 6 > 9$?

A.

B.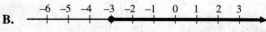

C.

D.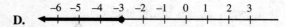

E.

2. What is the midpoint of the line segment whose endpoints are represented on the coordinate axis by the points (3,5) and (−4,3) ?

F. (−2, −5)

G. $(-\frac{1}{2}, 4)$

H. (1, 8)

J. $(4, -\frac{1}{2})$

K. (3, 3)

3. What is the slope of the line represented by the equation $10x + 2x = y + 6$?

A. 10
B. 12
C. 14
D. 15
E. 16

4. What is the length of the line segment whose endpoints are represented on the coordinate axis by the points (−2,−1) and (1,3) ?

F. 3
G. 4
H. 5
J. 6
K. 7

5. What is the slope of the line that contains the points (6,4) and (13,5) ?

A. $-\frac{1}{8}$

B. $-\frac{1}{9}$

C. $\frac{1}{7}$

D. 1

E. 7

6. Which of the following gives the center point and radius of circle O, represented by the equation $(x - 3)^2 + (y + 2)^2 = 9$?

	Center	Radius
F.	(−3, 2)	3
G.	(−3, 2)	9
H.	(2, 3)	9
J.	(3, −2)	3
K.	(3, −2)	9

7. The ellipse shown in the standard (x,y) coordinate plane below has the equation $\frac{x^2}{25} + \frac{(y-2)^2}{9} = 1$. Which of the following ordered pairs is one focus of this ellipse?

A. (−4, 2)
B. (−2, 1)
C. (0, 2)
D. (3, 5)
E. (4, −2)

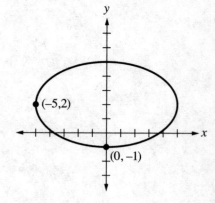

Summary

o   Coordinate geometry tests many of the same concepts you've seen elsewhere on the Math test.

o   If you are stuck on a coordinate geometry question, sketch a graph and draw in a few points.

o   Many coordinate geometry questions can be solved by putting them into the format $y + mx = b$, where m is the slope of the line and b is the y-intercept.

o   Review the midpoint equation.

$$\left(x[m], y[m]\right) = \frac{x_1 + x_2}{2}, \frac{y_1 + y_2}{2}$$

o   You can avoid using the confusing distance formula by drawing a right triangle and using the Pythagorean Theorem.

o   Review the circle equation.

$$(x - h)^2 + (y - k)^2 = r^2$$

$$(h, k) = \text{center of the circle}$$

$$r = \text{radius}$$

o   Every once in a while, ACT asks a question based on the equations of ellipses and parabolas. If you need a very high score, it might help to memorize these equations, but remember, these questions can frequently be done by using graphing to estimate the correct answer.

Chapter 15
Trigonometry

We've covered most of what you'll need to get a great score on the ACT Math test. This chapter will give a brief overview of one of the more advanced topics covered on the exam: trigonometry. Though we will be discussing the identities and rules you need, we will always have an eye on how we can crack some of these problems more strategically as well.

A NOTE ON ACT MATH "DIFFICULTY"

As we noted in the first Math chapter in this book, "difficulty" is kind of a weird thing on the ACT. Is a problem difficult because it tests an unfamiliar concept? Or is it difficult because it tests a very familiar concept in a long word problem? We've seen that Plugging In and PITA can make some of the toughest problems pretty easy, so this part of the exam is more about POOD than ever. In this chapter, we will review trigonometry. Trigonometry is one of the more advanced topics on the ACT, and ACT wants to make you think it and the other advanced topics are very difficult. Some of these questions *are* difficult, tapping some of the most advanced topics of Algebra II. But as you will see with trigonometry, most if not all of these questions can be answered correctly with a smart approach. We will review the relevant concepts, but we will also keep an eye on how to use the strategies from earlier chapters.

TRIGONOMETRY

It's easy to get freaked out by the trigonometry on the ACT. But remember there are usually only four questions on any given exam that deal with trig. What this means is that if you haven't learned trig before, it's not worth your time to try to do it now. If you are familiar with trig, on the other hand, here are a few topics that might come up. And don't worry, in four questions, there's no way all of these topics can come up!

Finally, as ever, remember that you don't get bonus points for doing anything the "real" way on the ACT. Always be on the lookout to use some of the great new techniques you've learned in this book.

SOHCAHTOA

There are four trig questions on any given ACT Math test, and typically two of them will ask about very basic trig concepts, covered by the acronym SOHCAHTOA. If you've had trig before, you probably know this acronym like the back of your hand. If not, here's what it means:

$$\mathbf{S}\text{ine} = \frac{\mathbf{O}\text{pposite}}{\mathbf{H}\text{ypotenuse}} \quad \mathbf{C}\text{osine} = \frac{\mathbf{A}\text{djacent}}{\mathbf{H}\text{ypotenuse}} \quad \mathbf{T}\text{angent} = \frac{\mathbf{O}\text{pposite}}{\mathbf{A}\text{djacent}}$$

Sine is **O**pposite over **H**ypotenuse. **C**osine is **A**djacent over **H**ypotenuse. **T**angent is **O**pposite over **A**djacent. So in the triangle below, the sine of angle θ [*theta*, a Greek letter] would be $\frac{4}{5}$. The cosine of angle θ would be $\frac{3}{5}$. The tangent of angle θ would be $\frac{4}{3}$.

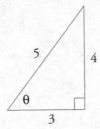

Sine, cosine, and tangent are often abbreviated as sin, cos, and tan, respectively.

The easier trig questions on this test involve the relationships between the sides of a right triangle. In the right triangle below, the trigonometric functions of the angle x can be expressed in terms of the ratios of different sides of the triangle.

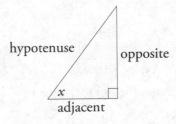

The **sine** of angle $x = \dfrac{\text{length of side opposite angle } x}{\text{length of hypotenuse}}$

The **cosine** of angle $x = \dfrac{\text{length of side adjacent angle } x}{\text{length of hypotenuse}}$

The **tangent** of angle $x = \dfrac{\text{length of side opposite angle } x}{\text{length of side adjacent angle } x}$

YOU'RE ALMOST DONE

There are three more relationships to memorize. They involve the reciprocals of the previous three.

$$\text{cosecant} = \frac{1}{\text{sine}}$$

$$\text{secant} = \frac{1}{\text{cosine}}$$

$$\text{cotangent} = \frac{1}{\text{tangent}}$$

Let's try a few problems.

_____◯_____

31. What is sin θ, if tan $\theta = \dfrac{4}{3}$?

A. $\dfrac{3}{4}$

B. $\dfrac{4}{5}$

C. $\dfrac{5}{4}$

D. $\dfrac{5}{3}$

E. $\dfrac{7}{3}$

Helpful Trig Identities

$$\sin^2 \theta + \cos^2 \theta = 1$$

$$\frac{\sin \theta}{\cos \theta} = \tan \theta$$

Here's How to Crack It

It helps to sketch out the right triangle and fill in the information we know.

What kind of right triangle is this? That's right—a 3-4-5. Now, we need to know the sine of angle θ: opposite over hypotenuse, or $\dfrac{4}{5}$, which is (B).

_____◯_____

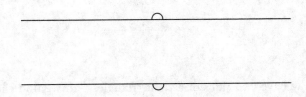

43. For all θ, $\dfrac{\cos \theta}{\sin^2 \theta + \cos^2 \theta} = ?$

  A. sin θ
  B. csc θ
  C. cot θ
  D. cos θ
  E. tan θ

Here's How to Crack It

Because $\sin^2 \theta + \cos^2 \theta$ always equals 1, $\dfrac{\cos \theta}{1} = \cos \theta$. The answer is (D).

50. In a right triangle shown below, sec θ is $\dfrac{25}{7}$. What is sin θ ?

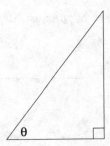

  F. $\dfrac{3}{25}$

  G. $\dfrac{5}{25}$

  H. $\dfrac{7}{25}$

  J. $\dfrac{24}{25}$

  K. $\dfrac{25}{7}$

Here's How to Crack It

The secant of any angle is the reciprocal of the cosine, so the cosine of angle θ is $\frac{7}{25}$.

Are you done? No! Cross off (H) because you know it's not the answer.

You need to find sine, which is opposite over hypotenuse. Let's sketch it.

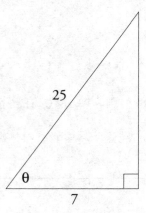

As you can see, we now have two sides of a right triangle. Can we find the third side? If you said this was one of the triples we told you about before, you are absolutely correct, although you also could have derived this by using the Pythagorean Theorem. The third side must be 24. The question asks for sin θ; sine = opposite over hypotenuse, or $\frac{24}{25}$, which is (J).

THE UNIT CIRCLE

When you see trig questions without triangles, you may need to use the *Unit Circle* instead of SOHCAHTOA. The Unit Circle is centered at (0, 0) in a coordinate plane and has a radius of 1. Angle measures are measured counterclockwise from the point (1, 0). A full revolution is 360°, or 2π in radian measure. You should familiarize yourself with the angle measures and coordinates in the figure on the next page.

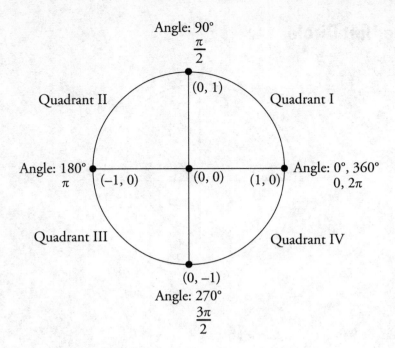

Since 360° = 2π, you can convert radian measures to degrees and vice versa using any of the equations below:

$$\frac{degree\ measure}{360} = \frac{radian\ measure}{2\pi}$$

$$radians = \frac{degrees\left(\pi\right)}{180} \text{ and } degrees = \frac{radians\left(180\right)}{\pi}$$

Negative angle measures are used to indicate that the angle moves clockwise from the point (1, 0) instead of counterclockwise. For example, –90° is 90° clockwise from (1, 0), which is the point (0, –1). This means that 270°, $\frac{3\pi}{2}$, –90°, and $-\frac{\pi}{2}$ all have the same coordinates!

Similarly, angle measures greater than 360° or 2π merely represent more than one revolution around the circle. For example, if θ = 450° (which is $\frac{5\pi}{2}$ in radians), this represents a full revolution of 360° (or 2π) and then an additional 90°, so the coordinates would be equal to those of θ = 90° and θ = $\frac{\pi}{2}$.

Trig in the Unit Circle

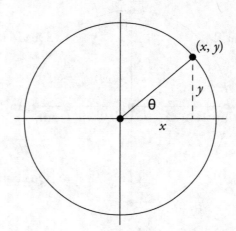

Consider the angle θ in the Unit Circle above.

Based on SOHCAHTOA, the sine of θ is $\frac{opposite}{hypotenuse} = \frac{y}{1} = y$. Likewise, the cosine of θ is $\frac{adjacent}{hypotenuse} = \frac{x}{1} = x$. Since the hypotenuse in the unit circle is always 1, the sine is always equal to the y-coordinate, and the cosine is always equal to the x-coordinate. The tangent is always $\frac{y}{x}$. You can use these ideas to determine the signs for sine, cosine, and tangent just by identifying the quadrant. Sine is positive when y is positive: Quadrants I and II only. Cosine is positive when x is positive: Quadrants I and IV only. Lastly, tangent is positive when x and y have the same sign: Quadrants I and III. Determining the signs can be a very useful tool for POE!

Let's try a problem.

47. If $\frac{5\pi}{6} \le \theta \le \frac{7\pi}{6}$, which of the following could be the value of cos θ ?

A. $\frac{\sqrt{3}}{2}$

B. $\frac{\sqrt{2}}{2}$

C. 0

D. $-\frac{\sqrt{3}}{2}$

E. $-\sqrt{3}$

Here's How to Crack It

Work this one step at a time. Start with the basics: sine and cosine are always between –1 and 1, inclusive. You can eliminate (E) since $-\sqrt{3}$ is outside of this range. Now determine the sign. $\theta = \pi$ falls on the border between Quadrants II and Quadrants III, so this range includes values from these two quadrants. Since $x < 0$ in both of these quadrants, $\cos \theta$ must be negative. Eliminate (A), (B), and (C), and you've now successfully—and correctly!—answered the question without even needing to calculate any values. Just for clarity, though, to test (D), punch $\cos^{-1}\left(\dfrac{-\sqrt{3}}{2}\right)$ into your calculator. If your calculator is in radians mode, it will return the value of $\dfrac{5\pi}{6}$, which is clearly within the range of $\dfrac{5\pi}{6} \le \theta \le \dfrac{7\pi}{6}$. Choice (D) is correct.

(Note that if your calculator is in degree mode, it will return 150°. Remember that you can convert this to radians with the formula:

$$\text{radians} = \frac{degrees\left(\pi\right)}{180} = \frac{150\pi}{180} = \frac{5\pi}{6}.)$$

ADVANCED TRIGONOMETRY

When graphing a trig function, such as sine, there are two important **coefficients**, A and B: A{sin (Bθ)}.

The two coefficients A and B govern the **amplitude** of the graph (how tall it is) and the **period** of the graph (how long it takes to get through a complete cycle), respectively. If there are no coefficients, then that means A = 1 and B = 1 and the graph is the same as what you'd get when you graph it on your calculator.

•   Increases in A increase the amplitude of the graph. It's a direct relationship.

That means if A = 2, then the amplitude is doubled. If A = $\dfrac{1}{2}$, then the amplitude is cut in half.

•   Increases in B decrease the period of the graph. It's an inverse relationship.

That means if B = 2, then the period is cut in half, which is to say the graph completes a full cycle faster than usual. If B = $\dfrac{1}{2}$, then the period is doubled.

You can add to or subtract from the function as a whole and also to or from the variable, but neither of those actions changes the shape of the graph, only its position and starting place.

Here's the graph of sin *x*. What are the amplitude and period?

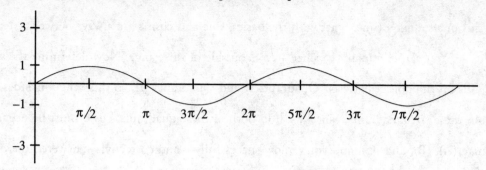

The simple function sin θ goes from −1 to 1 on the *y*-axis, so the amplitude is 1, while its period is 2π, which means that every 2π on the graph (as you go from side to side), the graph completes a full cycle. That's what you see in the graph above.

The graph below is also a sine function, but it's been changed. What is the function graphed here?

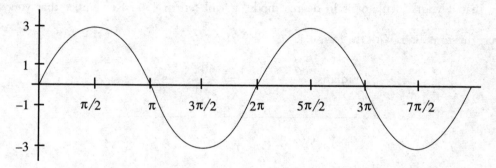

You have three things to check when looking at this graph: is it sin or cos, is the period changed, and is the amplitude changed?

- This is a sin graph because it has a value of 0 at 0; cos has a value of 1 at 0.
- It makes a complete cycle in 2π, so the period isn't changed. In other words, B = 1.
- The amplitude is triple what it normally is, so A = 3. The function graphed, therefore, is 3 sin θ.

How about here?

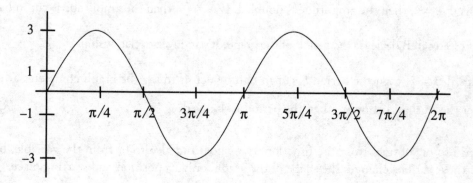

Once again, there are three things to check.

- This is a sin graph because it has a value of 0 at 0; cos has a value of 1 at 0.
- It makes a complete cycle in π, so the period has changed—it's half of what it usually is. B has an inverse effect, which means B = 2.
- The amplitude is triple what it normally is, so A = 3. The function graphed, therefore, is 3 sin 2θ.

Let's try some practice questions.

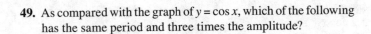

49. As compared with the graph of $y = \cos x$, which of the following has the same period and three times the amplitude?

 A. $y = \cos 3x$

 B. $y = \cos \dfrac{1}{2}(x + 3)$

 C. $y = 3 \cos \dfrac{1}{2}x$

 D. $y = 1 + 3 \cos x$

 E. $y = 3 + \cos x$

Here's How to Crack It

Recall that the coefficient on the outside of the function changes the amplitude, and the one on the inside changes the period. Because the question states that the period isn't changed, you can eliminate (A), (B), and (C). The amplitude is three times greater, you're told; because there's a direct relationship between A and amplitude, you want to have a 3 multiplying the outside of the function. That leaves only (D) as a possibility.

52. Which of the following equations describes the equation graphed below?

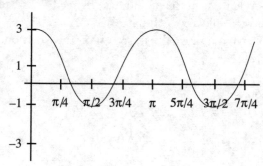

F. $2 \cos x$

G. $1 + 2 \cos x$

H. $\cos 2x$

J. $1 + \cos 2x$

K. $1 + 2 \cos 2x$

Here's How to Crack It

At first it looks like this graph has an amplitude of 3, but if you look closer, you'll see that though the top value is 3, the bottom value is –1, which means that the whole graph has been shifted up. Because (F) and (H) don't add anything to the function (which is how you move a graph up and down), they're out. The period of this graph is half of what it usually is, so B = 2, which eliminates (G). Because the amplitude is changed also, you can eliminate (J). The answer is (K).

Trigonometry Drill

For the answers to this drill, please go to Chapter 25.

1. In $\triangle ABC$ below, tan θ = ?

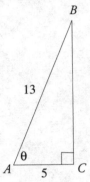

A. $\dfrac{5}{12}$

B. $\dfrac{12}{13}$

C. $\dfrac{17}{12}$

D. $\dfrac{12}{5}$

E. 3

2. If the cotangent of an angle θ is 1, then the tangent of angle θ is

F. -1
G. 0
H. 1
J. 2
K. 3

3. If $x + \sin^2 \theta + \cos^2 \theta = 4$, then x = ?

A. 1
B. 2
C. 3
D. 4
E. 5

4. If cos $\theta = \dfrac{-7}{25}$ and sin $\theta > 0$, then tan θ = ?

F. $\dfrac{24}{7}$

G. $\dfrac{24}{25}$

H. $\dfrac{7}{24}$

J. $-\dfrac{24}{25}$

K. $-\dfrac{24}{7}$

5. Which of the following angles has the same terminal side as $\dfrac{17\pi}{3}$?

A. $-720°$
B. $-300°$
C. $-60°$
D. $60°$
E. $720°$

Summary

- If you haven't had trigonometry in school, use your Letter of the Day on these trig problems. There are only a maximum of 4!

- Remember SOHCAHTOA!

$$\text{sine} = \frac{\text{opposite}}{\text{hypotenuse}} \; ; \; \text{cosine} = \frac{\text{adjacent}}{\text{hypotenuse}} \; ; \; \text{tangent} = \frac{\text{opposite}}{\text{adjacent}}$$

- For inverse functions, remember

$$\csc \theta = \frac{1}{\text{sine}} \qquad \sec \theta = \frac{1}{\text{cosine}} \qquad \cot \theta = \frac{1}{\text{tangent}}$$

- Remember the special trig identities.

$$\sin^2 \theta + \cos^2 \theta = 1 \qquad \frac{\sin \theta}{\cos \theta} = \tan \theta$$

- Remember that in the unit circle, sin = y, cos = x, and tan = $\frac{y}{x}$.

- For more advanced trig problems, remember A{sin (Bθ)}, where A is directly proportional to the amplitude and B is inversely proportional to the period of the function. These are usually the easiest to see on the graph.

Chapter 16
Advanced Math

You may see logs, vectors, or matrices on your test. It's good to be familiar with these topics if you're aiming for a 30+ on the Math test, but if any of these concepts make your head spin, don't sweat it: it's unlikely that you will see more than one question in each of these topics.

LOGARITHMS

A logarithm is an alternative way to express an exponent.

If no value is given for the base (b), then $b = 10$. For example, $\log 6 = x$ means $10^x = 6$.

$$\log_b n = x \text{ is the same as } b^x = n$$

Take a look at this problem.

45. If $\log_x 81 = 4$, then $x = ?$

- **A.** 2
- **B.** 3
- **C.** 9
- **D.** $\dfrac{81}{4}$
- **E.** $81\log_4$

Here's How to Crack It

Following the definition of logarithms, $\log_x 81 = 4$ can be rewritten as $x^4 = 81$. Take the fourth root of both sides to get $\sqrt[4]{x^4} = \sqrt[4]{81}$; which simplifies to $x = 3$, which is (B).

MADSPM

Since logs are used to express exponents, they follow the same MADSPM rules as exponents:

As with exponents, MADSPM rules apply only to logs with the same base.

Multiply → **A**dd	$\log xy = \log x + \log y$
Divide → **S**ubtract	$\log \left(\dfrac{x}{y}\right) = \log x - \log y$
Power → **M**ultiply	$\log (x^y) = y \log x$

Try an example problem.

---

53. Whenever x and y are positive real numbers, which of the following expressions is equal to $4\log_3 x - \log_3 5y$?

    A. $4\log_3(x - 5y)$

    B. $4\log_3\left(\dfrac{x}{y^5}\right)$

    C. $\log_3\left(\dfrac{4x}{5y}\right)$

    D. $\log_3(4x - 5y)$

    E. $\log_3\left(\dfrac{x^4}{5y}\right)$

Here's How to Crack It

Use bite-sized pieces. Since all of the logs in the expression and answers have the same base (3), you can use the MADSPM rules. Using the Power/Multiply rule, $4\log_3 x = \log_3 x^4$. The whole expression can therefore be written as $\log_3 x^4 - \log_3 5y$. Now, use the Divide/Subtract rule: $\log_3 x^4 - \log_3 5y = \log_3\left(\dfrac{x^4}{5y}\right)$, choice (E).

VECTORS

You may also come across a vector question on your test. Vectors are used to notate changes in the x- and y-values on a coordinate plane.

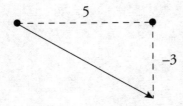

> Vectors are a measure of *displacement*, rather than absolute position on a coordinate plane.

The vector **v** above can be notated in either of the following manners:

Component Form:

$$\mathbf{v} = \langle x, y \rangle$$

Vector **v** has a component form of $\langle 5, -3 \rangle$ because it moves 5 units right and 3 units down. Note that the sign indicates the direction of the change: positive values signal shifts to the right and upward, while negative values denote changes to the left and downward.

To add two vectors in component form, add the *x* to the *x* and the *y* to the *y*:

$$\langle 5, -3 \rangle + \langle c, d \rangle = \langle 5 + c, -3 + d \rangle$$

To multiply a vector by a constant, multiply both the *x* and *y* values by the constant:

$$a\langle 5, -3 \rangle = \langle 5a, -3a \rangle$$

Unit Vector Notation:

$$\mathbf{i} = \langle 1, 0 \rangle \qquad \mathbf{j} = \langle 0, 1 \rangle$$

In unit vector notation, vectors are expressed as addition or subtraction of the unit vectors **i** and **j**.

Vector **v** above has the unit vector notation $\mathbf{v} = 5\mathbf{i} - 3\mathbf{j}$.

You can use the addition and multiplication rules to see how $\mathbf{v} = 5\mathbf{i} - 3\mathbf{j}$ and $\langle 5, -3 \rangle$ represent the same vector.

$$\mathbf{v} = 5\mathbf{i} - 3\mathbf{j} = 5\langle 1, 0 \rangle - 3\langle 0, 1 \rangle = \langle 5, 0 \rangle + \langle 0, -3 \rangle = \langle 5, -3 \rangle$$

Vectors in unit vector forms follow the same basic rules as component forms:

To add two vectors, add the **i** to the **i** and the **j** to the **j**:

$$(5\mathbf{i} - 3\mathbf{j}) + (c\mathbf{i} + d\mathbf{j}) = (5 + c)\mathbf{i} + (-3 + d)\mathbf{j}$$

To multiply a vector by a constant, multiply both the **i** and **j** values by the constant:

$$a\mathbf{v} = a(5\mathbf{i} - 3\mathbf{j}) = 5a\mathbf{i} - 3a\mathbf{j}$$

Let's try a problem:

45. Vectors $\vec{AB}$ and $\vec{CD}$ are shown in the standard xy-plane below. What is the component form of vector $\vec{AB} + \vec{CD}$?

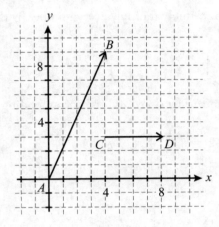

A. $\langle 0,4 \rangle$
B. $\langle 4,3 \rangle$
C. $\langle 4,9 \rangle$
D. $\langle 8,9 \rangle$
E. $\langle 8,12 \rangle$

Here's How to Crack It

The component form of a vector describes the vector in terms of the changes in the x and y values. Vector $\vec{AB}$ starts at $(0, 0)$ and ends at $(4, 9)$, so it increases the x value by 4 and the y value by 9. Therefore, the component form of vector $\vec{AB}$ is $\langle 4, 9 \rangle$. Vector $\vec{CD}$ starts at $(4, 3)$ and ends at $(8, 3)$, so the component form is $\langle 8 - 4, 3 - 3 \rangle = \langle 4, 0 \rangle$. When adding or subtracting vectors in component form, add or subtract the x values and the y values. $\vec{AB} + \vec{CD} = \langle 4 + 4, 9 + 0 \rangle = \langle 8, 9 \rangle$, which is (D).

MATRICES

An $m \times n$ matrix is an array of numbers organized in m rows and n columns.

Matrices may sound scary, but knowing a few basic rules will help you tackle many of the concepts with confidence.

To multiply a matrix by a constant, simply multiply every number by that constant:

$$a \begin{bmatrix} 3 & -2 \\ 4 & 1 \end{bmatrix} = \begin{bmatrix} 3a & -2a \\ 4a & 1a \end{bmatrix}$$

To add two matrices with the same dimensions, add the corresponding elements:

$$\begin{bmatrix} 3 & -2 \\ 4 & 1 \end{bmatrix} + \begin{bmatrix} 5 & -1 \\ -3 & 3 \end{bmatrix} = \begin{bmatrix} 3+5 & -2-1 \\ 4-3 & 1+3 \end{bmatrix} = \begin{bmatrix} 8 & -3 \\ 1 & 4 \end{bmatrix}$$

The determinant of a 2 × 2 matrix $\begin{bmatrix} a & b \\ c & d \end{bmatrix} = ad - bc$.

Let's try a problem.

> You will not be expected to solve for the determinant of anything other than 2 x 2 matrices.

43. If the determinant of the matrix below is 3, n = ?

$$\begin{bmatrix} 3 & n \\ -5 & 6 \end{bmatrix}$$

    A.   −5
    B.   −3
    C.   3
    D.   5
    E.   15

Here's How to Crack It

The determinant of this matrix is $3(6) - [(-5)n] = 18 + 5n$. The problem states that the determinant is 3, so $18 + 5n = 3$. Subtract 18 from both sides to get $5n = -15$; $n = -3$, which is (B).

MULTIPLYING MATRICES

Multiplying two matrices is more complicated than adding them. Let your calculator do the hard work when possible, but some questions will require you to understand the concepts. Brush up on your skills if you're familiar with matrices, but if you've never worked with matrices before, then your best bet on difficult multiplication questions is to use your LOTD and keep moving.

> To find the product, multiply the elements in each row of the first matrix by the elements in each column of the second and then add the products.
>
> $$\begin{bmatrix} a & b \\ c & d \\ e & f \end{bmatrix} \times \begin{bmatrix} u & v & w \\ x & y & z \end{bmatrix} = \begin{bmatrix} au+bx & av+by & aw+bz \\ cu+dx & cv+dy & cw+dz \\ eu+fx & ev+fy & ew+fz \end{bmatrix}$$

The product of two matrices is defined only when the number of columns in the first matrix is equal to the number of rows in the second. When you multiply an $m \times n$ matrix by an $n \times p$ matrix, the resulting product will be an $m \times p$ matrix.

Here's an example:

$$\begin{bmatrix} 3 & 2 \\ 1 & 5 \\ 4 & -1 \end{bmatrix} \begin{bmatrix} 6 & 7 \\ -2 & 8 \end{bmatrix} = \begin{bmatrix} 3(6)+2(-2) & 3(7)+2(8) \\ 1(6)+5(-2) & 1(7)+5(8) \\ 4(6)+-1(-2) & 4(7)+-1(8) \end{bmatrix} = \begin{bmatrix} 14 & 37 \\ -4 & 47 \\ 26 & 20 \end{bmatrix}$$

It's a little easier to remember this process when you consider that matrices can be used to represent linear equations. Consider the system of linear equations below:

$$2x + 3y = 10$$

$$6x - 5y = 13$$

This system can be represented by the following matrix equation:

$$\begin{bmatrix} 2 & 3 \\ 6 & -5 \end{bmatrix} \begin{bmatrix} x \\ y \end{bmatrix} = \begin{bmatrix} 10 \\ 13 \end{bmatrix}$$

Notice how solving the matrix equation using the matrix multiplication rule gives you $\begin{bmatrix} 2x+3y \\ 6x-5y \end{bmatrix} = \begin{bmatrix} 10 \\ 13 \end{bmatrix}$, which yields the two original equations $2x + 3y = 10$ and $6x - 5y = 13$!

Try this example:

47. The Wittenberg Boating Club sponsors a 2-day sailing excursion. 35 members and 15 nonmembers attend both days of the excursion. For the first day, members are charged $25 and nonmembers are charged $35. For the second day, members are charged $15 and nonmembers are charged $25. Which of the following product matrices represents the total charges each day made by the 35 members and 15 nonmembers who attended both days of the excursion?

A. $\begin{bmatrix} 35 & 35 \\ 15 & 15 \end{bmatrix}\begin{bmatrix} 25 & 15 \\ 35 & 25 \end{bmatrix}$

B. $\begin{bmatrix} 35 & 15 \\ 35 & 15 \end{bmatrix}\begin{bmatrix} 25 & 15 \\ 35 & 25 \end{bmatrix}$

C. $\begin{bmatrix} 15 & 35 \end{bmatrix}\begin{bmatrix} 25 & 15 \\ 35 & 25 \end{bmatrix}$

D. $\begin{bmatrix} 35 & 15 \end{bmatrix}\begin{bmatrix} 25 & 35 \\ 15 & 25 \end{bmatrix}$

E. $\begin{bmatrix} 35 & 15 \end{bmatrix}\begin{bmatrix} 25 & 15 \\ 35 & 25 \end{bmatrix}$

Here's How to Crack It

The product matrix should multiply the number of members by the prices charged for members and the number of nonmembers by the prices charged to nonmembers, giving a total for each day.

Because there should be a total for each day, there should be only two numbers in the resulting product matrix. Choices (A) and (B) multiply a 2 × 2 by a 2 × 2. The product matrix will have the same number of rows as the first matrix (2), and the same number of columns as the second matrix (2), resulting in a 2 × 2 matrix. These matrices will have four numbers, not two, so eliminate (A) and (B). Use POE on the remaining choices. For (C), the row $\begin{bmatrix} 15 & 35 \end{bmatrix}$ would first be multiplied by the first column $\begin{bmatrix} 25 \\ 35 \end{bmatrix}$, resulting in 15 × 25 + 35 × 35. This should represent the total charges for the first day, but this multiplies the number of nonmembers (15) by the price that the members paid (25) and the number of members (35) by the price the nonmembers paid (35). This is incorrect, so eliminate (C). Choice (D) multiplies the row $\begin{bmatrix} 35 & 15 \end{bmatrix}$ by the column $\begin{bmatrix} 25 \\ 15 \end{bmatrix}$.

The number of members (35) is multiplied by a price members paid the first day (25), but the number of nonmembers (15) should be multiplied by 35 not 15. This is incorrect; eliminate (D). The answer is (E).

You're In the Home Stretch!
You've tackled the Math section masterfully! Once you've completed the advanced math drill, give yourself a study break. Let these lessons sink in before diving into Part IV.

Advanced Math Drill

For the answers to this drill, please go to Chapter 25.

1. If $\log_3 x = 5$, then $x = ?$

  A. $\sqrt[5]{3}$

  B. $\sqrt[3]{5}$

  C. 15

  D. 125

  E. 243

2. The component forms of vectors **u** and **v** are given by $\mathbf{u} = \langle -3, 2 \rangle$ and $\mathbf{v} = \langle 7, 5 \rangle$. Given that $4\mathbf{u} + (-2\mathbf{v}) + \mathbf{w} = 0$, what is the component form of **w** ?

  F. $\langle -26, -2 \rangle$

  G. $\langle -10, -3 \rangle$

  H. $\langle -4, -7 \rangle$

  J. $\langle 10, 3 \rangle$

  K. $\langle 26, 2 \rangle$

3. What value of a satisfies the matrix equation below?

$$3\begin{bmatrix} 5 & a \\ 1 & 6 \end{bmatrix} + \begin{bmatrix} 2 & 7 \\ 3 & 4 \end{bmatrix} = \begin{bmatrix} 17 & 13 \\ 6 & 22 \end{bmatrix}$$

  A. 2

  B. 4

  C. 6

  D. 7

  E. 8

Summary

o   A logarithm is another way to express an exponent. The equation $b^x = n$ can also be written as $\log_b n = x$.

o   Logarithms follow the same MADSPM rules as exponents.

$$\log xy = \log x + \log y$$

$$\log\left(\frac{x}{y}\right) = \log x - \log y$$

$$\log\left(x^y\right) = y \log x$$

o   Vectors are a measure of displacement and can be used to notate changes in the x- and y-values on a coordinate plane.

o   The component form of vector **v** is $\langle x, y \rangle$ where x represents the movement in the horizontal direction and y represents the movement in the vertical direction. The sign of x or y indicates the direction of the movement, and the value indicates the number of units of the movement. A vector that moves 5 units to the right and 3 units down has a component form of $\langle 5, -3 \rangle$.

o   Vectors can also be written in unit vector notation, expressed as the addition or subtraction of unit vectors **i** and **j**. A vector with the component form of $\langle 5, -3 \rangle$ can be expressed in unit vector notation as **v** = 5**i** – 3**j**.

o   In either notation, vectors can be added or subtracted by adding or subtracting the two parts separately. Vectors can also be multiplied or divided by a constant by applying that operation to both parts of the vector.

o   Matrices are arrays of numbers arranged in rows and columns.

o   Matrices can be added or subtracted by adding or subtracting the corresponding numbers in each position. Matrices can also be multiplied or divided by a constant by applying that operation to the number in each position of the matrix.

o   The determinant of a 2 × 2 matrix $\begin{bmatrix} a & b \\ c & d \end{bmatrix}$ is $ad - bc$.

o   The product of two matrices can be found by multiplying the elements in each row of the first matrix by the elements in each column of the second matrix and then adding the products. The product will have the same number of rows as the first matrix and the same number of columns as the second matrix. If the number or rows in the first matrix does not match the number of columns in the second matrix, the product is undefined.

Part IV
How to Crack the ACT Reading Test

Chapter 17
Introduction to the ACT Reading Test

The ACT Reading test always comes third, after the Math test and before the Science test. Reading is a unique challenge on a timed standardized test: there are no rules and formulas to review, and the reading skills you've developed throughout your school career do not necessarily work as well on the ACT.

To maximize your score on the ACT Reading test, you need to develop reading skills specific to this test and learn how to use your time effectively.

We'll teach you how to work the passages in a personal order of difficulty that makes best use of the time allotted. We'll also teach you how to employ a strategic and efficient approach that will earn you your highest possible score.

The Format
You have 35 minutes for 4 passages and 40 questions.

WHAT'S ON THE READING TEST

On the Reading test, you have 35 minutes to work through 4 passages and a total of 40 questions. One of the passages will typically be split in two, with passages by different authors or from different works. The category, or genre, of the passages always appears in the same order: Prose Fiction (sometimes called Literary Narrative), Social Science, Humanities, and Natural Science. The passages are roughly the same length, 800–850 words, and each is followed by 10 questions.

The passages feature authors and topics that the ACT writers judge typical of the type of reading required in first-year college courses. And your goal, according to ACT, is to read the passages and answer questions that prove you understood both what was "directly stated" and what were the "implied meanings."

That's a pretty simple summary of the Reading test, but what is simple on paper can be more challenging in practice. In other words, the description from ACT doesn't really match the experience of trying to read 3,400 words and prove "your understanding" 40 times in less time than a typical English class in school.

Your reading comprehension skills and the challenge of the ACT format are intertwined. In Chapter 18, we'll teach you a Basic Approach that draws upon your skills to crack the Reading test. But first, let's pull both apart for further examination.

Passage Content

Within the 4 categories, ACT selects excerpts from books and articles to create one long passage or two shorter passages. For each test, they choose 5 new passages, but the topics are always chosen from the same content areas.

Prose Fiction (aka, Literary Narrative)

The passages can be excerpts from novels or short stories, or even short stories in their entirety. While there are occasional uses of historical fiction, most passages are contemporary, emphasize diversity, and often center on family relationships.

Social Science

Topics are drawn from the fields of anthropology, archaeology, biography, business, economics, education, geography, history, political science, psychology, and sociology.

Humanities

These passages are nonfiction, but they are usually memoirs or personal essays that can read much like fiction. Topics include architecture, art, dance, ethics, film, language, literary criticism, music, philosophy, radio, television, and theater.

Natural Science

Content areas include anatomy, astronomy, biology, botany, chemistry, ecology, geology, medicine, meteorology, microbiology, natural history, physiology, physics, technology, and zoology.

Reading Skills

For school, most of your reading is done with no time limits, at least theoretically. You have assignments of chapters, essays, and articles that you read, reread, highlight, and notate out of class. You may even make flashcards. In class, group discussions and even lectures from the teacher help you grasp the significance, meaning, and context of what you have read. You may need to "show your understanding" in a quiz, test, in-class essay, or paper, but you have had time to work with the text to develop a thorough understanding.

Outside of school, serious readers take time to process what they've read and form an opinion.

As a college student, you'll be asked not only to read but also to think about what you've read and offer an opinion. Any professor will tell you that understanding takes thought, and thought usually takes time, more than 35 minutes.

When you take the ACT, you don't have the luxury of time. You can't read thoroughly, much less reread, highlight, take notes, or make flashcards. There's certainly no group discussion to help elicit the meaning of each passage. So the first step in raising your score is to *stop treating the Reading test as a school assignment.* You need to read differently on the ACT, but you also need to know that a thorough, thoughtful grasp of the meaning isn't needed to answer the questions correctly.

In this section, we'll teach you how to read the passages and apply the Basic Approach to answer the questions correctly. But the next step in raising your scores is to apply your own personal order of difficulty to the order of the passages.

HOW TO CRACK THE READING TEST

Order the Passages

You shouldn't work the passages in the order ACT offers *just because they're in that order.* Always choose your own order, working first the passages that are easiest for you and leaving for last the most difficult. What if natural science is the easiest for you? If you did the four passages in the order ACT offers, you could easily run out of time before even getting to the natural science, or find yourself with so little time that you manage to answer correctly only half the number of questions you would have otherwise sailed through.

Now, Later, Never

When time is your enemy, as it is on the ACT, find and work Now the passages that are easiest for you. Leave for Later, or perhaps even Never, the passages that are the most difficult for you.

Every time you take an ACT, for practice and for real, pick your own order. In practice, you will likely build up a track record to determine your Personal Order of Difficulty (POOD). However, each ACT features all new passages, and certain characteristics may vary enough to affect the difficulty of a passage. Pay attention to the particulars of each test, and be willing to adapt your order for that day's test.

> **Passages start at 1**
> Each passage starts with a question number with a units digit of 1 - 1, 11, 21, or 31. On the ACT Online Test, you can use the navigation bar at the bottom of the screen to quickly jump between passages, both when determining your order and when doing the passages.

> Under the Pacing section of this chapter, we'll help you decide if you should mark any passages as Never.

- • **Your POOD**: categories and topics you like best
- • **Paragraphs**: about eight to twelve paragraphs is best
- • **Questions**: the more line references or questions with highlighted text in the passage, the better
- • **Answers**: short are better than long

Let's discuss what each of these mean.

Your Personal Order of Difficulty (POOD)

The best way to determine which categories you work the best is through repeated practice tests followed by self-analysis. Regardless of where it is in your order, do you consistently do the best on social science? Do you usually prefer the prose fiction and humanities over social science and natural science?

Before you've developed your POOD, identify your own likes and dislikes. For example, do you rarely read fiction outside of school? If so, then the prose fiction is unlikely to be a smart choice to do first. On the following pages, we've supplied brief excerpts of each category to give you an idea of what each is like.

Prose Fiction/Literary Narrative   On the fiction passages, facts typically matter less than do the setting, the atmosphere, and the relationships between characters. The plot and dialogue may even be secondary to the characters' thoughts and emotions, not all of which will be directly stated.

> Allen's grandmother was readying herself to leave. She was, in fact, putting the final touches on her makeup which, as always, looked to Allen as though someone had thrown it on her face with a shovel. As Mrs. Mandale placed her newly purchased
> 5 bracelet over her wrist, a look of troubled ambivalence came over her. "Perhaps this bracelet isn't right for me," she said. "I won't wear it."
>
> Waiting now for 30 minutes, Allen tried to be tolerant. "It is right for you," he said. "It matches your personality. Wear it."
> 10 The bracelet was a remarkable illustration of poor taste. Its colors were vulgar, and the structure lacked any sign of thoughtful design. The truth is, it did match his grandmother's personality. All that she did and enjoyed was tasteless and induced in Allen a quiet hopelessness.

The questions are more likely to involve identifying the implied meanings than what was directly stated.

1. Allen most likely encouraged his grandmother to wear her bracelet because he:

   A. found it colorful and approved of its appearance.
   B. found its appearance pathetic and wished his grandmother to look pretty.
   C. was impatient with his grandmother for spending time worrying about the bracelet.
   D. felt the bracelet matched his grandmother's bright personality.

If you like to read fiction for school assignments or for pleasure, you may find the prose fiction one of the easier passages. If you don't like to read fiction, you may find them unclear and confusing. Do the prose fiction later, or perhaps Never.

For the record, the answer is (C). Allen has been waiting and is trying "to be tolerant."

Social Science   Social science passages should remind you of the papers you write for school. The organization will flow logically with clear topic sentences and well-chosen transitions to develop the main idea. The author may have a point of view on the subject or may simply deliver informative facts in a neutral tone.

Religion is so fundamental a part of human existence that one might easily forget to ask how it started. Yet it had to start somewhere, and there had to be a time when human beings or their apelike ancestors did not entertain notions of the super-
5 natural. Hence the historian should want to probe the origins of religious belief.

It is doubtful that morality played a part in the beginnings of religious belief. Rather, religion is traceable to a far more fundamental human and animal characteristic. Storms, floods,
10 famine, and other adversities inspired *fear* in the hearts of primitive peoples as well they should have. Curiously, humankind early took the position that it might somehow subject such catastrophes to its control. Specifically, it believed it might control them by obedience and submission and by conforming its behavior to
15 their mandates. Worship, ritual, sacrifice of life, and property became means through which early peoples sought to cajole the powers and avoid the blights and miseries the peoples dreaded. As Petronius, in Lucretius's tradition remarked, "It was fear that first made the gods."

11. According to the passage, natural disasters contributed to the development of religion by:

A. motivating human beings to acquire some command over their environment.
B. making human beings distinguish themselves from animals.
C. causing human beings to sacrifice their lives and goods.
D. providing a need for ritual and tradition.

12. The author believes that the origins of religion:

F. are extremely easy to ascertain and understand.
G. should not be questioned by historians because religion is fundamental to civilized life.
H. are directly tied to apelike subhuman species.
J. should be the subject of serious historical inquiry.

The correct answer to 11 is (A), and the answer to 12 is (J).

Humanities   Humanities passages are nonfiction, but because they are memoirs or personal essays, they can feel similar to the fiction passages. The narrative may use a more organic development instead of a linear one, and the tone will be more personal and perhaps more emotional than the more objective tones found in social and natural science.

> I grew up thinking I hated tomatoes. I used to describe the raw fruit as tasting like curdled water and preferred tomato sauce from a can. But it was not by accident that the tomato rapidly insinuated
> 5 itself into the world's cuisines after 1492: it grows like a weed, and wherever this weed took root, locals fell in love with it. To grow a bad tomato takes careful planning. Unfortunately, careful planning is exactly what the North American food industry has
> 10 provided. It has carefully crafted tomatoes that can be hauled long distances and still look great, and the only casualty is taste. And it has done so for so long now that most of us have forgotten, or never learned, what tomatoes are supposed to taste like.

24. In the passage, the phrase "careful planning" (line 7) refers to the method of tomato cultivation that has:

   F.   allowed the plant to grow like a weed.
   G.   valued appearance and durability over taste.
   H.   failed to make the fruit taste less like curdled water.
   J.   made the narrator change his opinion of tomatoes.

The answer to 24 is (G).

Natural Science   Natural science passages feature a lot of details and sometimes very technical descriptions. Similar to the social science passage, the natural science passage features a linear organization with clear topic sentences and transitions to develop the main idea. The author may or may not have an opinion on the topic.

> It is further noteworthy that the terrestrial vertebrate's most significant muscles of movement are no longer located lateral to the vertebral column as they are in the fish but rather in ventral and dorsal relation to it. This trend in terrestrial evolution is highly
> 5 significant and means that the terrestrial vertebrate's principal movements are fore and back, not side to side. The trend is well documented in the whale, an aquatic animal whose ancestors are terrestrial quadrupeds. The whale, in other words, has "returned" to the sea secondarily after an ancestral stage on the land. Unlike
> 10 the fish, and in accordance with its ancestry, it propels itself by moving the tail up and down, not side to side. In a sense, the whale moves itself by bending up and down at the waist. Indeed, that very analogy is recalled by the mythical mermaid figure who seems to represent a humanlike line returned to the water
> 15 secondarily like the whale.

The questions usually track the text pretty closely and require you to make few inferences.

31. Which of the following best represents a general trend associated with mammalian evolution?

   A. Enhancement of bodily movement from right to left and left to right

   B. Minimization of muscle groups oriented lateral to the vertebral column

   C. The development of propulsive fins from paired limbs

   D. Secondary return to the sea

The answer to 31 is (B).

Order the Passages, Redux

As you take practice Reading tests, develop a consistent order that works for you, but always be willing to mix it up when you start each test, practice or real. The passages all run roughly the same number of words (800–850), and each features 10 questions each followed by 4 answer choices. But the chosen topics, revealed in the blurb, and the way the passages, questions, and answers look can provide valuable clues that should make you reconsider that day's order.

Need More Practice?
The Princeton Review's *English and Reading Workout for the ACT* has four more full-length Reading tests.

Paragraphs

Which passage would you rather work, one with 8–12 medium-sized paragraphs, or one with three huge paragraphs, or one with over 20 paragraphs, some only one line long? The overall length is the same, but the size and number of the paragraphs influence how easily you can navigate the passage and retrieve answers as you work the questions.

Some fiction passages can feature too many paragraphs, with each paragraph an individual line of dialogue. Too many paragraphs can make it just as difficult to locate the right part of the passage to find answers.

Ideally, a passage should feature 8–12 paragraphs, with each paragraph made up of 5–15 lines.

Questions

The questions on the Reading test don't follow a chronological order of the passage, and not every question comes with a line reference or highlighted text. Line references, paragraph references, and highlighted text are maps, pointing to the precise part of the passage where you can find the answer. You waste no time getting lost, hunting through the passage to find where to read. Therefore, a passage with only 1-2 questions with line references or highlighted text will be more challenging than one that features 4, 5, 6, or more (8 is the most we've ever seen).

On the ACT Online Test, don't click through all the questions when determining your passage order. It's not worth the time spent clicking through each question!

Answers

Compare the two "questions" and their answer choices below.

13. Blah blah blah blah:

   A. are caused primarily by humanity's overriding concern with acceptance and peace.
   B. are due in part to a faulty understanding of history.
   C. should make historians question the role of the individual in human affairs.
   D. should provoke historical inquiry into humanity's willingness to tolerate adversity.

14. Blah blah blah blah:

   F. more traditional.
   G. more formal.
   H. less rigid.
   J. less informative.

Which do you think is the easier question? Question 14, of course! Long answers usually answer harder questions, and short answers usually answer easier questions. A passage with lots of questions with short answers is a good sign.

Use Your Eye, Not Your Brain

Look at the passages to evaluate the paragraphs and, on the pencil-and-paper ACT, line references and answer choices. Don't thoughtfully ponder and consider each element, and don't read through the questions. Quickly check the blurb to see if you recognize the subject or author.

Use your eye to scan the paragraphs, look for numbers amidst the questions, and examine the length of answer choices. If you see lots of warning signs on what is typically your first passage, leave it for Later. If you see great paragraphs, line references, and lots of short answers on the passage you typically do third, consider bumping it up to second, maybe first. This should take no more than 1–2 seconds.

The Blurb

The blurb at the top of the passage will provide the title, author, copyright date, and publisher. The title may not make the subject clear, but it's always worth checking to see if it will or if you recognize the author.

Exercise: Pick Your Order

Put these passages in your own order: 1st, 2nd, 3rd, and 4th. We listed the number of paragraphs and questions with line references and short answers for the purpose of the exercise. This is not a hint that you need to be overly precise on a real test. You're looking for warning signs, a quick visual task.

Exercise I

Prose Fiction: _____

Unknown author and title, a ton of dialogue, over 20 paragraphs, many of them only one line, 2 line/paragraph references, and lots of long answers.

Social Science: _____

The title sounds technical, 6 paragraphs, 3 line/paragraph references, and 4 questions with short answers.

Humanities: _____

The title sounds deep, 9 paragraphs, 6 line/paragraph references, 1 question with short answers, and a dual passage.

Natural Science: _____

The title sounds kind of cool, 9 paragraphs, 4 line/paragraph references, and 4 questions with short answers.

Exercise II

Prose Fiction: _____

Familiar author, 7 paragraphs, 8 line/paragraph references, and 4 questions with short answers.

Social Science: _____

The title sounds sort of interesting, 6 paragraphs, 2 line/paragraph references, 2 questions with short answers, and a dual passage.

Humanities: _____

The title sounds sort of interesting, 11 paragraphs, 5 line/paragraph references, and 4 questions with short answers.

Natural Science: _____

The title sounds kind of dull, 9 paragraphs, 4 line/paragraph references, and 6 questions with short answers.

Order the Questions

In Chapter 18, we'll teach you the Basic Approach of how to attack the passage and the questions, and in that lesson we'll go into more depth about how you order the questions.

<aside>The order in which you do the questions will be somewhat different between the pencil-and-paper ACT and the ACT Online Test. However, the key ideas of "Easy to Answer" and "Easy to Find" apply to both formats.</aside>

The only order you need to know now is the one to avoid: ACT's. The questions aren't in chronological order, nor are they in any order of difficulty from easiest to hardest. You shouldn't work the questions in the order given *just because ACT numbered them in order.*

Now Questions

Work the questions in an order that makes sense for you.

> Do Now questions that are easy to answer or for which it's easy to *find* the answer.

Easy to Answer   A question that is easy to answer often simply asks what the passage says, or as ACT puts it, what is directly stated. ACT, in fact, calls these "Referring questions," requiring the use of your "referral skills" (ACT's words, not ours) to find the right part of the passage. Referring questions don't require much reasoning; the answer will be waiting in black and white, and the correct answer will be barely paraphrased, if at all. Most answers are also relatively short: that's why you look for plenty of questions with short answers in picking your order of passages.

<aside>On the ACT Online Test, Easy to Find is more important than Easy to Answer.</aside>

Easy to Find the Answer   A question with a line reference or highlighted text comes with a map, showing you where in the passage to find the answer. Some of these questions may be tough to answer, but as long as they come with line or paragraph references, they direct you where to read. Questions that come with a great lead word can also make finding the answer easy. Lead words are the nouns, phrases, and sometimes verbs that are specific to the passage. They're not the boilerplate language like "main idea" or "the passage characterizes."

Look at the following questions. All the lead words have been underlined.

11.   Jeremy Bentham probably would have said that lawyers:

12.   The author states that common law differs from civil law in that:

13.   According to the passage, the integrative movement produced:

31.   The main purpose of the passage is to:

35.   Which of the following statements most accurately summarizes how the passage characterizes edema and hypoproteinemia?

Lead words are words and phrases that can be found in the passage.

Great lead words are proper nouns, unusual words, and dates.

Your eye can spot great lead words in the passage just by looking and without reading. They leap off the page. In Chapter 18, we'll teach you how to use lead words as part of the Basic Approach.

Later Questions

Later questions are difficult to answer, and it's difficult to find the answer, like Question 31 in the last set of examples. Most questions that are difficult to answer require reasoning skills to "show your understanding of statements with implied meaning."

Reasoning Questions   Reasoning questions require more thought than do Referring questions, so they do not qualify as "easy to answer." However, they are Later only if they don't come with a line reference or highlighted text, which makes the answer easy to find.

In the description of the Reading test, ACT lists the various tasks that reasoning skills must be applied to.

- Determine main ideas
- Locate and interpret significant details
- Understand sequences of events
- Make comparisons
- Comprehend cause-effect relationships
- Determine the meaning of context-dependent words, phrases, and statements
- Draw generalizations
- Analyze the author's or narrator's voice and method

Any insight into the test writers' purpose and intent always benefits your preparation. However, you don't need to name the specific task when you come across it in a question. During the actual exam, identify questions as Now or Later, and don't forget that questions with line references or highlighted text are Now, regardless of the task assigned in the question.

Pace Yourself

It would be logical to assume that you must pace yourself to spend 8 minutes and 45 seconds on each passage. But to earn your best possible Reading score, you have to invest your time where it will do the most good and where its absence would create the most damage. To raise your score, you have to identify a pacing strategy that works for you.

> Focus on the number of questions that you need to answer correctly in order to earn your goal score.

Let's say you used 35 minutes to do all 4 passages, but because you had to hurry, you missed 2–3 questions per passage for a total of 10 wrong answers and therefore a raw score of 30. According to the score grid on page 22, 30 raw points would give you a scaled score of 28.

Let's say instead you used 35 minutes to do just 3 passages. With the extra time spent on your 3 best passages, you missed only 2 questions. And for that Never passage, you used your LOTD, choosing your favorite combination of answer choices to bubble in a nice straight line on the answer sheet. You picked up 2 correct answers, making your raw score 30, and your scaled score 28.

Letter of the Day (LOTD) Just because you don't work on a passage doesn't mean you don't choose an answer. Never leave any questions blank on the ACT. Choose your Letter of the Day for all the questions on your Never passages.

Which pacing strategy is better? Neither and both. Pacing strategies for Reading are just as personal as picking the order of the passages. You have to practice and find a pace that works for you. Some students are better off doing fewer passages, using the extra time per passage to answer most if not all questions correctly. Others find that even with all the time in the world, they'd never get all the questions right on one passage. They find the points they need across more passages, finding all the Now questions and guessing on the Never questions. Which type are you? That's what timed practice tests will help you discover.

Goal Score

Use the score grid on page 22 to find your goal score and determine how many raw points you need. This is the number of questions you need to answer correctly, whether by working them or lucky LOTD.

One Sample Pacing Strategy

This is only one way to use the 35 minutes. This is a possible strategy for anyone working all 4 passages.

- First Passage: *11 minutes*
- Second Passage: *10 minutes*
- Third Passage: *8 minutes*
- Fourth Passage: *6 minutes*

Just as there is no one pacing strategy for all students, there is no one pace for all passages. In practice, try varying the amount of time you spend on each passage. Some students do best by dividing the 35 minutes equally over all the passages. Other students do best by spending more time on the first one or two passages and less on the remaining passages. Experiment in practice until you find a pacing strategy that works for you.

Be Flexible

Flexibility is key to your ACT success, particularly on the Reading test. Picking the order of the passages rests on your willingness to flip your order when you see that day's test. The passages, after all, are new on each test you see, and you have to look at what you've been given and adapt.

Similarly, you have to be flexible in your pacing. Focus on the number of raw points you need, and don't drown in one particular passage or get stuck on one tough question. Get out of a passage on which you've already spent too much time. Force yourself to guess on the question you've been rereading for minutes, use LOTD on any questions still left, and move on.

We're not saying this is easy. In fact, changing your own instinctual behavior is the hardest part of cracking the Reading test. Everyone has made the mistake of ignoring that voice that's screaming inside your head to move on, and we've all answered back, "But I know I'm almost there and if I take just a little more time, I know l can get it."

You may in fact get that question. But that one right answer likely cost you 2–3 others. And even worse, you had probably already narrowed it down to two answer choices. You were down to a fifty-fifty chance of getting it right, and instead you wasted more time to prove the one right answer.

In these chapters, we'll show you how to use that time more effectively to begin with and what to do when you're down to two. But both skills depend on the Process of Elimination, POE.

POE

POE is a powerful tool on a multiple-choice, standardized test. On the Reading test, you may find several Now questions easy to answer and be able to spot the right answer right away among the four choices. There will be plenty of tough Reasoning questions, however, whose answers aren't obvious, either in your own words or among the four choices. You can easily fall into the trap of rereading and rereading to figure out the answer. Wrong answers, however, can be more obvious to identify. After all, they are there to hide the right answer. In fact, if you can cross off all the wrong ones, the right answer will be waiting there for you. Even if you cross off only one or two, the right answer frequently becomes more obvious.

We'll spend more time with POE in the following chapters. For now, just remember that we started this lesson with a reminder that the first step in raising your ACT Reading score is to stop treating this test as if it's a reading assignment for school. You don't get extra points for knowing the answer before you look at the answer choices. You get a point for a correct answer, and you need to get to as many questions as possible in order to answer them. Use POE to escape the death spiral questions that will hold you back.

> **Process of Elimination**
> Each time you eliminate a wrong answer, you increase your chance of choosing the correct answer.

Summary

- There are always 4 passages and 40 questions on the Reading test. One of these will be a "Dual Passage," that includes two shorter passages by different authors or from different works.

- The passages are always in the same order: Prose Fiction/Literary Narrative, Social Science, Humanities, Natural Science.

- Each passage has 10 questions.

- The passages, including the Dual Passages, are all roughly the same length, between 800–850 words.

- Follow your POOD to pick your own order of the passages.

- Look for passages to do Now: categories and topics you like best or find easier.

- Look for passages with 8–12 paragraphs of 5–15 lines.

- Look for passages with lots of line references.

- Look for passages with lots of questions with short answers.

- Pace yourself. Find the number of questions you need to answer correctly in order to reach your goal score.

- Be Flexible. Be ready to adapt your order, leave a tough passage, or guess on a tough question.

- Use Process of Elimination to cross off wrong answers and save time.

Chapter 18
The 6-Step Basic Approach

To earn your highest possible score on the Reading test, you need an efficient and strategic approach to working the passages. In this chapter, we'll teach you how to work the passages, questions, and answers.

HOW TO CRACK THE READING TEST

The most efficient way to boost your Reading score is to pick your order of the passages and apply our 6-Step Basic Approach to the passages. Use the Basic Approach to enhance your reading skills and train them for specific use on the ACT.

The 6-Step Basic Approach

Step 1: Preview. Read the blurb. On the pencil-and-paper ACT, map the questions.

Step 2: Work the Passage.
Up Front—read in 2–3 minutes
As You Go—Read as you answer the questions

Step 3: Select and Understand a Question. Use POOD to choose a question and determine what the question is asking

Step 4: Read What You Need. Most questions require 5–10 lines.

Step 5: Predict the Correct Answer. Predict the Answer based on the passage.

Step 6: Use POE.

Before we train you on each step in cracking the test the right way, let's talk about the temptations to attack the passages in the wrong way.

This Isn't School

In the Introduction, we discussed the reading skills you've spent your whole school career developing. You have been rewarded for your ability to develop a thorough, thoughtful grasp of the meaning and significance of the text. But in school, you have the benefit of time, not to mention the aid of your teachers' lectures, class discussions, and various tools to help you not only understand but also remember what you've read. You have none of those tools on the Reading test, but you walk into it with the instinct to approach the Reading test as if you do.

Where does that leave you on the ACT Reading test? You spend several minutes reading the passage, trying to understand the details and follow the author's main point. You furiously underline or highlight what you think may be important points that will be tested later in the questions. And when you hit a particularly confusing chunk of detailed text, what do you do? You read it again. And again. You worry you can't move on until you have solved this one detail. All the while, time is slipping by....

Now, on to the questions. Your first mistake is to do them in order. But as we told you in the Introduction, they are not written in order of difficulty, nor chronologically. You confront main-idea questions before specific questions. You try to answer the questions all from memory. After all, you've spent so much time reading the passage, you don't have the time to go back to find or even confirm an answer. And when you do occasionally go back to read a specific part of the passage, you still don't see the answer. So you read the chunk of the passage again and again.

If you approach the Reading test this way, you will likely not earn the points you need to hit your goal score.

The Passage

You don't earn points from reading the passage. You earn points from answering the questions correctly. And you have no idea what the questions will ask. You're searching desperately through the passage, looking for conclusions and main points. You stumble on the details, rereading several times to master them. But how do you even know what details are important if you haven't seen the questions?

The Questions

When you answer the questions from memory, you will either face answer choices that all seem right, or you will fall right into ACT's trap, choosing an answer choice that sounds right with some familiar words, but which in reality doesn't match what the passage said.

The test writers at ACT know everyone is inclined to attack the Reading test this way. They write deceptive answer choices that will tempt you because that's what wrong answers have to do. If the right answer were surrounded by three ridiculous, obviously wrong answers, everyone would get a 36. Wrong answers have to sound temptingly right, and the easiest way to do that is to use noticeable terms out of the passage. You gratefully latch onto them the way a drowning person clutches a life preserver.

THE 6-STEP BASIC APPROACH

The best way to beat the ACT system is to use a different one. The 6-Step Basic Approach will help you direct the bulk of your time to where you earn points, on the questions and answers. When you read the passage, you'll read knowing exactly what you're looking for.

Step 1: Preview

The first step involves one part on the ACT Online Test and two parts on the pencil-and-paper ACT. The first step is the same: read the blurb at the beginning of the passage to see if it offers any additional information. Ninety-nine percent of the time, all it will offer will be the title, author, copyright date, and publisher. There is even no guarantee that the title will convey the topic. But occasionally, the blurb will define an unfamiliar term, place a setting, or identify a character.

> **Passage III**
>
> **HUMANITIES:** This passage is adapted from the article "The Sculpture Revolution" by Michael Michalski (©1998 Geer Publishing).

True to form, this offers only the basic information.

Potholes
If you're out driving and you hit a pothole, do you back up and drive over it again? Rereading text you didn't understand is the literary equivalent of driving over and over the same pothole.

In this chapter, we've formatted the passage as if it were on the pencil-and-paper ACT. If you're taking the ACT Online Test, remember that the passage won't have line references, and that questions with line references would instead have the relevant parts of the passage highlighted.

Step 1

Second Time Around
You'll check the blurb twice. Once when you're confirming your order and now as part of Step 1.

On the ACT Online Test, you won't do the next step, as it takes too much time clicking between questions. Instead, skip to Step 2 after you read the blurb. On the pencil-and-paper ACT, the next part of Step 1 addresses the questions.

Map the Questions

Take no more than 30 seconds to map the questions. Underline the lead words. Star any line or paragraph references.

Lead Words

We introduced lead words in the Introduction. These are the specific words and phrases that you will find in the passage. They are not the boilerplate language of reading test questions like "main idea" or "author's purpose." They are usually nouns, phrases, or verbs.

Map the following questions that accompany the humanities passage. Even if a question has a line/paragraph reference, underline any lead words in the question.

21. The author expresses the idea that:

22. The information in lines 75–81 suggests that Quentin Bell believes that historians and critics:

23. Which of the following most accurately summarizes how the passage characterizes subjectivism's effect on Rodin?

24. According to the passage, academicism and mannerism:

25. Information in the fourth paragraph (lines 33–41) makes clear that the author believes that:

26. According to the passage, Renoir differs from Daleur in that:

27. According to the passage, Cézanne's work is characterized by:

28. Based on information in the sixth paragraph (lines 49–57), the author implies that:

29. In line 65, when the author uses the phrase "modern," he most nearly means sculpture that:

30. Which of the following statements would the author most likely agree with?

Your mapped questions should look like this:

21. The author expresses the idea that:

⭐ **22.** The information in lines 75–81 suggests that <u>Quentin Bell</u> believes that <u>historians</u> and <u>critics</u>:

23. Which of the following most accurately summarizes how the passage characterizes <u>subjectivism's effect</u> on <u>Rodin</u>?

24. According to the passage, <u>academicism</u> and <u>mannerism</u>:

⭐ **25.** Information in the fourth paragraph (lines 33–41) makes clear that the author believes that:

26. According to the passage, <u>Renoir differs from Daleur</u> in that:

27. According to the passage, <u>Cézanne's work</u> is characterized by:

⭐ **28.** Based on information in the sixth paragraph (lines 49–57), the author implies that:

⭐ **29.** In line 65, when the author uses the phrase "<u>modern</u>" he most nearly means <u>sculpture</u> that:

30. Which of the following statements would the author most likely agree with?

Two Birds, One Stone

Mapping the questions provides two key benefits. First, you've just identified (with stars) four questions that have easy-to-find answers. With all those great lead words, you have two more questions whose answers will be easy to find. Second, you have the main idea of the passage *before* you've read it. When you read the passage knowing what to look for, you *read actively*.

Look again at all the words you've underlined. They tell you what the passage will be about: modern sculpture, Renoir, Daleur, Cézanne, Rodin, and a bunch of "-isms" that you could safely guess concern art. There is also someone named Quentin Bell, historians, critics, and art. You're ready to move on to Step 2.

Read Actively

Reading actively means knowing in advance what you're going to read. You have the important details to look for, and you won't waste time on details that never appear in a question. Reading passively means walking into a dark cave, wandering in the dark trying to see what dangers or treasures await. Reading actively means walking into the cave with a flashlight and a map, looking for what you know is in there.

Step 2: Work the Passage

Your next step is to work the passage. You have two options: work the passage Up Front or As You Go through the questions. We'll look at the As You Go approach later. For now, work the passage Up Front. Spend no more than 2–3 minutes. Look for and underline the lead words, underlining each time any appear more than once. If you're taking the ACT Online Test, we *strongly* recommend you work the passage As You Go. If you do work the passage Up Front, your goal is to understand the overall structure and big ideas in the passage. You're not reading to understand every word and detail. You'll read smaller selections in depth when you work the questions. If you can't finish in three minutes, don't worry about it. We'll discuss time management strategies later in the chapter.

Passage III

HUMANITIES: This passage is adapted from the article "The Sculpture Revolution" by Michael Michalski (©1998 Geer Publishing).

If we were to start fresh in the study of sculpture or any art, we might observe that the record is largely filled by works of relatively few great contributors. Next to the influences of these great geniuses, time periods
5 themselves are of little significance. The study of art and art history are properly directed to the achievements of outstanding individual artists, not the particular decades or centuries in which any may have worked.

Nonetheless, when we study art in historical
10 perspective we select a convenient frame of reference through which diverse styles and talents are to be compared. Hence we write of "movements" and attempt to understand each artist in terms of the one to which he "belongs." Movements have limited use, but we should
15 not talk of realism, impressionism, cubism, or surrealism as though they genuinely had lives of their own to which the artist was answerable. We regard the movement as the governing force and the artist as its servant. Yet it is well to remember that the movements do not necessarily
20 present themselves in orderly chronological series, and the individual artist frequently weaves her way into one and out of another over the course of a single career.

Great artists are not normally confined by the "movements" that others may name for them. Rather, they
25 transcend the conventional structure working now in one style, then in another, and later in a third. Picasso's work, for example, echoes many of the artistic movements, and other artists too, moving from one style through another. Indeed, artists are people, and any may decide
30 to alter her style for no more complex a reason than that which makes most people want to "try something new" once in a while.

In studying modern sculpture one is tempted to begin a history with Auguste Rodin (1840–1917), who
35 was a contemporary of Paul Cézanne (1839–1906). Yet the two artists did not, in artistic terms, belong to the same period. Their strategies and objectives differed. Although Rodin was surely a great artist, he did not do for sculpture what Cézanne did for painting. In fact,
40 although Cézanne was a painter, he had a more lasting effect on sculpture than did Rodin.

Cézanne's work constitutes a reaction against impressionism and the confusion he thought it created. He searched persistently for the "motif." Cézanne strived
45 for clarity of form and was able to convert his personal perceptions into concrete, recognizable substance. He is justly considered to have offered the first glimmer of a new art—a new classicism.

Rodin was surely a great artist, but he was not an
50 innovator as was Cézanne; prevailing tides of subjectivism came over him. Rodin's mission was to reinvest sculpture with the integrity it lost when Michelangelo died. Rodin succeeded in this mission. His first true work, *The Age of Bronze* (1877), marked the beginning
55 of the end of academicism, mannerism, and decadence that had prevailed since Michelangelo's last sculpture, the *Rondanini Pietà*.

Yet it is largely Cézanne, not Rodin, who was artistic ancestor to Picasso, Gonzalez, Brancusi, Archipenko,
60 Lipchitz, and Laurens, and they are unquestionably the first lights in the "new art" of sculpture. This "new art," of course, is the sculpture we call "modern." It is modern because it breaks with tradition and draws little on that which preceded it.

65 When I speak of "modern" sculpture, I do not refer to every sculptor nor even to every highly talented sculptor of our age. I do not exclude, necessarily, the sculptors of an earlier time. Modern sculpture, as far as I am concerned, is any that consciously casts tradition
70 aside and seeks forms more suitable to the senses and values of its time. Renoir and Daumier are, in this light, modern sculptors notwithstanding the earlier time at which they worked. Daleur and Carpeaux are not modern, although they belong chronologically to the recent era.

75   Professor Quentin Bell argues that historians and critics name as "modern" those sculptors in whom they happen to be interested and that the term when abused in that way has no historical or artistic significance.

That, I think, is not right. The problem is that Profes-
80 sor Bell thinks "modern" means "now," when in fact it means "new."

Your passage should look like this. If you couldn't find all the lead words to underline, don't worry. You can do those questions Later. But did you notice that there is nothing underlined in the second and third paragraphs? If you hadn't mapped the questions first, you would have likely wasted a lot of time on details that ACT doesn't seem to care about.

Passage III

HUMANITIES: This passage is adapted from the article "The Sculpture Revolution" by Michael Michalski (©1998 Geer Publishing).

    If we were to start fresh in the study of sculpture or any art, we might observe that the record is largely filled by works of relatively few great contributors. Next to the influences of these great geniuses, time periods
5 themselves are of little significance. The study of art and art history are properly directed to the achievements of outstanding individual artists, not the particular decades or centuries in which any may have worked.

    Nonetheless, when we study art in historical
10 perspective we select a convenient frame of reference through which diverse styles and talents are to be compared. Hence we write of "movements" and attempt to understand each artist in terms of the one to which he "belongs." Movements have limited use, but we should
15 not talk of realism, impressionism, cubism, or surrealism as though they genuinely had lives of their own to which the artist was answerable. We regard the movement as the governing force and the artist as its servant. Yet it is well to remember that the movements do not necessarily
20 present themselves in orderly chronological series and the individual artist frequently weaves her way into one and out of another over the course of a single career.

    Great artists are not normally confined by the "movements" that others may name for them. Rather, they
25 transcend the conventional structure working now in one style, then in another, and later in a third. Picasso's work, for example, echoes many of the artistic movements, and other artists too, moving from one style through another. Indeed, artists are people, and any may decide
30 to alter her style for no more complex a reason than that which makes most people want to "try something new" once in a while.

    In studying modern sculpture one is tempted to begin a history with Auguste Rodin (1840–1917), who
35 was a contemporary of Paul Cézanne (1839–1906). Yet the two artists did not, in artistic terms, belong to the same period. Their strategies and objectives differed. Although Rodin was surely a great artist, he did not do for sculpture what Cézanne did for painting. In fact,

40 although Cézanne was a painter, he had a more lasting effect on sculpture than did Rodin.

    Cézanne's work constitutes a reaction against impressionism and the confusion he thought it created. He searched persistently for the "motif." Cézanne strived
45 for clarity of form and was able to convert his personal perceptions into concrete, recognizable substance. He is justly considered to have offered the first glimmer of a new art—a new classicism.

    Rodin was surely a great artist, but he was not an
50 innovator as was Cézanne; prevailing tides of subjectivism came over him. Rodin's mission was to reinvest sculpture with the integrity it lost when Michelangelo died. Rodin succeeded in this mission. His first true work, *The Age of Bronze* (1877), marked the beginning
55 of the end of academicism, mannerism, and decadence that had prevailed since Michelangelo's last sculpture, the *Rondanini Pietà*.

    Yet it is largely Cézanne, not Rodin, who was artistic ancestor to Picasso, Gonzalez, Brancusi, Archipenko,
60 Lipchitz, and Laurens, and they are unquestionably the first lights in the "new art" of sculpture. This "new art," of course, is the sculpture we call "modern." It is modern because it breaks with tradition and draws little on that which preceded it.

65   When I speak of "modern" sculpture, I do not refer to every sculptor nor even to every highly talented sculptor of our age. I do not exclude, necessarily, the sculptors of an earlier time. Modern sculpture, as far as I am concerned, is any that consciously casts tradition
70 aside and seeks forms more suitable to the senses and values of its time. Renoir and Daumier are, in this light, modern sculptors notwithstanding the earlier time at which they worked. Daleur and Carpeaux are not modern, although they belong chronologically to the recent era.

75   Professor Quentin Bell argues that historians and critics name as "modern" those sculptors in whom they happen to be interested and that the term when abused in that way has no historical or artistic significance. That, I think, is not right. The problem is that Profes-
80 sor Bell thinks "modern" means "now," when in fact it means "new."

Step 3: Select and Understand the Question

As we told you in the Introduction, you can't do the questions in the order ACT gives you. Question 21 has no stars or lead words and poses what seems to be a Reasoning question. Thus, it's neither easy to answer, nor is the answer easy to find. Question 22 is a great question to start with, however. It has a line reference (or highlight on the ACT Online Test), and it's a Referral question, asking directly what is stated in the passage.

When Selecting a Question on the ACT Online Test, if a question is Easy to Find (a portion of the text is highlighted or you Worked the Passage and know where in the passage the content you need is), do it Now. Understand the question and then move on to Step 4. If the question is not Easy to Find (in other words, you don't immediately know where in the passage to go), write down the question's lead words on your whiteboard next to the question number. Include EXCEPT/LEAST/NOT if the question includes those words. If there are no lead words, flag the question.

Select a Question
Do Now questions that are easy to answer, easy to find, or best of all, both.

☆ **22.** The information in lines 75–81 suggests that <u>Quentin Bell</u> believes that <u>historians</u> and <u>critics</u>:

Here's How to Crack It

Make sure you understand what the question is asking. Try rephrasing it as an actual question: What does Quentin Bell believe about historians and critics, based on lines 75–81?

Step 4: Read What You Need

Read what you need in the passage to find your prediction. The line reference points you to line 75, but you'll find your answer within a window of 5–10 lines around the line reference. Read the last paragraph to see what Quentin Bell believes about historians and critics.

You can use the Line Mask tool on the ACT Online Test to help you focus on your window. Don't feel obligated to use this tool, however—not everyone finds it helpful.

Step 5: Predict the Correct Answer

Predict the answer to the question using the passage. This is a Referral question, asking what is directly stated, so you can underline or highlight the prediction in the text. Lines 75–78 offer Bell's opinion. Do you see the importance of making sure you understand the question? We care what Quentin Bell thinks about historians and critics, not what the author thinks of them.

On the ACT Online Test, you can highlight portions of the text that are already highlighted. The color will change to "your" highlighter color.

Step 6: Use POE

If you can clearly identify the answer in the passage, look for its match among the answers. Eliminate any choice that talks about something not found in your window. If you aren't sure if an answer is right or wrong, leave it. You'll either find one better or three worse. If you're down to two, choose key words in the answer choices. See if you can locate them back in the passage, and determine whether the answer choice matches what the passage says.

Here's How to Crack It

F.   have no appreciation for the value of modern art.

Bell is critical of historians and critics, and value could refer to significance in the passage. This seems possible, so keep it.

G.   abuse art and its history.

The passage states that the term is abused, not art and its history. This is a trap, and it's wrong. Cross it off.

H.   should evaluate works of art on the basis of their merit without regard to the artist's fame.

There was nothing in the window about "fame." Cross it off.

J.   attach the phrase "modern art" to those sculptors that intrigue them.

Attach the phrase is a good match for *name* as *modern* and *sculptors that intrigue them* is a good match for *in whom they happen to be interested*. This answer is better than (F), and it is correct.

Steps 3–6: Repeat

Look for all the Now questions, and repeat Steps 3–6. Make sure you understand what each question is asking. Read what you need to find your answer, usually a window of 5–10 lines. Work the answers, using POE until you find your answer.

Referral Questions

Referral questions are easy to answer because they ask what was directly stated in the passage. Read the question carefully to identify what it's asking. The passage directly states something about what? Once you find your window to read, read to find the answer. The correct answers to Referral questions are barely paraphrased and will match the text very closely.

How to Spot Referral Questions
- Questions that begin with *According to the passage*
- Questions that ask what the passage or author states
- Questions with short answers

If the answer to a Referral question is also easy to find, they are great Now questions. Look for Referral questions with line references or great lead words.

On the ACT Online Test, you would likely do question 26 Later—no part of the text would be highlighted. Instead, write down the question number and lead words on your whiteboard (abbreviations and shorthand are fine—"26: Ren. differs from Dal."). Then, when you work the passage after doing all the questions with highlighted text, you can go directly to question 26 when you come across the lead words.

26. According to the passage, Renoir differs from Daleur in that:

    F. Daleur had no inspiration, while Renoir was tremendously inspired.

    G. Renoir's work was highly innovative, while Daleur's was not.

    H. Daleur was a sculptor, while Renoir was not.

    J. Renoir revered tradition, while Daleur did not.

65   When I speak of "modern" sculpture, I do not refer to every sculptor nor even to every highly talented sculptor of our age. I do not exclude, necessarily, the sculptors of an earlier time. Modern sculpture, as far as I am concerned, is any that consciously casts tradition
70 aside and seeks forms more suitable to the senses and values of its time. Renoir and Daumier are, in this light, modern sculptors notwithstanding the earlier time at which they worked. Daleur and Carpeaux are not modern, although they belong chronologically to the recent era.

Here's How to Crack It

Renoir and *Daleur* are great lead words, easy for your eye to spot in the eighth paragraph. On the pencil-and-paper ACT, you'll have the passage on the left and all your mapped questions on the right-hand page. (On the ACT Online Test, the passage will be on the left and one question on the right.) For convenience's sake and to avoid flipping back to the passage, we're printing the window to read with the question.

Lines 71–73 state that *Renoir was a modern sculptor* and *Daleur* is not. But that same sentence mentions four artists *in this light*. What light? Any time you see *this*, *that*, or *such* in front of a noun, back up to read the first mention of that topic. *This light* is the author's definition of modern, given in lines 68–71.

Now work the answers. Cross off answers that don't state Renoir is modern and Daleur is not. *Innovative* in (G) is a good match for modern and is the correct answer. *Inspiration* in (F) doesn't match modern. Choice (H) is disproven by the passage. Choice (J) tempts with *tradition* but compare it to the text, and the author states modern sculpture *consciously casts tradition aside*.

Try another Referral question with great lead words.

---

27. According to the passage, <u>Cézanne's work</u> is characterized by:

    A. a return to subjectivism.
    B. a pointless search for form.
    C. excessively personal expressions.
    D. rejection of the impressionistic philosophy.

> <u>Cézanne</u>'s work constitutes a reaction against im-
> pressionism and the confusion he thought it created. He
> searched persistently for the "motif." <u>Cézanne</u> strived
> 45 for clarity of form and was able to convert his personal
> perceptions into concrete, recognizable substance. He
> is justly considered to have offered the first glimmer of
> a new art—a new classicism.

Here's How to Crack It

Cézanne appears first in the fourth paragraph, but the question is about *Cézanne's work*, which is in the fifth paragraph. Choice (D) matches *reaction against impressionism* and is the correct answer.

Reasoning Questions

Reasoning questions require you to read between the lines. Instead of being directly stated, the correct answer is implied or suggested. In other words, look for the larger point that the author is making based on the text.

Reasoning questions aren't as easy to answer as Referral questions, but they're not *that* much harder. If they come with a line or paragraph reference or a great lead word, they should be done Now.

How to Spot Reasoning Questions

- Questions that use *infer*, *means*, *suggests*, or *implies*
- Questions that ask about the purpose or function of part or all of the passage
- Questions that ask what the author or a person written about in the passage would agree or disagree with
- Questions that ask you to characterize or describe all or parts of the passage
- Questions with long answers

☆ 25. Information in the fourth paragraph (lines 33–41) makes clear that the author believes that:

    A. Rodin was more innovative than Cézanne.
    B. Cézanne was more innovative than Rodin.
    C. Modern art is more important than classical art.
    D. Cézanne tried to emulate impressionism.

>   In studying <u>modern sculpture</u> one is tempted to begin a history with Auguste <u>Rodin</u> (1840–1917), who
> 35 was a contemporary of Paul <u>Cézanne</u> (1839–1906). Yet the two artists did not, in artistic terms, belong to the same period. Their strategies and objectives differed. Although <u>Rodin</u> was surely a great artist, he did not do for sculpture what <u>Cézanne</u> did for painting. In fact,
> 40 although <u>Cézanne</u> was a painter, he had a more lasting effect on sculpture than did <u>Rodin</u>.

Here's How to Crack It

The question doesn't provide specific clues about what to look for and instead asks what the author's point is in the fourth paragraph. The author is comparing the artists Cézanne and Rodin. The concluding sentence states that *Cézanne...had a more lasting effect on sculpture than did Rodin*. Choice (A) says the opposite. The paragraph does not mention either *classical art* or *impressionism,* so (C) and (D) can be eliminated. Choice (B) is a good paraphrase of the author's point and is the correct answer.

Work the Answers
Use POE heavily with Reasoning questions.

Work Now the Reasoning questions with line or paragraph references or great lead words. Use POE heavily as you work the answers.

☆ **28.** Based on information in the sixth paragraph (lines 49–57), the author implies that:

    F. mannerism reflects a lack of integrity.

    G. Rodin disliked the work of Michelangelo.

    H. Rodin embraced the notion of decadence.

    J. Rodin's work represented a shift in style different from the works of artists who preceded him.

        Rodin was surely a great artist, but he was not an
50 innovator as was Cézanne; prevailing tides of subjectivism came over him. Rodin's mission was to reinvest
sculpture with the integrity it lost when Michelangelo
died. Rodin succeeded in this mission. His first true
work, *The Age of Bronze* (1877), marked the beginning
55 of the end of academicism, mannerism, and decadence
that had prevailed since Michelangelo's last sculpture,
the *Rondanini Pietà*.

Here's How to Crack It

Use POE. Choices (F) and (H) use terms from the paragraph but change the meaning. Rodin wanted to restore elements of sculpture that had changed since the death of Michelangelo, which means he respected Michelangelo's work, so (G) is not supported. The last sentence states that Rodin's work *marked the beginning of the end* and therefore represented something new, as is stated in (J), which is the correct answer.

☆ **29.** In line 65, when the author uses the phrase "modern," he most nearly means sculpture that:

    A. postdates the *Rondanini Pietà*.

    B. is not significantly tied to work that comes before it.

    C. shows no artistic merit.

    D. genuinely interests contemporary critics.

---

65   When I speak of "modern" sculpture, I do not refer to every sculptor nor even to every highly talented
sculptor of our age. I do not exclude, necessarily, the
sculptors of an earlier time. Modern sculpture, as far as
I am concerned, is any that consciously casts tradition
70 aside and seeks forms more suitable to the senses and
values of its time. Renoir and Daumier are, in this light,
modern sculptors notwithstanding the earlier time at
which they worked. Daleur and Carpeaux are not modern,
although they belong chronologically to the recent era.

Here's How to Crack It

Use POE. The *Rondanini Pietà* is in the wrong window, so eliminate (A). Choice (B) is a good paraphrase of the art that *consciously casts tradition aside and seeks forms more suitable to the sense and values of its time*, and it is the correct answer. Choice (C) can't be proven by the passage; the author doesn't state that they have no worth at all. Choice (D) tempts with *contemporary* as a possible match for *modern* or *its time*, but *critics* are not in this window.

Later Questions

Once you have worked all the questions with line or paragraph references and great lead words, move to the Later questions. The answers to questions without a line or paragraph reference or any great lead words can be difficult to find, which is why you should do them Later. But the later you do them, the easier they become. You've either found them or you've narrowed down where to look. From the windows you've read closely to answer all the Now questions, you may have located lead words you missed when you worked the passage. And if you haven't, then they must be in the few paragraphs you haven't read since you worked the passage.

---

24. According to the passage, <u>academicism</u> and <u>mannerism</u>:

F. were readily visible in *The Age of Bronze*.
G. were partially manifest in the *Rondanini Pietà*.
H. were styles that Rodin believed lacked integrity.
J. were styles that Rodin wanted to restore into fashion.

> <u>Rodin</u> was surely a great artist, but he was not an
> 50 innovator as was <u>Cézanne</u>; prevailing tides of <u>subjectiv-</u>
> <u>ism</u> came over him. <u>Rodin</u>'s mission was to reinvest
> sculpture with the integrity it lost when Michelangelo
> died. <u>Rodin</u> succeeded in this mission. His first true
> work, *The Age of Bronze* (1877), marked the beginning
> 55 of the end of <u>academicism</u>, <u>mannerism</u>, and decadence
> that had prevailed since Michelangelo's last sculpture,
> the *Rondanini Pietà*.

Here's How to Crack It

According to the passage means that this is a Referral question and should be easy to answer. The challenge, however, is finding the lead words. But you read this paragraph when you answered 28. Not only would you find *academicism* and *mannerism* if you missed them when you worked the passage, but you also know the paragraph well from working question 28. Use POE to eliminate choices that don't match your correct answer from 28. Choices (F), (G), and (J) all contradict both the passage and your previous answer. Choice (H) matches, and it is the correct answer.

Now move on to question 23. Because you worked it Later, the answer is easy to find.

---

23. Which of the following most accurately summarizes how the passage characterizes <u>subjectivism's effect</u> on <u>Rodin</u>?

    A. It ended his affiliation with mannerism.
    B. It caused him to lose his artistic integrity.
    C. It limited his ability to innovate.
    D. It caused him to become decadent.

Here's How to Crack It

You know this paragraph well by now, but *subjectivism* didn't play a major role in the points made for questions 28 and 24. Use POE to eliminate (B) and (D) because they don't match what you've learned about Rodin. You know Rodin didn't like *mannerism*, but check the part of the window that specifically discusses *subjectivism*. Lines 49–51 give *subjectivism* as the explanation of why Rodin *was not an innovator*. That matches (C) perfectly.

Last

Questions 24 and 23 showed how your work on each question builds your understanding of the passage, making the Later questions easier to do than if you hadn't waited. The questions, after all, refer back to the same passage, so the answers should agree with each other. Some questions may ask about a relatively minor detail in the passage, but most should ask about important details, the ones that help the author make the main point.

Use what you've learned about the passage to answer last the questions that ask about the entire passage.

> On the ACT Online Test, you should have flagged these questions the first time the first time you went through the questions associated with the passage. Regardless of the test format, questions without lead words are much easier when answered last!

---

21. The author expresses the idea that:

    A. art should never be studied in terms of movements.
    B. art can be labeled as modern when it introduces a style that is different from those found in works that came earlier.
    C. lesser artists do not usually vary their styles.
    D. great artists are always nonconformists.

Here's How to Crack It

Question 29 helps the most with this question, but several questions echoed the theme of art making a break from the past. The correct answer is (B).

---

30. Which of the following statements would the author most likely agree with?
  F. Cézanne had greater influence on modern sculpture than did Rodin.
  G. Rodin made no significant contribution to modern sculpture.
  H. Daumier should not be considered a modern sculptor.
  J. Carpeaux should be considered a modern sculptor.

Here's How to Crack It

Questions 23, 24, 25, 26, 27, and 28 all help eliminate the wrong answers (G), (H), and (J), making (F) the correct answer.

The Basic Approach
1. Preview.
2. Work the Passage.
3. Select and Understand a Question.
4. Read What You Need.
5. Predict the Correct Answer.
6. Use POE.

THE 6-STEP BASIC APPROACH

Try a passage on your own. Give yourself up to 12 minutes, but don't worry if you go a little over. Use the passage on the next page to help you master the Basic Approach, and worry less about your speed. Later in the chapter and in the next, we'll discuss other strategies to help with time. The answers are given on the page following the questions.

Passage I

PROSE FICTION: This passage is adapted from the novel *Skyward* by Prakriti Basrai (©2012 by Prakriti Basrai).

Ever since I graduated from high school, I've worked at the company my father started, Singer Stations and Service, a gas station and car maintenance center that was the fulfillment of my father's American dream shortly after he arrived here in
5 the late 1960s and that, if all goes according to plan, will pass to my grandsons and their grandsons in perpetuity, and which is already making its way into the twenty-first century with a Facebook page and a sophisticated iPhone app.

Our family name is still Singh, but in our small town,
10 my father thought it would put a safer face on the business to change the name to Singer, a name which we've all unofficially adopted now that we're in the United States, as I suppose many of our more-established neighbors' ancestors must've done a few generations ago.

15 Also, Singer is just a nice name for a business: it's got a nice, musical ring to it, and the alliterative name of our gas station chain seems to churn up memories of great American businesses and the non-threatening pose that has been necessary to immigrant assimilation from the beginning. When drivers
20 pull up to our pumps, they do so with the sense that we'll smile back at them, whistling while we work, operating the pumps like expert musicians, and it'll cost them a song (a line, I'm sure you can imagine, that is emblazoned proudly on all of our public signage). All of the credit for this name has always gone
25 to my father, and I can believe that he was the one behind this smart change: he was always a good businessman, and he had that added penchant, almost a poetic sense for a clever, musical turn of phrase. My father has always loved his business, and although that love has been diluted as it has come through my
30 generation and my son's, it's nothing that the standard narrative of Americanization and the decline of hard work can't explain, and which I have no interest in rehashing here. We've all had our challenges, regardless of age, so who says one generation has it tougher than the next, and frankly, who cares?

35 When I really think about it, though, I think my son, Ravneet, whom everyone calls Richie, might have it hardest. Even for our relatively small business, Richie's public-relations responsibilities are those of any of the international stations. He's always

posting something new to the Internet or monitoring the price of
40 gas all over the world at once. It doesn't hurt that the kid knows how to make a buck—my father marvels every day at what his grandson has been able to do with the family business. You'd think with all that's gone wrong with the economy in the last few years, Richie would've sold his Italian sports car, but the
45 kid actually just bought another one.

Richie's success is undeniable, but sometimes I worry that he works too hard for all that he's got. It's nearly impossible to get him on the phone; he must work 80 hours a week, and he's spent more than one Thanksgiving Day stuck at the office balanc-
50 ing the books. My father at the very least had a family to come home to, and the saving grace of his religious observance forced him to take at least a day off every week. I was pulled neither to overwork nor underwork; I was always focused on maintaining what had been given to me. In later years, my mother told me
55 secretly that she thought I actually had it worst of all—I had no burning desire to enter this business, but I didn't really have any other choice. I did well enough, and if I might've been brilliant at something else, I guess we'll never know.

Even so, I was Raman (The Gas Man) Singer's son, but I
60 never quite shared his pioneer spirit at breaking new ground, nor his enviable belief that he did what he did because it had to be done. I did perfectly well at Singer Stations and Service. I wasn't the boss's lazy kid, and I worked just as hard as any of my employees making minimum wage. I stuck with it. When
65 you look at it this way, I did just fine.

When I fully handed the business over to Richie five years ago, I knew right away that my life couldn't simply be over at the age of 50. As a result, at the urging of my college-aged daughter Geeta, I decided to try something I always wished
70 that I had done. I enrolled in the business program at the State University, and before long, I realized that Geeta knew me better than I knew myself. I had fun like I never had before, and looking back, I came to see that the part of the business that always drew me in was learning: whether it was the stories of
75 my co-workers or the inner workings of a small business that is trying to grow. Now that I'm done with school, I'm starting my own business. In fact, Geeta and I are starting one, and while I've left to her what exactly it is we're selling, I'm brimming with excitement to find out.

1. The passage can be best described as primarily:

   A. one business owner's questioning of the direction his business has taken after he handed the management over to his son.
   B. a son's elegant praise of his father's skill and determination in creating a family business.
   C. a personal narrative that describes one man's role within a business started by his father and passed down through generations.
   D. a story of the changes in American immigrant businesses in the twentieth century.

2. Which of the following actions affecting the family business does the narrator NOT attribute to his father?

   F. A sophisticated iPhone app
   G. The founding of Singer Stations and Service
   H. A change in the family's last name
   J. An alliterative name for the business

3. The narrator explicitly declines to take a firm stand on which of the following issues?

   A. The personal preferences he had that enabled him to succeed in business
   B. The quality of the name Singer Stations and Service
   C. Which generation has had the most difficult time in the world of business
   D. Whether the family should have kept the name Singh rather than Singer

4. According to the passage, what is the narrator's father's attitude toward words?

   F. He treats them like a poet would.
   G. He believes business names should be alliterative.
   H. A man should keep his mouth closed and his ears open.
   J. He believes that advertisers work in the business of deception.

5. As it is used in line 40, the word *hurt* most nearly means:

   A. impede success.
   B. injure.
   C. sting.
   D. cause a bruise.

6. What or who is the "saving grace" referred to in the passage?

   F. Singer Stations and Service
   G. The narrator's mother
   H. The narrator's daughter
   J. Religious piety

7. What does the narrator state is his mother's view of his role in Singer Stations and Service?

   A. In actuality, the credit for the business's name should go to him because he was the real artist.
   B. He had the worst time of any of his family members because he ran a business in which he did not have a passionate interest.
   C. His hard work, though less public than his son's, was crucial to the company's success at the time.
   D. He should be more grateful for his inheritance and not insist on changing professions.

8. According to the passage, who or what is "Raman (The Gas Man)"?

   F. Singer's main gas supplier
   G. The business's main competitor
   H. The narrator's son
   J. The narrator's father

9. According to the passage, the narrator's daughter knows the narrator better than he knows himself because:

   A. the company's new Internet presence emerged after he retired.
   B. she suggested that he go back to school, and he enjoyed doing so.
   C. Richie bought a second Italian sports car.
   D. the history of Singer Stations and Service is a history of the immigrant experience.

10. As it is used in line 73, the phrase *came to see* most nearly means:

    F. arrived at.
    G. realized.
    H. attended.
    J. visited.

Score and Analyze Your Performance

The correct answers are (C), (F), (C), (F), (A), (J), (B), (J), (B), and (G). (For detailed explanations, see Chapter 25.) How did you do? Were you able to finish in 12 minutes or less? If you struggled with time, identify what step took up the most time. Identify any questions that slowed you down. Did you make good choices of Now and Later questions? Did you use *enough* time? If you finished in less than 12 minutes but missed several questions, next time plan to slow down to give yourself enough time to evaluate the answers carefully. In Chapter 19, we'll work on skills to help you work the questions and answers with more speed and greater accuracy. But first, we'll finish this chapter with strategies to help you increase your speed working the passage.

BEAT THE CLOCK

When you struggle with time, there are several places within the Basic Approach that are eating up the minutes.

Pacing the Basic Approach

If you spend 10–11 minutes on your first passage, use your time wisely.

Step 1: Preview. *30–60 seconds*
Step 2: Work the Passage. *3 minutes*
Steps 3 through 6: Work the Questions and Answers. *7 minutes*

Step 1: Preview

To move at the fastest speed when you preview, you can't read the questions. Let your eye *look* for lead words and numbers. Don't let your brain *read*.

Time yourself to see if you can preview the following questions and blurb in less than a minute.

Passage IV

NATURAL SCIENCE: This passage is adapted from the article "What Giotto Saw" by James Herndon (©2001 by Galaxy Press).

31. The author characterizes the comparison of the work of Sagdeev to that of Peale as:

32. The main point of the last paragraph (lines 43-48) is to show that Zdenek Sekanina:

33. In terms of their role in studying the rotational period, the 1920 photographs are described by the author as:

34. Lines 17–19 mainly emphasize what quality?

35. According to the passage, the nuclear surface of Halley's comet is believed to be:

36. As described in the passage, Giotto's camera was specifically programmed to:

37. As used in the passage, the word *resolution* (line 11) means:

38. The passage indicates that H. Use Keler:

39. Lines 25–28 are best summarized as describing a problem that:

40. According to the passage, the volume of Halley's comet is:

Step 2: Work the Passage

If you work the passage up front, this step should take no more than 3 minutes, and you should not be trying to read the passage thoroughly. Your only goal is to find as many of your lead words as you can and underline them.

Skimming, Scanning, and Reading

If we told you to skim the passage, would you know what that means? If you do, great. If you don't, don't worry. *Skimming* is something many readers feel they're supposed to do on a timed test, but they don't know what it means and therefore can't do it.

Reading needs your brain on full power. You're reading words, and your brain is processing what they mean and drawing conclusions. Reading is watching the road, searching for directional signs, and glancing at the scenery, all for the purpose of trying to figure out where the road is leading.

Skimming means reading only a few words. When you work the passage, your brain can try to process key parts that build to the main idea, but you don't necessarily need to identify the main idea just yet. Working the questions and answers tells you the main idea and all the important details. Skimming is reading only the directional signs and ignoring the scenery.

Scanning needs very little of your brain. Use your eyes. Look, don't think, and don't try to process for understanding. Scanning is looking for Volkswagen Beetles in a game of Slug Bug.

When you're working the passage, you can skim or scan, but you shouldn't be reading. Read windows of text when you work the questions.

> Depending on where you're from, Slug Bug might be known as Punch Buggy.

If you feel you can't turn your brain off when you work the passage, or you even skim and scan too slowly, then focus only on the first sentence of each paragraph. You may find fewer lead words, but you will give yourself more time to spend on working the questions and answers and can find the lead words then.

Time yourself to work the following passage, focusing only on the first sentence of each paragraph. We've actually made it impossible to do otherwise. Look for the lead words you underlined in Step 1 and underline any that you see.

Such relatively reliable insights as we have into the nature of Halley's comet's nucleus derive largely from the work done by the Giotto imaging team. Blah blah blah blah blah blah blah blah. Blah blah. Blah blah blah blah blah blah blah blah blah.
5 Blah blah blah. Blah blah blah blah blah blah blah blah blah. Blah blah blah blah blah blah blah blah blah. Blah blah blah blah blah blah blah blah.

Discernibility of detail varies at different points in the photograph. Blah blah blah blah blah blah blah blah. Blah blah. Blah
10 blah blah blah blah blah blah blah blah. Blah blah blah. Blah blah blah blah blah blah blah blah blah. Blah blah blah blah blah blah blah blah blah. Blah blah blah blah blah blah blah blah blah. Blah blah blah blah blah blah blah blah. Blah blah blah blah blah blah blah blah blah. Blah blah blah blah blah blah blah blah blah.

15 The Giotto photographs have allowed investigators to conclude that the surface of the nucleus is rough. Blah blah blah blah blah blah blah blah. Blah blah. Blah blah blah blah blah blah blah blah blah. Blah blah blah. Blah blah blah blah blah blah blah blah blah. Blah blah blah blah blah blah blah blah blah.
20 Blah blah blah blah blah blah blah blah blah. Blah blah blah blah blah blah blah blah blah.

On the other hand, the Giotto photographs reveal virtually nothing on the interior of the comet's nucleus or its rotational period. Blah blah blah blah blah blah blah blah. Blah blah. Blah
25 blah blah blah blah blah blah blah. Blah blah blah. Blah blah blah blah blah blah blah blah blah. Blah blah blah blah blah blah blah blah. Blah blah blah blah blah blah blah blah blah. Blah blah blah blah blah blah blah blah.

Moreover, the comet's overall dimensions were already
30 known to an approximation, and on this basis Rickman took the volume as 500–550 cubic centimeters. Blah blah blah blah blah blah blah blah. Blah blah. Blah blah blah blah blah blah blah blah blah. Blah blah blah. Blah blah blah blah blah blah blah blah blah. Blah blah blah blah blah blah blah blah blah. Blah blah blah blah
35 blah blah blah blah blah.

Using an analogous technique, R. Z. Sagdeev and colleagues arrived at a value of 0.2 to 1.5 grams per cubic centimeter. Blah blah blah blah blah blah blah blah. Blah blah. Blah blah blah blah blah blah blah blah blah. Blah blah blah. Blah blah blah blah blah
40 blah blah blah blah. Blah blah blah blah blah blah blah blah blah. Blah blah blah blah blah blah blah blah blah. Blah blah blah blah blah blah blah blah.

Finally, Zdenek Sekanina and Stephen M. Larson studied the rotational period by first processing images of 1920 photographs
45 in an attempt to improve the image of spiral dust features. Blah blah blah blah blah blah blah blah. Blah blah. Blah blah blah blah blah blah blah blah blah. Blah blah blah. Blah blah blah blah blah blah blah blah blah. Blah blah blah blah blah blah blah blah blah.

Let's see what you learned in less than three minutes.

Now Questions

You should have several Now questions.

- Questions 32, 34, 37, and 39 all have line references.
- Questions 31, 33, 35, 36, 38, and 40 all have lead words, great lead words in some.
- The lead words in 31 can be found in the first sentence of the sixth paragraph.
- The lead words in 33 can be found in the first sentence of the last paragraph.
- The lead words in 35 and 36 can be found in the first sentence of the first paragraph.
- The lead words in 40 can be found in the first sentence of the fifth paragraph.
- Nine of the ten questions have been located, and the great lead word in 38 should be easy to find when you're given the whole passage and not a lot of "blahs."

> ### The Pencil Trick
> When you have to look harder for a lead word, use your pencil or cursor to sweep each and every line from beginning to end. This will keep your brain from reading and let your eye look for the word.

The Passage

You also have a great outline of the passage. The topic sentences have drawn a map of the passage organization, and the transition words tell you how the paragraphs connect.

- What is the first paragraph about? The nucleus of Halley's Comet and the Giotto camera.
- The second paragraph? The details that the photographs show.
- The third? What scientists have learned from the photographs.
- How does the fourth paragraph relate to the third? *On the other hand* tells you that it is different from the third.
- How does the fifth paragraph relate to the fourth? *Moreover* tells you that they are similar.
- What is the sixth paragraph about? It's still on *volume*, which came up in the fifth paragraph.
- What is the last paragraph? It's the conclusion, which the transition word *Finally* makes clear.

Topic Sentences and Transition Words

Think of your own papers that you write for school. What does a good topic sentence do? It provides at worst an introduction to the paragraph and at best a summary of the paragraph's main idea. What follows are the details that clarify or prove the main idea. And do you care about the details at Step 2? No, you'll focus on the details if and when there is a question on them.

Look for Transition Words

Here are 15 transition words and/or phrases.

- *Despite*
- *However*
- *In spite of*
- *Nonetheless*
- *On the other hand*
- *But*
- *Rather*
- *Yet*
- *Ironically*
- *Notwithstanding*
- *Unfortunately*
- *On the contrary*
- *Therefore*
- *Hence*
- *Consequently*

Transition words are like great road signs. They show you the route, direct you to a detour, and get you back on the path of the main idea. When you *skim*, you're focusing on topic sentences and transition words.

In the next chapter, we'll cover more strategies for steps 3 through 6. But now it's time to try another passage.

Reading Drill 1

Use the Basic Approach on the following passage. Time yourself to complete it in 8–10 minutes. Check your answers in Chapter 25.

Passage III

HUMANITIES: This passage is adapted from the article "The Buzz in Our Pockets" by Danielle Panizzi (©2013 by Telephony Biquarterly).

To the extent that it has a creator at all, the text message, or SMS (short message service), was created in the early 1980s by Friedhelm Hillebrand and Bernard Ghillebaert, who wanted to find a way to send data over the parts of phone lines that were
5   not being used in normal telephony. The first text messages were 160 characters long. Hillebrand suggested that "160 characters was sufficient to express most messages succinctly," citing typical postcard and Telex lengths.

Although this form might seem to limit the way we commu-
10 nicate, the text message is the most widely used data application in the world, with about 80% of all cellphone users (3.5 billion people) using the medium. Text messages are already a part of the cultural landscape: they are mentioned in rap and rock songs; they show up in billboards and advertisements selling just
15 about anything; and they've even cropped up in serious novels like Jonathan Franzen's *Freedom* and David Foster Wallace's *The Pale King*. Text messages, in fact, move the whole plot of Martin Scorsese's 2006 film *The Departed,* a critical success and eventual Oscar winner for Best Picture.

20 But the text message is more than a cultural fad. It's part of a broader shift in the way we connect with one another. Speaking on an actual telephone is basically defunct in 2013, not only for the economic reason that "time is money" and a text is quicker than a call, but also for a much older desire in all of us for
25 permanence. With a text message, we've got a record of all our communications, and although we may cast them off quickly, even the shortest text message requires more pre-thought than a verbalized remark: we can't go back to our recorded calls, but our texts live on our phones for as long as we choose to keep
30 them there. The text message has made even our most fleeting conversations permanent—and in this way, the text harkens back to one of the earliest modes of communication, even before the telephone: the letter.

Although America was a sprawling, disparate place even
35 before the War for Independence in the 1770s, its residents always felt the need to communicate with those farther and farther away. Ships carried people back and forth across the Atlantic Ocean, but they also carried correspondence, and we could even say that our very nation was founded in these writ-
40 ten communiqués: much of what we know about that era comes from these letters. One day, text messages may provide a similar record of our own moment.

But it would be naïve to say that these quick notes are anything like the voluminous correspondence of ages past. In
45 her recent monograph *Write Me a Letter,* Kari Fields wonders if the sophisticated concentration of that historical correspondence is even available to us anymore. Fields warns not only that we may have been "dumbed down" by our technologies but also that we may have lost one of the essential elements of the human
50 experience. "The content of our communication with each other ('I'll be late to work today'; 'I'll be home at 10'; or even, 'I love you') may be ultimately the same," Fields concedes, "but the real communication lives in the form—the tone, the unsteady hand on a particular word, the hasty erasures." Perhaps Fields herself
55 is missing the point: naysayers have said that everything from the printing press, to the radio, to the movie screen, to Google, has compromised the way we think and understand. It makes no difference whether a letter takes a month by boat, two weeks by Pony Express, a few days by post, or a few seconds by email.
60 The medium, it seems safe to say, is not the message.

However, Fields is aware of all these earlier changes. She is as sophisticated a historian of these media as anyone working in the field today. We cannot deny that text messages and the Internet have isolated us from one another like never before. In
65 addition to placing us alone at our computers or on our phones, these new technologies also force us to spread our limited attention spans thinner and thinner. We may have to think about the text messages we send, but we typically do so while looking at something else on the web, listening to music or podcasts,
70 or seconds before or after sending messages to someone else. It's not merely that our communications are getting shorter and shorter; it's that the time we have for real interactions has shrunk. All of these new devices are supposed to be time-savers, but what they've really given us is more time to use the devices,
75 to the point that a year without seeing a dear friend seems less daunting than a few hours without the phone.

Still, text messages may be our last, best surrogate for the intimacy of "real" communication. As Herberth Chacon observes in *I Like You...on Facebook*, "Whatever the limitations of this
80 new medium of communication, people are interacting on a day-to-day basis with more people than their ancestors might have met in a lifetime." Text messages have gained such currency because, for all their flaws, they do bring us together. After all, even if the words "I love you" are flashing up impersonally on
85 a screen—stripped of all tone and affection—the words are nice to hear nonetheless, and even if our new definition of "friends" may not square with the old definition, it's nice to know there's a world out there that's paying attention to us.

21. The main idea of the passage is that:

    A. telephone conversations are defunct because they are so impermanent.
    B. telephones took the place of serious long-letter writing.
    C. text messages do not provide real interactions for the people who send them.
    D. text messaging is a popular medium whose social effects are debatable.

22. Based on the passage, with which of the following statements would Fields most likely agree?

    F. The frequent use of text messaging can limit people's other human experiences.
    G. Internet users lost their capacity for human experience when they started using Google.
    H. Text messages provide a quick, intimate way for people to communicate.
    J. Text messages force people to write more thoughtfully to one another.

23. How does the passage's author directly support her claim that the text message is more than a simple message?

    A. By citing examples from American culture in which text messaging plays a role
    B. By describing famous novels about the cultural role of texting in American society
    C. By listing the accomplishments of the two German men who created the medium of text messaging
    D. By showing that text messaging was initially limited to 160 characters

24. The passage's author most likely discusses the era before the War of Independence to:

    F. demonstrate how historical figures refused to use text-messaging technology.
    G. prompt the reader to do more research into the history of communication.
    H. give a fun digression in an otherwise dry discussion of communication media.
    J. show that forms of communication can provide historical records.

25. Which of the following people think or act in a way that is most similar to that of the naysayers described in the fifth paragraph (lines 43–60)?

    A. Scientists who see improvements in medicine as an improvement in the quality of life
    B. Sports journalists who say that a change in rules will destroy the integrity of a sport
    C. Novelists who prefer to write on computers rather than with pen and paper
    D. Historians who would prefer to read official documents rather than letters

26. According to the passage, of the following, who were the earliest contributors to the development of the medium of the text message?

    F. Fields and Chacon
    G. Scorsese and Franzen
    H. Franzen and Wallace
    J. Hillebrand and Ghillebaert

27. A character in a short story published in 1994 had this to say about text messages:

    > Say what you will about the "decline of real interaction"—I've had plenty of them that would've felt a lot more real if they'd happened in a sentence or two rather than a two-hour phone conversation.

    Based on the passage, would Hillebrand agree or disagree with this statement?

    A. Disagree, because 160 characters proved to be an inadequate number of characters.
    B. Disagree, because he ultimately believed that most communication should occur by letter.
    C. Agree, because he felt that the telephone was no longer an effective communicator.
    D. Agree, because he thought that 160 characters was adequate to express most messages concisely.

28. Based on the passage, why might *The Departed* have been considered a film interested in contemporary issues?

    F. It made a recent communication medium, text messaging, central to its story.
    G. Its actors spoke in favor of text messaging, and the medium exploded in popularity after the film's release.
    H. It won an important award in honor of the quality of the filmmaking.
    J. It showed that letter writing was no longer a sufficient way to communicate.

29. Based on the passage, when the author cites the saying "time is money" (line 23), she most likely means that a text message:

    A. is an inexpensive way to send a message.
    B. keeps a long-lasting record of people's conversations.
    C. is a quick way for people to communicate.
    D. allows an intimacy that can otherwise take a long time to develop.

30. Based on the passage, Chacon suggests the number of people with whom people's ancestors might have had interactions in order to:

    F. state that the family unit is no longer as important as it once was.
    G. suggest that new media can connect people in new ways.
    H. imply that people in older times should have traveled more.
    J. encourage readers to explore what their ancestors said in letters.

Summary

- Use the 6-Step Basic Approach.

- Step 1: Preview. Read the blurb, and map the questions. Star line and paragraph references and underline lead words.

- Step 2: Work the Passage.
  - Up Front: Finish in 2–3 minutes. Look for and underline lead words. One option is to focus on only the first sentence of each paragraph.
  - As You Go: Work the passage as you go through the questions.

- Step 3: Select and Understand a Question. Do Now questions that are easy to answer or whose answers are easy to find. Save for Later questions that are both hard to find and hard to answer. Make sure that you understand what each question is asking.

- Step 4: Read What You Need. Read a window of 5–10 lines to find your answer.

- Step 5: Predict the Correct Answer. Predict the answer based on the text. If possible, underline the prediction in the text.

- Step 6: Use POE. Eliminate answers that don't match the prediction.

- Skim and scan when you work the passage.

- Read windows of text when you work the questions.

- Look for topic sentences and transition words.

Chapter 19
Advanced Reading Skills

In this lesson, we'll help you hone your skills to crack specific question types and the most challenging of difficult text. We'll also build on your mastery of the 6-Step Basic Approach by teaching you advanced POE (Process of Elimination) strategies.

LATER QUESTIONS

On the Reading test, some questions appear in unique formats that make them stand out among the Referral and Reasoning questions. These questions still require you to show your understanding of what is directly stated or what is implied. However, it's useful to have specific strategies to crack these.

The 6-Step Basic Approach

Step 1: Preview. Check the blurb, and map the questions. Underline lead words and star line or paragraph references.

Step 2: Work the Passage.
- Up Front: Spend 2–3 minutes reading the passage.
- As You Go: Work the passage as you go through the questions.

Step 3: Select and Understand a Question. Use your POOD to find Now, Later, and Never questions. Make sure you understand what each question is asking.

Step 4: Read What You Need. Read 5–10 lines from the passage.

Step 5: Predict the Correct Answer. Predict the answer using the text.

Step 6: Use POE.

Negatives

The test writers can throw a curveball at you when they ask a question in the negative using EXCEPT, LEAST, or NOT to twist the task. These questions are inherently tricky. What's right is wrong, and the right answer is the one that's wrong. Clear as a bell, isn't it?

No wonder it's so easy for your brain to trip all over itself. You may even start off trying to find the one choice that is false. But you somehow lose sight of the trap, and when you come across one of the answers in the passage, you think, "Eureka! This answer is true. I found it right here." Of course it's "right" in the passage: two other answer choices are somewhere in the passage as well. It's the choice that isn't in the passage that is the "right" answer.

Here's a better approach. Let's take a look at a question after it has been previewed in Step 1.

33. The passage mentions transportation of bees by river in all of the following countries EXCEPT:

    A. Scotland.
    B. France.
    C. Poland.
    D. Egypt.

When you map the questions, underline *transportation of bees by river* and *countries,* but don't underline or mark *EXCEPT.* Wait until you work the question to deal with the trick.

This is a Referral question. If the negative weren't there, it would be easy to answer. What country transports bees by river? But it wouldn't be easy to find the answer, since there is no line or paragraph reference, and none of these lead words qualify as great.

Occasionally, an EXCEPT question will come with a line or paragraph reference to help narrow down your search, but most times they don't. The answers can be scattered throughout the passage or grouped together in one paragraph.

That's why you should always do a negative question Later. By the time you get to it, you should be able to identify where in the passage you'll find at least some of the answers, or you will have narrowed down where to look.

When you do work this question, mark the EXCEPT so your eye can help your brain. You could double underline it. You can circle it and jot down two double exclamation points. You can cross it out altogether and write "True/False," or "T/F." On the ACT Online Test, use your whiteboard, write down ABCD, and mark the answers T/F. Do whatever you need to keep yourself focused on the goal: identify the one answer that is not like the others.

33. The passage mentions <u>transportation of bees by river</u> in all of the following <u>countries</u> <u>EXCEPT</u>:

   A. Scotland.
   B. France.
   C. Poland.
   D. Egypt.

For question 33, the answers happen to be grouped into the same paragraph, something you would have found easier to spot by using the great lead words in the answers. Always let the answers help in an EXCEPT question.

> ### Answer Choice Lead Words
> In any type of question, lead words may be found in the answers instead of the question.

Now use POE. Locate the countries in the window of text, and read to find out which use rivers. When you find one, cross it off in the answers.

> In Scotland, after the best of the Lowland bloom is past, the bees are carried in carts to the Highlands and set free on the heather hills. In France, too, and in Poland, they are carried from pasture to pasture among orchards and fields in the same way and
> 5 along the rivers in barges to collect the honey of the delightful vegetation of the banks. In Egypt they are taken far up the Nile and floated slowly home again, gathering the honey-harvest of the various fields on the way, timing their movements in accord with the seasons. Were similar methods pursued in California,
> 10 the productive season would last nearly all the year.

The correct answer is (A). All four countries are listed, but only Scotland doesn't involve *rivers*.

Negative questions can be more complicated when the question type itself is Reasoning instead of Referral.

Particularly difficult are questions that ask what is NOT answered by the passage. These essentially require four times the amount of work, since you have to look for four answers instead of just one. Sometimes, the question is asked but not answered, and in others, the topic may not arise at all, both of which can frustrate you and make you waste a lot of time, scouring the passage over and over. That's why Negative questions can be good candidates for Never. If you do work a negative question, always use POE. Cross off the ones that you know are true. If you're stuck between two, or even among three, don't waste that much more time before forcing yourself to guess and move on.

These next two questions would both be the last questions you do, and you would have gained a good grasp of the passage, even the details, by reading small windows as you worked the rest of the questions.

For the purposes of this exercise, don't worry about time. Read the excerpt of the passage, and use POE.

36. Which of the following questions is NOT answered by information given in the passage?

F. How many bee ranches might be successfully established in the Sierra Mountains?
G. What types of flowers attract bees?
H. Where did the honeybees in the Sierra Mountains come from?
J. How much honey is produced by bee-trees in the Sierra Mountains?

38. Which of the following statements is LEAST supported by the passage?

F. The Sierra Mountains have the appropriate requirements to support bee ranching activities.
G. Bees flourish in the Sierra Mountains in part because the area is not hospitable to traditional cattle ranching.
H. The presence of bees in the Sierra Mountains prevents sheep from grazing in certain areas.
J. Bee-ranching is an economically viable and environmentally sound enterprise.

The Sierra region is the largest of the three main divisions of the bee-lands of the State, and the most regularly varied in its subdivisions, owing to its gradual rise from the level of the Central Plain to the alpine summits. Up through the forest region, to a height of about 9,000 feet above sea-level, there are ragged patches of manzanita and five or six species of ceanothus, called deer-brush or California lilac. These are the most important of all the honey-bearing bushes of the Sierra.

From swarms that escaped their owners in the lowlands, the honey-bee is now generally distributed throughout the whole length of the Sierra, up to an elevation of 8,000 feet above sea-level. At this height they flourish without care, though the snow every winter is deep. Even higher than this, several bee-trees have been cut, which contained over 200 pounds of honey. Wild bees and butterflies have been seen feeding at a height of 13,000 feet above the sea.

The destructive action of sheep has not been so general on the mountain pastures as on those of the great plain. Fortunately, neither sheep nor cattle care to feed on the manzanita, spiraea, or adenostoma; these fine honey-bushes are too stiff and tall or grow in places too rough and inaccessible to be trodden under foot. Also the canyon walls and gorges, which form so considerable a part of the area of the range, while inaccessible to domestic sheep, are well fringed with honey-shrubs and contain thousands of lovely bee-gardens, lying hidden in narrow side-canyons and recesses fenced with avalanche taluses, and on the top of flat, projecting headlands, where only bees would think to look for them.

The plow has not yet invaded the forest region to any appreciable extent, nor has it accomplished much in the foot-hills. Thousands of bee-ranches might be established along the margin of the plain and up to a height of 4,000 feet, wherever water could be obtained. The climate at this elevation admits of the making of permanent homes, and by moving the hives to higher pastures as the lower pass out of bloom, the annual yield of honey would be nearly doubled. The foot-hill pastures, as we have seen, fail about the end of May; those of the chaparral belt and lower forests are in full bloom in June, those of the upper and alpine region in July, August, and September.

Of all the upper flower fields of the Sierra, Shasta is the most honeyful, and may yet surpass in fame the celebrated honey hills of Hybla and hearthy Hymettus. In this flowery wilderness the bees rove and revel, rejoicing in the bounty of the sun, clambering eagerly through bramble and hucklebloom, ringing the myriad bells of the manzanita, now humming aloft among polleny willows and firs, now down on the ashy ground among gilias and buttercups, and anon plunging deep into snowy banks of cherry and buckthorn....

Here's How to Crack Them

Work questions 36 and 38 as your last questions. For 36, double underline, highlight, circle, or cross off the NOT when you work it. As you find the answers to the answer choices—that is, the answers to the questions in the answer choices—cross off those choices or mark them on your whiteboard. Choice (F) is answered in lines 30–32. Choice (G) is answered in lines 6–8 and again in 18–21. Choice (H) is answered in lines 9–11. Choice (J) is never answered, and it is therefore the correct answer.

Question 38 is less specific and less dependent on detail than is question 36. Remember, the answers to your questions should all agree with each other, at least in terms of reinforcing the main points. Double underline, highlight, circle, or cross off the LEAST, and use POE for any answer that doesn't reinforce the theme in the rest of the questions. Choice (H) is not supported by the passage and is therefore the correct answer. Choices (F) and (J) describe positive benefits of bees to the Sierra Mountains, and they would likely be the easiest choices to eliminate right away. Choice (G) is supported by lines 18–28.

○

Vocabulary in Context

In some Referral questions, you'll have to determine the meaning of a word or phrase as it's used in context. The level of the vocabulary can vary, and many of these questions test secondary meanings of relatively common words.

Don't Know the Word?

If the Vocabulary in Context question tests a more difficult word that you're familiar with, you can still try to read the context to see if you can come up with your own word that fits the meaning, and then use POE among the answers. But if you can't eliminate three choices, guess from what's left and move on. Similarly, if you are pressed for time and need to get to the next passage, mark this a Never. Choose your LOTD and move on.

You don't need to read a full window of 5–10 lines for Vocabulary in Context questions, but you do need to read at least the full sentence to determine the meaning in its context. Cross off the phrase (or simply ignore the word on the ACT Online Test), and try to substitute your own word. Then move to the answers, and use POE to eliminate choices that don't match your word. Beware the most common definition! Vocabulary in Context questions often test a secondary meaning.

Let's try an example.

―――――――――――――◯―――――――――――――

The plow has not yet invaded the forest region to any appreciable extent, nor has it accomplished much in the foot-hills.
30 Thousands of bee-ranches might be established along the margin of the plain and up to a height of 4000 feet, wherever water could be obtained. The climate at this elevation admits of the making of permanent homes, and by moving the hives to higher pastures as the lower pass out of bloom, the annual yield of honey would
35 be nearly doubled. The foot-hill pastures, as we have seen, fail about the end of May; those of the chaparral belt and lower forests are in full bloom in June, those of the upper and alpine region in July, August, and September.

37. As it is used in line 32, the phrase *admits of* most nearly means:

    A. makes possible.
    B. grants permission.
    C. confesses guilt.
    D. leaves out.

Here's How to Crack It

Admits is a common word, but it has different definitions depending on the context. The phrase *admits of* may be a less common phrase, but if you cross it out and read the sentence, you may come up with a word like "allows." Choice (A) works the same way "allows" does, and it's the correct answer. Choice (B) is close, but a climate can't literally *permit* something. Choice (C) is tempting if you don't use the context of the sentence, since *confessing guilt* is a correct definition of *admits* in another context. Choice (D), *leaves out*, does not match the meaning of "allows."

―――――――――――――◯―――――――――――――

Roman Numerals

Roman numeral questions show up on the Reading test very rarely. They can be used in a Referral question or in a Reference question. They may come with line references or great lead words, or they may not. Use those factors to determine when to work the question, but in general, Roman numeral questions are good choices for Later when you know the passage better.

When you do work a Roman numeral question, be efficient. Choose the easiest of the Roman numerals to look up in the passage. Once you know yes or no, go to the answer choices and use POE. Look up only the Roman numerals that are still in the running among the answers.

Let's try an example.

They consider the lilies and roll into them, and, like lilies, they toil not for they are impelled by sun-power, as water-wheels by water-power; and when the one has plenty of high-pressure water, the other plenty of sunshine, they hum and quiver alike.
5 Sauntering in the Shasta bee-lands in the sun-days of summer, one may readily infer the time of day from the comparative energy of bee-movements alone—drowsy and moderate in the cool of the morning, increasing in energy with the ascending sun, and, at high noon, thrilling and quivering in wild ecstasy, then gradually
10 declining again to the stillness of night.

39. The passage describes the movement of the bees during the day as which of the following?

I.   Drowsy and moderate
II. Thrilling and quivering
III. Cool and still

A. I only
B. III only
C. II and III only
D. I and II only

Here's How to Crack It

Work efficiently. Use the lead words in the Roman numerals to find them in the passage, beginning with I. *Drowsy* and *moderate* are used in line 7 to describe the bees in the morning. Eliminate all choices without I, which leaves you with just II to review: neither I nor III occurs in either of the remaining choices. *Trilling* and *quivering* are used in line 9 to describe the bees at high noon. Choice (D) is correct.

Dual Reading Passages

You will also see a "Dual Passage" in Reading. You'll see a passage like this on the Science test, too: they give two separate passages with questions about each passage individually and then questions about both together.

The Basic Approach still applies, but work the passages one at a time.

Here's the strategy we'll be using in this section:

1. **Preview.** Read the Blurb and decide which passage to do first. If you're taking the pencil-and-paper ACT, map the Questions for that passage.

2. **Work the Passage.** If you're working the passage Up Front, work the passage you're doing first.

3. **Select and Understand a Question.** As always, work the easier questions first.

4. **Read What You Need.** It can be easier to find the correct answer because the passages are short.

5. **Predict the Correct Answer.**

6. **Use POE.**

7. **Repeat.** If you're taking the pencil-and-paper ACT, map the Questions for the second passage; then repeat steps 2–6. Answer the questions about both passages last.

A NOTE ON THE GOLDEN THREAD

As you may have noticed, correct answers seem to repeat in a lot of ACT passages. It almost seems like sometimes if you get one answer, you can get three more with the same information. We call this phenomenon "The Golden Thread": some main idea or topic that threads through many of the answer choices.

On Dual Passages, it's more important than ever to find the Golden Thread. If you think about it, the questions that ask about both passages are really just variations on the theme, "What do these two passages have to do with each other?"

As you read through the two passages separately, try to answer this question even if only in a vague way. "What's the link between these two passages?" "Why are these passages on the same page together?" Any kinds of answers you can generate to these "Golden Thread"-type questions will help you down the line.

Here is what one of the passages will look like. Note how ACT has kindly separated the questions for you; on the ACT Online Test, the questions will be grouped together, but instead of a box above the first question for each passage, all the questions will have a label indicating if they ask about Passage A, Passage B, or both.

SOCIAL SCIENCE: Passage A is adapted from the 2015 *Time* Magazine article "What We Can Learn From Coca-Cola's Biggest Blunder" by James C. Cobb. Passage B is adapted from the 2007 *Washington Post* article "The Flop Heard Round the World" by Peter Carlson.

Passage A

Network executives had been understandably hesitant to interrupt the nation's most popular daytime soap opera. Yet viewers raised few complaints after ABC's Peter Jennings broke into General Hospital, on July 10, 1985, to tell them that, bow-
5 ing to public outrage and stunned by the anemic sales figures of its replacement, Coca-Cola was moving to put its original soft-drink formula back on the market.

This decidedly welcome news came just 79 days after the traditional version had been pulled abruptly to make way
10 for "New Coke." The almost palpable chagrin enveloping the company's official press briefing on the about-face was a far cry from the unrestrained bravado that had marked CEO Roberto Goizueta's announcement back on April 23 that Coca-Cola was scrapping its jealously guarded secret formula, which had
15 gone unchanged for almost a century, in favor of a new mixture that he promised would be a "bolder," "rounder" and more "harmonious" flavor. He failed to mention that it would also be markedly sweeter—doing so would have meant admitting that the more sugary appeal of Pepsi was steadily encroaching
20 on Coke's market share. The radical change struck consumer-marketing experts as more than a little risky, though Goizueta insisted at the time that he and his colleagues considered it "the surest move ever made."

Not for long, for company switchboards were soon drown-
25 ing in a torrent of as many as 8,000 calls a day from irate consumers suddenly deprived of the dependable drink that had always suited them just fine. Like the otherwise matronly lady interviewed by *Newsweek* at an Atlanta supermarket who needed but a single sip of New Coke to declare "it sucks," most who
30 rallied to pop-up protest groups like "Old Coca-Cola Drinkers of America" may have simply been taking their cue from their palates. Yet others appeared to be speaking more from their hearts as they likened Coke's switcheroo to a blasphemous assault on their most cherished icons and precepts. Some
35 compared it to burning the flag or rewriting the Constitution. "God and Coca Cola" had been "the only two things in my life," one complained in a letter, "now you have taken one of those things away from me."

Stunned by this fierce and unrelenting backlash, not to
40 mention New Coke's disappointing sales, Coke's spin-meisters scrambled to put the best possible face on the fiasco. Company President Donald Keough observed that, despite the extensive and expensive taste-testing that seemed to confirm New Coke's surefire appeal, there had simply been no way to gauge the
45 "deep and abiding emotional attachment to original Coca-Cola felt by so many people."

Passage B

Fifty years ago today, Don Mazzella skipped out of school to see the hot new car that everybody was talking about, the hot new car that almost nobody had actually seen.

50 Ford Motor Co. had proclaimed it "E-Day." Mazzella and two buddies sneaked out of East Side High School in Newark, N.J., and hiked 13 blocks to Foley Ford so they could cast their gaze upon the much-ballyhooed new car that had been kept secret from the American public until its release that day.

55 It was called the Edsel.

"The line was around the block," recalls Mazzella, now 66 and an executive in a New Jersey consulting firm. "People were coming from all over to see this car. You couldn't see it from the street. The only way you could see it was to walk into
60 the showroom and look behind a curtain."

Mazzella and his truant friends waited their turn, thrilled to be there. "Back then for teenagers, cars were the be-all and end-all," he explains. They'd read countless articles about the Edsel and seen countless ads that touted it as the car of the future. But
65 they hadn't seen the car. Ford kept it secret, building excitement by coyly withholding it from sight, like a strip-tease dancer.

Finally, Mazzella and his friends reached the showroom. Finally, they were permitted to peek behind the curtain. They saw a cream-colored car with a strange oval grille that looked
70 like a big chrome O.

"We looked at it and said, 'What?'" Mazzella recalls. "It was just a blah car. I remember my friend Joe Grandi, who later became a Newark cop—he had a gruff voice, and he said, 'This is what we waited all this time for?' We all felt betrayed."

75 They weren't alone. The rest of America was equally dis-appointed. The Edsel fizzled. It flopped. It tanked. It became a national joke, the car that launched a million punch lines. By November 1959, when Ford finally mercy-killed the Edsel, it had lost an estimated $250 million—nearly $2 billion in
80 today's dollars.

Forget New Coke or the Susan B. Anthony dollar or the over-hyped Segway scooter or those pathetic dot-coms that went belly up in the late '90s. The Edsel was the most colossal, stupendous, and legendary blunder in the history of American
85 marketing.

11. Which of the following statements regarding New Coke is best supported by Passage A?

- **A.** Despite record sales, New Coke was pulled from the market just 79 days after its release.
- **B.** New Coke was launched in an attempt to compete with a rival soft drink manufacturer.
- **C.** Coca-Cola executives were initially hesitant to launch New Coke.
- **D.** In public statements, Coca-Cola executives eventually admitted the failure of New Coke.

12. Which of the following explains how Passage A characterizes the failure of New Coke?

- **F.** It happened gradually and was initially unnoticed by Coca-Cola executives.
- **G.** It happened quickly and dramatically.
- **H.** It was spearheaded by underground consumer protest groups.
- **J.** It occurred only after the renewed success of the classic formula.

13. Passage A quotes Roberto Goizueta at the end of the second paragraph in order to

- **A.** support the idea that the launch of New Coke was inherently risky.
- **B.** suggest that consumers and executives rarely agree on matters of product innovation.
- **C.** emphasize the misguided sentiments of the promoters of New Coke.
- **D.** provide further evidence that Pepsi would continue to dominate the soft drink market.

14. Which of the following events referenced in Passage A occurred first chronologically?

- **F.** Peter Jennings's announcement to soap opera audiences
- **G.** The launch of New Coke
- **H.** New Coke's disappointing sales
- **J.** Increased market share by Pepsi

15. As used in lines 33–34, the "blasphemous assault" is most nearly similar to

- **A.** "a torrent of as many as 8,000 calls a day" (line 25).
- **B.** "pop-up protest groups" (line 30).
- **C.** "burning the flag" (line 35).
- **D.** "unrelenting backlash" (line 39).

16. Which of the following statements in Passage B is used to convey irony?

- **F.** "hot new car" (lines 48–49)
- **G.** "much-ballyhooed" (line 53)
- **H.** "strip-tease dancer" (line 66)
- **J.** "legendary blunder" (line 84)

17. Much of Passage B focuses on Don Mazzella because

- **A.** he was typical of the type of customer for whom the Edsel was created.
- **B.** he waited in line to buy the Edsel on the day of its unveiling.
- **C.** he was too young to properly appreciate the Edsel.
- **D.** his reaction to the Edsel was typical of that of many Americans in the 1950s.

18. A similarity between the two passages is that they both

- **F.** examine their topics in an objective manner.
- **G.** describe the reactions of ordinary people to new products.
- **H.** assert that product innovations are generally unwise ventures.
- **J.** incorporate advice to corporations about how to avoid product failure.

19. An element in Passage B that is not present in Passage A is a reference to

- **A.** specific information regarding product market share.
- **B.** public opinion.
- **C.** other failed products.
- **D.** quotations from experts.

20. If advertisers for New Coke had used tactics similar to those used to promote the Edsel, they would most likely have

- **F.** run ads promoting a new secret formula but not allowed anyone to taste it until the day it was launched.
- **G.** kept the launch day of New Coke a secret until its unveiling.
- **H.** limited the number of ads promoting New Coke.
- **J.** promised that it would improve upon an old formula.

How to Work Through a Dual-Passage Reading Section

Step 1: Preview

As the blurb indicates, these passages are adapted from a couple of essays. It doesn't tell much more than that. A quick count will show that there are more questions about Passage A than there are about Passage B. Let's do Passage A first!

If you're taking the pencil-and-paper ACT, map the questions for Passage A. Lead words include *New Coke*, *failure*, *Roberto Goizueta*, *Jennings*, *Pepsi*, and *blasphemous assault*.

Step 2: Work the Passage

Work Passage A either Up Front or As You Go. Let's work this one As You Go. Before you start reading, if you're taking the pencil-and-paper ACT, rearrange the line reference questions chronologically. In this case, the questions appear in this order: 13, 15. Then come the general questions 11, 12, and 14. If you're taking the ACT Online Test, do the questions with highlighted text first, then go back to the other questions; you'll do the questions in the same order for this passage. Either way, you'll be working the passage as you go through the questions, so move on to Step 3.

Step 3: Select and Understand a Question

Start with question 13 and make sure you understand what it is asking. Work the specific questions roughly in chronological order, but remember POOD!

Step 4: Read What You Need

On the pencil-and-paper ACT, for question 13, work the passage through the second paragraph. After you finish Steps 5 and 6 for question 13, continue to read through the passage and stop as you come to the lines in each question. Keep an eye out for lead words from the other questions as you work.

On the ACT Online Test, you'll work the second and third paragraphs as you work questions 13 and 15. Then, go back and work the rest of the passage, looking for lead words from the other questions. When you find a lead word, stop and answer the corresponding question; then return to working the passage.

Step 5: Predict the Correct Answer

After you read the window for the question, make a prediction based on the text.

Step 6: Use POE
Eliminate answers that don't match your prediction.

Step 7: Repeat
After you've worked the general questions for Passage A, repeat Steps 2–6 for Passage B, working questions 16 and 17.

By this point, you have hopefully noticed what unites these passages. Passage A describes the introduction of—and negative reaction to—New Coke. Passage B describes the introduction of—and negative reaction to—the Edsel. Use your POOD to answer questions 18–20, which ask about both passages.

Check your answers here:

11. B
12. G
13. C
14. J
15. C
16. F
17. D
18. G
19. C
20. F

CRITICAL READING
Your use of the 6-Step Basic Approach and your personal order of difficulty (POOD) of both passages and questions should by now make you feel more confident on the Reading test. But you also may still be struggling with time and feel that you just can't work fast enough to get to enough questions.

In Chapter 18, we discussed ways to use your time better when you preview and work the passage. But you may also be wasting time when you work the questions, reading and rereading the window of text, trying to figure out what it's saying. You may have eliminated two answers, but when you're still not sure what the correct answer is, what do you do? You read the window yet again, desperate to figure out the meaning and answer the question in your own words.

We've all been there. Part of what makes standardized tests so evil is how they encourage us to listen to our worst instincts. You can't treat the Reading test as you would a school assignment, and you can't fall prey to your own panicked responses. You have to develop both strategies and skills specific to *this* test.

Critical Thinking

The key to better reading skills is to *think* better, which means to think critically. Getting lost in even a small window of text that makes no sense is like getting lost on unfamiliar roads. You don't stare down at the yellow line. You look around, looking for landmarks and road signs, trying to figure out where you are and where the road is going.

When you're lost in a tough section of text, use topic sentences and transitions as your landmarks and road signs. Don't try to understand every single word. Use the topic sentences to identify what the main point of the paragraph is. Look for transitions to see if points are on the same side or different sides from each other.

Topic Sentences and Main Points

Think of how you write papers for school. A good topic sentence makes clear the main subject of the paragraph, and it may even provide the author's main point on the subject. The rest of the paragraph will be details or examples that explain that point, and it may also include a more explicit conclusion of the main point. If you don't understand the details, read the main point to know what they mean. Examples and details usually come right before or right after the main point. If you don't understand the details, read the sentence before or after to see if it gives you the main point. If you don't understand the main point, read the sentence before or after to see if the details explain it for you.

Let's see how this works. Read the following topic sentence.

> Studies of American middle and high school students have shown that there is considerable uncertainty among students about what behaviors count as cheating.

What's going to come next in the paragraph? It could be examples of the behaviors. It could be an explanation of why students are uncertain. It could even be a statement of a different study that contradicts this one. You would be safe anticipating any of those outcomes, but the anticipation is the key. Don't sit back and wait to see where the road is going. Lean forward and look for the fork in the road or the detour sign telling you to turn around. In other words, look for transitions.

Transitions

The first word or phrase after the topic sentence can tell you what direction you're heading.

Let's look at some choices for our cheating sentence.

If the next words were *In particular*, what does that tell you is coming next? Examples of the behavior.

If the next word were *However*, what does that tell you is coming next? A contradiction to this study.

Transitions play a key role in critical thinking. Look for transitions to announce additional points, contradictory points, cause-and-effect relationships, examples, or conclusions. Here are just a few common transitions.

Additional Points	Cause and Effect Relationships
And	Because
Also	Since
As well	So
In addition	
Furthermore	
Moreover	Examples
	For example
	In particular
Contradictory Points	Such as
Although	
But	
Even though	Conclusions
However	Consequently
Nevertheless	In other words
On the other hand	That is
Rather	Therefore
Yet	Thus

Modifiers

Nouns and verbs reliably give you the facts in a statement, but they don't necessarily provide the author's point. Look at the two adverbs in the prior sentence and see how they helped shape the point. *Reliably* means you can infer that nouns and verbs *almost always* give facts. *Necessarily* modifies the verb phrase *don't provide*. Without it, you could infer that nouns and verbs never give you the point. Adjectives and adverbs are just as useful as transitions, conveying the author's opinion on what would otherwise be a statement of fact.

Consider this sentence.

> Surprisingly, students do not consider sharing notes to be cheating.

The point of this sentence is that *sharing notes* is a form of *cheating*, and the author believes students should know this. If you removed *surprisingly* from the sentence, it's just a factual statement of what students think. On the Reading test, most Reasoning questions involve the author's opinion or main point, or as ACT puts it, "the implied meaning."

Try another.

> Students offered a refreshingly candid explanation for their behavior.

Refreshingly means that the author judged the admission as unexpected but welcome. *Candid* means the students were honest and open.

Translation

When you're struggling to make sense of a window of confusing text, look for transitions and modifiers to help you determine the main point. You may be in the thick of a body paragraph with the topic sentence in the rearview mirror. Instead of focusing on every single word, use the transitions and modifiers to get the general direction of points and the connections between them.

Let's look at a tough window to see how this works.

The strikingly tolerant attitudes demonstrated by the students toward cheating cannot be explained by mere immorality and laziness, but may rather point to a sobering conclusion that high-stakes tests have created a ruthless atmosphere in which
5 students are desperate to succeed at any cost.

Here's How to Crack It

Focus on the transitions and modifiers. *Strikingly* tells you that the author finds the students' tolerance of cheating noteworthy and unusual. The key verb phrase *cannot be explained* directs you away from what <u>is not</u> the cause and the transitions *but* and *rather* direct you to what <u>is</u> the cause. Even if you didn't understand all the vocabulary words, the transitions act as huge road signs that identify the most important part of the sentence. Students don't cheat because of *immorality* and *laziness* but because *high-stakes tests* have made things *ruthless* and *desperate*. Even just knowing which sentence, or which part of the sentence, to focus on will help, along with POE, to find the right answer.

ADVANCED POE SKILLS

When you're stuck on a confusing window of text, the best use of your time is spent working the answers. Reread your window, even to spot transitions and modifiers, in conjunction with working the answers.

In an ideal situation, you read a question, read the window of text looking for your answer, answer the question in your own words, and then work through the answer choices looking for the best match, using POE to get rid of those that don't.

But situations are seldom ideal on the Reading test. When you don't quite understand the window and therefore have no clue about the answer, go straight to working the answers.

The Art of Wrong Answers

If you worked for ACT, you'd have to sit in a cubicle all day writing test questions. The easy part of the job is writing the correct answer. You may even know that before you write the question. The harder part is coming up with three wrong answers. If you didn't write great wrong answers, everyone would get a 36. So you have to come up with temptingly wrong answers.

Let's take a look at some ways to make wrong answers.

Read the following question, correct answer, and text. We don't care about the right answer in this exercise, so you can read it before you read the window.

13. The main point of the fifth paragraph (lines 40–48) is that:

   A. cultural norms affect how students judge cheating behaviors.

The authors of one such study contend that differences between German students and the other students in the study regarding what constitutes cheating can be explained by differences
40 in social norms. In particular, German students viewed passive cheating more as "helping others" or "cooperation" rather than as unethical or immoral behavior. Costa Rican students also were more liberal than Americans in their views of passive cheating, also due to a cultural tendency toward cooperation rather than
45 competition.

Our goal here is to examine *why* the three wrong answers are wrong.

   B. German students consider passive cheating to be unethical and immoral.

Look carefully at lines 43–45. Choice (B) took tempting words out of the passage and garbled them. The passage disproves this answer.

   C. American students have a less liberal view of passive cheating than do Costa Rican students.

Since lines 45–46 say Costa Rican students are *more liberal than Americans*, (C) is true. But it's not the correct answer because it's not the main point of the paragraph.

   D. Russian students do not consider passive cheating to be unethical.

Russian students are not mentioned in this window and have instead been taken from a different window.

Answers can be wrong because they don't match what the passage says, because they answer the wrong question, or because they're not even found in the right window. But no matter how tempting or obvious wrong answers are, they are all easier to understand than 5–10 lines of text, simply because they're shorter. So when you're stuck on tough questions on tough windows, work backwards with the answers.

Work Backwards

Instead of rereading the window to try to determine the meaning, read the answer choices for their meaning. Then see if you can match each back into the passage.

> Read to understand the meaning of the answer choices instead of rereading the window.
>
> - Look for lead words or phrases in the answer choices.
> - Determine if the words match those found in the window.
> - Use POE to cross off choices that don't match the window.

Let's see how this works. Read the following question and window.

> The dictionary defines cheating as unfairly gaining advantage in a given situation by deliberately violating established rules. Cheating behaviors may include plagiarism, copying exam answers, using crib notes, obtaining test questions beforehand (all
> 5 active behaviors), as well as allowing others to copy from you, taking advantage of teacher scoring errors, and failing to report cheating (more passive behaviors). The definition of cheating is not under debate, but the way that students define their behavior, in relation to this definition, and how morally acceptable they
> 10 deem such behavior, is. In other words, there is a large variance regarding which behaviors students consider to be cheating.

13. It can reasonably be inferred that the author provides the dictionary definition of cheating (lines 1–2) in order to:

Take the answer choices one at a time. In each choice, we've put in bold a lead word or phrase in the answer. Can you match these words, or a paraphrased meaning of them, in the window of text?

A. argue that passive behaviors **are more morally acceptable** than active behaviors.

Morally acceptable appears in line 9, but the phrase isn't used to compare *passive* and *active behaviors*. Tempting, but wrong.

B. illustrate what behaviors will get students **expelled or suspended**.

Expelled and *suspended*, or any paraphrases of those words, don't appear anywhere in the window, so (B) can't be the right answer.

C. prove that students **deliberately violate established rules**.

Deliberately violating established rules appears in line 2, but it's used as part of the definition of cheating, not as proof of students' conduct. We've eliminated three answers, so (D) must be right. But always check all four answers to be sure the one you choose is better than the three you've eliminated.

D. show that students may not consider their own **behavior to be cheating**.

Students' *own behavior* is in the last sentence, and (D) matches well the point of that sentence.

Try another example. Choose your own words or phrases out of each answer to work backwards with. Does the passage match the answer?

Patterns of individual cheating behavior in different societies typically reflect their respective normative climates. Students recognize certain activities as cheating and may be able to provide
60 justifications for their unethical behavior in some way. Yet cheating, when identified as such, is overall felt to be wrong. However, an eye-opening study of Russian university students' cheating behaviors by Yulia Poltorak reveals a different type of normative climate that is a unique part of the Communist legacy. According
65 to this study, cheating behavior in Soviet Russia was not only very widespread, but also widely accepted as an appropriate response to social conditions.

12. It can reasonably be inferred by information in the seventh paragraph (lines 57–67) that:

F. cheating in Soviet Russia was widely rejected as an acceptable response.

G. the cold climate in Russian classrooms motivated students to cheat.

H. the normative climate that produced cheating in Soviet Russia may be explained by the role of the Communist legacy.

J. students in Soviet Russia failed to provide justifications for their unethical behavior.

Here's How to Crack It

In (F), you could choose *widely rejected* and try to place it in line 66. The passage disproves this, stating that cheating is *widely accepted*, so cross off (F). Choice (G) misuses the word *climate*, but it also discusses *classrooms*, which are nowhere to be found in the passage. Eliminate it. Choice (H) offers *Communist legacy*, an easy lead word phrase to locate in the passage. Choice (H) could match lines 62–64, so keep it. Choice (J) offers *justifications for their unethical behavior*, words right out of the passage. But the passage doesn't state that Russian students *failed to provide* them. The correct answer is (H).

Reading Drill 2

Use the 6-Step Basic Approach on the following passage, and apply your advanced reading skills. Time yourself to complete in 8–10 minutes. Check your answers in Chapter 25.

Passage III

HUMANITIES: The following passage is adapted from the article "Conquering Jazz" by Patrick Tyrrell (© 2006 by Patrick Tyrrell).

From the time I started playing instruments, I have been intrigued and slightly mystified by the world of jazz. I'm not talking about adventurous, atonal, confusing jazz that normal music listeners have a hard time following. I'm talking about the lively,
5 accessible, beautiful jazz that came of age in the swinging 1920s and 1930s: the simultaneously hip and regal symphonic swing of Duke Ellington and Count Basie; the carnival of contrapuntal melodies that inexplicably harmonize with each other in New Orleans' jazz; the buoyant, atmosphere-touching saxophone solos
10 of Charlie Parker and the young John Coltrane.

The one thing I had always heard about jazz but could never accept was that jazz was an improvised form of music. How could this be?

The trademark of beautiful jazz is the complexity of the
15 music. All the instrumentalists are capable of dizzying arrays of notes and rhythms. The soloists find seemingly impossible transitions from one phrase to the next that are so perfect one would think they had spent weeks trying to devise *just* the right route to conduct safe passage. To think they spontaneously craft
20 these ideas seems preposterous.

My first nervous jabs into the world of jazz came during college. I was in a rock band, but my fellow guitarist and bandmate, Victor, also played in a jazz ensemble. At our practices, I would sometimes show off a new chord I had just "invented" only to
25 have him calmly and confidently name it, "Oh, you mean C-sharp diminished?" Often, in between our band's simplistic rock songs, I would look over and see him playing chord shapes on his guitar I had never seen before. Were we playing the same instrument?

Of course, rock music, as well as most early classical mu-
30 sic, operates within a much simpler harmonic world than does jazz. There are 12 tones in Western music: A-flat, A, B-flat, B, C, D-flat, D, E-flat, E, F, G-flat, and G. There are major chords, which sound happy, and minor chords, which sound sad. Essentially, rock music requires only that you learn the major and
35 minor chord for each of the 12 tones. If you do, you can play 99 percent of all the popular radio songs from the 1950s onward.

Jazz uses the same twelve tones as do rock and classical, but it employs a much more robust variety of chords. Major sevenths, augmented fifths, flat ninths, and diminished chords all add to
40 the depth and detail of the music. These often bizarre-sounding chords toss in subtle hints of chaos and imbalance, adding a worldly imperfection to otherwise standard chord values. Jazz starts sounding better the older you get, just as candy starts tasting too sweet and a bit of bitterness makes for a more appealing flavor.

45 For the most part, Victor's elliptical personality prevented him from ever giving me straightforward explanations when I asked him to divulge the "magician's secrets" of jazz. But I did learn that jazz is only *partly* improvised. The musicians aren't inventing the structure of songs spontaneously, just the specific
50 details and embellishments. A sheet of jazz music doesn't look like a sheet of classical music. There aren't notes all over the page dictating the "ideas." There are just chord names spaced out over time, dictating the "topic of conversation."

There's a legendary book in the jazz world known as *The*
55 *Real Book*. It's a collection of a few hundred classic songs. Open it up in any room full of jazz musicians, and they could play in synchrony for a week. For years, I wanted my own copy, but I had always been too afraid to buy it, afraid that I wouldn't know how to use the book once I had it. Then, at age 30, more than a
60 decade since Victor and I had gone our separate ways, I bought myself a copy. I resolved to learn how to play all the chords on guitar and piano. For the next few months, I quietly plucked away at these strange, new combinations. F-sharp minor-7 flat-5? Each chord was a cryptic message I had to decode and then
65 understand. It felt like being dropped off alone in a country where I didn't speak the language.

But I made progress. Chords that initially took me twenty seconds to figure out started to take only a few. My left hand was becoming comfortable in its role of supplying my right hand
70 with a steady bass line. Meanwhile, to my amazement, my right hand began to improvise melodies that sounded undeniably *jazzy*.

It seemed like the hard work of figuring out the exotic jazz chords had sent new melodic understanding straight to my hand, bypassing my brain entirely. I felt like a witness to performances
75 by detached hands; I couldn't believe that I was the one creating these sounds. I'm sure this feeling will not last, but for now I'm enjoying the rare and miraculous feeling of improvising music that I still consider beyond my abilities.

21. Which chord, if any, does the author eventually conclude is the most confusing jazz chord to play?

   A. The passage does not indicate any such chord.
   B. C-sharp diminished
   C. Major sevenths
   D. F-sharp minor-7 flat-5

22. As it is used in line 47, "magician's secrets" most nearly means:

   F. information on how to play jazz.
   G. forbidden bits of knowledge.
   H. instances of harmless trickery.
   J. the true nature of a private person.

23. As portrayed by the author, Victor responds to the author's *invented* chord with what is best described as:

   A. amazement.
   B. jealousy.
   C. confusion.
   D. nonchalance.

24. The author states that *The Real Book* was something he explored for a few:

   F. years.
   G. months.
   H. weeks.
   J. days.

25. The details in lines 40–44 primarily serve to suggest the:

   A. aspects of jazz's complexity that more mature listeners enjoy.
   B. lack of depth and detail found in rock and classical music.
   C. confusion and awkwardness of standard jazz chord values.
   D. unpleasantly bitter taste of candy that develops with age.

26. In the context of the passage, the author's statement in lines 72–74 most nearly means that:

   F. he was so overworked that his hands could still move, but his thoughts were turned off.
   G. he had accidentally trained his hands to resist being controlled by his brain.
   H. it was easier to decode the exotic jazz chords by pointing at them with his hands.
   J. his hand was capable of playing music that his mind was incapable of fully comprehending.

27. The author implies that F-sharp minor-7 flat-5 is an example of a chord that he:

   A. had little trouble decoding now that he had "The Real Book."
   B. had previously only seen during his travels abroad.
   C. knew how to play on guitar but not on a piano.
   D. initially found confusing and struggled to understand.

28. The passage supports which one of the following conclusions about Victor?

   F. He played music with the author until the author turned 30 years old.
   G. He gave his copy of "The Real Book" to the author as a gift.
   H. He was at one time a member of multiple musical groups.
   J. He invented a chord and named it C-sharp diminished.

29. The passage is best described as being told from the point of view of someone who is:

   A. reviewing the chain of events that led to his career in jazz.
   B. discussing reasons why jazz is less complicated than it seems.
   C. relating his impressions of jazz music and his attempts to play it.
   D. highlighting an important friendship that he had in college.

30. Assessing his early and later experiences with *The Real Book*, the author most strongly implies that it was:

   F. pleasantly strange to begin with but annoyingly familiar by the end.
   G. initially difficult to decipher, but ultimately manageable following diligent practice.
   H. almost impossible to understand because its pages didn't look like sheets of classical music.
   J. very useful as a learning tool, but not useful for more profound study.

Summary

o   Work special question types Later. They require more work than a typical question, and they will become easier to do the later you do them.

o   Double underline, highlight, circle, or cross out negative words EXCEPT, LEAST, or NOT. Use POE to cross off answers that are found in the passage, or use your whiteboard to mark each answer choice "T/F."

o   For Vocabulary in Context questions, read the entire sentence. Cross off the word or phrase and come up with your own word. Use POE to eliminate answers that don't match your word.

o   Work Roman numeral questions efficiently, using POE.

o   Don't waste time on special question types if you can't eliminate three answers. Guess from the choices that are remaining and move on.

o   Use topic sentences, transitions, and modifiers to help translate confusing windows of text.

o   Work backwards with answer choices. Try to match the answer to the passage instead of the passage to the answer.

Part V
How to Crack the ACT Science Test

Chapter 20
Introduction to the ACT Science Test

The ACT Science test always comes fourth, after the Reading test and before the optional Writing test. Fatigue can negatively affect even the founding president of the I Heart Science Club. Even if the Science test were first, many students would find it the most intimidating and feel that they need to crack open their freshman bio textbooks. But this is not a test of science facts: it is instead a test of how well you look up and synthesize information from tables, graphs, illustrations, and passages.

To maximize your score on the Science test, you need to work the passages in a personal order of difficulty. We'll teach you how to order the passages, and we'll teach you how to employ a strategic and efficient approach that will earn you your highest possible score.

WHAT'S ON THE SCIENCE TEST

Remember when you had to study for that tough biology exam, memorizing dozens of facts about things like meiosis, mitosis, and mitochondria? When you sat down to take the test, you either knew the answers or you didn't. Well, that's not the case on the ACT Science test. Even though the word *science* appears in the title, this test doesn't look much like the tests you've taken in your high school science classes. Like the English and Reading tests, the Science test is passage-based, but most of the passages present the really important content in figures rather than in text.

The Format
You have 35 minutes to do 40 questions, usually split up among 6 passages.

On the Science test, you have 35 minutes to spend on probably 6, but possibly 7, passages and a total of 40 questions. There are 3 types of passages, but unlike in the Reading test, the order of the passages will vary every time. We'll go into more detail about the 3 types of passages later in this chapter.

What Do You Need to Know?

For the topics of the passages, ACT pulls content from biology, chemistry, physics, and Earth/space sciences such as astronomy, geology, and meteorology. While you won't be quizzed on specific facts, background familiarity with the topics certainly helps. If the passage is on genetics, you'll undoubtedly do better if you've recently finished that unit in school and know it cold. But the information you need in order to answer the questions is offered in the passage itself, most frequently presented in a table, graph, or illustration of some kind. The ACT Science test is an open-book test, and you do not need advanced knowledge of any science topic.

You may not need an encyclopedic knowledge of science facts. You *do* need good scientific reasoning skills, a personalized pacing strategy, and a smart, effective approach to working the passages. You also need to be flexible, ready to adapt your strategy or abandon a question you've already spent way too much time on: guess, and move on. Of all the tests on the ACT, Science is the most time-sensitive. Even the biggest science geeks find themselves barely finishing.

Outside Knowledge

Most of the questions can be answered from the information presented in the passages or figures, but be prepared for 3 to 4 questions that require outside knowledge. The outside-knowledge questions are nothing to stress over, however. There is no way to predict what the outside-knowledge questions will be on the next ACT, so there is nothing you can do to prepare; you cannot, and *should not*, try to review everything you've never learned or already forgotten. Besides, the outside-knowledge questions tend to ask about fairly basic facts, commonly addressed in intro-level high school science courses.

For example, you may need to know that a honey badger is a mammal, or you may need to identify a chemical formula as bleach, or you may need to know where acid falls on the pH scale. In any case, remember that for the overwhelming number of questions, everything that you need to answer them is right there in front of you. Use the Basic Approach we'll teach you in Chapter 22, and you'll do just fine.

On ACT.org, ACT identifies the skills you need for this test: "interpretation, analysis, evaluation, reasoning, and problem solving." We can boil this down to a more concise list.

You need to be able to:

- look up data and trends
- make predictions
- synthesize information

But before you learn how to work the passages, you need to learn how to order them. To understand the reasoning behind the method, it's helpful to know the 3 categories of passages.

The Passages

All of the passages fall within 3 categories. The order of the passages will vary on each test, but the distribution of types of passages is typically the same. To pick your order, it's less important what the passage is called than what it looks like. But it is important to know that there are 3 categories of passages and to know their similarities and differences. ACT has very formal-sounding names for the categories, so we made up our own. The distribution below represents the typical format of the Science test.

> This information about the number of questions in each category is based on a Science test with 6 passages. That will usually be what you get, but once in a while, there are 7 passages instead.

Charts and Graphs (aka Data Representation)

2 Passages with 6 Questions Each These passages will *always* come with figures: it's their purpose in life. You'll see one or more charts, tables, graphs, or illustrations. Charts and Graphs passages are intended to test your ability to understand and interpret the information that's presented. There is a total of 12 questions.

Experiments (aka Research Summaries)

3 Passages with 7 Questions Each These passages will *usually* come with figures. They're intended to describe several experiments, and they include more text than do the Charts and Graphs passages. But the results of the experiments are frequently presented in tables or in graphs, and you may have trouble distinguishing the Experiments passages from Charts and Graphs passages. That doesn't matter, however, because in Chapter 22 we'll teach you the basic approach that applies to both types of passages. You'll never need to identify one over the other when you're taking the test. For the record, however, Experiments passages come with more questions: a grand total of 21.

Dual Science Passages (aka Conflicting Viewpoints)

1 passage with 7 questions This passage *sometimes* comes with figures. Even when there are figures, however, the passage is fundamentally different from the Charts and Graphs passages and the Experiments passages. That means it also requires a different way to crack it, and we'll teach you how to do just that in Chapter 23. The Dual Science Passages involve much more reading than you'll need to do for the other 2 types. In fact, most of the Dual Science Passages will feel more like the passages on the Reading test, and you'll be able to use some of the skills you learned to crack the Reading test as you compare, contrast, and synthesize the different viewpoints.

When it comes to the topics, ACT may use arguments already resolved by the scientific community as well as more cutting-edge issues that are still contested. In either case, remind yourself again that the Science test is an open-book test, providing you the information you need to answer almost all the questions.

HOW TO CRACK THE SCIENCE TEST

Order the Passages

As always on the ACT, time is your enemy. With only 35 minutes to review 6 or 7 passages and answer 40 questions, you can't afford to spend too much time on the most difficult ones only to run out of time for the easiest. ACT doesn't present the passages in order of difficulty, but on every exam, some are easier than others, while some are truly tough. What would happen if on your ACT, the most difficult came first and the easiest last? If you did them in order, you could likely run out of time without a chance to correctly answer all the questions on the easiest passage.

That's why you can't do the passages in the order ACT picks—unless that happens to match your Personal Order of Difficulty (POOD). If time is going to run out, you want it to run out on the hardest passage, not the easiest.

Now, Later, Never

We're using the term "easier" only because we're grading the passages on a curve. "Easy" is a loaded term.

Therefore, it's more useful to think of the passages as those you'd do *Now*, those you'd do *Later*, and those you'd *Never* do.

Now Passages

Your goal with all the passages is to crack the main point. You don't necessarily need to know the topic, but you do need to spot the conclusions the content offers: trends, patterns, and relationships. You will spot the main point faster when those conclusions are presented in figures rather than in text. The easier the figures are to "read," the faster you'll crack the main point.

As we explained earlier, this is not a test of science knowledge. Instead, it's a test of your scientific reasoning skills. That means spotting the trends and patterns of variables and the relationships between figures and viewpoints.

The best passages to do Now have the most obvious patterns as well as a few other common characteristics.

Look for

> **Patterns**
> Look for trends *within* a figure. Look for relationships *between* figures and viewpoints.

- **Small graphs and tables:** A good Now passage can have only tables, only graphs, or both. Tables should be no more than 3–4 rows and columns, and graphs should have no more than 3–4 lines or curves.
- **Easy-to-spot consistent trends:** Look for graphs with all lines/curves heading in the same direction: all up, all down, or all flat.
- **Numbers in the figures:** To show a consistent trend, the figure has to feature numbers, not words or symbols.
- **Short answers:** Look for as many questions as possible with short answers, specifically answers with numbers and short relationship words like *increase* or *decrease*.

In Chapter 21, we'll show in greater detail how trends and patterns deliver the main point.

Personal Order of Difficulty (POOD)

There is one additional important characteristic you need to look for: topics you know. Even if the figures are really ugly and confusing, if a passage is on a topic you just finished in school and know cold, you'll get the main point of the passage quickly, and that's the goal of choosing a Now passage.

Pace Yourself

Unless you're shooting for a 27 or higher on the Science test, you're better off choosing at least one passage as Never. Take 35 minutes, and do fewer passages. You'll give yourself more time per passage and increase your accuracy. As you steadily increase your scoring goals in practice, target the number of questions you need to reach your goal. The more aggressively you can move through the passages finding all the Now questions you can answer—no matter how difficult the passage may be—the better you'll score.

Goal Score

Use the pacing strategies and score grid on pages 22-27 to find your goal score for each practice test and, eventually, the ACT.

Be Flexible

As we've mentioned before, to earn your best score on the ACT, you have to be flexible, and nowhere is this more true than on the Science test. The Science test shows the greatest change in level of difficulty from one administration to the next. There is no way to predict how difficult the Science test will be, nor what the particular topics will be. Certainly, if you know more about the topic, you'll find even an ugly-looking passage more understandable. But that doesn't mean you're relying on luck. The Princeton Review's Basic Approach works regardless of what the topics are. The goal is to practice using the Basic Approach so that the particulars of the passage are irrelevant.

However, you have to fight your own instincts, or at least retrain them into those of a great test taker. Always be prepared to adapt your order based on what you see, both in practice and on a real test. If you choose a passage that looked good and then find yourself struggling, leave it and find another. Ignore the voice in your head that says, "Well, I've put so much time into this incredibly hard passage already, all that time would be a waste if I didn't finish the passage." Nothing could be further from the truth. You're throwing away perfectly good time if you stick with a passage that you're just not grasping.

You have to be just as strict with a tough question. When you're stumped, your first instinct may be to go back and read the passage or stare at the figure *again*, waiting for a flash of inspirational genius to suddenly make everything clear. Instead, focus on using POE to get rid of answers that can't be right. Even if you can cross off only one answer, guess from what's left and move on. If you stick with one tough question too long, you may be robbing yourself of the time you need for 2–3 questions.

Process of Elimination (POE)

Just as in the other tests, POE is a powerful tool on the Science test. Particularly on tougher questions, use POE to eliminate wrong answers that are clearly contradicted by what you're looking at.

Let's see how POE works on the Science test.

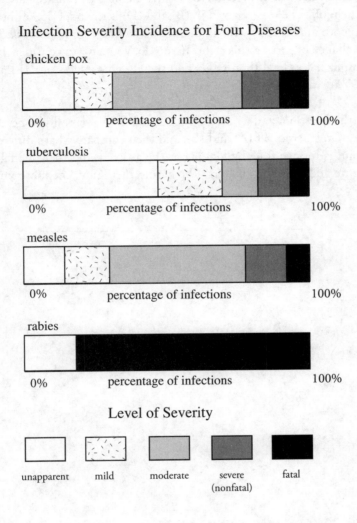

Infection Severity Incidence for Four Diseases

Level of Severity

unapparent   mild   moderate   severe   fatal
                                (nonfatal)

1. An epidemiologist claims that a patient infected with chicken pox faces the greatest risk of mortality for any of the diseases studied. Do the results of Experiment 1 support her claim?

   A. Yes; the percentage of fatal chicken pox infections is greater than the percentage of fatal rabies infections.

   B. Yes; the percentage of fatal chicken pox infections is less than the percentage of fatal rabies infections.

   C. No; the percentage of fatal chicken pox infections is greater than the percentage of fatal rabies infections.

   D. No; the percentage of fatal chicken pox infections is less than the percentage of fatal rabies infections.

POE
Each time you eliminate a wrong answer, you increase your chance of choosing the correct answer.

Here's How to Crack It

Don't waste time staring at the figure trying to look up the answer. Look at how descriptive the answer choices are: POE will be much faster. Ignore the "Yes" and "No," and focus on the reasons given. Do they accurately describe the figure? Choices (A) and (C) are disproven by the figure, so cross them off. The reason given in (B) and (D) is the opposite of the reason given in the other two, so both are proven by the figure. If you had no clue what *mortality* meant, you'd have a fifty-fifty chance of getting this right. If you do, you have to consider the claim and reason that chicken pox is less fatal than rabies and therefore poses less of a risk of mortality, i.e., death. The correct answer is (D).

Maybe you read the question, and a quick glance at the figure was all you needed to know the answer was "No." Great, cross off (A) and (B), and then compare what's different between (C) and (D). The point is to save time by looking at the answers and then the figure rather than staring at the figure and then the answers. The harder the figure, the more important POE is to your success.

Summary

o   There are always 40 questions on the Science test. They are split up into Charts and Graphs, Experiments, and Dual Science Passages passages.

o   You don't need to know science content, but you do need good scientific reasoning skills.

o   Look for trends within figures and relationships between figures and viewpoints.

o   Order your passages. Use your POOD to look for topics you know a lot about. Look for Now passages, which feature small graphs and tables, easy-to-spot consistent trends, numbers instead of words or symbols, and short answers made up of numbers or short relationship words like *increase* or *lower*.

o   Pace yourself. Slow down and do fewer passages, but work up to your goal score by focusing on the number of points you need to earn your goal score.

o   Be flexible. Be ready to adapt your order, leave a tough passage, or guess on a tough question.

o   Use Process of Elimination to cross off wrong answers and save time.

Chapter 21
Scientific Reasoning Skills

You don't need to know science facts for the ACT. For the most part, the Science test is an open-book test, with the passages offering the content you need to answer nearly all the questions. According to ACT, you do need scientific reasoning skills. But all this really means is that you need some common sense. Science may seem intimidating, but it's based on a lot more common sense than you may think.

YOU KNOW MORE THAN YOU THINK

It's easy to feel very intimidated by the content and even the figures on the Science test. But all of science is built on common sense. The key to building good scientific reasoning skills is to realize you *already have* those skills. You use common sense every day to figure things out, to solve problems, to make conclusions. A scientist does the same. When you solve a problem, you think critically, and that's the basis of scientific reasoning.

How to Solve a Problem

Let's try an experiment. Say you put on a wool sweater and go out to dinner one night. At the restaurant you order some delectable shrimp for dinner and then a beautiful bowl of strawberries for dessert.

The next morning, you wake up covered in red, itchy hives. What caused them? Do you jump to the conclusion it was the sweater? What about the shrimp? A lot of people have allergies to shellfish. But so, too, do a lot of people have allergies to strawberries. How are you supposed to know which one caused your hives? How do you know any of these options are the only possible culprits?

Assumption = Guess

An assumption is nothing more than a guess, and a lazy one at that, if you are willing to believe the riddle has been solved. A guess doesn't cut it in the scientific world: only proof does.

You don't. That's the first rule of scientific reasoning: make no assumptions. You can't assume it was the sweater, the shrimp, or the strawberries. But you have to prove it was one and only one of these, if any. So how do you set about finding out which one?

You design an experiment. You first need to narrow the list of suspects down to the sweater, shrimp, and strawberries. Begin with a baseline. You need to see what happens on a day with none of the possible causes in play to compare to the days with them. Wear a cotton T-shirt and eat cauliflower and cantaloupe. Do you still have hives? Then the three suspects have all been vindicated. But if your hives have cleared up, you've confirmed your first hypothesis that it was indeed the sweater, the shrimp, or the strawberries.

Hypothesis

A hypothesis is a theory. An assumption is a guess with no proof. A hypothesis is more advanced than that. It's a theory that tries to explain what happened, but it requires proof.

Now you have to figure out which one of the three caused your hives. We need a day with one, and one only, of the possibilities, or *variables*, in play. That's the second rule of scientific reasoning: change one variable at a time. On one day wear the sweater, but skip the shrimp and strawberries. On another lose the sweater, and eat the shrimp but not the strawberries. On yet another replace the shrimp with the strawberries. On each day check for hives. The itchy red bumps *depend* on whatever *independent* variable is causing them.

Independent and Dependent Variables

The independent variable affects or creates the dependent variable. Does *x* create or affect *y*? Some examples of independent variables include time, temperature, and depth. Dependent variables are the events possibly created or affected by an independent variable, and they can be whatever the scientist is studying. Some examples of dependent variables include volume, solubility, and pressure.

That's all well and good. But what about everything else in your life? Notice we said you couldn't wear the sweater on the days you ate the shrimp and strawberries. But other than the sweater, *you have to wear the exact same clothes on the day you eat shrimp and on the day you eat strawberries*. It's not just what you wear. Everything else in your life has to be exactly the same. If on the day you wore the sweater, you worked out at the gym, but on the day you ate shrimp, you lay on your sofa all day watching television, how much would you know? Not much. Certainly not much of anything with proof, and proof is what it's all about in science. The third rule of scientific reasoning is that you have to keep all the other variables in the experiment the same as you vary one and only one independent variable. In the hives experiment, this means that in order to conclusively prove the cause, you have to keep everything else the same on each day that you change one and only one independent variable. Do the same things. Wear the same clothes (except the sweater). Eat the same things (except the shrimp and strawberries).

And that's it. If you follow these three rules, you'll know what causes your hives.

Trends

In our first example, we looked at a dependent variable, hives, that were present only when an independent variable was present. You've undoubtedly faced other situations in which different amounts of a variable seem to have an effect on another variable. The more you study, the better your grades. The more you practice your free throws, the more you make on game day.

Let's look at another situation. You sleep only 5 hours a night, staying up late and getting up early to study, but you're consistently scoring in the high 70s on your daily math quizzes no matter how many hours you study. Suppose you had a hypothesis that if you slept more, your scores would improve. How would you design an experiment to test this? You already have a baseline of 5 hours and consistent scores in the high 70s. So beginning with the first night, you sleep longer, and then see how you score the next day.

The Three Rules of Scientific Reasoning

1. **Make no assumptions.** You need a standard of comparison to measure against your results. How does your dependent variable react without the presence of any of your independent variables?

2. **Change one variable at a time.** Vary each independent variable to see its effect on your dependent variable.

3. **Keep all other variables the same.** Your other independent variables *and everything else* have to be the same as you vary one and only one independent variable.

The next night, you sleep even longer, and check your quiz score the next day. Can you do anything else differently? No, you have to keep all the other variables in your life the same. Each day you eat the same things and study the same number of hours. You even track quiz scores in the same unit to eliminate any possibility that there is any other reason why your quiz scores improve.

To be organized, you record all your data in a simple table.

Table 1	
Hours of sleep	Quiz scores
5	78
6	83
7	88
8	93

Direct Proportion
As x increases,
y increases.
As x decreases,
y decreases.

As the number of hours of sleep increases, your quiz score increases. In this experiment, the number of hours of sleep is the independent variable, and the quiz score is the dependent variable. You've established that your quiz score is ***directly*** proportional to the number of hours you sleep.

Let's look at another experiment. Suppose your hypothesis this time is that the more cups of coffee you drink, the fewer hours you sleep. How would you design the experiment? Same rules as always. First, you need a baseline. You need to get all the caffeine out of your system and cut your consumption down to 0 cups each day. You establish a consistent routine of the same diet, exercise, studying, sports practice, and so on. Then, without changing any of those variables, you begin drinking coffee again—same size cup each day—increasing the number of cups and measuring the number of hours you sleep the following night.

Once again, you record your findings in a table.

Table 2	
Cups of coffee	Hours of sleep
0	8
1	7
2	6
3	5

Inverse Proportion
As x increases,
y decreases.
As x decreases,
y increases.

As the cups of coffee increase, the hours of sleep decrease. This time, the number of hours of sleep is the dependent variable, and the number of cups of coffee is the independent variable. You've established that the amount you sleep is ***inversely*** proportional to the amount of coffee you drink.

Many passages on the Science test feature passages whose main point is either a direct or inverse trend of the variables. In Chapter 20, we outlined characteristics of Now passages, such as small tables and graphs with easy-to-spot consistent trends.

When you look at the two tables above, the trend is pretty obvious from just a quick glance. You've already cracked the main point, and you will find all the questions that much easier to tackle as a result.

Graphs

Both tables and graphs show the trends of variables. Graphs are more visual, making the trends easier to spot.

If you graphed your data from Table 1, what would it look like?

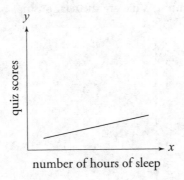

Remember that in math, the horizontal axis is always x: it's the independent variable. The vertical axis is always y: it's the dependent variable. Science follows the same rules. This graph shows you that as x increases, y increases. They have a direct relationship.

Let's stick with using math to understand the graphs on the Science test better. Think about slope. It's the change in y over the change in x. In this graph, the slope is positive. Direct relationships have positive slopes.

Let's graph Table 2.

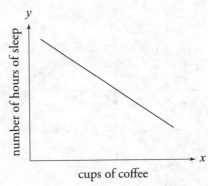

$$\text{Slope} = \frac{rise}{run}$$

$$\frac{y_2 - y_1}{x_2 - x_1}$$

This graph shows you that as x increases, y decreases. They have an inverse relationship, and the slope is negative. Inverse relationships have negative slopes.

TRENDS ON THE SCIENCE TEST

The key to cracking the Science test is to look for trends and patterns. Figures with consistent trends point to a Now passage because the figure has provided the main point of the passage—the relationship between the variables.

In the next chapter, we'll teach you a Basic Approach to cracking each passage, including passages that *don't* feature small tables and graphs with consistent trends. But we hope that this chapter has convinced you to look for passages featuring figures with consistent trends to do Now. You'll find even the hardest questions are easier to tackle when the figure tells you everything you need to know.

Look at each of the following figures. What are the relationships between the variables?

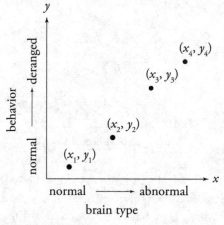

Dr. Frankenstein's Experiment

As the positive slope of the ordered pairs shows, it's a direct, linear relationship. The more abnormal the brain, the more deranged the behavior.

Try another.

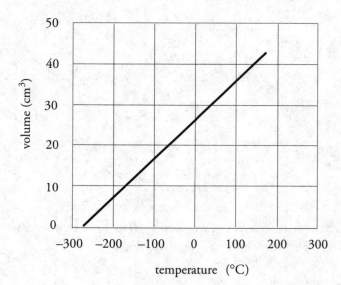

This, too, is a direct, linear relationship. As temperature increases, volume increases.

What about the next one?

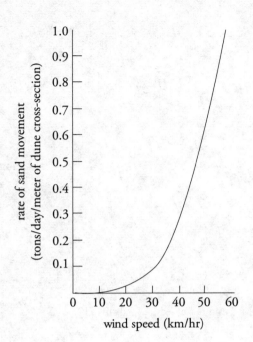

When the wind speed is 40 km/hr, what is the rate of sand movement? It's 0.3. When the wind speed is 50 km/hr, the rate of sand movement increases to 0.6, double the last reading even though the wind speed increased by only 10 km/hr. The relationship is direct, but the curve shows you it's an exponential relationship, not a linear one.

Try the next one.

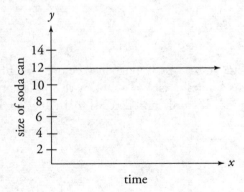

Does time actually affect the size of a soda can? Of course not. As a result, we get a flat line.

> **Curves = Exponential Change**
> When the dependent variable changes by an increasing or decreasing amount every time the independent variable changes, the result will be a curved line.

Try one more.

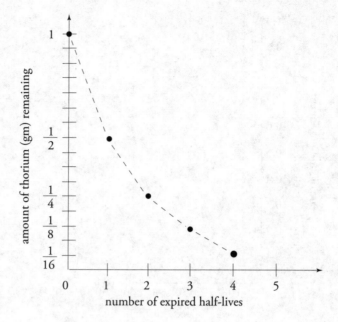

As the number of expired half-lives increases, the amount of thorium remaining decreases, so the two have an inverse relationship.

Do you need to know what "expired half-lives" and "thorium" are? No, you don't need to (but it's always helpful when you're familiar with the content). To answer the questions for this passage, everything you need to know comes from the relationships between the variables. The main point of the passage is just a summary of these relationships.

Tables

When we began this chapter, we showed you tables before switching to graphs. Everything we've discussed about graphs applies to tables. A table with consistent trends is just as helpful as a graph with consistent trends. The only difference is that tables are not as visual as graphs, so it's up to you to make them visual.

Look at the table below.

Number of half-lives expired for radioactive thorium	Amount of thorium (gm) remaining
0	1
1	$\frac{1}{2}$
2	$\frac{1}{4}$
3	$\frac{1}{8}$
4	$\frac{1}{16}$

This is the same information we saw in a graph. What direction is the number of half-lives headed? It's headed up. Draw an arrow to reflect the trend. What direction is the amount of thorium headed? It's headed down. Draw an arrow to reflect the trend. Your table should now look like this:

Number of half-lives expired for radioactive thorium	Amount of thorium (gm) remaining
0	1
1	$\frac{1}{2}$
2	$\frac{1}{4}$
3	$\frac{1}{8}$
4	$\frac{1}{16}$

↑ ↓

If you're taking the ACT Online Test, you can't mark the trends on the screen, but you can on your whiteboard. Use abbreviations and mark the trends:

1/2 lives expired ↑ thorium remaining ↓

You've just gotten a preview of the next chapter. Marking the trends in a figure is the first step in the Basic Approach to cracking Science passages.

Inconsistent Trends and No Relationships

Wouldn't it be great if you saw only tables and graphs with consistent trends on the ACT? Yes, it would, but there will be uglier figures as well. Now that you know how powerful consistent trends are, you can actually use that knowledge even when there is no consistency. The absence of consistency tells its own story.

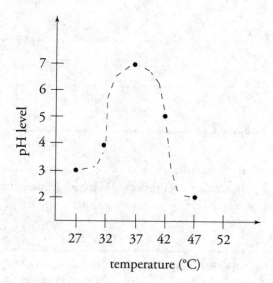

As temperature increases, what does pH do? It barely increases at first and then makes a sharp jump before an equally sharp fall to a point that is lower than where it began. You may have immediately identified this as a **bell curve**. Is a bell curve consistent?

A bell curve is certainly not as consistent as a straight line or even a curve that moves in a positive or negative direction. There is some consistency, however. It increases and then decreases. The problem is that we can't make a prediction of what it will do next. That's the real beauty of consistent lines and curves: we can predict what will happen outside the figure. But with a bell curve, we can't determine whether it will repeat its trend or if it will steadily decrease.

What about the next graph? What story does it tell?

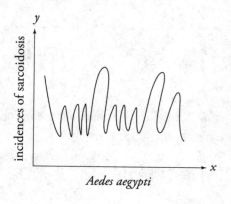

There is no relationship at all between *Aedes aegypti* and sarcoidosis. The incidence of sarcoidosis is *independent* of the *Aedes aegypti*, not *dependent*. And unlike the relationship in a flat line, the incidence of sarcoidosis is not constant. Instead, it fluctuates wildly.

That's a good deal of information from a confusing figure with two strange variables. But would you want to do the passage with this figure Now or Later? Definitely Later.

Multiple Variables

In many Experiments passages, you'll see multiple tables and graphs. Take a look at the following tables (Tables 3 and 4).

Table 3	
Length (m)	Resistance (Ω)
0.9	7.5
1.8	15.0
3.6	30.0

Table 4	
Cross-sectional area (mm^2)	Resistance (Ω)
0.8	35.0
1.6	18.0
3.2	7.5

First, mark the trends within each figure. In Table 3, as length increases, resistance increases. Length is the independent variable, resistance is the dependent variable, and the two have a direct relationship. In Table 4, as cross-sectional area increases, resistance decreases, and the two have an inverse relationship. What's the relationship between the figures? Look at the variable they have in common: resistance.

In Experiments passages—as well as in scientific studies in real life—it's common to test different independent variables to measure their effect on the same dependent variable. But recall our second and third rules of scientific reasoning skills:

- **Change one variable at a time.** Vary each independent variable to see its effect on your dependent variable.
- **Keep all other variables the same.** Your other independent variables *and everything else* have to be the same as you vary one and only one independent variable.

When length is varied, can cross-sectional area vary at the same time? No, it has to stay the same, that is, constant. And when cross-sectional area is varied, length has to stay constant.

On the Science test, you are likely to see a question that tests your ability to spot the constants.

1. Based on the results shown in Table 3 and Table 4, the cross-sectional area used in the first experiment (resulting in Table 3), was most likely:

   A. 0.8 mm^2.
   B. 1.6 mm^2.
   C. 3.2 mm^2.
   D. 4.8 mm^2.

Here's How to Crack It

Find the link between the two tables by looking at the variable they have in common, resistance. Look for a value of resistance that is the same in both tables. In Table 3, resistance is 7.5 Ω when length is 0.9 m. In Table 4, resistance is 7.5 Ω when cross-sectional area is 3.2 mm^2. Thus, we know that as length was varied, cross-sectional area was held constant at 3.2 mm^2, and as cross-sectional area was varied, length was held constant at 0.9 m. The correct answer is (C).

Graphs can also have multiple variables. Take a look at the following graph.

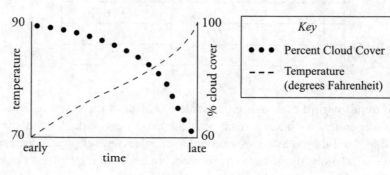

When there are multiple variables on a graph, you always need to be careful to look at the correct line and the correct axis. As time increases, temperature increases. As time increases, cloud cover decreases. Does this data mean that temperature and cloud cover have a direct relationship? Not necessarily. What's the variable they have in common? Time.

Try another question.

2. According to the figure above, what was the temperature, in degrees Fahrenheit, when cloud cover was at its highest?

   F. 100°
   G. 90°
   H. 70°
   J. 60°

Here's How to Crack It

Find the link between the two axes by looking at the variable they have in common, time. Be sure to look at the correct curve on the correct axis. Cloud cover is the bubbled line, and when it's at its highest, the time on the x-axis is early. When time is early, look at the dashed line for the temperature. When it's early, the temperature is 70°.

The correct answer is (H).

In the next lesson, we'll teach you how to use your scientific reasoning skills on ACT Science passages, which will feature plenty of tables and graphs with various trends and relationships.

Summary

- Scientific reasoning is based on common sense.

- The three rules of scientific reasoning skills are:
  - Make no assumptions.
  - Change one variable at a time.
  - Keep all other variables the same.

- A hypothesis is a theory that needs proof to become a conclusion.

- An independent variable creates or causes an effect on a dependent variable.

- In a direct relationship, as x increases, y increases.

- Direct linear relationships on a graph have positive slopes.

- In an inverse relationship, as x increases, y decreases.

- Inverse linear relationships on a graph have negative slopes.

- A flat line means the dependent variable is constant, and the independent variable has no effect. Keep in mind that "no effect" is still a consistent trend. Two variables with no consistent trends are said to have "no relationship."

- A steep slope means the independent variable has a drastic effect on the dependent variable.

- A shallow slope means the independent variable has a slight effect on the dependent variable.

- When the dependent variable changes by an increasing or decreasing amount each time the independent variable changes, the result is a curved line and the relationship is exponential.

Chapter 22
The Basic Approach

To earn your highest possible score on the Science test, you need an efficient and strategic approach to working the passages. In this chapter, we'll teach you how to apply your scientific reasoning skills to quickly assess the content of the passage and figures and make your way methodically through the questions.

HOW TO CRACK THE SCIENCE TEST

The most efficient way to boost your Science score is to pick your order of the passages and apply our 3-Step Basic Approach to the Charts and Graphs passages and Experiments passages. Follow our smart, effective strategy to earn as many points as you can.

Step 1: Work the Figures

Take 10–30 seconds to review the figures. In the last chapter, we taught you how to look for and identify trends, patterns, and relationships. Your goal in Step 1 is to quickly identify the main point of the passage and the relationships between the variables that convey the main point. Consistent trends are the fastest to assess, but all trends and patterns tell a story. In Chapter 20, we gave you a way to spot the Now passages, which are chiefly characterized by consistent trends.

Now Passages

1. **Small tables and graphs:** No more than 3–4 curves on a graph, no more than 3–4 rows and columns on a table.
2. **Easy-to-spot consistent trends:** All lines headed in same direction, numbers in a table in easy-to-spot order.
3. **Numbers, not words or symbols:** Look for tables and graphs with more numbers and fewer words and symbols.
4. **Short answers:** Numbers or trend words like *increase* and *decrease* or *higher* and *lower*.

Graphs

Graphs visually represent the relationship between the variables. When you work a graph, identify the relationship, and take note of the variables and their units.

Take a look at the graph on the next page.

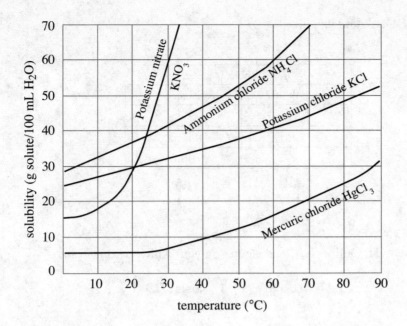

Figure 1

Dual Passages
The Dual Science passage is fundamentally different from the Charts and Graphs passages and Experiments passages, and it requires a different approach. In Chapter 23, we teach you the approach for Dual Science passages.

- Look at the direction of the curves: they are all headed up.
- Take note of the variables and their units. Temperature, in °C, is on the *x*-axis; solubility, in g solute/100 mL H_2O is on the *y*-axis.
- Identify the relationship. A positive slope means it's a direct relationship. As temperature increases, solubility increases.

Tables

For tables, you need to make the trends visual. Take a look at the table below. We saw this table in the last chapter, but now we'll show you how to mark the trends.

Table 1	
Length (m)	Resistance (Ω)
0.9	7.5
1.8	15.0
3.6	30.0

- What is length doing? It's increasing. Mark it with an arrow.
- What is resistance doing? It's increasing. Mark it with an arrow.
- What are the units of the variables? m and Ω.
- Identify the relationship. Both variables move in the same direction, so it's a direct relationship.

Here's what your table should look like.

Table 1	
Length (m)	Resistance (Ω)
0.9	7.5
1.8	15.0
3.6	30.0

↑　　　　　　↑

If you're taking the ACT Online Test, make notes on your whiteboard instead:

Table 1: Length (m) ↑ , Resist (Ω) ↑

Try another table from the same passage.

Table 2	
Cross-sectional area (mm^2)	Resistance (Ω)
0.8	30.0
1.6	15.0
3.2	7.5

- What is the cross-sectional area doing? It's increasing. Mark it with an arrow.
- What is resistance doing? It's decreasing. Mark it with an arrow.
- What are the units of the variables? mm^2 and Ω.
- Identify the relationship. As the cross-sectional area increases, resistance decreases. It's an inverse relationship.

Here's what your table should look like.

Table 2	
Cross-sectional area (mm^2)	Resistance (Ω)
0.8	30.0
1.6	15.0
3.2	7.5

↑　　　　　　↓

Make notes on your whiteboard instead if you're taking the test on a computer:

Table 1: Cross-sec area (mm^2) ↑ , Resist (Ω)↓

Last, identify the relationship between the tables. Each table has the variable **resistance** in common.

Step 2: Work the Questions

Once you've marked the figures, go straight to the questions.

Now, Later, Never

There is no set order of difficulty of these questions. Follow your Personal Order of Difficulty (POOD): if a question is fairly straightforward, do it Now. Most of the questions you consider straightforward will likely ask you to identify a trend, look up a value, or make a prediction. Now questions will have values or trend words like *increase* or *lower* in the answers. If a question strikes you as confusing or time-consuming, come back to it Later. Occasionally, you'll judge a question tough enough you may Never want to do it. Select your Letter of the Day (LOTD), and move on to the next passage. In Step 3, we'll address how smart use of Process of Elimination (POE) may eliminate the need for any Never questions on a Now passage. But for now, let's look at a sample Now question.

> **Acronyms Rule!**
> You've seen our favorite Princeton Review acronyms before and you'll see them again: POOD, LOTD, POE.

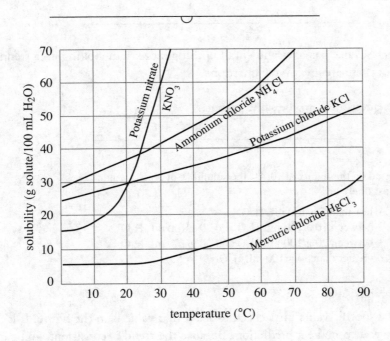

1. Based on the figure, as temperature increases, the solubility of $HgCl_3$:

   A. increases.
   B. decreases.
   C. increases, then decreases.
   D. decreases, then increases.

Here's How to Crack It

This question is asking you to identify a trend. You already cracked this question in Step 1, when you worked the figures and identified the trends. All the curves are headed up, so as temperature increases, the solubility of $HgCl_3$ increases. The correct answer is (A).

Try another.

---

2. According to Figure 1, KNO_3 and KCl have the same solubility at what temperature?

    F. Between 0° and 10°
    G. Between 10° and 20°
    H. Between 20° and 30°
    J. Between 30° and 40°

Here's How to Crack It

This question is asking you to look up a value in the figure. Find where KNO_3 and KCl have the same solubility. They have the same solubility when the lines intersect, at a solubility of 30 g/100 mL H_2O. Draw a line or carefully trace your finger down to the *x*-axis to see what the temperature is when solubility is 30; it's just over 20°, so the correct answer is (H).

Many questions on Science passages will entail nothing more than looking up a trend or value in a figure. Both of these are great Now questions.

Let's try one more question from the same passage.

---

3. Based on the figure, at 100°C the solubility of $HgCl_3$ would most likely be:

    A. less than 5 g/100 mL H_2O.
    B. between 10 g/100 mL H_2O and 20 g/100 mL H_2O.
    C. between 20 g/100 mL H_2O and 30 g/100 mL H_2O.
    D. greater than 30 g/100 mL H_2O.

Here's How to Crack It

If a question cites a specific value, first check to see if that value is in the figure. If it's not, the question is asking you to make a prediction. Because the trend is consistent, you can predict what the curve will do. At 90°C, the solubility of $HgCl_3$ is already more than 30 g/100 mL H_2O. Therefore, at 100°C, the solubility will be greater than 30 g/100 mL H_2O. The correct answer is (D).

Read If and Only When You Need To

On most of the questions, particularly on Now passages, you will be able to answer the questions based on the figures. Whether it's a Charts and Graphs passage or Experiments passage, waste no time reading any of the introduction, or in the case of the Experiments passages, the descriptions of each experiment/study. It's only when you can't answer a question from the figures that you should read.

Let's take a look at some questions from an Experiments passage. We've already marked the tables from this passage.

Passage III

The *resistance* of a material that obeys Ohm's Law can be calculated by setting up a potential difference at the ends of a wire made of that material and then measuring the current in the wire; the resistance is the ratio of potential difference to current. Because resistance is dependent on length and cross-sectional area, scientists created a standard measure, *resistivity*, which is the measure of how strongly a material opposes the flow of current. In the experiments below, scientists examined the factors affecting resistance in an Ohmic material that they invented.

Experiment 1

In their first experiment, scientists examined the relationship between the length of a wire and its resistance. The resistivity of the wires used in this experiment was 27.5 ρ, and the cross-sectional area of the wires was 3.2 mm^2.

Table 1	
Length (m)	Resistance (Ω)
0.9	7.5
1.8	15.0
3.6	30.0

↑ ↑

Experiment 2

In their second experiment, scientists examined the relationship between the cross-sectional area of a wire and its resistance. The resistivity of the wires used in this experiment was 27.5 ρ, and the length of the wires was 0.9 m. The results are shown in Table 2.

Table 2	
Cross-sectional area (mm^2)	Resistance (Ω)
0.8	30.0
1.6	15.0
3.2	7.5

↑ ↓

Opposites
Whenever there is only one pair of answers that are exact opposites, the correct answer is frequently one of the two opposites.

4. *Conductivity* measures a material's ability to conduct an electric current, and it is defined as the reciprocal of a material's ability to oppose the flow of electric current. If the scientists wanted to increase the conductivity of the material they invented, they would:

    F. increase the length.
    G. decrease the cross-sectional area.
    H. increase the resistivity.
    J. decrease the resistivity.

Here's How to Crack It

The question defines a new term, **conductivity,** and asks how the scientists would increase the conductivity of their specific material. As part of the definition, the question states that conductivity is the reciprocal of a material's ability to oppose the flow of current. The tables do not feature an obvious variable for this quality, so you have to read the introduction and studies.

When to Read
Read if and only when you can't answer a question from the figures. If a question introduces a new term that you can't identify as one of the variables on the figures, look for information about that term in the introduction and/or experiments.

In the introduction, the term **resistivity** is defined as a material's ability to oppose the flow of electric current. The question adds the information that conductivity is the reciprocal of resistivity. Therefore, to increase the conductivity, the scientists would decrease the resistivity. The correct answer is (J). Notice that (H) and (J) are exact opposites. Whenever there is only one pair of exact opposites, the correct answer is frequently one of the pair.

Step 3: Work the Answers

On more difficult questions, POE will be much faster and more effective than scouring the text or figures to find an answer. If the answers are wordy—that is, anything but a simple value or trend word like *increase* or *lower*—use POE. Read each answer choice, and eliminate any that are contradicted by the figures.

Let's try a question from a different passage.

Passage I

The term *solubility* refers to the amount of a substance (solute) that will dissolve in a given amount of a liquid substance (solvent). The solubility of solids in water varies with temperature. The graph below displays the water solubility curves for four crystalline solids.

This passage refers to the graph on page 335.

6. A solution is *saturated* when the concentration of a solute is equal to the solubility at that temperature. If a saturated solution of potassium chloride (KCl) at 10°C were heated to 80°C, would the solution remain saturated?

F. Yes, because solubility decreases with increasing temperature.

G. Yes, because the solubility of copper sulfate is greater than that of potassium nitrate (KNO_3) at those temperatures.

H. No, because solubility is unaffected by increasing temperature.

J. No, because concentration is unaffected by increasing temperature.

Here's How to Crack It

The question defines a new term, *saturated*, identifies KCl as saturated at a given temperature, and asks if KCl will remain saturated at a new temperature. If you're familiar with the topic of saturation, you may already know whether it's yes or no. If so, cross off the two answers you know to be wrong, and examine the reasons given in the two remaining answers.

But if you didn't understand the new information and can't process what will happen at a new temperature, use POE on all four answers. Ignore the yes/no, and focus on the reasons given in each answer.

Choice (F) says that solubility will decrease with increasing temperature, but the figure disproves this. No matter what the new information in the question is, this cannot be the correct answer. Cross it off. Choice (G) brings in a new solute, potassium nitrate. Check the figure to see whether what it says about the relationship of the two solutes is correct. At 10°C, the solubility of potassium nitrate is lower than that of KCl, but at 80°C, it is much higher—it is off the chart! Since the reason in (G) is not true, there is no need to worry about whether this answer is correct. However, it is unlikely in any case that the solubility of a different solute tells you something about the saturation of KCL.

Choice (H) is also disproven by the figure, which shows a clear relationship between solubility and temperature. Eliminate (H) as well and you are left with (J), which must be correct. POE got you there, but if more than one answer was left, this is the likely correct one anyway. In general, avoid picking an answer in Science that makes an assumption about a trend in an unknown variable if you have no proof of how that variable will behave. Concentration is the number of grams of the substance per unit volume, so that will not change with temperature. Choice (J) is correct.

POE and Pacing

POE is so powerful on Science, you should be able to eliminate at least one, sometimes two, wrong answers even on questions that look like Never questions. This is particularly true on a Now passage.

Depending on your pacing, you may try to reason between the remaining answers, or you may just guess and move on. Don't spend more than another minute. Even if you get the question right eventually, spending too much time on one question will likely cost 2–3 questions later on.

THE 3-STEP BASIC APPROACH AND LATER PASSAGES

The 3-Step Basic Approach works on all passages with figures, not just the Now passages featuring consistent trends in tables and graphs.

Take a look using the 3-Step Basic Approach at a Later passage in the following section.

Step 1: Work the Figures

Some ACT passages will feature an illustration, a diagram, or tables and graphs with no consistent trends. Take 10–15 seconds to review the figure. When there are no consistent trends, a figure doesn't reveal the main point as readily. You'll learn the main point as you work the questions and answers. Spend the limited time devoted to Step 1 looking for any patterns or terms.

Try this figure.

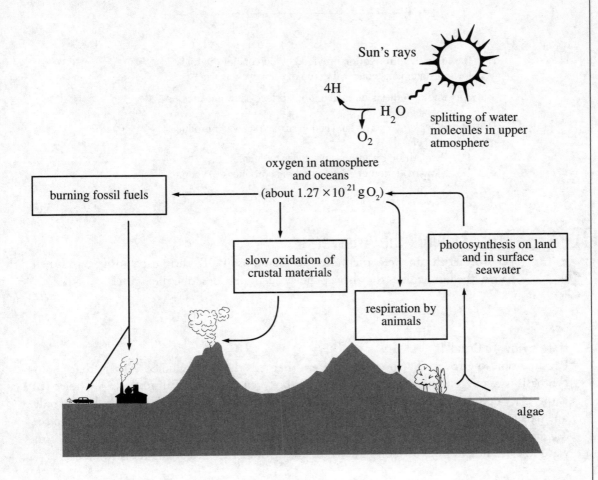

The terms **oxygen**, **fossil fuels**, **oxidation**, **respiration**, and **photosynthesis** all appear.

Step 2: Work the Questions

Even on Later passages, several questions will ask you to look something up in the figure. The more confusing the figure, however, the more likely you are to waste valuable time trying to figure everything out from staring at the figure, waiting for a flash of inspiration to hit. As we mentioned before, spend no more than 10–15 seconds looking for any patterns or terms. Your time is better spent moving to Steps 2 and 3. Working the questions and answers will help you crack the main point of the passage.

Step
2

Try a question.

---

13. Based on the information provided, which one of the following statements concerning the oxygen cycle is true?

    A. Photosynthesis on land and in surface seawater uses up oxygen.

    B. Photosynthesis on land and in surface seawater produces oxygen.

    C. Respiration by animals produces oxygen.

    D. Slow oxidation of crustal materials produces oxygen.

Step 3: Work the Answers

The wordier the answers, the more you should use POE. Read each answer, and then review the figure: does the answer choice accurately describe the figure?

Here's How to Crack It

Pay attention to arrows. They provide a pattern that tells the story. Choice (A) says that photosynthesis uses oxygen, but the arrows lead toward oxygen, not away. Eliminate (A). Choice (B) is the exact opposite and matches the direction of the arrows. Keep it. Whenever there is only one pair of exact opposites, the correct answer is frequently one of the two opposites. Choices (C) and (D) both describe producing oxygen, but the arrows move away from oxygen, not toward it. Both descriptions are contradicted by the arrows. The correct answer is (B).

Basic Approach Drill 1

Use the Basic Approach on the passage below. For the answers to this drill, please go to Chapter 25.

When introduced into H_2O, many solid substances are able to dissolve, or disperse evenly throughout the solvent. Salts have been found to dissolve easily when introduced into H_2O, since they readily dissociate to yield ions that may interact directly with H_2O. Molecular compounds, on the other hand, do not dissolve as easily. Two experiments were conducted to better understand the solubility of salts and molecular compounds in water at various temperatures. The solubility, S, was measured as follows:

$$S = (m_{sub}) / (m_{H_2O})$$

where m_{sub} was the mass of the substance dissolved in water, and m_{H_2O} was the mass of the water itself. ΔS, or the change in solubility (from 0° C), was calculated in the experiments for three salts and three molecular compounds with increasing temperature. The mass of water was held constant at 100 g for each of these experiments.

Figures 1 and 2 show the changes in solubility at different temperatures for three salts and three molecular compounds, respectively. Molecular masses (MM) are shown for each substance.

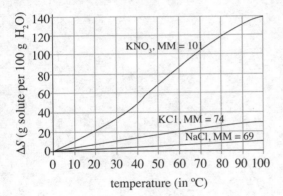

Figure 1

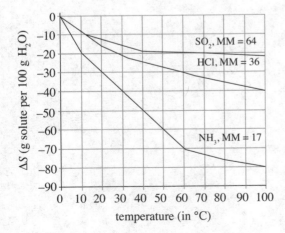

Figure 2

1. Based on Figure 1, at 40°C, as the molecular masses of the salts increase, the ΔS:

   A. decreases, because a greater mass of substance dissolves in the same mass of water.
   B. decreases, because a smaller mass of substance dissolves in the same mass of water.
   C. increases, because a greater mass of substance dissolves in the same mass of water.
   D. increases, because a smaller mass of substance dissolves in the same mass of water.

2. Consider the trials represented in Figure 2 that occurred at 60°C. As the molecular mass of the substance decreased, the observed ΔS:

   F. increased only.
   G. decreased only.
   H. increased, then decreased.
   J. decreased, then increased.

3. If an additional trial had been done in which a salt with a MM of 80 dissolved in H_2O at 50°C, the ΔS, in g solute per 100 g H_2O, most likely would have been:

   A. less than 10.
   B. between 10 and 20.
   C. between 20 and 60.
   D. greater than 60.

4. According to Figure 2, when a solution of NH_3 in water is heated from 0°C to 20°C, the solubility of the NH_3:

   F. increased, because ΔS was positive.
   G. increased, because ΔS was negative.
   H. decreased, because ΔS was positive.
   J. decreased, because ΔS was negative.

5. Based on Figures 1 and 2, which of the following combinations of solute and temperature at a known m_{H_2O} would produce the greatest increase in solubility?

   A. CH_4 (molecular compound, MM = 16) at 40°C
   B. CH_4 (molecular compound, MM = 16) at 80°C
   C. NaF (salt, MM = 42) at 40°C
   D. NaF (salt, MM = 42) at 80°C

6. The solubility of Compound X is 26.9 g per 100 g H_2O at 0°C and 37.1 g per 100 g H_2O at 25°C. Based on the information in the passage and figures, is Compound X most likely a salt or a molecular compound?

    F. Salt, because the solubility increases with increasing temperature.

    G. Salt, because the solubility decreases with increasing temperature.

    H. Molecular compound, because the solubility increases with increasing temperature.

    J. Molecular compound, because the solubility decreases with increasing temperature.

Basic Approach Drill 2

Use the Basic Approach on the passage below. For the answers to this drill, please go to Chapter 25.

Each element is arranged in the periodic table according to its atomic number, which represents the number of protons in the nucleus. In every neutrally charged atom, the number of electrons equals the number of protons. *Electronegativity* is a measure of the relative strength with which the atoms attract outer electrons. Elements with higher electronegativity have tighter bonding between protons and electrons than elements with lower electronegativity.

The different rows of the periodic table are called periods, and all elements in a period have the same number of electron shells. Table 1 shows the characteristics of the elements in Period 2.

Table 1				
Element	Atomic number	Atomic radius (pm)	Electro-negativity	Type
Li	3	167	0.98	metal
Be	4	112	1.57	metal
B	5	87	2.04	metalloid
C	6	67	2.55	nonmetal
N	7	56	3.04	nonmetal
O	8	48	3.44	nonmetal
F	9	42	3.98	nonmetal

The different columns of the periodic table are called groups. Elements in the same group share similar chemical behaviors. Table 2 shows some characteristics of several Group 2 elements.

Table 2				
Element	Period	Atomic radius (pm)	Electro-negativity	Type
Be	2	112	1.57	metal
Mg	3	145	1.31	metal
Ca	4	194	1.00	metal
Sr	5	219	0.95	metal
Ba	6	253	0.89	metal

1. Which of the following graphs best represents the relationship between atomic number and atomic radius for Period 2 elements?

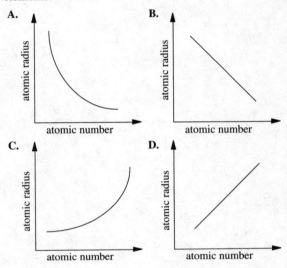

2. Based on Tables 1 and 2, the electronegativity of a Period 3 element in the same group as nitrogen (N) is most likely:

   F. less than 0.98.
   G. between 0.98 and 1.31.
   H. between 1.31 and 3.04.
   J. greater than 3.04.

3. Which of the following statements is supported by the information in both Table 1 and Table 2 ?

   A. As the atomic radius decreases, the electronegativity decreases.
   B. As the atomic radius decreases, the electronegativity increases.
   C. All metals have higher electronegativity values than nonmetals.
   D. All metals have smaller atomic radii than nonmetals.

4. Based on the information in the passage and Table 1, which of the following is true regarding the comparative electronegativity of fluorine (F) and lithium (Li) ?

   F. The electronegativity of F is greater than Li because F has fewer electrons in its outer shell.
   G. The electronegativity of F is greater than Li because F electrons are more tightly bound.
   H. The electronegativity of Li is greater than F because Li has fewer electrons in its outer shell.
   J. The electronegativity of Li is greater than F because Li electrons are more tightly bound.

5. Generally speaking, elements with a high electronegativity also have a high ionization energy. Based on Table 1, which of the following is a correct order of elements with *increasing* ionization energies?

   A. Be, O, Li
   B. F, N, Li
   C. B, N, Be
   D. Li, N, F

6. Potassium (K) is a Period 4 element with an electronegativity of 0.82. Based on the information in Tables 1 and 2, is K more likely to be a metal or a nonmetal?

   F. Metal, because K has a lower electronegativity than Ca.
   G. Metal, because K has a higher electronegativity than B.
   H. Nonmetal, because K has a higher electronegativity than Ca.
   J. Nonmetal, because K has a lower electronegativity than B.

Basic Approach Drill 3

Use the Basic Approach on the passage below. For the answers to this drill, please go to Chapter 25.

Amphibians are unique organisms that undergo drastic physical changes during the transformation from an immature organism into an adult form during a process called *metamorphosis*. The process begins with cell determination in the embryo stage. Figure 1 shows the stages of development in frogs.

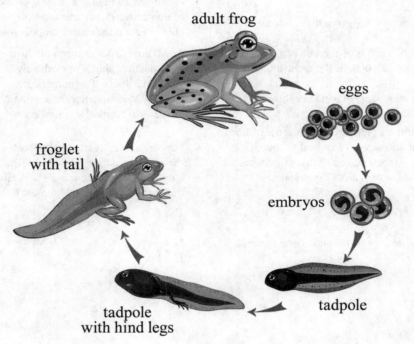

Figure 1

Experiment

An experiment was conducted using tadpoles to determine the influence of thyroxine (a hormone) on metamorphosis. The researchers predicted that increased levels of thyroxine would lead to an earlier appearance of adult characteristics such as lungs and hind legs and tail reabsorption. Twenty recently emerged tadpoles were divided into four treatment groups. Five tadpoles were placed into each of 3 aqueous solutions containing various concentrations of thyroxine. The remaining five tadpoles were placed in pure distilled water. The researchers measured the tail width of each tadpole every 12 hours and calculated the average percent decrease in tail width over the course of the study for each group (see Figure 2).

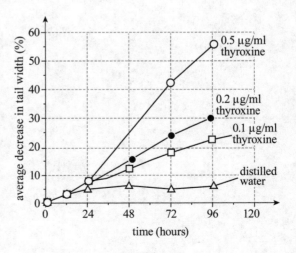

Figure 2

1. Suppose that an additional group of recently emerged tadpoles were immersed in a 0.3 μg/ml thyroxine solution for 72 hours. Based on Figure 2, the approximate average decrease in tail width would most likely have been closest to:

   A. 22%.
   B. 30%.
   C. 41%.
   D. 50%.

2. Which of the following assertions about tadpoles is supported by the results of the experiment?

   F. They will not undergo metamorphosis if they are not exposed to thyroxine.
   G. Metamorphosis in a tadpole not given thyroxine takes at least five days.
   H. The most rapid disappearance of the tail is associated with the immersion of tadpoles in the most dilute thyroxine solution.
   J. Temperature plays a major role in metamorphosis.

3. After four days of immersion, the tadpoles are checked for other signs of development. In all tadpoles exposed to thyroxine, at which of the following concentrations of thyroxine would the tadpoles be likely to show the LEAST development?

   A. 0.1 μg/ml
   B. 0.2 μg/ml
   C. 0.5 μg/ml
   D. All of the tadpoles would show the same development.

4. Based on the information in the passage and Figure 1, which of the following would be a correct order of the stages of frog development?

   F. Tadpole → hind leg development → reabsorption of tail → cell determination
   G. Tadpole → cell determination → reabsorption of tail → hind leg development
   H. Cell determination → reabsorption of tail → tadpole→ hind leg development
   J. Cell determination → tadpole → hind leg development → reabsorption of tail

5. According to Figure 2, after approximately how many hours of immersion does exposure to thyroxine first show a measurable effect on the rate of tadpole metamorphosis?

   A. 0 hours after immersion; the thyroxine affects the rate of metamorphosis immediately.
   B. 0–12 hours after immersion
   C. 12–24 hours after immersion
   D. 24–36 hours after immersion

6. Suppose a recently emerged tadpole is immersed in a 0.15 μg/ml thryroxine solution. Based on Figure 2, if after t hours, the tadpole has undergone a 22% decrease in tail width, which of the following is likely closest to he value of t ?

   F. 60
   G. 72
   H. 84
   J. 96

Summary

o   All Charts and Graphs passages and most Experiments passages come with figures.

o   Use the 3-Step Basic Approach on passages with figures.

   Step 1. Work the Figures. Look at the trends and patterns in the figure to identify the relationship between the variables. Mark trends in tables with arrows.

   Step 2. Work the Questions. Do Now the straightforward questions that involve looking up a trend or value on the figure or making a prediction of what a variable will do. Read if and only when you can't answer a question from the figures. Do Later any question that strikes you as more difficult or time-consuming.

   Step 3. Work the Answers. For tougher questions, POE should help you eliminate at least one wrong answer, if not three.

o   Pace yourself. If you've eliminated at least one wrong answer on a tough question, guess and move on.

Chapter 23
Dual Science
Passages

The third type of passage on the Science test is based on more than one passage. Two, three, or possibly more conflicting views on a scientific phenomenon will be presented. Make a plan of the order in which you will read the scientists, and work one theory at a time before tackling the questions that require comparing and contrasting all of the theories.

Think of it as a debate. Each debater proposes a hypothesis and then supports that hypothesis with facts, opinions, and assumptions. The ACT test writers want you to evaluate and compare the arguments made by each debater, but they don't care who wins the debate. We don't care either, but we do want you to correctly answer questions about the debate. In order to do that, you must understand each viewpoint and how it agrees and disagrees with the others. Some questions will ask about just one theory, but most of the questions will ask you to compare and contrast two or more. That's a lot to keep track of. Wouldn't it be easier to navigate this passage if you had a plan?

FOLLOW A PLAN

The Dual Science passage has a lot in common with the Reading test, and you might recognize some of the same strategies we taught you to employ for Reading. How would you fare if your boss assigned you the task of checking out an empty building? How well do you do when you don't know what you're looking for? Not very well. How well would you fare if you dived right into a passage on the Reading test if you didn't know what you're looking for? Right. So how can you succeed on the Dual Science passage if you don't know what you're looking for?

Step 1: Preview

Your first task is to map the order in which you will read the scientists. Just as on the Reading test, you should look at the questions first. On the Dual Science passage, the questions help you determine which hypothesis to read and which questions to answer first.

Let's try this with the questions below. Read each question, and mark it with a "1" if it asks about Hypothesis 1, a "2" if it asks about Hypothesis 2, and a "1 & 2" if it asks about both hypotheses. On the ACT Online Test, use your whiteboard instead: write the question number, then "1," "2," or "1 & 2" next to the number.

1. Hypotheses 1 and 2 agree that the dinosaurs:

2. The basis of Hypothesis 1 is that a meteorite striking Earth was the primary cause of the dinosaurs' demise. Which of the following discoveries would best support this theory?

3. Suppose a geologist discovered that the fossilized bones of dinosaurs contained traces of radioactive iridium. How would this evidence influence the two hypotheses?

4. The authors of the two hypotheses would disagree over whether the extinction of the dinosaurs was:

5. If current climatic changes turn out to be as dramatic as those described by the author of Hypothesis 2, which of the following would he say is most likely to occur?

6. Recent studies have shown that climatic conditions at the K-T boundary were interdependent. As conditions became less favorable for life in one locale, they improved in another. Do the results of these recent studies strengthen or weaken Hypothesis 2 ?

7. Both Hypothesis 1 and 2 would be supported by evidence showing that:

You should have a "1 & 2" next to questions 1, 3, 4, and 7. Question 2 should have a "1" next to it, and questions 5 and 6 should have a "2" next to them. What does this tell us? We should read Hypothesis 2 first.

Step 2: One Side at a Time

In order to compare and contrast multiple hypotheses, you need to understand each viewpoint and how it agrees and disagrees with the others. Reading and working the questions for one scientist at a time will give you the firm grasp of each theory you need.

Once the questions have provided a map, read the introduction to identify the disagreement.

> Approximately 65 million years ago (at the boundary between the Cretaceous and Tertiary periods, known as the K-T boundary), the dinosaurs became extinct.
>
> Here are two of the hypotheses that have been presented to explain their disappearance.

What will the hypotheses debate? They will debate what caused the extinction of the dinosaurs.

Next, read Hypothesis 2. You don't need to comprehend everything in the passage or remember every point of fact or argumentation, and until you read the other hypothesis, you have no basis for comparison. You do need to grasp the argument each is making, so as you read Hypothesis 2, find and underline or highlight the scientist's answer to the question—that is, what caused the extinction of the dinosaurs.

Hypothesis 2

This event at the K-T boundary was neither sudden nor isolated. It was a consequence of minor shifts in Earth's weather that spanned the K-T boundary. Furthermore, its effect was not as sweeping as some have suggested. While the majority of dinosaurs disappeared, some were able to adapt to the changing world. We see their descendants every day—the birds.

Alterations in Earth's *jet stream* (a steady, powerful wind that blows from west to east, circling the globe) shifted rains away from the great shallow seas that extended across much of what is now North America. As these late-Cretaceous seas began to dry up, a chain reaction of extinctions was set into motion. First affected was plant life. Next, animals that fed on plants began dying off. Ultimately, the lack of prey caused the demise of the majority of the dinosaurs. It was the mobility of the winged dinosaurs that saved them, allowing them to move to more favorable locations as conditions in their ancestral homes deteriorated.

What Are They Fighting About?

Some of the scientific theories you'll read about in a Dual Science passage were settled a long time ago. In reading a passage arguing that Earth is the center of the solar system, you may think, "Wait, Earth is NOT the center of the solar system—why in the world are they arguing about this?" For the ACT, the arguments presented are what count. Even though an argument may have been disproved a long time ago, it's still possible to evaluate it scientifically, and that's all you're being asked to do on this test.

What is the main point of Hypothesis 2?

According to Hypothesis 2, the extinction of dinosaurs was caused by a chain reaction prompted by changes in the weather.

Your Underlined Version Should Look Like This

Hypothesis 2

<u>This event at the K-T boundary was neither sudden nor isolated. It was a consequence of minor shifts in Earth's weather that spanned the K-T boundary.</u> Furthermore, its effect was not as sweeping as some have suggested. While the majority of dinosaurs disappeared, some were able to adapt to the changing world. We see their descendants every day—the birds.

Alterations in Earth's *jet stream* (a steady, powerful wind that blows from west to east, circling the globe) shifted rains away from the great shallow seas that extended across much of what is now North America. As these late-Cretaceous seas began to dry up, a chain reaction of extinctions was set into motion. First affected was plant life. Next, animals that fed on plants began dying off. Ultimately, the lack of prey caused the demise of the dinosaurs. It was the mobility of the winged dinosaurs that saved them, allowing them to move to more favorable locations as conditions in their ancestral homes deteriorated.

Did you notice that we didn't underline the details of the theory in the second paragraph? It's not that they are unimportant, but until we dive into the questions, we don't know what to pay attention to other than the main point. As we work the questions for Hypothesis 2, we'll gain a deeper understanding of the details of the theory.

Without further ado, let's go to the questions about Hypothesis 2.

---

5. If current climatic changes turn out to be as dramatic as those described by the author of Hypothesis 2, which of the following would he say is most likely to occur?

   A. A rapid extinction of most of Earth's life, beginning with sea dwellers such as krill (a microscopic crustacean) and progressing through the food chain

   B. A gradual and complete extinction of Earth's life forms that moves through the food chain from the bottom up

   C. An extinction of most life forms on Earth that is gradual and simultaneous, affecting predators as well as prey at roughly the same rates

   D. A progressive extinction that begins with vegetation and eventually reaches to the top of the food chain, affecting most dramatically those life forms least suited to relocation

Here's How to Crack It

The main point of Hypothesis 2 is that changes in the weather prompted a chain reaction of extinctions through the food chain until the dinosaurs were affected. We need to look for an answer that would predict a similar result from today's climatic changes. Use POE as you make your way through the answer choices.

Choice (A) is tempting because it mentions a progression *through the food chain*, but the word *rapid* contradicts the first sentence of Hypothesis 2: *The event at the K-T boundary was neither sudden nor isolated.* Choice (B) looks good, until we go back to the passage to confirm it and see that some dinosaurs survived: those that evolved into birds. Because of the word *complete*, we have to eliminate it. Choice (C) is out because of the word *simultaneous*, which we know from evaluating (A) is contradicted by the passage. The answer must be (D), since it paraphrases nicely what we underlined as the main point.

---

6. Recent studies have shown that climatic conditions at the K-T boundary were interdependent. As conditions became less favorable for life in one locale, they improved in another. Do the results of these recent studies strengthen or weaken Hypothesis 2 ?

F. Strengthen, because they support the assumption that there were some locations with more favorable conditions to which the winged dinosaurs could migrate.

G. Strengthen, because they support the assumption that worsening climatic conditions led to the extinction of dinosaurs before the Tertiary period.

H. Weaken, because they refute the assumption that there were some locations with more favorable conditions to which the winged dinosaurs could migrate.

J. Weaken, because the area of improving climatic conditions should have provided a means for the survival of the dinosaurs well into the Tertiary period.

Here's How to Crack It

We've learned a lot about Hypothesis 2. We read it and underlined the main point, and then we evaluated some of the nuances of the argument to eliminate wrong answers for question 5. When you consider the import of these new studies, you should draw upon the deeper understanding you've gained. The correct answer to question 5 reminded us that those *least* suited to relocation are more impacted by the changes in weather. Hypothesis 2 stated explicitly that some winged dinosaurs survived and evolved into birds because their mobility allowed *them to move to more favorable locations*. Eliminate (G) and (J) because both imply that Hypothesis 2 states that no dinosaurs survived into the Tertiary period. Eliminate (H) because the recent studies support rather than refute the idea that there were some locations in which conditions improved. The correct answer is (F).

Step 3: The Other Side

Now it's time to read Hypothesis 1, but we know more than we did before reading Hypothesis 2 and thus should read more proactively. When you read the second theory, you should look for and underline the following:

- the main idea

- how this hypothesis disagrees with the first

- how this hypothesis agrees with the first

Differentiate Between Theories
Questions on the Dual Science passages often ask about the areas of agreement as well as disagreement between the scientists' theories. Make sure you know what both the similarities and differences are.

Hypothesis 1

For many years, scientists have speculated about the cause of the extinction of the dinosaurs. Fossil records confirm that dinosaurs as well as other life forms were suddenly wiped out. The natural cause of extinction is the inability of an organism to adapt to environmental changes, yet the extinction of all life forms is unlikely. Chemical analysis of clay found from this era attributes the sweeping extinction of dinosaurs to the collision of a huge meteorite with Earth. These fossil records confirm the presence of a high concentration of iridium, a rare heavy metal that is abundant in meteorites. It is believed that a meteorite hit Earth and created a huge crater, which threw up a dust cloud that blocked the sun for several months. This event led first to the destruction of much plant life and eventually all other life forms that consumed plants and/or herbivores, including the dinosaurs.

> **Write, Write, Write**
> Underlining or highlighting and taking notes in the margins or on your whiteboard help you keep track of the differences between the scientists.

What is the main point? Hypothesis 1 believes a meteorite struck Earth and wiped out the dinosaurs.

How do the two hypotheses differ? Hypothesis 2 believes the extinction was gradual; Hypothesis 1 believes it was sudden.

How do they agree? Both hypotheses mention the food chain.

If you didn't come up with those points, look at the underlined portions of the passage below.

Hypothesis 1

For many years, scientists have speculated about the cause of the extinction of the dinosaurs. Fossil records confirm that dinosaurs as well as other life forms were suddenly wiped out. The natural cause of extinction is the inability of an organism to adapt to environmental changes, yet the extinction of all life forms is unlikely. Chemical analysis of clay found from this era attributes the sweeping extinction of dinosaurs to the collision of a huge meteorite with Earth. These fossil records confirm the presence of a high concentration of iridium, a rare heavy metal that is abundant in meteorites. It is believed that a meteorite hit Earth and created a huge crater, which threw up a dust cloud that blocked the sun for several months. This event led first to the destruction of much plant life and eventually all other life forms that consumed plants and/or herbivores, including the dinosaurs.

> **Dual Science (A Science Duel?)**
> In a Dual Science passage, you're given two or more opinions about a scientific phenomenon. Your job is to identify the differences between or among the viewpoints and the information the scientists use to support their points of view.

Now let's do the one question on Hypothesis 1 before we tackle the questions on both.

2. The basis of Hypothesis 1 is that a meteorite striking Earth was the primary cause of the dinosaurs' demise. Which of the following discoveries would best support this theory?

F. The existence of radioactive substances in the soil
G. The presence of other rare metals common to meteorites in the clay beds of the ocean from that period
H. Fossil records of land-dwelling reptiles that roamed Earth for an additional 10 million years
J. Evidence of dramatic changes in sea levels 65 million years ago

Here's How to Crack It

What type of evidence would support Hypothesis 1? Any evidence that shows that dinosaurs were wiped out as a result of the impact of a meteorite. Would the presence of radioactive substances in the soil support Hypothesis 1? It could support the passage only if the radioactive elements were from meteorites (like iridium). Choice (F) did not specify that. Would the fact that some land-dwelling reptiles survived past this period support Hypothesis 1? No, so (H) is out. We can also get rid of (J) because it supports Hypothesis 2. What about (G)? What if other rare metals that are known to be found in meteorites were discovered? Would this support Hypothesis 1? Yes. The correct answer is (G).

Step 4: Compare and Contrast
We are now armed with a clear understanding of the main point of each hypothesis, how the two differ, and how they agree.

1. Hypotheses 1 and 2 agree that the dinosaurs:

I. vanished because of a meteorite impact with Earth.
II. became extinct due to disruptions in their food chain.
III. became extinct due to some external force other than predation.

A. I only
B. I and II only
C. II and III only
D. III only

Here's How to Crack It

We've already identified the area in which the two agree: the impact on the food chain. Look for a statement that reflects that—it's Statement II. Eliminate the answers that do not include Statement II, which are (A) and (D). Now check either Statement I or III to decide between the remaining answer choices. Statement I is true only for Hypothesis 1, not both, so eliminate (B). The only answer that remains contains Statements II and III, so III must be true. Do both hypotheses state that dinosaurs became extinct because of some external force? Yes, so the correct answer is (C).

Study Break!
You're almost finished with Science! Tackle the Dual Science Drills, and then give yourself some downtime before diving into Part VI.

3. Suppose a geologist discovered that the fossilized bones of dinosaurs contained traces of radioactive iridium. How would this evidence influence the two hypotheses?

   A. It would support both hypotheses.
   B. It would support Hypothesis 1 and weaken Hypothesis 2.
   C. It would support Hypothesis 2 and weaken Hypothesis 1.
   D. It would not support Hypothesis 1 or Hypothesis 2.

Here's How to Crack It

Which of the hypotheses would be supported if a geologist found fossil bones that contained traces of radioactive iridium? Hypothesis 1, of course! The passage states that radioactive iridium is abundant in meteorites. If dinosaurs were exposed to the dust of meteorites, their bones would contain this metal. Hypothesis 2 didn't mention anything about iridium, so (B) is the correct answer.

4. The authors of the two hypotheses would disagree over whether the extinction of the dinosaurs was:

   F. a natural process.
   G. something that occurred rapidly.
   H. due to food chain disruptions.
   J. potentially avoidable.

Here's How to Crack It

The two hypotheses disagreed about the cause of the extinction, but they also disagreed on the pace. Hypothesis 1 believed it was sudden, whereas Hypothesis 2 believed it was gradual. Thus, (G) is the correct answer. Be careful with (H)—that's an issue on which both *agree*.

7. Both Hypotheses 1 and 2 would be supported by evidence showing that:

    A. pterodactyls (winged dinosaurs) survived well into the Tertiary period, adapted to changes in Earth's environment, and eventually evolved into a non-dinosaur life form.

    B. blockage of the sun's rays by particles measurable only on the microscopic scale can still have a significant effect on rates of photosynthesis.

    C. even apparently minor degradation of the plant population in a given ecosystem can have far-reaching effects on the animal population within that ecosystem.

    D. iridium is extremely likely to remain trapped in an ocean's bed when that ocean dries up.

Here's How to Crack It

On what point do the hypotheses agree? Look for an answer choice that provides evidence about the food chain. Eliminate any answer choice that supports only one hypothesis. Choice (A) is out because Hypothesis 1 never mentioned relocation or winged dinosaurs. Choice (B) looks good because it mentions photosynthesis, a necessary step in the food chain, so keep it. Choice (C) looks much better because it explicitly mentions the effects of plants on animals. Choice (D) is incorrect because Hypothesis 2 never mentioned iridium, and Hypothesis 1 never mentioned the ocean drying up. The test writers are trying to distract you with a switch, but you won't fall for it when you take the passages one at a time and learn each thoroughly before working the questions on both. The correct answer is (C).

Dual Science Passage Drill 1

How are natural gases extracted from reservoirs? Two differing views are presented below. For the answers to this drill, please go to Chapter 25.

Natural gas (a variable combination of methane and other heavier hydrocarbons) is extracted and brought to the surface from reservoirs located between 0 and 0.5 miles beneath Earth's surface. Two scientists discuss the origin of natural gas in a particular undersea reservoir.

Scientist 1

All of the natural gas present in the reservoir was formed within the last 500 million years from the decay of organic matter. Natural gas formation began when the remains of marine organisms and terrestrial plants piled up on land and on the seafloor over a long period. Mud and other sediments then buried the accumulated plants and organisms. Deep beneath the surface, at depths greater than 10 miles, high temperatures and pressure converted the buried organic matter into natural gas over millions of years.

After its formation, the natural gas rises toward the surface. Some is dissipated into the air, but a significant amount is trapped under the specific geological formation overlaying the reservoir. Fossils from the plants and marine organisms that provided the organic matter can be found in rocks brought to the surface from locations in Earth's crust where natural gas forms.

Because of the unique geological conditions and time required for formation of such reservoirs, Earth's crust contains only a small amount of natural gas formed in this manner.

Scientist 2

All of the natural gas present in the reservoir was formed by the action of microorganisms at depths from 2 to 10 miles beneath the surface of Earth. The supply of natural gas has been in constant production since soon after the reservoir's formation. The production begins as various microorganisms digest buried organic material to produce simple, inorganic carbon compounds. Other microorganisms convert the carbon compounds and water into the hydrocarbons of natural gas.

After its formation, the natural gas rises and subsequently amasses in significant quantities in the reservoir. Many natural gas deposits can be found in deep rock layers, where the gas can be released by procedures such as *hydraulic fracturing*, the fracturing of rock by a pressurized liquid. A carbon-13 isotope, commonly linked to natural gas produced from microorganism involvement, is contained in the natural gas brought up to the reservoir.

Since natural gas is always forming and rising towards reservoirs such as this one, there is an infinite amount obtainable.

1. Based on Scientist 1's discussion, the natural gas reservoir would most likely be found at or near sites where:

   A. a body of water had existed at some time in the past.
   B. a body of water exists where none had existed in the past.
   C. microorganisms produce carbon compounds.
   D. carbon compounds produce microorganisms.

2. A natural gas reservoir has been found at a depth of 20 miles below Earth's surface. Is this information consistent with the position expressed by Scientist 1 ?

   F. No, because Scientist 1 indicates that natural gas forms at depths greater than 10 miles below Earth's surface.
   G. No, because Scientist 1 indicates that natural gas forms at depths between 2 and 10 miles beneath Earth's surface.
   H. Yes, because Scientist 1 indicates that natural gas forms at depths greater than 10 miles beneath Earth's surface.
   J. Yes, because Scientist 1 indicates that natural gas forms at depths between 2 and 10 miles beneath Earth's surface.

3. Which scientist indicates that the natural gas found in the reservoir formed in the lower pressure environment?

   A. Scientist 1, because that scientist states that the natural gas formed at depths of more than 10 miles beneath Earth's surface.
   B. Scientist 1, because that scientist states that the natural gas formed at depths between 2 and 10 miles beneath Earth's surface.
   C. Scientist 2, because that scientist states that the natural gas formed at depths of more than 10 miles beneath Earth's surface.
   D. Scientist 2, because that scientist states that the natural gas formed at depths between 2 and 10 miles beneath Earth's surface.

4. Which of the following diagrams is most consistent with Scientist 2's description of the formation and migration of natural gas?

(Note: Diagrams are not to scale.)

F.

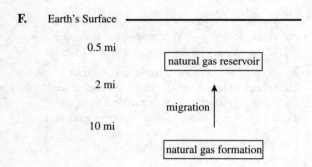

G.

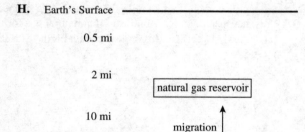

H.

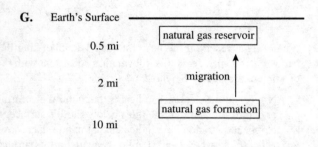

J.

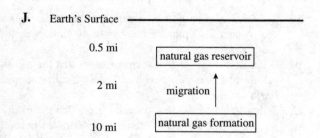

5. An experiment showed that natural gas can be formed through a reaction of carbon dioxide and water. Which scientist would most likely use this result to support his/her viewpoint?

A. Scientist 1, because it would demonstrate how, under high temperature and pressure, organic material can be converted into natural gas.

B. Scientist 1, because it would demonstrate a chemical reaction that microorganisms might carry out to convert organic material into natural gas.

C. Scientist 2, because it would demonstrate how, under high temperature and pressure, organic material can be converted into natural gas.

D. Scientist 2, because it would demonstrate a chemical reaction that microorganisms might carry out to convert organic material into natural gas.

6. Based on Scientist 2's discussion, which of the following statements describes two properties of natural gas that migrated to the reservoir in which it accumulated? The natural gas:

F. does not contain carbon-13 and is less dense than the material through which it migrates.

G. does not contain carbon-13 and is more dense than the material through which it migrates.

H. contains carbon-13 and is less dense than the material through which it migrates.

J. contains carbon-13 and is more dense than the material through which it migrates.

7. Based on Scientist 2's discussion, which of the following compounds is involved in the formation of natural gas?

I. F_2
II. KCl
III. CO_2

A. I only
B. III only
C. I and II only
D. II and III only

Dual Science Passage Drill 2

What affects effusion time of gases? Three differing views are presented. For the answers to this drill, please go to Chapter 25.

A professor placed 100 mL of Gas A at 25°C into a syringe. The syringe was then inserted into a rubber stopper placed in the top of an empty flask (see Figure 1). The escape of gas molecules from the syringe into the evacuated flask is known as *effusion*.

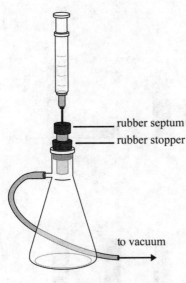

rubber septum

rubber stopper

to vacuum

Figure 1

After insertion of the syringe into the flask, the *total effusion time*, the time required for all 100 mL of the gas to effuse from the syringe into the flask, was measured and found to be 4 sec. The procedure was repeated with Gas B, which had a total effusion time of 16 sec.

Three students proposed explanations for why the total effusion time for the two gasses differed.

Student 1

Gas B effused more slowly than Gas A because it has greater *molecular mass* (the mass of each molecule) than Gas A. The temperature of a gas is a measure of the average kinetic energy of the molecules of that gas. If the temperature of each gas is the same, then the average kinetic energy of the molecules of both gasses is also equal. Since average kinetic energy depends on both the mass and the velocity of gas particles, gases with greater molecular masses travel with a smaller average velocity. Therefore, if two gases are at the same temperature, the gas with the greater molecular mass will effuse more slowly.

Student 2

Gas B effused more slowly than Gas A because it has greater *molecular volume* (the volume occupied by each molecule) than Gas A. Because of their greater molecular volume, fewer larger molecules are able to pass through the opening between the syringe and flask in a given period of time when compared to the number of smaller molecules that are able to pass through the opening in the same period of time. Therefore, if two gases are at the same temperature, the gas with the greater molecular volume will effuse more slowly.

Student 3

Gas B effused more slowly than Gas A because it has greater density than Gas A. Because Gas B has a greater density, its molecules are nearer one another than are the molecules of Gas A. The close proximity of the molecules of Gas B increases the likelihood of collisions, which slow the speed of the molecules. Therefore, if two gases are at the same temperature, the gas with the greater density will effuse more slowly.

Table 1 gives the molecular mass (in atomic mass units, amu), molecular volume (in cubic Angstroms ($Å^3$), where 10 billion $Å$ = 1 m), and density for several gases at 25°C.

Table 1			
Gas	Molecular mass (amu)	Molecular volume ($Å^3$)	Density (kg/L)
Oxygen	32.00	52.86	1.429
Hydrogen	2.016	37.54	0.089
Xenon	131.3	42.12	5.894
Krypton	83.80	34.45	3.749
Helium	4.003	11.46	0.179
Fluorine	38.00	21.17	1.696

1. In the professor's experiment using Gas A, as the 4 seconds of measured effusion time elapsed, the volume of gas in the flask:

   A. decreased only.
   B. increased only.
   C. decreased, then increased.
   D. increased, then decreased.

2. Based on Student 1's explanation, which of the gases listed in Table 1 would effuse most quickly at 25°C ?

F. Hydrogen
G. Xenon
H. Helium
J. Fluorine

3. Suppose that the professor had also tested nitrogen gas and found that it had an effusion time of 9 seconds. Student 1 would claim that nitrogen:

A. has a smaller molecular mass than Gas A but a greater molecular mass than Gas B.
B. has a greater molecular mass than Gas A but a smaller molecular mass than Gas B.
C. has a smaller molecular volume than Gas A but a greater molecular volume than Gas B.
D. has a greater molecular volume than Gas A but a smaller molecular volume than Gas B.

4. Is the claim "At 25°C, xenon effuses more quickly than krypton" consistent with Student 2's explanation?

F. No, because xenon has a larger molecular volume than krypton.
G. No, because xenon has a greater density than krypton.
H. Yes, because xenon has a larger molecular volume than krypton.
J. Yes, because xenon has a greater density than krypton.

5. Which of the following graphs of the relative effusion rates of oxygen, xenon, and krypton at 25°C is most consistent with Student 3's explanation?

A.

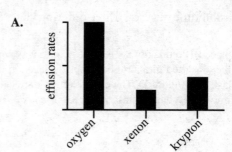

B.

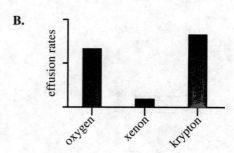

C.

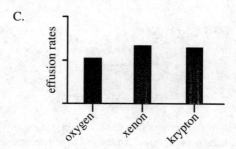

D.

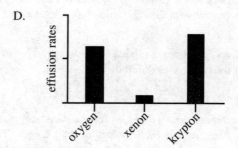

6. Suppose that Gas A had been hydrogen and Gas B had been helium. The results of the professor's experiment would have supported the explanation(s) provided by which student(s)?

F. Student 1 only
G. Student 2 only
H. Students 1 and 2 only
J. Students 1 and 3 only

7. Consider the data for carbon dioxide (a gas) at 25°C shown in the table below:

Molecular mass (amu)	Molecular volume ($\mathring{A}^3$)	Density (kg/L)
44.01	34.87	1.77

Which student(s) would predict that carbon dioxide would have a shorter effusion time than krypton?

A. Student 1 only
B. Student 1 and 2 only
C. Student 1 and 3 only
D. Students 1, 2, and 3

Summary

- In Dual Science passages, two, three, or more scientists present their differing views on a scientific subject.

- Don't pick a side. The ACT test writers want you to evaluate and compare the arguments presented, not decide which one is correct. Even if you know something about the topic, answer the questions using only what is presented in the passage.

- Start by using the questions to make a map of the order in which you will read the theories and answer questions on each, one at a time.

- Leave the questions on more than one theory for last.

- Don't forget to use your Letter of the Day if there are questions that you don't know how to do.

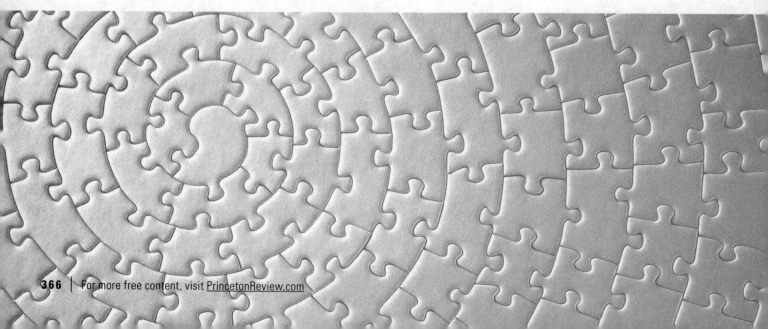

Part VI
How to Crack the ACT Writing Test

Chapter 24
Writing

The ACT includes an optional Writing Test. The Writing is optional because some schools want it, and some don't care either way. Unless you are 100% sure that everywhere you'll be applying doesn't need the Writing Test, we recommend that you sign up to take it when you take the ACT. Still, even though the writing task is kind of annoying, we've got some tips that will help you to get a great score.

THE OPTIONAL-ISH WRITING TEST

The ACT Writing Test is optional, but unfortunately, the "option" is not exactly yours. It's not whether you feel like taking an extra 40-minute section or not. Who would want to do that? Some of the schools you're applying to may require the Writing Test. Even if you're not sure, we still recommend that you take the additional test. We have two main reasons for saying so:

If you've purchased *ACT Elite 36,* then you already know The Princeton Review's approach to cracking the Essay section. Feel free to use this as a refresher, and then go to page 388 to hone those finely tuned writing skills you're developing.

- First, some schools require that you take the Writing Test. You wouldn't want to have to spend another Saturday taking the ACT because you opted out of the Writing when you shouldn't have.
- Second, a Writing score can make your college application more attractive, even to those schools that don't require it. Your essay score will appear on every score report you send to colleges. Every school you apply to will see that you took the initiative to opt in for the Writing Test, which is a good thing. Think of it like Honors or AP classes. You don't have to take them, but it looks good if you do.

The biggest reason of all is that it's just not that hard to get a good score on the Writing test. An impressive score is an impressive score, optional or not.

ALL RIGHT, YOU CONVINCED ME…NOW WHAT?

The ACT Writing Test consists of a single essay, which you are given 40 minutes to write. The big question will have to do with something ACT deems socially relevant. The question will not be relevant only for high-school students ("Are school uniforms the best, you guys?") nor so grandiose and abstract as to be basically unanswerable ("Is it always cruel to be kind in the right measure?").

A typical prompt will look something like this:

Education and the Workplace

Many colleges and universities have cut their humanities departments, and high schools have started to shift their attention much more definitively toward STEM (Science, Technology, Engineering, Mathematics) and away from ELA (English, Language Arts). Representatives from both school boards and government organizations suggest that the move toward STEM is necessary in helping students to participate in a meaningful way in the American workplace. Given the urgency of this debate for the future of education and society as a whole, it is worth examining the potential consequences of this shift in how students are educated in the United States.

Read and carefully consider these perspectives. Each suggests a particular way of thinking about the shift in American education.

Perspective One	Perspective Two	Perspective Three
ELA programs should be emphasized over STEM programs. Education is not merely a means to employment: ELA education helps students to live more meaningful lives. In addition, an exclusively STEM-based program cannot help but limit students' creativity and lead them to overemphasize the importance of money and other tangible gains.	ELA programs should be eradicated entirely, except to establish the basic literacy necessary to engage in the hard sciences, mathematics, and business. Reading and writing are activities that are best saved for the leisure of students who enjoy them.	ELA and STEM programs should always be in equal balance with one another. Both are necessary to providing a student with a well-rounded education. Moreover, equal emphasis will allow the fullest possible exposure to many subjects before students choose their majors and careers.

Essay Task

Write a unified, coherent essay in which you evaluate multiple perspectives on the issue of how schools should balance ELA and STEM subjects. In your essay, be sure to:

- analyze and evaluate the perspectives given
- state and develop your own perspective on the issue
- explain the relationship between your perspective and those given

Your perspective may be in full agreement with any of the others, in partial agreement, or wholly different. Whatever the case, support your ideas with logical reasoning and detailed, persuasive examples.

Here's How to Crack It

Your job is to write an essay in which you take some sort of position on the prompt, all while assessing the three perspectives provided in the boxes. ACT has hinted at the larger significance of the prompt, but you should also, if possible, give some indication of how you understand that significance.

This may be unlike essays you've written in your English classes. You're probably more used to answering some big question about a book or some ethical question. This time the question is, in a sense, already answered, so you need to be the moderator of the discussion. The idea behind such an exercise is that, in college, you will be required to take a variety of perspectives on some issue, assess those perspectives, and add your own. This is good practice: as you'll find in your college writing classes, essays are much less about coming up with the single correct answer than they are about *contributing to the conversation.*

Even if you have had to do something like this before, you probably haven't had to do it in 40 minutes. That's really not a lot of time, so throughout this chapter, we'll give you some tips for how to get a great score even with the time constraints.

A NOTE ON ARGUMENTS

You'll notice that ACT has placed a very explicit emphasis on the terms *argument* and *perspective*. These are terms that you assuredly already know, but the way these terms are used in everyday speech differs a lot from how they are used among English teachers and academics.

It's important to note that ACT is very careful to ask for your *perspective* rather than your *opinion*. That careful choice of language is there for your benefit. An argument can be a difficult thing to construct because it doesn't just take into account what you think: it requires a more complex understanding of the topic at hand.

The crucial thing about arguments is this:

> In order for a statement to be an *argument*, it must be possible to disagree with that statement.

Think about it this way. As you were reading the prompt above, you might have been thinking, "Great! I hate my English class!" or "Bummer! I hate my math class!" So you might think it would be good to center your essay on this kind of statement:

I don't like to read, so I like the idea of having to take fewer English classes.

That is an opinion, but it's not an argument. In order for it to be an argument, it would have to be possible to disagree with it. And go ahead and try to disagree with the italicized sentence. What could you say? "Yes, you do like to read!" or "No, you don't like the idea!" This isn't a real argument, and that's because the statement that started it (the italicized one) isn't a real argument itself.

The same goes for statements that are too vague, like this one:

The question of how to balance ELA and STEM classes is an interesting one.

Or this one:

All three of the perspectives provided are interesting.

Think about what kinds of conversations these statements begin. How would you respond? Probably something along the lines of, "Um…yep" or "Okay." Not much of a conversation, is it? That's because it hasn't started with an *argument*.

If you can find a way to anchor your essay with some argument, some unique perspective of your own that can be defended and debated, you are already in the upper echelon of scorers. Although it may seem like a minor point, the quality of the *argument* at the center of your essay will go a long way toward predicting your score.

WHAT THE GRADERS ARE GRADING

If you think you have a tough job writing an essay in only 40 minutes, have some sympathy for the graders. They have to grade each essay in a matter of minutes. Imagine how you would feel if you spent an entire day grading thousands of essays on the same topic. By essay number 50 or so, you probably wouldn't care much if a student used "except" instead of "accept."

ACT graders focus on the big picture. Your essay will be read by two graders, each of whom will assign it a series of four subscores, each from 1 to 6. Their scores will then be combined to give you a total score of 2–12. The scores will be based on how closely the essay adheres to the standards outlined on the following page.

Given the complexity of this grading system, it's best to think about these graders as grading *holistically*. In other words, they grade the essay as a whole, rather than keeping tabs on every little success or failure within the essay itself. To give one simple example, if you've got a few misspellings in the essay, that won't hurt you that much, but if your grammar and spelling are so messy that the grader doesn't know what you're saying, your Language Use and Conventions score will suffer.

ACT Graders vs. English Teachers

The graders who grade for ACT aren't like your English teachers. They don't have the time to focus on the little details of each essay, and frankly, they don't care about your grade the way your English teacher does. So don't sweat the small stuff! Focus on the big picture for the ACT: strong argument, engagement with multiple perspectives, solid examples, and (on the pencil-and-paper ACT) neatness.

According to the ACT guidelines, essay graders give scores in the following four categories.

1. **Ideas and Analysis:** Above all else, graders want to see that you can handle complex ideas. This essentially means how skilled you are at constructing an argument and assessing the arguments of others. You won't be graded on whether you pick the "right" answer (there isn't one). Instead, you'll be graded on how complex and sophisticated your answers are.

2. **Development and Support:** It's tough to make an argument without citing some examples. Graders want to see that you can justify the positions you're presenting in a given essay. This applies to how you assess the three given perspectives as well: nothing damages your interlocutor's argument like a killer counterexample.

3. **Organization:** In order to make sure that your graders can see the complexity of your ideas and the quality of the support you provide for them, you need to make sure your essay is organized in a way that makes that easy. Your essay should be a vehicle to help your readers see how smart you are. If you don't organize the essay well or effectively, your readers won't be able to see your brilliance in its full and effervescent luminousness.

4. **Language Use and Conventions:** Writing is all about *communication*. If your use of the language is coated with grammatical errors and misspellings, your writing won't communicate the way that it should. Graders will forgive a few stray errors, but if your grammar and spelling get in the way of what you're trying to say, those mistakes could cost you.

HOW TO GET A GOOD SCORE

The way to get a good score on the Writing Test is to make the graders' job easy. Show that you understand the perspectives and can generate one of your own. Show that you can support your ideas with examples, real or hypothetical. Show that you can arrange your essay in a way that makes sense. Show that you can use the English language correctly. This may seem like a tall order, but in the next few pages, we'll talk about how to write an essay that is most pleasing to your graders.

> Give the graders what they want! You may be a great writer, but the ACT graders are concerned with only a few very specific things.

It can be very intimidating to think that you have to keep all of this in mind as you write a 40-minute essay. It helps, though, if you remember that this essay is part of the ACT, and what do you typically have to do on the ACT? Fill in bubbles. Think of this essay as just another one of those bubbles: all the pieces should basically be in place before you even get to the test.

THE APPROACH

You may not know what the prompt will ask about, but you can at least go into the test with a consistent approach. You can approach each prompt the same way, and your essay can look very similar each time.

Just remember these four basic steps.

> The Basic Approach for the Writing Test
>
> 1. Work the Prompt.
> 2. Work the Perspectives.
> 3. Generate Your Own Perspective.
> 4. Consider Context.

Let's use each of these steps to break down the given prompt.

Step 1: Work the Prompt

Let's have another look at the prompt.

> Many colleges and universities have cut their humanities departments, and high schools have started to shift their attention much more definitively toward STEM (Science, Technology, Engineering, Mathematics) and away from ELA (English, Language Arts). Representatives from both school boards and government organizations suggest that the move toward STEM is necessary in helping students to participate in a meaningful way in the American workplace. Given the urgency of this debate for the future of education and society at as whole, it is worth examining the potential consequences of this shift in how students are educated in the United States.

In order to work the prompt, we'll need to clarify a few things.

First, we should identify the major *terms* of the prompt. Give this a try.

_____

_____

_____

The answers you came up with are probably some version of these terms: *education, schools, STEM, ELA,* and *workplace.*

The next task is a little more complex. Figure out the central relationship in those terms, and identify the possible points of *tension* within those terms. In other words, what in the prompt requires you to weigh in? Why is this relationship still the subject of debate and not a done deal?

_____

_____

_____

This task is a little tougher, but it's essential. Try to pick two or three of the terms you identified as key, and write a sentence describing their relationship.

You may come up with something like this:

If schools *prepare students for the* workplace, *what should students be learning in schools?*

Or like this:

Schools *should weigh* ELA *and* STEM *differently depending on what those schools care about teaching.*

You may have come up with something different, and that's fine. The real test will come in the next step when you read the three perspectives provided. If those seem to address the central tension you've described, you're in good shape.

Step 2: Work the Perspectives

Typically, the three perspectives will be split: one *for*, one *against*, and one *in the middle*. Your job in Step 2 is to identify these perspectives, and to try to figure out what they have to say to each other.

> It doesn't matter whether you agree or disagree with the perspectives. Assess them *as arguments* first and foremost.

Let's have another look at the perspectives before we get started.

Perspective One	Perspective Two	Perspective Three
ELA programs should be emphasized over STEM programs. Education is not merely a means to employment: ELA education helps students to live more meaningful lives. In addition, an exclusively STEM-based program cannot help but limit students' creativity and lead them to overemphasize the importance of money and other tangible gains.	ELA programs should be eradicated entirely, except to establish the basic literacy necessary to engage in the hard sciences, mathematics, and business. Reading and writing are activities that are best saved for the leisure of students who enjoy them.	ELA and STEM programs should always be in equal balance with one another. Both are necessary to providing a student with a well-rounded education. Moreover, equal emphasis will allow the fullest possible exposure to many subjects before students choose their majors and careers.

Which perspective is *for* emphasizing STEM programs over ELA programs? What does this perspective consider? What does it overlook?

_____

_____

_____

Which perspective is *against* emphasizing STEM programs over ELA programs? What does this perspective consider? What does it overlook?

_____

_____

_____

Which perspective is *in the middle* on the question of emphasizing STEM programs over ELA programs? What does this perspective consider? What does it overlook?

_____

_____

_____

You may have come up with something like this:

For (Perspective 2): This perspective takes fully seriously the idea that education leads to employment, and as a result, it sees no value in ELA programs at all because those programs do not have any tangible benefits in the workplace. What this perspective misses, however, is that ELA could have some applicability to the world of work (in marketing, for instance, or in other creative spheres). Nor does it give any serious consideration to the idea that education could be good on its own.

Against (Perspective 1): This perspective is absolutely against the idea of allowing STEM programs to take over, even if those programs do lead to more employability. Perspective 1 says that education should be independent of the workplace and should be more about how to live life. What this perspective misses, however, is that de-emphasis of STEM programs is not practical in the contemporary world, which privileges STEM and technical knowledge. Perspective 1 also severs the link between education and employability too definitively: they must have something to do with each other!

In the middle (Perspective 3): This perspective is in favor of the status quo, which has STEM and ELA programs in equal balance with one another. It says that only a variety of exposure will allow students to find their niches within the workplace. What this perspective misses, however, is that if there is a link between education and employment, this variety is potentially irrelevant. It also overlooks the idea that there is a crisis in education, which is the whole impetus for the previous two ideas.

Your working of the perspectives may not look exactly like this, but that's okay. As long as you've identified where each perspective stands (*for, against,* or *in the middle*) and then identified at least one shortcoming of each perspective, you're in good shape for the next step: generating your own perspective.

Step 3: Generate Your Own Perspective

Now that you've outlined the prompt and the perspectives, it's time to generate your own. You'll draw from each of the perspectives, and you may side with one of them, but your perspective should have something unique about it.

> Come up with your own perspective! If you merely restate one of the three given perspectives, you won't be able to get into the highest scoring ranges.

Start by describing your perspective.

_____

_____

_____

Just so you have a sense of how to build this perspective, we've included one of our own. This is not to say that this perspective is correct—remember, there is no correct answer! It's just an effective argument that would generate a high score.

In my view, the question of how education and the workplace are related to each other misses the point. The cause and effect is wrong, and the very fact that we can ask this question shows that a significant change has already taken place. The prompt asks us to explain what the most effective link between school and workplace is, but that already presumes that there is a link between school and workplace, which is not necessarily universally true. Before we can answer the question of whether STEM programs should be emphasized over ELA programs, we should first wonder whether we'd like to proceed with this linkage between education and workplace. Understanding this linkage is essential because if we find that social prejudices are shaping education without seeming to do so, we will likely find that the potential for innovation and creativity shrinks, and all the technical knowledge in the world won't save us.

Now that you've generated your own perspective, check it against the perspectives already given.

How does your perspective compare to Perspective One?

_____

_____

_____

My perspective is probably closest to Perspective One, but it differs from Perspective One in that it refuses to engage in the question of employment. Perspective One is limited because, especially at the end, it tries to make a case for ELA as employable skills, which is not particularly viable.

How does your perspective compare to Perspective Two?

_____

_____

_____

My perspective is furthest from Perspective Two, though the disagreement is not so explicit as to say, "Perspective Two, you're wrong!" Instead, my perspective shows that Perspective Two is wrapped up in all kinds of assumptions and prejudices of which the author of Perspective Two is seemingly unaware.

How does your perspective compare to Perspective Three?

_____

_____

_____

My perspective has a different aim from that of Perspective Three. Perspective Three is interested in maintaining a balance, but only because he or she sees that balance as advantageous in determining one's eventual employment. In my view, Perspective Three is the worst of both worlds: it has a loose grip on the status quo while at the same time accepting premises that there is no good reason to accept.

If you were able to differentiate your view from all three perspectives while your view remained intact, congratulations! You're on your way to a great score! There's just one more thing…the bigger picture.

Step 4: Consider Context

As you build your argument, remember that the graders are looking to see a complex mind at work. Examples are important, but they exist mainly to help you structure and discuss your perspective and why you have that perspective. Examples can come from anywhere, but they should be reasonable, and they should have a clear application to your argument.

To start, list the examples you'll use to make your argument, and identify how they will help you make that argument. Try to come up with at least two.

_____

_____

_____

_____

_____

I'm going to use one example that has a direct application to what's being discussed in the prompt: Albert Einstein. I'm going to use another that shows why the discussion may be irrelevant: the question of human happiness.

Now describe the order in which you'll discuss your examples and why.

_____

_____

_____

_____

I'm going to discuss the examples in the order I've given above. That way my essay will start by discussing the prompt directly and will then broaden out to show the larger question of which the prompt is part.

THE TEMPLATE

You've done a lot of pre-work, and now it's time to put it all in essay form. Remember, though, that you are taking a *standardized test,* so it will help you to be as *standardized* as possible in your presentation. If you come in knowing basically what your essay will look like, you'll have a much easier time saying all you need to say.

If you already know what your template will look like, great. The best essays always reveal something personal about the writer and his or her complex mind.

If you're not sure what your essay will look like, never fear! Below, we outline a basic template that will have space for all the good stuff you just did in your pre-writing.

Introduction

A good introduction will lay out the terms of the *conversation* in which the writer is planning to participate. It will give the reader a preview of what is to come and will, hopefully, encourage the reader to keep reading. In roughly three to five sentences, try out the following:

1. Identify *why* the question posed in the prompt is important.
2. Present your perspective on the question posed in the prompt.
3. Preview how you intend to give support to your perspective.

Based on the pre-writing we did above, here is an example of an effective introduction.

"We want our students to have the best education possible." We've heard enough politicians say it to know that this idea is more or less a truth universally acknowledged. The problem comes when we start to think in a real way about what that "best" education could be. Recently, the rhetoric surrounding educational policy has been all about the importance of STEM programs—improving them, foregrounding them, and making them more attractive to all students. The idea motivating this rhetoric is economic. School is preparation for the workplace; therefore, students should become best educated in the subjects that will make them most employable. This seems like sound logic, but it is not the only possible conclusion, nor even necessarily the best one. The more essential task, in my view, is to clarify what a "good education" is and, in a much larger sense, what we want from our lives.

This introduction is effective because it shows the broader context into which the prompt fits: that of education reform in the country as a whole. The introduction then goes on to show a potential problem with asking the question itself: the not-so-universal agreement on what a "good education" is. Then, the introduction is particularly effective at stating the essay's goal: to analyze the three perspectives, to show their limitations, and to show why a different question may get more squarely to the root of the problem.

Body Paragraphs

Body paragraphs provide your reader with the details and examples of your discussion. Try to generate one body paragraph for each example you discuss (usually two or three). Make sure that your body paragraphs do the following:

1. Provide a transition from the previous paragraph and a topic sentence that describes the new one.
2. Assess at least one of the perspectives given in the prompt as a way to strengthen your own perspective.
3. Use an example to develop your perspective or analyze one of the given perspectives.
4. Relate your discussion back to your position and the larger topic.

Based on the pre-writing exercises, here's an example of an effective body paragraph.

You may ask, then, which do I think is better? ELA or STEM? The idea that one would need to choose is part of the problem. Albert Einstein said, "Imagination is more important than knowledge." Now, you'd think that Einstein (the father of twentieth-century STEM, basically) would love the idea of turning all students into little scientists and mathematicians. What Einstein believed, and what his life showed, however, are far different. Einstein understood that all knowledge was valuable but that the imaginative things one does with that knowledge are even more valuable. One would be hard-pressed to find a great mind that was not richly educated across the subjects, from ELA to STEM and beyond. As a result, those who argue solely in favor of either ELA or STEM both miss the point in suggesting the overemphasis of one subject group over another. As Einstein's example shows, what one learns is less important than how one applies that knowledge, and one's possibilities for breadth and imagination necessarily increase with the acquisition of many types of knowledge.

This is an effective body paragraph because it analyzes two or three perspectives given in the prompt. Notice that you do not need to (nor should you) write "Perspective One...." The graders are looking for you to include the ideas of the perspectives but not to mention them directly. The paragraph gives an example, Albert Einstein, to show the limitations of both of those perspectives while supporting the author's own perspective.

The paragraph also contains an implied transition to the next paragraph, especially because the reader may now believe that if the author is neither *for* nor *against*, he or she must be *in the middle*. As we know from the introduction, however, this may not be the case, and we should read on to find out.

If you want to know what the author's next body paragraph says, good! That means the author has your interest. Think about some of the ways that has happened. What do you want to know? What questions has the author left unanswered? What else do you want to contribute to the *conversation*?

Try your own paragraph. Even if our perspective doesn't match yours, try to think along with us here. You'll find it's a useful exercise: ACT Writing is not the place to express your deepest thoughts but to develop your most complex argument.

_____

_____

_____

_____

_____

What did you do well in that argument? What could you have improved? Do you need a third paragraph before you hit the conclusion?

_____

_____

_____

Conclusion

Even though you may be running out of time, it's important to write a conclusion. It gives your essay a completeness that it might not otherwise have. An effective conclusion will usually do the following:

1. Recap your discussion as it has related to the prompt and perspectives
2. Restate your perspective and arguments
3. Provide a final overarching thought on the topic

Here's an example of an effective conclusion.

In short, the question of a STEM focus versus an ELA emphasis forces us to ask an even larger question. What is education? Is it job training? Is it life training? Education reform creates larger changes than many of us realize, and it therefore requires more reflection. While we are comfortable in the idea that education creates members of society, we should also see that society creates a certain type of education. Before we implement these changes, we need to be very certain what our goals are, especially in the very long term.

This conclusion is effective because it summarizes what the author has said without restating it outright. It also pushes the discussion toward a different, larger question, showing that the author has a broader understanding of what is going on in the prompt.

Now, here's the full essay in all its glory.

"We want our students to have the best education possible." We've heard enough politicians say it to know that this idea is more or less a truth universally acknowledged. The problem comes when we start to think in a real way about what that "best" education could be. Recently, the rhetoric surrounding educational policy has been all about the importance of STEM programs—improving them, foregrounding them, and making them more attractive to all students. The idea motivating this rhetoric is economic. School is preparation for the workplace; therefore, students should become best educated in the subjects that will make them most employable. This seems like sound logic, but it is not the only possible conclusion, nor even necessarily the best one. The more essential task, in my view, is to clarify what a "good education" is and, in a much larger sense, what we want from our lives.

You may ask, then, which do I think is better? ELA or STEM? The idea that one would need to choose is part of the problem. Albert Einstein said, "Imagination is more important than knowledge." Now, you'd think that Einstein (the father of twentieth-century STEM, basically) would love the idea of turning all students into little scientists and mathematicians. What Einstein believed, and what his life showed, however, are far different. Einstein understood that all knowledge was valuable but that the imaginative things one does with that knowledge are even more valuable. One would be hard-pressed to find a great mind that was not richly educated across the subjects, from ELA to STEM and beyond. As a result, those who argue solely in favor of either ELA or STEM both miss the point in suggesting the overemphasis of one subject group over another. As Einstein's example shows, what one learns is less important than how one applies that knowledge, and one's possibilities for breadth and imagination necessarily increase with the acquisition of many types of knowledge.

This is not to say, however, that education must involve an equal portion of STEM and ELA. While there is some value in maintaining a balance between ELA and STEM subjects, the idea that such balance is a necessity is wildly misdirected. While it is to be hoped that all adults will be gainfully employed once they leave school, the idea that school should be all geared towards employability is disappointing. As Einstein's example shows, there is more to learning than employability, and even if STEM programs were somehow foregrounded, the lack of ELA programs would limit how imaginatively and creatively students could interpret their data. And let's not overlook the biggest problem of all: if all knowledge acquisition is geared toward how much money it can make us, then to what have we reduced the meaning of our lives? This rhetoric of schools as training sites can lead to only one place: five-year-olds who believe that the only purpose anyone could have on this Earth is to get a good job and make money. Is that a world you'd want to live in? Consider yourself lucky to have the capacity to imagine such a world!

In short, the question of a STEM focus versus an ELA emphasis forces us to ask an even larger question. What is education? Is it job training? Is it life training? Education reform creates larger changes than many of us realize, and it therefore requires more reflection. While we are comfortable in the idea that education creates members of society, we should also see that society creates a certain type of education. Before we implement these changes, we need to be very certain what our goals are, especially in the very long term.

A CONCLUSION OF OUR OWN

We know that this can seem like a lot to do in 40 minutes, especially for something that won't count toward your composite. We can't help you with the composite part, but we can say this: the essay becomes easier with practice.

And now that you're an expert at the ACT Writing section, here are a few other things to keep in mind.

1. **Length.** ACT graders tend to reward longer essays. On the ACT Online Test, aim for at least 500 words (you won't have a word count function, so practice to learn about how long that is). On the pencil-and-paper ACT, make sure you get onto the second page and the third if possible. If your writing tends to be small, you may want to practice writing larger, especially because it will also make your essay a bit neater and easier to read. If your handwriting is large, make sure you write an extra page to compensate.

2. **Sentence structure.** Varying your sentence structure helps to improve the rhythm of your essay. If you write a really long sentence with lots of modifiers and dependent clauses, it sometimes helps to follow it with a shorter, more direct sentence. It really works. Don't try to be too fancy, though. The longer the sentence is, the more opportunity there is to confuse the reader or to make a grammatical mistake.

3. **Diction.** Diction refers to word choice. You certainly want to sprinkle some nice vocabulary words throughout your paper. But make sure to use and spell them correctly. If you're uncertain about the meaning or spelling of a word, it's best just to pick a different word. Using a big word incorrectly makes a worse impression than using a smaller word correctly.

4. **Neatness.** Use capital letters at the beginning of sentences. Break your writing into paragraphs. On the pencil-and-paper ACT, make sure you indent each new paragraph. Align your essay using the lines on the paper. Don't go over the lines or write down the side of the page. Avoid messy cross-outs. Although the grader should not take these kinds of things into consideration when determining your grade, a neat, legible essay will be easier to read. Your grader will read hundreds, if not thousands, of essays. A neat essay will make the grader happier.

PRACTICE ESSAY PROMPTS

Here are a few more sample essay prompts that you can use for practice. After you finish each essay, read it over—or better yet, have someone else read it—and see how well your essay conforms to the ACT's grading standards. When you practice writing the essay, it's best to limit your time to 40 minutes to experience how short the allotted time really is.

Prompt #1

Commercial Drones

One of the most exciting yet divisive technologies to become available to the public in the last few years is commercial drones. Commercial drones have been used by movie studios to cheaply and safely shoot action scenes for films. Scientists and researchers have used them in order to access the most restricted parts of the globe for observation. However, along with the beneficial uses of commercial drones come more detrimental ones. Several privacy concerns have surfaced over the use of commercial drones to spy on individuals, even on their personal property. Recently, a commercial drone interfered with the work of firefighter helicopters delivering water over a California forest fire. These events have prompted serious debate as to whether commercial drones should be regulated or restricted by the government and to what extent.

Read and carefully consider these perspectives. Each suggests a particular way of thinking about the manner in which the government should regulate commercial drone use.

Perspective One	Perspective Two	Perspective Three
The government can, and should, regulate the use of drones. If any behavior of an individual or business interferes with government and safety operations or violates the rights of an individual, that behavior is legally penalized. Drone use is no different.	Drones should absolutely be regulated when used for business purposes, as all aspects of business are regulated in this country. However, the regulation of personal drone use by private citizens seems to be an overreach of the government's power.	The very space that drones occupy implies that they should not be regulated: no one *owns* the sky. Just as an individual is free to take his boat into the ocean, so too should an individual or business be able to freely access the sky with a commercial drone.

Essay Task

Write a unified, coherent essay in which you evaluate multiple perspectives on the question of to what extent the government should regulate commercial drone use. In your essay, be sure to:

- analyze and evaluate the perspectives given
- state and develop your own perspective on the issue
- explain the relationship between your perspective and those given

Your perspective may be in full agreement with any of the others, in partial agreement, or wholly different. Whatever the case, support your ideas with logical reasoning and detailed, persuasive examples.

Prompt #2

Genetic Engineering

Since the 1970s, humans have directly altered the DNA of animals, plants, and bacteria to produce desired traits. Genetic engineering has been used by the medical industry to manufacture insulin for the treatment of diabetes. The agricultural industry has utilized genetic engineering to create pesticide-resistant crops, improve the health value of soybeans, and increase the size of cattle. If the scientific community generally sees genetic engineering as a massive step forward, why is there such widespread opposition to the practice? As the use of genetic engineering increases, it is important to examine the potential consequences of directly altering DNA.

Read and carefully consider these perspectives. Each suggests a particular way of thinking about genetic engineering.

Perspective One	Perspective Two	Perspective Three
Genetic engineering will have detrimental effects on the environment. Artificially strengthening particular organisms will upset the natural balance of ecosystems, with disastrous consequences.	Genetically modified organisms are superior to non-modified organisms in pest resistance, hardiness, and yield. Further genetic engineering of crops and livestock will help solve global food shortages.	Genetically modifying organisms is ultimately no different from the cross-breeding that farmers have been doing for thousands of years. While the technology has improved, it's still just combining favorable characteristics of organisms to produce a better plant.

Essay Task

Write a unified, coherent essay in which you evaluate multiple perspectives on the question of weighing the potential benefits versus consequences of genetic engineering. In your essay, be sure to:

- analyze and evaluate the perspectives given
- state and develop your own perspective on the issue
- explain the relationship between your perspective and those given

Your perspective may be in full agreement with any of the others, in partial agreement, or wholly different. Whatever the case, support your ideas with logical reasoning and detailed, persuasive examples.

Summary: An Essay Checklist

Now look at your essays and see whether you applied the strategies presented in this chapter.

- ○ The Introduction
  Did you
  - start with a topic sentence that paraphrases or restates the central issue?
  - clearly state your position on the issue?

- ○ Body Paragraph 1
  Did you
  - start with a transition/topic sentence that discusses the opposing side of your argument?
  - discuss the given perspective(s) that would support the opposing argument?
  - give a specific example that could be used to support the perspective(s)?
  - explain why you disagree with those perspectives?

- ○ Body Paragraph 2
  Did you
  - start with a transition/topic sentence that discusses your position on the central issue?
  - clearly explain your position including any of the given perspectives that support your position?
  - give a clear example that supports your position?
  - end the paragraph by restating your thesis?

- ○ Conclusion
  Did you
  - restate your position on the issue?
  - end with a flourish?

- ○ Overall
  Did you
  - write neatly if you hand-wrote the test?
  - avoid multiple spelling and grammar mistakes?
  - try to vary your sentence structure?
  - use a few impressive-sounding words?

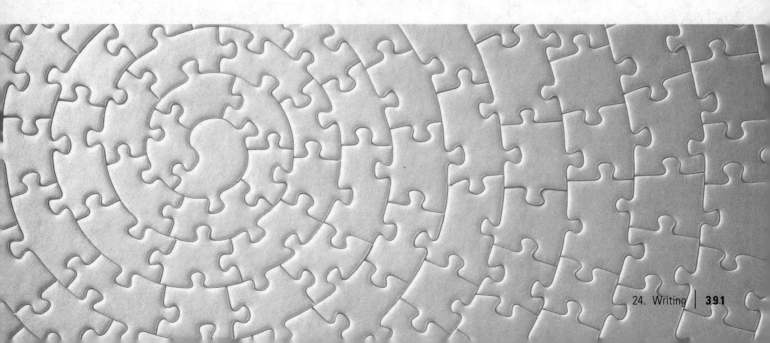

Part VII
Drill
Answers and
Explanations

Chapter 25
Drill Answers and
Explanations

PART II: ENGLISH

English Drill 1 (Chapter 6)

1. **C** This sentence requires a word that will go with the non-underlined object, *the many achievements.* Choices (A), (B), and (D) do not work with this phrase. Only (C) can work with the non-underlined portions of the sentence, creating the phrase *large canvases that celebrate the many achievements.*

2. **J** Apostrophes should be used only to indicate possession or contractions. Since *achievements* is not in possession of anything, and *achievement is* would not work in the context, eliminate all choices with apostrophes: (F), (G), and (H). Only (J), containing no apostrophe, can work in the context.

3. **A** Since there is Stop punctuation in the answer choices, use the Vertical Line Test. The first part of the sentence, *His portrait of Ice-T,* is not a complete idea, so (C) and (D) can be eliminated. Choice (A) is the correct answer because the comma sets off the unnecessary information that follows, *the rapper and reality-TV star.*

4. **H** As written, this sentence is incomplete, so eliminate (F). Choices (G) and (J) do not make the sentence complete, so those can also be eliminated. Only (H) creates a complete idea.

5. **A** Pay close attention to the non-underlined part of this sentence. The word *them* needs to refer back to a specific noun, and only (A) provides the appropriate one: *Wiley's subjects.* Choices (B), (C), and (D) do not make the meaning of the sentence clear.

6. **G** All four of the answer choices say essentially the same thing. In this case, choose the shortest one that makes the sentence complete, consistent, and clear. Choice (G) is the shortest, and it preserves the meaning of the sentence, so (G) is the correct answer.

7. **A** The underlined portion of this sentence is part of a pair of activities: the non-underlined portion says *mix the paints,* so the underlined portion must match the verb tense of the word *mix.* Only (A), the original answer, does so.

8. **J** As written, this sentence contains an ambiguous pronoun. The word *them* could refer to *assistants, materials,* or *paints,* none of which would work in context, eliminating (F). Choices (G) and (H) are unclear. Only (J) is adequately specific and is therefore the correct answer.

9. **C** All four of the answer choices say essentially the same thing. In this case, choose the shortest one that makes the sentence complete, consistent, and clear. Choice (C) is the shortest, and it preserves the meaning of the sentence, so (C) is the correct answer.

10. **J** Each sentence in this paragraph contains a description of Wiley's subjects: *various, anonymous men; common people; people from oppressed cultures;* and *those to whom history pays no attention.* Therefore, the first sentence must preview this theme of the "common" or "average" people whom Wiley paints. Choice (J) does so and is therefore the correct answer. Choices (F), (G), and (H) are true statements about Wiley himself, but they do not fit with the focus of this paragraph.

11. **D** The underlined portion does not fit where it is now, eliminating (A). The phrase *portray of Harlem various, anonymous men* does not make sense, eliminating (B). The phrase *Wiley of Harlem* does not make sense in context because, in addition to being awkwardly phrased, this phrase assumes that Wiley is from Harlem, which is not supported by the passage, eliminating (C). Only (D) can work, as it correctly situates the underlined portion in the phrase *the streets of Harlem*.

12. **F** The *recent work* is that of Kehinde Wiley, so the only pronoun that can be substituted here is *his*, as in (F). Choices (G), (H), and (J) do not work in this context.

13. **C** Each sentence in this paragraph contains a description of Wiley's subjects: *various, anonymous men; common people; people from oppressed cultures;* and *those to whom history pays no attention*. It would therefore not make sense to include a sentence that lists a museum where Wiley's paintings have been been shown, eliminating (A) and (B). Choice (D) can also be eliminated because this paragraph is not exclusively about Harlem. Only (C) correctly states that the sentence should not be included and gives the appropriate reason.

14. **J** The sentence is not complete as written, which immediately eliminates (F). Choices (G) and (H) also create incomplete sentences, so those too can be eliminated. Only (J) creates a complete idea, so it is the correct answer.

15. **B** This sentence states that *Wiley's works can be seen in galleries all over the world*, and the underlined portion offers one reason that Wiley's popularity is so broad. Therefore, there is no reason to delete the information, especially because it does not repeat or undermine earlier parts of the passage. Eliminate (C) and (D). The underlined portion does not contain information about Wiley's selection of subjects, so (A) can also be eliminated. Only (B) correctly states that the information should be kept and gives an appropriate reason.

English Drill 2 (Chapter 7)

1. **C** If you can't cite a reason to use a comma, don't use one. This particular comma separates the subject from its verb, so eliminate (A). Choice (B) adds a comma unnecessarily, so it can also be eliminated. Choice (D) uses a single dash, which requires a complete idea before it. *After school let out, my best friend, and I* is not a complete idea, so (D) can be eliminated. Only (C), containing no punctuation, remains.

2. **H** Stop punctuation is used in the answer choices, so use the Vertical Line Test. The first part of the sentence, *From the little trail beside the school, we'd climb down to the old railway tunnel that had gone dark many years before,* is complete. The second part of the sentence, *that pitch darkness was terrifying and mysterious,* is also complete. These ideas must therefore be separated by Stop punctuation, which eliminates (F) and (G). Choice (J) contains Stop punctuation (comma + FANBOYS), but it introduces a contrast with the word *yet* that does not make sense in this context. Only (H) works.

3. **B** Identify the purpose stated in the question that the correct choice is supposed to fulfill. It asks for a word that indicates that the narrator and his friend held their flashlights *nervously*. Choices (A) and (C) are neutral and therefore do not contain any hint of this nervousness. Choice (D) does not make sense in this context. Only (B), *clutching*, fulfills the purpose.

4. **H** Pay close attention to the question, which asks for *what happened during the summer walks*. Only (H) continues the narration in an appropriate way. Choices (F), (G), and (J) break the narrative flow. Also, the word *Sometimes* in (H) provides the necessary contrast to the word *always* in the following sentence.

5. **C** Since there are colons in the answer choices, use the Vertical Line Test to start. The first part of the sentence (up to the word *purpose*) is complete, as is the second part of the sentence (from *really* onward). Therefore, Go punctuation cannot work, eliminating (A) and (B). Choice (D) changes the meaning, so it can also be eliminated. Choice (C) can work because a colon requires only a complete idea before it: the idea after it can be complete or incomplete.

6. **F** Choices (F), (G), and (H) sound the same, but make sure you are using the correct pronoun for the context. *They're* is a contraction of *they are*, which cannot work in this context, and *their* is a possessive pronoun, which also cannot work, eliminating (G) and (H). Choice (J) does not make sense in this context, so only (F) remains as the correct answer.

7. **C** The word *though* in Sentence 6 indicates a contrast with whatever sentence comes before it. Therefore, look for a sentence that contains *aimless visits* with which this sentence will contrast. Sentence 1 provides these *aimless visits,* stating that the narrator and his friend didn't go down into the tunnel *with any specific purpose*. Therefore, the sentence should go before Sentence 2, as suggested in (C).

8. **J** The subject of this sentence is *history*, so the modifier that comes before it should modify that word. Choices (F), (G), and (H) all create modifiers that describe the narrator or something other than history, so they can be eliminated. Only (J) provides an appropriate modifier for *history*.

9. **D** As written, this sentence suggests that the history teacher gave this bit of information to his students four hundred years earlier, which can't work, eliminating (A). *Four centuries earlier* must refer to something about the Dutch settlers, and only (D) provides a placement that will create the appropriate reference.

10. **F** There is Stop punctuation in the answers, so use the Vertical Line Test. The first part of the sentence, *In fact...region,* is complete, but the second part of the sentence, *an area...New York,* is incomplete. Stop punctuation cannot work, eliminating (H), but there must be some pause, eliminating (G). Choice (J) makes the sentence incomplete, so it too can be eliminated. Only (F) works because a colon can be used only after a complete idea but can be followed by either an incomplete or complete idea.

11. **C** This sentence is incomplete as written, so (A) can be eliminated. Choice (D) creates the same problem. Of the remaining two choices, (C) is better because it indicates a contrast between the *ruthless* behavior of the Dutch and the fact that they *held on to many Lenape names*.

12. **J** All answer choices contain the word *the*. Choices (F), (G), and (H) put some information before that word, but none of that information is necessary. Therefore, in order to make the sentence as concise as possible, (J) is the correct answer.

13. **A** This part of the sentence describes the word *influence*, and (A) is appropriate because that influence is *commemorated by the names*. Choices (B), (C), and (D) cannot work in the context, so they can be eliminated.

14. **H** This sentence describes *corridors of the city* that are not well-known, and (F), (G), and (J) provide reasonable synonyms. Choice (H), *classified*, may be a synonym for secret, but it is not an appropriate synonym in this context. Choice (H) is therefore correct because it would NOT be acceptable.

15. **D** A colon must be preceded by a complete idea. Neither *we were invited to* nor *we were invited to give* is a complete idea, so (B) and (C) can be eliminated. Eliminate (A) because it inserts a comma where there is not a good reason to insert one. Only (D), containing no punctuation, remains and is the correct answer.

Rhetorical Skills Drill (Chapter 8)

1. **B** Cross off LEAST, and use POE. *Fame*, *stardom*, and *greatness* can all work the same way as *prominence* in the context of the sentence. *Projection* does not mean the same thing and is the correct answer.

2. **J** Try out each answer choice. *Live television* is the intended meaning.

3. **A** Try reading the paragraph without the sentence. The following sentence mentions "the remakes," which doesn't refer back to anything if this sentence is deleted. The sentence must be kept, so eliminate (C) and (D). Choice (A) is supported because this sentence does provide context for the next sentence. Choice (B) is not supported because the sentence doesn't mention why the show was a success. Choice (A) is the correct answer.

4. **G** Identify the purpose in the question. The correct choice must convey extreme skill. *Honing their craft* does just that, while all of the other choices contain no specific mention of skill.

5. **D** Use POE. Sentences 2 and 3 should go back to back, with Sentence 3 providing a list of the *young talents* mentioned in Sentence 2. Eliminate (B) and (C), and compare the difference between (A) and (D). Sentence 1 should directly precede Sentence 4, so (D) is correct.

6. **F** Identify the purpose in the question. The correct choice must introduce the paragraph. Finish reading the paragraph, and then return to the question. Since the topic involves problems with the live broadcast, (F) is the correct introduction.

7. **C** To crack this type of strategy question, use POE to consider which choice correctly describes the sentence to be deleted. Choice (C) is the correct description.

8. **F**   Identify the purpose in the question and connect it to the correct reason among the answers. Choices (G), (H), and (J) offer reasons that do not support the purpose well, nor describe the content of the essay accurately.

9. **D**   If you didn't see the warning at the beginning of the passage, you may have found the flow of the essay jarring. Even if you didn't, always use POE with order of paragraph questions. Look for topic and concluding sentences to make the flow of ideas consistent. The topic sentence of paragraph 2 makes a good transition after the discussion of accidents in paragraph 4.

PART III: MATH

Fundamentals Drill (Chapter 10)

1. **C**   You'll need to find the prime factorization of 54, so use a factor tree. In using this tree, you'll find the prime factorization of $54 = 6 \times 9 = (2 \times 3) \times (3 \times 3) = 2 \times 3^3$. The *distinct* prime factors of 54, therefore, are 2 and 3. The product of these two numbers is 6, (C). If you chose (E), you may have missed the word *distinct*! Read carefully!

2. **G**   Take this problem in bite-sized pieces. If x is the least odd prime number, x must be 3. If y is the least positive integer multiple of 10, y must be 10. The difference between these two numbers is therefore $10 - 3 = 7$, (G). If you selected (K), be careful: you may have thought that 20 was the first integer multiple of 10, but the first multiple of any number is that number itself!

3. **D**   Remember MADSPM, and don't forget Order of Operations, or PEMDAS. Do the parentheses first, and remember, when you raise an exponent to a *power*, you *multiply* those exponents: $(x^{-1}y^{-3})^{-2}(x^4y^7)^3 = (x^2y^6)(x^{12}y^{21})$. Now, combine like terms, and remember, when you *multiply* numbers with exponents, you *add* those exponents to one another: $(x^2y^6)(x^{12}y^{21}) = x^{14}y^{27}$, (D).

4. **H**   Although this problem involves an imaginary number, you can still use a traditional FOIL method to find the answer. You are asked to square the expression, so do so, and remember to multiply the First, Outer, Inner, and Last terms: $(i + 4)(i + 4) = i^2 + 8i + 16$. None of the answer choices look quite like this, but remember, $i^2 = -1$, so substitute this term: $i^2 + 8i + 16 = -1 + 8i + 16 = 8i + 15$, (H).

5. **C**   The prime numbers between 10 and 20 are as follows: 11, 13, 17, 19. You want the *least* sum of three *distinct* numbers, so the only possible answer is $11 + 13 + 17 = 41$, (C). If you chose (B), you may have missed the word *distinct*.

6. **F**   You may have solved this problem with your calculator. Alternately, using fraction rules and MADSPM, this scientific notation equation can be solved like this:

$$\frac{9.1 \times 10^{-7}}{1.3 \times 10^3} = \frac{9.1}{1.3} \times \frac{10^{-7}}{10^3} = \frac{9.1}{1.3} \times 10^{-7-3} = \frac{9.1}{1.3} \times 10^{-10} = 7.0 \times 10^{-10}$$

If you used your calculator to solve this problem and got the wrong answer, make sure that you entered the appropriate exponents, used parentheses around the numerator and denominator, and closed any parenthesis your calculator opened.

7. **C** You may have solved this problem using a graphing calculator by entering the answer choices in the Y= menu and graphing each one to see which graph does not intersect the x-axis. You may have also decided to check the discriminants for all the answers. All the equations are in standard form, so plug the values of a, b, and c into the discriminant, $b^2 - 4ac$, for each answer. The values for (C) are $a = 1$, $b = -3$, and $c = 10$. The discriminant is $(-3)^2 - 4(1)(10) = 9 - 40 = -31$. Since the discriminant is negative, the graph of the equation in (C) does not intersect the x-axis.

Algebra Drill (Chapter 11)

1. **C** This might look like a traditional plug-and-chug problem, but the problem is asking for a specific value, and the answer choices are all real numbers—a great indication that you can use PITA! This time, the problem is asking for the *largest*, so start with (E). Does the equation work if $x = 5$? $5^2 - 4(5) + 3 = 25 - 20 + 3 \neq 0$. Eliminate (E). Try (D): $4^2 - 4(4) + 3 = 16 - 16 + 3 \neq 0$. Try (C): $3^2 - 4(3) + 3 = 9 - 12 + 3 = 0$. It works, and because you're using PITA, you can stop once you've found a correct answer. If you selected (A), be careful: this is the *smallest* value of x that solves the equation!

2. **G** There are variables in the answer choices, so let's plug in. Let's say $x = 2$ and plug this in to the equation: $\dfrac{(2)^2 + 6(2) - 27}{(2 + 9)} = \dfrac{4 + 12 - 27}{11} = \dfrac{-11}{11} = -1$, which means your target answer is -1. Try $x = 2$ in the answer choices to see which one gives this target answer. Only (G) works.

3. **A** This problem is very confusingly worded, so let's make sure we use PITA to keep all the work manageable. We'll start with (C) and work out from there, so our number is 11. "2 less than 3 times 11" is $3(11) - 2 = 31$. "4 more than the product of 5 and 3" is $4 + (5 \times 3) = 19$. The problem tells us these numbers should be the same, and they're not here, so eliminate (C); you can also eliminate (D) and (E) because we know we need something smaller than 31. Try (B): 10. "2 less than 3 times 10" is $3(10) - 2 = 28$—still too big. You can actually stop here, because there's only one answer choice left, but let's check it just to be on the safe side. Try (A): 7. "2 less than 3 times 7" is $3(7) - 2 = 19$. Bingo! Choice (A) is the correct answer.

4. **G** There are no variables in this problem, but it deals with fractions of a "certain number," which means that this is a Hidden Plug-In. Let's plug something in for the number of books: it's usually a good idea to do some common multiple of the denominators, so let's say there are 30 books. $\dfrac{2}{5}$ of the books are distributed in the morning, which means $\dfrac{2}{5} \times 30 = 12$ books are distributed in the morning, leaving 18 books. $\dfrac{1}{3}$ of the remaining books are distributed in the afternoon, which

means $\frac{1}{3} \times 18 = 6$ books are distributed in the afternoon, leaving 12 books. We're looking for the fraction of remaining books, so find $\frac{12}{30} = \frac{6}{15} = \frac{2}{5}$, (G).

5. **B** We need to find out what happens as b increases, and there's no easier way to do that than to try it out. Let's start with $b = 2$. If $b = 2$, $a = \frac{3}{2}$. We want to see what happens when b increases, so let's try $b = 3$. If $b = 3$, $a = \frac{3}{3} = 1$. Therefore, we can see even from these two numbers, that as b increases, a decreases, so we can eliminate (A), (D), and (E). Now, the remaining question is whether a gets closer to 1 or if it continues to get closer to 0. Try $b = 4$. If $b = 4$, $a = \frac{3}{4}$. It has continued decreasing past 1, so eliminate (C). Only (B) works.

Geometry Drill (Chapter 12)

1. **B** Although this is a geometry problem, it is asking for a specific value and giving a list of numerical answer choices as possibilities. This means you can use PITA. Start with (C). If $m\angle A = 50$, then $m\angle B = 50$, and because it is twice as large as $\angle B$, $m\angle C = 100$. The sum of the three angle measures will then be $50 + 50 + 100 = 200$, which is too big, so you can eliminate (C), (D), and (E). Try (B). If $m\angle A = 45$, then $m\angle B = 45$, and because it is twice as large as $\angle B$, $m\angle C = 90$. The sum of the three angle measures will then be $45 + 45 + 90 = 180$, which is exactly what you need, so the answer is (B).

2. **F** When two parallel lines are intersected by a third line, it creates two kinds of angles: BIG angles and small angles. All the BIG angles are equal, and all the small angles are equal. Because $\angle D$ is on a separate line, you don't know anything about it, so it can't possibly be correct, eliminating (G) and (J). The BIG angles, therefore, are A and C. The small angles are B and E. Only (F) matches like angles, so it is the only possible correct answer.

3. **D** Deal with the two right triangles separately. We already have the two legs of $\triangle ABC$, so use the Pythagorean Theorem ($a^2 + b^2 = c^2$) to find the hypotenuse. In this case, $AB^2 + BC^2 = AC^2$, so $(20)^2 + (15)^2 = AC^2$, and $AC = 25$. Notice this is a special right triangle: it's a 3-4-5 with a multiplier of 5! Now that we have AC, we have two sides of the other right triangle and can find the third. This, too, is a special right triangle with sides 7-24-25, and since we have sides 7 and 25, the remaining side must be 24, or (D). If you don't spot these special right triangles, you can always use the Pythagorean Theorem.

4. **G** If you have one piece of information about a circle, you can find everything else you need. The area of circle A is 16π, and because $A = \pi r^2$, the radius of circle A must be 4. If the radius of circle B is half that of circle A, then the radius of circle B must be 2. Then find the circumference of circle B: $C = 2\pi r = 2\pi(2) = 4\pi$, (G).

5. **A** Separate the triangles and take this problem in bite-sized pieces. You know two sides of the left triangle, so find the third with the Pythagorean Theorem: $LO^2 + MO^2 = LM^2$. Substitute the values you know: $(4)^2 + MO^2 = (6)^2$, and $MO = 2\sqrt{5}$. Then because you know MO is equal to ON, ON must also be equal to $2\sqrt{5}$. You can either use the Pythagorean Theorem to find the third side, or note that this is a 45-45-90 triangle, which means its sides must be in a ratio of $x : x : x\sqrt{2}$, so the third side must be $2\sqrt{5} \times \sqrt{2} = 2\sqrt{10}$, (A).

Word Problems Drill (Chapter 13)

1. **C** The question is asking for a specific number and offering a list of numerical answer choices as options. Use PITA! Start with (C). If there are 12 boys in the class, then there must be $27 - 12 = 15$ girls. The ratio of boys to girls is therefore 12:15, which, when divided by 3, reduces to 4:5—exactly what you need! Choice (C) is the answer.

2. **J** Use the average formula to help Aubrie fix her mistake. She initially worked with only 5 items to get an average of 88. Multiply this average and this number of items to find the total score for these five tests: $T = (88)(5) = 440$. Now add the sixth score to the total to find a new total of 522. The new formula is $522 = A(6)$, so divide both sides by 6 to get an average of 87, (J). You're welcome, Aubrie.

3. **E** Read this problem carefully. Because both percentages are taken "of the original," add them together to find that 8% of the original amount is lost. Use the percentage translation to find how much is lost: *8% of 490 tons is how much?* In math terms, $\dfrac{8}{100} \times 490 = 39.2$ tons lost. The question asks for how much remains, so subtract $490 - 39.2 = 450.8$ tons, (E).

4. **J** There's no figure in this problem, so draw one! This problem has variables in the answer choices, which is a dead giveaway that you can Plug In. Let's say $a = 2$ and $b = 3$. To find the surface area, simply find the area of all the surfaces; remember that there will be six in all. The surfaces will have areas of 4, 4, 6, 6, 6, and 6. Add them together to find $4 + 4 + 6 + 6 + 6 + 6 = 32$, your target answer. Go to the answer choices to find the one that matches this answer when $a = 2$ and $b = 3$. Choice (F) gives 36. Choice (G) gives 12. Choice (H) gives 16. Choice (J) gives 32. Choice (K) gives 26. Only (J) works!

5. **C** This problem is asking for arrangements, so start by creating the number of slots you will need:

    ___ ___ ___ ___ ___

    There is a restriction on the last in that only one letter, W, can go there, so fill this one in first:

    ___ ___ ___ ___ 1

Then, fill the rest in as normal, remembering that W is already taken, so there are only four letters left:

<u> 4 </u> <u> 3 </u> <u> 2 </u> <u> 1 </u> <u> 1 </u>

Now that you've got the slots filled in, go ahead and multiply the numbers to find the number of possible arrangements:

<u> 4 </u> × <u> 3 </u> × <u> 2 </u> × <u> 1 </u> × <u> 1 </u> = 24 possible arrangements, (C).

6. **H** The question is asking for the expected value and provides both the number of quarters won and the probability that each value will happen. To find the expected value, simply multiply each number of quarters by its associated probability and sum the outcomes: (0)(0.5) + (1)(0.3) + (2)(0.15) + (3)(0.03) + (4)(0.02) = 0 + 0.3 + 0.3 + 0.09 + 0.08 = 0.77. The correct answer is (H).

7. **C** Plugging In is a great way to solve this question. Pick numbers for the sequence described that fit the criteria listed and work with real numbers! The first term is 11, and the easiest thing to do is to subtract 1 each time to get smaller numbers to work with for the list. Make the numbers 11, 10, 9, 8, 7, 6, and 5. The median is the middle number when the terms are listed in order, so the median is 8. Use the average formula $T = AN$. The total is 56 and there are 7 things, so this becomes 56 = A(7). Divide both sides by 7 to find that the average is 8. Therefore, the mean and median of this sequence are equal, and the answer is (C).

Graphing and Coordinate Geometry Drill (Chapter 14)

1. **E** First, use POE to eliminate some answer choices. Since this is only a > sign, we can eliminate (B) and (D) right off the bat. Now, let's use Plugging In to narrow down the rest. First, let's try $x = -2$: $-3(-2) - 6 > 9$. This equation doesn't work, because 0 is NOT greater than 9, so eliminate any answer choices that include –2, leaving only (E).

2. **G** Use the midpoint formula with the two given points. The midpoint formula is $\left(\dfrac{x_1 + x_2}{2}, \dfrac{y_1 + y_2}{2} \right)$, so plug the points into the equation to find $\left(\dfrac{3 + (-4)}{2}, \dfrac{5 + 3}{2} \right)$, resulting in a midpoint of $\left(-\dfrac{1}{2}, 4 \right)$, (G).

3. **B** In order to find the slope, put this equation into slope-intercept form, or $y = mx + b$. Combine the x-terms, and subtract 6 from each side to find $12x - 6 = y$, in which the m term must be 12, (B).

4. **H** Plot your points on a graph, and use them to draw a right triangle. The triangle will rise 4 units and run 3 units, meaning the legs of the triangle will be 3 and 4. You can then use the Pythagorean Theorem to find the third side, or if you notice this is a 3-4-5 Pythagorean triple, the third side of the triangle must be 5, (H).

5. **C**   Use the slope formula, $\dfrac{rise}{run}$ or $\dfrac{y_2 - y_1}{x_2 - x_1}$, with the given points to find that the slope is equivalent to $\dfrac{5-4}{13-6} = \dfrac{1}{7}$, (C). If you selected (E), you may have switched the x- and y-terms!

6. **J**   The circle formula is $(x - h)^2 + (y - k)^2 = r^2$, in which (h, k) is the center of the circle, and r is its radius. Since $r^2 = 9$, the radius of the circle must be 3, eliminating (G), (H), and (K). Then look at the first part of the equation: the $(x - 3)$ matches up without any manipulation with the $(x - h)$ part of the equation, so h must equal 3, eliminating (F). Only (J) is left, and we don't even need to solve for k!

7. **A**   The focus, by definition, is inside the ellipse. Eliminate (D) and (E), which are outside it. The center of the ellipse, determined using the equation of the ellipse or the graph, is located at $(0, 2)$. Eliminate (C). The foci must be on the horizontal axis, since this ellipse is wider than it is tall, and therefore will have a y-value of 2. Use that information to eliminate (B), leaving only (A). There was no need to calculate the foci using the formula $c^2 = a^2 - b^2$, where c is the distance from the center to the focus, a is half the length of horizontal axis, and b is half the length of the vertical axis. If it was necessary, for this ellipse a is 5 and b is 3, so $c^2 = 5^2 - 3^2 = 25 - 9 = 16$, $c = 4$. The distance from the center of the ellipse to the foci is 4 units along the longer axis in either direction. Count 4 to the left and right on the graph to find that $(4, 2)$ and $(-4, 2)$ are foci. Either through use of POE or calculating c, the answer is (A).

Trigonometry Drill (Chapter 15)

1. **D**   Use SOHCAHTOA to find that $\tan \theta = \dfrac{opp}{adj}$. Your first impulse here may be to solve for the unknown side, but take a close look at where the θ is. Its adjacent side is 5, meaning the tangent of that angle must have a denominator of 5. Only (D) has it, so it's the only answer that can work. If you *do* solve for the unknown side, remember your Pythagorean triples: this is a 5-12-13 triangle, so the unknown side must be 12.

2. **H** $\cot \theta$ is defined as $\dfrac{1}{\tan \theta}$. Therefore, because $\tan \theta = 1$, substitute to find $\cot \theta = \dfrac{1}{\tan \theta} = \dfrac{1}{1} = 1$. Only (H) works!

3. **C**   Remember the special trig identity which states $\sin^2 \theta + \cos^2 \theta = 1$. Substitute this into the equation $x + \sin^2 \theta + \cos^2 \theta = 4$ to find that $x + 1 = 4$, so x must be equal to 3. Choice (C) is the correct answer.

4. **K**   Start with POE. If $\cos \theta < 0$ and $\sin \theta > 0$, then θ has to be in Quadrant II, which means that $\tan \theta$ must be negative. Eliminate (F), (G), and (H). Now use SOHCAHTOA: $\cos = \dfrac{adjacent}{hypotenuse}$ and $\tan = \dfrac{opposite}{adjacent}$, so the numerator of the cos should be the denominator of the tan. Eliminate (J), and choose (K).

5. **C** Start by converting $\frac{17\pi}{3}$ into degrees: degrees $= \frac{radians(180)}{\pi} = \frac{17\pi(180)}{3\pi} = 1{,}020°$. Unfortunately, this is not an answer, so you need to do a little more work. Angles greater than 360° represent multiple rotations around the unit circle. All the answers are less than 1,020, so keep subtracting 360 until you hit one of the answer choices. $1{,}020 - 360 = 660 - 360 = 300 - 360 = -60$. The correct answer is (C).

Advanced Math Drill (Chapter 16)

1. **E** Rewrite $\log_3 x = 5$ as $3^5 = x$; $x = 243$.

2. **K** The component form of a vector describes the vector in terms of the changes in the x and y values. In other words, if $\mathbf{u} = \langle -3, 2 \rangle$, vector $\mathbf{u}$ changes x by -3 and y by 2. First, solve for the vector $4\mathbf{u} + (-2\mathbf{v})$. To do this, multiply $\mathbf{u}$ and $\mathbf{v}$ by 4 and -2, respectively: $4\mathbf{u} + (-2\mathbf{v}) = 4\langle -3, 2 \rangle + (-2\langle 7, 5 \rangle) = \langle -12, 8 \rangle + \langle -14, -10 \rangle$. Next, combine the vectors in component form by adding the x values and adding the y values to get $4\mathbf{u} + (-2\mathbf{v}) = \langle -12 + (-14), 8 + (-10) \rangle = \langle -26, -2 \rangle$. Substitute this back into the original equation to get $\langle -26, -2 \rangle + \mathbf{w} = 0$. Note that 0 represents a vector with x and y components of 0, so the equation is $\langle -26, -2 \rangle + \mathbf{w} = \langle 0, 0 \rangle$. Add $\langle 26, 2 \rangle$ to both sides to isolate $\mathbf{w}$ and get $\mathbf{w} = \langle 26, 2 \rangle$. The correct answer is (K).

3. **A** When multiplying a matrix by a constant, you multiply each element by that constant:

$$3\begin{bmatrix} 5 & a \\ 1 & 6 \end{bmatrix} = \begin{bmatrix} 15 & 3a \\ 3 & 18 \end{bmatrix}.$$

Substitute this matrix into the original equation to get

$$\begin{bmatrix} 15 & 3a \\ 3 & 18 \end{bmatrix} + \begin{bmatrix} 2 & 7 \\ 3 & 4 \end{bmatrix} = \begin{bmatrix} 17 & 13 \\ 6 & 22 \end{bmatrix}.$$

When adding matrices, you add the elements in the corresponding locations. This means that $3a + 7 = 13$. Subtract 7 from both sides to get $3a = 6$; $a = 2$. The correct answer is (A).

PART IV: READING

Passage I: Prose Fiction (Chapter 18)

1. **C** The passage as a whole describes the narrator's father's business, the narrator's own time as head of the business, and his son's current achievements as head of the business. Choice (C) correctly summarizes this narrative movement. Choice (A) suggests that the narrator does not like the direction in which his son has taken the business, which is untrue. Choice (B) is partially correct, though it is not as complete as (C). Choice (D) is too general for this very personal narrative.

2. **F** In the first paragraph, the narrator refers to Singer Stations and Service as *the company my father started*, eliminating (G). In the second paragraph, the narrator states that *my father thought it would put a safer face on the business to change the name to Singer*, eliminating (H). In the middle of the third paragraph, the narrator refers back to the name of the station (which he calls *alliterative*), and he adds, *All of the credit for this name has always gone to my father, and I can believe that he was the one behind this smart change*, eliminating (J). Only (F) remains, and although the first paragraph cites *a sophisticated iPhone app*, there is NOT a clear indication that his father was responsible for it.

3. **C** The end of the third paragraph says the following: *We've all had our challenges, regardless of age, so who says one generation has it tougher than the next, and frankly, who cares?* Therefore, the narrator does not take a firm stand on whether *one generation has it tougher than the next*. This agrees with (C). The narrator takes a specific stand about (A) in the final paragraph and (B) and (D) in the second paragraph.

4. **F** The middle of the third paragraph says of the narrator's father, *he had that added penchant, almost a poetic sense, for a clever, musical turn of phrase*. This *poetic sense* agrees with (F). The other choices are not specifically supported in the passage.

5. **A** The sentence in which the word appears reads as follows: *It doesn't hurt that the kid knows how to make a buck*. In this sentence, the word *hurt* does not have its primary meaning of to cause harm to a person. It is used idiomatically in the phrase *It doesn't hurt*, which means something like *It helps*. Only (A) points toward this secondary, idiomatic meaning.

6. **J** The third sentence of the fifth paragraph reads as follows: *My father at the very least had a family to come home to, and the saving grace of his religious observance forced him to take at least a day off every week*. This sentence establishes a clear link between *saving grace* and *religious observance*, meaning that (J) is the correct answer.

7. **B** The end of the fifth paragraph reads as follows: *In later years, my mother told me secretly that she thought I actually had it worst of all—I had no burning desire to enter this business, but I didn't really have any other choice*. This question asks for the narrator's mother's view, which appears only in these lines. Choice (B) gives a clear paraphrase of these lines. Choices (A) and (D) are not mentioned in the text, and although some words from the passage appear in (C), these reflect the narrator's view of himself, not his mother's view of him.

8.   **J**   The first line of the sixth paragraph reads, *Even so, I was Raman (The Gas Man) Singer's son.* Because the narrator is this man's son, the man in question must be the narrator's father, as in (J).

9.   **B**   The middle of the final paragraph states the following: *As a result, at the urging of my college-aged daughter Geeta, I decided to try something I always wished that I had done. I enrolled in the business program at the State University, and before long, I realized that Geeta knew me better than I knew myself. I had fun like I never had before.* Choice (B) paraphrases these lines. Choices (A), (C), and (D) may be true, but they do not answer the question regarding the narrator's daughter, nor the lines that the question indirectly references.

10. **G**   The lines in which the phrase appears read as follows: *I had fun like I never had before, and looking back, I came to see that the part of the business that always drew me in was learning.* These lines do not have anything to do with coming or going to a place but have more to do with the secondary meaning of *come to see*, which is a synonym for *realize*, as in (G).

Reading Drill 1 (Chapter 18)

21. **D**   While there are hints of (A), (B), and (C) in the passage, none can be called the main point. Each idea is mentioned in the passage, but the author is more interested in presenting many different perspectives. In other words, the author is interested in showing that texting's *social effects are debatable*, as (D) suggests.

22. **F**   As the fifth paragraph states, *Fields warns not only that we may have been 'dumbed down' by our technologies but also that we may have lost one of the essential elements of the human experience. "The content of our communication with each other…may be ultimately the same," Fields concedes, "but the real communication lives in the form…."* Choice (F) essentially restates these lines, so it is reasonable to infer that Fields would agree with this choice. Google is mentioned in the paragraph on Fields, but she does not offer any ideas on it, eliminating (G). Choices (H) and (J) contradict the lines quoted above.

23. **A**   In the second paragraph, the author claims, *Text messages are already a part of the cultural landscape.* She then goes on to offer many examples of places where the text message plays a role, as (A) suggests. Although she mentions two novels that discuss texting, she does not say that these novels are *about* texting, nor are novels the only examples given in this list, eliminating (B). Though (C) uses words from the first paragraph, it does not describe that paragraph accurately. Choice (D) may be true, but it does not answer the question.

24. **J**   The fourth paragraph states, *we could even say that our very nation was founded in these written communiqués: much of what we know about that era comes from these letters.* This idea of providing a historical record is restated in (J), making this the correct answer. Choice (F) does not make sense, and (G) and (H) have no support in the text.

25. **B**   Of the *naysayers*, the fourth paragraph states, *naysayers have said that everything from the printing press, to the radio, to the movie screen, to Google, has compromised the way we think and understand.* In other words, these *naysayers* speak out against any new technologies as impairing our ability to think. The sports journalists described in (B) provide the closest analogue, in that they warn against changes.

26. **J**   According to the first paragraph, Hillebrand and Ghillebaert, (J), were early contributors to the creation of the text message *to the extent that it has a creator at all*. Scorsese is a filmmaker; Wallace and Franzen are novelists; and Fields and Chacon are media theorists.

27. **D**   Hillebrand states, *160 characters was sufficient to express most messages succinctly*. Therefore, he would likely agree with the statement that prefers messages of *a sentence or two rather than…two-hour phone conversation[s]*, thus eliminating (A) and (B). Hillebrand nowhere states that the phone is no longer an effective communicator, eliminating (C). Choice (D) correctly states that Hillebrand would agree and gives a paraphrase of his quotation.

28. **F**   The last sentence of the second paragraph states, *Text messages, in fact, move the whole plot of Martin Scorsese's 2006 film* The Departed, *a critical success and eventual Oscar winner for Best Picture.* All we know about this film is that text messages play a central role in moving the plot, meaning that text messages must appear in the answer, eliminating (H) and (J). Choice (G) can also be eliminated because there is no support for the idea that *the medium exploded in popularity after the film's release.* Only (F) is supported by the passage.

29. **C**   The second sentence of the third paragraph reads, *Speaking on an actual telephone is basically defunct in 2013, not only for the economic reason that "time is money" and a text is quicker than a call, but also for a much older desire in all of us for permanence.* Only a portion of this sentence relates to "time is money": *the economic reason that "time is money" and a text is quicker than a call.* Choice (C) mentions this quickness, so it is the correct answer. Choice (A) is not discussed. Choice (B) is part of this sentence, but it is evidence that works against the idea that "time is money." Choice (D) is not discussed in this paragraph, and neither the author nor the later theorists argue that text messaging has any positive effects on *intimacy*.

30. **G**   In the final paragraph, Chacon observes, *Whatever the limitations of this new medium of communication, people are interacting on a day-to-day basis with more people than their ancestors might have met in a lifetime.* The words *Whatever the limitations* suggest that Chacon is about to say something positive about *this new medium of communication*, the text message. Choices (F), (H), and (J) focus too much on *ancestors* and lose the main point of the passage and paragraph. Only (G) adequately paraphrases the quote.

Reading Drill 2 (Chapter 19)

21. **A** Choice (A) is correct because, although the author discusses having great difficulty and confusion in learning jazz chords, he does not ever identify one that is *most* confusing. Choices (B), (C), and (D) are incorrect because none of the chords are ever identified as the *most* confusing chord.

22. **F** In the context of the passage as a whole, the author discusses Victor as a source of knowledge about jazz. The author states he did not get *straightforward explanations* from Victor but that he *did learn* some things. Choice (F) is correct because, given the context of the passage, it refers to the most likely subject matter the author would be trying to get from Victor. Choice (G) is incorrect because the idea that knowledge about jazz would be *forbidden* is too strong. There is no evidence that the author was being purposefully excluded from learning about jazz. Choice (H) is incorrect because there is no context to support the idea that the author was asking about literal magic tricks. Choice (J) is incorrect because there is no context to support the idea that the author was trying to learn more about Victor as a person, nor does the passage ever describe Victor as *private*.

23. **D** Upon seeing the author's *invented* chord, Victor *calmly* informs the author of the chord's proper name. Choice (D) is correct because *nonchalance* indicates a relaxed, unimpressed manner, which is how Victor responds. Choice (A) is incorrect because Victor would not be amazed by a chord for which he already knows the technical name. Choice (B) is incorrect because Victor would not be jealous that the author could play a chord that was already familiar to Victor. Choice (C) is incorrect because Victor does not show confusion; he shows immediate recognition of what chord the author is playing.

24. **G** In the eighth paragraph, the author states that *for the next few months, I quietly plucked away* at the music found in *The Real Book*. Hence, (G) is correct, and (F), (H), and (J) are incorrect.

25. **A** The passage describes the more complex chord types of jazz and describes the effects of using them as introducing *subtle hints of chaos and imbalance*, *adding a worldly imperfection*, and becoming more enjoyable as one's age starts making things like candy taste too sweet and "imperfections" like bitterness make *for a more appealing flavor*. Choice (A) provides the correct summary for these ideas. Choice (B) is incorrect because the description of jazz's complexity is not intended to be a critical comment about fundamental flaws in rock and classical music. Just because jazz's unique chords add *detail and depth to the music*, that doesn't mean the author thinks that other styles of music necessarily lack detail and depth. Choice (C) is incorrect because the passage does not specify anything about the confusion and awkwardness of *standard jazz chord values*; it describes what elements jazz chords add to *standard chord values*. Choice (D) is incorrect because the context explains that candy starts tasting unpleasantly *sweet* the older one gets.

26. **J** The end of the passage describes the author beginning to develop an ability to play jazz, but his newfound ability is still mentally surprising. Choice (J) summarizes this context best and is therefore correct. Choice (F) is incorrect because the passage does not support the idea that the author was *overworked*. Choice (G) is incorrect because, although the author is surprised by what his

hands can do musically, there is no context to support that the author is actually losing the ability to *control* his hands. Choice (H) is incorrect because there is no information to support the idea that the author *pointing* at chords was part of his learning process.

27. **D** Choice (D) is correct because the eighth paragraph describes the author's initial attempts to work through the *strange, new combinations* he found in *The Real Book*. He mentions F-sharp minor-7 flat-5 while speaking of chords that he *had to decode and then understand*. Choice (A) is incorrect because the context of this paragraph suggests that the author did indeed have some trouble with these unfamiliar chords. Choice (B) is incorrect because the remark about not knowing the language of a foreign country has no literal relation to this specific chord or the author's previous travels (about which we know nothing). Choice (C) is incorrect because the passage provides no evidence that the author knew how to play this chord on guitar.

28. **H** The fourth paragraph identifies Victor as a member of the author's rock band as well as a member of a jazz ensemble. This makes (H) correct. Choice (F) is incorrect because the passage states that at age 30, it had been *over a decade* since the author and Victor had gone their separate ways. Choice (G) is incorrect because the passage states that the author bought his own copy of *The Real Book*. Choice (J) is incorrect because the passage does not say that Victor invented this chord, rather that he told the author the name of the chord the author presumed to have invented.

29. **C** The passage begins with the author's love for jazz. It transitions into his own experiences learning how to play jazz and culminates with his early successes in doing so. Choice (C) is correct because it encompasses the various points of focus throughout the passage. Choice (A) is incorrect because the passage only occasionally refers to a chain of events and never establishes that the author has a jazz career. Choice (B) is incorrect because the author does not try to show that jazz is uncomplicated; he describes the hard work he put into learning its complexity. Choice (D) is incorrect because the central focus of the passage is the author's learning of jazz. Although the author's friendship with Victor relates to jazz, it is not the central focus of the author's discussion.

30. **G** In the last few paragraphs, the author describes the process by which he struggled to learn jazz. He begins by seeing jazz as *a cryptic message...to decode* but later describes himself as *becoming comfortable* and possessing a *new melodic understanding*. These details make (G) correct. Choice (F) is incorrect because the author never says that the book becomes *annoyingly familiar* by the end. Choice (H) is incorrect because the author identifies a difference between jazz sheet music and classical sheet music, but this detail does not enter his discussion of his experiences with "The Real Book." Choice (J) is incorrect because the author has not suggested that he has moved on to other learning tools or more profound study.

PART V: SCIENCE

Basic Approach Drill 1 (Chapter 22)

1. **C** The question asks, based on Figure 1, what the ΔS does at 40°C *as the molecular masses of the salts increase*. Look at Figure 1. All three of the lines on the graph show that, at any temperature, as temperature increases, ΔS is also increasing. Eliminate (A) and (B). Also, Figure 1 shows that the units for ΔS are g solute per 100 g H_2O. That means that if ΔS is increasing, the g solute per 100 g H_2O is increasing, which means there is a greater mass of the substance dissolved in the same mass of water. Eliminate (D). The correct answer is (C).

2. **G** The question asks what the observed ΔS did at 60°C as the molecular mass of the substance decrease during the trials represented in Figure 2. Look at Figure 2. The substance with the greatest molecular mass has the highest ΔS at every temperature above 15°C, and the substance with the smallest molecular mass has the lowest ΔS at each temperature above 15°C. Therefore, as the molecular mass decreased, the observed ΔS decreased. The correct answer is (G).

3. **C** The question asks what the ΔS would most likely have been if an additional trial had been done *in which a salt with a MM of 80 dissolved in H_2O at 50°C*. According to the passage, Figure 1 shows salts while Figure 2 shows molecular compounds, so look at Figure 1. KCl has a MM of 74 and the ΔS of KCl is approximately 18 g solute per 100 g H_2O at 50° C. KNO_3 has a MM of 101 and a ΔS of approximately 70 g solute per 100 g H_2O at 50°C. Therefore, *a salt with a MM of 80 dissolved in H_2O at 50° C* should have a ΔS between 18 and 70. Eliminate (A) as this is too small. Because a MM of 80 is much closer to 74 than it is to 101, the ΔS should be closer to 18 than to 70. Eliminate (D) as 60 is too high. Notice that as the MM increases from 69 for NaCl to 74 for KCl, the ΔS at 50° C increases by approximately 15 g solute per 100 g H_2O. Therefore, increasing the MM from 74 to 80 will likely increase the ΔS above 20. The correct answer is (C).

4. **J** The question asks, according to Figure 2, what happens to the solubility of NH_3 when a solution of NH_3 in water is heated from 0°C to 20°C. Look at Figure 2. The ΔS of NH_3 from 0°C to 20°C is negative. Eliminate (F) and (H). A negative ΔS would represent a negative change, which is a decrease in the solubility. Eliminate (G). The correct answer is (J).

5. **D** The question asks, based on Figures 1 and 2, which of the following combinations of solute and temperature at a known m_{H_2O} would produce the greatest increase in solubility. According to the passage, Figure 1 represents salts and Figure 2 represents molecular compounds. Notice that in Figure 2, the ΔS is negative, which represents a decrease in solubility rather than an increase. Therefore, Figure 2 shows that molecular compounds will not produce an increase in solubility. Eliminate (A) and (B) because these include a molecular compound. Choices (C) and (D) both contain NaF but at different temperatures. Since NaF is a salt, refer to Figure 1. For all of the salts in Figure 1, increasing temperature leads to greater ΔS. Eliminate (C) as this is a lower temperature. The correct answer is (D).

6. **F**   The question asks if Compound X, a compound that has a solubility of 26.9 g per 100 g H_2O at 0°C and 37.1 g per 100 g H_2O at 25°C, is *most likely a salt or a molecular compound*, based on the information in the passage and figures. The information given about Compound X in the question shows that the solubility of Compound X increases with increasing temperature. Eliminate (G) and (J) because both say that the solubility decreases with increasing temperature. Now, look at Figures 1 and 2. Figure 1 shows an increase in ΔS with increasing temperature, while Figure 2 shows a decrease in ΔS with increasing temperature. Therefore, Compound X matches Figure 1 but not Figure 2. According to the passage, Figure 1 represents salts. The correct answer is (F).

Basic Approach Drill 2 (Chapter 22)

1. **A**   The question asks which of the graphs given in the answer choices best represents the relationship between atomic number and atomic radius for Period 2 elements. The atomic numbers and atomic radii of the elements in Period 2 can be found in Table 1. As the atomic number increases, the atomic radius decreases. Eliminate (C) and (D) because they show the atomic radius increasing. As the atomic radius decreases, the differences between the values get smaller as well. Eliminate (B) because it shows a linear relationship which would mean the radius decreased at a steady rate. The correct answer is (A).

2. **H**   The question asks, based on Tables 1 and 2, what is most likely the electronegativity of a Period 3 element in the same group as N. Table 1 shows characteristics of several Period 2 elements, including N. According to Table 1, N is a nonmetal with an electronegativity of 3.04. Now, look at Table 2 and see that electronegativity decreases as period increases. Since the element is in the same group as N but the period is increased by 1, the electronegativity would decrease. This means that the electronegativity of that element would be less than 3.04. Eliminate (J). Also in Table 2, notice that Mg is a Period 3 metal with an electronegativity of 1.31. Table 1 shows that within a period, nonmetals have higher electronegativity values than metals. Since N is a nonmetal, then the Period 3 element in the same group as N must also be a nonmetal and would therefore have an electronegativity higher than Mg, a Period 3 metal. The correct answer is (H).

3. **B**   The question asks which of the statements listed in the answer choices is supported by the information in both Table 1 and Table 2. Look at Table 1 and use POE. As the atomic radius decreases, electronegativity increases. Eliminate (A) as this is the opposite, but keep (B). Check the remaining answers to be sure. Table 1 shows that metals have smaller electronegativity values than nonmetals. Eliminate (C). Table 1 shows that metals in Period 2 have larger atomic radii than nonmetals. Eliminate (D). The correct answer is (B).

4. **G**   The question asks, based on the information in the passage and Table 1, which of the statements regarding the comparative electronegativity of fluorine (F) and lithium (Li) is true. Both F and Li can be found in Table 1 so look at Table 1. The electronegativity of F is greater than the electronegativity of Li. Eliminate (H) and (J). Now, look at the passage for an explanation of elements with higher electronegativity. The last sentence of the first paragraph states that *Elements with*

higher electronegativity have tighter bonding between protons and electrons than elements with lower electronegativity. Eliminate (F). The correct answer is (G).

5. **D** The question asks, based on Table 1 and the statement that *elements with a high electronegativity also have a higher ionization energy*, which of the answer choices gives a correct order of elements with *increasing* ionization energies. If high electronegativity means high ionization energy, low electronegativity must mean low ionization energy. Therefore, in order to list the elements in order of increasing ionization energies, start with the lowest electronegativity. All of the elements listed in the answer choices appear in Table 1, so use Table 1. Notice Li has the smallest electronegativity of the elements listed. Therefore, it should be listed first if it is included in the list. Eliminate (A) and (B) because they have Li after other elements. The next lowest electronegativity is Be. Eliminate (C) because it includes Be after B and N, both of which have higher electronegativity values. The correct answer is (D).

6. **F** The question asks, based on the information in Tables 1 and 2 and the statement that K is *a Period 4 element with an electronegativity of 0.82*, whether K is more likely a metal or a nonmetal. Start by checking the electronegativity values of B and Ca. Table 1 shows that K has a lower electronegativity value than B. Eliminate (G), which incorrectly states that K has a higher electronegativity value. Table 2 shows that K also has a lower electronegativity than Ca, so eliminate (H). Now, look back at Table 1, which shows the electronegativity for both metals and nonmetals in Period 2. All the metals have lower electronegativity values than the nonmetals, so the low electronegativity of K indicates that it is most likely a metal. Eliminate (J). The correct answer is (F).

Basic Approach Drill 3 (Chapter 22)

1. **B** The question asks what the approximate average decrease in tail width would most likely have been closest to if *an additional group of recently emerged tadpoles was immersed in a 0.3 µg/ml thyroxine solution for 72 hours.* Look at Figure 2, which shows the percent average decrease in tail width over time. If an additional group were included in the study at 0.3 µg/ml, the results would fall between the results for the 0.2 µg/ml group and the 0.5 µg/ml group. For the 0.2 µg/ml group at 72 hours, the decrease was around 22%. The result for a group at 0.3 µg/ml should be more than that. Eliminate (A). For the 0.5 µg/ml group at 72 hours, the decrease was around 41%. The result for a group at 0.3 µg/ml should be less than that. Eliminate (C) and (D). The correct answer is (B).

2. **G** The question asks which of the assertions about tadpoles listed in the answer choices is supported by the results of the experiment. The results of the experiment are shown in Figure 2, so look at Figure 2 and use POE. The tadpoles that were exposed only to distilled water and no thyroxine still saw a decrease in tail width, just at a slower rate, which means that they are still experiencing metamorphosis. Eliminate (F). The data in Figure 2 ends a little before 120 hours, which is 5 days. At this point, the tadpoles not given thyroxine have only experienced a little over 10% decrease in tail width, so they have not come close to completing metamorphosis. This indicates that meta-

morphosis takes more than 5 days, so keep (G). Also in Figure 2, notice that the most concentrated solution of thyroxine, 0.5 μg/ml, produced the most rapid disappearance of the tail rather than the most dilute thyroxine solution. Eliminate (H). The experiment varied the concentration of the thyroxine solution and measured percent decrease in tail width over time; temperature was not a factor. Eliminate (J). The correct answer is (G).

3.   A   The question asks in which of the concentrations listed in the answer choices the tadpoles would show the LEAST development after four days of immersion. Look at Figure 2. For all times past 24 hours, as the concentration of thyroxine increases, the values for the average decrease in tail width percent also increase. The larger value of the average decrease in tail width indicate development as the tail is reabsorbed. Therefore, the least development occurs in the lowest thyroxine concentration, which the 0.1 μg/ml thyroxine solution. The correct answer is (A).

4.   J   The question asks which of the answer choices would be a correct order of the stages of frog development based on the information in the passage. The last sentence of the first paragraph of the passage states that *the process begins with cell determination in the embryo stage*, so we know cell determination is the first stage of frog development. Eliminate (F) and (G). Now look at Figure 1. The stage that follows cell determination in the embryo stage is the tadpole stage. The tail does not get reabsorbed until the final state before adulthood. Eliminate (H). The correct answer is (J).

5.   C   The question asks after how many hours of immersion does exposure to thyroxine first show a measurable effect on the rate of tadpole metamorphosis, according to Figure 2. Look at Figure 2. Look for the point in time that the thyroxine solution data first shows a different result than the distilled water data. That change happens somewhere after the 12-hour data point, where the data all overlap, and the 24-hour data points, where there is a difference between the distilled water and the thyroxine solutions. Therefore, the difference is first measurable somewhere from 12-24 hours. The correct answer is (C).

6.   H   The question asks, according to Figure 2, which of the following is closest to the value of *t* if after *t* hours, a tadpole immersed in a 0.15 μg/ml thyroxine solution *has undergone a 22% decrease in tail width*. A 0.15 μg/ml thyroxine solution will produce results somewhere between the results of the 0.1 μg/ml thyroxine solution and the 0.2 μg/ml. Use POE. Look at 60 hours, which is the hashmark halfway between 48 and 72 hours. Both the 0.1 and 0.2 lines have a percent decrease in tail width of less than 20% at this point, so a 0.15 solution would also be less than 20%. Eliminate (F). At 72 hours, the 0.1 μg/ml thyroxine solution is at about 17% and the 0.2 μg/ml thyroxine solution is at about 23%, so a 0.15 μg/ml thyroxine solution would likely produce results around 20%, which is too small. Eliminate (G). At 96 hours, notice that the 0.1 μg/ml thyroxine solution is just over 20% and the 0.2 μg/ml thyroxine solution is almost 30%, so a 0.15 μg/ml thyroxine solution would likely produce results around 25% which is too large. Eliminate (J). The correct answer is (H).

Dual Science Passage Drill 1 (Chapter 23)

1. **A** Scientist 1 argues that natural gas formed where the *remains of marine organisms and terrestrial plants piled up on land and on the seafloor over a long period. This indicates that the natural gas reservoir may have formed near the site of a past ocean, where the organic remnants of marine organisms could have been transformed into natural gas over a long period of time.* Therefore, (A) is the correct answer. Choice (B) indicates that the natural gas reservoirs would be found near the site of a present-day ocean, where none had existed in the past, leaving no time for the conversion process described by Scientist 1 to occur. Choice (C) is not mentioned by Scientist 1. Neither scientist's argument includes formation of microorganisms from nonliving carbon sources, eliminating (D).

2. **H** Scientist 1 mentions that natural gas would have formed at depths greater than 10 miles below Earth's surface. Natural gas formed 20 miles below the surface of Earth is consistent with the mechanism described by Scientist 1. Therefore, (H) is the correct answer.

3. **D** Pressure will increase as the depth below Earth's surface increases. Scientist 2 indicates that natural gas formed at depths of 2 to 10 miles below the surface. Scientist 1 indicates that natural gas formed at depths of more than 10 miles. As a result, Scientist 2, who indicates that natural gas formed at shallower depths, also indicates that natural gas formation occurred at lower pressures. Therefore, (D) is the correct answer.

4. **G** According to Scientist 2, natural gas formed at depths from 2 to 10 miles beneath the surface of Earth. This eliminates (F) and (H), which depict natural gas as forming at depths of greater than 10 miles beneath Earth's surface. The first paragraph of the passage explains that natural gas reservoirs are located between 0 and 0.5 miles beneath Earth's surface. As this information precedes the discussion of the individual scientists' specific arguments, this information is not disputed and is acknowledged by both scientists, so Scientist 2's description should be consistent with this information. Only (G) depicts a natural gas reservoir located between 0 and 0.5 miles beneath Earth's surface.

5. **D** According to Scientist 2, *microorganisms convert the carbon compounds and water into the hydrocarbons of natural gas.* The reaction of carbon dioxide (CO_2), a carbon-containing compound, and water would be an example of such a reaction and would therefore support Scientist 2's argument that microorganisms convert organic material into natural gas. Thus, (D) is the correct answer.

6. **H** Scientist 2 states that carbon-13 is contained in the natural gas brought up to the reservoir, eliminating (F) and (G). In order for the gas to rise upward through the material in which it migrates, it must be less dense than that material, eliminating (J). Therefore, (H) is the correct answer.

7. **B** According to Scientist 2, *microorganisms convert the carbon compounds and water into the hydrocarbons of natural gas.* Carbon dioxide (CO_2) (III) is a carbon-containing compound and could be involved in the formation of natural gas as described by Scientist 2. Neither F_2 (I) nor KCl (II) is water or a carbon compound, eliminating (A), (C) and (D). Therefore, (B) is the correct answer.

Dual Science Passage Drill 2 (Chapter 23)

1. **B** This paragraph is about three students' explanations for effusion rates. Since the students didn't perform the experiment for which they're offering competing explanations—the professor did—the question references the professor rather than the students. According to the passage, the time required for all 100 mL of the gas to effuse from the syringe into the empty flask was measured. As a result, the volume of gas in the flask continued to increase until all of the gas was emptied from the syringe. Therefore, the correct answer is (B).

2. **F** Student 1 proposes that gases with greater molecular masses diffuse more slowly. Therefore, gases with smaller molecular masses diffuse more quickly. Of the choices listed, hydrogen gas (2.016 amu) possesses the smallest molecular mass and will effuse most quickly. Thus, (F) is the correct answer.

3. **B** Student 1 proposes that gases with greater molecular masses diffuse more slowly. According to the results of the experiment, Gas A's total effusion time is 4 seconds, and Gas B's total effusion time is 16 seconds. The question states that nitrogen gas's effusion time is 9 seconds—longer than Gas A's total effusion time but shorter than Gas B's total effusion time. Consequently, nitrogen gas's molecular mass must be greater than Gas A's molecular mass and smaller than Gas B's molecular mass. Thus, (B) is the correct answer.

4. **F** According to Student 2, gases with greater molecular volumes effuse more slowly. Table 1 shows you that xenon's molecular volume is greater than krypton's. Based upon this, krypton should effuse more quickly than does xenon, which contradicts the claim made in the question. Thus, (F) is the correct answer.

5. **A** Student 3 proposes that gases with greater densities effuse more slowly than gases with lesser densities. Table 1 says that xenon is denser than krypton and that krypton is denser than oxygen. Xenon, the densest gas, should therefore have the smallest relative effusion rate, while oxygen, the least dense gas, should have the greatest relative effusion rate. The relative effusion rate of krypton should be between the relative effusion rates of xenon and oxygen. Choice (A) correctly demonstrates this relationship between effusion rates.

6. **J** Student 1 proposes that gases with greater molecular *masses* diffuse more slowly than gases with smaller molecular masses. Student 2 proposes that gases with greater molecular *volumes* effuse more slowly than gases with smaller molecular volumes. Student 3 proposes that gases with greater *densities* effuse more slowly than gases with lesser densities. According to Table 1, helium's molecular mass and density are greater than hydrogen's, while hydrogen's molecular volume is greater than helium's. Students 1 and 3, then, would predict that helium would effuse more slowly; Student 2 will predict that hydrogen will effuse more slowly. The professor's experiment finds that Gas B effuses more slowly than Gas A. If helium were Gas B and hydrogen were Gas A, then Student 1's prediction and Student 3's prediction would be consistent with the professor's finding, while Student 2's prediction would not be. Thus, (J) is the correct answer.

7. **C** Student 1 proposes that gases with greater molecular *masses* diffuse more slowly than gases with smaller molecular masses. Student 2 proposes that gases with greater molecular *volumes* effuse more slowly than gases with smaller molecular volumes. Student 3 proposes that gases with greater *densities* effuse more slowly than gases with lesser densities. According to the information provided in the table in the question and in Table 1, krypton's molecular mass and density are greater than carbon dioxide's, while carbon dioxide's molecular volume is greater than krypton's. Student 1 and Student 3 would predict that carbon dioxide effuses more quickly than krypton, yielding shorter effusion times for carbon dioxide. Student 2 would predict the opposite, that krypton would effuse more quickly than carbon dioxide, yielding shorter effusion times for krypton. Therefore, (C) is the correct answer.

Part VIII
The Princeton Review ACT Practice Exams

Chapter 26
Practice Exam 1

ACT Diagnostic Test Form

Use a No. 2 pencil only. Be sure each mark is dark and completely fills the intended oval. Completely erase any errors or stray marks.

1. **YOUR NAME:** _____

    (Print)   Last   First   M.I.

SIGNATURE: _____ **DATE:** _____ / _____ / _____

HOME ADDRESS: _____

    (Print)   Number and Street

_____

    City   State   Zip

E-MAIL: _____

PHONE NO.: _____
    (Print)

SCHOOL: _____

CLASS OF: _____

IMPORTANT: Please fill in these boxes exactly as shown on the back cover of your test book.

2. TEST FORM

_____

3. TEST CODE

⓪	⓪	⓪	⓪
①	①	①	①
②	②	②	②
③	③	③	③
④	④	④	④
⑤	⑤	⑤	⑤
⑥	⑥	⑥	⑥
⑦	⑦	⑦	⑦
⑧	⑧	⑧	⑧
⑨	⑨	⑨	⑨

4. PHONE NUMBER

⓪	⓪	⓪	⓪	⓪	⓪	⓪
①	①	①	①	①	①	①
②	②	②	②	②	②	②
③	③	③	③	③	③	③
④	④	④	④	④	④	④
⑤	⑤	⑤	⑤	⑤	⑤	⑤
⑥	⑥	⑥	⑥	⑥	⑥	⑥
⑦	⑦	⑦	⑦	⑦	⑦	⑦
⑧	⑧	⑧	⑧	⑧	⑧	⑧
⑨	⑨	⑨	⑨	⑨	⑨	⑨

5. YOUR NAME

First 4 letters of last name				FIRST INIT	MID INIT
Ⓐ	Ⓐ	Ⓐ	Ⓐ	Ⓐ	Ⓐ
Ⓑ	Ⓑ	Ⓑ	Ⓑ	Ⓑ	Ⓑ
Ⓒ	Ⓒ	Ⓒ	Ⓒ	Ⓒ	Ⓒ
Ⓓ	Ⓓ	Ⓓ	Ⓓ	Ⓓ	Ⓓ
Ⓔ	Ⓔ	Ⓔ	Ⓔ	Ⓔ	Ⓔ
Ⓕ	Ⓕ	Ⓕ	Ⓕ	Ⓕ	Ⓕ
Ⓖ	Ⓖ	Ⓖ	Ⓖ	Ⓖ	Ⓖ
Ⓗ	Ⓗ	Ⓗ	Ⓗ	Ⓗ	Ⓗ
Ⓘ	Ⓘ	Ⓘ	Ⓘ	Ⓘ	Ⓘ
Ⓙ	Ⓙ	Ⓙ	Ⓙ	Ⓙ	Ⓙ
Ⓚ	Ⓚ	Ⓚ	Ⓚ	Ⓚ	Ⓚ
Ⓛ	Ⓛ	Ⓛ	Ⓛ	Ⓛ	Ⓛ
Ⓜ	Ⓜ	Ⓜ	Ⓜ	Ⓜ	Ⓜ
Ⓝ	Ⓝ	Ⓝ	Ⓝ	Ⓝ	Ⓝ
Ⓞ	Ⓞ	Ⓞ	Ⓞ	Ⓞ	Ⓞ
Ⓟ	Ⓟ	Ⓟ	Ⓟ	Ⓟ	Ⓟ
Ⓠ	Ⓠ	Ⓠ	Ⓠ	Ⓠ	Ⓠ
Ⓡ	Ⓡ	Ⓡ	Ⓡ	Ⓡ	Ⓡ
Ⓢ	Ⓢ	Ⓢ	Ⓢ	Ⓢ	Ⓢ
Ⓣ	Ⓣ	Ⓣ	Ⓣ	Ⓣ	Ⓣ
Ⓤ	Ⓤ	Ⓤ	Ⓤ	Ⓤ	Ⓤ
Ⓥ	Ⓥ	Ⓥ	Ⓥ	Ⓥ	Ⓥ
Ⓦ	Ⓦ	Ⓦ	Ⓦ	Ⓦ	Ⓦ
Ⓧ	Ⓧ	Ⓧ	Ⓧ	Ⓧ	Ⓧ
Ⓨ	Ⓨ	Ⓨ	Ⓨ	Ⓨ	Ⓨ
Ⓩ	Ⓩ	Ⓩ	Ⓩ	Ⓩ	Ⓩ

6. DATE OF BIRTH

MONTH	DAY		YEAR	
◯ JAN				
◯ FEB				
◯ MAR	⓪	⓪	⓪	⓪
◯ APR	①	①	①	①
◯ MAY	②	②	②	②
◯ JUN	③	③	③	③
◯ JUL		④	④	④
◯ AUG		⑤	⑤	⑤
◯ SEP		⑥	⑥	⑥
◯ OCT		⑦	⑦	⑦
◯ NOV		⑧	⑧	⑧
◯ DEC		⑨	⑨	⑨

7. SEX

◯ MALE
◯ FEMALE

8. OTHER

1 Ⓐ Ⓑ Ⓒ Ⓓ Ⓔ
2 Ⓐ Ⓑ Ⓒ Ⓓ Ⓔ
3 Ⓐ Ⓑ Ⓒ Ⓓ Ⓔ

OpScan iNSIGHT™ forms by Pearson NCS EM-255315-1:654321   Printed in U.S.A.

THIS PAGE INTENTIONALLY LEFT BLANK

The Princeton Review
Diagnostic ACT Form

Completely darken bubbles with a No. 2 pencil. If you make a mistake, be sure to erase mark completely. Erase all stray marks.

ENGLISH

1 A B C D	21 A B C D	41 A B C D	61 A B C D
2 F G H J	22 F G H J	42 F G H J	62 F G H J
3 A B C D	23 A B C D	43 A B C D	63 A B C D
4 F G H J	24 F G H J	44 F G H J	64 F G H J
5 A B C D	25 A B C D	45 A B C D	65 A B C D
6 F G H J	26 F G H J	46 F G H J	66 F G H J
7 A B C D	27 A B C D	47 A B C D	67 A B C D
8 F G H J	28 F G H J	48 F G H J	68 F G H J
9 A B C D	29 A B C D	49 A B C D	69 A B C D
10 F G H J	30 F G H J	50 F G H J	70 F G H J
11 A B C D	31 A B C D	51 A B C D	71 A B C D
12 F G H J	32 F G H J	52 F G H J	72 F G H J
13 A B C D	33 A B C D	53 A B C D	73 A B C D
14 F G H J	34 F G H J	54 F G H J	74 F G H J
15 A B C D	35 A B C D	55 A B C D	75 A B C D
16 F G H J	36 F G H J	56 F G H J	
17 A B C D	37 A B C D	57 A B C D	
18 F G H J	38 F G H J	58 F G H J	
19 A B C D	39 A B C D	59 A B C D	
20 F G H J	40 F G H J	60 F G H J	

MATHEMATICS

1 A B C D E	16 F G H J K	31 A B C D E	46 F G H J K
2 F G H J K	17 A B C D E	32 F G H J K	47 A B C D E
3 A B C D E	18 F G H J K	33 A B C D E	48 F G H J K
4 F G H J K	19 A B C D E	34 F G H J K	49 A B C D E
5 A B C D E	20 F G H J K	35 A B C D E	50 F G H J K
6 F G H J K	21 A B C D E	36 F G H J K	51 A B C D E
7 A B C D E	22 F G H J K	37 A B C D E	52 F G H J K
8 F G H J K	23 A B C D E	38 F G H J K	53 A B C D E
9 A B C D E	24 F G H J K	39 A B C D E	54 F G H J K
10 F G H J K	25 A B C D E	40 F G H J K	55 A B C D E
11 A B C D E	26 F G H J K	41 A B C D E	56 F G H J K
12 F G H J K	27 A B C D E	42 F G H J K	57 A B C D E
13 A B C D E	28 F G H J K	43 A B C D E	58 F G H J K
14 F G H J K	29 A B C D E	44 F G H J K	59 A B C D E
15 A B C D E	30 F G H J K	45 A B C D E	60 F G H J K

The Princeton Review
Diagnostic ACT Form

READING

1	Ⓐ Ⓑ Ⓒ Ⓓ	11	Ⓐ Ⓑ Ⓒ Ⓓ	21	Ⓐ Ⓑ Ⓒ Ⓓ	31	Ⓐ Ⓑ Ⓒ Ⓓ
2	Ⓕ Ⓖ Ⓗ Ⓙ	12	Ⓕ Ⓖ Ⓗ Ⓙ	22	Ⓕ Ⓖ Ⓗ Ⓙ	32	Ⓕ Ⓖ Ⓗ Ⓙ
3	Ⓐ Ⓑ Ⓒ Ⓓ	13	Ⓐ Ⓑ Ⓒ Ⓓ	23	Ⓐ Ⓑ Ⓒ Ⓓ	33	Ⓐ Ⓑ Ⓒ Ⓓ
4	Ⓕ Ⓖ Ⓗ Ⓙ	14	Ⓕ Ⓖ Ⓗ Ⓙ	24	Ⓕ Ⓖ Ⓗ Ⓙ	34	Ⓕ Ⓖ Ⓗ Ⓙ
5	Ⓐ Ⓑ Ⓒ Ⓓ	15	Ⓐ Ⓑ Ⓒ Ⓓ	25	Ⓐ Ⓑ Ⓒ Ⓓ	35	Ⓐ Ⓑ Ⓒ Ⓓ
6	Ⓕ Ⓖ Ⓗ Ⓙ	16	Ⓕ Ⓖ Ⓗ Ⓙ	26	Ⓕ Ⓖ Ⓗ Ⓙ	36	Ⓕ Ⓖ Ⓗ Ⓙ
7	Ⓐ Ⓑ Ⓒ Ⓓ	17	Ⓐ Ⓑ Ⓒ Ⓓ	27	Ⓐ Ⓑ Ⓒ Ⓓ	37	Ⓐ Ⓑ Ⓒ Ⓓ
8	Ⓕ Ⓖ Ⓗ Ⓙ	18	Ⓕ Ⓖ Ⓗ Ⓙ	28	Ⓕ Ⓖ Ⓗ Ⓙ	38	Ⓕ Ⓖ Ⓗ Ⓙ
9	Ⓐ Ⓑ Ⓒ Ⓓ	19	Ⓐ Ⓑ Ⓒ Ⓓ	29	Ⓐ Ⓑ Ⓒ Ⓓ	39	Ⓐ Ⓑ Ⓒ Ⓓ
10	Ⓕ Ⓖ Ⓗ Ⓙ	20	Ⓕ Ⓖ Ⓗ Ⓙ	30	Ⓕ Ⓖ Ⓗ Ⓙ	40	Ⓕ Ⓖ Ⓗ Ⓙ

SCIENCE REASONING

1	Ⓐ Ⓑ Ⓒ Ⓓ	11	Ⓐ Ⓑ Ⓒ Ⓓ	21	Ⓐ Ⓑ Ⓒ Ⓓ	31	Ⓐ Ⓑ Ⓒ Ⓓ
2	Ⓕ Ⓖ Ⓗ Ⓙ	12	Ⓕ Ⓖ Ⓗ Ⓙ	22	Ⓕ Ⓖ Ⓗ Ⓙ	32	Ⓕ Ⓖ Ⓗ Ⓙ
3	Ⓐ Ⓑ Ⓒ Ⓓ	13	Ⓐ Ⓑ Ⓒ Ⓓ	23	Ⓐ Ⓑ Ⓒ Ⓓ	33	Ⓐ Ⓑ Ⓒ Ⓓ
4	Ⓕ Ⓖ Ⓗ Ⓙ	14	Ⓕ Ⓖ Ⓗ Ⓙ	24	Ⓕ Ⓖ Ⓗ Ⓙ	34	Ⓕ Ⓖ Ⓗ Ⓙ
5	Ⓐ Ⓑ Ⓒ Ⓓ	15	Ⓐ Ⓑ Ⓒ Ⓓ	25	Ⓐ Ⓑ Ⓒ Ⓓ	35	Ⓐ Ⓑ Ⓒ Ⓓ
6	Ⓕ Ⓖ Ⓗ Ⓙ	16	Ⓕ Ⓖ Ⓗ Ⓙ	26	Ⓕ Ⓖ Ⓗ Ⓙ	36	Ⓕ Ⓖ Ⓗ Ⓙ
7	Ⓐ Ⓑ Ⓒ Ⓓ	17	Ⓐ Ⓑ Ⓒ Ⓓ	27	Ⓐ Ⓑ Ⓒ Ⓓ	37	Ⓐ Ⓑ Ⓒ Ⓓ
8	Ⓕ Ⓖ Ⓗ Ⓙ	18	Ⓕ Ⓖ Ⓗ Ⓙ	28	Ⓕ Ⓖ Ⓗ Ⓙ	38	Ⓕ Ⓖ Ⓗ Ⓙ
9	Ⓐ Ⓑ Ⓒ Ⓓ	19	Ⓐ Ⓑ Ⓒ Ⓓ	29	Ⓐ Ⓑ Ⓒ Ⓓ	39	Ⓐ Ⓑ Ⓒ Ⓓ
10	Ⓕ Ⓖ Ⓗ Ⓙ	20	Ⓕ Ⓖ Ⓗ Ⓙ	30	Ⓕ Ⓖ Ⓗ Ⓙ	40	Ⓕ Ⓖ Ⓗ Ⓙ

I hereby certify that I have truthfully identified myself on this form. I accept the consequences of falsifying my identity.

_____

Your signature

_____

Today's date

The Princeton Review
Diagnostic ACT Form

ESSAY

Begin your essay on this side. If necessary, continue on the opposite side.

Continue on the opposite side if necessary.

The Princeton Review
Diagnostic ACT Form

Continued from previous page.

PLEASE PRINT
YOUR INITIALS

First   Middle   Last

THIS PAGE INTENTIONALLY LEFT BLANK

ENGLISH TEST
45 Minutes—75 Questions

DIRECTIONS: In the five passages that follow, certain words and phrases are underlined and numbered. In the right-hand column, you will find alternatives for the underlined part. In most cases, you are to choose the one that correctly expresses the idea, makes the statement appropriate for standard written English, or is worded most consistently with the style and tone of the passage as a whole. If you think the original version is correct, choose "NO CHANGE." In some cases, you will find in the right-hand column a question about the underlined part. You are to choose the correct answer to the question.

You will also find questions about a section of the passage, or about the passage as a whole. These questions do not refer to an underlined portion of the passage, but rather are identified by a number or numbers in a box.

For each question, choose the alternative you consider correct and fill in the corresponding oval on your answer document. Read each passage through once before you begin to answer the questions that accompany it. For many of the questions, you must read several sentences beyond the question to determine the answer. Be sure that you have read far enough ahead each time you choose an alternative.

PASSAGE I

The Special Ingredient

As the firstborn grandchild, I made the most to the years [1] when I had the undivided attention of my adult relatives. I especially loved spending the day with my grandmother. I was ready to "help" around the house with everything; weeding, [2]

changing sheets, even washing windows. Solitary jobs thrilled [3] me because I was spending time alone with her. She made

everyday chores meaningful, when she set to work, hard and [4] easy tasks alike were undertaken as acts of love.

1. A. NO CHANGE
   B. along
   C. of
   D. into

2. F. NO CHANGE
   G. house with, everything:
   H. house with everything:
   J. house. With everything

3. Which choice best suggests the potentially unusual nature of the narrator's enthusiasm for the kinds of housework she helped her grandmother with?
   A. NO CHANGE
   B. Mundane
   C. Exciting
   D. Necessary

4. F. NO CHANGE
   G. meaningful. When she set to work
   H. meaningful and when she set to work
   J. meaningful. When she set to work,

GO ON TO THE NEXT PAGE.

I loved dinner preparations. No tasks seemed more magical <u>then it.</u>
₅

<u>Cooking without</u> written recipes, conjuring complex dishes with
₆
the same ease with which a magician pulls a rabbit from

a hat. My favorite dish, <u>however,</u> was a simple one: chicken
₇

and dumplings. She always began by <u>teasingly</u> asking me to
₈
catch and pluck a chicken, the way she'd had to do growing up.
While a store-bought chicken cooked in the soup pot, Grandma
transformed a few ingredients into dough, which she let rest and
then cut into the thin strips that would plump up in the broth.
After my brother was born, I became even more determined to
keep some activities just for myself. To reduce the resulting

quarrels, we both met with Grandma, <u>whom promised us</u> that
₉
we'd each have special activities. I rejoiced that I got to keep
chicken and dumplings.

When I left for college and then began a career abroad,
"our dish" came to <u>signal</u> everything I missed about
₁₀

<u>home when I was far away from it.</u> In desperation, whenever
₁₁
I came across chicken and dumplings on a menu, I'd order it
with high hopes, but the restaurant's version never tasted as
good as Grandma's. Eventually I became resigned to the fact

---

5. A. NO CHANGE
   B. then those of the kitchen.
   C. than it.
   D. than those of the kitchen.

6. F. NO CHANGE
   G. Cooking as she did without
   H. Grandma cooked without
   J. Without

7. A. NO CHANGE
   B. moreover,
   C. naturally,
   D. then,

8. If the writer were to delete the underlined portion, the paragraph would primarily lose:

   F. a sense of the relationship between the narrator and her grandmother as they engaged in their cooking rituals.
   G. an insight into how the grandmother both loved and kept a distance from her granddaughter.
   H. a suggestion that sometimes the narrator felt her grandmother picked on her.
   J. a detail that keeps the narrator's reminiscences from seeming too perfect.

9. A. NO CHANGE
   B. who promised us
   C. who promised ourselves
   D. whom promised ourselves

10. F. NO CHANGE
   G. represent
   H. stand up for
   J. give anew

11. A. NO CHANGE
   B. home when I wasn't there.
   C. home.
   D. the place I loved a lot, which was home.

GO ON TO THE NEXT PAGE.

that my favorite food was only available over visits home or, after
Grandma's death, in my dreams.

After hearing this lament a few times over the years, my
mother finally challenged me to cook the dish myself. I objected

that none of Grandma's recipes were written down, but Mom
dismissed my concerns, insisting my memories would guide me—
especially since I already knew that the most important ingredient
was love.

It turned out Mom was right. It took some trial and error,
but with help from the internet, I found a recipe for chicken and
dumplings that I love.

12. F. NO CHANGE
    G. when
    H. before
    J. on

13. Which choice indicates most specifically how the narrator felt
    about her access to the dish she craved, prior to her mother's
    suggestion?
    A. NO CHANGE
    B. explanation
    C. story
    D. long tale

14. F. NO CHANGE
    G. Grandmas' recipes
    H. Grandmas recipes
    J. Grandmas recipe's

15. Which choice best concludes the essay by emphasizing the
    central point made in the first and second paragraphs?
    A. NO CHANGE
    B. Grandma wouldn't have wanted me to be a quitter.
    C. perfecting a recipe for a dish you love always takes some
        practice.
    D. memories of how safe, happy, and loved I felt in the kitchen
        with Grandma helped me remember what to do—and,
        more importantly, how to do it.

PASSAGE II

Ada Lovelace, Programming the Future

[1] In 1833, when Ada Lovelace was seventeen, she met the
inventor Charles Babbage at a party. [2] Lovelace's intelligence
seems to have fazed him, because he soon offered to show her a
device he'd been working on. [3] Babbage introduced Lovelace
to his complicated Difference Engine—a towering mechanical

16. F. NO CHANGE
    G. overawed
    H. impressed
    J. motivated

GO ON TO THE NEXT PAGE.

calculator. [4] <u>Such</u> was a pivotal moment, as it was only after
₁₇

seeing this machine that <u>Lovelace fully focused</u> her keen
₁₈
understanding on the subject that absorbed her thereafter. [5]
With the benefit of an unusually extensive education, Lovelace
had excelled in many subjects; after meeting <u>Babbage though,</u>
₁₉

she concentrated on mathematical theories and methods. [20]

Almost a decade later, Babbage delivered a lecture on a
new, more sophisticated machine—the Analytical Engine.
The transcript of this lecture was published only in French.
After reading that version, Lovelace decided to translate it into
English. As she did so, she wrote footnotes to contribute her
own additional insights, including <u>many</u> that greatly clarified the
₂₁
mechanism of Babbage's work and expanded on its vast

potential. [22] In 1801, Joseph-Marie Jacquard had invented
a weaving machine that "read" a series of punched cards to
determine which patterns to weave. Babbage proposed that,
in his machine, such a card could specify mathematical

17. A. NO CHANGE
  B. These
  C. There
  D. This

18. F. NO CHANGE
  G. Lovelace fully to engage with
  H. Lovelace—she was fully engaged with
  J. Lovelace, she focused fully on

19. A. NO CHANGE
  B. Babbage, though,
  C. Babbage though
  D. Babbage, though

20. For the sake of logic and cohesion, Sentence 2 should be placed:

  F. where it is now.
  G. before Sentence 4.
  H. after Sentence 4.
  J. after Sentence 5.

21. A. NO CHANGE
  B. a number of hers
  C. many of those insights
  D. a lot of her insights

22. At this point, the writer is considering dividing the paragraph into two. Making this change would help organize the essay by separating:

  F. a suggestion that Lovelace took unwarranted liberties in the act of translation from an explanation of why she did so.
  G. an overview of the limitations of Babbage's lecture from an explanation of how the Analytical Engine could improve industries such as weaving.
  H. details of how Lovelace translated the French text from an explanation of Babbage's response to that translation.
  J. an introduction to Lovelace's translation from details that establish why it was so extraordinary.

GO ON TO THE NEXT PAGE.

operations Lovelace quickly grasped. This idea's immense
23
potential and strove to demonstrate it. Today, her outline

of the input data needed to calculate certain numbers

have been widely regarded as the first computer program.
24

Further, she predicted that such a machine could be used to do
25
more than just manipulate numbers. Lovelace's suggestion that

such a machine could produce diverse things: scientific analysis,
26

visual images, and music) to foreshadow the digital revolution.
27

    Lovelace died in 1852, decades before the first "real" computer

was built, but recognition of her trailblazing role as

a woman in computing has grown. Naturally, in the 1970s, the
28
Department of Defense named a software language "Ada" in her

honor, and, on the second Tuesday of every October, Ada Lovelace

Day prompts us to notice women in STEM fields.
29

23. A. NO CHANGE
    B. operations. Lovelace quickly grasped this
    C. operations, Lovelace quickly grasped this
    D. operations Lovelace quickly grasped; this

24. F. NO CHANGE
    G. are widely regarded
    H. have wide regard
    J. is widely regarded

25. A. NO CHANGE
    B. could be employed and
    C. akin to that could be
    D. like that could be

26. F. NO CHANGE
    G. things (scientific analysis,
    H. things, scientific analysis,
    J. things (scientific analysis

27. A. NO CHANGE
    B. foreshadowed
    C. foreshadowing
    D. DELETE the underlined portion.

28. F. NO CHANGE
    G. However, in
    H. In
    J. By contrast, in

29. Which choice most strongly and specifically emphasizes that Ada Lovelace Day is intended to shine a light on often-overlooked work done by women in math and science fields?

    A. NO CHANGE
    B. think about the work of
    C. celebrate under-recognized contributions of
    D. honor efforts by

GO ON TO THE NEXT PAGE.

Question 30 asks about the preceding passage as a whole.

30. Suppose the writer's primary purpose had been to discuss a mathematician whose work was remarkable but did not receive great recognition during the mathematician's lifetime. Would this essay accomplish that purpose?

   F. Yes, because it proves that Lovelace improved on Babbage's work to change the course of computer science.

   G. Yes, because it recounts the story of Ada Lovelace's pioneering work in her field and of the recognition she has received decades after her death.

   H. No, because although it describes the program Lovelace wrote, it does not provide evidence that the program was remarkable.

   J. No, because the passage speculates that Babbage recognized Lovelace's intelligence.

PASSAGE III

On Volcano's Edge

[1]

The U.S. is home to approximately 170 active volcanoes. While some in Alaska and Hawaii are so active that they erupt daily, many more lie dormant for years—or even decades, between eruptions. Since some of these active volcanoes sit near populated towns and cities, predicting future eruptions is essential to public safety.

[2]

The National Volcano Early Warning System reports that approximately 54 U.S. volcanoes pose a high or very high risk to public safety. The field of volcanology is devoted to understanding the formation and dynamics of volcanoes. [A]

31. A. NO CHANGE
    B. years,
    C. years
    D. years;

32. Given that all the choices are true, which one would provide the most effective introduction to the paragraph?

   F. NO CHANGE
   G. This task is the responsibility of volcanologists.
   H. On average, approximately one volcano erupts per week somewhere around the world.
   J. The deadliest volcanic event in the United States occurred when Mount St. Helens erupted in 1980.

GO ON TO THE NEXT PAGE.

This work can focus on dead and dormant volcanoes, it can also require volcanologists to monitor volcanoes that are active or potentially "reawakening."

[3]

[B] Field research on dead or dormant volcanoes frequently involves analyzing the chemical makeup of the rocks around the

volcano site to determine the amounts of sulfur and iron in the rocks. At active sites,

however, volcanologists collect samples and measure lava temperatures, gas emissions, and ongoing earthquake activities. "Long-period" earthquakes can indicate

magma rising through Earth's crust. As

magma liquefied rock that eventually becomes lava, builds up under the surface, a volcano's shape often changes. Thus,

it's vital to monitor a volcano using GPS and precisely calibrated instruments to detect and react to such changes.

33. **A.** NO CHANGE
    B. volcanoes; since
    C. volcanoes
    D. volcanoes, but

34. **F.** NO CHANGE
    G. have involved
    H. involve
    J. are involving

35. The writer wants to end this sentence by emphasizing that analysis of dormant and dead volcanoes provides insights into the geological history of those sites. Which choice best accomplishes that goal?

    A. NO CHANGE
    B. establish when and how previous eruptions occurred.
    C. confirm that the volcanoes are unlikely to erupt again in the near future.
    D. test for evidence of ancient civilizations that might have lived there.

36. **F.** NO CHANGE
    G. in fact,
    H. therefore,
    J. furthermore,

37. **A.** NO CHANGE
    B. behind
    C. of
    D. with

38. **F.** NO CHANGE
    G. magma, liquefied rock that eventually becomes lava—
    H. magma—liquefied rock that eventually becomes lava—
    J. magma, liquefied rock that eventually becomes lava

39. **A.** NO CHANGE
    B. it was
    C. its'
    D. its

GO ON TO THE NEXT PAGE.

[4]

Volcanologists also help to prepare areas for the chance
that a volcano could erupt. Fast-moving lava, avalanches, and
sudden rocky explosions pose dire risks to nearby humans,
animals, and their homes. Even far from the eruption site,
plumes of ash can harm crops and air travel is disrupted in
places nowhere near the volcano. Advising the public about
when to evacuate and when to stay away from a site can save
thousands of lives. [C]

[5]

Because a career that involves camping by a soon-to-erupt
volcano might seem spectacularly dangerous, only two U.S.
geologists have ever died as a result of volcanic eruption. [D]
Recent advances in technology and methods of prediction
help volcanologists advise residents living near an active site
while greatly minimizing risks to the scientists themselves.

[6]

Like many applied science positions, a volcanologist's
job combines direct observation, theoretical modeling, and
analyzing of data.

40. **F.** NO CHANGE
G. the possibility that a volcano could erupt in a certain area.
H. a possible eruption.
J. a likelihood that a volcano will erupt nearby, since they know it could happen.

41. **A.** NO CHANGE
B. ash plumes can cause problems for farmers, crops, air traffic controllers, and airplanes.
C. ash that forms massive clouds in the sky can rain down on fields and affect airplane travel in faraway locales.
D. plumes of ash can disrupt air travel and affect agriculture.

42. **F.** NO CHANGE
G. Considering that
H. Since
J. While

43. **A.** NO CHANGE
B. has helped
C. is helping
D. helps

44. **F.** NO CHANGE
G. they analyze data.
H. data to be analyzed.
J. data analysis.

Question 45 asks about the preceding passage as a whole.

---

45. The writer wants to add the following sentence to the essay:

> Whatever a volcano's status, volcanologists must conduct much of this monitoring on site.

The sentence would most logically be placed at:

A. Point A in Paragraph 2.
B. Point B in Paragraph 3.
C. Point C in Paragraph 4.
D. Point D in Paragraph 5.

GO ON TO THE NEXT PAGE.

PASSAGE IV

Vermeer's Artistry

The following paragraphs may or may not be in the most logical order. Each paragraph is numbered in brackets, and question 59 will ask you to choose where Paragraph 4 should most logically be placed.

[1]

Johannes Vermeer's *The Art of Painting* combines realistic representation with metaphorical details to prompt the viewer to think about how art works. Vermeer is best known for
46

portraying women in everyday domestic moments, since he showed them making lace, reading, or doing chores. This
47

painting, however, centers on a male artist; critics believe
48
represents Vermeer himself, as he paints a female model. Thus, the painting seems to offer the artist's commentary on his art.

[2]

[1] Yet some details are inconsistent with the work's prevailing realism. [2] In one place, the painter's hair fades gradually into the background colors of the map behind him. [3] In another, blurring of background details, the folds of drapery
49
on the table are out of focus, creating an impressionistic effect.

46. Which choice best indicates where Vermeer was born and worked?
   F. NO CHANGE
   G. in one of the Dutch painter's most self-referential works.
   H. to produce a complex statement about the politics and practice of painting.
   J. in a painting owned by the Kunsthistorisches Museum in Vienna.

47. A. NO CHANGE
    B. showing
    C. in which he showed
    D. DELETE the underlined portion.

48. F. NO CHANGE
    G. artist, critics
    H. artist. Critics
    J. artist critics

49. A. NO CHANGE
    B. another blurring of background details,
    C. another, blurring of background details
    D. another blurring, of background details

GO ON TO THE NEXT PAGE.

[4] Basic tools which the painter would need access in order
to paint, like a palette, are absent from the image. [5] It also
appears that, were the painter to stand up, he'd bang

his head on the chandelier above him. [6] Suggesting the artist's
metaphorical stature within the scene and reaffirms his

significance. ▢52

[3]

Together, the realistic and metaphorical details make
Vermeer's work stand out even from other Dutch masterpieces
that also depict art being made. Emanuel de Witte's *Interior with
a Woman at the Clavichord*, for instance, also shows a domestic
space as the site of artistic performance. Yet de Witte's work
does not emphasize the role of an artist's decisions in creating
the semblance of realism the way Vermeer's does. Vermeer's
image directly reminds us that an artist's choices are based on
that artist's personal experiences.

50. **F.** NO CHANGE
G. to which
H. for
J. DELETE the underlined portion.

51. **A.** NO CHANGE
B. While this suggests
C. This detail suggests
D. Since suggesting

52. The writer wants to add the following statement to the paragraph:

> This omission has the paradoxical effect of directing
> attention to the elements of craft that are not shown or
> that go unnoticed.

This statement would most logically be placed after:

F. Sentence 1.
G. Sentence 3.
H. Sentence 4.
J. Sentence 5.

53. **A.** NO CHANGE
B. noticeably stand out
C. draw attention by standing out
D. stand out with prominence

54. Which choice both supports the claim the writer makes in the
preceding sentence about an artist's decisions and best emphasizes how significant those choices are to what we perceive?

F. NO CHANGE
G. are affected by a whole range of factors.
H. always shape what the viewer perceives in a work of art.
J. are not so different from the everyday choices people make.

GO ON TO THE NEXT PAGE.

[4]

The realistic precision of *The Art of Painting* is striking. Details are so clear that, for instance, historians have diagnosed
₅₅

the exact document Vermeer must have referenced in his
₅₆
depiction of a map that hangs on the wall in the painting. Vermeer's mastery of many of painting's components,

including such fundamental elements as light and color,
₅₇

result in an image that appears as accurate as a photograph.
₅₈

55. **A.** NO CHANGE
B. determined the identification of
C. identified
D. put a name to

56. **F.** NO CHANGE
G. referenced;
H. referenced—
J. referenced,

57. **A.** NO CHANGE
B. that are elements
C. elements as
D. DELETE the underlined portion.

58. **F.** NO CHANGE
G. are resulting
H. results
J. have resulted

Questions 59 and 60 ask about the preceding passage as a whole.

---

59. For the sake of logic and cohesion, Paragraph 4 should be placed:

A. where it is now.
B. before Paragraph 1.
C. before Paragraph 2.
D. after Paragraph 2.

60. Suppose the writer's primary purpose had been to examine how a work of art reshaped the way historians think about the role of the artist. Would this essay accomplish that purpose?

F. Yes, because it suggests that other painters were influenced by Vermeer's innovative approach.
G. Yes, because it indicates the role that historians have played in analyzing the painting.
H. No, because it states that Vermeer's subject in *The Art of Painting* was atypical for him.
J. No, because it focuses on the particulars of one painting but does not indicate what effect the painting has had on art criticism overall.

GO ON TO THE NEXT PAGE.

PASSAGE V

The Intricate Layers of *Matryoshka*

Natasha Pugaeva is a professional painter of *matryoshki*, the nesting dolls that rank among Russia's most recognizable national symbols. She painted her first *matryoshka* doll in 1990, while she was in Kazakhstan, who worked as a painting instructor. The *matryoshka* trade has flourished among former Soviet state employees who could produce the dolls from their homes. ▣62 Three years later, she and her husband moved to a city east of Moscow, where she has expanded

her *matryoshka* production.

All dolls in a set except the smallest are hollow, with "daughter" dolls nesting inside one another, so it's not surprising that the word *matryoshka* recalls the Russian word for "mother." While the exact origins of *matryoshki* are unclear,

one possibility, travel played a key role, is that a Russian who had visited Asia brought home a Japanese nesting doll in the 1890s. The development of a similar doll in Sergiev Posad—a

61. A. NO CHANGE
B. Kazakhstan, and worked
C. Kazakhstan, and having work
D. Kazakhstan working

62. The writer is considering deleting the preceding sentence. Should the sentence be kept or deleted?

F. Kept, because it places Natasha's painting in a broader social context.
G. Kept, because it explains why Natasha was one of many people to begin painting *matryoshka* dolls in the early 1990s.
H. Deleted, because it detracts from the paragraph's focus on the development of Natasha's *matryoshka*-painting practice.
J. Deleted, because it contradicts the paragraph's explanation of where Natasha learned to paint *matroyshka* dolls.

63. A. NO CHANGE
B. her production.
C. their production.
D. the production of them.

64. Which choice most clearly builds on the information provided earlier in the sentence about the relationship of the dolls' structure to their name?

F. NO CHANGE
G. but, while *matryoshka* dolls are more often female, it is possible to find male dolls as well.
H. and, as Russian speakers know, the plural of *matryoshka* is *matryoshki*.
J. which means the largest *matryoshka* doll is the one most people see.

65. A. NO CHANGE
B. possibility and
C. possibility, which
D. possibility, in which

GO ON TO THE NEXT PAGE.

Russian region famous for its folk art—resulted from, or perhaps simply coinciding with, that cross-cultural exchange. Soon, the lathes that were operated by local workers to craft various

wooden objects was used to produce great numbers of blank

matryoshka dolls (particularly games and nesting Easter eggs). Then came the painting. Over the years, amateur and

professional artists alike have hand-painted the smooth, curved surfaces, and brought beautiful images to life. Inspiration for these designs comes from Russian life, and less traditional subjects include fantastical fairy tales, politicians of great power, revered religious figures, and iconic works of art. Since an early *matryoshka* set was displayed in Paris in 1900, the dolls have had a long career as an evocative example of traditional

Russian goods.

66. **F.** NO CHANGE
    G. coincided
    H. as a coincidence
    J. it was to coincide

67. **A.** NO CHANGE
    B. used
    C. were used
    D. has been used

68. The best placement for the underlined portion would be:
    F. where it is now.
    G. after the word *lathes*.
    H. after the word *workers*.
    J. after the word *objects*.

69. **A.** NO CHANGE
    B. smooth curved surfaces,
    C. smooth curved, surfaces
    D. smooth, curved surfaces

70. Which choice best maintains the stylistic pattern of descriptions established earlier in the sentence?
    F. NO CHANGE
    G. art.
    H. famous artworks that are imitated.
    J. some famous artworks.

71. The writer is considering revising the underlined portion to the following:

    handicrafts.

    Should the writer make this revision?

    A. Yes, because the revision better indicates why there is so much variation in the decorations on the dolls.
    B. Yes, because the revision emphasizes the handmade nature of the dolls, which effectively reinforces the essay's framing discussion of an individual artisan.
    C. No, because the original word places the dolls within the larger context of a market in which souvenirs are bought and sold.
    D. No, because the original word more specifically describes the type of object that a *matryoshka* doll is.

GO ON TO THE NEXT PAGE.

For Natasha, her exceptional skills offer a means of engaging with her community. Instead, she runs a workshop in which <u>72</u> she instructs and collaborates with students. The students do not

pay for their lessons, and they receive a portion of the <u>profits.</u> <u>73</u>

<u>74</u> With artists like Natasha passing on their skills, Russia's

generation's-old folk tradition of *matryoshka* may well last for <u>75</u> generations more.

72. **F.** NO CHANGE
    G. She
    H. In fact, she
    J. Nevertheless, she

73. Which choice most clearly and concisely indicates that Natasha and her students mutually benefit from selling the *matryoshka* dolls they produce together?

    A. NO CHANGE
    B. money she earns from doll-making.
    C. profits generated by the workshop-made dolls.
    D. money.

74. Which of the following true statements, if added here, would best build on the ideas presented in this paragraph and connect to the final sentence of the essay?

    F. Two recent students have even gone on to establish their own doll businesses.
    G. Natasha's mother and sister are also associated with her workshop.
    H. Many people are surprised and delighted by the less traditional designs and themes found on some more recently made *matryoshka* dolls.
    J. Natasha's work is characterized by dazzlingly detailed faces and small dots of paint that look like gems.

75. **A.** NO CHANGE
    B. generations'-old
    C. generation's-oldest
    D. generations-old

END OF TEST 1
STOP! DO NOT TURN THE PAGE UNTIL TOLD TO DO SO.

MATHEMATICS TEST

60 Minutes—60 Questions

DIRECTIONS: Solve each problem, choose the correct answer, and then darken the corresponding oval on your answer sheet.

Do not linger over problems that take too much time. Solve as many as you can; then return to the others in the time you have left for this test.

You are permitted to use a calculator on this test. You may use your calculator for any problems you choose,

but some of the problems may best be done without using a calculator.

Note: Unless otherwise stated, all of the following should be assumed:

1. Illustrative figures are NOT necessarily drawn to scale.
2. Geometric figures lie in a plane.
3. The word *line* indicates a straight line.
4. The word *average* indicates arithmetic mean.

---

1. A child randomly selects a jellybean from a jar of jellybeans. The probability that the child selects a grape jellybean is $\frac{7}{23}$, and the probability that he selects a grape jellybean or a cherry jellybean is $\frac{13}{23}$. What is the probability that the child selects a cherry jellybean?

   A. $\frac{1}{23}$

   B. $\frac{6}{46}$

   C. $\frac{6}{23}$

   D. $\frac{20}{46}$

   E. $\frac{20}{23}$

DO YOUR FIGURING HERE.

GO ON TO THE NEXT PAGE.

2. The children at a birthday party range from 6 to 9 years old. The graph below shows the number of children of each age at the party. What is the probability that a child selected at random from the children at the party will be 7 years old?

DO YOUR FIGURING HERE.

F. $\dfrac{1}{24}$

G. $\dfrac{1}{8}$

H. $\dfrac{1}{7}$

J. $\dfrac{1}{4}$

K. $\dfrac{1}{3}$

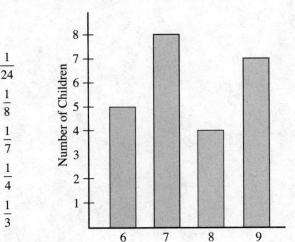

3. For all numbers p and q, $q = \dfrac{5}{3}p + 46$. What is the value of p when the value of q is 21 ?

A. -24

B. -15

C. $-\dfrac{125}{3}$

D. $\dfrac{63}{5}$

E. 35

GO ON TO THE NEXT PAGE.

DO YOUR FIGURING HERE.

4. What is the value of $|2+y|$ when $y = -6$?

   F.   –8
   G. –6
   H. –4
   J.   4
   K.   8

5. In 2015, the total rainfall in Central City was 13 inches less than the total annual rainfall in Central City in 2000. In 2016, the total rainfall in Central City was 33 inches greater than the total annual rainfall in Central City in 2000. If + indicates an increase in rainfall and – indicates a decrease in rainfall, what was the difference, in inches, in the yearly rainfall from 2015 to 2016 in Central City?

   A. –46
   B. –20
   C. +10
   D. +20
   E. +46

6. Ruben purchases a violin that is on sale for a total price of $1,250, which includes tax and all other fees. He makes an initial payment of $300 in cash and puts the remainder on his new credit card. He makes no other purchases on the card and pays off the credit card balance with 9 monthly payments of $150. What is the difference between the total amount Ruben pays for the violin, including the initial payment and the credit card payments, and the sale price of the violin?

   F. $ 100
   G. $ 250
   H. $ 400
   J. $1,350
   K. $1,650

7. The regular hexagon shown below has a perimeter of 30 and center C. What is the perimeter of $\triangle ABC$?

   A.   5
   B. 10
   C. 15
   D. 18
   E. $5 + 10\sqrt{3}$

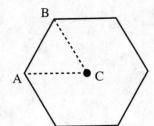

GO ON TO THE NEXT PAGE.

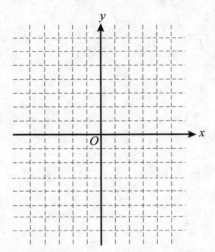

8. Shown below is the proposed layout for a driveway. The length of each side is marked in feet. What is the area of the driveway, in square feet?

(Note: Edges of the driveway meet at right angles.)

F.   85
G.   153
H.   265
J.   337
K.   350

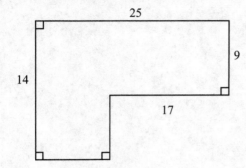

DO YOUR FIGURING HERE.

9. Three vertices of a parallelogram are located at the points (−1,2), (4,3), and (−3,−1) in the standard (x,y) coordinate plane shown below.

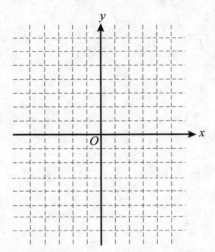

Which of the following could be the coordinates of the fourth vertex?

A.   (2, 0)
B.   (3, −2)
C.   (1, 1)
D.   (−2, −5)
E.   (−5, −1)

GO ON TO THE NEXT PAGE.

DO YOUR FIGURING HERE.

10. Consider two functions defined by the equations $m(x) = 2x - 2$ and $n(x) = \dfrac{\sqrt{x}}{3}$. When $x = 9$, what is the value of $m(n(x))$?

    F. 0

    G. 1

    H. $\dfrac{4}{3}$

    J. 3

    K. 16

11. Maria sells homemade holiday cards at a craft fair. The total cost of the supplies and the booth rental is $150. She sells n cards for $3 each. If she makes a profit, which of the following inequalities includes all possible values of n ?

    A. $n + 150 > 0$

    B. $n - 150 > 0$

    C. $n - 150 < 0$

    D. $3n - 150 > 0$

    E. $3n - 150 < 0$

12. What is the slope of the line $5x - 11y = 7$ in the standard (x,y) coordinate plane?

    F. -5

    G. $-\dfrac{5}{7}$

    H. $\dfrac{5}{11}$

    J. 5

    K. 7

13. The lines represented by the equations $x + 3y = 6$ and $-5x + y = 18$ intersect at point A in the standard (x,y) coordinate plane. Which of the following could be the coordinates of A ?

    A. $(-12, 6)$

    B. $(-3, 3)$

    C. $\left(-1, 2\dfrac{1}{3}\right)$

    D. $(0, 2)$

    E. $\left(1, 1\dfrac{2}{3}\right)$

GO ON TO THE NEXT PAGE.

14. In a blueprint for a new building, $\frac{1}{3}$ centimeter represents 9 meters in the finished building. If a hallway shown on the blueprint is $4\frac{2}{3}$ centimeters long, how long, in meters, will the hallway be in the finished building?

F. 9
G. 14
H. 27
J. 126
K. 378

DO YOUR FIGURING HERE.

15. The matrix $3\begin{bmatrix} 2 & -1 \\ 3 & 0 \end{bmatrix}$ is equivalent to which of the following matrices?

A. $[15 - 3]$

B. $\begin{bmatrix} 3 \\ 9 \end{bmatrix}$

C. $\begin{bmatrix} 6 & -3 \\ 9 & 0 \end{bmatrix}$

D. $\begin{bmatrix} 5 & 2 \\ 6 & 3 \end{bmatrix}$

E. $\begin{bmatrix} \frac{2}{3} & -\frac{1}{3} \\ 1 & 0 \end{bmatrix}$

16. In right triangle XYZ, shown below, what is the value of $\cos Z$?

F. $\frac{7}{25}$

G. $\frac{7}{24}$

H. $\frac{24}{25}$

J. $\frac{24}{7}$

K. $\frac{25}{7}$

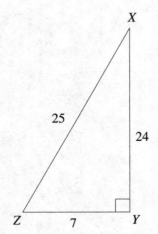

GO ON TO THE NEXT PAGE.

17. A snail travels 7 inches in one minute. At this rate, how many inches will the snail travel in 5 seconds?

DO YOUR FIGURING HERE.

A. $\dfrac{7}{20}$

B. $\dfrac{7}{12}$

C. $\dfrac{5}{7}$

D. $1\dfrac{2}{5}$

E. $1\dfrac{5}{7}$

18. Given that $g(x) = -\dfrac{x^2}{4}$, what is the value of $g(-8)$?

F. −16
G. −4
H. −1
J. 4
K. 16

19. In the figure shown below, Q lies on $\overline{PR}$ and T lies on $\overline{PS}$. What is the measure of $\angle TQR$?

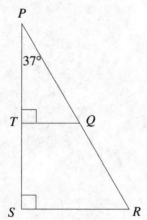

A. 53°
B. 107°
C. 127°
D. 137°
E. 153°

GO ON TO THE NEXT PAGE.

20. A line is graphed in the standard (x,y) coordinate plane. When x is equal to 3, y is equal to 8. When x is equal to 7, y is equal to 20. Which of the following expressions could be the equation of the line?

F. $y = \dfrac{x+1}{3}$

G. $y = \dfrac{3}{8}x$

H. $y = \dfrac{8}{3}x$

J. $y = 2x + 2$

K. $y = 3x - 1$

21. A park ranger records the height of a river at 7:00 A.M. and 7:00 P.M. daily. On Sunday at 7:00 P.M., the river was at a height of 14 feet. The river height fell at a rate of 1.5 feet per day from Sunday at 7:00 P.M. through Thursday at 7:00 P.M. At that time, heavy rains caused the water to rise at a constant rate of 3 feet per day. At what time will the park ranger first record a height over 14 feet?

A. Friday at 7 P.M.
B. Saturday at 7 A.M.
C. Saturday at 7 P.M.
D. Sunday at 7 A.M.
E. Sunday at 7 P.M.

22. Viviana is competing in a science fair and will receive 5 scores, each out of 60 points, from 5 separate judges. Different colored ribbons are awarded based on a participant's average score, A, from the five judges. The average scores necessary for each ribbon color are shown in the chart below.

Range	Ribbon
$A \geq 55$	Red
$50 \leq A < 55$	Blue
$40 \leq A < 50$	White
$30 \leq A < 40$	Yellow

The first three judges award Viviana scores of 37, 46, and 49. If p represents the combined total of the points that Viviana receives from the final two judges, which of the following is a possible value of p for which Viviana would earn a white ribbon?

F. 49
G. 66
H. 98
J. 118
K. 130

GO ON TO THE NEXT PAGE.

Use the following information to answer questions 23–25.

A rectangular swimming pool is divided into a free swim portion and a lap swimming portion with a double stranded lane line. The dimensions of the pool are shown below. Each strand of the lane line consists of 20 spherical buoys.

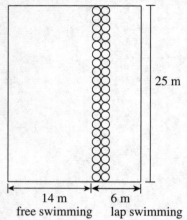

25 m

14 m
free swimming

6 m
lap swimming

(Note: Figure not drawn to scale.)

A four-person relay team is swimming a relay in the lap swimming portion. The first three members of the team complete their laps in 63, 65, and 59 seconds, respectively.

23. The diameter of each buoy in the lane line is 1.25 meters, and each buoy sits in the water such that its diameter is level with the pool's surface. What is the approximate area of the pool's surface, in square meters, that the double stranded lane line occupies?

   A.   20
   B.   49
   C.   98
   D.   126
   E.   196

24. What is the ratio of the area of the surface of the lap swimming portion (including the double lane line) to the area of the surface of the free swimming portion?

   F.   3:7
   G.   3:10
   H.   7:10
   J.   150:323
   K.   150:359

GO ON TO THE NEXT PAGE.

DO YOUR FIGURING HERE.

25. If the relay team finishes with an average time of 60 seconds per person, how long, in seconds, does it take the fourth member to finish his lap?

A. 52
B. 53
C. 58
D. 60
E. 61

26. The width of a rectangle is twice its length, and the area of the rectangle is 72. What is the length of the rectangle?

F. 3
G. 6
H. 12
J. 24
K. 36

27. Parallelogram *ABCD* has a perimeter of 64, and side $\overline{AB}$ has a length of 12. If it can be determined, what is the length of side $\overline{BC}$?

A. 20
B. 26
C. 32
D. 52
E. Cannot be determined from the information given

28. A pedestrian bridge used as an outdoor market is divided into an eastbound and westbound side. On each side, there is a 16-foot-wide lane dedicated to foot traffic, a 10-foot-wide lane for browsing and purchasing, and a 9-foot-wide row of wooden vendor stalls. How many total feet wide is the pedestrian bridge?

F. 35
G. 40
H. 51
J. 70
K. 85

GO ON TO THE NEXT PAGE.

29. In Culver City, there are 720 households. If 5 out of every 12 of these households own a dog, and 6 out of every 10 households that own a dog also have a fenced-in backyard, how many of the households in Culver City are dog owners with fenced-in backyards?

A. 86
B. 180
C. 228
D. 360
E. 464

DO YOUR FIGURING HERE.

30. If $\tan x = -\dfrac{7}{24}$ and $\dfrac{3\pi}{2} < x < 2\pi$, what is $\sin x$?

F. $-\dfrac{24}{25}$

G. $-\dfrac{7}{25}$

H. $\dfrac{7}{24}$

J. $\dfrac{24}{25}$

K. $\dfrac{25}{24}$

31. If $g(n) = \dfrac{-3}{n+2}$ and $h(n) = -n$, for what real value of x is $g(x) = h(x)$?

A. 1 only
B. 3 only
C. −1 and 3 only
D. 1 and −3 only
E. 1 and 3 only

GO ON TO THE NEXT PAGE.

Use the following information to answer questions 32–35.

The figure below shows two roads, Route 1 and Route 2, that both run directly north-south through a town. On Route 1, the library is located 14 miles due north of the town hall (at points Y and X respectively). The town is considering a proposal to build a new road that will begin at point W on Route 1, 5 miles south of Y, and run due east to Point Z on Route 2. The straight-line distance between point Z and the library is 13 miles, and the straight-line distance between Z and the town hall is 15 miles.

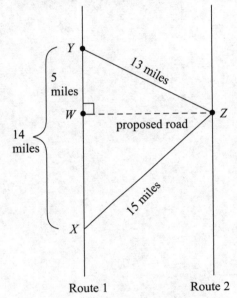

32. Which of the following is the length of the proposed road segment, in miles, connecting points W and Z ?

F. 9

G. 12

H. $12\frac{1}{2}$

J. 13

K. 14

DO YOUR FIGURING HERE.

33. If the roads are mapped in the standard (x,y) coordinate plane such that the coordinates of X and Y are $(0,0)$ and $(0,14)$, respectively, which of the following equations represents the line along which the proposed road would be drawn?

A. $y = 9$
B. $y = 14$
C. $x = 5$
D. $x = 9$
E. $x = 14$

34. A car located at point Z is driving due north on Route 2 at 20 miles per hour. At this rate, how long, in minutes, will it take the car to reach the point due east of the library located at point Y ?

F. 4
G. 9
H. 15
J. 27
K. 39

35. A city planner suggests that the proposed road be located farther south. If points W and Z are both relocated exactly three miles south of their current locations, which of the following describes how the measures of $\angle X$, $\angle Y$, and $\angle Z$ will be adjusted?

 I. The measure of angle $\angle X$ will increase.
 II. The measure of angle $\angle Y$ will decrease.
 III. The measure of angle $\angle Z$ will remain unchanged.

A. I only
B. II only
C. III only
D. I and II only
E. I, II, and III

36. In her living room, Christa has a rectangular rug that is 6 feet wide and 8 feet long. She decides that the rug is too small for the room, so she orders a new one that covers twice as much area. If the new rug is 1.5 times as wide as the original rug, how long, in feet, is the new rug?

F. $5\dfrac{1}{3}$
G. 9
H. $10\dfrac{2}{3}$
J. 12
K. 24

GO ON TO THE NEXT PAGE.

37. For which of the following values of x is the equation $4(x - 2) - 3x = x + 2$ true?

    A. The equation has no solution.
    B. 3
    C. 2
    D. −1
    E. All real numbers

DO YOUR FIGURING HERE.

38. A teacher plans to use a 40-inch long roll of string to form a border around a rectangular space on her bulletin board reserved for student use. What is the maximum amount of space, in square inches, that she can reserve on her bulletin board using this roll of string?

    F. 96
    G. 99
    H. 100
    J. 160
    K. 400

39. In 2010, there are 8 homes on a street and each home is valued somewhere between $250,000 and $350,000. Two new houses are built on the street in 2011. One of the new homes is valued at a little over $2,000,000, and the other is valued at less than $100,000. The value of the original 8 houses remains the same. If it can be determined, of the mean, median, standard deviation, and range, which of the following will increase the most?

    A. The standard deviation
    B. The median
    C. The mean
    D. The range
    E. Cannot be determined from the information given

40. A house painting company assigns three employees to a particular customer's house. The first employee paints $\frac{3}{7}$ of the house in her 4-hour shift. The second employee paints another $\frac{1}{4}$ of the house before the third employee takes over. If all three employees paint at the same rate, how many hours will it take the third employee to finish painting the remainder of the house by himself?

    F. 0.32
    G. 2.00
    H. 3.00
    J. 3.63
    K. 9.33

GO ON TO THE NEXT PAGE.

41. Which of the following expressions, where defined, is equivalent to $\dfrac{(3xy^{-3})^3}{\left(\sqrt{xy}\right)^{-2}}$?

DO YOUR FIGURING HERE.

A. $\dfrac{27x^4}{y^8}$

B. $\dfrac{27y^6}{x}$

C. $\dfrac{27x}{y^7}$

D. $\dfrac{9x}{y^8}$

E. $9xy^7$

42. A pet sitter knows that her client's five-digit alarm code contains the digits 2, 3, 1, 7, and 8. She cannot remember the order of the first four digits, but she knows that the last digit is 7. If she randomly guesses the order of the first four digits, what is the probability that she enters the correct alarm code on her first attempt?

F. $\dfrac{1}{4}$

G. $\dfrac{1}{5}$

H. $\dfrac{1}{6}$

J. $\dfrac{1}{24}$

K. $\dfrac{1}{120}$

43. For all real values of a, which of the following is equivalent to $\dfrac{\dfrac{1}{3}-\dfrac{1}{2}}{\dfrac{1}{3}+\dfrac{a}{4}}$?

A. $4 + 3a$

B. $\dfrac{-2}{4+3a}$

C. $\dfrac{4}{3+2a}$

D. $\dfrac{-2}{3+3a}$

E. $\dfrac{2}{3a}$

GO ON TO THE NEXT PAGE.

DO YOUR FIGURING HERE.

44. A library classifies each of its books using a five-character code. The first character denotes one of 15 different genres represented by the 15 letters A through O, and the second character denotes one of 11 different subgenres denoted by the 11 letters P through Z. The final 3 characters each consist of a single digit from 0 through 9. Digits can be repeated within a classification code. If every book must have a unique classification code, what is the maximum number of books that the library can own?

F. 260
G. 4,950
H. 120,285
J. 165,000
K. 225,000

45. The figure below shows the graph of the function $y = g(x)$ in the standard (x,y) coordinate plane.

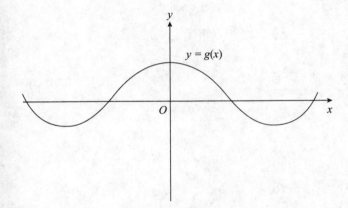

If every point on $y = g(x)$ is shifted 3 units to the left and 2 units down, the resulting graph would represent the function $y = h(x)$. Which of the following could be the equation for $h(x)$?

A. $h(x) = g(x - 3) - 2$
B. $h(x) = g(x + 3) - 2$
C. $h(x) = g(x - 2) + 3$
D. $h(x) = g(x + 2) - 3$
E. $h(x) = g(x - 2) - 3$

46. If $\log_n \dfrac{1}{27} = -3$, what is n ?

F. -9

G. $-\dfrac{1}{9}$

H. 3

J. $\dfrac{1}{9}$

K. $\dfrac{1}{3}$

GO ON TO THE NEXT PAGE.

DO YOUR FIGURING HERE.

47. Which of the following sets contains all the integer values of k for which $\dfrac{1}{6} < \dfrac{k}{5} < \dfrac{3}{4}$?

   A. $\{1, 2\}$
   B. $\{2\}$
   C. $\{1, 2, 3\}$
   D. $\{4\}$
   E. $\{3, 4, 5\}$

48. For all real numbers x, y, and z, $x < y < z$ and $xyz < 0$. Which of the following *must* be true?

   F. $xy < yz$

   G. $x + y > y + z$

   H. $\dfrac{x}{y} < \dfrac{y}{z}$

   J. $x < yz$

   K. $x + z < y$

49. The triangle shown below has side lengths x, y, and z such that $x < y < z$. Which of the following expressions could be used to find the measure of the smallest angle in the triangle?

   (Note: For every triangle with sides of length a, b, and c that are opposite $\angle A$, $\angle B$, and $\angle C$, respectively, $c^2 = a^2 + b^2 - 2ab \cos C$.)

   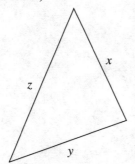

   A. $\cos^{-1}(x^2 - y^2 - z^2 - 2yz)$

   B. $\cos^{-1}(z^2 - y^2 - x^2 - 2xy)$

   C. $\cos^{-1}\left(-\dfrac{z^2 - y^2 - x^2}{2xy}\right)$

   D. $\cos^{-1}\left(-\dfrac{x^2 - y^2 - z^2}{2yz}\right)$

   E. $\cos^{-1}\left(-\dfrac{x^2 + y^2 - z^2}{2yz}\right)$

GO ON TO THE NEXT PAGE.

50. Kyle scores an average of p points per game in his first 9 basketball games of the season. After Kyle scores n points in his 10th game, his season average increases by 3 points per game. What is the value of $n - p$?

    F.   3
    G.   12
    H.   27
    J.   30
    K.   39

51. AB and CD are both diameters of a circle with center O. If the measure of $\angle AOD$ is 1.5 times the measure of $\angle AOC$, what is the measure of $\angle AOD$?

    A.   36°
    B.   54°
    C.   72°
    D.   96°
    E.   108°

52. The first term in sequence A is 6 and the third term is 72. Which of the following equations could define sequence A for all positive values of n ?

    F. $3\left(A_{n-1}\right) + 2n$
    G. $12\left(A_{n-1}\right)$
    H. $6\left(A_{n-1}\right) + 18n$
    J. $6\left(A_{n-1}\right) - 6$
    K. $3\left(A_{n-1}\right) + 2$

53. If $c^{-1} < c^2 < |c|$, which of the following describes all possible values of c ?

    A. $c < -2$
    B. $-2 < c < -1$
    C. $-1 < c < 0$
    D. $0 < c < 1$
    E. $c > 1$

54. On a game show, contestants blindly pull a marble out of a bag containing 6 colored marbles. Each color is worth a certain number of points. The bag contains 3 green marbles that are worth 6 points each, 2 purple marbles that are worth 3 points each, and 1 yellow marble that is worth 0 points. A contestant pulls one marble out of the bag at random. If the random variable P represents the number of points the contestant earns on this single marble draw, what is the expected value of P ?

    F.   0.5
    G.   1.5
    H.   3
    J.   3.5
    K.   4

DO YOUR FIGURING HERE.

GO ON TO THE NEXT PAGE.

55. If a, b, c, d, and e are consecutive integers such that $a < b < c < d < e$, which of the following is equivalent to the sum of a, b, c, d, and e ?

A. $5a + 5$

B. $5b$

C. $5b + 4$

D. $5c$

E. $\dfrac{a+e}{2}$

56. The set $\{13, 7, 22, 6, 4, a\}$ has a mean of 11 and a median of b. If it can be determined, what is the value of $a - b$?

F. -24
G. -4
H. 4
J. 24
K. Cannot be determined from the information given

57. A rectangular room has a width of n feet and a length of m feet, and $n \neq m$. If n and m are both integers and the perimeter of the room is 36 feet, which of the following CANNOT be the area of the room?

A. 45
B. 56
C. 72
D. 77
E. 81

58. The equation $(x - 5)^2 + (y + 2)^2 = 20$ defines a circle that lies in the standard (x,y) coordinate plane. The line with endpoints $(9,0)$ and (a,b) is a diameter of the circle. What is the value of a ?

F. -13
G. -7
H. -5
J. -2
K. 1

GO ON TO THE NEXT PAGE.

59. In 2012, a shipping company offered a large flat-rate shipping box with a length of 15 inches, a width of 20 inches, and a height of 10 inches. In 2013, the company decreased both the height and width of the flat-rate box by 20%. Which of the following is closest to the percent decrease in the volume of the flat-rate box between 2012 and 2013 ?

 A. 20%
 B. 36%
 C. 40%
 D. 49%
 E. 56%

DO YOUR FIGURING HERE.

60. Which of the following is true if the binomial $(x - 2)$ is a factor of the equation $3x^3 - 4x^2 + x - 10 = 0$?

 F. The equation has three real solutions.
 G. The equation has two real solutions and one complex solution.
 H. The equation has one real solution and three complex solutions.
 J. The equation has one real solution and two complex solutions.
 K. The equation has no real solutions and three complex solutions.

END OF TEST 2

STOP! DO NOT TURN THE PAGE UNTIL TOLD TO DO SO.

DO NOT RETURN TO A PREVIOUS TEST.

READING TEST

35 Minutes—40 Questions

DIRECTIONS: There are several passages in this test. Each passage is accompanied by several questions. After reading a passage, choose the best answer to each question and fill in the corresponding oval on your answer document. You may refer to the passages as often as necessary.

Passage I

LITERARY NARRATIVE: This passage is adapted from the short story "Simple Recipes" by Madeleine Thien (©2002 by Madeleine Thien). Publisher: Little, Brown.

There is a simple recipe for making rice. My father taught it to me when I was a child. Back then, I used to sit up on the kitchen counter watching him, how he sifted the grains in his hands, sure and quick, removing pieces of dirt or sand, tiny
5 imperfections. He swirled his hands through the water and it turned cloudy. When he scrubbed the grains clean, the sound was as big as a field of insects. Over and over, my father rinsed the rice, drained the water, then filled the pot again.

The instructions are simple. Once the washing is done, you
10 measure the water this way—by resting the tip of your index finger on the surface of the rice. The water should reach the bend of your first knuckle.

My father did not need instructions or measuring cups. He closed his eyes and felt for the waterline. Sometimes I still
15 dream of my father, his bare feet flat against the floor, standing in the middle of the kitchen. He wears old buttoned shirts and faded sweatpants drawn at the waist. Surrounded by the gloss of the kitchen counters, the sharp angles of the stove, the fridge, the shiny sink, he looks out of place. This memory of him is so
20 strong, sometimes it stuns me, the detail with which I can see it.

Every night before dinner, my father would perform this ritual—rinsing and draining, then setting the pot in the cooker. When I was older, he passed this task on to me but I never did it with the same care. I went through the motions, splashing the
25 water around, jabbing my finger down to measure the water level. Some nights the rice was a mushy gruel. I worried that I could not do so simple a task right. "Sorry," I would say to the table, my voice soft and embarrassed. In answer, my father would keep eating, pushing the rice into his mouth as if he never expected
30 anything different, as if he noticed no difference between what he did so well and I so poorly. He would eat every last mouthful, his chopsticks walking quickly across the plate. Then he would rise, whistling, and clear the table, every motion so clean and sure, I would be convinced by him that all was well in the world.

35 My father is standing in the middle of the kitchen. In his right hand he holds a plastic bag filled with water. Caught inside the bag is a live fish.

The fish is barely breathing, though its mouth opens and closes. I reach up and touch it through the plastic bag, trailing
40 my fingers along the gills, the soft, muscled body, pushing my finger overtop the eyeball. The fish looks straight at me, flopping sluggishly from side to side.

My father fills the kitchen sink. In one swift motion he overturns the bag and the fish comes sailing out with the water.
45 It curls and jumps. We watch it closely, me on my tiptoes, chin propped up on the counter. The fish is the length of my arm from wrist to elbow. It floats in place, brushing up against the sides of the sink.

I keep watch over the fish while my father begins the
50 preparations for dinner. The fish folds its body, trying to turn or swim, the water nudging overtop. Though I ripple tiny circles around it with my fingers, the fish stays still, bobbing side to side in the cold water.

For many hours at a time, it was just the two of us. While
55 my mother worked and my older brother played outside, my father and I sat on the couch, flipping channels. He loved cooking shows. We watched *Wok with Yan*, my father passing judgement on Yan's methods. I was enthralled when Yan transformed orange peels into swans. My father sniffed. "I can do that," he said. "You
60 don't have to be a genius to do that." He placed a sprig of green onion in water and showed me how it bloomed like a flower. "I know many tricks like this," he said. "Much more than Yan."

Still, my father made careful notes when Yan demonstrated Peking Duck. He chuckled heartily at Yan's punning. "Take a wok
65 on the wild side!" Yan said, pointing his spatula at the camera.

"Ha ha!" my father laughed, his shoulders shaking. "*Wok on the wild side!*"

In the mornings, my father took me to school. At three o'clock, when we came home again, I would rattle off everything

GO ON TO THE NEXT PAGE.

70 I learned that day. "The brachiosaurus," I informed him, "eats only soft vegetables."

My father nodded. "That is like me. Let me see your forehead." We stopped and faced each other in the road. "You have a high forehead," he said, leaning down to take a closer look. 75 "All smart people do."

I walked proudly, stretching my legs to match his steps. I was overjoyed when my feet kept time with his, right, then left, then right, and we walked like a single unit.

1. Based on the passage, it could be assumed that the narrator learned to make rice by:

   A. carefully following the complicated process her father taught her.

   B. studiously watching cooking shows with her father.

   C. following her father's steps in a half-hearted way that led to unsatisfying results.

   D. reading about the process in books her father left her.

2. In the context of the passage, which of the following statements most strongly foreshadows the joy and connection the narrator feels in the last paragraph?

   F. "There is a simple recipe for making rice" (line 1).

   G. "When I was older, he passed this task on to me but I never did it with the same care" (lines 23–24).

   H. "Then he would rise, whistling, and clear the table, every motion so clean and sure, I would be convinced by him that all was well in the world" (lines 32–34).

   J. "My father sniffed. 'I can do that,' he said. "You don't have to be a genius to do that" (lines 59–60).

3. The passage suggests that in walking to match her father, the daughter:

   A. folded her body, trying to turn away.

   B. found joy in copying his movements.

   C. felt inferior to her father in every way.

   D. did not find Yan's puns as amusing as her father did.

4. Which of the following is true of the fish after the father has put it into the sink?

    I. It does not respond to the narrator touching the water.

    II. It is as long as the narrator's arm from wrist to elbow.

    III. It looks straight at the narrator while flopping sluggishly.

    IV. It brushes against the sides of the sink.

   F. III and IV only

   G. I, II, and IV only

   H. II, III, and IV only

   J. I and II only

5. Which of the following best paraphrases the narrator's comments in lines 5–7?

   A. The rice her father made was better prepared than that of Chef Yan.

   B. She viewed the many rice kernels as so many individual insects.

   C. She was concerned that her father's repetitious actions signaled a mental disorder.

   D. Her father was very thorough in preparing the rice for cooking.

6. As it is used in line 39, the word *trailing* most nearly means:

   F. pursuing.

   G. tracing.

   H. losing.

   J. hanging.

7. The narrator suggests that her father ate her rice out of:

   A. pleasure; it was nearly as good as one of his own meals.

   B. obligation; it was important never to waste any food.

   C. consideration; he wanted his daughter to have the feeling that all was well.

   D. embarrassment; otherwise, he would have to admit her incompetence.

8. Based on the passage, it's most logical to conclude that the fish is:

   F. ill and dying.

   G. restless and fearful.

   H. confined and sluggish.

   J. alert and watchful.

9. According to the passage, the father regarded *Wok with Yan* as:

   A. providing some information worthy of his attention.

   B. irrelevant to an accomplished chef like himself.

   C. the primary source of his own cooking methods.

   D. the funniest cooking show on television.

10. The narrator states that she is sometimes stunned by:

   F. her father's ability to make rice without instructions or measuring cups.

   G. the way her father dressed when he cooked.

   H. the contrast between her father's appearance and that of the kitchen.

   J. how detailed her memory of her father is.

GO ON TO THE NEXT PAGE.

Passage II

SOCIAL SCIENCE: Passage A is adapted from "Fertilizer History" by Gary Hergert, Rex Nielsen, and Jim Margheim (© 2015 by University of Nebraska-Lincoln). Passage B is adapted from "Fertilizers, a Boon to Agriculture, Pose Growing Threat to U.S. Waterways" by Tatiana Schlossberg (© 2017 by The New York Times Company).

Passage A by Gary Hergert, Rex Nielsen, and Jim Margheim

For thousands of years after agriculture came into existence, manure was the main source of fertilizer. But sometime in the 18th century, it became common knowledge that ground-up bones provided crop nutrients. It wasn't until the 19th century
5 that ground-breaking research, done by several innovative scientists, finally ushered in the modern era of soil chemistry and plant nutrition. One of the most prominent of these chemists was Justus von Liebig (1803–1873), a German chemist who did pioneering research in organic and biological chemistry.

10 Ammonia and nitric acid, basic components of many chemical fertilizers, could be manufactured by the early 20th century, but until the middle of the century, use of chemical fertilizer was limited.

However, this would all change.

15 With the start of World War II, there was a tremendous increase in nitrogen production, mainly because nitrogen is a principal ingredient in explosives. After World War II, the need to manufacture war munitions was replaced with the need to restore food supplies in Europe and the United States.

20 The development of high-tech equipment has led to "precision" and "best-management" farming practices, which have resulted in the ability to apply various fertilizer types to a given crop in site-specific amounts. Technological advances in various fields of study, including crop genetics and breeding, plant and
25 soil testing, and the development of techniques to monitor the movement of nutrients and water within the soil profile have allowed today's farmers to use fertilizers more effectively and efficiently, in addition to being better stewards of the land and environment.

30 Manure is still an important source of plant nutrients; however, during the last 75 years, its use has been surpassed by the large-scale production and use of chemical fertilizers. In the mid- to late 1940s, about 2 million tons of chemical fertilizers were used per year. By 1960, over 7 million tons were used each
35 year and by 2014 over 20 million tons were used.

There is still much to learn about the complex interactions involving fertilizer use in differing soil and plant ecosystems; however, we have made historical progress since the first use of manure—progress that has been foundational to feeding our
40 nation and providing food and hope to other parts of the world.

Passage B by Tatiana Schlossberg

Nitrogen-based fertilizers, which came into wide use after World War II, helped prompt the agricultural revolution that has allowed the Earth to feed its seven billion people.

But that revolution came at a cost: artificial fertilizers, often
45 applied in amounts beyond what crops need to grow, are carried in runoff from farmland into streams, lakes and the ocean. New research suggests that climate change will substantially increase this form of pollution, leading to more damaging algae blooms and dead zones in American coastal waters.

50 A study published Thursday in *Science* concludes that eutrophication, excessive nutrient enrichment, is likely to increase in the continental United States as a result of the changes in precipitation patterns brought by climate change. Heavier rains caused by warmer temperatures will cause more agricultural
55 runoff, sluicing more nutrients into rivers, lakes and oceans.

The authors found that future climate change-driven increases in rainfall in the United States could boost nitrogen runoff by as much as 20 percent by the end of the century.

"When we think about climate change, we are used to think-
60 ing about water quantity—drought, flooding, extreme rainfall and things along those lines," said Anna Michalak, a professor of global ecology at the Carnegie Institution for Science in Stanford, Calif., and one of the authors of the study. "Climate change is just as tightly linked to issues related to water quality, and it's
65 not enough for the water to just be there, it has to be sustainable."

Excess nitrogen from the fertilizers can cause eutrophication in the ocean, which can lead to harmful algae blooms or hypoxia—reduced levels of oxygen that create conditions in which organisms can't survive.

GO ON TO THE NEXT PAGE.

11. In Passage A, the primary purpose of the details about the "ground-breaking research" (line 5) is to:

   A. show that few fertilizers were successful until the development of chemical fertilizers.

   B. demonstrate how manure replaced ground-up bones as the main source of fertilizer in the 18th century.

   C. connect prominent scientists to their contributions to the agricultural industry.

   D. provide details that show how knowledge of effective fertilizers grew over time.

12. According to Passage A, one reason for the development of chemical fertilizers was that:

   F. the United States needed a practical use for nitrogen left-over from the war.

   G. wartime industry created a way to mass-produce the components necessary for the fertilizer.

   H. soldiers coming home from the war were able to return to their jobs as chemists.

   J. farming practices provided crucial technologies which allowed nitrogen production to expand dramatically.

13. In the context of Passage A, the authors use the description of technological advances and techniques (lines 24–26) most nearly to:

   A. critique farmers for their reliance on technology.

   B. present factors that helped make chemical fertilizer use more efficient.

   C. list the strategies that farmers rely on to improve their harvests.

   D. explain different technologies that are used to monitor water usage on a farm.

14. The main idea of the sixth paragraph (lines 30–35) is that chemical fertilizers:

   F. are twice as effective as manure is for large-scale agricultural production.

   G. have only begun to be used by farmers in the last 75 years.

   H. are growing in how widely they are used compared to other common types of fertilizers.

   J. have become more important, but still have yet to surpass manure in annual usage.

15. It can reasonably be inferred from Passage B that a major factor in the reshaping of global agriculture was:

   A. an increase in the use of chemical fertilizers.

   B. a revolutionary fertilizing technique that maximized crop yields.

   C. the discovery of a farming method that encouraged crop growth while avoiding ecological consequences.

   D. a focus on lessening the impacts of the agricultural industry on climate change.

16. In the context of Passage B, the statement "But that revolution came at a cost" (line 44) most nearly refers to the way that chemical fertilizers:

   F. place financial burdens on those who commit to using them.

   G. increase the amount of money required to feed 7 billion people.

   H. have environmental disadvantages in addition to economic advantages.

   J. are less effective in coastal regions than in plains regions.

17. Passage B most nearly suggests that, compared to concerns about water quantity, concerns about water quality are:

   A. equally connected to effects of climate change.

   B. less important for those in urban areas than for those in rural areas.

   C. more important on a global scale.

   D. more heavily focused on salt water bodies.

18. Both passages suggest that the agricultural industry has been significantly impacted by types of fertilizer that were:

   F. impractical.

   G. artificially manufactured.

   H. naturally produced.

   J. ammonia-based.

GO ON TO THE NEXT PAGE.

19. Which of the following statements best compares the ways the authors of Passage A and Passage B use details about the effects of incorporating nitrogen-based fertilizers into agriculture?

A. Passage A looks to the fertilizer as a source of hope for the future while Passage B considers it a source of concern.

B. Passage A uses the fertilizer as one example in a discussion of farming advances, while Passage B focuses exclusively on the fertilizer.

C. Passage A considers the effects of the fertilizer on land, while Passage B considers the effects of the fertilizer on aquatic life.

D. Both passages discuss the effects of the increased fertilizer use on the environment.

20. To support their claims about the impact of increasing use of nitrogen-based fertilizers, the authors of both passages:

F. define key terms related to ecology.

G. quote experts in a related field.

H. provide statistics to support a point.

J. outline a specific timeline of development.

GO ON TO THE NEXT PAGE.

THIS PAGE IS INTENTIONALLY LEFT BLANK.

GO ON TO THE NEXT PAGE.

Passage III

HUMANITIES: This passage is adapted from the article "And where are the lilacs?" by Andrew Motion (©2004 by *The Guardian*).

Pablo Neruda couldn't hold a tune. "My ear," he admitted, "could never recognise any but the most obvious melodies, and even then, only with difficulty." This is remarkable: Neruda's cadences are crucial to his writing. No one reading his poems
5 in their original Spanish would want to separate their sense from their sound. Even translated into English, their meaning is inseparable from their melody.

Adam Feinstein's new biography is fuelled by an infectious enthusiasm for Neruda's poems, but it also has an admirable
10 patience with his life's dizzying details. It's difficult to think of a 20th-century poet who did more than Neruda. He wrote a huge number of books, he travelled like a man possessed, he loved and lost many women, he collected a host of famous friends. Some of these things are grist to the biographer's mill:
15 Feinstein's account is crammed with adventure stories, narrow scrapes, passionate encounters. Others are harder to deal with: globe-trottings have to be logged but risk becoming a list of place-names. By pacing the story so as to give pre-eminence to the writing and the adventuring, while recording the duller
20 passages more briefly, Feinstein creates his own sympathetic music. His book turns Neruda's life into an opera—a blend of aria and recitative.

Sensibly, he relies a good deal on Neruda's own *Memoirs*. These are packed with marvellous details that give colour to the
25 story, as well as providing a way of understanding how Neruda's fascination with real things gives shape to even his most vatic poems. At a parting with a grief-stricken girlfriend, for instance: "She kissed my arms, my suit, in a kind of ritual, and suddenly slipped down to my shoes, before I could stop her. When she
30 stood up again, the chalk polish of my white shoes was smeared like flour all over her face."

Feinstein is too thorough to accept the *Memoirs* at face value, wonderful as they are. He understands that an author's reminiscences are a way of creating disguises as well as revealing
35 secrets, and regularly checks them against available evidence, amplifying the many complicated or contentious issues hushed up by Neruda himself. Feinstein acknowledges, from the first, that Neruda grew up among secrets and was therefore likely to enjoy them later.

40 Leaving his hometown for the relatively cosmopolitan Santiago, Neruda's interests expanded to accommodate social as well as family matters, and to create a more suggestive style. He relied on French symbolist poetry to stretch his imagination, combining his own fidelity to facts with surrealist touches and
45 impressionistic overviews. The result was a fusion previously unseen in Chilean poetry—or poetry anywhere—and his success was meteoric. But his exploded imagination needed a larger canvas, and the cultural and economic conditions of Chile both compelled and exasperated him.

50 Consular activity served as his means of escape. By 1927 he was in Rangoon, then moved on through France, Japan, China, Ceylon and Java (where he met his first wife, Maria), before returning home in 1932. By this time his Spanish was apparently "quite odd...very much influenced by his solitude," and his
55 sense of himself much altered. But these were not changes which threatened his audience: they added authority to his originality.

They didn't, however, do much for his political conscience, which began to develop during his posting to Spain in the early 1930s, when he fell in love with Delia del Carril. Delia per-
60 suaded him to become a communist—a process which meant that he inflicted a great deal of pain on his first wife and their sickly daughter, while producing poems that exalted the suffering masses. It confronts Feinstein with the classic biographer's dilemma—how to respect the work while dealing with a con-
65 tradictory private life—and he copes with it by presenting the facts rather than wagging his finger, and by foregrounding the writing. As the scenery changes from France to Chile again, we see Neruda the romantic lyricist turning into Neruda the "truth-teller and exposer of the world's injustices."

70 Neruda spent the late 30s and early 40s travelling round South America, converting his experience of other people's suffering into poems, standing as a senator, and defending the new emphasis of his work. Given the political climate, it was bound to end in trouble—or rather, trouble and adventure. In
75 1949 Neruda made a daring escape from Chile over the Andes into Buenos Aires, then soon set off again, speaking for the oppressed everywhere while neglecting Delia in favour of Matilde, who eventually became his third wife.

These paradoxes bring their own difficulties—but their
80 tensions are intensified by fault-lines in Neruda's politics. Feinstein lets his readers draw their own conclusions about the moral muddle of Neruda's life, shining the same clear light on his politics that he turns on his private life (even Matilde was betrayed, when Neruda had a late fling with her niece). This is
85 as well. The faults and weaknesses are plain to see, but so is the undimmed exuberance and generosity of the work, which feeds hungrily off the life and yet stands as a thing apart.

21. The primary function of the first paragraph is to:
   A. clarify misunderstandings about what made Neruda so talented as a Spanish singer and musician.
   B. outline how Neruda wrote his poems.
   C. tell a story from Neruda's youth.
   D. contrast a statement of Neruda's with a characteristic of his poetry.

GO ON TO THE NEXT PAGE.

22. Based on the passage, which of the following best describes the passage author's opinion of Neruda's poetry?

F. He prefers Neruda's *Memoirs* to Neruda's poetry.
G. He considers Neruda's poetry to be original.
H. He thinks Neruda's poetry is too heavily based on his own life.
J. He believes that Neruda's poetry shows faults and weaknesses.

23. The "melody" mentioned in lines 6–7 most nearly refers to:

A. the aria for Neruda's opera that was discovered by Adam Feinstein.
B. the effect Neruda's word choice and pacing has on a reader's understanding of his poems.
C. the connection between Neruda's life and his poetry discussed by the passage author.
D. the many adventures, narrow scrapes, and passionate encounters Neruda had during his life.

24. The passage most strongly suggests that a reader might appreciate Feinstein's treatment of the "dizzying details" (lines 9–10) of Neruda's life because Feinstein:

F. is critical of Neruda's many travels and adventures.
G. concentrates on explaining Neruda's writing process rather than focusing on his life.
H. never elaborates on why Neruda was a globe-trotter and prolific writer.
J. keeps dull passages brief to ensure the reader does not lose interest.

25. As it is used in line 17, the word *logged* most nearly means:

A. cut.
B. completed.
C. recorded.
D. harvested.

26. According to the passage, Neruda's reminiscences as related in his autobiography:

F. amplified contentious issues.
G. should be studied as literature.
H. create disguises and reveal secrets.
J. were a guide for Feinstein's writing style.

27. The passage indicates that Feinstein addresses Neruda's conversion to communism by:

A. avoiding the topic of politics as much as possible.
B. contradicting Neruda's own account of that time period.
C. respecting Neruda's first wife and sickly daughter to ensure the biography does not cause pain.
D. recording information truthfully without passing judgment on it.

28. According to Feinstein, Neruda's Spanish became "quite odd" (line 54) during his:

F. travels to Rangoon and other countries.
G. studies of French symbolist poetry.
H. escape from consular activity.
J. marriage to Delia del Carril.

29. The passage author indicates that Feinstein's treatment of Neruda's contradictions allows Feinstein to:

A. muddle the picture of Neruda's life.
B. show the downside of Neruda's exuberance.
C. let readers draw their own conclusions.
D. make Neruda appear less noble.

30. As it is used in line 86 the word *work* refers to Neruda's:

F. poetry.
G. biography.
H. travels.
J. marriage.

GO ON TO THE NEXT PAGE.

Passage IV

NATURAL SCIENCE: This passage is adapted from the essay "The Higgs at Last" by Michael Riordan, Guido Tonelli, and Sau Lan Wu (©2013 by Scientific American).

The Higgs boson is the cornerstone of the Standard Model, an interwoven set of theories that constitute modern particle physics. This particle's existence had been suggested in 1964 by Peter W. Higgs of the University of Edinburgh as the result of a subtle
5 mechanism—independently conceived by François Englert and Robert Brout in Brussels plus three theorists in London—that endows elementary particles with mass. The Higgs boson is the physical manifestation of an ethereal fluid (called the Higgs field) that permeates every corner of the cosmos and imbues particles
10 with distinctive masses.

Although theorists asserted that the Higgs boson—or something like it—must exist, they could not predict what its mass might be. For this and other reasons, researchers had few clues about where to look for it. An early candidate, weighing
15 in at less than nine times the proton mass, turned up in 1984 at a refurbished, low-energy electron-positron collider in Hamburg, Germany. Yet the evidence withered away after further study.

Most theorists agreed that the Higgs mass should be 10 to 100 times higher. If so, discovering it would require a much larger
20 and more energetic particle collider than even the Fermi National Laboratory's Tevatron, a collider completed in 1983. That same year CERN began building the billion-dollar Large Electron Positron (LEP) collider, boring a 27-kilometer circular tunnel that crossed the French-Swiss border four times near Geneva.
25 Although LEP had other goals, the Higgs boson was high on its target list. Discoveries and precision measurements made at LEP and the Tevatron soon implied that the Higgs boson should be no more than 200 GeV, which put it potentially within reach of these colliders. (GeV is the standard unit of mass and energy in
30 particle physics, about equal to a proton mass.) In over a decade of searching, however, physicists found no lasting evidence for Higgs-like data bumps.

During the final LEP runs in the summer of 2000, physicists decided to push the collision energy beyond what the machine was
35 designed to handle. That is when hints of a Higgs boson began appearing. After a heated debate, CERN's then-director Luciano Maiani decided to shut LEP down and begin its planned conversion into the LHC, a machine designed to find the Higgs boson.

The LHC is the most spectacular collection of advanced
40 technology ever assembled. Built inside the original LEP tunnel, it uses little left from that collider. Its principal components include more than 1,200 superconducting dipole magnets—shiny, 15-meter-long cylinders worth nearly $1 million each. Probably the most sophisticated components ever mass-produced, by firms
45 in France, Germany and Italy, they harbor twin beam tubes that are flanked by niobium-titanium magnet coils bathed in liquid helium at 1.9 kelvins, or −271 degrees Celsius. Inside, twin proton

beams circulate in both directions at energies up to 7 TeV and velocities approaching light speed.

50 Although the LHC is a giant collider feeding multiple experiments, only the two largest ones—ATLAS and CMS—had been tasked with finding the Higgs boson. The ATLAS and CMS experiments couldn't observe a Higgs boson directly—it would decay into other particles far too quickly. They looked
55 for evidence that it was created inside. Depending on the Higgs boson's mass, it could decay into lighter particles in a variety of ways. In 2011, attention began to focus on its rare decays into two photons and four charged leptons, because these signals would stand out starkly against tremendous backgrounds of data. By
60 May 2012, the LHC was producing data 15 times faster than the Tevatron had ever achieved.

On June 15, 2012, CMS physicists began gathering to hear the preliminary reports. Signals from their data were occurring again in the same vicinity—near 125 GeV—that had
65 so tantalized researchers six months earlier. Scientists realized almost immediately that if they were to combine the new data with the 2011 results, chances were good that CMS could claim a Higgs discovery. Similar revelations occurred in the ATLAS experiment. At the thrilling moment of recognition, one ATLAS
70 group of about a dozen physicists erupted in loud clapping and cries of joy, which echoed down the hallway. CMS and ATLAS independently concluded that the chances that the apparition was a fluke, due to random fluctuations, were less than one in three million. It had to be real.

75 These results were shared at a public joint seminar at CERN on July 4, 2012. When the camera panned to Dr. Higgs, he could be seen pulling out a handkerchief to wipe his eyes.

Few physicists doubt that a heavy new particle has turned up at CERN, but there is still debate about its exact nature—since
80 July 2012, attention has focused on whether the new particle is indeed "the" Higgs boson predicted by the Standard Model. The particle opens up a fabulous new laboratory for further experimentation. Are its properties exactly as predicted? The apparent discrepancies in the early data could be random fluctuations that
85 disappear in months to come. Or perhaps they are offering subtle hints of intriguing new physics.

---

31. The overall organization of the passage is best described as a:

A. chronological account of scientists determining the correct mass of various elementary particles.

B. step-by-step explanation of how the Large Hadron Collider was constructed.

C. series of important events leading to the discovery of the Higgs boson.

D. collection of stories describing how the Standard Model of physics evolved over time.

GO ON TO THE NEXT PAGE.

32. The main function of the first paragraph is to:

    F. list the information discovered about the Higgs boson by research scientists in Hamburg.

    G. demonstrate what led scientists to build larger and more energetic particle colliders.

    H. summarize contributions made by theorists in London.

    J. explain the origin and importance of the Higgs boson theory.

33. Based on the passage, one similarity between the two particle colliders described in lines 19–32 is that:

    A. neither provided lasting evidence that definitively proved the existence of the Higgs boson.

    B. both cost upwards of one billion dollars to build.

    C. construction for both particle accelerators was completed in the same year.

    D. they both had the size and energy that enabled them to discover the Higgs boson.

34. The main idea of the last paragraph is that:

    F. the properties of the new particle were predicted by the Standard Model only recently and leave physicists' results in doubt.

    G. recent research by physicists makes earlier data gathered by scientists look faulty by comparison.

    H. few doubt a new heavy particle has been discovered and additional research should explain its properties.

    J. the heavy particle discovered weighs far more than originally predicted by scientists.

35. According to the passage, scientists in Brussels and London:

    A. suggested in 1964 that the Higgs boson exists.

    B. developed an interwoven set of theories for particle physics.

    C. discovered the cornerstone of the Standard Model.

    D. independently conceived of a subtle mechanism that endows elementary particles with mass.

36. Based on the passage, to make the particle collider functional, French, Italian, and German firms designed the dipole magnets to be capable of:

    F. utilizing the principal components from the LEP accelerator and fitting in the original tunnel.

    G. accelerating protons to velocities approaching light speed and having the protons circulate in two directions.

    H. floating in the air when filled with liquid helium and achieving energies up to 7 TeV.

    J. costing under one million dollars each and fitting into a fifteen meter long cylinder.

37. The passage indicates that physicists could not discover the Higgs boson until:

    A. they used a low-energy collider.

    B. a new collider was built.

    C. they applied Englert's mechanism.

    D. the Tevatron and LEP came online.

38. The passage suggests that compared to work at the LHC, work at the Tevatron was:

    F. less rapid.

    G. less reliable.

    H. more expensive.

    J. more insightful.

39. It can reasonably be inferred from the passage that the author includes the description of the scientists' reactions to data gained from the ATLAS and CMS experiments (lines 69–71) primarily to:

    A. illustrate how pleased the researchers were to meet Peter Higgs when he visited CERN.

    B. describe their reaction to data gained from the Tevatron experiments.

    C. suggest that the physicists' celebration may have disrupted other scientists in the building.

    D. highlight the magnitude of their discovery by showing their emotional reaction to the results.

40. As it is used in line 78, the phrase *turned up* most nearly means:

    F. been amplified.

    G. been discovered.

    H. arrived on site.

    J. grown in height.

END OF TEST 3

STOP! DO NOT TURN THE PAGE UNTIL TOLD TO DO SO.

DO NOT RETURN TO A PREVIOUS TEST.

SCIENCE TEST

35 Minutes–40 Questions

DIRECTIONS: There are several passages in this test. Each passage is accompanied by several questions. After reading a passage, choose the best answer to each question and fill in the corresponding oval on your answer document. You may refer to the passages as often as necessary.

You are NOT permitted to use a calculator on this test.

Passage I

As substrate is added to an enzyme, *enzyme velocity,* or the rate at which an enzyme can change substrate into products, varies with initial substrate concentration, temperature, and time since the reaction began. Table 1 shows, for each of 4 enzymes (A, B, C, and D), the enzyme velocity 10 seconds after addition of substrate for different substrate concentrations and temperatures.

Enzyme	Initial substrate concentration	Enzyme velocity (mmol/s) at a substrate temperature of:		
		20°C	30°C	60°C
A	5 mM	9.1	6.5	4.6
	10 mM	13.2	8.9	6.4
	15 mM	17.6	11.4	7.5
B	5 mM	13.1	7.3	4.9
	10 mM	20.3	10.9	6.9
	15 mM	25.5	13.8	8.6
C	5 mM	20.7	14.3	10.6
	10 mM	30.3	20.8	13.1
	15 mM	35.2	23.1	14.9
D	5 mM	50.2	23.5	14.6
	10 mM	57.6	28.3	18.6
	15 mM	63.3	30.7	19.9

Table 1

Figure 1 shows how each enzyme's velocity changes over time with an initial substrate concentration of 12 mM at a temperature of 40°C.

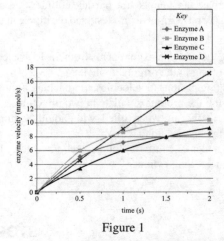

Figure 1

GO ON TO THE NEXT PAGE.

1. According to Table 1, which of the following graphs accurately depicts the velocities of Enzymes A, B, C, and D after 10 seconds at an initial substrate concentration of 5 mM and a temperature of 60°C ?

A.

B.

C.

D.

2. Based on Table 1, the enzyme velocity of Enzyme B after 10 seconds in a solution with a substrate concentration of 10 mM at a temperature of 35°C would most likely be:

F. less than 7 mmol/s.
G. between 7 and 11 mmol/s.
H. between 11 and 20 mmol/s.
J. greater than 20 mmol/s.

3. According to Figure 1, which of the following correctly orders the enzymes according to their enzyme velocities from highest to lowest after 1 second at a substrate concentration of 12 mM and a temperature of 40°C ?

A. Enzyme A, Enzyme B, Enzyme C, Enzyme D
B. Enzyme A, Enzyme C, Enzyme D, Enzyme B
C. Enzyme D, Enzyme A, Enzyme B, Enzyme C
D. Enzyme D, Enzyme B, Enzyme A, Enzyme C

4. According to Figure 1, at a substrate concentration of 12 mM and a temperature of 40°C, which of the enzymes had the highest enzyme velocity after 0.75 seconds?

F. Enzyme A
G. Enzyme B
H. Enzyme C
J. Enzyme D

5. Based on Table 1, the enzyme velocity for Enzyme C in a solution with an 8 mM substrate concentration at 60°C after 10 seconds would likely be approximately:

A. 12.0 mmol/s.
B. 13.5 mmol/s.
C. 14.5 mmol/s.
D. 16.0 mmol/s.

6. According to Figure 1, which enzyme takes the *shortest* amount of time to reach an enzyme velocity of 6 mmol/s in a solution with a substrate concentration of 12 mM at a temperature of 40°C ?

F. Enzyme A
G. Enzyme B
H. Enzyme C
J. Enzyme D

GO ON TO THE NEXT PAGE.

Passage II

Ozone (O_3) is an inorganic gas found primarily in the stratosphere of Earth's atmosphere. Stratospheric ozone is formed naturally when UV (*ultra-violet*) light breaks apart an oxygen molecule to form two highly reactive oxygen atoms. The oxygen atoms each then collide with another oxygen molecule to form ozone. Though ozone makes up a very small percentage of the gas in the stratosphere, it is the primary absorber of the sun's UV-B rays, allowing only a small percentage of these harmful rays to reach Earth's surface. Ozone also absorbs light in the infrared spectrum, as does carbon dioxide (CO_2).

A researcher performed three studies on the behavior of ozone and CO_2.

Study 1

The researcher modeled the transmittance of both O_3 and CO_2 at their average concentrations in the atmosphere at various wavelengths in the UV spectrum from 0.25–0.35 microns (μm) and in the infrared spectrum from 2.5–11 μm. The *transmittance* of a gas is the percent of incoming solar radiation that is transmitted through that gas towards Earth's surface. The model is shown below in Figure 1.

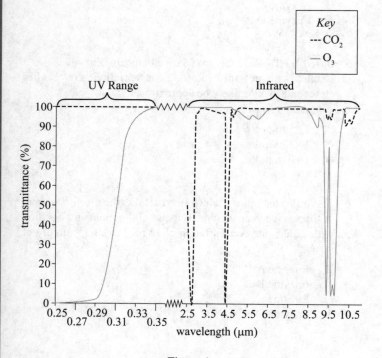

Figure 1

Study 2

Ozone levels vary throughout the stratosphere by both location and season. The researcher modeled the transmittance through the stratosphere at five different concentrations of ozone, in milligrams per cubic meter (mg/m^3), at a wavelength of 0.31 microns (see Figure 2).

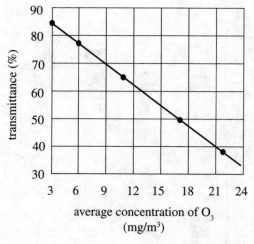

Figure 2

Study 3

The researcher also estimated the average stratospheric ozone concentration, in mg/m^3, at five different locations (Locations 1–5) on a particular day. The concentrations were estimated at standard temperature and pressure. The results are shown in Table 1.

Table 1	
Location	Concentration (mg/m^3)
1	10
2	6
3	21
4	14
5	9

GO ON TO THE NEXT PAGE.

7. Based on the data in Figure 2, the transmittance at 0.31 microns at a concentration of 18 mg/m^3 would most likely be:

    A. less than 45%.
    B. between 45 and 50%.
    C. between 50 and 55%.
    D. greater than 55%.

8. In Study 2, as the concentration of ozone increased from 3 to 24 mg/m^3, the transmittance at 0.31 microns:

    F. increased only.
    G. decreased only.
    H. increased and then decreased.
    J. decreased and then increased.

9. Based on the model in Study 2, which of the locations in Study 3 likely has the greatest transmittance at 0.31 microns?

    A. Location 1
    B. Location 2
    C. Location 3
    D. Location 5

10. According to the passage, which of the following pairs of equations represents the production of ozone in the stratosphere?

    F. O_2 + UV light = 2 O
       2 O + 2 O_2 = 2 O_3

    G. 2 O + UV light = O_3
       O_3 + 3 O_2 = 3 O_3

    H. O_2 + UV light = 2 O
       O_3 + O = 2 O_2

    J. O_2 + O = O_3
       O_3 + UV light = 3 O

11. The researcher plans to repeat Study 2, but this time he wants to study the effects on transmittance of different CO_2 concentrations instead of O_3 concentrations. Based on Figure 1, should he measure the transmittance at 4.3 microns or at 9.5 microns?

    A. At 4.3 microns; the transmittance of CO_2 is lower at this wavelength than it is at 9.5 microns.
    B. At 4.3 microns; the transmittance of CO_2 is higher at this wavelength than it is at 9.5 microns.
    C. At 9.5 microns; the transmittance of CO_2 is lower at this wavelength than it is at 4.3 microns.
    D. At 9.5 microns; the transmittance of CO_2 is higher at this wavelength than it is at 4.3 microns.

12. Planet Z has the same atmospheric make-up as Earth, except that the concentration of carbon dioxide is higher and there is no ozone. Would the total transmittance of sunlight on Planet Z at a wavelength of 0.3 microns likely be higher or lower than the transmittance on Earth at a wavelength of 0.3 microns?

    F. Higher; the transmittance of CO_2 is lower than the transmittance of O_3 at 0.3 microns.
    G. Higher; the transmittance of CO_2 is higher than the transmittance of O_3 at 0.3 microns.
    H. Lower; the transmittance of CO_2 is lower than the transmittance of O_3 at 0.3 microns.
    J. Lower; the transmittance of CO_2 is higher than the transmittance of O_3 at 0.3 microns.

13. Based on Table 1, assuming that the atmospheric gases are uniformly mixed in the stratosphere, what would be the approximate mass of O_3, in *grams*, in 100 cubic meters of stratospheric air at Location 3 on the date of the study?

    A. 0.21
    B. 2.1
    C. 210
    D. 2,100

GO ON TO THE NEXT PAGE.

Passage III

Ocean depth affects both temperature and dissolved oxygen levels. In Figure 1, the values of temperature, t, in degrees Celsius, and dissolved oxygen, $D.O.$, in milligrams per liter (mg/L), are graphed versus depth, d, in meters below the ocean's surface. Five distinct ocean zones are also identified in Figure 1.

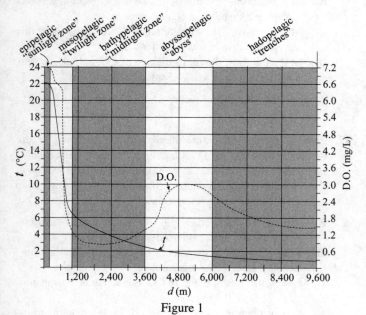

Figure 1

Approximately 98% of marine life is located in the epipelagic, mesopelagic, and bathypelagic zones. Figure 2 shows the percent of marine life that is located between sea level and a given depth within these three zones. For example, 20% of all marine life is located between sea level and a depth of 50 meters.

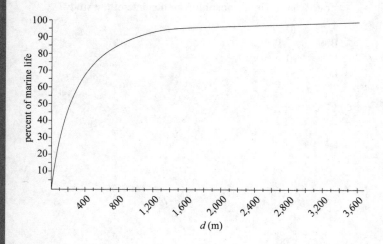

Figure 2

14. The range of a zone refers to the difference in depth between the top and the bottom of that zone. According to Figure 1, which two zones have similar ranges?

F. Epipelagic and mesopelagic
G. Mesopelagic and bathypelagic
H. Mesopelagic and abyssopelagic
J. Bathypelagic and abyssopelagic

15. Figure 2 indicates that approximately 35% of marine life lives between $d = 0$ m and:

A. $d = 50$ m.
B. $d = 100$ m.
C. $d = 300$ m.
D. $d = 500$ m.

16. According the information in Figures 1 and 2, the bathypelagic zone extends to a depth of approximately:

F. 1,000 m.
G. 1,500 m.
H. 3,600 m.
J. 6,000 m.

17. Based on Figure 1, the dissolved oxygen levels at $d = 10,000$ m would most likely be:

A. less than 0.3 mg/L.
B. between 0.3 and 0.9 mg/L.
C. between 0.9 and 1.2 mg/L.
D. between 1.2 and 1.5 mg/L.

18. Depths below 1,000 meters are considered *aphotic* because no sunlight penetrates that deep. Based on Figure 2, the aphotic zones account for approximately what percentage of marine life?

F. 2%
G. 10%
H. 90%
J. 98%

19. Colder ocean water is denser than warmer ocean water. A scientist compares the masses of two 1-liter samples of water: one collected at $d = 1,000$ m and one collected at $d = 3,600$ m. Based on Figure 1, which of the samples of water, if either, would have a lower mass?

A. The sample at $d = 3,600$ m has a lower mass because the water temperature is lower and the density is higher.
B. The sample at $d = 1,000$ m has a lower mass because the water temperature is higher and the density is lower.
C. Both samples have the same mass because the density is the same for both samples.
D. Both samples have the same mass because the volume is the same for both samples.

GO ON TO THE NEXT PAGE.

THIS PAGE IS INTENTIONALLY LEFT BLANK.

GO ON TO THE NEXT PAGE.

Passage IV

Fibromyalgia is a central nervous system disorder characterized by chronic widespread pain and a heightened pain response. Four students each propose a theory of what causes fibromyalgia.

Student 1

Fibromyalgia is caused only by an abnormal immune response to an infection or injury. When the body detects damaged tissue, white blood cells release chemicals called cytokines that direct blood flow to the damaged cells and cause inflammation. The inflammation aggravates the nerves and makes the infected area more sensitive to pain. Usually the increased sensitivity goes away after the inflammation subsides, but sometimes the inflammation causes irreparable physical damage to the nerve cells. Fibromyalgia is the result of the damaged nerve cells disrupting the normal functioning of the central nervous system.

Student 2

Fibromyalgia is caused only by the overproduction of excitatory neurotransmitters. Neurons transmit pain signals by firing chemicals called neurotransmitters that bind to pain receptors on another neuron. The most prevalent of these neurotransmitters is glutamate. When the nerve cells chronically overproduce glutamate, the pain receptors adapt by physically changing shape to more readily absorb the signals. This change makes neurons more sensitive to pain, which results in fibromyalgia. Injury and illness can cause nerve damage to specific neurons, but they do not create the widespread pain of fibromyalgia.

Student 3

Fibromyalgia is caused only by abnormal estrogen or thyroid hormone levels. These hormones affect the production of serotonin and norepinephrine, two inhibitory neurotransmitters that suppress pain transmission through the central nervous system. When levels of these inhibitory neurotransmitters are low, the body is unable to suppress pain transmission, and fibromyalgia is the result. While it is true that some people do overproduce glutamate, sufficient levels of serotonin and norepinephrine neutralize the excess glutamate before it interacts with any pain receptors.

Student 4

Fibromyalgia results only from a diet low in L-tryptophan, an essential amino acid necessary for the production of serotonin. Serotonin helps the brain interpret pain signals. When serotonin levels drop due to inadequate L-tryptophan intake, the brain is unable to properly interpret various pain signals, causing fibromyalgia. Nerve damage from injury only creates localized pain. Excess glutamate is harmless because it is not absorbed by the pain receptors. Estrogen and thyroid hormone imbalances do not limit the production of serotonin.

20. Which of the students theorized that fibromyalgia is triggered by neurons that are in some way physically altered?

F. Student 1 only
G. Student 4 only
H. Students 1 and 2 only
J. Students 2 and 3 only

21. A researcher discovers that female fibromyalgia patients report a higher incidence of pain during pregnancy and menopause when estrogen levels are rapidly changing. This discovery best supports which student's theory?

A. Student 1
B. Student 2
C. Student 3
D. Student 4

22. Based on the information provided by Student 4, people consume L-tryptophan through foods containing which of the following?

F. Carbohydrates
G. Protein
H. Saturated fat
J. Unsaturated fat

23. Substance P is an excitatory neurotransmitter similar in function to glutamate. Which student, if any, would be most likely to predict that people that produce higher than average levels of Substance P have a higher than average risk of developing fibromyalgia within their lifetimes?

A. None of the medical students
B. Student 1
C. Student 2
D. Student 3

24. Which of the students theorized that fibromyalgia is the result of low levels of certain neurotransmitters?

F. Students 1 and 2 only
G. Student 3 only
H. Students 2 and 3 only
J. Students 3 and 4 only

GO ON TO THE NEXT PAGE.

25. Which of the following research findings, if true, best supports Student 4's theory?

    A. The prevalence of fibromyalgia is lower than average among people who consume diets low in L-tryptophan.

    B. The prevalence of fibromyalgia is higher than average among people that consume diets low in L-tryptophan.

    C. Patients with fibromyalgia have lower levels of thyroid hormone than patients that do not have fibromyalgia.

    D. Patients with fibromyalgia have higher levels of thyroid hormone than patients that do not have fibromyalgia.

26. Prescription C is a powerful anti-inflammatory medication often prescribed to patients recovering from serious injury. A study examined the incidence of fibromyalgia following serious injury and found that the likelihood of developing fibromyalgia was the same among patients treated with Prescription C and patients that were not treated with any anti-inflammatory medications. These study results *weaken* the viewpoint(s) provided by which student(s)?

    F. Student 1 only

    G. Students 1 and 2 only

    H. Student 3 only

    J. Students 2 and 3 only

GO ON TO THE NEXT PAGE.

Passage V

Sufficient nitrogen levels in soil are necessary for crops to grow. Often, fertilizers rich in ammonium (NH_4^+) are applied to fields to increase crop yields, and nitrogen-fixing bacteria convert the applied ammonium into nitrate (NO_3^-) in a process known as *nitrification*. Nitrate is susceptible to loss through leaching before crops are able to use it, so nitrogen inhibitors are often used to prevent the conversion of ammonium into nitrate. Three studies examined the rates of nitrification in several regions using different nitrogen inhibitors: N-1, N-2, and N-3.

Soil samples of 3 cubic meters were collected from five different biomes (grassland, desert, tropical forest, coniferous forest, and deciduous forest). The samples were immediately placed in a sealed container in a cooler kept at a constant 20°C before they were transported to the same greenhouse. Each sample was thoroughly mixed, tested for the ammonium levels, and then divided evenly into three 1-cubic-meter plots in the same greenhouse. The plots had a mesh bottom to allow for drainage of the soils. The plots were each irrigated once with 2 L of water and then maintained at 20°C with constant humidity for one week before the fertilizer and nitrogen inhibitors were applied.

Study 1

The following procedures were performed for one plot from each biome. A 50 g sample of crystallized N-1 was added to 5 L of liquid fertilizer and the mixture was stirred until there were no remaining solids suspended in the mixture. The mixture was then sprayed uniformly along the top of each soil plot. For the next 8 weeks, the plots were watered once weekly with 2 L of water and the greenhouse remained at 20°C with constant humidity. After 8 weeks, the soil was analyzed to determine the percentage of the applied ammonium that was converted to nitrate over the 8-week period. The results are shown in Figure 1.

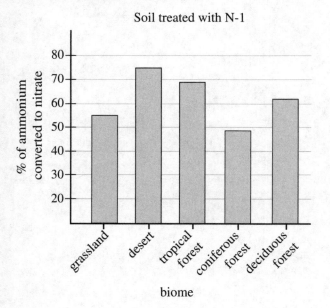

Soil treated with N-1

Figure 1

Study 2

Study 1 was repeated with a 50 g sample of crystallized N-2 substituted for the crystallized N-1 (see Figure 2).

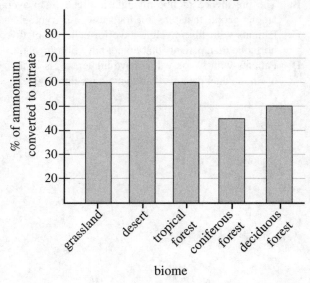

Soil treated with N-2

Figure 2

Study 3

Study 1 was repeated with a 50 g sample of crystallized N-3 substituted for the crystallized N-1 (see Figure 3).

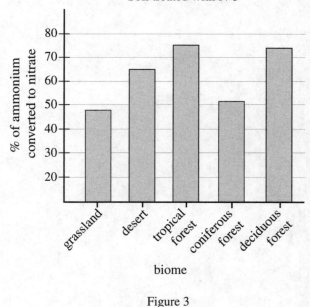

Soil treated with N-3

Figure 3

GO ON TO THE NEXT PAGE.

27. According to the results of the studies, the soil from which of the five biomes had the lowest percentage of ammonium converted to nitrate after treatment with N-1, N-2, and N-3, respectively?

	N-1	N-2	N-3
A.	coniferous forest	deciduous forest	grassland
B.	coniferous forest	coniferous forest	grassland
C.	desert	desert	tropical forest
D.	tropical forest	desert	deciduous forest

28. According to the results of Study 2, the percent of ammonium converted to nitrate in the soils treated with N-2, averaged across all 5 biomes, was closest to which of the following?

F. 40%
G. 50%
H. 60%
J. 70%

29. Do the results of Studies 1 and 3 support the statement "A greater percentage of applied ammonium was converted to nitrate in the tropical forest soil treated with N-3 than the same soil treated with N-1"?

A. Yes; 63% of the applied ammonium was converted to nitrate in N-3, whereas only 47% was converted to nitrate in N-1.
B. Yes; 75% of the applied ammonium was converted to nitrate in N-3, whereas only 68% was converted to nitrate in N-1.
C. No; 63% of the applied ammonium was converted to nitrate in N-1, whereas only 47% was converted to nitrate in N-3.
D. No; 75% of the applied ammonium was converted to nitrate in N-1, whereas only 68% was converted to nitrate in N-3.

30. Which of the following correctly identifies the independent (experimental) variable across the 3 studies?

F. Biome
G. Concentration of ammonia
H. Type of nitrogen inhibitor
J. Concentration of nitrate

31. The concentration of applied ammonium ions was reduced by less than 50% in the deciduous forest soil treated with which, if any, of the inhibitors?

A. None of the inhibitors
B. N-2 only
C. N-1 and N-3 only
D. All of the inhibitors

32. Is the mixture of N-1 and liquid fertilizer a solution when it is applied to the soil?

F. Yes, because the N-1 dissolved in the liquid fertilizer.
G. Yes, because the N-1 was suspended in the liquid fertilizer.
H. No, because the N-1 dissolved in the liquid fertilizer.
J. No, because the N-1 was suspended in the liquid fertilizer.

33. In soil, nitrogen-fixing bacteria are inactive in temperatures below 12°C. Which of the following steps was incorporated in the experimental design to ensure that the bacteria in all five soils were active?

A. The soil samples were all gathered when the outside temperature was 20°C.
B. The soil samples were tested for nitrate levels before the fertilizer was applied.
C. The soil samples were transported and maintained at 20°C throughout the study.
D. The soil samples were tested for ammonium levels before the fertilizer was applied.

GO ON TO THE NEXT PAGE.

Passage VI

Yeast cells exhibit *bipolar growth*: they grow in length from both tips in a straight-rod shape. However, the presence of an external electrical field can affect the growth patterns of yeast cells. Two researchers created a genetically modified strain of the fission yeast *Schizosaccharomyces pombe* (*S. pombe*). The genetically modified (GMO) strain was deficient in one of the proteins used to regulate the intracellular pH.

The researchers conducted two experiments to examine how an electric field affects the growth of both the non-GMO yeast cells (*S. pombe* – *N*) and the GMO yeast cells (*S. pombe* – *GM*).

Experiment 1

The researchers put a sugar-based agar into four square petri dishes (designated A, B, C, and D). Three *S. pombe* cells were placed into each of the dishes. The yeast placed in Dishes A and B were all *S. pombe* – *N* cells, and the yeast placed in Dishes C and D were all *S. pombe* – *GM*. A battery was used to generate a current through Dishes B and D. Figure 1 shows the growth of the cells in all four petri dishes and the direction of the electric fields (where present). The shaded portion of the cell represents the original shape of the cell when it was placed in the dish, while the dotted lines indicate the size and shape of the cell after 3 days at a constant temperature of 20°C. The nucleus is also shown for each cell.

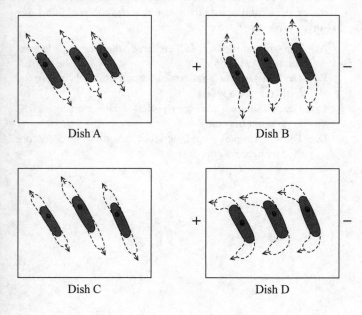

Figure 1

Experiment 2

A sugar-based agar was placed into four new petri dishes (designated W, X, Y, and Z). Three *S. pombe* cells were placed into each dish: *S. pombe* – *N* cells in Dishes W and X, and *S. pombe* – *GM* cells in Dishes Y and Z. A battery was used to generate a current through all four dishes. After 3 days at a constant temperature of 20°, the researchers measured the length, *L,* from tip to tip of each yeast cell along the axis parallel to the orientation of the cell body as shown for one particular yeast cell in Figure 2.

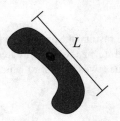

Figure 2

Dishes W and Y were moved to a room with a constant temperature of 15°C while Dishes X and Z were moved to a second room with a constant temperature of 30°C. The researchers measured each cell's length every 12 hours for the following three days. The results of the average cell lengths in each dish are shown in Figure 3.

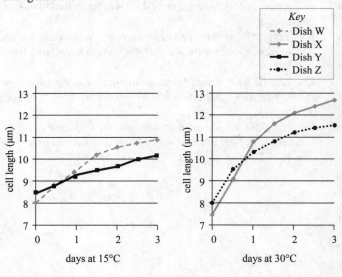

Figure 3

GO ON TO THE NEXT PAGE.

34. The cell shown in Figure 2 is oriented exactly how it appeared in its dish. Which of the following diagrams most likely represents the petri dish from which this cell is found?

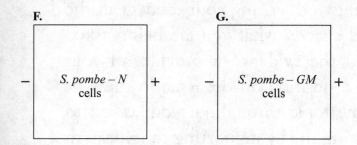

F.   – | S. pombe – N cells | +

G.   – | S. pombe – GM cells | +

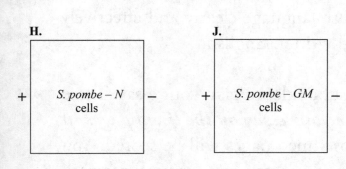

H.   + | S. pombe – N cells | –

J.   + | S. pombe – GM cells | –

35. Before Dish X was moved to a higher temperature room, the cells in Dish X likely exhibited growth most similar to the cells in which of the dishes in Experiment 1 ?

A.   Dish A
B.   Dish B
C.   Dish C
D.   Dish D

36. In Experiment 1, in the presence of an electrical field, did the *S. pombe – N* cells exhibit the same growth patterns as the *S. pombe – GM* cells?

F.   Yes; the yeast cells in both Dishes A and C exhibited bipolar growth with a straight-rod morphology.
G.   Yes; the yeast cells in both Dishes B and D exhibited bipolar growth with an s-shaped morphology.
H.   No; the yeast cells in Dish B exhibited bipolar growth with an s-shaped morphology, but the yeast cells in Dish D exhibited bipolar growth with a c-shaped morphology.
J.   No; the yeast cells in Dish A exhibited bipolar growth with an s-shaped morphology, but the yeast cells in Dish C exhibited bipolar growth with a c-shaped morphology.

37. The anode of the petri dishes in Experiment 2 is the positively charged electrode, and the cathode is the negatively charged electrode. Did the yeast cells in Dish Y likely grow towards the anode or towards the cathode?

A.   Cathode; the *S. pombe – N* cells in Dish B grew towards the negatively charged electrode.
B.   Cathode; the *S. pombe – GM* cells in Dish D grew towards the negatively charged electrode.
C.   Anode; the *S. pombe – N* cells in Dish B grew towards the positively charged electrode.
D.   Anode; the *S. pombe – GM* cells in Dish D grew towards the positively charged electrode.

38. Based on the information shown in Figure 1, is *S. pombe* a eukaryotic or prokaryotic cell?

F.   Prokaryotic; each cell has a nucleus.
G.   Eukaryotic; each cell has a nucleus.
H.   Prokaryotic; each cell does not have a nucleus.
J.   Eukaryotic; each cell does not have a nucleus.

39. In Experiment 2, how many times was the length of each cell measured?

A.   2
B.   3
C.   5
D.   7

40. If researchers wanted to examine the effects of different temperatures on the growth of *S. pombe – GM* cells, which two dishes should they compare?

F.   Dish W and Dish X
G.   Dish W and Dish Y
H.   Dish Y and Dish X
J.   Dish Y and Dish Z

END OF TEST 4

STOP! DO NOT RETURN TO ANY OTHER TEST.

DIRECTIONS

This is a test of your writing skills. You will have forty (40) minutes to write an essay. Before you begin planning and writing your essay, read the writing prompt carefully to understand exactly what you are being asked to do. Your essay will be evaluated on the evidence it provides of your ability to express judgments by taking a position on the issue in the writing prompt; to maintain a focus on the topic throughout your essay; to develop a position by using logical reasoning and by supporting your ideas; to organize ideas in a logical way; and to use language clearly and effectively according to the conventions of standard written English.

You may use the unlined pages in this test booklet to plan your essay. These pages will not be scored. **You must write your essay on the lined pages in the answer folder.** Your writing on those lined pages will be scored. You may not need all the lined pages, but to ensure you have enough room to finish, do NOT skip lines. You may write corrections or additions neatly between the lines of your essay, but do NOT write in the margins of the lined pages. **Illegible essays cannot be scored, so you must write (or print) clearly.**

If you finish before time is called, you may review your work. Lay your pencil down immediately when time is called.

DO NOT OPEN THIS BOOK UNTIL YOU ARE TOLD TO DO SO.

ACT Assessment Writing Test Prompt

Globalization

Improved travel and communication networks have the potential to transform the world population into a single, global society. We can now travel across the globe in a matter of hours. The internet enables us to spread ideas and share cultural norms instantly. Many of the products we use every day are produced on the other side of the world. Globalization can be seen as beneficial, but is generally thought of as a more complicated issue. Given the accelerating pace of globalization, what are the implications it could have for humanity?

Read and carefully consider these perspectives. Each suggests a particular way of thinking about increasing globalization.

Perspective One	Perspective Two	Perspective Three
As the development of a single world culture becomes a real possibility, we risk losing the diversity that makes life interesting. As people become more similar, the unique elements that identify various cultures will be lost in a global melting pot.	The ability to cheaply ship goods across the planet makes necessities and luxuries more affordable to all. Increased product affordability leads to an increase in the quality of life for millions of people globally.	Globalization brings greater interaction between countries, which could lead to more conflict. The more we interact with other cultures, the more our differences and disagreements will be emphasized. It would be better for cultures to be more isolated from one another in order to exist harmoniously.

Essay Task

Write a unified, coherent essay in which you evaluate multiple perspectives on the question of the implications increased globalization may have on humanity. In your essay, be sure to:

- analyze and evaluate the perspectives given
- state and develop your own perspective on the issue
- explain the relationship between your perspective and those given

Your perspective may be in full agreement with any of the others, in partial agreement, or wholly different. Whatever the case, support your ideas with logical reasoning and detailed, persuasive examples.

Chapter 27
Practice Exam 1:
Answers and
Explanations

English		Math		Reading		Science	
1. C	39. A	1. C	31. D	1. C	21. D	1. A	21. C
2. H	40. H	2. K	32. G	2. H	22. G	2. G	22. G
3. B	41. D	3. B	33. A	3. B	23. B	3. D	23. C
4. J	42. J	4. J	34. H	4. G	24. J	4. G	24. J
5. D	43. A	5. E	35. D	5. D	25. C	5. A	25. B
6. H	44. J	6. H	36. H	6. G	26. H	6. G	26. A
7. A	45. B	7. C	37. A	7. C	27. D	7. B	27. B
8. F	46. G	8. H	38. H	8. H	28. F	8. G	28. H
9. B	47. B	9. A	39. D	9. A	29. C	9. B	29. B
10. G	48. J	10. F	40. H	10. J	30. F	10. F	30. H
11. C	49. B	11. D	41. A	11. D	31. C	11. A	31. A
12. J	50. G	12. H	42. J	12. G	32. J	12. G	32. F
13. A	51. C	13. B	43. B	13. B	33. A	13. B	33. C
14. F	52. H	14. J	44. J	14. H	34. H	14. J	34. J
15. D	53. A	15. C	45. B	15. A	35. D	15. B	35. B
16. H	54. H	16. F	46. H	16. H	36. G	16. H	36. H
17. D	55. C	17. B	47. C	17. A	37. B	17. D	37. D
18. F	56. F	18. F	48. J	18. G	38. F	18. G	38. G
19. B	57. A	19. C	49. D	19. A	39. D	19. B	39. D
20. F	58. H	20. K	50. J	20. H	40. G	20. H	40. J
21. A	59. C	21. D	51. E				
22. J	60. J	22. H	52. F				
23. B	61. D	23. B	53. C				
24. J	62. H	24. F	54. K				
25. A	63. A	25. B	55. D				
26. G	64. F	26. G	56. H				
27. B	65. D	27. A	57. E				
28. H	66. G	28. J	58. K				
29. C	67. C	29. B	59. B				
30. G	68. J	30. G	60. J				
31. B	69. D						
32. G	70. F						
33. D	71. B						
34. F	72. G						
35. B	73. C						
36. F	74. F						
37. A	75. D						
38. H							

ENGLISH TEST

1. **C** Prepositions are changing in the answer choices, so the question is testing an idiom. Look at the phrase before the preposition to determine the correct idiom. Use POE to get rid of the answers that are inconsistent with the phrase. The correct idiom is *made the most of*. Eliminate (A), (B), and (D). The correct answer is (C).

2. **H** Punctuation is changing in the answer choices, so the question is testing STOP and GO punctuation. Use the Vertical Line Test and identify whether the ideas are complete or incomplete. Draw the vertical line between the words *everything* and *weeding*. *I was ready to "help" around the house with everything* is a complete idea, and *weeding, changing sheets, even washing windows* is an incomplete idea. To connect a complete idea to an incomplete idea, HALF-STOP or GO punctuation is needed. Eliminate (F) because a semicolon is STOP punctuation. Choice (J) has GO punctuation at the end of the underlined portion but adds a period between *house* and *everything,* so draw a line between those two words and repeat the Vertical Line Test. The first part of the sentence is still a complete idea, and the second half, *With everything weeding, changing sheets, even washing windows,* is still incomplete. Since a period is STOP punctuation, eliminate (J). Choices (G) and (H) both use a colon, which is HALF-STOP punctuation and works effectively to set up the list that follows, but (G) introduces a comma between *with* and *everything*. There is no reason to include this comma, so eliminate (G). The correct answer is (H).

3. **B** Note the question! The question asks which choice *best suggests the potentially unusual nature of the narrator's enthusiasm for the kinds of housework* she performed with her grandmother, so it's testing precision of word choice. The narrator states that she *was ready to "help" around the house with everything,* and the list of chores she gives includes *weeding, changing sheets*, and *washing windows;* the rest of the paragraph describes these chores as *everyday,* but also suggests that these kinds of jobs *thrilled me because I was spending time alone with her.* To be consistent with the narrator's description, the correct answer must mean something like "day-to-day" or "uninteresting." *Solitary* means "done or existing alone," which is not indicated in the passage; eliminate (A). *Mundane* means "humdrum" or "uninteresting," which is consistent with the suggestion that the *narrator's enthusiasm* is *potentially unusual,* so keep (B). *Exciting* means "causing great enthusiasm or eagerness." This does describe the narrator's feelings, but it does not emphasize the unusual nature of those feelings; eliminate (C). *Necessary* means "needed," which is inconsistent with how the passage characterizes the chores, so eliminate (D). The correct answer is (B).

4. **J** Punctuation is changing in the answer choices, so the question is testing STOP and GO punctuation. Use the Vertical Line Test and identify whether the ideas are complete or incomplete. Draw the vertical line between the words *meaningful* and *when*. *She made everyday chores meaningful* is a complete idea, and *when she set to work, hard and easy tasks alike were undertaken as acts of love* is also a complete idea. To connect two complete ideas, STOP or HALF-STOP punctuation is needed. Eliminate (F) because a comma is GO punctuation. Eliminate (H) because the word *and* without a comma is GO punctuation. In the context of the sentence, *when she set to work* is unnecessary

information because the sentence already specifies that the tasks she performs *were undertaken*; as a result, the phrase *when she set to work* should be surrounded by commas. In (G) and (J), the period after *meaningful* takes the place of one of the necessary commas, so only the comma after *work* is still needed; eliminate (G) because it omits that comma. The correct answer is (J).

5. **D** The wording of a term in a comparison is changing in the answer choices, so the question is testing precision and consistency. The sentence states that *no tasks seemed more magical* compared to whatever the underlined portion represents. Since the narrator begins the paragraph by asserting that she loved *dinner preparations, no tasks* is being compared to *preparations*. A pronoun must be consistent in number with the noun it is replacing; because the pronoun is replacing *preparations*, which is a plural noun, the correct answer must include a plural pronoun. Eliminate (A) and (C), because *it* is a singular pronoun. The words *than* and *then* are what change between (B) and (D). The correct accompanying word for comparisons like *more* is *than*, so eliminate (B). The correct answer is (D).

6. **H** The description of the grandmother's actions is changing in the answer choices, so the question is testing precision. Though the answer choices do not include STOP or HALF-STOP punctuation, this question is testing complete and incomplete ideas. To be consistent, the first part of the sentence should be a complete idea that can be modified by the incomplete idea of the second part of the sentence. *Cooking without* does not make the first part of the sentence a complete idea, so eliminate (F). *Without* also makes the first part of the sentence incomplete, so eliminate (J). While (G) includes a subject for the sentence, *cooking*, it does not include a main verb, so it also makes the first part of the sentence incomplete; eliminate (G). Only (H) includes both a subject, *Grandma*, and a main verb, *cooked*, to make the first part of the sentence a complete idea. The correct answer is (H).

7. **A** Transitions are changing in the answer choices, so the question is testing consistency of ideas. Select the word that reflects the correct relationship between the ideas. In the previous sentence, the narrator describes how her grandmother prepared *complex dishes* with extraordinary *ease*. In the next sentence, the narrator states that her *favorite dish*, by comparison, *was a simple one*. The second sentence offers a contrasting example to the trend described in the first sentence, so the correct answer must be consistent with that relationship. *However* suggests a contrast, so keep (A). *Moreover* and *naturally* both indicate that the second idea is a logical continuation or effect of the first idea, which is not consistent with the contrast between the ideas, so eliminate (B) and (C). *Then* indicates that the second idea follows, either in logic or in chronology, after the first idea, but it does not clearly indicate a contrast, so eliminate (D). The correct answer is (A).

8. **F** Note the question! The question asks what *the paragraph would primarily lose* if the underlined portion were deleted, so it's testing consistency. The sentence describes how the narrator's grandmother *always began* making chicken and dumplings by asking the narrator *to catch and pluck a chicken, the way she'd had to do growing up*, but the next sentence notes that it is a *store-bought chicken* that *cooked in the soup pot*. Therefore, the grandmother's request was not a serious one—which the

underlined portion, *teasingly*, makes clear. The correct answer should be consistent with the sense that omitting the word *teasingly* would take away the paragraph's indication that the narrator and grandmother had light-hearted interactions as they cooked together. Choice (F) states that the paragraph would lose *a sense of the relationship between the narrator and her grandmother as they engaged in their cooking rituals*, which is consistent with the tone and evidence of the passage; keep (F). There is no indication that the Grandmother's teasing resulted in her keeping *a distance from her granddaughter* or that the narrator felt that *her grandmother picked on her*, so eliminate (G) and (H). Because the exchange has a light-hearted tone, it does nothing to detract from the positive nature of the narrator's reminiscences, so (J) can be eliminated. The correct answer is (F).

9. **B** Pronouns are changing in the answer choices, so the question is testing consistency of pronouns. A pronoun must be consistent in case with the noun it is replacing. The first pronoun in the underlined phrase is referring to the noun *Grandma*, which is the subject of the phrase, so the pronoun should also be in the subject case. *Who* is the subject case, while *whom* is the object case, so eliminate (A) and (D). The second pronoun in the underlined phrase is referring to the narrator and her brother; in the phrase, they are the object of the grandmother's promising, not the object of something they are doing to themselves. *Us* and *ourselves* are both object case, but only *us* makes it clear that they were receiving someone else's action. Eliminate (C). The correct answer is (B).

10. **G** Vocabulary is changing in the answer choices, so the question is testing precision of word choice. The sentence discusses how the narrator thought of chicken and dumplings after she had *left for college and then began a career abroad,* and she links the dish to *everything I missed about home,* so the correct answer must mean something like "symbolize" or "be a reminder of." *Signal* means "send a message about," which is not consistent with the meaning of the sentence, so eliminate (F). *Represent* means "symbolize," which is consistent with the rest of the sentence and paragraph, so keep (G). *Stand up for* means "defend," so eliminate (H). *Give anew* means "offer again," so eliminate (J). The correct answer is (G).

11. **C** The description of *home* is changing in the answer choices, so the question is testing concision and precision. The narrator states that when she *left for college and then began a career abroad, "our dish"* came to signify *everything* the narrator *missed* about her home and family. The sentence already explains that the dish became significant when the narrator *left* and then was *abroad*, so it is unnecessary to repeat that idea. Eliminate (A) and (B) because they repeat the idea that the narrator was away from home. Choice (C) concisely states that the dish signified *home* when the narrator was away, so keep (C). Choice (D) is an overly wordy definition of the narrator's home as *the place I loved a lot*: eliminate (D). The correct answer is (C).

12. **J** Prepositions are changing in the answer choices, so the question is testing idioms. Look at the phrase before the preposition to determine the correct idiom. Use POE to get rid of the answers that are inconsistent with the phrase. In this case, the narrator is describing the *only* times her *favorite food* was *available*, explaining that she had the food only during *visits home*. While the sentence itself is indicating *when* the narrator had the dish, the word *when* is not a preposition and

should be followed by a complete thought, so it does not work to connect the ideas; eliminate (G). She can't have been having the food *before* her visits home, so eliminate (H). The correct idiom is *on visits*, so eliminate (F). The correct answer is (J).

13. **A** Note the question! The question is asking which word *indicates most specifically how the narrator felt about her access to the dish she craved*, so it's testing precision of word choice. The previous paragraph describes the narrator's attempts to eat comparably delicious chicken and dumplings as *desperation*, and when she could not find a comparable version she became *resigned to the fact* that her favorite food was not readily available, so the correct answer should reflect the sadness of her reaction. *Lament* means "mournful statement," which is consistent with the idea of the passage, so keep (A). *Explanation* means "summary of facts or logic," which does not match the tone of the narrator's description, so eliminate (B). *Story* is a general word for a "narrative" or "description of events," which does not indicate the narrator's feelings *most specifically*, so eliminate (C). Similarly, *long tale* specifies the duration of the narrator's story but not her feelings *about her access to the dish*, so eliminate (D). The correct answer is (A).

14. **F** Apostrophes are changing in the answer choices, so the question is testing apostrophe usage. The sentence states that the narrator *objected* to the idea that she should make the dish herself because her grandmother had not written down any of her cooking directions. When used with a noun, an apostrophe signifies possession: in this case, *Grandma* is the noun that is possessing things, the *recipes*, so *Grandma* should be in the possessive case. Because *Grandma* is only one person, the apostrophe should go before the *s*. Eliminate (G), (H), and (J), because none of them has the correct form of *Grandma's*. The correct answer is (F).

15. **D** Note the question! The question asks for the answer that *best concludes the essay by emphasizing the central point made in the first and second paragraphs*, so it's testing consistency. The first and second paragraphs emphasize how *thrilled* the narrator was to spend time doing *everyday chores* with her grandmother, and how particularly *magical* the *tasks* of *dinner preparations* felt. Choice (A) explains that the narrator used *help from the internet* to find a recipe she loves, which does not mention the narrator's memories of cooking with her grandmother and so is not consistent with the central point of the essay's beginning: eliminate (A). Choice (B) makes an assertion about how the narrator's grandmother *wouldn't have wanted me to be a quitter*; there is no mention of the grandmother's attitude toward *quitting* earlier in the passage, so eliminate (B). Choice (C) is consistent with the idea that the recipe is for a dish the narrator *loves*, but it does not mention experience with her grandmother, so eliminate (C). Choice (D) references the narrator's memories *of how safe, happy, and loved I felt in the kitchen with Grandma*, which is consistent with the central point of the essay's early paragraphs, so keep (D). The correct answer is (D).

16. **H** Vocabulary is changing in the answer choices, so the question is testing precision of word choice. The sentence describes how Lovelace's *intelligence* had an effect on Babbage that led him to *show her a device he'd been working on*, so the correct answer must mean something like "interested." *Fazed* means "disturbed," so eliminate (F). *Overawed* means "overwhelmed with awe," which is a

stronger effect than Lovelace's intelligence seems to have had, so eliminate (G). *Impressed* means "had an effect on" or "was favorable to," which is consistent with the tone of the passage, so keep (H). *Motivated* means "inspired" or "encouraged," so eliminate (J). The correct answer is (H).

17. **D** Pronouns are changing in the answer choices, so the question is testing consistency of pronouns. A pronoun must be consistent in number and case with the noun it is replacing. The pronoun is replacing the noun *moment*, which is singular, so the correct answer must also be singular: eliminate (B). The sentence is identifying which moment was a pivotal one, not stating that the moment occurred, so adding the pronoun *there* to the phrase *was a pivotal moment* is inconsistent with the idea of the sentence: eliminate (C). *Such* is a pronoun that describes the quality of the *moment*, not the identity of which moment it was, so eliminate (A). The correct answer is (D).

18. **F** Many things are changing in the answer choices, so focus on one thing at a time. Punctuation is changing, so the question is partly testing STOP and GO punctuation. In (H), there is a dash, which is HALF-STOP punctuation, after an incomplete idea. Eliminate (H). In (J), there is a comma joining an incomplete idea with a complete idea. However, it does not make sense to say *this machine that Lovelace she focused fully on,* as it has both *Lovelace* and *she* as the subject of the verb *focused*. Eliminate (J). Between (F) and (G), the vocabulary is changing, so the question is also testing clarity of word choice. It makes more sense to say that Lovelace *focused her keen understanding* on something, rather than *engaged with* her own understanding. Eliminate (G). The correct answer is (F).

19. **B** Commas are changing in the answer choices, so the question is testing the four ways to use a comma. The word *though* is unnecessary information, so it should be surrounded by commas. Eliminate (A), (C), and (D) because they do not include commas in the correct positions. Choice (B) correctly surrounds the word with commas. The correct answer is (B).

20. **F** Note the question! The question asks where *Sentence 2 should be placed*, so it's testing consistency of ideas. Note the subject matter of the sentence and find other sentences that also reference that information. Sentence 2 describes how Lovelace's *intelligence* prompted Babbage to offer to *show her a device he'd been working on*. Sentence 3 explains that Babbage *introduced* her to *his complicated Difference Engine*. The invitation to show her the device must have come before her introduction to it, so Sentence 2 must come before Sentence 3. Choices (G), (H), and (J) all place Sentence 2 after Sentence 3, so eliminate them. The correct answer is (F).

21. **A** The combination of pronouns and nouns is changing in the answer choices, so the question is testing precision and concision. Determine the term to which the pronoun is referring and choose an answer that makes the idea consistent and concise. The phrase is describing the *additional insights* that Lovelace contributed to her translation of Babbage's *lecture*, so the correct answer will be the shortest phrase that is consistent with the meaning of the sentence. *Many* is both consistent and concise, so keep (A). The sentence has already indicated that the *additional insights* were *her own*, so there is no need to repeat the idea that the insights belonged to Lovelace; eliminate (B) and

(D) because they repeat the pronoun *her* or *hers*. The sentence has also already indicated that what Lovelace contributed were *insights*, so there is no need to repeat that idea: eliminate (C). The correct answer is (A).

22. **J**   Note the question! The question asks which choice best articulates how *dividing the paragraph into two* would *help organize the essay*, so it is testing consistency of ideas. The first part of the paragraph states that *Babbage delivered a lecture on a new, more sophisticated machine*, and when *Lovelace decided to translate* that lecture *into English*, she contributed *her own additional insights* to the publication. The second part of the paragraph explains a particular insight of Babbage's—that a *card* like those invented by Joseph-Marie Jacquard *could specify mathematical operations*—and outlines Lovelace's additional theorizing on that topic, theorizing that led to what is *widely regarded as the first computer program*. Dividing the paragraph into two, then, would separate the explanation of Lovelace's translation and additional work from an example of how Lovelace's work was an important expansion of Babbage's ideas. Look for an answer choice that is consistent with that relationship between the two components of the paragraph. Choice (F) characterizes the first part of the paragraph as *a suggestion that Lovelace took unwarranted liberties in the act of translation*, which is inconsistent with the evidence in the passage; eliminate (F). Choice (G) characterizes the second part of the paragraph as *an explanation of how the Analytical Engine could improve industries such as weaving*, which is also inconsistent with the evidence in the passage; eliminate (G). Choice (H) says that the paragraph includes *an explanation of Babbage's response* to Lovelace's *translation*, which the passage does not, so eliminate (H). Choice (J) suggests that dividing the paragraph would separate *an introduction to Lovelace's translation* from *details that establish* why Lovelace's work *was so extraordinary*, which is consistent with the evidence in the paragraph. The correct answer is (J).

23. **B**   Punctuation is changing in the answer choices, so the question is testing STOP and GO punctuation. Use the Vertical Line Test and identify whether the ideas are complete or incomplete. Draw a vertical line between the words *grasped* and *this*. *Babbage proposed that, in his machine, such a card could specify mathematical operations Lovelace quickly grasped* is an incomplete idea, and *this idea's immense potential and strove to demonstrate it* is also an incomplete idea. To connect two incomplete ideas, GO punctuation is needed; eliminate (A) and (D), because a period and a semicolon are STOP punctuation. The difference between (B) and (C) is also a difference of STOP and GO punctuation, so repeat the Vertical Line Test, this time drawing the line between *operations* and *Lovelace*. The first part is a complete idea, and the second part is also a complete idea. To connect two complete ideas, STOP punctuation is needed, so eliminate (C), which uses GO punctuation. The correct answer is (B).

24. **J**   Verbs are changing in the answer choices, so the question is testing consistency of verbs. A verb must be consistent with its subject and with the other verbs in the sentence. The subject of the verb is *outline*, which is a singular noun, so the correct answer must also be singular. *Have been widely regarded*, *are widely regarded*, and *have wide regard* all contain plural verbs, so eliminate (F), (G), and (H). *Is widely regarded* contains a singular verb, so keep (J). The correct answer is (J).

25. **A** The descriptive phrases surrounding *could be* are changing in the answer choices, so the question is testing concision and precision. The sentence states that Lovelace intuited the potential for *such a machine* to *do more than just manipulate numbers*. First, determine whether the phrases are necessary. The sentence states that Lovelace was considering *such a machine*, so there is no need to repeat the idea that the machine she was proposing was *akin to* or *like* Babbage's: eliminate (C) and (D). After the underlined portion, the sentence states that Lovelace's suggestion was about how the machine might be *used*, so there is no need to repeat the idea that it would be put to work in a certain way: the word *employed* in (B) is redundant, so eliminate (B). The correct answer is (A).

26. **G** The punctuation used to set off items in a list is changing in the answer choices, so the question is testing consistency and the four ways to use a comma. The sentence contains a list of three things: 1) *scientific analysis,* 2) *visual images,* and 3) *music.* Because the list ends with a closing parenthesis after *music,* the list should also begin with an opening parenthesis before *scientific,* so eliminate (F) and (H). Inside the parentheses, there should be a comma separating each item in the list. Eliminate (J) because it does not include a comma after *analysis.* The correct answer is (G).

27. **B** The forms of the verb are changing in the answer choices, so the question is testing consistency of verbs. There is also the option to DELETE the underlined portion; consider this choice carefully, as it's often the correct answer. The sentence states that *Lovelace's suggestion* had some relationship to *the digital revolution,* so the verb in the underlined portion is necessary: eliminate (D). The verb forms in (A) and (C) make the sentence an incomplete idea, so eliminate (A) and (C). The correct answer is (B).

28. **H** Transitions are changing in the answer choices, so the question is testing consistency of ideas and concision. Look for an answer that is consistent with the relationship between the two sentences. The previous sentence states that although Lovelace died *decades before the first "real" computer was built,* general *recognition of her trailblazing role…has grown,* and the next sentence explains that *in the 1970s, the Department of Defense named a software language "Ada" in her honor.* The second sentence provides an example in support of the claim made in the first sentence, so the correct answer must be consistent with that relationship. *Naturally* indicates that the second idea is an inevitable or necessary consequence of the first idea; since Lovelace's *recognition* did not necessarily have to include having a coding language named after her, eliminate (F). *However* and *by contrast* suggest that the second idea is in opposition to the first idea, which is not consistent with the evidence in the passage, so eliminate (G) and (J). The correct answer is (H).

29. **C** Note the question! The question asks which choice *strongly and specifically highlights that Ada Lovelace Day is intended to shine a light on often-overlooked work by women,* so it is testing consistency of ideas. The sentence states that *Ada Lovelace Day prompts us to* behave a certain way toward *women in STEM fields,* and the description of *Ada Lovelace Day* follows a claim that the *recognition* of Lovelace's *trailblazing role…has grown.* To be consistent, therefore, the correct answer should mean something like "recognize" or "appreciate." *Notice* means "become aware of," and *Think about the work of* mentions the *work* of women in STEM fields, but neither answer highlights

how that work is *often-overlooked* or how Ada Lovelace Day encourages us to *shine a light* on it, so eliminate (A) and (B). *Celebrate under-recognized contributions of* is consistent with the phrasing of the question and the content of the passage, so keep (C). *Honor efforts by* focuses on attempts, rather than accomplishments, so it is not consistent with the main ideas of the passage; eliminate (D). The correct answer is (C).

30. **G** Note the question! The question asks whether the essay accomplishes the purpose of discussing *a mathematician whose work was remarkable but did not receive great recognition during the mathematician's lifetime*, so it's testing consistency. Determine whether the stated purpose is consistent with the main ideas of the essay. The essay discusses the work Ada Lovelace did in the 19th century, and it emphasizes that even though she died *decades before the first "real" computer was built, recognition of her trailblazing role as a woman in computing has grown*; these ideas are consistent with the purpose outlined in the question, so the essay does accomplish the stated purpose. Eliminate (H) and (J). While the essay discusses the additions Lovelace made to her translation of Babbage's lecture, it does not demonstrate that she *improved on Babbage's work to change the course of computer science*, so eliminate (F). Choice (G) accurately notes that the essay accomplishes the stated purpose by telling *the story of Ada Lovelace's pioneering work* and noting *the recognition she has received decades after her death*. The correct answer is (G).

31. **B** Punctuation is changing in the answer choices, so the question is testing the four ways to use a comma. Notice the non-underlined punctuation elsewhere in the sentence. *Or even decades* is unnecessary information, so it should be surrounded by commas; since there is already a comma after *decades*, there needs to be a comma after *years*. Eliminate (A), (C), and (D) because the dash, no punctuation, or semicolon will not correctly separate the unnecessary information. The correct answer is (B).

32. **G** Note the question! The question asks which choice gives *the most effective introduction to the paragraph*, so it's testing consistency of ideas. The previous sentence notes that *some* of the *active volcanoes* in the U.S. are *near populated towns and cities*, which means that *predicting future eruptions is essential to public safety*. The paragraph being introduced defines *the field of volcanology* and explains that volcanology can focus either *on dead and dormant volcanoes* or on *active or potentially "reawakening"* sites. To be consistent, the first sentence of the paragraph should connect the main ideas of the two paragraphs. Choice (F) describes the number of *U.S. volcanoes* that *pose a high or very high risk to public safety*, which is not consistent with the main ideas of the second paragraph, so eliminate (F). Choice (G) asserts that *this task is the responsibility of volcanologists*, which links the previous paragraph's mention of the *essential* job of *predicting future eruptions* to the new paragraph's focus on what volcanologists do; keep (G). Choice (H) enumerates how many volcanoes erupt *per week somewhere around the world*, which is not relevant to the main idea of the new paragraph; eliminate (H). Choice (J) gives details about the *deadliest volcanic event in the United States*, which is not relevant to the main idea of the new paragraph, so eliminate (J). The correct answer is (G).

33. **D** Punctuation and transition words are changing in the answer choices, so the question is testing STOP and GO punctuation. Use the Vertical Line Test and identify whether the ideas are complete or incomplete. Draw the vertical line between the words *volcanoes* and *it*. *This work can focus on dead and dormant volcanoes* is a complete idea, and *it can also require volcanologists to monitor volcanoes that are active or potentially "reawakening"* is also a complete idea. To connect complete ideas, STOP punctuation is needed. Eliminate (A) and (C) because the comma and no punctuation are GO punctuation. The difference between (B) and (D) is the direction of the transitional words, so choose the answer that most closely matches the relationship between the ideas in the sentence. The first part of the sentence explains that volcanologists can focus on *dead and dormant* volcanoes, and the second part of the sentence notes that volcanology *can also require* scientists to monitor *active or potentially "reawakening"* volcanoes. The second part of the sentence provides an alternative to the work circumstances described in the first part, so the transition should reflect that change in direction. *Since* suggests that the second part of the sentence explains the idea in the first part, which does not match the relationship between the ideas; eliminate (B). *But* reflects the contrast between the two parts of the sentence. The correct answer is (D).

34. **F** Verbs are changing in the answer choices, so the question is testing consistency of verbs. A verb must be consistent in number with its subject. The subject of the underlined verb is *research*, which is a singular noun, so the correct answer must also be singular. *Involves* is a singular verb, so keep (F). *Have involved, involve,* and *are involving* are all plural verbs, so eliminate (G), (H), and (J). The correct answer is (F).

35. **B** Note the question! The question asks which choice provides the best emphasis on the idea *that analysis of dormant and dead volcanoes provides insights into the geological history of those sites*, so it is testing consistency of ideas. Choice (A) mentions that the analysis allows scientists to *determine the amounts of sulfur and iron in the rocks*, which is consistent with the idea of the sites' *chemical makeup* but not of their *geological history*, so eliminate (A). Choice (B) states that the analysis can *establish when and how previous eruptions occurred*, which is consistent with the idea of *geological history*, so keep (B). Choice (C) focuses on whether the volcanoes are *unlikely to erupt again in the near future*, which does not establish anything about their *history*, so eliminate (C). Choice (D) mentions *evidence of ancient civilizations that might have lived* at the volcano sites, which is consistent with the idea of history but not with the topic of *geological* history, so eliminate (D). The correct answer is (B).

36. **F** Transitional phrases are changing in the answer choices, so the question is testing consistency of ideas. Select the phrase that reflects the correct relationship between the ideas. The previous sentence describes the activities *frequently* involved in *field research on dead or dormant volcanoes*, and the new sentence describes what happens *at active sites*. The new sentence provides information that is in contrast to the ideas discussed in the previous sentence, so the correct answer should signal the difference between the two ideas. *However* signals a contrast between ideas, so keep (F). *In fact* indicates that the second idea is a clarification or specific example of the first idea, which is not consistent with the relationship between ideas, so eliminate (G). *Therefore* suggests that the first

idea explains the reason for the second idea, which is inconsistent with the passage, so eliminate (H). *Furthermore* indicates that the second idea is a continuation of the first idea, which is also inconsistent with the passage, so eliminate (J). The correct answer is (F).

37. **A**   Prepositions are changing in the answer choices, so the question is testing an idiom. Look at the phrase before the preposition to determine the correct idiom. Use POE to get rid of the answers that are inconsistent with the phrase. The sentence is describing how *magma* rises to the surface of Earth. *Through* indicates that the magma is traveling from underneath the crust to the surface, which is consistent with the description, so keep (A). Since the magma is rising up from below horizontal layers of Earth, it does not make sense to use the word *behind,* so eliminate (B). *Of* suggests that the rising is somehow possessed by *Earth's crust,* which doesn't make sense, so eliminate (C). *With* suggests that both the *crust* and the *magma* are *rising,* which is inconsistent with the content of the paragraph, so eliminate (D). The correct answer is (A).

38. **H**   The punctuation is changing between commas and dashes in the answer choices, so the question is testing variations in the four ways to use a comma. The sentence is describing how a volcano's shape changes as magma accumulates underground; the phrase *liquefied rock that eventually becomes lava* is a modifier defining *magma.* To set off a piece of unnecessary information, the phrase can be surrounded by either a pair of commas or a pair of dashes (or a set of parentheses). Eliminate (F) and (J), because they include punctuation after only one word in the phrase. Choice (G) uses a comma to separate the first part of the phrase and a dash to separate the second part, which is inconsistent; eliminate (G). Choice (H) correctly uses two dashes, like commas, to surround the modifying phrase. The correct answer is (H).

39. **A**   Apostrophes and pronouns are changing in the answer choices, so the question is testing precision and apostrophe usage. The sentence is describing the importance of monitoring *a volcano using GPS and precisely calibrated instruments.* The rest of the sentence lacks a subject or a verb, so in order for the sentence to be a complete idea, the underlined portion must include a verb and the *it* pronoun in the subject case. Eliminate (C) and (D) because *its'* places an unnecessary apostrophe after the pronoun and *its* is in the possessive case, not the subject case. The apostrophe in (A), *it's,* signals a contraction of the phrase *it is,* so the difference between (A) and (B) is a difference of verb tense. A verb must be consistent with the other verbs in the sentence. Because there are no other main verbs in the sentence, look at the previous sentence: verbs like *builds up* and *changes* indicate that to be consistent, the correct answer must be a present tense verb. *It was* uses a past tense verb, so eliminate (B). The correct answer is (A).

40. **H**   Descriptions of the probability of a volcanic eruption are changing in the answer choices, so the question is testing concision and precision. The sentence is describing volcanologists' work in preparing communities for the possibility of volcanic activity. All four answer choices use a word like *chance, possibility,* or *likelihood* to signal that the timing of a volcano's eruption cannot be predicted with total certainty, so there is no reason to repeat that idea. Choices (F), (G), and (J) all include redundant phrases noting that the possible eruption *could* happen, so eliminate them. Choice (H) only describes the eruption as *possible,* so it is the most concise option. The correct answer is (H).

41. **D** The description of the consequences of ash plumes is changing in the answer choices, so the question is testing concision and precision. The non-underlined portion of the sentence already states that the effects it is describing take place *far from the eruption site*, so there is no need to repeat that idea. Choices (A) and (C) mention that ash plumes have effects *nowhere near the volcano* and *in faraway locales*, so they are redundant; eliminate (A) and (C). The difference between (B) and (D) is wordiness: (B) mentions that ash plumes can affect *farmers, crops, air traffic controllers, and airplanes*, while (D) more concisely notes that the plumes *can disrupt air travel and affect agriculture*. Choose the shortest answer that retains the precise meaning the sentence needs: eliminate (B). The correct answer is (D).

42. **J** Transitional phrases are changing in the answer choices, so the question is testing consistency of ideas. Select the word that reflects the correct relationship between the ideas. The first part of the sentence states that *a career that involves camping by a soon-to-erupt volcano might seem spectacularly dangerous*, and the second part of the sentence notes that *only two U.S. geologists have ever died as a result of volcanic eruption*. The second idea is in contrast to what *might seem spectacularly dangerous*, so the correct answer should indicate that contrast. Choice (F), *because*, indicates that the first idea is the reason for the second idea, which is inconsistent with the relationship between the phrases: eliminate (F). *Considering that* indicates that the first idea is a condition that makes sense of the second idea, which is also inconsistent with the contrast between the ideas in the sentence: eliminate (G). Choice (H), *since*, also indicates that the first idea explains the situation in the second idea: eliminate (H). Choice (J), *while*, reflects the contrast between the two ideas. The correct answer is (J).

43. **A** Verbs are changing in the answer choices, so the question is testing consistency of verbs. A verb must be consistent with its subject and the other verbs in the sentence. The subject of the underlined verb is *advances*, which is a plural noun, so the correct answer must also be plural. *Help* is a plural verb, so keep (A). *Has helped, is helping*, and *helps* are all singular verbs, so eliminate (B), (C), and (D). The correct answer is (A).

44. **J** The wording of a term in a list is changing in the answer choices, so the question is testing consistency. The other two items in the sentence's list are *direct observation* and *theoretical modeling*, so the correct answer should be consistent with those items. *Analyzing of data* adds a prepositional phrase that is absent in the wording of the other items, so eliminate (F). Choices (G), *they analyze data*, and (H), *data to be analyzed*, include verbs, which is inconsistent with the phrasing of the other items in the list, so eliminate (G) and (H). Choice (J), *data analysis*, is consistent with the wording of the other items because its second word describes a scientific process (*analysis*) and its first word clarifies what kind of information is being processed (*data*). The correct answer is (J).

45. **B** Note the question! The question asks where the new sentence should be placed, so it's testing consistency of ideas. Note the subject matter of the sentence and find other sentences that also reference that information. The sentence says that no matter what *a volcano's status* may be, *much of* the *monitoring* volcanologists do occurs *on site*. Choice (A) places the sentence in Paragraph 2, before

the essay explains the various statuses a volcano may have; the sentence is not consistent with the organization of Paragraph 2, so eliminate (A). Choice (B) places the sentence in Paragraph 3, which describes *field research on dead or dormant volcanoes* as well as the work done *at active sites*; these references are consistent with the statement in the new sentence, so keep (B). Choice (C) places the sentence in Paragraph 4, which outlines the *dire risks* that erupting volcanoes can pose to *humans, animals, and their homes*; the sentence is not consistent with the main ideas of Paragraph 4, so eliminate (C). Choice (D) places the sentence in Paragraph 5, which describes how *advances in technology and methods of prediction* are involved in protecting *residents* near volcanoes as well as *scientists*; the sentence focuses on *monitoring*, which is consistent with the focus of the paragraph, but it mentions that this *monitoring* occurs *whatever a volcano's status*, while Paragraph 5 focuses specifically on about-to-erupt volcanic sites. Eliminate (D). The correct answer is (B).

46. **G** Note the question! The question is asking which choice best *indicates where Vermeer was born and worked*. Choice (F), *to prompt the viewer to think about how art works,* provides no information about where Vermeer was born or worked, so eliminate (F). Choice (G) describes the painter as *Dutch*, which does indicate that Vermeer was born in the Netherlands, so keep (G). Choice (H) makes no mention of Vermeer himself and does not given any indication of where he was born and worked, so eliminate (H). While (J) does make reference to a location, the fact that the painting is owned by a museum in Vienna does not necessarily indicate that Vermeer was from Austria, so eliminate (J). The correct answer is (G).

47. **B** Verbs are changing in the answer choices, so the question is testing consistency of verbs. There is also the option to DELETE; consider this choice carefully, as it's often the correct answer. In this case, the verb in the underlined phrase contributes necessary information to the phrase *them making lace, reading, doing chores,* so the portion should not be deleted; eliminate (D). A verb must be consistent with its subject and with the other verbs in the sentence. The sentence states that Vermeer *is best known for portraying women in everyday domestic moments,* so the correct answer must also be a present-tense verb. *Since he showed* is a phrase in the past tense, so eliminate (A). Choice (B), *showing*, is present tense and is consistent with the verb *portraying* earlier in the sentence, so keep (B). The pronoun in (C), *in which he showed*, does not have a clear noun to replace earlier in the sentence, and the verb in (C) is in the past tense, so eliminate (C). The correct answer is (B).

48. **J** Punctuation is changing in the answer choices, so the question is testing STOP and GO punctuation. Use the Vertical Line Test and identify whether the ideas are complete or incomplete. Draw the vertical line between the words *artist* and *critics*. *This painting, however, centers on a male artist* is a complete idea, and *critics believe represents Vermeer himself, as he paints a female model* is an incomplete idea. To connect a complete idea and an incomplete idea, GO or HALF-STOP punctuation is needed. The semicolon and the period are STOP punctuation, so eliminate (F) and (H). None of the four ways to use a comma applies to the comma after *artist*, so eliminate (G). No punctuation is GO punctuation, which can connect a complete idea to an incomplete idea. The correct answer is (J).

49. **B** Commas are changing in the answer choices, so the question is testing the four ways to use a comma. The phrase *blurring of background details* is not unnecessary information, so it should not be surrounded by commas: eliminate (A). The adjective *another* refers to *blurring*, so there is no reason to insert a comma between those two words: keep (B) and eliminate (C). There is no reason to insert a comma between *blurring* and *of,* so eliminate (D). The correct answer is (B).

50. **G** Prepositions are changing in the answer choices, so the question is testing idioms. There is an option to delete the underlined portion, so consider that option carefully. When something is being accessed, the preposition used with access is *to*, as in *to need access to the exit*. If the underlined portion were removed, there would be no preposition to connect *tools* with *access*. Eliminate (J). Eliminate (F) and (H) as well, as they also do not use the correct preposition with the expression. Choice (G) does include the necessary *to*, by inserting the phrase *to which* at the underlined section; *to which the painter would need access* works, so keep (G). The correct answer is (G).

51. **C** Transitions are changing in the answer choices, so the question is testing consistency of ideas. (It is also a sneaky way to test complete and incomplete ideas.) The previous sentence states that *were the painter to stand up, he'd bang his head on the chandelier above him*, and the new sentence claims that this fact does something about *the artist's metaphorical stature* and also *reaffirms his significance*. The new sentence agrees with the claim made in the previous sentence and uses that claim to make new observations about the painting, so the correct answer must be consistent with that relationship. *While* indicates a contrast between the ideas, not an agreement, so eliminate (B). *Since* indicates a causal relationship, which is not consistent with the logic of the sentences, so eliminate (D). The difference between (A) and (C) is that (C) introduces a subject/verb combination that makes the entire phrase that contains the underlined portion into a compete idea. The previous sentence is also a complete idea, so STOP punctuation is needed. A period is found right before the underlined portion, so adding the subject and verb in the underlined portion, as (C) does, is necessary. Keep (C) and eliminate (A), since (A) does not create a complete idea. The correct answer is (C).

52. **H** Note the question! The question asks where the new sentence should be placed, so it's testing consistency of ideas. Note the subject matter of the sentence and find other sentences that also reference that information. The new sentence refers to *this omission* and claims that it *has the paradoxical effect of directing attention* to certain *elements of craft*, so it should follow a sentence that identifies a particular omission. Sentence 4 explains that *basic tools* of painting, *like a palette, are absent from the image*, which is consistent with the idea that the omission paradoxically emphasizes elements of craft. Because the new sentence refers to those *absent* tools as *this omission*, the new sentence must come after the description of the absences in Sentence 4. The correct answer is (H).

53. **A** The description of how *details* make *Vermeer's work stand out* is changing in the answer choices, so the question is testing concision and precision. First, determine whether the phrases are necessary. All four answer choices include that the details make Vermeer's work *stand out*, so there is no need to repeat the idea that his work is distinct from others'. Choices (B), (C), and (D) all include ad-

ditional descriptions of the work's distinction—*noticeably, draw attention,* and *with prominence*—that make them redundant. Eliminate (B), (C), and (D). The correct answer is (A).

54. **H** Note the question! The question asks which choice *supports the claim the writer makes in the preceding sentence about an artist's decisions* and also *best emphasizes how significant those choices are to what we perceive,* so it's testing consistency. The previous sentence suggests that Vermeer's work emphasizes *the role of an artist's decisions in creating the semblance of realism,* so the correct answer must be consistent with the idea that what an artist chooses to include in a painting affects *what we perceive.* Choices (F) and (G) focus on the factors on which an artist's choices are *based* or by which the choices are *affected,* and they do not mention the choices' effects on *the semblance of realism,* so eliminate (F) and (G). Choice (H) states that the choices *shape what the viewer perceives,* which is consistent with the idea that *those choices* are *significant* to *what we perceive,* so keep (H). Choice (J) compares an artist's choices to *the everyday choices people make,* which does not connect the artist's choices to a viewer's perceptions, so eliminate (J). The correct answer is (H).

55. **C** Vocabulary is changing in the answer choices, so the question is testing concision and precision of word choice. The sentence states that the details in Vermeer's painting are *so clear* that *historians* have been able to specify *the exact document* Vermeer used as a model in *his depiction of a map;* the correct answer must mean something like "found" or "identified." *Diagnosed* means "determined the nature of a disease," so eliminate (A). *Determined the identification of, identified,* and *put a name to* are all consistent with the idea of the sentence, but (B) and (D) are much wordier than (C), so eliminate them. The correct answer is (C).

56. **F** Punctuation is changing in the answer choices, so the question is testing STOP and GO punctuation. Use the Vertical Line Test and identify whether the ideas are complete or incomplete. Draw the vertical line between the words *referenced* and *in. Details are so clear that, for instance, historians have identified the exact document Vermeer must have referenced* is a complete idea, and *in his depiction of a map that hangs on the wall in the painting* is an incomplete idea. To connect a complete idea and an incomplete idea, GO or HALF-STOP punctuation is needed. Eliminate (G) because a semicolon is STOP punctuation. Because the context in which Vermeer *referenced* the document is necessary to the sentence, there is no reason to separate *referenced* from *in* with either a dash or a comma: eliminate (H) and (J). The correct answer is (F).

57. **A** The description of *elements* in Vermeer's paintings is changing in the answer choices, so the question is testing concision and precision. (The question is also a sneaky way to test the four ways to use a comma.) The answers include an option to DELETE the underlined portion, so check to see whether the sentence remains clear and concise without that portion. When the underlined portion is removed, the phrase *light and color* is set off by commas and immediately follows the phrase *many of painting's components.* While *light* and *color* are *components* of painting, they are not *many* components, so the underlined portion cannot be deleted; eliminate (D). Choice (B), *that are elements,* changes the section that is set off by commas to *that are elements light and color.* This phrase is missing an *of* to link the parts; without it, the phrase does not make sense in context, so elimi-

nate (B). Between (A) and (C), (A) is the longer answer, but the additional words serve to clarify that *such fundamental elements as light and color* are included in *painting's components.* Choice (C) is shorter but not effective in showing the relationship between *components* and *elements.* Eliminate (C). The correct answer is (A).

58.　**H**　Verbs are changing in the answer choices, so the question is testing consistency of verbs. A verb must be consistent with its subject and with the other verbs in the sentence. This verb's subject is *mastery,* which is singular, so the correct answer must be a singular verb. Eliminate (F), (G), and (J), because *result, are resulting,* and *have resulted* are all plural verbs. *Results* is a singular verb. The correct answer is (H).

59.　**C**　Note the question! The question asks where Paragraph 4 should be placed *for the sake of logic and cohesion,* so it's testing consistency of ideas. Note the subject matter of the paragraph and find other paragraphs that also reference that information. Paragraph 4 describes the effects of *the realistic precision* in Vermeer's work *The Art of Painting,* claiming that Vermeer's techniques lead to *an image that appears as accurate as a photograph.* The first sentence of Paragraph 2 notes that *some details are inconsistent with the work's prevailing realism,* and the rest of the paragraph describes those unrealistic details; in order for that contrast to make sense, Paragraph 4 and its description of *realistic precision* should be placed before Paragraph 2. Eliminate (A) and (D). Paragraph 1 introduces the painter, title, and subject of the painting, so the first sentence of Paragraph 4, *The realistic precision of* The Art of Painting *is striking,* cannot appear before Paragraph 1's introduction of the painting. Eliminate (B). The correct answer is (C).

60.　**J**　Note the question! The question asks whether the essay accomplishes the purpose of examining *how a work of art reshaped the way historians think about the role of the artist.* Determine whether the content of the stated purpose is consistent with the main ideas of the essay. While the essay does suggest that a single work of art, *The Art of Painting,* works to *offer the artist's commentary on his art,* there is no evidence that the painting *reshaped how historians think about the role of the artist.* The only mention of *historians* in the passage suggests that the details of Vermeer's painting allowed them to identify *the exact document* he referenced—not that the painting caused them to rethink artistic practice or intentions. The essay is not consistent with the purpose stated in the question, so eliminate (F) and (G). While the essay says that Vermeer is *best known* for subject matter other than that seen in *The Art of Painting,* it does not say that the subject was *atypical* for him, so there is no evidence that the painting's atypicality is why the essay does not accomplish the stated purpose: eliminate (H). Choice (J) correctly notes that the passage does *focus on the particulars of one painting* but also correctly notes that the passage does not accomplish the stated purpose because it *does not indicate what effect the painting has had on art criticism overall.* The correct answer is (J).

61.　**D**　Verbs and punctuation are changing in the answer choices, so the question is testing consistency and complete and incomplete ideas. In (A), *who* should refer to *Pugaeva,* but the closest noun is *Kazakhstan.* This is a misplaced modifier; eliminate (A). Choices (B) and (C) have the STOP punctuation of a comma plus FANBOYS, but the second part of both answers is incomplete. Eliminate (B) and (C). The correct answer is (D).

62. **H** Note the question! The question asks whether the sentence should be deleted, so it's testing consistency. If the content of the sentence is consistent with the ideas surrounding it, then it should be kept. The sentence describes how the production of *matryoshka* dolls *flourished among former Soviet state employees*. The rest of the paragraph focuses on introducing the development of one individual's *matryoshka*-painting practice, so the sentence is not consistent with the rest of the paragraph. The sentence should be deleted, so eliminate (F) and (G). Choice (H) correctly emphasizes that the sentence *detracts from the paragraph's focus* on Natasha's development as a doll painter, so keep (H). The sentence does not *contradict the paragraph's explanation of where Natasha learned to paint* matryoshka *dolls*, so (J) is inconsistent with both the sentence and the paragraph: eliminate (J). The correct answer is (H).

63. **A** Pronouns are changing in the answer choices, so the question is testing precision and consistency of pronouns. A pronoun must be consistent in number and gender with the noun it is replacing. Two pronouns are at issue here: in the context of the paragraph, only one singular female noun is introduced, so *she* clearly refers to Natasha, but there are several plural nouns to which *their* and *them* might be referring. Because the plural pronouns are imprecise, eliminate (C) and (D). Choice (B) leaves unclear what kind of *production* Natasha is undertaking; the added word *matryoshka* makes (A) more precise, so eliminate (B). The correct answer is (A).

64. **F** Note the question! The question asks which choice *most clearly builds on the information provided earlier in the sentence about the relationship of the dolls' structure to their name*, so it is testing consistency and precision. The beginning of the sentence explains that *all the dolls in a set except the smallest are hollow*, and that each set features *"daughter" dolls nesting inside one another*. Choice (F) relates the dolls' *name* to the *Russian word for "mother,"* which builds on the description of the successively smaller dolls as *"daughter"* dolls, so keep (F). The focus of (G) is on the gender of the figures painted on the dolls, which doesn't relate *the dolls' structure to their name*, so eliminate (G). Choice (H) describes *the plural of* matryoshka, so it provides more information about the dolls' name, but it does not mention anything related to *the dolls' structure*, so eliminate (H). Choice (J) focuses on *the dolls' structure*, clarifying that *the largest* matryoshka *doll is the one most people see*, but it does not mention *their name*, so eliminate (J). The correct answer is (F).

65. **D** Commas and pronouns are changing in the answer choices, so the question is testing the four ways to use a comma and modifiers. In (B), the phrase *travel played a key role* is complete, so it would need to be joined by a comma plus a FANBOY. There is no comma in (B), so eliminate it. In (A), (C), and (D), commas surround a phrase, indicating that is it unnecessary. The phrase is next to *one possiblility,* so the phrase must modify or further describe the possibility. *In which* is the proper phrase to introduce a description of something. The correct answer is (D).

66. **G** Verbs are changing in the answer choices, so the question is testing consistency of verbs. A verb must be consistent with its subject and with the other verbs in the sentence. This sentence is presenting two options: the *development of a similar doll* either *resulted from* the exchange or *perhaps simply* happened at the same time. To be consistent, the underlined verb must be in the same form

as *resulted*. Choices (F), (H), and (J) are not consistent with the other verb in the sentence, so eliminate them. The correct answer is (G).

67. **C** Verbs are changing in the answer choices, so the question is testing consistency of verbs. A verb must be consistent with its subject and with the other verbs in the sentence. The subject of the underlined verb in this sentence is *lathes*, which is a plural noun; to be consistent, the correct answer must also be plural. Eliminate (A) and (D) because *was used* and *has been used* are singular verbs. The verb in (B), *used*, creates an incomplete idea in the sentence. Eliminate (B). The correct answer is (C).

68. **J** Note the question! The question asks for the *best placement for the underlined portion*, so it's testing consistency of ideas. The underlined portion is a modifying phrase, so it should be placed as close as possible to the word it is modifying. The parenthetical is modifying *objects*, so eliminate (F), (G), and (H). The correct answer is (J).

69. **D** Commas are changing in the answer choices, so the question is testing the four ways to use a comma. The phrase *curved surfaces* is not unnecessary information, so it should not be surrounded by commas: eliminate (A). Including a comma after *surfaces* creates STOP punctuation in the form of comma plus FANBOYS, but the idea after the *and* is incomplete. Eliminate (B). The remaining two answer choices are testing where a comma should be placed when a noun is modified by two adjectives—in this case, *smooth* and *curved*. The comma should go between the adjectives, not after them, so eliminate (C). The correct answer is (D).

70. **F** Note the question! The question asks which choice *best maintains the stylistic pattern of descriptions* in the sentence, so it's testing consistency. Earlier in the sentence, the descriptions are *fantastical fairy tales, politicians of great power*, and *revered religious figures*, so the correct answer should include a noun and at least one specific adjective or descriptive phrase. Choice (F), *iconic works of art*, maintains the pattern of pairing a specific adjective (*iconic*) with a noun (*works of art*), so keep (F). Choice (G), *art*, does not maintain the pattern because it is too brief, so eliminate (G). Choice (H), *famous artworks that are imitated*, breaks with the pattern by adding a verb to the description, so eliminate (H). Choice (J), *some famous artworks*, describes both the quality (*famous*) and the quantity (*some*) of the artworks, which is not consistent with the pattern of descriptions; eliminate (J). The correct answer is (F).

71. **B** Note the question! The question asks whether the vocabulary should be changed, so it's testing precision of word choice. The vocabulary should be changed if the new word will be more precise. *Handicrafts* are "objects made by hand," which is consistent with the paragraph's earlier description of the dolls' being made on *lathes operated by local workers* and later *hand-painted*. *Goods* means "things that are for sale," which is a much more general term. Because *handicrafts* is more precise, the vocabulary should be changed: eliminate (C) and (D). The revision does not further explain *why there is so much variation in the decorations* on *matryoshka* dolls, so eliminate (A). The revision does *emphasize the handmade nature of the dolls*. The correct answer is (B).

72.   **G**   Transitions are changing in the answer choices, so the question is testing consistency of ideas. Select the phrase that correctly connects the ideas. The previous sentence explains that Natasha's *skills offer a means of engaging with her community*, and the next sentence describes *a workshop in which she instructs and collaborates with students*. The new sentence is in agreement with the previous sentence and is providing an example of how Natasha's skills facilitate community engagement, so the correct answer must reflect that relationship between the ideas. *Instead* indicates that the two ideas are in opposition to one another, so (F) is not consistent with the relationship between the ideas; eliminate (F). Choice (G) does not introduce a specific directional transition, so the second idea appears as the logical continuation of the first idea; keep (G). *In fact* suggests that the second idea is counterintuitive or unexpected, which is not consistent with the *workshop* acting as an example of *engaging with her community*, so eliminate (H). *Nevertheless* indicates that Natasha *runs a workshop* in spite of her engagement with the community, which is not consistent with the ideas of the sentences, so eliminate (J). The correct answer is (G).

73.   **C**   Note the question! The question asks which choice *most clearly and concisely indicates that Natasha and her students mutually benefit from selling the* matryoshka *dolls they produce together*, so it's testing concision and precision. Choices (A), *profits*, and (D), *money*, do not clearly indicate what is being sold, so eliminate (A) and (D). Choice (B) describes the *money* as something *she earns*, which suggests that only Natasha earns money *from doll-making*, so eliminate (B). Choice (C) may be the wordiest answer, but its reference to *workshop-made dolls* makes it the only choice that is consistent with the idea that Natasha and her students share profits generated from dolls *they produce together*. The correct answer is (C).

74.   **F**   Note the question! The question asks which statement *would best build on the ideas* of the paragraph and *connect to the final sentence of the essay*, so it's testing consistency of ideas. The paragraph is describing how Natasha's workshop is *a means of engaging with her community* where she *instructs and collaborates with students*, and the final sentence of the passage connects Natasha's workshop to the possibility that the *folk tradition of* matryoshka *may well last for generations more*. Choice (F) states that two of Natasha's *students have even gone on to establish their own doll businesses*, which is consistent with the description of the workshop and the positive influence of the workshop on the future of the tradition; keep (F). Choice (G) explains that two of Natasha's relatives *are also associated with her workshop*, which builds on the description of the workshop but does not connect the workshop's composition to the future of *matryoshka*-making; eliminate (G). Eliminate (H) because it does not mention Natasha's workshop; instead, it describes a general phenomenon in which *people are surprised and delighted* by the different designs found on *more recently made* matryoshka *dolls*. Choice (J) focuses on the characteristic designs in *Natasha's work*, not on the workshop or the future production of *matryoshka* dolls, so eliminate (J). The correct answer is (F).

75.   **D**   Apostrophes are changing in the answer choices, so the question is testing apostrophe usage. The underlined phrase describes the tradition of *matryoshka* dolls as being so old that it has lasted through multiple generations. When used with a noun, on the ACT, an apostrophe indicates possession. Because generations are not possessing anything, no apostrophe is needed: eliminate (A), (B), and (C). The correct answer is (D).

MATH TEST

1.   **C**   The question asks for the probability that the child selects a cherry jellybean. Probability is defined as $probability = \dfrac{part}{whole}$. The question states that the probability of selecting a grape jellybean is $\dfrac{7}{23}$ and the probability of selecting a grape or a cherry jellybean is $\dfrac{13}{23}$. The probability of one of two or more events occurring is the sum of the individual probabilities of each event. To find the probability of selecting a cherry jellybean, take the total probability and subtract the probability of selecting a grape jellybean: $P_{grape} + P_{cherry} = P_{grape\ or\ cherry}$; $\dfrac{7}{23} + x = \dfrac{13}{23}$; $x = \dfrac{13}{23} - \dfrac{7}{23} = \dfrac{6}{23}$. The correct answer is (C).

2.   **K**   The question asks for the probability that a child selected at random from the children at the party will be 7 years old. Probability is defined as $probability = \dfrac{part}{whole}$. To find the numerator, refer to the x-axis of the graph and locate the age 7. The y-axis provides the number of children, which is 8. Put this number in the numerator. To find the denominator, add up the total numbers of 6-, 7-, 8-, and 9-year-olds, which are 5, 8, 4, and 7, respectively. This will go in the denominator: $P = \dfrac{7\ year\ olds}{total\ children} = \dfrac{8}{5+8+4+7} = \dfrac{8}{24} = \dfrac{1}{3}$. The correct answer is (K).

3.   **B**   The question asks for the value of p when q is 21. The question provides the equation $q = \dfrac{5}{3}p + 46$. Plug 21 in for q, and solve for p: $(21) = \dfrac{5}{3}p + 46$. Then $21 - 46 = \dfrac{5}{3}p$ or $-25 = \dfrac{5}{3}p$. Multiply both sides by 3 to get $-75 = 5p$, and then divide both sides by 5 to get $-15 = p$. The correct answer is (B).

4.   **J**   The question asks for the value of $|2 + y|$ when $y = -6$. First ballpark out (F), (G), and (H) since the result must be positive or zero. Plug -6 in for y and simplify: $|2 + (-6)| = |-4| = 4$. The correct answer is (J).

5.   **E**   The question asks for the difference, in inches, in the yearly rainfall from 2015 to 2016. The question states that the total rainfall in Central City in 2015 was 13 inches less than the total annual rainfall in 2000, and the total rainfall in Central City in 2016 was 33 inches greater than the total annual rainfall in 2000. Use this data, along with the statement that + indicates an increase in

rainfall and – indicates a decrease in rainfall, to calculate the difference: yearly rainfall 2016 minus yearly rainfall 2015 = (+33) – (–13) = 33 + 13 = +46. The correct answer is (E).

6. **H** The question asks for the difference between the total amount Ruben pays for the violin, including the initial payment and the credit card payments, and the sale price of the violin. The question states that the violin has a total price of $1,250, which includes tax and all other fees. To find the total amount that Ruben pays, add the initial payment of $300 to the 9 monthly payments of $150: $300 + 9($150) = $300 + $1,350 = $1,650. Subtract the sale price of the violin from the total amount that Ruben pays to arrive at the difference: $1,650 – $1,250 = $400. The correct answer is (H).

7. **C** The question asks for the perimeter of $\triangle ABC$. The question states that the regular hexagon has a perimeter of 30. A regular hexagon means that all sides are equal in length, so find the length of each side by dividing the perimeter by the number of sides: side length = $\dfrac{30}{6}$ = 5. In a regular hexagon, when two lines are extended from the center to the vertices to create a triangle, that triangle is an equilateral triangle with equal side lengths and equal angle measures. Since $AB = 5$, AC and BC must also equal 5. Find the perimeter of the triangle by adding the three side lengths together: 5 + 5 + 5 = 15. The correct answer is (C).

8. **H** The question asks for the area of the driveway in square feet. The provided figure is not a familiar shape with a formula, but it can be carved up into two individual rectangles. Extend the line labeled 17 over to the left side labeled 14, creating an upper rectangle with a length of 25 and a width of 9. The area of a rectangle can be calculated by $A = l \times w$, so the area of the upper rectangle is $A = (25) \times (9) = 225$. At this point, (F) and (G) can safely be ballparked out. To calculate the area of the lower rectangle, the dimensions need to be calculated. To find the length, use the length of the upper rectangle and subtract the opposite side length of 17: 25 – 17 = 8. To find the width, use the width of the upper rectangle and subtract it from the opposite side length of 14: 14 – 9 = 5. Calculate the area of the lower rectangle: $A = (8) \times (5) = 40$. Find the total area of the driveway by adding the individual areas: 225 + 40 = 265. The correct answer is (H).

9. **A** The question asks for the possible coordinates of the fourth vertex of the parallelogram. A parallelogram is a 4-sided figure that has opposite sides that are parallel. Use the given xy-plane to sketch out the given points and ballpark. The fourth coordinate must be near the x-axis around 2 or 3, so eliminate (C), (D), and (E). For the opposite sides, or lines, to be parallel, they must have the same slope. Use $slope = \dfrac{rise}{run}$ to count up-and-over from the upper left coordinate to the upper right coordinate, a rise of 1 and a run of 5. To find the fourth vertex, count up-and-over the same increments from the lower left coordinate. The new y-coordinate becomes –1 + 1 = 0. At this point, (B) can safely be eliminated. The new x-coordinate becomes –3 + 5 = 2. The correct answer is (A).

10. **F** The question asks for the value of $m(n(x))$ when $x = 9$. For calculations involving compound functions, start with the inner function and work outward. The inner function is $n(x)$, and the question provides that $n(x) = \dfrac{\sqrt{x}}{3}$, so plug 9 in for x and calculate the value: $n(9) = \dfrac{\sqrt{9}}{3} = \dfrac{3}{3} = 1$. The question also provides $m(x) = 2x - 2$, so use that in conjunction with $n(9) = 1$ to calculate the final value: $m(n(9)) = m(1) = 2(1) - 2 = 2 - 2 = 0$. The correct answer is (F).

11. **D** The question asks for the inequality that includes all possible values of n. The question states that the total cost of the supplies and the booth rental is \$150. Maria sells n holiday cards for \$3 each and makes a profit. Use bite-sized pieces to translate and set up an inequality. For Maria to make a profit, the total sales of cards, \$3 × n, must be greater than the total cost, or \$150: $3n > 150$. Subtract 150 from both sides to match an answer choice: $3n - 150 > 0$. Alternatively, plug in values of n to see which values will allow Maria to make a profit. The correct answer is (D).

12. **H** The question asks for the slope of the provided line. When given a line in the standard form of $Ax + By = C$, the slope is equal to $-\dfrac{A}{B}$. The provided line is $5x - 11y = 7$, so $A = 5$ and $B = -11$. Plug these values in, paying close attention to any sign changes, to get $slope = -\dfrac{A}{B} = -\dfrac{5}{(-11)} = \dfrac{5}{11}$. Alternatively, the equation could be rewritten in slope-intercept form, $y = mx + b$, where m is the slope. The correct answer is (H).

13. **B** The question asks for the coordinates of A, the point of intersection of two lines. The question provides that $x + 3y = 6$ and $-5x + y = 18$. When two lines intersect at a point, they are equal at that point. All the given points have different x-coordinates, so solve the system of equations for x. Multiply the second equation by -3 to get $15x - 3y = -54$. Now stack the equations and add them together and the y-values will disappear.

$$
\begin{array}{rcr}
x + 3y & = & 6 \\
15x - 3y & = & -54 \\
\hline
16x \quad\;\; & = & -48
\end{array}
$$

Divide both sides by 16 to get $x = -3$. Alternatively, PITA could be used as the question is asking for a specific value. The correct answer is (B).

14. **J** The question asks for the length, in meters, of the hallway in the finished building. The question states that in a blueprint, $\dfrac{1}{3}$ centimeter represents 9 meters in the finished building. The question also states that the hallway shown on the blueprint is $4\dfrac{2}{3}$ centimeters long. Convert $4\dfrac{2}{3}$ to an improper fraction to make it easier to work with: $4\dfrac{2}{3} = 4 + \dfrac{2}{3} = \dfrac{12}{3} + \dfrac{2}{3} = \dfrac{14}{3}$. Set up a proportion using the provided conversion of centimeters to meters, making sure to keep consistent units in

the numerators and denominators: $\dfrac{\frac{1}{3}\ \text{centimeter}}{9\ \text{meters}} = \dfrac{\frac{14}{3}\ \text{centimeters}}{x\ \text{meters}}$. Cross multiply and solve for x:

$\frac{1}{3}x = \left(\frac{14}{3}\right)(9)$, so $x = (3)\left(\frac{14}{3}\right)(9)$, or $x = 126$ meters. The correct answer is (J).

15. **C** The question asks for an equivalent matrix to the provided matrix. The provided matrix, $\begin{bmatrix} 2 & -1 \\ 3 & 0 \end{bmatrix}$,

is multiplied by 3, so distribute the 3 to each term inside the matrix to get $\begin{bmatrix} 3(2) & 3(-1) \\ 3(3) & 3(0) \end{bmatrix} =$

$\begin{bmatrix} 6 & -3 \\ 9 & 0 \end{bmatrix}$. The correct answer is (C).

16. **F** The question asks for the value of $\cos Z$ in right triangle XYZ. According to SOHCAHTOA,

$\text{cosine} = \dfrac{adjacent}{hypotenuse}$. The side adjacent to Z is 7, and the hypotenuse is 25, so $\cos Z = \dfrac{7}{25}$. The correct

answer is (F).

17. **B** The question asks for how many inches the snail will travel in 5 seconds. The question states that

the snail travels 7 inches in one minute, but the question asks about seconds. Use the conversion

of 1 minute = 60 seconds and set up a proportion, making sure to keep consistent units in numera-

tors and denominators: $\dfrac{7\ \text{inches}}{60\ \text{seconds}} = \dfrac{x\ \text{inches}}{5\ \text{seconds}}$. Cross multiply to solve for x: $(7)(5) = (60)(x)$, so

$\dfrac{(7)(5)}{60} = x$, and $x = \dfrac{7}{12}$ inches. The correct answer is (B).

18. **F** The question asks for the value of $g(-8)$. The question provides that $g(x) = -\dfrac{x^2}{4}$, which will be

negative whether x is positive or negative. Eliminate (J) and (K). To find the exact value of $g(-8)$,

plug -8 in for x, paying close attention to any sign changes. The function becomes $g(-8) = -\dfrac{(-8)^2}{4}$

$= -\dfrac{(64)}{4} = -16$. The correct answer is (F).

19. **C** The question asks for the measure of $\angle TQR$. The angle is clearly obtuse (greater than 90°), so

eliminate (A). The figure provides a large right triangle, $\triangle PRS$, and a small right triangle, $\triangle PQT$.

In $\triangle PQT$, two of the three angles are known. Since there are 180° in a triangle, solve for the

third angle: $90° + 37° + \angle PQT = 180°$, so $127° + \angle PQT = 180°$, and $\angle PQT = 53°$. Since $\overline{PR}$ is a

straight line, and a straight line has 180°, use $\angle PQT$ to arrive at $\angle TQR$: $\angle TQR + \angle PQT = 180°$, so

$\angle TQR + 53° = 180°$, and $\angle TQR = 127°$. The correct answer is (C).

20. **K** The question asks for the expression that could be the equation of the line described. The question

states that when $x = 3$, $y = 8$, and when $x = 7$, $y = 20$. This information provides the coordinates of

$(3, 8)$ and $(7, 20)$, so the slope can be calculated using $slope = \dfrac{y_2 - y_1}{x_2 - x_1}$: $slope = \dfrac{20 - 8}{7 - 3} = \dfrac{12}{4} = 3$.

The answer choices are provided in slope-intercept form, $y = mx + b$, where m is the slope. Therefore,

(F), (G), (H), and (J) can be eliminated for not matching the calculated slope of 3. The correct answer is (K).

21. **D** The question asks for the time that the park ranger will first record a height over 14 feet. The question states that on Sunday at 7:00 P.M., the river was at a height of 14 feet and that the river height fell at a rate of 1.5 feet per day from Sunday, 7:00 P.M., to Thursday, 7:00 P.M., or 4 days. Calculate the total decrease in height: (4 days) × (1.5 feet per day) = 6 feet. This means on Thursday, at 7:00 P.M., the river height was 14 − 6 = 8 feet. The question then states that heavy rains caused the water to rise at a constant rate of 3 feet per day. So, from Thursday, 7:00 P.M., to Friday, 7:00 P.M., the new height would be 8 + 3 = 11 feet, and (A) can be eliminated. From Friday, 7:00 P.M., to Saturday, 7:00 P.M., the new height would be 11 + 3 = 14 feet. However, the question asks for a time *over* 14 feet, so (B) and (C) can be eliminated. The first time the park ranger records a height of over 14 will be the next time the park rangers checks, which will be the next day at 7:00 A.M., so the correct answer is (D).

22. **H** The question asks for a possible value of p for which Viviana would earn a white ribbon. The question states that p represents the combined total of the points that Viviana receives from the final two judges, and the first three judges award her scores of 37, 46, and 49. According to the table, to get a white ribbon, the range of $40 \leq A < 50$ is needed. Since the question is asking for a specific value, p, PITA will be helpful in solving. Label the answers as p and start with (H), 98. If the final two judges provided a total of 98, calculate the average using the equation $T = AN$. The *Total* is 37 + 46 + 49 + 98 = 230, and the *Number of things* is 5 for the 5 judges. The equation becomes 230 = A(5). Divide both sides by 5 to get 46, which qualifies for a white ribbon. The correct answer is (H).

23. **B** The question asks for the approximate area of the pool's surface, in square meters, that the double stranded lane line occupies. Since the question asks for an approximation, and the answers are fairly spread apart, Ballparking can be helpful in solving. The accompanying information states that each strand of the lane line consists of 20 spherical buoys, and the question states that each buoy in the lane line has a diameter of 1.25 meters. The double-stranded lane line is approximately in the shape of a rectangle, and the area can be found by $A = l \times w$. The length of the lane line is the same as the length of the pool, 25 meters. The width of the lane line can be found by doubling the diameter: 1.25 × 2 = 2.5 meters. Calculate the approximate area of the double stranded lane line: $A = 25 \times 2.5 = 62.5$, so (C), (D), and (E) can be eliminated. Since this represents the area of a complete rectangle, and the spherical buoys will fill most of the rectangle, pick the largest remaining answer. The correct answer is (B).

24. **F** The question asks for the ratio of the area of the surface of the lap swimming portion (including the lane line) to the area of the surface of the free swim portion. Use bite-sized pieces to tackle this question. Begin with the lap swimming portion with measurements of 25 m by 6 m and calculate the area: $A = l \times w$, so $A = 25 \times 6$. Next, find the area of the free swim portion with dimensions of 25 m by 14 m: $A = l \times w$, so $A = 25 \times 14$. Finally, find the ratio and reduce. Lap swimming:free swimming is (25 × 6):(25 × 14), which can be divided by 25 to get 6:14 and then reduced by 2 to 3:7. Alternatively, since the width is the same for both, simply compare the lengths to get 6:14 or 3:7. The correct answer is (F).

25. **B** The question asks for the time, in seconds, that it takes the fourth member to finish his lap. The question states that the relay team finishes with an average of 60 seconds per person, and the accompanying information states that the first three members of the team complete their laps in 63, 65, and 59 seconds, respectively. To get an average of 60 seconds, the 4th member must have a time that is less than 60 seconds, so (D) and (E) can be eliminated. When the question asks for a specific value, PITA can be helpful with solving. Label the answers as 4th swimmer and start with the middle of the remaining answers, (B), which is 53. Calculate the average of the four members using this value and the equation $T = AN$. The *Total* is $63 + 65 + 59 + 53 = 240$, and the *Number of things* is 4 for the 4 swimmers. The equation becomes $240 = A(4)$. Divide both sides by 4 to get $A = 60$ seconds. The correct answer is (B).

26. **G** The question asks for the length of the rectangle. When the question asks for a specific value, PITA can be helpful with solving. Label the answers as length and start with (H), 12. The question states that the width is twice its length, so $w = 12 \times 2 = 24$. The area is $A = l \times w = 12 \times 24 = 288$. This is larger than the required area of 72, so eliminate (H), (J), and (K). Check (G) next. If the length is 6, then the width is $6 \times 2 = 12$. The area is $A = 6 \times 12 = 72$. The correct answer is (G).

27. **A** The question asks for the length of side $\overline{BC}$, if it can be determined. The question states that side $\overline{AB}$ has a length of 12, and the total perimeter of the parallelogram is 64. Perimeter can be found by adding the lengths of all sides together. Parallelograms have opposite sides that are not only parallel, but also equal in length. Therefore, the length of side $\overline{BC}$ can be determined, and (E) can be eliminated. Use the provided information to calculate the length of side $\overline{BC}$: $P = 12 + 12 + x + x = 64$, or $24 + 2x = 64$. Therefore, $2x = 40$, and $x = 20$. The correct answer is (A).

28. **J** The question asks for the total width of the pedestrian bridge. The question states that on each side of the pedestrian bridge, there is a 16-foot-wide lane for foot traffic, a 10-foot-wide lane for browsing and purchasing, and a 9-foot-wide row of wooden vendor stalls. Since these are on each side, each number can be doubled and added together to get the total width: $2(16) + 2(10) + 2(9) = 32 + 20 + 18 = 70$ feet. The correct answer is (J).

29. **B** The question asks for the number of households in Culver City that are dog owners with fenced-in backyards. Use bite-sized pieces to help tackle this question. The question states that there are 720 households, and 5 out of every 12, or $\frac{5}{12}$, own a dog. Calculate the number of households that own a dog: $720 \times \frac{5}{12} = 300$ households. The question then states that 6 out of every 10, or $\frac{6}{10}$, households that own a dog have a fenced-in backyard. Calculate the number of dog-owning households that have fenced-in backyards: $300 \times \frac{6}{10} = 180$ households. The correct answer is (B).

30. **G** The question asks for the value of sin x. The question states that tan $x = -\frac{7}{24}$ and provides a restriction of $\frac{3\pi}{2} < x < 2\pi$. That restriction puts the angle in Quadrant IV, making the sine and tangent negative. Eliminate (H), (J), and (K). Because tan $= \frac{opposite}{adjacent}$, let opposite be 7 and adjacent be 24.

The question asks for sine, which is $\dfrac{opposite}{hypotenuse}$. Both remaining choices have 25 as the hypotenuse. However, only (G) has *opposite* equal to 7, so eliminate (F). The correct answer is (G).

31. **D** The question asks for the value of x that makes $g(x) = h(x)$. When the question asks for a specific value, PITA can be helpful with solving. The answers contain repetitive elements, so label the answers as x and start by checking $x = 1$. The question provides that $g(n) = \dfrac{-3}{n+2}$, so calculate $g(x)$, or $g(1) = \dfrac{-3}{(1)+2} = \dfrac{-3}{3} = -1$. Next, check that the same value is obtained in $h(n) = -n$. Calculate $h(x)$, or $h(1) = -(1) = -1$. Since $g(1) = h(1)$, the correct answer must contain 1. Choices (B) and (C) can be eliminated. Next, check $x = -3$ in the same manner: $g(-3) = \dfrac{-3}{(-3)+2} = \dfrac{-3}{-1} = 3$ and $h(-3) = -(-3) = 3$. These are also equal, and now (A) and (E) can be eliminated. Alternatively, the equations could have been set equal and solved algebraically. The correct answer is (D).

32. **G** The question asks for the length of the proposed road segment connecting points W and Z. In right triangle WYZ, the length of $\overline{WY}$ is 5 miles, and the length of $\overline{YZ}$ is 13 miles. Recognize that this is a common Pythagorean triple of 5-12-13, or use the Pythagorean Theorem to calculate the length of the proposed road: $a^2 + b^2 = c^2$, so $(5)^2 + b^2 = (13)^2$, and $25 + b^2 = 169$. Therefore, $b^2 = 144$, and $b = 12$ miles. The correct answer is (G).

33. **A** The question asks for the equation that would represent the line along which the proposed road would be drawn in the standard (x, y) coordinate plane. Since the proposed road is horizontal, the y-coordinate remains constant, and the equation would be "$y =$", not "$x =$". Choices (C), (D), and (E) can safely be eliminated. The question states that the coordinates of X and Y in the coordinate plane are $(0, 0)$ and $(0, 14)$, respectively. The proposed road begins at point W. The accompanying information states that point W is located 5 miles south of point Y, so the y-coordinate of point W is $14 - 5 = 9$. The correct answer is (A).

34. **H** The question asks for the time, in minutes, that it will take the car to reach the point due east of the library at point Y. The question states that a car located at point Z is driving due north on Route 2 at 20 miles per hour. To solve for time, use the formula *distance = rate × time*. The distance the car needs to travel north is 5 miles. Plug in the rate and the distance to solve for time: $5 = 20 \times t$, so $t = \dfrac{5}{20} = \dfrac{1}{4}$ hour. To find the time in minutes, convert using 60 minutes = 1 hour: $\dfrac{1}{4}(60) = 15$ minutes. The correct answer is (H).

35. **D** The question asks for which of the statements describe how the measures of $\angle X$, $\angle Y$, and $\angle Z$ will be adjusted. The question states that a city planner suggests that the proposed road be located farther south, and that points W and Z both be relocated exactly three miles south of their current locations. Visual inspection could be used to credit or discredit the statements, or, if needed, the figure can be redrawn to help see the changes in the angles. Consider statement (I): if the pro-

posed road is moved south, then $\angle X$ will open, increasing in measure. Since statement (I) is true, (B) and (C) can be eliminated. Consider statement (II): if the proposed road is moved south, then $\angle Y$ will close, decreasing in measure. Since statement (II) is true, (A) can be eliminated. Consider statement (III): moving the proposed road south would change $\angle Z$. If the proposed road was half-way between the town hall and library, $\angle Z$ would be at its widest, and then moving the road south of this would decrease the angle again. Since $\angle Z$ would change, statement (III) is false, and (E) can be eliminated. The correct answer is (D).

36. **H** The question asks for the length, in feet, of the new rug. Tackle this question in bite-sized pieces to help with solving. The question states that Christa has a rectangular rug with dimensions 6 by 8 and orders a new one that covers twice as much area. Calculate the area of the current rug: $A = l \times w$, so $A = 8 \times 6 = 48$. This means that the area of the new rug must be $48 \times 2 = 96$. Since the question asks for a specific value, PITA can be helpful with solving. Label the answers as length, and start with (H), $10\frac{2}{3}$. First, rewrite $10\frac{2}{3}$ as $\frac{32}{3}$ and use it with the area formula to calculate the new width: $96 = \left(\frac{32}{3}\right)w$, or $w = 96\left(\frac{3}{32}\right) = 3(3) = 9$. The question states that the width of the new rug is 1.5 times the width of the original rug. Check whether 9 is 1.5 times 6: $6(1.5) = 9$. The correct answer is (H).

37. **A** The question asks for the value of x that makes the equation true. When the question asks for a specific value, PITA can be helpful with solving. Label the answers as x, and start with (C), 2. Plug $x = 2$ into the provided equation to check if it's valid: $4[(2) - 2] - 3(2) = (2) + 2$ simplifies to $4(0) - 6 = 4$, or $-6 = 4$. Since $x = 2$ is not a solution, (C) and (E) can be eliminated. Check (B), $x = 3$: $4[(3) - 2] - 3(3) = (3) + 2$ simplifies to $4(1) - 9 = 5$ or $-5 = 5$. Since $x = 3$ is not a solution, (B) can be eliminated. Check (D), $x = -1$: $4[(-1) - 2] - 3(-1) = (-1) + 2$ simplifies to $4(-3) + 3 = 1$ or $-9 = 1$. Since $x = -1$ is not a solution, (D) can be eliminated. Alternatively, the equation can be solved algebraically to arrive at an untrue statement proving no solutions. The correct answer is (A).

38. **H** The question asks for the maximum amount of space, in square inches, that the teacher can reserve on her bulletin board using the roll of string. When a question asks for a specific value, PITA can be helpful with solving. However, in this case, there are too many possible values for the lengths of the sides to use the answer choices. Instead, use the perimeter of 40 to determine the possible side lengths and the resulting areas. One possible set of dimensions for the rectangle is 2 inches by 18 inches, with an area of 36. Another possibility is a rectangle that is 4 by 16 inches, with an area of 64. As the values for the length and width get closer together, the area increases. If the dimensions of the rectangle were 10 by 10 inches, the area would be 100. No other combination of side lengths would result in a greater area. The correct answer is (H).

39. **D** The question asks which, of the mean, median, standard deviation, and range, will increase the most. Since the question describes a relationship, plugging in can be helpful with solving. The question states that 8 homes each are valued somewhere between $250,000 and $350,000. Each of the homes could be valued the exact same (like $300,000). From this set, determine the required data. The mean (average) would be $\frac{8(\$300,000)}{8}$ = $300,000, and the median would be the average of the middle two elements, or $\frac{\$300,000+\$300,000}{2}$ = $300,000. The standard deviation, or spread of data, would be zero since the values are the exact same, and the range would be $300,000 – $300,000 = $0. If two more houses are built on the street, say the lower priced one is $90,000 and the higher priced one is $2,100,000; then the required data can be calculated from the new set of $90,000, $300,000, $300,000, $300,000, $300,000, $300,000, $300,000, $300,000, $300,000, and $2,100,000. The average of the set would be $\frac{\$90,000+8(\$300,000)+\$2,100,000}{10}$ = $\frac{\$4,590,000}{10}$ = $459,000. This makes an increase in the average of $459,000 – $300,000 = $159,000. The median would be the exact same since the middle two elements didn't change, so (B) can be eliminated. The range would be $2,100,000 – $90,000 = $2,010,000, which is a larger increase than the average, so (C) can be eliminated. The standard deviation would change some with the new set, but there are still a lot of numbers grouped close to the mean. The standard deviation would not change as much as the range, so (A) can be eliminated. The correct answer is (D).

40. **H** The question asks how many hours it will take the third employee to finish painting the remainder of the house by himself. The question states that all three employees paint at the same rate. Use the equation *work* = *rate* × *time* with the first employee to determine the rate: $w = r \times t$, so $\frac{3}{7} = r \times 4$, and $r = \left(\frac{3}{7}\right)\left(\frac{1}{4}\right) = \frac{3}{28}$ of the house painted per hour. The next step is to figure out how much of the house remains to be painted. Add the completed portions of the first two employees to figure out how much is completed: $\frac{3}{7} + \frac{1}{4} = \frac{12}{28} + \frac{7}{28} = \frac{19}{28}$. The amount of the house that is left to be painted is $1 - \frac{19}{28} = \frac{28}{28} - \frac{19}{28} = \frac{9}{28}$. Knowing how much work is left to do, and the rate of the employee, solve for time: $\frac{9}{28} = \frac{3}{28} \times t$, so $t = \frac{9}{28} \times \frac{28}{3} = \frac{9}{3}$ = 3 hours. The correct answer is (H).

41. **A** The question asks for an equivalent expression to the provided expression. Use bite-sized pieces, MADSPM rules, and POE to tackle this question. Start with the numbers first: $\dfrac{(3)^3}{(1)^{-2}} = (3)^3(1)^2 = (27)(1) = 27$. Choices (D) and (E) can be eliminated because they don't include 27. Next, work with the variable x: $\dfrac{(x)^3}{\left(\sqrt{x}\right)^{-2}} = \dfrac{(x)^3}{\left(x^{\frac{1}{2}}\right)^{-2}} = \dfrac{x^3}{x^{-1}} = (x^3)(x) = x^4$. Choices (B) and (C) can be eliminated. The correct answer is (A).

42. **J** The question asks for the probability that the sitter enters the correct alarm code on her first attempt. Probability is defined as $probability = \dfrac{part}{whole}$. The sitter wants to get the code on the first attempt, and there is only one correct code, so the numerator will be 1. To figure out the total number of possibilities, create 4 spaces to represent the first, second, third, and fourth digits, since the sitter knows for sure what the fifth digit is. The first digit can be 2, 3, 1, or 8 for a total of 4 options, the second digit can be any of the remaining 3 digits after the first is entered, the third can be any of the remaining 2, and the fourth digit can only be the remaining 1. Multiply the determined possibilities to get the total number: $4 \times 3 \times 2 \times 1 = 24$ total possibilities. Plug the determined numbers into the probability definition: $P = \dfrac{1}{24}$. The correct answer is (J).

43. **B** The question asks for an equivalent expression to the provided expression. When the question and answers contain variables, plugging in can be helpful with solving. Choose an easy number for a, like $a = 3$. The expression becomes $\dfrac{\frac{1}{3} - \frac{1}{2}}{\frac{1}{3} + \frac{(3)}{4}} = \dfrac{\frac{2}{6} - \frac{3}{6}}{\frac{4}{12} + \frac{9}{12}} = \dfrac{-\frac{1}{6}}{\frac{13}{12}} = -\dfrac{1}{6} \times \dfrac{12}{13} = -\dfrac{2}{13}$. Circle $-\dfrac{2}{13}$ as the target value and check the answers using $a = 3$ to see what matches. Choice (A) can be eliminated as it is not a fraction, so check (B): $\dfrac{-2}{4+3(3)} = \dfrac{-2}{4+9} = -\dfrac{2}{13}$. Keep (B) for now and check the other answers just in case. Choice (C) becomes $\dfrac{4}{3+2(3)} = \dfrac{4}{3+6} = \dfrac{4}{9}$ and can be eliminated. Choice (D) becomes $\dfrac{-2}{3+3(3)} = \dfrac{-2}{3+9} = \dfrac{-2}{12}$ and can be eliminated. Choice (E) becomes $\dfrac{2}{3(3)} = \dfrac{2}{9}$ and can be eliminated. Alternatively, the expression could have been manipulated algebraically to arrive at the same result. The correct answer is (B).

44. **J** The question asks for the maximum number of books that the library can own. Use bite-sized pieces to help tackle this question. The question states that a library classifies each of its books using a 5-character code. To begin, create 5 spaces to represent each of the characters. For the first character, the question states that this is one of 15 different genres. Since there are 15 possibilities, place 15 in the first space. The question then states that the second character denotes one of 11 different subgenres, so place 11 in the second space. For the final 3 characters, the question states that they each consist of a single digit from 0 through 9, and these digits can be repeated. Since there are 10 digits total to select from, the final three spaces should each be assigned a 10. To calculate the maximum number of books, multiply the possibilities together: $\underline{15} \times \underline{11} \times \underline{10} \times \underline{10} \times \underline{10} = 165{,}000$. The correct answer is (J).

45. **B** The question asks for the possible equation for $h(x)$. Use bite-sized pieces and POE to help tackle this question. The question states that every point on $y = g(x)$ is shifted 3 units to the left. Horizontal shifts affect the x-coordinate, so the 3 must be inside the parentheses, and (C), (D), and (E) can be safely eliminated. Since the shift is left, the inside of the parentheses must be $(x + 3)$, and (A) can be eliminated. Alternatively, the vertical shift could be handled first to arrive at the same result. The correct answer is (B).

46. **H** The question asks for the value of n. When dealing with logarithms, $\log_b n = x$ means $b^x = n$ in exponential form. Rewrite the provided equation in exponential form to get $n^{-3} = \dfrac{1}{27}$. Since the question is asking for a specific value, PITA can be helpful with solving. Label the answers as n and start with (H), 3. Plug $n = 3$ into the exponential form to check: $(3)^{-3} = \dfrac{1}{27}$, or $\dfrac{1}{3^3} = \dfrac{1}{27}$, so $\dfrac{1}{27} = \dfrac{1}{27}$. The correct answer is (H).

47. **C** The question asks for the set that contains all integer values of k. When the question asks for a specific value, PITA can be helpful with solving. Label the answers as k. Since the answers contain sets with repeated values, start with a number that shows up multiple times, such as $k = 2$, and use the calculator to verify. First, $\dfrac{1}{6} = 0.1\overline{6}$ and $\dfrac{3}{4} = 0.75$. Plug $k = 2$ into $\dfrac{k}{5}$ to check if that value is between these values: $\dfrac{(2)}{5} = 0.4$. Since $k = 2$ is a possible value, (D) and (E) can be safely eliminated for not including 2. Next, check $k = 3$: $\dfrac{(3)}{5} = 0.6$. This means that 3 must be included in the set, and (A) and (B) can be eliminated. The correct answer is (C).

48. **J** The question asks for what *must* be true. Since the question and answers contain variables, plugging in can be helpful with solving. The question states that x, y, and z are real numbers. The question also provides the restrictions that $x < y < z$ and $xyz < 0$. Plug in easy numbers that qualify the

restrictions, like $x = -1$, $y = 1$, and $z = 2$, and check the answers to see which choices are true. Choice

(F) becomes $(-1)(1) < (1)(2)$, or $-1 < 2$. This is a true statement, so keep (F), but continue check-

ing. Choice (G) becomes $(-1) + (1) > (1) + (2)$, or $0 > 3$, which is not true and can be eliminated.

Choice (H) becomes $\frac{(-1)}{(1)} < \frac{(1)}{(2)}$, a true statement. Keep (H) for now. Choice (J) becomes

$(-1) < (1)(2)$, or $-1 < 2$, a true statement. Keep (J) for now. Choice (K) becomes $(-1) + (2) < (1)$,

or $1 < 1$, which is not true and can be eliminated. Since 3 answers remain, and x, y, and z are

all real numbers, plug in some fractions. Let $x = -2$, $y = -\frac{2}{3}$, and $z = -\frac{1}{3}$. Choice (F) becomes

$(-2)\left(-\frac{2}{3}\right) < \left(-\frac{2}{3}\right)\left(-\frac{1}{3}\right)$, or $\frac{4}{3} < \frac{2}{9}$, which is not true and can be eliminated. Choice (H)

becomes $\frac{(-2)}{\left(-\frac{2}{3}\right)} < \frac{\left(-\frac{2}{3}\right)}{\left(-\frac{1}{3}\right)}$, or $3 < 2$, which is not true and can be eliminated. Choice (J) becomes

$-2 < \left(-\frac{2}{3}\right)\left(-\frac{1}{3}\right)$, or $-2 < \frac{2}{9}$, a true statement. The correct answer is (J).

49. **D** The question asks for the expression that could be used to find the measure of the smallest angle in the triangle. The question states that the side lengths, x, y, and z, compare to each other by $x < y < z$. In any triangle, the smallest angle measure is directly opposite the shortest side length. Use the provided identity to plug in the information and get the expression: $c^2 = a^2 + b^2 - 2ab \cos C$ becomes $(x)^2 = (y)^2 + (z)^2 - 2(y)(z) \cos (X)$ or $x^2 - y^2 - z^2 = -2yz \cos X$. Divide both sides by $-2yz$ to get $\frac{x^2 - y^2 - z^2}{-2yz} = \cos X$. At this point, (A), (B), (C), and (E) could safely be eliminated as the expressions in the parentheses do not match. To finish, take the inverse cosine of both sides to get $\cos^{-1}\left(-\frac{x^2 - y^2 - z^2}{2yz}\right) = X$. The correct answer is (D).

50. **J** The question asks for the value of $n - p$. When the question asks about relationships between variables, plugging in can help with solving. The question states that Kyle scores an average of p points per game in his first 9 basketball games. Let $p = 2$. This means that 2 points × 9 games = 18

points scored. Because p represents Kyle's average for the first 9 games, the average is 2. The question states that Kyle's season average increases by 3 points as a result of scoring n points in his 10th game. The resulting average is now $2 + 3 = 5$. Since this represents the average for all 10 games, calculate the total points for all 10 games: $5 \times 10 = 50$. To find the number of points scored in the 10th game, n, subtract the total points in the first 9 games from the total points for all 10 games: $n = 50 - 18 = 32$. Finally, calculate the value of $n - p$ by plugging in $n = 32$ and $p = 2$: $32 - 2 = 30$. The correct answer is (J).

51. **E** The question asks for the measure of $\angle AOD$. When the question asks for a specific value, PITA can be helpful with solving. Label the answers as $\angle AOD$ and start with (C), $72°$. The question states that $\angle AOD$ is 1.5 times the measure of $\angle AOC$, so translate and solve for $\angle AOC$: $\angle AOD = 1.5 \times \angle AOC$, so $72° = 1.5 \times \angle AOC$. Divide both sides by 1.5 to get $48° = \angle AOC$. Since the two angles lie on the diameter, a straight line, the total must be $180°$, but $72° + 48° = 120°$. Since the calculated angle measure was smaller than needed, eliminate (C), (B), and (A) and check a larger angle. Check (D), $96°$, the same way: $96° = 1.5 \times \angle AOC$, so $64° = \angle AOC$. Add the two values to get $96° + 64° = 160°$, which is still not $180°$. Choice (D) can be eliminated. The correct answer is (E).

52. **F** The question asks for the equation that could define the sequence A for all positive values of n. The question states that the first term in the sequence is 6 and the third term is 72. This means that $A_1 = 6$ and $A_3 = 72$. Plug $A_1 = 6$ into each of the answer choices to get A_2 and then A_3 to see whether A_3 is 72. Start with (F). $A_2 = 3(6) + 2(2) = 22$. $A_3 = 3(22) + 2(3) = 72$. This gives the provided value of A_3, so stop here. The correct answer is (F).

53. **C** The question asks for all possible values of c that satisfy the inequality $c^{-1} < c^2 < |c|$. It may be difficult to find values that satisfy the inequality, so use the choices as a guide. None of the answer choices have overlapping ranges, so start with the most straightforward answer to plug in for. Choice (E) includes everything greater than 1, so make $c = 2$. This makes the inequality $(2)^{-1} < 2^2 < |2|$. Since $2^{-1} = \frac{1}{2}$ and $2^2 = 4$, the first part of the inequality works. However, $|2| = 2$, so the inequality as a whole is false. Eliminate (E). Next, try (A). Make $c = -3$. The inequality becomes $(-3)^{-1} < (-3)^2 < |-3|$, which is $-\frac{1}{3} < 9 < 3$. This is false; eliminate (A). The remaining answers require using fractions. Try (D). Make $c = \frac{1}{2}$. The inequality becomes $\left(\frac{1}{2}\right)^{-1} < \left(\frac{1}{2}\right)^2 < \left|\frac{1}{2}\right|$, or $2 < \frac{1}{4} < \frac{1}{2}$. This is false; eliminate (D). Try (C). Make $c = -\frac{1}{2}$. The inequality becomes $\left(-\frac{1}{2}\right)^{-1} < \left(-\frac{1}{2}\right)^2 < \left|-\frac{1}{2}\right|$, or $-2 < \frac{1}{4} < \frac{1}{2}$.

This is true; keep (C). Finally, try (B). Make $c = -\dfrac{3}{2}$. The inequality becomes $\left(\dfrac{3}{2}\right)^{-1} < \left(\dfrac{3}{2}\right)^{2} < \left|\dfrac{3}{2}\right|$, or $-\dfrac{2}{3} < \dfrac{9}{4} < \dfrac{3}{2}$. This is false; eliminate (B). Only one answer remains. The correct answer is (C).

54.　**K**　The question asks for the expected value of P, the number of points the contestant earns on a single marble draw. The question states that there is a total of 6 marbles: 3 green marbles worth 6 points each, 2 purple marbles worth 3 points each, and 1 yellow marble worth 0 points. To calculate the estimated value of an outcome, use $P =$ (Probability of Outcome 1)(Value of Outcome 1) + (Probability of Outcome 2)(Value of Outcome 2) + … for as many outcomes as needed. Calculate the individual probabilities using $P = \dfrac{part}{whole}$: Green $= \dfrac{3}{6} = \dfrac{1}{2}$, Purple $= \dfrac{2}{6} = \dfrac{1}{3}$, and Yellow $= \dfrac{1}{6}$. Use the individual probabilities in conjunction with the corresponding values to determine the value of P: $P = \dfrac{1}{2}(6) + \dfrac{1}{3}(3) + \dfrac{1}{6}(0) = 3 + 1 + 0 = 4$. The correct answer is (K).

55.　**D**　The question asks for the value equivalent to the sum of a, b, c, d, and e. When the question and answers contain variables, plugging in can help with solving. The question states that a, b, c, d, and e are consecutive integers such that $a < b < c < d < e$. Plug in easy numbers that meet the restrictions, like $a = 1$, $b = 2$, $c = 3$, $d = 4$, and $e = 5$, and calculate the sum: $1 + 2 + 3 + 4 + 5 = 15$. Circle 15 as the target value and check the answers using the assigned values. Choice (A) becomes $5(1) + 5 = 5 + 5 = 10$, which does not match the target and can be eliminated. Choice (B) becomes $5(2) = 10$, which does not match the target and can be eliminated. Choice (C) becomes $5(2) + 4 = 10 + 4 = 14$, which does not match the target and can be eliminated. Choice (D) becomes $5(3) = 15$. This matches the target, so keep (D), but check (E) to be sure. Choice (E) becomes $\dfrac{(1)+(5)}{2} = \dfrac{6}{2} = 3$, which does not match the target and can be eliminated. The correct answer is (D).

56.　**H**　The question asks for the value of $a - b$, if it can be determined. The question states that the set $\{13, 7, 22, 6, 4, a\}$ has a mean, or average, of 11. Average can be found using the formula $T = AN$, in which T is the total, A is the average, and N is the number of things. There are 6 numbers in the list, so $T = (11)(6) = 66$. Another way to write the total is $13 + 7 + 22 + 6 + 4 + a$ or $52 + a$. Set these totals equal to get $66 = 52 + a$, so $a = 14$. Next, determine the median, the middle-most number of a set. First, arrange the elements in increasing order: $\{4, 6, 7, 13, 14, 22\}$. When a set consists of an even number of elements, find the median by taking the average of the middle two elements. Calculate the value of b using $b = \dfrac{7+13}{2} = \dfrac{20}{2} = 10$. Finally, use the determined values to arrive at the value of $a - b = (14) - (10) = 4$. The correct answer is (H).

57. **E** The question asks for the value that CANNOT be the area of the room. PITA can be helpful with solving this question, but look for the answer that *cannot* work. Label the answers as area and start with (A), 45. The area of a rectangle is $A = l \times w$, so determine the possible combinations to get an area of 45: $45 = 1 \times 45$, $45 = 3 \times 15$, and $45 = 5 \times 9$. The question states that the perimeter is 36 feet. The formula for perimeter of a rectangle is $P = 2l + 2w$. When $n = 3$ and $m = 15$, $P = 2(3) + 2(15) = 6 + 30 = 36$ feet. Since this works, (A) can be eliminated. For (B), determine the possible combinations to get an area of 56: $56 = 1 \times 56$, $56 = 2 \times 28$, $56 = 4 \times 14$, and $56 = 7 \times 8$. When $n = 4$ and $m = 14$, $P = 2(4) + 2(14) = 8 + 28 = 36$. Since this works, (B) can be eliminated. Repeat the process for (C): $72 = 1 \times 72$, $72 = 2 \times 36$, $72 = 3 \times 24$, $72 = 4 \times 18$, $72 = 6 \times 12$, and $72 = 8 \times 9$. When $n = 6$ and $m = 12$, $P = 2(6) + 2(12) = 12 + 24 = 36$. Choice (C) can be eliminated. Repeat the process for (D): $77 = 1 \times 77$, and $77 = 7 \times 11$. When $n = 7$ and $m = 11$, $P = 2(7) + 2(11) = 14 + 22 = 36$. Choice (D) can be eliminated. The correct answer is (E).

58. **K** The question asks for the value of a. The question states that the line with endpoints (9, 0) and (a, b) is a diameter of a circle. The question provides the equation of the circle as $(x - 5)^2 + (y + 2)^2 = 20$. This equation is in the standard form $(x - h)^2 + (y - k)^2 = r^2$ with the center defined by (h, k) and the radius equal to r. The center of the circle is $(5, -2)$, so count up-and-over to arrive at (9, 0), one of the endpoints of the diameter. The y-coordinate moves up 2 units, and the x-coordinate moves to the right 4 units. To get to the other endpoint, (a, b), move in the opposite direction from the center: 2 units down and 4 units to the left. That endpoint is at $(1, -4)$, so the value of a is 1. The correct answer is (K).

59. **B** The question asks for the percentage that is closest to the percent decrease in the volume of the flat-rate box from 2012 to 2013. Use bite-sized pieces to help tackle this question. The question states that a shipping company offered a large flat-rate shipping box with dimensions 15 by 20 by 10. The volume of a box can be determined using $V = l \times w \times h$: $V = 15 \times 20 \times 10 = 3{,}000$ cubic inches. In 2013, the company decreased *both* the height and the width of the flat-rate box by 20%. The new height is $10 - 0.20(10) = 10 - 2 = 8$, and the new width is $20 - 0.20(20) = 20 - 4 = 16$. Calculate the new volume: $V = 15 \times 16 \times 8 = 1{,}920$ cubic inches. To find the percent decrease, use *percent change* $= \dfrac{difference}{original} \times 100$: *percent change* $= \dfrac{3{,}000 - 1{,}920}{3{,}000} \times 100$; $\dfrac{1{,}080}{3{,}000} \times 100$; $0.36 \times 100 = 36\%$. The correct answer is (B).

60. **J** The question asks for the statement that is true. The question provides the equation $3x^3 - 4x^2 + x - 10 = 0$ and states that $(x - 2)$ is a factor. Since $(x - 2)$ is a factor, it follows that there exists a real solution of $x = 2$ and (K) can be eliminated. Since the polynomial has a degree of 3, it can have at most 3 solutions, so (H) can be eliminated. Use polynomial long division to determine the resulting quadratic: $\dfrac{3x^3 - 4x^2 + x - 10}{x - 2} = 3x^2 + 2x + 5$. Use the discriminant, $d = b^2 - 4ac$, with $a = 3$, $b = 2$, and $c = 5$ to determine the number of roots. When $d > 0$, the quadratic has 2 real solu-

tions, when $d = 0$, the quadratic has 1 real solution, and when $d < 0$, the quadratic has 2 complex

solutions. The calculated discriminant is $d = (2)^2 - 4(3)(5) = 4 - 60 = -54$. This means that there

are 2 complex solutions, along with the 1 real solution provided, so (F) and (G) can be eliminated.

The correct answer is (J).

READING TEST

1. **C** The question asks about the way in which the narrator learned to make rice. Lines 1–14 describe the father's method of making rice without giving any specific measurements. The passage states that the father *closed his eyes and felt for the waterline*. When it was the author's turn to make rice, she states *I never did it with the same care. I went through the motions, splashing the water around, jabbing my finger down to measure the water level. Some nights the rice was a mushy gruel.* Choice (A) indicates that the author *carefully followed* the method her father taught her, but this is not true. Eliminate (A). Choice (B) mentions *watching cooking shows,* which is discussed starting in line 55. These lines, however, are not related to the method of making rice, so eliminate (B). Choice (C) matches the references in the text to not making the rice *with the same care* and the *mushy gruel* that resulted. Keep (C). Choice (D) refers to books the author's father left to her, but this is not mentioned in the passage. Eliminate (D). The correct answer is (C).

2. **H** The question asks for the statement that foreshadows the joy and connection the narrator feels at the end of the passage. The last sentence of the passage says, *I was overjoyed when my feet kept time with his, right, then left, then right, and we walked like a single unit.* The statement in (F) has no emotion in it, so eliminate it. The statement in (G) has no positive emotion, so eliminate it. The statement in (H) has the phrase *all was well in the world*, which connects with the joy in the last paragraph, so keep it. The statement in (J) has no positive emotion in it, so eliminate it. The correct answer is (H).

3. **B** The question asks about the daughter walking with her father. In the last paragraph, it says, *I was overjoyed when my feet kept time with his, right, then left, then right, and we walked like a single unit.* There is no mention of her folding her body, so eliminate (A). Joy is mentioned, so keep (B). There is no evidence that she felt inferior, so eliminate (C). Yan's puns are not mentioned in this part of the passage, so eliminate (D). The correct answer is (B).

4. **G** The question asks for the true statements after the fish is put into the sink. The fish is put into the sink at the beginning of paragraph seven. The passage says, *though I ripple tiny circles around it with my fingers, the fish stays still,* so (I) is true. Eliminate (F) and (H), which do not include (I). Both (G) and (J) include (II), so it must be true, and they do not include (III), so it must be false. Check if (IV) is true. The passage says that the fish is *brushing up against the sides of the sink,* so (IV) is true. The correct answer is (G).

5. **D** The question asks for the best paraphrase of the statement, *He swirled his hands through the water and it turned cloudy. When he scrubbed the grains clean, the sound was as big as a field of insects.*

The sentences are describing the sights and sounds of the father cleaning the rice. There is no mention of Chef Yan, so eliminate (A). The sound is compared to insects, not the rice, so eliminate (B). There is no evidence that she thought he may have a mental disorder, so eliminate (C). Choice (D) is about the cleaning of the rice, so it matches the statement. The correct answer is (D).

6. **G** The question asks what *trailing* most nearly means. The passage says, *I reach up and touch it through the plastic bag, trailing my fingers along the gills, the soft, muscled body, pushing my finger overtop the eyeball.* *Trailing* means something like "touching" or "tracing." Only (G) matches those words. Eliminate (F), (H), and (J). The correct answer is (G).

7. **C** The question asks why the father ate the narrator's rice. The passage says, *my father would keep eating, pushing the rice into his mouth as if he never expected anything different, as if he noticed no difference between what he did so well and I so poorly.* The rice was not as good as his own, so eliminate (A). There is no mention of wasting food, so eliminate (B). Later on in the paragraph, it says *I would be convinced by him that all was well in the world*, suggesting that the father would do things to reassure his daughter. This matches (C), so keep it. There is no evidence that her father is embarrassed, so eliminate (D). The correct answer is (C).

8. **H** The question asks about a logical conclusion about the fish. There is no evidence that the fish is *ill and dying*, so eliminate (F). The fish *floats in place* and *stays still*, which suggests it's not *restless,* so eliminate (G). The fish is described as *flopping sluggishly* and is *confined* in the sink, so keep (H). Although the fish watches the narrator, it does not react when she swirls water around it, suggesting that it is not *alert*, so eliminate (J). The correct answer is (H).

9. **A** The question asks how the father regarded *Wok with Yan*. The narrator says that her father was *passing judgement on Yan's methods,* saying, *"You don't have to be a genius to do that."* However, he also *made careful notes when Yan demonstrated Peking Duck.* Since the father took notes, keep (A). Not everything was irrelevant to him, as he took notes about the Peking Duck, so eliminate (B). There is no mention of the show being *the primary source of his own cooking methods*, so eliminate (C). Although he laughs at the Yan's puns, there is no evidence that he thinks it's the funniest show, so eliminate (D). The correct answer is (A).

10. **J** The question asks what stuns the narrator about her father. In the third paragraph, it says, *this memory of him is so strong, sometimes it stuns me, the detail with which I can see it.* The detailed memory stuns the narrator. Only (J) mentions memory. The correct answer is (J).

11. **D** The question asks why the author provides details about the research. The paragraph provides a timeline of advancements in fertilizers. Eliminate (A) because the author doesn't say that previous fertilizers were unsuccessful. Choice (B) contradicts what the passage says because according to the passage, manure use came before the use of bones; eliminate (B). Eliminate (C) because the passage mentions only one scientist. Keep (D) because the paragraph discusses how our knowledge *grew over time.* The correct answer is (D).

12. **G** The question asks why chemical fertilizer was developed. The author states that *use of chemical fertilizer was limited* until World War II when there was a *tremendous increase in nitrogen production, mainly because nitrogen is a principal ingredient in explosives.* Eliminate (F) because the passage does not state that there was nitrogen *leftover.* The *wartime industry* did *mass-produce* nitrogen, so keep (G). Eliminate (H) because the author never mentions soldiers working as chemists. Choice (J) contradicts the passage because the passage states that nitrogen production increased due to the wartime production of explosives, not due to farming; eliminate (J). The correct answer is (G).

13. **B** The question asks why the description of technological advances and techniques is included. The paragraph states that the techniques allowed modern farmers to *use fertilizers more effectively and efficiently.* Eliminate (A) because the author has a positive tone rather than critiquing. The passage discusses the *efficiency of chemical fertilizers,* so keep (B). This is not a list of *strategies that farmers rely on*; rather they led to the farmer's effective use of fertilizer; eliminate (C). Eliminate (D) because monitoring water usage is not mentioned in this window. The correct answer is (B).

14. **H** The question asks for the paragraph's main point about the chemical fertilizers. The paragraph compares the use of manure to that of chemical fertilizers, indicating that chemical fertilizer use has grown and surpassed the use of manure. Eliminate (F) because the author doesn't compare the effectiveness of the two types of fertilizer in this paragraph. Choice (G) has some of the same words as the paragraph, but the author only says that in the last 75 years chemical fertilizer use has surpassed that of manure—not that chemical fertilizers weren't used at all until 75 years ago; eliminate (G). The passage says that the use of manure *has been surpassed by...chemical fertilizers,* and gives numbers that certainly show growth in the use of chemical fertilizers, so keep (H). Eliminate (J) because it is contradicted by the paragraph when it says that the use of manure *has been surpassed by the large-scale production and use of chemical fertilizers.* The correct answer is (H).

15. **A** The first paragraph of Passage B states that *Nitrogen-based fertilizers* were a revolutionary advancement that *has allowed Earth to feed its seven billion people.* This indicates a global scope that supports (A). Choice (B) is incorrect because the passage states that artificial fertilizers are *often applied in amounts beyond what crops need to grow* but does not talk about the size of crop yields. Choice (C) contradicts the main point of Passage B, which focuses on negative environmental consequences. Passage B points out the harmful results of an earlier revolutionary change in the agricultural industry, which makes (D) incorrect. The correct answer is (A).

16. **H** The question asks why the chemical fertilizers came with a cost. The paragraph states that fertilizers are *carried in runoff from farmland into streams, lakes and the ocean* and may lead to *more damaging algae blooms and dead zones in American coastal waters.* The correct answer will address this environmental cost. Eliminate (F) because the consequences are environmental, not financial. Eliminate (G) because it doesn't mention the environmental consequences. Keep (H) because it mentions the *environmental disadvantages.* Eliminate (J) because this part of the passage doesn't compare coastal to plains regions. The correct answer is (H).

17.   **A**   The question asks for a comparison between the concerns of water quantity and water quality. The paragraph provides the quote *we are used to thinking about water quantity* and goes on to say that *climate change is just as tightly linked to issues related to water quality*. Therefore, quantity and quality are both important. They are *equally as connected,* so keep (A). Eliminate (B) because no comparison between urban and rural areas is made in this paragraph. Eliminate (C) because it contradicts the quoted statement. Eliminate (D) because the paragraph doesn't mention *salt water bodies*. The correct answer is (A).

18.   **G**   The question asks for what is common to both passages about the way that fertilizers have impacted the agricultural industry. Passage A is focused on the rise and influence of chemical fertilizers, which are *manufactured*. Passage B focuses on the impact of *artificial fertilizers*. Eliminate (F) because Passage A views the fertilizer in a positive light, saying it *has been foundational to feeding our nation and providing food and hope to other parts of the world*. Both discuss fertilizer that is *artificially manufactured,* so keep (G). Eliminate (H) because it's the opposite of what the passages state. Eliminate (J) because Passage B doesn't mention ammonia. The correct answer is (G).

19.   **A**   The question asks how each passage uses details about the effects of incorporating nitrogen-based fertilizers into agriculture. The author of Passage A focuses on the positive effects, stating that fertilizer *has been foundational to feeding our nation and providing food and hope to other parts of the world*. The author of Passage B focuses on the negative effects, stating that fertilizer use *comes with a cost* including creating *conditions in which organisms can't survive*. Keep (A) because Passage A takes a positive tone toward chemical fertilizers and their benefits, while Passage B expresses strong environmental concerns. Eliminate (B) because Passage A is focused on chemical fertilizers, not farming advances as a whole. Eliminate (C) because Passage A doesn't mention the effects of fertilizers on land. Eliminate (D) because only Passage B discusses environmental effects. The correct answer is (A).

20.   **H**   The question asks how both authors support their claims. Passage B defines *eutrophication,* but Passage A doesn't define a term, so eliminate (F). Eliminate (G) because only Passage B provides a quote. Passage A states *In the mid- to late 1940s, about 2 million tons of chemical fertilizers were used per year,* and Passage B states *The authors found that future climate change-driven increases in rainfall in the United States could boost nitrogen runoff by as much as 20 percent by the end of the century*. Both include statistics, so keep (H). Eliminate (J) because only Passage A includes a specific timeline. The correct answer is (H).

21.   **D**   The question asks about the function of the first paragraph. The first paragraph says *Pablo Neruda couldn't hold a tune* but that his *cadences are crucial to his writing*. Pablo Neruda is a writer, not a singer, so eliminate (A). The paragraph does not discuss how he wrote his poems, so eliminate (B). There is no mention of Neruda's youth, so eliminate (C). The paragraph does contrast his inability to hold a tune and the melody in his writing, so keep (D). The correct answer is (D).

22.   **G**   The question asks about the passage author's opinion of Neruda's poetry. The author says that Neruda's work has an *undimmed exuberance and generosity* and that *it feeds hungrily off the life and yet stands as a thing apart*. The passage mentions Neruda's *Memoirs*, but not in comparison to his poetry, so eliminate (F). The author has a positive view of Neruda's poetry, so keep (G). The pas-

sage author says that Neruda's work is influenced by his life, but also that it *stands as a thing apart*, so eliminate (H). The passage mentions *faults and weaknesses*, but that is in reference to Neruda's life, not his work, so eliminate (J). The correct answer is (G).

23. **B** The question asks about *melody* in the first paragraph. The first paragraph says that *Neruda's cadences are crucial to his writing* and that no one would *want to separate their sense from their sound*, so *melody* refers to the sound of his writing. Neruda did not write an opera, so eliminate (A). Choice (B) matches the idea of the sound of Neruda's writing, so keep it. The paragraph does not discuss Neruda's life, so eliminate (C) and (D). The correct answer is (B).

24. **J** The question asks why a reader might appreciate Feinstein's treatment of the "dizzying details." The second paragraph says that Feinstein paces the *story so as to give pre-eminence to the writing and the adventuring, while recording the duller passages more briefly*. There is no evidence that he is critical of Neruda's travels, so eliminate (F). Feinstein writes about both Neruda's writing and adventuring, so eliminate (G). There is no mention of whether Feinstein elaborates on why Neruda was prolific in writing and travel, so eliminate (H). He does keep the dull passages brief, so keep (J). The correct answer is (J).

25. **C** The question asks what *logged* most nearly means. Find *logged* in the second paragraph. The paragraph is discussing Feinstein writing a biography of Neruda. The sentence says *Others are harder to deal with: globe-trottings have to be logged but risk becoming a list of place-names* so *logged* means something like "written down." Eliminate (A), (B), and (D) since those words do not match "written down." The correct answer is (C).

26. **H** The question asks about Neruda's reminiscences in his autobiography. Paragraphs three and four discuss Neruda's *Memoirs*. The fourth paragraph says that Feinstein *understands that an author's reminiscences are a way of creating disguises as well as revealing secrets*. There is no evidence that the reminiscences *amplified contentious issues*, so eliminate (F). There is no mention that they should be *studied as literature*, so eliminate (G). Choice (H) matches the content of paragraph four, so keep it. Although the passage says that Feinstein *relies a good deal on Neruda's own Memoirs*, he relies on it for the content, not the writing style, so eliminate (J). The correct answer is (H).

27. **D** The question asks how Feinstein addresses Neruda's conversion to communism. The seventh paragraph says that Neruda's conversion to communism confronts Feinstein *with the classic biographer's dilemma—how to respect the work while dealing with a contradictory private life—*and that Feinstein *copes with it by presenting the facts rather than wagging his finger, and by foregrounding the writing*. Feinstein doesn't avoid the topic, so eliminate (A). He doesn't contradict Neruda's account, so eliminate (B). There's no evidence that he tried to protect Neruda's wife and daughter, so eliminate (C). He does present the facts, so keep (D). The correct answer is (D).

28. **F** The question asks about Neruda's Spanish becoming quite odd. The sixth paragraph says that Neruda was in Rangoon in 1927, *then moved on through France, Japan, China, Ceylon and Java*, and returned home in 1932. His Spanish became odd due to his travels, so keep (F). There is no mention of *French symbolist poetry* in the sixth paragraph, so eliminate (G). He didn't escape from

consular activity, but instead it was a way to escape, so eliminate (H). There is no mention of his marriage in the sixth paragraph, so eliminate (J). The correct answer is (F).

29. **C** The question asks about Feinstein's treatment of Neruda's contradictions. The last paragraph says *Feinstein lets his readers draw their own conclusions about the moral muddle of Neruda's life.* Feinstein is not muddling Neruda's life, so eliminate (A). Feinstein does not show the downside to Neruda's exuberance, so eliminate (B). Choice (C) matches the passage, so keep it. There is no mention of Neruda appearing less noble, so eliminate (D). The correct answer is (C).

30. **F** The question asks what *work* refers to. The last sentence of the passage says, *The faults and weaknesses are plain to see, but so is the undimmed exuberance and generosity of the work, which feeds hungrily off the life and yet stands as a thing apart.* Neruda is a writer, so his *work* is writing. Choice (F) matches writing. Eliminate (G), (H), and (J). The correct answer is (F).

31. **C** The question asks for the organization of the passage. The passage proceeds chronologically, starting with 1964 in the first paragraph and leading to 2012 in the end of the passage. It describes the events leading up to and the eventual discovery of the Higgs boson. The passage is *chronological,* but the focus isn't finding the *mass of various particles,* so eliminate (A). The focus of the passage is not the *construction* of the LHC, so eliminate (B). The events *leading to the discovery of the Higgs boson* is a close match, so keep (C). There's no *collection of stories,* so eliminate (D). The correct answer is (C).

32. **J** The question asks for the main function of the first paragraph. The first paragraph states that scientists suggested that the Higgs boson existed in 1964 and explains briefly what it is, calling it the *cornerstone of the Standard Model.* Eliminate (F) because Hamburg is mentioned in the second, not first, paragraph. Eliminate (G) because the first paragraph doesn't talk about scientists building anything. The paragraph is focused on the *Higgs boson,* not the *theorists,* so eliminate (H). The focus is the Higgs boson and its *importance,* so keep (J). The correct answer is (J).

33. **A** The question asks for the similarity between the two particle colliders. The paragraph states that the Tevatron and LEP both used *discoveries and precision measurements* to determine that the Higgs boson *should be no more than 200 GeV.* But according to the last sentence, the scientists *found no lasting evidence.* Keep (A), which is similar to the passage. Eliminate (B) because this cost is stated about the LEP but not the Tevatron. Eliminate (C) because the Tevatron was completed in 1983 but the LEP only began to be built that year. The passage doesn't say whether it was completed that year. Eliminate (D) because it contradicts the last sentence of the paragraph. The correct answer is (A).

34. **H** The question asks for the main idea of the last paragraph. The first sentence of the last paragraph indicates that scientists don't doubt that the particle has been discovered, but *there is still debate about its exact nature.* Eliminate (F) because the paragraph doesn't say its properties were predicted *only recently.* In fact, earlier in the passage it states that the Higgs boson was predicted decades ago. Eliminate (G) because the paragraph doesn't mention *recent research.* Choice (H) is consistent with the paragraph, so keep it. Eliminate (J) because the paragraph doesn't say that the particle weighs *more than originally predicted.* The correct answer is (H).

35.   **D**   The question asks for information about the scientists in Brussels and London. The first paragraph states that they *independently conceived of the subtle mechanism…that endows elementary particles with mass.* Eliminate (A) because Peter W. Higgs suggested the particle's existence, not the scientists from Brussels and London. Eliminate (B) because it describes the Standard Model, which isn't credited to these scientists. The *cornerstone of the Standard Model* is the Higgs boson, and that isn't what these scientists discovered, so eliminate (C). Choice (D) is consistent with the paragraph, so keep it. The correct answer is (D).

36.   **G**   The question asks what the dipole magnets were capable of. The fifth paragraph states that inside the dipole magnets, *twin proton beams circulate in both directions…approaching light speed.* Eliminate (F) because it contradicts the passage, which says that there was *little left from that collider.* Keep (G) because it's consistent with the passage. Eliminate (H) because it is the proton beams that circulate at energies up to 7 TeV, not the dipole magnets. Eliminate (J) because the dipole magnets are cylinders; they don't fit inside cylinders. The correct answer is (G).

37.   **B**   The question asks what was needed for the physicists to discover the Higgs boson. The passage is structured to describe colliders that were built over time. Eventually scientists were able to discover the particle through the use of a more advanced collider, the LHC. Eliminate (A) because it contradicts the passage, which notes that an earlier collider used energy *beyond what the machine was designed to handle* yet still only found *hints of a Higgs boson.* Keep (B) because it's consistent with the passage. *Englert's mechanism* is mentioned in the first paragraph as something that was used from the very beginning, so it wasn't the final thing that was needed to discover the Higgs boson; eliminate (C). Choice (D) contradicts the passage because it says that the Tevatron and LEP weren't successful in discovering the Higgs boson, so eliminate it. The correct answer is (B).

38.   **F**   The question asks how the work at Tevatron compares with the work at the LHC. At the end of the sixth paragraph, the author states that *the LHC was producing data 15 times faster than the Tevatron had ever achieved,* so the correct answer will address the speed. Eliminate (G), (H), and (J), which do not relate to speed. The correct answer is (F).

39.   **D**   The question asks why the author includes the scientists' reactions. The passage states that they *erupted in loud clapping and cries of joy.* This demonstrates how excited they were by the discovery. Eliminate (A) because they were not excited to meet Peter. Eliminate (B) because the it was the LHC, not the Tevatron, that produced the exciting results. Eliminate (C) because the passage doesn't say that the cheers *which echoed down the hallway* disturbed anyone. They were excited about *the magnitude of their discovery*, so keep (D). The correct answer is (D).

40.   **G**   The question asks what the phrase *turned up* means. The author says that *few scientists doubt that a heavy new particle has turned up at CERN,* and this is after the passage explains the discovery of the particle. So, *turned up* means something like "been discovered." Eliminate (F), (H), and (J) because they don't mean "discovered." The correct answer is (G).

SCIENCE TEST

1. **A** The question asks which graph best represents the enzyme velocities of Enzymes A, B, C, and D in solutions with *an initial substrate concentration of 5 mM* at *60°C* after *10 seconds,* based on Table 1. According to the description above Table 1, 10 seconds is a constant for all measurements in Table 1. Look at Table 1 and find the enzyme velocity of each enzyme at 60°C with an initial substrate concentration of 5 mM. Under these conditions, Enzymes A, B, C, and D have velocities of 4.6, 4.9, 10.6, and 14.6 mmol/s, respectively, so Enzyme A has the smallest enzyme velocity. Eliminate (B), (C), and (D) because these graphs do not show Enzyme A as having the smallest enzyme velocity. The correct answers is (A).

2. **G** The question asks for the most likely enzyme velocity if Enzyme B solution had *a substrate concentration of 10 mM* at *35°C,* based on Table 1. Look for the data for Enzyme B at an initial substrate concentration of 10 mM. The enzyme velocity is listed for substate temperatures of 20°C, 30°C, and 60°C. The enzyme velocity decreases with higher temperatures. Thus, the enzyme velocity at 35°C will fall between the values for 30°C and 60°C. At 30°C the enzyme velocity is 10.9 mmol/s, and at 60°C the enzyme velocity is 6.9 mmol/s. Therefore, the enzyme velocity at 35°C will be between 10.9 mmol/s and 6.9 mmol/s. The correct answer is (G).

3. **D** The question asks for the enzyme velocities from *highest to lowest* after 1 second with a *substrate concentration of 12 mM* at *40°,* based on Figure 1. The description for Figure 1 states that the graph shows the change in enzyme velocity over time at a substrate concentration of 12 mM and a temperature of 40°C. Find 1 second on the horizontal axis and draw a vertical line from 1 second on the *x*-axis to the enzyme velocity curves for all four enzymes. Enzyme D has the highest enzyme velocity at 1 second, so eliminate (A) and (B). Enzyme B has the second highest enzyme velocity, so eliminate (C). The correct answer is (D).

4. **G** The question asks which enzyme *had the highest enzyme velocity after 0.75 seconds* with a *substrate concentration of 12 mM* at *40°,* according to Figure 1. The description for Figure 1 states that the graph shows the change in enzyme velocity over time at a substrate concentration of 12 mM and a temperature of 40°C. Find 0.75 seconds on the horizontal axis, and draw a vertical line from 0.75 seconds on the *x*-axis to the enzyme velocity curves for all four enzymes. Enzyme B has the highest enzyme velocity at 0.75 seconds. The correct answer is (G).

5. **A** The question asks for the enzyme velocity for Enzyme C *after 10 seconds* at an *8 mM substrate concentration at 60°C,* based on Table 1. According to the description above Table 1, 10 seconds is a constant for all measurements in Table 1. Look for the data for Enzyme C at 60°C. The enzyme velocity is listed for initial substrate concentrations of 5 mM, 10 mM, and 15 mM. The enzyme velocity increases with higher substrate concentrations. Thus, the enzyme velocity at an 8 mM substrate concentration will fall between the values for 5 mM and 10 mM. At 5 mM the enzyme velocity is 10.6 mmol/s, and at 10 mM the enzyme velocity is 13.1 mmol/s. Therefore, the enzyme velocity will be between 10.6 mmol/s and 13.1 mmol/s. The only value between 10.6 mmol/s and 13/1 mmol/s is 12.0 mmol/s in (A). The correct answer is (A).

6. **G** The questions asks for the enzyme that *takes the shortest amount of time to reach an enzyme velocity of 6 mmol/s*, given that the substrate concentration is 12 mM and the temperature is 40°C, according to Figure 1. The description for Figure 1 states that the graph shows the change in enzyme velocity over time at a substrate concentration of 12 mM and a temperature of 40°C. Find the enzyme velocity of 6 mmol/s on the vertical axis. Draw a horizontal line from 6 mmol/s on the *y*-axis. The first enzyme to reach an enzyme velocity of 6 mmol/s is Enzyme B at 0.5 seconds. The correct answer is (G).

7. **B** The question asks for *the transmittance at 0.31 microns at a concentration of 18 mg/m³*, based on Figure 2. According to the description for Study 2, Figure 2 shows the transmittance at 0.31 microns at various average concentrations of O_3. Look at Figure 2 for the transmittance at a concentration of 18 mg/m³. At 18 mg/m³ the transmittance is approximately 48%, which is between 45 and 55%. The correct answer is (B).

8. **G** The question asks how *the transmittance at 0.31 microns varied* as *the concentration of ozone increased from 3 to 24 mg/m³*, based on Study 2. According to the description for Study 2, Figure 2 shows the transmittance at 0.31 microns at various average concentrations of O_3. Use Figure 2 and look for the relationship between transmittance and average concentration of O_3. Figure 2 shows an inverse relationship between concentration and transmittance. As the concentration increased, the transmittance decreased. The correct answer is (G).

9. **B** The question asks which of the five locations has the *greatest transmittance at 0.31 microns*, according to Studies 2 and 3. According to the description for Study 2, Figure 2 shows the transmittance at 0.31 microns at various average concentrations of O_3. Study 3 shows the *average stratospheric ozone concentration*, and the results of Study 3 are shown in Table 1. Use Figure 2 and look for the relationship between transmittance and average concentration of O_3. Figure 2 shows an inverse relationship between concentration and transmittance. As the concentration increased, the transmittance decreased. The question asks for the *greatest transmittance*, so this would be found at the location with the lowest concentration. Table 3 indicates that the lowest concentration is at Location 2. The correct answer is (B).

10. **F** The question asks which equations represent *the production of ozone in the stratosphere*, based on the passage. Use the information in the first paragraph to determine the equations. The passage states that *ozone is formed naturally when UV light breaks apart an oxygen molecule to form two highly reactive oxygen atoms.* Eliminate (G) and (J) because ozone (O_3) is not involved in same reaction as UV light. The passage then states that *oxygen atoms collide with another oxygen molecule to form ozone.* This means that the oxygen atoms (O) and the oxygen molecules (O_2) should be on one side of the equation and ozone (O_3) should be alone on the other side of the equation. Eliminate (H) since ozone (O_3) should be the only product. The correct answer is (F).

11. **A** The question asks, based on Figure 1, whether the researcher should measure the transmittance at *4.3 microns or at 9.5 microns*, given that the researcher wants to repeat Study 2 to study the effects on transmittance of different CO_2 *concentrations instead of* O_3 *concentrations*. Look at Figure

1 and determine the CO_2 transmittance at 4.3 microns and 9.5 microns. The CO_2 transmittance is approximately 0% at 4.3 microns and approximately 95% at 9.5 microns. Eliminate (B) and (C) because these incorrectly state that the transmittance is lower at 9.5 microns. Now, consider the original wavelength used in Study 2. The transmittance of O_3 varied from approximately 0% to 100% between 0.27 and 0.35 microns, and the researchers used a wavelength in the middle of this range. Similarly, a wavelength of 4.3 microns is in the middle of a range of wavelengths where the transmittance of CO_2 varies from approximately 0% to 100%. The correct answer is (A).

12. **G** The question asks whether *the total transmittance of sunlight* on Planet Z at a *wavelength of 0.3 microns* would be higher or lower than the transmittance on *Earth at a wavelength of 0.3 microns*, given that Planet Z has a *higher* concentration of carbon dioxide and there is *no ozone*. The relationship between wavelength and transmittance is shown in Figure 1. Look at Figure 1 to determine the transmittance of CO_2 and O_3 at 0.3 microns. According to Figure 1, at a wavelength of 0.3 microns the transmittance of CO_2 is approximately 100%, and the transmittance of O_3 is approximately 20%. Eliminate (F) and (H) because both indicate that the transmittance of CO_2 is lower than the transmittance of O_3. Since Planet Z has no O_3 and more CO_2 and CO_2 has a higher transmittance at 0.3 microns than O_3, the total transmittance of sunlight on Planet Z would likely be higher overall. The correct answer is (G).

13. **B** The question asks for the mass of O_3, in *grams*, in 100 cubic meters of stratospheric air at Location 3, based on Table 1. Look at Table 1 and find the concentration of O_3 at Location 3. Table 1 shows that Location 3 has a concentration of 21 mg/m³. Therefore, 100 cubic meters would contain 21 mg/m³ × 100 m³ = 2,100 mg of O_3 per 100 cubic meters of stratospheric air. Be careful! The question asks for *grams* not milligrams, so eliminate (D). Since 1 g = 1,000 mg, a volume of 2,100 mg would be equal to 2.1 g. The correct answer is (B).

14. **J** The question asks, according to Figure 1, *which two zones have similar ranges*. The question states that the *range refers to the difference in depth between the top and bottom of that zone*. The horizontal axis in Figure 1 shows the depth, so the width of each zone along the horizontal axis would correspond to the range. Use POE. The epipelagic zone is very narrow, indicating a much smaller range than any of the other zones. Eliminate (F). The mesopelagic zone is larger than the epipelagic zone, but still much smaller than any others, so it is not close in range to any other zone. Eliminate (G) and (H) because both include mesopelagic. Only bathypelagic and abyssopelagic have approximately the same width for their zones in Figure 1. The correct answer is (J).

15. **B** The question asks, according to Figure 2, for which value of *d* does *approximately 35% of marine life lives between 0 m and d*. Figure 2 shows the percent of marine life between sea level (0 m) and a given value of *d*. Find 35% on the vertical axis of Figure 2 and draw a horizontal line over until you reach the curve and then down to the horizontal axis. It's hard to tell exactly what the depth is at 35%, but it is definitely less than 200 m, so eliminate (C) and (D) because they are too large. In the description preceding Figure 2, the passage states that *20% of all marine life is located between sea level and a depth of 50 m*. Eliminate (A) since 20% is not 35%. The depth must be somewhere between 50 m and 200 m. The correct answer is (B).

16. **H** The question asks, according to Figures 1 and 2, to what depth does the bathypelagic zone extend. Figure 1 shows the depths of the different zones of the ocean, so look at Figure 1. The bathypelagic zone (the third zone from the left) starts at 1,000 m and extends to 3,600 m on the horizontal axis (*d*). The correct answer is (H).

17. **D** The question asks, based on Figure 1, what the dissolved oxygen level is at *d* = 10,000 m. In Figure 1, there are two vertical axes, and two curves, *t* and D.O. To answer this question, use the D.O. curve and make sure to use the vertical axis on the right-hand side of the graph. At *d* = 9,600 m, the D.O. is between 1.2 and 1.5 mg/L. The curve is increasing very slightly at 9,600 m, so eliminate (A), (B), and (C), which would all indicate a substantial decrease between 9,600 m and 10,000 m. Since the rate of increase is so small, the values will stay between 1.2 and 1.5 mg/L at 10,000 m. The correct answer is (D).

18. **G** The question asks for the approximate *percentage of marine life* that *the aphotic zones account for*. The question defines *the aphotic zones* as *depths below 1,000 m*. Figure 2 shows *the percent of marine life located between sea level and a given depth*. Find 1,000 m on the horizontal axis and draw a straight line up until the curve and then over to the vertical axis. Approximately 90% of marine life is located between sea level and 1,000 m. The question asked for the percentage of marine life *below* 1,000 m, so there is 10% of marine life remaining at a depth below 1,000 m. The correct answer is (G).

19. **B** The question asks, based on Figure 1, *which of the samples of water, if either, would have a lower mass*. The two samples are both *1-liter samples of water collected*, and one was *collected at* d = *1,000 m* and the other was *collected at* d = *3,600 m*. Refer to Figure 1. Notice that the temperature, represented by the solid line, is decreasing as the depth increases. Therefore, the water gets colder as the depth increases. The question states that *colder ocean water is denser than warmer ocean water*, so the water at 1,000 m is less dense than the colder water at 3,600 m. Eliminate (C) because the density of the two samples is not the same. To choose between the remaining answers, outside knowledge is necessary: density is equal to mass divided by volume. Since both of these samples have the same volume, the less dense sample, which is the sample from 1,000 m, must have the smaller mass. The correct answer is (B).

20. **H** The question asks *which of the students theorized that fibromyalgia is triggered by neurons that are in some way physically altered*. Student 1 states that fibromyalgia results after *irreparable physical damage to nerve cells*, so the answer must include Student 1. Eliminate (G) and (J) because they do not include Student 1. Student 2 states that when there is a chronic excess of glutamate, the pain receptors on neurons *adapt by physically changing shape* and this change *results in fibromyalgia*. Therefore, Student 2 also believes that fibromyalgia is triggered by physically altered neurons. The correct answer is (H).

21. **C** The question asks which student's theory is best supported by evidence that *female fibromyalgia patients report a higher incidence of pain during pregnancy and menopause when estrogen levels are rapidly changing*. Student 3 states that *fibromyalgia is caused only by abnormal estrogen or thyroid*

hormone levels. None of the other students believe that estrogen contributes to fibromyalgia. The correct answer is (C).

22. **G** The question asks which types of foods provide L-tryptophan, based on Student 4's description. Find L-trytophan in Student 4's description. Student 4 states that L-tryptophan is *an essential amino acid.* Outside knowledge is necessary here: amino acids are the building blocks of proteins. The correct answer is (G).

23. **C** The question asks which student *would be most likely to predict that people that produce higher than average levels of Substance P have a higher than average risk of developing fibromyalgia.* The question describes Substance P as an *excitatory neurotransmitter similar in function to glutamate.* Student 2 states that *fibromyalgia is caused only by the overproduction of excitatory transmitters, such as glutamate.* If Substance P is similar to glutamate, then Student 2 would believe that higher levels of Substance P would make someone more likely to develop fibromyalgia. The correct answer is (C).

24. **J** The question asks *which of the students theorized that fibromyalgia is the result of low levels of certain neurotransmitters.* Use POE. Student 3 is in 3 of the answers, so check Student 3's explanation for mention of neurotransmitters. Student 3 states that serotonin and norepinephrine are *two inhibitory neurotransmitters* and that fibromyalgia results *when the levels of these inhibitory neurotransmitters are low.* Therefore, the answer must include Student 3. Eliminate (F) because it does not include Student 3. Student 2 states that *fibromyalgia is caused by the overproduction of neurotransmitters.* Overproduction is the opposite of low levels, so Student 2 cannot be in the correct answer. Eliminate (H). Now, determine if the answer needs to include Student 4 or not. Student 4 says that fibromyalgia is caused *when serotonin levels drop.* Serotonin was previously defined as an *inhibitory neurotransmitter* in Student 3's description, so Student 4 also believes that fibromyalgia is the result of *low levels of neurotransmitters.* The correct answer is (J).

25. **B** The question asks which of the findings, if true, *best supports Student 4's theory.* Student 4 states that *Fibromyalgia results only from a diet low in L-tryptophan.* This would mean that diets low in L-tryptophan would be associated with a higher number of cases of fibromyalgia. Eliminate (A) which states that *the prevalence of fibromyalgia is* lower *than average* for people who consume diets low in L-tryptophan. Keep (B) as it states the prevalence is higher. Choices (C) and (D) deal with levels of thyroid hormone. Student 4 states that *estrogen and thyroid hormone imbalances do not limit the production of serotonin.* Eliminate (C) and (D). The correct answer is (B).

26. **A** The question asks which of the students' viewpoints would be weakened by the results of a study involving Prescription *C, a powerful anti-inflammatory medication often prescribed to patients recovering from serious injury.* Since the question states that *the likelihood of developing fibromyalgia was the same among patients treated with Prescription* C *and patients that were not treated with any anti-inflammatory medications*, viewpoints attributing fibromyalgia to inflammation would be weakened by these results. Scan the viewpoints to see which ones mention inflammation or injury. Student 3 does not mention inflammation or injury, so eliminate (H) and (J). Student 2 mentions injury, but says that injury and illness *do not create the widespread pain of fibromyalgia.* Eliminate

(B). Student 1 states that fibromyalgia results when *inflammation causes irreparable physical damage to the nerve cells.* The correct answer is (A).

27. **B** The question asks which soil samples had *the lowest percentage of ammonium converted to nitrate after treatment with N-1, N-2, and N-3*, according to the results of the studies. Figure 1 shows the results soil samples treated with N-1, Figure 2 shows the results of soil samples treated with N-2, and Figure 3 shows the results of soil samples treated with N-3. Start by looking at Figure 1 to determine which biome sample had the lowest percent of ammonium converted to nitrate for N-1. Figure 1 shows that the coniferous forest had the smallest percent of ammonium converted to nitrate in soil treated with N-1. Eliminate (C) and (D). Figure 2 shows that the coniferous forest had the lowest percentage of ammonium converted to nitrate for N-2. Eliminate (A). The correct answer is (B).

28. **H** The question asks for the approximate *percent of ammonium converted to nitrate in the soils treated with N-2, averaged across all 5 biomes*, according to the results of Study 2. The results of Study 2 are shown in Figure 2, so look at Figure 2. In Figure 2, the highest percentage of ammonium converted to nitrate is 70% and the lowest percentage is 45%. Eliminate (F) since the average cannot be less than the smallest value. Eliminate (J) because the average must be smaller than the greatest value. Since the majority of the values are 60% or greater and only one value is less than 50% (45% for the coniferous forest), the average must be closer to 60% than 50%. Eliminate (G). The correct answer is (H).

29. **B** The question asks whether *a greater percentage of ammonium was converted to nitrate in the tropical forest soil treated with N-3 than the same soil treated with N-1,* based on Studies 1 and 3. Figure 1 shows the soil samples treated with N-1, and Figure 3 shows the soil samples treated with N-3. Start by looking at Figure 1 to determine percent of ammonium converted to nitrate in the tropical forest soil treated with N-1. According to Figure 1, tropical forest soil treated with N-1 had approximately 68% of the ammonium converted to nitrate. Eliminate (A), (C), and (D) because these answers do not identify 68% as the value for the soil sample treated with N-1. The correct answer is (B).

30. **H** The question asks for the *independent (experimental) variable across the 3 studies.* This question requires outside knowledge. An *independent variable* is also known as a manipulated variable because it is the variable that is manipulated by the experimenter in order to measure the effect on the dependent variable. Since the question asks for the independent variable *across the 3 studies,* consider which variable is different among the 3 studies. The same 5 biomes were used for each study, so eliminate (F). The concentration of ammonia and the concentration of nitrate are both dependent variables, so eliminate (G) and (J). Each of these studies uses a different nitrogen inhibitor, so the experimental variable is the type of nitrogen inhibitor. The correct answer is (H).

31. **A** The question asks which inhibitor reduced the concentration of applied ammonium ions by less than 50% in the deciduous forest soil. The reduction in the percentage of ammonium ions is another way of saying the percentage of ammonium converted to nitrate, so determine the percent of

ammonium converted to nitrate in the deciduous forest soil treated with N-1, N-2, and N-3. These values in the deciduous forest soil are approximately 61% in soil treated with N-1, 50% in soil treated with N-2, and 73% in soil treated with N-3. None of these values are *less* than 50%, so the answer is none of the inhibitors. The correct answer is (A).

32. **F** The question asks whether *the mixture of N-1 and liquid fertilizer is a solution.* Use POE. Notice that two answers says N-1 was dissolved in the fertilizer while the other two say that N-1 was suspended. Study 1 uses N-1, so look in the description of Study 1 for reference to *dissolved* or *suspended.* The description of Study 1 states that the *mixture was stirred until there were no remaining solids suspended in the mixture.* Therefore, the N-1 was not suspended; eliminate (G) and (J). To choose between (F) and (H), outside knowledge is needed. In chemistry, a solution is a homogenous mixture in which all solids are dissolved in the mixture. Since the N-1 was stirred until there were no remaining solids, the mixture is a solution. The correct answer is (F).

33. **C** The question asks which *step was incorporated in the experimental design to ensure that the bacteria in all five soils were active.* Since the question states that *nitrogen-fixing bacteria are inactive in temperatures below 12°C,* the correct answer must relate to the temperature of the soil. Eliminate (B) and (D), which do not relate to soil temperature. Look at the introduction and study description for information regarding soil temperature. The passage states that the soil samples were *maintained at 20°C* for one week before the studies began and *remained at 20°C* during the studies. The passage never specifies the outside temperature at the time of collection, so eliminate (A). The correct answer is (C).

34. **J** The question asks which diagram most likely represents the petri dish where the cell in Figure 2 would be found, given that *the cell shown in Figure 2 is oriented exactly how it appeared in its dish.* Look at Figure 1 and determine which cells are most similar in shape to the cell in Figure 2. The cell in Figure 2 most resembles the cells in Dish D in Experiment 1. Eliminate (F) and (G) because the direction of the electric field is reversed from that in Dish D. According to the description for Experiment 1, *the yeast placed in Dishes C and D were all* S. pombe – GM. The correct answer is (J).

35. **B** The question asks which dish of cells in Experiment 1 had the most similar growth to the cells in Dish X *before Dish X was moved to a higher temperature room.* Look at the description of Experiment 2. The passage states that Dish X contained *S. pombe – N* cells, so eliminate (C) and (D), which both contained *S. pombe – GM* cells. The passage also states that *a battery was used to generate a current through all four dishes.* Since Dish A in Experiment 1 did not have an electric field, eliminate (A). The correct answer is (B).

36. **H** The question asks whether *the* S. pombe – N *cells exhibit the same growth patterns as the* S. pombe – GM *cells in presence of an electrical field,* according to Experiment 1. The growth pattern of the *S. pombe* cells is shown in Figure 1. Look at Figure 1 and determine the shape of the *S. pombe – N* and *S. pombe – GM* *cells in presence of an electrical field.* In Experiment 1, Dish B contained *S. pombe – N* cells in an electric field, and Dish D contained *S. pombe – GM* cells in an electric field. Eliminate (F) and (J) because these answers refer to the wrong dishes. Based on Figure 1, the

shapes of the cells in Dish B and Dish D differ after 3 days of growth, so eliminate (G). The correct answer is (H).

37. **D**   The question asks whether *the yeast cells in Dish Y likely grew towards the anode or towards the cathode,* according to Experiment 2. The question also states that *the anode of the petri dish is the positively charged electrode, and the cathode is the negatively charged electrode.* Look at the description of Experiment 2. The passage states that Dish Y contained *S. pombe – GM* cells. The passage also states that *a battery was used to generate a current through all four dishes.* Since the yeast cells in Dish Y were *S. pombe – GM* in the presence of an electric field, the cells in Dish Y would exhibit growth similar to Dish D, which also contained *S. pombe – GM* in the presence of an electric field. Eliminate (A) and (C) because these answers refer to Dish B, rather than Dish D. According to Figure 1, the yeast cells in Dish D grew toward the positively charged electrode, so this is the anode. The correct answer is (D).

38. **G**   The question asks whether *S. pombe* is *a eukaryotic or prokaryotic cell,* based on Figure 1. Look at the description of Experiment 1. The description of Experiment 1 states that *the nucleus is shown for each cell.* Eliminate (H) and (J). To choose between the remaining choices, outside knowledge is necessary. Eukaryotic cells have a nucleus while prokaryotic cells do not. The correct answer is (G).

39. **D**   The question asks *how many times* the length of each cell was measured in Experiment 2. The results of Experiment 2 are shown in Figure 3, so look at Figure 3. Figure 3 shows a data point for each time data was collected during Experiment 2. Each dish has 7 data points, so each cell was measured 7 times. The correct answer is (D).

40. **J**   The question asks which two dishes researchers should compare if they want to *examine the effects of different temperatures on the growth of* S. pombe – GM *cells.* In Experiment 1, the dishes were held *at a constant temperature of 20°C,* and in Experiment 2, the temperature was varied, so look at the description for Experiment 2. Dishes Y and Z contained *S. pombe – GM,* and Dishes W and X contained *S. pombe – N* cells. Since the researchers want to examine *the growth of* S. pombe – GM *cells,* eliminate (F), (G), and (H), which refer to Dishes W and/or X. The correct answer is (J).

SCORING YOUR PRACTICE EXAM

Step A

Count the number of correct answers for each section and record the number in the space provided for your raw score on the Score Conversion Worksheet below.

Step B

Using the Score Conversion Chart on the next page, convert your raw scores on each section to scaled scores. Then compute your composite ACT score by averaging the four subject scores. Add them up and divide by four. Don't worry about the essay score; it is not included in your composite score.

Score Conversion Worksheet		
Section	**Raw Score**	**Scaled Score**
1	_____/75	_____
2	_____/60	_____
3	_____/40	_____
4	_____/40	_____

Step C

To grade your essay, see the Essay Checklist and an example of a top scoring essay online on your Student Tools.

SCORING YOUR PRACTICE EXAM

SCORE CONVERSION CHART

Scaled Score	Raw Scores			
	English	Math	Reading	Science
36	75	60	40	40
35	73–74	59	39	39
34	72	58	38	38
33	71	57	37	37
32	70	56	36	—
31	69	54–55	34–35	36
30	68	53	33	35
29	67	51–52	32	34
28	65–66	49–50	30–31	33
27	64	46–48	29	32
26	62–63	44–45	28	30–31
25	60–61	41–43	27	28–29
24	58–59	39–40	26	27
23	55–57	37–38	24–25	25–26
22	53–54	35–36	23	23–24
21	50–52	33–34	22	21–22
20	47–49	31–32	21	19–20
19	44–46	28–30	19–20	17–18
18	42–43	25–27	18	15–16
17	40–41	22–24	17	14
16	37–39	18–21	16	13
15	34–36	15–17	15	12
14	31–33	11–14	13–14	11
13	29–30	9–10	12	10
12	27–28	7–8	10–11	9
11	25–26	6	8–9	8
10	23–24	5	7	7
9	21–22	4	6	6
8	18–20	3	5	5
7	15–17	—	—	4
6	12–14	2	4	3
5	9–11	—	3	2
4	7–8	1	2	—
3	5–6	—	—	1
2	3–4	—	1	—
1	0–2	0	0	0

Chapter 28
Practice Exam 2

*Make sure to download a bubble sheet for this test via your online Student Tools.

ENGLISH TEST

45 Minutes—75 Questions

DIRECTIONS: In the five passages that follow, certain words and phrases are underlined and numbered. In the right-hand column, you will find alternatives for each underlined part. In most cases, you are to choose the one that correctly expresses the idea, makes the statement appropriate for standard written English, or is worded most consistently with the style and tone of the passage as a whole. If you think the original version is correct, choose "NO CHANGE." In some cases, you will find in the right-hand column a question about the underlined part of the passage. You are to choose the correct answer to the question.

You will also find questions about a section of the passage or the passage as a whole. These questions do not refer to an underlined portion of the passage, but rather are identified by a number or numbers in a box.

For each question, choose the alternative you consider correct and blacken the corresponding oval on your answer document. Read each passage through once before you begin to answer the questions that accompany it. For many of the questions, you must read several sentences beyond the question to determine the answer. Be sure that you have read far enough ahead each time you choose an alternative.

PASSAGE I

Crocheting Makes a Good Hobby

Crocheting is the art of making fabric by twisting yarn or thread with a hook. Although many associate it by older people,
<ins>1</ins>

crocheting can be a fun hobby for people of all ages. Once you
<ins>2</ins>
start crocheting, you won't be able to put down the hook; you'll have a hobby for life. ☐ 3

1. A. NO CHANGE
   B. to
   C. on
   D. with

2. F. NO CHANGE
   G. people of all ages, young and old.
   H. young and old people of all ages.
   J. people of all ages, both young and old people alike.

3. At this point, the author is considering adding the following true statement:

> Irish nuns helped save lives with crocheting when they used it as a way to make a living during the Great Irish Potato Famine of 1846.

Should the writer add this sentence here?

   A. Yes, because it is essential to know when crocheting became internationally prominent and how it did so.
   B. Yes, because the reference to the Great Irish Potato Famine demonstrates that the author is conscious of historical events.
   C. No, because the reference to the Great Irish Potato Famine is not relevant to the main topic of this essay.
   D. No, because many people who left Ireland in 1846 brought crocheting with them to the United States and Australia.

GO ON TO THE NEXT PAGE.

Time-honored and easily taught to all, crocheting is an easy
hobby to pick up. Instructional books are readily available, and

once you've learned a few basic stitches. Picking up the more
advanced ones is a snap. Once you learn how to crochet, you can

purchase store-bought books that detail crocheting patterns that
tell you exactly how to make the projects that interest you. Even
if you want to try several projects, the supplies required for

it's completion are minimal; all you need are a crochet hook,
yarn, and a pair of scissors. You don't need to worry about
making a big investment, either; fifteen dollars will buy you no
fewer than three starter kits!

[1] As you grow more proficient, you can expand your
supplies by purchasing hooks of different types to vary the
size of your stitches. [2] Crochet hooks are available in all

sizes, ranging, from very small to very large, with everything in
between. [3] Some are so big that you need to use two strands of
yarn. [4] Other hooks are very tiny, so small that you must use
thread. [5] These hooks are suitable for making smaller, more
delicate things such as lace doilies, tablecloths, and bedspreads.
[6] These hooks make big stitches, so you can finish a project
with them very quickly. [7] It is best to start with hooks that are
medium in size; these are the easiest to manipulate and require
only one strand of yarn. [11]

4. F. NO CHANGE
   G. teaches
   H. taughted
   J. teached

5. A. NO CHANGE
   B. stitches; picking
   C. stitches, picking
   D. stitches since picking

6. F. NO CHANGE
   G. buy books and other pamphlets at craft and book stores detailing certain specific patterns
   H. buy pattern books
   J. acquire store-bought pattern books

7. A. NO CHANGE
   B. its
   C. its'
   D. their

8. F. NO CHANGE
   G. fewer then
   H. less than
   J. less then

9. A. NO CHANGE
   B. types;
   C. types:
   D. types,

10. F. NO CHANGE
    G. sizes, ranging
    H. sizes; ranging
    J. sizes ranging,

11. For the sake of the logic and coherence of this paragraph, Sentence 6 should be placed:
    A. where it is now.
    B. after Sentence 1.
    C. after Sentence 3.
    D. after Sentence 7.

GO ON TO THE NEXT PAGE.

Because it seems like there are a million hooks to keep
track of, crocheting makes a good hobby because it requires only
time and patience, not attention or tremendous investment. You
can crochet while watching television, listening to music, or
visiting with other people. It is fun and relaxing and allows you
to express your creative side in an easy way. Also, you have
finished a project, you have a cherished keepsake. Whether you

have made an afghan to keep you warm on cold winter nights or
a lace tablecloth to add a touch of elegance to your dining room,
your creation is sure to be cherished for a long time to come.

12. Given that all the choices are true, which one provides the most effective transition from the preceding paragraph to this one?
   F. NO CHANGE
   G. Because it can take a long time to finish a project,
   H. With such a simple and inexpensive set of materials,
   J. No longer a field dominated primarily by older women,

13. A. NO CHANGE
    B. finally you
    C. despite the fact you
    D. once you

14. F. NO CHANGE
    G. at
    H. of
    J. within

Question 15 asks about the preceding passage as a whole.

15. Suppose the writer's goal had been to write an essay that demonstrates the commercial potential of crocheting. Would this essay successfully accomplish that goal?

   A. Yes, because it gives examples of end products of crocheting and shows the different kinds of materials needed to produce a wide range of products.
   B. Yes, because it discusses the supplies necessary to create crocheted products, and it shows the usefulness of many of them during the cold winter months.
   C. No, because it does not mention the market value of crocheted products or how one might go about selling them.
   D. No, because it describes other industries and hobbies that would be more commercially successful.

PASSAGE II

Seurat's Masterpiece

[1] How can I describe the wonder I felt the first time I saw
my favorite painting, Georges Seurat's *A Sunday on La Grande
Jatte*? [2] I had admired the work for years in art books, but I
never thought I saw the actual painting, which was housed in
Chicago, many miles from where I lived. [3] I finally got my

16. F. NO CHANGE
    G. would see
    H. had seen
    J. was seeing

GO ON TO THE NEXT PAGE.

chance to when I met someone else who loved the painting as
much as I did. [4] We both had three days off at the same time,
so we decided to make a road trip to Chicago so we could see
the painting in all it's grandeur. [5] We packed our bags,

jumped into the car, and headed on our way toward Chicago. [20]

[1] The first thing that struck me as we entered the room
where the painting was displayed; was the size of the painting.
[2] A common size for canvases is 24 by 36 inches. [3] It was
enormous! [4] It covered a large part of an even larger wall. [5]
The painting's size amazed me since it was painted with dots, a
technique called pointillism. [6] To create a painting of such
magnitude using this technique seemed an almost impossible
task. [7] Seurat had done it, though, and had made it look easy! [23]

17. A. NO CHANGE
B. at the moment
C. just to
D. DELETE the underlined portion.

18. F. NO CHANGE
G. our
H. its
J. its'

19. A. NO CHANGE
B. jumped into the car, and had headed
C. jumped into the car, and head
D. had jumped into the car, and headed

20. Upon reviewing this paragraph and noticing that some information has been left out, the writer composes the following sentence, incorporating the information:

> Her name was Lisa; she lived in my dorm, and a mutual friend had introduced us to each other, knowing how much both of us loved art.

For the sake of the logic of this paragraph, this sentence should be placed after Sentence:

F. 2.
G. 3.
H. 4.
J. 5.

21. A. NO CHANGE
B. displayed:
C. displayed,
D. displayed

22. F. NO CHANGE
G. task and difficult to complete.
H. task, difficult to complete.
J. task, overwhelming in its difficulty.

23. Which of the following sentences is LEAST relevant to the development of this paragraph and therefore could be deleted?

A. Sentence 2
B. Sentence 4
C. Sentence 5
D. Sentence 6

GO ON TO THE NEXT PAGE.

Even more impressive, however, was the beauty of the
painting. Viewed from a distance, the colors looked muted,
capturing the idyllic mood of a summer day in the park.

When I approached the painting, though, its colors exploded into
myriad hues, illustrating the artist's skill in combining colors to
create a mood. Even the parts of the painting that appeared white
from a distance were vibrantly multicolored when viewed up

close. 26 The effect was incredible;

he sat and stared at the painting in wonder for a good portion of

the afternoon. 28

My friend and I saw many other sights, on our trip to
Chicago, but the best part by far was being able to see our favorite
work of art. The image is forever imprinted in my mind

24. Given that all of the choices are accurate, which provides the most effective and logical transition from the preceding paragraph to this one?

- **F.** NO CHANGE
- **G.** One thing that struck me was
- **H.** Many art critics have written about
- **J.** The debate rages on over

25. Which of the following alternatives to the underlined portion would NOT be acceptable?

- **A.** As I approached the painting, though,
- **B.** However, as I approached the painting,
- **C.** I approached the painting, though,
- **D.** However, when I approached the painting,

26. If the writer were to delete the phrase "from a distance" from the preceding sentence, the paragraph would primarily lose:

- **F.** an essential point explaining the author's love of the painting.
- **G.** the first part of the contrast in this sentence, which the author uses to describe viewing the painting.
- **H.** a further indication of the length of the road trip taken by the author and her friend.
- **J.** nothing, because the information provided by this phrase is stated more clearly elsewhere in the paragraph.

27. A. NO CHANGE
B. one
C. they
D. we

28. At this point, the writer is considering adding the following true statement:

> The Art Institute of Chicago contains many other famous paintings, among them Edvard Munch's *The Scream* and Grant Wood's *American Gothic*.

Should the writer make this addition here?

- **F.** Yes, because it gives additional details essential to understanding the collection at the museum.
- **G.** Yes, because it demonstrates a contrast between the author's favorite painting and those in this sentence.
- **H.** No, because it provides information that is not relevant at this point in the paragraph and essay.
- **J.** No, because it is contradicted by other information presented in this essay.

29. A. NO CHANGE
B. sights, which
C. sights;
D. sights

GO ON TO THE NEXT PAGE.

at the museum gift shop, even when I'm not looking at the
$\underline{\text{souvenir print}}$ I bought.
₃₀

PASSAGE III

The Language of Cats

Many people believe that language is the domain of human

beings. However, cats have $\underline{\text{developed an intricate language}}$ not
₃₁

for each other, but for the human beings who

$\underline{\text{have adopted them as pets.}}$
₃₂

When communicating with each other, $\underline{\text{cats' "talk" is a}}$
₃₃
$\underline{\text{complex system of nonverbal signals.}}$ In particular, their tails,
₃₃

rather than any kind of "speech," $\underline{\text{provide}}$ cats' chief means of
₃₄
expression. They also use physical contact to express their

feelings. With other cats, cats will use their voices only to

express pain. $\boxed{35}$

Next, incredibly, all of that changes when a human walks
₃₆
into the room. Cats use a wide range of vocal expressions when

they communicate with a person, from affectionate meows to

30. The best placement for the underlined portion would be:

    F. where it is now.
    G. after the word *image*.
    H. after the word *looking*.
    J. after the word *bought* (ending the sentence with a period).

31. **A.** NO CHANGE
    B. developed, an intricate language
    C. developed an intricate language,
    D. developed; an intricate language

32. Which choice would most clearly and effectively express the ownership relationship between humans and cats?

    F. NO CHANGE
    G. like to have cats around.
    H. often have dogs as well.
    J. are naturally inclined to like cats.

33. **A.** NO CHANGE
    B. a complicated system of nonverbal signals is used by cats to "talk."
    C. cats "talk" with a complex system of nonverbal signals.
    D. "talking" is done by them with a system of complex nonverbal signals.

34. **F.** NO CHANGE
    G. having provided
    H. has provided
    J. were provided by

35. If the preceding sentence were deleted, the essay would primarily lose:

    A. a redundant point made elsewhere in the essay.
    B. another description of the ways in which cats communicate nonverbally.
    C. an exception to the general trend described in this paragraph.
    D. a brief summary of the information contained in the essay up to this point.

36. **F.** NO CHANGE
    G. (Do NOT begin new paragraph) Incredibly,
    H. (Begin new paragraph) Next incredibly,
    J. (Begin new paragraph) Incredibly,

GO ON TO THE NEXT PAGE.

menacing hisses. Since cats verbal expressions are not used to
<u>   </u>
                    37

communicate with other cats, it is logical and reasonable
                                    <u>   </u>
                                              38
to conclude that cats developed this "language" expressly to

communicate with their human owners.

This fact is demonstrated more clear since observing
                                    <u>   </u>
                                         39
households that have only one cat. An only cat is usually very

vocal, since the only creature around with whom the cat can

communicate is its owner. Cats with other feline companions,

though, are much quieter. If they want to have a conversation, they

need only go to their fellow cats and communicate in their natural

way. 40

Since cats learned to meow for the sole purpose of

communicating with human beings, owners should take the time

to learn what their different meows mean. If an owner

knows, to name just a few examples, which meow means the cat is
<u>   </u>
   41
hungry, which means the cat wants to be petted, and which means

the cat wants to have a little "conversation," the bond between cat

and owner will grow deeper. 42 Certainly, after a time, owners

will see that communicating with their pets, not just cats, is every

bit as important to forging good relationships

as to communicate with other humans. Once, as an owner,
<u>   </u>
         43
you know that the cat is not just

37. A. NO CHANGE
   B. cat's verbal expressions
   C. cats' verbal expressions
   D. cats verbal expressions,

38. F. NO CHANGE
   G. logical and well-reasoned
   H. logical to a startling degree
   J. logical

39. A. NO CHANGE
   B. clear when
   C. clearly since
   D. clearly when

40. At this point, the writer is considering adding the following true statement:

> On the other hand, the natural way for most birds to communicate is vocally, by way of the "bird song."

Should the writer add this sentence here?

   F. Yes, because it shows that cats are truly unique in communicating nonverbally.
   G. Yes, because it adds a relevant and enlightening detail about another animal.
   H. No, because it basically repeats information given earlier in the essay.
   J. No, because it does not contribute to the development of this paragraph and the essay as a whole.

41. A. NO CHANGE
   B. knows, to,
   C. knows to,
   D. knows to

42. If the writer wanted to emphasize that cats communicate vocally with their owners to express a large number of different emotions in addition to those listed in the previous sentence, which of the following true statements should be added at this point?

   F. Many animals communicate hunger similarly to cats.
   G. Cats will tell their owners when they feel pain, sadness, irritation, or love.
   H. Cats communicate these emotions differently to other cats.
   J. Humans have the easiest time communicating with other mammals.

43. A. NO CHANGE
   B. as being communicative
   C. as communicating
   D. through communicating

GO ON TO THE NEXT PAGE.

making senseless noises without any rhyme or reason but is
makingenseless noises without any rhyme or reason but is
<u>making senseless noises without any rhyme or reason</u> but is
making an attempt to communicate, you can make an effort to

communicate back. After all, your cat isn't meowing just for the

sake of making noise; <u>however, cats are less communicative than</u>

<u>many other animals.</u>

44. F. NO CHANGE
G. making senseless noises
H. senselessly making noises with no thought involved
J. making senseless noises, having no idea what they mean,

45. Which choice would best summarize the main point the essay makes about cats' communication with their human owners?
A. NO CHANGE
B. rather, there's a good chance your cat is trying to tell you something.
C. instead, your cat is probably trying to communicate with other cats by meowing.
D. on the other hand, it is better to have more than one cat so they can undergo a natural development.

PASSAGE IV

Visiting Mackinac Island

Visiting Mackinac (pronounced "Mackinaw") Island is like
<u>taking a step back to the past in time.</u> Victorian

<u>houses'</u> and a fort dating back to the War of 1812 surround the

historic downtown, where horses and buggies still pull

passengers down the road.

The only way to get to <u>Mackinac Island is by boat or private</u>

plane, and you may not bring your car. Automobiles are

outlawed on the little, <u>isolated, Michigan, island,</u> so visitors can

see the sights only by horse, carriage, or <u>by riding a bicycle,</u> or

on foot. Luckily, the island is small enough that cars are not

<u>necessary, Mackinac</u> measures only a mile and a half in

diameter.

46. F. NO CHANGE
G. moving in a past-related direction
H. going back to the past, not the future,
J. stepping back

47. A. NO CHANGE
B. house's
C. houses
D. houses,

48. F. NO CHANGE
G. your sweet self over to
H. yourself on down to
J. over to

49. A. NO CHANGE
B. isolated Michigan island
C. isolated Michigan island,
D. isolated, Michigan, island

50. F. NO CHANGE
G. by bicycle,
H. riding on a bicycle,
J. bicycle,

51. A. NO CHANGE
B. necessary, furthermore, Mackinac
C. necessary. Mackinac
D. necessary Mackinac

GO ON TO THE NEXT PAGE.

There are many things to see while visiting Mackinac Island. The majestic Grand Hotel is a popular tourist spot, as are the governor's mansion and Arch Rock, a towering limestone arch formed naturally by water erosion. [52] Fort Mackinac, where they still set off cannons every hour, is also a popular place to visit. Visible from parts of the island are Mackinac Bridge—the longest suspension bridge ever built—and a picturesque old lighthouse.

Shopping is also a favorite pastime on Mackinac Island. The island's biggest industry is tourism, [53] For the island's many tourists, the most popular item of sale on Mackinac Island is
                                                    54

fudge. The downtown streets are lined with fudge shops, where
                                                             55
tourists can watch fudge of all different flavors being made before lining up to buy some for themselves. These fudge shops are so numerous and abundant that the local residents have even
        56

developed a special nickname for these tourists: I call the
                                                     57
tourists "fudgies."

Apart from sightseeing and shopping, Mackinac Island is a great place to just sit back and relax. In the summer, a gentle lake breeze floats through the air, when it creates a beautiful,
                                              58
temperate climate. It is peaceful to sit in the city park and watch the ferries and private boats float into the harbor. The privacy of

52. If the writer were to delete the phrase "formed naturally by water erosion" (placing a period after the word *arch*), this sentence would primarily lose:

F. a detail describing the unique formation of the Arch Rock.

G. factual information concerning the geological formations of the tourist attractions on Mackinac Island.

H. a contrast to the governor's mansion, which was constructed by human hands.

J. nothing; this information is detailed elsewhere in this paragraph.

53. Given that all the following are true, which one, if added here at the end of this sentence, would provide the most effective transition to the topic discussed in the sentence that follows?

A. so there are many souvenir stores, T-shirt shops, and candy and ice cream parlors.

B. so Mackinac Island has not been negatively affected by outsourcing.

C. which is a big change from the island's eighteenth-century use in the fur trade.

D. but it's not a tourist attraction like many others with theme parks and chain restaurants.

54. F. NO CHANGE
G. for selling
H. for sale
J. of selling

55. Which of the following alternatives to the underlined portion would NOT be acceptable?

A. which
B. so
C. and
D. in which

56. F. NO CHANGE
G. abundantly numerous
H. numerous
J. of an abundance truly numerous

57. A. NO CHANGE
B. one calls
C. it calls
D. they call

58. F. NO CHANGE
G. creating
H. once it creates
J. as if it had created

GO ON TO THE NEXT PAGE.

the island's environs certainly <u>don't give</u> it the hustle-bustle
₅₉
quality of a city, but the relaxing atmosphere makes Mackinac
Island the perfect place to visit to get away from the hectic pace
of everyday life.

59. A. NO CHANGE
   B. isn't giving
   C. hasn't given
   D. doesn't give

Question 60 asks about the preceding passage as a whole.

---

60. Suppose the writer had intended to write an essay on the difficulty the residents of Mackinac Island have had prohibiting automobile traffic from the historic island. Would this essay have successfully fulfilled that goal?

   F. Yes, because the automobile has become such an essential part of American tourist travel that the residents are clearly threatened.
   G. Yes, because this essay discusses the fact that automobiles are outlawed and goes on to detail many of the reasons this was possible.
   H. No, because the essay focuses instead on other aspects of Mackinac Island, mentioning automobiles in only one part of the passage.
   J. No, because this essay describes the ways the residents of Mackinac Island have sought to bring automobiles back to the island, not to outlaw them.

PASSAGE V

Fun with Karaoke

[1]

[1] Karaoke is one of the most popular forms of entertainment in the world. [2] What defies understanding, though, is why so many ordinary people insist on getting up on stage in public, humiliating themselves in front of both their <u>friends; and peers.</u> [3] Whether practiced at home, in a
₆₁
restaurant, or at a party, karaoke is a form of <u>entertainment</u>
₆₂
<u>that provides</u> people with a great time and a positive feeling. [4]
₆₂
It is understandable that people would enjoy singing in the

61. A. NO CHANGE
   B. friends and
   C. friends, and
   D. friends and,

62. Which of the following alternatives to the underlined portion would NOT be acceptable?

   F. entertainment that can provide
   G. entertainment, providing
   H. entertainment, one which provides
   J. entertainment that having provided

GO ON TO THE NEXT PAGE.

privacy of their homes. [5] There are many different ways to respond to this question. ⬚63

[2]

Looking more closely, and you'll see a main reason for karaoke's success is its glitz and glamour. Karaoke provides people with a moment when they are more than just everyday folks—they are stars. Even though their performances may be heard only in dimly lit bars or busy restaurants, but karaoke singers are still performing as if in a true concert with such

concert-hall staples, as microphones, lights, and applause. Even though the singers' voices are not spectacular, the audience

has known that it's all for fun and responds anyway. And in the

end, everyone would like to be a rock star. Karaoke is as close as many people will get to fame and stardom, but this is not the only reason for its enduring popularity.

[3]

There is another, more obvious reason why karaoke is so popular and singing in public is such fun. The average person allows his or her singing to be heard only in the shower or in the car as the radio plays. Karaoke, by contrast, allows the average person the opportunity to share that ordinarily solitary

experience with other people. In lieu of how good or bad their voices are, people can experience the sheer joy of music with

63. For the sake of logic and coherence, Sentence 2 should be placed:
A. where it is now.
B. after Sentence 3.
C. after Sentence 4.
D. after Sentence 5.

64. F. NO CHANGE
G. Having looked
H. To look
J. Look

65. A. NO CHANGE
B. restaurants which
C. restaurants,
D. restaurants but

66. F. NO CHANGE
G. staples:
H. staples
J. staples;

67. A. NO CHANGE
B. is knowing
C. knew
D. knows

68. Given that all the choices are true, which one would most effectively conclude this paragraph while leading into the main focus of the next paragraph?
F. NO CHANGE
G. This is why AudioSynTrac and Numark Electronics were so successful in debuting the first sing-along tapes and equipment back in the 1970s.
H. Japan's lasting influence on karaoke is obvious all the way down to its name—the Japanese word karaoke translates roughly to "empty orchestra."
J. Singing in front of people is more fun for many people than singing in the shower or in the car.

69. A. NO CHANGE
B. furthermore,
C. moreover,
D. as a result,

70. F. NO CHANGE
G. Regardless of
H. However
J. Because of

GO ON TO THE NEXT PAGE.

others, whose singing is mostly a private affair as well, through
 ̄71
karaoke.

[4]

The effect karaoke has on people may also provide an
explanation for its popularity: it helps bring people who are
ordinarily shy out of their shells. ⟨72⟩ Karaoke helps them
overcome stage fright, build their self-confidence, and conquer

their fears. The singers may feel nervous or silly if they first take
 ̄73
the stage, but when the audience breaks out into applause, the

singers are sure to feel rewarded.

[5]

Whatever the reason, karaoke continues to grow in
popularity. Last year, karaoke made no less than $7 billion in
 ̄74
profit in Japan. Many dismiss it as a fad, but as long as karaoke
is fun and leaves people feeling good, it will not disappear.

71. A. NO CHANGE
  B. who
  C. whom
  D. who's

72. If the writer were to delete the clause "who are ordinarily shy"
from the preceding sentence, the essay would primarily lose:

  F. a detail that explains why karaoke is so popular in the
  international community.
  G. a detail meant to indicate that karaoke is popular among
  those not normally inclined to sing in public.
  H. information that emphasizes the possible psychological
  benefits of karaoke for the chronically shy.
  J. an indication that karaoke may be used at some future time
  to help singers overcome stage fright.

73. A. NO CHANGE
  B. when
  C. unless
  D. where

74. F. NO CHANGE
  G. lesser than
  H. fewer then
  J. few than

> Question 75 asks about the preceding passage
> as a whole.

75. Upon reviewing notes for this essay, the writer comes across
some information and composes the following sentence incorporating that information:

> While different regions of the United States prefer
> different artists, the most popular karaoke requests
> are invariably for country artists, varying from the
> modern Carrie Underwood to the classic Johnny Cash.

For the sake of the logic and coherence of this essay, this
sentence should be:

  A. placed at the end of Paragraph 3.
  B. placed at the end of Paragraph 4.
  C. placed at the end of Paragraph 5.
  D. NOT added to the essay at all.

END OF TEST 1

STOP! DO NOT TURN THE PAGE UNTIL TOLD TO DO SO.

MATHEMATICS TEST

60 Minutes—60 Questions

DIRECTIONS: Solve each problem, choose the correct answer, and then darken the corresponding oval on your answer sheet.

Do not linger over problems that take too much time. Solve as many as you can; then return to the others in the time you have left for this test.

You are permitted to use a calculator on this test. You may use your calculator for any problems you choose, but some of the problems may best be done without using a calculator.

Note: Unless otherwise stated, all of the following should be assumed:

1. Illustrative figures are NOT necessarily drawn to scale.
2. Geometric figures lie in a plane.
3. The word *line* indicates a straight line.
4. The word *average* indicates arithmetic mean.

---

1. Point *X* is located at –15 on the real number line. If point *Y* is located at –11, what is the midpoint of line segment *XY* ?

   A. –13
   B. –4
   C. –2
   D. 2
   E. 13

DO YOUR FIGURING HERE.

2. Given triangle *CDE* (shown below) with a right angle at point *E*, what is the length of leg *DE* ?

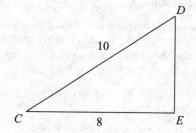

   F. $\sqrt{2}$
   G. 2
   H. 6
   J. $\sqrt{164}$
   K. 16

GO ON TO THE NEXT PAGE.

DO YOUR FIGURING HERE.

3. Lucy is studying her ant farm. She needs to approximate the number of ants in the population, and she realizes that the number of ants, N, is close to 50 more than double the volume of the ant farm, V. Which of the formulas below expresses that approximation?

A. $N \approx \frac{1}{2}V + 50$

B. $N \approx \frac{1}{2}(V + 50)$

C. $N \approx 2V + 50$

D. $N \approx 2(V + 50)$

E. $N \approx V^2 + 50$

4. Lisa has 5 fiction books and 7 nonfiction books on a table by her front door. As she rushes out the door one day, she takes a book at random. What is the probability that the book she takes is fiction?

F. $\frac{1}{5}$

G. $\frac{5}{7}$

H. $\frac{1}{12}$

J. $\frac{5}{12}$

K. $\frac{7}{12}$

5. In the spring semester of her math class, Katie's test scores were 108, 81, 79, 99, 85, and 82. What was her average test score in the spring semester?

A. 534

B. 108

C. 89

D. 84

E. 80

GO ON TO THE NEXT PAGE.

DO YOUR FIGURING HERE.

6. Given parallel lines *l* and *m*, which of the following choices lists a pair of angles that must be congruent?

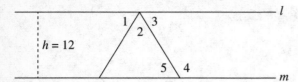

F. ∠1 and ∠2
G. ∠1 and ∠3
H. ∠2 and ∠3
J. ∠2 and ∠5
K. ∠3 and ∠5

7. Gregor works as a political intern and receives a monthly paycheck. He spends 20% of his paycheck on rent and deposits the remainder into a savings account. If his deposit is $3,200, how much does he receive as his monthly pay?

A. $ 4,000
B. $ 5,760
C. $ 7,200
D. $ 8,000
E. $17,000

8. Given parallelogram *ABCD* below and parallelogram *EFGH* (not shown) are similar, which of the following statements must be true about the two shapes?

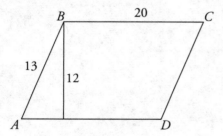

F. Their areas are equal.
G. Their perimeters are equal.
H. Side *AB* is congruent to side *EF*.
J. Diagonal *AC* is congruent to diagonal *EG*.
K. Their corresponding angles are congruent.

9. A size 8 dress that usually sells for $60 is on sale for 30% off. Victoria has a store credit card that entitles her to an additional 10% off the reduced price of any item in the store. Excluding sales tax, what is the price Victoria pays for the dress?

A. $22.20
B. $24.75
C. $34.00
D. $36.00
E. $37.80

GO ON TO THE NEXT PAGE.

10. Erin and Amy are playing poker. At a certain point in the game, Erin has 3 more chips than Amy. On the next hand, Erin wins 4 chips from Amy. Now how many more chips does Erin have than Amy?

   F.   −1
   G.   4
   H.   7
   J.   11
   K.   14

11. If $y = 4$, then $|1 - y| = $?

   A.   −5
   B.   −3
   C.   3
   D.   4
   E.   5

12. $(3a + 2b)(a - b^2)$ is equivalent to:

   F. $4a + b^2$
   G. $3a^2 - 2b^3$
   H. $3a^2 + 2ab + 2b^3$
   J. $3a^2 - 3ab^2 + a^2b^2$
   K. $3a^2 - 3ab^2 + 2ab - 2b^3$

13. For all real values of y, $3 - 2(4 - y) = $?

   A. $-2y - 9$
   B. $-2y + 8$
   C. $-2y - 1$
   D. $2y - 5$
   E. $2y + 11$

14. Which of the following is equivalent to $(y^3)^8$?

   F. y^{11}
   G. y^{24}
   H. $8y^3$
   J. $8y^{11}$
   K. $24y$

15. If the first day of the year is a Monday, what is the 260th day?

   A.   Monday
   B.   Tuesday
   C.   Wednesday
   D.   Thursday
   E.   Friday

DO YOUR FIGURING HERE.

GO ON TO THE NEXT PAGE.

DO YOUR FIGURING HERE.

16. If a square has an area of 64 square units, what is the area of the largest circle that can be inscribed inside the square?

    F. 4π
    G. 8π
    H. 16π
    J. 64
    K. 64π

17. What is the product of the solutions of the equation $x^2 - 5x - 14 = 0$?

    A. -14
    B. -2
    C. 0
    D. 5
    E. 7

18. Factoring the polynomial $x^{12} - 9$ reveals a number of factors for the expression. Which of these is NOT one of the possible factors?

    F. $x^6 + 3$
    G. $x^{12} - 9$
    H. $x^3 + \sqrt{3}$
    J. $x^3 - \sqrt{3}$
    K. $x - \sqrt{3}$

19. What is the value of $\dfrac{2x+4}{3x}$ when $x = \dfrac{1}{6}$?

    A. $4\dfrac{1}{3}$
    B. 2
    C. $\dfrac{26}{3}$
    D. 12
    E. 24

20. If you drive 60 miles at 90 miles an hour, how many minutes will the trip take you?

    F. 15
    G. 30
    H. 40
    J. 60
    K. 90

GO ON TO THE NEXT PAGE.

21. The area of a trapezoid is found by multiplying the height by the average of the bases: $A = \frac{1}{2}h(b_1 + b_2)$. Given the side measurements below, what is the area, in square inches, of the trapezoid?

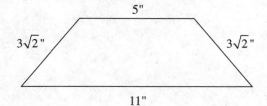

A. $15\sqrt{2}$
B. 22
C. 24
D. $24\sqrt{2}$
E. $30\sqrt{2}$

DO YOUR FIGURING HERE.

22. If $x = -\frac{2}{3}$ and $x = \frac{1}{4}$ are the roots of the quadratic equation $ax^2 + bx + c = 0$, then which of the following could represent the two factors of $ax^2 + bx + c$?

F. $(3x + 2)$ and $(4x - 1)$
G. $(3x + 1)$ and $(4x - 2)$
H. $(3x - 1)$ and $(4x + 2)$
J. $(3x - 2)$ and $(4x + 1)$
K. $(3x - 2)$ and $(4x - 1)$

23. In the rhombus below, diagonal $AC = 6$ and diagonal $BD = 8$. What is the length of each of the four sides?

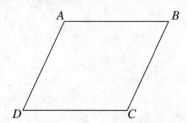

A. $\sqrt{7}$
B. $\sqrt{14}$
C. 5
D. 7
E. 10

GO ON TO THE NEXT PAGE.

24. A rectangular rug has an area of 80 square feet, and its width is exactly 2 feet shorter than its length. What is the length, in feet, of the rug?

F. 8
G. 10
H. 16
J. 18
K. 36

DO YOUR FIGURING HERE.

25. In the standard (x,y) coordinate plane, a line runs through points $(1,-5)$ and $(5,10)$. Which of the following represents the slope of that line?

A. $\dfrac{4}{15}$

B. $\dfrac{4}{5}$

C. 1

D. $\dfrac{5}{4}$

E. $\dfrac{15}{4}$

26. The equation of a circle in the standard (x,y) coordinate plane is given by the equation $(x+5)^2 + (y-5)^2 = 5$. What is the center of the circle?

F. $\left(-\sqrt{5},\ \sqrt{5}\right)$
G. $(\ -5,\quad 5)$
H. $\left(\ \sqrt{5},\ -\sqrt{5}\right)$
J. $(\ 5,\ -5)$
K. $(\ 5,\quad 5)$

27. The graph below shows the function $f(x)$ in the the standard (x,y) coordinate plane. Which of the following choices best describes the *domain* of this function?

A. $\{0, 1, 2, 3, 4\}$
B. $\{0, 1, 2\}$
C. $\{x : 0 < x < 2\}$
D. $\{x : 0 < x < 4\}$
E. All real values of x

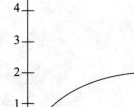

GO ON TO THE NEXT PAGE.

28. Amber decides to graph her office and the nearest coffee shop in the standard (x,y) plane. If her office is at point $(-1,-5)$ and the coffee shop is at point $(3,3)$, what are the coordinates of the point exactly halfway between those of her office and the shop? (You may assume Amber is able to walk a straight line between them.)

F. $(1, -1)$
G. $(1, 4)$
H. $(2, -1)$
J. $(2, 4)$
K. $(2, 0)$

29. For a chemistry class, Sanjay is doing an experiment that involves periodically heating a container of liquid. The graph below shows the temperature of the liquid at different times during the experiment. What is the average rate of change of temperature (in degrees Celsius per minute) during the times in which the temperature is increasing?

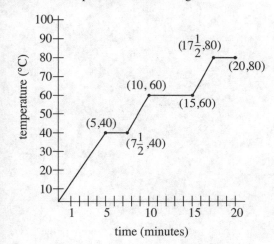

A. 4
B. 5
C. 8
D. 10
E. 20

30. If $\dfrac{a^x}{a^y} = a^5$, for $a \neq 0$, which of the following statements must be true?

F. $x \neq 0$ and $y \neq 0$

G. $x + y = 5$

H. $x - y = 5$

J. $xy = 5$

K. $\dfrac{x}{y} = 5$

GO ON TO THE NEXT PAGE.

31. What is the slope of the line given by the equation $8 = 3y - 5x$?

    A. -5

    B. $-\dfrac{5}{3}$

    C. $-\dfrac{3}{5}$

    D. $\dfrac{3}{5}$

    E. $\dfrac{5}{3}$

DO YOUR FIGURING HERE.

32. When adding fractions, a useful first step is to find the least common denominator (LCD) of the fractions. What is the LCD for these fractions?

$$\frac{2}{3^2 \times 5}, \frac{13}{5^2 \times 7 \times 11}, \frac{2}{3 \times 11^3}$$

    F. $3 \times 5 \times 7 \times 11$
    G. $3^2 \times 5^2 \times 7 \times 11$
    H. $3^2 \times 5^2 \times 11^3$
    J. $3^2 \times 5^2 \times 7 \times 11^3$
    K. $3^3 \times 5^3 \times 7 \times 11^4$

33. $\dfrac{1}{4} \times \dfrac{2}{5} \times \dfrac{3}{6} \times \dfrac{4}{7} \times \dfrac{5}{8} \times \dfrac{6}{9} \times \dfrac{7}{10} = ?$

    A. $\dfrac{1}{720}$

    B. $\dfrac{1}{360}$

    C. $\dfrac{1}{120}$

    D. $\dfrac{27}{49}$

    E. 1

GO ON TO THE NEXT PAGE.

34. Dave is in Pikeston and needs to go to Danville, which is about 110 miles due south of Pikeston. From Danville, he'll head east to Rocketville, about 200 miles from Danville. As he sets out on his trip, a plane takes off from the Pikeston airport and flies directly to Rocketville. Approximately how far, in miles, does the plane fly?

DO YOUR FIGURING HERE.

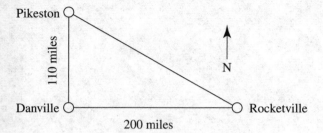

F. 310

G. $\sqrt{310}$

H. $\sqrt{27,900}$

J. $\sqrt{30,000}$

K. $\sqrt{52,100}$

35. The figure below is a pentagon (5-sided figure). Suppose a second pentagon were overlaid on this pentagon. At most, the two figures could have how many points of intersection?

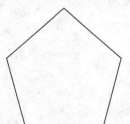

A. 1
B. 2
C. 5
D. 10
E. Infinitely many

36. MicroCorp will hold its annual company picnic next week and will assign planning duties to 3 of its employees. One person selected will reserve a venue, another will arrange catering, and a third will plan activities. There are 10 employees eligible to fulfill these duties, and no employee can be assigned more than one duty. How many different ways are there for duties to be assigned to employees?

F. 7^3

G. 9^3

H. 10^3

J. $9 \times 8 \times 7$

K. $10 \times 9 \times 8$

GO ON TO THE NEXT PAGE.

37. In the (x,y) coordinate plane below, points P (6,2) and Q (1,4) are two vertices of △PQR. If ∠PQR is a right angle, then which of the following could be the coordinates of R ?

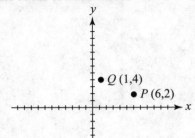

A. (4, −3)
B. (3, 0)
C. (2, 1)
D. (2, 4)
E. (3, 9)

38. If $y = 0.25(100 - y)$, then what is the value of y ?

F. 200
G. 75
H. 25
J. 20
K. 18

39. If $0° \le x \le 180°$ and $4\cos^2 x = 1$, then $x = $?

A. 0°
B. 60°
C. 90°
D. 150°
E. 180°

40. Danielle's living room is a rectangle with the dimensions 16 feet by 18 feet. If she partially covers the bare floor with a circular throw rug with a diameter of 12 feet, what is the approximate area of bare floor, in square feet, that remains exposed?

(Note: Assume the rug lies completely flat and does not touch any wall.)

F. 113
G. 144
H. 175
J. 288
K. Cannot be determined without knowing the exact position of the rug

GO ON TO THE NEXT PAGE.

41. A portion of a parabola is shown below. Over which of the following intervals is the average rate of change the greatest?

A. $0 \leq x \leq 2$
B. $2 \leq x \leq 5$
C. $5 \leq x \leq 10$
D. $10 \leq x \leq 13$
E. $13 \leq x \leq 14$

DO YOUR FIGURING HERE.

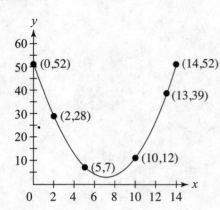

42. In the figure given below, what is $\sin \theta$?

F. $\dfrac{1}{2}$

G. $\dfrac{\sqrt{3}}{3}$

H. $\dfrac{\sqrt{3}}{2}$

J. 1

K. $\sqrt{3}$

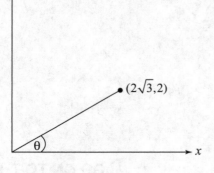

GO ON TO THE NEXT PAGE.

DO YOUR FIGURING HERE.

43. The magnitude of an earthquake on the Richter Scale is determined by the equation $R = \log\left(\dfrac{A}{A_0}\right)$, in which A is the maximum amplitude measured at a sensor and A_0 is the threshold amplitude, dependent only on the sensor distance from the epicenter. What is the approximate magnitude, on the Richter Scale, of an earthquake with a measured amplitude 3,000 times the value of A_0?

    A. 2.5
    B. 3
    C. 3.5
    D. 4
    E. 4.5

44. Set $P = \{2, 3, 5.5, 6\}$ Set $Q = \{1, 2, 3, 4\}$

    If m is randomly selected from Set P and n is randomly selected from Set Q, what is the probability that mn is an even integer?

    F. $\dfrac{3}{4}$
    G. $\dfrac{11}{16}$
    H. $\dfrac{9}{16}$
    J. $\dfrac{1}{4}$
    K. $\dfrac{3}{16}$

45. Which choice below is the complete solution set of $|2z - 3| \geq 7$?

    A. $z \geq 5$
    B. $z \leq -2$ or $z \geq 5$
    C. $-5 \leq z \leq 5$
    D. $z \leq -6$ or $z \geq 2$
    E. $z \leq -5$ or $z \geq 2$

GO ON TO THE NEXT PAGE.

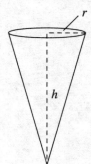
46. Which trigonometric function (where defined) is equivalent to

$$\frac{\sin^2 x}{\cos x \tan x}?$$

DO YOUR FIGURING HERE.

- **F.** $\dfrac{\cos x}{\sin^2 x}$

- **G.** $\dfrac{1}{\cos x}$

- **H.** $\sin x$

- **J.** $\dfrac{1}{\sin x}$

- **K.** $\dfrac{1}{\sin^2 x}$

47. When $a \neq b$, $\dfrac{ax - bx}{4a - 4b} < 0$. Which of the following describes the complete set of x values that make this inequality true?

- **A.** $x = -4$ only

- **B.** $x = 4$ only

- **C.** $x = -\dfrac{1}{4}$ only

- **D.** $x < 0$

- **E.** $x > 0$

48. The volume of a cone, which is derived by treating it as a pyramid with infinitely many lateral faces, is given by the formula $V = \dfrac{1}{3}\pi r^2 h$, where r is the radius of the base, and h is the height. If the radius is halved and the height is doubled, what will be the ratio of the new volume to the old volume?

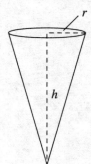

- **F.** 4:1
- **G.** 2:1
- **H.** 1:1
- **J.** 1:2
- **K.** 1:4

GO ON TO THE NEXT PAGE.

DO YOUR FIGURING HERE.

49. Al bikes a trail to the top of a hill and back down. He bikes up the hill in *m* minutes, and then returns twice as quickly downhill on the same trail. What is the total time, in hours, that Al spends biking up the hill and back down?

A. $\dfrac{m}{60}$

B. $\dfrac{m}{40}$

C. $\dfrac{m}{30}$

D. $\dfrac{3m}{2}$

E. $2m$

50. A cylindrical cup with an interior radius of 5 centimeters has a cube of ice with side length 3 centimeters inside of it. The cup is then filled with lemonade until the lemonade reaches a height of 9 centimeters. Assuming the ice cube is fully submerged, which of the following expressions gives the volume, in cubic centimeters, of the lemonade poured into the cup?

F. $9(10^2)\pi - 3^3$
G. $9(5^2)\pi - 3^3$
H. $3(9^2)\pi - 5^3$
J. $9(3^2)\pi - 5^3$
K. $2(5)(9)\pi - 3^3$

51. A circle is inscribed in a square, as shown below. If *x* is the distance from the center of the circle to a vertex of the square, then what is the length of the radius of the circle, in terms of *x* ?

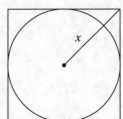

A. $2x$

B. $x\sqrt{2}$

C. x

D. $\dfrac{x\sqrt{2}}{2}$

E. Cannot be determined from the information given

GO ON TO THE NEXT PAGE.

DO YOUR FIGURING HERE.

52. $\begin{bmatrix} 4a & 3 & -1 \\ 2 & 1 & 5 \end{bmatrix} \begin{bmatrix} 2 & 7 \\ 4 & 3 \\ 1 & 5 \end{bmatrix} = \begin{bmatrix} 35 & 88 \\ 13 & 42 \end{bmatrix}$

What value of *a* satisfies the matrix equation above?

F.   12

G.   7

H.   5

J.   4

K.   3

53. A pipe of radius $4\sqrt{2}$ feet sends water to two smaller pipes of equal size. If the cross-sectional area of each of the smaller pipes is exactly one-fourth that of the larger pipe, what is the radius of one of the smaller pipes?

A.   2

B. 2π

C. $2\sqrt{2}$

D. $4\sqrt{2}$

E. $2\pi\sqrt{2}$

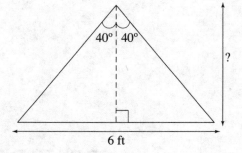

54. The cross-sectional view of a tent is shown below. If the tent is 6 feet wide at its base, then which of the following expressions could be used to calculate the height of the tent, in feet?

F. $\dfrac{3}{\tan 80°}$

G. $3\tan 40°$

H. $\dfrac{3}{\tan 40°}$

J. $6\tan 40°$

K. $3\tan 80°$

GO ON TO THE NEXT PAGE.

55. Which of the following sets has the lowest standard deviation?

DO YOUR FIGURING HERE.

- **A.** $\{-10, -5, 0, 5, 10\}$
- **B.** $\{100, 200, 300, 400, 500\}$
- **C.** $\{2, 4, 6, 8, 10\}$
- **D.** $\{100, 100, 101, 102, 102\}$
- **E.** $\{1, 2, 3, 4, 5\}$

56. For all integer values of a and b such that $a > 0$ and $b < 0$, which of the following must also be an integer?

F. 3^{a+b}

G. 3^{a-b}

H. 3^{ab}

J. 3^{-a}

K. $3^{\frac{a}{b}}$

57. If x and y are real numbers and $0 < x < y < \dfrac{y}{x}$, which of the

following gives the set of all values which $\dfrac{y}{x}$ could have?

A.

B.

C.

D.

E.

GO ON TO THE NEXT PAGE.

58. A circular running track is being built in a fenced-in athletic field 100 feet wide and 150 feet long. If a border of 10 feet is needed between the outside edge of the track and the fence, what is the radius of the largest track that can be built?

 F. 40
 G. 45
 H. 65
 J. 90
 K. 110

DO YOUR FIGURING HERE.

59. If a sphere is cut by two different planes, dividing it into sections, how many sections is it possible to end up with?

 A. 2 only
 B. 2 or 4 only
 C. 3 only
 D. 3 or 4 only
 E. 2, 3, or 4 only

60. For all real values of a and b, the equation $|a - b| = 5$ can be interpreted as "the positive difference of a and b is 5." What is the positive difference between the 2 solutions for a ?

 F. b

 G. $b + 5$

 H. $2b$

 J. $\sqrt{b^2 - 25}$

 K. 10

END OF TEST 2

STOP! DO NOT TURN THE PAGE UNTIL TOLD TO DO SO.

DO NOT RETURN TO A PREVIOUS TEST.

READING TEST

35 Minutes—40 Questions

DIRECTIONS: There are several passages in this test. Each passage is accompanied by several questions. After reading a passage, choose the best answer to each question and fill in the corresponding oval on your answer document. You may refer to the passages as often as necessary.

Passage I

LITERARY NARRATIVE: Passage A is adapted from the essay "What Baseball Taught Us" by Richard Brown (©2007 by Richard Brown). Passage B is adapted from the essay "The Major Leagues" by Jack Bryant (©1998 by Jack Bryant).

Passage A by Richard Brown

April 15, 1947: I happen to be home sick from school, and my grandfather is delighted to have someone to share his anticipation with. He's been pacing the house all morning, occasionally sitting down but quickly hopping back up, adjusting the TV
5 antennas, cleaning his glasses, flicking an imaginary piece of lint off the television screen. Amidst my mother's protestations, I am brought out of my stuffy, dark bedroom where I have been confined to fight my fever and propped up on the sofa with four quilts over me, at least three more than I really need. Fever or
10 no, my grandfather wants me to witness history.

Jackie Robinson is making his major league debut for the Brooklyn Dodgers, the first African-American player in the Major League Baseball. I'm not sure what's more stifling, the quilts, or my grandfather's tense excitement that has us all on edge. I'm
15 proud that Robinson is playing—there's been a long build-up to this day, and he has taken people's prejudice and abuse like a gentleman, never losing his cool. I know he'll do the same today. I wonder, through my fever and quilts, just what my grandfather thinks will happen.

20   We were not Dodgers fans before Jackie Robinson. Our team was the Memphis Red Sox, in the Negro League. But now we are watching the small, jerky figures take the field hundreds of miles away in Brooklyn. At first base, number 42, is a black man. My grandfather has finally settled down, staring at the tele-
25 vision in disbelief. My mother has tears in her eyes. The Braves are at bat, and Robinson gets the first man out, on a ground ball thrown from third. The crowd cheers. In the bottom of the first inning, he grounds out. I let out a loud groan. My grandfather turns to look at me, his eyes ablaze. He quietly tells my mother
30 to take me back to bed.

Later, I try to apologize to my grandfather, and I blame my outburst on the fever. It's partly true—I needed to break the tension, which I probably felt more keenly because of my illness, but he doesn't buy it. *He needs our support, son. Take a cue from*
35 *the way he's stood up to his critics, and stand up for him. What matters is how he plays the whole game, not an occasional out.* I realize then that I had been nervous, too. I had expected the impossible—I had wanted him to bat a thousand.

Passage B by Jack Bryant

Opening Day, 1947—some friends and I cut school and in-
40 stead made our way to Ebbets Field to see Jackie Robinson make his major league debut. We hadn't expected to get in; everyone thought the game would be sold out, with crowds overflowing into the streets near the stadium. We just wanted to be part of that crowd. We had been saving up money, just in case, and it paid
45 off. The game was not sold out, and we got in. I hadn't been to a major league game before, and inside the stadium I felt I was in some utopian society that existed without segregation and racism. The crowd, which was more than half black, cheered as Jackie made the first out of the game at first base. Though
50 he didn't get a hit in the game, he scored a run after drawing a walk, and got eleven put-outs at first base.

My friends and I were flying high as we left the stadium. If a black man was now playing for the Brooklyn Dodgers, we felt there was nothing we couldn't do. Later that same season,
55 Larry Doby signed with the Cleveland Indians to become the first African American player in the American league. Change, we thought, was rapidly coming. To a certain extent that was true, but racism and injustice also persisted. Other teams treated Jackie badly, calling him names, threatening to strike if he played, and
60 handling him roughly. When the Dodgers were on the road, he often was not allowed to stay at the hotels where the rest of the team stayed. These injustices weren't new, but somehow I had thought they would go away when he took the field, that when Branch Rickey had offered him a contract, he was extending
65 an olive branch to all African Americans on behalf of white Americans.

GO ON TO THE NEXT PAGE.

Twenty-one years later, I remembered that day as I grieved the death of Dr. Martin Luther King, Jr., a victim of the struggle for racial equality that was ongoing. I had been so young, and so hopeful, and so hopelessly naïve. At times it felt like nothing had been accomplished in those 21 years. But that isn't entirely true. In baseball, getting a hit three out of every ten at bats is considered a good record. While I wish the struggle for equality were more like golf, in which the professionals hit the ball every time, we have come a long way since that day in 1947. But the season is 162 games long, and we are only part way through it.

Questions 1–3 ask about Passage A.

1. The last paragraph of Passage A (lines 31–38) marks a shift in the passage from:

A. the time when baseball was segregated to after African Americans started playing in the major leagues.

B. the narrator seeing things through a fever-induced delirium to his understanding of how he had misinterpreted events.

C. a description of the experience of a historical moment to a lesson learned from that moment.

D. the narrator's grandfather's happy anticipation of an event to his anger at how the event unfolded.

2. In Passage A, the narrator's descriptions of Jackie Robinson suggest that he sees him as ultimately:

F. a gentleman and a hero.

G. capable of doing the impossible.

H. a disappointing player.

J. overly excited and tense.

3. The narrator of Passage A most nearly suggests that his grandfather is annoyed with him for groaning because:

A. his grandfather believes the narrator shouldn't have criticized Robinson.

B. his grandfather was disappointed that Robinson grounded out but didn't want to say so.

C. the noise disturbed his grandfather's concentration on the game.

D. the narrator was too sick to be out of bed and watching baseball.

Questions 4–7 ask about Passage B.

4. The narrator's statement "inside the stadium I felt I was in some utopian society that existed without segregation and racism" (lines 46–48) is most nearly meant to:

F. describe the way people interact with each other inside a baseball stadium.

G. express the narrator's feelings of the momentousness of the occasion.

H. illustrate the way that Jackie Robinson changed society by playing in the major leagues.

J. foreshadow the way the narrator would feel 21 years later.

5. Passage B indicates that compared to the narrator's expectation about how Jackie Robinson's appearance in Major League Baseball would affect segregation, its actual effect was:

A. different; the narrator had thought the crowd at the game would be bigger than it was.

B. different; the narrator had thought segregation would quickly disappear.

C. similar; the narrator had thought Robinson was a good choice for the Dodgers.

D. similar; the narrator had thought racism and injustice would last for a long time.

6. Based on the passage, the information about Dr. Martin Luther King, Jr. provided in lines 67–69 is most likely included to:

F. show that not all of the narrator's role models were baseball players.

G. provide historical context for the importance of Jackie Robinson's role in baseball.

H. illustrate how little progress the narrator felt had been made in the struggle for racial equality.

J. convey the idea that Jackie Robinson's influence was felt far beyond the world of sports.

7. The narrator of Passage B makes a comparison between:

A. the struggle for racial equality and the baseball season.

B. professional golf and major league baseball.

C. tense excitement and bed covers.

D. striking out in baseball and experiencing injustice.

GO ON TO THE NEXT PAGE.

Questions 8–10 ask about both passages.

8. Which of the following statements provides the most accurate comparison of the tone of each passage?
   F. Passage A is hopeful and cheery, while Passage B is dreary and pessimistic.
   G. Passage A is objectively factual, while Passage B is descriptive and detailed.
   H. Both passages maintain a sense of disappointment throughout.
   J. Both passages begin with a sense of optimism and end with a sense that expectations had been too high.

9. Compared to the narrator of Passage A, the narrator of Passage B provides more information about:
   A. the play-by-play analysis of Jackie Robinson's first major league game.
   B. the long-term effects of Jackie Robinson's appearance in the major leagues.
   C. Jackie Robinson's baseball career before signing with the Dodgers.
   D. the role of Negro League baseball in the early 20th century.

10. It can reasonably be inferred that after seeing Jackie Robinson play, compared to the narrator of Passage B, the narrator of Passage A felt:
   F. less optimistic about how race relations would change.
   G. less interested in continuing to follow the Dodgers.
   H. more disappointed that he hadn't played better.
   J. more excited about the future for African-American baseball players.

GO ON TO THE NEXT PAGE.

THIS PAGE IS INTENTIONALLY LEFT BLANK.

GO ON TO THE NEXT PAGE.

Passage II

SOCIAL SCIENCE: This passage is adapted from T. H. Watkins' *The Great Depression* (©1993, Little, Brown and Co.; Blackside Inc.).

One of the most durable and well regarded of all the New Deal's programs came from President Roosevelt himself, who had his own share of inventiveness. If the president cared about the fate of people, he also cared about the fate of trees, having
5 practiced the art of silviculture on his Hyde Park estate with such enthusiasm that on various official forms he was fond of listing his occupation as "tree farmer." It was in early March, 1933, that he proceeded to bring the two concerns together—enlisting young unemployed men in a kind of volunteer "army" to be put to
10 work in the national forests, national parks, and on other federal public lands. When he went to Congress for authorization of the program, he called the new agency the Civilian Corps Reforestation Youth Rehabilitation Movement, but before sinking under the weight of an acronym like CCRYRM, it was soon changed
15 to the Civilian Conservation Corps (known forever after as the CCC). Congress chose not to handle the details itself. It simply authorized the president to create the program and structure it as he saw fit by executive order; it was to last two years. Responsibility was divided up among the Labor Department, which was
20 to screen and select the enrollees, the War Department, which would house and feed them in their nonworking hours, and the Departments of Agriculture and Interior, which would design and supervise projects in regional and national forests, national parks, and other public lands. The men would be paid $30 a
25 month, anywhere from $23 to $25 of it to be sent to their families.

The CCC officially began on April 5, 1933, calling for an enrollment of 250,000 to be housed in 1,468 camps around the country. The cost for the first year was estimated at $500 million. The men had to be US citizens between the ages of seventeen
30 and twenty-seven (later, twenty-four), out of school, out of work, capable of physical labor, over 60 inches but under 78 inches in height, more than 107 pounds in weight, and had to possess no fewer than "three serviceable natural masticating teeth above and below." They would serve terms of no more than nine months
35 so that as many as possible could be accommodated over the course of time.

Among the earliest enrollees were some veterans who had returned to Washington, setting up camp and demanding payment of their bonuses for service during the war. While making
40 it clear that he opposed the payments on economic grounds, FDR provided tents, showers, mess halls, and latrines, and, waiving the age restriction for them, invited the members of this new Bonus Army to join his new agency. What was more, Eleanor Roosevelt dropped by one rainy day for a visit, slogging through
45 ankle-deep mud to meet and talk with the men. "Hoover sent the army," said one veteran of the previous summer's BEF disaster, "Roosevelt sent his wife." When it became clear that no bonus would be forthcoming, about twenty-five hundred of the men took Roosevelt up on his offer and joined the CCC.

50 In the summer of 1934, Roosevelt expanded the size of the CCC to 350,000 and would raise it to 500,000 in 1935. Congress continued to reauthorize it faithfully over the next seven years, and by the time it was closed out in 1942, the CCC had put more than three million young "soil soldiers" to work. In the national
55 forests alone they built 3,470 fire towers, installed 65,100 miles of telephone lines, scraped and graded thousands of fire breaks, roads, and trails, and built 97,000 miles of truck trails and roads, spent 4.1 million man-hours fighting fires, and cut down and hauled out millions of diseased trees and planted more than 1.3
60 billion young trees in the first major reforestation campaign in the country's history. For the National Park Service, they built roads, campgrounds, bridges, and recreation and administration facilities; for the Biological Survey (a predecessor of today's Fish and Wildlife Service), they conducted wildlife surveys
65 and improved wildlife refuge lands; and for the Army Corps of Engineers, they built flood control projects in West Virginia, Vermont, and New York State.

In return, the CCC, at its best, took at least some young men out of the urban tangle of hopelessness where so many resided,
70 introduced them to the intricacies and healing joy of the outdoors, and clothed and fed them better than many had been for years. Moreover, the program taught more than a hundred thousand to read and write, passed out twenty-five thousand eighth-grade diplomas and five thousand high-school diplomas, gave structure and
75 discipline to lives that had experienced little of either, strengthened bodies and minds, and for many provided a dose of self-esteem they had never known.

11. The main idea of the passage is that:

A. the CCC forced unemployed young men to work in the national forests, national parks, and on other federal public lands for no payment or bonus.

B. it was only after President Roosevelt created the CCC that veterans had suitable employment during the Great Depression.

C. research into the history of the New Deal shows that the idea for the CCC came from Congress.

D. among the programs of the New Deal, the CCC employed young men to build public works projects on public lands in return for modest wages, food, clothing, and some education.

GO ON TO THE NEXT PAGE.

12. The main idea of the third paragraph (lines 37–49) is that:

   F. President Hoover had dispatched the army to meet with disgruntled veterans, but President Roosevelt sent his wife, Eleanor, to meet with the Bonus Army.

   G. when they realized President Roosevelt would not pay the bonus, many veterans abandoned the Bonus Army and accepted his invitation to join the CCC.

   H. President Roosevelt supplied shelter and food to the veterans before paying the bonus the veterans demanded.

   J. many of the veterans were above the age requirement of the CCC.

13. As it is used in line 7 to describe President Roosevelt, the term *tree farmer* most nearly means that Roosevelt:

   A. had supported his family by growing trees before he entered politics.

   B. believed in an agrarian economy over urban industrialization.

   C. continued his successful business selling trees while in office.

   D. had a great interest in trees and knew a good deal about them.

14. According to the passage, which of the following was a project the CCC performed for the National Park Service?

   F. Building fire towers

   G. Building campground facilities

   H. Installing telephone lines

   J. Conducting wildlife surveys

15. According to the passage, which of the following statements is true about the CCC?

   A. The agency provided enrollees with academic instruction.

   B. The agency provided enrollees with urban job training.

   C. The agency accepted only men with six teeth.

   D. The agency offered courses in nutrition and self-esteem.

16. Information in the fourth paragraph (lines 50–67) makes it clear that the CCC:

   F. was voluntary and therefore did not pay members anything.

   G. ran for more years and employed more men than was originally intended.

   H. employed 4.1 million men.

   J. battled fires in West Virginia, Vermont, and New York.

17. The passage most strongly suggests that before the 1930s, the national forests:

   A. received no federal support or aid for projects to clear diseased trees.

   B. included land reserved for wildlife refuges.

   C. had never undergone a major reforestation campaign.

   D. experienced more floods than forest fires.

18. According to the passage, when did the CCC change its name?

   F. After President Roosevelt received authorization from Congress

   G. After Congress protested that CCRYRM was too difficult to say

   H. In the same year the size expanded to 500,000 men

   J. After the Bonus Army disbanded

19. The passage states that the same year the CCC was authorized enrollees had to be:

   A. over 78 inches in height.

   B. in school.

   C. between the ages of seventeen and twenty-seven.

   D. between the ages of seventeen and twenty-four.

20. According to the passage, CCC programs in national parks and forests were:

   F. conducted far from where the members were fed and housed.

   G. under the control of the Departments of Agriculture and the Interior.

   H. supervised by the Labor Department.

   J. minimum-wage jobs.

GO ON TO THE NEXT PAGE.

Passage III

HUMANITIES: This passage is adapted from John Gattuso, ed., Native America (©1993, Houghton Mifflin Co.).

Northwest natives are carvers by tradition, but it was the natives of the far north, in what is now British Columbia and Alaska, who first carved totem poles. The history of these fasci- nating works is surprisingly brief, for it wasn't until the mid-18th
5 century, when European explorers first encountered these remote tribes, that the unique sculptures began to appear. Although the natives were already expert carvers of canoes, tools, longhouses, and furniture, they lacked the iron tools necessary to fell a mas- sive tree in one piece and carve its entire length.

10 With the iron axes they got in trade for their baskets, boxes, and pelts, the coastal tribes of the far north could take advantage of the trees that grew so tall and straight in their wet climate. Initially, the poles were made to stand against the front of a house, with figures facing out and a door cut through the base, so all
15 would enter the house through the pole. In this case, the totem pole functioned as a family crest, recounting genealogies, stories, or legends that in some way identified the owner. Towards the end of the 19th century, the poles stood free on the beach or in the village outside the carvers' homes. Some villages were virtual
20 forests of dozens, sometimes hundreds, of poles.

The family that carved the pole gave a potlatch with feast- ing, games, and much gift-giving. The guests, in return, raised the pole. These gatherings were costly and required a great deal of preparation and participation. The custom frustrated whites
25 trying to "civilize" the Indians, especially missionaries who solved the problem by knocking the poles down. Employers, too, complained that their Indian workers were unreliable when a pole was being carved or a potlatch planned. Eventually, both the Canadian and United States governments banned potlatches,
30 and pole carving nearly died out. The ban was lifted in the 1950s.

The Tlingit, on the southeastern coast of Alaska, and the Haidas and Tsimshian of western Canada are known for their pole carving. On a tour in 1899, a group of Seattle businessmen visited the Tlingit village of Tongas and, finding no one there, took
35 one of the poles. They erected it in Seattle where, at a towering 50 ft., it became one of the city's most distinctive monuments. In 1938, Tlingit carvers copied the pole after the original was destroyed by fire, and it remains in Pioneer Square today.

Poles serve the important purpose of recording the lore of
40 a clan, much as a book would. The top figure on the pole identi- fies the owner's clan, and succeeding characters (read from top to bottom) tell their stories. Raven, the trickster, might tell the story of how he fooled the Creator into giving him the sun, or Frog might tell how he wooed a human woman. With slight
45 variations between villages, everyone knew these stories, and potlatch guests dramatized them at the pole-raising with masks, drumming, and songs. And so the legends were preserved from one generation to the next.

There is a story behind almost every image on the pole. For
50 example, if an animal had the power to transform itself into other beings, the carver would portray it in all its forms. If Raven were sometimes bird, sometimes human, he would be carved with both wings and limbs, or have a human face with a raven's beak. Other images are used to describe the spirits' special abilities.
55 Eyes are frequently used to suggest acuteness or skill. So, for example, if an eye appears in an animal's ear, it might indicate that that animal has a sharp sense of hearing. And human figures in unexpected places, like an ear or nose, might mean that the animal has great powers.

60 Learning to read totem poles is like learning to read a lan- guage. They speak of history, mythology, social structure, and spirituality. They serve many purposes and continue to be carved by the descendants of the original carvers.

Today, Haida, Tlingit, Tsimshian, Kwakiutl and other na-
65 tive craftsmen carve, predominantly for the tourist trade, small "souvenir" totem poles in wood and black slate (or argillite). They also carve extraordinarily beautiful masks, effigies, boxes, house posts, and fixtures....

21. Which of the following statements best expresses the main idea of the passage?

  A. Many Native American tribes created totem poles with meaningful symbols, but these poles were less important than the canoes carved before the mid-18th century.

  B. Although the Tlingit village was deserted, the Seattle businessmen who took the totem pole were not right to take it without permission.

  C. The history of totem pole carving dates back to only the mid-18th-century, but these poles have played an impor- tant role in Native American culture since that time.

  D. The ban issued by the Canadian and United States governments against potlatches was lifted in the 1950s, but interest in totem-pole carving had diminished by that time.

22. Which of the following questions is NOT answered in the passage?

  F. In terms of geographical region, which were the first groups to carve totem poles?

  G. What is the tallest totem pole in North America?

  H. What is the predominant use of the small totem poles carved today?

  J. What prevented Native American tribes from carving totem poles before the 18th century?

GO ON TO THE NEXT PAGE.

23. The passage suggests that one of the main purposes of totem poles is the way in which they:

   A. demonstrate the artistic skill of the carvers.
   B. function as landmarks in major North American cities.
   C. document the history and mythology of various clans.
   D. complement the festivities of the potlatch.

24. The main function of the sixth paragraph (lines 49–59) is to:

   F. identify the origins of the stories behind every image on a totem pole.
   G. describe and explain some of the images that might appear on a totem pole.
   H. contrast the images on the totem poles of the Northwest natives with those of British Columbia and Alaska.
   J. explain the role of the Raven in Native American mythology.

25. All of the following are used in the passage as illustrations of the role totem poles play in Native American culture EXCEPT the:

   A. function of the top figure on the pole.
   B. descriptions of the Raven and Frog as characters on the pole.
   C. reference to the popularity of totem poles in the tourist industries of many tribes.
   D. placement of the Tlingit totem pole in Seattle's Pioneer Square.

26. The second paragraph (lines 10–20) establishes all of the following about the totem poles carved by the coastal tribes of the far north EXCEPT that they were:

   F. initially used as the entryways of houses.
   G. fashioned from tall, straight trees.
   H. used to identify the owners of the poles.
   J. produced only by clans with family crests.

27. One of the main points of the fifth paragraph (lines 39–48) is that the various characters on a totem pole are meant to represent:

   A. the owner of the totem pole.
   B. the lore of the owner's clan.
   C. Raven, the trickster, fooling the Creator.
   D. Frog wooing a human woman.

28. According to the passage, which of the following places is home to the Tlingit?

   F. Seattle
   G. Western Canada
   H. Pioneer Square
   J. Alaska

29. The author most likely includes the information in lines 60–63 to suggest that:

   A. totem poles are notable for reasons beyond physical beauty.
   B. totem poles have replaced books for Native American tribes.
   C. Native American tribes have no spoken or written language.
   D. the descendants of the original carvers of totem poles carve copies of older poles.

30. Which of the following words best describes the attitude of the employers referred to in the third paragraph (lines 21–30) in reaction to potlatches?

   F. Patient
   G. Accepting
   H. Irritated
   J. Civilized

GO ON TO THE NEXT PAGE.

Passage IV

NATURAL SCIENCE: This passage is adapted from the article "The Pioneer Mission to Venus" by Janet G. Luhmann, James B. Pollack, and Lawrence Colin (©1994, Scientific American).

Venus is sometimes referred to as the Earth's "twin" because it resembles the Earth in size and in distance from the sun. Over its 14 years of operation, the National Aeronautics and Space Administration's *Pioneer Venus* mission revealed that the relation
5 between the two worlds is more analogous to Dr. Jekyll and Mr. Hyde. The surface of Venus bakes under a dense carbon dioxide atmosphere, the overlying clouds consist of noxious sulfuric acid, and the planet's lack of a magnetic field exposes the upper atmosphere to the continuous hail of charged particles from the
10 sun. Our opportunity to explore the hostile Venusian environment came to an abrupt close in October 1992, when the *Pioneer Venus Orbiter* burned up like a meteor in the thick Venusian atmosphere. The craft's demise marked the end of an era for the U.S. space program; in the present climate of fiscal austerity, there is no
15 telling when humans will next get a good look at Earth's nearest planetary neighbor.

The information gleaned by *Pioneer Venus* complements the well-publicized radar images recently sent back by the *Magellan* spacecraft. *Magellan* concentrated on studies of Venus's surface
20 geology and interior structure. *Pioneer Venus*, in comparison, gathered data on the composition and dynamics of the planet's atmosphere and interplanetary surroundings. These findings illustrate how seemingly small differences in physical conditions have sent Venus and the Earth hurtling down very different evo-
25 lutionary paths. Such knowledge will help scientists intelligently evaluate how human activity may be changing the environment on the Earth.

Well before the arrival of *Pioneer Venus*, astronomers had learned that Venus does not live up to its image as Earth's near-
30 twin. Whereas Earth maintains conditions ideal for liquid water and life, Venus's surface temperature of 450 degrees Celsius is hotter than the melting point of lead. Atmospheric pressure at the ground is some 93 times that at sea level on Earth.

Even aside from the heat and the pressure, the air on Venus
35 would be utterly unbreathable to humans. The Earth's atmosphere is about 78 percent nitrogen and 21 percent oxygen. Venus's much thicker atmosphere, in contrast, is composed almost entirely of carbon dioxide. Nitrogen, the next most abundant gas, makes up only about 3.5 percent of the gas molecules. Both planets
40 possess about the same amount of gaseous nitrogen, but Venus's atmosphere contains some 30,000 times as much carbon dioxide as does Earth's. In fact, Earth does hold a quantity of carbon dioxide comparable to that in the Venusian atmosphere. On Earth, however, the carbon dioxide is locked away in carbonate
45 rocks, not in gaseous form in the air. The crucial distinction is responsible for many of the drastic environmental differences that exist between the two planets.

The large *Pioneer Venus* atmospheric probe carried a mass spectrometer and gas chromatograph, devices that measured the
50 exact composition of the atmosphere of Venus. One of the most stunning aspects of the Venusian atmosphere is that it is extremely dry. It possesses only a hundred thousandth as much water as Earth has in its oceans. If all of Venus's water could somehow be condensed onto the surface, it would make a global puddle
55 only a couple of centimeters deep.

Unlike Earth, Venus harbors little if any molecular oxygen in its lower atmosphere. The abundant oxygen in Earth's atmo- sphere is a by-product of photosynthesis by plants; if not for the activity of living things, Earth's atmosphere also would be
60 oxygen poor. The atmosphere of Venus is far richer than Earth's in sulfur-containing gases, primarily sulfur dioxide. On Earth, rain efficiently removes similar sulfur gases from the atmosphere.

Pioneer Venus revealed other ways in which Venus is more primordial than Earth. Venus's atmosphere contains higher con-
65 centrations of inert, or noble, gases—especially neon and isotopes of argon—that have been present since the time the planets were born. This difference suggests that Venus has held on to a far greater fraction of its earliest atmosphere. Much of Earth's primi- tive atmosphere may have been stripped away and lost into space
70 when our world was struck by a Mars-size body. Many planetary scientists now think the moon formed out of the cloud of debris that resulted from such a gigantic impact.

31. With regard to the possibility of returning to the planet Venus, information presented in the passage makes it clear that the authors are:

   A. cheerful and optimistic.
   B. sarcastic and contentious.
   C. doubtful and pragmatic.
   D. uncertain and withdrawn.

32. Which of the following statements most accurately summarizes how the passage characterizes the state of scientific knowledge about Venus before the *Pioneer* mission?

   F. The scientific community was hesitant to return to Venus after an earlier mission had ended in disaster.
   G. Scientists saw Earth and Venus as near polar opposites in atmospheric conditions.
   H. The common belief that Earth and Venus were "twins" had been eroding under the weight of scientific evidence.
   J. Scientists knew little about the planet Venus because they were more interested in other planets.

GO ON TO THE NEXT PAGE.

33. Based on the passage, Earth may have retained less of its early atmosphere than Venus did due to:

   A. the impact that occurred when Earth was struck by Mars.
   B. a cloud of debris that stripped the atmosphere away.
   C. rain that removes sulfur gases from the atmosphere.
   D. a collision between Earth and another massive object.

34. The main point of the second paragraph (lines 17–27) is to:

   F. account for the failure of the *Magellan* mission and to show the superiority of the *Pioneer* mission.
   G. suggest that information from both the *Magellan* and *Pioneer* missions can bring the scientific community to a deeper understanding of Venus.
   H. show that the *Magellan* had sent back information regarding physical characteristics while the *Pioneer* had not.
   J. hypothesize that the findings of the *Pioneer* mission will help scientists to approach problems more intelligently.

35. The passage indicates that if humans were to attempt to live on the planet Venus, survival would not be possible because:

   A. of the mistaken belief that Venus and Earth are "twin" planets.
   B. carbon dioxide is locked away in bicarbonate rocks, not in gaseous form.
   C. the atmospheric pressure, heat, and air are not suitable for human life.
   D. all of the water on Venus is condensed onto the surface.

36. According to the passage, some evidence gained before the *Pioneer Venus* mission suggesting that Earth and Venus are not near-twins stated that:

   F. Venus produces no lead on or underneath its surface.
   G. Earth was found to be much farther from the sun than was previously thought.
   H. the atmosphere of Venus contains 78 percent nitrogen and 21 percent oxygen.
   J. the surface temperature of Venus is 450 degrees Celsius and thus unlivable for humans.

37. As it is used in line 56, the word *harbors* most nearly means:

   A. shelters.
   B. hides.
   C. holds.
   D. cherishes.

38. According to the passage, "primordial" most nearly refers to planets that:

   F. are oxygen-poor due to a lack of activity by living things.
   G. are not hospitable to humans because they have thick atmospheres and high surface temperatures.
   H. have preserved many of the characteristics present when the planets were formed.
   J. have been struck by large bodies which have altered the planets' atmospheres.

39. It can reasonably be inferred that the "activity of living things" described in line 59 directly refers to organisms on Earth that:

   A. produce oxygen by their own natural processes and influence the contents of Earth's atmosphere.
   B. remove sulfur gases from the atmosphere during heavy rainfall.
   C. lock away carbon dioxide in carbonate rocks and maintain a reserve of the gas.
   D. could easily live in oppressive atmospheres similar to the atmosphere of Venus.

40. According to the passage, the *Pioneer Venus* mission to Venus involved investigating details relating to the planet's:

   F. surface geology and interior structure.
   G. atmosphere as it has been changed by the influence of photosynthesis.
   H. similarities to the planet Earth.
   J. atmospheric contents.

END OF TEST 3
STOP! DO NOT TURN THE PAGE UNTIL TOLD TO DO SO.
DO NOT RETURN TO A PREVIOUS TEST.

SCIENCE TEST

35 Minutes–40 Questions

DIRECTIONS: There are several passages in this test. Each passage is followed by several questions. After reading a passage, choose the correct answer to each question and fill in the corresponding oval on your answer document. You may refer to the passages as often as necessary.

You are NOT permitted to use a calculator on this test.

Passage I

Metallic *alloys*, solid mixtures of metal, are useful for coin production when they contain a high percentage of zinc. When electric current is applied to zinc in the presence of precious metal solutions of *silver nitrate, copper sulfate,* or *potassium gold cyanide*, the precious metals *plate* (form a coating) on the zinc surface.

- Silver nitrate, formed when silver dissolves in *nitric acid*, reacts with zinc to form solid silver and *zinc nitrate*.
- Copper sulfate, formed when copper dissolves in *sulfuric acid*, reacts with zinc to form solid copper and *zinc sulfate*.
- Potassium gold cyanide contains reactive gold ions.

A chemist performed experiments on precious metal plating.

Experiment 1

The chemist obtained 4 coin-like samples of a high percentage zinc alloy. All samples were circular, had a radius of 1 cm, and had the same thickness. The mass of each coin was recorded. Each coin was wired via a battery to a strip of either pure silver or copper metal. Coins wired to silver were placed in dilute nitric acid and coins wired to copper were placed in dilute sulfuric acid. An electric current of either 1,000 milliamperes (mA) or 2,000 mA was applied for 30 minutes to each sample. The coins were removed and the increase in mass from precious metal plating was recorded in milligrams. Results of the experiment are shown in Table 1.

	Table 1		
	Precious metal solution		Increased mass from plating (mg)
Coin sample	Identity	Electric current (mA)	
I	silver nitrate	1,000	2.0
II	silver nitrate	2,000	4.0
III	copper sulfate	1,000	1.2
IV	copper sulfate	2,000	2.4

Experiment 2

The chemist completely dissolved equal amounts of pure silver in 4 beakers of nitric acid. He then placed equivalent coin-like samples of zinc into the beakers for different lengths of time measured in minutes (min). The coin surfaces developed a silver metal coating without any electric current applied. The concentrations of silver coating on the coin and zinc nitrate in the surrounding solution were determined in parts per billion (ppb) and recorded in Table 2.

	Table 2		
Coin sample	Time (min)	Silver coating concentration (ppb)	Zinc nitrate concentration (ppb)
V	5	75	30
VI	15	125	55
VII	30	200	75
VIII	60	500	85

1. A comparison of the results for coin samples II and IV supports the hypothesis that zinc is plated more extensively when exposed to:

   A. silver nitrate and a current of 1,000 mA than silver nitrate and a current of 2,000 mA.
   B. copper sulfate and a current of 1,000 mA than copper sulfate and a current of 2,000 mA.
   C. silver nitrate than when exposed to copper sulfate.
   D. copper sulfate than when exposed to silver nitrate.

GO ON TO THE NEXT PAGE.

2. If the chemist were to repeat Experiment 1, but compress each coin sample to a radius of 0.5 cm to decrease the surface area exposed to the surrounding solution, how would the mass of precious metal plated most likely be affected?

   F. The mass of precious metal plated would decrease for all coin samples.
   G. The mass of precious metal plated would decrease for coin samples I and III and increase for coin samples II and IV.
   H. The mass of precious metal plated would remain constant for all coin samples.
   J. The mass of precious metal plated would increase for all coin samples.

3. According to the information in the passage, a zinc alloy coin sample exposed to which of the following conditions would result in the greatest concentration of zinc nitrate?

   A. 6 minutes in a solution with a high initial concentration of silver nitrate
   B. 6 minutes in a solution with a low initial concentration of silver nitrate
   C. 10 minutes in a solution with a high initial concentration of silver nitrate
   D. 10 minutes in a solution with a low initial concentration of silver nitrate

4. In Experiment 1, if the chemist had applied 1,580 mA to a 1 cm radius zinc alloy coin sample in a copper sulfate solution, approximately how much copper would have plated after 30 minutes?

   F. 0.6 mg
   G. 1.1 mg
   H. 1.9 mg
   J. 4.6 mg

5. In Experiment 1, which of the following variables was the same for all 4 zinc alloy coin sample trials?

   A. Change in mass from plating
   B. Electric current applied
   C. Type of precious metal solution used
   D. Initial radius of the sample

6. According to the passage, if a chemist wants to study the effect of plating zinc alloys with silver, the chemist should monitor the concentration of which of the following substances in the surrounding solution?

   F. Potassium gold cyanide
   G. Zinc nitrate
   H. Copper sulfate
   J. Sulfuric acid

7. One of the ways in which Experiment 2 differed from Experiment 1 is that in Experiment 2:

   A. Zinc was used to plate the coins, whereas in Experiment 1 only silver was used.
   B. The mass of the coins increased only, whereas in Experiment 1 the mass of the coins increased and then decreased.
   C. Only silver was used to plate the coins, whereas in Experiment 1 copper was also used.
   D. The mass of the coins increased and then decreased, whereas in Experiment 1 the mass of the coins increased only.

GO ON TO THE NEXT PAGE.

Passage II

Organic compounds are molecules that frequently contain carbon (C), hydrogen (H), and oxygen (O) joined together by covalent bonds (symbolized by straight lines in chemical notation). As the number of bonds to oxygen atoms increases in a carbon chain, the overall molecule is increasingly oxidized. For example, aldehydes are more oxidized than alcohols, which are more oxidized than alkanes, as shown in Table 1. The melting points of these compounds are listed in Table 2, and their *viscosities* (resistance to flow) are listed in Table 3.

Table 1

Carbons in the chain	Name prefix	Structure		
		alkane (suffix -ane)	alcohol (suffix -anol)	aldehyde (suffix -analdehyde)
4	but-			
5	pent-			
6	hex-			
7	hept-			
8	oct-			

Table 2

Carbons in the chain	Melting point (K)		
	alkane	alcohol	aldehyde
4	135	183	174
5	143	194	213
6	178	221	217
7	182	239	231
8	216	257	285

Table 3

Carbons in the chain	Viscosity (cP)		
	alkane	alcohol	aldehyde
4	0.01	3.0	0.4
5	0.24	5.1	0.5
6	0.29	5.4	0.8
7	0.39	5.8	1.0
8	0.54	8.4	1.2

GO ON TO THE NEXT PAGE.

8. Based on Table 1, which of the following is the chemical formula for pentanol?

   F. C_4H_{10}
   G. $C_4H_{12}O$
   H. C_5H_{12}
   J. $C_5H_{12}O$

9. Which organic compounds in Table 2 are solids at 215 K ?

   A. All alkanes, alcohols, and aldehydes with 5 carbons or fewer
   B. Alcohols and aldehydes with 6 or more carbons and octane
   C. The 4- and 5-carbon alcohols and aldehydes, and all alkanes with 7 or fewer carbons
   D. The 5-carbon pentane and pentanol compounds and the 4-carbon butane, butanol, and butanaldehyde

10. According to Tables 1 and 3, which organic compound has the highest viscosity?

   F. Octanol
   G. Octanaldehyde
   H. Hexanol
   J. Butane

11. According to Table 3, how do the different types of 5-carbon molecules differ with respect to their viscosity?

   A. The alkane has a higher viscosity than the aldehyde, and the aldehyde has a higher viscosity than the alcohol.
   B. The alkane has a higher viscosity than the alcohol, and the alcohol has a higher viscosity than the aldehyde.
   C. The alcohol has a higher viscosity than the alkane, and the alkane has a higher viscosity than the aldehyde.
   D. The alcohol has a higher viscosity than the aldehyde, and the aldehyde has a higher viscosity than the alkane.

12. For each type of organic compound, what is the relationship between the length of the carbon chain to the melting point and viscosity? As the number of carbons in the chain increases, the melting point:

   F. decreases, and the viscosity decreases.
   G. increases, and the viscosity increases.
   H. increases, but the viscosity decreases.
   J. decreases, but the viscosity increases.

13. According to Table 2, the difference in melting point between an alkane and an alcohol with the same number of carbons is approximately how much?

   A. 25 K
   B. 35 K
   C. 50 K
   D. 65 K

GO ON TO THE NEXT PAGE.

Passage III

A mass suspended by a lightweight thread and swinging back and forth approximates the motion of a *simple gravity pendulum*, a system in which gravity is the only force acting on the mass, causing an acceleration of 9.8 m/sec^2. The time to complete one cycle of swinging back and forth is the *period* and is inversely related to gravitational acceleration.

Using the same type and length of thread, 2 cubes were suspended, lifted to the same starting angle, and let go. The amount of time required for each pendulum to complete one swinging cycle (1 period) was recorded with a timer capable of reading to the nearest 0.01 sec. The measured times were used to calculate acceleration.

Experiment 1

A cube of lead (11.3 grams) and a cube of tin (7.4 grams) were suspended from a 0.5 m length of thread. Both cubes had the same length. (Note: A cube's volume is proportional to its length cubed; its surface area is proportional to its length squared.) The cubes were set in motion from a fixed starting angle, and the period for each was recorded.

Table 1		
Trial	Measured period (sec)	
	lead cube	tin cube
1	1.48	1.51
2	1.45	1.47
3	1.46	1.42
4	1.49	1.45
5	1.39	1.53

The average periods were 1.46 sec and 1.48 sec for the lead and tin cubes, respectively. The average accelerations were 9.3 m/sec2 for lead and 9.1 m/sec2 for tin.

Experiment 2

The same procedures used in Experiment 1 were repeated using a thread length of 1.0 m and the same fixed starting angle. Results were recorded in Table 2.

Table 2		
Trial	Measured period (sec)	
	lead cube	tin cube
6	2.10	2.12
7	2.04	2.06
8	2.05	2.07
9	2.12	2.11
10	2.00	2.10

The average periods were 2.06 sec and 2.09 sec for the lead and tin cubes, respectively. The average accelerations were 9.3 m/sec^2 for lead and 9.0 m/sec^2 for tin.

Experiment 3

Given the results of the first 2 experiments, the accuracy of the timer was tested. The procedures of Experiment 1 were repeated using only the lead cube. The trials were recorded on digital video at 100 frames per second. The video was then reviewed to obtain precise measurements of the period for each trial and results are shown in Table 3.

Table 3	
Trial	Measured period (sec)
11	1.47
12	1.42
13	1.49
14	1.50
15	1.46

The average period recorded in Table 3 was 1.47 sec.

GO ON TO THE NEXT PAGE.

14. To demonstrate that a pendulum's acceleration is reduced by drag force from air resistance, which additional experiment can be performed in addition to those in the passage?

F. The cubes are suspended by 0.5 m and 1.0 m springs and set in motion by extending the spring 9.8 cm and letting go in a vacuum chamber with no air pressure.
G. The cubes are suspended by 0.5 m and 1.0 m threads and set in motion from the same starting angle in a vacuum chamber with no air pressure.
H. The cubes are suspended by 0.5 m and 1.0 m springs and set in motion by extending the spring 9.8 cm and letting go in a vacuum chamber at 1 atmosphere of pressure.
J. The cubes are suspended by 0.5 m and 1.0 m threads and set in motion from the same starting angle in a vacuum chamber at 1 atmosphere of pressure.

15. In Experiment 1, could a timer that reads to the nearest half second be used to obtain similar results, and why?

A. No, because the period of both pendulums was approximately 1.5 seconds.
B. No, because the pendulums would not have completed a full swinging cycle in 1.5 seconds.
C. Yes, because the period of both pendulums was approximately 1.5 seconds.
D. Yes, because the pendulums would have completed more than one swinging cycle in 1.5 seconds.

16. The results of the experiments indicate that forces other than gravity are acting on the pendulums because the calculated values of acceleration were:

F. the same for pendulums of different lengths.
G. the same for cubes of different mass.
H. lower than the expected 9.8 m/sec^2 from gravity alone.
J. greater than the expected 9.8 m/sec^2 from gravity alone.

17. Based on the passage, if a tin cube is suspended from a 2.0 m thread and set in motion multiple times from the same starting angle, the average measured period will most likely be:

A. less than 1.48 sec.
B. approximately 1.48 sec.
C. approximately 2.09 sec.
D. greater than 2.09 sec.

18. In Experiment 2, if an additional trial were conducted using the lead cube, the cube's measured period would most likely be nearest to:

F. 1.90 sec.
G. 2.05 sec.
H. 2.15 sec.
J. 2.20 sec.

19. Experiments 1 and 2 were conducted using lead and tin cubes most likely to determine whether a pendulum's period was altered by the cube's:

A. length.
B. mass.
C. starting angle.
D. surface area.

20. Based on the results of Experiments 1 and 2, which cube most likely had a larger drag coefficient?

F. The lead cube, because the average period of the lead cube was shorter than the average period of the tin cube in both experiments.
G. The lead cube, because the mass of the lead cube was smaller.
H. The tin cube, because the average period of the tin cube was longer than the average period of the lead cube in both experiments.
J. The tin cube, because the mass of the tin cube was greater.

GO ON TO THE NEXT PAGE.

Passage IV

Accepted classification systems of life do not include *viruses*. Although viruses possess certain features of cellular organisms, including genetic material that codes for making new viral particles, they cannot *replicate* (make copies of) themselves without first infecting a living cell. Biologists agree that viruses originated from genetic material called *nucleic acid*, but it is difficult to prove any single theory regarding how this occurred. Three scientists present their hypotheses of viral origin.

Scientist 1

Viruses evolved alongside other organisms over billions of years. Simple molecules of *ribonucleic acid* (RNA), a *nucleotide* that forms the genetic code for proteins, joined to form more complex sequences. These RNA sequences developed enzyme-like abilities including the ability to self-replicate and insert themselves into other nucleotide sequences. While some RNA sequences became incorporated into membrane-bound cells, others were packaged inside proteins as the first viral particles that could replicate after infecting cellular organisms (see Figure 1).

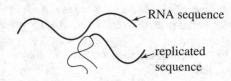

ancestral self-replicating RNA

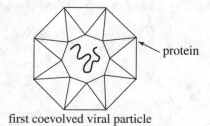

first coevolved viral particle

Figure 1

Scientist 2

Nucleotide sequences within *prokaryotic* (non-nucleated) and *eukaryotic* (nucleated) cellular organisms incorporated into a protein coating and escaped from the cells as viral particles. Initially, DNA or RNA nucleotide sequences gained the code required for other cells to replicate them. Next, these sequences associated with proteins to form an outer *capsid*. Finally, the *virion* (viral particle) became capable of passing through the cell membrane and infecting other cells where it could be replicated. After the initial escape, viruses evolved independently from their initial host and ultimately could infect either prokaryotic or eukaryotic cells.

Scientist 3

Viruses evolved from cellular organisms. Some cellular organisms, particularly certain bacteria, are *obligate intracellular parasites* because they must infect a host cell in order to reproduce. Regressive evolution suggests that some bacterial parasites gradually lost the structures required for survival outside of a cell. The result was a virus particle containing only nucleotides, a capsid (protein coating), and at times an outer membrane or envelope. This would account readily for viruses that contain complex *deoxyribonucleic acid* (DNA) similar to that found in bacteria and other cellular organisms (see Figure 2).

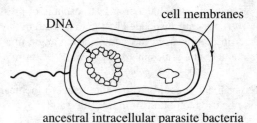

ancestral intracellular parasite bacteria

first regressive evolved virus

Figure 2

21. The development of which of the following is addressed in the passage by Scientist 1 but not by Scientist 3 ?

A. Self-replication
B. Capsid
C. Deoxyribonucleic acid
D. Cell membrane transit

22. All three scientist would agree with the conclusion that the first viruses:

F. evolved from bacteria.
G. could self-replicate outside a cell.
H. were enclosed within a membrane.
J. contained nucleic acid.

23. Scientist 1 does NOT provide an explanation for the earliest virus particles possessing:

A. protein.
B. enzyme-like activity.
C. nucleotides.
D. DNA.

GO ON TO THE NEXT PAGE.

24. If Scientist 2 is correct, which of the following conclusions can be made about modern T4 DNA viruses, which infect *Escherichia coli* bacteria, and modern PP7 RNA viruses, which infect *Pseudomonas aeruginosa* bacteria?

F. T4 and PP7 are more closely related to each other than to bacteria genetically.

G. T4 and PP7 are only distantly related genetically through a cellular organism.

H. T4 and PP7 both evolved from prokaryotic organisms.

J. T4 and PP7 both evolved from eukaryotic organisms.

25. The discovery of which of the following living organisms would provide the most support for Scientist 3's theory?

A. Extracellular parasites with DNA resembling a known virus

B. Extracellular parasites with unique RNA nucleotide sequences

C. Intracellular parasites with DNA resembling a known virus

D. Intracellular parasites with unique RNA nucleotide sequences

26. All three scientists would agree with which of the following conclusions about the origin of viruses?

F. Viral capsids contain a protein structure similar to the cell walls of modern bacteria.

G. The first viruses did not originate before the first cellular organisms.

H. RNA viruses are more advanced than DNA viruses.

J. The first virus contained DNA and was surrounded by an envelope similar to a cell membrane.

27. Which of the following questions is raised by Scientist 1, but is NOT answered in the passage?

A. Why were some RNA sequences packaged into protein structures and others incorporated into cell structures?

B. Why did obligate intracellular parasites lose their ability to survive outside of cells?

C. How could two different types of cellular organisms account for the origin of viruses?

D. How did virions develop the ability to pass through the cell membrane out of the cell?

GO ON TO THE NEXT PAGE.

Passage V

Wind causes *topsoil deflation*, a type of erosion that is affected by plant and organic cover as well as water content of the soil. Scientists performed 2 experiments using equal-sized fields containing the same volume of soil. The soil samples were primarily a mixture of sand and silt, but differed in the percentage of clay they contained. Soil X was composed of 5% clay and Soil Y was composed of 40% clay. Large fans were used to simulate wind. Topsoil deflation was measured in kilograms per hectare (kg/ha) following 10 hours of wind.

Experiment 1

A mixture of compost and straw was used to represent plant and organic cover. The percentage of soil covered with the mixture was considered to approximate an equivalent percentage of natural vegetative cover. One field remained uncovered, and the other fields were covered with different percentages of compost and straw. The topsoil deflation from each field was recorded in Table 1.

Table 1				
Soil	Topsoil deflation (kg/ha) by percentage of organic cover			
	0%	25%	50%	75%
X	105,000	68,000	46,000	20,000
Y	65,000	42,000	28,500	12,000

Experiment 2

Rainfall was simulated using a sprinkler system. Sprinklers were turned on for either 4 hours or 8 hours for fields of each kind of soil. Two additional fields composed of each type of soil were left unwatered. Afterward, soil samples were taken from all of the fields to determine their water content percentage, which was recorded in Table 2. Wind was applied as in Experiment 1 and topsoil deflation for all fields was recorded in Table 3.

Table 2			
Soil	Water content of soil following various sprinkler times		
	0 hours	4 hours	8 hours
X	10%	13%	16%
Y	10%	14%	22%

Table 3			
Soil	Topsoil deflation (kg/ha) following various sprinkler times		
	0 hours	4 hours	8 hours
X	89,250	66,000	14,000
Y	53,400	40,100	10,300

28. A third soil, Soil Z, contains 45% clay. One field with Soil Z is covered with a mixture of compost and straw and subjected to 10 hours of simulated wind in the same procedure used in Experiment 1. At the conclusion of the trial, the topsoil deflation in the field was determined to be 26,000 kg/ha. The percentage of organic cover used on the field was most likely closest to:

F. 0%.
G. 25%.
H. 50%.
J. 75%.

29. According to the results of Experiments 1 and 2, topsoil deflation will be minimized by:

A. decreased organic cover, increased amount of rainfall, and the use of either Soil X or Y as topsoil.
B. decreased organic cover, decreased amount of rainfall, and the use of Soil Y as topsoil.
C. increased organic cover, increased amount of rainfall, and the use of Soil Y as topsoil.
D. increased organic cover, increased amount of rainfall, and the use of Soil X as topsoil.

30. If Experiment 1 were repeated using a soil containing 10% clay with 0% organic cover, which of the following would be the most likely topsoil deflation amount?

F. 60,200 kg/ha
G. 70,700 kg/ha
H. 99,800 kg/ha
J. 110,200 kg/ha

31. To further investigate the effect of water content on erosion from topsoil deflation, the scientists should repeat Experiment:

A. 1, using a different type of topsoil.
B. 1, using plastic covers over the fields.
C. 2, using no sprinklers.
D. 2, using fields exposed to various amounts of rainfall.

GO ON TO THE NEXT PAGE.

32. Which of the following assumptions was made in the design of Experiment 1 ?

F. The quantity of topsoil deflation is independent of the percentage of clay present in the soil.

G. The presence of straw on the soil does not accurately simulate vegetation and organic cover.

H. Air movement from fans provides an accurate simulation of the wind responsible for topsoil deflation.

J. Compost is more effective than water content in the prevention of topsoil erosion.

33. In Experiment 2, the water content in the two soil types was similar after 4 hours of sprinkling, yet the topsoil deflation was significantly different. Which of the following statements provides the best explanation for these findings?

A. Topsoil erosion is independent of the water content found in the soil.

B. Fields are susceptible to topsoil deflation only when water completely evaporates from the topsoil.

C. Soil with a lower percentage of clay is more prone to erosion from topsoil deflation than one with a higher percentage of clay.

D. Water is trapped in the topsoil by wind and this increases the rate of topsoil deflation.

34. If Experiment 2 were repeated with soil containing 10% clay, which of the following values would be expected for water content and topsoil deflation in a field following 8 hours of water sprinkling?

F. Water content of 21%; topsoil deflation of 9,700 kg/ha

G. Water content of 17%; topsoil deflation of 13,400 kg/ha

H. Water content of 15%; topsoil deflation of 10,900 kg/ha

J. Water content of 14%; topsoil deflation of 101,000 kg/ha

GO ON TO THE NEXT PAGE.

Passage VI

The oceans of Earth are exposed to various climates and consequently have different physical properties. Deep oceans can be divided into zones based on temperature gradient and penetration of sunlight. Figure 1 shows the zones of a typical deep-water ocean, the depth of the zone boundaries in meters (m), and the overall pressure at those depths in kilopascals (kPa). Figure 2 shows the water temperature in degrees Celsius (°C) in warmer tropical oceans and cooler temperate oceans at varying depths. Sound waves are used to measure water temperature at depth, and readings from two different ocean regions are recorded in Table 1.

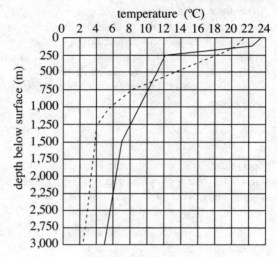

Figure 2

Zone of ocean			Depth (m)	Total pressure (kPa)
	surface		0	101
epipelagic	continental shelf	mixed	100	1,107
			140	1,509
			200	2,112
mesopelagic		thermocline		
	continental rise		1,000	10,153
bathypelagic				
			4,000	4.0×10^4
abyssopelagic		deep water		
	abyss		6,000	6.0×10^4
hadopelagic				

Figure 1

(Note: Figure is NOT drawn to scale)

Table 1			
Total pressure (kPa)	Depth (m)	Ocean temperature (°C)	
		Region 1	Region 2
101	0.0	24	21
200	9.8	22	20
300	19.8	14	11
400	29.7	11	9
500	39.7	10	8
600	49.6	9	6
700	59.6	7	5
800	69.5	5	5
900	79.5	4	6

GO ON TO THE NEXT PAGE.

35. According to Figure 1, the regions of several ocean zones overlap. Which of the following pairs of ocean zones share part of a common depth range?

    A. Bathypelagic and thermocline
    B. Bathypelagic and epipelagic
    C. Epipelagic and thermocline
    D. Epipelagic and mesopelagic

36. According to Figure 1, an oceanographic reading taken at a total pressure of 1,700 kPa is most likely from which of the following zones?

    F. Abyss
    G. Continental shelf
    H. Mixed
    J. Thermocline

37. According to Figure 2, a sonographic measurement of temperature would be unable to distinguish the difference between tropical and temperate oceans at which of the following depths?

    A. 250 m
    B. 500 m
    C. 625 m
    D. 750 m

38. According to Table 1, the relationship between depth and ocean temperature is best described by which of the following statements?

    F. The water temperature increased with increasing depth in Region 1 only.
    G. The water temperature decreased with increasing depth in Region 1 only.
    H. The water temperature increased with increasing depth in Region 2 only.
    J. The water temperature decreased with increasing depth in Region 2 only.

39. According to Figure 1 and Table 1, if water temperature measurements were taken at depths greater than 79.5 m, the total pressure at those depths would most likely:

    A. increase to 101 kPa.
    B. increase to more than 900 kPa.
    C. stay at 900 kPa.
    D. decrease to less than 101 kPa.

40. According to Figures 1 and 2, the range of depths at which the temperate ocean is warmer than the tropical ocean occurs within which of the following ocean zones?

    F. Mixed
    G. Thermocline
    H. Bathypelagic
    J. Deep water

END OF TEST 4

STOP! DO NOT RETURN TO A PREVIOUS TEST.

DIRECTIONS

This is a test of your writing skills. You will have forty (40) minutes to write an essay. Before you begin planning and writing your essay, read the writing prompt carefully to understand exactly what you are being asked to do. Your essay will be evaluated on the evidence it provides of your ability to express judgments by taking a position on the issue in the writing prompt; to maintain a focus on the topic throughout your essay; to develop a position by using logical reasoning and by supporting your ideas; to organize ideas in a logical way; and to use language clearly and effectively according to the conventions of standard written English.

You may use the unlined pages in this test booklet to plan your essay. These pages will not be scored. *You must write your essay on the lined pages in the answer folder.* Your writing on those lined pages will be scored. You may not need all the lined pages, but to ensure you have enough room to finish, do NOT skip lines. You may write corrections or additions neatly between the lines of your essay, but do NOT write in the margins of the lined pages. *Illegible essays cannot be scored, so you must write (or print) clearly.*

If you finish before time is called, you may review your work. Lay your pencil down immediately when time is called.

DO NOT OPEN THIS BOOK UNTIL YOU ARE TOLD TO DO SO.

Population Growth

Since the Industrial Revolution, the growth rate of Earth's human population has increased dramatically. It took mankind until the 1800s to reach one billion, but only 120 years after that to reach two billion, and less than 40 years after that to reach three billion. We continue to increase our numbers, currently measuring in at 7.3 billion in 2015. Some express a great deal of concern about this trend, arguing that the increasing population uses more resources than the planet can provide and encourages harmful practices such as deforestation and industrial pollution. Others say that while our population is at higher numbers than ever before and the subsequent problems are very real, the issues are caused less by the actual number of people and more by the unequal distribution of resources.

Read and carefully consider these perspectives. Each suggests a particular way of thinking about human population growth.

Perspective One	**Perspective Two**	**Perspective Three**
Overpopulation is one of the most serious environmental issues humans face. Our increasing numbers are causing myriad problems from loss of fresh water to extinction of species to lowered life expectancy in developing countries.	The number of people on Earth is not a problem. We only have 7 billion, while scientists predict our planet can support up to 10 billion. The real problem is the unequal distribution of resources. A more equitable use of water, land, food, and fuel would eliminate many of the problems we currently face.	Though our population numbers are higher than they've ever been, this is not a cause for alarm. Our growth rate is already beginning to slow. As we approach critical mass, that decrease in rate will continue until we're at "replacement" levels of reproduction, allowing the human race to continue without drastically increasing the overall numbers.

Essay Task

Write a unified, coherent essay in which you evaluate multiple perspectives on the issues connected with population growth. In your essay, be sure to:

- analyze and evaluate the perspectives given
- state and develop your own perspective on the issue
- explain the relationship between your perspective and those given

Your perspective may be in full agreement with any of the others, in partial agreement, or wholly different. Whatever the case, support your ideas with logical reasoning and detailed, persuasive examples.

Chapter 29
Practice Exam 2:
Answers
and Explanations

*Note on scoring: please refer to the Scoring Conversion Worksheet and Score Conversion Chart on pages 539 and 540.

To grade your essay, see the Essay Checklist and an example of a top scoring essay online on your Student Tools.

English		Math		Reading		Science	
1. D	39. D	1. A	31. E	1. C	21. C	1. C	21. A
2. F	40. J	2. H	32. J	2. F	22. G	2. F	22. J
3. C	41. A	3. C	33. C	3. A	23. C	3. C	23. D
4. F	42. G	4. J	34. K	4. G	24. G	4. H	24. G
5. C	43. C	5. C	35. E	5. B	25. D	5. D	25. C
6. H	44. G	6. K	36. K	6. H	26. J	6. G	26. G
7. D	45. B	7. A	37. E	7. A	27. B	7. C	27. A
8. F	46. J	8. K	38. J	8. J	28. J	8. J	28. H
9. A	47. C	9. E	39. B	9. B	29. A	9. B	29. C
10. G	48. F	10. J	40. H	10. H	30. H	10. F	30. H
11. C	49. C	11. C	41. E	11. D	31. C	11. D	31. D
12. H	50. J	12. K	42. F	12. G	32. H	12. G	32. H
13. D	51. C	13. D	43. C	13. D	33. D	13. C	33. C
14. F	52. F	14. G	44. G	14. G	34. G	14. G	34. G
15. C	53. A	15. A	45. B	15. A	35. C	15. A	35. C
16. G	54. H	16. H	46. H	16. G	36. J	16. H	36. J
17. D	55. A	17. A	47. D	17. C	37. C	17. D	37. C
18. H	56. H	18. K	48. J	18. F	38. H	18. G	38. G
19. A	57. D	19. C	49. B	19. C	39. A	19. B	39. B
20. G	58. G	20. H	50. G	20. G	40. J	20. H	40. G
21. D	59. D	21. C	51. D				
22. F	60. H	22. F	52. K				
23. A	61. B	23. C	53. C				
24. F	62. J	24. G	54. H				
25. C	63. C	25. E	55. D				
26. G	64. J	26. G	56. G				
27. D	65. C	27. D	57. A				
28. H	66. H	28. F	58. F				
29. D	67. D	29. C	59. D				
30. J	68. F	30. H	60. K				
31. A	69. A						
32. F	70. G						
33. C	71. A						
34. F	72. G						
35. C	73. B						
36. J	74. F						
37. C	75. D						
38. J							

ENGLISH TEST

1. **D** Connecting words are changing in the answer choices, so the question is testing consistency. The part before the underlined portion contains the word *associate*. The correct idiom is *associate…with*. Eliminate (A), (B), and (C) because they do not contain the word *with*. The correct answer is (D).

2. **F** The phrase surrounding *people of all ages* is changing in the answer choices, so the question could be testing concision. First determine whether the phrase is necessary. The sentence already states *people of all ages*, so there is no need to repeat that idea. Eliminate any choices that are redundant. The phrase *young and old* means the same as *all ages*, so eliminate (G), (H), and (J). The correct answer is (F).

3. **C** Note the question! The question asks whether the sentence should be added, so it's testing consistency. If the content of the new sentence is consistent with the ideas surrounding it, then it should be added. The paragraph discusses the widespread appeal of *crocheting* to modern audiences. The new sentence discusses *Irish nuns* who crocheted during the *Great Irish Potato Famine*, so it is not consistent with the ideas in the text; the sentence should not be added. Eliminate (A) and (B). Keep (C) because it states that the new sentence is irrelevant. Eliminate (D) because it doesn't state that the new sentence is inconsistent with the text. The correct answer is (C).

4. **F** Vocabulary is changing in the answers, so the question is testing word choice. Determine what meaning of the underlined portion would be consistent with the sentence. The underlined word is part of a phrase that describes *crocheting*, so look for a word that can work in context. Keep (F) because *crocheting* can be *easily taught*. Eliminate (G) because it is not correct to say that crocheting *easily teaches*; this changes the meaning of the sentence. Eliminate (H) and (J) because *taughted* and *teached* are incorrect forms of *taught*. The correct answer is (F).

5. **C** Punctuation is changing in the answer choices, so the question is testing STOP and GO punctuation. Use the vertical line test, and identify the ideas as complete or incomplete. Draw the vertical line between the words *stitches* and *picking*. The phrase *Instructional books are readily available, and once you've learned a few basic stitches* is an incomplete idea, and the phrase *picking up the more advanced ones is a snap* is a complete idea. To connect an incomplete idea to a complete idea, GO punctuation is needed. The period and the semicolon are STOP punctuation, so eliminate (A) and (B). The comma is GO punctuation, so keep (C). A lack of punctuation is GO punctuation, but (D) adds an extra word. Adding the word *since* without a punctuation mark makes the sentence incomplete; eliminate (D). The correct answer is (C).

6. **H** The length of the phrase is changing in the answer choices, so the question could be testing concision. Determine what parts of the phrase are necessary. Choice (F) says *purchase* and describes the books as *store-bought*. Since both mean the same thing in context, (F) is redundant. Eliminate (F). Likewise, *acquire* and *bought* have the same meaning in context, so eliminate (J). Eliminate (G) because *certain* and *specific* mean the same thing in context. Keep (H) because it is the most concise choice. The correct answer is (H).

7. **D** Pronouns are changing in the answer choices, so the question is testing consistency of pronouns. A pronoun must be consistent in number with the noun it is replacing. The pronoun refers to the noun *projects*, which is plural. To be consistent, the pronoun in the answer choice must also be plural. Eliminate (A), (B), and (C) because none of these contains a plural pronoun. Keep (D) because *their* is plural. The correct answer is (D).

8. **F** Vocabulary is changing in the answers, so the question is testing word choice. Determine what meaning of the underlined portion would be consistent with the sentence. The underlined portion should mean that *fifteen dollars will buy* "at least" *three starter kits*. Keep (F) because *no fewer than* means the same as "at least." Eliminate (G) and (J) because *then* refers to time, not a comparison of quantities. Eliminate (H) because the word *less* must be used for a quantity that is not countable, but *kits* are countable and therefore should go with the word *fewer*. The correct answer is (F).

9. **A** Punctuation is changing in the answer choices, so the question is testing STOP and GO punctuation. Use the vertical line test, and identify the ideas as complete or incomplete. Draw the vertical line between the words *types* and *to*. The phrase *As you grow more proficient, you can expand your supplies by purchasing hooks of different types* is a complete idea, and the phrase *to vary the size of your stitches* is an incomplete idea. To connect a complete idea to an incomplete idea, HALF-STOP or GO punctuation is needed. Keep (A) because a lack of punctuation is GO punctuation. Eliminate (B) because the semicolon is STOP punctuation. A colon is HALF-STOP punctuation, but there is no reason to use a colon here, since the second part of the sentence does not contain a list or an explanation of a concept from the first part. Eliminate (C). A comma is GO punctuation, but there is no reason to use a comma here, so eliminate (D). The correct answer is (A).

10. **G** Punctuation is changing in the answer choices, so the question is testing STOP and GO punctuation. Use the vertical line test, and identify the ideas as complete or incomplete. Draw the vertical line between the words *sizes* and *ranging*. The phrase *Crochet hooks are available in all sizes* is a complete idea, and the phrase *ranging from very small to very large, with everything in between* is an incomplete idea. To connect a complete idea to an incomplete idea, HALF-STOP or GO punctuation is needed. A comma is GO punctuation, but there is no reason to use a comma after *ranging*, so eliminate (F). Likewise, eliminate (J) because it also contains an unnecessary comma after *ranging*. Keep (G) because a comma is GO punctuation. Eliminate (H) because a semicolon is STOP punctuation. The correct answer is (G).

11. **C** Note the question! The question asks where Sentence 6 should be placed, so it's testing consistency. Look for a clue in the sentence to determine what idea it needs to come before or after. Sentence 6 says, *These hooks make big stitches*. Sentence 6 must come after some mention of a specific type of hook. Sentences 5 and 1 do not mention a specific type of hook, so eliminate (A) and (B). Sentence 3 mentions *big* hooks, so keep (C). Sentence 7 mentions *medium* hooks, so keep (D). To choose between (C) and (D), consider which sentence is most consistent with Sentence 6. Sentence 6 mentions hooks that make *big stitches*, so Sentence 3, which mentions *big* hooks, is more consistent than Sentence 7, which mentions *medium* hooks. Therefore, Sentence 6 should follow Sentence 3. Eliminate (D). The correct answer is (C).

12. **H** Note the question! The question asks which option *provides the most effective transition*. A transition must be consistent with the relationship between the ideas it connects, so look at the two paragraphs to determine how they are related. The preceding paragraph discusses the variety of materials available to people who crochet, and the paragraph beginning with the transition discusses the relatively inexpensive cost of crocheting in relation to its benefits. Eliminate (F) and (G) because neither mentions the relatively low cost of crocheting. Keep (H) because it relates the *materials* discussed in the previous paragraph to the idea that crocheting is an *inexpensive* hobby. Eliminate (J) because who dominates the *field* does not relate to the cost of crocheting. The correct answer is (H).

13. **D** Vocabulary is changing in the answers, so the question is testing word choice. Determine what meaning of the underlined portion would be consistent with the sentence. *Also, you have finished a project* and *you have a cherished keepsake* are both complete ideas. A comma without a FANBOYS word is GO punctuation, so it cannot connect two complete ideas. Eliminate (A). Choice (B) also makes the first part of the sentence complete, so eliminate it. Eliminate (C) because the word *despite* introduces a conflict that isn't consistent with the ideas in the sentence. Keep (D) because *once* makes the first part of the sentence incomplete, allowing it to be followed by the comma, and provides a consistent meaning. The correct answer is (D).

14. **F** Connecting words are changing in the answer choices, so the question is testing consistency. The part before the underlined portion contains the word *warm*, and the part after the underlined portion contains the words *cold winter nights*. When describing something that happens on certain days or nights, the correct preposition is *on*. Keep (F) because it contains the word *on*. Eliminate (G), (H), and (J) because they do not contain the word *on*. The correct answer is (F).

15. **C** Note the question! The question asks whether the essay demonstrates the *commercial potential of crocheting*. Consider the main idea of the passage and use Process of Elimination. The passage is about the personal benefits of adopting crocheting as a hobby. Eliminate (A) and (B) because, though the author did discuss *end products* and *supplies*, these concepts were discussed on a personal, not a commercial, level. Keep (C) because it is true that the author does not mention the *market value of crocheted products*. Eliminate (D) because the author does not compare crocheting to *other industries and hobbies that would be more commercially successful*. The correct answer is (C).

16. **G** Verbs are changing in the answer choices, so the question is testing consistency of verbs. The answer choices are in different tenses, so look for a clue in the sentence or surrounding sentences to identify the appropriate tense. The beginning of the sentence uses *never thought* to indicate an action that the narrator didn't believe would occur in the future, so the action refers to a possible future action from a point of view in the past. Therefore, the underlined portion needs to be in past tense but also needs to indicate that it was a possible action in the future. Eliminate (F) because *saw* is past tense, indicating that this action happened in the past. Keep (G) because *would see* is past tense describing an action that may happen in the future. Eliminate (H) because *had seen* indicates an action that has already happened. Eliminate (J) because *was seeing* indicates an action that has already happened. The correct answer is (G).

17. **D** Vocabulary is changing in the answer choices, so this question is testing word choice. There is also the option to DELETE; consider this choice carefully as it's often the correct answer. The phrase *got my chance to* must be followed by an action. Since no action is provided, there is no need to use the word *to* or the phrase *just to*. Eliminate (A) and (C). The sentence already says *when*, so there is no need to use the phrase *at the moment*. Eliminate (B). The phrase should be deleted to make the sentence more concise. The correct answer is (D).

18. **H** Pronouns are changing in the answer choices, so the question is testing consistency of pronouns. A pronoun must be consistent in number with the noun it is replacing. The pronoun refers to the noun *painting*, which is singular. To be consistent, the pronoun in the answer choice must also be singular. Eliminate (G) because *our* is plural and refers to people. The *grandeur* belongs to *the painting*, so the pronoun must also be possessive. Eliminate (F) because *it's* is a contraction, not a

possessive pronoun. Keep (H) because *its* is singular and possessive. Eliminate (J) because *its'* is an incorrect pronoun. The correct answer is (H).

19. **A**   The phrase surrounding *jumped into the car* is changing, and the underlined portion is part of a list, so the question is testing consistency with lists. All items in a list must be consistent in structure, and all items must be separated by a comma. The unchanging items in the list—*packed our bags* and *jumped into the car*—begin with a simple past tense verb. To be consistent, the third item must also begin with a simple past tense verb. Keep (A) because *headed* is a simple past tense verb. Eliminate (B) because *had headed* is not in the correct tense to be consistent with *packed* and *jumped*. Eliminate (C) because *head* is present tense. Eliminate (D) because *had jumped* is not in the correct tense to be consistent with *packed* and *jumped*. The correct answer is (A).

20. **G**   Note the question! The question asks where a new sentence should be placed, so it's testing consistency. Look for a clue in the sentence to determine what idea it needs to come before or after. The new sentence says *Her name was Lisa*. Therefore, this sentence must come after some introduction of a person. Sentence 3 introduces *someone else who loved the painting*. Therefore, the new sentence should follow Sentence 3. The correct answer is (G).

21. **D**   Punctuation is changing in the answer choices, so the question is testing STOP and GO punctuation. Use the vertical line test, and identify the ideas as complete or incomplete. Draw the vertical line between the words *displayed* and *was*. The phrase *The first thing that struck me as we entered the room where the painting was displayed* is an incomplete idea, and the phrase *was the size of the painting* is an incomplete idea. To connect an incomplete idea to an incomplete idea, GO punctuation is needed. The semicolon is STOP punctuation, so eliminate (A). The colon is HALF-STOP punctuation, so eliminate (B). The comma is GO punctuation, but there is no reason to use a comma here since the second idea is a continuation of the first, so eliminate (C). A lack of punctuation is GO punctuation, so keep (D). The correct answer is (D).

22. **F**   The phrase after *task* is changing in the answer choices, so the question could be testing concision. First determine whether the phrase is necessary. The sentence already states, *To create a painting... seemed an almost impossible task*, meaning the task is difficult. There is no need to repeat that idea. Eliminate any choices that are redundant. Choices (G), (H), and (J) each repeat the idea that the task is *difficult*, so eliminate them. The correct answer is (F).

23. **A**   Note the question! The question asks for the sentence that is *LEAST relevant to the development of this paragraph*, so it's testing consistency. Cross off the word *LEAST*, and mark each answer as Yes/No. The paragraph describes the narrator's reaction when he or she saw *the painting* in person. Sentence 2 discusses *a common size for canvases*. This is not consistent with the paragraph, so mark (A) as No. Sentences 4, 5, and 6 each describe a reaction that the narrator had when seeing the painting, so mark (B), (C), and (D) as Yes. Choice (A) is the odd one out. The correct answer is (A).

24. **F**   Note the question! The question asks which option *provides the most effective and logical transition from the preceding paragraph to this one*. A transition should be consistent with the relationship between the ideas it connects. The previous paragraph says that the narrator is struck by the *size* of the painting. The paragraph beginning with the transition phrase discusses the *beauty* of the painting, which the narrator seems even more fascinated by. Keep (F) because *Even more impressive*

indicates that the narrator will draw a comparison between the information in the previous paragraph and the information in this paragraph. Eliminate (G) because it does not draw a comparison between the information in the preceding paragraph and the information in this paragraph. Eliminate (H) because the writing of *art critics* is not consistent with either paragraph. Eliminate (J) because neither paragraph indicates that the beauty of the painting is subject to harsh *debate*. The correct answer is (F).

25. **C** Note the question! The question asks which alternative *would NOT be acceptable*, so it's testing consistency. Cross off the word *NOT*, and mark each answer as Yes/No. The underlined portion uses an opposite-direction transition word to imply that something changed when the narrator *approached the painting*. Mark (A), (B), and (D) as Yes because each is consistent with the underlined portion. Mark (C) as No because it is not consistent in meaning with the underlined portion: this phrase makes the sentence incomplete. The odd one out is (C). The correct answer is (C).

26. **G** Note the question! The question asks what the paragraph would lose if the phrase *from a distance* were deleted. Consider the purpose of the phrase. The sentence containing the phrase compares the appearance of the painting *from a distance* to its appearance *up close*. Therefore, the phrase is part of a contrast. Check the answers and eliminate any choice that is not consistent with this purpose. Eliminate (A) because the phrase does not convey *the author's love of the painting*. Keep (G) because the *contrast* is consistent with the purpose of the phrase. Eliminate (H) because the phrase does not refer to a *road trip*. Eliminate (J) because the phrase is necessary to the meaning of the statement, and the information it provides is not *stated more clearly elsewhere in the paragraph*. The correct answer is (G).

27. **D** Pronouns are changing in the answer choices, so the question is testing consistency of pronouns. A pronoun must be consistent in number and case with the noun it is replacing. The pronoun refers to the subject of the sentence––both the narrator and Lisa––which is plural. Additionally, the pronoun must be a first-person pronoun, since the narrator uses it to refer to a memory. To be consistent, the pronoun in the answer choice must also be first-person and plural. Eliminate (A) and (B) because neither *he* nor *one* is first-person or plural. Eliminate (C) because *they* is not first-person. Keep (D) because *we* is first-person and plural. The correct answer is (D).

28. **H** Note the question! The question asks whether the sentence should be added, so it's testing consistency. If the content of the new sentence is consistent with the ideas surrounding it, then it should be added. The paragraph discusses the narrator's reaction to the *beauty of the painting* with regard to its coloration. The new sentence discusses *other famous paintings* in the *Art Institute of Chicago*, so it is not consistent with the ideas in the text; the sentence should not be added. Eliminate choices (F) and (G). Keep choice (H) because it states that the new sentence is irrelevant. Eliminate (J) because it doesn't state that the new sentence is inconsistent with the text. The correct answer is (H).

29. **D** Punctuation is changing in the answer choices, so the question is testing STOP and GO punctuation. Use the vertical line test, and identify the ideas as complete or incomplete. Draw the vertical line between the words *sights* and *on*. The phrase *My friend and I saw many other sights* is a complete idea, and the phrase *on our trip to Chicago, but the best part by far was being able to see our favorite work of art* is an incomplete idea. To connect a complete idea to an incomplete idea, HALF-STOP or GO punctuation is needed. The comma is GO punctuation, but no comma is needed here, so

eliminate (A). Eliminate (B) because the addition of the word *which* makes the sentence incomplete. Eliminate (C) because a semicolon is STOP punctuation. Keep (D) because a lack of punctuation is GO punctuation. The correct answer is (D).

30. **J** Note the question! The question asks where the underlined portion should be placed, so it's testing consistency. Look for a clue in the sentence to determine what idea the underlined portion needs to come before or after. The underlined portion says, *at the museum gift shop*. Therefore, this phrase refers to an event that happened at the gift shop, so it must come after a mention of some event. The narrator's *mind* was not an event at the gift shop, so eliminate (F). The *image* imprinted in the narrator's mind is not an event at the gift shop, so eliminate (G). Eliminate (H) because it makes the sentence incomplete. Keep (J) because it states an event: the narrator *bought* the *souvenir print* at the gift shop. The correct answer is (J).

31. **A** Punctuation is changing in the answer choices, so the question is testing STOP and GO punctuation. Use the vertical line test, and identify the ideas as complete or incomplete. Draw the vertical line between the words *developed* and *an*. The phrase *However, cats have developed* is a complete idea, and the phrase *an intricate language not for each other, but for the human beings who have adopted them as pets* is an incomplete idea. To connect a complete idea to an incomplete idea, HALF-STOP or GO punctuation is needed. A lack of punctuation is GO punctuation, so keep (A). A comma is GO punctuation, but there is no reason to use a comma here, so eliminate (B). A lack of punctuation is GO punctuation, but there is no reason to use a comma after *language*; eliminate (C). A semicolon is STOP punctuation, so eliminate (D). The correct answer is (A).

32. **F** Note the question! The question asks which option would *most clearly and effectively express the ownership relationship between humans and cats*. Check each answer choice to see whether it has to do with the *ownership relationship* between *humans and cats*. Keep (F) because *adopted them as pets* means that humans have ownership of cats. Eliminate (G) because the idea that humans *like* to have cats around doesn't reflect an *ownership relationship*. Eliminate (H) because the idea that humans *often have dogs* does not relate to their ownership relationship with cats. Eliminate (J) because a statement about the natural inclination of humans toward cats does not express an *ownership relationship*. The correct answer is (F).

33. **C** The order of the words is changing in the answer choices, so the question is testing consistency with a modifier. The non-underlined portion contains the modifier *When communicating with each other*. The communication is being done by the cats, so the word that directly follows the modifying phrase should be "cats." Eliminate (B) and (D) because neither begins with the word *cats*. Eliminate (A) because, though *cats'* follows the modifying phrase, the phrase incorrectly modifies *cats' "talk"* rather than cats themselves. Keep (C) because the word *cats* directly follows the modifying phrase. The correct answer is (C).

34. **F** Verbs are changing in the answer choices, so the question is testing consistency of verbs. The answer choices are in different tenses, so look for a clue in the sentence or surrounding sentences to identify the appropriate tense. The underlined verb refers to the word *tails*, which is plural, so the verb in the underlined portion also needs to be plural to be consistent. Furthermore, the sentence continues a thought expressed in the preceding sentence, which has verbs in the simple present tense, so the underlined verb should be in simple present tense to be consistent. Keep (F)

because *provide* is both plural and in simple present tense. Eliminate (G) because *having provided* is not simple present tense. Eliminate (H) because *has provided* is not plural or simple present tense. Eliminate (J) because *were provided by* is not simple present tense. The correct answer is (F).

35. **C** Note the question! The question asks what the paragraph would lose if the sentence were deleted. Consider the purpose of the sentence. The paragraph describes nonverbal communication used when cats communicate with each other. The sentence explains the only time when *cats will use their voices* while communicating with *other cats*. This is an exception to the earlier idea that cats communicate with each other through nonverbal signals. Check the answers and eliminate any choice that is not consistent with this purpose. Eliminate (A) because the idea that cats use their voices with other cats is not mentioned elsewhere. Eliminate (B) because the sentence mentions verbal, not nonverbal, communication. Keep (C) because the *exception to the general trend* is consistent with the purpose of the sentence. Eliminate (D) because the sentence doesn't provide a *summary of the information*. The correct answer is (C).

36. **J** Transitions are changing in the answer choices, so the question is testing consistency with transitions. Note that each choice also contains the option to either begin a new paragraph or continue the previous paragraph. A new paragraph should be started when a new idea is discussed. Look at the previous sentence to determine how the two ideas are related; then determine whether the information that follows is consistent with the preceding paragraph. The sentences prior to the underlined portion discuss how cats communicate with one another, and the sentences after the underlined portion discuss how cats communicate with humans. Since these ideas are different, they should not be part of the same paragraph. Eliminate (F) and (G). *Next* implies a series. Since there is no series in the paragraph, there is no need to use *Next*. Eliminate (H). The correct answer is (J).

37. **C** Apostrophes are changing in the answer choices, so the question is testing apostrophe usage. When used with a noun, on the ACT, the apostrophe indicates possession. In this sentence, the *cats* are possessing the *verbal expressions*. Therefore, the apostrophe is needed, and because *cats* is plural, the apostrophe should be placed after the *s*. Eliminate (A) and (D) because neither contains the apostrophe. Eliminate (B) because the apostrophe is before the *s*, which indicates a singular noun. Keep (C) because the apostrophe is after the *s*. The correct answer is (C).

38. **J** The phrase after *logical* is changing in the answer choices, so the question could be testing concision. First determine whether the phrase is necessary. The sentence already uses the word *logical*, so there is no need to repeat that idea. Eliminate any choices that are redundant. Eliminate (F) and (G) because *reasonable* and *well-reasoned* both have the same meaning as *logical*. Eliminate (H) because adding *to a startling degree* is not necessary to the main idea and does not change the meaning of the sentence; (J) is more concise. The correct answer is (J).

39. **D** Vocabulary is changing in the answer choices, so this question is testing word choice. The underlined phrase is explaining how the fact was *demonstrated*; therefore, the underlined portion needs an adverb to describe how the fact is *demonstrated*. Eliminate (A) and (B) because *clear* is an adjective (a word describing a noun) rather than an adverb (a word describing a verb). To choose between (C) and (D), consider the meaning of the sentence with each choice. The word *since* implies that the *fact is demonstrated* more clearly now that *households* with *only one cat* have been observed. The word *when* implies that the fact is demonstrated more clearly whenever *households* with *only one cat*

are observed. Since the paragraph suggests that the *fact* may still be demonstrated, eliminate (C). The correct answer is (D).

40. **J** Note the question! The question asks whether the sentence should be added, so it's testing consistency. If the content of the new sentence is consistent with the ideas surrounding it, then it should be added. The paragraph discusses the differences in communication between cats *in households that have only one cat* and *cats with other feline companions*. The new sentence discusses communication in *birds*, so it is not consistent with the ideas in the text; the sentence should not be added. Eliminate (F) and (G). Eliminate (H) because it doesn't repeat information given earlier in the essay. Keep (J) because it states that the new sentence *does not contribute to the development of the paragraph and the essay as a whole*. The correct answer is (J).

41. **A** Commas are changing in the answer choices, so the question is testing comma rules. The phrase *to name just a few examples* is unnecessary information, so it needs a comma before and after. There is already a comma after the phrase, so eliminate choices that do not have a comma before the phrase. Keep (A) because it has a comma before the phrase. Eliminate (B) because, though it has a comma before the phrase, there is no reason to have a comma after *to*. Eliminate (C) and (D) because each lacks a comma before the phrase. The correct answer is (A).

42. **G** Note the question! The question asks which option would emphasize that *cats communicate vocally with their owners to express a large number of different emotions*. Check each answer choice to see whether it has to do with *cats* communicating *different emotions* with their *owners*. Eliminate (F) because this choice compares *cats* to other *animals*. Keep (G) because it states that *cats will tell their owners* when they feel a variety of emotions. Eliminate (H) because it expresses how cats communicate with *other cats*, not with their owners. Eliminate (J) because it discusses *humans*, not cats. The correct answer is (G).

43. **C** Connecting words and verbs are changing in the answer choices, so the question is testing consistency. The part before the underlined portion contains the phrase *every bit as important*, which implies a comparison between two items. The two items being compared must have the same structure. The non-underlined item is *forging good relationships*, so the underlined item must be consistent with this structure. Eliminate (A) and (B) because *communicate* and *communicative* aren't in the correct form to be consistent with *forging*. Since the sentence is making a comparison, the correct phrasing *is every bit as important…as* because of the *as…as* idiom. Eliminate (D) because it does not include the word *as*. The correct answer is (C).

44. **G** The phrase after *making senseless noises* is changing in the answer choices, so the question could be testing concision. First determine whether the phrase is necessary. The sentence already states *senseless*, so there is no need to repeat that idea. Eliminate any choices that are redundant. Choices (F), (H), and (J) each repeat the idea that the noises are *senseless*, or made without thought and reason, so eliminate them. The correct answer is (G).

45. **B** Note the question! The question asks which option would *summarize the main point the essay makes about cats' communication with their human owners*. The essay suggests that cats make noises for specific reasons, and that each time they communicate with their human owners, it's to convey something. Check each answer choice to see whether it is consistent with this idea. Eliminate (A)

because this choice compares *cats* to *other animals*. Keep (B) because it states that cats will communicate with their owners when they want to express *something*. Eliminate (C) because it expresses how cats communicate with *other cats*, not with their owners. Eliminate (D) because it discusses a benefit of having *more than one cat*. The correct answer is (B).

46. **J** Phrase length is changing in the answer choices, so this question is testing concision. The sentence already uses the phrase *in time*, so there's no need to include another reference to time. Eliminate (F), (G), and (H) because each of these mentions the *past*, which is redundant with the idea of stepping or moving back in time. Keep (J) because it is the most concise. The correct answer is (J).

47. **C** Apostrophes are changing in the answer choices, so the question is testing apostrophe usage. When used with a noun, on the ACT, the apostrophe indicates possession. In this sentence, nothing belongs to the *houses*. Therefore, no apostrophe is needed, so eliminate (A) and (B). To choose between (C) and (D), consider the function of the comma. The word *houses* is part of a list with two items—*Victorian houses* and *a fort*. A comma should be used only in a list with three or more items, so no comma is needed. Eliminate (D). The correct answer is (C).

48. **F** The phrase before *to* is changing in the answer choices, so the question could be testing concision. First determine whether the phrase is necessary. The sentence already states *get to*, and it is implied that *you* are the person traveling, so there is no need to repeat that idea. Eliminate any choices that are redundant. Choices (G), (H), and (J) each repeat the idea that *you* will *get to* the island, so eliminate them. Keep (F) because it is the most concise. The correct answer is (F).

49. **C** Commas are changing in the answer choices, so the question is testing comma rules. The word *Michigan* is necessary information, so it does not need a comma before and after. Eliminate (A) and (D) because each contains a comma before and after the word. To choose between the remaining choices, consider the difference between them: (C) contains a comma and (B) does not. Since a comma with a FANBOYS word is STOP punctuation and a lack of punctuation is GO punctuation, use the vertical line test. Draw vertical lines after the word *island* and before the word *visitors*, and identify the ideas as complete or incomplete. The phrase *Automobiles are outlawed on the little, isolated Michigan island* is a complete idea, and the phrase *visitors can see the sights only by horse, carriage, bicycle, or on foot* is a complete idea. To connect a complete idea to a complete idea, STOP or HALF-STOP punctuation is needed. Eliminate (B) because a lack of punctuation is GO punctuation. Keep (C) because a comma with a FANBOYS word is STOP punctuation. The correct answer is (C).

50. **J** The phrase before *bicycle* is changing in the answer choices, so the question could be testing concision. However, the underlined portion is also part of a list, so the question is also testing consistency. All items in a list must be consistent, so the underlined item must be consistent with the non-underlined items in the list—*horse, carriage,* and *foot*. Eliminate (F) and (H) because each of these includes a verb, *riding*; none of the other items in the list uses a verb. Eliminate (G) because none of the other items in the list repeats the word *by*. Keep (J) because it is consistent with the other items in the list. The correct answer is (J).

51. **C** Punctuation is changing in the answer choices, so the question is testing STOP and GO punctuation. Use the vertical line test, and identify the ideas as complete or incomplete. Draw the vertical

line between the words *necessary* and *Mackinac*. The phrase *Luckily, the island is small enough that cars are not necessary* is a complete idea, and the phrase *Mackinac measures only a mile and a half in diameter* is a complete idea. To connect a complete idea to a complete idea, STOP or HALF-STOP punctuation is needed. The comma is GO punctuation, so eliminate (A). Even with the word *furthermore* added, the second part of the sentence is still a complete idea. A comma cannot link two complete ideas, so eliminate (B). The period is STOP punctuation, so keep (C). A lack of punctuation is GO punctuation, so eliminate (D). The correct answer is (C).

52. **F** Note the question! The question asks what the paragraph would lose if the phrase were deleted. Consider the purpose of the phrase. The sentence containing the phrase describes *popular tourist spots*, one of which is *Arch Rock*. The phrase explains how the *arch* was formed. Check the answers and eliminate any choice that is not consistent with this purpose. Keep (F) because the *unique formation of Arch Rock* is consistent with the purpose of the sentence. Eliminate (G) because the phrase discusses the *geological formations* of only one, not multiple, *tourist attractions*. Eliminate (H) because the phrase does not compare *Arch Rock* to the *governor's mansion*. Eliminate (J) because information about Arch Rock's formation is not *detailed elsewhere in the paragraph*. The correct answer is (F).

53. **A** Note the question! The question asks which option would *provide the most effective transition to the topic discussed in the sentence that follows*. The sentence containing the transition says that *the island's biggest industry is tourism*, and the following sentence says that *the most popular item* to buy is *fudge*. Check each answer choice to see whether it has to do with items that tourists buy. Keep (A) because it mentions stores at which tourists may purchase items. Eliminate (B) because it discusses *outsourcing*, not shopping opportunities for tourists. Eliminate (C) because *the island's eighteenth-century use in the fur trade* does not relate to shopping opportunities for tourists. Eliminate (D) because it compares Mackinac Island to other vacation destinations; it does not discuss shopping opportunities for tourists. The correct answer is (A).

54. **H** Connecting words are changing in the answer choices, so the question is testing consistency. The part before the underlined portion contains the phrase *most popular item*, and the sentence, as a whole, discusses an item sold to tourists on the island. The correct idiom is *for sale*. Eliminate (F), (G), and (J) because they do not contain the correct idiom. The correct answer is (H).

55. **A** Note the question! The question asks which alternative would *NOT* be acceptable, so it's testing consistency. Cross off the word *NOT*, and mark each answer with Yes/No. The first part of the sentence says, *The downtown streets are lined with fudge shops*, and the second part says that at these fudge shops, *tourists can watch fudge of all different flavors being made*. The underlined word, *where*, indicates that the tourists' actions are happening at the fudge shops. Mark (A) as No because it makes the sentence incomplete. Mark (B), (C), and (D) as Yes because they all are consistent with the original meaning. Choice (A) is the odd one out. The correct answer is (A).

56. **H** The phrase surrounding *numerous* is changing in the answer choices, so the question could be testing concision. First determine whether the phrase is necessary. The sentence already states *numerous*, so there is no need to repeat that idea. Eliminate any choices that are redundant. Choices (F), (G), and (J) use *numerous* and a form of *abundant*, which have the same meaning in context, so eliminate each. Keep (H) because it is the most concise. The correct answer is (H).

57. **D** Pronouns and nouns are changing in the answer choices, so the question is testing clarity with pronouns. Determine who or what the pronoun refers to, and choose an answer that makes the meaning 100% clear. The subject of the phrase *call the tourists "fudgies"* is *local residents*. The narrator does not call the tourists *"fudgies,"* so eliminate (A). Eliminate (B) because one implies that the nickname *"fudgies"* is universally accepted, but the sentence indicates that it is used only by *local residents*. The subject *local residents* is plural. Eliminate (C) because *it* is a singular pronoun used to describe an object. Keep (D) because *they* is a plural pronoun. The correct answer is (D).

58. **G** Vocabulary is changing in the answer choices, so this question is testing word choice. The sentence says that a *gentle lake breeze floats through the air in the summer*, and when that happens, the result is *a beautiful, temperate climate*. Eliminate answer choices that are not consistent with this meaning. Eliminate (F) because the sentence already says that this phenomenon occurs in the *summer*, so there is no need to refer to time again with the word *when*. Keep (G) because it is consistent with the meaning of the sentence. Eliminate (H) because it suggests that *the gentle lake breeze floats through the air* only after it creates *a beautiful, temperate climate*. Eliminate (J) because it suggests that the *beautiful, temperate climate* is hypothetical. The correct answer is (G).

59. **D** Verbs are changing in the answer choices, so this question is testing consistency of verbs. Notice that verbs are also changing, so eliminate answers that are not consistent with the subject and with other verbs in the sentence. The subject of the underlined verb is *privacy*, which is singular, so the underlined verb must also be singular. Eliminate (A) because *don't* (or *do not*) is plural. To choose between the remaining choices, consider the form of the verb. The second part of the sentence is a comparison to an idea in the first part of the sentence, so the verbs used should be consistent. The second part of the sentence uses the verb *makes*, and the underlined verb must be consistent. Eliminate (B) and (C) because *giving* and *given* are not consistent in form with *makes*. Keep (D) because *doesn't give* is consistent in form with *makes*. The correct answer is (D).

60. **H** Note the question! The question asks whether the essay conveys the *difficulty the residents of Mackinac Island have had prohibiting automobile traffic from the historic island*. Consider the main idea of the passage and use Process of Elimination. The passage describes the features of Mackinac Island that may appeal to tourists. Eliminate (F), (G), and (J) because the main point of the essay is not to discuss issues related to *automobiles* on the island. Keep (H) because it is true that the author focuses on *other aspects of Mackinac Island, mentioning automobiles in only one part of the passage*. The correct answer is (H).

61. **B** Punctuation is changing in the answer choices, so the question is testing STOP and GO punctuation. However, notice that the non-underlined portion of the sentence contains the word *both* and the underlined portion contains a list—*friends* and *peers*—so this question is also testing comma rules. Commas should be used to separate items only in a list of three or more items. Since this list contains only two items, commas should not be used. Eliminate (C). Since (A) includes STOP punctuation, try the vertical line test. Draw a vertical line between the words *friends* and *and*. Notice that the phrase *and their peers*, after the semicolon, is an incomplete idea. A semicolon can be used only to connect two complete ideas, so eliminate (A). Keep (B) because it does not use commas between items in the list. Eliminate (D) because there is no reason to use a comma after *and*. The correct answer is (B).

62. **J** Note the question! The question asks which alternative to the *underlined portion would NOT be acceptable*. Cross off the word *NOT* and mark each choice as Yes/No. Choices (F), (G), and (H) each preserve the meaning of the sentence: *karaoke* provides *people with a great time and a positive feeling*. Mark (F), (G), and (H) as Yes. Mark (J) as No because it makes the sentence incomplete. Choice (J) is the odd one out. The correct answer is (J).

63. **C** Note the question! The question asks where Sentence 2 should be placed, so it's testing consistency. Look for a clue in the sentence to determine what idea it needs to come before or after. Sentence 2 discusses an aspect of karaoke that *defies understanding* and uses the word *though* to indicate that this contrasts with a prior statement regarding something understandable about karaoke. Sentence 4 discusses an *understandable* action. Therefore, Sentence 2 should follow Sentence 4. The correct answer is (C).

64. **J** Verbs are changing in the answer choices, so the question is testing consistency of verbs. The answer choices are in different tenses, so look for a clue in the sentence or surrounding sentences to identify the appropriate tense. The sentence lists two actions directed toward the reader. The first is the underlined verb, and the second is the verb *see*. Since both verbs must be consistent, and *see* is in the simple present tense, the underlined portion must be consistent in form with *see*. Eliminate (F) because *Looking* is the *-ing* form of a verb, which is not consistent with *see*. Eliminate (G) and (H) because *Having looked* and *To look* are not consistent with *see*. Keep (J) because *Look* is consistent with *see*. The correct answer is (J).

65. **C** Vocabulary after *restaurants* is changing in the answer choices, so the question is testing word choice. Punctuation also changes, so use the vertical line test. A comma with a FANBOYS word is STOP punctuation, so draw vertical lines after *restaurants* and before *karaoke*. The phrase *Even though their performances may be heard only in dimly lit bars or busy restaurants* is an incomplete idea, and the phrase *karaoke singers are still performing as if in a true concert with such concert-hall staples as microphones, lights, and applause* is a complete idea. To connect an incomplete idea to a complete idea, GO punctuation is needed. The comma with a FANBOYS word is STOP punctuation, so eliminate (A). Eliminate (B) because the word *which* makes the sentence incomplete. Keep (C) because a comma is GO punctuation. Eliminate (D) because the word *but* makes the sentence incomplete and there is no need for another opposite-direction word since the sentence begins with *Even though*. The correct answer is (C).

66. **H** Punctuation is changing in the answer choices, so the question is testing STOP and GO punctuation. Use the vertical line test, and identify the ideas as complete or incomplete. Draw the vertical line between the words *staples* and *as*. The phrase *Even though their performances may be heard only in dimly lit bars or busy restaurants, karaoke singers are still performing as if in a true concert with such concert-hall staples* is a complete idea, and the phrase *as microphones, lights, and applause* is an incomplete idea. To connect a complete idea to an incomplete idea, HALF-STOP or GO punctuation is needed. The comma is GO punctuation, but there is no reason to use a comma, so eliminate (F). The colon is HALF-STOP punctuation, but there is no need to use a colon. A colon can introduce an explanatory phrase or a list. There is a list after the colon in this sentence, but since the phrase *such...as* precedes the list, a colon is redundant; eliminate (G). A lack of punctuation is GO punctuation, so keep (H). A semicolon is STOP punctuation, so eliminate (J). The correct answer is (H).

67. **D** Verbs are changing in the answer choices, so the question is testing consistency of verbs. The answer choices are in different tenses, so look for a clue in the sentence or surrounding sentences to identify the appropriate tense. The beginning of the sentence says *the singers' voices are not spectacular*, which includes the simple present tense verb *are*. Since verbs in a sentence should be consistent with other verbs, the underlined portion needs to be in simple present tense to be consistent. Eliminate (A) because *has known* is not simple present tense. Eliminate (B) because *is knowing* is not simple present tense. Eliminate (C) because *knew* is past, not simple present, tense. Keep (D) because *knows* is simple present tense. The correct answer is (D).

68. **F** Note the question! The question asks which option would *effectively conclude this paragraph while leading into the main focus of the next paragraph*. Since this question asks about a transition, check each answer choice to see whether it is consistent with ideas in both paragraphs. The paragraph ending with the underlined sentence discusses one reason karaoke is successful, and the following paragraph discusses *another, more obvious reason*. Keep (F) because it summarizes the reason from the preceding paragraph while introducing the idea that there is another reason karaoke is popular. Eliminate (G) because neither paragraph discusses *AudioSynTrac* or *Numark Electronics*. Eliminate (H) because neither paragraph discusses *Japan's lasting influence on karaoke*. Eliminate (J) because, though the previous paragraph does mention that *singing in front of people is more fun*, it does not compare this to *singing in the shower or in the car*. The correct answer is (F).

69. **A** Transitions are changing in the answer choices, so the question is testing consistency with transitions. Look at the previous sentence to determine how the two ideas are related. The previous sentence indicates that the *average person* generally sings alone, and this sentence explains that *karaoke* gives people a chance to sing together. Therefore, the two ideas contrast. Keep (A) because *by contrast* indicates that the two ideas contrast. Eliminate (B) and (C) because *furthermore* and *moreover* indicate that the two ideas agree. Eliminate (D) because *as a result* indicates that the second idea is an effect caused by the first idea. The correct answer is (A).

70. **G** Vocabulary is changing in the answers, so the question is testing word choice. Determine what meaning of the underlined portion would be consistent with the sentence. The underlined portion should mean something like "no matter." Eliminate (F) because *In lieu of* means "instead of." Keep (G) because *Regardless of* means "no matter." Eliminate (H) because *However* means "by contrast." Eliminate (J) because *Because of* means "as a result of." The correct answer is (G).

71. **A** Pronouns are changing in the answer choices, so the question is testing consistency of pronouns. A pronoun must be consistent in number with the noun it is replacing. The pronoun refers to the noun *others*, which is plural. To be consistent, the pronoun in the answer choice must also be plural. In addition, since the *singing* belongs to the *others*, the pronoun must also be possessive. Keep (A) because *whose* can be plural and is possessive. Eliminate (B) and (C) because *who* and *whom* are not possessive. Eliminate (D) because *who's* is a contraction that means "who is," so it is also not a possessive pronoun. The correct answer is (A).

72. **G** Note the question! The question asks what the paragraph would lose if the phrase were deleted. Consider the purpose of the phrase. The sentence explains that *karaoke* helps to bring certain people *out of their shells*. The phrase specifies the group of people that karaoke helps: *people who*

are ordinarily shy. Without the phrase, the sentence would imply that karaoke helps all people. Check the answers and eliminate any choice that is not consistent with this purpose. Eliminate (F) because the phrase does not focus on the *international community*. Keep (G) because the phrase does specify a detail about a group with whom *karaoke is popular*. Eliminate (H) because, while it does talk about *chronically shy* people, the *psychological benefits of karaoke* are not consistent with the purpose of the phrase. Eliminate (J) because the phrase does not mention *stage fright*. The correct answer is (G).

73. **B**   Vocabulary is changing in the answers, so the question is testing word choice. Determine what meaning of the underlined portion would be consistent with the sentence. The sentence talks about singers' feelings at the time that they *take the stage*, so the underlined portion should mean something like "at the time." Eliminate (A) because *if* indicates a possibility rather than a point in time. Keep (B) because *when* means "at the time." Eliminate (C) because *unless* changes the meaning of the sentence. Eliminate (D) because *where* refers to a physical place, not a time. The correct answer is (B).

74. **F**   Vocabulary is changing in the answers, so the question is testing word choice. Determine what meaning of the underlined portion would be consistent with the sentence. The sentence says that *karaoke* made at least *$7 billion in profit in Japan*, so the underlined portion should mean something like "at least." Keep (F) because *no less than* means the same as "at least" in context. Eliminate (G) because *lesser* is an adjective that means "inferior to" and usually refers to the quality, not the quantity, of an object. Eliminate (H) because *then* refers to time rather than to a comparison of quantities. Eliminate (J) because *few* is a descriptive adjective that makes the sentence incomplete. The correct answer is (F).

75. **D**   Note the question! The question asks where a new sentence should be placed, so it's testing consistency. Look for a clue in the sentence to determine what idea it needs to come before or after. The new sentence says that *the most popular karaoke requests are invariably for country artists*, though regional preferences vary. None of the paragraphs discusses music preference among those who sing karaoke, so the new sentence is not consistent with information in any paragraph. Therefore, it should not be added to the essay. Eliminate (A), (B), and (C). The correct answer is (D).

MATHEMATICS TEST

1. **A**   The question asks for the *midpoint of line segment XY* given that point X is located at –15 on the number line and point Y is located at –11. To find the midpoint, average the coordinates to get $\left(\dfrac{-15+(-11)}{2}\right) = \dfrac{-26}{2} = -13$. The correct answer is (A).

2. **H**   The question asks for *the length of leg DE* in the given right triangle with hypotenuse of 10 and leg of 8. Either recognize the Pythagorean triple 6-8-10, or use the Pythagorean Theorem, $a^2 + b^2 = c^2$, to solve for side DE. Fill in the known sides to get $a^2 + 8^2 = 10^2$. Simplify the equation to $a^2 + 64 = 100$ and subtract 64 from both sides to get $a^2 = 36$. Finally take the square root of both sides to get $a = 6$. The correct answer is (H).

3. **C** The question asks which formula expresses the approximation of the calculation given in the question. Use the Word Problem Basic Approach and break the question into bite-sized pieces. Start with the most straightforward piece of information, *50 more than*, and eliminate any choices that do not add 50. Eliminate (B) and (D) since they multiply 50 by $\frac{1}{2}$ and 2, respectively. Now look for the next piece of information, *double the volume of the ant farm*. The question states that the volume of the ant farm is V, so double the volume would be $2V$. Eliminate choices (A) and (E) because they do not include $2V$. The correct answer is (C).

4. **J** The question asks for the *probability that the book Lisa takes is fiction*. Probability is defined as $\frac{part}{whole}$. There are 5 fiction books, so 5 is the *part*, or the number of outcomes that fit the requirements. The *whole* is the total number of outcomes, or the total available books: $5 + 7 = 12$ total books. The probability is $\frac{5}{12}$. The correct answer is (J).

5. **C** The question asks for Katie's *average test score*. To find an average, use the formula $T = AN$ where T is the total of the items in the list, A is the average, and N is the number of things. For this question, $T = 108 + 81 + 79 + 99 + 85 + 82 = 534$, and $N = 6$. Plug the numbers into the equation to get $534 = A(6)$. Divide both sides by 6 to get $89 = A$. The correct answer is (C).

6. **K** The question asks for a *pair of angles that must be congruent*. Use the Geometry Basic Approach. Start by labeling the figure with the given information. Mark lines l and m as parallel. When parallel lines are cut by third line, two kinds of angles are formed—big and small. All big angles are equal, and all small angles are equal. For the line that goes between angles 2 and 3 and angles 4 and 5, the big angles are the one labeled 4 and the sum of the two labeled 1 and 2. The small angles are 3 and 5. Let the answers help; no answer refers to the sum of 1 and 2, so focus on the 3 and 5. Those angles are equal, as indicated in (K). There is not enough information provided to say that any other pair of angles *must* be congruent, so eliminate (F), (G), (H), and (J). The correct answer is (K).

7. **A** The question asks how much Gregor *receive(s) as his monthly pay*. Since the question asks for a specific value and the answers contain numbers in increasing order, plug in the answers. Begin by labeling the answers as "monthly pay" and start with (C), $7,200. The question states that Gregory spends 20% of his monthly pay on rent and deposits, so calculate 20% of $7,200: $\frac{20}{100}(\$7,200) = \$1,440$. Subtract $1,440 from the total pay, $7,200, to get $7,200 − $1,440 = $5,760. This is bigger than the value of $3,200 that the question says he deposits in his savings account, so eliminate (C). Eliminate (D) and (E) because they would give larger values than (C). Now try (A) since the result from (C) was significantly larger than $3,200. Calculate 20% of $4,000: $\frac{20}{100}(\$4,000) = \$800$. Subtract $800 from the total pay, $4,000, to get $4,000 − $800 = $3,200, which matches the value given in the question, so stop here. The correct answer is (A).

8. **K** The question asks for the statement in the answers that must be true given similar parallelograms *ABCD* and *EFGH*. To be similar, figures will have corresponding sides in proportion and corresponding angles that are equal in measure, or congruent. Eliminate (F) and (G) because similar figures do not need to be the same size. Congruent means equal in measure, so eliminate (H) and (J) because the lengths of sides and diagonals in similar figures are proportional but do not need to be equal. By definition, similar shapes must have congruent angles; therefore (K) will always be true. The correct answer is (K).

9. **E** The question asks for the *price Victoria pays for* a dress that was initially $60. Although this question asks for a specific value, the answers reflect the result of a few operations. Instead of plugging in the answers, use bite-sized pieces to tackle this question. Start by calculating the cost of the dress on sale by multiplying $60 by 30% to get $\$60\left(\dfrac{30}{100}\right) = \$18$. This is the amount by which the price of the dress was reduced, so subtract $18 from the initial price of the dress to get the sale price of the dress: $60 − $18 = $42. Victoria also receives an additional discount of 10% off the sales price for using her store credit card. Calculate this cost by multiplying $42 by 10% to get $\$42\left(\dfrac{10}{100}\right) = \$4.20$; then subtract $4.20 from $42 to get the final price: $42 − $4.20 = $37.80. The correct answer is (E).

10. **J** The question asks *how many more chips* Amy has compared to Erin after the next hand. The question is asking for numbers in relation to one another. Because no actual numbers of chips are given, this is a hidden plug in question. Start by plugging in a value for the amount of chips Erin and Amy have initially. Because the question states that at *a certain point in the game, Erin has 3 more chips than Amy*, let Erin have 10 chips and Amy have 7 chips. The question also states that *on the next hand, Erin wins 4 chips from Amy*; in other words, Amy lost 4 of her chips to Erin. Subtract 4 chips from Amy's 7, so Amy has 7 − 4 = 3 chips remaining. The 4 chips Amy lost are added to Erin's chips, so Erin has 10 + 4 = 14 chips remaining. To find how many more chips Erin has than Amy, subtract Amy's 3 chips from Erin's 14 to get 14 − 3 = 11. The correct answer is (J).

11. **C** The question asks for the value of an expression with an absolute value. Taking the absolute value of an expression will yield a positive result, so eliminate (A) and (B). When working with absolute values, do the calculations inside the absolute value symbols as if they are parentheses; then take the absolute value. Plug in the value of $y = 4$ given in the question to get $|1 − 4| = |−3| = 3$. The correct answer is (C).

12. **K** The question asks for an equivalent form of an expression. There are variables in the answer choices, so Plugging In is an option. However, with two variables and many exponents, it is probably quicker to use FOIL to expand the expression, pausing after each bite-sized piece to eliminate answers. Multiply the First values to get $3a(a) = 3a^2$. There will be no other a^2 terms, so eliminate (F), which does not start with this term. Next, multiply the Outer values to get $3a(−b^2) = −3ab^2$. Multiply the Inner values next to get $2b(a) = 2ab$. The Outer and Inner terms cannot be combined. Eliminate (G) and (H), which do not contain $−3ab^2$, and (J), which does not contain $2ab$. To see why (K) is correct, multiply the Last values to get $2b(−b^2) = −2b^3$. The correct answer is (K).

13. **D** The question asks for an equivalent form of an expression. There is a variable in the answer choices, so Plug In. Make $y = 2$. The expression becomes $3 - 2(4 - 2) = 3 - 2(2) = 3 - 4 = -1$. This is the target value; circle it. Now plug $y = 2$ into the answer choices to see which one matches the target value. Choice (A) becomes $-2(2) - 9 = -4 - 9 = -13$. This does not match the target, so eliminate (A). Choice (B) becomes $-2(2) + 8 = -4 + 8 = 4$. Eliminate (B). Choice (C) becomes $-2(2) - 1 = -4 - 1 = -5$. Eliminate (C). Choice (D) becomes $2(2) - 5 = 4 - 5 = -1$. Keep (D), but check (E) just in case. Choice (E) becomes $2(2) + 11 = 15$. Eliminate (E). The correct answer is (D).

14. **G** The question asks for an equivalent form of an expression. When dealing with questions about exponents, remember the MADSPM rules. The PM part of the acronym indicates that raising a base with an exponent to another Power means to Multiply the exponents. The expression $(y^3)^8$ can be rewritten as $y^{(3 \times 8)} = y^{24}$. The correct answer is (G).

15. **A** The question asks for the 260th day of the year given that *the first day of the year is a Monday*. The days of the year happen in a 7-day repeating pattern. In this case, Monday is day 1, Tuesday day 2, … and Sunday is day 7. Counting out 260 days would be time consuming and impractical, so divide 260 by 7 to determine how many full weeks have passed and use that information to determine what day of the week the 260th day is. Start by dividing $260 \div 7 \approx 37.143$. This indicates that 37 full weeks and some fraction of a week have passed. Find the number of days in 37 weeks by multiplying 37 weeks × 7 days = 259 days. The 259th day is a multiple of 7, which indicates that the 259th day is a Sunday. That means that the 260th day of the year is one more day, or a Monday. The correct answer is (A).

16. **H** The question asks for *the area of the largest circle that can be inscribed inside the square* with *an area of 64 square units*. Use the Geometry Basic Approach. Start by drawing and labeling a figure with the given information. Draw a square with a circle inscribed inside it that touches all four sides of the square. Next, write down the formulas needed. The area of a square is given in the question, and the question asks for the area of a circle, so write down the formula for the area of a square, $A = s^2$, and the formula for the area of a circle, $A = \pi r^2$. Now, put the given value for the area of the square into the area formula to get $64 = s^2$; then take the square root of both sides to find the side of the square is 8. Label that on the drawing. Notice that the side of the square is the same length as the diameter of the circle, so $s = d = 8$. The radius is half the diameter, so $r = 4$. Label that. Finally, use the radius to find the area of the circle: $A = \pi(4)^2 = 16\pi$. The correct answer is (H).

17. **A** The question asks for the product of the solutions to the given quadratic equation. The formula to find the products of the roots when the quadratic is in the standard form of $ax^2 + bx + c = 0$ is $\frac{c}{a}$. In this quadratic, $c = -14$ and $a = 1$. Therefore, the product of the roots will be $\frac{-14}{1} = -14$. Alternately, factor the equation to find the solutions. The first term of each binomial factor will be x since the first term of the quadratic is x^2. The last term of the quadratic is formed by multiplying the last terms of the binomials, so look for factors of -14 that will add up to -5. For this quadratic, those factors of -14 are -7 and 2. The factored form of the quadratic is $(x + 2)(x - 7) = 0$. The solutions can be found by setting each binomial equal to zero to get $x = -2$ and $x = 7$. Now multiply those solutions to get $-2 \times 7 = -14$. Either way, the correct answer is (A).

18. **K** The question asks which of the answers is NOT a factor of the given polynomial. An expression is always a factor of itself, so eliminate (G). There are variables in the answer choices, but Plugging In could get messy with such large exponents, so try factoring the expression first. The polynomial $x^{12} - 9$ is in the format $a^2 - b^2 = (a - b)(a + b)$, so it can be factored to $(x^6 - 3)(x^6 + 3)$. Eliminate (F), which is a factor of the polynomial. The factor $x^6 + 3$ cannot be factored further. The other factor, $x^6 - 3$, is in the same format as the initial expression and can be factored to get $\left(x^3 - \sqrt{3}\right)\left(x^3 + \sqrt{3}\right)$. Eliminate (H) and (J), as these are factors of the polynomial. Only the expression in (K) cannot be obtained by factoring the polynomial. The correct answer is (K).

19. **C** The question asks for the value of an expression given the value of x. Plug the value of x into the given expression and solve. Since $\dfrac{1}{6}$ is a fraction, pay special attention to the work on the page or in the calculator; close all open parentheses and notice whether the work is in the numerator or denominator. Plug the value of x into the expression to get $\dfrac{2x + 4}{3x} = \dfrac{2\left(\frac{1}{6}\right) + 4}{3\left(\frac{1}{6}\right)} = \dfrac{\frac{1}{3} + 4}{\frac{1}{2}}$. To eliminate the fraction in the denominator, multiply the numerator and denominator of the main fraction by 2 and simplify to get $\dfrac{2\left(\frac{1}{3} + 4\right)}{2\left(\frac{1}{2}\right)} = \dfrac{2\left(\frac{1}{3} + 4\right)}{1} = \dfrac{2}{3} + 8$. To combine these terms, use a common denominator of 3. This becomes $\dfrac{2}{3} + 8 = \dfrac{2}{3} + \dfrac{24}{3} = \dfrac{2 + 24}{3} = \dfrac{26}{3}$. The correct answer is (C).

20. **H** The question asks for the amount of time given the rate and distance traveled. Use a proportion to solve for the requested time. The question states that the rate is 90 miles an hour. The question also gives the number of miles the trip covers, 60 miles. Set up the proportion using that information: $\dfrac{90 \text{ miles}}{1 \text{ hour}} = \dfrac{60 \text{ miles}}{x \text{ hours}}$. Cross-multiply to get $90x = 60$; then divide both sides by 60 to get $x = \dfrac{60}{90}$ *hours* or $x = \dfrac{2}{3}$ *hours*. The question asks for the number of minutes, not the number of hours, the trip will take. Eliminate (J) and (K) because they represent a full hour or more. It is also possible to eliminate (F) and (G) since they are a half an hour or less, but if that was not obvious, multiply the total number of minutes in an hour, 60, by the fraction of the hour the trip will take, $\dfrac{2}{3}$, to find the exact number of minutes the trip will take: $60\left(\dfrac{2}{3}\right) = 40$ minutes. The correct answer is (H).

21. **C** The question asks for the area of the trapezoid in square inches based on the given measurements. The formula for the area of a trapezoid is provided, but the height of the trapezoid is not, so start by calculating the height of the trapezoid. Draw a line down from one of the top vertices perpendicular to the bottom base of the trapezoid: this is the height of the trapezoid. This also forms a right triangle with a known hypotenuse.

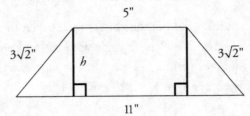

The trapezoid is symmetrical, which means the bottom base is the sum of the top base and the bases of the two equal triangles. Thus, the base of the right triangle can be calculated by finding the difference between the top base and the bottom base and dividing that difference by 2: $\frac{11-5}{2} = 3$. Label the base of the right triangle as 3. Now, use the Pythagorean theorem $a^2 + b^2 = c^2$ to solve for the height of the triangle. The height of the triangle is h. Plug the known values into the theorem to get $h^2 + 3^2 = \left(3\sqrt{2}\right)^2$. Simplify to get $h^2 + 9 = 9(2)$, then $h^2 + 9 = 18$. Subtract 9 from both sides to get $h^2 = 9$, then take the square root of both sides to get $h = 3$. The height of the triangle and therefore the height of the trapezoid is 3. Label this on the figure. Now use the provided formula for the area of a trapezoid to find the area: $A = \frac{1}{2}h(b_1 + b_2) = \frac{1}{2}(3)(5+11) = \frac{1}{2}(3)(16) = 24$. The correct answer is (C).

22. **F** The question asks for the factors of a quadratic equation in standard form. Factors of a quadratic equation are binomials. To find the roots, those binomials are set equal to 0 and solved for the value of x. The question provides the roots, so it is just a matter of plugging in the answers to see which binomials, when set equal to 0, provide the roots $x = -\frac{2}{3}$ and $x = \frac{1}{4}$ given in the question. Take things in bite-sized pieces and start with the first binomial in (F); set it equal to 0, and solve for x. This becomes $3x + 2 = 0$. Subtract 2 from both sides to get $3x = -2$. Finally, divide both sides by 3 to get $x = -\frac{2}{3}$. This value of x matches one of the roots given in the equation. Eliminate (G), (H), (J), (K) because they do not contain the binomial $(3x + 2)$. The correct answer is (F).

23. **C** The question asks for the length of the sides of the given rhombus. A rhombus has four equal sides and the diagonals bisect one another and meet at right angles. Use the Geometry Basic Approach and draw and label the lengths of AC and BD. Label the point at which the diagonals intersect as E.

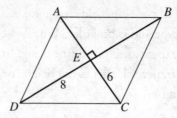

Since it is known that diagonals of a rhombus bisect each other, lines AE and BE can be labeled 3 and 4, respectively. Triangle ABE is a right triangle with legs of known length, and AB is a side of the rhombus. Use the Pythagorean triple 3-4-5 or the Pythagorean theorem $a^2 + b^2 = c^2$ to solve for the hypotenuse AB. This becomes $4^2 + 3^2 = AB^2$, or $16 + 9 = AB^2$, so $25 = AB^2$ and $5 = AB$. The correct answer is (C).

24. **G** The question asks for the length of a rectangular rug with a given area. Use the Geometry Basic Approach: draw a rectangle and write the formula for the area of a rectangle, $A = bh$. Since the question asks for a specific value and the answers contain numbers in increasing order, plug in the answers. Begin by labeling the answers as "length" and start with (H), 16 feet. The rug has a width that is 2 feet shorter than its length, so create and label a second column for "width." Calculate the width of a rug with length of 16 feet as $16 - 2 = 14$ feet. The area of a rug with these dimensions is $A = (16)(14) = 224$ square feet. This does not match the 80 square feet provided in the question, so eliminate (H). The result is too big, so also eliminate (J) and (K). Now repeat the steps with (G), 10 feet. The width is $10 - 2 = 8$ feet, and the area is $A = (8)(10) = 80$ square feet. This matches the value given in the question, so stop here. The correct answer is (G).

25. **E** The question asks for the slope of a line given two points. To calculate the slope given two points, use the formula $slope = \dfrac{y_2 - y_1}{x_2 - x_1}$. Let $(1, -5) = (x_1, y_1)$ and $(5, 10) = (x_2, y_2)$. Now solve for the slope: $\dfrac{10 - (-5)}{5 - 1} = \dfrac{10 + 5}{4} = \dfrac{15}{4}$. The correct answer is (E).

26. **G** The question asks for the center of the circle given the equation in standard form. The equation of a circle in standard form is $(x - h)^2 + (y - k)^2 = r^2$, where (h, k) is the center and r is the radius. In the given equation, $(x + 5)^2 + (y - 5)^2 = 5$, the value of $h = -5$ and the value of $k = 5$. Therefore, the center of the circle is point $(-5, 5)$. The correct answer is (G).

27. **D** The question asks for the *domain* of $f(x)$ on the provided graph. The domain of a function is all the x-values that provide a real number answer when plugged into the function, or, when represented on a graph, the x-values that the graph passes through. On this graph, the x-values start at, but do not include, zero and include every x-value up to, but not including, 4. The choice that represents the x-values described is (D). The correct answer is (D).

28. **F** The question asks for the midpoint of a line given the endpoints. Use bite-sized pieces and find the value of the x-coordinate first. To do so, average the x-coordinates of the endpoints to get $x = \dfrac{-1 + 3}{2} = \dfrac{2}{2} = 1$. Eliminate (H), (J), and (K) because they do not have an x-coordinate of 1.

Now, find the average of the *y*-coordinates of the endpoints to get $y = \dfrac{-5+3}{2} = \dfrac{-2}{2} = -1$. Eliminate (G). The correct answer is (F).

29. **C** The question asks for the average rate of change for the experiment described. Be sure to read the question carefully and note that the rate of change shouldbe calculated ONLY for *the times in which the temperature is increasing*. To find the average rate of change, divide the total change in temperature by the total time that the temperature was increasing. The change in temperature is calculated by subtracting the final temperature from the initial temperature, which is 80 − 0 = 80. There is an 80-degree change in temperature. To find the amount of time that this change happens over, calculate the change in the *x*-values for each of the 3 periods in which the line is going up and add those together to get the total time of change as follows: 5 − 0 = 5 minutes of heating for the first increase, 10 − 7.5 = 2.5 minutes for the second increase, and 17.5 − 15 = 2.5 minutes for the final increase. Add those together to get a total time of temperature increase of 5 + 2.5 + 2.5 = 10 minutes. Now divide the change in temperature, 80, by the amount of time that changed happened over, 10 minutes, to get a rate of change of $\dfrac{80}{10} = 8$. The correct answer is (C).

30. **H** The question asks for a true statement given an equation with exponents. When dealing with questions about exponents, remember the MADSPM rules. The DS part of the acronym indicates that Dividing matching bases means to Subtract the exponents. Since the base of all the components of this equation is *a*, then $\dfrac{a^x}{a^y} = a^{(x-y)} = a^5$ and *x* − *y* = 5. The correct answer is (H).

31. **E** The question asks for the slope of a given line. The standard form of a linear equation is $Ax + By = C$, and the slope of a line in standard form is $-\dfrac{A}{B}$. The given equation, 8 = 3*y* − 5*x*, can easily be rearranged into the standard form of a linear equation, −5*x* + 3*y* = 8. The *A*-value is −5, and the *B*-value is 3. Therefore, the slope of the line is $-\left(\dfrac{-5}{3}\right) = \dfrac{5}{3}$. The correct answer is (E).

32. **J** The question asks for the least common denominator of 3 fractions. The least common denominator, or LCD, is the smallest number that is a multiple of all the denominators. Stated another way, the LCD includes all the common factors of the numbers given. Because these denominators are already in a factored form, first look at 3 and find the largest exponent associated with 3, which in this case is 2. That means that 3^2 is part of the LCD. Eliminate (F) and (K), which have 3 and 3^3, respectively. Compare the remaining answers. All have the term 5^2, so that must be part of the LCD. Now work with the 7. There must be a 7 in the LCD, as it is in the middle fraction, so eliminate (H) which does not include 7. Repeat this process with the 11 to see that 11^3 is required in the LCD. Eliminate (K), which has 11^4. The correct answer is (J).

33. **C** The question asks for the solution to the expression given. Notice that it is possible to simplify this expression before multiplying by eliminating any common numerators and denominators. This can be done with the 4s, 5s, 6s, and 7s to get $\frac{1}{\cancel{4}_1} \times \frac{2}{\cancel{5}_1} \times \frac{3}{\cancel{6}_1} \times \frac{\cancel{4}^1}{\cancel{7}_1} \times \frac{\cancel{5}^1}{8} \times \frac{\cancel{6}^1}{9} \times \frac{\cancel{7}^1}{10}$. The expression can be simplified further by cancelling out the 2 and 3 in the numerators with multiples of those factors in the denominators to get $\frac{1}{1} \times \frac{\cancel{2}^1}{1} \times \frac{\cancel{3}^1}{1} \times \frac{1}{1} \times \frac{1}{\cancel{8}_4} \times \frac{1}{\cancel{9}_3} \times \frac{1}{10}$. Multiply the numerators and the denominators separately to get $\frac{1 \times 1 \times 1 \times 1 \times 1 \times 1 \times 1}{1 \times 1 \times 1 \times 4 \times 3 \times 10} = \frac{1}{120}$. The correct answer is (C).

34. **K** The question asks for the distance the plane flies. The question describes a right triangle and has already provided a labeled figure. Use the Geometry Basic Approach and write down the Pythagorean Theorem, $a^2 + b^2 = c^2$, to solve for the distance the plane flies. This distance is represented by the length of the hypotenuse, c, and the legs are $a = 110$ miles and $b = 200$ miles. Plug in these values to get $110^2 + 200^2 = c^2$, which becomes $12{,}100 + 40{,}000 = c^2$, and then $52{,}100 = c^2$. Take the square root of each side to get $\sqrt{52{,}100} = c$ miles. The correct answer is (K).

35. **E** The question asks how many points are in common when one pentagon is overlaid on another pentagon. Start by drawing another pentagon that intersects the provided pentagon in some way. One possibility looks like this:

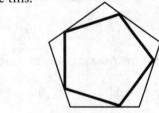

The two pentagons have 5 points of intersection, one on each side. Eliminate any choices that are smaller than 5, which are (A) and (B). Consider the remaining answers. Choice (D) indicates 10 points of intersection, which can happen if one pentagon cuts off each corner of the other one, like so:

Eliminate (C). Choice (E) states that there are *infinitely many* points of intersection. To have infinitely many points of intersection, the shapes would have to be identical and directly on top of one another. Since there are no rules in the question that prevent that scenario, it represents the most points that the two pentagons can have in common. The correct answer is (E).

36. **K** The question asks for the number of different ways that 10 employees can be assigned to 3 duties. Each employee can be assigned to only one duty. Because each employee can be assigned to only

one distinct duty, it will not be necessary to divide by the factorial of the number of spaces to eliminate duplicate groups. There are 10 employees available for the first duty, then only 9 available for the second, and only 8 available for the third. To find the number of ways that employees could be selected to complete those duties, multiply $10 \times 9 \times 8$. Since the answers are expressions and don't multiply the numbers together, stop here. The correct answer is (K).

37. **E** The question asks for the point that completes the right triangle with the right angle at point Q. Some points can be eliminated by plotting them and visually noting that they do not form right angles.

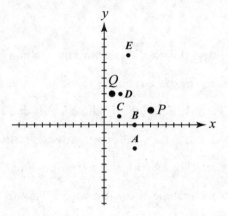

Eliminate (A), (B), (C), and (D) because points at those locations do not appear to form a right triangle with the right angle at point Q. To check that the point at $(3, 9)$ does create a right angle at point Q, check the slopes. Lines that meet at a right angle in the coordinate plane are perpendicular, which means they have slopes that are opposite reciprocals. Calculate the slope of line EQ using the formula $slope = \dfrac{y_2 - y_1}{x_2 - x_1} = \dfrac{9-4}{3-1} = \dfrac{5}{2}$. Now do the same for line segment QP: $\dfrac{y_2 - y_1}{x_2 - x_1} = \dfrac{2-4}{6-1} = \dfrac{-2}{5}$. The slopes are opposite reciprocals; therefore, the lines are perpendicular. The correct answer is (E).

38. **J** The question asks for the value of y in an equation. Since the question asks for a specific value and the answers contain numbers in decreasing order, plug in the answers. Begin by labelling the answers as "y" and start with (H), 25. The equation becomes $25 = 0.25(100 - 25)$, then $25 = 0.25(75)$, and finally $25 = 18.75$. This is not true, so eliminate (H). It may not be clear if a larger or smaller value of y is needed, so pick a direction and go with it. Try (J), 20. The equation becomes $20 = 0.25(100 - 20)$, then $20 = 0.25(80)$, and finally $20 = 20$. This is true. The correct answer is (J).

39. **B** The question asks for the value of x in a trigonometric equation. Since the question asks for a specific value and the answers contain numbers in increasing order, plug in the answers. Begin by labeling the answers as "x" and start with (C). Plug $90°$ into the left side of the equation to get $4\cos^2(90°)$. This can also be written as $4 \times (\cos 90°)^2$. Use a calculator in degree mode to determine that $\cos(90°) = 0$, so the left side of the equation becomes $4 \times (0)^2 = 4(0) = 0$. This does not equal 1, so eliminate (C). It may be difficult to determine if a larger or smaller angle measure is needed, so just pick a direction. For (B), $\cos 60° = 0.5$, so the left side of the equation becomes $4(0.5)^2 = 4(0.25) = 1$. This equals 1. The correct answer is (B).

40. **H** The question asks for the area of the floor not covered by the rug. Use the Geometry Basic Approach to draw a rectangle containing a circle that does not touch any of the sides of the rectangle. Label the dimensions of the rectangle 16 feet and 18 feet and label the diameter of the circle as 12 feet. Write the formula for the area of a rectangle, $A = lw$, and the area of a circle, $A = \pi r^2$. The area of floor exposed will be the area of the rectangle minus the area of the circle. Start by calculating the area of the rectangle: $A = 16$ feet $\times 18$ feet $= 288$ ft^2. Next, find the radius of the circle by taking half the diameter to get a radius of 6 feet. Now calculate the area of the circle, $A = \pi(6)^2 = 36\pi$ ft^2. The exposed area of the bare floor is $288 - 36\pi \approx 288 - 113.1 \approx 174.9$, which is closest to 175 ft^2. The correct answer is (H).

41. **E** The question asks for the interval with the greatest rate of change. The rate of change is the change in the y-value over the change in the x-value, or the slope of the line between the indicated points. Let the answer choices help and eliminate any choices that don't make sense. The slope of the line from the x values of 0 to 2 and 2 to 5 will be negative. Eliminate (A) and (B) because there are intervals listed in the answer choices with positive slopes and the greatest rate of change will be positive. Ballpark to see that the slope of the line from $x = 5$ to $x = 10$ is not as large as the slope of the other answers, so eliminate (C). It may be hard to visually determine the larger slope from the remaining answers, so calculate those. Start with (D). Use the slope formula $slope = \dfrac{y_2 - y_1}{x_2 - x_1}$ to get $\dfrac{39 - 12}{13 - 10} = \dfrac{27}{3} = 9$. Repeat for (E) to get $\dfrac{52 - 39}{14 - 13} = \dfrac{13}{1} = 13$. Eliminate (D) because the slope for that interval is smaller than the one for (E). The correct answer is (E).

42. **F** The question asks for the sine of the given angle. Note that the given coordinate indicates the x- and y-values of that point. Use the Geometry Basic Approach and create a right triangle with the x-axis. Label the vertical leg 2 and the horizontal leg $2\sqrt{3}$. Write out SOHCAHTOA to remember the trig functions. The SOH part defines the sine as $\dfrac{opposite}{hypotenuse}$, and the leg with length 2 is the side opposite θ. Use the Pythagorean Theorem $a^2 + b^2 = c^2$ to determine the hypotenuse. This becomes $2^2 + \left(2\sqrt{3}\right)^2 = c^2$, then $4 + 4(3) = c^2$. This further simplifies to $4 + 12 = c^2$ or $16 = c^2$. Take the square root of both sides to determine that the hypotenuse measures 4. Therefore, $\sin\theta = \dfrac{2}{4} = \dfrac{1}{2}$. The correct answer is (F).

43. **C** The question asks for the approximate magnitude of an earthquake. An equation is given, but there are no exact numbers to use. Since the relationship between two values is given, it is a hidden plug in question. First determine which values to plug in: A is the maximum amplitude measured at a sensor and A_0 is the threshold amplitude. The question asks for the value of R when A is 3,000 times bigger that A_0. Let $A_0 = 2$ and $A = 6,000$ to meet that requirement. Plug those into the given

equation and solve with a calculator to get $R = \log\left(\dfrac{6{,}000}{2}\right) = \log(3{,}000) \approx 3.477$. This is closest to 3.5. The correct answer is (C).

44. **G** The question asks for a probability which is defined as $\dfrac{part}{whole}$. First determine the *whole*, which is the number of outcomes that are possible, by multiplying the number of elements in Set P by the number of elements in Set Q to get $4 \times 4 = 16$ total outcomes. Next determine the *part*, which is the number of products of elements from Set P and Set Q that are even. To do this, multiply the first element in Set P, 2, by each of the elements in Set Q to get values of $2 \times 1 = 2$, $2 \times 2 = 4$, $2 \times 3 = 6$ and $2 \times 4 = 8$. Now repeat the process for each element in Set P to get the following: $3 \times 1 = 3$, $3 \times 2 = 6$, $3 \times 3 = 9$, $3 \times 4 = 12$; $5.5 \times 1 = 5.5$, $5.5 \times 2 = 11$, $5.5 \times 3 = 16.5$, $5.5 \times 4 = 22$; $6 \times 1 = 6$, $6 \times 2 = 12$, $6 \times 3 = 18$, $6 \times 4 = 24$. Now count the number of even answers; there are 11. That is the number of outcomes that fit the requirements, so the probability that mn is an even integer is $\dfrac{11}{16}$. The correct answer is (G).

45. **B** The question asks for the complete solution set for an inequality. There is an absolute value and an inequality, making this difficult to set up and solve. Instead, tackle this question by plugging in values from the ranges in the answer choices, eliminating those that contain numbers that make the inequality false. Choices (A) and (B) contain the inequality $z \geq 5$. Plug in $z = 6$ to test this. The inequality in the question becomes $|2(6) - 3| \geq 7$, which simplifies to $|12 - 3| \geq 7$ or $|9| \geq 7$. This is true, so eliminate answers that do not include 6 as a possible value of z. Eliminate (C). Compare the remaining answer choices to see that one difference is that (B) contains values of $z \leq -2$. Plug in $z = -3$ to see if it works. This becomes $|2(-3) - 3| \geq 7$, which simplifies to $|-6 - 3| \geq 7$, and then $|-9| \geq 7$. This becomes $9 \geq 7$, which is true, so -3 must also be included in the solution set. Eliminate (A), (D), and (E) which do not include -3. The correct answer is (B).

46. **H** The question asks for an equivalent to the given trigonometric expression. There is a variable in the answer choices, so plugging in is an option. Pick a value for x such as 30°; then use a calculator in degree mode to find the target value. This becomes $\dfrac{(\sin 30°)^2}{\cos 30° \tan 30°} = \dfrac{(0.5)^2}{(0.866)(0.577)} = \dfrac{0.25}{0.5} = 0.5$. Circle this target value; then plug $x = 30$ into the answer choices to see which one matches. Choice (F) becomes $\dfrac{\cos 30°}{(\sin 30°)^2} = \dfrac{0.866}{(0.5)^2} = \dfrac{0.866}{0.25} = 1.732$. This does not match the target, so eliminate (F). Choice (G) becomes $\dfrac{1}{\cos 30°} = \dfrac{1}{0.866} \approx 1.155$. Eliminate (G). Choice (H) becomes $\sin 30° = 0.5$. Keep (H) but check the remaining answers just in case. Choice (J) becomes $\dfrac{1}{\sin 30°} = \dfrac{1}{0.5} = 2$ and (K) becomes $\dfrac{1}{(\sin 30°)^2} = \dfrac{1}{(0.5)^2} = \dfrac{1}{0.25} = 4$. Eliminate (J) and (K). It is also possible to solve

this by using trigonometric identities. Start by rewriting $\tan x$ as $\dfrac{\sin x}{\cos x}$, so the expression becomes

$\dfrac{\sin^2 x}{\cos x \left(\dfrac{\sin x}{\cos x} \right)}$. Simplify the denominator to get $\dfrac{\sin^2 x}{\sin x}$. Then simplify the fraction to get $\sin x$.

Either way, the correct answer is (H).

47. **D** The question asks for all the x-values that make the given inequality true. There are several unde-fined variables in the inequality, so plugging in the answers will be tricky. Note that both the numerator and the denominator on the left side of the inequality can be simplified to have $(a - b)$ as a factor. Simplify to get $\dfrac{ax - bx}{4a - 4b} = \dfrac{x(a-b)}{4(a-b)} = \dfrac{x}{4}$ on the left side of the inequality. Multiply both sides of the new inequality, $\dfrac{x}{4} < 0$, by 4 to get $x < 0$. The correct answer is (D).

48. **J** The question asks about the change to the volume of a cone that will result from a change to the dimensions of the cone. The question involves a relationship between unknown numbers, so plug in. Working in bite-sized pieces, plug in values for the "old" cone first: $r_o = 4$ and $h_o = 3$. The volume of the "old" cone is $V_o = \dfrac{1}{3}\pi\left(4^2\right)(3) = 16\pi$. According to the question, the dimensions of the "new" cone halve the radius and double the height, so the new dimensions are $r_n = 2$ and $h_n = 6$. The vol-ume of the "new" cone is $V_n = \dfrac{1}{3}\pi\left(2^2\right)(6) = 8\pi$. The ratio of the new volume to the old volume is $8\pi : 16\pi$, which simplifies to 1:2. The correct answer is (J).

49. **B** The question asks for the time in hours that Al spends on his bike. Note that the question asks for the answer in hours but gives the time biked in minutes. There is a variable in the answer choices, so plug in. Let the time it took Al to bike up the hill be $m = 120$ minutes. The time it took Al to bike back down the hill is half that, or 60 minutes. The total time it took Al to bike up and down the hill is 120 minutes + 60 minutes = 180 minutes. Since the question asks for the time in hours, divide 180 minutes by 60 to find that it took Al 3 hours to bike up and down the hill. Circle 3 hours; that is the target value. Now plug $m = 120$ into the answer choices to see which one matches the target value. Choice (A) becomes $\dfrac{120}{60} = 2$. This does not match the target, so eliminate (A). Choice (B) becomes $\dfrac{120}{40} = 3$. This matches the target value, so keep (B) but check the remaining answers just in case. Choice (C) becomes $\dfrac{120}{30} = 4$. Eliminate (C). Choice (D) becomes $\dfrac{3(120)}{2} = 180$. Elimi-nate (D). Choice (E) becomes $2(120) = 240$. Eliminate (E). The correct answer is (B).

50. **G** The question asks for the volume of liquid poured into a cylinder. Use the Geometry Basic Approach and write down the formulas needed: the volume of a cylinder: is $V_{cylinder} = \pi r^2 h$, and the volume of a cube is $V_{cube} = s^3$. The question states that a cube with side length 3 cm is placed into a cylindri-cal cup and that cup is then filled with liquid. Therefore, the volume of the liquid would be the

volume of the cylindrical cup minus the volume of the ice cube, or $V_{cylinder} - V_{cube}$. Find the volume of the cylinder first. Plug in the radius of 5 cm and the height of 9 cm given in the question to get $V_{cylinder} = (9)(5^2)\pi$. Note that the answers do not simplify this, so don't spend extra time multiplying it out. Now find the volume of the cube by plugging in the side length of 3 cm to get $V_{cube} = 3^3$, and subtract the volume of the cube from the volume of the cylinder to get $(9)(5^2)\pi - 3^3$. The correct answer is (G).

51. **D** The question asks for the radius of the circle inscribed in the square. There is a variable in the answer choices, so plug in. The line labeled x is half the diagonal of the square. Extend x to get the entire diagonal of the square, which is also the hypotenuse of a 45-45-90 triangle with a length of $2x$. A 45-45-90 triangle has sides with lengths of s, s, and $s\sqrt{2}$, so the math will work out well if $x = \sqrt{2}$. Now the diagonal measures $2\sqrt{2}$, and the sides of the square are 2. The side of the square is equal to the diameter of the inscribed circle, so $d = 2$ and $r = 1$. Since the question asks for the radius, circle 1 as the target value. Eliminate (E) because a value has been determined from the information provided. Now plug $x = \sqrt{2}$ into the remaining answer choices to see which one matches the target value. Choice (A) becomes $2\sqrt{2}$. This does not match the target, so eliminate (A). Choice (B) becomes $(\sqrt{2})(\sqrt{2}) = 2$. Eliminate (B). Choice (C) becomes $\sqrt{2}$. Eliminate (C). Choice (D) becomes $\dfrac{(\sqrt{2})(\sqrt{2})}{2} = \dfrac{2}{2} = 1$. This matches the target value. The correct answer is (D).

52. **K** The question asks for the value of the variable that satisfies the matrix equation given. When multiplying matrices, the resulting matrix is determined as follows: $\begin{bmatrix} a & b & c \\ d & e & f \end{bmatrix} \begin{bmatrix} g & h \\ j & k \\ l & m \end{bmatrix} = \begin{bmatrix} ag + bj + cl & ah + bk + cm \\ dg + ej + fl & dh + ek + fm \end{bmatrix}$. Using that information, it can be determined that multiplying the values in the first row of the first matrix by the corresponding values in the first column of the second matrix and then adding the results will equal the value in the upper left of the resulting matrix. Doing so for the given matrices produces the equation $4a(2) + 3(4) + (-1)(1) = 35$. Simplify the equation to get $8a + 12 - 1 = 35$. Combine like terms to get $8a + 11 = 35$; then subtract 11 from both sides to get $8a = 24$. Divide both sides by 8 to get $a = 3$. The correct answer is (K).

53.   **C**   The question asks for the radius of one of the smaller pipes. Use the Word Problem Basic Approach and break the question into bite-sized pieces. Start by noting that the cross-sectional area of each pipe is the area of the circle formed when the pipe is cut. Use the geometry basic approach and write the formula for the area of a circle, $A = \pi r^2$. The question gives the radius of the large pipe as $4\sqrt{2}$ feet, so the area of the large pipe is $\pi\left(4\sqrt{2}\right)^2 = \pi(16)(2) = 32\pi$ ft^2. The area of each of the smaller cross-sections is one-fourth that, so the cross-sectional area of each smaller pipe is $\frac{32\pi}{4} = 8\pi$ ft^2. To find the radius of the smaller pipe, use the formula for the area of a circle again: $A = 8\pi = \pi r^2$. Divide both sides by π to get $8 = r^2$. Finally, take the square root of each side to get $\sqrt{8} = r$, then simplify to get $\sqrt{(4)(2)} = 2\sqrt{2} = r$. The correct answer is (C).

54.   **H**   The question asks for the height of the tent as a trigonometric function. Letting the answers help shows that tangent will be used to answer this question. Write out SOHCAHTOA to remember the trig functions. The TOA part defines the tangent as $\frac{opposite}{adjacent}$. In relation to the 40° angle, the height labeled with a question mark is the adjacent side. Now find the side opposite the 40° angle, which is part of the side labeled as the 6 ft base. Because the line representing the height bisects the base, the portion of the base of the large triangle from the height to one of the bottom vertices has a length of $\frac{6}{2} = 3$ feet. Now set up the tangent equation as $\tan 40° = \frac{3}{h}$, where h is the height. Solve for h by first multiplying each side by h to get $h(\tan 40°) = 3$, then divide both sides by $\tan 40°$ to get $h = \frac{3}{\tan 40°}$. The correct answer is (H).

55.   **D**   The question asks for the set with the lowest standard deviation. Standard deviation is a measure of the spread of the data from the average, so look for the set of data most closely grouped around the average value. Choice (A) has a list of numbers that are evenly spread apart by 5, so the middle number 0 is the average. The extremes are each 10 away from 0. Choice (B) has an average of 300 with extremes that are 200 away from that. Eliminate (B) since its extremes are further spread apart from the average than are those in (A). Choice (C) has an average of 6 with extremes that are 4 away from that. Eliminate (A) since its extremes are further spread apart from the average than are those in (C). Choice (D) has two values equally spaced on either side of the middle value, so the middle number 101 is the average. The extremes are only 1 away from this average. Eliminate (C). Finally, (E) has an average of 3 with extremes 2 away from that average. Eliminate (E). The correct answer is (D).

56.   **G**   The question asks which answer choice must be an integer. Since there are variables in the answer choices, plug in for a and b. The question notes that $a > 0$, or positive, and $b < 0$, or negative. Let

$a = 2$ and $b = -3$. Choice (F) becomes $3^{2+(-3)} = 3^{-1} = \frac{1}{3}$. Eliminate (F) because it is not an integer. Choice (G) becomes $3^{2-(-3)} = 3^5 = 243$. Keep (G) but check the remaining answers just in case. Choice (H) becomes $3^{2(-3)} = 3^{-6} = \frac{1}{3^6} = \frac{1}{729}$. Eliminate (H). Choice (J) becomes $3^{-2} = \frac{1}{3^2} = \frac{1}{9}$. Eliminate (J). Choice (K) becomes $3^{-\frac{2}{3}} = \frac{1}{3^{\frac{2}{3}}} = \frac{1}{\sqrt[3]{3^2}} = \frac{1}{\sqrt[3]{9}}$. Eliminate (K). The correct answer is (G).

57.   **A**   The question asks for a set of numbers given variables in relationship to one another. Plug in values for x and y that fit the rules given in the question: $0 < x < y < \frac{y}{x}$. Let $x = 0.1$ and $y = 0.2$, so $\frac{y}{x} = \frac{0.2}{0.1} = 2$. Therefore, 2 must be part of the solution. Eliminate (C), (D), and (E) because they do not contain 2 in the sets. Plug in another set of numbers, or compare the remaining answers to see that the range $0 < \frac{y}{x} \le 1$ is included in (B) but not in (A). In order for a fraction to be between 0 and 1, the numerator of the fraction must be smaller than the denominator of the fraction. Since the question states that $x < y$, that will never be the case for this set of rules. Eliminate (B). The correct answer is (A).

58.   **F**   The question asks for the radius of the largest circle that can be contained within a rectangle. Use the Geometry Basic Approach and draw a picture of the proposed track. Draw a rectangle with sides labeled 100 feet and 150 feet to represent the fence. Draw a second rectangle inside that one that is 10 feet from each side of the rectangle to represent the maximum area that the circular track can use. Label the sides of the new rectangle 80 feet and 130 feet since it will be 10 feet away from the fence on all 4 sides. Now draw a circle that touches the sides of the interior rectangle. The diameter of that circle will be the smaller of the two sides of the rectangle in which it is contained, which is 80 feet. The radius of the circle will be half that measurement, or 40 feet. The correct answer is (F).

59.   **D**   The question asks for the possible number of sections created when a sphere is cut by 2 different planes. Use the Geometry Basic Approach and draw a sphere. Let the answers help by noting that the planes can cut the sphere into only 2, 3, or 4 sections. First draw a horizontal plane and a vertical plane intersecting the sphere to see that it is possible to split the sphere into 4 sections with 2 planes. Eliminate (A) and (C) since they do not contain that possibility. Now draw 2 different vertical planes to see that the sphere can also be split into 3 sections. Eliminate (B). Attempt additional configurations of planes intersecting the sphere to determine if there is a way for 2 *different* planes to intersect the sphere and cut it into only 2 sections. There is not, so eliminate (E). The correct answer is (D).

60.   **K**   The question asks for the positive difference between the two values of a variable, or the absolute value of the difference of those two values. There are variables in the answer choices, so start by plugging in values of a and b. Let $a = 6$ and $b = 1$, to make 5 the positive difference of those

numbers as given in the question. Since the question asks for the different values of *a*, keep *b* = 1 and solve for the second value of *a* by solving $|a-1| = 5$ for the negative value inside the absolute value sign: $a - 1 = -5$. Add 1 to both sides of the equation to find the other value of $a = -4$. The positive difference between 6 and −4 is 6 − (−4) = 10. Circle that because it is the target value. Now plug *b* = 1 into the answers. Choice (F) is 1. That does not match the target value, so eliminate (F). Choice (G) is 1 + 5 = 6. Eliminate (G). Choice (H) is 2(1) = 2. Eliminate (H). Choice (J) is $\sqrt{1^2 - 25} = \sqrt{1 - 25} = \sqrt{-24}$, which is an imaginary number, so eliminate (J). Choice (K) is 10 and matches the target. The correct answer is (K).

READING TEST

1. **C** This reasoning question asks about the *shift in the passage* found in the last paragraph of Passage A. Because this is a general question, it should be done after all the specific questions. Look for the Golden Thread. Once you identify the Golden Thread, read the last paragraph. While the majority of the passage describes watching Jackie Robinson *making his major league debut* as the first African-American to play in Major League Baseball, the last paragraph finds the narrator apologizing for his actions and starting to understand that his expectations had been unrealistic. Eliminate answers that don't match this prediction. Eliminate (A), as the passage begins with the end of segregation in baseball. Eliminate (B), as while the narrator does blame his outburst on his fever, he admits it's only *partly true*. Choice (C) matches the prediction, so keep it. While the narrator's grandfather's *anticipation* is mentioned early in the passage, *anger* doesn't fit the grandfather's tone in the last paragraph, so eliminate (D). The correct answer is (C).

2. **F** This reasoning question asks what the narrator's ultimate opinion was of *Jackie Robinson*. Look for the lead words *Jackie Robinson* to find the window for the question in Passage A. In the second paragraph, the narrator describes Robinson as a *gentleman, never losing his cool*. Additionally, he mentions that he is *proud that Robinson is playing*. Eliminate answers that don't match this prediction. Choice (F) matches the prediction, so keep it. Choice (G) is mentioned in the passage, but it answers the wrong question: while the narrator initially thinks Robinson is *capable of doing the impossible*, the question asks how he *ultimately* sees Robinson; eliminate (G). While the narrator is at one point disappointed in a play by Robinson, he learns that *what matters is how he plays the whole game*, so eliminate (H). Eliminate (J) because the passage describes the narrator and his grandfather as *excited and tense*, but the question asks about *Robinson*. The correct answer is (F).

3. **A** This reasoning question asks what the passage suggests about why the narrator's grandfather is *annoyed* when the narrator groans. Look for the lead word *groan* to find the window for the question in Passage A. In lines 27–28, the narrator lets out a *loud groan* when another player gets Robinson out. In lines 31–36, the narrator apologizes to his grandfather, who tells him that Robinson *needs our support*. Eliminate answers that don't match this prediction. Choice (A) states that the narrator's grandfather believes the narrator *shouldn't have criticized Robinson*, which is consistent with the text. The text contradicts (B), so eliminate it. There is no indication that the grandfather is concerned with his ability to concentrate on the game, so eliminate (C). Choice (D) doesn't reflect the grandfather's response to the narrator's apology, so eliminate it. The correct answer is (A)

4. **G** This reasoning question asks for the purpose of the *narrator's statement* in lines 46-48. Although this question includes a line reference, it asks about the purpose of the statement in relationship to the passage as a whole; it is a general question and should be done after all of the specific questions about Passage B. Look for the Golden Thread. In Passage B, the narrator notes a change in how he felt about progress toward racial equality: he felt excited and hopeful at the game, but disappointed by the slow pace of change outside the stadium. This question asks about the narrator's description of how he felt *inside the stadium*. He says, *I felt I was in some utopian society that existed without segregation and racism.* Eliminate answers that don't match this prediction. Eliminate (F) because the narrator is describing the feelings he has about the significance of the event; it is not a literal description of how people were interacting in the stadium. Choice (G) matches the prediction, so keep it. Choice (H) uses words from the passage but doesn't match what the passage says; while the narrator believed that Jackie Robinson playing in the major leagues would change the world, the rest of the passage shows that society was not free from *segregation and racism.* Eliminate (H). Eliminate (J) as the statement in the window is largely positive and does not reflect the negative feelings of the narrator 21 years later. The correct answer is (G).

5. **B** This referral question asks how the *narrator's expectations about how Jackie Robinson's appearance in Major League Baseball would affect segregation* compared to its *actual effect*, based on Passage B. Because this is a general question, it should be done after all the specific questions. Look for the Golden Thread. In lines 52–58, the narrator recounts, *My friends and I were flying high as we left the stadium. If a black man was now playing for the Brooklyn Dodgers, we felt there was nothing we couldn't do…Change, we thought, was rapidly coming. To some extent that was true, but racism and injustice also persisted.* In lines 67–70, as he recounts the death of Martin Luther King, Jr., the narrator describes his earlier sentiments as *hopelessly naïve.* This indicates that the effect of Robinson's playing in the Major Leagues was different than anticipated, so eliminate (C) and (D). Eliminate (A) as the size of the *crowd* is not related to the effect on segregation. Choice (B) aligns closely with the narrator's statement: *Change, we thought, was rapidly coming.* The correct answer is (B).

6. **H** This reasoning question asks why *the information about Dr. Martin Luther King, Jr. in lines 67–69* was included. Read a window around the given line reference. As the narrator contrasts the death of Martin Luther King, Jr. with Jackie Robinson's first major league game, he says *at times it felt like nothing had been accomplished* regarding the struggle for racial equality in the 21 years since the baseball game. Eliminate answers that don't match this prediction. Nothing is said about *role models*, so eliminate (F). Eliminate (G) as the mention of King does not point to Robinson's importance *in baseball.* Choice (H) matches the prediction about the narrator's feeling that *nothing had been accomplished* with regard to racial equality; keep (H). Eliminate (J) because the lines referenced in the question do not touch on *Robinson's influence.* Eliminate (J). The correct answer is (H).

7. **A** This reasoning question asks what the *narrator of Passage B makes a comparison between.* There is not a good lead word in this question, so work the question later. Choice (A) mentions comparing *the struggle for racial equality* and *the baseball season.* In the final paragraph, the narrator states that *the season is 162 games long, and we are only part of the way through it,* and compares that to the slow pace of change in equality issues. Keep (A). Choice (B) uses words from the passage but does not match what the passage says: the passage brings up both *baseball* and *golf,* but there is no direct

comparison between the two. Eliminate (B). The references to *tense excitement* and *bed covers* are made only in Passage A, so eliminate (C). Eliminate (D) as Passage B never mentions *striking out*. The correct answer is (A).

8. **J**   This reasoning question asks for a *comparison of the tone of each passage*. Because this question asks about both passages, it should be done after the questions that ask about each passage individually. Consider the Golden Thread of both passages. Passage A starts with a tone of excitement but finishes with a more somber tone, which is similar to the positivity in the first half of Passage B followed by disappointment in the latter half. Eliminate answers that don't match this prediction. Eliminate (F), as *hopeful and cheery* doesn't describe the full progression of Passage A; nor does *dreary and pessimistic* reflect the tone of Passage B. Eliminate (G) because Passage A is not objectively factual; it is a story which includes subjective descriptions such as, *I realize then that I had been nervous, too. I had expected the impossible—I had wanted him to bat a thousand*. Eliminate (H) as it disregards the positive aspects of both passages. Choice (J) matches the prediction, so keep (J). The correct answer is (J).

9. **B**   This referral question asks what *the narrator of Passage B provides more information about* than *the narrator of Passage A* does. Because this question asks about both passages, it should be done after the questions that ask about each passage individually. Eliminate any answer choices that misrepresent either passage. While Passage A describes the events of only one day, Passage B relays the events of that day along with future events. Eliminate (A), as a *play-by-play* is not included in either passage. Keep (B) as the narrator of Passage B relates Jackie Robinson's actions to the long-term *struggle for racial equality*. Eliminate (C) since Passage B does not discuss Robinson's career prior to that day's events. Eliminate (D) as only Passage A mentions the *Negro League*. The correct answer is (B).

10. **H**   This reasoning question asks how the narrator of Passage A felt *after seeing Jackie Robinson play*, compared to the way the narrator of Passage B felt. Because this question asks about both passages, it should be done after the questions that ask about each passage individually. The narrator of Passage A says that he *let out a loud groan* when another player got Robinson out, and realizes that he had wanted Robinson *to bat a thousand*. The narrator of Passage B describes himself as *flying high* after seeing Robinson play. In other words, the narrator of Passage B was excited, and the narrator of Passage A was disappointed. Eliminate any answer choices that misrepresent either passage. Eliminate (F), as the narrator for Passage B focuses more on race relations than the narrator for passage A does. Eliminate (G) as there is no indication that the narrator of Passage A is likely to stop following the Dodgers. Keep (H) because it matches the prediction. Eliminate (J) as the narrator of Passage A does not mention excitement about *the future for African American baseball players*. The correct answer is (H).

11. **D**   This reasoning question asks about the *main idea of the passage*. Because this is a general question, it should be done after all the specific questions. Look for the Golden Thread. The passage focuses on the CCC, a program that arose from the New Deal that put many young men to work in forests, parks, and other public lands in return for pay, housing, education, food, and clothing. Eliminate answers that don't match this prediction. Eliminate (A) because the CCC never *forced unemployed young men to work*. Eliminate (B) because the passage does not suggest that there was no *suitable employment* for *veterans* before the CCC. Eliminate (C) because the passage states that the *idea for*

the CCC came from *President Roosevelt*, not from *Congress*. Keep (D) because it is consistent with the main idea of the text. The correct answer is (D)

12. **G**   This reasoning question asks about the main idea of the third paragraph. Read the third paragraph. The paragraph states that the *earliest enrollees were some veterans who returned to Washington…demanding pay…When it became clear that no bonus would be forthcoming, about twenty-five hundred of the men took Roosevelt up on his offer and joined the CCC*. Eliminate answers that don't match this prediction. Choice (F) includes a statement that is mentioned in the passage, but it answers the wrong question: while the paragraph mentions that *Eleanor Roosevelt* met with the Bonus Army, this is not the main idea of the paragraph. (Also, *Hoover* was not President, but ACT doesn't expect you to know information that is not included in the passage.) Keep (G) because it matches the prediction. Eliminate (H) because the fact that *Roosevelt* provided *food* and *shelter* is not the main idea of the paragraph. Additionally, the passage doesn't indicate that Roosevelt paid the veterans a *bonus*. Eliminate (J) because the paragraph does not mention the *age requirement*. The correct answer is (G).

13. **D**   This reasoning question asks why President Roosevelt described himself as a *tree farmer* in line 7. Read a window around the line reference. The passage states that the president *cared about the fate of the trees* and *was fond of listing his occupation as "tree farmer."* The phrase *"tree farmer"* means he enjoyed caring for the trees on his estate. Eliminate answers that don't match this prediction. Eliminate (A) because the passage never mentions Roosevelt growing trees to support his *family*. Eliminate (B) because the passage never states that he *believed in agrarian economy over urban industrialization*. Eliminate (C) because the passage does not mention a *successful business selling trees*. Note that (A) and (C) take the description *tree farmer* literally, which is not supported by the text. Keep (D), which is consistent with the passage. The correct answer is (D).

14. **G**   This referral question asks for a project *the CCC performed for the National Park Service*. Look for the lead words *National Park Service* to find the window for the question. In lines 61–63 the passage states, *For the National Park Service, they built roads, campgrounds, bridges, and recreation and administration facilities*. Choices (F), (H), and (J) all include details that are mentioned in the passage but that answer the wrong question: they describe projects that were done in the *national forests* or for the *Biological Survey*, instead of for the *National Park Service*. Keep (G), which is consistent with the passage. The correct answer is (G).

15. **A**   This referral question asks for a true statement *about the CCC*. There is not a good lead word in this question, so work the question later. Eliminate answers that are not consistent with the passage. Keep (A) since lines 72–74 state that the program *taught more than a hundred thousand to read and write* and passed out eighth grade and high school diplomas. Eliminate (B) because the CCC did not focus on *urban job training*. Eliminate (C), which uses words from the passage but doesn't match what the passage says: lines 32–34 indicate that the CCC required enrollees to have at least six teeth; it does not say that the CCC accepted *only men with six teeth*. Eliminate (D) because the passage never mentions *courses in nutrition and self-esteem*. The correct answer is (A).

16. **G**   This referral question asks what the fourth paragraph *makes clear* about the CCC. Read the fourth paragraph. Lines 51–54 state that *Congress continued to reauthorize [the CCC program] faithfully over the next seven years* and that *the CCC had put more than three million young "soil soldiers" to*

work. Eliminate answers that don't match this prediction. Eliminate (F), which is only partially true; the organization was *voluntary*, but workers were compensated. Keep (G) because Congress kept reinstating the program year after year, and line 18 states that the CCC was originally *to last two years*. Eliminate (H) because the number *4.1 million* refers to the *man-hours fighting fires*, not the number of men *employed*; this answer uses words from the passage but doesn't match what the passage says. Eliminate (J), which also uses words from the passage but doesn't match what the passage says: the passage mentions *flood controls* in West Virginia, Vermont, and New York, rather than fighting *fires* in these states. The correct answer is (G).

17. **C** This reasoning question asks what the passage suggests about *national forests before the 1930s*. Look for the lead words *national forests* to find the window for the question. Lines 54-61 describe the work the CCC did in the *national forests*. According to the passage, the CCC existed from *1933 to 1942*, but this question asks about the period *before the 1930s*. Lines 59-61 say that the CCC *planted more than 1.3 billion young trees in the first major reforestation campaign in the country's history*. This implies that before the 1930s, there had not been a major reforestation campaign. Eliminate answers that don't match this prediction. Choices (A) and (B) use words from the passage, but neither matches what the passage says: the passage doesn't give any information about *diseased trees* or *wildlife refuges* in the national parks before the 1930s. Eliminate (A) and (B). Keep (C) because it matches the prediction. Eliminate (D), which uses words from the passage but doesn't match what the passage says: the passage does not indicate that there were *floods* in the national forests before the 1930s. The correct answer is (C).

18. **F** This referral question asks *when the CCC changed its name*. Work backwards and use lead words from the answers to find the window for this question. The lead words *CCRYRM* and *Congress* appear in the first paragraph. Lines 11–15 state that when President Roosevelt *went to Congress for authorization of the program, he called the new agency the Civilian Corps Reforestation Youth Rehabilitation Movement, but before sinking under the weight of an acronym like CCRYRM, it was soon changed to the Civilian Conservation Corps*. Eliminate any answers that do not match this prediction. Keep (F), as the name was *soon changed* after the program was approved by Congress. Eliminate (G) because Congress never *protested that CCRYRM was too difficult to say*. This answer uses words from the passage but doesn't match what the passage says. Eliminate (H) because lines 7–16 imply that *the CCC changed its name* in 1933, soon after Roosevelt *went to Congress for authorization of the program*, and lines 50–51 state that Roosevelt *expanded the size of the CCC...to 500,000 in 1935*. Eliminate (J), which uses words from the passage but doesn't match what the passage says: the passage never states that the *Bonus Army disbanded*, and lines 47–49 state that men from the Bonus Army *joined the CCC*, suggesting that the name had already been changed when they joined. The correct answer is (F).

19. **C** This referral question asks what requirements enrollees had to meet *the same year the CCC was authorized*. Work backwards and use lead words from the answers to find the window for the question. Lines 29–34 state, *The men had to be US citizens between the ages of seventeen and twenty-seven...out of school, out of work, capable of physical labor, over 60 inches but under 78 inches in height, more than 107 pounds in weight, and had to possess no fewer than "three serviceable natural masticating teeth above and below."* Eliminate answers that don't match this prediction. Eliminate

(A) because the passage states that the men should be *over 60 inches but under 78 inches*, not *over 78 inches*. Eliminate (B) because the passage states that the men needed to be *out of school*, not *in school*. Keep (C) because it matches the prediction. Eliminate (D) because, according to line 30, the age limit changed *later*, not in *the same year the CCC was authorized*. Choices (A), (B), and (D) each use words from the passage but don't match what the passage says. The correct answer is (C).

20. **G** This referral question asks about *CCC programs in national parks and forests*. Look for the lead words *national parks and forests*. Lines 21–24 state that the *Departments of Agriculture and Interior… would design and supervise projects in regional and national forests, national parks, and other public lands*. Eliminate answers that don't match this prediction. Eliminate (F) because the passage does not indicate that the CCC programs were *conducted far from where the members were fed and housed*. Keep (G), which matches the prediction. Eliminate (H), since it contradicts lines 21–24. Eliminate (J), as the passage does not indicate that these were *minimum-wage jobs*. The correct answer is (G).

21. **C** This reasoning question asks for the *main idea of the passage*. Because this is a general question, it should be done after all the specific questions. Look for the Golden Thread. This passage deals with the importance of the totem pole and the role the totem pole plays in Native American culture. Eliminate answers that don't match this prediction. Choice (A) stresses the importance of *canoes* over *totem poles*. Eliminate (A). Choice (B) focuses too narrowly on the history of a single totem pole, so eliminate (B). Choice (C) matches the prediction, so keep it. Like (B), (D) focuses too narrowly on one detail (specifically on the potlatch ban) and can be eliminated. The correct answer is (C).

22. **G** This referral question asks for a question that is *NOT answered in the passage*. When a question asks what is **not** mentioned in the text, eliminate answers that are mentioned. Work backwards and use lead words from the answers to find the window for this question. Lines 1–3 state that it was the *natives of the far north, in what is now British Columbia and Alaska, who first carved totem poles*, so eliminate (F). Lines 64–66 state, *Today, Haida, Tlingit, Tsimshian, Kwakiutl and other native craftsmen carve, predominantly for the tourist trade, small "souvenir" totem poles*, so eliminate (H). Lines 3–9 indicate that totem poles were not carved before *the mid-18th century* because the Native Americans *lacked the iron tools necessary to fell a massive tree in one piece and carve its entire length*. Eliminate (J). Only the question posed in (G) goes unanswered in the passage. The correct answer is (G).

23. **C** This referral question asks for *one of the main purposes of totem poles*. Look for the lead words *poles* and *purpose* to find the window for this question. Lines 39–40 state that *poles serve the important purpose of recording the lore of a clan, much as a book would*. Eliminate answers that don't match this prediction. Choice (A) is stated in the passage but answers the wrong question; the idea that the totem poles display the carvers' *artistic skill* is stated in the passage, but the passage doesn't indicate that this is a main purpose of totem poles. Eliminate (A). While (B) is mentioned in the passage, it similarly answers the wrong question: the passage does not state that serving as a landmark is a main purpose of totem poles. Eliminate (B). Choice (C) matches the prediction, so keep it. Choice (D) is stated in the passage but answers the wrong question: totem poles are associated with potlatches, but only lines 39–40 identify an *important purpose* of totem poles. Eliminate (D). The correct answer is (C).

24. **G** This reasoning question asks how the sixth paragraph functions in the context of the passage. Read the sixth paragraph. Lines 49–59 describe the meanings of some of the symbols used on totem poles. Eliminate answers that don't match this prediction. Choice (F) uses words from the passage but doesn't match what the passage says: the passage indicates that there is a story behind *almost every*, not *every*, image. Eliminate (F). Choice (G) matches the prediction, so keep it. There are no comparisons of regional totem poles in the paragraph, so eliminate (H). Eliminate (J), as the paragraph describes how Raven is depicted, but not Raven's *role* in *mythology*; this answer comes from the wrong window, since Raven's role in mythology is mentioned in the fifth paragraph. The correct answer is (G).

25. **D** This referral question asks which example of *the role totem poles play in Native American culture* is NOT used in the passage. When a question asks what is **not** mentioned in the text, eliminate answers that are mentioned. Work backwards and use lead words from the answers to find the window for this question. Choice (A) is addressed in lines 40–41, which *state that the top figure on the pole identifies the owner's clan*. Eliminate (A). Choice (B) is addressed in lines 42–44, which state that *Raven, the trickster, might tell [a] story…while Frog might tell how he wooed a human woman*. Eliminate (B). Choice (C) is addressed in lines 64–66, which state that *native craftsmen carve, predominantly for the tourist trade, small "souvenir" totem poles*. Eliminate (C). Choice (D) is mentioned in the passage, but it answers the wrong question. According to line 33, the pole was placed by *Seattle businessmen*, not the *Tlingit*. The correct answer is (D).

26. **J** This referral question asks which fact about the *totem poles carved by coastal tribes of the far north* is NOT included in the second paragraph. Read the second paragraph. When a question asks what is **not** mentioned in the text, eliminate answers that are mentioned. Choice (F) is addressed in lines 13–15, which state that *initially, the poles were made to stand against the front of a house…so all would enter the house through the pole*. Eliminate (F). Choice (G) is addressed in lines 11–12, which state that the coastal tribes of the far north *used trees that grew so tall and straight in their wet climate*. Eliminate (G). Choice (H) is addressed in lines 15–17, which state that the totem poles in *some way identified the owner*. Eliminate (H). Choice (J) uses words from the passage but doesn't match what the passage says; the *family crest* is mentioned in line 16, but there is no evidence in the passage that the poles were constructed *only* by clans who had family crests. The correct answer is (J).

27. **B** This referral question asks what *the various characters on a totem pole* represent according to the fifth paragraph. Read the fifth paragraph. Lines 40–42 indicate that the *top figure on the pole identifies the owner's clan, and succeeding characters…tell their stories*. Eliminate answers that don't match this prediction. Choice (A) uses words from the passage but doesn't match what the passage says, as the *owner's clan* is identified only by the top figure on the totem pole, not by the *various characters* underneath it. Eliminate (A). Choice (B) matches the prediction, so keep it. Eliminate (C) and (D), which are stated in the passage but answer the wrong question. *Raven* and *Frog* are specific examples (lines 42–44) of the *various characters*; neither answers the question about what the *various characters* represent. The correct answer is (B).

28. **J** This referral question asks for the *home* of the *Tlingit*. Look for the lead word *Tlingit* to find the window for the question. Line 31 indicates that the Tlingit are from *the southeastern coast of Alaska*. Eliminate (F), (G), and (H) because they do not match the prediction. The correct answer is (J).

29. **A** This reasoning question asks why the author includes the information in lines 60–63. Read a window around the given line reference. This paragraph suggests that the broad importance of totem poles is related to the poles' *history, mythology, social structure, and spirituality*. Eliminate answers that don't match this prediction. Choice (A) matches the prediction, so keep it. Choice (B) uses words from the passage but doesn't match what the passage says: while totem poles can function *as* books do, there is no evidence in the passage that the poles have *replaced* books. Eliminate (B). Like (B), (C) and (D) use words from the passage but don't match what the passage says. Lines 60–61 say, *Learning to read totem poles is like learning to read a language.* The passage does not say that *Native American tribes have no spoken or written language.* Eliminate (C). Lines 62–63 state that *totem poles continue to be carved by the descendants of the original carvers*, but there is no indication in the passage that these *descendants* carve *copies*. Eliminate (D). The correct answer is (A).

30. **H** This reasoning question asks for a word to describe the employers' attitude toward *potlatches* in the third paragraph. Read the third paragraph. Lines 26–28 state, *Employers, too, complained that their Indian workers were unreliable when a pole was being carved or a potlatch planned.* Eliminate answers that don't match this prediction. Eliminate (F) and (G), as there is no evidence that the employers were *patient* or *accepting* regarding the potlatches. Choice (H) matches the prediction, so keep it. Eliminate (J) because the mention of the employers' complaints offers no evidence of civility. The correct answer is (H).

31. **C** This reasoning question asks for the authors' attitude about the *possibility of returning to the planet Venus*. There is not a good lead word in this question (the word *Venus* appears throughout the passage), so work the question later. Lines 14–16 say, *in the present climate of fiscal austerity, there is no telling when humans will next get a good look at Earth's nearest planetary neighbor.* Based on those lines, the authors are unsure about the possibility of returning to Venus for financial reasons. Eliminate answers that don't match this prediction. Eliminate (A) because there is no indication that the authors are *cheerful and optimistic* about the possibility of returning to Venus. Eliminate (B) because *sarcastic and contentious* are not supported by the passage. Choice (C) matches the prediction; *doubtful* is supported by the phrase *there is no telling when* and *pragmatic* (which means "practical") is supported by the mention of *fiscal austerity*. Although *uncertain* matches the prediction, *withdrawn* is not supported, so eliminate (D). The correct answer is (C).

32. **H** This reasoning question asks how the passage describes the *state of scientific knowledge about Venus before the Pioneer mission*. Look for the lead words before the Pioneer mission to find the window for the question. Lines 28–30 say, *Well before the arrival of Pioneer Venus, astronomers had learned that Venus does not live up to its image as Earth's near-twin.* Eliminate answers that don't match this prediction. Eliminate (F) because it doesn't mention any *scientific knowledge*. Additionally, the passage does not mention an *earlier mission* that *ended in disaster*, nor does it support the idea that the scientific community was *hesitant to return to Venus* before the Pioneer mission. Eliminate (G) because it goes beyond what is stated in the passage: although the prediction does support the idea that Earth and Venus are not twins, it doesn't indicate that the planets are *polar opposites in atmospheric conditions*. Keep (H) because it matches the prediction; in addition, lines 30–34 give *scientific evidence* of how Earth and Venus are different. Eliminate (J) because there is no mention of scientists' interest in *other planets* in the window for the question. The correct answer is (H).

33.   **D**   This referral question asks why *Earth may have retained less of its early atmosphere than Venus did*. Look for the lead words *early atmosphere* to find the window for this question. Lines 67–70 state that *Venus has held on to a far greater fraction of its earliest atmosphere. Much of Earth's primitive atmosphere may have been stripped away and lost into space when our world was struck by a Mars-size body*. Eliminate answers that do not match this prediction. Eliminate (A), which uses words from the passage but doesn't match what the passage says: the passage states that Earth was *struck by a Mars-size body*, not by Mars itself. Eliminate (B), which also uses words from the passage but doesn't match what the passage says: the passage mentions a *cloud of debris* that resulted from the impact but does not say that the cloud of debris stripped the atmosphere away. Eliminate (C) because *rain* that removes *sulfur gases* is not mentioned in the window for the question, nor does the passage indicate that rain removed Earth's early atmosphere. Keep (D), which matches the prediction. The correct answer is (D).

34.   **G**   This reasoning question asks about the *main point* of the second paragraph. Read the second paragraph. The paragraph discusses what *Magellan* and *Pioneer Venus* studied on Venus. Lines 22–25 state, *These findings illustrate how seemingly small differences in physical conditions have sent Venus and the Earth hurtling down very different evolutionary paths*. Eliminate answers that don't match this prediction. Choice (F) uses words from the passage but doesn't match what the passage says; although the paragraph discusses both *Magellan* and *Pioneer Venus*, there is no indication that one mission was better than the other. Eliminate (F). Keep (G) because it matches the prediction; it says that information from both *Magellan* and *Pioneer Venus* contributed to a *deeper understanding of Venus*. Eliminate (H) because both missions, not just the *Magellan*, studied *physical characteristics*. Choice (J) uses words from the passage but doesn't match what the passage says; the paragraph says that the *knowledge will help scientists intelligently evaluate how human activity may be changing the environment on the Earth*; it does not say that the knowledge will help them *approach problems*, in general, more intelligently. Additionally, this sentence is a detail, rather than the main point of the paragraph. Eliminate (J). The correct answer is (G).

35.   **C**   This referral question asks what makes it impossible for *humans to live on the planet Venus*. Work backwards and use lead words from the answers to find the window for this question. For (A), look for the lead words *"twin" planets* in the passage. Lines 1–2 say, *Venus is sometimes referred to as the Earth's "twin" because it resembles the Earth in size and in distance from the sun*, and lines 28–30 say, *astronomers had learned that Venus does not live up to its image as Earth's near-twin*. Although these lines support (A), (A) answers the wrong question; the fact that Venus and Earth are not twin planets does not answer the question about why humans cannot live on Venus. Eliminate (A). For (B), look for the lead words *carbon dioxide* and *bicarbonate rocks*. Lines 43–45 say, *On Earth, however, the carbon dioxide is locked away in carbonate rocks, not in gaseous form in the air*. Choice (B) uses words from the passage but doesn't match what the passage says; the lines are about Earth, but the question is about Venus. The passage also says *carbonate rocks*, rather than *bicarbonate rocks*. Eliminate (B). For (C), look for the lead words *heat, temperature*, and *atmosphere*. Lines 34–35 say, *Even aside from the heat and the pressure, the air on Venus would be utterly unbreathable to humans*. These lines support (C) and answer the question, so keep (C). For (D), look for the lead words *water* and *condensed*. Lines 53–55 say, *If all of Venus's water could somehow be condensed onto the surface, it would make a global puddle only a couple of centimeters deep*. Choice (D) uses words from the passage but doesn't match what the passage says; the passage discusses the water on Venus being

condensed on the surface as a hypothetical situation, not the actual condition on Venus. Eliminate (D). The correct answer is (C).

36. **J** This referral question asks for evidence gathered before *Pioneer Venus* that supports the idea that *Earth* and *Venus* are *not near-twins*. Look for the lead words *near-twins* to find the window for the question. Lines 28–30 say, *Well before the arrival of Pioneer Venus, astronomers had learned that Venus does not live up to its image as Earth's near-twin*. Lines 30–33 contrast conditions on Earth, which *maintains conditions ideal for liquid water and life*, with the high *surface temperature* and *atmospheric pressure* of Venus. Eliminate answers that don't match this prediction. Choice (F) uses words from the passage but doesn't match what the passage says; although the paragraph mentions *lead*, it says that Venus's surface temperature is *hotter than the melting point of lead*, not that Venus does not produce *lead*. Eliminate (F). Eliminate (G) because it doesn't mention evidence gathered about Venus and Earth that shows they are different. Furthermore, the passage never mentions a new discovery about Earth's distance from the *sun*. Choice (H) uses words from the passage but doesn't match what the passage says; *78 percent nitrogen and 21 percent oxygen* describe Earth's atmosphere, not Venus's. Eliminate (H). Keep (J) because it matches the prediction; the paragraph says, *Venus's surface temperature is 450 degrees Celsius*. The correct answer is (J).

37. **C** This vocabulary-in-context question asks what the word *harbors* most nearly means as it is used in line 56. Go back to the text, find the word *harbors*, and cross it out. Carefully read the surrounding text to determine another word that would fit in the blank based on the context. Lines 56–57 say, *Unlike Earth, Venus harbors little if any molecular oxygen in its lower atmosphere*. In the context of the sentence, *harbors* means something like "contains." *Shelters* does not match "contains," so eliminate (A). *Hides* does not match "contains," so eliminate (B). *Holds* matches "contains," so keep (C). *Cherishes* does not match "contains," so eliminate (D). Note that (A), (B), and (D) are other meanings of *harbors*, but they answer the wrong question because they do not match the way the word *is used in line 56*. The correct answer is (C).

38. **H** This referral question asks what kinds of planets the word *primordial refers to*. Look for the lead word *primordial* to find the window for the question. Lines 63–64 state, *Pioneer Venus revealed other ways in which Venus is more primordial than Earth*. The paragraph goes on to say that *Venus's atmosphere* contains gases *that have been present since the time the planets were born* and that this *difference suggests that Venus has held on to a far greater fraction of its earliest atmosphere*. Therefore, *primordial* describes a planet where current conditions are similar to conditions that existed near the time the planet was formed. Eliminate answers that don't match this prediction. Choices (F) and (G) are true statements about Venus, but they answer the wrong question. The passage does indicate that Venus's atmosphere is *oxygen-poor* and that *activity by living things* generates oxygen; however, this is not the meaning of *primordial*. Eliminate (F). The passage indicates that Venus has a thick atmosphere and high surface temperature, and that it is not hospitable to humans, but this is not the meaning of *primordial*. Eliminate (G). Keep (H) because it matches the prediction. Eliminate (J) because it describes a characteristic of *Earth*, which the passage does not characterize as a *primordial* planet. The correct answer is (H).

39. **A** This reasoning question asks what the *activity of living things* in line 59 refers to. Read a window around the given line reference. Lines 57–60 say, *The abundant oxygen in Earth's atmosphere is a by-*

product of photosynthesis by plants; if not for the activity of living things, Earth's atmosphere also would be oxygen poor. Eliminate answers that don't match this prediction. Keep (A) because it matches the prediction. Choice (B) uses words from the passage but doesn't match what the passage says. The paragraph says that on Earth, *rain* removes *sulfur gases*; it does not say that the *living things* remove sulfur gases. Eliminate (B). Eliminate (C) because *carbon dioxide* is not mentioned in the window for the question, nor does the passage state that living things store *carbon dioxide* in *carbonate rocks*. Eliminate (D) because the passage does not indicate that living things could *easily live* in atmospheres like the one on *Venus*. The correct answer is (A).

40. **J** This referral question asks what details the *Pioneer Venus* studied. There is not a good lead word in this question (*Pioneer Venus* appears throughout the passage), so work the question later. Lines 20–22 say, *Pioneer Venus…gathered data on the composition and dynamics of the planet's atmosphere and interplanetary surroundings.* Eliminate answers that don't match this prediction. Choice (F) includes details that are mentioned in the passage, but it answers the wrong question; *surface geology and interior structure* were studied by *Magellan*, not *Pioneer Venus*. Eliminate (F). Eliminate (G) because the passage does not indicate that *photosynthesis* was studied on Venus. Eliminate (H) because the window mentions *differences*, not *similarities*, between Earth and Venus. Keep (J) because it matches the prediction. The correct answer is (J).

SCIENCE TEST

1. **C** The question asks which hypothesis about the conditions under which zinc is plated more extensively is supported by a comparison of the results for coin samples II and IV. Table 1 shows the results of coin samples II and IV, so compare the results in Table 1 of coin samples II and IV. For coin sample II, the chemist used silver nitrate and an electric current of 2,000 mA for a 4.0 mg increased mass from plating. For coin sample IV, the chemist used copper sulfate and an electric current of 2,000 mA for a 2.4 mg increased mass from plating. Since the same electric current was used for both coins, eliminate (A) and (B), which indicate different currents between the two coins. Coin II (silver nitrate) had a greater increase in mass with the same electric current. Eliminate (D), which states that the copper sulfate plated more extensively than the silver nitrate. The correct answer is (C).

2. **F** The question asks how the mass of the metal plating would be affected if Experiment 1 were to be repeated with a coin radius that was compressed to a radius of 0.5 cm to decrease the surface area. Since all the coins were altered in the same way and are still identical to each other, it makes sense that an identical change would happen to all the coins. Eliminate (G), which states that the mass of plated metal would increase on some coins and decrease on others. The compressed coins have a smaller surface area, so it is logical to assume that there would be a smaller amount of precious metal that would coat the smaller surface area of the coin. Therefore, the mass of precious metal would decrease. Eliminate (H) and (J) because neither mentions the mass decreasing. The correct answer is (F).

3. **C** The question asks which answer choice conditions would result in the greatest concentration of zinc nitrate from interaction with a zinc alloy coin. Table 2 contains the words *zinc nitrate*, so look

at Table 2. The first part of the answer choices refers to time, so look at the relationship between time and zinc nitrate concentration. As time increases from 5 minutes to 60 minutes, the amount of zinc nitrate also increases. Therefore, 10 minutes will have a greater zinc nitrate concentration than 6 minutes. Eliminate (A) and (B) because both say 6 minutes. The second part of the answer refers to the initial concentration of silver nitrate. The initial concentration of silver nitrate is not shown in either table, so look through the passage text for reference to silver nitrate. The introduction states that *silver nitrate, formed when silver dissolves in nitric acid, reacts with zinc to form solid silver and zinc nitrate.* Since zinc nitrate is formed when silver nitrate reacts with zinc, it makes sense that a higher initial silver nitrate concentration will lead to more zinc nitrate. Eliminate (D) as it mentions a low initial concentration of silver nitrate. The correct answer is (C).

4. **H** The question asks how much copper would have plated after 30 minutes in Experiment 1 if, hypothetically, the chemist had applied 1,580 mA to a 1 cm radius zinc alloy coin sample in a copper sulfate solution. According to the description of Experiment 1, the coins used were zinc alloy coins with a radius of 1 cm. The results of Experiment 1 are shown in Table 1. Coin samples III and IV were plated in copper sulfate, so look at the results for these two coins. For coin III, the scientist applied a current of 1,000 mA and there was an increased mass of 1.2 mg. For coin IV, the scientist applied a current of 2,000 mA and there was an increased mass of 2.4 mg. The results for the application of 1,580 mA would be between 1.2 mg and 2.4 mg, as 1,580 mA is between 1,000 mA and 2,000 mA. Eliminate (F), (G), and (J) as they are not between 1.2 mg and 2.4 mg. The only answer choice between these values is 1.9 mg. The correct answer is (H).

5. **D** The question asks which variable was the same in Experiment 1 for all coin sample trials. Look at the columns in Table 1 to see which variables did or did not change in Experiment 1. The mass from plating increased some amount for every coin sample. Eliminate (A). The electric current applied was not the same in every experiment. Eliminate (B). Some experiments used silver nitrate and others used copper sulfate. Eliminate (C). The experiment description states that all samples *had a radius of 1 cm.* The initial radius of the sample was the same for all sample trials. The correct answer is (D).

6. **G** The question asks which substance's concentration the chemist should monitor if the chemist wants to study the effect of plating zinc alloys with silver. Experiment 2 plates zinc alloy coins with silver and measures the zinc nitrate concentration in the surrounding solution. Additionally, the introduction to the passage states that *silver nitrate, formed when silver dissolves in nitric acid, reacts with zinc to form solid silver and zinc nitrate.* Therefore, zinc nitrate is formed when silver plating occurs, which matches (G). None of the other answer choices are mentioned in relation to the production of silver or measured in Experiment 2. The correct answer is (G.)

7. **C** The question asks how Experiment 2 differed from Experiment 1. Use Process of Elimination. Both (B) and (D) mention the mass increasing in one experiment and increasing and then decreasing in the other. However, the coins in Experiment 1 all increased in mass and the chemist did not even measure final mass in Experiment 2, so neither of these statements is supported by the data. Eliminate (B) and (D). The remaining answers address the type of material used to plate the coins, so look at Table 1 for the type of material used in Experiment 1. Coins I and II used a silver nitrate solution, but coins III and IV used a copper sulfate solution. Since Experiment 1 used both silver and copper,

eliminate (A), which says that Experiment 1 used silver only. In Experiment 2, the chemist *dissolved equal amounts of pure silver* to plate all four of the coins. The correct answer is (C).

8. **J** The question asks for the *chemical formula for pentanol*, based on Table 1. Find the prefix pent in the column titled *Name prefix* in Table 1. The row for *pent* indicates that molecules with the prefix *pent* have 5 carbons. Eliminate (F) and (G) because they both incorrectly indicate that there are 4 carbons in pentanol. The difference between the remaining answers is the presence or absence of oxygen. Use the suffix *anol* to determine the correct structure for pentanol. The chemical structure of pentanol is shown in the middle column of structures. On the right side of the chain there is an O atom present. Eliminate (H) since there is no O in the chemical formula in (H). Choice (J) correctly shows one oxygen atom in the chemical formula. The correct answer is (J).

9. **B** The question asks which compounds *are solid at 215 K*, according to Table 2. Table 2 shows the melting points (the temperatures at which substances change from a solid to a liquid) of alkanes, alcohols, and aldehydes. In order for a compound to be *solid at 215 K*, its melting point must be above 215 K. Look at Table 2 and determine which compounds have a melting point above 215 K. In the column for alkanes, only the 8-carbon alkane has a melting point above 215 K. Eliminate (A) and (C) because both include alkanes with less than 8-carbons in the list. Also notice that in Table 2, there are no 4-carbon compounds with melting points above 215 K. Eliminate (D) as it includes a 4-carbon compound in the list. Only the alcohols and aldehydes with 6-carbons or more and the 8-carbon alkane, which is identified as octane in Table 1, have melting points above 215 K. The correct answer is (B).

10. **F** The question asks which *compound has the highest viscosity*, based on Tables 1 and 3. Viscosity is shown only in Table 3, so look at Table 3 to find the compound with the highest value for viscosity. According to Table 3, the 8-carbon alcohol has the highest value for viscosity. Refer to Table 1 to determine the name of the compound. An 8-carbon compound has the prefix *oct*, and an alcohol has the suffix *anol*. Therefore, the compound name is octanol. The correct answer is (F).

11. **D** The question asks how the viscosity of the *5-carbon molecules* differ, according to Table 3. Refer to Table 3 and look at the viscosities for compounds with 5 carbons. The 5-carbon alkane has a viscosity of 0.24, the 5-carbon alcohol has a viscosity of 5.1, and the 5-carbon aldehyde has a viscosity of 0.5. Eliminate (A), (B), and (C) since the viscosity of the alkane is the lowest. The correct answer is (D).

12. **G** The questions asks for the *relationship between the length of the carbon chain* and *melting point* and *the relationship between the length of the carbon chain* and *viscosity*. Table 2 shows the relationship between the number of carbons in the chain and melting point. Note the trends in Table 2. As the number of carbons in the chain increases, the melting point increases. Eliminate (F) and (J) because they indicate that the melting point decreases. Table 3 shows the relationship between the number of carbons in the chain and viscosity. Note the trends in Table 3. As the number of carbons in the chain increases, the viscosity increases. Eliminate (H) because it indicates that the viscosity decreases. The correct answer is (G).

13. **C** The question asks for the *difference in melting point between an alkane and an alcohol with the same number of carbons*, based on Table 2. Use Table 2 to approximate the difference in melting points between the alkanes and alcohols with the same number of carbons. For the 4-carbon chain, the

alkane has a melting point of 135 K and the alcohol has a melting point of 183 K. The difference between these values is 183 − 135 = 48 K. For the 5-carbon chain, the difference between melting points is 51 K. Look through all of the carbon chains. The largest difference is 57 K, between the 7-carbon alkane and the 7-carbon alcohol. The smallest difference is 41 K between the 8-carbon compounds. Therefore, the average difference must be between 41 K and 57 K. Eliminate (A) and (B) because 25 K and 35 K are less than 41 K. Eliminate (D) because 65 K is greater than 57 K. The only value between 41 K and 57 K is 50 K in (C). The correct answer is (C).

14. **G** The question asks which additional experiment could be used to demonstrate that air resistance decreases the pendulum's acceleration. The passage makes no mention of air resistance or drag force, so the experiment is most likely done at normal indoor conditions. Eliminate (F) and (H) because altering the experiment to include a spring doesn't account for air resistance. To negate air resistance, using a vacuum with no air pressure would be best. The correct answer is (G).

15. **A** The question asks if *a timer that reads to the nearest second* can be used to obtain similar results. Paragraph 2 mentions the timer used in the passage is *capable of reading to nearest 0.01 sec.* Look to Table 1 for the results of Experiment 1. The trials for the lead cube would all round down to 1 second (with an average of 1 second overall). Eliminate (C) and (D) because this is significantly different than the results shown in Table 1. Eliminate (B) because both pendulums have average periods less than 1.5 seconds. Thus, both pendulums will have completed a full swinging cycle within 1.5 seconds. The correct answer is (A).

16. **H** The question asks for a reason why *forces other than gravity are acting on the pendulums*. Use POE. Eliminate (F) because the periods in Table 1 and Table 2 are not the same, so the periods for different lengths do differ. The two materials have different masses and different periods as well, so eliminate (G). Both of the remaining answers reference the acceleration due to gravity, so determine if the acceleration is greater or less than 9.8 m/sec^2. The description of Experiment 1 states that *the average accelerations were 9.3 m/sec^2 for lead and 9.1 m/sec^2 for tin*. The description of Experiment 2 states that *the average accelerations were 9.3 m/sec^2 for lead and 9.0 m/sec^2 for tin*. Eliminate (J) as the values obtained for the acceleration are less than 9.8 m/sec^2. The correct answer is (H).

17. **D** The question asks for the best answer for the period of the *tin cube suspended from a 2.0 m thread*. Experiments 1, 2, or 3 do not mention a length of 2.0 m. Rather, Experiments 1 and 2, the length of the thread is 0.5 m and 1.0 m respectively. The measured periods in Table 2 are greater than those in Table 1. Therefore, the conclusion can be made that if the string gets longer, then the period should also increase. Thus, the period of a tin cube suspended from a 2.0 m thread should be greater than the average period in Experiment 2 (2.09 seconds). The correct answer is (D).

18. **G** The question asks for the nearest estimate of the period of the lead cube if another trial was run in Experiment 2. Look to Table 2 for the results of Experiment 2. Using Table 2, all values, although not showing a consistent trend, fall between 2.00 and 2.12 seconds. Eliminate (F), (H) and (J) as these are not between 2.00 and 2.12 seconds. The correct answer is (G).

19. **B** The question asks why the experiments were conducted using lead and tin cubes. In Experiments 1 and 2, the length of the lead cube is equal to the length of the tin cube. Since the length is the same, the surface area would also be the same. Eliminate (A) and (D). The passage also states that the same

starting angle was used for both cubes. Eliminate (C). Only the mass differed between the cubes, so the different materials were used to investigate the effect of mass on the period. The correct answer is (B).

20.   **H**   The question asks which cube had a larger drag coefficient based on the results of Experiments 1 and 2. Look to Experiments 1 and 2 and use POE. The description of Experiment 1 states that the mass of the lead cube is 11.3 grams and the mass of the tin cube is 7.4 grams. Eliminate (G) and (J) because both incorrectly indicate that the mass of the tin cube is higher. Both of the remaining answers agree with the results of Experiments 1 and 2 that the lead cube has a shorter period than the tin cube. According to the passage, the period is *inversely related to gravitational acceleration*. Therefore, the tin cube has a longer period and a smaller acceleration. Since drag force slows an object, the smaller acceleration of the tin cube must be caused by a larger drag coefficient. Eliminate (F), which incorrectly identifies the lead cube as the cube with the larger drag coefficient. The correct answer is (H).

21.   **A**   The question asks which answer choice reflects something mentioned by Scientist 1 but not by Scientist 3. To answer this question, first use the answer choices to identify information that is mentioned by Scientist 1 and then see whether that information is mentioned by Scientist 3. Choice (A) is self-replication. Scientist 1 mentions the development of self-replication: *these RNA sequences developed enzyme-like abilities including the ability to self-replicate and insert themselves into other nucleotide sequences*. Scientist 3 does not mention anything about self-replication. Keep (A). Scientist 1 does not mention capsid, deoxyribonucleic acid, or cell membrane transit, so eliminate (B), (C), and (D). The correct answer is (A).

22.   **J**   The question asks what information all three scientists would agree with. Look at all three theories, as well as the introduction, to find information that is shared by all the scientists. Choice (F) is that viruses evolved from bacteria. Only Scientist 3 believes that viruses evolved from bacteria. Eliminate (F). Choice (G) is that the first viruses could self-replicate outside a cell. Only Scientist 1 mentions that the first viruses could self-replicate outside a cell. Eliminate (G). Choice (H) is that the first viruses were enclosed in a membrane. Scientist 2 does not mention a membrane enclosure around the first viral particles. Eliminate (H). Choice (J) is that the first viruses contained nucleic acid. The introduction states *biologists agree that viruses originated from genetic material called nucleic acid*. The correct answer is (J).

23.   **D**   The question asks which feature Scientist 1 *does NOT provide an explanation for the earliest virus particles possessing*. Scientist 1 states that some RNA sequences *were packaged inside proteins as the first viral particles that could replicate after infecting cellular organisms*. Scientist 1 does mention proteins, so eliminate (A). Scientist 1 also states that *these RNA sequences developed enzyme-like abilities including the ability to self-replicate and insert themselves into other nucleotide sequences*. Since this provides an explanation for enzyme-like activity and nucleotides, eliminate (B) and (C). Scientist 1 never mentions DNA, so Scientist 1 does not give an explanation for its presence in early virus particles. The correct answer is (D).

24.   **G**   The question asks which conclusion could be made about the modern T4 DNA viruses and modern PP7 RNA viruses if Scientist 2 is correct. Scientist 2 states that *viruses evolved independently from their initial host and ultimately could infect either prokaryotic or eukaryotic cells*. Since the passage specifically mentions prokaryotic and eukaryotic cells, start with the two answer choices that

address these terms. Since the viruses ultimately could infect either type of cell, knowing what type of cell the viruses infect now does not provide any information about which type of cell they originally evolved from. Eliminate (H) and (J). The remaining two answers address how closely the viruses are related. The idea that *viruses evolved independently* best matches the idea that they are distantly related rather than closely related. Eliminate (F). The correct answer is (G).

25. **C** The question asks for the discovery of a living organism that would provide the most support for Scientist 3's theory. Use Process of Elimination. Scientist 3 states that *some cellular organisms, particularly certain bacteria, are obligate intracellular parasites because they must infect a host cell in order to reproduce.* Intracellular parasites are an important part of this theory. Scientist 3 does not mention extracellular parasites. Eliminate both (A) and (B), as both answers mention extracellular parasites. The passage further states that it accounts for *viruses that contain complex deoxyribonucleic acid (DNA) similar to that found in bacteria and other cellular organisms.* This matches (C). Eliminate (D) as Scientist 3 does not mention RNA. The answer is (C).

26. **G** The question asks which conclusion about the origin of viruses would be agreed upon by all three scientists. Look at the introduction and all three theories for an answer choice that would be supported. Choice (F) states that *viral capsids contain a protein structure similar to the cell walls of modern bacteria.* Scientist 1 does not discuss capsids. Eliminate (F). Choice (G) states that the *first viruses did not originate before the first cellular organisms.* Scientist 1 states that viruses evolved alongside other organisms over billions of years. This agrees with the idea that viruses did not originate before organisms. Scientist 2 states that that *nucleotide sequences within prokaryotic (non-nucleated) and eukaryotic (nucleated) cellular organisms incorporated into a protein coating and escaped from the cell as a viral particle.* The viral particles developed inside a cellular organism, so viruses did not originate before cellular organisms. Scientist 3 states *viruses evolved from cellular organisms*, which would mean that they did not originate before cellular organisms. All three scientists agree that the first cellular organisms existed either at the same time as or after the first cellular organisms. Keep (G). None of the theories compare the advancement levels of RNA viruses to those of DNA viruses. Eliminate (H). Scientist 1 does not mention DNA, so eliminate (J). The correct answer is (G).

27. **A** The question asks which question is mentioned by Scientist 1, but not answered by the passage. Look at the hypothesis of Scientist 1 to learn the details of this theory. Use Process of Elimination. Choice (A) asks why some RNA sequences are packaged into protein structures and others are incorporated into cell structures. The passage mentions *while some RNA sequences became incorporated into membrane-bound cells, others were packaged inside proteins as the first viral particles that could replicate after infecting cellular organisms.* However, the passage does not explain why this occurred. Keep (A). Scientist 1 does not mention *obligate intracellular parasites*, two different types of cellular organisms, or virions passing through membranes. Eliminate (B), (C), and (D). The correct answer is (A).

28. **H** The question asks for the most likely *percentage of organic cover used on the field* with Soil Z, given that *the topsoil deflation in the field was determined to be 26,000 kg/ha.* The question states that Soil Z *contains 45% clay* and the same procedure as Experiment 1 was used. The results of Experiment 1 are shown in Table 1. Since clay content is not shown in Table 1, first skim the introduction for information regarding clay content for Soil X and Soil Y. The introduction states that *Soil X was*

composed of 5% clay and Soil Y was composed of 40% clay. Based on Table 1, the topsoil deflation of Soil Y is lower than Soil X, so increasing the clay content of the soil decreases topsoil deflation. Since the clay content of Soil Z is only slightly higher than Soil Y, the topsoil deflation at each percentage of organic cover should be only slightly lower than that of Soil Y. A topsoil deflation of 26,000 kg/ha is slightly less than the 28,500 kg/ha for Soil Y at 50% organic cover. The correct answer is (H).

29. **C** The question asks what will *minimize* topsoil deflation, based on Experiments 1 and 2. Topsoil deflation for Experiments 1 and 2 is shown in Tables 1 and 3 respectively. Look at Table 1 to determine when the minimum topsoil deflation occurs. Table 1 shows that topsoil deflation decreases as the percentage of organic cover increases. Eliminate (A) and (B) because both incorrectly state that topsoil deflation will be minimized by *decreased* organic cover. Choices (C) and (D) both state that increased rainfall will reduce erosion as shown in Table 3. The only difference between the two remaining answers is the type of topsoil. Use Tables 1 and 3 to determine whether Soil X or Soil Y had less topsoil deflation. Tables 1 and 3 consistently show that at every percentage of organic cover and every sprinkler time, Soil Y had less topsoil deflation than Soil X had. Eliminate (D), which incorrectly states that topsoil deflation will be minimized by using Soil X as topsoil. The correct answer is (C).

30. **H** The question asks what *the most likely topsoil deflation amount* would be *if Experiment 1 were repeated using a soil containing 10% clay with 0% organic cover*. The results of Experiment 1 are shown in Table 1. Since clay content is not shown in Table 1, first skim the introduction for information regarding clay content for Soil X and Soil Y. The introduction states that *Soil X was composed of 5% clay and Soil Y was composed of 40% clay*. Since 10% clay is between 5% clay and 40% clay, a soil with 10% clay and 0% organic cover should have a topsoil deflation value between the topsoil deflation values for Soil X and Soil Y with 0% organic cover. According to Table 1, at 0% organic cover, Soil X has a topsoil deflation value of 105,000 kg/ha, and Soil Y has a value of 65,000 kg/ha. Therefore, a soil with 10% clay and 0% organic cover should have topsoil deflation between 65,000 kg/ha and 105,000 kg/ha. Eliminate (F) and (J), because they are not between 65,000 kg/ha and 105,000 kg/ha. Since 10% clay is closer to 5% clay found in Soil X than the 40% clay found in Soil Y, the topsoil deflation value of soil with 10% clay should be closer to the 105,000 kg/ha value for Soil X. Eliminate (G) as this is closer to the value for Soil Y. The correct answer is (H).

31. **D** The question asks which experiment should be repeated to *investigate the effect of water content on the erosion from topsoil deflation*. Experiment 1 focuses on percentage of organic cover, rather than water content. Eliminate (A) and (B), which both state that the scientists should repeat Experiment 1. Eliminate (C) because using no sprinklers would not investigate the effect of any water content on erosion. Only (D), *using fields exposed to various amounts of rainfall*, provides a clear method to study the *effect of water content on erosion from topsoil deflation*. The correct answer is (D).

32. **H** The question asks about the *assumptions...in the design of Experiment 1*. Look at Experiment 1 and determine what is being tested. Experiment 1 investigates the topsoil erosion due to wind for Soil X, composed of 5% clay, and Soil Y, composed of 40% clay, with varying amounts of organic cover. The results of Experiment 1 are shown in Table 1. Table 1 shows that topsoil deflation decreases as the percentage of organic cover increases and at every percentage of organic cover, Soil Y had less topsoil deflation than Soil X had. Eliminate (F), which incorrectly states that the quantity of

topsoil deflation is independent of the percentage of clay present in the soil. Eliminate (G), which states that the presence of straw on the soil does *not* accurately simulate vegetation and organic cover. This is the opposite of the assumption made in Experiment 1, which is that that the presence of straw on the soil *does* accurately simulate vegetation and organic cover. If the presence of straw on the soil *did not* accurately simulate plant and organic cover, then it would have been a poor choice to use it in the experimental design. The introduction states that *large fans were used to simulate wind*. Thus, it is assumed that the air movement from fans provides an accurate simulation of the wind responsible for topsoil deflation, as (H) states. If the fans did not adequately simulate the effects of real wind, it would be difficult to apply the findings to any practical situation. Keep (H). Eliminate (J) since water content is not addressed in Experiment 1. The correct answer is (H).

33. **C** The question asks why there was a difference in topsoil deflation when both fields were sprinkled for 4 hours and the water content between the two soils was similar, based on Experiment 2. The results of Experiment 2 are shown in Tables 2 and 3. Table 2 shows the relationship between sprinkler times and water content for Soils X and Y, and Table 3 shows the relationship between sprinkler times and topsoil deflation. Look at the introduction to determine the difference between Soil X and Soil Y. The introduction states that *Soil X was composed of 5% clay and Soil Y was composed of 40% clay*. Since the only difference between Soil X and Soil Y is the percentage of clay, that is the most likely cause of the difference in topsoil deflation. Only (C) mentions the percentage of clay. The correct answer is (C).

34. **G** The question asks, *if Experiment 2 were repeated with soil containing 10% clay, which of the following values would be expected for water content and topsoil deflation following 8 hours of water sprinkling*. The results of Experiment 2 are shown in Tables 2 and 3. Since clay content is not shown in Tables 2 or 3, first skim the introduction for information regarding clay content for Soil X and Soil Y. The introduction states that *Soil X was composed of 5% clay and Soil Y was composed of 40% clay*. The question concerns a soil with 10% clay. Since 10% clay is between 5% clay and 40% clay, a soil with 10% clay following 8 hours of water sprinkling should have water content and topsoil deflation values between the water content and topsoil deflation values for Soil X and Soil Y following 8 hours of water sprinkling. According to Table 2, after 8 hours, Soil X had 16% water content and Soil Y had 22% water content. Therefore, a soil with 10% clay should have water content between 16% and 22%. Eliminate (H) and (J) they do not include values between 16% and 22%. According to Table 3, after 8 hours, Soil X had 14,000 kg/ha of topsoil deflation and Soil Y had 10,300 kg/ha of topsoil deflation. Eliminate (F) because 9,700 kg/ha does not fall between 10,300 kg/ha and 14,000 kg/ha. The correct answer is (G).

35. **C** The question asks which pair of ocean zones shares parts of a common depth range, based on information in Figure 1. Look at the *Zone of Ocean* and *Depth* columns in Figure 1 to learn the depths of the various ocean zones. All of the zones that end in -pelagic are in the same column with no overlap. Eliminate (B) and (D) as these both include two -pelagic zones. Check the zones in (A). The bathypelagic zone extends from 1,000 m to 4,000 m and the thermocline extends from 140 m to 1,000 m. These do not overlap, so eliminate (A). The epipelagic zone extends from 0 m to 200 m. This overlaps the thermocline between 140 m and 200 m. The correct answer is (C).

36. **J** The question asks which zone would most likely include a total pressure of 1,700 kPa in an oceano-graphic reading, according to Figure 1. Look at the *Pressure* columns in Figure 1 to see where 1,700 kPa would fall. 1,700 kPa is between the listed values of 1,509 kPa at 140 m and 2,112 kPa at 200 m, so the depth would be between 140 and 200 m. Read horizontally across Figure 1 to learn that a depth between 140 and 200 is part of the thermocline, continental rise, and epipelagic zones. Eliminate (F), (G), and (H) because they do not refer to any of these three zones. The only possible zone that is an answer choice is thermocline. The correct answer is (J).

37. **C** The question asks at what depth, according to Figure 2, would it be impossible to distinguish the difference between tropical and temperature oceans by temperature. The sonographic measure-ment of temperature would not be able to distinguish the difference if the temperatures were the same, so look at Figure 2 to find the points at which the lines intersect. The lines intersect at two depths: at approximately 175 m and 625 m. Eliminate (A), (B), and (D) because they do not match either of these two depths. Choice (C), 625 m, is the only option that lists one of the places where the lines intersect. The correct answer is (C).

38. **G** The question asks what the relationship is between depth and ocean temperature in Table 1. Look at the depth and ocean temperature columns in Table 1. As the depth increased, the ocean tem-perature in Region 1 decreased only. Eliminate (F) because this says that the water temperature increased with increasing depth. Eliminate (J) because it says that the temperature decreased in Region 2 only. Now, look at the water temperature in Region 2. In Region 2, the ocean temperature decreased at first, but then increased from 5°C to 6°C. Eliminate (H) as Region 2 did not maintain a consistent trend between depth and temperature. Choice (G) correctly states that the water tem-perature consistently decreased with increasing depth in Region 1 only. The correct answer is (G).

39. **B** The question asks what the total pressure would be, according to Figure 1 and Table 1, *if water temperature measurements were taken at depths greater than 79.5 m*. Look at Table 1 first. At a depth of 79.5 m, the total pressure is 900 kPa. Both Figure 1 and Table 1 show that as the depth increases, the pressure increases. Therefore, measurements taken at depths greater than 79.5 m would have a pressure greater than 900 kPa. The correct answer is (B).

40. **G** The question asks, based on Figures 1 and 2, which ocean zone includes *the range of depths at which the temperate ocean is warmer than the tropical ocean*. Figure 2 illustrates the relationship between temperature and depth. Look at the key to see that the solid line represents the tropical ocean and the dashed line represents the temperate ocean. According to the information, the temperate ocean is warmer than the tropical ocean between the approximate depths of 150 m and 600 m. Look at Figure 1 to find the names of the zones at those depths. The zones that include the range between 150 m and 600 m are the mesopelagic zone and the thermocline. Eliminate (F), (H), and (J), as none of them mention either of the zones that extend between 150 m and 600 m. The correct answer is (G).

Chapter 30
Practice Exam 3

*Make sure to download a bubble sheet for this test via your online Student Tools.

ENGLISH TEST

45 Minutes—75 Questions

DIRECTIONS: In the five passages that follow, certain words and phrases are underlined and numbered. In the right-hand column, you will find alternatives for each underlined part. In most cases, you are to choose the one that correctly expresses the idea, makes the statement appropriate for standard written English, or is worded most consistently with the style and tone of the passage as a whole. If you think the original version is correct, choose "NO CHANGE." In some cases, you will find in the right-hand column a question about the underlined part of the passage. You are to choose the correct answer to the question.

You will also find questions about a section of the passage or the passage as a whole. These questions do not refer to an underlined portion of the passage, but rather are identified by a number or numbers in a box.

For each question, choose the alternative you consider correct and blacken the corresponding oval on your answer document. Read each passage through once before you begin to answer the questions that accompany it. For many of the questions, you must read several sentences beyond the question to determine the answer. Be sure that you have read far enough ahead each time you choose an alternative.

PASSAGE I

The Rat Race

When I was a little girl, my family was deciding to move
from suburban Southern California to rural Northern California.
All of my friends lived in the neighborhood where I had grown

up but I didn't want to move. Classes starting in the fall and

unfamiliar faces looked at me with curiosity scared me stiff.

For example, I asked my parents why they were doing

this to me. I pleaded; begging to be allowed to stay behind
and live with my grandparents. My mother, trying to explain to
me, said, "Daddy needs to get away from the rat race." I
imagined my father in his car, surrounded by giant rats racing

1. **A.** NO CHANGE
   B. were deciding and moving
   C. were deciding to move
   D. decided to move

2. **F.** NO CHANGE
   G. up, because
   H. up, so
   J. up, but

3. **A.** NO CHANGE
   B. having looked
   C. looking
   D. DELETE the underlined portion.

4. **F.** NO CHANGE
   G. Nevertheless, I
   H. I, however,
   J. I

5. **A.** NO CHANGE
   B. pleaded, begging to be allowed
   C. pleaded, begging to be allowed,
   D. pleaded begging to be allowed

GO ON TO THE NEXT PAGE.

him home and was blocking his way. In my imagination
                    6

he didn't look scared so much as frustrated.
                    7

     I finally asked my father why he wanted us to move so far
                                                    8
away from home. One of his main reasons, he said, was the long
8

drive home after work. For him, the worst and most terrible thing,
                                    9
about living in Southern California was having no time to go

fishing, one of his favorite hobbies.

     [1] My parents eventually picked Redding for our new home,

partly because there were two lakes within an hour's drive, and

we made the move. [2] Since my father's new commute was

only fifteen minutes, he would be able to go fishing after work

sometimes. [3] I was sad to say goodbye to my friends when we

finally did move. [4] However, I had to admit that my father

looked happier than he had in years. [5] Before the move, he
       10
used to complain about crazy drivers while eating reheated

leftovers. [6] After the move, we had dinner and, talked about
                                        11

the weekend calmly as a family. ⬚12

6. **F.** NO CHANGE
   G. blocking
   H. were blocking
   J. DELETE the underlined portion.

7. At this point, the author would like to give the reader a better
   idea of how she thought her father felt. Given that all the
   choices are true, which one best accomplishes this purpose?

   A. NO CHANGE
   B. he was stuck on the highway for hours and hours.
   C. he couldn't see the rats even though I could.
   D. he looked so small compared to the giant rats.

8. Given that all the choices are true, which one provides the
   best opening to this paragraph?

   F. NO CHANGE
   G. The rats seemed like more of an annoyance than a danger.
   H. I didn't really understand what my mom meant by the "rat
   race" until years later.
   J. During holidays and long weekends, my father loved to
   go fishing.

9. **A.** NO CHANGE
   B. most awfully terrible part
   C. worst, most terrible thing
   D. worst part

10. **F.** NO CHANGE
    G. more happier then
    H. happier then
    J. the happiest than

11. **A.** NO CHANGE
    B. dinner and talked,
    C. dinner, and talked
    D. dinner and talked

12. For the sake of the logic and coherence of this paragraph,
    Sentence 5 should be placed:

    F. where it is now.
    G. after Sentence 1.
    H. after Sentence 2.
    J. after Sentence 3.

GO ON TO THE NEXT PAGE.

As I got older, when we visited family and friends in
Southern California. I could see the difference from the traffic at
home in Redding. There weren't any huge rats on the highway,

but as I sat in the car watching the endless lines of cars, I got a
glimpse of what my parents had meant. Redding might have
been unpleasantly empty of familiar associations for me but that
same emptiness was more pleasant for my parents, because it
included empty roads, empty skies, and empty days to fill as
they pleased.

13. **A.** NO CHANGE
    B. California;
    C. California,
    D. California and

14. **F.** NO CHANGE
    G. unending and interminable lines
    H. endlessly, continuing forever, lines
    J. lines, going on into eternity without end

> Question 15 asks about the preceding passage as a whole.

15. Suppose the writer's goal had been to write a short essay telling the reader why, in her opinion, her family moved to Redding. Would this essay successfully fulfill that goal?

    A. Yes, because it describes her father's reasons for wanting to move, as the author understands them.
    B. Yes, because it demonstrates that children sometimes have misconceptions about the reasons for a move.
    C. No, because it fails to explain why the author was frightened by the prospect of the move.
    D. No, because it focuses more heavily on the feelings of a party other than the author.

PASSAGE II

The Latino Murals of Los Angeles

The Mexican-American artist Judith Baca credits her family
for her artistic inspiration. She was raised by her mother and
grandmother, themselves in a vibrant Latino community in East
Los Angeles. Her art is thus a tribute to her family's past as well

as to her cultural heritage, which she believes her art embodies
the spirit of Los Angeles.

Baca studied art both in Los Angeles and Cuernavaca,
Mexico. Her chosen field of art, the mural, has long been a part
of Mexican artistic culture and has experienced a popular

16. **F.** NO CHANGE
    G. grandmother, themselves,
    H. grandmother related to her
    J. grandmother

17. **A.** NO CHANGE
    B. heritage;
    C. heritage,
    D. heritage, but

18. **F.** NO CHANGE
    G. art, the mural—
    H. art the mural—
    J. art the mural,

GO ON TO THE NEXT PAGE.

revival in Los Angeles in recent years. She has gained fame for
her colorful murals depicting episodes from Latino history, many

of which can be found in the Los Angeles area. [20]

Moreover, the recent popularity of the mural as a form of
art is often linked to the prevalence of graffiti in urban areas.
Some of the earliest examples of modern murals, such as

Willie Herrón's *The Wall That Cracked Open*, was treated
as graffiti, rather than art. Many muralists remain

anonymous, and their works tend to be in public places.

Some murals political messages also made people uneasy
about this art form in the early days of its resurgence.

Today, however, city officials often hire known

muralists such as Baca to create masterpieces on

government property. Because of their size, murals often

require the assistance of other artists and, as evidence,

sometimes become community efforts. Murals are also

a way for people to connect their cultural past with their present

reality, by using traditional figures to tell modern stories.

It is this community involvement that has helped sway the

minds of officials, as well as the realization that many

murals convey positive messages. Some depict scenes

19. The underlined phrase could be placed in all the following
locations EXCEPT:

   A. where it is now.
   B. after the word *revival*.
   C. after the word *popular*.
   D. before the word *experienced*.

20. If the writer were to delete the preceding sentence, the essay
would primarily lose:

   F. an artistic evaluation of Baca's techniques compared to
traditional techniques.
   G. an explanation of the historical circumstances that led to
the development of murals as an art form.
   H. an analysis of Baca's place in the rebirth of murals with
themes from Latino history.
   J. a piece of information regarding Baca's success and one
region in which her work is popular.

21. A. NO CHANGE
   B. However, the
   C. The
   D. Therefore, the

22. F. NO CHANGE
   G. was mistakenly treated
   H. were treated
   J. was treated, by mistake,

23. A. NO CHANGE
   B. murals political messages,
   C. mural's political messages
   D. murals' political messages

24. F. NO CHANGE
   G. stated
   H. a result
   J. imagined

25. Given that all the choices are true, which one provides the
most relevant information at this point in the essay?

   A. NO CHANGE
   B. more accessible to members of the public than most art is,
because they are located in the heart of the community.
   C. often funded by government agencies that want to cover
up abandoned factories and warehouses.
   D. particularly effective for telling allegorical stories, in part
because their large size gives artists so much room.

GO ON TO THE NEXT PAGE.

of multicultural harmony, they are inspired by the
neighborhoods in which they are situated. Others show

scenes of past successes by members of the community. Still
others strive to depict the historic achievements of the generations
past.

By creating beautiful murals in her neighborhood,
Baca is working to create a sense of community pride. The bright

faces of the people, she paints signal the bright possibilities

available to the viewer. They're successes, Baca suggests, can be
yours.

26. F. NO CHANGE
G. harmony, it was prompted
H. harmony, that was inspired
J. harmony, inspired

27. A. NO CHANGE
B. by members of the community of past successes
C. of past successes of the community by members
D. of the community by members of past successes

28. F. NO CHANGE
G. a sense of community pride is being created by Baca.
H. the community is developing a sense of pride.
J. a sense of community pride, which Baca is working to create.

29. A. NO CHANGE
B. people she paints:
C. people; she paints
D. people she paints

30. F. NO CHANGE
G. Its
H. Their
J. It's

PASSAGE III

The Birth of the Video Game

The last decade had saw increasingly sophisticated video
gaming consoles that allow players to compete at great distances,
control characters through body movements, and much more. The
possibilities of video gaming, taken for granted today, were
mind-blowing in 1972 when Nolan Bushnell and Ted Dabney
introduced the public to their new creation: *Pong*.

There had been other video games before *Pong*, of course. The
necessary technology had been developed as early as 1952, and
Pong were preceded by several other games, such as *Tennis for
Two*, *Spacewar!*, and *Computer Science*.

31. A. NO CHANGE
B. has seen
C. has saw
D. would of seen

32. F. NO CHANGE
G. 1972, where
H. 1972, in which
J. 1972, that

33. A. NO CHANGE
B. precede
C. was preceding
D. was preceded

GO ON TO THE NEXT PAGE.

However, it was not until *Pong*, with its simple interface and addictive nature, that the concept of home video gaming systems really took off. [34]

[1] Looking back on *Pong* today, it seems ridiculously old-fashioned, so it's easy to contrast it with modern games. [2] It's not that *Pong* was the most advanced game of the

era: several earlier games, in fact; were actually more technologically advanced. [3] *Pong*'s strength was its

combination of novelty and accessibility. [4] The other games, sophisticated as they were, simply proved too difficult for

the average consumer or person considering making a purchase.

[5] However, it was groundbreaking in its day, in it's own way. [40]

34. The writer is considering deleting the preceding sentence from the essay. The sentence should NOT be deleted because it:

F. serves as a transition from the more general discussion about *Pong* to the more specific description of what made *Pong* successful.

G. describes the technical skill required to play *Pong*, which is important to understanding the essay.

H. demonstrates which elements of *Pong* led to its ultimate ascendance over other, more technologically sophisticated games.

J. shows that those who claim that *Pong* was the first modern video game are basing their claim on insufficient information.

35. Given that all the choices are true, which one would best complete the sentence so that it most clearly explains the writer's reasons for calling *Pong* "old-fashioned"?

A. NO CHANGE

B. with its basic graphics, simplistic game play, and repetition.

C. and some people like for things to stay that way.

D. because of the lack of technological development and complex game-play.

36. F. NO CHANGE

G. games in fact,

H. games, in fact,

J. games, in fact

37. Which of the following alternatives to the underlined word would be LEAST acceptable?

A. uniqueness

B. complexity

C. innovation

D. freshness

38. F. NO CHANGE

G. consumer or individual possibly purchasing it.

H. consumer or someone making a purchase, possibly.

J. consumer.

39. A. NO CHANGE

B. they're

C. their

D. its

40. For the sake of the logic and coherence of this paragraph, Sentence 5 should be placed:

F. where it is now.

G. after Sentence 1.

H. after Sentence 2.

J. after Sentence 3.

GO ON TO THE NEXT PAGE.

The history of the video game becomes more understandable when it is remembered that the creators of early games were primarily engineers and mathematicians, developing these games for their own amusement, they paid little attention to popular marketing. These pioneering developers saw the games they created as "doodling," more or less. Even when they introduced their products to the public, they usually did so as part of a showpiece, on a temporary basis.

So just think of how far video game technology has come, and don't forget that the technology continues to advance every day. In *Pong*, a player uses a single knob to send a "ball" back and forth across the screen, gaining points and trying to prevent the ball from slipping past the "paddle," a bar at the bottom of the screen. Compared to high complex games like *Super Mario Galaxy* and *Halo*, *Pong* may seem laughable.

But anyway, I still think *Pong* is fun to play sometimes.

41. A. NO CHANGE
    B. mathematicians only developing
    C. mathematicians. Developing
    D. mathematicians, only developing

42. F. NO CHANGE
    G. public, whom they met at special events,
    H. public, who wouldn't normally see their products,
    J. public, with whom they spoke at events,

43. A. NO CHANGE
    B. high complexity
    C. highly complexity
    D. highly complex

44. Given that all the choices are true, which one would most effectively express the writer's attitude towards the future of the video game industry?

    F. NO CHANGE.
    G. The men who created *Pong* are truly to be thanked for introducing the world to one of its most entertaining hobbies.
    H. At its core, *Pong* represents the ultimate goal of all video games: just having a good time.
    J. Still, it opened the door to all of the advances that have come since, and that will no doubt continue until the games of today seem just as ridiculous as *Pong*.

Question 45 asks about the preceding passage as a whole.

---

45. Suppose the writer's goal had been to write an essay demonstrating the impact a single invention can have on the development of an industry. Would this essay fulfill that goal?

    A. No, because the essay focuses too heavily on the other games that preceded *Pong* rather than its actual impact.
    B. No, because the essay concludes that *Pong* was ultimately not as influential as some assert.
    C. Yes, because the essay explains how *Pong* was able to gain widespread acceptance for video games.
    D. Yes, because the essay demonstrates that *Pong* was the first video game released to the public.

GO ON TO THE NEXT PAGE.

PASSAGE IV

The Life of a Hero

During a weekend visit a while back, I decided to show my
nephew, Paul, my old comic books. The pristine copies of
Superman, *Spider-Man*, and my favorite, *Green Lantern*, were
all stored neatly in a box. I thought it would be fun to introduce
him to my favorite handful of characters. I knew Superman and
Spider-Man were still popular, but I figured the Green Lantern of
my youth had probably went the way of other long-forgotten
heroes.

John Stewart, the first African-American to serve
as the Green Lantern was one of the first African-
American superheroes to become widely popular. A

former Marine and a practiced and fearsome warrior. With

his ring, he was almost unstoppable. He was a fighter,
leading, and, on top of everything else, acting cool. Stewart

seemed to embody everything I could have wanted for my
future: the respect of others, the power to control himself,

and he was known for having a great sense of style.

46. Which choice provides the most specific information?
- **F.** NO CHANGE
- **G.** a few years ago
- **H.** last summer
- **J.** some time ago

47. A. NO CHANGE
- **B.** gone
- **C.** left
- **D.** went out

48. F. NO CHANGE
- **G.** Lantern, was one,
- **H.** Lantern, was one
- **J.** Lantern was one,

49. A. NO CHANGE
- **B.** Marine, he practiced
- **C.** Marine, he was a practiced
- **D.** Marine, practicing

50. F. NO CHANGE
- **G.** was good at fighting,
- **H.** had an ability to fight,
- **J.** could fight,

51. A. NO CHANGE
- **B.** could of wanted
- **C.** could of been wanting
- **D.** DELETE the underlined portion

52. F. NO CHANGE
- **G.** he dressed with great personal style.
- **H.** the best sense of style ever.
- **J.** his sense of personal style was really great.

GO ON TO THE NEXT PAGE.

Growing up in the 1970s, I idolized Stewart. [53] I devoured the comics featuring Stewart, not just because he was a true superhero but because of his back-story. Unlike Superman, Stewart seemed like a hero I could understand.

His life had its ups and its downs; his problems were real life problems that I could relate to. He got in trouble sometimes and fought with his friends and family. He came from a bad neighborhood and hadn't always been on the road to superhero status.

For a little while in the early 1990s, there was a series that focused solely on Stewart as the Green Lantern, but after it ended, Stewart was replaced and seemed likely to be

forgotten. Much to my surprise, however, Paul knew exactly who Stewart was. He was just as big a fan as I had been, but

for different reasons. For me, Stewart's rocky, life story was central to his appeal. For Paul, however, Stewart's past didn't matter as much as did his actions; Paul admired Stewart because he was such a strong role model.

When I was young, Stewart was a role model that I could identify with. I assumed Paul would either have his own role models or would share my feelings about my role models.

---

53. At this point, the writer is considering adding the following true statement:

> Each Green Lantern was chosen by a group called The Guardians, whose members took into consideration a number of personal qualities, including physical strength, moral fiber, and a strong sense of duty to all living beings.

Should the writer make this addition here?

A. Yes, because it provides important background information that helps the reader understand the essay.

B. Yes, because it contributes to the writer's discussion of Stewart's positive attributes.

C. No, because it undermines the author's claim that Stewart was a more realistic role model.

D. No, because it provides information that is irrelevant to the main point of the paragraph.

54. Given that all of the choices are true, which one best explains the author's belief that Stewart was a more understandable character and shows a more realistic image of Stewart?

F. NO CHANGE

G. Stewart was a more sympathetic character and I had an easier time imagining myself in his shoes.

H. The Green Lantern ring allowed Stewart to fly into space, create weapons out of thin air, and protect his friends.

J. Unlike Superman, Stewart couldn't fly without his ring because he didn't naturally have superpowers.

55. A. NO CHANGE

B. after;

C. after:

D. after,

56. Which of the following alternatives to the underlined portion would be LEAST acceptable?

F. though,

G. furthermore,

H. on the contrary,

J. DELETE the underlined portion

57. A. NO CHANGE

B. Stewarts rocky

C. Stewarts' rocky,

D. Stewart's rocky

58. Which choice most effectively supports the point being made in the first part of this sentence?

F. NO CHANGE

G. of what he did, not who he was.

H. of what he represented.

J. he was able to overcome his past.

GO ON TO THE NEXT PAGE.

Instead, he shared my role models but not my reasons. To him,
Stewart was simply a superhero, just like Superman. He admired
them both without worrying about that. In Paul's worldview, all
₅₉

superheroes are simply superheroes they're heroes, regardless of
₆₀
their pasts, not because of them.

59. A. NO CHANGE
   B. their back-stories.
   C. all that.
   D. those.

60. F. NO CHANGE
   G. superheroes; they're
   H. superheroes, they're
   J. superheroes being

PASSAGE V

Into the Trenches

It has often been suggested that, contrary to the
worn-out time saying, the ocean, rather than space, is the true
₆₁

final frontier. There is the immense pressure that poses a serious
₆₂
danger to unknown geography that can injure people and vessel
alike, various factors make sending human explorers very risky.
Deep-sea expeditions also tend to incur prohibitive costs, with
₆₃
the cost increasing as the expedition ventures into deeper
regions. The deepest section of the ocean is the *Marianas
Trench*. ☐64 Due primarily to its depth and the potential for
danger, the *Marianas Trench* remains largely unexplored to
this day.

61. A. NO CHANGE
   B. timeworn
   C. timed out
   D. out of time

62. F. NO CHANGE
   G. From
   H. Just like
   J. Between

63. Given that all the choices are true, which one is the most
relevant to the statement that follows in this sentence?

   A. NO CHANGE
   B. are known for being rather difficult,
   C. are dangerous to diver and sea-life alike,
   D. often cause damage to human life and to equipment,

64. The writer is considering adding the following true information to the end of the preceding sentence (placing a comma
after the word *Trench*):

> which begins at 20,000 feet and has points where the
> depth approaches seven miles and pressure reaching eight
> tons per square inch.

Should the writer make this addition?

   F. Yes, because it provides specific information about the
   Marianas Trench that explains why the author included
   this sentence.
   G. Yes, because it demonstrates how valuable human-led
   explorations of the depths of the ocean are likely to be.
   H. No, because it detracts from the writer's discussion of the
   potential dangers of deep-sea exploration.
   J. No, because it weakens the writer's point about the cor-
   relation between increasing depth and increasing cost.

GO ON TO THE NEXT PAGE.

The shallow portions of the oceans also hold many fascinating species of plants and animals. The environment, hostile though it may be to man, is hospitable to others,

allowing for the development of creatures not found anywhere else on the planet. The first and last exploration of the *Marianas*

Trench's floor took place in 1960. Therefore, the cost of sending people back has been seen as too great, the danger as too serious.

The goal, then, has been to find a way to learn about this frontier without risking the lives of scientist-explorers. One way that scientists had discovered new information is through the use

of sonar. As sonar—which is far less expensive than a human-led diving expedition is—capabilities have improved, scientists have been able to get more accurate maps of the ocean's floor based on sound-imaging.

Another method of exploration that has become more common in recent years, as technology has advanced revolves around the use of unmanned submersibles. These include devices

as simple for cameras and as advanced as underwater robots able to perform a wide-range of functions. The latter have become increasingly common in recent years as they have become ever more advanced.

The question faced today is why these underwater robots will be sufficient, eliminating the need to send humans back

65. Given that all the choices are true, which one best leads from the preceding paragraph to the subject of this paragraph?
- **A.** NO CHANGE
- **B.** One danger of deep-sea diving is a medical condition caused by an abrupt change in outside pressure.
- **C.** Some argue that the bottom of the ocean isn't truly any more dangerous than the deep rainforest or highest mountain peaks.
- **D.** Even knowing about all of the obstacles, however, some scientists feel the draw of the ocean's depths.

66. **F.** NO CHANGE
- **G.** to which development has been allowed
- **H.** which allows for the developing of
- **J.** development has been allowed

67. **A.** NO CHANGE
- **B.** Nevertheless,
- **C.** In contrast,
- **D.** Since then,

68. **F.** NO CHANGE
- **G.** could of discovered
- **H.** were discovering
- **J.** have discovered

69. Given that all the choices are true, which one most effectively describes what sonar is?
- **A.** NO CHANGE
- **B.** initially developed during World War I—
- **C.** a sound-based method of determining surroundings—
- **D.** not completely unlike the echolocation used by certain animals—

70. **F.** NO CHANGE
- **G.** advanced,
- **H.** advanced—
- **J.** advanced:

71. **A.** NO CHANGE
- **B.** as
- **C.** than
- **D.** DELETE the underlined portion

72. **F.** NO CHANGE
- **G.** what
- **H.** whether
- **J.** DELETE the underlined portion

GO ON TO THE NEXT PAGE.

into the depths. Most of the robots used thus far have been
73
"tethered," or attached in some way to a larger device with

people aboard, the day when the robots can move independently

may not be far off. Given the extreme depths of some locations,

however, it seems likely that self-propelled robots will become

more useful and handy. If that is the case, one is forced to
74
wonder: are more complex robots truly the key, or will humans

need to venture back into the ocean's inky depths? 75

73. A. NO CHANGE
   B. Most, if not all,
   C. Although most
   D. All or most

74. F. NO CHANGE
   G. practically useful.
   H. useful.
   J. effectively useful.

75. The writer is considering ending the essay with the following sentence:

> Perhaps one day humans will be able to create a robot able to simulate the emotional responses of a human, or even a robot with the ability to experience feelings.

Should the writer add this sentence here?

   A. Yes, because it expands the essay to encompass the ethical concerns raised by the development of artificial intelligence.
   B. Yes, because it explains one reason for continued reliance on robots in deep-sea explorations.
   C. No, because it fails to consider the usefulness of robots in present and future deep-sea exploration, as well as whether their use is cost-effective.
   D. No, because it distracts from the essay's central topic of deep-sea exploration and the issues preventing humans from leading expeditions.

END OF TEST 1
STOP! DO NOT TURN THE PAGE UNTIL TOLD TO DO SO.

MATHEMATICS TEST

60 Minutes—60 Questions

DIRECTIONS: Solve each problem, choose the correct answer, and then darken the corresponding oval on your answer sheet.

Do not linger over problems that take too much time. Solve as many as you can; then return to the others in the time you have left for this test.

You are permitted to use a calculator on this test. You may use your calculator for any problems you choose, but some of the problems may best be done without using a calculator.

Note: Unless otherwise stated, all of the following should be assumed:

1. Illustrative figures are NOT necessarily drawn to scale.
2. Geometric figures lie in a plane.
3. The word *line* indicates a straight line.
4. The word *average* indicates arithmetic mean.

DO YOUR FIGURING HERE.

1. If $\dfrac{5y-1}{3} = -6$, then which of the following must be true?

   A. $y = -18$

   B. $y = -\dfrac{19}{5}$

   C. $y = -\dfrac{17}{5}$

   D. $y = -1$

   E. $y = \dfrac{17}{5}$

2. The expression $\dfrac{12z^{10}}{4z^2}$ is equivalent to:

   F. $3z^5$
   G. $8z^5$
   H. $3z^8$
   J. $8z^8$
   K. $8z^{12}$

3. If $f(x) = \dfrac{x^2 - 18}{x + 2}$, then $f(12) = ?$

   A. -4
   B. 3
   C. 9
   D. 12
   E. 126

GO ON TO THE NEXT PAGE.

4. In one month, Rebecca, an entertainment journalist, recorded how many movies she watched and how many articles she wrote. She plotted this data in the graphs below: Graph 1 shows the relationship between the time elapsed and the number of movies watched; Graph 2 shows the relationship between the number of movies watched and the number of articles written. According to this data, how many articles did she write in the first 3 weeks of this month?

DO YOUR FIGURING HERE.

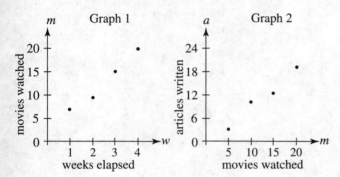

F. 3
G. 5
H. 8
J. 12
K. 15

5. What is the value of $117 - 54 + 6$, rounded to the nearest ten?

A. 40
B. 50
C. 60
D. 70
E. 80

6. A restaurant has 4 napkins at each table, plus 20 extra napkins held in reserve. If the restaurant has a total of 100 napkins, how many tables are in the restaurant?

F. 15
G. 20
H. 25
J. 30
K. 35

7. If $4(w-2) - w = 46$, then $w = ?$

A. 8
B. 10
C. 16
D. 18
E. 20

GO ON TO THE NEXT PAGE.

8. Six points (U, V, W, X, Y, Z) appear on a number line in that order, as shown in the figure below. Which of the following rays does NOT contain $\overline{WX}$?

$$U \quad V \quad W \quad X \quad Y \quad Z$$

F. $\overrightarrow{UY}$

G. $\overrightarrow{VZ}$

H. $\overrightarrow{YV}$

J. $\overrightarrow{YZ}$

K. $\overrightarrow{ZV}$

9. If $ab = 32$, $bc = 40$, and $c = 5$, then which of the following is the value of a ?

A. 4

B. 6

C. 8

D. 10

E. 12

10. Yunyun swam 4 laps, and her coach recorded her time for each as 43.4 seconds, 44.1 seconds, 42.9 seconds, and 45.4 seconds, respectively, for a total of 175.8 seconds. If Yunyun must swim her 5th lap in x seconds in order to make her average time for all 5 laps 43 seconds, then which of the following equations could be solved for the correct value of x ?

F. $\dfrac{175.8 + x}{5} = \dfrac{43}{60}$

G. $\dfrac{175.8 + x}{5} = 43$

H. $\dfrac{175.8 + x}{4} = 43$

J. $\dfrac{175.8}{5} + x = 43$

K. $\dfrac{175.8}{4} + x = 43$

11. For how many integers from 123 to 132 is the tens digit greater than the ones digit?

A. 2

B. 3

C. 4

D. 9

E. 10

GO ON TO THE NEXT PAGE.

12. The number of points Julie scores in a basketball game is proportional to the amount of time she practiced that week. Last week, Julie scored 20 points after practicing for 12 hours. How many hours should Julie practice this week if she wants to score 35 points?

F. 7
G. 14
H. 16
J. 20
K. 21

13. Rectangle *ABCD* is graphed in the (*x*,*y*) coordinate plane below. What fraction of rectangle *ABCD* lies in Quadrant IV ?

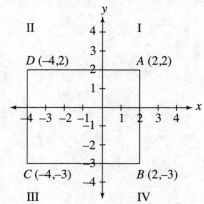

A. $\dfrac{2}{15}$

B. $\dfrac{1}{5}$

C. $\dfrac{4}{15}$

D. $\dfrac{1}{3}$

E. $\dfrac{2}{5}$

GO ON TO THE NEXT PAGE.

14. Which of the following is equivalent to the expression

$$\frac{2(z+3)-9}{5+4(z+3)}?$$

   F. $-\dfrac{9}{5}$

   G. $-\dfrac{9}{10}$

   H. $-\dfrac{7}{9}$

   J. $\dfrac{-7z-21}{9z+15}$

   K. $\dfrac{2z-3}{4z+17}$

15. A circle with the equation $x^2 + y^2 = 49$ is graphed in the standard (x,y) coordinate plane. At which 2 points does this circle intersect the x-axis?

   A. $(-1, 0)$ and $(1, 0)$
   B. $(-7, 0)$ and $(7, 0)$
   C. $(-14, 0)$ and $(14, 0)$
   D. $(-21, 0)$ and $(21, 0)$
   E. $(-49, 0)$ and $(49, 0)$

16. $\begin{bmatrix} 4 & -3 & | & 13 \\ 5 & 2 & | & 45 \end{bmatrix}$

   The augmented matrix above could represent which of the following systems of linear equations?

   F. $4m + 3n = 13$
   $5m - 2n = 45$

   G. $5m - 3n = 13$
   $4m + 2n = 45$

   H. $4m - 3n = 13$
   $5m + 2n = 45$

   J. $4m + 5n = 13$
   $-3m + 2n = 45$

   K. $4m + 3n = 13$
   $-5m - 2n = 45$

GO ON TO THE NEXT PAGE.

17. In 1905, the distance between the edge of a lake and Marker X was 75 meters. In 2005, the distance between the edge of this lake and Marker X was 825 meters. If the edge of this lake withdrew from Marker X at a linear rate, then what was the distance, in meters, between the edge of the lake and Marker X in 1985 ?

- **A.** 675
- **B.** 682.5
- **C.** 690
- **D.** 705
- **E.** 750

DO YOUR FIGURING HERE.

18. For a decorating project, Beatrice found the area and perimeter of a drawing she made of a beach scene. She found that the area of her rectangular drawing was 144 square inches and that the perimeter was 80 inches. When she arrived at the craft store to purchase a frame for her drawing, she discovered that she had forgotten to write down the dimensions of her drawing. What are the dimensions of Beatrice's drawing, in inches?

- **F.** 4 by 36
- **G.** 6 by 24
- **H.** 8 by 18
- **J.** 9 by 16
- **K.** 12 by 12

19. Which of the following is equivalent to $\dfrac{6.0 \times 10^5}{1.5 \times 10^7}$?

- **A.** 4.0×10^2
- **B.** 4.0×10^{-2}
- **C.** 4.0×10^{12}
- **D.** 4.5×10^{12}
- **E.** 4.5×10^{-2}

20. All 7-digit phone numbers at a university start with the same 3-digit prefix. How many phone numbers can be generated for the university before a new prefix must be used?

- **F.** 10^7
- **G.** 7^{10}
- **H.** 4^9
- **J.** 9^4
- **K.** 10^4

GO ON TO THE NEXT PAGE.

DO YOUR FIGURING HERE.

21. The cost to rent headphones at the listening library is $3.50 for the first hour (or any fraction thereof), $2.50 for the second hour (or any fraction thereof), and $1.25 for each additional hour (or any fraction thereof) beyond the first two. If you rent headphones at 2:12 P.M. and are charged $9.75 when you return them, then which of the following could be the time you return the headphones?

(Note: Assume that this listening library does not charge additional taxes or fees.)

A. 5:30 P.M.
B. 6:30 P.M.
C. 7:30 P.M.
D. 8:00 P.M.
E. 8:30 P.M.

22. The degree measures of the 4 angles of quadrilateral *LMNO*, not shown, form a geometric sequence with a common ratio of 2. What is the last term of the sequence?

F. 24°
G. 96°
H. 160°
J. 192°
K. 216°

23. Ray $\overrightarrow{FH}$ bisects $\angle EFG$ and the measure of $\angle EFH$ is $(2n + 34)$. If the measure of $\angle EFG$ is 140°, what is the value of *n* ?

A. 17°
B. 18°
C. 36°
D. 52°
E. 70°

GO ON TO THE NEXT PAGE.

24. If $6x + 10y = 14$ and $3x + 4y = 2$, then what is the value of $5x + 7y$?

F.   5
G.   2
H.   −5
J.   −7
K.   −12

25. Which of the following correctly solves the equation $\dfrac{a-b}{2} = 6$

for any b ?

A. $b = 12a$
B. $b = 12 - a$
C. $b = 3 - a$
D. $b = a - 3$
E. $b = a - 12$

26. The product of which of the following results in a negative odd number?

F.   A positive even number and a negative even number
G.   Two negative odd numbers
H.   A positive even number and a negative odd number
J.   A negative even number and a negative odd number
K.   A positive odd number and a negative odd number

27. A bag contains 11 purple marbles, 11 yellow marbles, 11 red marbles, and 11 black marbles. John begins removing marbles at random from the bag, and the first 4 marbles removed are all purple. What is the probability that the fifth marble removed will also be purple?

A. $\dfrac{7}{44}$

B. $\dfrac{7}{40}$

C. $\dfrac{1}{4}$

D. $\dfrac{5}{11}$

E. $\dfrac{7}{11}$

GO ON TO THE NEXT PAGE.

28. A student in Miss Ruane's class must repeat a test if that student earns less than 70% of the points available on that test. There were 30 points available on the first test of this semester. If Oliver scored p points on this test and therefore must repeat it, then which of the following must be true?

F. $p < 20$

G. $p > 20$

H. $p < 21$

J. $p = 21$

K. $p > 21$

29. A work crew paints a broken yellow line down the middle of a straight road $16\frac{1}{9}$ miles long over the course of 3 days. On Day 1, the crew records $5\frac{8}{27}$ miles of road painted. On Day 2, the crew forgets to measure how much road was painted, but on Day 3, the crew records $3\frac{2}{3}$ miles painted to finish the job. According to the measurements available, how many miles of road did the crew paint on Day 2 ?

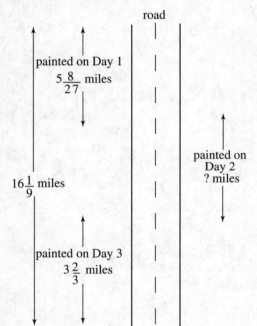

A. $7\frac{7}{27}$

B. $7\frac{4}{27}$

C. 7

D. $6\frac{7}{27}$

E. $6\frac{4}{27}$

DO YOUR FIGURING HERE.

GO ON TO THE NEXT PAGE.

30. The owners of the Movie Palace use the *Illuminator 100* light bulb in their projectors, but are now considering switching to the *Illuminator 100 Plus*, a more powerful light bulb that projects movies onto larger screens farther away. The *Illuminator 100 Plus* projects movies onto screens 108 feet wide and 180 feet from the projector, while the *Illuminator 100* projects movies onto screens only 81 feet wide, as shown in the figure below. How much farther from the projector, in feet, is the screen for the *Illuminator 100 Plus* than the screen for the *Illuminator 100* ?

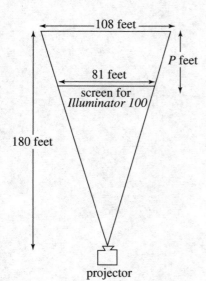

projector

F. 27
G. 40
H. 45
J. 50
K. 55

31. What is the distance, in coordinate units, between points $J(-5,4)$ and $K(6,-2)$ in the standard (x,y) coordinate plane?

A. $\sqrt{15}$
B. $\sqrt{17}$
C. $\sqrt{157}$
D. 10
E. 17

GO ON TO THE NEXT PAGE.

DO YOUR FIGURING HERE.

32. Cynthia decorates the ceiling of her bedroom with stars that glow in the dark. She puts 1 star on the ceiling on the 1st day of decorating, 2 stars on the ceiling on the 2nd day of decorating, 3 stars on the 3rd day, and so on. If she puts stars on the ceiling in this pattern for 30 days (so she puts 30 stars on the ceiling on the 30th day), then what will be the total number of stars on the ceiling at the end of the 30 days?

- **F.** 155
- **G.** 435
- **H.** 450
- **J.** 465
- **K.** 480

33. In $\triangle PQR$, side $\overline{PQ}$ is 12 inches long and side $\overline{QR}$ is 41 inches long. Which of the following CANNOT be the length, in inches, of side $\overline{PR}$?

- **A.** 17
- **B.** 30
- **C.** 38
- **D.** 44
- **E.** 52

34. Which of the following is equivalent to the expression $\dfrac{5d^2 - 2}{20d}$?

- **F.** $\dfrac{3}{20}$
- **G.** $\dfrac{1}{5d^2}$
- **H.** d
- **J.** $\dfrac{d}{4} - \dfrac{1}{10d}$
- **K.** $\dfrac{d^2 - 1}{10d}$

GO ON TO THE NEXT PAGE.

DO YOUR FIGURING HERE.

Use the following information to answer questions 35–37.

Merav's school has an Olympic-size pool that is 50 meters long, 25 meters wide, and 2 meters deep. The pool is surrounded by special non-slip tiles, as shown in the figure below.

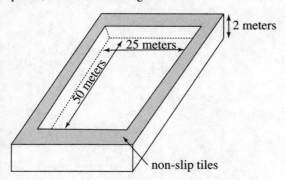

non-slip tiles

35. Merav's school laid non-slip tiles on the floor around its pool to reduce injuries among its athletes. These non-slip tiles extend 5 meters beyond the pool on all sides. What is the area, in square meters, of the floor space that has the non-slip tiles?

A.   800
B.   850
C.   900
D.   950
E.   1,000

36. For the synchronized swimming team, each swimmer needs an area within the pool to perform her routine without colliding with a teammate. Each area is 5 meters wide and 5 meters long. What is the maximum number of synchronized swimmers in the pool who can perform the routine without any collisions?

F. 75
G. 50
H. 25
J. 15
K. 10

37. Merav pays $4.00 for a ticket to her school's first swim meet to watch her classmates compete. While there, Merav buys a slice of pizza and a soda. She pays $3.75 for the pizza and $1.75 for the soda, plus 10% sales tax for both of these items. What is the total amount Merav pays for her ticket, pizza, and soda?

A. $ 3.75
B. $ 9.50
C. $10.05
D. $10.45
E. $10.75

GO ON TO THE NEXT PAGE.

38. Points *G* and *H* lie on circle *F* as shown below. If the measure of ∠*FGH* is 40°, then what is the measure of central angle ∠*GFH* ?

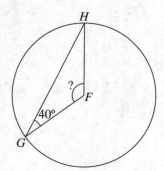

F. 60°
G. 80°
H. 100°
J. 120°
K. Cannot be determined from the information given

39. The pie chart below shows the operating expenses of Stephanie's office for the month of July, during which time the expenses totaled $10,000.

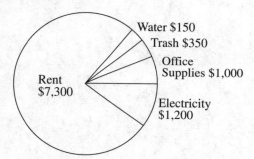

Stephanie tries to reduce her operating expenses for August by making her office more energy efficient and asking her landlord to lower her rent. She hopes to reduce her electricity expenses by $700 and her rent by $1,300. If she is successful in both of these goals and the rest of her expenses are unchanged, then what percent of her August expenses will be for office supplies?

A. 5.0%
B. 7.5%
C. 10.0%
D. 12.5%
E. 15.0%

40. Assuming *q* is a positive integer, then the difference between 14*q* and 5*q* is always divisible by:

F. 5
G. 9
H. 14
J. 19
K. 70

GO ON TO THE NEXT PAGE.

41. Ron earns $1,800 for a 6-week assignment. While working a 6-week assignment, Ron works a minimum of 20 hours each week. Ron's hourly rate of pay, therefore, depends upon how many hours he works. If r is Ron's average hourly pay, in dollars, for a 6-week assignment, then which of the following best describes r ?

A. $r \leq$ $15.00
B. $r \geq$ $15.00
C. $r \leq$ $90.00
D. $r \geq$ $90.00
E. $r \geq$ $180.00

42. P and Q both represent complex numbers. If $P = 2 + i$ and $Q = 6 + 4i$, what is the distance in coordinate units between P and Q in the complex plane?

F. $\sqrt{5}$
G. $\sqrt{7}$
H. 4
J. 5
K. 7

43. Two wires connect the top of a flagpole to the ground, as shown below. Each wire has a length of 23 feet and attaches to the ground at a point 8 feet from the flagpole. Which of the following expressions gives the angle measure, in degrees, of the angle that the wire makes with the ground?

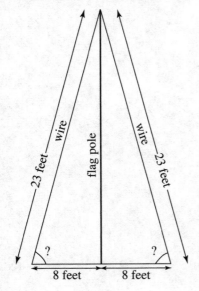

A. $\tan^{-1}\left(\dfrac{23}{8}\right)$

B. $\tan^{-1}\left(\dfrac{8}{23}\right)$

C. $\cos^{-1}\left(\dfrac{8}{23}\right)$

D. $\cos^{-1}\left(\dfrac{23}{8}\right)$

E. $\sin^{-1}\left(\dfrac{8}{23}\right)$

DO YOUR FIGURING HERE.

GO ON TO THE NEXT PAGE.

Use the following information to answer
questions 44–46.

As shown in the figure below, ΔXYZ is a right triangle with legs
of length x units and y units and hypotenuse of z units, such that
$0 < x < y$. Quadrilaterals $ABYX$, $CDZY$, and $EFXZ$ are squares.

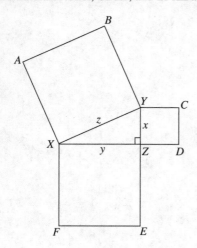

44. What is the perimeter, in units, of polygon $CDZXY$?

   F. $3x + y + z$
   G. $3x + 2y + z$
   H. $3x + 3y + 3z$
   J. $4x + y + z$
   K. $4x + 4y + 4z$

45. Given that $0 < x < y$, which of the following correctly lists the
angles $\angle BYC$, $\angle AXF$, and $\angle EZD$ in order of their measures
from least to greatest?

   A. $\angle AXF, \angle EZD, \angle BYC$
   B. $\angle BYC, \angle EZD, \angle AXF$
   C. $\angle BYC, \angle AXF, \angle EZD$
   D. $\angle EZD, \angle AXF, \angle BYC$
   E. $\angle EZD, \angle BYC, \angle AXF$

46. If $2x = z$, then what is the value of $\cos(\angle XYZ)$?

   F. $\dfrac{1}{2}$

   G. $\dfrac{\sqrt{3}}{2}$

   H. $\dfrac{2\sqrt{3}}{3}$

   J. $\sqrt{3}$

   K. 2

GO ON TO THE NEXT PAGE.

47. The sum of 4 consecutive even integers is t. What is the sum, in terms of t, of the 2 largest of these integers?

A. $\dfrac{t}{2} - 4$

B. $\dfrac{t}{2}$

C. $\dfrac{t}{2} + 4$

D. $t + 2$

E. $t + 4$

48. Figure 1 below shows the graph of $y = x^2$ in the standard (x,y) coordinate plane. Which of the following is the equation for the graph in Figure 2 ?

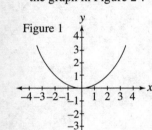
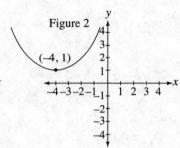

F. $y = (x - 4)^2 - 1$

G. $y = (x - 4)^2 + 1$

H. $y = (x + 1)^2 - 4$

J. $y = (x + 4)^2 - 1$

K. $y = (x + 4)^2 + 1$

49. In a piggy bank, there are pennies, nickels, dimes, and quarters that total $5.29 in value. If there are 3 times as many dimes as there are pennies, 1 more dime than nickels, and 2 more quarters than dimes, then how many nickels are in the piggy bank?

A. 11
B. 13
C. 17
D. 21
E. 23

GO ON TO THE NEXT PAGE.

50. The mean of 5 numbers is 87. The smallest of the 5 numbers is 75. What is the mean of the other 4 numbers?

F.   72

G.   87

H. $88\dfrac{2}{5}$

J.   90

K. $108\dfrac{3}{4}$

DO YOUR FIGURING HERE.

51. "If Jenny is home, then her car is in the driveway." If the previous statement is true, then which of the following must also be true?

A.   "If Jenny's car is in the driveway, then she is home."
B.   "If Jenny is not home, then her car is in the driveway."
C.   "If Jenny is not home, then her car is not in the driveway."
D.   "If Jenny's car is not in the driveway, then she is home."
E.   "If Jenny's car is not in the driveway, then she is not home."

52. If $\left(y^{0.2}\right)^{a^2-20} = y$ and $y \neq 0$, then what is the solution set of a ?

F. $\{1\}$
G. $\{-\sqrt{10}, \sqrt{10}\}$
H. $\{5\}$
J. $\{-5, 5\}$
K. $\{25\}$

53. If $g(x) = \csc x \tan x$, then which of the following trigonometric functions is equivalent to $g(x)$?

(Note: $\csc x = \dfrac{1}{\sin x}$, $\sec x = \dfrac{1}{\cos x}$, and $\cot x = \dfrac{1}{\tan x}$)

A. $g(x) = \sin x$
B. $g(x) = \cos x$
C. $g(x) = \tan x$
D. $g(x) = \csc x$
E. $g(x) = \sec x$

GO ON TO THE NEXT PAGE.

54. Evan and Ron play a game of Rock, Paper, Scissors. Each round has three equally likely outcomes for Evan: win, lose, or tie. Evan earns 2 points for a win, but he earns nothing for a loss or a tie. Let the random variable N represent the total number of points he has after 5 rounds. What is the expected value of N ?

DO YOUR FIGURING HERE.

F. $\dfrac{5}{3}$

G. 2

H. 3

J. $\dfrac{10}{3}$

K. 5

55. If the volume of a sphere is 288π cubic inches, then which of the following is the surface area, in square inches, of the same sphere?

(Note: For a sphere with radius r, the volume is $\dfrac{4}{3}\pi r^3$ and the surface area is $4\pi r^2$.)

A. 6π
B. 8π
C. 24π
D. 36π
E. 144π

56. When $x > 1$, $3\log_x x^{-2} = ?$

F. -6

G. $-\dfrac{2}{3}$

H. $\dfrac{2}{3}$

J. 1

K. $\dfrac{3}{2}$

GO ON TO THE NEXT PAGE.

57. Jamie drew a triangle bounded by the lines $y = -x$, $x = -2$, and $y = 8$ and shaded the interior, as shown in the figure below. Then Jamie decided to reflect this triangle across the y-axis and shade the interior of the new triangle. Which of the following would describe the shaded region of Jamie's new triangle?

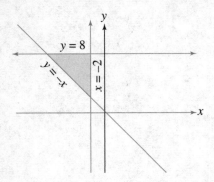

DO YOUR FIGURING HERE.

- **A.** $x \geq 2$, $y \leq 8$, $y \leq x$
- **B.** $x \geq 2$, $y \leq 8$, $y \geq x$
- **C.** $x \geq 2$, $y \leq -8$, $y \leq x$
- **D.** $x \geq -2$, $y \leq 8$, $y \geq x$
- **E.** $x \leq -2$, $y \leq -8$, $y \leq x$

58. An angle with vertex at the origin and measure θ is shown in the standard (x,y) coordinate plane below. If one side of the angle includes the positive x-axis and the other side passes through $(-12,-5)$, then what is the sine of θ ?

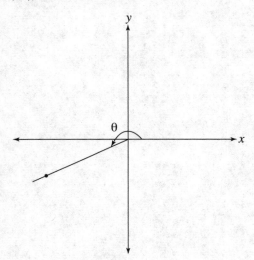

- **F.** $-\dfrac{12}{5}$
- **G.** $-\dfrac{12}{13}$
- **H.** $-\dfrac{5}{13}$
- **J.** $\dfrac{5}{12}$
- **K.** $\dfrac{13}{12}$

GO ON TO THE NEXT PAGE.

59. Side $\overline{AB}$ of parallelogram $ABCD$ is shown in the figure below. If the coordinates of A are $(7,6)$ and those of B are $(5,1)$, then $\overline{CD}$ could lie on which of the following lines?

DO YOUR FIGURING HERE.

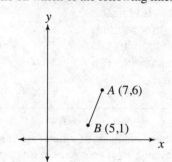

A. $y = \dfrac{5}{2}x + 9$

B. $y = x + 5$

C. $y = \dfrac{2}{5}x - 4$

D. $y = -\dfrac{2}{5}x + 4$

E. $y = -\dfrac{5}{2}x - 9$

60. If the function $f(x,y)$ is defined as $f(x,y) = (x - y)^2 + (x + y)^2$, then, for all values of c and d, $f(c^2, d^2) = $?

F. $4c^2d^2$

G. $2c^4 + 2d^4$

H. $2c^4 - 2d^4$

J. 1

K. $-4c^2d^2$

END OF TEST 2

STOP! DO NOT TURN THE PAGE UNTIL TOLD TO DO SO.

DO NOT RETURN TO A PREVIOUS TEST.

READING TEST

35 Minutes — 40 Questions

DIRECTIONS: There are several passages in this test. Each passage is accompanied by several questions. After reading a passage, choose the best answer to each question and fill in the corresponding oval on your answer document. You may refer to the passages as often as necessary.

Passage I

PROSE FICTION: This passage is adapted from the novel *Thick Skinned* by Grace McCloud, (©2005 by Grace McCloud). The setting is a forest in Oregon in 1935.

The dusk descends upon the earth like a series of linens slowly tucking a child into bed. The first sheet is just a soft lens that dampens the harsh glow of sunlight and reveals the untainted essence of the landscape. Colors seem richer, and subtle details
5 are easier to perceive. The final layer of dusk comes on thick like a quilt, burrowing the world in darkness and allowing all the daytime creatures the glorious serenity in letting go.

As my father and I gathered twigs and leaves for our campfire, it was still the earliest stage of evening. The vibrant forms
10 of daytime—flowers, trees, and radiant water—still flooded our eyes, but all the earth's activity took on the falling action of a story that had passed its climax. The tension had been resolved; the expectations now clear; the progression calm. My mother was playing her role, setting up tents and laying out pillows and
15 sleeping bags inside of them. Here, amid these familiar habits, the possibility of Dad losing his job at the plant, as so many of his friends had, began to evaporate with the disappearing sunlight.

The Wood River rolled by our campsite with a gentle gurgle. My father taught me to look at the river as he does: a metaphor
20 for the human body. "The shape of it basically stays the same," he said, "even though the underlying substance is always changing."

My father was now attempting to start the fire with the first load of kindling. As he teased bits of leaves, sticks, and dry pine needles into a stack underneath the firewood, I went to look a
25 second time for more of the same. Whenever you're trying to ignite damp, untreated wood, you need to keep some tiny flame alive by finding a steady supply of easier things to burn.

I set off from the campsite in the opposite direction from the one I had gone before, just as a fisherman would sail down-
30 stream after catching the first load of fish. The snaps and pops of the burning tinder started to come with greater frequency. Then, without even turning to look towards the campsite, I knew things were under way.

Just like the grand finale of a 4th of July fireworks display,
35 the sound of a blazing fire is a conversation of too many individual sparks to hear each of them speak.

"Honey, do you want me to start boiling some water?" my father yelled.

Even though it sounded like a question, it was really a re-
40 quest for my mother to hand him the pot. We always boil some water for the sake of the hot cocoa we would eventually sip by the fire, once all the work had been done to prepare the campsite for sleeping and the campfire for burning.

"Are you ready for your sandwich?" responded my mother,
45 as she began pulling the water pot and other food supplies out of a paper bag.

I sometimes marveled at the well-grooved partnership my parents had carved out. It seemed so familiar to both of them. Often, I considered it a sign that the once-heaving seas of young
50 love had quieted within them to something more like the standing water of a pond. However, right now the familiar habit of camping with my family was a welcome reprieve from the strange new presence at home: fear of the uncertain future. What sort of job would Dad get if he needed to find work? Would we have to
55 move away from Eugene or back into the dusty basements of my aunts' and uncles' houses where I had spent my earliest years?

"Myra, do you want your usual two?" my mom asked as she measured the amount of water we would need for our cocoa into the cooking pot. I used to sigh so mournfully at the end of
60 my cup that my mom would offer me the rest of hers. Soon, she realized she could just make me extra so that she didn't have to sacrifice her own.

"Yes, please," I replied.

After my mom had set the pot down on the flames, she stood
65 up, handed a sandwich to my father and leaned in with the same motion to get a kiss on the lips.

"Nice fire," she complimented.

GO ON TO THE NEXT PAGE.

My dad smiled in return, his face illuminated by firelight but projecting its own warmth. This time, the familiarity exchanged
70 between my parents seemed like a wonderful gift they had earned by being together for so long. Like a river, their relationship maintained a constant appearance while the substance that flowed through it continually changed.

The river next to our campsite began to disappear into thicker
75 darkness, while its sound continued throughout the night. Drifting off to sleep, I felt some peace knowing my worries would be carried away by the current.

1. As it is used in line 3, the word *untainted* can reasonably be said to mean all of the following EXCEPT:

A. natural.
B. non-toxic.
C. undistorted.
D. true.

2. The passage does NOT mention which of the following as something that at least one member of the family is doing?

F. Wading in the Wood River
G. Setting up a tent
H. Gathering pine needles
J. Igniting damp wood

3. The narrator describes her father as doing all of the following EXCEPT:

A. sharing his hot cocoa with Myra during past camping excursions.
B. exuding a sense of warmth once the campfire is ignited.
C. describing to Myra a similarity between a river and a human body.
D. helping to gather materials for use with starting the campfire.

4. The point of view from which the passage is told is best described as an adolescent girl who:

F. knows her father only has a limited amount of time left at his job and worries that her life will fall apart once his job ends.
G. hopes that her father's unemployment situation will have the upside of allowing her parents to repair their troubled marriage.
H. realizes that her father's job is in jeopardy but feels like he worries too much about things that are beyond his control.
J. recognizes the possibility of her father's unemployment and speculates about the effects it may have on the family.

5. In order to help light a fire, the passage most strongly suggests that the family has gathered:

A. dry pine needles only.
B. dry pine needles and sticks only.
C. dry pine needles, sticks, and leaves only.
D. dry pine needles, sticks, leaves, and twigs.

6. Which of the following does the narrator NOT directly mention as something seen during the earliest stages of dusk?

F. Shining water
G. Fish
H. Flowers
J. Trees

7. When the narrator's mother hands her husband a sandwich and compliments him on the fire, the narrator reacts to this interaction with a feeling of familiarity that:

A. she often finds depressing.
B. distracts her from the river.
C. she worries will not last.
D. thoroughly comforts her.

8. As it is used in line 33, the word *things* most precisely refers to:

F. 4th of July fireworks.
G. water boiling.
H. the campfire fully igniting.
J. the snaps and pops of kindling.

9. As it is used in line 10, the word *flooded* most nearly means:

A. spilled.
B. devastated.
C. filled.
D. soaked.

10. The narrator's statement in lines 49–51 most nearly means she believes her parents' relationship has:

F. not been the same since the threat of her father losing his job began to put a strain on their marriage.
G. become more stable and predictable than it was in the earlier part of their relationship.
H. degraded into something disease ridden and murky, like a mosquito infested pond.
J. somehow managed to grow more passionate and spontaneous with each passing year.

GO ON TO THE NEXT PAGE.

Passage II

SOCIAL SCIENCE: This passage is adapted from the article, "When Charities Need Help" by Ellen Wurtner, (©2009 by Ellen Wurtner).

Traditionally, when people think of charitable giving, there are only a few images that spring to mind. They probably envision dropping change into the Salvation Army basket outside retail stores around the holidays, or into a basket passed around at their
5 places of worship, or even into the hands of a homeless person whose pitiable appearance and humble request for "anything you can spare" is hard to deny. But can't we do better?

Religious institutions have typically been the societal force that drives philanthropy. This is most likely because religion
10 is vitally intertwined with morality, and charitable generosity has forever been exalted as one of the highest forms of moral behavior. Typically, churches collect alms for the poor at their church services and organize such hunger relief activities as soup kitchens.

15 Ted Stumbacher, head of the Global Empowerment Initiative, believes that truly effective philanthropy will need to have at its roots a more economic mindset. He feels religious organizations often provide only a temporary reprieve from suffering related to food, clothing, or shelter. While a noble end, this type of
20 charity succeeds more in establishing a life-long commitment to philanthropy among the churchgoing public than it does in remedying any of the systemic problems that face the world's impoverished masses.

Stumbacher points to several transformations taking place
25 over the past two decades as harbingers of the new paradigm of philanthropic organizations. Some organizations are devoting increased attention to their marketing images, using meticulous branding and celebrity endorsements to solidify consumer awareness. Despite the fact that charities are nonprofit entities, they
30 can still approach the task of maximizing their "market share" the way that other big corporations do. More commonly, nonprofits are finding non-monetary forms of assistance to tap, such as stationing clothing-recycling drop boxes around dense cities. These drop boxes not only allow used clothing to be funneled
35 to those in need but also prevent needless environmental stress by keeping these textiles out of the world's trash.

Similarly, Stumbacher notes the way charities are looking to increase the consumer choice aspect of giving. Rather than
40 using the traditional model of citizens simply dropping money into a basket intended for some generic form of relief to the poor, organizations like Donors Choose are giving philanthropists much more decision-making power in how their money is used. The website for Donors Choose allows donors to sift through a list of
45 charitable projects, enabling them to fund the cause they find most worthy. This model has proven to motivate giving by providing the giver with concrete imagery of where his money is going.

Other philanthropists, such as Karen Pitts, founder of Taste of Giving, say they are, "seeking to engage donors by merging
50 their charitable giving with other activities they enjoy." Ms. Pitts has organized wine tastings that successfully raise tens of thousands of dollars for charities. This is essentially a win-win-win situation. The wineries receive the excellent promotional context of a charitable event, the affluent wine drinkers are delighted to
55 help others while enjoying themselves, and the charities enjoy a healthy slice of the financial proceeds.

Perhaps the most forward-minded approach is that of Jacqueline Novogratz, founder of the Acumen Fund. Endeavoring to extinguish poverty at its roots, the Acumen Fund collects
60 donations in a typical way but then treats its pool of resources as investment capital. Instead of providing immediate relief of suffering, the Acumen Fund provides micro-loans to small businesses throughout third-world countries. Novogratz believes that this capitalistic approach is a more tenable form of long-term aid.

65 The old Chinese proverb, "give a man a fish and you'll feed him for a day; teach a man to fish and you'll feed him for a lifetime" seems to be at the root of Novogratz's philosophy. By providing poor people with investment capital rather than food or clothing, she hopes to nourish and sustain them economically
70 so that they can provide for themselves. Moreover, the Acumen Fund is a very hands-on enterprise, making regular inspections of the businesses they fund to verify that money is being spent shrewdly, efficiently, and honestly.

Unfortunately, what makes so many of these innovative
75 philanthropic approaches inspiring and effective is their adaptation to the specific needs of their locales. Naysayers are quick to point out that these progressive business models will not be tenable on a large scale. As these ambitious charities grow with success, they may ultimately become lumbering organizational
80 giants, such as UNICEF and the Rockefeller Foundation, and lose the flexibility, creativity, and personality that made them great.

However, even if these new tactics cannot be used in all contexts, they are still very valuable. By redefining what forms charity can take, these new approaches are widening the base of
85 donors. By employing innovative methods, these philanthropic entrepreneurs are helping larger charitable organizations to reexamine and refine their own approach.

11. The passage indicates that in their attempt to promote philanthropy, religious institutions provide all of the following benefits or services EXCEPT:

A. instructing homeless people on how to live moral lives.
B. collecting alms for the poor from churchgoers.
C. organizing events that feed those who are hungry.
D. providing temporary relief from suffering related to lack of shelter.

GO ON TO THE NEXT PAGE.

12. The author mentions clothing-recycling drop boxes and celebrity endorsements as two examples of:

F. philanthropic approaches that are gaining popularity.

G. problems Stumbacher cites with modern philanthropy.

H. ways Karen Pitts has raised money for the needy.

J. the best way to reverse environmental problems.

13. The main function of the first paragraph is to:

A. urge people to feel sympathy for and generosity towards homeless people.

B. cause the reader to picture himself in a charitable giving context.

C. discuss typical methods of charity and imply an alternative.

D. argue that the traditional methods of charity do nothing.

14. As described in the passage, philanthropy organized by religious institutions:

F. provides solutions to systemic problems that cause poverty.

G. is an example of the highest form of morality.

H. is more flexible than efforts spearheaded by other nonprofit organizations are.

J. encourages long-term dedication to charity among those who attend church.

15. When Karen Pitts talks about "other activities they enjoy" (line 49), she is most likely referring to:

A. finding positive promotional contexts for wineries in their community.

B. partaking in social events such as that of a wine tasting.

C. giving tens of thousands of dollars to charities that Pitts represents.

D. finding win-win opportunities with other donors in the wine industry.

16. The author most likely places the words "market share" in quotation marks in (line 30) to:

F. suggest that only big corporations understand how to build a successful business model.

G. imply a different sense of market share from that of corporations seeking to maximize their profits.

H. emphasize that nonprofit entities must learn to coexist with each other to avoid collective failure.

J. caution readers that nonprofits can also sometimes attain a monopoly in their markets.

17. Stumbacher feels that "religious organizations often provide only a temporary reprieve from suffering" (lines 17–18) due to their:

A. inability to boost the self-esteem of the impoverished.

B. failure to address the systemic roots of poverty.

C. overemphasis on noble ends.

D. lack of branding and celebrity endorsements.

18. According to the passage, which of the following is true about the practices of the Acumen Fund?

F. Its method of distributing funds is less typical than its method of collecting funds.

G. It attempts but fails to treat the systemic roots of poverty.

H. It endeavors to temporarily relieve impoverished people of their suffering.

J. It collects most of its donations from small third-world businesses.

19. The passage mentions which of the following as a reason some innovative philanthropic approaches are effective?

A. They integrate charity with activities the recipients enjoy.

B. They exalt charitable giving as one of the highest forms of moral behavior.

C. They are less expensive than traditional methods.

D. They can adapt to specific local needs.

20. In the context of the tenth paragraph (lines 81–86), the statement in lines 75–77 most nearly means that:

F. new modes of providing charity will succeed only in large measures.

G. philanthropists do not have a realistic sense of the scale of some problems.

H. the value of innovative business models is not based on their ability to work globally.

J. progressive philanthropic approaches ultimately will not provide any benefit.

GO ON TO THE NEXT PAGE.

Passage III

HUMANITIES: Passage A is adapted from "The Original Native Son" by Alain C. Tuppence. Passage B is adapted from "Their Eyes Were Watching Richard Wright" by Abel Cooper Tay.

Passage A

Richard Wright's achievement as an author is almost inconceivable. Although slavery ended in 1865, the period from the 1880s to the beginning of the Second World War in the 1940s might have been even worse for African-Americans in the United
5 States. There was a certain additional cruelty to the fact that African-Americans had been given their freedom from bondage but were still isolated and alienated from American political and cultural life. Richard Wright managed to rise above this oppression to become the first major African-American writer and still
10 one of the best loved.

Wright was born near Natchez, Mississippi, in 1908, and his early family life was tumultuous. His father left when he was 6, his mother was incapacitated with a stroke, and Richard moved in with his uncle. Because of all these moves and his family's difficult
15 economic circumstances, Richard did not complete a full year of school until he was 12 years old. The fact that he was valedictorian of his junior high only three years later is just one in a long string of truly stunning events in this exceptional man's life.

Wright's writing career also began around this time, when
20 as a 15-year-old he published his first story, "The Voodoo of Hell's Half-Acre," in the *Southern Register*. In 1927, Wright left the south for Chicago, where he worked as a postal clerk and read the great works during free moments. Here he also became involved with the Communist Party, which was one of the more
25 racially progressive institutions of the time. His association with left-wing politics brought him into contact with the work of Bertolt Brecht, a German playwright and theorist. The particular political slant of Brecht's plays and essays shaped the course that Wright's work would take in the next few years.

30   It was thus seemingly out of nowhere that Wright became an overnight success with the publication of his great novel *Native Son* in 1940. The novel's reception exceeded any reasonable expectation for an African-American author of the time. Rising theater and film star Orson Welles bought the rights to bring the
35 dramatized version of the book to stage and screen. The national Book of the Month Club selected *Native Son* in 1941, the first time in its then fifteen-year history that it had selected a book by an African-American author.

Wright's career only grew larger from there. French celebrity
40 philosopher Jean-Paul Sartre began to champion Wright's works abroad, and *Native Son* was translated into many languages throughout the world. A boy with no formal schooling before the age of 12, whose race seemed to expressly forbid his access to the world of letters, that such a person could achieve Wright's
45 level of success and admiration, which have now outlived him by more than 50 years, is awe-inspiring.

Passage B

No one will dispute that Richard Wright is a great author or that his success was groundbreaking. The idea, however, that Richard Wright emerged from some kind of void would be pre-
50 posterous if it were not for the fact that Wright himself seemed to believe it. Studying Wright's works can bear a good deal of fruit, but studying his life can lead us to only one conclusion: Wright was one of the greatest and most image-conscious strategists of 20th-century letters. His capacity for self-mythologizing rivals
55 only that of Ernest Hemingway, whose adventurous, romantic lifestyle abroad continues to inspire many who read him, and just as many who don't.

Although Richard Wright was clearly influenced by the works of white authors Gertrude Stein, Bertolt Brecht, and, of
60 course, Karl Marx, he was also writing into a tradition of African-American literature that, by the 1930s, was over a century old. Wright's story of his impoverished childhood and his sudden and full-fledged entry into the world of letters was actually a theme extending back to Frederick Douglass in the 1840s and Booker
65 T. Washington in the 1890s. All three of these men achieved a kind of "freedom," whether from slavery, sharecropping, or simply the oppressive shackles of race prejudice, through their education and literacy. Wright was surely cognizant of those who had come before him, but he must have been equally cognizant
70 of the fact that citing them would dilute his own myth.

Then, as anyone familiar with early 20th century literature knows, Wright was publishing shortly after one of the greatest moments in African-American literature: the Harlem Renaissance. In fact, Wright was a vibrant presence within the Harlem
75 scene. Indeed, the success of Wright's first book *Uncle Tom's Children* (1938) gave him the means to move to the epicenter of African-American culture, Harlem, New York. In fact, *Native Son*, that work we are led to believe had emerged from a vacuum, emerged from precisely this close contact Wright had with the
80 other great minds of his generation.

Literary critics, in fact, should know better. Anyone who studies the history of African-American literature knows that it was critics themselves who were out of the loop, not the writers. Critics were unaware of Hurston's *Their Eyes Were Watching God*,
85 for instance, for forty years, and now it is universally acknowledged as one of the great books of the century. As a result, critics should know how self-serving this attitude of Wright's should be, but they should also know how dreadfully wrong critics of the past had a tendency to be. Indeed, it was not that Wright was
90 working in a void; it was instead that the critics themselves were unprepared, or downright unwilling, to see the rich tapestry of influences that had produced him.

GO ON TO THE NEXT PAGE.

21. The fourth paragraph of Passage A (lines 30–38) marks a shift in the passage from:

A. an extended metaphor of the author's difficulties to a literal description of his biography.

B. a discussion of the author's background to a discussion of his public successes.

C. a biographical sketch to a piece of detailed literary criticism and analysis.

D. an analysis of the author's motives to an explanation of the author's results.

22. In Passage A, the author's descriptions of Wright suggest that the author sees Wright as ultimately:

F. impressive and brave.

G. troubled and derivative.

H. gifted and sociable.

J. shrewd and calculating.

23. The author of Passage A most nearly suggests that Bertolt Brecht was an important influence on Wright because Brecht:

A. worked with Wright during Wright's travels in Germany.

B. introduced Wright to national audiences and high-profile publishers.

C. inspired Wright to write in a particular way.

D. was one of the first people to introduce Wright to communism.

24. The author's statement "Literary critics, in fact, should know better" (line 81) is most nearly meant to:

F. indicate the author's irritation with some critics for perpetuating a falsehood.

G. state the author's approval of those who do not work in literary criticism.

H. support Wright's bold claim that he worked entirely without influences.

J. reflect Wright's position toward the literary establishment that analyzed his works.

25. Passage B indicates that compared to how Richard Wright has traditionally been understood within literary history, Wright's context and influences were:

A. dissimilar; Wright was exceptionally intelligent, but he had more formal schooling than was initially believed.

B. dissimilar; Wright did achieve a great deal, but he did not do so without influences and support.

C. similar; Wright was a brilliant author, and he worked with virtually no influences.

D. similar; Wright had a troubled childhood, and his writing explored and expressed his conflicted feelings.

26. Based on the passage, the information about *Their Eyes Were Watching God* provided in lines 83–85 is most likely meant to represent:

F. the risk of pairing authors of fiction with their fictional characters.

G. the difficulty of identifying the sources of influence in the arts.

H. an example of the ways that critics can leave obvious gaps in literary history.

J. an author whose influence is much more powerful and more widely accepted than Wright's.

27. According to the passage, Richard Wright is similar to Ernest Hemingway in that both authors:

A. were misunderstood for many years by critics who were unaware of their works.

B. stated openly that they had no literary influences and no formal education.

C. wrote their greatest works shortly after the Harlem Renaissance.

D. had public personalities that were separate from the books they wrote.

GO ON TO THE NEXT PAGE.

Questions 28–30 ask about both passages.

28. Which of the following statements provides the most accurate comparison of the tone of each passage?

   F. Passage A is respectful and reverential, while Passage B is measured and skeptical.

   G. Passage A is elated and amicable, while Passage B is pessimistic and contrarian.

   H. Both passages begin artistic and loose but conclude with technical and precise arguments.

   J. Both passages begin by doubting conventional wisdom but conclude by accepting that wisdom.

29. Compared to the author of Passage A, the author of Passage B provides more detail about:

   A. Wright's immediate context and professional strategy.

   B. Wright's background and education.

   C. the direct influences of Bertolt Brecht and Ernest Hemingway.

   D. the contemporary political influences on Wright's life.

30. It can reasonably be inferred that when thinking about Richard Wright's success as an author, compared to the author of Passage B, the author of Passage A feels:

   F. less skeptical of how political events shape authors' professional lives.

   G. less dismissive of the literary career of Ernest Hemingway.

   H. more impressed that Wright was able to overcome his difficult past.

   J. more neutral as to whether Wright's success could properly be called his own.

GO ON TO THE NEXT PAGE.

THIS PAGE IS INTENTIONALLY LEFT BLANK.

GO ON TO THE NEXT PAGE.

Passage IV

NATURAL SCIENCE: This passage is adapted from the article "Unearthing the Greatest Fossil Ever Found" by Stanley Walsh, (©2009 by Stanley Walsh).

Evolutionary biologists can finally breathe a sigh of relief. Those who have been bursting at the seams to blurt out the "big secret" can finally shout it from the mountaintops, and those who have been hunting tirelessly for a "missing link" to solidify the
5 Darwinian theory of evolution can finally rest easily.

The "big secret" and "missing link" are one and the same: a 47-million-year-old, uncannily preserved fossil of an ancient ancestor of the primate family, nicknamed Ida. After two years of secretly performing research on the fossil, experts are ready
10 to present their findings to the world. They firmly believe that the lemur monkey they have preserved in polyester resin is conclusive evidence of a transitional species, a fork in the road where the genetic tree branches off in the direction that eventually gives rise to such simian species as monkeys, apes, and humans.

15 Two things make this particular specimen so valuable. It is older than any previously found primate fossil, vastly predating the previous record-holder, Lucy, which is a 3.18-million-year-old fossil. Furthermore, it is one of the most complete fossils ever found, with 95% of the skeleton preserved. In fact, the fos-
20 silization conditions were so perfect in Ida's case that scientists could actually still analyze the last meal Ida had before apparently falling into a crater and dying of carbon dioxide poisoning. By contrast, Lucy's remains were only 40% complete, lacking a skull among other important features.

25 Ironically, for such a monumentally important fossil, Ida has actually been flying under the radar for the past 25 years. An amateur fossil hunter first discovered her in 1983, in a volcanic crater-lake called the Messel Pit, just outside of Frankfurt, Germany. Because the Messel Pit was already considered a bounti-
30 ful source of fossils, Ida's discoverer did not assume there was anything distinctive about the discovery and hung Ida on his wall as a display piece for the next 20 years. He revered it as a piece of natural art, not recognizing its exceedingly old age as a fossil.

Eventually, the piece made its way to a display in the 2006
35 Hamburg Fossil and Mineral Fair in Germany. A researcher from Norway's National History Museum, Professor Jorn Hurum, was immediately entranced upon seeing Ida. Unfortunately, his enthusiasm meant that the fossil dealer could charge an outlandish price of roughly 1 million dollars. Determined to secure this
40 landmark specimen for the sake of scientific inquiry, Professor Hurum quickly raised the needed bounty and brought Ida home to Oslo, Norway.

For the next two years, a team of top scientists studied Ida's features and attempted to integrate the information into the
45 genetic tree of the primates. All the while, the scientists knew they were on the cusp of providing the most conclusive evidence yet of the accuracy of Darwin's theory of evolution. However, they had all signed non-disclosure agreements that prevented them from discussing these tentative findings with others in the
50 field or the media.

Charles Darwin's revolutionary book *The Origin of Species*, published in 1859, first detailed the theory of natural selection. It was extremely controversial in its time, and its contention that humans evolved from a lineage of monkeys remains an uncom-
55 fortable idea to many even to this day. Despite the 98.4% genetic similarity that humans have to chimpanzees, many of Darwin's skeptics have routinely rested their cases on the fact that there was a gigantic hole in the fossil evidence that relates to where the branch of higher primates begins.

60 Around 50 million years ago, the first primates are thought to have emerged, two different species called *tarsidae* and *adapidae*. Scientists have been unsure which species ultimately led to the higher primates (monkeys and humans). The discovery of Ida, an *adapid* with several human-like features, suggests that
65 *adapidae* are the ancestors of modern humans.

With so many anatomical features vividly preserved in Ida's fossilized remains, scientists have been able to identify several telltale similarities Ida has to modern humans. One feature that distinguishes Ida's species from non-anthropoid primates is
70 the talus bone, a bone that turns the corner between the leg and the foot. Her eyes face forward, which makes her visual fields overlap, a requirement for accurate depth perception. Her hands and feet have nails, rather than claws, and opposable thumbs. Both characteristics allow for the use of appendages in a more
75 refined way, whether it be peeling fruit, climbing, or, in the case of humans and their closer ancestors, using tools.

The debate over evolution is likely to continue for many years. However, the discovery of Ida has given evolutionary scientists a stronger supporting piece of evidence than they ever dreamed
80 was possible. As Harold Zemeckels, a professor of evolutionary biology at Emerson University, puts it, "This fossil is essentially a prayer answered, a perfect time capsule that's been miraculously gift-wrapped for posterity."

31. The language of the first paragraph is most likely intended to convey a sense of:

A. warning that a secret will be revealed.
B. anguish for an ongoing scientific struggle.
C. reluctance to accept a theory of evolution.
D. anticipation for the topic the passage will discuss.

GO ON TO THE NEXT PAGE.

32. According to the passage, the "big secret" and the "missing link" refer to:

- **F.** Ida only.
- **G.** Lucy only.
- **H.** Ida, and the more recently discovered Lucy.
- **J.** Lucy, and the more recently discovered Ida.

33. The passage characterizes the idea that Ida was a transitional species which later resulted in simians as:

- **A.** a conclusion that results from an extended period of studying the fossil.
- **B.** a conclusion that stems from analyzing the polyester resin.
- **C.** a speculation based on ruling out *tarsidae* as simian ancestors.
- **D.** a speculation that springs from scientists' desire to find a "missing link."

34. The passage implies that the price that was paid to obtain Ida's fossil from the private collector was:

- **F.** outlandish because Lucy, an even older fossil, was cheaper.
- **G.** higher than is customary due to the buyer's obvious interest.
- **H.** unusual given how little the private collector valued it.
- **J.** high due to its being discovered in a rare site for fossils.

35. In the passage, the amateur fossil hunter who found Ida in the Messel Pit is said to have:

- **A.** not immediately assumed Ida was special and so kept it for himself.
- **B.** not immediately assumed Ida was special and so showed it to fellow scientists.
- **C.** immediately assumed Ida was special and so brought it to the Fossil and Mineral Fair.
- **D.** immediately assumed Ida was special and so brought it to Oslo, Norway.

36. Which of the following best summarizes the objection of those who remain skeptical of Darwin's theory of evolution?

- **F.** 98.4% is not a close enough genetic similarity to suggest genetic relation.
- **G.** They are uncomfortable with the idea that chimpanzees evolved from lemurs.
- **H.** There are not enough fossils available that date before 1859.
- **J.** There is some explanation missing as to how and when higher primates evolved.

37. The passage states that Lucy was not:

- **A.** at one point the oldest fossil known to man.
- **B.** found in worse condition than was Ida.
- **C.** found with a well preserved head.
- **D.** only 40% complete as a fossil.

38. It can most reasonably be inferred that the word *enthusiasm* in line 38 refers to Professor Hurum's enthusiasm for:

- **F.** the fossil dealer.
- **G.** the specimen.
- **H.** his home in Oslo.
- **J.** the Fossil and Mineral Fair.

39. The author points out that scientists "could actually still analyze the last meal Ida had" (line 21) primarily to:

- **A.** foreshadow the valuable clues scientists derived from her last meal.
- **B.** explain why comparatively little was learned from Lucy's fossil.
- **C.** underscore how well preserved Ida's fossil was by its environment.
- **D.** argue for a new theory on the diets of early primates.

40. As it relates to the passage, the eighth paragraph (lines 60–65) serves mainly to:

- **F.** explain the misconceptions that led some to doubt Darwin's theory.
- **G.** demonstrate the confusion that results from classifying ancient fossils.
- **H.** illustrate a scientific context in which Ida's fossil has proven helpful.
- **J.** argue against the prevailing theory that humans came from *tarsidae*.

END OF TEST 3

STOP! DO NOT TURN THE PAGE UNTIL TOLD TO DO SO.

DO NOT RETURN TO A PREVIOUS TEST.

SCIENCE TEST

35 Minutes–40 Questions

DIRECTIONS: There are several passages in this test. Each passage is followed by several questions. After reading a passage, choose the correct answer to each question and fill in the corresponding oval on your answer document. You may refer to the passages as often as necessary.

You are NOT permitted to use a calculator on this test.

Passage I

Hamsters forage and hoard many types of seeds and nuts. Scientists hypothesized that the European hamster (*Cricetus cricetus*) would be more drawn to hoard seeds soaked in certain fruit juices over seeds soaked in other fruit juices. Three experiments were performed to test this hypothesis.

Experiment 1

Seeds from pumpkins (*Cucurbita pepa*) were soaked in juice from one of five different fruits (mango, lemon, coconut, apple, and orange) so that the seeds would absorb the fruit juice scent and flavor. The seeds were removed from the juice and dried, and 10 seeds soaked in each fruit juice were equally spaced throughout a glass cage. Then, a *C. cricetus* hamster that was recently captured in Belgium was placed in the center of the cage. Over the next 30 minutes, for each seed the hamster collected, the fruit juice in which it was soaked was recorded. For each seed the hamster placed in its cheek, an additional seed soaked in the same juice was added to the cage. This process was repeated with an additional 24 recently captured *C. cricetus* hamsters from Belgium. Figure 1 shows the average number of seeds collected from each type of fruit juice in 30 minutes.

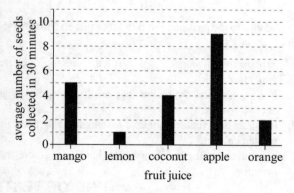

Figure 1

Experiment 2

The procedure for Experiment 1 was repeated with the same set of 25 hamsters from Belgium, which had been kept in captivity in the research facility for 2 months. Figure 2 shows the average number of seeds collected from each type of fruit juice in 30 minutes.

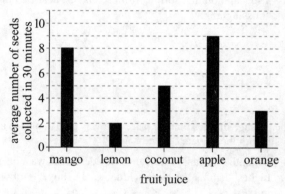

Figure 2

Experiment 3

The procedure for Experiment 1 was repeated except with 25 recently captured *C. cricetus* hamsters from Russia. Figure 3 shows the average number of seeds collected from each type of fruit juice in 30 minutes.

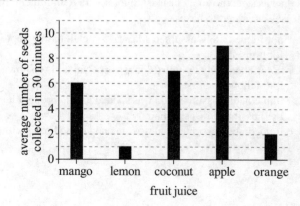

Figure 3

GO ON TO THE NEXT PAGE.

1. Suppose that an additional experiment was performed in which the scientists repeated Experiment 1 except that they recorded the fruit juice of the seeds collected by the hamsters over ten minutes. Assuming that the hamsters collected seeds for the entirety of Experiment 1, would the total number of seeds collected in the new experiment more likely have been greater than or less than the total number of seeds collected in Experiment 1 ?

    A. Greater, because the amount of time the hamsters spent collecting seeds would have been three times as great.
    B. Greater, because the amount of time the hamsters spent collecting seeds would have been twice as great.
    C. Less, because the amount of time the hamsters spent collecting seeds would have been one-half as great.
    D. Less, because the amount of time the hamsters spent collecting seeds would have been one-third as great.

2. Was the scientists' hypothesis supported by the results of the experiments?

    F. No; in each experiment, on average, the hamsters collected more seeds soaked in apple juice than any other fruit juice in 30 minutes.
    G. No; in each experiment, on average, the hamsters collected the same number of seeds soaked in each fruit juice in 30 minutes.
    H. Yes; in each experiment, on average, the hamsters collected more seeds soaked in apple juice than any other fruit juice in 30 minutes.
    J. Yes; in each experiment, on average, the hamsters collected the same number of seeds soaked in each fruit juice in 30 minutes.

3. How many total hamsters were needed to complete Experiments 1–3 ?

    A. 25
    B. 40
    C. 50
    D. 75

4. Which of the following experiments could be used to determine if the fruit juice preferences of recently captured European hamsters from Russia are the same for a different species of food source?

    F. Repeat Experiment 2 with *C. pepa* as the food source.
    G. Repeat Experiment 2 with a species other than *C. pepa* as the food source.
    H. Repeat Experiment 3 with *C. pepa* as the food source.
    J. Repeat Experiment 3 with a species other than *C. pepa* as the food source.

5. Which of the following calculations was most likely used to calculate each of the values in Figure 3 ?

    A. $\dfrac{\text{Number of seeds of each fruit juice collected by hamsters from Russia}}{\text{Number of hamsters from Russia}}$

    B. $\dfrac{\text{Number of seeds of each fruit juice collected by hamsters from Belgium}}{\text{Number of hamsters from Belgium}}$

    C. $\dfrac{\text{Total number of seeds collected by hamsters from Russia}}{\text{Number of hamsters from Russia}}$

    D. $\dfrac{\text{Total number of seeds collected by hamsters from Belgium}}{\text{Number of hamsters from Belgium}}$

6. Which of the following statements regarding the hamsters used in Experiments 1 and 3 is consistent with the information provided in the passage?

    F. The hamsters used in Experiment 1 are neither members of the same genus nor species as those used in Experiment 3.
    G. The hamsters used in Experiment 1 are members of the same genus as those used in Experiment 3, but they are not members of the same species.
    H. The hamsters used in Experiment 1 are members of the same species as those used in Experiment 3, but they are not members of the same genus.
    J. The hamsters used in both Experiments 1 and 3 are members of the same genus and species.

7. Which of the following statements is most consistent with the results of Experiments 1 and 2 ? After the captured hamsters from Belgium spent 2 months in captivity, they collected, on average:

    A. fewer seeds in 30 minutes than did the recently captured hamsters from Russia.
    B. more seeds in 30 minutes than they did when they were recently captured.
    C. fewer apple juice soaked seeds in 30 minutes than did the recently captured hamsters from Russia.
    D. more apple juice soaked seeds in 30 minutes than they did when they were recently captured.

GO ON TO THE NEXT PAGE.

Passage II

Dye-sensitized solar cells (DSSCs) are a cost-effective way of producing electricity from sunlight. One advantage of DSSCs compared to other types of solar cells is that they are composed of readily available materials, such as titanium dioxide. Scientists studied the effectiveness of DSSCs using mixtures of two metal oxides.

Experiment

In each trial, the following steps were performed:

1. A mixture of titanium dioxide (TiO_2) and zinc oxide (ZnO) was combined with 20 mL dilute nitric acid in a 100 mL beaker and stirred to form a paste.

2. The paste was applied with a spatula to a negative electrode made of a conductive glass slide and then left to dry for 10 minutes.

3. The coated glass slide was placed into a preheated oven and heated at a high temperature for 5 minutes, then removed from the oven and left to cool for 1 hour.

4. Blackberry juice, a dark-colored natural dye, was applied to the side of the glass slide containing the oxide paste and left to dry for 30 minutes until the dye was adsorbed onto the oxide surface.

5. A positive electrode made of glass coated with graphite was pressed onto the dye-coated slide.

6. The two electrodes were connected by wires to the two ends of a multimeter and the assembly was exposed to sunlight to measure the *conversion efficiency,* the energy produced by the cell as a percentage of the total incident solar energy.

For any given combination of conditions (identity of primary oxide, concentration of secondary oxide, and heating temperature), 3 trials were conducted. The table shows, for each set of trials, the experimental conditions and the average conversion efficiency of the solar cells.

Set of trials	Primary oxide	Concentration of secondary oxide (% by mass)	Temperature (°C)	Average conversion efficiency (%)
1–3	TiO_2	10	400	14.4
4–6	TiO_2	20	400	12.6
7–9	TiO_2	40	400	10.7
10–12	ZnO	10	400	5.6
13–15	ZnO	20	400	7.0
16–18	ZnO	40	400	9.2
19–21	TiO_2	20	300	9.5
22–24	TiO_2	20	500	15.9
25–27	TiO_2	20	600	17.8
28–30	ZnO	20	300	6.1
31–33	ZnO	20	500	9.4

8. Which step was most likely performed to ensure that the solar cell would absorb a sufficient amount of sunlight once it was exposed to light?

F. Step 1
G. Step 2
H. Step 3
J. Step 4

9. According to the table, which combination of primary oxide, concentration of secondary oxide, and temperature resulted in the *lowest* average conversion efficiency?

	primary oxide	secondary oxide concentration	temperature
A.	TiO_2	20%	300°C
B.	TiO2	20%	400°C
C.	ZnO	40%	400°C
D.	ZnO	20%	500°C

GO ON TO THE NEXT PAGE.

10. Consider the results for each combination of secondary oxide concentration and temperature that was tested. Compared with the average conversion efficiency in the ZnO trials, the average conversion efficiency in the TiO_2 trials was:

F. always higher.
G. always lower.
H. always the same.
J. sometimes higher and sometimes lower.

11. Which of the following gives the volume of dilute nitric acid used in the experiment?

A. 11 trials × $\dfrac{(20\ mL\ nitric\ acid)}{trial}$

B. 11 trials × $\dfrac{(100\ mL\ nitric\ acid)}{trial}$

C. 33 trials × $\dfrac{(20\ mL\ nitric\ acid)}{trial}$

D. 33 trials × $\dfrac{(100\ mL\ nitric\ acid)}{trial}$

12. The average conversion efficiency in Trials 4–6 differed from that in Trials 19–21 because the 2 sets of trials differed with respect to the:

F. identity of the primary oxide.
G. concentration of the secondary oxide.
H. temperature.
J. time for which the slide was heated.

13. For the trials conducted with TiO_2 as the primary oxide and 20% secondary oxide by mass, as the temperature increased, the average conversion efficiency:

A. decreased only.
B. increased only.
C. decreased and then increased.
D. increased and then decreased.

14. The mixture formed in Step 1 of each trial had a mass of 21 g. Based on this information and the table, the mass of the secondary oxide added to the mixture in Step 1 of Trial 14 was closest to which of the following?

F. 0.2 g
G. 0.4 g
H. 2 g
J. 4 g

GO ON TO THE NEXT PAGE.

Passage III

In order to estimate the irrigation needs, groundwater recharge rates, and flash flood risks for a region, it is necessary to examine the distribution of precipitation throughout the year. A researcher calculated the total precipitation over each 5-day period for a year in 9 cities. When the 5-day precipitation, P_5, exceeded the North American average of 10 mm, the 5-day excess (FDE) was calculated by subtracting 10 mm from P_5. When P_5 was less than 10 mm, the 5-day shortfall (FDS) was calculated by subtracting P_5 from 10 mm.

Table 1 lists the longitude, the sum of the FDE values, and the sum of the FDS values for the year 2018 for 9 North American cities.

		Annual sum of:	
City	Longitude	FDE (mm)	FDS (mm)
Philadelphia, PA	75.17° W	1,158	205
Toronto, ON	79.38° W	522	323
New Orleans, LA	90.07° W	1,068	233
Oklahoma City, OK	97.52° W	501	474
Cheyenne, WY	104.82° W	189	461
Tucson, AZ	110.97° W	167	536
Boise, ID	116.20° W	69	528
Reno, NV	119.81° W	107	553
San Francisco, CA	122.42° W	232	570

Table 1

Note: FDE = P_5 – 10 mm for all $P_5 > 10$ mm;
FDS = 10 mm – P_5 for all $P_5 < 10$ mm

For the city of New Orleans, the annual sums of both the FDE values and FDS values were determined for each of the years 1995–2015 (see Figure 1).

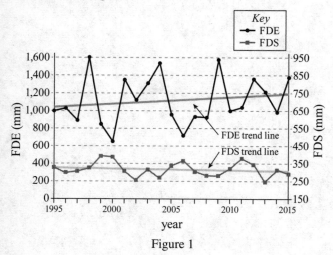

Figure 1

15. According to Figure 1, did the maximum FDE occur during the same year as the minimum FDS ?

A. Yes; the maximum FDE and the minimum FDS both occurred in 1998.
B. Yes; the maximum FDE and the minimum FDS both occurred in 2013.
C. No; the maximum FDE occurred in 1998, whereas the minimum FDS occurred in 2013.
D. No; the maximum FDE occurred in 2013, whereas the minimum FDE occurred in 1998.

16. Based on Table 1, in Tucson, the total FDS was approximately how many times as great as the total FDE ?

F. $\frac{1}{6}$

G. $\frac{1}{3}$

H. 3

J. 6

17. Based on Table 1, for all the cities between 95° W and 120° W longitude, which of the following statements describing FDE or FDS is accurate? In 2018, the total:

A. FDE was always greater than the total FDS.
B. FDE was always greater than 100.
C. FDS was always greater than the total FDE.
D. FDS was always greater than 450.

18. For a particular 5-day period, the P_5 = 10 mm. For this period, what FDE value would be calculated and what FDS value would be calculated?

	FDE	FDS
F.	−1	1
G.	0	0
H.	1	0
J.	1	1

GO ON TO THE NEXT PAGE.

19. Which of the following graphs best illustrates the longitude and the FDE for each of the cities listed in Table 1 ?

A.

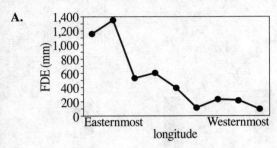

B.

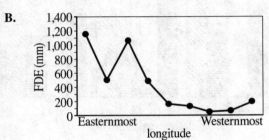

C.

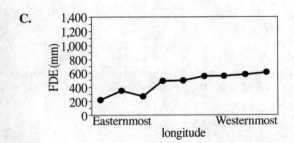

D.

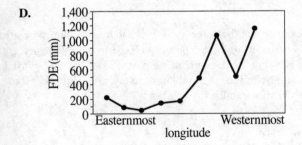

20. Consider the FDS equation and the FDS trend line shown in Figure 1. The slope of the trend line is negative, which indicates that, over the 21 yr period, the average value of P_5:

F. increased only.
G. decreased only.
H. remained constant.
J. increased then decreased.

GO ON TO THE NEXT PAGE.

Passage IV

The plant *Toxicodendron vernix* can cause contact dermatitis. Scientists conducted 2 experiments to study the *herbicidal* (plant-killing) activity of a particular natural weed killer.

Experiment 1

One hundred liters of an *aqueous solution* (AS) that was 10% NaCl by volume was sprayed onto a 5 m by 5 m square plot of land containing 50 *T. vernix* plants. This procedure was performed twice more on two additional plots of land, except that the percents by volume of NaCl were 20% and 30%, respectively. One hundred liters of pure distilled water was sprayed on a fourth plot of land. Next, a second set of land plots was similarly prepared, except that weed killer was substituted for NaCl. All 8 plots of land were exposed to 3 hours of sunlight at the same intensity and then covered with tarps. The land plots were then observed again after 2 days, and the *percent survival* (percent of the *T. vernix* that were still alive) was determined for each land plot.

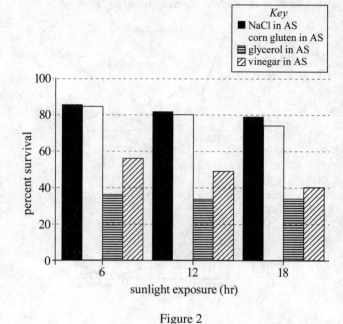

Figure 2

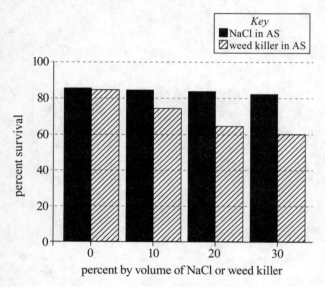

Figure 1

Experiment 2

A sample of the weed killer was separated into its three ingredients: corn gluten, *glycerol* (a sugar alcohol), and vinegar. One hundred liters of an AS that was 35% NaCl by volume was sprayed onto a 5 m by 5 m square plot of land containing 50 *T. vernix* plants. This process was repeated 3 times, except that each time a different ingredient from the weed killer was substituted for NaCl. Then, 2 more sets of 4 land plots were similarly treated. Each set of 4 land plots was exposed to sunlight of the same intensity for a different number of hours: 6 hours, 12 hours, 18 hours. After 2 days, the percent survival was determined for each plot (see Figure 2).

21. In Experiment 2, at each sunlight exposure, which AS mixture resulted in the *fewest* surviving *T. vernix*?

   A. NaCl in AS
   B. Corn gluten in AS
   C. Glycerol in AS
   D. Vinegar in AS

22. Suppose that the percent survival had been documented after 24 hours of sunlight exposure in Experiment 2. The percent survival of the *T. vernix* in the plot of land that was sprayed with glycerol in AS would most likely have been closest to which of the following values?

   F. 5%
   G. 35%
   H. 45%
   J. 65%

23. In Experiment 2, for which of the sunlight exposures did the scientists include a control to determine whether a substantial decrease in *T. vernix* survival occurred in the absence of a natural weed killer ingredient?

   A. 6 hours only
   B. 12 hours only
   C. 18 hours only
   D. All 3 sunlight exposures

GO ON TO THE NEXT PAGE.

24. In Experiment 1, which of the following questions were the researchers most likely attempting to answer?

F. Does the percent survival for *T. vernix* sprayed with corn starch differ from the percent survival for *T. vernix* sprayed with glycerol?

G. Does the percent survival for *T. vernix* sprayed with weed killer differ from the percent survival for *T. vernix* sprayed with NaCl ?

H. Is the percent survival of *T. vernix* sprayed with NaCl and *T. vernix* sprayed with vinegar affected by increasing the sunlight exposure from 3 hours to 6 hours?

J. Is the percent survival of *T. vernix* sprayed with NaCl and *T. vernix* sprayed with weed killer affected by increasing the sunlight exposure from 3 hours to 6 hours?

25. In Experiment 1, the scientists used a knife to make a 1 cm cut into the *cambium layer* of each plant. Living *T. vernix* have a green cambium layer; dead *T. vernix* do not. Approximately what percent of the *T. vernix* in the plot of land that was sprayed with 10% weed killer in AS did not have a green cambium layer?

A. 25%
B. 35%
C. 75%
D. 80%

26. To best compare the herbicidal ability of each of the 3 natural weed killer ingredients tested in Experiment 2 to the herbicidal ability of natural weed killer that has not been separated into its ingredients, the scientists should repeat the procedures of:

F. Experiment 1, except include a plot of land sprayed with weed killer in AS for each set of land plots.

G. Experiment 1, except include a plot of land sprayed with a glycerol in AS for each set of land plots.

H. Experiment 2, except include a plot of land sprayed with weed killer in AS for all three days.

J. Experiment 2, except include a plot of land sprayed with glycerol in AS for all three days.

27. A *T. vernix* cell possesses which of the following sets of characteristics?

A. Has a nucleus; has a cell wall
B. Has a nucleus; does not have a cell wall
C. Does not have a nucleus; has a cell wall
D. Does not have a nucleus; does not have a cell wall

GO ON TO THE NEXT PAGE.

Passage V

To demonstrate static electricity, a teacher had students suspend 2 identical acrylic bars from each of 3 wooden beams. Then, the students rubbed each acrylic bar with a piece of fabric (either silk cloth or faux fur) as shown in Figure 1.

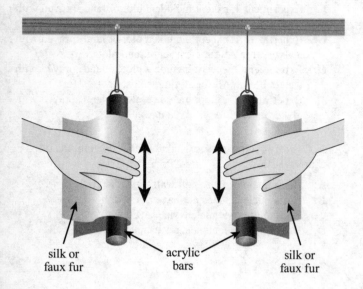

silk or faux fur   acrylic bars   silk or faux fur

Figure 1

On the first beam, a student used a silk cloth on both bars, and the bars moved away from each other. On the second beam, a student used a piece of faux fur on both bars, and the bars moved away from each other. On the last beam, a student used a piece of silk cloth on the acrylic bar on the left and faux fur on the acrylic bar on the right, and the bars moved towards each other. See Figure 2.

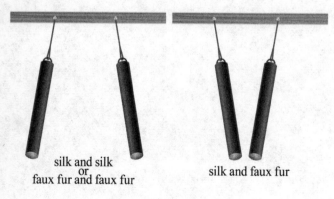

silk and silk
or
faux fur and faux fur   silk and faux fur

Figure 2

The teacher asked each of 3 students to explain these results.

Student 1

Rubbing the acrylic bar with a piece of fabric generated static electricity because negatively charged subatomic particles were transferred between the two materials. The type of fabric affected the direction of transfer: negative charges were transferred out of the bar to the silk and into the bar from the faux fur.

In an atom, the positive charges are contained in the nucleus, while the negative charges orbit the nucleus. When two materials come into contact, the negative charges can move from the atoms on one material to the atoms on the other material, creating both positively and negatively charged ions. Ions of like charges repel each other, while ions of opposite charges attract each other.

Student 2

Static electricity was generated, and the type of fabric affected the direction of transfer as Student 1 said, except that the charges transferred were positive.

When two materials come into contact, the positive charges can move from the atoms on one material to the atoms on the other material. The material that receives positive charges will contain positive ions that are attracted to negative ions and repulsed by other positive ions. The material that loses positive charges will form negative ions that are attracted to positive ions and repulsed by other negative ions.

Student 3

Static electricity was created when charged ions transferred from one material to the other.

Silk has a lot of positive ions, so when the silk cloth was rubbed on the bar, some of these positive ions transferred onto the bar. Faux fur, on the other hand, has a lot of negative ions, so when the faux fur was rubbed on a bar, some of the negative ions were transferred onto the bar. Ions of like charges repel each other, while ions of opposite charges attract each other.

28. Which of the following statements, each of which was stated by or implied by Student 2, is scientifically *inaccurate*?

   F. Rubbing two materials together can generate static electricity.
   G. Charges of like sign are repulsed by each other.
   H. Ions can be either positively or negatively charged.
   J. The subatomic particles that orbit the nucleus of an atom are positively charged.

29. Assume that an individual atom on the acrylic bar becomes charged after the transfer of a charged particle from an atom on the faux fur. If Student 1's explanation is correct, the charged particle transferred to the atom on the bar was most likely:

   A. an electron.
   B. a proton.
   C. a photon.
   D. a neutron.

GO ON TO THE NEXT PAGE.

30. If Student 1's explanation is correct, then a neutral atom has:

   F. more positive charges orbiting the nucleus than negative charges inside the nucleus.

   G. fewer negative charges orbiting the nucleus than positive charges inside the nucleus.

   H. the same number of positive charges orbiting the nucleus as negative charges inside the nucleus.

   J. the same number of negative charges orbiting the nucleus as positive charges inside the nucleus.

31. Based on Student 1's explanation, when a silk cloth was used on the acrylic bar on the left and faux fur was used on the acrylic bar on the right, did the bars experience an attractive or repulsive force towards each other?

   A. Attractive, because negative charges moved into the bar on the left and charges moved out of the bar on the right.

   B. Attractive, because the negative charges moved out of the bar on the left moved into the bar on the right.

   C. Repulsive, because negative charges moved into both bars.

   D. Repulsive, because negative charges moved out of both bars.

32. Which of the following figures is consistent with both Student 3's explanation and Figure 2?

F.
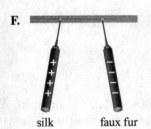
silk   faux fur

G.
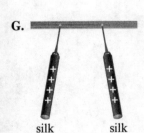
silk   silk

H.

silk faux fur

J.

faux fur faux fur

33. In regard to the transfer of charges between materials, how does Student 2's explanation differ from Student 3's explanation? Student 2 believes that:

   A. either positively or negatively charged subatomic particles are transferred, while Student 3 believes that only positive ions are transferred.

   B. either positively or negatively charged ions are transferred, while Student 3 believes only positive subatomic particles are transferred.

   C. only positively charged subatomic particles are transferred, while Student 3 believes either positive or negative ions are transferred.

   D. only positive ions are transferred, while Student 3 believes that either positively or negatively charged subatomic particles are transferred.

34. Which of the following procedures would best test Student 3's explanation? Using the same types of fabric as used in the three experiments, determine if:

   F. a piece of silk cloth and a piece of faux fur that have not yet been used on the acrylic bars move towards each other when held near each other.

   G. a piece of silk cloth that has not yet been used on the acrylic bars moves towards an uncharged acrylic bar when held near it.

   H. a piece of faux fur that has not yet been used on the acrylic bars moves towards an uncharged acrylic bar when held near it.

   J. two pieces of silk cloth and faux fur that have already been in contact with the acrylic bars move towards an uncharged acrylic bar when held near it.

GO ON TO THE NEXT PAGE.

Passage VI

Figure 1 shows how an aqueous solution's *resistivity* (a measure of a material's ability to resist electrical current) varies with its electrical conductivity. Figure 2 shows how the current produced by a particular battery at room temperature (20 °C) varies with the resistivity of the aqueous solution used in the battery.

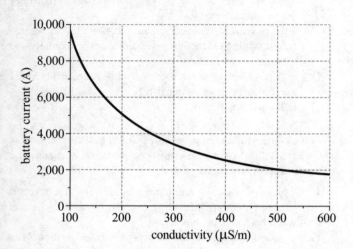

Figure 1

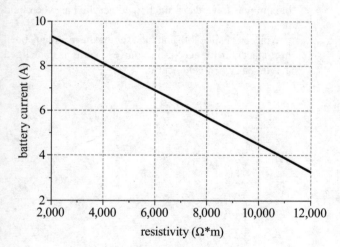

Figure 2

At room temperature, an aqueous solution has a constant electrical conductivity. Figure 3 shows, for 3 salts, how the electrical conductivities of aqueous solutions at room temperature vary with the molar concentrations of the dissolved salts.

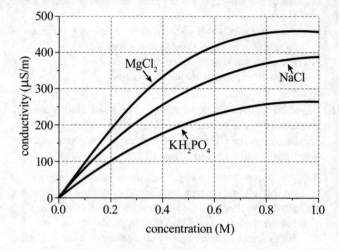

Figure 3

35. Based on Figures 1 and 2, as conductivity increases from 200 µS/m to 500 µS/m at room temperature, battery current:

A. decreases only.
B. increases only.
C. decreases, then increases.
D. increases, then decreases.

36. Based on Figure 2, a battery that produces a current of 2 A will contain an aqueous solution with a resistivity closest to which of the following?

F. 10,000 Ω·m
G. 12,000 Ω·m
H. 14,000 Ω·m
J. 16,000 Ω·m

GO ON TO THE NEXT PAGE.

37. According to Figure 3, at room temperature, pure H_2O has a conductivity of:

A. 0 μS/m.
B. 200 μS/m.
C. 400 μS/m.
D. 500 μS/m.

38. Based on Figure 2, will the battery supply more power if it contains a solution with a resistivity of 5,000 Ω·m or 10,000 Ω·m?

F. 5,000 Ω·m, because it will produce a higher current.
G. 5,000 Ω·m, because it will produce a lower current.
H. 10,000 Ω·m, because it will produce a higher current.
J. 10,000 Ω·m, because it will produce a lower current.

39. Consider a battery containing a 0.5 M aqueous solution of $MgCl_2$. Based on Figures 1–3, if the battery is at room temperature, the current produced by the battery will be closest to which of the following?

A. 0 A
B. 2 A
C. 7 A
D. 9 A

40. Consider two 0.2 M aqueous solutions, one of $MgCl_2$ and one of KH_2PO_4, each kept at room temperature. A student claimed that the KH_2PO_4 solution will have a higher resistivity than the $MgCl_2$ solution. Do Figures 1 and 3 support this claim?

F. Yes, because a lower conductivity results from the $MgCl_2$ solution.
G. Yes, because a lower conductivity results from the KH_2PO_4 solution.
H. No, because a lower conductivity results from the $MgCl_2$ solution.
J. No, because a lower conductivity results from the KH_2PO_4 solution.

GO ON TO THE NEXT PAGE.

Chapter 31
Practice Exam 3:
Answers
and Explanations

*Note on scoring: please refer to the Scoring Conversion Worksheet and Score Conversion Chart on pages 539 and 540.

English		Math		Reading		Science	
1. D	39. D	1. C	31. C	1. B	21. B	1. D	21. C
2. H	40. G	2. H	32. J	2. F	22. F	2. H	22. G
3. C	41. C	3. C	33. A	3. A	23. C	3. C	23. D
4. J	42. F	4. J	34. J	4. J	24. F	4. J	24. G
5. B	43. D	5. D	35. B	5. D	25. B	5. A	25. A
6. G	44. J	6. G	36. G	6. G	26. H	6. J	26. H
7. A	45. C	7. D	37. C	7. D	27. D	7. B	27. A
8. F	46. H	8. J	38. H	8. H	28. F	8. J	28. J
9. D	47. B	9. A	39. D	9. C	29. A	9. C	29. A
10. F	48. H	10. G	40. G	10. G	30. H	10. F	30. J
11. D	49. C	11. B	41. A	11. A	31. D	11. C	31. B
12. F	50. G	12. K	42. J	12. F	32. F	12. H	32. G
13. C	51. A	13. B	43. C	13. C	33. A	13. B	33. C
14. F	52. H	14. K	44. F	14. J	34. G	14. J	34. F
15. A	53. D	15. B	45. E	15. B	35. A	15. C	35. B
16. J	54. F	16. H	46. F	16. G	36. J	16. H	36. H
17. B	55. A	17. A	47. C	17. B	37. C	17. D	37. A
18. F	56. G	18. F	48. K	18. F	38. G	18. G	38. F
19. C	57. D	19. B	49. A	19. D	39. C	19. B	39. D
20. J	58. G	20. K	50. J	20. H	40. H	20. F	40. G
21. C	59. B	21. B	51. E				
22. H	60. G	22. J	52. J				
23. D	61. B	23. B	53. E				
24. H	62. G	24. F	54. J				
25. B	63. A	25. E	55. E				
26. J	64. F	26. K	56. F				
27. A	65. D	27. B	57. B				
28. F	66. F	28. H	58. H				
29. D	67. D	29. B	59. A				
30. H	68. J	30. H	60. G				
31. B	69. C						
32. F	70. G						
33. D	71. B						
34. F	72. H						
35. B	73. C						
36. H	74. H						
37. B	75. D						
38. J							

ENGLISH TEST

1. **D** Verbs are changing in the answer choices, so the question is testing consistency of verbs. A verb must be consistent with its subject and with the other verbs in the sentence. The subject of the verb is *family*, which is singular. To be consistent, the verb in the answer choices must also be singular. Eliminate (B) and (C) because *were* is plural. Eliminate (A) because *was deciding* is not concise and indicates that the decision was ongoing. Choice (D) is consistent with the subject, is concise, and indicates the decision was a one-time event. The correct answer is (D).

2. **H** Transitions are changing in the answer choices, so the question is testing consistency with transitions. Look at the first part of the sentence to determine how the two ideas are related. The first part of the sentence is a cause, and the second part of the sentence is an effect. Eliminate (F) and (J) because *but* indicates a contrast, but there is not a contrast in the sentence. Eliminate (G) because *because* needs to be placed before the cause, not the effect. Keep (H) because *so* correctly indicates the cause-effect relationship between the two ideas. The correct answer is (H).

3. **C** Verbs are changing in the answer choices, so this question is testing consistency of verbs. There is also the option to DELETE; consider this choice carefully as it's often the correct answer. Deleting the underlined portion results in the phrase *unfamiliar faces at me*, which is not clear, so eliminate (D). The answer choices are in different tenses, so look for a clue in the sentence or surrounding sentences to identify the appropriate tense. The sentence contains two things that *scared* the narrator, so these two items should be consistent in tense. The first is *Classes starting in the fall*, which uses an -ing form of a verb. The second, *unfamiliar faces looked at me*, should be consistent with the first phrase. Eliminate (A) and (B) because *looked* and *having looked* are not consistent with *starting*. Keep (C) because *looking* is consistent with *starting*. The correct answer is (C).

4. **J** Transitions are changing in the answer choices, so the question is testing consistency with transitions. Look at the previous sentence to determine how the two ideas are related. The previous sentence describes things that would scare the narrator, and this sentence describes the narrator asking her parents why they were moving. Eliminate (F) because the current sentence is not an example. Eliminate (G) and (H) because *nevertheless* and *however* indicate a contrast, and there is no contrast between the two sentences. Keep (J) because a transition is not necessary. The correct answer is (J).

5. **B** Punctuation is changing in the answer choices, so the question is testing STOP and GO punctuation. Use the vertical line test, and identify the ideas as complete or incomplete. Draw the vertical line between the words *pleaded* and *begging*. The phrase *I pleaded* is a complete idea, and the phrase *begging to be allowed to stay behind and live with my grandparents* is an incomplete idea. To connect a complete idea to an incomplete idea, HALF-STOP or GO punctuation is needed. The semi-colon is STOP punctuation, so eliminate (A). The pair of commas in (C) implies that *begging to be allowed* is an unnecessary phrase. The phrase is necessary to the sentence, so eliminate (C). Keep (B) and (D) because a comma and no punctuation are both GO punctuation. A pause is needed between *pleaded* and *begging* in order to separate the ideas, so a comma is needed. Eliminate (D). The correct answer is (B).

6. **G** Verbs are changing in the answer choices, so this question is testing consistency of verbs. There is also the option to DELETE; consider this choice carefully as it's often the correct answer. Deleting the underlined portion results in the phrase *surrounded by giant rats racing him home and his way*, which is not clear, so eliminate (J). A verb must be consistent with its subject and with the other verbs in the sentence. The *giant rats* are doing two things; the first is *racing*, so the second should be consistent in tense with *racing*. Eliminate (F) and (H) because *was blocking* and *were blocking* are not consistent with *racing*. Keep (G) because *blocking* is consistent with *racing*. The correct answer is (G).

7. **A** Note the question! The question asks which option would *give the reader a better idea of how* the author *thought her father felt*. Check each answer choice to see whether it has to do with *how her father felt*. Keep (A) because *frustrated* is a feeling. Eliminate (B) because being *stuck on the highway* does not tell the reader how the author's father felt. Eliminate (C) because *he couldn't see the rats* is not a description of feelings. Eliminate (D) because comparing the size of her father to that of the rats is a physical description, not an emotional one. The correct answer is (A).

8. **F** Note the question! The question asks which option *provides the best opening to this paragraph*. Read the paragraph and pick the option that is consistent with the topic of the paragraph. The paragraph says, *One of his main reasons, he said, was the long drive home after work*. It also mentions the narrator's father *having no time to go fishing*. Keep (F) because it provides a question that the paragraph answers: why the narrator's father wants to move. Eliminate (G) because *rats* are not discussed in this paragraph. Eliminate (H) because the paragraph does not mention the narrator's mother or the phrase *"rat race."* Although the paragraph does mention *fishing*, the paragraph is not about when the narrator's father likes to go fishing, so eliminate (J). The correct answer is (F).

9. **D** The number of words is changing in the answer choices, so the question could be testing concision. Eliminate any choices that are redundant. *Worst* and *most terrible* mean the same thing, so including both in the phrase is redundant; eliminate (A) and (C). *Awfully* and *terrible* are also redundant, so eliminate (B). Choice (D) is clear and concise. The correct answer is (D).

10. **F** Comparison words are changing in the answer choices, so the question is testing consistency. The sentence is comparing how the father currently looks to how the father had looked before. When making a comparison, the correct word to use is *than*. *Then* is a word used to indicate a sequence, not a comparison, so eliminate (G) and (H). When comparing two things, *more, less*, or an adjective ending in *-er* is used. Eliminate (J) because *happiest* is not consistent with the comparison of two things. The correct answer is (F).

11. **D** Punctuation is changing in the answer choices, so the question is testing STOP and GO punctuation. Use the vertical line test, and identify the ideas as complete or incomplete. Draw two vertical lines around the word *and*. The phrase *After the move, we had dinner* is a complete idea, and the phrase *talked about the weekend calmly as a family* is an incomplete idea. To connect a complete idea to an incomplete idea, HALF-STOP or GO punctuation is needed. A comma with a FANBOYS word is STOP punctuation, so eliminate (C). Keep (D) because a lack of punctuation is GO punc-

tuation. Choices (A) and (B) have commas after *and* and *talked*, respectively. There is no reason to use a comma in either of these locations, so eliminate (A) and (B). The correct answer is (D).

12. **F** Note the question! The question asks where Sentence 5 should be placed, so it's testing consistency. Look for a clue in the sentence to determine what idea it needs to come before or after. Sentence 5 says that *Before the move, he used to complain about crazy drivers while eating reheated leftovers.* Sentence 6 completes the comparison by starting with *After the move.* Therefore, Sentence 5 should stay before Sentence 6. The correct answer is (F).

13. **C** Punctuation is changing in the answer choices, so the question is testing STOP and GO punctuation. Use the vertical line test, and identify the ideas as complete or incomplete. Draw the vertical line between the words *California* and *I.* The phrase *As I got older, when we visited family and friends in Southern California* is an incomplete idea, and the phrase *I could see the difference from the traffic at home in Redding* is a complete idea. To connect an incomplete idea to a complete idea, GO punctuation is needed. A period and a semicolon are both STOP punctuation, so eliminate (A) and (B). Keep (C) because a comma is GO punctuation. The phrase *when we visited family and friends in Southern California* is unnecessary, so it needs a comma after the phrase. Choice (D) lacks a comma after the phrase, so eliminate it. The correct answer is (C).

14. **F** The number of words is changing in the answer choices, so the question could be testing concision. Eliminate any choices that are redundant. Keep (F) because it is concise. Eliminate (G) because *interminable* means *unending*, so it is redundant. Eliminate (H) because *endlessly* means *continuing forever*, so it is redundant. Eliminate (J) because *eternity* means *without end*, so it is redundant. The correct answer is (F).

15. **A** Note the question! The question asks whether the essay would fulfill the goal of *telling the reader why* the writer's *family moved to Redding.* Consider the main idea of the passage and use Process of Elimination. The passage describes why the narrator's family moved to Redding, so it agrees with the goal stated in the question. Eliminate (C) and (D). Keep (A) because the narrator learns her father's reasons for moving. Eliminate (B) because the essay is about one family, not *children* in general. The correct answer is (A).

16. **J** The phrase after *grandmother* is changing in the answer choices, so the question could be testing concision. First determine whether the phrase is necessary. The pronoun *themselves* is redundant, since the sentence already says that *she was raised by her mother and grandmother*, so eliminate (F) and (G). *Grandmother* is a family relation, so it is redundant to say *related to her*. Eliminate (H). Choice (J) is clear and concise. The correct answer is (J).

17. **B** Punctuation is changing in the answer choices, so the question is testing STOP and GO punctuation. Use the vertical line test, and identify the ideas as complete or incomplete. Draw the vertical line after the word heritage. The phrase *Her art is thus a tribute to her family's past as well as to her cultural heritage* is a complete idea. The phrase *which she believes her art embodies the spirit of Los Angeles* is not a correct phrasing because the word *which* would refer back to *heritage*, but the second part of the sentence doesn't include a reference to *heritage*. Eliminate (A). For (B) and (C), the second part of the sentence is a complete idea. To connect a complete idea to a complete idea, STOP or

HALF-STOP punctuation is needed. Keep (B) because a semicolon is STOP punctuation. Eliminate (C) because a comma is GO punctuation. Although a comma and a FANBOYS word is STOP punctuation, there is no contrast in the sentence, so eliminate (D). The correct answer is (B).

18. **F** Commas are changing in the answer choices, so the question is testing comma rules. The phrase *the mural* is unnecessary information, so it needs either a comma before and after or a dash before and after. Keep (F) because it has a comma before and after the phrase. Eliminate (G) because, while either commas or dashes can be used to surround unnecessary information, there can't be one of each. Eliminate (H) because there is no dash before the phrase. Eliminate (J) because there is no comma before the phrase. The correct answer is (F).

19. **C** Note the question! The question asks where *in recent years* CANNOT be placed. Cross out EXCEPT and decide Yes/No for each option, and then choose the odd one out. Mark (A) as Yes since the meaning of the sentence is clear when *in recent years* follows *in Los Angeles*. Mark (B) as Yes since the meaning of the sentence is clear when *in recent years* follows *revival*. Mark (C) as no since the phrase *a popular in recent years revival* is not clear. Mark (D) as Yes since the meaning of the sentence is clear when *in recent years* is placed before *experienced*. Choice (C) is the odd one out. The correct answer is (C).

20. **J** Note the question! The question asks what the essay would lose if the sentence were deleted. Consider the purpose of the sentence. The sentence explains that Baca *has gained fame for her colorful murals depicting episodes from Latino history* and that many murals are in *Los Angeles*. Check the answers and eliminate any choice that is not consistent with this purpose. Eliminate (F) because there is no mention of *techniques* in the sentence. Eliminate (G) because the sentence does not discuss the *development of murals as an art form*. Eliminate (H) because the sentence does not discuss *the rebirth of murals*. Keep (J) because the sentence does mention *Baca's success* and where *her work is popular*. The correct answer is (J).

21. **C** Transitions are changing in the answer choices, so the question is testing consistency with transitions. Look at the previous sentence to determine how the two ideas are related. The previous sentence mentions Baca's success and where her murals can be found. This sentence introduces the connection between *murals* and *graffiti*. Eliminate (A) because *moreover* indicates continuing to an additional point, and the current sentence is not an additional point. Eliminate (B) because *however* indicates a contrast, and there is no contrast between the two sentences. Keep (C) because the meanings of both sentences are clear without a transition. Eliminate (D) because *therefore* indicates a conclusion, and the current sentence is not a conclusion that follows from the previous one. The correct answer is (C).

22. **H** Verbs are changing in the answer choices, so the question is testing consistency of verbs. A verb must be consistent with its subject and with the other verbs in the sentence. The subject of the verb is *examples*, which is plural. To be consistent, the verb in the answer choices must also be plural. Eliminate (F), (G), and (J) because *was* is singular. Keep (H) because *were* is plural. The correct answer is (H).

23. **D** Apostrophes are changing in the answer choices, so the question is testing apostrophe usage. When used with a noun, on the ACT, the apostrophe indicates possession. In this sentence, the *political*

messages belong to the *murals*. Therefore, the apostrophe is needed, and because *murals* is plural, the apostrophe should be placed after the *s*. Eliminate (A) and (B) because they don't have an apostrophe after *murals*. Eliminate (C) because the apostrophe is placed before the *s*, which would indicate a singular noun (*mural*). Keep (D) because it correctly places the apostrophe after the *s*. The correct answer is (D).

24. **H** Vocabulary is changing in the answers, so the question is testing word choice. Determine what meaning of the underlined portion would be consistent with the sentence. The underlined portion should mean something like "consequence." Eliminate (F) because *evidence* means "proof." Eliminate (G) because *stated* means "expressed." Keep (H) because *a result* means "consequence." Eliminate (J) because *imagined* means "pictured." The correct answer is (H).

25. **B** Note the question! The question asks which option *provides the most relevant information at this point in the essay*. Check each answer choice to see whether it is consistent with the sentences around it. The previous sentence says that murals can *become community efforts*. The following sentence says, *It is this community involvement that has helped sway the minds of officials*. The *most relevant information* will be consistent with the discussion of murals and community. Eliminate (A) because the connection of *cultural past* and *present reality* is not consistent with the idea that murals may become *community efforts*. Keep (B) because it says murals *are located in the heart of the community*, which is consistent with the surrounding sentences. Eliminate (C) because government funding for murals is not consistent with the idea of *community*. Eliminate (D) because *telling allegorical stories* is not consistent with the idea of *community*. The correct answer is (B).

26. **J** Subjects and verbs are changing in the answer choices, so the question is testing complete sentences. Determine which answer choice would produce a complete sentence. The phrase *Some depict scenes of multicultural harmony* is a complete idea. Each answer choice has a comma between the two ideas of the sentence. A comma is GO punctuation, which can be used to connect a complete idea to an incomplete idea. The idea after the comma must be an incomplete idea. Eliminate (F), (G), and (H) because they all have a subject and verb, making the second idea complete. Keep (J) because it makes the second part of the sentence incomplete. The correct answer is (J).

27. **A** The order of the words is changing in the answer choices, so the question is testing consistency with a modifier. The non-underlined portion contains the word *scenes*. The underlined phrase is modifying *scenes*, so the words immediately after *scenes* should describe what is in the *scenes*. Keep (A) and (C) because *of past successes* correctly modifies *scenes* by coming directly after *scenes*. Eliminate (B) and (D) because *of past successes* does not come immediately after *scenes*. The phrase *of the community* describes *members*, so it should come immediately after *members*. Eliminate (C) because *of the community* does not come directly after *members*. The correct answer is (A).

28. **F** The order of the words is changing in the answer choices, so the question is testing consistency with a modifier. The non-underlined portion contains the modifier *By creating beautiful murals in her neighborhood*. The beautiful murals are created by someone, so the word or phrase that directly follows the modifying phrase should be the person who created the murals. Keep (F) because Baca

is an artist who creates murals. Eliminate (G) and (J) because *a sense of community pride* is not creating the murals. Eliminate (H) because the sentence refers to *her*, not to a *community* creating the murals. The correct answer is (F).

29. **D**   Punctuation is changing in the answer choices, so the question is testing STOP and GO punctuation. Use the vertical line test, and identify the ideas as complete or incomplete. Draw the vertical line between the words *people* and *she*. The phrase *The bright faces of the people* is an incomplete idea, and the phrase *she paints signal the bright possibilities available to the viewer* is an incomplete idea. To connect an incomplete idea to an incomplete idea, GO punctuation is needed. Keep (A) and (D) because a comma and a lack of punctuation are both GO punctuation. A semicolon is STOP punctuation, so eliminate (C). For (B), repeat the vertical line test by drawing the vertical line between *paints* and *signal*. The phrase *The bright faces of the people, she paints* is an incomplete idea. A colon is HALF-STOP punctuation and can be used only when the first idea is a complete idea. Since the first idea is incomplete, eliminate (B). There is no reason to use a comma between *people* and *she*, so eliminate (A). The correct answer is (D).

30. **H**   Pronouns and apostrophes are changing in the answer choices, so the question is testing consistency of pronouns and apostrophe usage. A pronoun must be consistent in number with the noun it is replacing. The pronoun refers to the noun *people*, which is plural. To be consistent, the pronoun in the answer choice must also be plural. Eliminate (G) and (J) because *its* and *it's* are both singular. When used with a pronoun, the apostrophe indicates a contraction. Expand the contraction in (F) to get *They are successes, Baca suggests, can be yours.* The sentence is not saying the *people* are *successes*, but rather that they are possessing the *successes*, so an apostrophe is not needed. Eliminate (F). Keep (H) because it uses the possessive pronoun *Their*. The correct answer is (H).

31. **B**   Verbs are changing in the answer choices, so the question is testing consistency of verbs. The answer choices contain different verb forms with helping verbs, so use Process of Elimination to remove any pairs that are incorrect. The non-underlined portion of the sentence refers to an event that began happening in the *last decade* and is still happening, so the underlined verb must be consistent with this idea. Eliminate (A) and (C) because *saw* is the simple past tense form of *see* and cannot be used with helping verbs like *had* and *has*. Keep (B) because *seen* is the form of the verb that is used with a helping verb such as *has*. Eliminate (D) because the correct phrase is *would have*, not *would of*. The correct answer is (B).

32. **F**   Transitions are changing in the answer choices, so the question is testing consistency with transitions. Look at the previous phrase to determine how the two ideas are related. The previous phrase mentions the *possibilities of video gaming* in *1972*, and the following phrase indicates an event in 1972 that led to these *possibilities* being *mind-blowing*. Keep (F) because *when* makes it clear that *Nolan Bushnell and Ted Dabney* introduced Pong in 1972. Eliminate (G) because *where* is used with places, not time. Eliminate (H) because *in which* is not used for time. Eliminate (J) because *that* is used to refer to something; the second phrase is not about 1972 but rather what happened in 1972. The correct answer is (F).

33. **D** Verbs are changing in the answer choices, so the question is testing consistency of verbs. A verb must be consistent with its subject and with the other verbs in the sentence. The subject of the verb is *Pong*, which is singular. To be consistent, the verb in the answer choice must also be singular. Eliminate (A) because *were* is plural. Eliminate (B) because *precede* is plural. Eliminate (C) because it uses the *-ing* form of the verb and is not the correct form of the idiom *preceded by*. Keep (D) because *was* is singular and the idiom is in the correct form. The correct answer is (D).

34. **F** Note the question! The question asks why the preceding sentence *should NOT be deleted*. Consider the purpose of the sentence. The sentence explains that *Pong* was unique and helped launch *the concept of home video gaming systems*. Check the answers and eliminate any choice that is not consistent with this purpose. Keep (F) because the sentence does discuss *Pong* generally and the next paragraph describes *Pong* in more detail. Eliminate (G) because the sentence says that *Pong* had a *simple interface*, not that it required *technical skill*. Eliminate (H) because the sentence says *Pong* contributed to *home video gaming systems*, not that *Pong* had *ultimate ascendance* over other games. Eliminate (J) because the sentence does not call *Pong* a *modern video game*. The correct answer is (F).

35. **B** Note the question! The question asks which choice *explains the writer's reasons for calling Pong "old-fashioned."* Check each answer choice to see whether it has to do with *Pong* being *old-fashioned*. Eliminate (A) because it mentions *modern video games* without giving reasons why Pong is *old-fashioned*. Keep (B) because it describes aspects of *Pong* that support the writer calling it *old-fashioned*. Eliminate (C) because it doesn't describe *Pong*. Eliminate (D) because *lack of technological development* describes the time when *Pong* was created, not the game itself. The correct answer is (B).

36. **H** Punctuation is changing in the answer choices, so the question is testing STOP and GO punctuation. Use the vertical line test, and identify the ideas as complete or incomplete. Draw the vertical line between the words *fact* and *were*. The phrase *It's not that Pong was the most advanced game of the era: several earlier games, in fact* is an incomplete idea, and the phrase *were actually more technologically advanced* is an incomplete idea. To connect an incomplete idea to an incomplete idea, GO punctuation is needed. The semicolon is HALF-STOP punctuation and can be used only if the first idea is complete, so eliminate (F). Commas are changing in the remaining answer choices, so the question is testing comma rules. The phrase *in fact* is unnecessary information, so it needs a comma before and after. Eliminate (G) because it doesn't include a comma before the unnecessary phrase. Keep (H) because it has a comma before and after the unnecessary phrase. Eliminate (J) because it doesn't include a comma after the unnecessary phrase. The correct answer is (H).

37. **B** Note the question! The question asks what alternative would be LEAST acceptable. Cross out LEAST and decide Yes/No for each option, and then choose the odd one out. The underlined word is *novelty*, which refers to something that is "new and unusual." Mark (A) as Yes since *uniqueness* matches with "unusual." Mark (B) as No since *complexity* means "intricate" or "complicated," neither of which matches any of the meanings for *novelty*. Mark (C) as Yes since *innovation* means "newness." Mark (D) as Yes since *freshness* means "newness." Choice (B) is the odd one out. The correct answer is (B).

38. **J**   The phrase after *consumer* is changing in the answer choices, so the question could be testing concision. First determine whether the phrase is necessary. The sentence already states *average consumer*, so there is no need to repeat that idea. Eliminate any choices that are redundant. Choices (F), (G), and (H) each repeat the idea of a consumer, or a person who makes a purchase, so eliminate them. The correct answer is (J).

39. **D**   Pronouns and apostrophes are changing in the answer choices, so the question is testing consistency of pronouns and apostrophe usage. A pronoun must be consistent in number with other pronouns in the sentence. The pronoun *it* is used twice earlier in the sentence. To be consistent, the pronoun in the answer choice must also be *it*. Eliminate (B) and (C) because *they're* and *their* are not consistent with *it*. When used with a pronoun, the apostrophe indicates a contraction. Expand the contraction in (A) to get *in it is own way*. Since *it* is possessing *own way*, the pronoun should be possessive and no apostrophe is needed. Eliminate (A). The correct answer is (D).

40. **G**   Note the question! The question asks where Sentence 5 should be placed, so it's testing consistency. Look for a clue in the sentence to determine what idea it needs to come before or after. Sentence 5 says *However, it was groundbreaking in its day, in its own way*. Sentence 5 should follow a sentence that makes it clear what *it* is and contrasts with *groundbreaking*. Sentence 1 is about *Pong* and calls the game *old-fashioned*, which contrasts with *groundbreaking in its day*. Therefore, Sentence 5 should follow Sentence 1. The correct answer is (G).

41. **C**   Punctuation is changing in the answer choices, so the question is testing STOP and GO punctuation. Use the vertical line test, and identify the ideas as complete or incomplete. Draw the vertical line between the words *mathematicians* and *developing*. The phrase *The history of the video game becomes more understandable when it is remembered that the creators of early games were primarily engineers and mathematicians* is a complete idea, and the phrase *developing these games for their own amusement, they paid little attention to popular marketing* is a complete idea. To connect a complete idea to a complete idea, STOP or HALF-STOP punctuation is needed. The comma is GO punctuation, so eliminate (A) and (D). A lack of punctuation is GO punctuation, so eliminate (B). A period is STOP punctuation, so keep (C). The correct answer is (C).

42. **F**   The phrase after *public* is changing in the answer choices, so the question could be testing concision. First determine whether the phrase is necessary. The sentence already states that developers introduced *products to the public as part of a showpiece* at events, *on a temporary basis*, so there is no need to repeat that idea. Eliminate any choices that are redundant. Choices (G), (H), and (J) each repeat the idea that developers introduced their products to audiences at special events, so eliminate them. The correct answer is (F).

43. **D**   Descriptive words are changing in the answer choices, so the question is testing consistency. First determine what is being described. The phrase is describing *games*, which is a noun. Eliminate (B) and (C) because *complexity* is a noun and cannot be used to describe another noun. Eliminate (A) because *high* is an adjective and cannot be used to describe another adjective, *complex*. The correct descriptive phrase is *highly complex*. The correct answer is (D).

44. **J** Note the question! The question asks which option *would most effectively express the writer's attitude towards the future of the video game industry*. Check each answer choice to see whether it has to do with the *future of the video game industry*. Eliminate (F) because the writer thinking that *Pong is fun to play sometimes* does not give any information about the video game industry. Eliminate (G) because the *men who created Pong* are from the industry's past, not the future. Eliminate (H) because the *ultimate goal of all video games* does not reveal how the writer feels about future video games. Keep (J) because the writer says that the *advances* in video games will continue *until the games of today seem just as ridiculous as Pong*, which is looking at the future of the video game industry. The correct answer is (J).

45. **C** Note the question! The question asks whether the essay demonstrates *the impact a single invention can have on the development of an industry*. Consider the main idea of the passage and use Process of Elimination. The passage is about *Pong* and how it changed the video game industry. Eliminate (A) and (B) because the writer does focus on a single invention, *Pong*, and its contribution to the development of the video game industry. Keep (C) because the essay discusses the aspects of *Pong* that helped it *gain widespread acceptance for video games*. Eliminate (D) because *Pong* was not *the first video game released to the public*. The correct answer is (C).

46. **H** Note the question! The question asks which option *provides the most specific information*. Check each answer choice to see whether it is specific. Eliminate (F) because *a while back* is not specific. Eliminate (G) because *a few years ago* is not specific. Keep (H) because *last summer* refers to a specific time period. Eliminate (J) because *some time ago* is not specific. The correct answer is (H).

47. **B** Verbs are changing in the answer choices, so the question is testing consistency of verbs. The answer choices are in different forms, so use Process of Elimination to remove any incorrect verbs. The word before *probably* is *had*, so the underlined verb must go along with the helping verb *had*. Eliminate (A) and (D) because *went* is the simple past tense of *go* and cannot be used with the helping verb *had*. Keep (B) because *gone* is the form of *go* that is used with a helping verb such as *had*. Eliminate (C) because the correct idiom is *go the way of*, not *leave the way of*. The correct answer is (B).

48. **H** Commas are changing in the answer choices, so the question is testing comma rules. The phrase *the first African-American to serve as the Green Lantern* is unnecessary information, so it needs a comma before and after. Eliminate (F) and (J) because they do not include a comma after *Lantern*. The phrase *was one* is necessary information, so it does not need a comma after *one*; eliminate (G). The correct answer is (H).

49. **C** Subjects and verbs are changing in the answer choices, so the question is testing complete sentences. Determine which answer choice would produce a complete sentence. The sentence has a subject, and it needs a verb to be complete. Eliminate (A) and (D) because *a practiced* and *practicing* are descriptions, not verbs. Eliminate (B) because *he practiced and fearsome warrior* makes the sentence unclear. Keep (C) because *he was a practiced and fearsome warrior* is a complete and clear idea. The correct answer is (C).

50. **G** Verbs and nouns are changing in the answer choices, so the question is testing consistency of verbs and nouns. Since the sentence contains a list, every item in the list must be consistent in form. The non-underlined parts of the list are *leading* and *acting cool*. The third item must be consistent in form. Eliminate (F) because a *fighter* is not consistent with the rest of the list. Keep (G) because *fighting* is consistent with *leading* and *acting cool*. Eliminate (H) because *to fight* is not consistent. Eliminate (J) because *could fight* is not consistent. The correct answer is (G).

51. **A** Verbs are changing in the answer choices, so the question is testing consistency of verbs. There is also the option to DELETE; consider this choice carefully as it's often the correct answer. Deleting the underlined portion creates the phrase *Stewart seemed to embody everything I for my future*, which makes the sentence unclear, so eliminate (D). The correct phrase is *could have*, not *could of*, so eliminate (B) and (C). The correct answer is (A).

52. **H** The order of the words is changing in the answer choices, so the question is testing consistency. Since the sentence contains a list, every item in the list must be consistent in form. The non-underlined parts of the list are *the respect of others* and *the power to control himself*. The third item must be consistent in form. Eliminate (F), (G), and (J) because each starts with *he* or *his*, not a noun preceded by *the*. Choice (H) is consistent because it starts with *the best style*. The correct answer is (H).

53. **D** Note the question! The question asks whether the sentence should be added, so it's testing consistency. If the content of the new sentence is consistent with the ideas surrounding it, then it should be added. The paragraph discusses how the writer viewed Stewart and why the writer liked him. The new sentence discusses how *each Green Lantern was chosen by a group called The Guardians*, so it is not consistent with the ideas in the text; the sentence should not be added. Eliminate (A) and (B). Eliminate (C) because it doesn't state that the new sentence is inconsistent with the text. Keep (D) because it states that the new sentence is irrelevant. The correct answer is (D).

54. **F** Note the question! The question asks which choice *explains the author's belief that Stewart was a more understandable character and shows a more realistic image of Stewart*. Check each answer choice to see whether it has to do with Stewart being *understandable* and *realistic*. Keep (F) because *His life had its ups and its downs* is consistent with *a realistic image of Stewart* and *his problems were real life problems that I could relate to* is consistent with Stewart being *a more understandable character*. Although *I had an easier time imagining myself in his shoes* is consistent with *a more understandable character*, there is no support for *a more realistic image of Stewart*; eliminate (G). Eliminate (H) because flying *into space* and creating *weapons out of thin air* are not consistent with *understandable* and *realistic*. Eliminate (J) because Stewart's *ring* and *superpowers* are not consistent with *realistic*. The correct answer is (F).

55. **A** Punctuation is changing in the answer choices, so the question is testing STOP and GO punctuation. Use the vertical line test, and identify the ideas as complete or incomplete. Draw the vertical line between the words *after* and *it*. The phrase *For a little while in the early 1990s, there was a series that focused solely on Stewart as the Green Lantern, but after* is an incomplete idea, and the phrase *it ended, Stewart was replaced and seemed likely to be forgotten* is an incomplete idea. To connect an incomplete idea to an incomplete idea, GO punctuation is needed. Keep (A) because a lack of

punctuation is GO punctuation. A semicolon is STOP punctuation, so eliminate (B). A colon is HALF-STOP punctuation, so eliminate (C). Although a comma is GO punctuation, there is no reason to use a comma between *after* and *it*, so eliminate (D). The correct answer is (A).

56. **G** Note the question! The question asks what alternative would be LEAST acceptable. Cross out LEAST and decide Yes/No for each option, and then choose the odd one out. The underlined word is *however*, which is used to indicate a contrast. Mark (F) as Yes since *though* is also used to indicate a contrast and is consistent with *however*. Mark (G) as No since *furthermore* is used to indicate an additional point, not a contrast, and makes the sentence unclear. Mark (H) as Yes since *on the contrary* is used to indicate a contrast and is consistent with *however*. Mark (J) as Yes since the meaning of the sentence is still clear without *however*. Choice (G) is the odd one out. The correct answer is (G).

57. **D** Commas and apostrophes are changing in the answer choices, so the question is testing comma rules and apostrophe usage. There is no reason to use a comma after *rocky*, so eliminate (A) and (C). When used with a noun, on the ACT, the apostrophe indicates possession. In this sentence, *Stewart* is possessing the *rocky life*. Therefore, the apostrophe is needed. Eliminate (B) because it does not have an apostrophe. The correct answer is (D).

58. **G** Note the question! The question asks which option *supports the point being made in the first part of this sentence*. Check each answer choice to see whether it supports the idea that Paul liked Stewart for *his actions*. Eliminate (F) because *strong role model* does not support an idea about Stewart's actions. Keep (G) because *what he did* supports an idea about actions. Eliminate (H) because *what he represented* does not support an idea about actions. Eliminate (J) because *his past* does not support an idea about actions. The correct answer is (G).

59. **B** Pronouns and nouns are changing in the answer choices, so the question is testing clarity with pronouns. Determine who or what the pronoun refers to, and choose an answer that makes the meaning 100% clear. As the sentence is written, it is not clear what Paul is not *worrying about*. Eliminate (A), (C), and (D) because the pronouns *that* and *those* do not make the sentence clear. *Their backstories* makes it clear what Paul is not worrying about, so keep (B). The correct answer is (B).

60. **G** Punctuation is changing in the answer choices, so the question is testing STOP and GO punctuation. Use the vertical line test, and identify the ideas as complete or incomplete. Draw the vertical line between the words *superheroes* and *they're*. The phrase *In Paul's worldview, all superheroes are simply superheroes* is a complete idea, and the phrase *they're heroes, regardless of their pasts, not because of them* is a complete idea. To connect a complete idea to a complete idea, STOP or HALF-STOP punctuation is needed. A lack of punctuation is GO punctuation, so eliminate (F). The semicolon is STOP punctuation, so keep (G). The comma is GO punctuation, so eliminate (H). Changing *they're* to *being* makes the sentence less clear, so eliminate (J). The correct answer is (G).

61. **B** Phrases are changing in the answer choices, so the question is testing word choice. Determine what meaning of the underlined portion would be consistent with the sentence. The underlined portion should mean something like "old" and should describe the *saying*. Eliminate (A) because *worn-out* is describing *time*, not the *saying*. Keep (B) because *timeworn* means "old." Eliminate (C) because *timed out* means "paused." Eliminate (D) because *out of time* does not mean "old." The correct answer is (B).

62. **G**   Connecting words are changing in the answer choices, so the question is testing consistency. The part after the underlined portion links the factors—*the immense pressure that poses a serious danger* and *unknown geography that can injure people and vessel alike*—with the word *to*. The correct idiom is *from…to*. Eliminate (F), (H), and (J). The correct answer is (G).

63. **A**   Note the question! The question asks which option is *most relevant to the statement that follows in this sentence*. The statement that follows says, *with the cost increasing as the expedition ventures into deeper regions*. Check each answer choice to see whether it has to do with the *cost increasing*. Keep (A) because *prohibitive costs* are relevant to increasing costs. Eliminate (B), (C), and (D) because *difficult*, *dangerous*, and *damage* are not relevant to the statement about the *cost increasing*. The correct answer is (A).

64. **F**   Note the question! The question asks whether the phrase should be added, so it's testing consistency. If the content of the new phrase is consistent with the ideas surrounding it, then it should be added. The sentence introduces the *Marianas Trench*, and the following sentence references the trench's *depth* and *potential for danger*. The phrase gives specific information about the *Marianas Trench*, so it is consistent with the ideas in the text; the phrase should be added. Eliminate (H) and (J). Keep (F) because it states that the information in the phrase is relevant. Eliminate (G) because the phrase is not about *human-led explorations*. The correct answer is (F).

65. **D**   Note the question! The question asks which option *best leads from the preceding paragraph to the subject of this paragraph*. Determine the topics of the preceding paragraph and this paragraph. The preceding paragraph discusses deep-sea exploration and the deepest section of the ocean, the *Marianas Trench*. This paragraph discusses *creatures not found anywhere else on the planet* and an exploration of the *Marianas Trench* in *1960*. Check each answer choice to see whether it is consistent with both of these topics. Eliminate (A) because *shallow parts of the ocean* is not consistent with the discussion of the *Marianas Trench*. Eliminate (B) because *a medical condition* related to *deep-sea diving* is not consistent with the information about *creatures* in the ocean trenches. Eliminate (C) because arguing about how *dangerous* it is *at the bottom of the ocean* is not consistent with the information about ocean *creatures*. Keep (D) because *obstacles* is consistent with the earlier discussion of deep-sea exploration and *scientists* feeling *the draw of the ocean's depths* is consistent with the ocean's depths having *creatures not found anywhere else on the planet*. The correct answer is (D).

66. **F**   Connecting words are changing in the answer choices, so the question is testing consistency. The correct idiom is *development of*. Eliminate (G) and (J) because they do not contain the word *of*. Eliminate (H) because it uses *developing* instead of *development*. The correct answer is (F).

67. **D**   Transitions are changing in the answer choices, so the question is testing consistency with transitions. Look at the previous sentence to determine how the two ideas are related. The previous sentence mentions the only expedition to the *Marianas Trench*; this sentence is a continuation of that idea and says that the cost and danger have prevented people from going back. Eliminate (A) because *therefore* is used for a conclusion, but this sentence is not a conclusion that follows from the previous sentence. Eliminate (B) and (C) because *nevertheless* and *in contrast* are used to con-

trast ideas, but there is no contrast between the two ideas. Keep (D) because *since then* connects the expedition in 1960 to the idea that no one has gone back. The correct answer is (D).

68. **J** Verbs are changing in the answer choices, so the question is testing consistency of verbs. The answer choices are in different tenses, so look for a clue in the sentence or surrounding sentences to identify the appropriate tense. Eliminate (F) because *had* + verb is used to compare two events that both occurred in the past, but there is only one event in the sentence. Eliminate (G) because the correct phrase is *could have*, not *could of*. Eliminate (H) because *were discovering* indicates that the *scientists* are no longer using *sonar* for discovery, and the paragraph indicates that *sonar* is still being used. Keep (J) because it uses the correct tense and makes the sentence clear. The correct answer is (J).

69. **C** Note the question! The question asks which option *most effectively describes what sonar is*. Check each answer choice to see whether it defines *sonar*. Eliminate (A) because it describes how *expensive* sonar is. Eliminate (B) because it describes when *sonar* was developed. Keep (C) because *a sound-based method of determining surroundings* describes what sonar is. Eliminate (D) because it introduces a new concept, *echolocation*. The correct answer is (C).

70. **G** Punctuation is changing in the answer choices, so the question is testing STOP and GO punctuation. Use the vertical line test, and identify the ideas as complete or incomplete. Draw the vertical line between the words *advanced* and *revolves*. The phrase *Another method of exploration that has become more common in recent years, as technology has advanced* is an incomplete idea, and the phrase *revolves around the use of unmanned submersibles* is an incomplete idea. To connect an incomplete idea to an incomplete idea, GO punctuation is needed. The single dash and the colon are HALF-STOP punctuation and can be used only after a complete idea, so eliminate (H) and (J). Commas are changing in the remaining answer choices, so the question is testing comma rules. The phrase *as technology has advanced* is unnecessary information, so it needs a comma before and after. Eliminate (F) because it does not have a comma after *advanced*. The correct answer is (G).

71. **B** Connecting words are changing in the answer choices, so the question is testing consistency. There is also the option to DELETE; consider this choice carefully as it's often the correct answer. Deleting the connecting word changes the meaning of the sentence, so eliminate (D). The part before the underlined portion contains the word *as*. The correct idiom is *as…as*. Eliminate (A) and (C) because they do not contain the word *as*. The correct answer is (B).

72. **H** Connecting words are changing in the answer choices, so the question is testing consistency. There is also the option to DELETE; consider this choice carefully as it's often the correct answer. Deleting the connecting word changes the meaning of the sentence, so eliminate (J). The question is, will these underwater robots be sufficient? *Why* and *what* change the meaning of the question, so eliminate (F) and (G). *Whether* these underwater robots will be sufficient preserves the meaning of the question and makes the sentence clear. The correct answer is (H).

73. **C** Transitions are changing in the answer choices, so the question is testing complete sentences. Look at the structure of the sentence and the type of punctuation used to connect ideas. The sentence has a comma between the two ideas. The comma is GO punctuation and can be used to connect

everything except two complete ideas. The second idea, *the day when the robots can move independently may not be far off*, is a complete idea, so the first idea must be incomplete for the punctuation to be correct. Eliminate (A), (B), and (D) because they all make the first idea complete. Choice (C) adds the transition word *although*, which makes the first idea incomplete. The correct answer is (C).

74. **H** The words around *useful* are changing in the answer choices, so the question could be testing concision. First determine whether the additional words are necessary. The additional words—*handy*, *practically*, and *effectively*—are all redundant with *useful*. Eliminate (F), (G), and (J). The correct answer is (H).

75. **D** Note the question! The question asks whether the sentence should be added, so it's testing consistency. If the content of the new sentence is consistent with the essay and the ideas before it, then it should be added. The essay discusses deep-sea exploration and how robots can assist with that. The previous sentence asks, *are more complex robots truly the key, or will humans need to venture back into the ocean's inky depths?* The new sentence discusses robots simulating emotional responses, so it is not consistent with the ideas in the text; the sentence should not be added. Eliminate (A) and (B). Eliminate (C) because it doesn't state that the new sentence is inconsistent with the text. Keep (D) because it states that the new sentence is irrelevant. The correct answer is (D).

MATHEMATICS TEST

1. **C** The question asks for the value of y in the equation. Since the question asks for a specific value and the answers contain numbers in increasing order, Plugging In the Answers is an option. The equation is not too complicated, though, so it may be faster to solve for y. Begin by multiplying both sides of the equation by 3 to get $5y - 1 = -18$. Add 1 to both sides to get $5y = -17$. Divide both sides by 5 to get $y = -\frac{17}{5}$. The correct answer is (C).

2. **H** The question asks for an equivalent expression. Use bite-sized pieces and Process of Elimination. The result of dividing the coefficients is $\frac{12}{4} = 3$. Eliminate (G), (J), and (K) which have a different coefficient. When dealing with questions about exponents, remember the MADSPM rules. The DS part of the acronym indicates that Dividing matching bases means to Subtract the exponents. The result of subtracting the exponents of the z terms is $z^{10-2} = z^8$. Eliminate (F). The correct answer is (H).

3. **C** The question asks for the value of a function. In function notation, the number inside the parentheses is the x-value that goes into the function, and the value that comes out of the function is the y-value. Plug $x = 12$ into the function to get $f(12) = \frac{12^2 - 18}{12 + 2} = \frac{144 - 18}{14} = \frac{126}{14} = 9$. The correct answer is (C).

4. **J** The question asks for the number of articles Rebecca writes in the first 3 weeks of the month. Read carefully and use bite-sized pieces to tackle this question. Graph 2 relates number of articles written to movies watched, so first determine how many movies she watched. Graph 1 indicates that at week 3, Rebecca had watched 15 movies. Graph 2 then indicates that when Rebecca had watched 15 movies, she had written 12 articles. The correct answer is (J).

5. **D** The question asks for the value of an expression rounded to the nearest tenth. First find the value of the expression, which is 117 − 54 + 6 = 69. Round 69 to the nearest ten to get 70. The correct answer is (D).

6. **G** The question asks for the number of tables in a restaurant given information about napkins and tables. Since the question asks for a specific value and the answers contain numbers in increasing order, plug in the answers. Begin by labeling the answers as "tables" and start with (H), 25. The question states there are 4 napkins at each table, so with 25 tables the restaurant would have 4(25) = 100 napkins at tables. The restaurant also has 20 napkins in reserve, so the total number of napkins would be 100 + 20 = 120 napkins. Since the question says the restaurant has 100 napkins total, this is too many, and the restaurant must have fewer tables. Eliminate (H), (J), and (K). Try (G), 20. With 20 tables the restaurant would have 4(20) = 80 napkins at tables. With the 20 napkins in reserve, that means the restaurant would have 80 + 20 = 100 napkins total. This matches the information in the question, so stop here. The correct answer is (G).

7. **D** The question asks for the value of w in the equation. Since the question asks for a specific value and the answers contain numbers in increasing order, plug in the answers. Begin by labeling the answers as "w" and start with (C), 16. The equation becomes 4[(16) − 2] − (16) = 46, which simplifies to 4(14) − 16 = 46 or 56 − 16 = 46. This becomes 40 = 46, which is not true, so eliminate (C). The left side of the equation was too small, so try a larger number next. Try (D), 18. The equation becomes 4[(18) − 2] − (18) = 46, which simplifies to 4(16) − 18 = 46 and finally 64 − 18 = 46. This is true, so stop here. The correct answer is (D).

8. **J** The question asks which ray does NOT contain $\overline{WX}$. A ray is part of a line which has an endpoint and extends infinitely from that endpoint in only one direction. The first letter in the name of a ray is the endpoint. For each choice, put a pencil on the first letter listed and travel toward the second letter to see if the pencil passes over $\overline{WX}$. The pencil will pass over $\overline{WX}$ for every choice except (J), $\overrightarrow{YZ}$. The correct answer is (J).

9. **A** The question asks for the value of a in a set of equations. Since the question asks for a specific value and the answers contain numbers in increasing order, Plugging In the Answers is an option. The equations are not too complicated, though, so it may be faster to solve for a. The third equation specifies that $c = 5$. Plug this value into the second equation to get $b(5) = 40$. Divide both sides of the equation by 5 to get $b = 8$. Plug this value into the first equation to get $a(8) = 32$. Divide both sides by 8 to get $a = 4$. The correct answer is (A).

10. **G** The question asks for an equation that models a specific situation. Translate the information in bite-sized pieces and eliminate after each piece. The question asks about Yunyun's average time.

For averages, use the formula $T = AN$, in which T is the total, A is the average, and N is the number of things. Calculate the total of the original set of numbers, using x for the missing 5th number. In this situation, the total time is the sum of the first four laps plus the time of the fifth lap, which is $175.8 + x$. Choices (J) and (K) do not contain this expression, so eliminate them. In this situation, the number of things is the number of laps being averaged, which is 5. This does not appear in (H), so eliminate it. The last part of the equation for average is A, which is 43. Eliminate (F) which divides 43 by another number. The correct answer is (G).

11. **B** The question asks how many integers in a certain range of numbers have a tens digit that is greater than the ones digit. There are not many numbers in the range, so list them all out. They are 123, 124, 125, 126, 127, 128, 129, 130, 131, and 132. Circle the numbers that have a tens digit greater than the ones digit. There are only three: 130, 131, and 132. The correct answer is (B).

12. **K** The question asks how many hours Julie must practice in order to score 35 points. Use Ballparking to eliminate incorrect answers. Since it takes 12 hours of practice for Julie to score 20 points, she will have to practice longer than that to score 35 points. Eliminate (F) which is less than 12 hours. Set up a proportion being sure to match up units. The proportion is $\dfrac{20 \text{ points}}{12 \text{ hours}} = \dfrac{35 \text{ points}}{x \text{ hours}}$. Cross-multiply to get $20x = 420$. Divide both sides of the equation by 20 to get $x = 21$. The correct answer is (K).

13. **B** The question asks for the fraction of a rectangle drawn on the coordinate plane that is in Quadrant IV. Begin by writing out the formula for the area of a rectangle, which is $A = lw$. Since the lines forming left and right sides of the rectangle are parallel to the y-axis, the length of the large rectangle can be found by subtracting the y-coordinates of the end points of those sides. This is $(2) - (-3) = 5$. The lines forming the top and bottom sides of the rectangle are parallel to the x-axis, so the width of the large rectangle can be found by subtracting the x-coordinates of the end points of those sides. This is $(2) - (-4) = 6$. Plug these into the formula for area to get $A = (5)(6) = 30$. The portion of the rectangle in Quadrant IV is also a rectangle; its area can be found by the same method. The length of this portion is $(0) - (-3) = 3$, and the width is $2 - 0 = 2$. Plug this into the formula for area to get $A = (3)(2) = 6$. The fraction this area is of the large rectangle is then $\dfrac{6}{30}$, which reduces to $\dfrac{1}{5}$. The correct answer is (B).

14. **K** The question asks for an equivalent form of an expression. There is a variable in the answer choices, so plug in. Make $z = 2$. The expression in the question becomes $\dfrac{2(2+3)-9}{5+4(2+3)}$. This simplifies to $\dfrac{2(5)-9}{5+4(5)} = \dfrac{10-9}{5+20} = \dfrac{1}{25}$. This is the target value; circle it. Now plug $z = 2$ into the answer choices to see which one matches the target value. Choices (F), (G), and (H) do not contain a variable and do not match the target value, so eliminate them. Choice (J) becomes $\dfrac{-7(2)-21}{9(2)+15} = \dfrac{-14-21}{18+15} = \dfrac{-35}{33}$. Eliminate (J). Choice (K) becomes $\dfrac{2(2)-3}{4(2)+17} = \dfrac{4-3}{8+17} = \dfrac{1}{25}$. The correct answer is (K).

15. **B** The question asks at what two points a circle crosses the *x*-axis. A point on the *x*-axis must have a *y*-coordinate of 0, so set $y = 0$ in the circle's equation. This becomes $x^2 - (0)^2 = 49$, or $x^2 = 49$. Take the square root of both sides of the equation, remembering to consider both the positive and negative roots. This gives $x = 7$ or $x = -7$. Therefore, the two points at which the circle crosses the *x*-axis are $(7, 0)$ and $(-7, 0)$. The correct answer is (B).

16. **H** The question asks for a system of linear equations represented by an augmented matrix. Each line in an augmented matrix represents a different equation in a system of equations. Compare the numbers in each row of the matrix with the equations, and eliminate choices that do not match. The first line of the matrix contains the numbers 4, –3, and 13. Only (H) includes an equation with these three numbers, which is $4m - 3n = 13$. Note that the other equation in (H) matches the three numbers in the other row of the augmented matrix. The correct answer is (H).

17. **A** The question asks the distance between the edge of a lake and a marker it is withdrawing from. Set up a proportion relating the change in distance to the change in years. Since the rate is linear, the proportion doesn't change. For the period from 1905 to 2005, this proportion is $\dfrac{825 - 75}{2005 - 1905} = \dfrac{750}{100}$ which reduces to $\dfrac{15}{2}$. Let *d* represent the distance between the marker and the lake in 1985. The proportion for the time between 1905 and 1985 is then $\dfrac{d - 75}{1985 - 1905} = \dfrac{d - 75}{80}$. Now the two proportions can be set equal to get $\dfrac{15}{2} = \dfrac{d - 75}{80}$. Cross-multiply to get $(15)(80) = 2(d - 75)$. Simplify to get $1{,}200 = 2d - 150$. Add 150 to both sides of the equation to get $2d = 1{,}350$. Divide both sides by 2 to get $d = 675$. The correct answer is (A).

18. **F** The question asks for the dimensions of a drawing given information about its area and perimeter. Use the Geometry Basic Approach. Start by drawing a figure and labeling it with the given information like this:

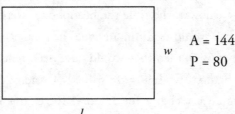

Write down the formula for the area of a rectangle, which is $A = lw$, and for the perimeter of a rectangle, which is $P = 2l + 2w$. Since the question asks for specific values and the answers contain numbers, plug in the answers. Begin by labeling the answers as "dimensions." Since the first dimension is increasing but the second is decreasing, just start with (F). Plug these numbers into the formula for area to get $A = (4)(36) = 144$. This matches the area given in the question, but the perimeter has to be checked as well. Plug the values into the formula for perimeter to get $P = 2(4) + 2(36) = 8 + 72 = 80$. Since all the information matches, these are the correct dimensions. Checking other choices would show that they either do not give the proper area or do not give the proper perimeter. The correct answer is (F).

19. **B** The question asks for a number equivalent to a fraction with numbers in scientific notation. Begin by dividing the digits before the multiplication sign to get $\frac{6.0}{1.5} = 4.0$. Eliminate (D) and (E) since they do not start with the correct digits. When dealing with exponents, remember the MADSPM rules. The DS part of the acronym indicates that Dividing matching bases means to Subtract the exponents. The result of subtracting the exponents on the 10's is $10^{(5-7)} = 10^{-2}$. Eliminate (A) and (C) which have the wrong exponent. The correct answer is (B).

20. **K** The question asks for the number of 7-digit phone numbers that can be generated which all have the same 3-digit prefix. Since digits can be any number from 0 to 9, there are 10 possibilities for each digit that is not in the prefix. Because digits can be selected independently of each other, simply multiply the number of possibilities for each digit together. The three digits in the prefix cannot change, so there are $10 - 7 = 4$ digits that can be selected. The number of possible combinations for these digits is $10 \times 10 \times 10 \times 10$, or 10^4. The correct answer is (K).

21. **B** The question asks for the time headphones could have been returned given the amount charged for rental. Since the question asks for a specific value and the answers are in increasing order, plug in the answers. Begin by labeling the answers as "return time" and start with (C), 7:30 p.m. If the headphones were returned at 7:30, then they would have been rented for the difference in time between 2:12 and 7:30. The difference between those two times is 5 hours plus $30 - 12 = 18$ minutes. For the first hour, the charge is $3.50. For the second hour, the charge is $2.50. That leaves 3 hours and 18 minutes remaining. For that time, the charge is $1.25 per hour or fraction thereof. Therefore, the last 3 hours and 18 minutes counts the same as 4 hours. The charge for that time would be 4($1.25) = $5.00. Add the amounts together to get $3.50 + $2.50 + $5.00 = $11.00. This doesn't match the amount charged specified in the question, $9.75, so eliminate (C). Since the amount actually charged was lower, the time the headphones were rented must have been less, so eliminate (D) and (E) as they would result in an equal or greater charge. Try (B), 6:30 p.m. If the headphones were returned at 6:30, then they would have been rented for 4 hours and $30 - 12 = 18$ minutes. The charges for the first two hours are still $3.50 and $2.50. The remaining 2 hours and 18 minutes would be the same as a charge for 3 hours. The charge for that time would be 3($1.25) = $3.75. Therefore, the total charge would be $3.50 + $2.50 + $3.75 = $9.75. This matches the information in the question, so stop here. The correct answer is (B).

22. **J** The question asks for the last term in a geometric sequence consisting of the measure of the angles in a quadrilateral. Any quadrilateral, or four-sided figure, will have 4 angles that add up to 360°. Since the question asks for a specific value and the answers are in increasing order, plug in the answers. Begin by labeling the answers as "last term" and start with (H), 160°. If the last term is 160, and the common ratio between the degree measures is 2, then the degree measure of the third angle is $160 \div 2 = 80°$. The measure of the second angle is then $80 \div 2 = 40°$, and the measure of the first

angle in the sequence is 40 ÷ 2 = 20°. The sum of these angles would be 160 + 80 + 40 + 20 = 300°. This doesn't match the sum of the angles in a quadrilateral, so eliminate (H). Since the sum was not large enough, the largest angle must be even larger, so eliminate (F) and (G) as well. Try (J), 192°. The other three angles would be 96°, 48°, and 24°. Add these angles to get 192 + 96 + 48 + 24 = 360°, which is the correct sum. The correct answer is (J).

23. **B** The question asks for the value of *n* in an expression representing the measure of an angle. Use the Geometry Basic Approach. Start by drawing a figure and labeling it with the given information like this:

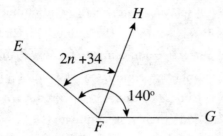

Since the question asks for a specific value and the answers contain numbers in increasing order, plug in the answers. Begin by labeling the answers as "*n*," and start with (C), 36°. Plug the value into the expression for ∠EFG to get 2(36) + 34 = 72 + 34 = 108°. The question states that $\overrightarrow{FH}$ bisects ∠EFG. Therefore, the measure of ∠EFG would be 108 × 2 = 216°. This does not match the angle in the question, 140°, so eliminate (C). Since the measure was too large, *n* must be smaller, so eliminate (D) and (E) as well. Try (B). The measure of ∠EFG becomes 2(18) + 34 = 36 + 34 = 70°. The measure of ∠EFG becomes 70 × 2 = 140°. This matches the information in the question, so stop here. The correct answer is (B).

24. **F** The question asks for the value of an expression with two variables given two equations containing the variables. First solve the system of equations to get the values of *x* and *y*. One way to do this is to stack and add the equations to eliminate a variable. To eliminate *x*, multiply the second equation by −2 so that the equations have the same *x* coefficient with opposite signs. The second equation becomes − 2(3*x* + 4*y*) = −2(2) or −6*x* − 8*y* = −4. Then stack the equations and add:

$$6x + 10y = 14$$
$$\underline{-6x - 8y = -4}$$
$$2y = 10$$

Divide both sides of the result by 2 to get *y* = 5. Plug this into one of the equations and solve for *x*. The original version of the second equation becomes 3*x* + 4(5) = 2. This simplifies to 3*x* + 20 = 2. Subtract 20 from both sides to get 3*x* = −18. Divide both sides by 3 to get *x* = −6. Plug the values for *x* and *y* into the expression 5*x* + 7*y* in the question to get 5(−6) + 7(5) = −30 + 35 = 5. The correct answer is (F).

25. **E** The equation asks for the form of an equation solved for *b*. There are variables in the answer choices, so Plugging In on this question is an option. It would be tricky to find numbers that make the equation true, though, so it may be faster to solve for *b*. Start by multiplying both sides of the equa-

tion by 2 to get $a - b = 12$. Subtract a from both sides to get $-b = 12 - a$. Multiply both sides by -1 to get $b = -12 + a$, or $b = a - 12$. The correct answer is (E).

26. **K**   The question asks for a product that results in a negative odd number. A product is the result of multiplying two values together. Plug in some values to determine what kind of numbers work. Select numbers that satisfy the conditions in the answer choices and multiply them together to see if the result is a negative odd number. Choice (F) specifies a positive even number and a negative even number. Try 2 and -4. The product of these is $(2)(-4) = -8$. This is not an odd number, so eliminate (F). Choice (G) specifies two negative odd numbers. Choose -3 and -5. The product of these is $(-3)(-5) = 15$. This is not a negative number, so eliminate (G). Choice (H) specifies a positive even number and a negative odd number. Choose 2 and -3. The product of these is $(2)(-3) = -6$. This is not an odd number, so eliminate (H). Choice (J) specifies a negative even number and a negative odd number. Choose -2 and -3. The product of these is $(-2)(-3) = 6$. This is neither a negative number nor an odd number, so eliminate (J). Choice (K) specifies a positive odd number and a negative odd number. Choose 3 and -3. The product of these is $(3)(-3) = -9$. This is a negative odd number. The correct answer is (K).

27. **B**   The question asks for the probability that the fifth marble removed from a bag will be purple. Probability is defined as $\frac{part}{whole}$. The *part*, or the number of outcomes that fit the requirements, is the number of purple marbles available when the fifth marble is removed. The bag initially contained 11 purple marbles, but 4 are removed, so the number of purple marbles currently in the bag is $11 - 4 = 7$. The *whole* is the total number of marbles that can be selected. The bag started out with $11 + 11 + 11 + 11 = 44$ marbles, but 4 are removed. Therefore, before the fifth marble is removed there are $44 - 4 = 40$ marbles available. Plug these numbers into the expression for probability to get $\frac{7}{40}$. The correct answer is (B).

28. **H**   The question asks for an inequality describing the number of points Oliver got if he must repeat a test. Use Ballparking to eliminate answers that do not make sense. Since a high score would mean that a test doesn't have to be repeated, choices that allow the score to be as high as possible cannot be correct. Eliminate (G) and (K) which allow p to be as high as possible. There is a variable in the answer choices, so plug in. Examine the remaining answer choices to determine what number to plug in. Try $p = 20$. If Oliver scores 20 points on a test with 30 available points, the percentage of points he earned is $\frac{20}{30} \times 100 = 66.\overline{6}\%$. This is less than 70%, so it means that Oliver would have to repeat the test. Eliminate (J) since it is not necessarily true that $p = 21$. Also eliminate (F) since it is not necessarily true that $p < 20$. The correct answer is (H).

29. **B**   The question asks how many miles of road were painted on a certain day. Since the entire line was painted in three days, the amount painted on Day 2 is the entire length of the road minus the amount

painted on Day 1 and Day 3. In order to subtract the distances, convert them all to improper fractions with a common denominator. Since 3 and 9 are both factors of 27, 27 is the lowest common denominator for the three fractions. Make all the fractions have a denominator of 27. The total length of the road becomes $16\frac{1}{9} = \frac{145}{9} = \frac{435}{27}$. The length painted on Day 1 becomes $5\frac{8}{27} = \frac{143}{27}$. The length painted on Day 3 becomes $3\frac{2}{3} = \frac{11}{3} = \frac{99}{27}$. The distance painted on Day 2 is $\frac{435}{27} - \frac{143}{27} - \frac{99}{27} = \frac{193}{27}$. Converted to a mixed fraction, this is $7\frac{4}{27}$. Another option to answer this question would be to use a calculator to get a decimal for each of the mixed numbers and then do the calculations. The result will be $16.\overline{11} - 5.\overline{296} - 3.\overline{66} = 7.\overline{148}$. This eliminates (C), (D), and (E). The values in (A) and (B) can then be converted to decimals to see which one is closer to this value. Either way, the correct answer is (B).

30. **H** The question asks for the distance in feet between two different screens and the projectors used for each one. Whenever dealing with relationships between parts of triangles, look for similar triangles and then set up proportions between corresponding sides. The diagram contains two triangles sharing a common angle at the projector. Since the screens are parallel, the angles formed by the left sides of the triangles and the two screens are equal. Also, the angles formed by each of the right sides of the two triangles and the two screens are equal. Since all the angles between the two triangles are equal, the two triangles are similar. Set up proportions involving corresponding lengths of the two triangles. The widths of the screens represent corresponding sides on the triangles, so one proportion that can be formed, putting the value for the smaller triangle on top, would be $\frac{81}{108}$. The other value in the question, 180, represents the distance to the screen for the *Illuminator 100 Plus* and is also the height of the larger triangle. The height of the smaller triangle, which represents the distance from the projector to the screen for the *Illuminator 100*, is unknown, so call it x. Another proportion that can be set up, again putting the value for the smaller triangle on top, is $\frac{x}{180}$. Set these proportions equal to get $\frac{81}{108} = \frac{x}{180}$. Cross-multiply to get $(81)(180) = 108x$. This simplifies to $14,580 = 108x$. Divide both sides by 108 to get $x = 135$. This is the distance from the *Illuminator 100* to the screen. To get the distance between the screens, subtract this from the distance between the projector and the *Illuminator 100 Plus*. This is $180 - 135 = 45$. The correct answer is (H).

31. **C** The question asks for the distance between two points in the standard coordinate plane. Draw the points on the coordinate plane. Add two lines to form a right triangle with $\overline{JK}$ as the hypotenuse. Then use the Pythagorean theorem, $a^2 + b^2 = c^2$, to calculate the length of the hypotenuse:

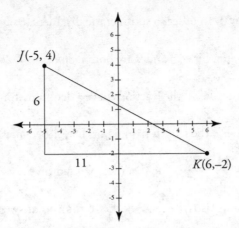

The height of the triangle is 4 − (−2) = 6 units. The base of the triangle is 6 − (−5) = 11 units. Put these into the Pythagorean theorem to get $6^2 + 11^2 = c^2$. This simplifies to $c^2 = 36 + 121$, or $c^2 =$ 157. Take the square root of both sides to get $c = \sqrt{157}$. The correct answer is (C).

32. **J** The question asks for the total number of stars Cynthia places on her bedroom ceiling after 30 days. This total is just the sum of the number of stars Cynthia places each day, or 1 + 2 + 3 + ... + 30. Because there are only 30 numbers to be added, just carefully add them up on a calculator. The total is 465. The correct answer is (J).

33. **A** The question asks which number CANNOT be the length of a side of a triangle given the lengths of the other two sides. The sum of the lengths of any two sides of a triangle must be greater than the third side. In particular, the lengths of the two smaller sides of a triangle must be greater than the largest side. Add $\overline{PQ}$ and $\overline{QR}$ to get 12 + 41 = 53. Since this is larger than the largest choice, none of the answers is too large. To see if any are too small, plug in the answers. Start with the smallest choice which is (A), 17. If $\overline{PR}$ is 17, the three sides of the triangle are 12, 41, and 17. Verify that the sum of the two smaller numbers is greater than the third: 12 + 17 = 29. This is not greater than 41, so these three sides cannot be the lengths of the sides of a triangle. The correct answer is (A).

34. **J** The question asks for an equivalent form of an expression. There is a variable in the answer choices, so plug in. Make $d = 2$. The expression becomes $\dfrac{5(2)^2 - 2}{20(2)} = \dfrac{5(4) - 2}{40} = \dfrac{18}{40} = \dfrac{9}{20}$. This is the target value; circle it. Now plug $d = 2$ into the answer choices to see which one matches the target value. Choice (F) is simply $\dfrac{3}{20}$. This doesn't match the target value, so eliminate (F). Choice (G) becomes $\dfrac{1}{5(2)^2} = \dfrac{1}{5(4)} = \dfrac{1}{20}$. Eliminate (G). Choice (H) becomes 2. Eliminate (H). Choice (J) becomes $\dfrac{2}{4} - \dfrac{1}{10(2)} = \dfrac{2}{4} - \dfrac{1}{20} = \dfrac{10}{20} - \dfrac{1}{20} = \dfrac{9}{20}$. This matches the target, so keep (J), but check the remaining answer just in case. Choice (K) becomes $\dfrac{(2)^2 - 1}{10(2)} = \dfrac{4 - 1}{20} = \dfrac{3}{20}$. Eliminate (K). The correct answer is (J).

35. **B** The question asks for the area of the floor space, in square meters, covered by non-slip tiles laid around the pool. Use the Geometry Basic Approach. A figure is given, but it represents the 3D

volume of the pool. Start by drawing a 2D figure of the tile-covered area and labeling it with the given information like this:

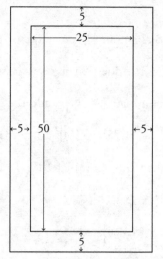

Write down the formula for the area of a rectangle, which is $A = lw$. The area of the floor space around the pool is equal to the area of the larger rectangle minus the area of the smaller rectangle. The length of the smaller rectangle is 50 meters. The width of the smaller rectangle is 25 meters. Plug these into the formula for area to get $A = (50)(25) = 1,250$ square meters. The length of the larger rectangle is $50 + 5 + 5 = 60$ meters. The width of the larger rectangle is $25 + 5 + 5 = 35$ meters. Plug these into the formula for area to get $A = (60)(35) = 2,100$ square meters. Therefore, the area of the floor space around the pool is $2,100 - 1,250 = 850$ square meters. The correct answer is (B).

36.   **G**   The question asks the maximum number of swimmers that can perform in a pool given that they need each need a certain amount of area. Use the Geometry Basic Approach. Start by drawing a figure of the pool area and labeling it with the given information like this:

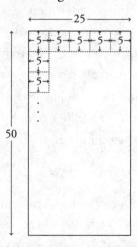

The rectangle representing the area of the pool can be filled with a grid of squares, each representing the area needed by a different swimmer. The number of swimmers that swim side by side along the width of the pool is 5 since 5 meters goes into 25 meters 5 times. In other words, $25 \div 5 = 5$. The number of swimmers that can swim along the length of the pool is $50 \div 5 = 10$. Note that no space is left over, so the number of squares in the grid must be the maximum number of swimmers that can perform in the pool. Since this grid is 5 squares by 10 squares, the maximum number of swimmers that can fit is 5 × 10 = 50. The correct answer is (G).

37. **C** The question asks for the total amount Merav pays for a ticket, pizza, and soda. Use bite-sized pieces and Process of Elimination. The question states that Merav pays $4.00 for the ticket alone. This is already more than (A), so eliminate (A). Next add the price of the pizza and soda to the price of the ticket to get $4.00 + $3.75 + $1.75 = $9.50. Since that doesn't yet include the sales tax, the price Merav pays will be more than this. Eliminate (B). To calculate the 10% sales tax, take 10% of the total of the taxed items. This is $($3.75 + 1.75) \times 10\% = \$5.50 \times \dfrac{10}{100} = \dfrac{\$55}{100} = \$0.55$. Add this to the total of the three items already calculated to get $9.50 + $0.55 = $10.05. The correct answer is (C).

38. **H** The question asks for the measure of a central angle of a circle. Start with Process of Elimination. The angle is a large angle—larger than a right angle, which is 90°. Eliminate (F) and (G) because they are less than 90°. Note that the diagram includes a triangle. Two of the sides of that triangle are radii of the circle and must be the same length. That means the angles opposite those sides are also equal. Therefore, the triangle has two 40° angles. Use the fact that the three angles of a triangle always add up to 180° to determine the measure of the third. Let x be the measure of the third angle, so 40 + 40 + x = 180. This becomes 80 + x = 180, so the central angle, x, is 100°. The correct answer is (H).

39. **D** The question asks what percent of Stephanie's August expenses will be for office supplies. Translate the English into math in bite-size pieces. The question states Stephanie will *reduce her electricity expenses by $700* in August. The pie chart indicates that she spent $1,200 on electricity in July so she will spend $1,200 − $700 = $500 on electricity in August. The question states she will reduce her rent *by $1,300* in August, and it was $7,300 in July, so she will spend $7,300 − $1,300 = $6,000 on rent. The question states that *the rest of her expenses are unchanged*. Add all her expenses for August, taking into account those adjustments, to calculate her total expenses for August: $150 + $350 + $1,000 + $500 + $6,000 = $8,000. The amount she will spend on office supplies will still be $1,000. Find the percent of her total expenses for August that will be for office supplies: $\dfrac{\$1,000}{\$8,000} \times 100 = 12.5\%$. The correct answer is (D).

40. **G** The question gives two expressions and asks for a number by which their difference will always be divisible. The question involves a relationship between unknown numbers, so plug in. Make $q = 2$. Plug 2 in for q to find that the difference between $14q$ and $5q$ is $14(2) − 5(2) = 28 − 10 = 18$. Of the answer choices, 18 is only divisible by (B), 9, so that is the answer. Alternatively, use algebra to find that the difference between $14q$ and $5q$ is $14q − 5q = 9q$, which is always divisible by 9. Either way, the correct answer is (G).

41.   **A**   The question asks for an inequality representing a specific situation. Translate the English into math in bite-size pieces. There is a variable in the answer choices, so plug in. As the question states, Ron's hourly rate of pay, r, is dependent on how many hours Ron works, so select a number of hours Ron could have worked. The question says he works for a minimum of 20 hours per week, so for 6 weeks he works at least $6(20) = 120$ hours. If Ron works for 120 hours, his hourly rate of pay will be $r = \$1,800 \div 120 = \$15$ per hour. Eliminate (C), (D), and (E) as they do not have $15 as an extreme. To determine whether (A) or (B) is correct, select another number of work hours. Try 30. If Ron works for 30 hours per week, he works for $6(30) = 180$ hours total, and his hourly rate of pay will be $r = \$1,800 \div 180 = \$10$ per hour. Eliminate (B). The correct answer is (A).

42.   **J**   The question asks for the distance between two points in the complex plane. The complex number $a + bi$ is plotted in the complex plane as (a, b) with a representing the real part of the complex number, and b representing the imaginary part. This means that $P = 2 + i$ would be plotted as the point $(2, 1)$, and $Q = 6 + 4i$ would be plotted as the point $(6, 4)$. Draw these points on a coordinate plane. Add two lines to form a right triangle with $\overline{PQ}$ as the hypotenuse. Then use the Pythagorean Theorem, $a^2 + b^2 = c^2$, to calculate the length of the hypotenuse:

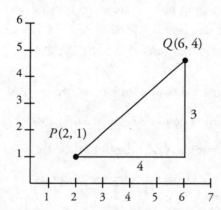

The height of the triangle is $4 - 1 = 3$ units. The base of the triangle is $6 - 2 = 4$ units. Plug these values into the Pythagorean equation, $a^2 + b^2 = c^2$, and solve for c to get the hypotenuse, or simply note that the triangle is a 3-4-5 right triangle with a hypotenuse of 5. Either way, the distance between the points is 5. The correct answer is (J).

43.   **C**   The question asks for the inverse trigonometric expression that represents an angle on the figure. Write out SOHCAHTOA to remember the trig functions. Let θ represent the angle. The 8 in the figure corresponds to the length of the side adjacent to θ, and the 23 in the figure corresponds to the hypotenuse. The CAH part of SOHCAHTOA defines the cosine as $\dfrac{adjacent}{hypotenuse}$, so $\cos\theta = \dfrac{8}{23}$. The answers choices contain inverse trig functions, which are simply the functions that take a ratio of the sides of a triangle and return the appropriate angle. Therefore, $\cos\theta = \dfrac{8}{23}$ means $\cos^{-1}\left(\dfrac{8}{23}\right) = \theta$. The correct answer is (C).

44. **F** The question asks for the perimeter of a polygon. The perimeter of a shape is simply the measure of the line around the shape. The perimeter of polygon *CDZXY* is the sum of the lengths of all the individual sides. Since *CDZY* is a square, all its sides are equal. This means that $\overline{CD} = x$. Another side of the square is $\overline{DZ}$, so it also has a length of *x*. The length of $\overline{ZX}$ is given as *y*. The length of $\overline{XY}$ is given as *z*. Continuing around the polygon, $\overline{YC}$ is another side of the square, so its length is again *x*. Add these all together to get the perimeter of *CDZXY* as *x + x + y + z + x*, which simplifies to 3*x + y + z*. The correct answer is (F).

45. **E** The question asks which list correctly orders the three angles on a figure from least to greatest. Use the Geometry Basic Approach. Start by labeling the figure with the given information. $\angle EZD$ is opposite $\angle XZY$, which is a right angle, so $\angle EZD$ is a right angle as well. Label $\angle EZD$ as 90°. Both $\angle AXF$ and $\angle BYC$ are larger than 90°, so $\angle EZD$ must be the smallest of the three angles. Eliminate (A), (B), and (C) which do not list $\angle EZD$ as the smallest angle. Examining the angles in the diagram, $\angle AXF$ appears larger than $\angle BYZ$. Since the diagram satisfies the inequality of 0 < *x* < *y* given in the question, this must be the case, and thus the answer is (E). To be convinced of this, note that *x* < *y* indicates that $\angle YXZ < \angle XYZ$. Also note that the sums of the angles around point *X* and point *Y* are equal because both of those sums are 360°. Lastly, note that $\angle AXY$ and $\angle FXZ$ are equal to $\angle BYX$ and $\angle CYZ$ since all of these angles are right angles. Therefore, $\angle YXZ < \angle XYZ$ indicates that $\angle BYC < \angle AXF$. Either way, the correct answer is (E).

46. **F** The question asks for the value of a trigonometric expression given a relationship between the sides. When dealing with trigonometric expressions, write out SOHCAHTOA to remember the trig functions. In relation to $\angle XYZ$, the line labeled *x* is the adjacent side, and the side labeled *z* is the hypotenuse. The CAH part defines the cosine as $\dfrac{adjacent}{hypotenuse}$. Therefore, $\cos(\angle XYZ) = \dfrac{x}{z}$. Since the question states 2*x* = *z*, substitute 2*x* for *z* in the expression to get $\cos(\angle XYZ) = \dfrac{x}{2x}$, which simplifies to $\cos(\angle XYZ) = \dfrac{1}{2}$. The correct answer is (F).

47. **C** The question asks for the sum of the two largest integers in a series of four consecutive even numbers. There is a variable in the answer choices, so plug in. Since *t* must be the sum of four consecutive, even integers, select four such integers and add them together. Use the numbers 2, 4, 6, and 8. This means *t* = 2 + 4 + 6 + 8 = 20. Take care to identify what the question asks for. The question asks for the sum of the 2 larger integers, which is 6 + 8 = 14. This is the target value; circle it. Now plug *t* = 20 into the answer choices to see which one matches the target value. Choice (A) becomes $\dfrac{20}{2} - 4 = 10 - 4 = 6$. This does not match the target value, so eliminate (A). Choice (B) becomes $\dfrac{20}{2} = 10$. Eliminate (B). Choice (C) becomes $\dfrac{20}{2} + 4 = 10 + 4 = 14$. This matches the target, so keep (C) but check the remaining answers just in case. Choice (D) becomes 20 + 2 = 22. Eliminate (D). Choice (E) becomes 20 + 4 = 24. Eliminate (E). The correct answer is (C).

48. **K** The question asks for the equation shown in the graph in Figure 2. The graph in Figure 2 has a labeled point. Since that point must satisfy the equation, plug its coordinates into the answer choices. For point $(-4, 1)$, $x = -4$, and $y = 1$. Choice (F) becomes $1 = (-4 - 4)^2 - 1$, which simplifies to $1 = (-8)^2 - 1$. This becomes $1 = 64 - 1$ or $1 = 63$. This is not true, so eliminate (F). Choice (G) becomes $1 = (-4 - 4)^2 + 1$. This simplifies to $1 = (-8)^2 + 1$, which becomes $1 = 64 + 1$ or $1 = 65$. Eliminate (G). Choice (H) becomes $1 = (-4 + 1)^2 - 4$. This simplifies to $1 = (-3)^2 - 4$, which becomes $1 = 9 - 4$ or $1 = 5$. Eliminate (H). Choice (J) becomes $1 = (-4 + 4)^2 - 1$. This simplifies to $1 = (0)^2 - 1$, which becomes $1 = 0 - 1$ or $1 = -1$. Eliminate (J). Choice (K) becomes $1 = (-4 + 4)^2 + 1$. This simplifies to $1 = (0)^2 + 1$, which becomes $1 = 0 + 1$, or $1 = 1$. The correct answer is (K).

49. **A** The question asks the number of nickels in a piggy bank. Since the question asks for a specific value and the answers contain numbers in increasing order, plug in the answers. Begin by labeling the answers as "nickels" and start with (C), 17. The question states that there is one more dime there are than nickels, so there are $17 + 1 = 18$ dimes. The question states that there three times as many dimes as pennies, so there are $18 \div 3 = 6$ pennies. The question says there are two more quarters than dimes, so there are $18 + 2 = 20$ quarters. Multiply the number of each type of coin by its value to get the total amount of money in the piggy bank as $17(0.05) + 18(0.10) + 6(0.01) + 20(0.25) = \$7.71$. This doesn't match the amount in the question, $\$5.29$, so eliminate (C). Since more nickels would only increase the amount of money in the bank, there must be fewer nickels. Eliminate (D) and (E). Try (B). If there are 13 nickels, then there are 14 dimes. There are supposed to be three times as many dimes as pennies, but since 14 is not divisible by 3, this is impossible. Eliminate (B). Try (A). If there are 11 nickels, then there are 12 dimes, 4 pennies, and 14 quarters. The total in the piggy bank is then $11(0.05) + 12(0.10) + 4(0.01) + 14(0.25) = \$5.29$. This matches the information in the question. The correct answer is (A).

50. **J** The question asks for the mean of a set of numbers given information about how the set relates to another set. For averages, use the formula $T = AN$, in which T is the total, A is the average, and N is the number of things. The average is 87, and the number of things is 5, so $T = (87)(5) = 435$. The new set removes the number 75, so the new total is $435 - 75 = 360$. To find the new average, plug $T = 360$ and $N = 4$ into the formula to get $360 = A(4)$. Divide both sides of the equation by 4 to get $A = 90$. The correct answer is (J).

51. **E** The question asks which statement is true given another true statement. For any true if-then statement, the statement's contrapositive is also true. The original statement is *"If Jenny is home, then her car is in the driveway."* Determine the contrapositive of this by flipping the two parts of the statement and reversing those parts. This means that the contrapositive is *"If Jenny's car is not in the driveway, then she is not home."* The correct answer is (E).

52. **J** The question asks for the solution set of an equation with exponents. When dealing with questions about exponents, remember the MADSPM rules. The PM part of the acronym indicates that when a number raised to a Power is raised to another Power, Multiply the exponents. The result of multiplying the exponents makes the equation $y^{0.2(a^2-20)} = y$. Since the question asks for a specific value and the answers contain numbers in increasing order, plug in the answers. Begin by labeling the answers

as "*a*" and start with a value that is in more than one answer choice, such as 5. Plug 5 in for *a*, and the equation becomes $y^{0.2(5^2-20)} = y$. This simplifies to $y^{0.2(25-20)} = y$, which becomes, $y^{0.2(5)} = y$, or $y^1 = y$. Since this is true, 5 is in the solution set of *a*. Since (F), (G), and (K) do not include 5, eliminate those answers. Choice (J) includes 5, but also includes −5, so check to see if −5 is also a valid solution. Plug −5 into the equation to get $y^{0.2[(-5)^2-20]} = y$. This simplifies to $y^{0.2(25-20)} = y$, which becomes $y^{0.2(5)} = y$, or $y^1 = y$. Since this is true, −5 is in the solution set of *a* as well. Since −5 is not included in (H), eliminate it. The correct answer is (J).

53. **E** The question asks for an equivalent equation involving trig functions. When dealing with trigonometric expressions, write out SOHCAHTOA to remember the trig functions. The question includes functions that are not defined in SOHCAHTOA, but it also includes some definitions to relate those functions to SOHCAHTOA functions. Use those definitions to convert the equation to SOHCAHTOA functions. The function $g(x) = \csc x \tan x$ becomes $g(x) = \left(\dfrac{1}{\sin x}\right)(\tan x)$. The SOH part of SOHCAHTOA defines the sine as $\dfrac{opposite}{hypotenuse}$. The TOA part of SOHCATOA defines the tangent as $\dfrac{opposite}{adjacent}$. The function includes the reciprocal of sine, so take the reciprocal of the expression to get $\dfrac{1}{\sin x} = \dfrac{hypotenuse}{opposite}$. Substitute these definitions into the equation to get $g(x) = \left(\dfrac{hypotenuse}{opposite}\right)\left(\dfrac{opposite}{adjacent}\right)$. The *opposite* sides cancel to give $g(x) = \dfrac{hypotenuse}{adjacent}$. Use SOHCAHTOA one more time to turn this back into a trig function. The CAH part of SOHCAHTOA defines the cosine as $\dfrac{adjacent}{hypotenuse}$. Since the equation now contains the reciprocal of this, the equation can be rewritten as $g(x) = \dfrac{1}{\cos x}$. Per the definitions in the question, this is the same as $\sec x$. The correct answer is (E).

54. **J** The question asks for the expected value of a random variable representing the total number of points in five rounds of a game. Expected value is calculated by multiplying each possible outcome by the probability of its occurrence and then adding the products. As stated in the question, each round of the game has three possible outcomes: win, lose, or tie. Since the question says that the outcomes are all equally likely, they each have a probability of $\dfrac{1}{3}$. Multiply the probability of each one by the point value each one earns and add the results. The result is $2\left(\dfrac{1}{3}\right) + 0\left(\dfrac{1}{3}\right) + 0\left(\dfrac{1}{3}\right) = \dfrac{2}{3}$. This is the expected result of one round. To get the expected result of five rounds, multiply by 5 to get $5\left(\dfrac{2}{3}\right) = \dfrac{10}{3}$. The correct answer is (J).

55. **E** The question asks for the surface area of a sphere given the volume. The question gives the equations for the surface area and volume of a sphere. Both involve radius, so find the radius of the sphere. Set the volume given for the sphere equal to the expression for volume to get $\dfrac{4}{3}\pi r^3 = 288\pi$.

Multiply both sides by 3 to get $4\pi r^3 = 864\pi$. Divide both sides by 4π to get $r^3 = 216$. Take the cube root of both sides to get $r = 6$. Plug this value for the radius into the expression for surface area to get $4\pi(6)^2 = 4\pi(36) = 144\pi$. The correct answer is (E).

56. **F** The question asks for the value of x in an equation involving a logarithm. Logarithms are another way of expressing exponents such that $\log_b = x$ can be written as $b^x = n$. First set the expression equal to a variable, such as y. Therefore $3\log_x x^{-2} = y$. Divide both sides by 3 to get $\log_x x^{-2} = \frac{y}{3}$. Using the identity for logs, this becomes $x^{\frac{y}{3}} = x^{-2}$. Since the bases are the same, the exponents are equal, so $\frac{y}{3} = -2$. Multiply both sides by 3 to get $y = -6$. The correct answer is (F).

57. **B** The question asks for the inequalities that describe a shaded area that has been reflected across the y-axis. Use the Geometry Basic Approach. Start by labeling the figure with the given information. Draw the reflected triangle on the figure like this:

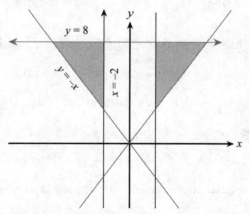

The top of the reflected triangle is still bounded by $y = 8$, meaning $y \le 8$. Eliminate (C) and (E) which do not have this inequality. The left side of the reflected triangle will be bounded by line $x = 2$, and the points will have an x-coordinate greater than this, meaning $x \ge 2$. Eliminate (D). The third side of the triangle is bounded by the line $y = x$. The points in the reflected triangle are above this line, meaning they have a larger y value, so $y \ge x$. If this isn't easy to see, pick a point that will be in the shaded region, such as $(3, 6)$. For this point, $x = 3$ and $y = 6$, so $y > x$. Eliminate (A). The correct answer is (B).

58. **H** The question asks for the sine of an angle depicted in the coordinate plane. Start with Process of Elimination. Using the mnemonic device All Students Take Calculus, determine the sign of the trig functions in Quadrant III, where θ terminates. This indicates that only tangent is positive in Quadrant III, so the sine must be negative. Eliminate (J) and (K). When dealing with trigonometric expressions, write out SOHCAHTOA to remember the trig functions. The SOH part defines the sine as $\frac{opposite}{hypotenuse}$. Trigonometric functions relate to right triangles, so draw a line from the point $(-12, -5)$ to the x-axis to create a right triangle like this:

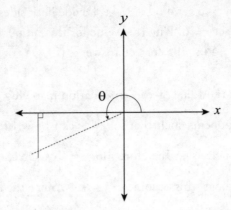

Even though θ includes the angle measure from the positive *x*-axis to the negative *x*-axis, sin θ will have the same value but the opposite sign as the angle that is formed with the negative *x*-axis. The side opposite that angle is represented by the distance between the point and the *x*-axis, which is 5. To find the hypotenuse, use the Pythagorean Theorem or realize this is a 5-12-13 triangle, so the hypotenuse is 13. The sine of this angle is $\frac{5}{13}$, but it must be negative. The correct answer is (H).

59. **A** The question asks which line could contain the side of a parallelogram with one side given. Since the given side, $\overline{AB}$, and the side in question, $\overline{CD}$, have no points in common, they are opposite sides of the parallelogram and so are parallel to each other. Two lines containing the two line segments would also be parallel. Lines that are parallel have the same slope. Calculate the slope of the line through $\overline{AB}$. The formula for slope is $\frac{y_2 - y_1}{x_2 - x_1}$. Plug in the values from the two endpoints of $\overline{AB}$ to get $\frac{6-1}{7-5} = \frac{5}{2}$. The answer choices are already in slope-intercept form, $y = mx + b$, where *m* represents the slope. The only one with a slope of $\frac{5}{2}$ is (A). The correct answer is (A).

60. **G** The question asks for the evaluation of a function with two variables. Since there are variables in the answers, plug in. Make *c* = 2 and *d* = 3, so c^2 = 4 and d^2 = 9. Plug these into the function for *x* and *y* to get $(4 - 9)^2 + (4 + 9)^2 = (-5)^2 + (13)^2 = 25 + 169 = 194$. This is the target value; circle it. Now plug *c* = 2 and *d* = 3 into the answer choices to see which matches the target value. Choice (F) becomes $4(2)^2(3)^2 = 4(4)(9) = 144$. This doesn't match the target value, so eliminate (F). Choice (G) becomes $2(2)^4 + 2(3)^4 = 32 + 162 = 194$. This matches the target, so keep (G) but check the remaining answers just in case. Choice (H) becomes $2(2)^4 - 2(3)^4 = 32 - 162 = -130$. Eliminate (H). Choice (J) is simply 1. Eliminate (J). Choice (K) becomes $-4(2)^2(3)^2 = -4(4)(9) = -144$. Eliminate (K). The correct answer is (G).

READING TEST

1. **B**   This vocabulary-in-context question asks what the word *untainted* in line 3 does NOT mean. Go back to the text, find the word *untainted*, and cross it out. Carefully read the surrounding text to determine another word that would fit in the blank based on the context. According to the narrator, dusk *reveals the untainted essence of the landscape*, and *subtle details are easier to perceive*, meaning that it is easier to see things as they truly are at dusk. Therefore, the word *untainted* could be replaced with something like "unaltered" or "true." When a question asks what is **not** supported, eliminate answers that are supported. Choices (A), (C), and (D) all closely match the prediction, so eliminate them. Keep (B) because *non-toxic* does not match *unaltered*. The correct answer is (B).

2. **F**   This referral question asks which activity is NOT taken on by at least one family member in the passage. When a question asks what is **not** mentioned in the text, eliminate answers that are mentioned. Work backwards and use lead words from the answers to find the windows for this question. Choice (F) mentions the *Wood River*, which the author does discuss. However, there is no discussion of the family *wading*. Keep (F). Choice (G) is *setting up a tent*, so look for the lead word *tent* in the passage. In lines 13–14, the author states *my mother was playing her role, setting up tents*. Eliminate (G). Choice (H) is *gathering pine needles*, so look for the lead words *pine needles* in the passage. In lines 23–25, the author states *as he teased bits of leaves, sticks, and dry pine needles into a stack underneath the firewood, I went to look a second time for more of the same*. Eliminate (H). Choice (J) is *igniting damp wood*, so look for the lead words *damp wood* in the passage. In lines 25–26, the author refers to *trying to ignite damp, untreated wood*. Eliminate (J). The correct answer is (F).

3. **A**   This referral question asks which activity the narrator does NOT describe her father doing. When a question asks what is **not** mentioned in the text, eliminate answers that are mentioned. Work backwards and use lead words from the answers to find the windows for this question. Choice (A) refers to *hot cocoa*, so look for those lead words in the passage. In lines 57–62, the author describes drinking *hot cocoa*, but says that Myra's mother, not her father, would share her hot cocoa with Myra. Keep (A). Choice (B) talks about Myra's father *exuding a sense of warmth*. Look in the text to see where her father is showing *warmth*. In lines 68–69, the narrator states that *my dad smiled in return, his face illuminated by firelight, but projecting its own warmth*. As the campfire has already been built and her father is *exuding warmth*, eliminate (B). Choice (C) mentions *a similarity between a river and a human body*. Look for the lead words *river* and *human body*. In lines 19–20, the narrator states that *my father taught me to look at the river as he does: a metaphor for the human body*. Eliminate (C). Choice (D) mentions *gathering materials* to start the campfire, so look to see where the narrator's father is gathering materials in the passage. In lines 8-9, the narrator states that *my father and I gathered twigs and leaves for our campfire*. Eliminate (D). The correct answer is (A).

4. **J**   This reasoning question asks which answer choice best describes the *point of view* from which the story is told. Because this is a general question, it should be done after all the specific questions. Eliminate answers that contradict the passage. Choice (F) asserts that Myra *knows her father only has a limited amount of time left at his job*. In lines 15–16 the narrator thinks about *the possibility of Dad losing his job*. Myra believes that her father may lose his job, but she does not *know* that it will happen. Eliminate (F). Choice (G) states that Myra's parents have a *troubled marriage*. Myra's par-

ents' marriage is actually referred to as a *well-grooved partnership*. Eliminate (G). Choice (H) states that the narrator's father *worries too much about things that are beyond his control*. While Myra and her family are certainly worried about the prospect of her father losing his job, she never states that she believes that her father should worry less. Eliminate (H). Choice (J) states that Myra *recognizes the possibility of her father's unemployment and speculates about the effects it may have on the family*. In lines 51–52, the narrator states that *right now the familiar habit of camping with my family was a welcome reprieve from the strange new presence at home: fear of the uncertain future. What sort of job would Dad get if he needed to find work?* Myra is clearly worried about the possibility of her father losing his job and the consequences of that, so keep (J). The correct answer is (J).

5. **D** This referral question asks what *the family has gathered* to *help light the campfire*. Work backwards and use lead words from the answers to find the window for this question. Lines 23–25 state, *As he teased bits of leaves, sticks, and dry pine needles into a stack underneath the firewood, I went to look a second time for more of the same.* As *leaves, sticks*, and *dry pine needles* are all mentioned, eliminate (A) and (B). The lead word *twigs* can be found in lines 8–9, which state that *my father and I gathered twigs and leaves for our campfire.* Eliminate (C). The correct answer is (D).

6. **G** This referral question asks what the narrator does NOT mention as *something seen during the earliest stages of dusk*. When a question asks what is **not** mentioned in the text, eliminate answers that are mentioned. Look for the lead words *earliest stages of dusk* to find the window for the question. In lines 9–11, the narrator states that *it was still the earliest stages of evening. The vibrant forms of daytime—flowers, trees, and radiant water—still flooded our eyes.* As the narrator mentions *radiant water*, eliminate (F). The narrator also mentions *flowers* and *trees*. Eliminate (H) and (J). The author does not mention *fish* in this window, so keep (G). The correct answer is (G).

7. **D** This reasoning question asks for a description of the *feeling of familiarity* the narrator experiences when her mother hands her father *a sandwich and compliments him on the fire*. Look for the lead words *sandwich, compliments*, and *fire* to find the window for the question. The interaction described in the question takes place in lines 64–67. In lines 69–71, the narrator states *the familiarity exchanged between my parents seemed like a wonderful gift they had earned.* The narrator views her parents' interaction in a positive manner. Eliminate answers that don't match this prediction. Choice (A) uses the negative word *depressing*, which does not match the prediction. Eliminate (A). Choice (B) uses a word from the passage, *river*, but the answer doesn't match what the passage says: the parents' interaction does not distract Myra from the river. Nothing in the window shows that the narrator is worried that her feelings *will not last*. Eliminate (C). Choice (D) matches the positive tone of the window. The correct answer is (D).

8. **H** This reasoning question asks what the word *things* refers to in line 33. Read a window around the given line reference. Lines 22–23 state that Myra's father was *attempting to start the fire with the first load of kindling*, and lines 30–33 state, *The snaps and pops of the burning tinder started to come with greater frequency. Then, without even turning to look towards the campsite, I knew things were under way.* The word *things* refers to the campfire. Eliminate answers that don't match this prediction. Eliminate (F) and (G) as they are not related to the campfire. Choice (H) closely matches the

prediction, so keep (H). Choice (J) uses a word from the passage, *kindling*, but the answer doesn't match what the passage says: the narrator describes the *snaps and pops* of the *tinder*, and refers to the *kindling* as something distinct added to the campfire to help it light. Additionally, the sounds of the *snaps and pops* are what alerts her that *things are underway*, but the word *things* refers to the campfire itself, not to the sounds of the campfire. Eliminate (J). The correct answer is (H).

9. **C** This vocabulary-in-context question asks what the word *flooded* most nearly means as it is used in line 10. Go back to the text, find the word *flooded*, and cross it out. Carefully read the surrounding text to determine another word that would fit in the blank based on the context. In the second half of the sentence, the narrator states, *but all the earth's activity took on the falling action of a story that had passed its climax.* This part of the sentence is saying that the day is winding down, but the word *but* after the comma means that the correct answer should be the opposite of winding down. The word *flooded* could be replaced with the word "overwhelmed." *Spilled* does not match "overwhelmed," so eliminate (A). *Devastated* means "destroyed"; it does not match "overwhelmed," so eliminate (B). *Filled* matches "overwhelmed," so keep (C). *Soaked* does not match "overwhelmed," so eliminate (D). Choices (A) and (D) are other possible meanings of *flooded*, but they answer the wrong question: this question asks for the meaning of the word as it is *used in line 10*. The correct answer is (C).

10. **G** This reasoning question asks what belief about *her parents' relationship* the narrator's statement in lines 49–51 reveals. Read a window around the given line reference. In lines 49–51, the narrator describes her parents' relationship: *the once-heaving seas of young love had quieted within them to something more like the standing water of a pond.* This means that her parents' relationship has gotten more settled over time. Eliminate answers that don't match this prediction. Choice (F) talks about the *strain on their marriage*, but the narrator states *I sometimes marveled at the well-grooved partnership my parents had carved out*, showing their relationship to be anything but *strained*. Eliminate (F). Choice (G) closely matches the prediction, as their relationship has gotten *more stable and predictable*. Keep (G). Choice (H) uses words from the passage—the *standing water of a pond*—but the answer does not match what the passage says. The narrator spoke mostly of the strength of her parents' relationship, and she never says that it has *degraded*. Eliminate (H). Choice (J) is actually the opposite of what is stated in the text: the narrator implies that her parents' relationship was more *passionate and spontaneous* when they were younger but grew more settled over time. Eliminate (J). The correct answer is (G).

11. **A** This referral question asks for the *benefit or service* that is NOT provided by *religious institutions*, according to the passage. When a question asks what is **not** mentioned in the passage, eliminate answers that are mentioned. Look for the lead words *religious institutions* to find the window for the question. Lines 8–9 mention *Religious institutions*; the following two paragraphs discuss benefits and services provided by religious institutions. The passage does not say that religious institutions instruct *homeless people on how to live moral lives*, so keep (A). Lines 12–14 say that *churches collect alms for the poor* and *organize such hunger relief activities as soup kitchens.* Eliminate (B) and (C) because they are supported by these lines. Lines 17–19 say that *religious organizations* provide a *reprieve from suffering* related to *shelter*, so eliminate (D). The correct answer is (A).

12. **F** This reasoning question asks what *clothing-recycling drop boxes* and *celebrity endorsements* are *examples of*. Look for the lead words *clothing-recycling drop boxes* and *celebrity endorsements* to find the window for the question. Lines 26-29 say that some organizations devote attention to their *marketing image* by using *celebrity endorsements to solidify consumer awareness*. Lines 31–33 say that some non-profits *station clothing-recycling drop boxes around dense cities* as a form of *non-monetary assistance*. The beginning of the paragraph discusses *the new paradigm of philanthropic organizations*. Therefore, these are examples of philanthropic actions that have recently become popular. Eliminate answers that don't match this prediction. Keep (F) because it matches the prediction. Choice (G) uses words from the passage but doesn't match what the passage says: *Stumbacher* does discuss acts of *modern philanthropy*, but he doesn't *cite* these acts as *problems*. Eliminate (H) because *Karen Pitts* is not mentioned in the window for the question. Eliminate (J) because it uses words from the passage but doesn't match what the passage says: the passage mentions preventing *needless environmental stress*, but it does not say that *celebrity endorsements* are intended to *reduce environmental problems*, nor does it indicate that *clothing-recycling drop boxes* are the *best way* to do so. The correct answer is (F).

13. **C** This reasoning question asks for *the main function of the first paragraph*. Read the first paragraph as the window. In the paragraph, the author discusses several examples of *charitable giving* and then asks if we can *do better* than these acts, implying that there is an alternative. Eliminate answers that don't match this prediction. Choice (A) is stated in the passage, but it answers the wrong question: although the paragraph mentions *a homeless person whose pitiable appearance and humble request... is hard to deny*, the function of the paragraph is not to *urge people to feel sympathy for and generosity towards homeless people*; eliminate (A). Eliminate (B) because, though the author mentions a *few images that spring to mind*, the function of the paragraph is not to *cause the reader to picture himself* in a specific way. Keep (C) because it matches the prediction. Choice (D) uses words from the passage but doesn't match what the passage says: the paragraph discusses *traditional methods of charity*, but the idea that these methods *do nothing* is not supported; eliminate (D). The correct answer is (C).

14. **J** This referral question asks what the passage states about *philanthropy organized by religious institutions*. Look for the lead words *religious institutions* to find the window for the question. Religious institutions are discussed in the second and third paragraphs (lines 8–23). Eliminate answers that aren't supported by the passage. Choice (F) uses words from the passage, but it doesn't match what the passage says. Lines 19–23 say that charity provided by religious organizations *succeeds more in establishing a life-long commitment to philanthropy among the churchgoing public than it does in remedying any of the systemic problems that face the world's impoverished masses*. In other words, philanthropy organized by religious institutions is **not** very successful at solving *systemic problems*. Eliminate (F). Choice (G) also uses words from the passage but doesn't match what the passage says. The passage says that *charitable generosity* has been praised *as one of the highest forms of moral behavior*, but it doesn't say that charity organized by religious institutions is the *highest* form of moral behavior. Eliminate (G). Eliminate (H) because *other nonprofit organizations* aren't mentioned in the window for the question, nor does the passage discuss how *flexible* religious organizations are in comparison with other organizations. Keep (J) because it matches the statement that charity organized by religious institutions succeeds in *establishing a life-long commitment to philanthropy among the churchgoing public*. The correct answer is (J).

15. **B** This reasoning question asks what *Karen Pitts* most likely refers to when she talks about *"other activities they enjoy."* Read a window around the given line reference. Lines 47–52 say that *Karen Pitts* seeks to *engage donors* by enabling them to merge *charitable giving* with *other activities they enjoy.* The author then gives *wine tasting* as an example of an activity. Eliminate answers that don't match this prediction. Choice (A) is stated in the passage, but it answers the wrong question: though the passage discusses *wine tastings that successfully raise* money, it does not indicate that the donors find *positive promotional contexts for wineries*; eliminate (A). Keep (B) because it matches the prediction. Choice (C) is stated in the passage, but it answers the wrong question: the paragraph mentions *tens of thousands of dollars for charities*, but raising money is *charitable giving*, rather than another activity that donors enjoy; eliminate (C). Likewise, (D) is stated in the passage, but it answers the wrong question: the paragraph indicates that Pitts's strategy is a *win-win-win situation*, but it does not support the idea that donors enjoy *finding win-win opportunities with other donors in the wine industry*; eliminate (D). The correct answer is (B).

16. **G** This reasoning question asks why the author *places the words "market share" in quotation marks.* Read a window around the given line reference. Lines 26–31 say that some charities devote *increased attention to their marketing image* in order to *solidify consumer awareness*, and that, despite being *nonprofit entities*, they can still *maximize their "market share" the way that big corporations do.* In other words, when a for-profit business tries to increase its market share, the goal is to attract customers in order to increase profits. When a charity tries to increase its market share, the goal is to attract supporters to their causes. The author uses quotation marks around the phrase *market share* because it is a term usually associated with for-profit businesses, and although the author is making a comparison between charities and businesses, she is suggesting that the term means something different when applied to charities. Eliminate answers that don't match this prediction. Choice (F) uses words from the passage but doesn't match what the passage says: though the passage discusses *big corporations*, it does not discuss the success of their *business models*; eliminate (F). Keep (G) because it matches the prediction. The passage does not suggest that *nonprofit entities must learn to coexist with each other*, nor does it indicate that *nonprofits can sometimes attain a monopoly* (in a *monopoly*, one company exclusively controls a market). Eliminate (H) and (J). The correct answer is (G).

17. **B** This referral question asks why *Stumbacher* feels that *religious organizations often provide only a temporary reprieve from suffering.* Read a window around the given line reference. Lines 19–23 indicate that charitable actions performed through religious organizations do not succeed at *remedying… the systemic problems that face the world's impoverished masses.* Therefore, the charitable work provides only temporary relief because it does not address the systemic problems that cause poverty. Eliminate answers that don't match this prediction. Choice (A) uses words from the passage but doesn't match what the passage says: though the passage discusses *the impoverished*, it does not discuss boosting their *self-esteem*; eliminate (A). Keep (B) because it matches the prediction. Choice (C) uses words from the passage but doesn't match what the passage says: the author indicates that the charitable work of churchgoers is a *noble end*, not that there is an *overemphasis on noble ends*; eliminate (C). Eliminate (D) because the passage does not relate the temporary reprieve to a *lack of branding and celebrity endorsements*. The correct answer is (B).

18. **F** This referral question asks for a true statement *about the practices of the Acumen Fund*. Look for the lead words *Acumen Fund* to find the window for the question. Lines 58–60 say that *the Acumen Fund collects donations in a typical way but then treats its pool of resources as investment capital*. Rather than provide *immediate relief of suffering* (as the passage suggests most nonprofits do), the *Acumen Fund* uses donations to fund small business loans, supplying *long-term aid*. Eliminate answers that don't match this prediction. Keep (F) because it matches the prediction. Eliminate (G) because the passage does not indicate that the Acumen Fund *fails to treat the systemic roots of poverty*. Eliminate (H) because the author indicates that the Acumen Fund aims to provide *long-term aid* rather than temporary relief. Choice (J) uses words from the passage but doesn't match what the passage says: the passage indicates that the *Acumen Fund provides micro-loans* to small *third-world* businesses, not that it collects donations from these businesses; eliminate (J). The correct answer is (F).

19. **D** This referral question asks why *some innovative philanthropic approaches are effective*, according to the passage. Look for the lead words *innovative philanthropic approaches* to find the window for the question. Lines 73–75 say that what makes these approaches effective is *their adaptation to the specific needs of their locales*. Eliminate answers that don't match this prediction. Choice (A) is stated in the passage, but it answers the wrong question: the author does not suggest that innovative philanthropic approaches are effective because they *integrate charity with activities the recipients enjoy*; eliminate (A). Choice (B) is stated in the passage, but it answers the wrong question: lines 10–12 say that *charitable generosity* is *one of the highest forms of moral behavior*, but this refers to a long-held view rather than an approach taken by *innovative* philanthropists. It also isn't mentioned in the window for the question; eliminate (B). Eliminate (C) because the passage does not compare the costs of innovative and *traditional methods*. Keep (D) because it matches the prediction. The correct answer is (D).

20. **H** This reasoning question asks for the meaning of lines 75–77 *in the context of the tenth paragraph*. Read a window around the given line reference and then read the tenth paragraph. Lines 75–77 say that the *progressive*, local *business models* may not work on a *large scale*. The tenth paragraph says that the *new tactics* are *very valuable*, even if they *cannot be used in all contexts*. In other words, lines 75–77 suggest that the innovative business models work well locally but may not succeed on a larger, global scale. However, the tenth paragraph states that the innovative models are still valuable, even if they don't work on a global scale. Eliminate answers that don't match this prediction. Choice (F) uses words from the passage but doesn't match what the passage says: though the passage discusses *new modes of providing charity* and *large measures*, it does not support the idea that these new modes *will succeed in large measures*. In fact, it implies the opposite; eliminate (F). Eliminate (G) because the passage does not indicate how realistically *philanthropists* view the *scale of some problems*. Keep (H) because it is supported by the passage: since the progressive models are valuable even though they don't work on a global scale, then their value must not *be based on their ability to work globally*. Eliminate (J) because it contradicts the tenth paragraph, which states that the progressive approaches are *very valuable*. The correct answer is (H).

21. **B** This reasoning question asks what *shift* occurs in the fourth paragraph of Passage A. Although this question references a specific paragraph, it asks about a shift that concerns most of the passage; it is a general question and should be done after all the specific questions about Passage A. Compare the first three paragraphs to the fourth paragraph. The first three paragraphs contain biographical

information about Richard Wright's childhood and the beginning of his writing career. In the fourth paragraph, lines 30–32 say, *Wright became an overnight success with the publication of his great novel* Native Son *in 1940*, and the paragraph goes on to give details about the novel's success. Eliminate answers that don't match this prediction. Eliminate (A) because there is no *extended metaphor* in the first part of the passage. Keep (B) because *background* matches the description of his childhood and *public successes* matches the success of *Native Son*. Although the first part of (C) matches the passage, the fourth paragraph does not include any *literary criticism and analysis*. Eliminate (C). Eliminate (D) as the passage does not analyze *the author's motives*. The correct answer is (B).

22. **F** This reasoning question asks how the author views *Wright*. Because this is a general question, it should be done after all the specific questions about Passage A. Look for the Golden Thread. Lines 1–2 say, *Richard Wright's achievement as an author is almost inconceivable*. Lines 8–10 say, *Richard Wright managed to rise above this oppression to become the first major African-American writer and still one of the best loved*. Lines 16–18 say that becoming valedictorian *is just one in a long string of truly stunning events in this exceptional man's life*. Lines 44–46 say, *that such a person could achieve Wright's level of success and admiration, which have now outlived him by more than 50 years, is awe-inspiring*. The author's view of Wright is positive. Eliminate answers that don't match this prediction. Eliminate (G) and (J) because neither is a positive view. Keep (F) because it matches the prediction. Though (H) is positive, and *gifted* is supported by the passage, there is no support for *sociable*. Eliminate (H). The correct answer is (F).

23. **C** This reasoning question asks why *Brecht was an important influence on Wright*. Look for the lead word *Brecht* in Passage A to find the window for the question. *Brecht* is mentioned in line 27. Lines 25–29 say, *His association with left-wing politics brought him into contact with the work of Bertolt Brecht, a German playwright and theorist. The particular political slant of Brecht's plays and essays shaped the course that Wright's work would take in the next few years*. Therefore, Brecht's political themes influenced Wright's writing. Eliminate answers that don't match this prediction. Choice (A) uses words from the passage but doesn't match what the passage says; Brecht was a German playwright, but there is no evidence in Passage A that Wright traveled to Germany. Eliminate (A). Eliminate (B) because, although Brecht's novel became well-known later, the passage does not indicate that *Brecht introduced Wright* to any *audiences* or *publishers*. Keep (C) because the phrase *inspired Wright* matches the prediction that Brecht influenced Wright's writing. Choice (D) uses words from the passage but doesn't match what the passage says; the passage says that Wright became involved with the Communist Party and that led to his contact with Brecht's work. Eliminate (D). The correct answer is (C).

24. **F** This reasoning question asks about the meaning of the author's statement, *Literary critics, in fact, should know better*. Read a window around the given line reference. Lines 82–83 say, *it was critics themselves who were out of the loop*. Lines 89–92 say, *Indeed, it was not that Wright was working in a void; it was instead that the critics themselves were unprepared, or downright unwilling, to see the rich tapestry of influences that had produced him*. Therefore, the critics were unaware of the environment of other writers who influenced Wright. Eliminate answers that don't match this prediction. Keep (F) as *irritation* is supported by the negative phrases the author uses to describe critics—*out of the loop, unprepared, unwilling*—and the *falsehood* is that *Wright was working in a void*. Eliminate

(G) as the window does not mention the author's attitude toward people who *do not work in literary criticism*. Eliminate (H) because *Wright's claim* is not supported; the author says the opposite. Eliminate (J) as the statement is the author's position, not *Wright's*. The correct answer is (F).

25. **B** This reasoning question asks how *Wright's context and influences* compared to how he *has traditionally been understood within literary history*. Because this is a general question, it should be done after all the specific questions about Passage B. Look for the Golden Thread. Lines 48–51 say, *The idea, however, that Richard Wright emerged from some kind of void would be preposterous if it were not for the fact that Wright himself seemed to believe it.* Lines 77–80 say, *In fact,* Native Son, *that work we are led to believe had emerged from a vacuum, emerged from precisely this close contact Wright had with the other great minds of his generation.* Lines 89–92 say, *Indeed, it was not that Wright was working in a void; it was instead that the critics themselves were unprepared, or downright unwilling, to see the rich tapestry of influences that had produced him.* Therefore, the traditional understanding is that Wright produced his work in a vacuum or void, but the author argues that this view is incorrect because Wright was influenced by the context of the *Harlem Renaissance* and other *African-American literature*. Eliminate answers that don't match this prediction. Eliminate (C) and (D) because the traditional understanding and Wright's actual context are not similar. Eliminate (A) because the discussion of Wright's schooling is in Passage A, not Passage B. Keep (B) because it matches the prediction. The correct answer is (B).

26. **H** This reasoning question asks what the information about *Their Eyes Were Watching God* represents. Read a window around the given line reference. Lines 81–83 say, *Anyone who studies the history of African-American literature knows that it was critics themselves who were out of the loop, not the writers.* The paragraph then mentions *Their Eyes Were Watching God* as an example, saying that *critics were unaware* of the book for *40 years*, and now it is *acknowledged as one of the great books of the century*. Therefore, *Their Eyes Were Watching God* is an example of a now-monumental book that critics were unaware of for a long time. Eliminate answers that don't match this prediction. Eliminate (F) because there is no mention of *fictional characters* in the window. Eliminate (G) because, according to the author, Wright's influences were not difficult to identify; the author says that the critics were *unprepared, or downright unwilling*, to see the influences. Keep (H) because it matches the prediction. Eliminate (J) because the passage doesn't compare *Hurston* to *Wright*. The correct answer is (H).

27. **D** This referral question asks how *Richard Wright* and *Ernest Hemingway* are similar, according to Passage B. Look for the lead words *Ernest Hemingway* to find the window for the question. Lines 54–57 say that Wright's *capacity for self-mythologizing rivals only that of Ernest Hemingway, whose adventurous, romantic lifestyle abroad continues to inspire many who read him, and just as many who don't*. The sentence before says that Wright was an *image-conscious strategist*. Therefore, Wright is similar to Hemingway in that they both created images of and myths about themselves. Eliminate (A) because *critics* are not mentioned in the window. Eliminate (B) because Wright's education is not discussed in detail in Passage B. The passage also doesn't say that Hemingway claimed he had *no literary influences and no formal education*. Eliminate (C) because the *Harlem Renaissance* is not mentioned in the window for the question, and the passage does not suggest that Hemingway wrote at that time. Keep (D) because the idea that they *had public personalities* that were not

based solely on their books matches the prediction that both authors were *image-conscious* and *self-mythologizing*. The correct answer is (D).

28. **F** This reasoning question asks how the tones of the passages compare. Because this question asks about both passages, it should be done after the questions that ask about each passage individually. Consider the Golden Thread of both passages. Passage A has a positive tone; the author of Passage A says that Richard Wright's achievement is *almost inconceivable*, his success is *awe-inspiring*, and he is *exceptional*. Passage B has a more critical tone; the author of Passage B disagrees with the previous characterization of Wright's success, saying *In fact*, Native Son, *that work we are led to believe had emerged from a vacuum, emerged from precisely this close contact Wright had with the other great minds of his generation* and criticizes literary critics, saying that they *should know better*. Keep (F) because it matches the prediction. Eliminate (G) because, while Passage A's tone is positive, it is not *elated*, and Passage B's tone is not *pessimistic* or *contrarian*. Eliminate (H) because the description of the passages starting *loose* but ending with *precise arguments* is not supported by either passage. Eliminate (J) because the passages reach different conclusions about the belief that Wright wrote *Native Son* without influences. The correct answer is (F).

29. **A** This reasoning question asks what Passage B *provides more detail about* than Passage A does. Because this question asks about both passages, it should be done after the questions that ask about each passage individually. Eliminate any answer choices that misrepresent Passage B. Keep (A) because Passage B includes information about Wright's context, including the *Harlem Renaissance*, and information about his strategy, comparing it to those of authors such as *Hemingway*. Eliminate (B) because Passage A provides more details about *Wright's background and education*; this answers the wrong question, since question 29 asks what Passage B provides more details about. Choice (C) uses words from the passages, but doesn't match what the passages say: *Brecht* is mentioned only in Passage A, and neither author discusses Hemingway's direct influence on Wright. Eliminate (D) because it answers the wrong question: Passage A discusses *political influences* more than Passage B does. The correct answer is (A).

30. **H** This reasoning question asks how the author of Passage A feels about *Wright's success as an author* compared to how the author of Passage B feels. Because this question asks about both passages, it should be done after the questions that ask about each passage individually. Consider the Golden Thread of both passages. The author of Passage A describes Richard Wright's achievements as *almost inconceivable*, *awe-inspiring*, and *exceptional*. The author of Passage B also acknowledges Wright's success but emphasizes that Wright was influenced *by other great minds of his generation* and that Wright had a *capacity for self-mythologizing*. Eliminate answers that misrepresent either passage. Eliminate (F) because Passage B doesn't mention *political events*. Eliminate (G) because Passage A doesn't discuss *Ernest Hemingway*. Keep (H) because the author of Passage A has a more positive view of how Wright overcame obstacles, saying *Richard Wright managed to rise above this oppression to become the first major African-American writer and still one of the best loved*, compared to the author of Passage B, who doesn't focus as much on Wright's past or demonstrate admiration of Wright for overcoming it. Eliminate (J) because the author of Passage A is more supportive of the idea that Wright's success was his own, saying, *It was thus seemingly out of nowhere that Wright*

became an overnight success, compared to the author of Passage B, who discusses the other authors who influenced Wright. The correct answer is (H).

31. **D** This reasoning question asks what *the language of the first paragraph* is *intended to convey*. Read the first paragraph as the window. Lines 2–3 say that those *who have been bursting at the seams to blurt out the "big secret" can finally shout it from the mountaintops*, creating a sense of excitement to draw the reader into the topic. Eliminate answers that don't match this prediction. Choice (A) uses a word from the passage, *secret*, but doesn't match what the passage says: *warning* does not match the prediction. Eliminate (A). Eliminate (B) because *anguish* does not match the prediction. Choice (C) uses words from the passage but doesn't match what the passage says. The paragraph mentions the *theory of evolution*, but *reluctance* does not match the prediction; eliminate (C). Choice (D) mentions *anticipation*, which matches the prediction. The correct answer is (D).

32. **F** This referral question asks what the *"big secret"* and *"missing link"* refer to. Look for the lead words *"big secret"* and *"missing link"* to find the window for the question. Lines 6–8 state that the *"big secret"* and *"missing link"* refer to the *uncannily preserved fossil of an ancient ancestor of the primate family, nicknamed Ida*. Eliminate answers that don't match this prediction. Choice (F) mentions *Ida*, so keep it. Choice (G) fails to include *Ida* and can be eliminated. Choices (H) and (J) mention *Ida* but can be eliminated as the passage does not include *Lucy* in the description of the *"big secret"* or *"missing link."* The correct answer is (F).

33. **A** This referral question asks how the passage *characterizes the idea that Ida was a transitional species to simians*. Look for the lead words *Ida* and *transitional species* to find the window for the question. Lines 6–12 state, *After two years of secretly performing research on* Ida, researchers *firmly believe that the lemur monkey they have preserved in polyester resin is conclusive evidence of a transitional species.* Eliminate answers that don't match this prediction. Choice (A) matches the prediction, so keep it. Eliminate (B) because it uses words from the passage but doesn't match what the passage says: the window mentions the *polyester resin*, but the resin is not what is being analyzed. Choice (C) can be eliminated as *tarsidae* is not discussed in the window for the question, nor does the passage suggest that ideas about Ida were based on discoveries about *tarsidae*. Choice (D) uses words from the passage but doesn't match what the passage says: the passage suggests that Ida was the *"missing link,"* but it does not suggest that ideas about Ida were based on *scientists' desire to find* a missing link. Eliminate (D). The correct answer is (A).

34. **G** This reasoning question asks what is implied about the *price that was paid to obtain Ida's fossil*. Look for the lead word *price* to find the window for this question. Lines 36–39 state that Professor Jorn Hurum's *enthusiasm meant that the fossil dealer could charge any outlandish price*. Eliminate answers that don't match this prediction. Choice (F) uses words from the passage but doesn't match what the passage says: the passage does not state that the fossil *Lucy* was *cheaper*. Additionally, it is not true that Lucy is an *older fossil*. Eliminate (F). Choice (G) matches the prediction, so keep (G). Eliminate (H) because the passage does not discuss the fossil's price in relation to how much the *private collector* valued the fossil. Choice (J) is partially true as the price was high, but the passage does not suggest that the price was related to where the fossil was found. Additionally, the passage

says that the Messel Pit, where Ida was found, was a *bountiful source of fossils*, which means that many fossils were discovered there. Eliminate (J). The correct answer is (G).

35. **A** This reference question asks what *the amateur fossil hunter who found Ida in the Messel Pit* did. Look for the lead words *Messel Pit* to find the window for the question. Lines 30–32 state that the amateur fossil hunter *did not assume there was anything distinctive* about Ida, and that he *hung Ida on his wall as a display piece*. Eliminate answers that don't match this prediction. Choices (C) and (D) both contradict the passage because they say that the fossil hunter *immediately assumed Ida was special*. Eliminate (C) and (D). Keep (A), which matches the prediction. Choice (B) states that the fossil hunter *showed the fossil to scientists*, which is not stated in the passage; eliminate (B). The correct answer is (A).

36. **J** This reasoning question asks for a summary of *the objection of those who remain skeptical of Darwin's theory of evolution*. Look for the lead word *skeptical* to find the window for the question, or look for the numbers *1859* and *98.4%* from the answer choices. Lines 56–59 suggest that *many of Darwin's skeptics* questioned the theory of evolution because *there was a gigantic hole in the fossil evidence that relates to where the branch of higher primates begins*. Eliminate answers that don't match this prediction. Choice (F) uses words from the passage but doesn't match what the passage says: the passage says that some people question the fossil evidence *[d]espite the 98.4% genetic similarity* between humans and chimpanzees. The word *despite* indicates that the 98.4% genetic match was not the reason for the objection; eliminate (F). Choice (G) can be eliminated because the window discusses the relationship *humans have to chimpanzees* but does not mention *lemurs*. Choice (H) also uses words from the passage but doesn't match what the passage says. The year *1859* is mentioned as the date when the theory of evolution was published; the passage does not discuss a lack of *fossils* from *before 1859*. Eliminate (H). Keep (J) because it states that there *is some explanation missing*; this is a good paraphrase of the idea that there was *a gigantic hole in the fossil evidence*. The correct answer is (J).

37. **C** This reference question asks which of the answer choices does not apply to *Lucy*. When a question asks what is **not** supported by the text, eliminate answers that are supported. Choice (A) is supported by lines 15–17, which state that Ida *is older than any previously found primate fossil, vastly predating the previous record-holder, Lucy*. Since Lucy was the *previous record-holder* with regard to age, it must have been the oldest known fossil at one point. Eliminate (A). Choice (B) can be eliminated; lines 18–19 state that Ida *is one of the most complete fossils ever found*, which implies that Ida was found in better condition than Lucy. Choice (C) is contradicted by lines 23–24, which state that Lucy was *lacking a skull among other important features*. Since (C) is false, keep it. Choice (D) is supported by line 23, which states that *Lucy's remains were only 40% complete*; eliminate (D). The correct answer is (C).

38. **G** This reasoning question asks what the word *enthusiasm* refers to in line 38. Read a window around the given line reference. Lines 36–37 state that the professor was *immediately entranced upon seeing Ida*. Therefore, Professor Hurum's *enthusiasm* was for the fossil called Ida. Eliminate answers that don't match this prediction. Choice (F) is mentioned in the window, but it answers the wrong question. The professor was enthusiastic about the fossil, not the *fossil dealer*; eliminate (F). Choice (G) matches the prediction: the word *specimen* is used in line 40 to refer to the fossil. Keep (G).

Choice (H) is mentioned in the window but answers the wrong question. The passage doesn't mention that the professor was enthusiastic about his *home*; eliminate (H). Choice (J) also answers the wrong question. The professor found Ida at the *Fossil and Mineral Fair*, but the fair is not what he was enthusiastic about. Eliminate (J). The correct answer is (G).

39. **C** This reasoning question asks why the author says that scientists *could actually still analyze the last meal Ida had* in line 21. Read a window around the given line reference. Lines 18–21 say that the fossil called Ida is *one of the most complete fossils ever found*, and that *the fossilization conditions were so perfect in Ida's case that scientists could actually still analyze the last meal Ida had*. Therefore, the fact that scientists could analyze Ida's last meal emphasizes how well the fossil was preserved. Choice (A) uses words from the passage but doesn't match what the passage says: the passage never discusses *valuable clues* that scientists learned from Ida's *last meal*. Eliminate (A). Choice (B) also uses words from the passage but doesn't match what that passage says: the passage doesn't discuss how *little* scientists learned from *Lucy's fossil*. Eliminate (B). Keep (C) because it matches the prediction (the word *underscore* means "emphasize"). Eliminate (D) because the passage does not discuss a theory about *the diet of early primates*. The correct answer is (C).

40. **H** This reasoning question asks for the purpose of the *eighth paragraph* in relationship to the rest of the passage. Because this question asks about the context of the passage as a whole, answer it after the specific questions. Read the eighth paragraph as the window. Lines 60–63 mention two species, *adapidae* and *tarsidae*, and say that *scientists have been unsure which species ultimately led to the higher primates*. Then the paragraph says that the discovery of Ida helped scientists answer this question. The passage as a whole is about the discovery of Ida. Therefore, the purpose of the eighth paragraph is to discuss a scientific question that Ida's discovery helped answer. Eliminate answers that don't match this prediction. Choice (F) can be eliminated; while the passage states that *scientists have been unsure*, that doesn't mean that the scientists were wrong or had *misconceptions*. Eliminate (G) because the paragraph's purpose is to show something that scientists learned, not to demonstrate *confusion*. Additionally, the passage doesn't state that the scientists' lack of certainty resulted from *classifying fossils*. Choice (H) matches the prediction, so keep it. Choice (J) mentions the *prevailing theory that humans came from tarisdae*, but the passage states that scientists were not sure which species led to humans. Therefore, there is no *prevailing theory* to *argue against*. Eliminate (J). The correct answer is (H).

SCIENCE TEST

1. **D** The question asks whether the number of seeds collected by the hamsters in Experiment 1 would have been less or greater if the experiment had been run for 10 minutes. The answer choices mention the amount of time the hamsters spent collecting seeds, which is not shown in the figures, so scan the passage's description of Experiment 1 and look for a mention of time. According to the passage, after a hamster was placed in the cage, the fruit juice of the seeds it collected was recorded *over the next 30 minutes*. Eliminate (A) and (B) because if the experiment had been run for 10 minutes, the time the hamsters spent collecting seeds would have been less, rather than greater, than in Experiment 1. Eliminate (C) because 10 minutes is one-third and not one-half of 30 minutes. The correct answer is (D).

2. **H** The question asks whether the scientists' hypothesis was supported by the experiments. The answer choices mention data about seeds soaked in apple juice in all three experiments, so use Figures 1–3 to find the bar that represents apple juice seeds in each experiment. In all three figures, the apple juice bar is the largest, meaning that the hamsters collected more seeds soaked in apple juice compared to any other type of juice. Eliminate (G) and (J) because they incorrectly state that the hamsters collected the same number of seeds soaked in each fruit juice. To choose between the remaining answers, scan the passage to find the scientists' hypothesis. According to the passage, the scientists hypothesized that *hamsters would be more drawn to hoard seeds soaked in certain fruit juices over seeds soaked in other fruit juices*, which is supported by the findings that the seeds soaked in apple juice were collected the most. Eliminate (F) since it states that the hypothesis was not supported by these findings. The correct answer is (H).

3. **C** The question asks how many hamsters, in total, were used in all three experiments. This information is not shown in the figures, so scan the passage to find the number of hamsters used in each experiment. According to the passage, in Experiment 1, *a* C. cricetus *hamster that was recently captured in Belgium was placed in the center of the cage*. Then, after the experiment was conducted, the *process was repeated with an additional 24 recently captured* C. cricetus *hamsters from Belgium*, for a total of 25 hamsters. In Experiment 2, *the procedure for Experiment 1 was repeated with the same set of 25 hamsters*. However, Experiment 3 used *25 recently captured* C. cricetus *hamsters from Russia*. So, Experiments 1 and 2 used the same 25 hamsters from Belgium and Experiment 3 used 25 hamsters from Russia, for a total of 50 hamsters. The correct answer is (C).

4. **J** The question asks which experimental setup could be used to determine whether hamsters from Russia have the same fruit juice preferences with a different species of food source. According to the passage, the food source used in the experiments was *seeds from pumpkins* (Cucurbita pepa). To obtain data for a different food source, a different species must be used. Eliminate (F) and (H), since they propose using the same species of food source, *C. pepa*. To choose between the remaining answer choices, refer back to Experiments 2 and 3. Experiment 2 used *25 hamsters from Belgium*, while Experiment 3 used *25 recently* captured C. cricetus *hamsters from Russia*. Eliminate (G), since the hamsters from Belgium used in Experiment 2 should not be used to determine the preferences of hamsters from Russia. The correct answer is (J).

5. **A** The question asks which expression represents the calculation performed to determine each value in Figure 3. Figure 3 shows the results of Experiment 3, which used *25 recently captured* C. cricetus *hamsters from Russia*. Eliminate (B) and (D), which both incorrectly mention hamsters from Belgium. Next, look at the values in Figure 3. There are 5 different values for seeds covered in each of 5 different kinds of fruit juice. Eliminate (C) since the values represent average seeds of each fruit juice rather than average total seeds. The correct answer is (A).

6. **J** The question asks which statement about the genus and species of the hamsters used in Experiments 1 and 3 is correct. Experiment 1 used C. cricetus *hamsters from Belgium*, while Experiment 3 used *25 recently captured* C. cricetus *hamsters from Russia*. Since the only difference between the two types of hamsters is the location of origin, eliminate (F), which mentions multiple differences

between them. To choose between the remaining answers, outside knowledge is necessary. The scientific name of an animal species is a two-word description consisting of the animal's genus followed by the species name. Since both experiments involved *C. cricetus* hamsters, both the genus and the species of the hamsters were the same. The correct answer is (J).

7. **B** The question asks which statement is correct based on Experiments 1 and 2. Use POE. Notice that the answer choices differ in the types of hamsters, so check the descriptions of Experiment 1 and Experiment 2 to see which types of hamsters were used. Experiment 1 used *recently captured* C. cricetus *hamsters from Belgium* and Experiment 2 used *the same set of 25 hamsters from Belgium, which had been kept in captivity in the research facility for 2 months.* Eliminate (A) and (C) because neither of the experiments mentioned in the question uses hamsters from Russia. The results of Experiments 1 and 2 are shown in Figures 1 and 2, so look at Figures 1 and 2 to use POE with the remaining answers. Notice that both Figure 1 and Figure 2 show an average of 9 apple juice soaked seeds collected. Since the number of apple juice soaked seeds is the same for both groups, eliminate (D). For all other fruit juices, the number of seeds collected in Figure 2 is higher than the number collected in Figure 1. Therefore, the hamsters collected a larger total amount of seeds after they had been kept in captivity. The correct answer is (B).

8. **J** The question asks for the step of the experimental procedure that is done to *ensure that the solar cell would absorb a sufficient amount of sunlight once it was exposed to light.* This question requires outside knowledge. Objects that are dark-colored absorb more light than light-colored objects. In Step 4, the glass slide is coated with blackberry juice, a *dark-colored natural dye.* Eliminate (F), (G), and (H) because Steps 1–3 do not contain any procedures relevant to increasing light absorption. The correct answer is (J).

9. **C** The question asks which experimental conditions *resulted in the* lowest *average conversion efficiency.* Look at the table to find the trials that correspond to each set of experimental conditions. Choice (A) matches up with Trials 19–21, which had a conversion efficiency of 9.5%. Choice (B) corresponds with Trials 4–6, which yielded a conversion efficiency of 12.6%. This is higher than that in Trials 19–21, so eliminate (B). Choice (C) matches up with Trials 16–18, which had a conversion efficiency of 9.2%. This is lower than the efficiency in Trials 19–21, so eliminate (A) and keep (C). Choice (D) represents Trials 31–33, which produced a conversion efficiency of 9.4%. Eliminate (D) since this conversion efficiency is higher than that in Trials 16–18. The correct answer is (C).

10. **F** The question asks whether the trials with TiO_2 produced a higher or lower conversion efficiency than those with ZnO *for each combination of secondary oxide concentration and temperature that was tested.* Look at the table to find sets of trials where the only difference is the primary oxide and the conversion efficiency. Trials 4–6 used TiO_2 as the primary oxide, 20% secondary oxide by mass, and a temperature of 400°C, and produced a conversion efficiency of 12.6%. Trials 13–15 used ZnO as the primary oxide and the same secondary oxide concentration and temperature as Trials 4–6, but the conversion efficiency was 7.0%. Since the conversion efficiency for the set of trials using TiO_2 was higher than that for the ZnO trials, eliminate (G), which states that it will always be lower, and (H), which claims that it will always be the same as that for the ZnO trials. Trials 1–3 and Trials 10–12 also have the same secondary oxide concentration and temperature as each

other, as do Trials 19–21 and Trials 28–30. For both of these sets of trials, the trials with TiO_2 have a higher conversion efficiency than the ZnO trials, so eliminate (J) since it states that the conversion efficiency for the TiO_2 trials will sometimes be lower. The correct answer is (F).

11. **C** The question asks for the expression that *gives the volume of dilute nitric acid used in the experiment*. Look for the term *nitric acid* in the passage. According to Step 1 in the experimental procedure, *20 mL of dilute nitric acid* was added in each trial. Eliminate (B) and (D) because these contain a volume of 100 mL dilute nitric acid in each trial, which does not match the experimental procedure. According to the table, there were 11 sets of 3 trials each, for a total of 33 trials. Eliminate (A) as it incorrectly mentions 11 total trials. The correct answer is (C).

12. **H** The question asks for the difference between Trials 4–6 and Trials 19–21. Look at the table to find both sets of trials. According to the table, both sets of trials used TiO_2 as the primary oxide. Eliminate (F), which indicates that the identity of the primary oxide differed. Both sets of trials used a concentration of 20% by mass of the secondary oxide. Eliminate (G) since it states that the two sets of trials used different secondary oxide concentrations. Trials 4–6 used a temperature of 400°C, while Trials 19–21 used a temperature of 300°C. These are different, so keep (H). The time for which the slides were heated is not found on the table, but according to the experimental procedure, for each trial the slides were *heated at a high temperature for 5 minutes*, so eliminate (J) since it states that the heating time differed for the two sets of trials. The correct answer is (H).

13. **B** The question asks how the conversion efficiency of solar cells *with TiO_2 as the primary oxide and 20% secondary oxide by mass* changed *as the temperature increased*. Look at the table to find trials that fit the criteria in the question. Trials 19–21, 22–24, and 25–27 all use TiO_2 as the primary oxide and 20% secondary oxide. In these trials, as the temperature increases from 300°C to 500°C to 600°C, the conversion efficiency increases from 9.5% to 15.9% to 17.8%. The correct answer is (B).

14. **J** The question asks for *the mass of the secondary oxide added to the mixture in Step 1 of Trial 14*. Look at the table to find that Trial 14 used 20% by mass of the secondary oxide. According to the question, the mixture of the two oxides had a mass of 21 g. When working with a percent without a calculator, it is often easiest to start by calculating 10%: 10% of 21 is "21÷10" = 2.1 Therefore, 20% of 21 is 2.1 × 2 = 4.2. The correct answer is (J).

15. **C** The question asks whether the maximum FDE occurred in the same year as the minimum FDS in Figure 1. Refer to Figure 1. The darker line with circles represents the FDE. The maximum FDE, which is approximately 1,600, occured in 1998. Eliminate (B) and (D) because both say the maximum FDE occured in 2013. The FDS is the lighter line with squares. The minimum value for the dashed line occured in 2013. Eliminate (A) because it incorrectly states that the minimum FDS occured in 1998. The correct answer is (C).

16. **H** The question asks, based on Table 1, for a comparison of the total FDE in terms of the total FDS in Tucson. Table 1 shows the total FDS and FDE for various cities. In Tucson, the total FDE was 167, and the FDS was 536. The FDS is higher, so eliminate (F) and (G), which would mean that the FDS was smaller. Ballpark with the remaining answers. Eliminate (J) as 6 times 167 would be much higher than 536. The total FDS is a little more than 3 times as great as the total FDE. The correct answer is (H).

17. **D**   The question asks which statement regarding FDE or FDS in 2018 is true, based on Table 1, for all of the cities between 95° W and 120° W longitude. Refer to Table 1 and use POE. The cities between 95° W and 120° W longitude are Oklahoma City, Cheyenne, Tucson, Boise, and Reno. Choice (A) says the FDE is always greater than the FDS, but this is true only for Oklahoma City. Eliminate (A). Eliminate (C) because the FDS is *not* greater for Oklahoma City. Eliminate (B) because the FDE in Boise is less than 100. Only (D) is true for all of the relevant cities. The correct answer is (D).

18. **G**   The question asks for the FDE and FDS that would be calculated for a particular 5-day period in which the P_5 = 10 mm. The note at the bottom of Table 1 gives the formula for the calculation of FDE and FDS, so look at these formulas. The FDE = P_5 – 10 mm for all P_5 > 10 mm, and the FDS = 10 mm – P_5 for all P_5 < 10 mm. When P_5 = 10 mm, neither of these formulas is applicable, so the values for FDE and FDS must both be 0. According to the passage, the FDE represents the excess over *the North American average of 10 mm*, while FDS represents the shortfall compared to *the North American average of 10 mm*. Therefore, when the P_5 = 10 mm, there is neither an excess nor a shortfall. The correct answer is (G).

19. **B**   The question asks *which of the following graphs best illustrates the longitude and the FDE for each of the cities listed in Table 1*. Refer to Table 1 and use POE. The western coordinates given in the longitude column increase from top to bottom in Table 1, so the cities are listed from Easternmost to Westernmost. Philadelphia, the Easternmost city in Table 1, has an FDE of 1,158. Eliminate (C) and (D) as both show an FDE of less than 300 for the Easternmost city. The next city is Toronto, which has an FDE of 522. Eliminate (A) because it shows an FDE of almost 1,400 for the second-most Eastern city. The correct answer is (B).

20. **F**   The question asks what happened to the average value of P_5 over the 21 years portrayed in Figure 1 based on the FDS equation and the fact that the slope of the trend line is negative. Refer to the FDS equation in the note at the bottom of Table 1: FDS = 10 mm – P_5 for all P_5 < 10 mm. Since FDS is calculated by subtracting the value of P_5 from 10, the FDS and P_5 have an inverse relationship. When a larger P_5 is subtracted, the resulting FDS is lower. Therefore, as the FDS decreases over the 21-yr period, the average P_5 must have increased. The correct answer is (F).

21. **C**   The question asks which aqueous solution resulted in the fewest surviving *T. vernix* in Experiment 2. The results of Experiment 2 are shown in Figure 2. Look for the lowest bar, representing lowest percent survival of *T. vernix*, at each sunlight exposure. At 6, 12, and 18 hours of sunlight exposure, the lowest bar is that for glycerol in AS. The correct answer is (C).

22. **G**   The question asks what the percent survival of *T. vernix* sprayed with glycerol in AS would be for a sunlight exposure of 24 hours in Experiment 2. The results of Experiment 2 are shown in Figure 2. Look for the data for glycerol in AS. The percent survival is listed for sunlight exposures of 6 hours, 12 hours, and 18 hours. The percent survival values stay nearly constant at about 35% with increasing sunlight exposure. Thus, the percent survival at 24 hours will also most likely be 35%. The correct answer is (G).

23. **D**   The question asks which of the sunlight exposures in Experiment 2 included a control that served to determine percent survival of *T. vernix* in the absence of weed killer ingredients. The results of

Experiment 2 are shown in Figure 2, which has bars at each sunlight exposure representing aqueous solutions of NaCl, corn gluten, glycerol, and vinegar. According to the description of Experiment 2, the weed killer had *three ingredients: corn gluten, glycerol (a sugar alcohol), and vinegar.* The NaCl is not an ingredient of the weed killer and thus must be the control. Since all three sunlight exposures included a bar for NaCl, all three used a control. The correct answer is (D).

24. **G** The question asks which question the researchers were trying to answer by conducting Experiment 1. The results of Experiment 1 are shown in Figure 1, which shows bars for solutions of different concentrations of NaCl and weed killer and the percent survival of *T. vernix* sprayed with these solutions. According to the description of Experiment 1, *all 8 plots of land* used in the experiment *were exposed to 3 hrs of sunlight.* Eliminate (H) and (J) since results for 6 hours of sunlight exposure are not featured in Figure 1, and thus hours of sunlight exposure was not a factor that was changed in Experiment 1. Also, eliminate (F) since neither corn starch solutions nor glycerol solutions are shown in Figure 1. The correct answer is (G).

25. **A** The question asks what percent of the *T. vernix* in Experiment 1 that have been sprayed with 10% weed killer in AS would not have a *green cambium layer*, given that *living T. vernix have a green cambium layer* and *dead T. vernix do not.* The results of Experiment 1 are shown in Figure 1. Look for the bar at 10 percent by volume that represents weed killer. The percent survival of *T. vernix* at this concentration of weed killer is 75%. This means that, after exposure, 75% of the *T. vernix* plants were still alive. Thus, 100% − 75% = 25% of the *T. vernix* were dead and would not have a green cambium layer. The correct answer is (A).

26. **H** The question asks which experimental procedure should be conducted to compare the herbicidal activity of each of the components of the weed killer used in Experiment 2 with that of the unseparated weed killer. Look for information about the components of the weed killer in the description of Experiment 2. In Experiment 2, the weed killer had *three ingredients: corn gluten, glycerol (a sugar alcohol), and vinegar.* The herbicidal activity of each component is shown in Figure 2. Eliminate (F) and (G) because Experiment 1, as shown in Figure 1, does not examine the herbicidal activity of the three components. To compare the weed killer to its components, Experiment 2 must also include the unseparated weed killer. Eliminate (J) since glycerol is only one component of the weed killer and a plot sprayed with glycerol is already included in Experiment 2. The correct answer is (H).

27. **A** The question asks whether a *T. vernix* cell has a nucleus or a cell wall. This question requires outside knowledge. All plant cells have a cell wall while animal cells lack a cell wall. Also, all animal, plant, fungal, and protist cells have a nucleus. Since *T. vernix* is in the plant kingdom, its cells have both a nucleus and a cell wall. The correct answer is (A).

28. **J** The question asks which of Student 2's statements is scientifically inaccurate. This question relies on outside knowledge: the subatomic particles that orbit the nucleus of an atom are electrons, which are negatively charged. This is inconsistent with Student 2's claim that positively charged particles orbit the nucleus. However, without knowing this outside knowledge, there is still some POE that can be done. Common knowledge and all three students agree that rubbing materials

together can generate static electricity, so eliminate (F). All three students also mentioned that like charges repel each other and discuss both positive and negative ions. Eliminate (G) and (H). Only Student 2 states that there are positively charged particles orbiting the nucleus, so this is the answer that doesn't match. The correct answer is (J).

29. **A** The question asks which charged particle was transferred to the atoms in the bar according to Student 1. This question requires outside knowledge. Electrons are negatively charged, while neutrons and photons have no charge and protons have a positive charge. Student 1 claims that *negatively charged subatomic particles were transferred between the two materials*. The correct answer is (A).

30. **J** The question asks which statement correctly describes a neutral atom *if Student 1's explanation is correct*. According to Student 1, *in an atom, the positive charges are contained in the nucleus, while the negative charges orbit the nucleus*. Eliminate (F) and (H) since both incorrectly state that the positive charges orbit the nucleus. To choose between the remaining answers, outside knowledge is needed. A neutral atom has no charge and thus has equal numbers of positively and negatively charged particles. Eliminate (G), which states that a neutral atom has fewer negative than positive charges. The correct answer is (J).

31. **B** The question asks whether a bar rubbed with silk and a bar rubbed with faux fur would attract or repel each other based on Student 1's explanation. The answer choices mention the movement of negative charges. According to Student 1, *negative charges were transferred out of the bar to the silk and into the bar from the faux fur*. Eliminate (C) and (D) since they incorrectly state that the negative charges would move in the same direction with respect to both bars. In the question, *silk cloth was used on the acrylic bar on the left*, so Student 1 would expect negative charges to move from this bar to the silk. Eliminate (A) because it claims that the charges would move from the silk into the bar on the left. The correct answer is (B).

32. **G** The question asks which figure is consistent with Student 3's explanation and Figure 2. Look at Figure 2 first. Figure 2 shows that the bars move away from each other when the same fabric is used on both and towards each other when different fabrics are used. Eliminate (F) and (J) which both reverse the relationships in Figure 2. The remaining two answers show different charges for the bar treated with silk, so check Student 3's explanation for mention of the charge on the bar rubbed with a silk cloth. According to Student 3, *when the silk cloth was rubbed on the bar, some of these positive ions transferred onto the bar*, making it positively charged. Eliminate (H), which shows the bar rubbed with silk having a negative charge. The correct answer is (G).

33. **C** The question asks how Student 2's explanation differs from that of Student 3. The answers all mention charges of particles that are transferred, so look in both explanations for mentions of positive or negative charge. Student 2 claims that *positive charges can move from the atoms on one material to the atoms on the other material*, but does not mention transfer of negative charges. Eliminate (A) and (B) since they incorrectly state that Student 2 believes that both positive and negative charges can be transferred. Student 3 claims that *when the silk cloth was rubbed on the bar, some of these positive ions transferred onto the bar*, while *when the faux fur was rubbed on a bar, some of the nega-*

tive ions were transferred onto the bar. This is consistent with (C). Eliminate (D), since Student 3's explanation mentions transfer of ions and not of subatomic particles. The correct answer is (C).

34. **F** The question asks which experimental procedure would best test the explanation of Student 3. According to Student 3, *silk has a lot of positive ions* while faux fur *has a lot of negative ions.* This explanation is different from those of the other students, since the other two students claimed that, through rubbing, *charged subatomic particles were transferred* between the silk or faux fur and the acrylic bars, causing an excess of either positive or negative charges in the bars. Since *ions of opposite charges attract each other,* if Student 3's explanation is correct, the silk and the faux fur should attract each other without being rubbed on the acrylic bars. This is consistent with (F). Eliminate (G), (H), and (J) because these all mention an uncharged acrylic bar, which should not attract either positively or negatively charged objects based on Student 3's explanation. The correct answer is (F).

35. **B** The question asks, based on Figures 1 and 2, what happens to the battery current *as conductivity increases from 200 μS/m to 500 μS/m at room temperature.* Figure 1 shows the relationship between conductivity and resistivity, so start there. As conductivity increases, the resistivity decreases from approximately 5,000 Ω·m to approximately 2,000 Ω·m. Now, look at Figure 2, which shows the relationship between resistivity and battery current at room temperature. Figure 2 shows an inverse relationship between resistivity and battery current: current decreases as resistivity increases. Therefore, as the resistivity decreases from 5,000 Ω·m to 2,000 Ω·m, the current will increase only. The correct answer is (B).

36. **H** The question asks for the approximate resistivity of the aqueous solution in a battery that produces a current of 2 A, based on Figure 2. Figure 2 shows the relationship between resistivity and battery current. Notice that battery current decreases as resistivity increases. At a resistivity of 12,000 Ω·m, the battery current is a little higher than 3 A. Therefore, the resistivity must be higher than 12,000 Ω·m to produce a battery current of only 2 A. Eliminate (F) and (G). In order to choose between (H) and (J), extend the horizontal axis, which represents 2 A, to the right and then extend the trend line until it intersects the extended axis. The line would intersect 2 A at approximately 14,000 Ω·m. Eliminate (J) because 16,000 Ω·m is too large. The correct answer is (H).

37. **A** The question asks for the conductivity of pure H_2O at room temperature, based on Figure 3. According to the passage, Figure 3 shows *how the electrical conductivities of aqueous solutions at room temperature vary with the molar concentrations of the dissolved salts.* An aqueous solution is a solution of a substance dissolved in H_2O. The molar concentration is a measure of the concentration of salt added to the H_2O. Therefore, a molar concentration of 0 represents pure H_2O with no salt added. For all three salts, at a molar concentration of 0, the electrical conductivity is 0 μS/m. The correct answer is (A).

38. **F** The question asks, based on Figure 2, *if the battery will supply more power if it contains a solution with a resistivity of 5,000 Ω·m or 10,000 Ω·m.* Refer to Figure 2 and use POE. Figure 2 shows that a battery with a resistivity of 5,000 Ω·m has a higher current than one with a resistivity of 10,000 Ω·m. Eliminate (G) and (H) because they contradict this fact. Batteries with a higher current gen-

erate more power, so the higher current at 5,000 $\Omega \cdot$m will generate more power. Eliminate (J). The correct answer is (F).

39. **D** The question asks, based on Figures 1–3, which value would likely be closest to the current that would be produced by *a battery containing a 0.5 M aqueous solution of MgCl$_2$* at room temperature. Start with Figure 3, which shows the electrical conductivity of MgCl$_2$ at various molar concentrations. Find 0.5 M on the horizontal axis of Figure 3. At this point, the conductivity of MgCl$_2$ is approximately 400 μS/m. Figure 1 compares conductivity to resistivity, so look at Figure 1 now. At a conductivity of 400 μS/m, the resistivity is approximately 2,500 $\Omega \cdot$m. Finally, look at Figure 3, which compares resistivity to battery current. At a resistivity of 2,500 $\Omega \cdot$m, the battery current is approximately 9 A. The correct answer is (D).

40. **G** The question asks whether Figures 1 and 3 support the claim that a 0.2 M KH$_2$PO$_4$ solution at room temperature will have a higher resistivity than a 0.2 M MgCl$_2$ solution at room temperature. Figure 3 shows the conductivity of various molar solutions *at room temperature*, so find 0.2 M on the horizontal axis of Figure 3. At a concentration of 0.2 M, the KH$_2$PO$_4$ solution has a lower conductivity than the MgCl$_2$ solution. Eliminate (F) and (H) because both state that KH$_2$PO$_4$ solution has a higher conductivity than the MgCl$_2$ solution. Now, refer to Figure 1, which compares the conductivity to resistivity. Figure 1 show an inverse relationship between resistivity and conductivity: resistivity decreases as conductivity increases. Therefore, since the KH$_2$PO$_4$ solution has a lower conductivity, it will have a higher resistivity. The data does support the claim. Eliminate (J). The correct answer is (G).

Chapter 32
Practice Exam 4

*Make sure to download a bubble sheet for this test via your online Student Tools.

ENGLISH TEST

45 Minutes—75 Questions

DIRECTIONS: In the five passages that follow, certain words and phrases are underlined and numbered. In the right-hand column, you will find alternatives for each underlined part. In most cases, you are to choose the one that correctly expresses the idea, makes the statement appropriate for standard written English, or is worded most consistently with the style and tone of the passage as a whole. If you think the original version is correct, choose "NO CHANGE." In some cases, you will find in the right-hand column a question about the underlined part of the passage. You are to choose the correct answer to the question.

You will also find questions about a section of the passage or the passage as a whole. These questions do not refer to an underlined portion of the passage, but rather are identified by a number or numbers in a box.

For each question, choose the alternative you consider correct and blacken the corresponding oval on your answer document. Read each passage through once before you begin to answer the questions that accompany it. For many of the questions, you must read several sentences beyond the question to determine the answer. Be sure that you have read far enough ahead each time you choose an alternative.

PASSAGE I

Lou Gehrig, All-American

Since their inception in 1913, the New York Yankees have long been regarded as a force in Major League Baseball. Love them or hate them, there is no denying the tradition of excellence that they have leveraged in order to win 26 World Series

¹

championships, a league record.

1. Which of the following alternatives to the underlined portion would NOT be acceptable?
   A. so as
   B. as a means
   C. so that
   D. DELETE the underlined portion.

The Yankees have had many great baseball players contribute

²

to the team, but one man stands out for his fortitude and good spirit: Lou Gehrig. Born to poor German immigrants in 1903, Gehrig received no encouragement to pursue baseball as a career. His mother considered business a better line of work for

³

her son, wanting him to excel academically, not physically. Gehrig followed her wishes, at least at first. He attended Columbia University, but after only two years, and without a degree, Gehrig left school.

2. F. NO CHANGE
   G. players;
   H. players,
   J. players and

3. A. NO CHANGE
   B. His mother, considering business
   C. Business was considered by his mother to be
   D. Business considered his mother

GO ON TO THE NEXT PAGE.

However, he did have a job lined up before he withdrew from college. A Yankee scout had seen an intercollegiate game Gehrig played in—coincidentally, on the very day Yankee Stadium first opened to the public in 1923—and immediately signed him to a contract. He played well in his first three years in the majors, but he did not become a true superstar until 1926. He broke many, long-standing records, including those for runs batted in and extra-base hits, and even played in 2,130 consecutive games! His formidable skills and unflinching dedication to the sport interested his teammates and the fans alike.

[1] The prognosis was a veritable death sentence. [2] Then suddenly, Gehrig's amazing stamina and talent seemed to

dissipate, leading one sports reporter to speculate that something was physically wrong with the athlete. [3] Unfortunately, that reporter was right: Gehrig was diagnosed with amyotrophic lateral sclerosis, a degenerative disease that leads to paralysis of both voluntary muscles and involuntary muscles, like those needed to control breathing and swallowing. [9]

Most people faced with such daunting news would of withdrawn from society and mourned their fates.

4. Which of the following alternatives to the underlined portion would be LEAST acceptable?

   F. that featured Gehrig
   G. that Gehrig played in
   H. in which Gehrig played
   J. and played Gehrig

5. A. NO CHANGE
   B. many long-standing records,
   C. many, long-standing, records
   D. many long-standing records

6. Given that all the choices are true, which one most clearly communicates how positively Gehrig was viewed as a player?

   F. NO CHANGE
   G. impressed
   H. offended
   J. confused

7. A. NO CHANGE
   B. suddenly Gehrig's
   C. suddenly Gehrigs
   D. suddenly, Gehrigs

8. Which of the following alternatives to the underlined portion would be LEAST acceptable?

   F. writer to infer
   G. sports reporter to infer
   H. writer to speculate
   J. sports reporter to imply

9. Which of the following sequences of sentences makes this paragraph most logical?

   A. NO CHANGE
   B. 1, 3, 2
   C. 2, 1, 3
   D. 2, 3, 1

10. F. NO CHANGE
   G. of withdrew
   H. have withdrawn
   J. have withdrew

GO ON TO THE NEXT PAGE.

[11] However, on the day of

Gehrig's retirement from baseball, he delivered one of
$\overline{\qquad}$
12
the most famous speeches of the time. He acknowledged his

grim fate but paid tribute to the life-affirming support he'd

received from his fans: "The ballplayer who loses his head, who
$\overline{\qquad\qquad\qquad\qquad\qquad\qquad}$
13
can't keep his cool, is worse than no ballplayer at all." He spoke
$\overline{\qquad\qquad\qquad\qquad\qquad\qquad}$
13
highly of the encouragement his fans always provided and

proudly proclaimed that, despite his fate, he didn't regret

anything in his life or career. He was a man who's eternal
$\overline{\qquad\qquad}$
14
optimism and good spirit lived on as a legacy of hope and

kindness for fans everywhere. We would all do well to learn that

lesson.

11. At this point, the writer is thinking about adding the following true statement:

> I know when I had to put my dog to sleep when he got cancer, all I could do was cry in my room for days.

Should the writer make this addition here?

A. Yes, because it provides a personal example comparable to the experience Lou Gehrig faced.
B. Yes, because it helps clarify the concept of mourning mentioned in the previous sentence.
C. No, because it detracts from the overall flow of the paragraph by adding irrelevant information.
D. No, because Gehrig did not have cancer.

12. F. NO CHANGE
G. Gehrig's retirement,
H. Gehrigs retirement
J. Gehrigs' retirement

13. Given that all the choices are quotations attributed to Gehrig, which one would most effectively support the preceding statement in this sentence?

A. NO CHANGE
B. "They're wishing me luck—and I'm dying."
C. "I don't know if we're going to be successful or not, but we're going to give her a go."
D. "Yet today I consider myself the luckiest man on the face of the earth."

14. F. NO CHANGE
G. man whose
H. man, who's
J. man who

Question 15 asks about the preceding passage as a whole.

15. After reviewing this essay, the writer is thinking about deleting its opening phrase—"Since their inception in 1913,"—and revising the capitalization accordingly. Should this phrase be kept or deleted?

A. Kept, because it explains why the New York Yankees have been so successful.
B. Kept, because it establishes when in Yankees' history Gehrig lived and played.
C. Deleted, because it provides information that is presented effectively later in the passage.
D. Deleted, because it does not provide the years in which the Yankees won the World Series.

GO ON TO THE NEXT PAGE.

PASSAGE II

A Quarter for Your Thoughts

Ever since I was a little girl, I could always count on my grandmother to initiate a wonderful field trip. We lived in Virginia and so had immediate access to hundreds of famous places. <u>Nonetheless, she</u> took me to Civil War battlefields,
₁₆
historic homes, national monuments, anywhere that had a story

to tell. <u>Old lighthouses can be dangerous, with rickety stairs and</u>
₁₇
<u>rotting floorboards.</u>
₁₇

My <u>love of history has only grown over the years.</u> History
₁₈
was always so real for me, not the dull, dusty stuff other people

seemed to think it was. My <u>trips'</u> with my grandmother made me
₁₉
feel as if I were shivering with George Washington at Valley
Forge, where the Revolutionary Army endured a brutal winter, or
hearing the words to the Gettysburg Address from Abraham

---

16. F. NO CHANGE
G. She
H. However, she
J. On the contrary, she

17. Given that all the choices are true, which one best identifies a personal connection the narrator feels to the locations she visits?
A. NO CHANGE
B. National monuments are especially fun to visit, but the lines can be quite long.
C. Civil War battlefields feel so alive when you walk through them; you almost expect to see a soldier around every corner.
D. The historic homes we visited are so nice they have been featured in decorating magazines.

18. Given that all the choices are true, which one introduces the subject of this paragraph and reinforces the essay's presentation of the relationship between the narrator and her grandmother?
F. NO CHANGE
G. My grandmother never visited Washington, D.C. until she was in her twenties, even though she lived so close.
H. A proper understanding of history requires extensive reading.
J. My grandmother indulged my love of history and deepened my appreciation for all there is to learn from it.

19. A. NO CHANGE
B. trip's
C. trips,
D. trips

GO ON TO THE NEXT PAGE.

Lincoln himself. 20 How could that ever be boring?

One day when I was visiting her, my grandmother took out a
big, flat box. "This is for you. I thought we could begin a new
project," she told me, handing me a pamphlet to read. The U.S.
Mint was starting a project, minting brand new quarters for each
of the 50 states bearing images significant and unique to each
state's history. The box contained a map of the country, and each
state had a space where we could insert its quarter.

My enthusiasm caused laughter for a "quarter collection"
project, my friends didn't understand my eagerness when I
eagerly tromped to the bank every couple of months when a new
quarter came out. I was so excited when the first three were
released Delaware, Pennsylvania, and New Jersey. My
grandmother and I would insert each quarter in its proper place
and look up the story behind each new image we
saw. Amusingly, as time progressed, even my friends liked to
look at the growing collection of quarters on my map, asking

---

20. The writer is considering deleting the phrase "where the Revolutionary Army endured a brutal winter" from the preceding sentence (deleting the comma following the phrase). Should the phrase be kept or deleted?

  F. Kept, because it maintains the passage's focus on history.

  G. Kept, because it explains the significance of Valley Forge, which might otherwise cause confusion.

  H. Deleted, because the narrator has already established her interest in history.

  J. Deleted, because the information overstates the severity of the weather during the Revolution.

21. Given that all the choices are true, which one best introduces the subject of this paragraph?

  A. NO CHANGE

  B. In my opinion, anything that has happened in the last century isn't history; it's current events.

  C. My grandmother originally wanted to be a history teacher.

  D. Studying history has really encouraged me in my other studies, too.

22. F. NO CHANGE

  G. told me to hand her a pamphlet to read.

  H. read a pamphlet, telling me to hold it.

  J. handed me a pamphlet, holding it.

23. A. NO CHANGE

  B. and when each

  C. for which each

  D. each

24. F. NO CHANGE

  G. Laughing at my enthusiasm

  H. So as to laugh about my enthusiasm

  J. Finding humor

25. A. NO CHANGE

  B. released;

  C. released:

  D. released,

26. Which of the following alternatives to the underlined portion would NOT be acceptable?

  F. saw. I was amused to see that,

  G. saw. To my utter amusement,

  H. saw; amusingly,

  J. saw, amusingly,

GO ON TO THE NEXT PAGE.

questions and <u>appreciating with admiration</u> the pristine
                            27
collection.

When the final quarter came out last year, my grandmother,

my friends, and I had a small <u>party, we wanted</u> to celebrate the
                                        28
complete collection. I think it is safe to say that

<u>the party was a smashing success.</u> Now, my grandmother says
            29

we'll have to start planning to visit all 50 states. <u>I wonder</u> where
                                                              30
we'll go first!

27. A. NO CHANGE
   B. admiring
   C. lauding the high estimation of
   D. adoring and praising

28. F. NO CHANGE
   G. party, everyone wanted to
   H. party to
   J. party, let's

29. Given that all the choices are true, which one best makes a connection between the narrator's view of history and that of her friends?

   A. NO CHANGE
   B. my friends enjoyed themselves at the party.
   C. my friends now firmly believe that history can be fun, just like me.
   D. my friends are a little less negative about the study of history.

30. Which of the following alternatives to the underlined portion would be LEAST acceptable?

   F. am curious
   G. am anxious to see
   H. am nervous about
   J. can't wait to know

PASSAGE III

Aviation Princess

My daughter just turned nine last week. We went to the mall,

and I gave her the best gift I could imagine: free rein to pick out

anything she <u>wanted and desired to have.</u> I expected her to pick
                        31
out some clothes, a new video game, maybe even a

<u>doll. However, she</u> insisted the only thing she wanted was a
          32
model airplane.

I guess <u>about her request</u> I shouldn't be surprised. My
              33

31. A. NO CHANGE
   B. wanted, so that she could pick out her desire.
   C. wanted.
   D. wanted and had come to desire.

32. Which of the following alternatives to the underlined portion would NOT be acceptable?

   F. doll; however, she
   G. doll, but she
   H. doll however she
   J. doll. She

33. The best placement for the underlined phrase would be:

   A. where it is now.
   B. before the word *shouldn't*.
   C. after the word *shouldn't*.
   D. after the word *surprised* (ending the sentence with a period).

GO ON TO THE NEXT PAGE.

daughter has grown up in a military household, the pride and joy
₃₄

of her overly doting father. He finds it perfectly appropriate that,
₃₅

from a very early age, she has shared his love of aviation. I'll

never forget my utter dismay when he taught her to jump off the

swing set in our backyard, pretending she was a pilot and
₃₆

shouting, "Airborne!" I believe she was four at the time, but even

then she would play pilot more than play house.
₃₇

Yet soon stories and pictures of aircraft weren't enough;
₃₈

she wanted to see the real thing. So my husband started

taking her to the annual air show at the local military base

that happens every year. Most other children her age admired
₃₉

how fast the planes flew or how nicely they were painted, but not

my daughter. [40] She would ask, "Daddy, when are they going

to upgrade the avionics system in that F-22 Raptor?" or "Do you

think unmanned drones will ever be as useful as manned

aircraft?" I once overhead her correcting an older gentleman

whom was mistaken about the planned retirement date of the
₄₁

---

34. **F.** NO CHANGE
    G. has been growing
    H. would have grown
    J. had grown

35. Which of the following alternatives to the underlined portion would NOT be acceptable?

    A. believes it appropriately
    B. believes it appropriate
    C. considers it entirely appropriate
    D. deems it perfectly appropriate

36. **F.** NO CHANGE
    G. backyard pretending,
    H. backyard; pretending
    J. backyard. Pretending

37. Which of the following alternatives to the underlined portion would NOT be acceptable?

    A. house.
    B. she would play house.
    C. house was.
    D. she played house.

38. **F.** NO CHANGE
    G. Therefore,
    H. Although
    J. Instead,

39. **A.** NO CHANGE
    B. that takes place each year.
    C. which occurs every twelve months.
    D. DELETE the underlined portion and end the sentence with a period.

40. The writer is considering deleting the phrase *other children her age* from the preceding sentence. Should this phrase be kept or deleted?

    F. Kept, because it clarifies the types of questions children should be asking at air shows.
    G. Kept, because it emphasizes how different the narrator's daughter is from other children her age.
    H. Deleted, because it introduces information about aircraft but does not provide enough specific details.
    J. Deleted, because it interrupts the flow of passage.

41. **A.** NO CHANGE
    B. who
    C. which
    D. DELETE the underlined portion.

GO ON TO THE NEXT PAGE.

F-15 Eagle. I would have been embarrassed about her

presumption, if she hadn't been <u>absolute and unequivocal right.</u>
₄₂

Of course, my husband has <u>big dreams</u> for his little
₄₃
aviatrix. She is going to be a military pilot, graduating at the

top of her class from the Naval Academy. Then she's going

<u>to be the individual who design</u> the next-generation supersonic
₄₄
fighter personally, while lecturing at Harvard about the history of

fixed-wing aircraft. <u>Otherwise, how</u> she's going to fit that in
₄₅
between being a surgeon and the president, I'll never know!

42. **F.** NO CHANGE
   G. absolute and unequivocally
   H. absolutely and unequivocal
   J. absolutely and unequivocally

43. Which of the following alternatives to the underlined portion would be LEAST acceptable?

   A. ambitious aims
   B. impossible hopes
   C. great aspirations
   D. impressive plans

44. **F.** NO CHANGE
   G. to
   H. to individually accept a task in order to
   J. to take the initiative to

45. **A.** NO CHANGE
   B. In contrast, how
   C. How
   D. Despite this, how

PASSAGE IV

**Light Bright, Light Bright:
Turn on the Magic of Colored Light**

As a child, I used to catch fireflies at dusk <u>when I was young.</u> I
₄₆

remember feeling a strange excitement <u>which,</u> looking into my
₄₇
cupped hands, I would see the light grow brighter then dimmer

as the fly flitted from one side to the other, trying to find an

escape. What I should have felt, however, was amazement at the

biological wonder I saw before me: bioluminescence.

Bioluminescence literally means "living light," <u>and it refers</u>
₄₈
to a strange adaptation found in some organisms. It allows these

organisms to create a chemical reaction that generates and emits

46. **F.** NO CHANGE
   G. when I was a youth.
   H. before I grew up.
   J. DELETE the underlined portion and end the sentence with a period.

47. **A.** NO CHANGE
   B. when,
   C. in which,
   D. DELETE the underlined portion.

48. **F.** NO CHANGE
   G. simultaneously,
   H. consider that
   J. in addition,

GO ON TO THE NEXT PAGE.

light. Even though scientists know that this light is not intended
to be a heat source, they're not totally certain what it is intended
to do, either. Theorists hypothesize that organisms use their

self-manufactured light for camouflaging themselves, illuminate
their surroundings, attract mates and prey, repulse predators, and

even communicate. 51 How the same adaptation can be
designed to both attract and repulse, however, is still a matter of
contention.

The number of terrestrial or land-based, organisms
that exhibit bioluminescence is rather small, and many,

such as fireflies and spiders, are fairly small in stature. In

fact, the vast majority are single-cell organisms that cannot be

seen with the naked eye. Unlike these smaller organisms,

researchers are puzzled as to why most animals and humans did

not evolve this unique trait. Apparently the adaptation was not

universally necessary, given the bright rays of the sun that bathed

the surface year-round.

However, sunlight clearly doesn't stop the development
of bioluminescence. In total, ninety percent of all deep-sea
marine lifeforms experience some sort of bioluminescence. Fish,

sharks, eels, and octopi, to name only a few, have all been seen

to bioluminesce in the murky depths. The most commonly

emitted colors are blue and green, but red and yellow have also

been observed. Its a veritable rainbow of color 1,800 meters

49. **A.** NO CHANGE
  B. Scientists
  C. In fact, scientists
  D. Understand that scientists

50. **F.** NO CHANGE
  G. in camouflaging theirselves,
  H. to camouflage itself,
  J. to camouflage themselves,

51. The writer is considering deleting the phrase "repulse predators" from the preceding sentence (deleting the comma after
the phrase). Should the phrase be kept or deleted?

  A. Kept, because it is an essential detail referred to directly
    in the next sentence.
  B. Kept, because the evolutionary trait of repulsing predators
    is critical to survival of the fittest.
  C. Deleted, because it repeats information previously pro-
    vided in the essay.
  D. Deleted, because it makes the sentence long and difficult
    to understand.

52. **F.** NO CHANGE
  G. terrestrial or, land-based
  H. terrestrial, or land-based,
  J. terrestrial, or land-based

53. **A.** NO CHANGE
  B. most animals
  C. animal researchers seek to discover why most animals
  D. researchers do not know why most animals

54. Given that all the choices are true, which one best indicates
the focus of this paragraph?

  F. NO CHANGE
  G. conditions are quite different in the ocean.
  H. there is no evidence that bioluminescence has ever devel-
    oped anywhere other than on planet Earth.
  J. humans do not need bioluminescence, because we can use
    our intellect to manipulate our surroundings.

55. **A.** NO CHANGE
  B. green but
  C. green; but
  D. green but,

56. **F.** NO CHANGE
  G. In it's
  H. Its'
  J. It's

GO ON TO THE NEXT PAGE.

below the surface thanks to these <u>organism's lights,</u> even though
₅₇
almost no visible light can penetrate to that level.

The extreme depth at which most of these organisms exist
represents the biggest obstacle researchers face in determining
the primary function of bioluminescence. Undoubtedly, this will
slow the pace of exploration more <u>then lack of money.</u> For that
₅₈
reason, it may be some time before this mysterious

adaptation is <u>clarified.</u>
₅₉

57. A. NO CHANGE
   B. organism's lights',
   C. organisms' lights,
   D. organisms lights,

58. F. NO CHANGE
   G. then lack of money will.
   H. than lack of money.
   J. as lack of money.

59. Which of the following alternatives to the underlined word
would be LEAST acceptable?

   A. fully explained.
   B. accounted for.
   C. transmitted.
   D. cleared up.

> Question 60 asks about the preceding passage
> as a whole.

60. Suppose the writer's goal had been to write a brief essay
focusing on a fascinating evolutionary adaptation that can be
found in multiple habitats. Would this essay accomplish this
goal?

   F. Yes, because fireflies exhibit the adaptation and live in trees.
   G. Yes, because bioluminescence is described, and it occurs
in both marine and non-marine habitats.
   H. No, because fireflies cannot live in both air and water.
   J. No, because all the habitats described exist on the same
planet.

PASSAGE V

Doctors Without Borders

In America, we take many things for granted. If we don't feel
well, we see a doctor. If we're hungry, we eat something. If
we're thirsty, we drink some water. <u>These very basic actions can</u>
₆₁
be amazingly difficult, if not impossible, in some parts of the

world. That is why a group of French <u>physicians, started</u> Doctors
₆₂
Without Borders in 1971.

61. A. NO CHANGE
   B. (Do NOT begin new paragraph) Yet these
   C. (Begin new paragraph) These
   D. (Begin new paragraph) Yet these

62. F. NO CHANGE
   G. physicians started,
   H. physicians; started
   J. physicians started

GO ON TO THE NEXT PAGE.

Doctors Without Borders started as a humanitarian aid
organization designed to reach out to the innocent victims of wars
in lesser-developed parts of the world. The doctors who first
started the organization had been working in Nigeria during the
country's very bloody civil war in the late 1960s. There, they saw

everything from starvation, and disease, to death and outright
murder happening in the streets, and neither the United Nations

nor the Red Cross seemed to do anything to stop these atrocities.

66 The doctors felt that, although they couldn't put an end to
the fighting itself, they could at least help to alleviate the

suffering, thus they declared themselves neutral in the conflict
and entered war-torn areas to provide aid to anyone who needed
it, regardless of which side of the conflict the person was on.

In contrast, the original mission was simply to provide health
care as well as medical training to up-and-coming doctors

63. Which choice most effectively introduces the basic goal of
Doctors Without Borders, as described elsewhere in the
essay?

A. NO CHANGE
B. tends to specialize in trauma treatment, which helps the
doctors in their personal medical practices when they
return home.
C. has never sought political support from the United States
or other countries, because it wants to remain completely
neutral.
D. has never operated within the United States, although
arguably there are many people here who could benefit
from its services.

64. F. NO CHANGE
G. starvation, and disease
H. starvation and disease
J. starvation and disease,

65. Which of the following alternatives to the underlined portion
would be LEAST acceptable?

A. horrors.
B. offenses.
C. wrongs.
D. alarms.

66. The writer is considering deleting the preceding sentence.
Should this sentence be kept or deleted?

F. Kept, because readers are used to hearing about murders
and starvation anyway.
G. Kept, because it provides a specific example of the type of
actions that provoked the doctors to take action.
H. Deleted, because it does not explain how the doctors actu-
ally stopped the fighting in Nigeria.
J. Deleted, because it detracts from the actual foundation of
Doctors Without Borders.

67. A. NO CHANGE
B. suffering thus
C. suffering. Thus
D. suffering and thus

68. F. NO CHANGE
G. The
H. Meanwhile, the
J. Finally, the

GO ON TO THE NEXT PAGE.

in the various regions. ⟦69⟧ In desperate need of medical

attention suffering in war-torn regions certainly felt the aid
—––
70
Doctors Without Borders supplied was important. When not in

the direct line of fire between two opposing military groups,
—–––
71
however, the organization puts special emphasis on the

preventative aspects of health care, especially vaccinations, good

nutrition, and sanitation. These seeming simple goals have made
—––––
72
substantial strides in the overall quality of health in Africa,

where most of the work of Doctors Without Borders has been

focused over the last 40 years.

Sadly, the noble effort expended by these selfless doctors have
——————————————————————
73
not met universal support. In some conflicts, the aid workers—

despite their political neutrality—have found themselves the

victims of kidnappings, arrests, even murder. Doctors who

volunteer to serve in Doctors Without Borders know the dangers
—–––
74

they face, yet they choose to try to help anyway. We can only hope
————————————
75
that eventually their dignified actions will become unnecessary.
————————————————————————————
75

69. The writer is considering deleting the phrase "to up-and-
coming doctors" from the preceding sentence. Should the
phrase be kept or deleted?

   A. Kept, because it clarifies to whom the medical training is
   being provided.
   B. Kept, because it is important to specify that there are doctors already practicing in the region.
   C. Deleted, because a person who has not successfully graduated from medical school cannot be considered a doctor.
   D. Deleted, because Doctors Without Borders should not take
   such a grandiose task on themselves without government
   sanction.

70. F. NO CHANGE
   G. attention who
   H. attention, and
   J. attention, individuals

71. A. NO CHANGE
   B. among
   C. across
   D. next

72. F. NO CHANGE
   G. more seemingly
   H. seemingly
   J. more seeming

73. A. NO CHANGE
   B. efforts expended by these selfless doctors have
   C. efforts expended by these selfless doctors has
   D. effort expended by these selfless doctors had

74. F. NO CHANGE
   G. distribute
   H. provide
   J. deliver

75. Given that all the choices are true, which one most clearly
shows that the self-sacrifice of the doctors deserves praise?

   A. NO CHANGE
   B. I don't know if I would have that depth of conviction or
   level of courage.
   C. Such unsung courage truly speaks to the depth of human
   kindness, and should be a lesson to us all.
   D. It is truly a shame that they are put into dangerous positions.

END OF TEST 1

STOP! DO NOT TURN THE PAGE UNTIL TOLD TO DO SO.

MATHEMATICS TEST

60 Minutes—60 Questions

DIRECTIONS: Solve each problem, choose the correct answer, and then darken the corresponding oval on your answer sheet.

Do not linger over problems that take too much time. Solve as many as you can; then return to the others in the time you have left for this test.

You are permitted to use a calculator on this test. You may use your calculator for any problems you choose, but some of the problems may best be done without using a calculator.

Note: Unless otherwise stated, all of the following should be assumed:

1. Illustrative figures are NOT necessarily drawn to scale.
2. Geometric figures lie in a plane.
3. The word *line* indicates a straight line.
4. The word *average* indicates arithmetic mean.

DO YOUR FIGURING HERE.

1. In a geometric sequence, the quotient of any two consecutive terms is the same. If the third term of a geometric sequence is 8 and the fourth term is 16, then what is the second term?

   A. −8
   B. −4
   C. 2
   D. 4
   E. 8

2. If the function $f(a, b)$ is defined as $f(a, b) = 2ab - (a + b)$, then $f(3, 4) = ?$

   F. 7
   G. 17
   H. 21
   J. 24
   K. 31

3. The Korean BBQ taco truck sells short rib tacos for 99¢. Christine has only pennies, nickels, dimes, and quarters in her purse. If she wants to pay with exact change, then what is the least number of coins Christine can use to buy a 99¢ taco?

   (Note: Assume any sales tax is included in the price.)

   A. 6
   B. 7
   C. 8
   D. 9
   E. 10

4. What is the area, in square inches, of a square with a side length of 8 inches?

   F. 8
   G. 16
   H. 24
   J. 32
   K. 64

GO ON TO THE NEXT PAGE.

DO YOUR FIGURING HERE.

5. If $x = 3$, then the expression $\dfrac{(x+1)^2}{x^2-1}$ is equal to:

   A.   2

   B. $\dfrac{1}{2}$

   C.   0

   D. $-\dfrac{1}{2}$

   E. -8

6. Which of the following is NOT a factor of 1,776 ?

   F.   12
   G.   16
   H.   18
   J.   24
   K.   37

7. Lauren's world history teacher needs to select one of his 19 students to lead the class in song. Lauren's teacher decides that the song leader, who will be chosen at random, CANNOT be any of the 4 seniors in the class. What is the probability that Lauren, who is NOT a senior, will be chosen?

   A.   0

   B. $\dfrac{1}{19}$

   C. $\dfrac{1}{15}$

   D. $\dfrac{4}{19}$

   E. $\dfrac{15}{19}$

8. If $4(x-5) + x = 45$, then $x = $?

   F.   5
   G.   8
   H.   9
   J.   10
   K.   13

9. Joe rents a car to drive across the state to visit his family for Thanksgiving. The car rental company charges Joe $112 for the weekend rental, plus $0.99 for each mile he drives. If Joe drives the rental car m miles, then which of the following expressions gives Joe's total cost, in dollars, for renting the car?

   A. $0.99m - 112$
   B. $0.99m + 112$
   C. $49.95m$
   D. $112m + 0.99$
   E. $112.99m$

GO ON TO THE NEXT PAGE.

DO YOUR FIGURING HERE.

10. Stella wants to buy a scooter for $4,800. A loan company offers to finance the purchase in return for payments of $130 a month for 4 years. If Stella were to finance the scooter, then how much more than the purchase price of the scooter will Stella have paid at the end of the 4-year period?

   F. $ 520
   G. $ 780
   H. $1,040
   J. $1,300
   K. $1,440

11. The expression $\dfrac{20y^8}{4y^2}$ is equivalent to:

   A. $5y^4$
   B. $5y^6$
   C. $5y^8$
   D. $16y^4$
   E. $16y^6$

12. Which of the following is equal to $\dfrac{3-\dfrac{1}{2}}{2+\dfrac{3}{4}}$?

   F. $\dfrac{10}{11}$
   G. 2
   H. 12
   J. 20
   K. $\dfrac{55}{2}$

13. Point C is at 3.5 on the real number line. If Point D is also on the real number line and is 8.5 units from C, then which of the following are the possible locations of D ?

   A. −12 and −5
   B. −12 and 5
   C. −5 and 5
   D. 12 and −5
   E. 12 and 5

14. The mean of 4 numbers in a data set is 7. If 3 of these numbers are 2, 4, and 10, then which of the following is the fourth number?

   F. 4
   G. 7
   H. 8
   J. 10
   K. 12

GO ON TO THE NEXT PAGE.

15. Motorcars, Inc. made $1,489,000 in net profit in 2007. In 2009, Motorcars, Inc. made $1,725,000 in net profit. If the net profit increased linearly from 2007 through 2009, then what was the net profit earned in 2008 ?

    A. $1,607,000
    B. $1,698,000
    C. $1,724,000
    D. $1,779,000
    E. $1,842,000

DO YOUR FIGURING HERE.

16. The art teacher at Valley High School is decorating her classroom by reproducing famous pictures on her walls. She has a picture 8 inches wide and 10 inches tall that she wants to replicate to scale on the wall. If the painting on the wall will be 6 feet tall, then approximately how wide will the painting be, in feet?

    F. 5
    G. 7
    H. 9
    J. 11
    K. 13

17. The formula for line l in standard form is $5x - y = 2$. Which of the following gives the formula for line l in slope-intercept form?

    A. $y = 5x + 2$
    B. $y = 5x - 2$
    C. $y = 2x - 5$
    D. $y = -5x - 2$
    E. $y = -5x + 2$

18. The expression $|2 - 14| - |-25|$ is equal to:

    F. 41
    G. 37
    H. 13
    J. −13
    K. −37

19. In $\triangle JKL$ the measure of $\angle J$ is exactly 37°, and the measure of $\angle K$ is less than or equal to 63°. Which of the following phrases best describes the measure of $\angle L$?

    A. Exactly 120°
    B. Exactly 100°
    C. Exactly 80°
    D. Greater than or equal to 80°
    E. Less than or equal to 80°

GO ON TO THE NEXT PAGE.

20. If $3x - 1 > 26$, then which of the following is the smallest possible integer value of x ?

F. 6
G. 7
H. 8
J. 9
K. 10

21. Paul is tying red and white ribbons around a gift box. He begins by tying the white ribbon and one red ribbon around the box. These two ribbons intersect on one face of the box at a 62° angle, as shown in the figure below. Now Paul wants to tie a second red ribbon onto the box so that the two red ribbons are parallel. What is the degree measure of the angle, indicated below, between the white ribbon and the bottom red ribbon?

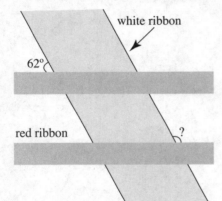

A. 62°
B. 76°
C. 90°
D. 104°
E. 118°

22. In right triangle *PRS* shown below, Q is the midpoint of $\overline{PR}$. What is the length of $\overline{QR}$, to the nearest inch?

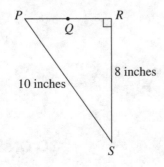

F. 2
G. 3
H. 4
J. 6
K. 36

GO ON TO THE NEXT PAGE.

Use the following information to answer questions 23–24.

Katie notices that the textbooks for her past 3 math courses have the same length and width, but each year's textbook has more pages and weighs more than the previous year's textbook. Katie weighs the textbooks, to the nearest 0.1 ounce, for her past 3 math courses and wonders about the relationship between the number of pages in math textbooks and the weights of those textbooks. She graphs the number of pages and corresponding weights of her 3 math textbooks in the standard (x,y) coordinate plane, as shown below, and discovers a linear relationship among these 3 points. She concludes that the equation of the line that passes through these 3 points is $y = 0.1x + 2.2$.

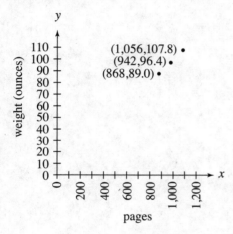

23. How much more, in ounces, does a math textbook with 1,056 pages weigh than one with 868 pages?

    A.   18.8
    B.   19.8
    C.   54.1
    D.   77.3
    E.   107.8

24. According to Katie's equation, how much would a math textbook with 1,338 pages weigh, in pounds?

    (Note: 16 ounces = 1 pound)

    F.   7.4
    G.   8.5
    H.   10.2
    J.   13.6
    K.   14.1

GO ON TO THE NEXT PAGE.

DO YOUR FIGURING HERE.

25. All line segments that intersect in the polygon below do so at right angles. If the dimensions given are in centimeters, then what is the area of the polygon, in square centimeters?

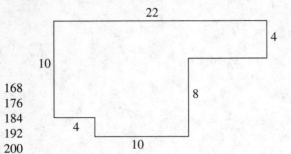

   A. 168
   B. 176
   C. 184
   D. 192
   E. 200

26. Mr. Baylor spent 6 days grading 996 essays. He averaged 178 essays per day for the first 3 days. Which of the following is closest to his average speed, in essays graded per day, for the final 3 days?

   F. 154
   G. 157
   H. 160
   J. 163
   K. 166

27. For all values of y, which of the following is equivalent to $(y+1)(y^2-3y+2)$?
   A. y^3+y^2-y-2
   B. y^3+y^2+2y+2
   C. y^3-2y^2-y+2
   D. y^3-2y^2+y-2
   E. y^3+2y+2

28. For $\angle D$ in $\triangle DEF$ below, which of the following trigonometric expressions has value $\dfrac{4}{5}$?

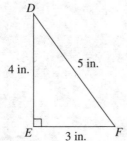

   F. $\sin D$
   G. $\tan D$
   H. $\cos D$
   J. $\sec D$
   K. $\csc D$

GO ON TO THE NEXT PAGE.

29. Over the weekend, Shawn bought 22 songs from an online music store. He spent a total of $17.90 on contemporary and classical songs. If contemporary songs cost $0.95 each and classical songs cost $0.75 each, then how many contemporary songs did Shawn buy?

(Note: There is no sales tax charged on these songs because they were purchased online.)

A. 7
B. 9
C. 10
D. 13
E. 15

30. If the operation # is defined as $x \# y = \dfrac{x^2 - y^2}{x + y}$, where x and y are real numbers such that $x \neq -y$, then what is the value of $(-3) \# (-7)$?

F. 10
G. 4
H. 1
J. −4
K. −10

31. Esther is making $2\dfrac{1}{4}$ gallons of punch for a large party. While mixing the punch, she uses $\dfrac{1}{2}$ gallon of pineapple juice. What fraction of the punch consists of pineapple juice?

A. $\dfrac{1}{9}$

B. $\dfrac{1}{6}$

C. $\dfrac{2}{9}$

D. $\dfrac{1}{3}$

E. $\dfrac{2}{3}$

32. Point O is the center of the circle shown below, and $\overline{XZ}$ is the diameter of the circle. If $XZ = 8$ ft, Y lies on the circle, and $\overline{OX} \cong \overline{XY}$, then what is the area, in square feet, of $\triangle XYZ$?

F. $4\sqrt{2}$
G. $8\sqrt{3}$
H. 16
J. 32
K. 64

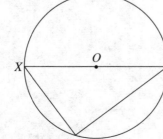

GO ON TO THE NEXT PAGE.

33. Which of the following values provides one of the roots for the equation $y^2 - 4y - 5 = 7$?

   A.   −12
   B.   −6
   C.   −2
   D.   −1
   E.   5

DO YOUR FIGURING HERE.

34. The plastic model house shown below consists of a right pyramid atop a right rectangular prism. The length and width of the prism and of the pyramid are 20 millimeters. The height of the prism is 16 millimeters, and the height of the pyramid is 12 millimeters. Which of the following is closest to the volume of the plastic model house, in cubic millimeters?

(Note: The volume of a right pyramid is given by $\frac{1}{3}lwh$, where l is the length, w is the width, and h is the height. The volume of a right rectangular prism is given by lwh, where l is the length, w is the width, and h is the height.)

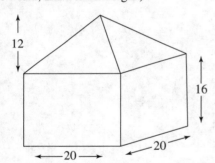

   F.   6,900
   G.   8,000
   H.   9,100
   J.   12,300
   K.   25,600

35. An isosceles trapezoid has bases of length 5 inches and 11 inches. The area of the trapezoid is 40 square inches. What is the height of the trapezoid, in inches?

   A.   4
   B.   5
   C.   7.5
   D.   17.5
   E.   35

GO ON TO THE NEXT PAGE.

36. What is the slope of the line that passes through the points (–2,6) and (3,–9) in the standard (*x*,*y*) coordinate plane?

F. $\dfrac{1}{15}$

G. $-\dfrac{1}{3}$

H. $-\dfrac{3}{5}$

J. –3

K. –5

37. Right triangle *WXY* is isosceles and has its right angle at Point *X*. Point *Z* is collinear with points *X* and *Y*, with *Y* between *X* and *Z*. What is the measure of ∠*WYZ* ?

A. 45°
B. 90°
C. 120°
D. 135°
E. 145°

38. The decimal construction of $\dfrac{5}{13}$ repeats and can be written as

0.384615384615.... What is the 99th digit to the right of the

decimal point in this decimal construction?

F. 1
G. 3
H. 4
J. 5
K. 6

GO ON TO THE NEXT PAGE.

39. In unit vector notation, **u** = a**i** + 5**j**, **v** = 2**i** + b**j**, and **u** + **v** = 4**i** − 3**j**. What is the ordered pair (a,b) ?

A. (−2, −5)
B. (2, −8)
C. (2, 5)
D. (4, −8)
E. (5, 2)

DO YOUR FIGURING HERE.

40. Which of the following equations represents the vertical asymptote of the function $y = \dfrac{3x+2}{2x-6}$?

F. $x = 1$

G. $x = \dfrac{3}{2}$

H. $x = 3$

J. $x = 5$

K. $x = -4$

41. In the figure below, $\overline{JK} \parallel \overline{MN}$, and $\overline{JM}$ and $\overline{KN}$ intersect at L. Which of the following statements must be true?

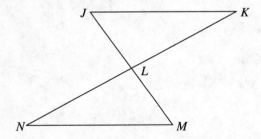

A. $\overline{JK} \cong \overline{MN}$
B. $\overline{JL} \cong \overline{LM}$
C. $\triangle JKL \cong \triangle MNL$
D. $\triangle JKL$ is similar to $\triangle MNL$
E. $\overline{JM}$ bisects $\overline{KN}$

GO ON TO THE NEXT PAGE.

DO YOUR FIGURING HERE.

Use the following information to answer questions 42–44.

The Wildcat athletic department at Wilson High School needs to raise $3,000.00 to fill a gap in its annual budget. The athletic department can choose 1 of the 2 options below to raise the needed funds.

Sell "Wildcat baseball caps" option: After paying a one-time fee of $23.00 to rent the necessary equipment, the athletic department can sell baseball caps featuring the school's logo. The athletic department will buy plain caps and print the school logo on each, at a cost of $3.50 per cap. The athletic department will sell each cap for $5.00.

Sell "Wildcat T-shirts" option: After paying a one-time fee of $19.00 to rent the necessary equipment, the athletic department can sell T-shirts featuring the school's logo. The athletic department will buy plain T-shirts and print the school logo on each, at a cost of $2.25 per T-shirt. The athletic department will sell each T-shirt for $4.00.

42. For the "Wildcat baseball caps" option, at least how many baseball caps must be sold in order to cover the one-time fee of renting the necessary equipment?

   F. 14
   G. 15
   H. 16
   J. 17
   K. 23

43. The Wildcat athletic department sold 540 tickets to Friday's football game. Of those tickets, 60% were adult tickets and the remainder were student tickets. The revenue from these ticket sales had already been factored into the annual budget. Jordan suggested raising the price of the adult tickets $2.00 to help fill the budget gap. If the athletic department had raised the price of each adult ticket $2.00, then by approximately what percent would the budget gap have been filled?

   A. 22%
   B. 23%
   C. 24%
   D. 25%
   E. 26%

GO ON TO THE NEXT PAGE.

DO YOUR FIGURING HERE.

44. The Wildcat athletic department chose the "Wildcat T-shirt" option and successfully filled the budget gap. What is the minimum number of T-shirts the athletic department must have sold?

   F. 1,480
   G. 1,664
   H. 1,709
   J. 1,726
   K. 1,812

45. The graph of $y^2 = x$ is shown in the standard (x,y) coordinate plane below for values of x such that $0 \le x \le 4$. The x-coordinates of points D and E are both 4. What is the area of $\triangle DEO$, in square coordinate units?

   A. $\dfrac{5}{2}$

   B. 4

   C. 8

   D. 12

   E. 16

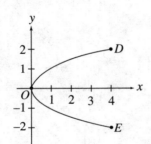

46. In $\triangle XYZ$ below, the length of $\overline{XY}$ is 12 centimeters. How long is $\overline{YZ}$, to the nearest tenth of a centimeter?

   (Note: $\sin 53° \approx 0.799$, $\sin 59° \approx 0.857$, $\sin 68° \approx 0.927$)

   F. 9.6
   G. 10.3
   H. 11.1
   J. 12.9
   K. 13.9

GO ON TO THE NEXT PAGE.

47. Jacob used the quadratic equation to find that the solutions to an equation are $x = 3 \pm \sqrt{-16c^2}$, where c is a positive real number. Which of the following expressions gives these solutions as complex numbers?

A. $3 \pm 1ci$
B. $3 \pm 2ci$
C. $3 \pm 4ci$
D. $3 \pm 8ci$
E. $3 \pm 16ci$

48. Points C and D are on the circle with center O as shown in the figure below. The length of $\overline{CD}$ is 12 millimeters and the measure of $\overset{\frown}{CD}$ is 60°. What is the length of the diameter of this circle?

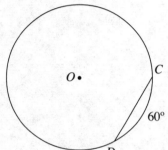

F. 12
G. 16
H. 20
J. 24
K. 28

49. A nylon cord is stretched from the top of a vertical playground pole to the ground. The cord is 25 feet long and makes a 19° angle with the ground. Which of the following expressions gives the horizontal distance, in feet, between the pole and the point where the cord touches the ground?

A. $\dfrac{\sin 19°}{25}$

B. $\dfrac{\cos 19°}{25}$

C. $25\tan 19°$

D. $25\sin 19°$

E. $25\cos 19°$

50. What are the coordinates of the center of the circle with the equation $x^2 + 8x + y^2 - 2y + 8 = 0$ in the standard (x,y) coordinate plane?

F. $(-4, \ 1)$
G. $(-1, -4)$
H. $(\ 1, -4)$
J. $(\ 4, -1)$
K. $(\ 4, \ 1)$

GO ON TO THE NEXT PAGE.

51. Scott's swimming pool has a depth of 8 feet and holds 13,000 gallons of water when full. Because of the warm weather, 10% of the water in the pool evaporates each day. Scott fills the pool with water and comes back the next day to measure the amount of water remaining in the pool. He considers this "Day 1" because it was taken 1 day after the pool was filled, and he labels his measurement as such. The next day, he measures the amount of water again, and he labels the results "Day 2" because it is now 2 days after he filled the pool. If Scott continues, on which day will he first measure that the pool is less than half full?

A. 5
B. 6
C. 7
D. 8
E. 9

52. What is the determinant of the matrix below?

$$\begin{bmatrix} 3 & -5 \\ -4 & 9 \end{bmatrix}$$

F. −33
G. −21
H. 7
J. 18
K. 47

53. The figure below shows 4 congruent circles, each tangent to 2 other circles and to 2 sides of the square. If the length of a side of the square is 24 inches, then what is the area, in square inches, of 1 circle?

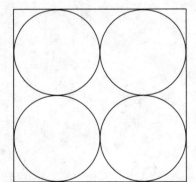

A. 9
B. 9π
C. 36
D. 36π
E. 144

54. Andy has 30 collectible comic books, which he bought in 2005 for $28.95 each. These comic books are currently valued at $34.35 each. Andy will sell these 30 comic books when their combined value is exactly $600.00 more than he paid for them. How much more will the average value per comic book have risen when Andy sells these 30 comic books?

F. $14.60
G. $12.72
H. $10.05
J. $ 7.84
K. $ 5.40

GO ON TO THE NEXT PAGE.

DO YOUR FIGURING HERE.

DO YOUR FIGURING HERE.

55. Circles with centers G and K intersect at points C and F, as shown below. Points B, G, H, J, K, and D are collinear. The lengths of $\overline{AC}$, $\overline{CE}$, and $\overline{HJ}$ are 18 cm, 10 cm, and 3 cm, respectively. What is the length, in centimeters, of $\overline{BD}$?

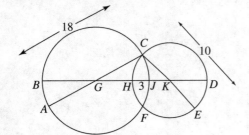

- **A.** 22
- **B.** 25
- **C.** 26
- **D.** 28
- **E.** 29

56. A parabola with vertex $(-3,-2)$ and axis of symmetry $y = -2$ crosses the y-axis at $\left(0,-2 + 3\sqrt{3}\right)$. At what other point does the parabola cross the y-axis?

- **F.** No other point
- **G.** $\left(0, 2 + 3\sqrt{3}\right)$
- **H.** $\left(0, 2 - 3\sqrt{3}\right)$
- **J.** $\left(0, -2 - 3\sqrt{3}\right)$
- **K.** Cannot be determined from the given information

57. If $z \neq 4$ and $z \neq -4$, then which of the following is equivalent to the expression $\dfrac{3z}{4-z} + \dfrac{3z}{z^2 - 16}$?

- **A.** $\dfrac{3z^2 + 15z}{z^2 - 16}$
- **B.** $\dfrac{9z^2 - 12z}{z^2 - 16}$
- **C.** $\dfrac{-12z}{z^2 - 16}$
- **D.** $\dfrac{-3z^2}{z^2 - 16}$
- **E.** $\dfrac{-3z^2 - 9z}{z^2 - 16}$

GO ON TO THE NEXT PAGE.

58. The point (a,b) is on the terminal side of an angle with radian measure θ. Which of the following is equal to the tangent of $\pi + \theta$?

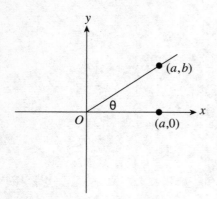

F. $\dfrac{a}{b}$

G. $\dfrac{-b}{a}$

H. $\dfrac{b}{a}$

J. $-b$

K. b

59. The nth term of an arithmetic sequence, a_n, is given by $a_n = a_1 + dn - d$, where a_1 is the 1st term, and d is the common difference between terms. Which of the following expressions gives d in terms of a_n, a_1, and n ?

A. $\dfrac{a_n - a_1}{n - 1}$

B. $\dfrac{n - 1}{a_n - a_1}$

C. $\dfrac{a_n - a_1}{n}$

D. $\dfrac{a_n}{a_1 + n}$

E. $a_n - a_1 - n$

GO ON TO THE NEXT PAGE.

60. A deck of 54 cards has 4 suits, each with 13 cards and 2 jokers. Each suit has cards labeled 2 through 10, and an ace, jack, queen, and king. Susan draws five cards without replacement. What is the probability that Susan draws a ten, jack, queen, king, and then ace, all of the same suit and in that order?

F. $\dfrac{4}{4(54)(53)(52)(51)(50)}$

G. $\dfrac{1}{(13)(12)(11)(10)(9)}$

H. $\dfrac{4}{(54)(53)(52)(51)(50)}$

J. $\dfrac{4^5}{(54)(53)(52)(51)(50)}$

K. $\dfrac{4(13)(12)(11)(10)(9)}{54^5}$

DO YOUR FIGURING HERE.

END OF TEST 2

STOP! DO NOT TURN THE PAGE UNTIL TOLD TO DO SO.

DO NOT RETURN TO A PREVIOUS TEST.

READING TEST

35 Minutes—40 Questions

DIRECTIONS: There are several passages in this test. Each passage is accompanied by several questions. After reading a passage, choose the best answer to each question and fill in the corresponding oval on your answer document. You may refer to the passages as often as necessary.

Passage I

PROSE FICTION: This passage is adapted from the novel *Oklahoma Sunrise* by Jack Elwyn Prouty (©2007 Jack Elwyn Prouty).

Rebecca stood and gazed out across the fields, into the unending horizon.

A warm breeze caressed the fields, causing the ears of the wheat to bend homeward, looking for all the world like they were
5 listening to a conversation none but they could hear. The ears bent and bobbed as the breeze eddied about them. She stood, inhaling the fresh and savory scent of the almost-ripe wheat, mixed with the rich scent of the earth. Someone had plowed nearby; the newly uncovered earth always smelled more alive. She could
10 hear bees—there was a hive somewhere not far away—and birds and men, all faintly but as much a part of the image in her mind as was the wheat itself. And underneath everything else, that slight tang in the air that said it would rain soon. Not even a tang, really—almost a feeling but somehow a smell, too.

15 The evening, just as dusk was falling, was always the best time to visit the fields alone. Earlier in the day there were too many people, and too many chores to do to justify standing silently in the middle of the field. Later it was too still, too quiet. It felt as if the field itself had gone to sleep; not an unpleasant feeling,
20 really, but not the feeling of being embraced by a living, breathing entity that she had wanted today. That she liked best of all.

Of course, the earth hadn't always been a friend to the people that cultivated it. Any farmer knows that there will be good years and bad years, and that sometimes one bad year will
25 follow another and then another, to the point where you wonder if a good year will ever come again. Growing up far away from the soil that had held her people for generations, Rebecca had known all of that. Known how the land had turned on her parents and driven them far from the only home they knew, seeking
30 work on a stranger's land, doing unfamiliar work. Still, she had felt the draw. Even as a child, she had known that someday, she would return. It was in her blood, really. Her great-grandparents had claimed the land as their own, poured their blood, sweat, and tears into it, and turned it from a wild tract of prairie into

35 productive fields of wheat and corn. Her grandparents had inherited the fields, and her parents in their turn had as well. They would have gone to Rebecca next, had her parents been able to hold on to what was theirs. Even when they had left, they had claimed the land as their own and had sworn that they'd return
40 to it someday. Both her mother and father had been prevented from returning home, but now Rebecca was here in their place, trying to reclaim her family's heritage.

She stood still, thinking about the past and the present, breathing in the heat and the life that surrounded her. The land
45 might not always be kind, but it is always good. She flinched a little bit as a bee landed on her cheek, inspecting this large thing that didn't seem to be a part of the field. She let it explore her face, knowing it would move on once it had ascertained that she was no flower. The feel of the bee's feet tramping across her nose
50 made her want to sneeze but she held her breath, not wanting to frighten it into stinging her.

When the bee ventured on in pursuit of more profitable discoveries, she opened her eyes and gazed out across her fields. They were hers, in truth if not writing, and would one day be
55 hers in every sense. For a moment, her stomach began to clench as her mind turned unwillingly but naturally to the realities of what lay ahead. The loans, the mortgage payments, the possibility of a bad crop ruining all her plans. Firmly, she pushed those thoughts aside. She had acknowledged them before and would
60 acknowledge them again, when she sat before her ledger or reviewed the accounts. This moment was for enjoying the sheer bounty of life, not for fears and numbers. Without the former, she could never face the latter. It was for the warm reality of the growing, breathing crops that she was determined to deal with
65 the men from the bank, to go without new things, and work until her back ached every day, only to get up and do the same the next morning, before the sun was up.

She breathed deeply, trying to take in the strength and life that surrounded her, trying to store it inside herself. This was her
70 people's land; she knew that in her bones. Whatever else might happen, that would not change.

GO ON TO THE NEXT PAGE.

1. Which of the following statements best expresses Rebecca's feelings during her visit to the fields, as expressed in lines 1–42 ?

   A. Overjoyed by the idea of ownership
   B. Connected with the land and her heritage
   C. Dismayed by her looming financial problems
   D. Exhausted and frustrated from hard work

2. The word *that* in line 28 most directly refers to:

   F. "someday, she would return " (lines 31–32).
   G. "far away from the soil" (lines 26–27).
   H. "it would move on once it had ascertained that she was no flower" (lines 48–49).
   J. "sometimes one bad year will follow another" (lines 24–25).

3. The main purpose of the information in lines 30–42 is to explain why Rebecca believes that the land is:

   A. her rightful heritage, passed down through her family, whose hard work forms the foundation for her claim.
   B. an entity unto itself, alive and free, and beyond the control of anyone.
   C. not worth the trouble that she and her predecessors have gone to in an attempt to claim it.
   D. beautiful, whether wild or cultivated, and filled with creatures that create a harmonious whole.

4. In the first four paragraphs (lines 1–42), the narrator describes all of the following aspects of Rebecca's surroundings EXCEPT the:

   F. different scents in the evening air.
   G. feel of freshly plowed earth.
   H. reason her family had left the area.
   J. best time of day to visit the fields.

5. The passage can best be described as a fictional depiction of a woman's impression of the land that:

   A. uses rich, suggestive detail to show that the land is a vital and cherished component of her personal life and family heritage.
   B. reveals a painful family history and explains why her ancestors had opted to give up all claims on the land.
   C. offers metaphors and similes to convey a deeper meaning than the one suggested by the events narrated in the story.
   D. explains exactly how one family can lose everything due to circumstances beyond the control of its members.

6. The narrator's statement in lines 62–63 ("Without the former, she could never face the latter") most directly refers back to Rebecca's:

   F. opinion about different times of the day and how that changes the atmosphere (lines 15–21).
   G. concern about the bee described in the fifth paragraph (lines 43–51).
   H. anxiety over financial matters being outweighed by her love of the land (lines 54–61).
   J. enjoyment of the scents described in the second paragraph (lines 3–14).

7. One of the main purposes of the last two paragraphs (lines 52–71) is for the narrator to describe Rebecca's attitude towards the land in a way that:

   A. explains the importance of the stranger's land that is mentioned previously in the passage.
   B. purposefully identifies the mistakes made by Rebecca's parents, referenced earlier in the passage, which Rebecca cannot correct.
   C. deepens the reader's understanding of the challenges and rewards the land presents to Rebecca.
   D. invites the reader to draw a parallel between Rebecca and the land itself and perhaps the reader as well.

8. The point of view from which the passage is told can best be described as that of a narrator who:

   F. is aware of what Rebecca is thinking and feeling.
   G. suspects that Rebecca is not sincere in her plans.
   H. is personally involved in the events being described.
   J. is Rebecca's close relative who didn't move.

9. As it is used in line 34, the word *wild* most nearly means:

   A. unconquerable.
   B. unrestrained.
   C. uncultivated.
   D. irrepressible.

10. When Rebecca realized that "a bee landed on her cheek" (line 46), her first response is to:

   F. brush it away from her face.
   G. worry that it might sting her.
   H. hope that it will fly away.
   J. flinch, then try not to respond.

GO ON TO THE NEXT PAGE.

Passage II

SOCIAL SCIENCE: This passage is adapted from the article "Illuminating the Dark Ages" by Krista Correa (©2003 Krista Correa).

The period that began with the fall of the Roman Empire in the fifth century and ended with the Renaissance in the fourteenth century has been referred to by many names: the Medieval period, the Middle Ages, and the Dark Ages. The writer Petrarch
5 coined the latter name in the fourteenth century in an attempt to differentiate the culture of Medieval Europe from his own time. The popular conception at that time was that Europe was finally emerging from a cultural wasteland during which much of the ancient learning had been lost; Petrarch, like many other writers
10 and artists of his time, wanted to connect his studies with those of antiquity, rather than those of more recent years. The name stuck, as did the idea that very little of cultural or intellectual importance took place during the years so described.

Recent scholars have begun to challenge that idea, however,
15 asserting that while it is true that certain fields of study did go into decline during the Middle Ages (the term they prefer), other areas flourished. These historians advocate the more neutral term "Middle Ages" because they feel that it more accurately describes the centuries during which Europe began to transition slowly
20 from a Rome-based, empire-dominated system into the modern states that exist today. According to them, using a negative term like "Dark Ages" serves only to underscore misconceptions about the era. This argument represents a sharp break from the past.

Many scholars have used the term "Dark Ages" to identify
25 the lack of information available about the years between the fall of Rome and the Renaissance. Few written records exist from the early years and the documents that do exist don't always shed a great deal of light on the larger picture of what was happening in Europe. Some scholars, such as William Jordan in his new
30 edition of the Dictionary of the Middle Ages, have argued that the term "Dark Ages" needn't be negative—it simply refers to the darkness caused by this lack of information.

That view, however, has been largely discredited. Even when used in a seemingly neutral way, "Dark Ages" has an inherently
35 negative connotation in most people's minds. Moreover, other scholars point out that it is no longer accurate. Research continues to uncover information about the era that allows scholars to gain an ever more accurate idea of what life was like during the Middle Ages, while other research has helped historians gain
40 a better understanding of the evidence they already possessed.

Other scholars have preferred the term "Dark Ages" to describe the decline in learning that they believe to have taken place during this era. These scholars assumed that without the advances of Roman society, learning must have virtually halted.
45 Modern historians such as David Lindberg and Ronald Numbers, however, point out that this view is very far from the truth. Evidence abounds that, although some knowledge was indeed lost, much was retained and that intellectual studies continued throughout the Middle Ages. Their books, such as Lindberg's
50 Science in the Middle Ages and Numbers's Galileo Goes to Jail and Other Myths about Science and Religion, debunk many popular misconceptions about the Middle Ages, such as that people widely believed the Earth was flat (they didn't) and that they largely abandoned the field of mathematics (they didn't).

55 The goal of scholars such as Lindberg and Numbers is not to idealize the medieval world, or claim that it was filled with light and learning, but rather to balance the overly pessimistic views that are held by so many even today. No one would seriously dispute that, in some areas, learning did go into a decline
60 after the fall of Rome. What modern medievalists, or medieval scholars, would point out is that while some areas diminished, others were able to flourish. For example, three-dimensional, realistic art certainly became less common, and the ability to build a self-sustaining dome was lost for hundreds of years. However,
65 symbolic art developed to such a level that a skilled artist could convey an entire legend in a single picture. Architects in the Middle Ages developed the flying buttress along with some of the most intricate stonework ever seen before or since. The key to understanding the Middle Ages is to avoid making assumptions
70 based on prior assertions or possibly biased historians from the past, and to instead look at what was actually created.

Perhaps it is finally time, then, for the term "Dark Ages" to pass out of not only scholarly but also casual speech. If the goal of historical study is to illuminate, not judge, a descriptive
75 yet neutral term like "Middle Ages" might well serve more effectively. In the meantime, medievalists will continue studying the evidence they have in an attempt to understand the era that saw Western European culture transition into the modern era.

11. Based on the passage, which of the following scholars most directly contributed to the popularity of the term "Dark Ages"?

A. Jordan
B. Lindberg
C. Petrarch
D. Numbers

12. The passage most strongly implies that which of the following activities flourished during the Middle Ages?

F. The construction of free-standing domes
G. Skilled and detailed stonework
H. Three-dimensional, realistic art
J. The field of mathematics

GO ON TO THE NEXT PAGE.

13. The passage indicates that, contrary to the historians with a traditional view of the Middle Ages, scholars today believe the Middle Ages were:

A. a transitional period between the classical era and the modern.

B. an era in which significant scientific discoveries were made.

C. an epoch that suffered a decline in learning, art, and architecture.

D. a time when much of the world lived in ignorance.

14. The passage states that an accurate picture of the Middle Ages will likely develop as a result of:

F. reconsidering existing evidence and discovering new evidence.

G. relying on written documents from the Renaissance.

H. new excavations throughout the European countryside.

J. disregarding all Renaissance accounts.

15. According to the passage, people during the Middle Ages did NOT:

A. keep written documents.

B. study advanced mathematics.

C. know how to carve stone well.

D. believe the world was flat.

16. The main purpose of the first paragraph (lines 1–13) is to:

F. compare the advances of the Renaissance and the classical period with the failings of the Middle Ages.

G. list all of the terms used to describe the period between the fifth and fourteenth century.

H. demonstrate that Petrarch and other writers of the Renaissance lived in a cultural wasteland.

J. introduce the era under discussion and some of the ways it has been described.

17. The passage identifies which of the following as two areas in which learning truly did go into decline during the Middle Ages?

A. Symbolic art and architecture

B. Astronomy and mathematics

C. Dome-building and three-dimensional art

D. Stonework and science

18. It can reasonably be inferred from the first paragraph (lines 1–13) that Renaissance writers such as Petrarch believed that their work would benefit from:

F. association with the classical era.

G. an in-depth study of science.

H. the creation of a well-educated middle class.

J. the new culture of the Renaissance.

19. As it is used in line 5, the word *coined* most nearly means:

A. counterfeited.

B. plagiarized.

C. spent.

D. created.

20. It can reasonably be inferred from the fourth and fifth paragraphs (lines 33–54) that before the work of modern scholars such as Numbers and Lindberg, some scholars tended to see educational pursuits during the Middle Ages as:

F. insignificant.

G. scientific.

H. advanced.

J. well-documented.

GO ON TO THE NEXT PAGE.

Passage III

HUMANITIES: Passage A is adapted from the essay "Much Ado About Shakespeare" by Arthur Coyle Thompson. Passage B is adapted from the essay "No Kidding This Theory Is Looney" by Amanda Combs Truelove.

Passage A

Since his death, the 17th century playwright William Shakespeare has been considered one of the greatest, if not the greatest, writers in the English language. His many plays have not only shaped the course of the arts and the theater, they may
5 have shaped the way that people in the modern world think of themselves. But when we talk about all that this playwright has done, we cannot help but notice that the playwright himself remains a mystery. Certainly there was a man named William Shakespeare who lived in Stratford-upon-Avon, but could this
10 man, who came from these humble origins, possibly have written all the great works that are attributed to him?

A group of critics and scholars known as the Anti-Stratfordians believe that Shakespeare's authorship of these great plays is nearly impossible. They argue that Shakespeare couldn't
15 have had the education, aristocratic sensibility, or the familiarity with the royal court that pervade his many works. Shakespeare's works were much more likely written by someone, or some group of people, that had these qualities, someone like Shakespeare's contemporary Christopher Marlowe or the English philosopher
20 and statesman Francis Bacon. There are even some who surmise that Shakespeare's oceanic grasp of the totality of Elizabethan England means that his works could only have come from one source: Queen Elizabeth herself.

According to these Anti-Stratfordians, Shakespeare's sole
25 authorship is the stuff of myth, a belief that has either been lazily accepted since Shakespeare's lifetime or a vast conspiracy to hide the true identity of the author. Because the historical record obviously contains no account of Sir Francis Bacon writing *Hamlet*, for instance, the Anti-Stratfordians rely instead upon
30 what they call a "rhetoric of accumulation." In other words, the Anti-Stratfordians seek to decode Shakespeare's texts for hints as to the author's true identity.

The controversy began in the mid-1800s, when a slew of books and articles began to question Shakespeare's authorship.
35 The first comprehensive theory of alternate authorship was formulated by Delia Bacon, who suggested that the plays were written by a group of authors under the direction of Sir Francis Bacon. The group, according to this theory, was constructed to promote philosophical and political ideas that were too danger-
40 ous for any one man to espouse publicly.

Other theories have emerged since. Since the 1920s and the publication of J. Thomas Looney's *Shakespeare Identified*, the second leading candidate has been Edward de Vere, 17th-century Earl of Oxford. The "Oxfordians," as they are known, cite certain
45 passages from *Hamlet* that depict the author as an eccentric aristocrat and poet who had traveled extensively in Italy. Oxford had some poetry of his own, which Looney used to identify parallels with Shakespeare's sonnets and some of his plays.

While it may be impossible for anyone to know for sure, the
50 Anti-Stratfordians nonetheless raise some interesting questions about Shakespeare's authorship and the question of authorship in general. How reasonable is it to think that the average townsman could have written the generation-defining, even language-defining, works for which William Shakespeare has
55 been given credit?

Passage B

Arthur Coyle Thompson asks, "How reasonable is it to think that the average townsman could have written the…works for which William Shakespeare has been given credit?" The answer is simple: it's not reasonable, but that is the nature of genius, espe-
60 cially genius of Shakespeare's magnitude. As difficult as it might be to believe, all evidence points toward William Shakespeare as the sole author of Shakespeare's works. If the authorship of Shakespeare's work was in doubt, why did no one identify this doubt until 200 years after Shakespeare's death? Why did none,
65 not a single one, of Shakespeare's contemporaries speak up? The theater world is a small but collaborative one: if something had been suspicious about the authorship of Shakespeare's plays, someone would certainly have said something.

If anything, the Anti-Stratfordians, whether explicitly or
70 implicitly, have been making a blatantly classist argument. The idea that a man of Shakespeare's level of genius must have come from the upper echelons of society is snobbish at best. All of these Anti-Stratfordians are teachers—do they assume that their most intelligent students are also the wealthiest? In our own age, when
75 the greatest discoveries are made in some eighteen-year-old's garage, we should see the fallacy in the argument that William Shakespeare "could not have" written his plays. One does not need money, after all, to feel emotions deeply or to observe the behaviors of others. And Shakespeare's work is so powerful, and
80 it continues to resonate today, precisely because of his eloquence in describing the indescribable. One does not need a fluency in Ancient Greek or the natural sciences to read Shakespeare, so why would Anti-Stratfordians suppose that Shakespeare himself must have needed it or that he couldn't have acquired it on his own?

85 In addition, these Anti-Stratfordians must understand how misleading it is to identify "parallels" in the texts of Shakespeare and the authors whom the Anti-Stratfordians propose. Certainly these texts should have parallel vocabularies: they were written in the same place in the same era! Words like "app" and "iPhone"
90 are spoken all the time: can we really suppose that those who speak them are all the same technological expert?

GO ON TO THE NEXT PAGE.

No, the Anti-Stratfordians must instead resort to accusations of conspiracy and deception. Why, they ask, have generations hidden the real story from us? Why has all the evidence of our
95 claims been destroyed? Well, because the claims of these Anti-Stratfordians amount to what King Lear would've called "an O without a figure." The evidence for an alternate author is tough to find for a simple reason: it doesn't exist.

Questions 21–24 ask about Passage A.

21. Based on the passage, the primary reason that some critics and scholars doubt the identity of the playwright William Shakespeare is that:

   A. the most accomplished playwrights in the 16th century were also the most successful and wealthy.
   B. a man of Shakespeare's relatively humble station is not likely to have produced works with such breadth.
   C. some of the ideas that Shakespeare's plays advanced were too dangerous to appear in novels.
   D. some readers in the 19th century wanted to connect the plays of Shakespeare to their own lives.

22. According to Thompson, critics cite Queen Elizabeth as the possible author of Shakespeare's plays because the plays:

   F. have unusually strong female characters.
   G. demonstrate an intimate knowledge of natural sciences.
   H. depict the era of Elizabeth's reign with notable breadth.
   J. were popular among dukes and other royalty of the time.

23. Thompson refers to Shakespeare as "the average townsman" (lines 52–53) in order to suggest that Shakespeare:

   A. may have been too unsophisticated to have written such sophisticated plays.
   B. was active in civic affairs as well as in theatrical ones.
   C. was probably too well-liked by his neighbors to be revealed as a fraud.
   D. may have disguised himself in his daily life in Stratford-upon-Avon.

24. As it is used in line 21, the word *oceanic* most nearly means:

   F. natural.
   G. informal.
   H. salty.
   J. comprehensive.

Questions 25–27 ask about Passage B.

25. Based on Truelove's account, the main reason that Shakespeare's authorship is difficult to understand is that Shakespeare:

   A. was only one of many authors who wrote under the name Shakespeare.
   B. appeared in the literary world before plays were considered serious works of art.
   C. is a genius who cannot be characterized in normal terms.
   D. disapproved of royalty and other nobles without sufficient knowledge of how they lived.

26. According to Truelove, the Anti-Stratfordians give a classist account of Shakespeare's authorship in that they:

   F. insist that only a royal or noble could have written a good play.
   G. assume that literary ability is based on the author's economic class.
   H. disapprove of their own low-income students.
   J. show that Shakespeare did not earn sufficient royalties from his plays.

27. Truelove critiques arguments against Shakespeare's authorship that are based on "parallels" with other authors' writing by suggesting that:

   A. the Anti-Stratfordians have been focusing on the wrong texts in their analysis.
   B. the Anti-Stratfordians have not sufficiently spoken of economics in their books and articles.
   C. the evidence used for such claims is not as meaningful as Anti-Stratfordians believe.
   D. the evidence for Francis Bacon's authorship is far less compelling than the evidence for Edward de Vere's.

GO ON TO THE NEXT PAGE.

Questions 28–30 ask about both passages.

---

28. One of the most obvious differences between Thompson's and Truelove's points of view is that Thompson:

   F. believes the theories of the Anti-Stratfordians, while True-love is more compelled by the theories of the Oxfordians.

   G. criticizes the authors he describes, while Truelove is more interested in finding the merits in Looney's and Bacon's arguments.

   H. doubts the claims of the Anti-Stratfordians, while Truelove considers them interesting intellectual exercises.

   J. presents a skeptical view on Shakespeare's authorship, while Truelove criticizes such skepticism as misguided.

29. By which of the following means does Truelove disagree with the theories presented in Thompson's passage?

   A. Personal attack and intellectual banter

   B. Direct response and rhetorical questions

   C. Emotional appeal and ironic exaggeration

   D. Historical data and archival research

30. Based on the passages, which pair of phrases best compares Thompson's and Truelove's responses to alternative theories of Shakespeare's authorship?

   F. Understated approval versus firm neutrality

   G. Dramatic appeal versus scholarly debate

   H. Staunch advocacy versus tentative support

   J. Receptive exploration versus decisive critique

GO ON TO THE NEXT PAGE.

THIS PAGE IS INTENTIONALLY LEFT BLANK.

GO ON TO THE NEXT PAGE.

Passage IV

NATURAL SCIENCE: This passage is adapted from the article "Does an Amoeba Have a Choice?" by Wilbur Stewart (©2007 Wilbur Stewart).

The question of how much freedom of choice humans exercise has long vexed scientists. Once the model of humans as the only thinking beings on the planet was abandoned, a new model of humans as higher-level animals took its place as the dominant
5 theory. According to the new theory, certain organisms, such as amoebas and plants, act unconsciously, according to almost mechanical impulses. Other organisms, such as dogs or horses, display a certain level of consciousness combined with instinct. Above them all stand humans—maybe not the only thinking
10 beings but still the most highly evolved, exercising "free will" when determining life choices.

Today, however, scientists are beginning to question that model as well. Could it be that much of what we take for conscious decision-making can actually be accounted for biologically? Are
15 we in truth not all that different from animals that act largely out of instinct? How separate are humans, really, from the rest of the natural world?

The human ability to form lasting romantic bonds is one of the primary proofs given in support of free will. Some theorists
20 argue that remaining with a single partner because of an emotional commitment is clearly unnatural and thus a sign of our higher development: social and emotional needs overpowering a base, animal instinct. Evolutionary biologists, however, have recently uncovered evidence that suggests that working as a
25 pair has many evolutionary advantages that may outweigh the disadvantages. Pair-bonding allows one party to remain behind and guard the offspring while the other seeks food and shelter; it increases the odds that an injured party will be cared for and thus survive; it even increases the chances that offspring will live
30 long enough to mature and become self-sufficient. Moreover, recent research seems to indicate that many of the feelings that humans experience when falling in love are in fact biologically motivated and that other animals finding a mate experience similar physical symptoms.

35 The truly staggering aspect of this new realization, however, is that it could extend not only to individuals but also to societies as a whole. If humans are instinctual animals, driven by biological imperatives much of the time, then the interplay between cities and even nations might also be open to biological
40 interpretation. After all, governments are composed of humans. The possible repercussions that such a discovery could have on international relations are truly astonishing. For example, perhaps in time scientists will determine which hormones cause humans to feel friendship, along with a way to administer those hormones
45 to a nation. Decade-long wars could be ended, amicably, in a matter of days.

Still other scientists, mainly chemists and physicists, have asserted that it's not so much that humans are like other animals as that all living things are relatively predictable on a cellular
50 level. Those scientists believe that all human interaction is, on some level, based in the laws of physics. Strange as that may sound at first, it's not as outrageous as it seems. Hormones and other natural chemicals are released in response to some kind of stimulus, causing biological impulses. In order for the body to
55 process those stimuli, however, a whole array of reactions has to take place. At the most basic level, those reactions are caused by cells sending out and responding to electrical impulses. Those electrical impulses become chemical impulses, or neurotransmitters, which eventually trigger biological impulses. All matter is
60 made up of protons, neutrons, and electrons, so by extension, all matter reacts to electrical impulses on some level. Advocates of the electro-chemical theory claim that studies involving large groups of people demonstrate their point most effectively. Human interaction can be compared to the interaction between differ-
65 ent particles—some are attracted to each other while others are repulsed, while the whole mass moves as a single entity. If it's true that group interactions can be compared to the mingling of different particles, then an entirely new background could be created against which national and international dynamics could
70 be newly considered.

One practical example of the convergence of scientific theory and human practice is the increasing involvement of scientists in the arena of criminal pursuit. Many police departments have realized that human behavior, even in flight, is startlingly pre-
75 dictable, if one knows how to find the patterns. That's where the academics come in; they're hired to look at the data accumulated by detectives and apply their knowledge of science to the case, trying to identify patterns. These academics consider the behavior of other animals, but they also compare the data to the movement
80 of particles and perform complex mathematical calculations. And, more often than might be expected, they help solve the cases.

31. According to the author of the passage, "free will" describes behavior such as:

A. falling in love by a series of natural and biological processes.

B. the study of pattern behavior to understand criminal behavior.

C. the choice of one mate based on a mutual emotional connection.

D. group efforts by all members of a city to improve that city.

GO ON TO THE NEXT PAGE.

32. Based on the passage, what relationship does the recent discovery described in the third paragraph (lines 30–34) have to the electro-chemical theory?

   F. It directly supports the electro-chemical theory.
   G. It supports another theory that is connected to the electro-chemical theory.
   H. It undermines the central claims of the electro-chemical theory.
   J. It is unrelated to the electro-chemical theory.

33. The author characterizes scientific contributions to police work as:

   A. charming but ultimately useless.
   B. mundane but logically unconvincing.
   C. alarming but theoretically persuasive.
   D. new and potentially helpful.

34. The supporters of the electro-chemical theory claim that humans are like particles in that both:

   F. are ultimately driven to action by electrical impulses.
   G. are potentially capable of conscious decision-making.
   H. can more adequately be understood in groups than individually.
   J. respond to outside stimuli without intermediate thought.

35. In terms of where and how frequently they occur, electrical impulses are described by the author of the passage as:

   A. possible in humans and animals but not in other types of matter.
   B. common to humans, animals, and other types of matter.
   C. present in cellular interactions but absent from human interactions.
   D. the basis of a theory of group activity for non-human matter.

36. The chemists and physicists define biological impulses as:

   F. apparently unconnected to decisions based in free will.
   G. apparently central to whether humans exercise free will.
   H. the basis for chemical impulses, which in turn cause electrical impulses.
   J. caused by chemical impulses, which are caused by electrical impulses.

37. Lines 26–30 are best characterized as describing an explanation that:

   A. slowly developed as the primary method of childrearing among all higher-level organisms.
   B. rapidly emerged as the leading cause of the successful evolution of lower-level animals.
   C. alternatively offers a reason for behavior that had previously been attributed to free will.
   D. recently undermined the traditional belief that human behavior was biologically motivated.

38. The main point of the sixth paragraph (lines 71–81) is that:

   F. the new theories discussed in the passage have been put into practice effectively in at least one field.
   G. recent research has indicated that academic theories tend to be difficult to put into practice.
   H. academic theories can be evaluated more fully when they are put into practice.
   J. police work has relied on academic help since before the debates over free will.

39. The passage states that in response to the suggestion that the tendency to remain with a single mate demonstrates humanity's free will, evolutionary biologists:

   A. added several new elements to their theory.
   B. accepted that their initial idea was deeply flawed.
   C. redefined the term "free will" to fit their theory.
   D. suggested an alternative interpretation of pair-bonding.

40. Lines 12–17 mainly emphasize what quality?

   F. Confidence
   G. Uncertainty
   H. Ignorance
   J. Contentment

END OF TEST 3

STOP! DO NOT TURN THE PAGE UNTIL TOLD TO DO SO.

DO NOT RETURN TO A PREVIOUS TEST.

SCIENCE TEST

35 Minutes–40 Questions

DIRECTIONS: There are several passages in this test. Each passage is followed by several questions. After reading a passage, choose the correct answer to each question and fill in the corresponding oval on your answer document. You may refer to the passages as often as necessary.

You are NOT permitted to use a calculator on this test.

Passage I

The *apoptotic index* (*AI*) for a group of dividing cells is calculated as shown below:

$$AI = \frac{\text{number of cells undergoing } apoptosis \text{ (cell death)}}{\text{total number of cells}}$$

Figure 1 shows the *AI* for a culture of fibroblast cells as a function of the surrounding concentration, in parts per million (ppm), of a cell toxin.

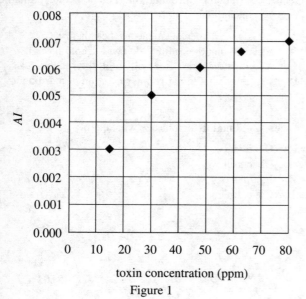

Figure 1

One thousand actively dividing fibroblast cells in culture were studied. Figure 2 shows the distribution of the cells in each of the stages of the dividing cell cycle.

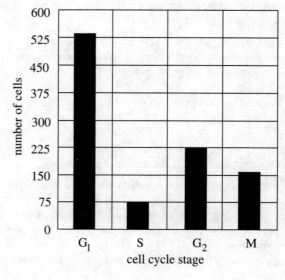

Figure 2

GO ON TO THE NEXT PAGE.

Electron micrographs were taken of the fibroblasts in culture. Figure 3 shows an example of cells in each of the 4 stages of the dividing cell cycle. Although the cells are *not* arranged in the sequence of the cell cycle, each stage is shown only once.

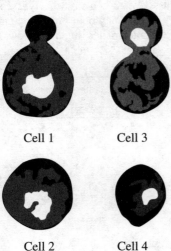

Cell 1   Cell 3

Cell 2   Cell 4

Figure 3

1. Which cell in Figure 3 is most likely in the stage of the cell cycle during which cytokinesis is occurring as mitosis nears completion?

   A. Cell 1
   B. Cell 2
   C. Cell 3
   D. Cell 4

2. Based on Figure 1, if a culture of fibroblast cells was surrounded by a toxin concentration of 90 ppm, the percent of those cells that would undergo apoptosis is most likely:

   F. less than 0.5%.
   G. between 0.5% and 0.6%.
   H. between 0.6% and 0.7%.
   J. greater than 0.7%.

3. Which of the following cells in Figure 3 is most likely in the first stage of the actively dividing cell cycle?

   A. Cell 1
   B. Cell 2
   C. Cell 3
   D. Cell 4

4. According to Figure 2, how did the number of fibroblast cells in stage G_2 compare with the number of cells in stage S? The number in G_2 was approximately:

   F. $\frac{1}{4}$ as great as the number in S.
   G. $\frac{1}{3}$ as great as the number in S.
   H. 3 times as great as the number in S.
   J. 4 times as great as the number in S.

5. Based on Figure 2, of the fibroblast cells that were in the actively dividing cell cycle, the proportion that were in G_1 is closest to which of the following?

   A. $\frac{540}{1,000}$
   B. $\frac{300}{540}$
   C. $\frac{1,000}{540}$
   D. $\frac{540}{300}$

6. Suppose that 3,000 cells are cultured in a surrounding toxin concentration of 30 ppm. Based on Figure 1, the number of these cells undergoing apoptosis is most likely closest to:

   F. 1.5.
   G. 15.
   H. 150.
   J. 1,500.

GO ON TO THE NEXT PAGE.

Passage II

A *polymorphism* is the persistent occurrence of different appearances for a particular trait in a species. All humans have slight differences in their *genotypes* (genetic code) that result in different *phenotypes* (observable characteristics). Genetic polymorphisms are persistent variations in gene sequences at a particular location in chromosomes, such as those accounting for different blood types. Variations that cannot be observed with the naked eye require techniques such as *capillary electrophoresis* (the separation of genetic or protein material based on charge characteristics using an electric field).

The label on a vial of blood from a hospital patient was lost. The sample just tested positive for a disease of the blood protein hemoglobin that is very common in the hospital population. The sample was traced to a room with 4 patients who were subsequently tested to determine the source of the initial vial.

Tests and Results

Smears of the blood from the unidentified patient (P) and from the 4 newly tested patients (1–4) were observed under the microscope for the presence of any cells with an abnormal appearance (target or sickle cells). Results are shown in Table 1.

Table 1	
Patient	Blood smear findings
P	Sickle cells
1	Target cells
2	Sickle cells
3	No abnormal cells
4	Sickle cells

Serum was isolated from the blood of Patient P and from Patients 1–4 and placed in separate tubes. A buffer was added to each vial to establish a pH of 8.6. One at a time, samples from each tube were injected into the capillary electrophoresis device set at 7.5 kilovolts (kV) to separate the types of hemoglobin present into peaks. The hemoglobin proteins composing a peak had similar charge characteristics. Figure 1 shows the peaks that resulted from all 5 samples.

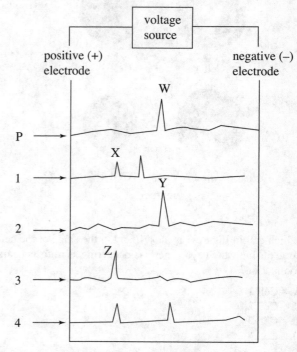

Note: Each peak is made up of hemoglobin proteins. W, X, Y, and Z are 4 specific peaks.

Figure 1

GO ON TO THE NEXT PAGE.

7. What is the most likely reason that the serum samples were treated with a buffer to bring pH to 8.6 ?

A. Hemoglobin protein breaks down at that pH.
B. All bacteria and viruses are destroyed at that pH.
C. Capillary electrophoresis separation of hemoglobin functions best at that pH.
D. Capillary electrophoresis separation of hemoglobin does not function at that pH.

8. Are the data in Table 1 consistent with the hypothesis that Patient 4 and Patient P are the same person?

F. Yes; Patient 4 has the same blood cell appearance as Patient P.
G. Yes; Patient 4 has different blood cell appearance than Patient P.
H. No; Patient 4 has the same blood cell appearance as Patient P.
J. No; Patient 4 has different blood cell appearance than Patient P.

9. Based on the information in the introduction and test results, do Patients 2 and 4 likely have the same genotype?

A. Yes, because the blood smear findings of Patients 2 and 4 are the same.
B. Yes, because Patients 2 and 4 have the same protein peak patterns.
C. No, because the blood smear findings of Patients 2 and 4 are different.
D. No, because Patients 2 and 4 have different protein peak patterns.

10. Sickle cells are caused by certain hemoglobin genotype combinations of 3 different alleles. The Hb^A allele is responsible for normal hemoglobin, the Hb^S allele is responsible for one variant that results in sickle cells, and the Hb^C allele is responsible for a different variant also resulting in sickle cells. Based on Table 1, the genotype of Patient 4 could be which of the following?

    I. $Hb^A Hb^A$
    II. $Hb^A Hb^S$
    III. $Hb^A Hb^C$

F. II only
G. I or III only
H. II or III only
J. I, II, or III

11. According to Figure 1, the pattern of protein peaks produced by serum from Patient P most closely resembles the pattern produced by the serum sample from:

A. Patient 1.
B. Patient 2.
C. Patient 3.
D. Patient 4.

12. Based on Figure 1, the hemoglobin proteins in which of the following two peaks were most likely closest in charge characteristics?

F. W and X
G. W and Z
H. X and Y
J. X and Z

13. During the capillary electrophoresis, all the hemoglobin proteins started with some quantity of charge before migrating from left to right in Figure 1. Therefore, the proteins resulting in peaks furthest to the left must have been the most:

A. negative, as opposite charges attract each other.
B. negative, as opposite charges repel each other.
C. positive, as opposite charges attract each other.
D. positive, as opposite charges repel each other.

GO ON TO THE NEXT PAGE.

Passage III

Carboxylic acids are organic compounds containing a carboxyl (–COOH) group. These molecules are acidic since they are able to donate protons in solution. The acidity and other physical properties of carboxylic acids are affected by the composition of the atoms bound to the carboxyl group. Table 1 lists the freezing points and boiling points for several carboxylic acids.

Table 1			
Formula	Name	Freezing point (°C)	Boiling point (°C)
CHOOH	Formic acid	8.4	101
CH$_3$COOH	Acetic acid	16.6	118
CH$_3$CH$_2$COOH	Propionic acid	–20.8	141
CH$_3$(CH$_2$)$_2$COOH	Butyric acid	–5.5	164
CH$_3$(CH$_2$)$_3$COOH	Valeric acid	–34.5	186

Figure 1 shows how the vapor pressure (in mm Hg) of 3 carboxylic acids changes as a function of temperature.

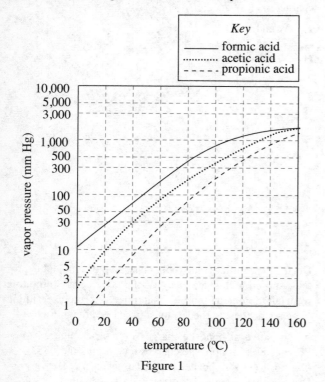

Figure 1

Figure 2 shows how the vapor pressure of the same 3 carboxylic acids changes as a function of concentration when mixed with water at 20°C.

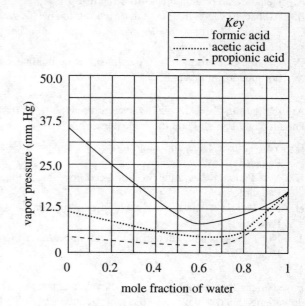

mole fraction of water

Figure 2

14. Which of the carboxylic acids listed in Table 1 has the *highest* melting point?

F. Propionic acid
G. Valeric acid
H. Acetic acid
J. Formic acid

15. A carboxylic acid not listed in Table 1, pyruvic acid, has a boiling point of 165°C. Based on Table 1 and Figure 1, the vapor pressure of pyruvic acid at 40°C is most likely:

A. less than 10 mm Hg.
B. between 10 and 100 mm Hg.
C. between 100 and 500 mm Hg.
D. greater than 500 mm Hg.

GO ON TO THE NEXT PAGE.

16. According to Figure 2, the vapor pressure of a 0.5 mole fraction solution of water in formic acid is closest to the vapor pressure of which of the following water in formic acid solutions?

    F. 0.4 mole fraction
    G. 0.6 mole fraction
    H. 0.8 mole fraction
    J. 0.9 mole fraction

17. According to Figure 2, as the mole fraction of water in an acetic acid and water solution increases from 0 to 1, the vapor pressure:

    A. decreases, then increases.
    B. increases, then decreases.
    C. decreases only.
    D. increases only.

18. $CH_3(CH_2)_4COOH$ is the chemical formula for the carboxylic acid named hexanoic acid. Based on Table 1, this compound most likely boils at a temperature:

    F. lower than 180°C.
    G. between 180°C and 215°C.
    H. between 215°C and 250°C.
    J. higher than 250°C.

19. According to Figure 1, does acetic acid or formic acid resist vaporization more at 60°C ?

    A. Formic acid, because formic acid has the lower vapor pressure.
    B. Formic acid, because formic acid has the higher vapor pressure.
    C. Acetic acid, because acetic acid has the lower vapor pressure.
    D. Acetic acid, because acetic acid has the higher vapor pressure.

GO ON TO THE NEXT PAGE.

Passage IV

A solenoid is a device that creates a magnetic field from electric current and can be used to exert a force on a nearby bar magnet to activate a mechanical device.

Scientists performed experiments on the solenoid apparatus shown in Figure 1.

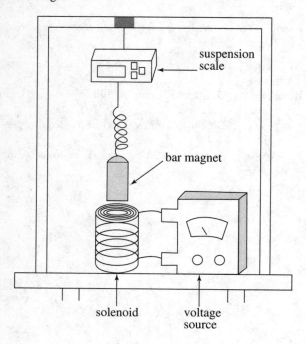

Figure 1

A wire carrying current from a voltage source was coiled into a hollow cylinder to form a solenoid with a length of XY. A solid cylinder bar magnet was suspended near the top of the solenoid as shown in Figure 2.

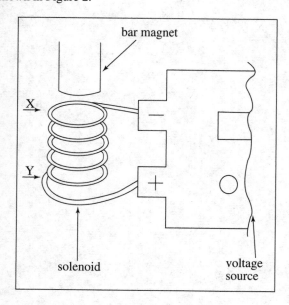

Figure 2

When the voltage source was turned on, the solenoid exerted a measurable force on the suspended bar magnet.

The bar magnet was attached to a digital suspension scale that measured weight in newtons (N). With the voltage source off, the scale read 4.7000 N. Prior to the start of each experimental trial, the scale was adjusted to read 5.0000 N.

Experiment 1

The scientists applied various levels of voltage in volts (V) to the circuit and recorded the weight indicated by the suspension scale for each trial. Results were recorded in Table 1.

Table 1	
Voltage (V)	Weight (N)
7.25	5.0078
8.00	5.0095
8.75	5.0113

Experiment 2

The scientists removed the bar magnet, inverted it, and reattached it to the suspension scale so that the opposite end was now facing the solenoid. The procedures of Experiment 1 were repeated and results were recorded in Table 2.

Table 2	
Voltage (V)	Weight (N)
7.25	4.9922
8.00	4.9905
8.75	4.9887

Experiment 3

The bar magnet was returned to the original alignment it was in during Experiment 1. The length XY of the solenoid coil was varied while a voltage of 8.00 V was applied to the circuit. Weights were recorded in Table 3.

Table 3	
Solenoid length XY (cm)	Weight (N)
7.50	5.0169
8.50	5.0131
9.50	5.0105

GO ON TO THE NEXT PAGE.

20. Based on the results of Experiments 1 and 3, the length XY of the solenoid coil in Experiment 1 was most likely:

   F. shorter than 7.50 cm.
   G. between 7.50 cm and 8.50 cm.
   H. between 8.50 cm and 9.50 cm.
   J. longer than 9.50 cm.

21. In Experiments 1 and 2, the orientation of the bar magnet relative to the solenoid opening determined which of the following?

   A. Solenoid length XY
   B. Direction of the force exerted by the solenoid on the bar magnet
   C. Density of the bar magnet
   D. Magnetic field strength of the solenoid

22. Which of the following provides the best explanation for the results of Experiment 3 ? The force exerted on the bar magnet by the solenoid magnetic field:

   F. increased as the voltage applied to the circuit increased.
   G. decreased as the voltage applied to the circuit increased.
   H. increased as the length XY of the solenoid increased.
   J. decreased as the length XY of the solenoid increased.

23. Suppose the scientists maintained the same bar magnet orientation in Experiment 3 as in Experiment 2. Based on the results of Experiments 1 and 2, with the solenoid length XY equal to 9.50 cm, the weight on the scale would most likely have been:

   A. 4.9831 N.
   B. 4.9895 N.
   C. 5.0105 N.
   D. 5.0169 N.

24. Prior to all experiments, the suspension scale was calibrated to read exactly 0 N when nothing was attached. Once the bar magnet was attached, the scientists made which of the following adjustments to the scale reading for each of the experimental trials?

   F. The displayed weight was adjusted downward by approximately 1.3 N.
   G. The displayed weight was adjusted upward by approximately 1.3 N.
   H. The displayed weight was adjusted downward by approximately 0.3 N.
   J. The displayed weight was adjusted upward by approximately 0.3 N.

25. Which of the following graphs best depicts the results of Experiment 3 ?

A.
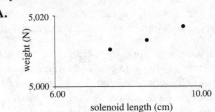

B.
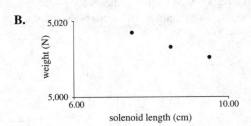

C.
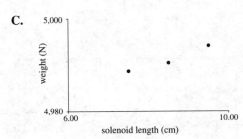

D.
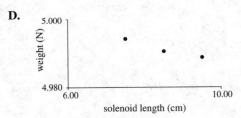

26. Suppose another trial had been conducted in Experiment 2 in which the voltage was 6.50 V. The weight measured on the scale would most likely have been closest to which of the following?

   F. 4.9908 N
   G. 4.9918 N
   H. 4.9928 N
   J. 4.9938 N

GO ON TO THE NEXT PAGE.

Passage V

Biodiversity is a measure of the variety of life in the world, and it can vary both due to natural factors and human activities.

Biodiversity is largely affected by the amount of available oxygen in the environment. When oxygen is plentiful, the number of species increases, but when oxygen levels are low, mass extinctions lower Earth's biodiversity. The marine biodiversity over time can be estimated by analyzing sediment and fossils found beneath the ocean floor. Figure 1 shows the global marine biodiversity, measured in the number of invertebrate genera, from the year 1500 to the year 2000.

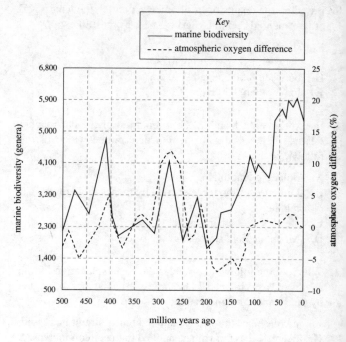

Figure 2

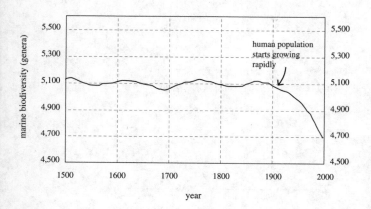

Figure 1

Figure 2 shows the global marine biodiversity and the atmospheric oxygen difference over the past 500 million years. The atmospheric oxygen difference is equal to:

(atmospheric oxygen concentration at a specific time) – (current atmospheric oxygen concentration)

Two ecology students describe their theories on the loss of marine biodiversity since 1900.

Student 1

The rapid loss in marine biodiversity since 1900 is caused by human activities. Figure 1 shows that the marine biodiversity was stable for centuries until the human population surged upward, quadrupling between 1900 and present day. The deforestation and large-scale industry necessary to support the large population has led to a decrease of 0.50% in the atmospheric oxygen concentration since 1900. As a result, marine biodiversity has decreased at a rate faster than any other time in the past 500 million years. Since 2000, marine biodiversity has fallen by approximately 2% per decade.

Student 2

The loss in marine biodiversity is part of a natural cycle of growth and loss that has occurred many times over the past 500 million years. As natural processes such as volcanic eruptions, asteroid impacts, and weathering cause decreases and increases in the atmospheric oxygen levels, marine biodiversity follows the same trend (see Figure 2). Human activities have very little effect on the atmospheric oxygen concentration, so the human impact on marine biodiversity is negligible.

GO ON TO THE NEXT PAGE.

27. Given Figure 1, Student 1 would most likely claim that from the year 1500 to the year 1900, the atmospheric oxygen concentration:

A. increased by more than 1.0%.
B. decreased by more than 1.0%.
C. changed by 1.0%.
D. changed by less than 1.0%, remaining relatively constant.

28. According to Figure 2, over which of the following time intervals did the atmospheric oxygen concentration decrease more than 10 times as much as Student 1 claims it has decreased since 1900?

F. 440 to 420 million years ago
G. 330 to 310 million years ago
H. 260 to 240 million years ago
J. 30 to 10 million years ago

29. Student 1 claims that current marine biodiversity is falling at a faster rate than it did at any time in the past 500 million years. Does Figure 1 give sufficient basis for that claim?

A. No; Figure 1 shows the marine biodiversity level for the past few centuries only.
B. No; Figure 1 shows the marine biodiversity for the past 500 million years.
C. Yes; Figure 1 shows the marine biodiversity level for the past few centuries only.
D. Yes; Figure 1 shows the marine biodiversity for the past 500 million years.

30. According to Student 1, marine biodiversity has been decreasing at a constant rate since 2000. Given the marine biodiversity level in the year 2000 in Figure 1, Student 1 would most likely conclude that the marine biodiversity in the year 2020 was closest to which of the following?

F. 4,500 genera
G. 4,600 genera
H. 4,800 genera
J. 4,900 genera

31. Suppose Student 2 stated that there have been times over the past 500 million years at which the atmospheric oxygen concentration has been lower than it is today. To support this statement, Student 2 would most likely cite oxygen data in Figure 2 for which of the following times?

A. 405 million years ago
B. 330 million years ago
C. 180 million years ago
D. 70 million years ago

32. Assume that the current atmospheric oxygen concentration is 21%. Given Figure 2, the two students would most likely claim that the atmospheric oxygen concentration 300 million years ago was closest to which of the following?

F. 15%
G. 19%
H. 24%
J. 27%

33. Which of the following statements about marine biodiversity would Student 2 most likely agree with?

A. Marine biodiversity generally increases as the oxygen concentration decreases.
B. Marine biodiversity generally decreases as the oxygen concentration decreases.
C. Marine biodiversity is affected only by human activities.
D. Marine biodiversity has remained constant for the past 500 million years.

GO ON TO THE NEXT PAGE.

Passage VI

The force per unit area resulting from the separation of solutions of different concentrations by a selectively permeable membrane is called *osmotic pressure*. Molecules, including water, have a tendency to move from regions of high concentration to regions of low concentration. Selectively permeable membranes act as filters, only allowing molecules below a certain threshold size to pass through. Osmotic pressure is the pressure required to stop water from moving across such a membrane from a region of high to low water concentration.

Cupric ions (Cu_2+) and glucose were dissolved separately in equal volumes of water to make two solutions. The glucose solution was more dilute, meaning that it had a higher percentage of water molecules than the cupric ion solution. Of the three molecules used for the solutions, water is the smallest and glucose is the largest. Water and glucose solutions are colorless while cupric ion solutions are blue. However, mixing glucose and cupric ions results in a red solution.

Experiment 1

A U-shaped tube contains a selectively permeable membrane, dividing it into equal halves. Glucose solution is poured in the left and an equal volume of cupric ion solution is poured in the right. Over 2 hours, the water level fell on the left and rose on the right. At this time, the left-sided solution was red and the right-sided was blue.

Experiment 2

Cupric ion solution is poured in the left side of the U-shaped tube and an equal volume of pure water is poured in the right. Over 2 hours, the water level fell on the right and rose on the left. At this time, both sides of the tube contained blue-colored solutions.

Experiment 3

Glucose solution is poured in the left side of the U-shaped tube and an equal volume of pure water is poured in the right. Over 2 hours, the water level fell on the right and rose on the left. At this time, both sides of the tube contained colorless solutions.

34. Which of the following diagrams could represent the results of Experiment 1 after the two hours had passed?

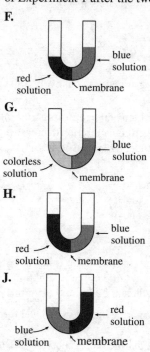

F.
red solution / blue solution / membrane

G.
colorless solution / blue solution / membrane

H.
red solution / blue solution / membrane

J.
blue solution / red solution / membrane

35. Albumin molecules do not pass through the selectively permeable membrane used in Experiments 1–3 and form clear solutions in water. If Experiment 2 were repeated, but the left side was filled with an albumin solution, the solution levels would:

   A. fall on the left and rise on the right, resulting in a left-sided red solution and right-sided clear solution.
   B. rise on the left and fall on the right, resulting in red solutions on both sides.
   C. fall on the left and rise on the right, resulting in red solutions on both sides.
   D. rise on the left and fall on the right, resulting in clear solutions on both sides.

36. In Experiments 1 and 2, cupric ion particles were able to move:

   F. through the membrane into both the glucose solution and pure water.
   G. through neither membrane into neither the glucose solution nor the pure water.
   H. only through the membrane separating it from the glucose solution.
   J. only through the membrane separating it from pure water.

GO ON TO THE NEXT PAGE.

37. In Experiments 2 and 3, what did the left side of the U-tube contain at the start of the experiment?

Experiment 2	Experiment 3
A. cupric ion solution	pure water
B. glucose solution	pure water
C. cupric ion solution	glucose solution
D. glucose solution	cupric ion solution

38. In Experiment 1, if a selectively permeable membrane that cupric ions, glucose, and water molecules could all pass through had been used, how, if at all, would the results have differed?

F. The water level would have fallen on the right and risen on the left.

G. A red color would have appeared on both sides of the U-tube.

H. A blue color would have appeared on both sides of the U-tube.

J. The same results would have been observed.

39. After watching Experiment 1 only, an observer asserted that since the left-sided solution ended up red, cupric ions must be bigger than water molecules. Is this a valid assertion?

A. No; the results show only that cupric ions and water molecules are smaller than glucose molecules.

B. No; the results show only that cupric ions and water molecules are larger than glucose molecules.

C. Yes; the results show that water molecules but not cupric ions can pass through the selectively permeable membrane.

D. Yes; the results show that both water molecules and cupric ions can pass through the selectively permeable membrane.

40. In Experiment 1, before the molecules began to move through the semi-permeable membrane, the appearance of the right-sided solution in the U-tube was:

F. clear.

G. blue.

H. red.

J. purple.

END OF TEST 4

STOP! DO NOT RETURN TO ANY OTHER TEST.

Chapter 33
Practice Exam 4:
Answers
and Explanations

*Note on scoring: please refer to the Scoring Conversion Worksheet and Score Conversion Chart on pages 539 and 540.

English		Math		Reading		Science	
1. C	39. D	1. D	31. C	1. B	21. B	1. C	21. B
2. F	40. G	2. G	32. G	2. J	22. H	2. J	22. J
3. A	41. B	3. D	33. C	3. A	23. A	3. D	23. B
4. J	42. J	4. K	34. G	4. G	24. J	4. H	24. J
5. B	43. B	5. A	35. B	5. A	25. C	5. A	25. B
6. G	44. G	6. H	36. J	6. H	26. G	6. G	26. J
7. A	45. C	7. C	37. D	7. C	27. C	7. C	27. D
8. J	46. J	8. K	38. H	8. F	28. J	8. F	28. H
9. D	47. B	9. B	39. B	9. C	29. B	9. D	29. A
10. H	48. F	10. K	40. H	10. J	30. J	10. H	30. F
11. C	49. A	11. B	41. D	11. C	31. C	11. B	31. C
12. F	50. J	12. F	42. H	12. G	32. G	12. J	32. J
13. D	51. A	13. D	43. A	13. A	33. D	13. A	33. B
14. G	52. H	14. K	44. J	14. F	34. F	14. H	34. F
15. B	53. B	15. A	45. C	15. D	35. B	15. A	35. D
16. G	54. G	16. F	46. K	16. J	36. J	16. H	36. F
17. C	55. A	17. B	47. C	17. C	37. C	17. A	37. C
18. J	56. J	18. J	48. J	18. F	38. F	18. G	38. G
19. D	57. C	19. D	49. E	19. D	39. D	19. C	39. A
20. G	58. H	20. K	50. F	20. F	40. G	20. J	40. G
21. A	59. C	21. E	51. C				
22. F	60. G	22. G	52. H				
23. A	61. B	23. A	53. D				
24. G	62. J	24. G	54. F				
25. C	63. A	25. D	55. B				
26. J	64. H	26. F	56. J				
27. B	65. D	27. C	57. E				
28. H	66. G	28. H	58. H				
29. C	67. C	29. A	59. A				
30. H	68. G	30. G	60. H				
31. C	69. A						
32. H	70. J						
33. D	71. A						
34. F	72. H						
35. A	73. B						
36. F	74. F						
37. C	75. C						
38. F							

ENGLISH TEST

1. **C** Note the question! The question asks which option *would NOT be acceptable* to replace the underlined portion. Cross out NOT and decide Yes/No for each option, and then choose the odd one out. Connecting words are changing in the answer choices, so the question is testing consistency. The part before the underlined portion contains the words *the tradition of excellence that they have leveraged*, and the part after the underlined portion contains the words *to win 26 World Series championships*. Choices (A) and (B) are both consistent with the cause-and-effect relationship indicated by *in order to*: (A) utilizes the correct idiom *so as to*, and (B) utilizes the correct idiom *as a means to*. Mark (A) and (B) as Yes. Choice (C) uses an incorrect idiom, so mark (C) as No. The correct idiom is *so that*, and the word *to* after the underlined portion makes the idiom incorrect. Choice (D) deletes the underlined portion and is also consistent with the passage since the word *to* after the underlined portion indicates the same cause-and-effect relationship as (A) and (B). Mark (D) as Yes. Choice (C) is the odd one out. The correct answer is (C).

2. **F** Punctuation is changing in the answer choices, so the question is testing STOP and GO punctuation. Use the vertical line test, and identify the ideas as complete or incomplete. Draw the vertical line between the words *players* and *contribute*. The phrase *The Yankees have had many great baseball players* is a complete idea, and the phrase *contribute to the team* is an incomplete idea. To connect a complete idea to an incomplete idea, GO or HALF-STOP punctuation is needed. A lack of punctuation is GO punctuation, so keep (F) and (J). The semicolon is STOP punctuation, so eliminate (G). The comma is GO punctuation, but there is no reason to include a comma after *players*, so eliminate (H). Compare (F) and (J). Choice (J) contains the word *and*, which is used to connect words of the same part of speech and changes the meaning of the sentence. The word *players* is a noun, and the word *contribute* is a verb, so *and* is not needed. Eliminate (J). The correct answer is (F).

3. **A** Subjects and verbs are changing in the answer choices, so the question is testing complete sentences. Determine which answer choice would produce a complete sentence. The sentence needs a subject that clarifies what is a *better line of work* for Gehrig. Eliminate (D) because *his mother* is not a line of work. The sentence also needs a verb tense that is consistent with the phrase *wanting him to excel academically* after the underlined portion. Eliminate (B) because it would require the word *and* in order for both verbs to be in the same tense and it makes the sentence incomplete. Compare (A) and (C). Choices (A) and (C) both convey the same information, but (A) is in active voice and (C) is in passive voice. Since active voice is more concise than passive voice, eliminate (C). The correct answer is (A).

4. **J** Note the question! The question asks which option *would be LEAST acceptable* to replace the underlined portion. Cross out LEAST and decide Yes/No for each option, and then choose the odd one out. The order of the words is changing in the answer choices, so the question is testing consistency with a modifier. The non-underlined portion contains the phrase *an intercollegiate game*. Gehrig is the one who played in the game, so the modifier should directly reference Gehrig's participation in the game. Choices (F) and (G) both use the word *that* to indicate that Gehrig played

in the game. Mark (F) and (G) as Yes. Choice (H) uses the words *in which* to reference the game. Mark (H) as Yes, since it displays the same consistency as (F) and (G). Choice (J) uses the words *and played* to reference the Yankee scout. This is the only answer choice not consistent with the passage, so mark (J) as No. Choice (J) is the odd one out. The correct answer is (J).

5. **B**   Commas are changing in the answer choices, so the question is testing comma rules. The phrase *long-standing* is necessary information, so it does not need a comma before or after. Eliminate (A) because it contains a comma before the phrase, and eliminate (C) because it contains commas before and after the phrase. The phrase *including those for runs batted in and extra-base hits* is unnecessary information, so it needs a comma before and after. Eliminate (D) because it lacks a comma before the phrase. The correct answer is (B).

6. **G**   Note the question! The question asks which option *most clearly communicates how positively Gehrig was viewed as a player*. Check each answer choice to see whether it is positive or negative. Keep (F) because *interested* could be positive. Keep (G) because *impressed* is positive. Eliminate (H) and (J) because both *offended* and *confused* indicate a negative view of Gehrig. Compare (F) and (G). Eliminate (F) because (G) is more strongly positive. The correct answer is (G).

7. **A**   Apostrophes are changing in the answer choices, so the question is testing apostrophe usage. When used with a noun, on the ACT, the apostrophe indicates possession. In this sentence, *Gehrig* possesses *amazing stamina and talent*, and because *Gehrig* is singular, the apostrophe should be placed before the *s*. Therefore, the apostrophe is needed. Eliminate (C) and (D) because they do not contain the apostrophe. Compare (A) and (B). The phrase *then suddenly* is unneeded information, so a comma is needed after the phrase. Eliminate (B). The correct answer is (A).

8. **J**   Note the question! The question asks which option *would be LEAST acceptable* to replace the underlined portion. Cross out LEAST and decide Yes/No for each option, and then choose the odd one out. Vocabulary is changing in the answer choices, so this question is testing word choice. The underlined portion contains the phrase *sports reporter to speculate*. Choices (F) and (G) use the word *infer* to replace *speculate*. *Infer* and *speculate* are synonyms, so mark (F) and (G) as Yes because both are consistent with the passage. Choice (H) uses the word *writer* to replace *sports reporter*. A sports reporter could be referred to as a writer, so mark (H) as Yes, since it is also consistent with the passage. Choice (J) uses the word *imply* to replace *speculate*. *Imply* and *speculate* have different meanings, so mark (J) as No because it is not consistent with the passage. Choice (J) is the odd one out. The correct answer is (J).

9. **D**   Note the question! The question asks for the *most logical* sequence of sentences in the paragraph, so it's testing consistency. Look for a clue in one sentence that indicates what idea that sentence needs to come before or after. Sentence 3 begins by saying *Unfortunately, that reporter was right*, so it must follow a sentence that introduces the reporter. Only Sentence 2 discusses a *sports reporter*. Therefore, Sentence 3 should directly follow Sentence 2. Eliminate (B) since it says Sentence 2 follows Sentence 3, and eliminate (C) because Sentence 3 does not directly follow Sentence 2. Sen-

tence 1 says *The prognosis was a veritable death sentence*, so it must follow a sentence discussing an illness or disease. Only Sentence 3 discusses a disease: *amyotrophic lateral sclerosis*. Therefore, Sentence 1 should follow Sentence 3. Eliminate (A) because it says that Sentence 3 follows Sentence 1. The correct answer is (D).

10. **H** Connecting words are changing in the answer choices, so the question is testing consistency. The part before the underlined portion contains the word *would*. The correct verb phrase is *would have*, not *would of*. Eliminate (F) and (G) because they do not contain the word *have*. The word *have* requires the verb to be in the past participle form *withdrawn*, not *withdrew*. Eliminate (J) because it uses the word *withdrew* instead of *withdrawn*. The correct answer is (H).

11. **C** Note the question! The question asks whether the statement should be added, so it's testing consistency. If the content of the new sentence is consistent with the ideas surrounding it, then it should be added. The paragraph discusses how Gehrig lived after his diagnosis. The new sentence discusses a personal experience of the author, so it is not consistent with the ideas in the text; the sentence should not be added. Eliminate (A) and (B). Keep (C) because it states that the new sentence is irrelevant. Eliminate (D) because it doesn't state that the new sentence is inconsistent with the text. The correct answer is (C).

12. **F** Apostrophes are changing in the answer choices, so the question is testing apostrophe usage. When used with a noun, on the ACT, the apostrophe indicates possession. In this sentence, *Gehrig* possesses his *retirement*. Therefore, the apostrophe is needed, and because *Gehrig* is singular, the apostrophe should be placed before the *s*. Eliminate (H) because it does not contain the apostrophe. Eliminate (J) because the apostrophe is after the *s*, which indicates a plural noun. Compare (F) and (G). There is no reason to include a comma after *retirement*, so eliminate (G). The correct answer is (F).

13. **D** Note the question! The question asks which quotation would support the preceding sentence, which says that Gehrig *paid tribute to the life-affirming support he'd received*. Check each answer choice to see whether it reflects Gehrig paying tribute to his fans. Eliminate (A) because a ballplayer who *can't keep his cool* does not reflect Gehrig's tribute to his fans. Eliminate (B) because although it discusses that Gehrig is dying from his illness, it does not present his fans in a positive light. Eliminate (C) because it does not reflect Gehrig's tribute to his fans. Choice (D) says Gehrig considers himself to be the *luckiest man on the face of the earth*, and this could convey that Gehrig appreciates his fans despite his diagnosis. The correct answer is (D).

14. **G** Pronouns are changing in the answers, so the question is testing consistency of pronouns. A pronoun must be consistent in number and case with the noun it is replacing. The pronoun refers to the noun *man*, which is singular and possesses the *eternal optimism and good spirit*. To be consistent, the pronoun in the answer choice must also be singular and demonstrate possession. Eliminate (F) and (H) because *who's* is a contraction meaning "who is." Keep (G) because *whose* is possessive. Eliminate (J) because *who* is not possessive. The correct answer is (G).

15. **B** Note the question! The question asks whether the phrase should be deleted, so it's testing consistency. If the content of the phrase is consistent with the ideas surrounding it, then it should be kept. The passage discusses Lou Gehrig's journey throughout his baseball career before and after a terminal diagnosis. The phrase includes *since their inception in 1913*, so it provides information about a point in time and is consistent with the ideas in the text; the sentence should not be deleted. Eliminate (C) and (D). Eliminate (A) because the year in which the Yankees were successful did not directly cause the Yankees to be successful. Keep (B) because it is consistent with the purpose of the phrase. The correct answer is (B).

16. **G** Transitions are changing in the answer choices, so the question is testing consistency with transitions. Look at the previous sentence to determine how the two ideas are related. The previous sentence explains that the author lived near many *famous places*, and this sentence explains that the author visited many of these places with her grandmother. The second sentence is adding detail to the prior one, so these sentences agree. Eliminate (F), (H), and (J) because all three choices include a contrasting transition. Keep (G) because the lack of transition implies that the sentences directly relate to each other, which is the correct relationship between them. The correct answer is (G).

17. **C** Note the question! The question asks which sentence *identifies a personal connection the narrator feels to the locations she visits*. Check each answer choice to see whether it refers to a personal connection. Eliminate (A) and (B) because descriptions of a lighthouse and national monuments are not personal connections. Keep (C) because an opinion of the impact of *Civil War battlefields* is a personal connection. Eliminate (D) because explaining how the *historic homes* ended up *featured in decorating magazines* is not a personal connection. The correct answer is (C).

18. **J** Note the question! The question asks which sentence *introduces the subject of this paragraph and reinforces the essay's presentation of the relationship between the narrator and her grandmother*. Check each answer choice to see whether it fulfills the purpose stated in the question. Eliminate (F) because a *love of history* does not refer to the narrator's grandmother. Eliminate (G) because although it does mention the narrator's grandmother, there is no reference to their relationship. Eliminate (H) because an *understanding of history* does not refer to the narrator's grandmother. Keep (J) because it explains how the narrator's *grandmother indulged* the narrator's *love of history*, which reflects their relationship. The correct answer is (J).

19. **D** Apostrophes are changing in the answer choices, so the question is testing apostrophe usage. When used with a noun, on the ACT, the apostrophe indicates possession. In this sentence, the *trips* are not possessing anything. Therefore, the apostrophe is not needed. Eliminate (A) and (B) because both contain an apostrophe. Compare (C) and (D). There is no reason to use a comma after *trips*, so eliminate (C). The correct answer is (D).

20. **G** Note the question! The question asks whether the phrase should be deleted, so it's testing consistency. If the content of the new sentence is not consistent with the ideas surrounding it, then it should be deleted. The paragraph discusses how the narrator's trips with her grandmother influenced her love of history. The phrase *where the Revolutionary Army endured a brutal winter* is used to describe

Valley Forge, so it is consistent with the ideas in the text; the sentence should be kept. Eliminate (H) and (J). Eliminate (F) because the passage's focus is on the narrator's love for history. Keep (G) because the phrase explains why Valley Forge is historically significant. The correct answer is (G).

21. **A** Note the question! The question asks which sentence *introduces the subject of this paragraph*. The paragraph discusses a coin collection for each of the 50 states. Check each answer choice to see whether it introduces this collection. Keep (A) because it references *a big, flat box* that contains the map used to display the coins. Eliminate (B), (C), and (D) because none of these references the coin collection. The correct answer is (A).

22. **F** Subjects and verbs are changing in the answer choices, so the question is testing complete sentences. Determine which answer choice would produce a complete sentence. The sentence needs something that clarifies who is saying *I thought we could begin a new project*. Keep (F) because it specifies that the grandmother is speaking to the narrator. Eliminate (G) because it says the narrator's grandmother told her to do something, not that she spoke the previous statement. Eliminate (H) because it says the grandmother is reading from the pamphlet. Eliminate (J) because it says the narrator's grandmother handed her the pamphlet while still holding it. The correct answer is (F).

23. **A** Connecting words are changing in the answer choices, so the question is testing consistency and complete sentences. Determine which answer choice would produce a complete sentence. Notice that the answer choices change around a comma, and some of the words after the comma are FANBOYS, so use the vertical line test. Draw two vertical lines around the word *and*, and identify the ideas before and after as complete or incomplete. The phrase *The box contained a map of the country* is a complete idea, and the phrase *each state had a space where we could insert its quarter* is a complete idea. To connect two complete ideas, HALF-STOP or STOP punctuation is needed. Keep (A) because a comma + *and* is STOP punctuation. Eliminate (D) because a comma without a FANBOYS word is GO punctuation. Though (B) and (C) have a FANBOYS word following the comma, both include an extra word before *each*, which makes the second part of the sentence incomplete. A comma + FANBOYS can only connect two complete ideas, so eliminate (B) and (C). The correct answer is (A).

24. **G** The order of the words is changing in the answer choices, so the question is testing consistency with a modifier. The underlined portion contains part of a modifier that ends with *for a "quarter collection" project*. The modifier describes an action done by the narrator's friends, so the phrase that begins the modifying phrase should include a verb. Eliminate (F) and (H) because they do not begin with a verb. Compare (G) and (J). The word after the underlined portion is *for*. Keep (G) because it utilizes the correct idiom *enthusiasm for*. Eliminate (J) because it uses the incorrect idiom *finding humor for* instead of *finding humor in*. The correct answer is (G).

25. **C** Punctuation is changing in the answer choices, so the question is testing STOP and GO punctuation. Use the vertical line test, and identify the ideas as complete or incomplete. Draw the vertical line between the words *released* and *Delaware*. The phrase *I was so excited when the first three were released* is a complete idea, and the phrase *Delaware, Pennsylvania, and New Jersey* is an incomplete

idea. To connect a complete idea to an incomplete idea, HALF-STOP or GO punctuation is needed. A lack of punctuation is GO punctuation, so keep (A). The semicolon is STOP punctuation, so eliminate (B). The colon is HALF-STOP punctuation, so keep (C). The comma is GO punctuation, but there is no reason to use a comma after the word *released*, so eliminate (D). Compare (A) and (C). The three states listed in the second phrase are an explanation of *the first three* identified in the first phrase, so a colon is needed. The correct answer is (C).

26. **J**   Note the question! The question asks which option *would NOT be acceptable* to replace the underlined portion. Cross out NOT and decide Yes/No for each option, and then choose the odd one out. Punctuation is changing in the answer choices, so the question is testing STOP and GO punctuation. Use the vertical line test, and identify the ideas as complete or incomplete. Draw the vertical line between the words *saw* and *amusingly*. The phrase *My grandmother and I would insert each quarter in its proper place and look up the story behind each new image we saw* is a complete idea, and the phrase *Amusingly, as time progressed, even my friends liked to look at the growing collection of quarters on my map* is also a complete idea. To connect two complete ideas, STOP or HALF-STOP punctuation is needed. The period is STOP punctuation, and the statements after the period in (F) and (G) preserve the meaning of *Amusingly*. Mark (F) and (G) as Yes because they both are consistent with the passage. The semicolon is also STOP punctuation, so mark (H) as Yes because it is also consistent with the passage. The comma is GO punctuation, so mark (J) as No because it is not consistent with the passage. Choice (J) is the odd one out. The correct answer is (J).

27. **B**   Vocabulary is changing in the answer choices, so this question is testing word choice. The four choices are all grammatically correct and mean the same thing, so choose the most concise one. The correct answer is (B).

28. **H**   Commas and the phrase after *party* are changing in the answer choices, so the question is testing comma rules. Notice that commas are used to connect ideas in most choices, so consider when commas can connect ideas. A comma can connect two complete ideas if it's followed by a FANBOYS word, and it can connect anything except for two complete ideas if it's not followed by a FANBOYS word. Use the vertical line test, and identify the ideas as complete or incomplete. Draw the vertical line after the word *party*. The phrase *When the final quarter came out last year, my grandmother, my friends, and I had a small party* is a complete idea, and the phrase *we wanted to celebrate the complete collection* is a complete idea. A comma not followed by a FANBOYS word cannot connect two complete ideas, so eliminate (F). Choices (G) and (J) alter the second part of the sentence, but in both cases the second part is still a complete idea. Eliminate (G) and (J) because each uses a comma without a FANBOYS word to connect two complete ideas. Keep (H) because it makes the second part of the sentence incomplete, and thus no punctuation is needed. The correct answer is (H).

29. **C**   Note the question! The question asks which sentence *best makes a connection between the narrator's view of history and that of her friends.* Check each answer choice to see whether it relates the narrator's opinion to her friends' viewpoints. Eliminate (A) and (B) because neither the *success* of nor the enjoyment at

the party indicates a *view of history*. Keep (C) because the narrator's friends' opinions are referenced in relation to the narrator's own opinions. Eliminate (D) because, while it mentions the narrator's friends' opinions, it does not compare them to the narrator's opinions. The correct answer is (C).

30. **H** Note the question! The question asks which option *would be LEAST acceptable* to replace the underlined portion. Cross out LEAST and decide Yes/No for each option, and then choose the odd one out. Vocabulary is changing in the answer choices, so this question is testing word choice. The underlined portion contains the phrase *wonder*. Choice (F) uses the words *am curious* and (J) uses the words *can't wait to know* to replace *wonder*. Mark (F) and (J) as Yes because both choices mean the same thing as *wonder*. Compare (G) and (H). Choice (G) uses the words *am anxious to see* and (H) uses the words *am nervous about* to replace *wonder*. The word *wonder* conveys that the narrator is excited about the next state she will visit. Mark (G) as Yes because *anxious* can refer to a positive emotion, so (G) is consistent with the passage. Mark (H) as No because *nervous* is typically negative, so (H) is not consistent with the passage. Choice (H) is the odd one out. The correct answer is (H).

31. **C** Vocabulary is changing in the answer choices, so this question is testing word choice. Since *want* and *desire* have the same meaning in context, the four choices are all grammatically correct and mean the same thing. Choose the most concise one. The correct answer is (C).

32. **H** Note the question! The question asks which option *would NOT be acceptable* to replace the underlined portion. Cross out NOT and decide Yes/No for each option, and then choose the odd one out. Punctuation is changing in the answer choices, so the question is testing STOP and GO punctuation. Use the vertical line test, and identify the ideas as complete or incomplete. Draw the vertical line between the words *doll* and *however*. The phrase *I expected her to pick out some clothes, a new video game, maybe even a doll* is a complete idea, and the phrase *However, she insisted the only thing she wanted was a model airplane* is also a complete idea. To connect two complete ideas, STOP or HALF-STOP punctuation is needed. The semicolon is STOP punctuation, so (F) is consistent with the passage. A comma + *but* is STOP punctuation, so (G) is also consistent with the passage. Mark (F) and (G) as Yes. A lack of punctuation is GO punctuation, so mark (H) as No because it is not consistent with the passage. The period is STOP punctuation, so mark (J) as Yes because it is consistent with the passage. Choice (H) is the odd one out. The correct answer is (H).

33. **D** Note the question! The question asks where the phrase *about her request* should be placed in a sentence, so it's testing consistency. Look for a clue in the sentence to determine what idea it needs to come before or after. The word *about* indicates that the phrase should immediately follow something referencing the *request*. Eliminate (A) because the *guess* is not referencing the *request*. Eliminate (B) because the narrator is not referencing the *request*. Eliminate (C) because the word *shouldn't* is not referencing the *request*. Keep (D) because the *surprised* is referencing the *request*. The correct answer is (D).

34. **F** Verbs are changing in the answer choices, so the question is testing consistency of verbs. The answer choices are in different tenses, so look for a clue in the sentence or surrounding sentences to identify the appropriate tense. The beginning of the passage says *My daughter just turned nine last*

week, so the underlined portion refers to an event that began happening in the past and is still happening. It needs a tense that indicates that the growing up is still happening. Keep (F) and (G) because both use the present-tense verb *has*. Eliminate (H) because *would have* is not the correct tense. Eliminate (J) because *had* is in past tense. Compare (F) and (G). Both could work, but (F) is more concise and does not use an -*ing* verb, so eliminate (G). The correct answer is (F).

35. **A** Note the question! The question asks which option *would NOT be acceptable* to replace the underlined portion. Cross out NOT and decide Yes/No for each option, and then choose the odd one out. Vocabulary is changing in the answer choices, so this question is testing word choice. The underlined portion contains the phrase *finds it perfectly appropriate*. Choice (A) uses the adverb *appropriately* in place of *appropriate*. Adverbs describe verbs or adjectives. *Appropriate* is an adjective that refers to a noun, the daughter's *love of aviation*, so an adverb is not consistent with the passage. Mark (A) as No. Choice (B) removes the adverb *perfectly* from the phrase, but the sentence is still grammatically correct and has the same meaning. Mark (B) as Yes. Choices (C) and (D) both preserve the meaning of the underlined portion, so mark both as Yes. Choice (A) is the odd one out. The correct answer is (A).

36. **F** Punctuation is changing in the answer choices, so the question is testing STOP and GO punctuation. Use the vertical line test, and identify the ideas as complete or incomplete. Draw the vertical line between the words *backyard* and *pretending*. The phrase *I'll never forget my utter dismay when he taught her to jump off the swing set in our backyard* is a complete idea, and the phrase *pretending she was a pilot and shouting "Airborne!"* is an incomplete idea. To connect a complete idea to an incomplete idea, HALF-STOP or GO punctuation is needed. The comma is GO punctuation, so keep (F). A lack of punctuation is GO punctuation, so keep (G). The semicolon is STOP punctuation, so eliminate (H). The period is STOP punctuation, so eliminate (J). Compare (F) and (G). The phrase *pretending she was a pilot and shouting "Airborne!"* is a separate idea from the idea before it, so it needs a comma before. Eliminate (G) because it doesn't have a comma before this phrase. The correct answer is (F).

37. **C** Note the question! The question asks which option *would NOT be acceptable* to replace the underlined portion. Cross out NOT and decide Yes/No for each option, and then choose the odd one out. Vocabulary is changing in the answer choices, so this question is testing word choice. The underlined portion contains the phrase *play house*. Choice (A) removes the word *play*, but it is still consistent with the passage because it mirrors the structure used earlier in the sentence. Mark (A) as Yes. Choice (B) adds the words *she would play*, but it is still consistent with the passage because it mirrors the structure used earlier in the sentence. Mark (B) as Yes. Choice (C) uses *than* to compare *play pilot* to *house was*. This is not consistent with the passage because it does not mirror the structure used earlier in the sentence. Mark (C) as No. Choice (D) uses *she played house* to replace the underlined phrase. This is also consistent with the passage because the narrator is describing a time from the past. Mark (D) as Yes. Choice (C) is the odd one out. The correct answer is (C).

38. **F** Transitions are changing in the answer choices, so the question is testing consistency with transitions. Look at the previous sentence to determine how the two ideas are related. The previous sentence describes how the narrator's daughter enjoyed pretending to be a pilot, and this sentence explains that, at a certain point, pretending wasn't good enough. The two ideas disagree, so an opposite-direction transition is needed. Keep (F) because *yet* implies a contrast between the two ideas and suggests that the idea in the first sentence was once true, but it did not remain true. Eliminate (G) because *therefore* implies that pretending to be a pilot caused the narrator's daughter to want to see real airplanes, and there is no cause-and-effect relationship mentioned in the passage. Eliminate (H) because *although* makes the first part of the sentence incomplete, which does not work with the semicolon later on. Eliminate (J) because *instead* suggests that the second idea happened in place of the first idea, or that the narrator's daughter did not pretend to play pilot. The correct answer is (F).

39. **D** Vocabulary is changing in the answer choices, so this question is testing word choice. There is also the option to DELETE; consider this choice carefully as it's often the correct answer. The three choices—*happens every year, takes place every year,* and *occurs every 12 months*—basically mean the same thing. The sentence already uses the word *annual*, so there's no need to repeat the idea. The phrase should be deleted to make the sentence more concise. The correct answer is (D).

40. **G** Note the question! The question asks whether the phrase should be deleted, so it's testing consistency. If the content of the new sentence is not consistent with the ideas surrounding it, then it should be deleted. The paragraph discusses how the narrator's daughter's questions about aircraft differed from those of other children. The phrase *other children her age* is consistent with the ideas in the text; the sentence should be kept. Eliminate (H) and (J). Eliminate (F) because the passage makes a claim about only the types of questions that are asked and not the types of questions that *should* be asked. Keep (G) because it states that the phrase compares the narrator's daughter to other children. The correct answer is (G).

41. **B** Pronouns are changing in the answer choices, so the question is testing clarity with pronouns. Determine who or what the pronoun refers to, and choose an answer that makes the meaning 100% clear. The subject is *an older gentleman*, so the pronoun must refer to the gentleman. Eliminate (C) because *which* refers to an object instead of a person. Eliminate (D) because the meaning of the sentence changes if the pronoun is removed. Compare (A) and (B). The pronoun *whom* is used when it could be replaced by "him" or "her," and the pronoun *who* is used when it could be replaced by "he" or "she." The sentence could be rewritten as "he" *was mistaken about the planned retirement date of the F-15 Eagle*, so the appropriate pronoun is *who*. Eliminate (A). The correct answer is (B).

42. **J** Vocabulary is changing in the answer choices, so this question is testing word choice. The underlined portion contains the phrase *absolute and unequivocal*. The words *absolute* and *unequivocal* are both describing how *right* the narrator's daughter was. *Right* is an adjective describing the narrator's daughter, and words describing adjectives must be adverbs. Eliminate (F) because neither word is

in adverb form. Eliminate (G) because *absolute* is not in adverb form. Eliminate (H) because *unequivocal* is not in adverb form. The correct answer is (J).

43. **B** Note the question! The question asks which option *would be LEAST acceptable* to replace the underlined portion. Cross out LEAST and decide Yes/No for each option, and then choose the odd one out. Vocabulary is changing in the answer choices, so this question is testing word choice. Determine what meaning of the underlined portion would be consistent with the sentence. The underlined portion contains the phrase *big dreams*. Choice (A) uses the phrase *ambitious aims*. The word *ambitious* is synonymous with *big* and *aims* is synonymous with *dreams*, so (A) is consistent with the passage. Mark (A) as Yes. Choice (B) uses the phrase *impossible hopes*. *Hopes* is synonymous with *dreams*, but *impossible* does not mean the same thing as *big*, so (B) is not consistent with the passage. Mark (B) as No. Choice (C) uses the words *great aspirations*, and (D) uses the words *impressive plans*. The words *great* and *impressive* are both synonyms for *big*, and the words *aspirations* and *plans* are both synonyms for *dreams*. Both (C) and (D) are also consistent with the passage, so mark both as Yes. Choice (B) is the odd one out. The correct answer is (B).

44. **G** Vocabulary is changing in the answer choices, so this question is testing word choice. The four choices are all grammatically correct and mean the same thing, so choose the most concise one. The correct answer is (G).

45. **C** Transitions are changing in the answer choices, so the question is testing consistency with transitions. Look at the previous sentence to determine how the two ideas are related. The previous sentence describes some of the narrator's husband's goals for their daughter, and this sentence gives examples of equally lofty goals for the narrator's daughter. The relationship between the two sentences is a continuation of the idea that the narrator's husband has lofty goals in mind for their daughter. Eliminate (A), (B), and (D) because all three choices use a contrasting transition, but the second sentence is building upon the prior one. Keep (C) because the lack of transition implies that the sentences directly relate to each other, which is the correct relationship between them. The correct answer is (C).

46. **J** Vocabulary is changing in the answer choices, so this question is testing word choice. There is also the option to DELETE; consider this choice carefully as it's often the correct answer. The three choices—*when I was young, when I was a youth,* and *before I grew up*—basically mean the same thing. The sentence already uses the phrase *as a child*, so there's no need to repeat the idea. The phrase should be deleted to make the sentence more concise. The correct answer is (J).

47. **B** Pronouns are changing in the answer choices, so the question is testing clarity with pronouns. Determine who or what the pronoun refers to, and choose an answer that makes the meaning 100% clear. The subject is *a strange excitement*, so the pronoun must refer to this moment of excitement. Eliminate (A) and (C) because *which* refers to an object instead of a moment in time. Eliminate (D) because it creates a sentence with just a comma between two complete ideas. Keep (B) because *when* refers to time. The correct answer is (B).

48.   **F**   Punctuation and word choice are changing in the answer choices, so the question is testing complete sentences. Use the vertical line test, and identify the ideas as complete or incomplete. Draw the vertical line after the word *light*. The phrase *Bioluminescence literally means "living light"* is a complete idea, and the phrase *it refers to a strange adaptation found in some organisms* is also a complete idea. To connect two complete ideas, STOP or HALF-STOP punctuation is needed. A comma with a FANBOYS word is STOP punctuation, so keep (F). A comma is GO punctuation, so eliminate (G) and (J). No punctuation is also GO punctuation, so eliminate (H). The correct answer is (F).

49.   **A**   Transitions are changing in the answer choices, so the question is testing consistency with transitions. Look at the ideas in the sentence to determine how the two ideas are related. The first idea is that *this light is not intended to be a heat source*, and the second idea is that scientists are *not totally certain what it is intended to do*. The relationship between the two ideas is a contrast between what scientists do and do not know about bioluminescence. Keep (A) because it uses a contrasting transition. Eliminate (B) and (D) because the lack of transitions in these choices does not support the contrast implied by the two ideas. Eliminate (C) because the transition implies that the sentences directly relate to each other instead of contrasting. The correct answer is (A).

50.   **J**   Pronouns and connecting words are changing in the answer choices, so the question is testing consistency of pronouns. A pronoun must be consistent in number with the noun it is replacing. The pronoun refers to the noun *organisms*, which is plural. To be consistent, the pronoun in the answer choice must also be plural. Eliminate (G) because it is the incorrect plural form of *themselves*, and eliminate (H) because *itself* is singular. Compare (F) and (J). The correct idiom is *use to*, so eliminate (F) because it uses the word *for* instead of *to*. The correct answer is (J).

51.   **A**   Note the question! The question asks whether the phrase should be deleted, so it's testing consistency. If the content of the phrase is consistent with the ideas surrounding it, then it should be kept. The paragraph discusses possible functions of bioluminescence in organisms. The phrase includes *repulse predators* as part of a list of possible functions, so it is consistent with the ideas in the text; the sentence should not be deleted. Eliminate (C) and (D). Keep (A) because the sentence following the underlined portion says *how the same adaptation can be designed to both attract and repulse*. Eliminate (B) because the paragraph does not directly explain how the ability to *repulse predators* would be beneficial to survival or fitness. The correct answer is (A).

52.   **H**   Commas are changing in the answer choices, so the question is testing comma rules. The phrase *or land-based* is unnecessary information, so it needs a comma before and after. Eliminate (F) because it lacks a comma before the phrase, eliminate (G) because it lacks commas before and after the phrase, and eliminate (J) because it lacks a comma after the phrase. The correct answer is (H).

53.   **B**   The order of the words is changing in the answer choices, so the question is testing consistency with a modifier. The non-underlined portion contains the modifier *Unlike these smaller organisms*, so the word or phrase that directly follows the modifying phrase should be a noun that is compa-

rable to small organisms. Eliminate (A), (C), and (D) because all three choices compare *researchers* to *smaller organisms*, which is not the correct meaning of the sentence. The correct answer is (B).

54. **G** Note the question! The question asks which sentence *best indicates the focus of the paragraph*. The paragraph discusses bioluminescence uniquely in *deep-sea marine lifeforms*. Check each answer choice to see whether it introduces this topic. Eliminate (F) because it references *sunlight*, which is not mentioned in the rest of the paragraph. Keep (G) because it mentions *conditions…in the ocean*, which is synonymous with the word *marine*. Eliminate (H) because it contradicts the following idea about bioluminescence being found in the ocean. Eliminate (J) because while it does mention bioluminescence, it discusses the phenomenon in terms of humans instead of *deep-sea marine lifeforms*. The correct answer is (G).

55. **A** Punctuation is changing in the answer choices, so the question is testing STOP and GO punctuation. Use the vertical line test, and identify the ideas as complete or incomplete. Draw vertical lines before and after the FANBOYS word *but*. The phrase *The most commonly emitted colors are blue and green* is a complete idea, and the phrase *red and yellow have also been observed* is also a complete idea. To connect two complete ideas, STOP or HALF-STOP punctuation is needed. A comma + *but* is STOP punctuation, so because the word *but* is in all four answers, a comma is needed. Eliminate (B), (C), and (D) because they don't contain a comma before the FANBOYS word. The correct answer is (A).

56. **J** Vocabulary is changing in the answers, so the question is testing word choice. Determine what meaning of the underlined portion would be consistent with the sentence. The underlined portion should mean something like "it is." Eliminate (F) because *its* is the possessive form of "it." Eliminate (H) because *its'* is not a word at all. Compare (G) and (J). Eliminate (G) because the word *in* should not immediately precede the words "it is." Keep (J) because the contraction *it's* means "it is." The correct answer is (J).

57. **C** Apostrophes are changing in the answer choices, so the question is testing apostrophe usage. When used with a noun, on the ACT, the apostrophe indicates possession. In this sentence, the *organisms* are possessing the *lights*. Therefore, the apostrophe is needed, and because *organisms* is plural, the apostrophe should be placed after the *s*. Eliminate (A) and (B) because both place the apostrophe before the *s*, which indicates a singular noun. Keep (C) because it places the apostrophe after the *s*. Eliminate (D) because it does not include the apostrophe. The correct answer is (C).

58. **H** Vocabulary is changing in the answers, so the question is testing word choice. Determine what meaning of the underlined portion would be consistent with the sentence. Several of the options contain either *then* or *than*, so consider which is appropriate in this sentence. The sentence uses the word *more*, so the comparison word *than* is needed. Eliminate (F) and (G) because they use *then* instead of *than*. Compare (H) and (J). The correct idiom is *more…than*, not *more…as*, so eliminate (J). The correct answer is (H).

59. **C** Note the question! The question asks which option *would be LEAST acceptable* to replace the underlined portion. Cross out LEAST and decide Yes/No for each option, and then choose the odd one out. Vocabulary is changing in the answers, so the question is testing word choice. Determine what meaning of the underlined portion would be consistent with the sentence. The underlined portion contains the word *clarified*. Choices (A) and (B) use the phrases *fully explained* and *accounted for* to replace *clarified*. Both phrases are synonymous with *clarified* and are consistent with the passage, so mark (A) and (B) as Yes. Choice (C) uses the word *transmitted* to replace *clarified*. The words *transmitted* and *clarified* have different meanings, so (C) is not consistent with the passage. Mark (C) as No. Choice (D) uses the words *cleared up* to replace *clarified*. The words *cleared up* and *clarified* have similar meanings, so (D) is also consistent with the passage. Mark (D) as Yes. Choice (C) is the odd one out. The correct answer is (C).

60. **G** Note the question! The question asks whether the essay would fulfill the goal of *focusing on a fascinating evolutionary adaptation that can be found in multiple habitats*. Consider the main idea of the passage and use Process of Elimination. The passage is about bioluminescence's prevalence in a variety of habitats and organisms. Eliminate (H) and (J) because the author does meet the goal. Eliminate (F) because while the passage does discuss fireflies, this would not demonstrate *multiple habitats*. Keep (G) because it is true that the author focuses on *marine and non-marine habitats*, which corresponds to *multiple habitats*. The correct answer is (G).

61. **B** Transitions and paragraph structure are changing in the answer choices, so the question is testing consistency with transitions. Look at the previous sentences to determine how the ideas are related and whether a new paragraph is necessary. The previous sentences describe how *we take many small things for granted* and provide examples of these *small things*, and this sentence explains how this is not the case *in some parts of the world*. The relationship between the two sentences is a contrast between *America* and other *parts of the world*. A new paragraph should be started when a new main idea is introduced. Eliminate (C) and (D) because both ideas are closely related, even though they contrast, and should remain in the same paragraph. Eliminate (A) because the lack of transition does not support the contrast between the two ideas. Keep (B) because *yet* is a contrasting transition. The correct answer is (B).

62. **J** Punctuation is changing in the answer choices, so the question is testing STOP and GO punctuation. Use the vertical line test, and identify the ideas as complete or incomplete. Draw the vertical line between the words *physicians* and *started*. The phrase *That is why a group of French physicians* is an incomplete idea, and the phrase *started Doctors Without Borders in 1971* is also an incomplete idea. To connect two incomplete ideas, GO punctuation is needed. The comma is GO punctuation, so keep (F). A lack of punctuation is GO punctuation, so keep (G) and (J). The semicolon is STOP punctuation, so eliminate (H). Compare (F), (G), and (J). There is no reason to use a comma after *physicians* or *started*, so eliminate (F) and (G). The correct answer is (J).

63. **A** Note the question! The question asks which sentence *introduces the basic goal of Doctors Without Borders*. The following paragraph says that doctors felt that they could *help to alleviate the suf-*

fering of those in *war-torn areas*. Check each answer choice to see whether it refers to the goal of the organization. Keep (A) because *humanitarian aid organization* matches the ideas later in the passage. Eliminate (B) because an organization that *helps the doctors* would not address the lack of basic needs outlined in the first paragraph. Eliminate (C) and (D) because neither *political support* nor the location of operation is relevant to the idea of helping those who are suffering. The correct answer is (A).

64. **H** Commas are changing in the answer choices, so the question is testing comma rules. The phrase *starvation and disease* is necessary information, so it does not need a comma before or after. Eliminate (F) and (J) because they contain a comma after the phrase. Compare (G) and (H). There is no reason to use a comma after *starvation*, so eliminate (G). The correct answer is (H).

65. **D** Note the question! The question asks which option *would be LEAST acceptable* to replace the underlined portion. Cross out LEAST and decide Yes/No for each option, and then choose the odd one out. Vocabulary is changing in the answers, so the question is testing word choice. Determine what meaning of the underlined portion would be consistent with the sentence. The underlined portion contains the word *atrocities*. Choices (A), (B), and (C) use the words *horrors, offenses,* and *wrongs*. All three words are synonyms for *atrocities* and are consistent with the passage. Mark (A), (B), and (C) as Yes. Choice (D) uses the word *alarms*. The word *alarms* is not synonymous with *atrocities*, so mark (D) as No. Choice (D) is the odd one out. The correct answer is (D).

66. **G** Note the question! The question asks whether the sentence should be deleted, so it's testing consistency. If the content of the sentence is consistent with the ideas surrounding it, then it should be kept. The passage discusses how *the doctors who first started the organization* did so in response to the suffering they witnessed during the civil war in Nigeria. The sentence includes information about the suffering and the lack of resources available from the *United Nations* and the *Red Cross*, so it is consistent with the ideas in the text; the sentence should not be deleted. Eliminate (H) and (J). Eliminate (F) because the topics *readers are used to hearing about* does not affect whether or not the sentence should be kept or deleted. Keep (G) because it explains that the sentence provides examples of the suffering that prompted the doctors to form *Doctors Without Borders*. The correct answer is (G).

67. **C** Punctuation is changing in the answer choices, so the question is testing STOP and GO punctuation. Use the vertical line test, and identify the ideas as complete or incomplete. Draw the vertical line between the words *suffering* and *thus*. The phrase *The doctors felt that, although they couldn't put an ending to the fighting itself, they could at least help to alleviate the suffering* is a complete idea, and the phrase *thus they declared themselves neutral in the conflict and entered war-torn areas to provide aid to anyone who needed it, regardless of which side of the conflict the person was on* is also a complete idea. To connect two complete ideas, STOP or HALF-STOP punctuation is needed. The comma is GO punctuation, so eliminate (A). A lack of punctuation is GO punctuation, so eliminate (B) and (D). The period is STOP punctuation, so keep (C). The correct answer is (C).

68. **G** Transitions are changing in the answer choices, so the question is testing consistency with transitions. Look at the previous sentence to determine how the two ideas are related. The previous paragraph describes why *Doctors Without Borders* was initially formed, and this sentence describes *the original mission* of the organization. The two ideas agree, and the second idea is a continuation of the first. Eliminate (F) because it uses a contrasting transition, but the sentence is building upon the prior paragraph. Keep (G) because the lack of transition implies that the sentences directly relate to each other, which is the correct relationship between them. Eliminate (H) and (J) because *meanwhile* and *finally* indicate that the two ideas occurred at certain moments in time, but the text does not support either. The correct answer is (G).

69. **A** Note the question! The question asks whether the phrase should be deleted, so it's testing consistency. If the content of the phrase is consistent with the ideas surrounding it, then it should be kept. The passage discusses the purpose and founding of *Doctors Without Borders*. The phrase *to up-and-coming doctors* clarifies who is receiving the *medical training,* so it is consistent with the ideas in the text; the phrase should not be deleted. Eliminate (C) and (D). Keep (A) because the phrase gives specific detail about the *original mission* of the organization and who is receiving the medical treatment. Eliminate (B) because the work of other doctors in the region is not pertinent to the mission of *Doctors Without Borders.* The correct answer is (A).

70. **J** Commas are changing in the answer choices, so the question is testing comma rules. The phrase *In desperate need of medical attention* is a modifier, so it needs a comma after it. Eliminate (F) and (G) because they both lack a comma after the phrase. Compare (H) and (J). Use the vertical line test, and identify the ideas as complete or incomplete. Draw the vertical line after the word *attention.* The phrase *In desperate need of medical attention* is an incomplete idea. HALF-STOP or GO punctuation is required to connect an incomplete idea to either a complete or an incomplete idea. A comma with a FANBOYS word is STOP punctuation, so eliminate (H). The correct answer is (J).

71. **A** Vocabulary is changing in the answer choices, so the question is testing word choice. Determine what meaning of the underlined portion would be consistent with the sentence. The underlined portion should mean something like "in the middle of." Keep (A) because *between* means "in the middle of." Eliminate (B) because *among* is used in a situation with more than two parties, and this sentence refers to *two groups.* Eliminate (C) and (D) because *across* and *next* do not mean "in the middle of." The correct answer is (A).

72. **H** Vocabulary is changing in the answer choices, so this question is testing word choice. The underlined portion describes the simplicity of the goals—more specifically, that the goals seem simple. The word *simple* is an adjective, and words describing adjectives must be adverbs. The correct adverb is *seemingly.* Eliminate (F) and (J) because neither includes *seemingly.* Compare (G) and (H). The word *more* is not necessary to convey the meaning of the adverb, so it is not needed. Eliminate (G). The correct answer is (H).

73. **B** Verbs are changing in the answer choices, so the question is testing consistency of verbs. To be consistent, the verb must match the subject in terms of number and tense. The subject of the verb is either *effort*, which is singular, or *efforts*, which is plural. For each choice, consider whether the verb at the end matches the subject at the beginning. Eliminate (A) because it includes the singular subject *effort* and the plural verb *have*. Keep (B) because it includes the plural subject *efforts* and the plural verb *have*. Eliminate (C) because it includes the plural subject *efforts* and the singular verb *has*. Eliminate (D) because it includes the past-tense verb *had*, but the other verbs in the paragraph are in present tense. The correct answer is (B).

74. **F** Vocabulary is changing in the answers, so the question is testing word choice. Determine what meaning of the underlined portion would be consistent with the sentence. The underlined portion should mean something like "work." Keep (F) because *serve* means "work." Eliminate (G) and (J) because *distribute* and *deliver* both mean "hand out." Eliminate (H) because *provide* means "supply." The correct answer is (F).

75. **C** Note the question! The question asks which option *most clearly shows that the self-sacrifice of the doctors deserves praise*. Check each answer choice to see whether it references *praise* for the doctors' actions. Eliminate (A) because while the doctors' *dignified actions* are mentioned, the focus is on eliminating the need for *Doctors Without Borders*. Eliminate (B) because while the doctors' *conviction* and *courage* are mentioned, the focus is on the narrator's personal opinions. Keep (C) because it references the *courage* of the doctors and how it *should be a lesson to us all*. Eliminate (D) because while the doctors are referenced, the focus is on the doctors' safety instead of their *sacrifice*. The correct answer is (C).

MATHEMATICS TEST

1. **D** The question asks for the second term in a geometric sequence. The question states that, in such a sequence, *the quotient of any two consecutive terms is the same*. The third term is 8 and the fourth term is 16. The *quotient* is the result of division, so $\frac{3rd}{4th} = \frac{8}{16}$. This reduces to $\frac{1}{2}$, and this will also be the quotient of the second and third terms. This becomes $\frac{2nd}{3rd} = \frac{1}{2}$ or $\frac{x}{8} = \frac{1}{2}$. Cross-multiply to get $2x = 8$, then divide both sides by two to get $x = 4$. It is also possible to plug in the answers to see which gives the quotient of $\frac{1}{2}$ when the answer is divided by 8. Either way, the correct answer is (D).

2. **G** The question asks for the value of a function. In function notation, the number inside the parentheses is the x-value that goes into the function, and the value that comes out of the function is the y-value. This function is defined in terms of a and b and the question asks for the value of $f(3,4)$. Plug 3 for a and 4 for b into the f function to get $f(3,4) = 2(3)(4) - (3 + 4)$. This simplifies to $24 - 7 = 17$. The correct answer is (G).

3. **D** The question asks for the fewest number of coins that can be used to make a purchase. In order to minimize the number of coins, Christine must use as many high-value coins as she can. The highest value coins she has are quarters, worth 25 cents each. Find the greatest multiple of 25 that is less than 99: $25 \times 1 = 25$; $25 \times 2 = 50$; $25 \times 3 = 75$; $25 \times 4 = 100$. Thus, Christine can use at most 3 quarters, for a total of 75 cents. She now has $99 - 75 = 24$ cents left to pay. The next highest value coins she has are dimes, worth 10 cents each. Find the greatest multiple of 10 that is less than 24: $10 \times 2 = 20$. Thus, she can use at most 2 dimes, for an additional 20 cents. She needs $99 - 75 - 20 = 4$ more cents to get to the 99 cents she needs, so she cannot use any nickels. She must use 4 pennies, bringing her number of coins to $3 + 2 + 4 = 9$. The correct answer is (D).

4. **K** The question asks for the area of a square with a side length of 8 inches. Use the Geometry Basic Approach. Start by drawing a square and labeling it with the given information. Label all four sides as 8. Then write out the formula for the area of a square: $A = s^2$. Plug in $s = 8$ to get $A = 8^2 = 64$. The correct answer is (K).

5. **A** The question asks for the value of the expression if $x = 3$. Plug $x = 3$ into the expression to get $\dfrac{(3+1)^2}{3^2-1}$. This simplifies to $\dfrac{4^2}{9-1} = \dfrac{16}{8} = 2$. The correct answer is (A).

6. **H** The question asks for the choice that is NOT a factor of 1,776. The question asks for a specific value and the answers contain numbers in increasing order, so plug in the answers. A factor divides evenly into the given number, so go through the choices and determine whether the result of dividing 1,776 by that choice results in an integer. Choice (F) becomes $1,776 \div 12 = 148$. This means that 12 is a factor of 1,776, so eliminate (F). Choice (G) becomes $1,776 \div 16 = 111$. Eliminate (G). Choice (H) becomes $1,776 \div 18 = 98.\overline{66}$. This is not an integer, so 18 is not a factor of 1,776. The correct answer is (H).

7. **C** The question asks for a probability, which is defined as $\dfrac{want}{total}$. Read the question carefully to find the numbers for *want* and *total*. There is only one student, Lauren, that the probability refers to, so the number for *want* is 1. The student selected must NOT be a senior. Of the students in the class, 4 are seniors, so $19 - 4 = 15$ are NOT seniors. Lauren is NOT a senior, so the *total* is 15. Therefore, the probability that Lauren is chosen is $\dfrac{1}{15}$. The correct answer is (C).

8. **K** The question asks for the value of x. Since the question asks for a specific value and the answers contain numbers in increasing order, Plugging In the Answers is an option. Begin by labeling the answers as "x" and start in the middle with (H), 9. The equation becomes $4(9 - 5) + 9 = 45$. Simplify the left side of the equation to $4(4) + 9 = 45$, then to $16 + 9 = 45$, and finally $25 = 45$. This is not true, so eliminate (H). Because the result was too small, try a larger number like (K), 13. The equation becomes $4(13 - 5) + 13 = 45$, which simplifies to $4(8) + 13 = 45$, and then to $32 + 13 = 45$. This is true, so stop here. Another way to answer this is to solve for x algebraically. Start by distributing on the left side of the equation to get $4x - 20 + x = 45$. Then combine like terms to get $5x - 20 = 45$. Add 20 to both sides of the equation to get $5x = 65$; then divide both sides by 5 to get $x = 13$. Either way, the correct answer is (K).

9. **B**   The question asks for an expression that models a specific situation. Translate the English to math in bite-sized pieces and eliminate after each piece. The number of miles will be represented as m, and Joe pays *$0.99 for each mile he drives*. Therefore, the cost for the miles can be represented as $0.99m$. Eliminate (C), (D), and (E), because these don't include this expression. The question also states that there is a charge of *$112 for the weekend*, so that must be added to the cost. Choice (A) subtracts 112 instead of adding it, so eliminate (A). The correct answer is (B).

10. **K**   The question asks how much more than the purchase price Stella will pay with the payment plan. Calculate her cost with the plan, on which she pays *$130 a month for 4 years*. There are 12 months in a year, so Stella will make payments for $4 \times 12 = 48$ months. Multiply the amount per month by the number of months to get a total payment of $130(48) = \$6,240$. The phrase *how much more* means to subtract, so subtract the purchase price from the amount Stella pays with the payment plan. This results in a difference of $\$6,240 - \$4,800 = \$1,440$. The correct answer is (K).

11. **B**   The question asks for an equivalent expression with exponents. Work in bite-sized pieces and use Process of Elimination. Start with the coefficients. The 20 in the numerator will be divided by the 4 in the denominator to get a coefficient of 5. Eliminate (D) and (E), because those do not include 5. Now work with the exponents, remembering the MADSPM rules. The DS part of the acronym indicates that Dividing matching bases means to Subtract the exponents. The y term becomes $y^{8-2} = y^6$. Eliminate (A) and (C). The correct answer is (B).

12. **F**   The question asks for a value that is equal to the given fraction. The most accurate way to handle this is to turn the fractions within the numerator and the denominator into decimals and use a calculator to find the value of the fraction. The $\frac{1}{2}$ in the numerator can be written as 0.5, and the $\frac{3}{4}$ in the denominator can be written as 0.75. The entire fraction becomes $\frac{3-0.5}{2+0.75} = \frac{2.5}{2.75}$. Use a calculator to find that this is equal to $0.\overline{90}$. This is less than 1, so the answer must be (F). To verify that (F) is less than 1, calculate $\frac{10}{11}$, which does equal $0.\overline{90}$. The correct answer is (F).

13. **D**   The question asks for the possible locations of D on a number line. Use the Geometry Basic Approach. Start by drawing a number line and labeling it with Point C at 3.5. Add 8.5 to find the point to the right of C at $3.5 + 8.5 = 12$. Eliminate (A), (B), and (C), because these do not contain the value 12. Now subtract 8.5 from 3.5 to find the point to the left of C at $3.5 - 8.5 = -5$. Eliminate (E). The correct answer is (D).

14. **K**   The question asks for the fourth number in a set with a mean of 7. Since the question asks for a specific value and the answers contain numbers in increasing order, Plugging In the Answers is an option. Begin by labeling the answers as "fourth number" and start in the middle with (H), 8. Use the formula $T = AN$, in which T is the total, A is the average, and N is the number of things to calculate the average with the answer choice as the fourth number. If the four numbers are 2, 4, 8, and 10, the total is $2 + 4 + 8 + 10 = 24$. There are 4 numbers, so the formula becomes $24 = A(4)$. Divide both sides of the equation by 4 to get $A = 6$. According to the question, the average is 7, so this is wrong.

Eliminate (H). The result was too small, so try a larger number, like (K), 12. Now the total becomes 2 + 4 + 10 + 12 = 28. The number of things is still 4, so the formula becomes 28 = A(4). Divide both sides by 4 to get A = 7. This matches the value given in the question, so stop here. Another option is to use T = AN to find the total. The average is 7, and the number of things is 4, so T = (7)(4) = 28. The three numbers already on the list are 2, 4, and 10, which add up to 16. The fourth number must be the difference between the total of the given three numbers and the total of all four numbers, so the fourth number is 28 − 16 = 12. Either way, the correct answer is (K).

15. **A** The question asks for the net profit in 2008 given the trend from 2007 to 2009. The net profit in 2007 was $1,489,000, and the net profit in 2009 was $1,725,000. If the net profit *increased linearly*, then the net profit for 2008 must be between these two values. Eliminate (D) and (E), both of which are greater than $1,725,000. Now find the value exactly in between the given ones by adding those together and dividing the sum by 2. This becomes $\frac{\$1,489,000 + \$1,725,000}{2} = \frac{\$3,214,000}{2} = \$1,607,000$. The correct answer is (A).

16. **F** The question asks for a measurement and gives lengths in inches and feet. When dealing with scale maps or models, make a proportion, being sure to match up dimensions. The proportion is $\frac{10 \text{ inches tall}}{6 \text{ feet tall}} = \frac{8 \text{ inches wide}}{x \text{ feet wide}}$. Cross-multiply to get 10x = 48. Divide both sides of the equation by 10 to get x = 4.8 feet wide. The question asks for the approximate width, so round to 5 feet. The correct answer is (F).

17. **B** The question asks for the equation of a line in *slope-intercept form*. In this form, y = mx + b, so solve the given equation for y. Start by adding y to both sides of the equation to get 5x = y + 2. Subtract 2 from both sides to get 5x − 2 = y, and then switch the sides of the equation to get y = 5x − 2. The correct answer is (B).

18. **J** The question asks for a value equal to the given expression, so simplify the expression. With absolute values, work inside the absolute value symbol first. The expression becomes |−12| − |−25|. Next, make the values inside the absolute values positive. This becomes 12 − 25 = −13. The correct answer is (J).

19. **D** The question asks for the best descriptor of an angle in a triangle. Use the Geometry Basic Approach. Start by drawing a triangle and labeling it with the given information. Make ∠K exactly 63° for simplicity. It will look like this:

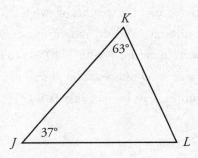

There are 180° in a triangle, so the measure of $\angle L$ is 180° – 37° – 63° = 80°. Eliminate (A) and (B) based on this calculation. Choices (C), (D), and (E) all include the possibility that $\angle L$ is 80°, so try a different measure for $\angle K$, such as 60°. The new measure of $\angle L$ is 180° – 37° – 60° = 83°. Eliminate (C) and (E). The correct answer is (D).

20. **K** The question asks for the least possible integer value of x. One option is to solve the inequality for x. Start by adding 1 to both sides of the inequality to get $3x > 27$. Divide both sides by 3 to get $x > 9$. The only choice that is greater than 9 is 10, which is (K). Since the question asks for a specific value and the answers contain numbers in increasing order, Plugging In the Answers is also an option. Begin by labeling the answers as "x" and start with (F), 6, because that is the least value. The inequality becomes $3(6) – 1 > 26$, which simplifies to $18 – 1 > 26$ or $17 > 26$. This is not true, so eliminate (F). The value on the left of the inequality was much too small, so consider skipping (G) and trying a greater number next, such as 8 in (H). The inequality becomes $3(8) – 1 > 26$, which becomes $24 – 1 > 26$, or $23 > 26$. This is not true and is still too small on the left side, so try (J) next. If $x = 9$, the inequality becomes $3(9) – 1 > 26$, then $27 – 1 > 26$, or $26 > 26$. This is still not true, so the value of x must be greater than 9. Try 10 just to be certain: the inequality becomes $3(10) – 1 > 26$, then $30 – 1 > 26$, and finally $29 > 26$. This is true. Either way, the correct answer is (K).

21. **E** The question asks for the measure of an angle on a figure. Use the Geometry Basic Approach. Start by Ballparking. The angle labeled 62° is smaller than the one asked for, so the answer must be greater than 62. Eliminate (A). The angle in question also looks to be obtuse, or greater than 90°, so it is likely safe to eliminate (B) and (C) as well. Next, label the figure with the given information, which is that the two gray bars representing red ribbons are parallel. When parallel lines are cut by a third line (or a set of parallel lines such as the edges of the white ribbon), two kinds of angles are created: big and small. All small angles are equal, and all big angles are equal. The sum of any big angle and any small angle is 180°. The angle labeled 62° is a small angle, and the angle labeled with the question mark is a big angle, which can be called x. Therefore, $x + 62° = 180°$. Subtract 62° from both sides of the equation to get $x = 118°$. The correct answer is (E).

22. **G** The question asks for the length of $\overline{QR}$ on the figure. Use the Geometry Basic Approach. Start by Ballparking: the hypotenuse of the triangle is 10 inches, so the length of $\overline{PR}$ must be less than that. Eliminate (J) and (K), as both are too long to be half the length of one leg on the triangle. Use the Pythagorean Theorem ($a^2 + b^2 = c^2$) or recognize that this triangle is a Pythagorean triple (6-8-10) to find that $\overline{PR}$ is 6 inches long. Label $\overline{PR}$ as 6. Because point Q is the midpoint of $\overline{PR}$, it divides this length in half, so $\overline{QR} = 6 \div 2 = 3$. The correct answer is (G).

23. **A** The question asks for the difference in the weights of two textbooks. Look up the values on the graph. The number of pages is on the x-axis, and the weight in ounces is on the y-axis. For a book with an x-value of 1,056 pages, the corresponding y-value is 107.8 ounces. For a book with an x-value of 868 pages, the corresponding y-value is 89 ounces. The phrase *how much more* means to subtract, so this becomes $107.8 – 89 = 18.8$ ounces. The correct answer is (A).

24. **G**   The question asks for the weight of a textbook in pounds given an equation relating the number of pages to the weight in ounces. Start by plugging the number of pages into the equation $y = 0.1x + 2.2$ to get the weight in ounces. The x-value is the number of pages, so the equation becomes $y = 0.1(1,338) + 2.2 = 133.8 + 2.2 = 136$ ounces. The question asks for the weight in pounds, so convert ounces to pounds. The note below the question states that there are 16 ounces in a pound, so set up a proportion, being sure to match the units: $\dfrac{16 \text{ ounces}}{1 \text{ pound}} = \dfrac{136 \text{ ounces}}{x \text{ pounds}}$. Cross-multiply to get $16x = 136$; then divide by 16 to get $x = 8.5$. The correct answer is (G).

25. **D**   The question asks for the area of a polygon. Use the Geometry Basic Approach. There is a figure provided and it is labeled, so use the formulas for area. There is no formula for the area of an irregular shape like this, so divide the figure into rectangles. One way to do it is like this:

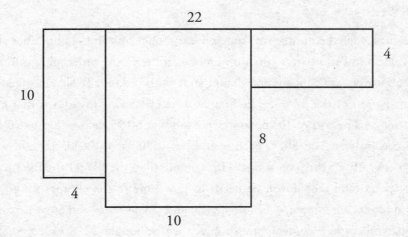

Then write out the formula for the area of a rectangle: $A = lw$. For the rectangle on the left side of the figure, the formula becomes $A = (10)(4) = 40$. Now figure out the other dimensions. The length across the top of the figure is 22. Since all lines meet at right angles, the horizontal lengths across the lower part of the figure must all be parallel to the top and must cover the same distance. Therefore, for the rectangle on the right side of the figure, the width will be $22 - 4 - 10 = 8$. Label the figure with this information. For that rectangle, the area formula becomes $A = (8)(4) = 32$. Now find the missing dimension on the rectangle in the middle of the figure. Just as the horizontal dimensions of the overall figure were the same, the vertical dimensions will all be the same. Therefore, the sum of the vertical sides on the right have the same measurement as the missing side of the middle rectangle. This becomes $4 + 8 = 12$, and the area of that rectangle becomes $A = (12)(10) = 120$. Now add the areas of all three rectangles to get the total area as $40 + 32 + 120 = 192$. The correct answer is (D).

26. **F**   The question asks for the average speed for part of the time Mr. Baylor spent grading essays. Use the formula $T = AN$, in which T is the total, A is the average, and N is the number of things. For the first 3 days, the average is 178 and the number of things is 3, so $T = (178)(3) = 534$. The total for all 6 days is 996, so subtract the total he graded over the first 3 days to find that he graded $996 - 534 = 462$ essays

in the final 3 days. Use the average formula again with a total of 462 and a number of things of 3 to get $462 = A(3)$; then divide both sides of the equation by 3 to get $A = 154$. The correct answer is (F).

27. **C** The question asks for an equivalent expression. Although there are variables in the answer choices, plugging in on this question might be difficult, given several terms and negative signs. Instead, distribute each term in the first set of parentheses to each in the second set, being careful with the signs. The result is $y^3 - 3y^2 + 2y + y^2 - 3y + 2$. Combine like terms to get $y^3 - 2y^2 - y + 2$. The correct answer is (C).

28. **H** The question asks for a trigonometric expression that relates to angle D and has a value of $\dfrac{4}{5}$. In relation to angle D, the side labeled as 4 is the adjacent side, and the side labeled as 5 is the hypotenuse. Write out SOHCAHTOA to remember the trig functions. The CAH part defines cosine as $\dfrac{adjacent}{hypotenuse}$, so $\cos D = \dfrac{4}{5}$. The correct answer is (H).

29. **A** The question asks for the number of contemporary songs Shawn bought. Since the question asks for a specific value and the answers contain numbers in increasing order, plug in the answers. Begin by labeling the answers as "contemporary" and start with (C), 10. If Shawn bought 10 contemporary songs, then the rest of the 22 songs he bought were classical. This means that he bought $22 - 10 = 12$ classical songs. The cost of 10 contemporary songs at \$0.95 each would be $10(\$0.95) = \$9.50$. The cost of 12 classical songs at \$0.75 each would be $12(\$0.75) = \$9.00$. Together, Shawn would have spent $\$9.50 + \$9.00 = \$18.50$ on songs. This is more than the \$17.90 that he spent, so eliminate (C). To bring Shawn's total cost down, he needs to buy more of the cheaper songs, which means more classical and fewer contemporary. Eliminate (D) and (E), as these will only increase Shawn's cost. Try (B), 9. If Shawn bought 9 contemporary songs, then he bought $22 - 9 = 13$ classical songs. The cost of 9 contemporary songs would be $9(\$0.95) = \$8.55$. The cost of 13 classical songs would be $13(\$0.75) = \$9.75$. Together, Shawn would have spent $\$8.55 + \$9.75 = \$18.30$ on songs. This is still more than the \$17.90 that he spent, so eliminate (B). Because the result of (B) was less than the result of (C), a smaller starting value is needed. Only one smaller answer remains. The correct answer is (A).

30. **G** The question asks for the value of operation $(-3)\#(-7)$ as defined as $x \# y = \dfrac{x^2 - y^2}{x + y}$. Because the x value is to the left of the # sign and the y value is to the right, $x = -3$ and $y = -7$. Plug these values into the operation to get $\dfrac{(-3)^2 - (-7)^2}{(-3) + (-7)}$, which simplifies to $\dfrac{9 - 49}{-10} = \dfrac{-40}{-10} = 4$. The correct answer is (G).

31. **C** The question asks for the fraction of the punch that is pineapple juice. To make this fraction, put the quantity of pineapple juice in the numerator and the quantity of punch in the denominator. Making a fraction with mixed numbers and fractions in both the numerator and denominator can be tricky, so convert both numbers to decimals. The quantity of pineapple juice can be written as 0.5 gallons, and the quantity of punch can be written as 2.25 gallons. The fraction becomes $\dfrac{0.5}{2.25}$. Use a calculator

to find that this is $0.\overline{2}$. Now use the calculator to see which answer choice also has this value. Choice (A) becomes $0.\overline{1}$, so eliminate (A). Choice (B) becomes $0.\overline{16}$, so eliminate (B). Choice (C) becomes $0.\overline{2}$. This matches the calculation above, so stop here. The correct answer is (C).

32. **G**   The question asks for the area of a triangle inscribed in a circle. Use the Geometry Basic Approach. Start by labeling the figure with the given information. Label $\overline{XZ}$ as 8 and $\overline{OX}$ as equal to $\overline{XY}$. Next, write the formula for the area of a triangle: $A = \frac{1}{2}bh$. A base and a height are needed for the triangle, so try to determine some of the other measurements. If $\overline{XZ}$ is a diameter, then $\overline{OX}$ is a radius and is half the diameter, or 4. Label $\overline{OX}$ and $\overline{XY}$ as 4. When a triangle is drawn in a circle such that one side of the triangle is also the diameter of the circle, and the point opposite that side is on the circle, a right triangle is created with the diameter as the hypotenuse. This means that angle Y is 90° and, because $\overline{XY}$ and $\overline{YZ}$ meet at a right angle, they can be used as the base and the height of the triangle. $\overline{XY}$ has already been marked with a length of 4, so the height is 4. The hypotenuse $\overline{XZ}$ has also been marked with a length of 8. Use the Pythagorean Theorem ($a^2 + b^2 = c^2$) or the fact that the measures of $\overline{XY}$ and $\overline{XZ}$ indicate that this is a 30°-60°-90° triangle to find that the length of $\overline{YZ}$ is $4\sqrt{3}$. The area formula becomes $A = \frac{1}{2}\left(4\sqrt{3}\right)(4) = 8\sqrt{3}$. The correct answer is (G).

33. **C**   The question asks for one of the roots of the quadratic equation, or the value of y that will make the equation true. Since the question asks for a specific value and the answers contain numbers in increasing order, Plugging In the Answers is an option. Begin by labeling the answers as "y" and start with (C), –2. The equation becomes $(-2)^2 - 4(-2) - 5 = 7$. This simplifies to $4 + 8 - 5 = 7$ or $7 = 7$. This is true, so stop here. Another option is to get the equation into the standard form, $ax^2 + bx + c = 0$, and then solve it. Subtract 7 from both sides of the equation to get $y^2 - 4y - 12 = 0$. To factor this, look for a pair of numbers that multiply to –12 and add to –4. These values are –6 and 2. The equation becomes $(y - 6)(y + 2) = 0$. Setting each binomial equal to 0 and solving results in roots of $y = 6$ and $y = -2$. Only one of these is an answer choice. Either way, the correct answer is (C).

34. **G**   The question asks for the volume of a plastic model of a house. Use the Geometry Basic Approach. There is a figure provided and it is labeled, so use the formulas for volume. There is not a formula for this shape, but formulas are given for the shape of the pyramid and the rectangular prism it sits on. Start with the rectangular prism, for which $V = lwh$. The length and width are both 20, and the height is 16, so the formula becomes $V = (20)(20)(16) = 6,400$. Now focus on the pyramid, for which $V = \frac{1}{3}lwh$. For this shape, the length and width are also 20, and the height is 12, so the formula becomes $V = \frac{1}{3}(20)(20)(12) = 1,600$. The volume of the model will be the sum of the volumes of the rectangular prism and the pyramid, so this becomes $6,400 + 1,600 = 8,000$. The correct answer is (G).

35. **B** The question asks for the height of a trapezoid. Use the Geometry Basic Approach. Start by drawing a trapezoid and labeling it with the given information. It will look like this:

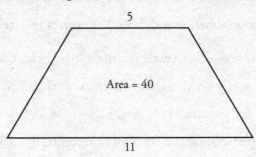

Solve for the area by dividing the trapezoid into a rectangle and two triangles. The base that is 11 inches long can be divided into 3 + 5 + 3 inches. It will look like this:

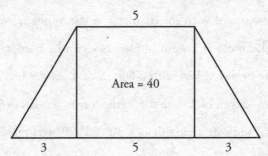

The formula for the area of a rectangle is $A = lw$ or bh, and the formula for the area of a triangle is $A = \frac{1}{2}bh$. The area of the trapezoid will be the area of the rectangle plus the area of the two triangles. Both the rectangle and the triangles have the same height. Plug in the known information to get $40 = 5h + \frac{1}{2}(3)h + \frac{1}{2}(3)h$. This simplifies to $40 = 5h + 3h$ or $40 = 8h$. Divide both sides of the equation by 8 to get $h = 5$. The correct answer is (B).

36. **J** The question asks for the slope of a line in the coordinate plane given two points $(-2, 6)$ and $(3, -9)$. Use the formula $slope = \frac{y_2 - y_1}{x_2 - x_1}$ with the given points to get $slope = \frac{6 - (-9)}{-2 - 3} = \frac{15}{-5} = -3$. The correct answer is (J).

37. **D** The question asks for the measure of an angle in a triangle. Use the Geometry Basic Approach. Start by drawing an isosceles right triangle, which has two equal legs. Label it with the given information. The question states that there is a right angle at X, so legs $\overline{WX}$ and $\overline{XY}$ are equal. The figure will look like this:

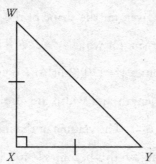

The question states that point Z is *collinear with points X and Y*. The word *collinear* means "on the same line," and the question states that Y is *between X and Z*. Add point Z to the figure.

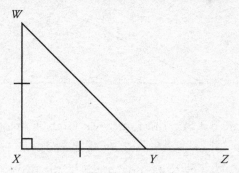

The question asks for the measure of $\angle WYZ$, which makes up a straight line with $\angle XYW$. There are $180°$ in a line, so find the measure of $\angle XYW$ and subtract it from $180°$. Because $\triangle WXY$ is isosceles, the two smaller angles are equal and measure $45°$ each. Therefore, $\angle XYW$ is $45°$ and $\angle WYZ = 180° - 45° = 135°$. The correct answer is (D).

38. **H**   The question asks for a certain digit in a repeating decimal. Determine the pattern of the repeating decimal rather than trying to write it out to the 99th place to the right of the decimal. There are 6 numbers before the pattern repeats: 384615. This pattern of 6 numbers will repeat, so every 6th digit will be the last number in the pattern: 5. Look for a multiple of 6 that is near 99. The closest one is 96, so the 96th digit is 5. Following the pattern, the 97th digit is 3, the 98th digit is 8, and the 99th digit is 4. The correct answer is (H).

39. **B**   The question asks for the ordered pair (a, b), in which a and b are part of the notation of vectors $\mathbf{u}$ and $\mathbf{v}$. In unit vector notation, $\mathbf{i}$ represents the change in the x value, and $\mathbf{j}$ represents the change in the y value. The coefficients of $\mathbf{i}$ and $\mathbf{j}$ are known for $\mathbf{u} + \mathbf{v}$, so find that sum. To add $\mathbf{u}$ and $\mathbf{v}$, add the $\mathbf{i}$ values and the $\mathbf{j}$ values: $\mathbf{u} + \mathbf{v} = (a + 2)\mathbf{i} + (5 + b)\mathbf{j}$. The question states that $\mathbf{u} + \mathbf{v} = 4\mathbf{i} - 3\mathbf{j}$, so $(a + 2)\mathbf{i} + (5 + b)\mathbf{j} = 4\mathbf{i} - 3\mathbf{j}$. Look at the $\mathbf{i}$ terms first: $(a + 2)\mathbf{i} = 4\mathbf{i}$, so $(a + 2) = 4$, and $a = 2$. Eliminate (A), (D), and (E), which do not have this value for a. Now, look at the $\mathbf{j}$ terms: $(5 + b)\mathbf{j} = -3\mathbf{j}$, so $5 + b = -3$, and $b = -8$. The ordered pair (a, b) is $(2, -8)$. The correct answer is (B).

40. **H**   The question asks for the vertical asymptote of a function. An asymptote is a line that a function approaches but never reaches. A rational function has a vertical asymptote anywhere that the function is undefined, which occurs when the denominator is zero. Set the denominator equal to zero and solve for x. This becomes $2x - 6 = 0$, so $2x = 6$, and $x = 3$. The correct answer is (H).

41. **D**   The question asks for a true statement based on a geometric figure. Use the Geometry Basic Approach. A figure is provided, but when determining what *must be true*, it is often necessary to redraw it based on the information given. The question states that $\overline{JK}$ is parallel to $\overline{MN}$. A new figure with the same information could look like the one on the following page.

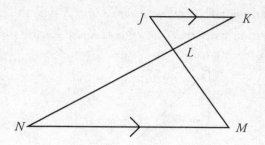

When parallel lines are cut by a third line, two kinds of angles are created: big and small. All small angles are equal, and all big angles are equal. Because $\overline{JK}$ is parallel to $\overline{MN}$, $\angle K$ is equal to $\angle N$, and $\angle J$ is equal to $\angle M$. The remaining angles in the two triangles are also equal, because they are opposite one another. Now use Process of Elimination on the answer choices. Choice (A) says that $\overline{JK}$ and $\overline{MN}$ are equal. Though they appear to be in the original drawing, the new drawing shows that they are not necessarily equal. Eliminate (A). Choice (B) says that $\overline{JL}$ and $\overline{LM}$ are equal, but this is not necessarily true either. Eliminate (B). Choice (C) says that the two triangles are congruent. Again, the new drawing shows that while they could be, they don't have to be. Eliminate (C). Choice (D) says that the two triangles are *similar*. Similar triangles have the same angles and proportional sides, and this is true of the triangles in the figure. Keep (D), but check (E) just in case. Choice (E) says that $\overline{JM}$ *bisects* $\overline{KN}$, which means it divides $\overline{KN}$ into two equal pieces. This could be true but could be false. Eliminate (E). The correct answer is (D).

42. **H** The question asks for the minimum number of caps that must be sold to cover the one-time rental fee. Since the question asks for a specific value and the answers contain numbers in increasing order, plug in the answers. Begin by labeling the answers as "number of caps" and start with the smallest value, which is 14 in (F). Each cap costs the athletic department $3.50 and is sold for $5.00. The profit on one hat is $5.00 − $3.50 = $1.50. If 14 caps were sold, the profit would be 14($1.50) = $21.00. The question states that the one-time fee is $23.00, so this is not enough to cover the fee. Eliminate (F). Try (G) next. The profit on 15 caps would be 15($1.50) = $22.50, which is still not quite enough. Eliminate (G). Try (H). The profit on 16 caps would be 16($1.50) = $24, which makes the profit enough to cover the $23 fee, so stop here. The correct answer is (H).

43. **A** The question asks for the percent by which the budget gap would have been filled if the price of each adult ticket had been raised by $2.00. Translate the English to math, read carefully, and use bite-sized pieces. The department sold 540 tickets, and 60% of those were adult tickets. Take 60% of 540 to find that the number of adult tickets sold was $\frac{60}{100}(540) = 324$. An increase of $2 per ticket would result in increased revenue of $2(324) = $648. The question states that the budget gap was $3,000. To find the percent that 648 is out of 3,000, divide the numbers and multiply by 100 to get $\frac{648}{3,000} \times 100 = 21.6\%$. The question asks for an approximate percent, so round this to 22%. The correct answer is (A).

44. **J**   The question asks for the minimum number of T-shirts the athletic department sold if they filled the budget gap. Since the question asks for a specific value and the answers contain numbers in increasing order, plug in the answers. Begin by labeling the answers as "number of T-shirts" and, because the question asks for the minimum, start with the least value, which is 1,480 in (F). Each T-shirt costs the athletic department $2.25 and is sold for $4.00. The profit on one T-shirt is $4.00 – $2.25 = $1.75. If 1,480 T-shirts were sold, the profit would be 1,480($1.75) = $2,590.00. The question states that the budget gap is $3,000, and they must also pay the one-time rental fee of $19.00. This is not enough to fill the gap and cover the fee. Eliminate (F). Because the result using the value in (F) is much too small, consider skipping (G) and trying the value in (H) next. If 1,709 T-shirts were sold, the profit would be 1,709($1.75) = $2,990.75, which is still not enough. Eliminate (G) and (H). Try (J). If 1,726 T-shirts were sold, the profit would be 1,726($1.75) = $3,020.50, which is enough to cover the budget gap and the fee, so stop here. The correct answer is (J).

45. **C**   The question asks for the area of a triangle formed within a parabola in the coordinate plane. Use the Geometry Basic Approach. A figure is provided, but the triangle is not drawn, so start by connecting points D, E, and O. Then write out the formula for the area of a triangle: $A = \frac{1}{2}bh$. The base and height must be perpendicular, so make $\overline{DE}$ the base, and make the distance on the x-axis from O to $\overline{DE}$ the height. The base goes from $y = 2$ to $y = -2$, so the base is $2 - (-2) = 2 + 2 = 4$. Points D and E appear to have y-coordinates of 2 and –2, respectively, but check by plugging $x = 4$ into the equation. If $y^2 = 4$, then $y = \pm 2$. Thus, the height is also $2 - (-2) = 2 + 2 = 4$. Now plug the values for the base and height into the formula to get $A = \frac{1}{2}(4)(4) = 8$. The correct answer is (C).

46. **K**   The question asks for the length of $\overline{YZ}$ in the triangle. The note below the question relates to sines, and the law of sines can be used when two pairs of angles and the sides opposite them are known or needed. The law of sines states that in a triangle, the ratio of the sine of any angle to the length of the side opposite that angle is equal to the same ratio for any other angle in the triangle. Here, that means that $\frac{\sin X}{YZ} = \frac{\sin Y}{XZ} = \frac{\sin Z}{XY}$. The length of $\overline{XY}$ is given as 12, and the length of $\overline{YZ}$ is needed, so use the first and third fractions in the ratios. Thus, $\frac{\sin X}{YZ} = \frac{\sin Z}{XY}$ becomes $\frac{68}{YZ} = \sin \frac{53}{12}$. Cross-multiply to get $(0.799)(YZ) = 11.124$; then divide both sides by 0.799 to get $XY \approx 13.9$. The correct answer is (K).

47. **C**   The question asks for solutions to $x = 3 \pm \sqrt{(-1)(16c^2)}$ expressed as complex numbers. Use bite-sized pieces and Process of Elimination to tackle this question. All the answers start with 3 ±, so focus on the square root. To make it easier to see what can come out from under the root, factor the expression

under the root symbol to $\sqrt{(-1)(16)(c^2)}$. The 16 and the c^2 are perfect squares, so these become 4 and c, respectively. Eliminate any answer that does not contain 4 and c, and only (C) remains. To check, bring those two terms in front of the root to leave $4c\sqrt{-1}$. The imaginary number i is defined as $\sqrt{-1}$, so this becomes $4ci$. The correct answer is (C).

48. **J** The question asks for the length of the diameter of a circle. Use the Geometry Basic Approach. Start by labeling the figure with the given information. Label CD as 12. It may be difficult to determine how to find the diameter, but this value is equal to 2 times the radius. The most useful radii to draw will be the ones that connect O to C and O to D, as this creates a triangle. To solve difficult geometry questions, it is often necessary to use the information about one shape to determine the measurements of another shape. For the new triangle, the measure of the central angle COD equals the measure of the arc it creates, so $\angle COD = 60°$. The radii CO and DO are equal, so angles OCD and ODC are equal. There are 180° in a triangle, so there are $180° - 60° = 120°$ left for angles OCD and ODC. Because the angles are equal, each angle is $120° \div 2 = 60°$, so triangle COD is equilateral. Therefore, $CD = CO = DO = 12$. If the radius is 12, then the diameter is $2(12) = 24$. The correct answer is (J).

49. **E** The question asks for the distance between the pole and the point where the cord touches the ground. Use the Geometry Basic Approach. Start by drawing a pole and the cord and labeling it with the given information. Label the length of the cord as 25 feet and the angle it makes with the ground as 19°. It will look like this:

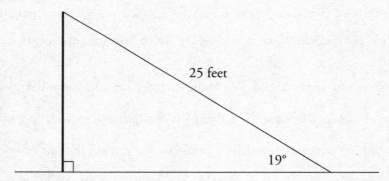

The question asks for the distance between the pole and the cord on the ground, so this is the base of the triangle. Label that as x. There are trigonometric expressions in the answer choices, so write out SOHCAHTOA to remember the trig functions. In relation to the angle that is 19°, the base of the triangle is the adjacent side, and the side labeled as 25 is the hypotenuse. The CAH part defines cosine as $\dfrac{adjacent}{hypotenuse}$, so $\cos 19° = \dfrac{x}{25}$. Multiply both sides of the equation by 25 to get $25 \cos 19° = x$. The correct answer is (E).

50. **F** The question asks for the coordinates of the center of a circle in the coordinate plane. The equation of a circle in standard form is $(x - h)^2 + (y - k)^2 = r^2$, in which (h, k) is the center and r is the radius. To get the given equation into this form, it is necessary to complete the square for the x terms and the y terms.

Start by moving the constant 8 to the right side by subtracting it from both sides of the equation to get $x^2 + 8x + y^2 - 2y = -8$. To complete the square for x, take half the coefficient on the x term, square it, and then add it to both sides. The coefficient is 8, half that is 4, and the square of that is 16. Adding 16 to both sides results in $x^2 + 8x + 16 + y^2 - 2y = -8 + 16$. The x terms can now be written as $(x + 4)^2$. Set this equal to $(x - h)^2$ to find the x-coordinate of the center, h. This becomes $(x - h)^2 = (x + 4)^2$, so take the square root of both sides to get $x - h = x + 4$. Subtract x from both sides to get $-h = 4$, so $h = -4$. Eliminate (G), (H), (J), and (K), which do not have this as the x-coordinate. The correct answer is (F).

51. **C** The question asks for the day on which the measurement of the pool will indicate that it is less than half full. For long word problems, read carefully and use bite-sized pieces. The question states that the depth of the pool is 8 feet and the volume of the pool is 13,000 gallons. Either measurement can be used to determine when the pool is *half full*: it will be when the water is at a depth of 4 feet or when the volume is 6,500 gallons. It may be easier to use smaller numbers, so focus on the depth. When Scott measures it on Day 1, it is 10% less than it was when full, so the depth is $8 - \dfrac{10}{100}(8) = 8 - 0.8 = 7.2$ feet. Another way to think about this is that each day, the depth of the pool is 90% of the depth from the previous day. This can simplify the calculation that needs to be made for each day. When Scott measures it on Day 2, the depth is $(7.2)(0.9) = 6.48$ feet. On Day 3, the depth is $(6.48)(0.9) = 5.832$ feet. On Day 4, the depth is $(5.832)(0.9) = 5.2488$ feet. On Day 5, the depth is $(5.2488)(0.9) = 4.72392$ feet. This is still not *less than half full*, so eliminate (A), which indicates Day 5. On Day 6, the depth is $(4.72392)(0.9) = 4.251528$ feet. Eliminate (B). On Day 7, the depth is $(4.251528)(0.9) = 3.8263752$ feet. This is the first value less than 4, so the pool is *less than half full* on Day 7. The correct answer is (C).

52. **H** The question asks for the determinant of the matrix $\begin{bmatrix} 3 & -5 \\ -4 & 9 \end{bmatrix}$. Given a matrix $\begin{bmatrix} a & b \\ c & d \end{bmatrix}$, the determinant is $ad - bc$. For this matrix, 3 is in the upper left corner and 9 is in the lower right, so these are the a and d values from the definition, respectively. Similarly, -5 corresponds to b and -4 corresponds to c in the definition matrix. Plug in the appropriate values to get $ad - bc = (3)(9) - (-5)(-4) = 27 - 20 = 7$. The correct answer is (H).

53. **D** The question asks for the area of one circle within the figure. Use the Geometry Basic Approach. Start by labeling the figure with the given information. Label all four sides of the square as 24. Then write out the formula for the area of a circle: $A = \pi r^2$. To solve difficult geometry questions, it is often necessary to use the information about one shape to determine the measurements of another shape. The circles are tangent to the square, which means that the length of a side of the square is equivalent to the sum of the diameters of two circles. All the circles are congruent, so each has a diameter of

$24 \div 2 = 12$. The radius is half the diameter, so the radius is $12 \div 2 = 6$. Plug $r = 6$ into the area formula to get $A = \pi(6)^2 = 36\pi$. The correct answer is (D).

54. **F** The question asks *how much more* one average value will be than another. For long word problems, read carefully and use bite-sized pieces. The question says that Andy bought 30 comics at $28.95 each. The total he paid for them was 30($28.95) = $868.50. He will sell them when the value is *$600 more than he paid for them.* Add this to the total he paid to get $868.50 + $600 = $1,468.50. To find the average value at that time, use the formula $T = AN$, in which T is the total, A is the average, and N is the number of things. The total is $1,468.50, and the number of things is 30, so $1,468.50 = A(30)$. Divide both sides of the equation by 30 to get $48.95 = A$. Finally, to find *how much more* the average value has risen, find the difference between this and the current value of $34.35. The result is $48.95 – $34.35 = $14.60. The correct answer is (F).

55. **B** The question asks for the length of $\overline{BD}$ on the figure. Use the Geometry Basic Approach. There is a figure provided and it is labeled, so see what else can be determined from the figure. Since B, D, and all the points between them are *collinear*, $\overline{BD}$ is a straight line. This line is made up of the diameter of circle G and the diameter of circle K, but there is some overlap in the middle. For circle G, diameter $\overline{AC}$ is labeled as 18, so diameter $\overline{BJ}$ is also 18. Label this on the figure. For circle K, diameter $\overline{CE}$ is labeled as 10, so diameter $\overline{HD}$ is also 10. Label this on the figure as well. Now it is possible to see that the overlap is the length of $\overline{HJ}$, which has a length of 3. Therefore, the length of $\overline{BD}$ is the sum of the length of $\overline{BJ}$ and only the part of $\overline{HD}$ that is not already contained in $\overline{BJ}$. This second part is $10 – 3 = 7$, so $\overline{BD} = 18 + 7 = 25$. The correct answer is (B).

56. **J** The question asks for the other point at which the parabola crosses the y-axis. Start by drawing a coordinate plane and plotting the given points. Use a calculator to determine that $\left(0, -2 + 3\sqrt{3}\right)$ is approximately (0, 3.2). Connect the points and use them to sketch the parabola. Also draw the line of symmetry at $y = -2$. It will look like this:

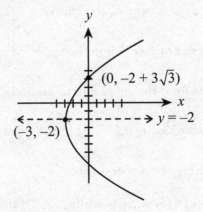

As shown in the sketch, the other point at which the parabola crosses the y-axis has a negative y-value. Eliminate (F), which indicates that there is not another y-intercept, and (G), which makes the second y-intercept positive. Choice (K) also cannot be correct, because there is a line of symmetry and both y-intercepts will be an equal distance from that line. Eliminate (K). Rather than trying to calculate the exact value of the missing y-intercept, use a calculator to estimate the locations of the points in the remaining answers. Choice (H) becomes approximately (0, –3.2). Eliminate (H). Choice (J) becomes approximately (0, –7.2). This is the only point that could work. The correct answer is (J).

57. **E** The question asks for an equivalent expression to the one given. There is a variable in the answer choices, so plug in. Make $z = 2$. The expression becomes $\dfrac{3(2)}{4-2}+\dfrac{3(2)}{2^2-16}$, which simplifies to $\dfrac{6}{2}+\dfrac{6}{-12}$. To combine the fractions, move the negative in the second denominator to the front of that fraction and reduce that fraction. The expression becomes $\dfrac{6}{2}-\dfrac{1}{2}=\dfrac{5}{2}$. This is the target value; circle it. Now plug $z = 2$ into the answer choices to see which one matches the target value. Choice (A) becomes $\dfrac{3(2)^2+15(2)}{2^2-16}=\dfrac{3(4)+30}{4-16}=\dfrac{12+30}{4-16}=\dfrac{42}{-12}=-\dfrac{14}{4}$. This does not match the target value. Eliminate (A). The remaining choices all have the same denominator, so focus on the numerators. The numerator in (B) becomes $9(2)^2 - 12(2) = 9(4) - 24 = 36 - 24 = 12$. With a denominator of –12, this becomes $\dfrac{12}{-12}=-1$. Eliminate (B). The numerator in (C) becomes $-12(2) = -24$. With a denominator of –12, this becomes $\dfrac{-24}{-12}=2$. Eliminate (C). The numerator in (D) becomes $-3(2)^2 = -3(4) = -12$. With a denominator of –12, this becomes $\dfrac{-12}{-12}=1$. Eliminate (D). The numerator in (E) becomes $-3(2)^2 - 9(2) = -3(4) - 18 = -12 - 18 = -30$. With a denominator of –12, this becomes $\dfrac{-30}{-12}=\dfrac{5}{2}$, which matches the target value. The correct answer is (E).

58. **H** The question asks for the tangent of $\pi + \theta$ in terms of a and b, the coordinates of a point on the terminal side of an angle measuring θ. The tangent function has a fundamental period of π, so the value of $\tan(\pi + \theta)$ would be equal to $\tan\theta$. Without this knowledge, sketching it out is a good way to approach this question. Use the concept of a unit circle. A radian degree measure of π represents half a revolution along the unit circle, so the angle $\pi + \theta$ is in Quadrant III, as shown below.

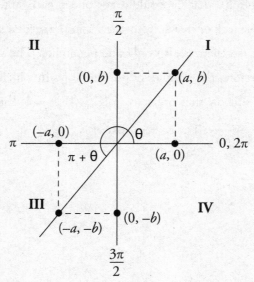

The mnemonic device All Students Take Calculus indicates that tangent is always positive in Quadrants I and III, so eliminate (G) and (J). The angle $\pi + \theta$ is a reflection of the original angle across $y = -x$, so the coordinates will be $(-a, -b)$. Write out SOHCAHTOA to remember the trig functions. The TOA part indicates that tangent $= \dfrac{opposite}{adjacent}$, which would equate to the vertical length, $-b$, divided by the horizontal length, $-a$, or $\dfrac{-b}{-a} = \dfrac{b}{a}$. The correct answer is (H).

59. **A** The question asks for the expression that gives d in terms of the other variables. Although there are variables in the answer choices, plugging in on this question would be difficult, given the four different variables. Solve this algebraically by isolating d instead. Start by subtracting a_1 from both sides of the equation to get $a_n - a_1 = dn - d$. Factor d out of both terms on the right side to get $a_n - a_1 = d(n - 1)$; then divide both sides by $(n - 1)$ to get $\dfrac{a_n - a_1}{n - 1} = d$. The correct answer is (A).

60. **H** The question asks for the probability that Susan draws a ten, jack, queen, king, and then ace from a deck of cards. Probability is defined as $\dfrac{part}{whole}$. In order to determine the total number of possible outcomes, set this problem up like a combination problem. Draw 5 spaces for the five cards she will draw. The first card could be any of the 54 cards, so put a 54 in the first spot. Since she does not replace the card that she just drew, the second card will be any of the remaining 53 cards, so place a 53 in the second spot. Using the same logic, the third space should be 52, the fourth should be 51, and the fifth should be 50. To determine the total number of possible outcomes, multiply these numbers together: there are $(54)(53)(52)(51)(50)$ possible outcomes. Now find the number of outcomes that match the outcome the question mentions. There are only four possible favorable outcomes: she could draw this combination and order of cards in any of the four suits. It is also possible to calculate the numerator by setting up another combination problem. Draw 5 spaces for the five cards. In the first space there are 4 possible 10s that she could draw: one of each suit. Once she has drawn a 10 though, there is only one possible jack of that suit, so put a 1 in the second space. The third space must be the queen of the same suit, so there is also only one possibility. The same idea applies to the spaces for the king and ace. Therefore, the number of possible ways in which she could draw a 10, jack, queen, king, ace of the same suit, in that order, is $(4)(1)(1)(1)(1) = 4$. Either way, the probability becomes $\dfrac{part}{whole} = \dfrac{4}{(54)(53)(52)(51)(50)}$. The correct answer is (H).

READING TEST

1. **B**   This reasoning question asks for a description of *Rebecca's feelings during her visit to the fields*. Read the paragraphs in the given line reference. Lines 3–14 include positive imagery, such as *a warm breeze caressed the fields* and *the fresh and savory scent* of the wheat. Lines 15–16 say, *The evening, just as dusk was falling, was always the best time to visit the fields alone*, and the paragraph goes on to say that she liked *the feeling of being embraced by a living, breathing entity*. Lines 30–42 state that Rebecca had *felt the draw* of the land and that she was here *trying to reclaim her family's heritage*. Eliminate answers that do not match this prediction. Choice (A) may be tempting, but it is incorrect because *overjoyed* is too strong to describe Rebecca's feelings: in lines 22–30, she indicates that there can be bad years on the farm. Additionally, Rebecca is not focused purely on *ownership* in those lines, but rather on her connection to the land. Eliminate (A). Keep (B) because it matches the prediction. Eliminate (C) because it is too negative to match the tone of the passage. Furthermore, although the text indicates that Rebecca's family struggled in the past, there is no indication that Rebecca faces *looming financial problems* now. Eliminate (D) because it uses words from the passage but doesn't match what the passage says: although lines 22–30 indicate that working the land can be challenging, this answer choice does not capture the positive tone conveyed in the rest of the window for the question. The correct answer is (B).

2. **J**   This reasoning question asks what the word *that* refers to, as used in line 28. Read a window around the given line reference. Lines 23–28 state, *Any farmer knows that there will be good years and bad years, and that sometimes one bad year will follow another and then another, to the point where you wonder if a good year will ever come again…Rebecca had known all of that*. The word *that* refers to the facts that were stated previously: that there will be both good and bad years and that sometimes one bad year will follow another. Eliminate answers that do not match this prediction. Eliminate (F) because although this answer is stated in the passage, it answers the wrong question: *someday, she would return* is mentioned after the word *that* and is not what the word refers to. Eliminate (G) because the phrase *far away from the soil* describes where Rebecca grew up; it does not describe what Rebecca knew. Choice (H) is not mentioned in the window for the question: it comes from another part of the passage and is not related to the phrase *Rebecca had known all of that*. Eliminate (H). Choice (J) matches the prediction, so keep it. The correct answer is (J).

3. **A**   This reasoning question asks what lines 30–42 are intended to convey about what *Rebecca believes about the land*. Read a window around the given line reference. Lines 32–36 state that Rebecca's *great-grandparents had claimed the land as their own, poured their blood, sweat, and tears into it,* and passed it down to Rebecca's parents. Lines 41–42 indicate that Rebecca intends to *reclaim her family's heritage*. Eliminate answers that do not match this prediction. Keep (A) because it matches the prediction. Eliminate (B) because the window for this question does not include evidence that the land is *beyond the control of* anyone. Eliminate (C) because the text states that Rebecca intends to reclaim the land; therefore, she does not believe that it is *not worth the trouble* to claim it. Eliminate (D) because the text gives no indication that the land is *filled with creatures*. The correct answer is (A).

4. **G** This referral question asks which aspect of *Rebecca's surroundings* is NOT mentioned within the first four paragraphs. When a question asks what is **not** mentioned in the text, eliminate answers that are mentioned. Eliminate (F) because the scents are described in lines 6–14: Rebecca inhales *the fresh and savory scent of almost-ripe wheat*, the smell of the *earth*, and the smell of coming *rain*. Keep (G) because there is no mention of how the plowed earth *feels* (only its *smell* is mentioned). Eliminate (H) because lines 28–29 state that *the land had turned on her parents and driven them far from the only home they knew*. Eliminate (J) because the *best time to visit the fields alone* is described in lines 15–16. The correct answer is (G).

5. **A** This reasoning question asks how the *passage can best be described*. Because this is a general question, it should be done after all the specific questions. Look for the Golden Thread. The passage describes the land and plants as if they were living things: for example, lines 3–5 say that *a warm breeze caressed the fields, causing the ears of the wheat to bend homeward, looking for all the world like they were listening to a conversation none but they could hear*. Lines 18–20 say, *It felt as if the field itself had gone to sleep*. Then, the passage describes Rebecca's family's history with the land and Rebecca's feeling of commitment to it. For example, lines 69–70 state, *This was her people's land; she knew that in her bones*. Therefore, the passage can be described as Rebecca's vivid description of land that is connected to her and her family. Eliminate answers that do not match this prediction. Keep (A) because it matches the prediction. Eliminate (B) because her family does not give up its claim on the land; rather, lines 38–40 state that even when her parents left, *they had claimed the land as their own*. Choice (C) may seem plausible, but the comparisons used in the passage support the meaning *suggested by the events narrated in the story*; there is no indication of another, deeper meaning. Eliminate (C). Eliminate (D) because, although the passage briefly mentions why the family had to leave the land, it does not go into detail about *exactly* why nor does it indicate that the family *lost everything*. Additionally, (D) does not reflect Rebecca's positive impressions of the land nor her commitment to reclaim it. The correct answer is (A).

6. **H** This reasoning question asks what the lines *Without the former, she could never face the latter* refer back to. Read a window around the given line reference. Lines 61–62 state, *This moment was for enjoying the sheer bounty of life, not for fears and numbers*. Therefore, the *former* refers to the phrase *enjoying the sheer bounty of life*, and the *latter* refers to the phrase *fears and numbers*. The phrase *the sheer bounty of life* refers to the fact that Rebecca has regained her family's land, which she loves. Lines 53–55 support this: *she opened her eyes and gazed out across her fields. They were hers, in truth if not writing, and would one day be hers in every sense*. The *fears and numbers* are described in lines 55–59: *her stomach began to clench as her mind turned…to the realities of what lay ahead. The loans, the mortgage payments, the possibility of a bad crop ruining all her plans*. Therefore, the *former* is Rebecca's connection with the land, while the *latter* is Rebecca's financial concerns. Eliminate answers that do not match this prediction. Choices (F), (G), and (J) mention details from other parts of the passage; none of them matches the prediction, and they are not mentioned in the window for the question. Eliminate (F), (G), and (J). Keep (H) because it matches the prediction. The correct answer is (H).

7. **C** This reasoning question asks what the description of *Rebecca's attitude toward the land* in the last two paragraphs is intended to convey. Read the last two paragraphs. In lines 52–71, Rebecca ponders both negative and positive aspects of owning the land. She worries about *loans, mortgage payments,* and a *bad crop ruining all her plans,* but she chooses to focus on the *warm reality of the growing, breathing crops.* Eliminate answers that do not match this prediction. Eliminate (A) because the *stranger's land* (mentioned in line 30) is land where Rebecca's parents worked, not the land that is described in the last two paragraphs. This answer uses words from the passage but does not match what the passage says. Eliminate (B) because the passage does not identify *mistakes* that Rebecca's parents made. Furthermore, the passage suggests that Rebecca is determined to reclaim the land, so the statement that she *cannot correct* past mistakes is not supported. Choice (C) matches the prediction, as it includes both *challenges and rewards* presented by the land. Choice (D) may be tempting because a story can do this, but there is no such parallel drawn in this passage; eliminate (D). The correct answer is (C).

8. **F** This reasoning question asks about the narrator's *point of view.* Because this is a general question, it should be done after all the specific questions. Look for the Golden Thread. Throughout the passage, the narrator describes Rebecca's thoughts and feelings. Eliminate answers that do not match this prediction. Keep (F) because it matches the prediction. Eliminate (G) because the narrator gives no indication that Rebecca is *not sincere* about her plans. Eliminate (H) because there is no evidence that the narrator is *personally involved* in these events; in fact, it's unlikely that the narrator is another person involved, since the narrator knows Rebecca's thoughts and feelings. For the same reason, eliminate (J)—a *relative* would not have the kind of insight into Rebecca's private thoughts and feelings that the narrator shows. The correct answer is (F).

9. **C** This vocabulary-in-context question asks what the word *wild* most nearly means as it is used in line 34. Go back to the text, find the word *wild,* and cross it out. Carefully read the surrounding text to determine another word or phrase that would fit in the blank based on the context. Lines 32–35 state that Rebecca's grandparents turned the *wild* prairie into *productive fields of wheat and corn.* Therefore, *wild* could be replaced with "not producing crops." Eliminate answers that do not match this prediction. *Unconquerable* means "not able to be conquered," which doesn't match "not producing crops." In fact, the text indicates that Rebecca's grandparents turned the land into productive fields, so this answer is contradicted. Eliminate (A). *Unrestrained* means "uncontrolled," and *irrepressible* means "impossible to control." Neither of these matches "not producing crops," so eliminate (B) and (D). *Uncultivated* matches "not producing crops," so keep (C). Choices (A), (B), and (D) are all possible meanings of *wild,* but they don't answer the question that was asked about the meaning of the word in context. The correct answer is (C).

10. **J** This referral question asks for Rebecca's *first response* when she realized that *a bee landed on her cheek.* Read a window around the given line reference. Lines 45–51 state that Rebecca *flinched a little bit as a bee landed on her cheek,* and that the feeling of the bee on her face *made her want to sneeze but she held her breath, not wanting to frighten it into stinging her.* Eliminate answers that do not match this prediction. Eliminate (F) because Rebecca does not *brush* the bee *away from her*

face. Eliminate (G), which uses words from the passage but doesn't match what the passage says. Although the text says that Rebecca did not want to frighten the bee into *stinging* her, it also says that she *let it explore her face, knowing it would move on*, indicating that she was calm, not worried. Eliminate (H) because, although the text describes Rebecca *knowing* the bee would *move on*, it does not describe her as hoping that the bee will fly away. Keep (J) because it matches the prediction. The correct answer is (J).

11. **C** This referral question asks which scholar *most directly contributed to the popularity of the term "Dark Ages."* Work backwards and use lead words from the answers to find the window for this question. *Petrarch* is mentioned in the first paragraph; lines 4–13 indicate that *Petrarch coined* the name "Dark Ages" and that the *name stuck*. Therefore, Petrarch directly contributed to the popularity of the name *Dark Ages*. Keep (C). William *Jordan* is mentioned in line 29; lines 29–32 indicate that in a book he wrote recently, Jordan *argued that the term "Dark Ages" needn't be negative*. Although he supported the use of the term *Dark Ages*, the term had already been popularized by Petrarch, so Jordan did not contribute as directly to the term's popularity as Petrarch did. Eliminate (A). David *Lindberg* and Ronald *Numbers* are mentioned in lines 45–46; lines 43–46 state that Lindberg and Numbers pointed out that learning did not stop during the Middle Ages. Lindberg and Numbers argued against using the term *Dark Ages*, so they did not contribute to its popularity. Eliminate (B) and (D). The correct answer is (C).

12. **G** This referral question asks which activity flourished during the Middle Ages. Work backwards and use lead words from the answers to find the window for this question. The lead words *dome, stonework*, and *three-dimensional, realistic art* all appear in lines 62–68. Lines 62–64 state that during the Middle Ages, *three-dimensional, realistic art became less common, and the ability to build a self-sustaining dome was lost for hundreds of years*. Eliminate (F) and (H). Lines 66–68 state, *Architects in the Middle Ages developed...some of the most intricate stonework seen before or since*. This indicates that *stonework* flourished during the Middle Ages, so keep (G). *Mathematics* appears in line 54; lines 49–54 indicate that the idea that people *abandoned the field of mathematics* during the Middle Ages is a misconception, but the text does not indicate that the field of mathematics flourished during this time, so eliminate (J). The correct answer is (G).

13. **A** This referral question asks what *scholars today* believe about the Middle Ages, in contrast with *historians with a traditional view of the Middle Ages*. There is not a good lead word in this question, so work the question later. Lines 1–14 explain that, beginning in the 14th century, a *popular conception* of the Medieval period in Europe was that *very little of cultural or intellectual importance took place during* that time. Lines 14–21 state that today, *scholars have begun to challenge that idea*, and that they *advocate the more neutral term "Middle Ages" because they feel that it more accurately describes the centuries during which Europe began to transition...into the modern states that exist today*. Eliminate answers that do not match this prediction. Keep (A) because it matches the prediction. Choice (B) may be tempting, but it goes beyond what is stated about the recent scholars' beliefs. The scholars discussed in the passage note that some *areas flourished* during the Middle Ages, but they do not mention *significant scientific discoveries*. Eliminate (B). Choices (C) and (D) describe

beliefs that contradict the views of the recent scholars discussed in the passage. The views in these two answers are more in keeping with the traditional view of the Medieval period as the *Dark Ages*. Therefore, although (C) and (D) include ideas that are mentioned in the passage, they answer the wrong question. Eliminate (C) and (D). The correct answer is (A).

14. **F** This referral question asks what will likely result in the development of *an accurate picture of the Middle Ages*. There is not a good lead word in this question (the phrase *Middle Ages* appears throughout the passage), so work the question later. Lines 36–40 state, *Research continues to uncover information about the era that allows scholars to gain an ever more accurate idea of what life was like during the Middle Ages, while other research has helped historians gain a better understanding of the evidence they already possessed.* Eliminate answers that don't match this prediction. Choice (F) mentions *reconsidering existing evidence*, which matches *gain a better understanding of the evidence they already possessed.* It also mentions *discovering new evidence*, which matches *[r]esearch continues to uncover information about the era.* Keep (F). Eliminate (G) because *written documents from the Renaissance* are not mentioned in the window for the question, and the first two paragraphs indicate that the author disagrees with Renaissance writers' views about the Middle Ages. Choice (H), *new excavations* in the *European countryside*, is a plausible way that researchers could study the Middle Ages, but the passage doesn't mention *new excavations.* The answer is not supported by the passage, so eliminate (H). Eliminate (J) because it goes beyond what is stated in the passage: the author disagrees with the Renaissance writers discussed in the first paragraph, but the passage doesn't suggest that researchers should disregard *all Renaissance accounts.* The correct answer is (F).

15. **D** The question asks what was NOT characteristic of *people during the Middle Ages.* When a question asks what is **not** supported by the text, eliminate answers that are supported. Eliminate (A) because lines 26–29 mention *written records* from the Middle Ages, which indicates that people during the Middle Ages did *keep written documents.* Although the passage says that *few* written records from that period exist now, that does not necessarily mean that people at that time did not typically keep written records; it simply means that few have survived to the present day. Eliminate (B) because lines 49–54 indicate that *mathematics* was not abandoned during the Middle Ages. Eliminate (C) because lines 66–68 indicate that *intricate stonework* was created during the Middle Ages. Keep (D) because lines 59–64 indicate that people in the Middle Ages did **not** widely believe that *the Earth was flat.* The correct answer is (D).

16. **J** This reasoning question asks for the *main purpose of the first paragraph.* Read the first paragraph. Lines 1–4 introduce the *period that began with the fall of the Roman Empire* and *ended with the Renaissance* and state that this time has been called the *Medieval Period, the Middle Ages, and the Dark Ages.* Lines 4–13 describe how the name *Dark Ages* was created: Petrarch, a Renaissance writer, created the name in order to *differentiate the culture of Medieval Europe from his own time* and to *connect his studies with those of antiquity.* Eliminate answers that don't match this prediction. Choice (F) is mentioned in the passage, but it answers the wrong question: it describes Petrarch's goal, rather than the purpose of the paragraph. Eliminate (F). Eliminate (G) because the passage does not indicate that the three terms listed are *all of the terms* used to describe the Medieval pe-

riod. Choice (H) uses words from the passage but doesn't match what the passage says: the text states that during the Renaissance, the *popular conception* of the Middle Ages was that it was a *cultural wasteland*. It does not say that *writers of the Renaissance lived in a cultural wasteland*. Eliminate (H). Keep (J) because it matches the prediction. The correct answer is (J).

17. **C** This referral question asks for areas *in which learning truly did go into decline during the Middle Ages*, according to the passage. Look for the lead words *learning* and *decline* to find the window for the question. Lines 58–64 indicate that *in some areas, learning did go into a decline after the fall of Rome*; these lines also give two examples: *three-dimensional, realistic art* and *the ability to build a self-sustaining dome*. Eliminate answers that don't match this prediction. Choice (A) includes references that are mentioned in the window, but they answer the wrong question. Lines 64–68 indicate that *symbolic art* and some aspects of *architecture* were highly developed during the Middle Ages, but the question asks for areas that went into *decline*, so eliminate (A). Eliminate (B) because lines 49–54 indicate that the study of *mathematics* was not abandoned during the Middle Ages. Keep (C) because it matches the prediction. Eliminate (D) because lines 66–68 indicate that *some of the most intricate stonework ever seen before or since* was developed during the Middle Ages. The correct answer is (C).

18. **F** This reasoning question asks what *Renaissance writers such as Petrarch* thought *their work would benefit from*, based on the first paragraph. Read the first paragraph. Lines 9–11 state that *Petrarch, like many other writers...of his time, wanted to connect his studies with those of antiquity*. Eliminate answers that don't match this prediction. Keep (F) because it matches the prediction: *antiquity* and the *classical era* are both ways of describing the same period. Neither (G) nor (H) is mentioned in the window for the question; eliminate (G) and (H). Eliminate (J) because the paragraph states that Petrarch wanted to relate his studies to those of antiquity; it does not say that he thought his work would benefit from *the new culture of the Renaissance*. The correct answer is (F).

19. **D** This vocabulary-in-context question asks what the word *coined* means as used in line 5. Go back to the text, find the word *coined*, and cross it out. Carefully read the surrounding text to determine another word that would fit in the blank based on the context. Lines 1–6 list some of the different names for the Middle Ages and state that Petrarch *coined* one of the terms. Therefore, *coined* must mean something like "invented." *Counterfeited* means "copied with the intention to deceive;" it does not match "invented," so eliminate (A). *Plagiarized* means "presented another's words as one's own"; it does match "invented," so eliminate (B). *Spent* does not match "invented," so eliminate (C). *Created* matches "invented," so keep (D). The correct answer is (D).

20. **F** This reasoning question asks what the fourth and fifth paragraphs suggest about how some scholars viewed *educational pursuits during the Middle Ages, before the work of modern scholars such as Numbers and Lindberg*. Read the fourth and fifth paragraphs. Lines 41–46 indicate that some scholars believed that *learning must have virtually halted* during the Middle Ages, before *Lindberg* and *Numbers* showed that this view was incorrect. Eliminate answers that don't match this prediction. Keep (F) because the description of educational pursuits as *insignificant* is supported by the

phrase *learning must have virtually halted*. Eliminate (G) and (H) because the description of educational pursuits as *scientific* and *advanced* is contradicted by the statement that scholars believed learning *virtually halted*. Eliminate (J) because the passage does not discuss scholars' beliefs about education being *well-documented*. The correct answer is (F).

21. **B**   This referral question refers to Passage A and asks for *the primary reason that some critics and scholars doubt the identity of the playwright William Shakespeare*. There is not a good lead word in this question (the word *Shakespeare* appears throughout the passage), so work the question later. Lines 12–23 outline the reasons that a *group of critics and scholars…believe that Shakespeare's authorship of these great plays is nearly impossible*. The arguments include the claim that *Shakespeare couldn't have had the education, aristocratic sensibility, or the familiarity with the royal court that pervade his many works* and that Shakespeare was not a likely source for the *oceanic grasp of the totality of Elizabethan England* demonstrated in the plays attributed to him. Eliminate answers that do not match this prediction. Eliminate (A) because the passage does not discuss other *accomplished playwrights* of Shakespeare's time who were also *successful and wealthy*. Keep (B) because it matches the prediction: Shakespeare's *relatively humble station* matches the claim that Shakespeare lacked *aristocratic sensibility* and *familiarity with the royal court*, and *works of such breadth* matches the *oceanic grasp of the totality of Elizabethan England*. Choice (C) uses words from the passage but does not match what the passage says: the passage indicates that some scholars believe that the ideas in Shakespeare's plays *were too dangerous for any one man to espouse publicly*, but it does not say that the ideas *were too dangerous to appear in novels*. Eliminate (C). Choice (D) may be tempting because the passage mentions that *Delia Bacon* proposed that Shakespeare's plays were written under the direction of *Sir Francis Bacon*—a person who shares her last name. However, the passage does not directly support the idea that *readers* wanted to *connect the plays of Shakespeare to their own lives*. Furthermore, this answer is only connected to one person mentioned in the passage and doesn't answer the question about *the primary reason* for the doubts of *critics and scholars*. Eliminate (D). The correct answer is (B).

22. **H**   This referral question asks why *critics cite Queen Elizabeth as the possible author of Shakespeare's plays*. Look for the lead words *Queen Elizabeth* to find the window for the question in Passage A. Lines 20–23 indicate that some critics believe that *Shakespeare's oceanic grasp of the totality of Elizabethan England means that his works could only have come from one source: Queen Elizabeth herself*. In other words, Shakespeare's plays demonstrate a broad knowledge about England during the time that Elizabeth was queen, and some critics believe that kind of knowledge could have belonged only to someone with the queen's perspective. Eliminate answers that don't match this prediction. Eliminate (F) because the passage does not discuss the *female characters* in Shakespeare's plays. Eliminate (G) because the passage does not mention the *natural sciences*. Keep (H) because it matches the prediction. Eliminate (J) because the passage does not discuss the popularity of Shakespeare's plays among *royalty*. The correct answer is (H).

23. **A**   This reasoning question asks why *Thompson refers to Shakespeare as "the average townsman."* Read a window around the given line reference. In lines 49–55, Thompson says that *the Anti-Stratfordians…raise some interesting questions about Shakespeare's authorship*. Then he asks, *How reasonable is it to think*

that the average townsman could have written the…works for which William Shakespeare has been given credit? Earlier in the passage, Thompson discusses the Anti-Stratfordians' belief that *Shakespeare couldn't have had the education, aristocratic sensibility, or the familiarity with the royal court that pervade his many works* (lines 12–16). Therefore, the reference to Shakespeare as *the average townsman* reflects uncertainty about whether Shakespeare was educated and aristocratic enough to have written the plays attributed to him. Eliminate answers that don't match this prediction. Choice (A) matches the prediction, so keep it. Choice (B) mentions that Shakespeare *was active in civic affairs,* but the passage does not discuss Shakespeare's involvement in *civic affairs.* Eliminate (B). Choice (C) states that Shakespeare was *too well liked by his neighbors to be revealed as a fraud,* but the passage does not discuss Shakespeare's *neighbors.* Eliminate (C). Choice (D) states that Shakespeare *may have disguised himself,* but the passage does not suggest this. Eliminate (D). The correct answer is (A).

24. **J** This vocabulary-in-context question asks what the word *oceanic* means in line 21. Go back to the text, find the word *oceanic,* and cross it out. Carefully read the surrounding text to determine another word that would fit in the blank based on the context. Lines 21–22 mention Shakespeare's understanding *of the totality of Elizabethan England,* so *oceanic* could be replaced with "complete." *Natural* does not match "complete," so eliminate (F). *Informal* does not match "complete," so eliminate (G). *Salty* does not match "complete," so eliminate (H). *Comprehensive* matches "complete," so keep (J). The correct answer is (J).

25. **C** This reasoning question asks why it is *difficult to understand* that Shakespeare is the sole author of his works, according to the author of Passage B. There is not a good lead word for this question, so work the question later. In lines 56–60, the author indicates that *it's not reasonable* to think that Shakespeare wrote the plays that are credited to him, but says, *that is the nature of genius, especially genius of Shakespeare's magnitude.* In other words, it's difficult to understand how an ordinary person could have written Shakespeare's plays, but Shakespeare was a genius, not an ordinary person. Choice (A) states that Shakespeare *was only one of many authors who wrote under the name Shakespeare.* Although the author of Passage A discusses this theory, the question is about Passage B. Eliminate (A). Eliminate (B) because Truelove never discusses a time *before plays were considered serious works of art.* Choice (C) matches the prediction, so keep it. Eliminate (D) because Truelove does not state that Shakespeare *disapproved of royalty and other nobles.* The correct answer is (C).

26. **G** This referral question asks why Truelove believes that *the Anti-Stratfordians give a classist account of Shakespeare's authorship.* Look for the lead word *classist* to find the window for this question in Passage B. Lines 69–72 state that the *Anti-Stratfordians…have been making a blatantly classist argument. The idea that a man of Shakespeare's level of genius must have come from the upper echelons of society is snobbish at best.* In other words, their account is *classist* because they assume that a man of Shakespeare's genius must have an upper-class background. Eliminate answers that don't match this prediction. Choice (F) uses words from the passage but doesn't match what the text says. In fact, the author would disagree with this statement. Eliminate (F). Keep (G) because it matches the prediction. Choice (H) uses words from the passage but doesn't match what the passage says.

Though Truelove questions the Anti-Stratfordians' beliefs about their students' wealth and intelligence, she never states that the Anti-Stratfordians *disapprove* of their *low-income students*. Eliminate (H). Eliminate (J) because the passage does not mention *royalties*. The correct answer is (G).

27. **C** This reasoning question asks what faults Truelove points out about arguments that are based on *"parallels"* between Shakespeare's writing and the writing of other authors. Look for the lead word *parallels* to find the window for the question in Passage B. Lines 85–91 indicate that it is *misleading* to *identify "parallels"* between *the texts of Shakespeare* and other authors. Truelove argues that these parallels are very likely because Shakespeare and the other authors *lived in the same place in the same era*. In other words, the *"parallels"* are not effective support for the Anti-Stratfordians' argument. Eliminate answers that don't match this prediction. Eliminate (A) because Truelove doesn't critique the Anti-Stratfordians' choice of *texts*, just their methodology. Eliminate (B) because the passage does not discuss *economics*. Keep (C) because it matches the prediction. Eliminate (D) because Truelove does not compare the evidence about *Bacon* and *de Vere*. The correct answer is (C).

28. **J** This reasoning question asks for a difference between *Thompson's and Truelove's points of view*. Because this question asks about both passages, it should be done after the questions that ask about each passage individually. Consider the Golden Thread of each passage. In Passage A, Thompson discusses the Anti-Stratfordians' theory that Shakespeare did not write the plays that are attributed to him, and states that *the Anti-Stratfordians...raise some interesting questions about Shakespeare's authorship*. Passage A identifies the *Oxfordians* as one particular group of Anti-Stratfordians. Therefore, Thompson believes that the Anti-Stratfordians' (and Oxfordians') theories are interesting and worth exploring. In Passage B, Truelove states, *as difficult as it might be to believe, all evidence points toward William Shakespeare as the sole author of Shakespeare's works*. In other words, Truelove disagrees with the Anti-Stratfordians (and the Oxfordians). Eliminate answers that misrepresent either passage. Eliminate (F) because Truelove is not compelled by *the theories of the Oxfordians*. Eliminate (G) because Thompson does not *criticize* the authors he discusses, and Truelove does not believe that *Looney's and Bacon's arguments* hold any *merit* at all. Eliminate (H) as it mixes up the viewpoints of Thompson and Truelove. Keep (J) because it matches the prediction. The correct answer is (J).

29. **B** This reasoning question asks how Truelove went about disagreeing with the theories Thompson presented. Because this question asks about both passages, it should be done after the questions that ask about each passage individually. Eliminate answers that misrepresent either passage. Choice (A) states that Truelove uses *personal attacks*, but Truelove does not attack those she disagrees with personally; instead, she attacks their theories. Eliminate (A). Choice (B) is supported by the passage: Passage B begins with a *direct response* that explicitly mentions Arthur Coyle Thompson. Passage B also includes many *rhetorical questions*, including lines 62–65, lines 72–74, and lines 90–91. Keep (B). Eliminate (C) because Truelove's arguments are logical, rather than *emotional*, and Passage B doesn't include any examples of *exaggeration*. Eliminate (D) because Truelove uses neither *historical data* nor *archival research* to make her argument. The correct answer is (B).

30. **J** This reasoning question asks for the best comparison of Thompson's and Truelove's views on *the alternative theories of Shakespeare's authorship*. Because this question asks about both passages, it should be done after the questions that ask about each passage individually. Consider the Golden Thread of each passage. In Passage A, Thompson states that *the Anti-Stratfordians nonetheless raise some interesting questions about Shakespeare's authorship*. The Anti-Stratfordians believe that Shakespeare did not write the plays he is credited with, so Thompson believes the theories of alternative authorship are interesting and worth looking into. In Passage B, Truelove states, *as difficult as it might be to believe, all evidence points toward William Shakespeare as the sole author of Shakespeare's works*. In other words, Truelove does not believe the claims about alternative authorship of Shakespeare's plays. Eliminate answers that misrepresent either passage. Eliminate (F) because Truelove firmly disagrees with the theories; she does not show *neutrality*. Eliminate (G) because Thompson does not use *dramatic appeal* in his response. Eliminate (H) because it misrepresents both passages: Thompson is open to the theories, but is not a *staunch* (strong) advocate for them, and Truelove disagrees with the theories. Keep (J) because it matches the prediction. The correct answer is (J).

31. **C** This referral question asks what *behavior* is described as *free will* in the passage. Look for the lead words *free will* to find the window for this question. Lines 18–19 identify the *human ability to form lasting romantic bonds* as an example of *free will*. Eliminate answers that don't match this prediction. Choice (A) is mentioned in the passage, but it answers the wrong question. The passage indicates that scientists are beginning to question the model of free will, and lines 30–34 indicate that *falling in love* may actually be *biologically motivated*. This is offered as evidence against free will, rather than as an example of free will. Eliminate (A). Choice (B) is not mentioned in the window for the question: the discussion of *trying to identify patterns* for the purposes of *criminal pursuit* appears in the last paragraph and is not an example of *free will*. Eliminate (B). Choice (C) matches the prediction, so keep it. Eliminate (D) because *group efforts* to *improve a city* are not mentioned in the passage. The correct answer is (C).

32. **G** This reasoning question asks how the *recent discovery* in lines 30–34 is related to the *electro-chemical theory*. Look for the lead words *electro-chemical theory* to find the first window for the question. Lines 50–51 describe a theory that *all human interaction is, on some level, based in the laws of physics*. Lines 57–63 describe the *electro-chemical theory*—the idea that *electrical impulses* in the human body *become chemical impulses...which eventually trigger biological impulses*. Then, read a window around lines 30–34. These lines state that *recent research* suggests that *falling in love* is *biologically motivated*. Therefore, the *recent discovery* supports the theory that all human behavior (such as *falling in love*) is *based in the laws of physics*. This theory, in turn, is connected to the electro-chemical theory, which explains how the laws of physics underlie biological impulses. Eliminate answers that don't match this prediction. Choice (F) is incorrect because the *recent discovery* does not support the *electro-chemical theory* directly. Instead, it supports a theory that is related to the electro-chemical theory. Eliminate (F). Choice (G) matches the prediction, so keep it. Choice (H) is incorrect because both the new research and the *electro-chemical theory* incorporate the idea that

human behavior has roots in biology. Eliminate (H). Since the research has a clear link to the *electro-chemical theory*, eliminate (J). The correct answer is (G).

33. **D** This referral question asks how *the author characterizes scientific contributions to police work*. Look for the lead word *police* to find the window for the question. Lines 71–78 discuss the *increasing involvement of scientists in the arena of criminal pursuit*. This paragraph indicates that *police* departments now bring in scientists to *identify patterns* and that the scientists *help solve the cases*. Eliminate answers that don't match the prediction. Eliminate (A) and (B) because the author says that the scientists *help solve the cases*; therefore, their contributions are not characterized as *useless* or *unconvincing*. Eliminate (C) because there is no indication that the help from scientists is *alarming*, and the research is applied to case work, so it is not only *theoretically persuasive*. Choice (D) matches the prediction. The correct answer is (D).

34. **F** This referral question asks how *humans are like particles*, according to *supporters of the electro-chemical theory*. Look for the lead words *electro-chemical theory* and *particles* to find the window for the question. According to lines 59–65, *all matter reacts to electrical impulses* and *advocates of the electro-chemical theory claim that…[h]uman interaction can be compared to the interaction between particles*. Therefore, advocates of the electro-chemical theory claim that both humans and particles react to electrical impulses. Eliminate answers that don't match this prediction. Choice (F) matches the prediction, so keep it. Eliminate (G) because, while it is true that humans are *capable of conscious decision-making*, the passage does not indicate that particles are. Furthermore, *conscious decision-making* is not mentioned in the window for the question. Choice (H) uses words from the passage but doesn't match what the passage says: *group interactions* between humans are mentioned, but there is no evidence that humans are better understood *in groups than individually*. Eliminate (H). Choice (J) uses words from the passage but doesn't match what the passage says: the passage discusses responses to *stimuli*, but it does not indicate that humans respond to stimuli *without intermediate thought*. Eliminate (J). The correct answer is (F).

35. **B** This referral question asks how *electrical impulses* are described by the author *in terms of where and how frequently they occur*. Look for the lead words *electrical impulses* to find the window for the question. Lines 59–61 indicate that *all matter reacts to electrical impulses on some level*. Eliminate answers that don't match this prediction. Since the passage states that *electrical impulses* affect *all matter*, eliminate (A). Choice (B) matches the prediction, so keep it. Like (A), (C) does not include *all matter*. Lines 64–66 state that *human interaction can be compared to the interaction between different particles*; therefore, the author includes humans in *all matter*. Eliminate (C). Eliminate (D) because it includes only *non-human matter*, rather than *all matter*. The correct answer is (B).

36. **J** This referral question asks how *chemists and physicists define biological impulses*. Look for the lead words *chemists and physicists* and *biological impulses* to find the window for the question. The *chemists and physicists* first mentioned in line 47 believe that *electrical impulses become chemical impulses… which eventually trigger biological impulses* (lines 57–59). Eliminate answers that don't match this prediction. *Free will* is not mentioned in the window for the question; the *chemists and physicists*

don't state whether *biological impulses* are connected to *free will*, so eliminate both (F) and (G). Choice (H) uses words from the passage but doesn't match what the passage says: it reverses the causes and effects described in the text. Eliminate (H). Choice (J) matches the prediction, so keep it. The correct answer is (J).

37. **C** This reasoning question asks for the best characterization of the *explanation* in lines 26–30. Read a window around the given line reference. Lines 18–19 indicate that forming *lasting romantic bonds* has been considered evidence that humans have *free will*. Lines 23–30, however, acknowledge the idea that *working as a pair has many evolutionary advantages*, improving the likelihood of survival for a pair and its offspring. Therefore, the explanation of pair bonding in lines 26–30 provides evidence for an alternative to the theory of *free will*. Eliminate answers that don't match this prediction. The window only discusses *human ability* to form pair bonds, as opposed to that of *all higher-level organisms*, so eliminate (A). Eliminate (B) because it focuses on *lower-level animals* instead of humans. Choice (C) matches the prediction, so keep it. Choice (D) is the reverse of the prediction, as the idea that pair bonding is *biologically motivated* actually counters the traditional idea that pair bonding is a demonstration of *free will*. Eliminate (D). The correct answer is (C).

38. **F** This reasoning question asks for the *main point of the sixth paragraph.* Read the sixth paragraph. Lines 71–81 describe *one practical example of the convergence of scientific theory and human practice*, specifically *criminal pursuit*. The paragraph describes how scientists *help solve cases* by applying data analysis and patterns to police work. Eliminate answers that don't match this prediction. Choice (F) matches the prediction, so keep it. Eliminate (G) because the paragraph indicates that specific *academic theories* have been applied successfully in police work, not that it has been *difficult* to apply them. Eliminate (H) because the paragraph does not focus on evaluating theories; it also focuses on a specific set of theories, rather than *academic theories* in general. Eliminate (J), since the time *before the debates over free will* is not discussed in the window for the question. The correct answer is (F).

39. **D** This referral question asks how *evolutionary biologists* responded *to the suggestion that the tendency to remain with a single mate demonstrates humanity's free will.* Look for the lead words *evolutionary biologists* to find the window for the question. Line 18–23 discuss the theory that the pair-bonding demonstrates humans' free will. Lines 23–30 state, *Evolutionary biologists, however, have recently uncovered evidence that suggests that pair-bonding has many evolutionary advantages.* In other words, evolutionary biologists responded to the theory that pair-bonding demonstrates free will by suggesting another explanation of pair-bonding. Eliminate answers that don't match this prediction. Choices (A) and (B) both suggest that the evolutionary biologists changed their own theory in response to the free-will theory, either by adding to their theory or accepting that their theory was flawed. However, the passage indicates that the evolutionary biologists disagreed with the free-will theory. Eliminate (A) and (B). Choice (C) is not supported by the passage, as the *evolutionary biologists* did not include *free will* in their theory at all. Eliminate (C). Choice (D) matches the prediction, so keep it. The correct answer is (D).

40. **G** This reasoning question asks for the *quality* that is most emphasized in lines 12–17. Read a window around the given line reference. The first paragraph discusses *free will*, and lines 12–13 indicate that scientists have started to *question* the free will model. Lines 13–17 pose a series of questions about what truly underlies our decision-making. Therefore, lines 12–17 can be described as "questioning." Eliminate answers that don't match this prediction. Eliminate (F) because *confidence* does not match "questioning." Choice (G) matches the prediction, so keep it. Eliminate (H) because, while *ignorance* is a possible cause of questioning, the fact that the scientists are discussing other possible theories indicates that they are not ignorant of the subject matter. Eliminate (J) because *contentment* means "happiness" or "satisfaction"; it doesn't match "questioning." The correct answer is (G).

SCIENCE TEST

1. **C** The question asks for the cell in Figure 3 that is most likely in the stage of the cell cycle in which mitosis is nearing completion. Read the description of Figure 3 to learn more about the images. The passage says the four images represent *cells in each of the 4 stages of the dividing cell cycle.* Since the question asks for a cell near the end of mitosis, look for the cell that has almost finished dividing into two cells. Cell 3 shows the clearest division into two cells. The correct answer is (C).

2. **J** The question asks for the percent of the cells in a *culture of fibroblast cells* in a toxin concentration of 90 ppm *that would undergo apoptosis*, based on Figure 1. Figure 1 shows the toxin concentration on the horizontal axis and *AI* on the vertical axis. Look for the definition of *AI* to see how it relates to the percent of cells that undergo apoptosis. Above Figure 1, *AI* is defined as $\frac{\text{number of cells undergoing } apoptosis}{\text{total number of cells}}$. Therefore, the question is asking for an *AI* value expressed as a percent. Look at the horizontal axis that shows toxin concentration in Figure 1. A concentration of 90 ppm is beyond the range of the graph, so extrapolate the pattern. At a toxin concentration of 80 ppm, the *AI* is approximately 0.007. To convert this *AI* to a percentage, multiply the *AI* by 100% to get 0.007(100%) = 0.7%. The *AI* increases as toxin concentration increases, so the percentage for 90 ppm would be a little higher than 0.7%. Eliminate (F), (G), and (H) as these are not higher than 0.7%. The correct answer is (J).

3. **D** The question asks for the cell that is in the first stage of the cell cycle based on Figure 3. Read the description of Figure 3 to learn more about the images. The passage states that the four images represent *cells in each of the 4 stages of the dividing cell cycle.* Since the question asks for a cell in the *first stage* of the cycle, use POE to determine the correct cell. Cells 1 and 3 show visible signs of division with two distinct cells, so they represent stages near the end of the cell cycle. Eliminate (A) and (C). Compare the remaining answer choices. Cells 2 and 3 are similar in appearance, but Cell 2 is larger. Cell 2 is also more similar in appearance to Cell 1, which is beginning to divide. Therefore, it is logical that Cell 2 is

closer in the cycle to the division stage than Cell 1. Therefore, Cell 1 must be closer to the beginning of the cycle. The correct answer is (D).

4. **H**   The question asks how the number of fibroblast cells in stage G_2 compares to the number of cells in stage S based on Figure 2. Look for the data for the number of cells in each cell cycle stage in Figure 2. Approximately 75 cells are in stage S, and approximately 225 cells are in stage G_2. There are more cells in stage G_2, so eliminate (F) and (G) because they show less cells in stage G_2. Try (H): 75 times 3 is 225. The correct answer is (H).

5. **A**   The question asks for the proportion of cells in the cell cycle that were in stage G_1 based on Figure 2. Look for the data for the number of cells in the G_1 stage in Figure 2. Approximately 540 cells are in stage G_1. Use POE. The proportion must have the number of cells in stage G_1 in the numerator, so eliminate (B) and (C). The proportion must have the total number of cells in the denominator, which must be greater than the number of cells in stage G_1, so eliminate (D). The correct answer is (A).

6. **G**   The question asks for the number of cells out of a sample of 3,000 cells that are undergoing apoptosis in a toxin concentration of 30 ppm. Figure 1 shows the toxin concentration on the horizontal axis and *AI* on the vertical axis. Look for the definition of *AI* in the passage. Above Figure 1, *AI* is defined as $\dfrac{\text{number of cells undergoing } apoptosis}{\text{total number of cells}}$, so this is a proportion. Look at the horizontal axis that shows toxin concentration in Figure 1. At a toxin concentration of 30 ppm, the *AI* is 0.005, which is a very small fraction. Use POE to eliminate (J) because 1,500 cells would be half of the cells, which is not a very small fraction. Now use the *AI* formula to solve for the number of cells undergoing apoptosis out of the total number of cells. The formula becomes $0.005 = \dfrac{\text{number of cells undergoing } apoptosis}{\text{3,000 total cells}}$. Multiply both sides by 3,000, being careful with the decimal places, to get 15 = number of cells undergoing *apoptosis*. The correct answer is (G).

7. **C**   The question asks for the rationale behind treating samples with a buffer to reach a pH of 8.6. Since pH is not mentioned in either figure, look for where pH is mentioned in the passage. In the 4th paragraph, the passage states that *a buffer was added to each vial to establish a pH of 8.6*. Immediately after adding the buffer, the passage says *samples from each tube were injected into the capillary electrophoresis device.* Since the buffer is added right before the samples are run through the capillary electrophoresis device, the buffer must have something to do with this process. Eliminate (A) and (B) since they don't mention capillary electrophoresis. If a pH of 8.6 did not allow the electrophoresis separation to occur, there would be no purpose for the scientists to add the buffer. Eliminate (D). If electrophoresis occurs best at a pH of 8.6, this explains why the buffer would have been added. The correct answer is (C).

8. **F** The question asks if the information in Table 1 is *consistent with the hypothesis that Patient 4 and Patient P are the same person*. Refer to Table 1 and use POE. Since Patient P's blood smear and Patient 4's blood smear both contain sickle cells, they have the same blood cell appearance. Eliminate (G) and (J). Since the blood cell appearance is the same, they could be the same person. Eliminate (H). The correct answer is (F).

9. **D** The question asks whether the information and data in the passage indicate that Patient 2 and Patient 4 likely have the same genotype. Look for information about genotypes in the passage. The first paragraph states that *all humans have slight differences in their genotypes (genetic code) that result in different phenotypes (observable characteristics)*. Since genotypes *cannot be observed with the naked eye*, scientists must rely on *capillary electrophoresis* to analyze the genetic code of different patients. Therefore, the data that will support or contradict a claim on genotypes must be in Figure 1, since that is the data from the capillary electrophoresis process. Eliminate (A) and (C) since they use data from Table 1 instead of Figure 1. Patient 2 has one large peak labeled Y, and Patient 4 has two smaller peaks in different locations. Eliminate (B) because the patients do not have protein peaks in the same locations. The correct answer is (D).

10. **H** The question asks for possible genotypes of Patient 4. Look for information about genotypes in the passage. The first paragraph says *all humans have slight differences in their genotypes (genetic code) that result in different phenotypes (observable characteristics)*. Table 1 says Patient 4 has sickle cells in his or her blood smear. Therefore, Patient 4 must have a genotype that results in sickle cells. The question says that the Hb^A allele results in normal cells, and both the Hb^S and Hb^C alleles result in sickle cells. Genotype I has two copies of the normal Hb^A allele, so this genotype cannot result in sickle cells. Eliminate (G) and (J). Both alleles Hb^S and Hb^C cause sickle cells, so Patient 4 could have either genotype II or genotype III. Therefore, the correct answer is (H).

11. **B** The question asks for a comparison between two samples represented in Figure 1. Patient P has one large peak labeled *W*. The only other sample with a single peak in a similar location is Patient 2. The correct answer is (B).

12. **J** The question asks which protein peaks are *closest in charge characteristics* based on Figure 1. Look for the term *charge characteristics* in the description of Figure 1. The passage says *the hemoglobin proteins composing a peak had similar charge characteristics*, so the proteins with similar charge characteristics should be located in a similar location on the figure. Peaks X and Z are in similar locations, and peaks W and Y are in similar locations. Out of these two pairs, only X and Z are linked in an answer choice. The correct answer is (J).

13. **A** The question asks for the charge of the proteins that resulted in peaks *furthest to the left* in Figure 1. Refer to Figure 1. The electrode on the left of the diagram is labeled *positive*, and the electrode on the right of the figure is labeled *negative*. Use POE to eliminate the illogical answers. Since the electrode on the left is positive, the proteins nearest to that electrode would be negative only if opposite charges attract. If opposite charges repel, the proteins would be positive. Eliminate (B) and (D) because they reverse this logic. To choose between the remaining answers, use some outside knowledge. Opposite charges

attract each other, so the proteins located closest to the positive electrode would be negatively charged. Eliminate (C) since it says the proteins on the left are positive. The correct answer is (A).

14. **H** The question asks for the acid with the highest melting point based on data in Table 1. Look at the variables in Table 1. Melting point is not listed, but freezing point is. Melting and freezing occur at the same temperature since both processes transition between liquids and solids at this temperature. Therefore, the acid with the highest freezing point also has the highest melting point. The highest freezing point listed on Table 1 is for acetic acid at 16.6°C. The correct answer is (H).

15. **A** The question asks for the value of the vapor pressure of an additional acid at 40°C based on its boiling point and the data in Table 1 and Figure 1. Look for the trends for boiling point and vapor pressure in Table 1 and Figure 1. In Table 1, formic acid has the lowest boiling point and propionic acid has the highest boiling point. In Figure 1, formic acid has the highest vapor pressure and propionic acid has the lowest vapor pressure. Therefore, boiling point and vapor pressure exhibit an inverse relationship: as one variable increases, the other variable decreases. The 165°C boiling point of pyruvic acid is greater than the boiling point of any of the three acids in Table 1 and Figure 1. Since vapor pressure decreases as boiling point increases, pyruvic acid should have a lower vapor pressure than any of the three acids. Find 40°C on the horizontal axis of the graph, and trace up to the dashed line for propionic acid. Read across to the vertical axis and note that propionic acid has a vapor pressure between 9 and 10 mm Hg. Pyruvic acid must have an even lower vapor pressure. The correct answer is (A).

16. **H** The question asks, based on Figure 2, for the concentration of the formic acid solution that has the vapor pressure closest to that of a 0.5 mole fraction formic acid solution. Look for the vapor pressure of a 0.5 mole fraction of water formic acid solution in Figure 2. A 0.5 mole fraction of water formic acid solution, represented by the solid line, has a vapor pressure of approximately 10 mm Hg. Draw a horizontal line at this vapor pressure to see where else the formic acid solution has this value. The formic acid solution line intersects the 10 mm Hg vapor pressure line again at a mole fraction of 0.8. The correct answer is (H).

17. **A** The question asks how the vapor pressure changes as the mole fraction of water increases from 0 to 1 in an acetic acid solution, based on Figure 2. Look for the trend between vapor pressure and mole fraction of water in Figure 2, making sure to use the dotted line for acetic acid. As the concentration increases from a mole fraction of 0 to 0.6, the vapor pressure decreases, and then from a mole fraction of 0.6 to 1, the vapor pressure increases. The correct answer is (A).

18. **G** The question asks for the boiling point of an additional acid based on its chemical formula and the data in Table 1. Look for the trend between chemical formula and boiling point in Table 1. As the number of CH_2 groups increases, the boiling point increases. In Table 1, valeric acid has the highest boiling point of 186°C and the greatest number of CH_2 groups. The chemical formula of hexanoic acid has one more CH_2 group than valeric acid, so hexanoic acid has a higher boiling point than valeric acid. Eliminate (F). For each additional CH_2 group added to the chemical formula, the boiling point increases by just over 20°C. Hexanoic acid has one more CH_2 group than valeric acid, so the boiling point of hexanoic acid should be approximately 23°C more than the boiling point of valeric

acid, or 186°C + 23°C = 209°C. This boiling point falls within the range of 180°C and 215°C. The correct answer is (G).

19. **C** The question asks whether acetic acid or formic acid resists vaporization more at 60°C, based on Figure 1. Figure 1 does not mention vaporization, but it does show vapor pressure, which is mentioned in the second half od each answer choice. Look for the data for vapor pressure in Figure 1, making sure to use the appropriate lines for each acid based on the key. At 60°C, the solid line for formic acid shows a vapor pressure of approximately 200 mm Hg, and the dotted line for acetic acid shows a vapor pressure of approximately 80 mm Hg. Eliminate (A) and (D) since both indicate that formic acid has a lower vapor pressure than acetic acid. Compare the remaining answer choices, using some outside knowledge about the relationship between vapor pressure and vaporization. For an acid to *resist* vaporization more, it must have the lower vapor pressure. Since acetic acid has the lower vapor pressure, the correct answer is (C).

20. **J** The question asks for the length of the solenoid coil in Experiment 1 based on the results of Experiments 1 and 3. Table 1 shows the results of Experiment 1, and Table 3 shows the results of Experiment 3. Since the question asks to synthesize information from two tables, look for the link between the data. Table 3 shows the weights for various solenoid lengths, while Table 1 shows the weights at various voltages. Read the description of Table 3 to find the voltage used in Experiment 3. The passage says *a voltage of 8.00 V was applied to the circuit.* Look for the weight for a voltage of 8.00 V in Table 1. At this voltage, the weight exerted on the suspension scale is 5.0095 N. Next, look at Table 3 to determine how solenoid length affects weight. As the solenoid length increases, the weight decreases. A weight of 5.0095 N is lower than any weight listed on Table 3, so the solenoid length must be longer than any length listed on Table 3. Since the maximum solenoid length listed is 9.50 cm, the solenoid length used in Experiment 1 must be longer than 9.50 cm. The correct answer is (J).

21. **B** The question asks which variable was determined by the orientation of the bar magnet in Experiments 1 and 2. Look for where bar magnet orientation is mentioned in the passage. In the description for Experiment 2, the passage says *the scientists removed the bar magnet, inverted it, and reattached it*, but everything else stayed the same as Experiment 1. Compare the data from Experiment 2 to Experiment 1 to see how the change in bar magnet orientation affected the data. In Experiment 1, as the voltage increases, the weight increases. In Experiment 2, as the voltage increases, the weight decreases. Use POE. Choice (A) mentions *solenoid length*. Since the procedures are kept the same except for changing the orientation of the bar magnet, solenoid length is not affected. Eliminate (A). Choice (B) mentions *direction of the force exerted by the solenoid on the bar magnet*. Since Experiment 1 shows an increasing force, and Experiment 2 shows a decreasing force, this is consistent with the data. Keep (B), but check the other answers just in case. Choice (C) mentions the *density of the bar magnet* which is calculated by dividing mass by volume. Reorienting the bar magnet will not change its mass or volume, so eliminate (C). Choice (D) mentions the *magnetic field strength of the solenoid*. Since only the direction of the magnet changed, the magnetic field strength would not change. Eliminate (D). The correct answer is (B).

22. **J**   The question asks how the force exerted on the magnet by the solenoid magnetic field is changed as another variable is changed in Experiment 3. The results of Experiment 3 are shown in Table 3. The description of Table 3 states that *a voltage of 8.00 V was applied to the circuit.* Since the voltage is constant, eliminate (F) and (G). Since weight is a measure of force, look for the data in Table 3 to determine how solenoid length affects weight. As the solenoid length increases, the weight decreases. A lower weight indicates a smaller force is pulling the magnet in a downward direction. Therefore, the force decreased as the solenoid length increased. The correct answer is (J).

23. **B**   The question asks what the weight on the scale for a solenoid length of 9.50 cm would have been if Experiment 3 used the same bar magnet orientation as Experiment 2. In the description for Experiment 2, the passage says *the scientists removed the bar magnet, inverted it, and reattached it,* but everything else stayed the same as Experiment 1. Compare the data from Experiment 2, found in Table 2, to the data from Experiment 1, found in Table 1, to see how the change in bar magnet orientation affected the data. In Experiment 1, the weight increases from 5.000 N as voltage increases, while in Experiment 2, it decreases from 5.000 N as voltage increases. Therefore, the bar magnet orientation in Experiment 2 causes weight to decrease instead of increase. In the description for Experiment 3, the passage says *the bar magnet was returned to the original alignment it was in during Experiment 1.* If Experiment 3 had used the bar magnet orientation from Experiment 2 instead, Experiment 3 would have exhibited the same pattern of decreasing weight instead of increasing weight. Eliminate (C) and (D) because they are greater than 5.000 N. At a solenoid length of 9.50 cm, the weight recorded in Experiment 3 was 5.0105 N, which is an increase of 0.0105 N from 5.000 N. The new orientation should cause a decrease of 0.0105 N instead: 5.0000 N – 0.0105 N = 4.9895 N. The correct answer is (B).

24. **J**   The question asks how scientists performed a calibration on the suspension scale. Look for where adjustment of the suspension scale is mentioned in the passage. In the fifth paragraph, the passage says *with the voltage source off, the scale read 4.7000 N.* The passage then states that *prior to the start of each experimental trial, the scale was adjusted to read 5.0000 N.* Eliminate (F) and (H) because they mention a downward adjustment, and the value of the scale reading increases. Find the difference between the two weights to determine the adjustment, or 5.0000 N – 4.7000 N = 0.3 N. The procedure would require an adjustment upward of approximately 0.3 N. The correct answer is (J).

25. **B**   The question asks for a graph that best conveys the results of Experiment 3. The results of Experiment 3 are in Table 3. In Table 3, as the solenoid length increases, the weight decreases. Eliminate (A) and (C), since these graphs show weight increasing as solenoid length increases. Compare the remaining answer choices. Choice (D) shows all of the weights below 5.000 N, but Table 3 shows all of the weights above 5.000 N. Eliminate (D). The correct answer is (B).

26. **J**   The question asks for the likely weight if an additional trial had been performed in Experiment 2 with a voltage of 6.50 V. Experiment 2 is represented by Table 2. As the voltage increases in Table 2, the weight decreases. An additional trial at 6.50 V is lower than any of the voltages listed in the table, so the additional trial should have a higher weight than the highest weight in the table, which is 4.9922 N. Eliminate (F) and (G). Compare the values in Table 2 to determine how much higher

the weight should be. A voltage of 6.50 V is 0.75 V below the first voltage listed on Table 2. To find the corresponding weight increase, determine the pattern of weight differences between voltages that are 0.75 V apart. As the voltage decreases from 8.75 V to 8.00 V, the weight increases from 4.9887 to 4.9905, which is an increase of 0.0018 N. As the voltage decreases from 8.00 V to 7.25 V, the weight increases from 4.9905 to 4.9922, which is an increase of 0.0017 N. Therefore, the approximate increase in weight from 7.50 V to 6.75 V should be 0.0016 N. Add this value to the weight at 7.25 V: 4.9922 + 0.0016 = 4.9938 N. The correct answer is (J).

27. **D** The question asks what Student 1 would most likely claim about the atmospheric oxygen concentration from 1500 to 1900 based on Figure 1. Figure 1 shows the biodiversity over time. Based on Figure 1, marine biodiversity was relatively stable between 1500 and 1900. Look at Student 1's theory. Student 1 states that *the marine biodiversity was stable for centuries until the human population surged upward, quadrupling between 1900 and present day*. Student 1 goes on to say that this population surge caused *a decrease of 0.50% in the atmospheric oxygen concentration since 1900*, which resulted in a decrease in biodiversity. If the change in oxygen concentration caused the change in marine biodiversity, then when the marine biodiversity is stable, the oxygen concentration should also be stable. Therefore, the student believes atmospheric oxygen concentrations were relatively stable prior to the population surge after the year 1900. The correct answer is (D).

28. **H** The question asks for an interval on Figure 2 that shows an oxygen concentration decrease that is *more than 10 times* the amount mentioned by Student 1. Look for information about oxygen concentration decreases in Student 1's theory. Student 1 says human actions have led to *a decrease of 0.50% in the atmospheric oxygen concentration since 1900*. The question asks for a time interval that shows an *atmospheric oxygen concentration decrease more than 10 times* this, so multiply 0.50% by 10 to get a 5% decrease. Look at Figure 2. Atmospheric oxygen difference, which is the difference between atmospheric oxygen concentration at a given time and current atmospheric oxygen concentration, corresponds to the *y*-axis on the right side of the graph and the dotted line. Use POE. Choice (F) refers to the period from 440 to 420 million years ago. At that time, atmospheric oxygen concentration was increasing, not decreasing. Eliminate (F). Choice (G) refers to the period from 330 to 310 million years ago. During that time, atmospheric oxygen decreased from 2.5% more than present day to approximately 1% more than present day. This is only a 1.5% difference, so eliminate (G). Choice (H) refers to the period from 260 to 240 million years ago. During that time, atmospheric oxygen concentration ranged from about 11% more than present day to about 1% less than present day for a decrease of about 12%. Keep (H), but check (J) just in case. Choice (J) refers to the period from 30 to 10 million years ago. During that time, atmospheric oxygen concentration ranged from about 2.5% to about 1% more than present day. Eliminate (J). The correct answer is (H).

29. **A** The question asks if Figure 1 supports a student's claim that marine biodiversity is falling at a rate faster than it has at any point over the last 500 million years. Look for the data for marine biodiversity in Figure 1. The *x*-axis ranges from the years 1500 to 2000, which is only a period of 500 years. Eliminate (B) and (D) since both say the figure describes the last 500 *million* years. Compare the

remaining answer choices. Since Figure 1 covers only approximately 500 years, it can't be used to provide evidence for the last 500 million years. Eliminate (C). The correct answer is (A).

30. **F**   The question asks what Student 1 would conclude about marine biodiversity in 2020 based on Figure 1. Look at the marine biodiversity values in Figure 1. Trace up from the year 2000 to determine the biodiversity in 2000: just under 4,700 genera. Student 1 states that *since 2000, marine biodiversity has fallen by approximately 2% per decade.* Eliminate (H) and (J) since both show an increase in the number of genera. Since 1% of 4,700 is 47, then 2% of 4,700 is 47 × 2 = 94. Therefore, the number of genera will drop to almost 100 between 2000 and 2010 to approximately 4,600. The question asks about 2020 not 2010, so eliminate (G). The number of genera would fall by a little less than 100 again between 2010 and 2020. The correct answer is (F).

31. **C**   The question asks for the time period in Figure 2 that Student 2 would most likely cite the oxygen data for in order to support the claim that there have been times over the past 500 million years in which oxygen concentration was lower than it is today. Look for the data for atmospheric oxygen difference in Figure 2. Atmospheric oxygen difference corresponds to the *y*-axis on the right side of the graph and the dotted line. Atmospheric oxygen difference is calculated by subtracting the current atmospheric oxygen concentration from the atmospheric oxygen concentration at a specific time. For the atmospheric oxygen concentration to be *lower than it is today*, the difference must be negative. Look for where the dotted line dips below 0%, which is between 200 and 120 million years ago. Eliminate (A), (B), and (D) because they do not fall in this range. The correct answer is (C).

32. **J**   The question asks for the value of atmospheric oxygen concentration 300 million years ago based on Figure 2, given that the current atmospheric oxygen concentration is 21%. Figure 2 graphs *atmospheric oxygen difference.* The equation in the introduction defines atmospheric oxygen difference as *(atmospheric oxygen concentration at a specific time) – (current atmospheric oxygen concentration).* Look at Figure 2 to find 300 million years ago along the *x*-axis. Draw a vertical line upward to reach the dotted line, which represents oxygen level. Now draw a line to the right to reach the vertical axis. The atmospheric oxygen difference at 300 million years ago is approximately 6%. Plug this value and the 21% present day value into the atmospheric oxygen difference equation to solve for the atmospheric oxygen concentration: 6% = (atmospheric oxygen concentration 300 million years ago) – 21%. The atmospheric oxygen concentration 300 million years ago is equal to 27%. The correct answer is (J).

33. **B**   The question asks which statement about marine biodiversity Student 2 would most likely agree with. Use POE. Student 2 believes that *the loss in marine biodiversity is part of a natural cycle of growth and loss* and *the human impact on marine biodiversity is negligible.* Eliminate (D) because a cycle of growth and loss means the biodiversity is not constant. Eliminate (C) as Student 2 believes the loss is natural rather than caused by humans. Compare the remaining answer choices. The only difference between (A) and (B) is how marine biodiversity changes as oxygen concentration decreases. Student 2 states that *as natural processes such as volcanic eruptions, asteroid impacts, and weathering cause decreases and increases in the atmospheric oxygen levels, marine biodiversity follows the same trend,* which means that

marine biodiversity and oxygen concentration exhibit a direct relationship: as one increases, so does the other. Eliminate (A). The correct answer is (B).

34. **F**   The question asks for a diagram that represents the results of Experiment 1 after two hours. Read the description for Experiment 1 to determine the results. The passage states that *the water level fell on the left and rose on the right.* Eliminate (G) and (H) because they do not show a higher water level on the right. The passage also states that *the left-sided solution was red and the right-sided was blue.* Eliminate (J) because it has the colors reversed. The correct answer is (F).

35. **D**   The question asks how repeating Experiment 2 with an albumin solution on the left would affect the results. Use POE. According to the description of Experiment 2, Experiment 2 uses cupric ion solution on the left side and water on the right side. If the cupric ion solution on the left was replaced with an albumin solution, then only albumin and water would be in the tube. The question states that albumin molecules *form clear solutions in water,* so both sides would have to be clear. Eliminate (B) and (C). In the first paragraph, the passage says *molecules, including water, have a tendency to move from regions of high concentration to regions of low concentration.* The albumin particles cannot pass through the membrane, but the water molecules on the right side of the tube will move to the lower concentration on the left side, so the water level will rise on the left. Eliminate (A). The correct answer is (D).

36. **F**   The question asks how cupric ion particles move in Experiments 1 and 2. In Experiment 1, *glucose solution is poured in the left and an equal volume of cupric ion solution is poured in the right.* At the end of the experiment, *the left-sided solution was red and the right-sided was blue.* The introduction states that *mixing glucose and cupric ions results in a red solution.* Therefore, the only way the left solution would end up red is if cupric ion particles passed through the selectively permeable membrane into the glucose solution. Eliminate (G) and (J) since both contradict this idea. Compare the remaining two answer choices. The only difference is whether the cupric ions were also able to move into pure water. Read the description for Experiment 2. In Experiment 2, *cupric ion solution is poured in the left side and an equal volume of pure water is poured in the right.* At the end of the experiment, *both sides of the tube contained blue-colored solutions.* The introduction states that *cupric ion solutions are blue,* so the only way both solutions would be blue is if cupric ions passed through the selectively permeable membrane into the pure water. Eliminate (H). The correct answer is (F).

37. **C**   The question asks for the substance in the left half of the U-tube at the start of Experiments 2 and 3. Read the description for Experiment 2 to determine the substance. In Experiment 2, *cupric ion solution is poured in the left side.* Eliminate (B) and (D) since they say the substance on the left was glucose. Next, read the description for Experiment 3. In Experiment 3, *glucose solution is poured in the left side,* so eliminate (A). The correct answer is (C).

38. **G**   The question asks how the results of Experiment 1 would have been different if a selectively permeable membrane that allows cupric ions, water, and glucose to pass had been used. Read the description for Experiment 1 to determine the solutions used for the experiment. In Experiment 1, *glucose solution is poured in the left and an equal volume of cupric ion solution is poured in the right.* In the original experiment, *the left-sided solution was red and the right-sided was blue* after two hours. According to

the introduction, *mixing glucose and cupric ions results in a red solution*. The only way the solution on the left would end up red is if cupric ion particles passed through the selectively permeable membrane into the glucose solution. The glucose particles must not have passed from the left to the right side. In the new experiment, glucose can also pass through the selectively permeable membrane, resulting in a mixture of cupric and glucose ions on both sides of the membrane. This would cause red solutions to occur on both sides. The correct answer is (G).

39. **A**   The question asks if the assertion that cupric ions are bigger than water molecules is valid based on Experiment 1. In Experiment 1, *glucose solution is poured in the left and an equal volume of cupric ion solution is poured in the right*. At the end of the experiment, *the left-sided solution was red and the right-sided was blue* after two hours. According to the introduction, *mixing glucose and cupric ions results in a red solution*. The only way the left solution would end up red is if cupric ion particles passed through the selectively permeable membrane into the glucose solution. Eliminate (C) because it says cupric ion particles can't pass through the membrane. Look through the introduction for a reference to the size of molecules. The introduction states that *selectively permeable membranes act as filters, only allowing molecules below a certain threshold size to pass through* and *of the three molecules used for the solutions, water is the smallest and glucose is the largest*. Eliminate (B), as it says water molecules and cupric ions are larger than glucose molecules. Consider the remaining choices. Choice (D) says that both water and cupric ions can pass through the selectively permeable membrane. If both can pass through the membrane, then that would not provide any evidence about whether cupric ions were larger than water molecules. Eliminate (D). Experiment 1 shows only that both cupric ions and water are small enough to pass through the membrane, but that glucose is too large to pass through the membrane. The correct answer is (A).

40. **G**   The question asks for the color of the substance in the right side of the tube at the beginning of Experiment 1. Read the description for Experiment 1 to determine the substance. In Experiment 1, *cupric ion solution is poured in the right*. Read the introduction to determine the color of cupric ion solution. The passage says *cupric ion solutions are blue*. The correct answer is (G).

NOTES

NOTES

NOTES

NOTES

NOTES

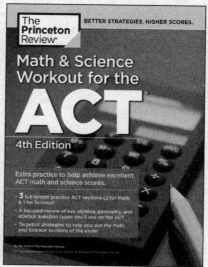